PHILIP'S

STREET ATLAS

UNRIVALLED DETAIL BEST-S ATLAS

CW00540468

NAVIGATOR® SOMERSET

NORTH SOMERSET AND
BATH AND NORTH EAST SOMERSET

www.philips-maps.co.uk

Published by Philip's a division of Octopus Publishing Group Ltd
www.octopusbooks.co.uk
Carmelite House
50 Victoria Embankment
London EC4Y 0DZ
An Hachette UK Company
www.hachette.co.uk

First edition 2022
SOMEA

ISBN 978-1-84907-588-6

© Philip's 2022

Map data

This product includes mapping data licensed from Ordnance Survey® with the permission of the Controller of Her Majesty's Stationery Office. © Crown copyright 2022. All rights reserved. Licence number 100011710.

CONTENTS

III **Key to map symbols**

IV **Key to map pages**

VI **Route planning**

X Major administrative and Postcode boundaries

1 **Street maps** at 3½ inches to 1 mile

122 **Street maps** at 1¾ inches to 1 mile

200 **Street maps** at 3½ inches to 1 mile

226 **Street maps of Bristol and Bath city centres** at 7 inches to 1 mile

229 **Index** of towns, villages, streets, hospitals, industrial estates, railway stations, schools, shopping centres, universities and places of interest

Key to map symbols

Motorway with junction number
Primary route – dual/single carriageway
A road – dual/single carriageway
B road – dual/single carriageway
Minor road – dual/single carriageway
Other minor road – dual/single carriageway
Road under construction
Tunnel, covered road
Rural track, private road or narrow road in urban area
Gate or obstruction to traffic – may not apply at all times or to all vehicles
Path, bridleway, byway open to all traffic, restricted byway
Pedestrianised area
BS22 Postcode boundaries
County and unitary authority boundaries
Railway with station
Tunnel
Railway under construction
Metro station
Private railway station
Miniature railway
Tramway, tram stop
Tramway, tram stop under construction
Bus, coach station

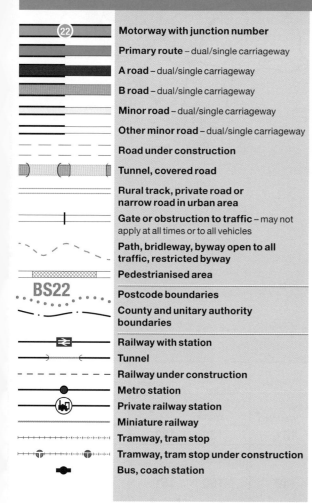

Ambulance station
Coastguard station
Fire station
Police station
Accident and Emergency entrance to hospital
H Hospital
+ Place of worship
i Information centre – open all year
P Shopping centre, parking
P&R PO Park and Ride, Post Office
Camping site, caravan site
Golf course, picnic site
Church ROMAN FORT Non-Roman antiquity, Roman antiquity
Univ Important buildings, schools, colleges, universities and hospitals
Woods, built-up area
River Medway Water name
River, weir
Stream
Canal, lock, tunnel
Water
Tidal water

58 ◄ **87** Adjoining page indicators and overlap
246 bands – the colour of the arrow and band indicates the scale of the adjoining or overlapping page (see scales below)

The dark grey border on the inside edge of some pages indicates that the mapping does not continue onto the adjacent page

The small numbers around the edges of the maps identify the 1-kilometre National Grid lines

Abbreviations

Acad	Academy		Meml	Memorial
Allot Gdns	Allotments		Mon	Monument
Cemy	Cemetery		Mus	Museum
C Ctr	Civic centre		Obsy	Observatory
CH	Club house		Pal	Royal palace
Coll	College		PH	Public house
Crem	Crematorium		Recn Gd	Recreation ground
Ent	Enterprise			
Ex H	Exhibition hall		Resr	Reservoir
Ind Est	Industrial Estate		Ret Pk	Retail park
IRB Sta	Inshore rescue boat station		Sch	School
			Sh Ctr	Shopping centre
Inst	Institute		TH	Town hall / house
Ct	Law court		Trad Est	Trading estate
L Ctr	Leisure centre		Univ	University
LC	Level crossing		W Twr	Water tower
Liby	Library		Wks	Works
Mkt	Market		YH	Youth hostel

Enlarged maps only

Railway or bus station building

Place of interest

Parkland

The map scale on the pages numbered in green is 1¾ inches to 1 mile
2.76 cm to 1 km • 1:36 206

0	½ mile	1 mile	1½ miles	2 miles
0	500m	1 km	1½ km	2km

The map scale on the pages numbered in blue is 3½ inches to 1 mile
5.52 cm to 1 km • 1:18 103

0	¼ mile	½ mile	¾ mile	1 mile
0	250m	500m	750m	1km

The map scale on the pages numbered in red is 7 inches to 1 mile
11.04 cm to 1 km • 1:9051

0	220yds	440yds	660yds	½ mile
0	125m	250m	375m	500m

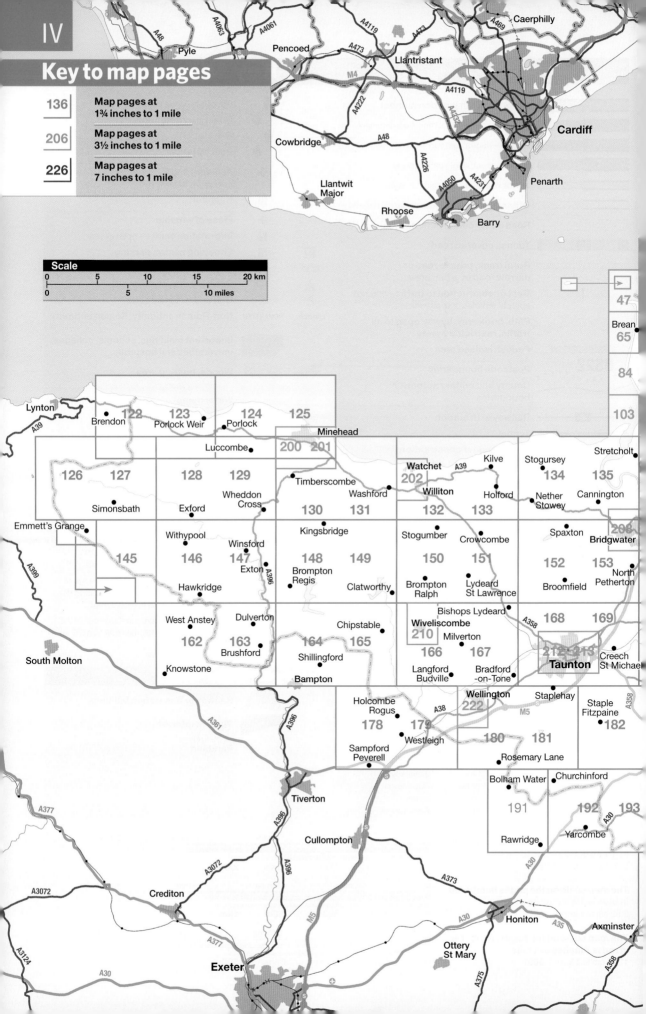

IV

Key to map pages

136	Map pages at 1¾ inches to 1 mile
206	Map pages at 3½ inches to 1 mile
226	Map pages at 7 inches to 1 mile

Scale

0   5   10   15   20 km
0   5   10 miles

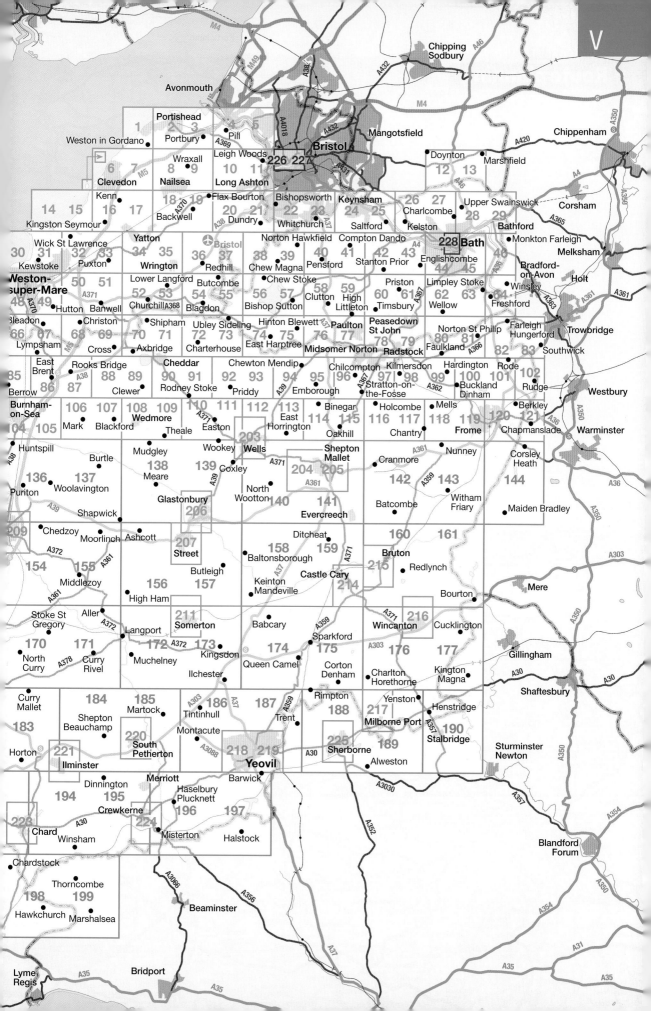

Chipping Sodbury

Avonmouth

Portishead
1
2 3
Portbury
Pill
5
Weston in Gordano
A369
Leigh Woods
226 227
Bristol
Mangotsfield
Doynton
12 13
Marshfield
Chippenham
Corsham
Wraxall
6 7
8 9
10 11
Keynsham
26 27
Charlcombe
28
Upper Swainswick
Bathford
Clevedon
Nailsea
Long Ashton
24 25
Saltford
Kelston
29
Bath

Kenn
Flax Bourton
18 19
20 21
Bishopsworth
22 23
Whitchurch
Dundry

14 15
16 17
Backwell
Norton Hawkfield
Compton Dando
42 43
228 Bath
44 45
Monkton Farleigh
Melksham
Kingston Seymour

Wick St Lawrence
Yatton
34 35
36 37
Redhill
38 39
Chew Magna
40
Pensford
41
Stanton Prior
Englishcombe
46
Bradford-on-Avon
Holt
30 31 32 33
Puxton
Wrington
Chew Stoke
Priston
Limpley Stoke
62 63
64
Winsley
Kewstoke
Lower Langford
Butcombe
Chew Stoke
58 59
60 61
Wellow
Freshford
Weston-super-Mare
50 51
52 53
54 55
56 57
Clutton
High Littleton
Timsbury
Farleigh Hungerford
Trowbridge
Churchill
Blagdon
Bishop Sutton

48 49
Hutton Banwell
Shipham
Ubley Sideling
72 73
Hinton Blewett
74 75
76
Paulton
77
Peasedown St John
78 79
80 81
Norton St Philip
Faulkland
82 83
Southwick
Bleadon
Christon
Cross
Axbridge
Charterhouse
East Harptree
Midsomer Norton
Radstock
66 67
68 69
70 71
Lympsham
Rooks Bridge
Cheddar
Chewton Mendip
Chilcompton Kilmersdon
Hardington
Rode
East Brent
88 89
90 91
92 93
94 95
96
97 98
99 100 101
102
Berrow
Clewer
Rodney Stoke
Priddy
Emborough
Stratton-on-the-Fosse
Buckland Dinham
Rudge
85
86 87
Westbury
Burnham-on-Sea
106 107
108 109
110 111
112 113
Binegar
Holcombe
Mells
Berkley
Warminster
Mark Blackford
Wedmore
Theale
Easton
East Horrington
114 115
116 117
118 119
120 121
Chantry
Frome
Chapmanslade
104 105
Oakhill

Huntspill
Burtle
Mudgley
138
Wookey
203
Wells
Shepton Mallet
Cranmore
Nunney
Corsley Heath
Meare
139
Coxley
Puriton
136 137
Woolavington
204 205
142
143
144
Shapwick
Glastonbury
North Wootton
Batcombe
Witham Friary
Maiden Bradley
206
140 141
Evercreech

Chedzoy
Ashcott
Ditcheat
160 161
209
Moorlinch
207
158
159
Bruton
154 155
Street
Baltonsborough
215
Redlynch
Middlezoy
Butleigh
Castle Cary
Mere
156 157
Keinton Mandeville
214
Bourton
High Ham
Stoke St Gregory
Aller
211
Babcary
216
Wincanton
Cucklington
Langport
Somerton
Sparkford
170 171
172 173
174
175
176
177
Gillingham
North Curry
Curry Rivel
Kingsdon
Queen Camel
Corton Denham
Kington Magna
Muchelney
Ilchester
Charlton Horethorne
Shaftesbury
Curry Mallet
184 185
Martock
186 187
Rimpton
Yenston
217
Henstridge
183
Shepton Beauchamp
220
Tintinhull
Trent
188
Milborne Port
190
Stalbridge
Horton
221
South Petherton
218 219
225
Sherborne
189
Sturminster Newton
Ilminster
Yeovil
Alweston
Merriott
Barwick
194 195
Dinnington
Haselbury Plucknett
196 197
Blandford Forum
Crewkerne
228
224
Chard
Misterton
Halstock
Winsham
Chardstock
198 199
Thorncombe
Beaminster
Hawkchurch Marshalsea
Bridport
Lyme Regis

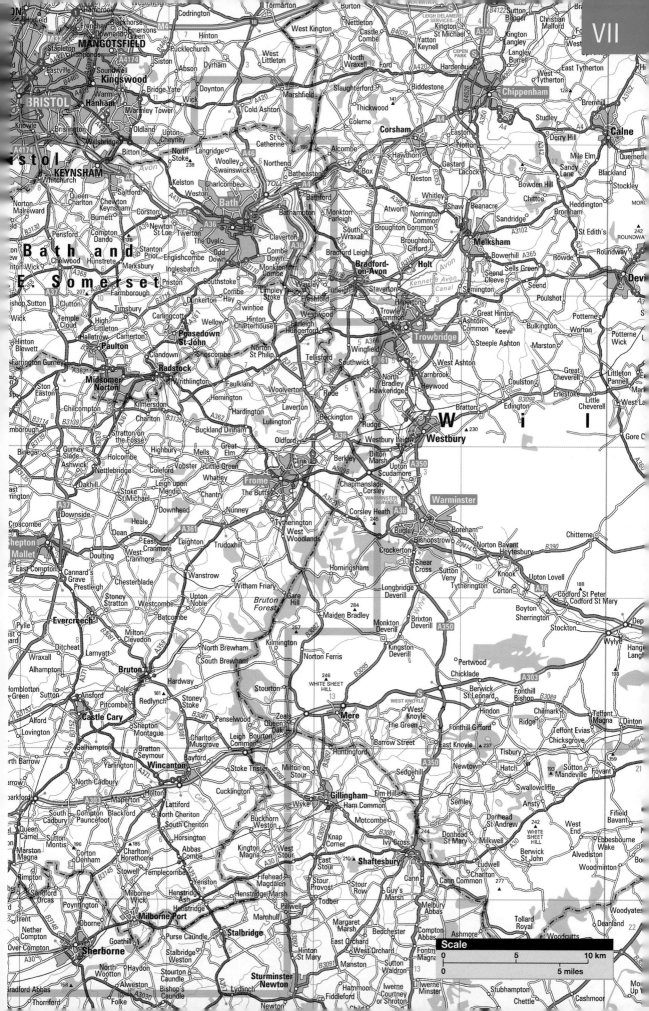

Major administrative and Postcode boundaries

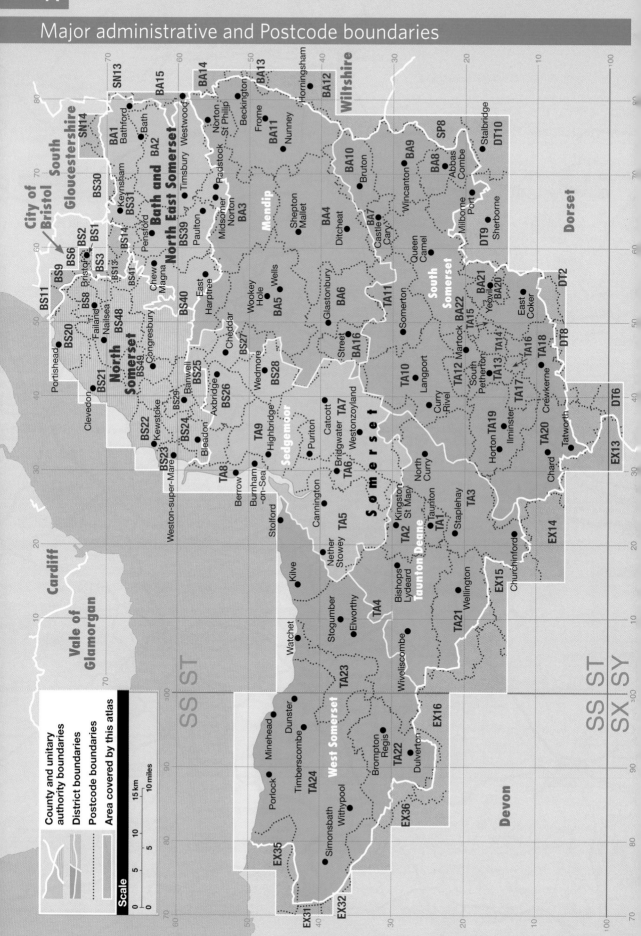

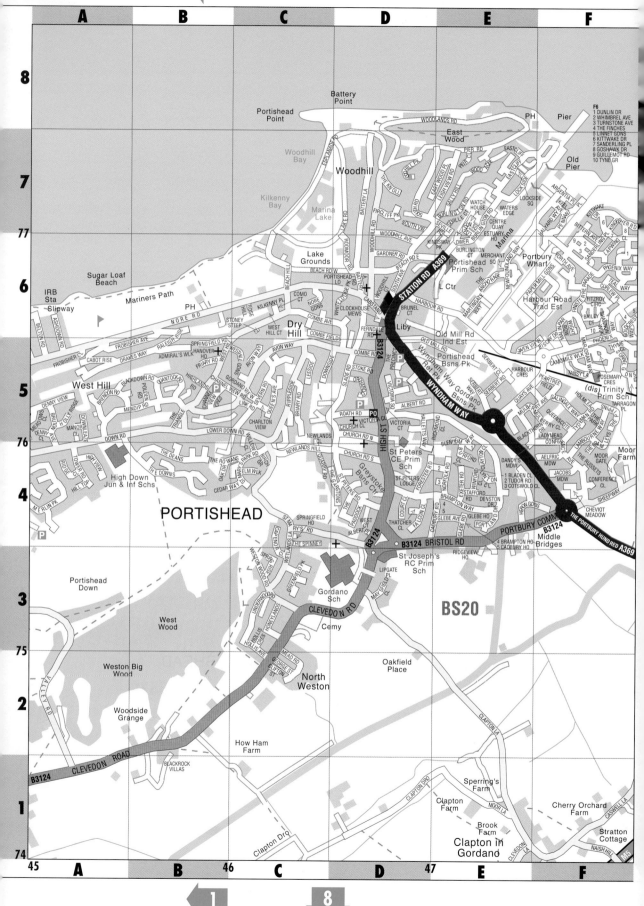

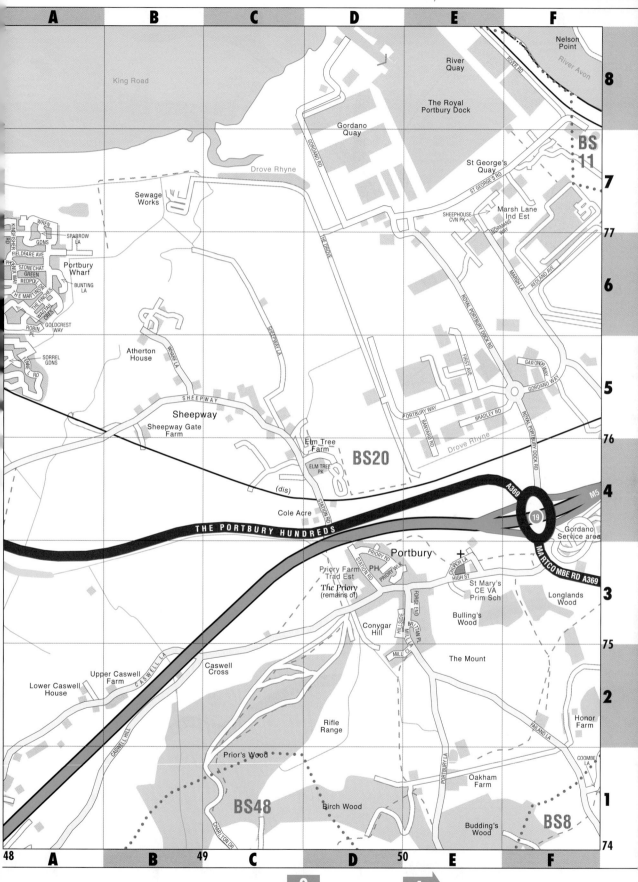

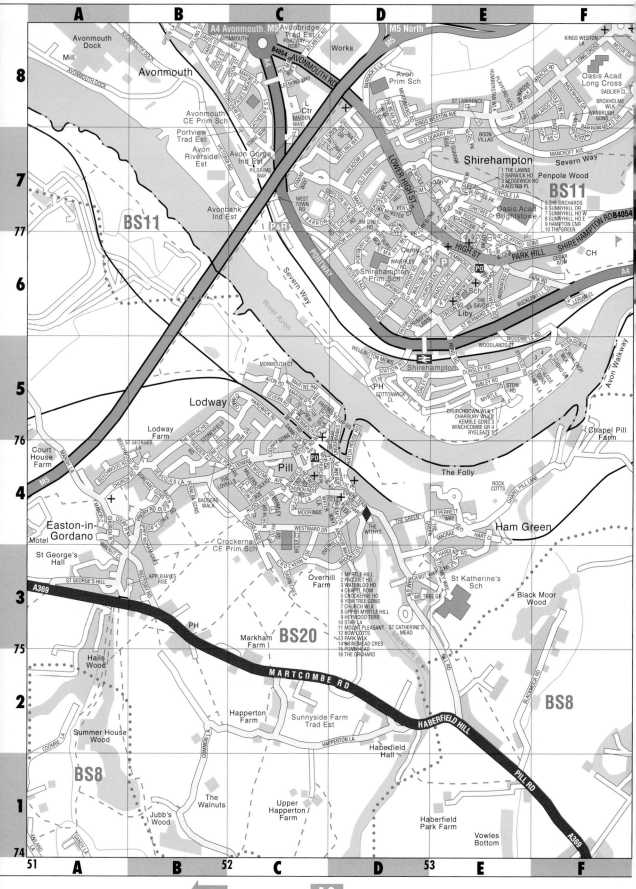

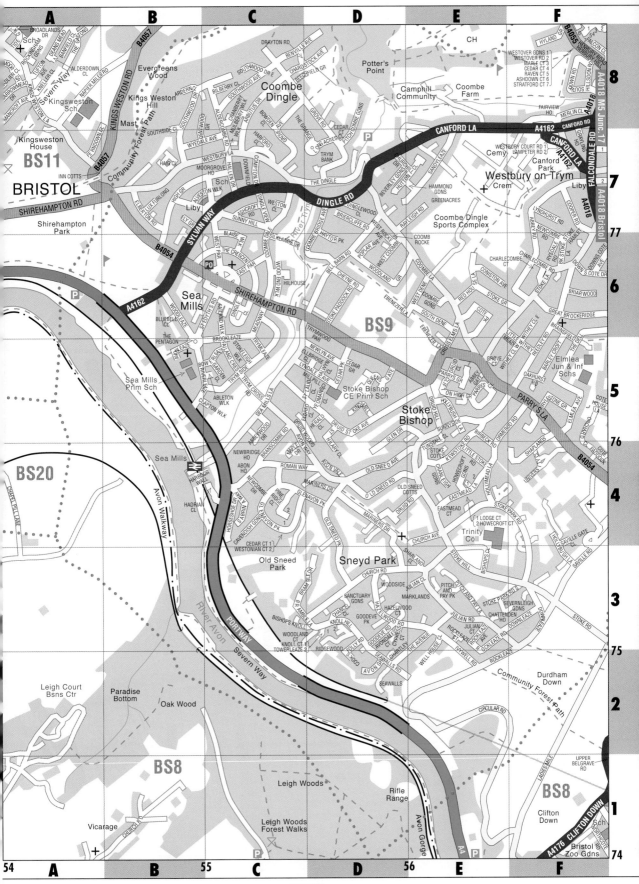

B1
1 CRAWFORD CL
2 SANDFORD CL
3 HEDGES CL
4 SOUTHERN RING PATH
5 LADYCROFT
6 LONGACRE
7 GARSTONS
8 BAKER CL

C1
1 Carey Developments
2 Tweed Rd Ind Est
3 St John the Evangelist CE Prim Sch

C2
1 Speedwell Ind Est
2 COLERIDGE VALE RD W
3 WAINS CL
4 HANSON'S WAY
5 CHURCHILL CL
6 COPPACK HO
7 GARLAND HO
8 SHOPLAND HO
9 BRIDGE HO

10 CLIFTON CT

D2
1 COLERIDGE VALE RD E
2 MELBOURNE TERR
3 PENNYWELL EST

E1
1 OTTER RD
2 TIVERTON RD
3 PORLOCK CL
4 PLUMERS CL

F3
1 STREAMSIDE
2 WOODVIEW
3 GREENWAY PK
4 MAYNARD CL
5 HOLLYMAN WLK
6 FRESHMOOR

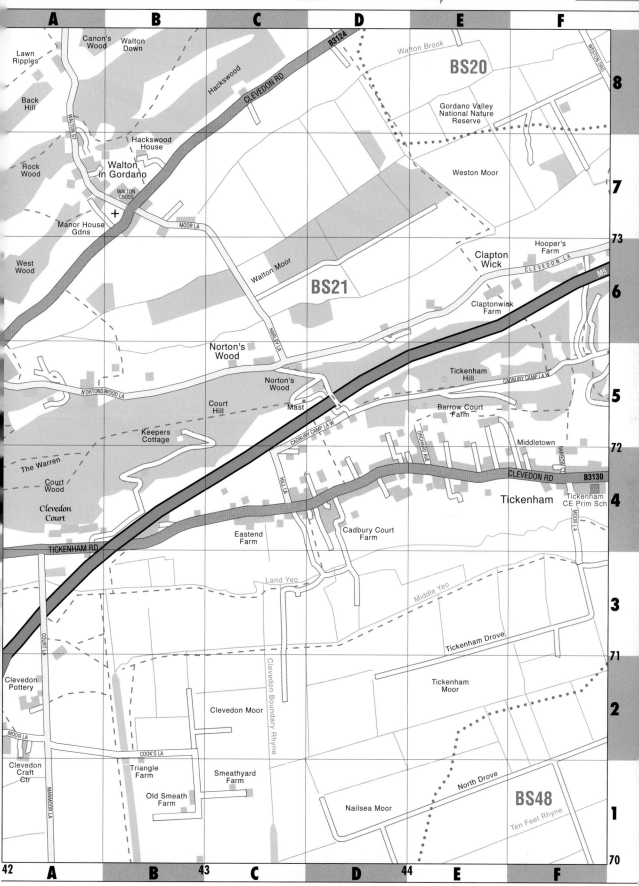

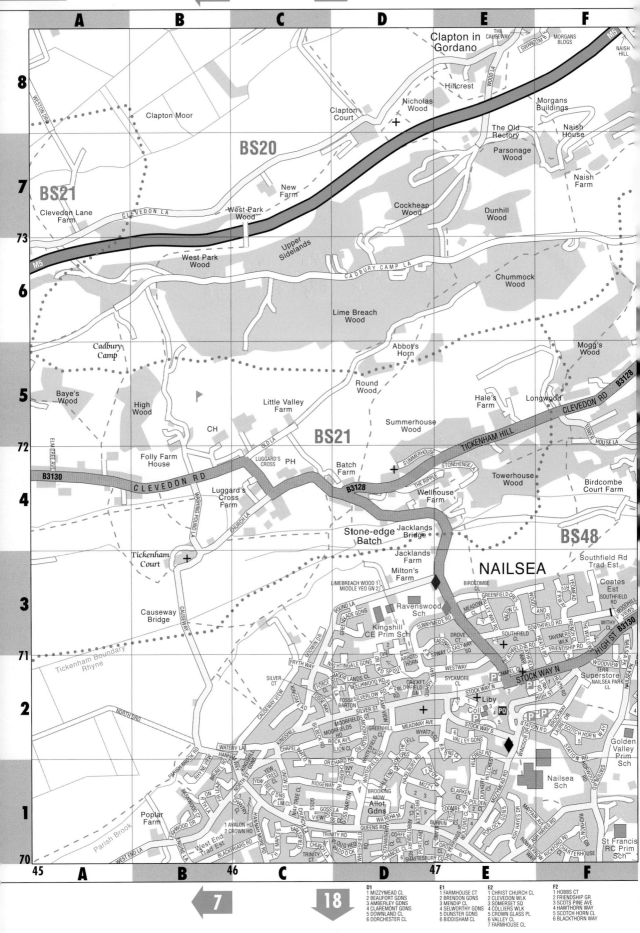

A B C D E F

8

Clapton in Gordano

THE CAUSEWAY
SWINGCOM
MORGANS BLDGS
M5
NAISH HILL

Hillcrest

Nicholas Wood

Clapton Court
Clapton Moor

Morgans Buildings

WOOD LA

The Old Rectory
Naish House

BS20

7

New Farm

CLEVEDON LA
West Park Wood

Cockheap Wood

Parsonage Wood

Dunhill Wood

Naish Farm

BS21

73

Clevedon Lane Farm

West Park Wood

Upper Sidelands

CADBURY CAMP LA

Chummock Wood

M5

6

Lime Breach Wood

Abbot's Horn

Mogg's Wood

Cadbury Camp

Round Wood

5

Baye's Wood

High Wood

Little Valley Farm

Summerhouse Wood

Hale's Farm

Longwood

CLEVEDON RD

B3128

BS21

CH

TICKENHAM HILL

TOWER HOUSE LA

72

ELM TREE AVE

Folly Farm House

OLD LA

Luggard's Cross

PH

SUMMERHOUSE

STONEHENGE LA

Towerhouse Wood

Birdcombe Court Farm

B3130

CLEVEDON RD

Luggard's Cross Farm

Batch Farm

B3128

THE RIPPLE

Wellhouse Farm

BS48

4

WASHING POUND LA

CHURCH LA

Tickenham Court

Stone-edge Batch

Jacklands Bridge

Jacklands Farm

NAILSEA

Southfield Rd Trad Est

3

CAUSEWAY

Causeway Bridge

Milton's Farm

LIMEBREACH WOOD 1
MIDDLE YEO GN 2

Ravenswood Sch

Kingshill CE Prim Sch

Birdcombe CL

Coates Est

SOUTHFIELD RD

WOODHILL VIEWS

B3130

71

Tickenham Boundary Rhyne

FRYTH WAY

NIGHTINGALE GDNS

OREN SPOUT

Abbots Horn

EASTWAY CLEASTWAY
CLEASTWAY SQ
WESTWAY

STOCK WAY N

WOODVIEW TERR
Superstore
NAILSEA PARK CL

2

NORTH DRO

SILVER CT

MOOR LANDS CL

BEECHWOOD RD

FOSSE WAY

SILVER ST

CRICKET GN

SYCAMORE CL

Stock Way N

COL
Liby
P PO

STATION RD

SCOTCH HORN WAY

Golden Valley Prim Sch

1

WATERY LA

KINGSHILL

PARISH BROOK RD

RHYNE VIEW

HANHAM WAY

CHAPEL BARTON

MOORFIELDS HO

GILCROSS

ROCK AVE

LION CL

GREENHILL

Stock Ways S

VALLEY GDNS

HILLCREST

Nailsea Sch

STATION RD

70

Poplar Farm

WEST END LA

Parish Brook

West End Trad Est

BLACKFRIARS RD

YEW TREE CL

MAY TREE CL

TRINITY RD

GOSS LA

BARTON

QUEENS RD

CORFE

ABBOTS

PORLOCK GDNS

ASH HAYES RD

ROWBERROW WAY

RICKFORD RD

CHARTERHOUSE

St Francis RC Prim Sch

45 A   B 46 C   D 47 E   F

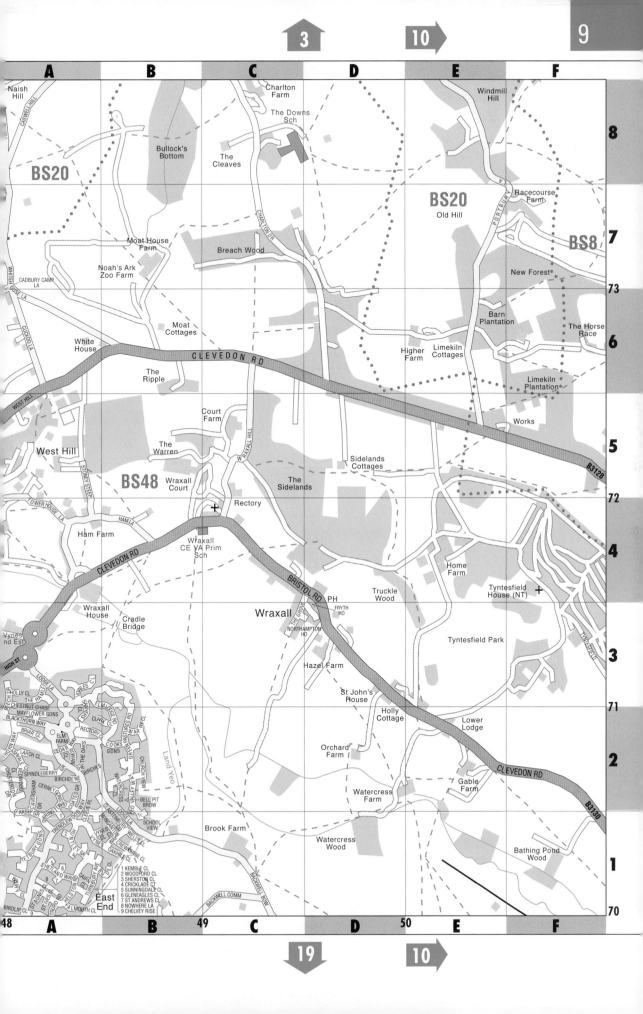

9 | 4

A | B | C | D | E | F

BS20

8

Lower Failand
Jubbs Court

Leigh Wood

Lower Failand Farm

Old Park

Old Park Wood

Poundbatch Farm

FAILAND LA
SANDY LA
DENNYVIEW RD
PILL RD A369
HARRIS LA
KNIGHTCOTT RD
GLEN AVE
MANOR LA

Home Farm

7

Failand Court

Mulberry Farm

Three Cornered Wood

Old Park House

Glen Farm

Fish Pond Wood

73

BS8

Failand Hill House

West Tanpit Wood

East Tanpit Wood

Scutche's Plantation

Yew Tree Plantation

MANOR RD

Durbans Batch

6

HORSE RACE LA
OXHOUSE LA

Failand Hill Farm

Ox House Bottom

Ferney Row

Failand Farm

Orchard Lodge

Round Hill Clump

WEIR LA

5

Failand Lodge Farm

Manor Farm

CH

Fifty Acre Wood

72

B3128

PH

B3129

BEGGAR BUSH LA

4

Works

PO

CLEVEDON RD

Green La

Wraxall Piece

North Longwood

Redwood Lodge Hotel & Country Club

REDWOOD DR

Durnford Quarry

LONGWOOD LA

MONARCH'S WAY

JUBILEE
WOODLAND WAY
WOODLAND DR
FLAX BOURTON RD
BOWDEN WAY
SIXTY ACRES CL
OLD CHELSEA LA
MANOR WAY
HILL DR
BELMONT DR
BIRCHWOOD DR
WESTON RD

Long Wood

LONGWOOD HO

Round Plantation

3

Tyntesfield Plantation

Belmont Combe

Clifton Lodge

P

Failand Lawn

Failand

B3128

CLARKEN COOMBE

CH

71

Iron Plantation

2

Belmont House

Mon

BELMONT HILL

TYNTESFIELD

Ashton Hill Plantation

The Brake

BS41

MIKES CL
PROVIDENCE LA
PROVIDENCE RISE
SHORT LA

Kingcot Farm

George's Hill Plantation

Fenn's Wood

1

BS48

CLEVEDON RD

B3130
B3129

Belmont Farm

Belmont Lodge

Cook's Wood

Shipley Brake

Land Yeo
GATCOMBE MILL LA

Rudge Farm

LOVELINCH GDNS 1
BRADVILLE GDNS 2
RAYMORE RISE 3
HOLDERS WLK 4
ELMHURST GDNS 5

ORCHARD RD
KEEDWELL HILL
WILLOW CL
CHERRY HILL
CE STAFF CL
BRACKEN
KEEDS LA
RAYENS CROSS RD
RAYENS CL
ARCH
WESTON RD
ARCHBROOK
BREWELL LA
BIRDWELL LA
BRICKS
YEOMEADS
LYNBROOK
LAMPTON RD

FENSWOOD CL
FENSWOOD CT
FENSWOOD MEAD
MEAD RD
FISHERS MEAD
KINGS
WARREN LA
WARREN CL
FENNEL LA

Liby

PO

70

51 | A | 52 | B | C | 53 | D | E | F

9 | 20

F5	F5	F6	7 CARRICK HO	F6	F7	7 BEAUFORT BLDGS	**11**
1 BRISTOL GATE	7 GRENVILLE PL	1 HABERFIELD HO	8 SOUTH GREEN ST	14 VICTORIA TERR	1 CLIFTON CL	8 GLOUCESTER ST	
2 FARADAY RD	8 ASHMEAD WAY	2 DAWES CT	9 ALBERMARLE ROW	15 THE POLYGON	2 HARLEY MEWS	9 WATERLOO ST	
3 DOWRY PL	9 CUMBERLAND RD	3 CLEVE CT	10 HOPECHAPEL HILL	16 GLENDALE	3 HARLEY CT	10 BEAUFORT MEWS	
4 LITTLE CAROLINE PL	10 BRUNSWICK PL	4 BROWNE CT	11 NORTH GREEN ST	17 PRINCE'S BLDGS	4 HARLEY PL		
5 GRANVILLE CHAPEL		5 ADAMS CT	12 HINTON LA	18 WELLINGTON TERR	5 CLIFTON DOWN RD		
6 HUMPHRY DAVY WAY		6 CUMBERLAND PL	13 WINDSOR CT	19 OXFORD PL	6 GLOUCESTER ROW		

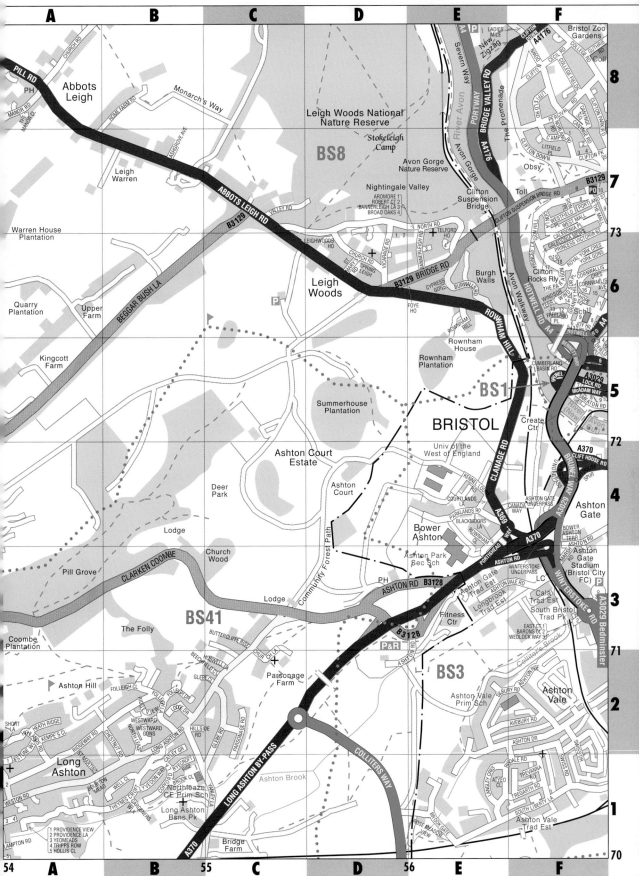

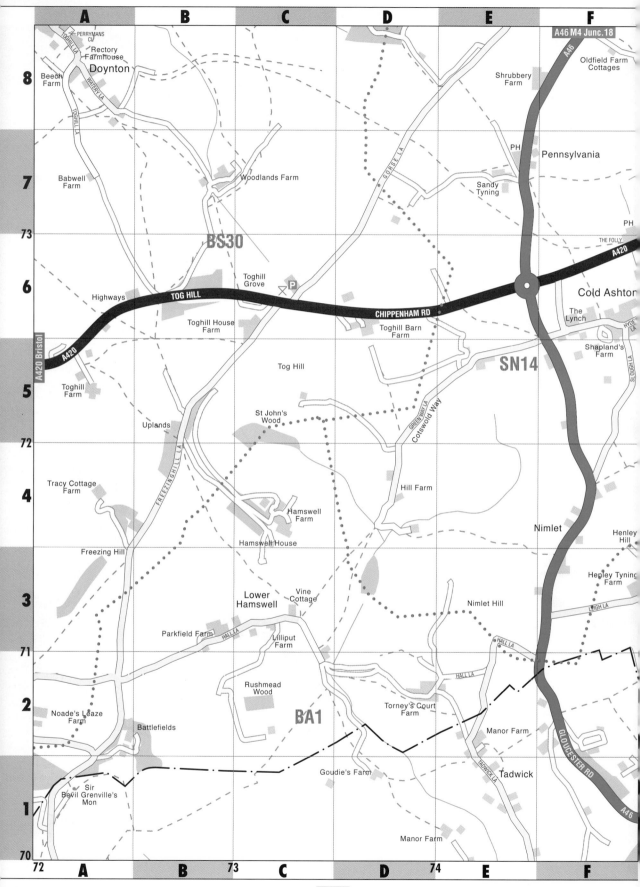

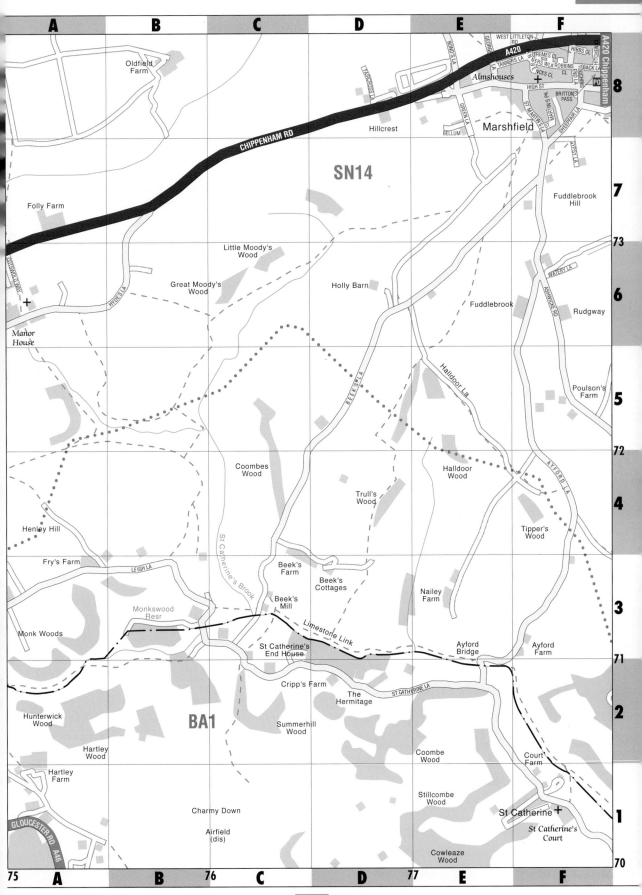

A B C D E F

Oldfield Farm

WEST LITTLETON RD
A420
GEORGE
BOND S LA
TANNERS LA
HIBBS CL
TOUCHING
NEPCOTE
A420 Chippenham
P O

FRANCROSS LA
EVERS WLK
ROBBINS
CL
NCES CL
BACK LA
HIGH ST
BRITTON'S PASS

CHIPPENHAM RD
Hillcrest

Almshouses

ST MARTIN'S LA
S MILLYFD PK
GREEN LA
BELLUM
Marshfield

SHEEPFAIR LA
SYPESS LA

SN14

Folly Farm

Fuddlebrook Hill

COTSWOLD WAY
HYDE'S LA
Little Moody's Wood

73

Great Moody's Wood
Holly Barn
WATERY LA
ASHWICKE RD

Fuddlebrook
Rudgway

6

Manor House

BEEK'S LA
Halldoor La
Poulson's Farm

5

Coombes Wood
Halldoor Wood
AYFORD LA

72

St Catherine's Brook
Trull's Wood

4

Henley Hill
Tipper's Wood

Fry's Farm
LEIGH LA
Beek's Farm
Beek's Cottages
Nailey Farm

Monkswood Resr
Beek's Mill

Monk Woods
Limestone Link
Ayford Bridge
Ayford Farm

71

St Catherine's End House
St Catherine La
Cripp's Farm
The Hermitage

BA1
Hunterwick Wood
Summerhill Wood

Coombe Wood
Court Farm

2

Hartley Wood
Stillcombe Wood

Hartley Farm
St Catherine

GLOUCESTER RD A46
Charmy Down
St Catherine's Court

Airfield (dis)
Cowleaze Wood

70

75 A B 76 C D 77 E F

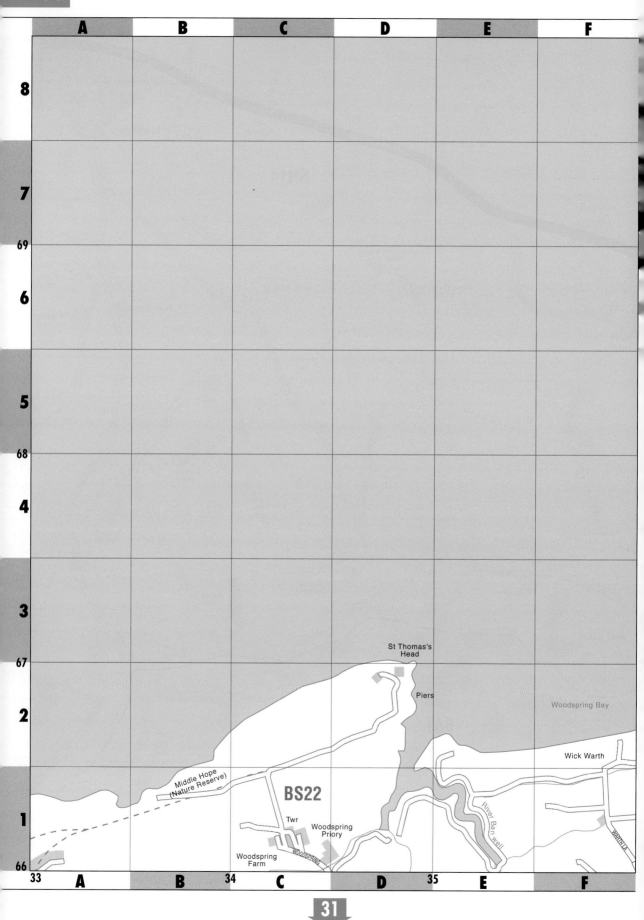

St Thomas's
Head

Piers

Woodspring Bay

Wick Warth

Middle Hope
(Nature Reserve)

BS22

River Banwell

Twr

Woodspring
Priory

WOODSPRING

Woodspring
Farm

A B C D E F

8

7

69

Dowlais Ditch

Kingston Pill

Seawall Farm
6

Hook's Ear

Treble House Farm

BACK LA
5

Sewage Works

68

Channel View Farm
4

BS21

Broadstone Rhyne

MIDDLE LA

MIDDLE LA

Broadstone Farm
3

BROADSTONE LA

Wharf Farm

67

New House Farm

HAM LA

Ham Farm
2

Pool Farm

Ham Rhyne

Sewage Works

BS22

Mendip View Farm

Yeo Bank Farm

YEO BANK LA

Mill Leaze Rhyne
1

MIDDLE LA

BS22

66

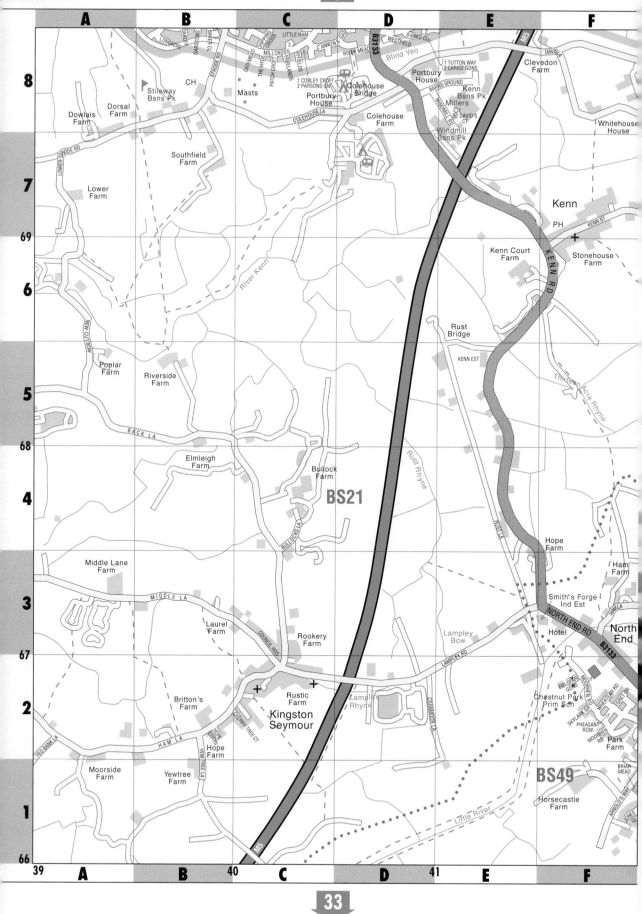

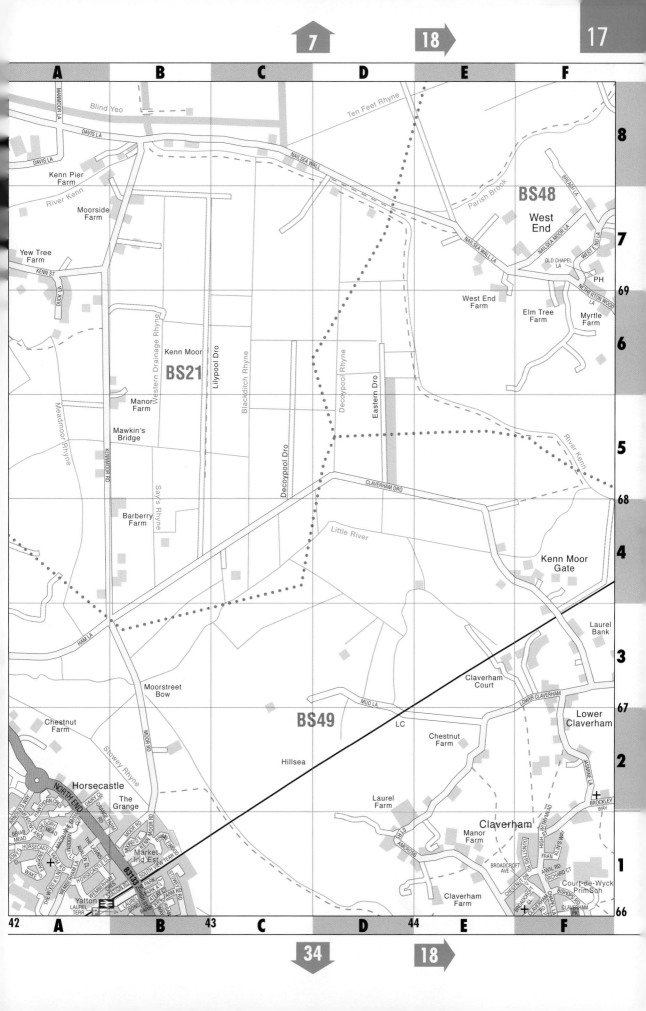

A B C D E F

8
7
69
6
5
68
4
3
67
2
1
66

Blind Yeo
Ten Feet Rhyne
DAVIS LA
MANMOOR LA
NAILSEA WALL
Parish Brook
BS48
West End
NAILSEA WALL LA
BREACH LA
OLD CHAPEL LA
NAILSEA MOOR LA
WEST END LA
PH
NETHERTON WOOD LA

Kenn Pier Farm
DAVIS LA
River Kenn
Moorside Farm
Yew Tree Farm
KENN ST
DUCK LA
West End Farm
Elm Tree Farm
Myrtle Farm

Western Drainage Rhyne
Kenn Moor
BS21
Lilypool Dro
Blackditch Rhyne
Decoypool Rhyne
Eastern Dro
River Kenn

Manor Farm
Mawkin's Bridge
KENNMOOR RD
Say's Rhyne
Meadmoor Rhyne
Decoypool Dro

Barberry Farm
CLAVERHAM DRO

Little River
Kenn Moor Gate
Laurel Bank

HAM LA
Claverham Court
LOWER CLAVERHAM
3

Moorstreet Bow
MUD LA
Lower Claverham

Chestnut Farm
MOOR RD
Stowey Rhyne
BS49
LC
Chestnut Farm
JASMINE LA

Hillsea
Horsecastle
The Grange
NORTH END
Laurel Farm
Claverham
Manor Farm
BROCKLEY WAY

Market Ind Est.
B3133
HIGH ST
WITHY MEAD
S ALLY WAY
FRAN
DUNSTERS RD
BROADCROFT AVE
ANVIL RD
ORCHARD CT
BISHOPS RD
CLAVERHAM PK
Court-de-Wyck Prim Sch

Yatton
LAUREL TERR
Claverham Farm
CHESTNUT DR
BROADCROFT
CHAPEL LA

42 43 44

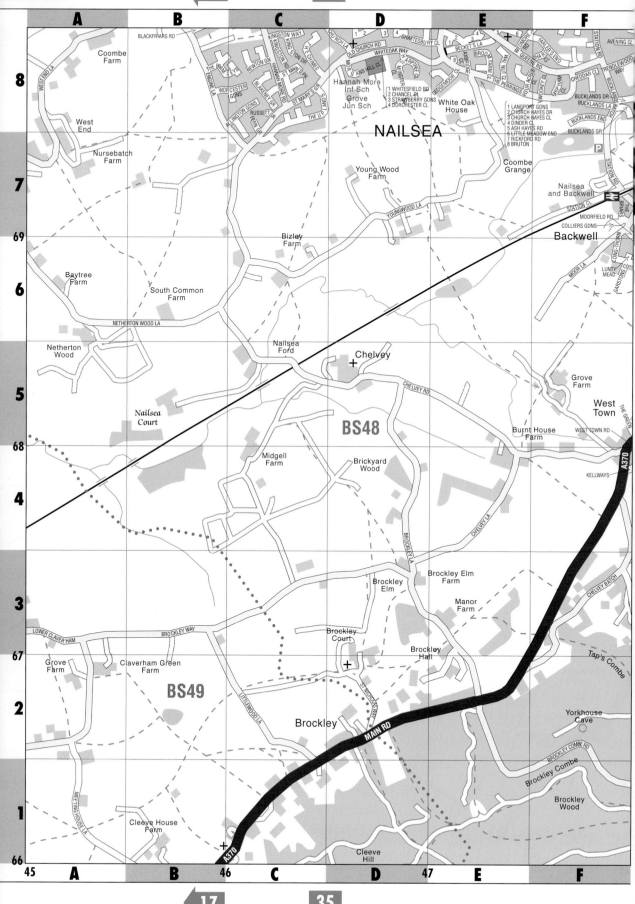

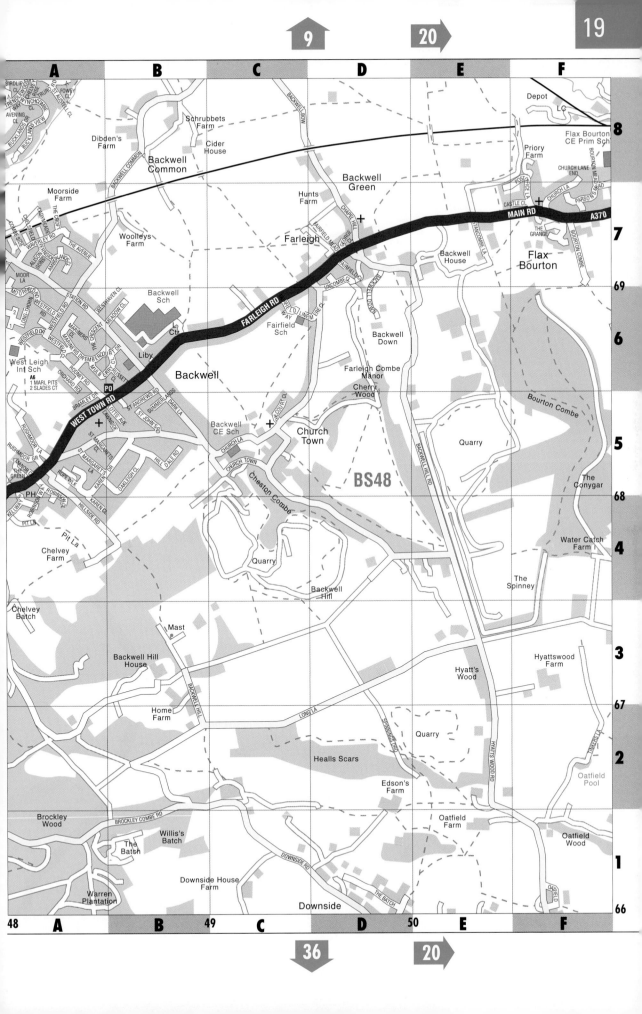

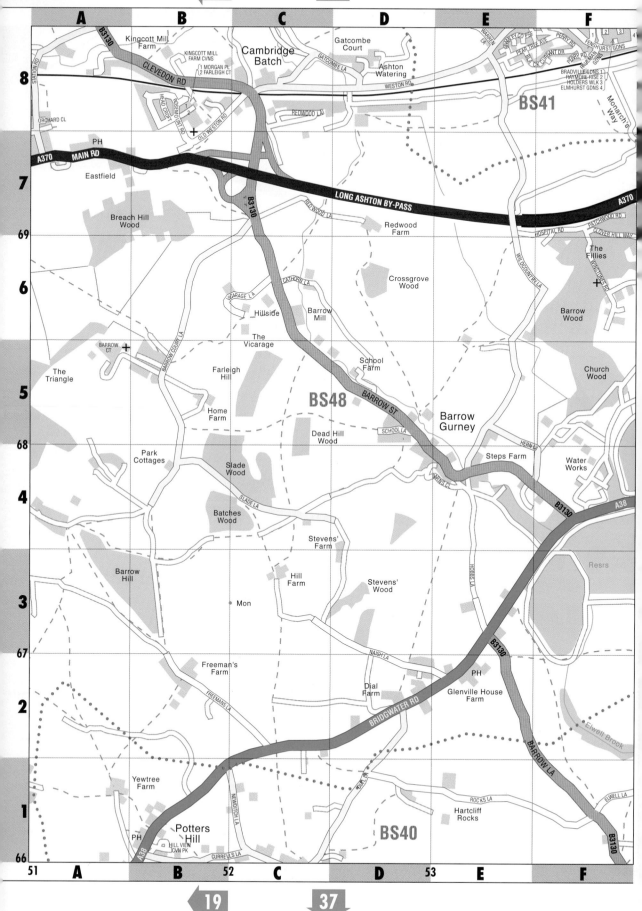

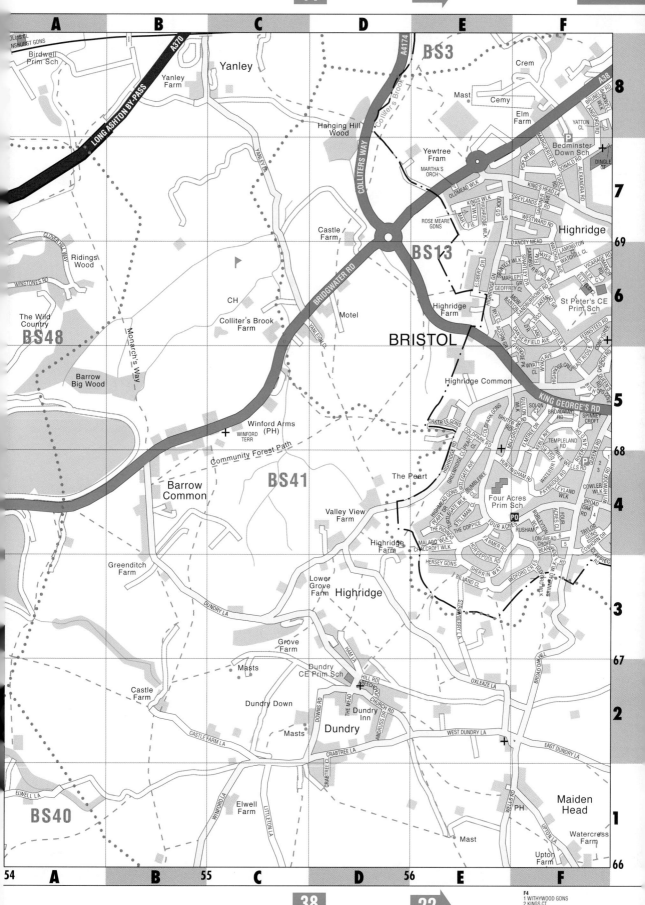

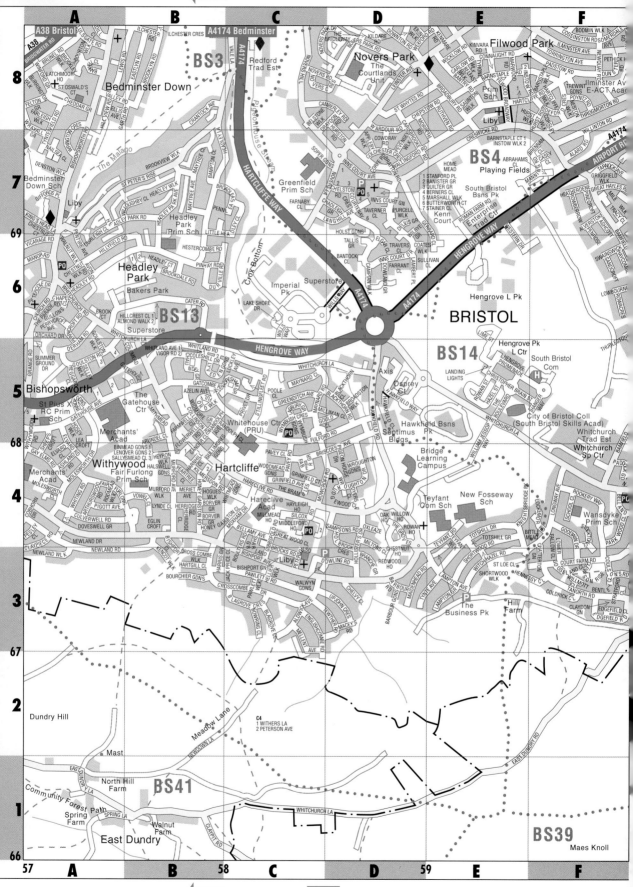

22

A8
1 Cheddar Gr
Prim Sch

A5
1 GATEHOUSE CL
2 GATEHOUSE WAY
3 CORNLEAZE
4 ACRESBUSH CL
5 QUEENS RD

21

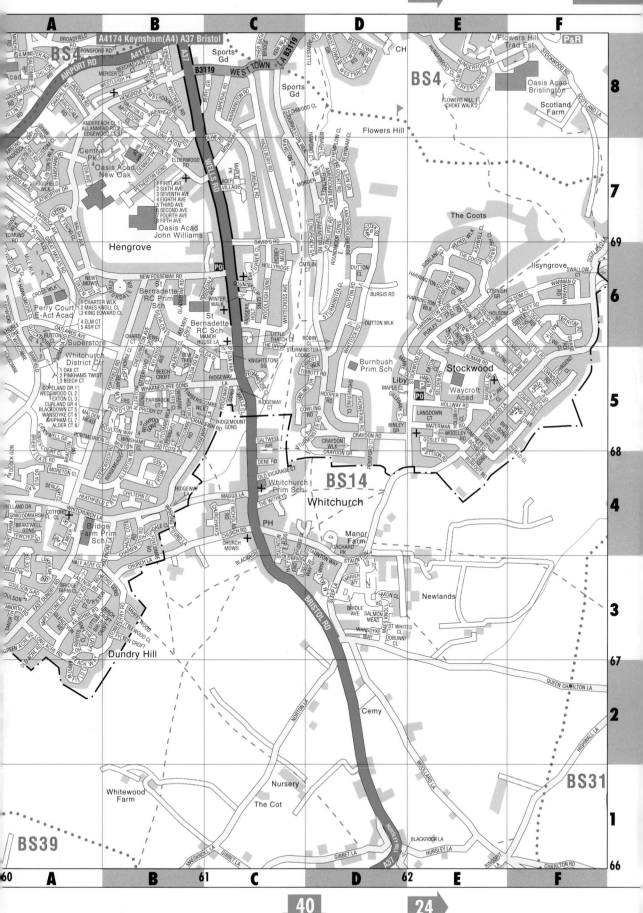

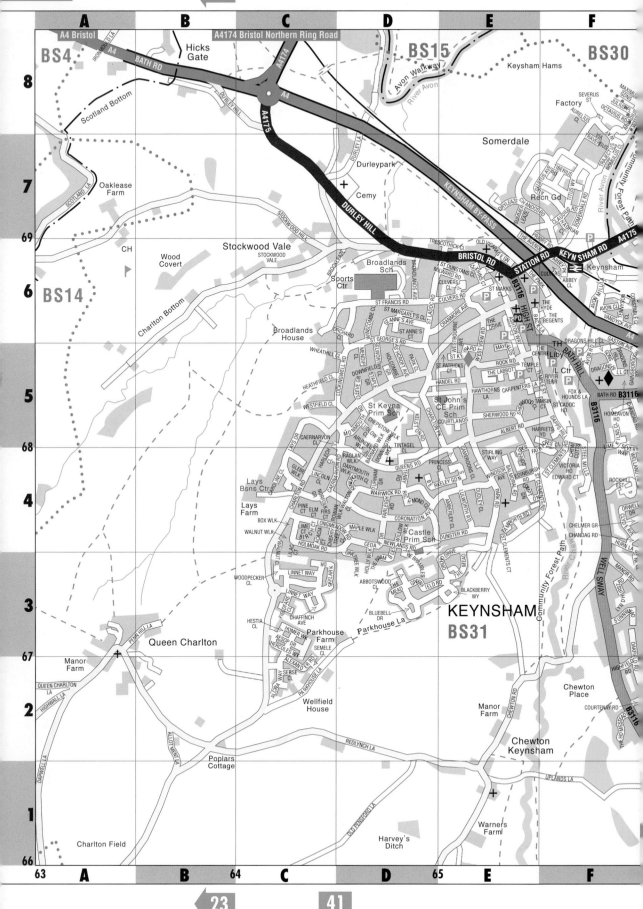

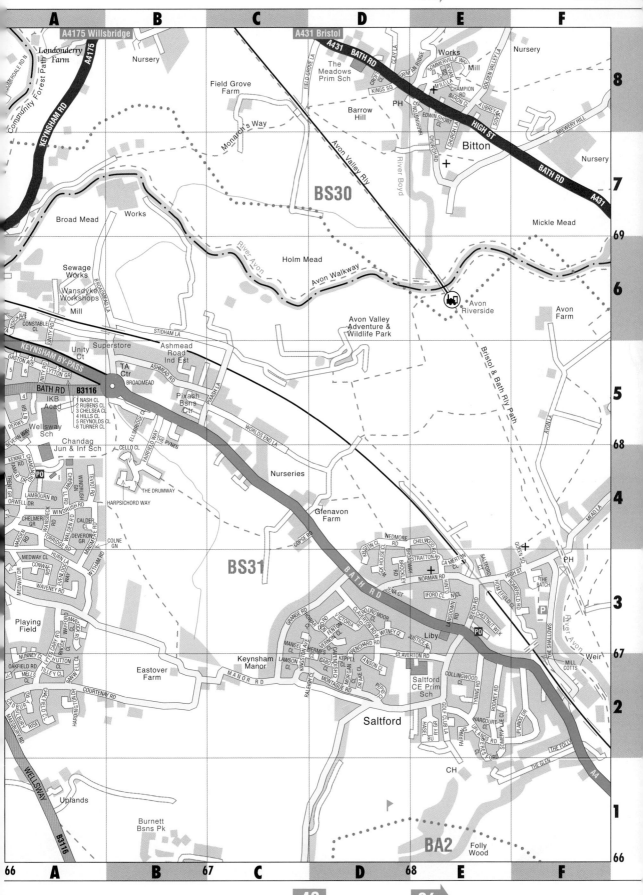

A B C D E F

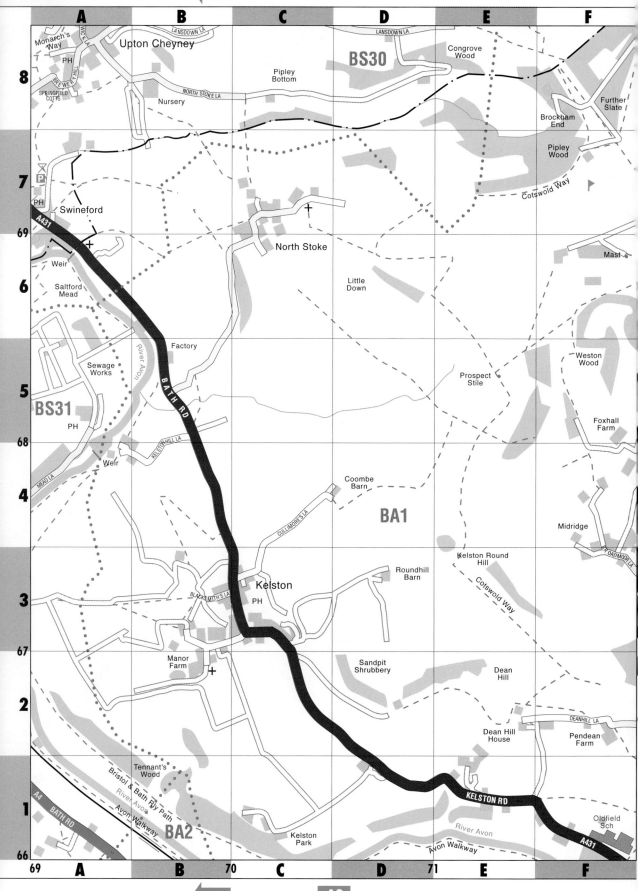

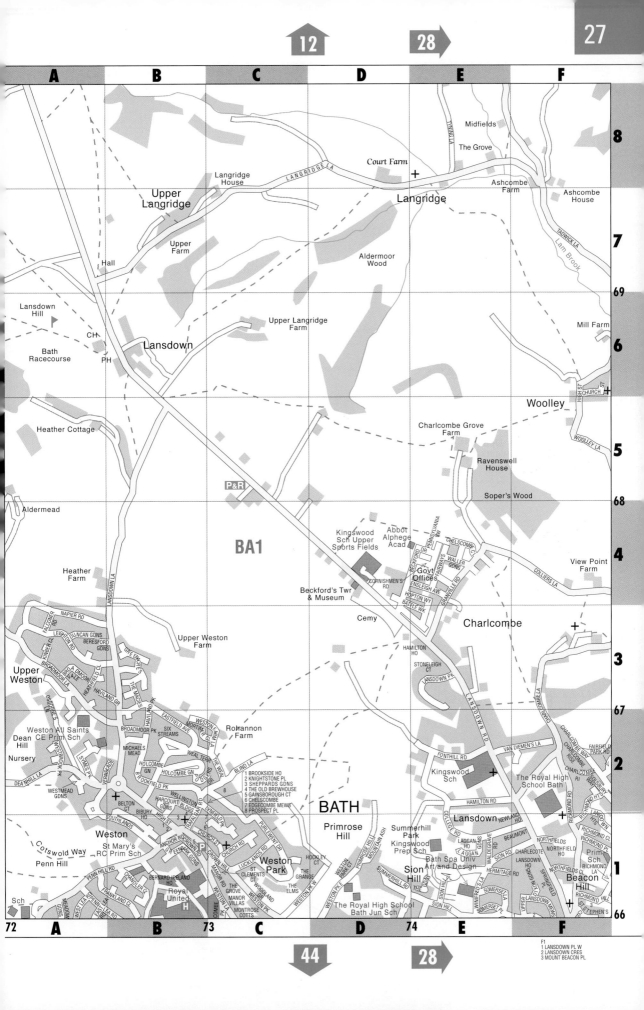

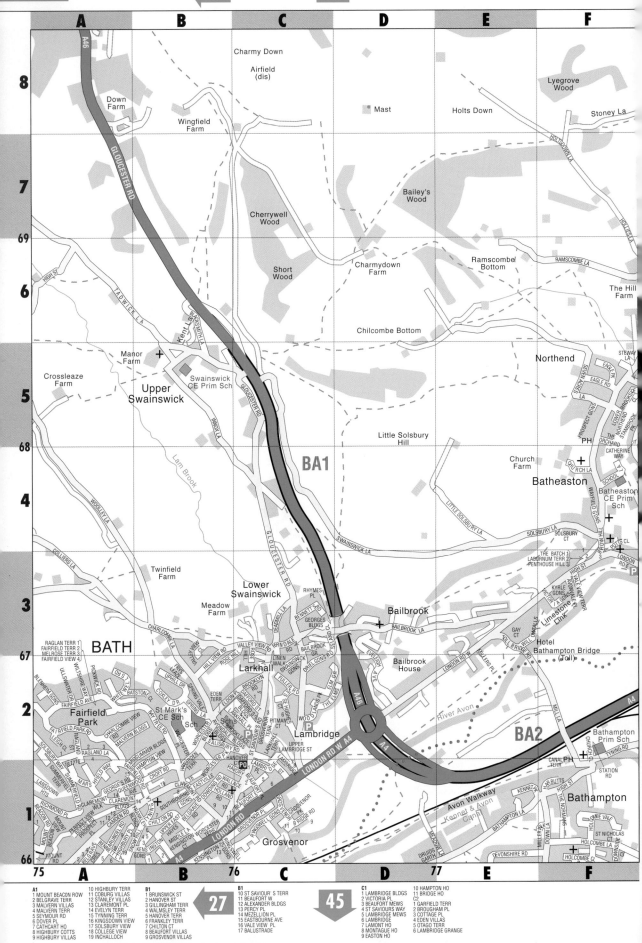

A1
1 MOUNT BEACON ROW
2 BELGRAVE TERR
3 MALVERN VILLAS
4 MALVERN TERR
5 SEYMOUR RD
6 DOVER PL
7 CATHCART HO
8 HIGHBURY COTTS
9 HIGHBURY VILLAS
10 HIGHBURY TERR
11 COBURG VILLAS
12 STANLEY VILLAS
13 CLAREMONT PL
14 EVELYN TERR
15 TYNNING TERR
16 KINGSDOWN VIEW
17 SOLSBURY VIEW
18 COLLEGE VIEW
19 INCHALLOCH

B1
1 BRUNSWICK ST
2 HANOVER ST
3 GILLINGHAM TERR
4 WALMSLEY TERR
5 HANOVER TERR
6 FRANKLEY TERR
7 CHILTON CT
8 BEAUFORT VILLAS
9 GROSVENOR VILLAS

B1
10 ST SAVIOUR'S TERR
11 BEAUFORT W
12 ALEXANDER BLDGS
13 PERCY PL
14 MEZELLION PL
15 EASTBOURNE AVE
16 VALE VIEW PL
17 BALUSTRADE

C1
1 LAMBRIDGE BLDGS
2 VICTORIA PL
3 BEAUFORT MEWS
4 ST SAVIOURS WAY
5 LAMBRIDGE MEWS
6 LAMBRIDGE ST
7 LAMONT HO
8 MONTAGUE HO
9 EASTON HO
10 HAMPTON HO
11 BRIDGE HO

C2
1 GARFIELD TERR
2 BROUGHAM PL
3 COTTAGE PL
4 EDEN VILLAS
5 OTAGO TERR
6 LAMBRIDGE GRANGE

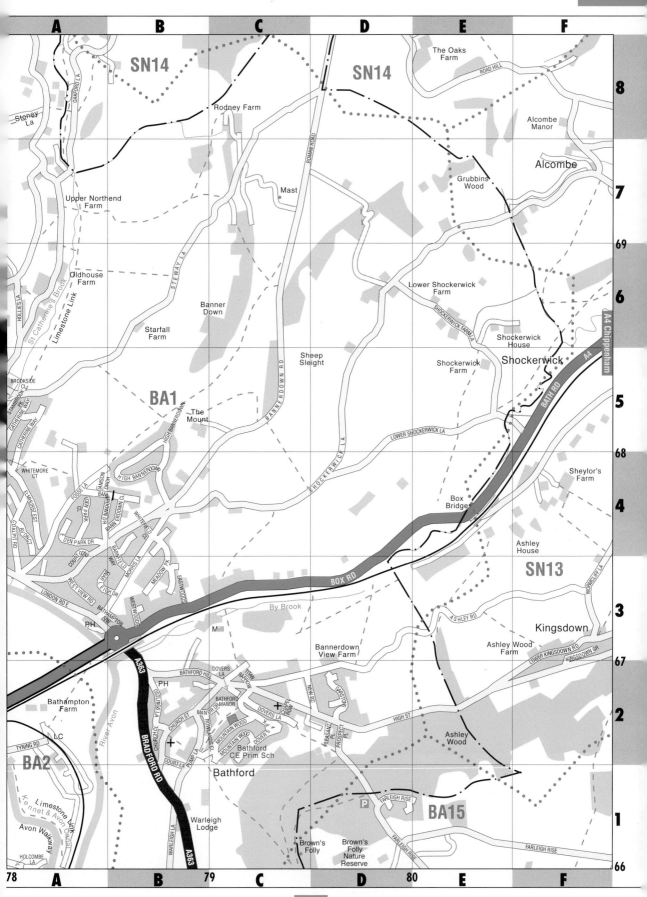

BS22

8

7

9

65

BS22

Swallow Cliff

Middle Hope (Nature Reserve)

66

32

E

F

33

6

Sand Bay

5

64

4

3

BEACH RD

P

63

BS22

Bathing Cove

KEWSTOKE RD

Worlebury Hill

Mast

2

Spring Cove

CAPRI VILLAS

Weston Woods

Wr Twr

WORLEBURY HILL RD

Birnbeck Island

Pier

FORELANDS 1 CAMP RD N 2

Worlebury

1 GLENWOOD MANS
2 SHRUBBERY WLK W
3 STUART HO
4 COACH HOUSE MEWS
5 KNIGHTSTONE CT
6 WOODLANDS

BS23

IRB Sta

1 KINGSHOLME CT
2 EASTERN HO
3 SYCAMORES

HIGHCROFT

EASTCOMBE GDNS

THE RETREAT

1

TRINITY RD

SOUTH RD

ST MATTHEW'S CL

GROVE PARK RD

CECIL RD

ALBANY

EASTFIELD PK

EASTCOMBE RD

Anchor Head

ATLANTIC RD

KNIGHTSTONE CT

9

ATLANTIC VIEW CT

SHRUBBERY AVE

ER'S AVE

GROVE PARK

QUEEN'S RD

ALL SAINTS RD

TICHFIELD RD

BRISTOL ROAD LOWER

SEDGEMOOR RD

1

ATLANTIC RD S

11

SHRUBBERY RD

ST JOHN'S CL

TREWARTHA PK

DUNCERY

LB Sta

MANILLA CRES

HIGHBURY PAR

SHRU

VICTORIA PK

COOMBE RD

LANGEMANN

ARUNDELL

ST JOSEPH'S RD

Cerny

MONTPELIER E

62

UPPER CHURCH RD

C1
1 PEMBROKE HO
2 RAINHAM CT
3 LEAWOOD CT
4 TRINITY PL
5 MORETON MANS
6 GOSFORD MANS
7 FRANKFORD MANS
8 HAMILTON RD
9 MAPLE CT
10 ROCKHALL HO

11 SHRUBBERY TERR
12 ROCKLEAZE MANS
13 PARAGON CT
14 ROZEL HO
15 HIGHBURY CT
16 VILLA ROSA
17 BADMINTON CT
18 CAIRO CT
19 GLENTWORTH CT
20 RAGLAN PL
21 MANILLA CRES

48

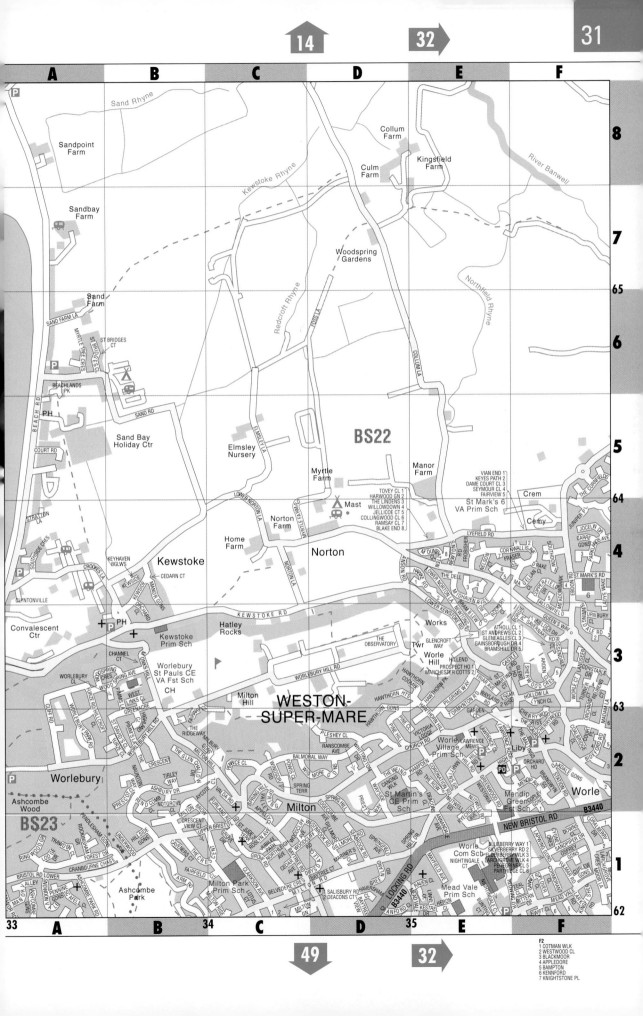

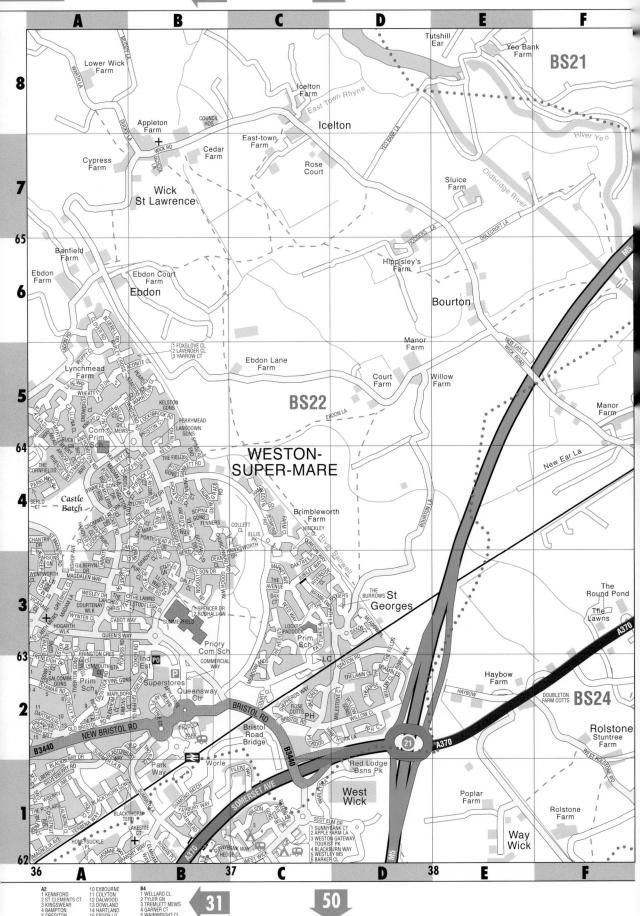

A2
1 KENNFORD
2 ST CLEMENTS CT
3 KINGSWEAR
4 BAMPTON
5 CREDITON
6 FENITON
7 INSTOW
8 IVYBRIDGE
9 HONITON
10 EXBOURNE
11 COLYTON
12 DALWOOD
13 DOWLAND
14 HARTLAND
15 EBDEN LO

B4
1 WELLARD CL
2 TYLER GN
3 TREMLETT MEWS
4 GARNER CT
5 WAINWRIGHT CL
6 EMLYN CL
7 THE SAFFRONS

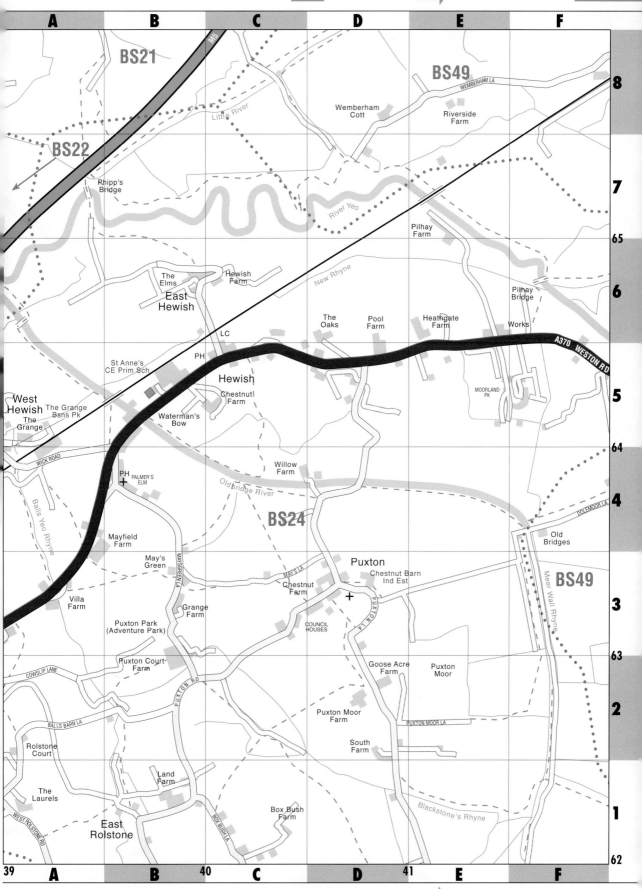

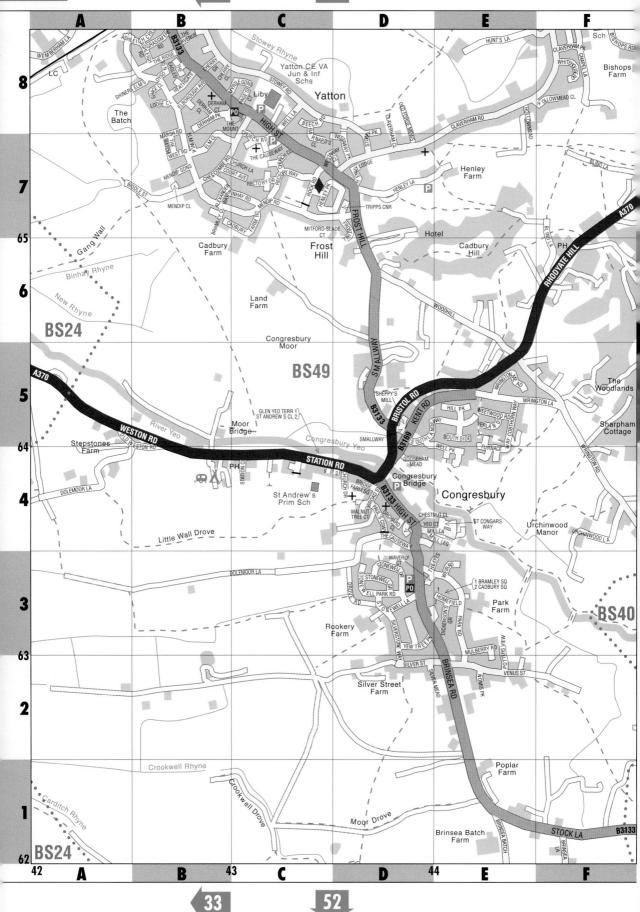

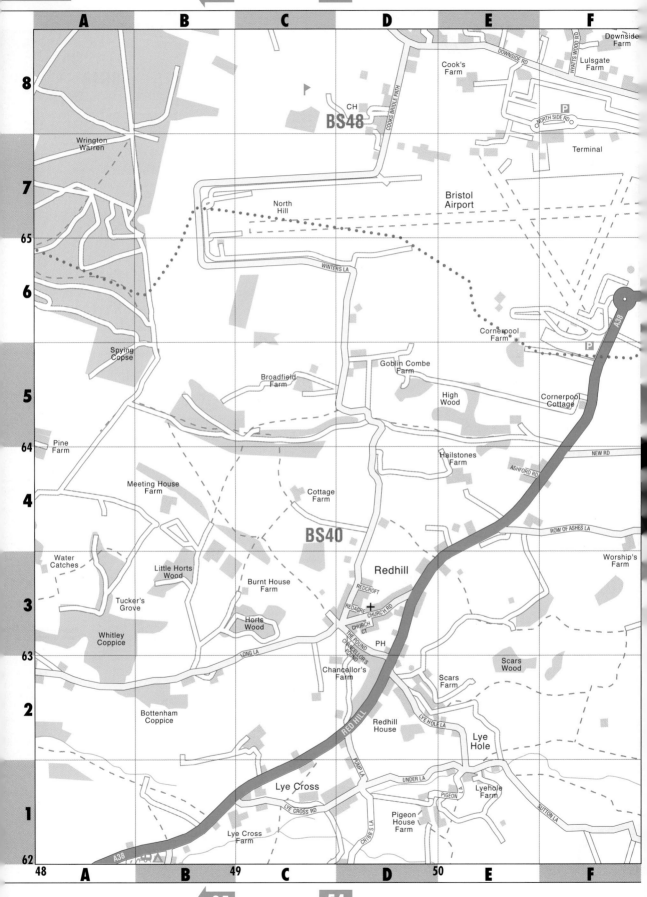

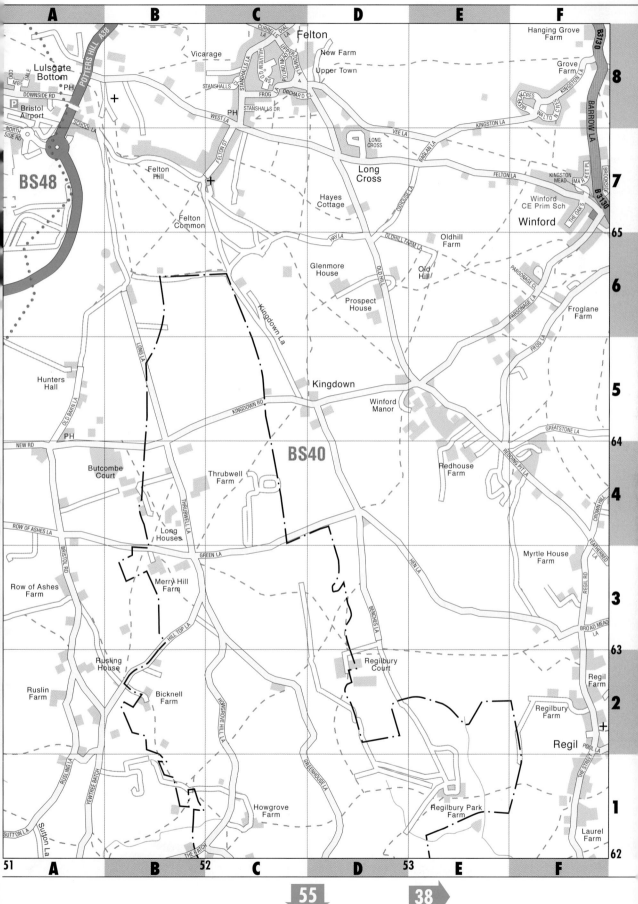

A B C D E F

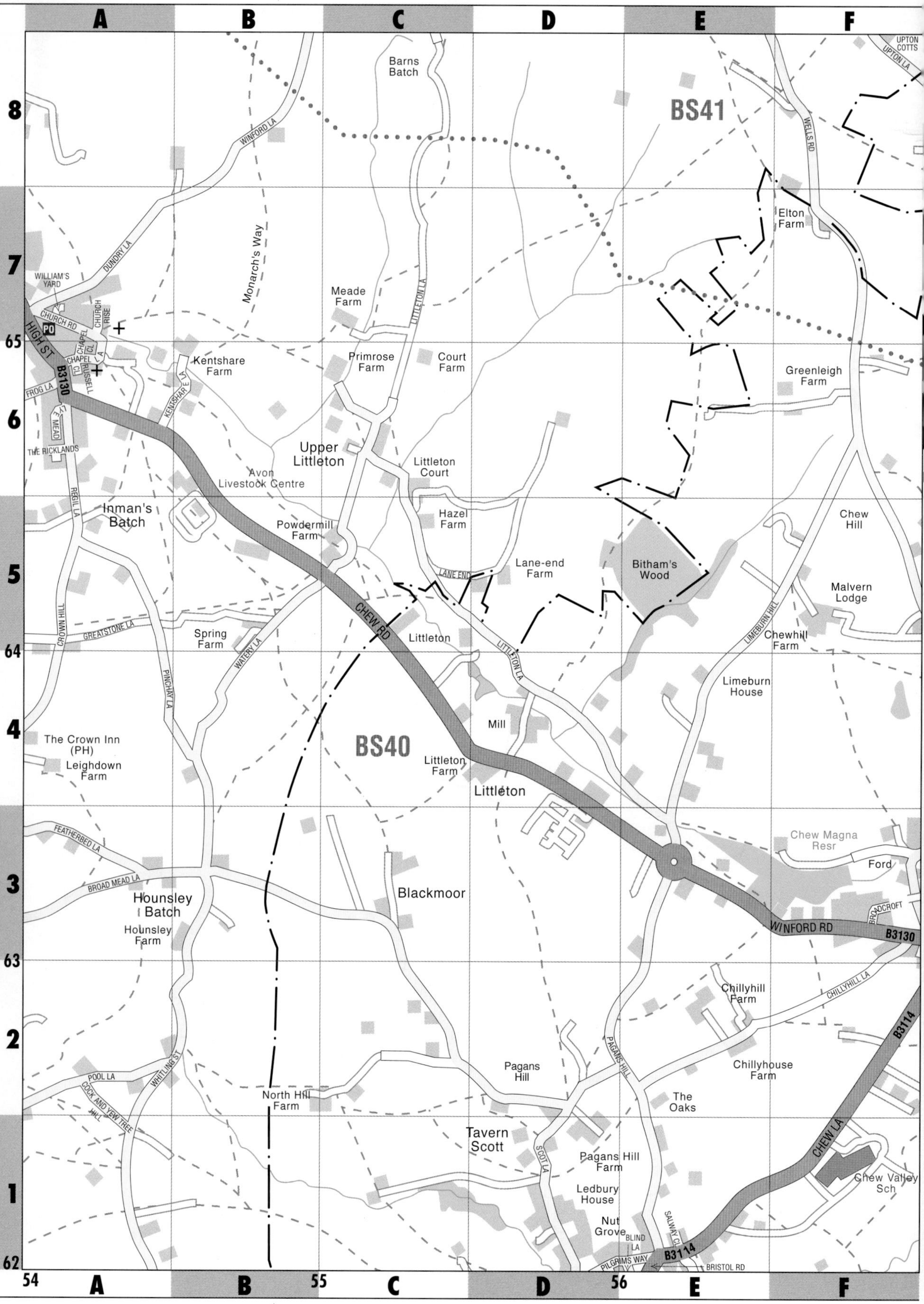

8

BS41

UPTON COTTS
UPTON LA

Barns
Batch

WINFORD LA

Monarch's Way

LITTLETON LA

WELLS RD

Elton
Farm

7

WILLIAM'S
YARD

DUNDRY LA

CHURCH RD

CHURCH RISE

Meade
Farm

65

HIGH ST

PO

CHAPEL CL

CHAPEL LA

RUSSELL

Kentshare
Farm

KENTSHARE LA

Primrose
Farm

Court
Farm

Greenleigh
Farm

6

B3130

FROG LA

A1

MEAD

REGIL LA

THE RICKLANDS

Upper
Littleton

Avon
Livestock Centre

Littleton
Court

Hazel
Farm

Chew
Hill

Inman's
Batch

Powdermill
Farm

Lane-end
Farm

Bitham's
Wood

Malvern
Lodge

LIMEBURN HILL

Chewhill
Farm

5

CROWN HILL

GREATSTONE LA

Spring
Farm

WATERY LA

CHEW RD

LANE END

Littleton

LITTLETON LA

64

PINCHAY LA

Littleton
Farm

Mill

Limeburn
House

4

The Crown Inn
(PH)

Leighdown
Farm

BS40

Littleton

Chew Magna
Resr

Ford

FEATHERBED LA

3

BROAD MEAD LA

Hounsley
Batch

Blackmoor

WINFORD RD

B3130

BROADCROFT

63

Hounsley
Farm

Chillyhill
Farm

CHILLYHILL LA

B3114

2

POOL LA

WHITLONG ST

North Hill
Farm

Pagans
Hill

PAGANS HILL

Chillyhouse
Farm

CHEW LA

COCK AND YEW TREE
HILL

The
Oaks

Tavern
Scott

SCOT LA

Pagans Hill
Farm

Chew Valley
Sch

1

Ledbury
House

Nut
Grove

BLIND
LA

SALWAY CL

B3114

PILGRIMS WAY

BRISTOL RD

62

54 A B 55 C D 56 E F

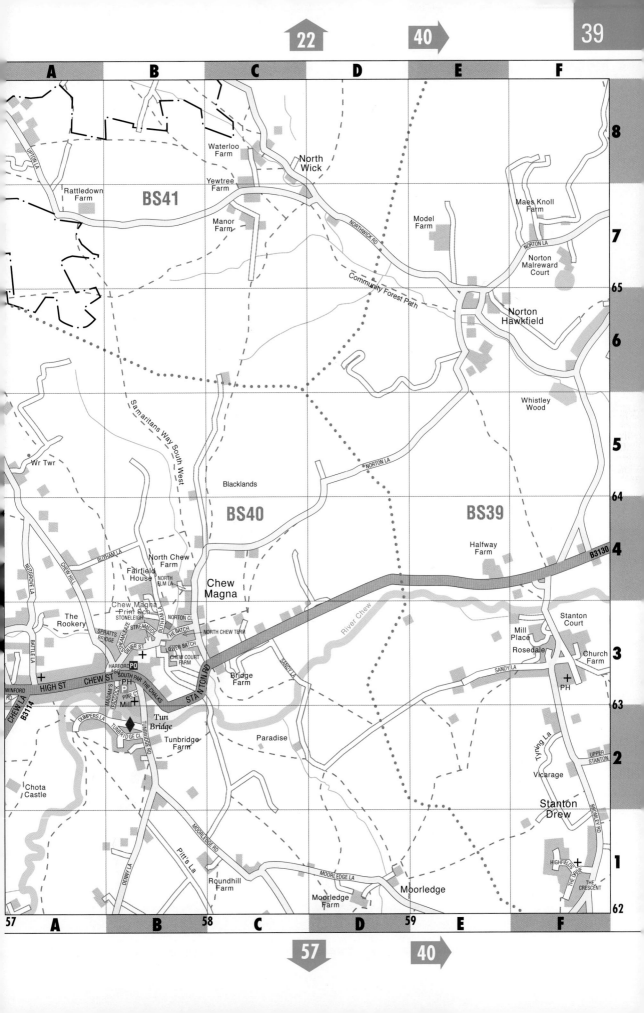

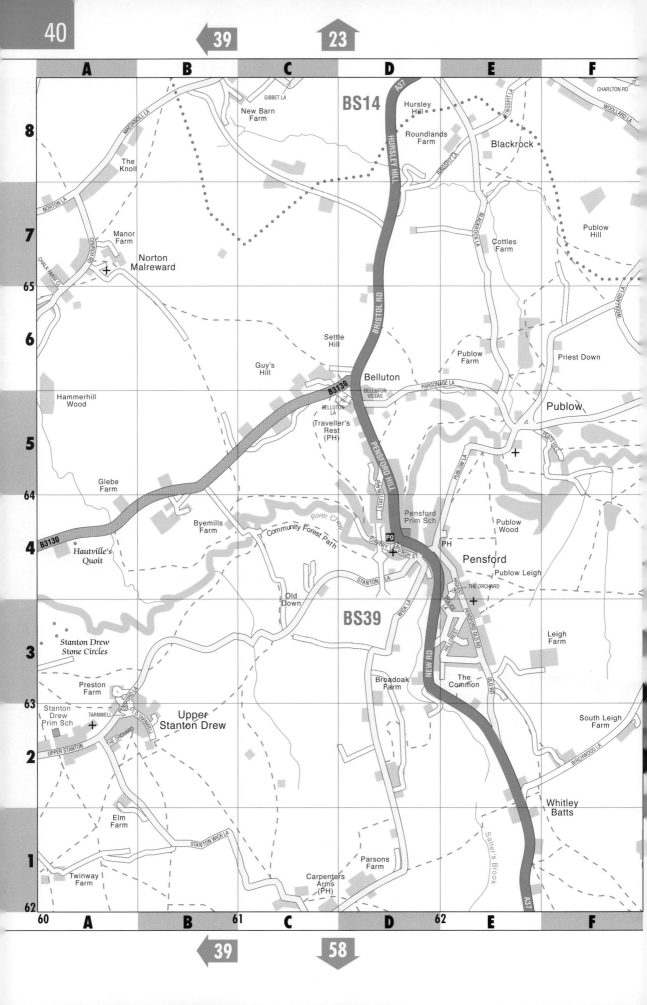

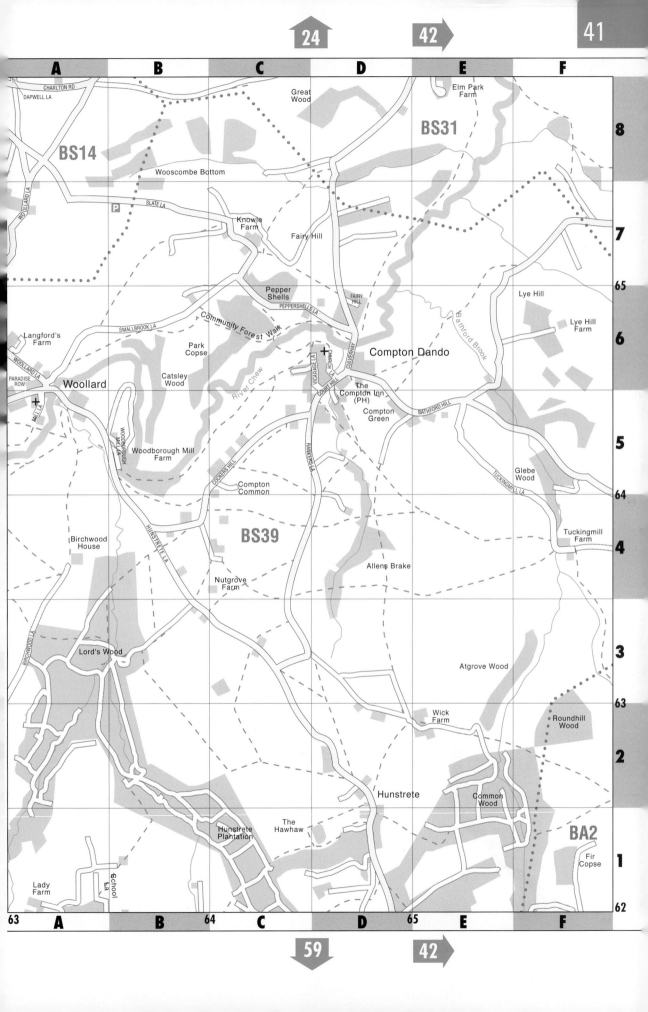

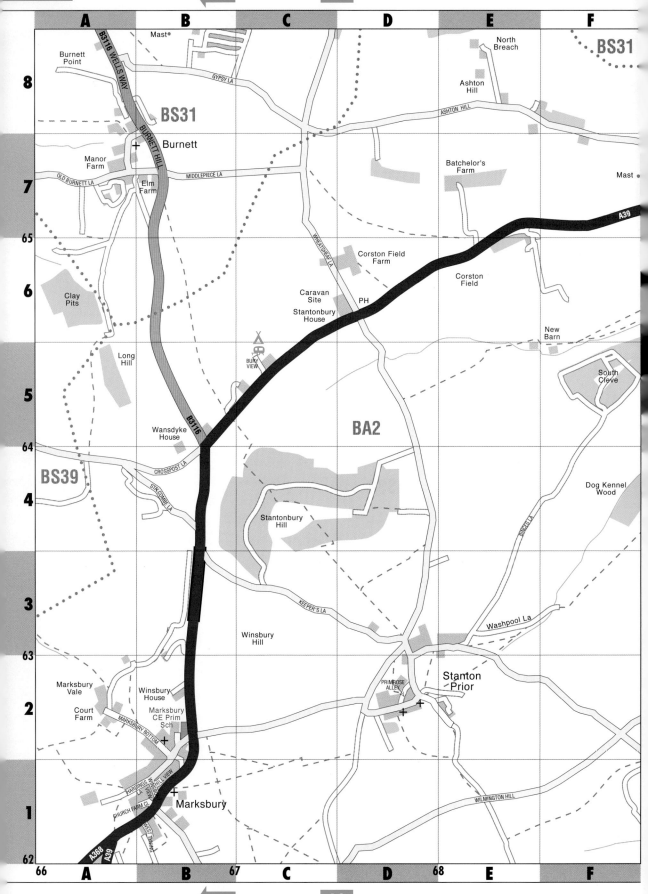

A B C D E F

BS31

8

BS31

Burnett Point

Mast

GYPSY LA

B3116 WELLS WAY

North Breach

Ashton Hill

7

Burnett

Manor Farm

Elm Farm

OLD BURNETT LA

MIDDLEPIECE LA

BURNETT HILL

Batchelor's Farm

ASHTON HILL

Mast

A39

65

WHEATSHEAF LA

Corston Field Farm

6

Clay Pits

Caravan Site

Stantonbury House

PH

Corston Field

New Barn

South Cleve

Long Hill

BURY VIEW

5

BA2

Dog Kennel Wood

64

Wansdyke House

B3116

CROSSPOST LA

STANCOMBE LA

BS39

4

Stantonbury Hill

BINCKS LA

3

Winsbury Hill

KEEPER'S LA

Washpool La

63

Marksbury Vale

Winsbury House

PRIMROSE ALLEY

Stanton Prior

2

Court Farm

Marksbury CE Prim Sch

MARKSBURY BOTTOM

1

HARDINGS
WINSHILL VIEW
CHURCH FARM CL
WEST HANG

Marksbury

WILMINGTON HILL

A368
A39

62

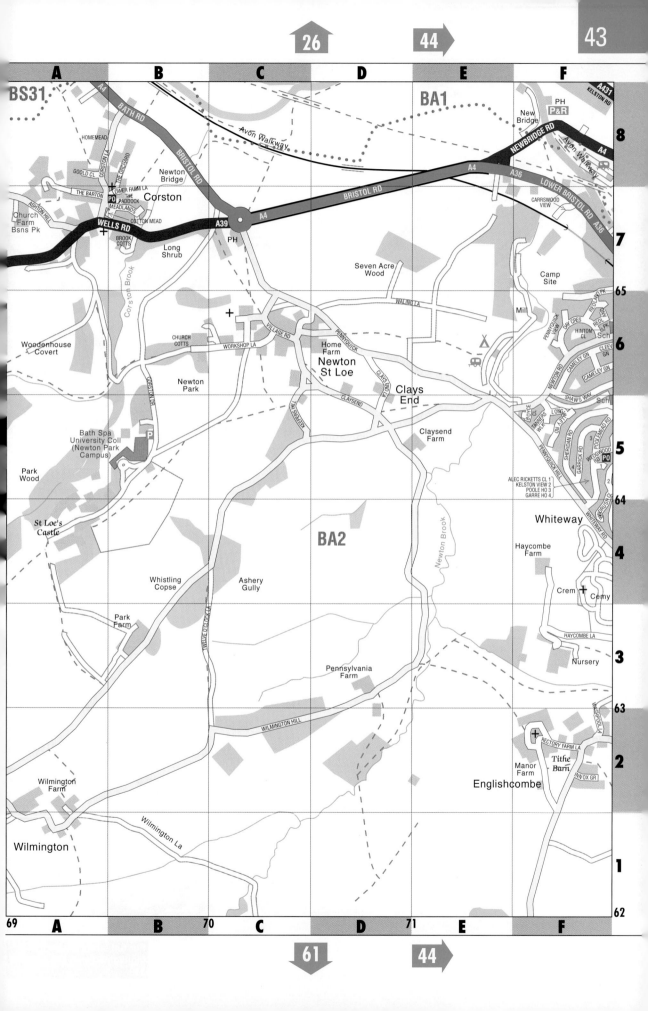

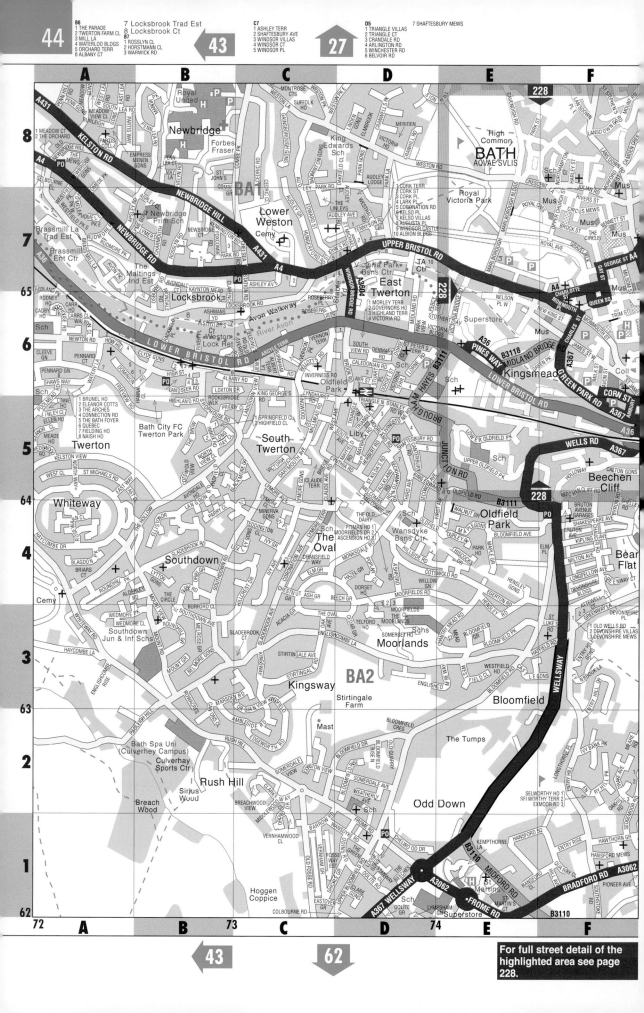

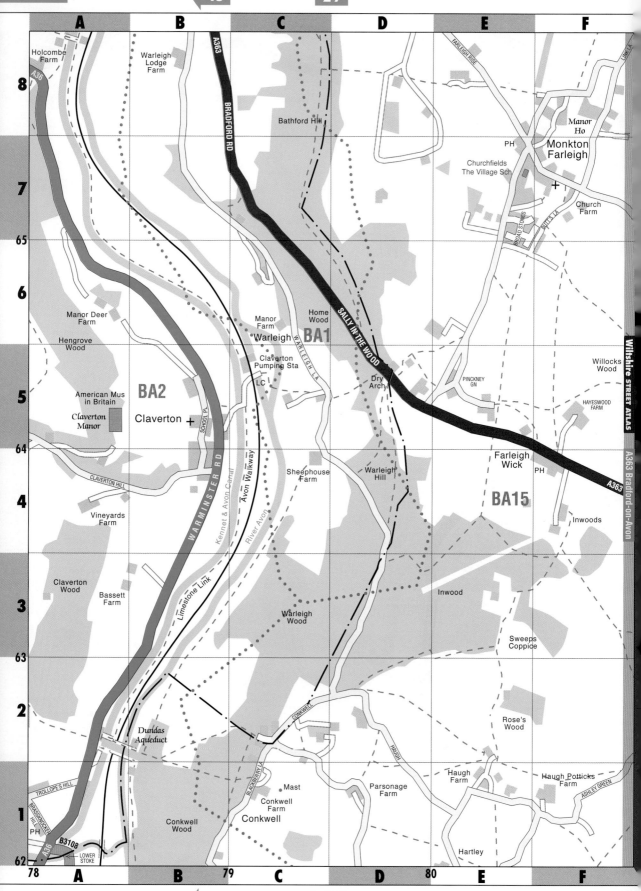

A B C D E F

8

7

65

6

5

64

4

3

63

2

1

62

78 A B 79 C D 80 E F

Holcombe Farm
Warleigh Lodge Farm
BRADFORD RD
A363
Bathford Hill
FARLEIGH RISE
LINK LA
Manor Ho
PH
Monkton Farleigh
Churchfields The Village Sch
Church Farm
BROAD STONES
BUTTS LA
Manor Deer Farm
Hengrove Wood
Manor Farm
Home Wood
Warleigh
BA1
SALLY IN THE WOOD
WARLEIGH LA
Willocks Wood
American Mus in Britain
BA2
Claverton Pumping Sta
LC
Dry Arch
PINCKNEY GN
HAYESWOOD FARM
Claverton Manor
Claverton
SCHOOL PL
WARMINSTER RD
Kennet & Avon Canal
Avon Walkway
River Avon
Sheephouse Farm
Warleigh Hill
Farleigh Wick
PH
CLAVERTON HILL
BA15
Vineyards Farm
Inwoods
Claverton Wood
Bassett Farm
Limestone Link
Warleigh Wood
Inwood
Sweeps Coppice
Dundas Aqueduct
CONKWELL
Rose's Wood
HAUGH
TROLLOPE'S HILL
BRASSKNOCKER HILL
A36
PH
B3108
LOWER STOKE
BLACKBERRY LA
Mast
Conkwell Farm
Conkwell
Conkwell Wood
Parsonage Farm
Haugh Farm
Haugh Potticks Farm
ASHLEY GREEN
Hartley

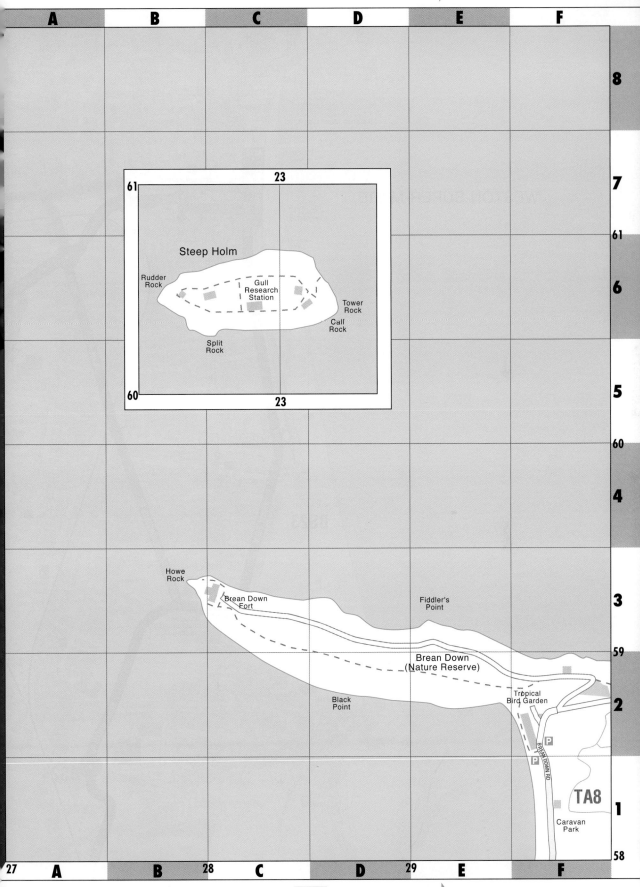

A   B   C   D   E   F

8

7

61

6

5

60

4

3

59

2

1

58

Steep Holm

23

61

60

23

Rudder
Rock

Gull
Research
Station

Tower
Rock

Call
Rock

Split
Rock

Howe
Rock

Brean Down
Fort

Fiddler's
Point

Brean Down
(Nature Reserve)

Tropical
Bird Garden

Black
Point

BREAN DOWN RD

P

P

TA8

Caravan
Park

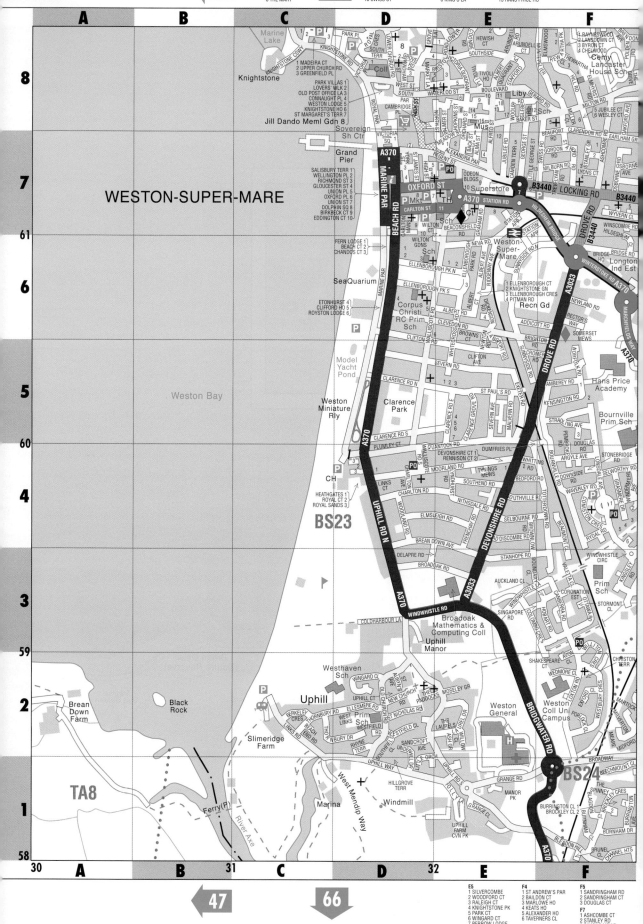

E7
1 ORCHARD PL
2 NORTH LA
3 CROSS ST
4 ALFRED CT
5 ALEXANDER MEWS
6 THE MART

7 FRANCIS FOX RD
8 STATION LODGE
9 HILDESHIEM CT
10 THE CENTRE
11 WALLISCOTE GROVE RD
12 TRAFALGAR CT
13 SWISS CT

E8
1 EDINBURGH PL
2 LANDEMANN CIRCUS
3 LONGTON GROVE RD
4 WORTHY PL
5 WORTHY LA
6 KING'S LA

7 PALMER ROW
8 JASMINE CT
9 PROSPECT PL
10 SAFFRON PL
11 HENRY BUTT HO
12 CHRIST CHURCH PATH S
13 HANS PRICE HO

14 MEADOW VILLAS
15 BURLINGTON ST
16 POPLAR PL
17 PAYNES HO
18 HANS PRICE CL

E5
1 SILVERCOMBE
2 WOODFORD CT
3 RALEIGH CT
4 KNIGHTSTONE PK
5 PARK CT
6 WINGARD CT
7 BERROW LODGE

F4
1 ST ANDREW'S PAR
2 BALLDON CT
3 MARLOWE HO
4 KEATS HO
5 ALEXANDER HO
6 TAVERNERS CL

F5
1 SANDRINGHAM RD
2 SANDRINGHAM CT
3 DOUGLAS CT

F7
1 ASHCOMBE CT
2 STANLEY RD
3 SIMONS MEWS
4 ASHCOMBE PL
5 WYVERN MEWS

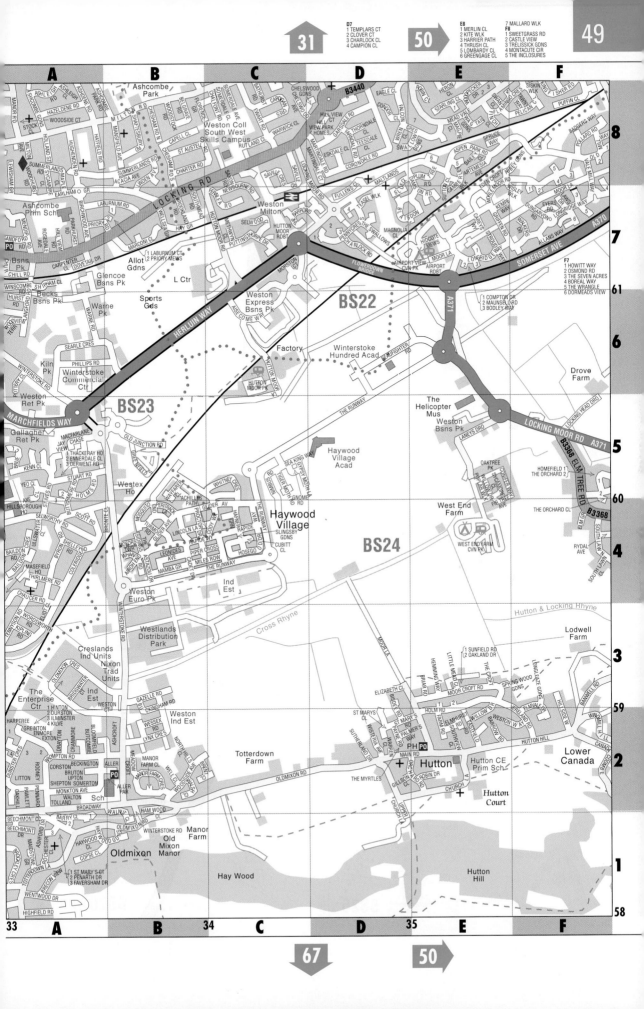

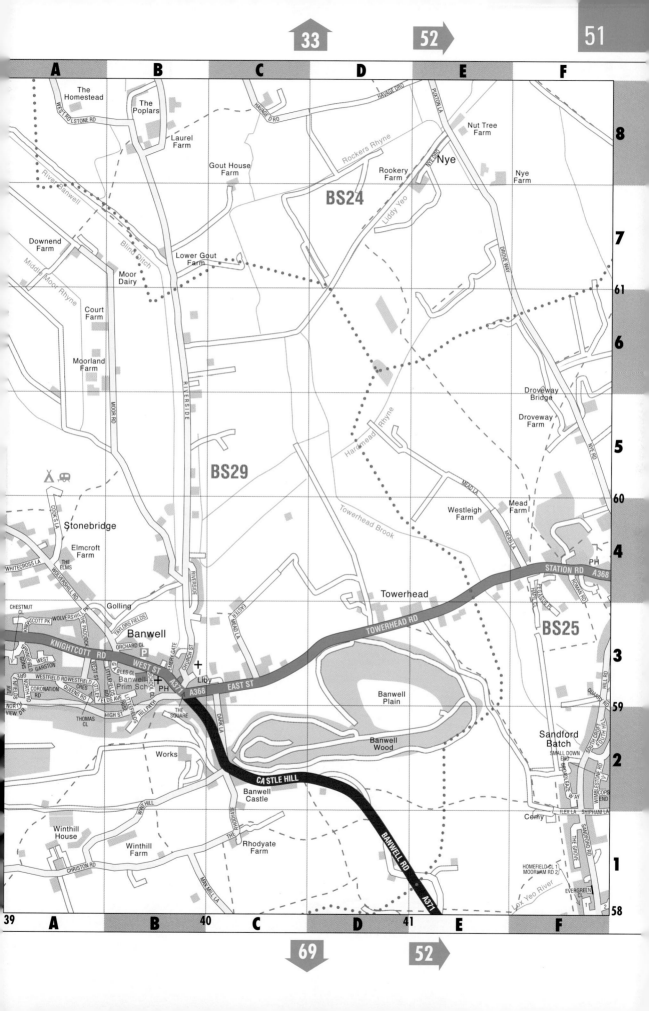

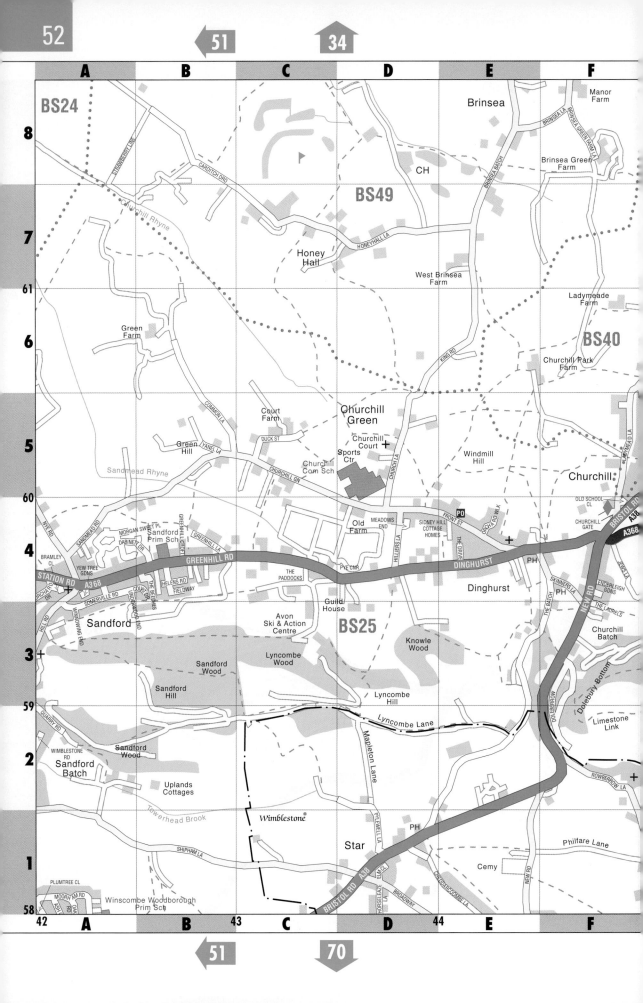

A B C D E F

BS24

8

Manor Farm

Brinsea

BRINSEA LA

BRINSEA GREEN FARM LA

CARDITCH DRO

STRAWBERRY LINE

CH

Brinsea Green Farm

BS49

7

Churchill Rhyne

HONEYHALL LA

BRINSEA BATCH

61

Honey Hall

West Brinsea Farm

Ladymeade Farm

6

Green Farm

KING RD

BS40

Churchill Park Farm

COMMON LA

Court Farm

Churchill Green

Windmill Hill

Churchill

5

Green Hill

YANEL LA

DUCK ST

Churchill Com Sch

Churchill Court

Sports Ctr

CHURCHILL LA

Sandmead Rhyne

CHURCHILL GN

OLD SCHOOL CL

60

Old Farm

MEADOWS END

Sidney Hill Cottage Homes

FRONT ST

PO

ORCH'A RD WLK

CHURCHILL GATE

BRISTOL RD

A38

NYE RD

MORGAN SWEET PL

Sandford Prim Sch

GREENHILL CROFT

GREENHILL LA

THE DRIVE

HILLIERS LA

A368

4

BRAMLEY CL

YEW TREE GDNS

DABINET DR

SANDMEAD RD

GREENHILL RD

PYE CNR

DINGHURST

PH

NEW RD

LENDERLEIGH GDNS

THE LAURELS

STATION RD

A368

ORCHARD DR

SOMERVILLE RD

HELENS RD

THE BEECHES

FIELDWAY

THE PADDOCKS

Dinghurst

SKINNERS LA

PH

THE BATCH

Churchill Batch

HILL RD

WINDWHISTLE END

COURT DOWN

UNDERWOOD END

Guild House

BS25

Knowle Wood

Doleberry Bottom

Sandford

Avon Ski & Action Centre

Lyncombe Wood

3

Sandford Wood

Sandford Hill

Lyncombe Hill

Limestone Link

59

QUARRY RD

Sandford Wood

Lyncombe Lane

MAPLETON LANE

DOLEBERROW

WIMBLESTONE RD

2

Sandford Batch

Uplands Cottages

ROWBERROW LA

Towerhead Brook

Wimblestone

PYLEWELL LA

PH

Philfare Lane

Star

ELM CL

CHEDDAR COMBE LA

BROADWAY

Cemy

NEW RD

SHIPHAM LA

1

BRISTOL RD A38

HORSELEAZE LA

PLUMTREE CL

MOORHAM RD

OAK RD

ASH RD

Winscombe Woodborough Prim Sch

58

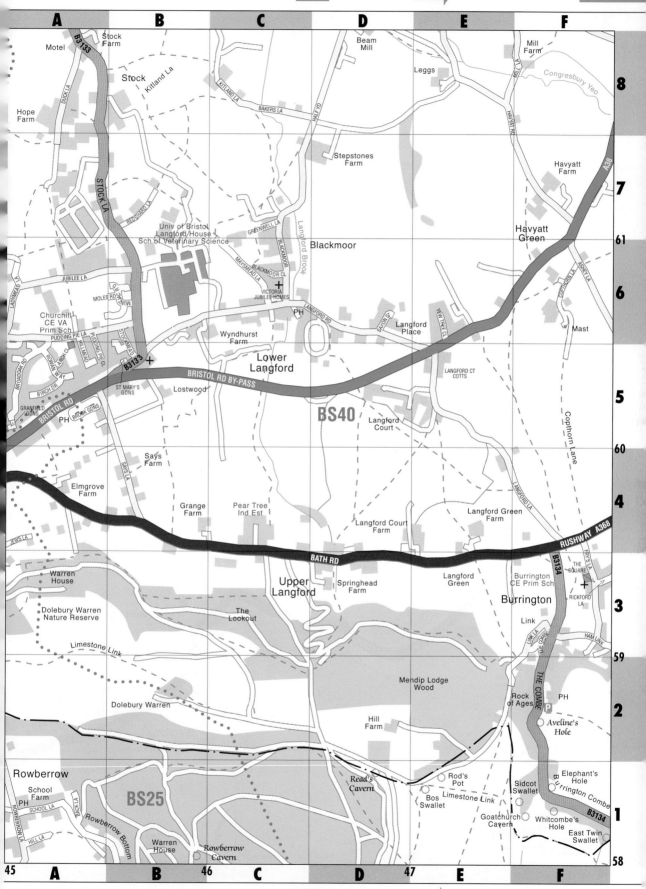

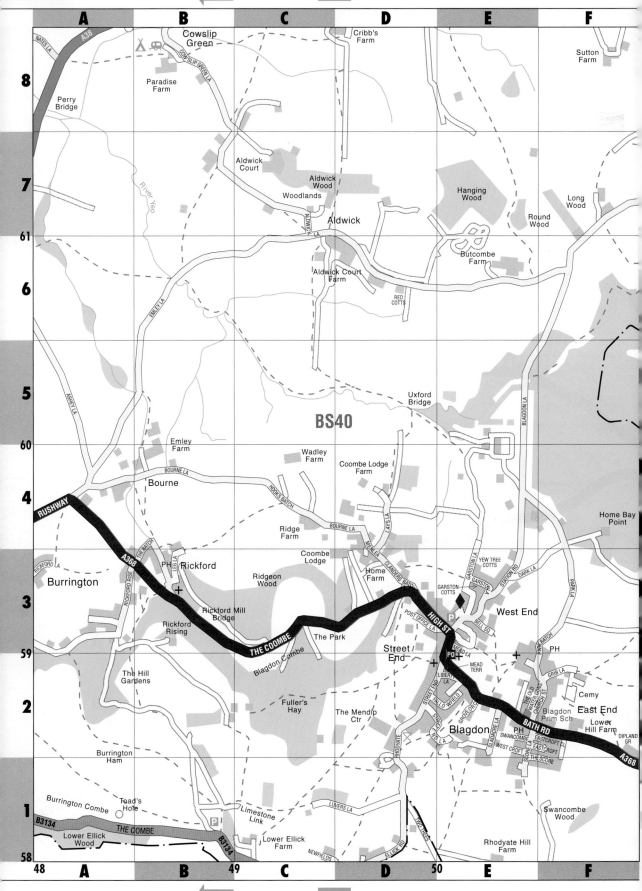

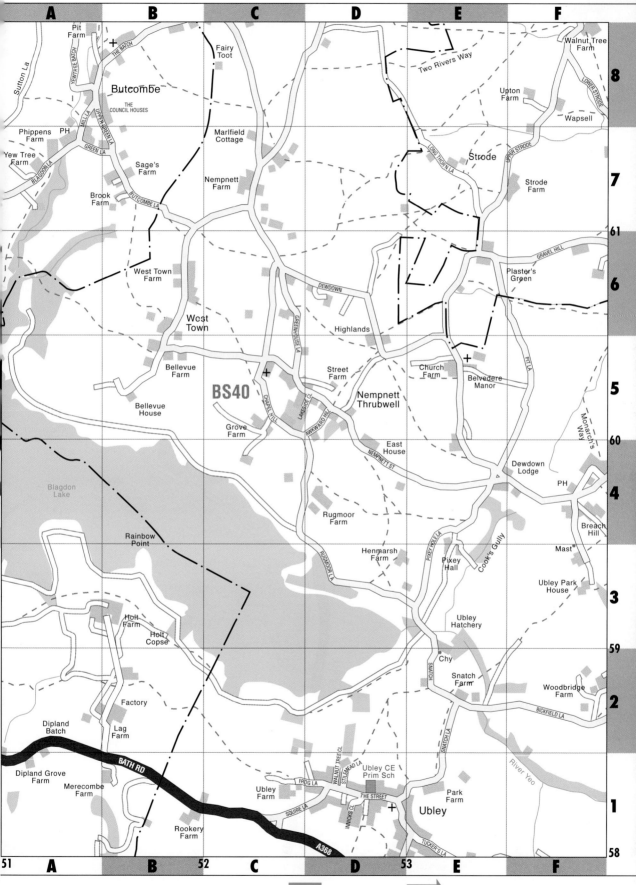

55
38

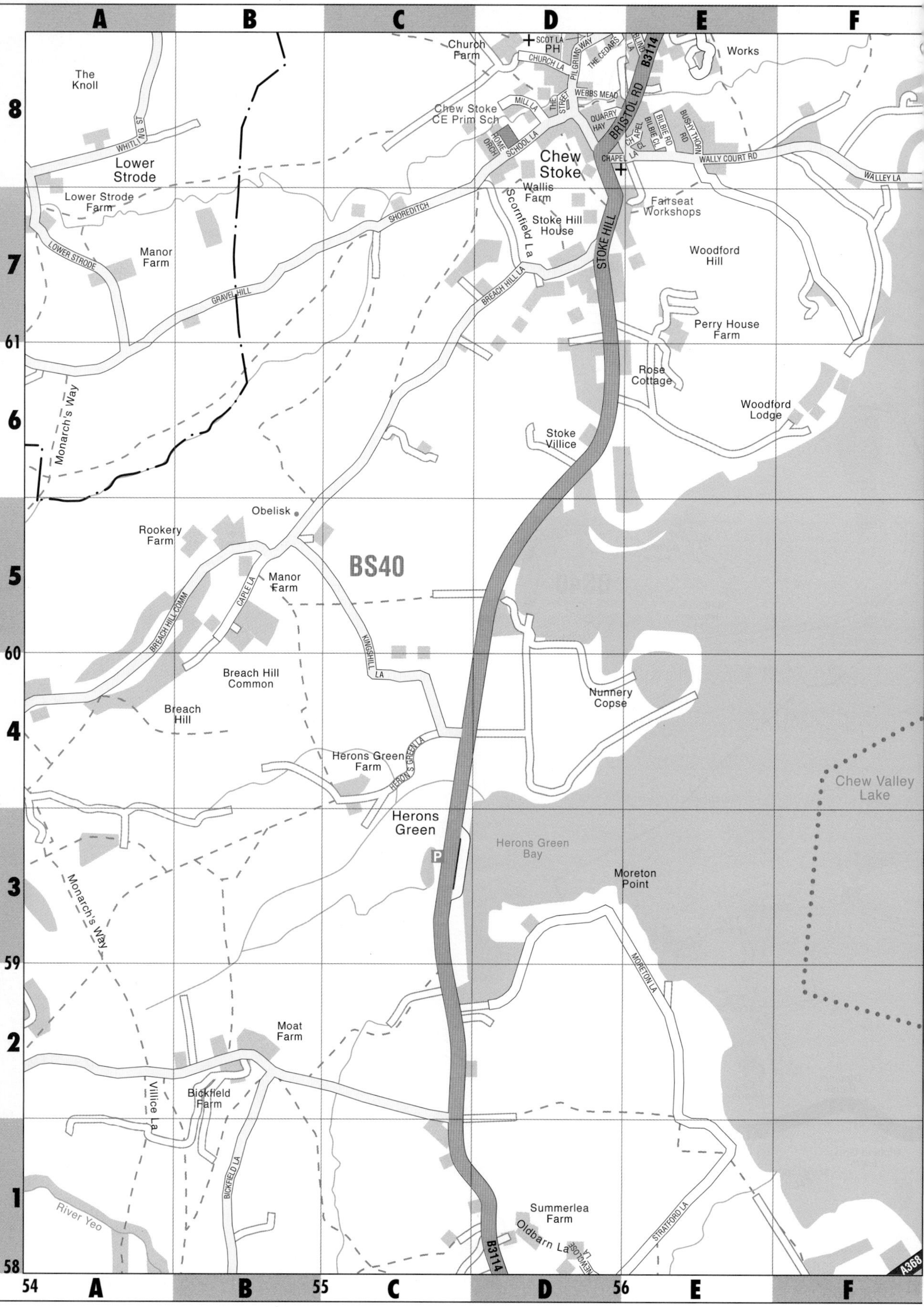

A
B
C
D
E
F
8
7
61
6
5
60
4
3
59
2
1
58
54
55
56
The Knoll
WHITLING ST
Lower Strode
Lower Strode Farm
LOWER STRODE
Manor Farm
GRAVEL HILL
SHOREDITCH
Church Farm
SCOT LA
PH
CHURCH LA
PILGRIMS WAY
THE CEDARS
BLIND LA
B3114
Works
MILL LA
THE STREET
WEBBS MEAD
BRISTOL RD
Chew Stoke CE Prim Sch
HOME ORCH
SCHOOL LA
QUARRY HAY
CHAPEL CL
BILBIE CL
BILBIE RD
BUSHY THORN RD
Chew Stoke
CHAPEL LA
WALLY COURT RD
WALLEY LA
Wallis Farm
Scornfield La
Stoke Hill House
Fairseat Workshops
STOKE HILL
Woodford Hill
BREACH HILL LA
Perry House Farm
Rose Cottage
Woodford Lodge
Monarch's Way
Stoke Villice
Obelisk
Rookery Farm
BS40
Manor Farm
BREACH HILL COMM
CAPLE LA
KINGSHILL LA
Breach Hill Common
Breach Hill
Nunnery Copse
Herons Green Farm
HERON'S GREEN LA
Chew Valley Lake
Herons Green
P
Herons Green Bay
Moreton Point
Monarch's Way
MORETON LA
Moat Farm
Bickfield Farm
Villice La
BICKFIELD LA
River Yeo
Summerlea Farm
Oldbarn La
NEWCLOSE LA
STRATFORD LA
B3114
A368

55
74

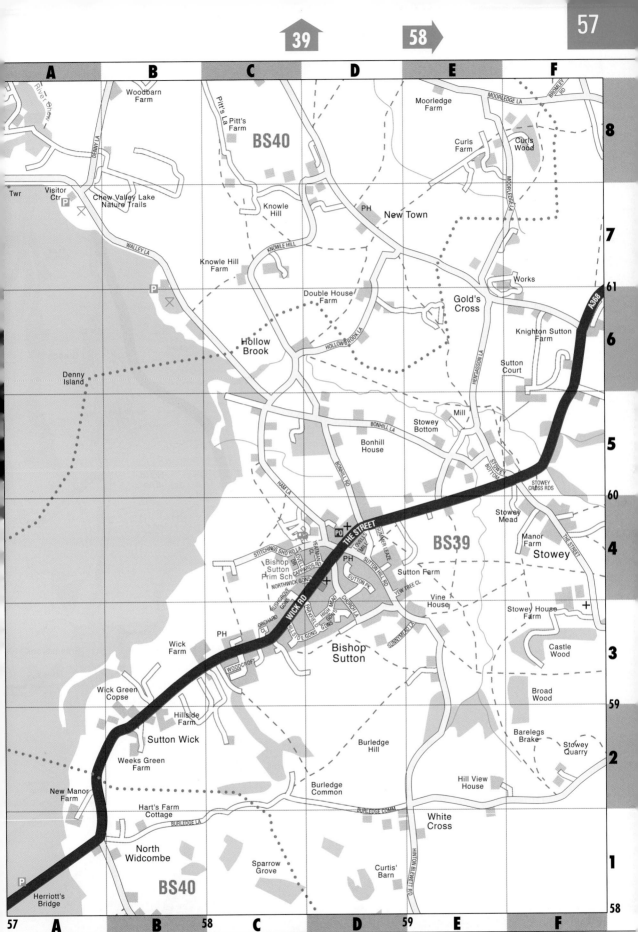

River Chew

Twr

Visitor Ctr

Chew Valley Lake Nature Trails

DENNY LA

Woodbarn Farm

Pitt's La

Pitt's Farm

BS40

Knowle Hill

WALLEY LA

Knowle Hill Farm

Knowle Hill

Double House Farm

Moorledge Farm

MOORLEDGE LA

BROMLEY RD

Curls Farm

Curls Wood

PH

New Town

Gold's Cross

Works

MOORLEDGE LA

A368

61

Hollow Brook

HOLLOW BROOK LA

Denny Island

Knighton Sutton Farm

Sutton Court

HERGASSON LA

6

BONHILL LA

Stowey Bottom

Mill

Bonhill House

BONHILL RD

HAM LA

STOWEY BOTTOM

Stowey Cross Rds

5

60

Stowey Mead

Manor Farm

THE STREET

Stowey

BS39

4

STITCHINGS SHD RD LA

Bishop Sutton Prim Sch

LOVELL DR

CAPPARDS RD

NORTHWICK GDNS

ASHGROVE GDNS

WICK RD

YEATMAN CL

THE STREET

PO

LOVELLS MEAD

SUMMER LEAZE

PH

SUTTON HILL RD

SUTTON PK

Sutton Farm

YEW TREE CL

Vine House

Stowey House Farm

ORCHARD CL

HIGH MEAD

PARKFIELD GDNS

CHURCH LA

SUNNYMEAD LA

PH

Wick Farm

WOODCROFT

HILLSIDE GDNS

Bishop Sutton

Castle Wood

3

Wick Green Copse

Hillside Farm

Sutton Wick

59

Broad Wood

Barelegs Brake

Stowey Quarry

Weeks Green Farm

Burledge Hill

Hill View House

2

New Manor Farm

Hart's Farm Cottage

BURLEDGE LA

Burledge Common

BURLEDGE COMM

White Cross

HINTON BLEWETT RD

P

North Widcombe

BS40

Sparrow Grove

Curtis' Barn

1

Herriott's Bridge

58

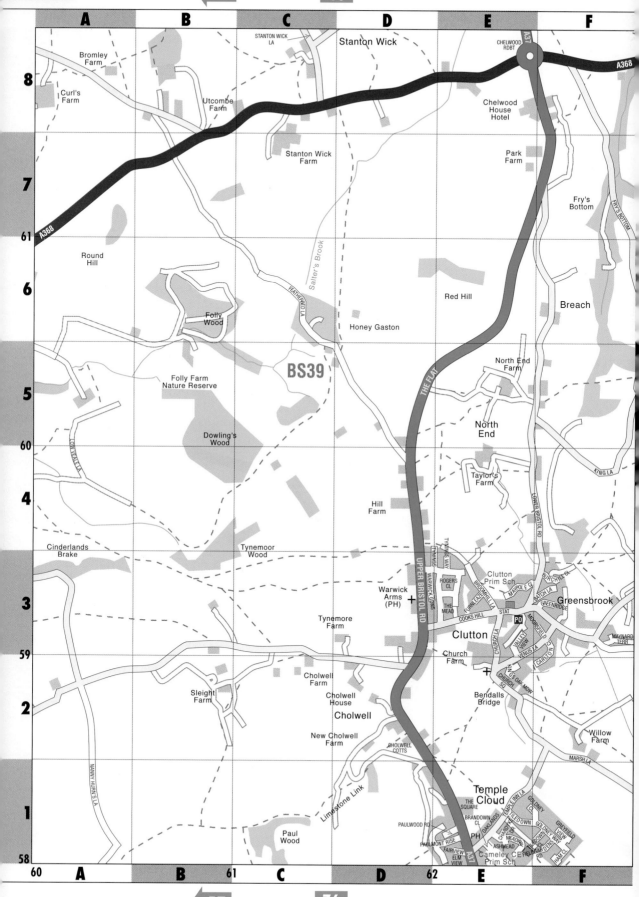

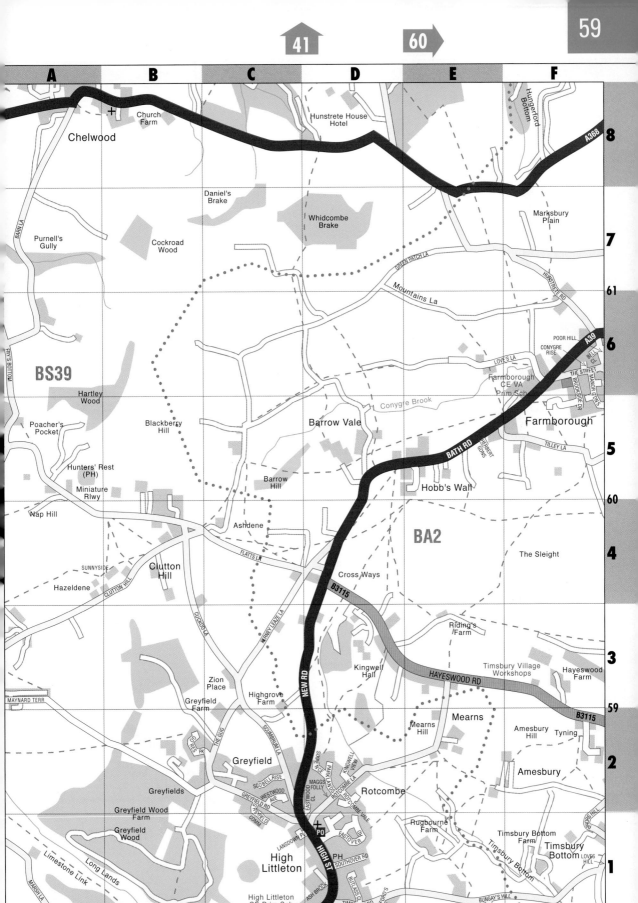

A   B   C   D   E   F

8

Hungerford
Bottom

A368

Chelwood
Church
Farm
Daniel's
Brake
Whidcombe
Brake
Hunstrete House
Hotel
Marksbury
Plain

7

Purnell's
Gully
Cockroad
Wood

61

GREEN PATCH LA

Mountains La

HUNSTRETT RD

6

POOR HILL
CONYGRE
RISE
A39
BELL
CL
THE STREET
BROOKSIDE DR
MANOR CLOSE

BS39

Hartley
Wood

Conygre Brook
LOVE'S LA
Farmborough
CE VA
Prim Sch

Farmborough

Poacher's
Pocket
Blackberry
Hill
Barrow Vale
TILLEY LA

5

Hunters' Rest
(PH)
Miniature
Rlwy
Barrow
Hill
Hobb's Wall
BATH RD
HERBERT
GDNS

60

Nap Hill
Ashdene
FLATTS LA

BA2

The Sleight

4

Clutton
Hill
Hazeldene
SUNNYSIDE
CLUTTON HILL
Cross Ways
B3115
Riding's
Farm
Timsbury Village
Workshops
Hayeswood
Farm

3

CLICKSON LA
Zion
Place
Highgrove
Farm
Kingwell
Hall
HAYESWOOD RD

MAYNARD TERR
Greyfield
Farm
NEW RD
Mearns
Hill
Mearns
Amesbury
Hill
Tyning
B3115

59

THE GUG
SCUMBRUM LA
Greyfield
Amesbury

2

Greyfields
PB RES PK
SCOBELL RISE
GREYFIELD RD
WESTWOOD AVE
MAGGS
FOLLY
EASTWOOD
CL
PARKLANDS RD
KINGWELL VIEW
ROTCOMBE VALE
Rotcombe
Rugbourne
Farm
Timsbury Bottom
Farm
Timsbury
Bottom

Greyfield Wood
Farm
Greyfield
Wood
GREYFIELD
COMN
LANGDOWN PL
PO
EASTOVER
Timsbury Bottom
LOVES
HILL

1

Long Lands
Limestone Link
High
Littleton
HIGH ST
PH
SOUTHOVER RD
BUNGAY'S HILL
BROOM HILL LA

MARSH LA
ASH BROOK
A39
High Littleton
CE Prim Sch
BUTT ASS CL
TIMSBURY RD
GOOSARD LA
LANGFORD'S

58

63   A   64   B   C   65   D   E   F

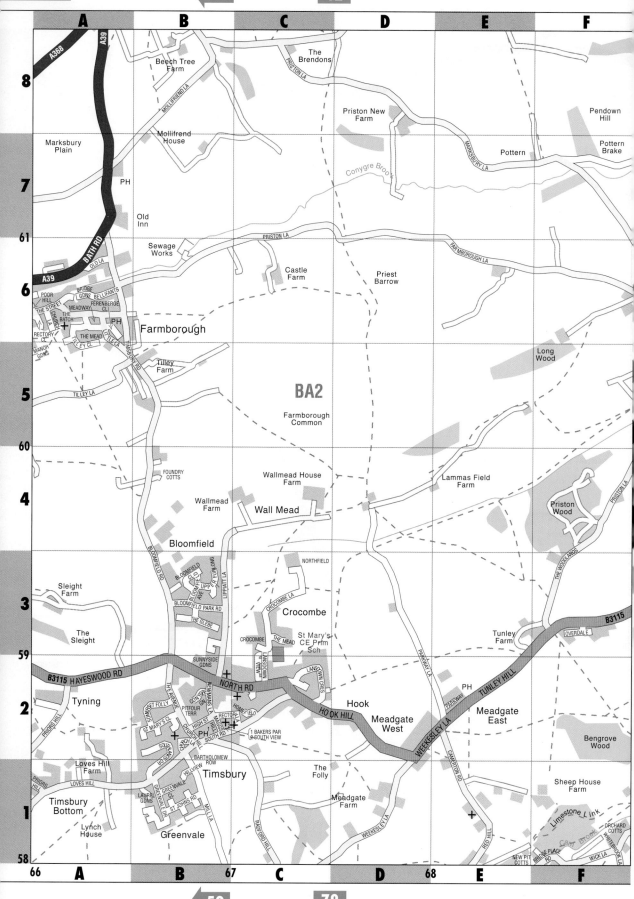

A B C D E F

8

7

61

6

5

60

4

3

59

2

1

58

A368

A39

BATH RD

A39

OLD LA

Marksbury
Plain

Beech Tree
Farm

MOLLIFRIEND LA

Mollifrend
House

The Brendons

PRISTON LA

Priston New
Farm

Pendown
Hill

Pottern

Pottern
Brake

MARKSBURY LA

Conygre Brook

PH

Old
Inn

Sewage
Works

PRISTON LA

Castle
Farm

Priest
Barrow

FARMBOROUGH LA

POOR
HILL

BRIDGE
GDNS

BELLIFANTS

THE STREET

MEADWAY

FERENBERGE
CL

THE
BATCH

CHURCH LA

PH

RECTORY
CL

MANOR
GDNS

THE MEAD

TILLEY CL

LITTLE LA

TIMSBURY RD

Farmborough

Tilley
Farm

Long
Wood

TILLEY LA

BA2

Farmborough
Common

FOUNDRY
COTTS

Wallmead House
Farm

Lammas Field
Farm

Priston
Wood

PRISTON LA

Wallmead
Farm

Wall Mead

BLOOMFIELD RD

Bloomfield

BLOOMFIELD DRIVE

BLOOMFIELD PARK RD

UPPER FURLONG

LIPPIATT LA

NORTHFIELD

THE WOODLANDS

Sleight
Farm

THE GLEBE

CROCOMBE LA

Crocombe

OVERDALE

B3115

The
Sleight

CROCOMBE

THE MEAD

St Mary's
CE Prim
Sch

Tunley
Farm

Tunley Hill

SUNNYSIDE
GDNS

LANSDOWN

59

B3115 HAYESWOOD RD

THE AVENUE

NORTH RD

LANSDOWN CHES

PARKWAY LA

PH

TUNLEY HILL

Tyning

SOMERSET FOLLY

CONYGRE

NEWMANS LA

PITFOUR TERR

HIGH ST

RECTORY LA

HOME FIELD

HOOK HILL

Hook

PARKWAY

Meadgate
East

PRIORS HILL

ST MARY'S CL

SQUARE

CHURCH RD

SOUTH RD

PH

1 BAKERS PAR
2 SOUTH VIEW

Meadgate
West

WEEKESLEY LA

CAMERTON RD

Bengrove
Wood

Loves Hill
Farm

BARTHOLOMEW
ROW

Timsbury

The
Folly

RED HILL

Sheep House
Farm

Limestone Link

PRIORS
HILL

LOVES HILL

HILLVIEW

LAUREL
GDNS

GREENVALE
CL

ST JOHNS RD

MILL LA

Meadgate
Farm

ORCHARD
COTTS

Timsbury
Bottom

Lynch
House

Greenvale

RADFORD HILL

WEEKESLEY LA

NEW PIT
COTTS

BRIDGE PLACE
RD

WHITEOAR LA

Carr Brook

WICK LA

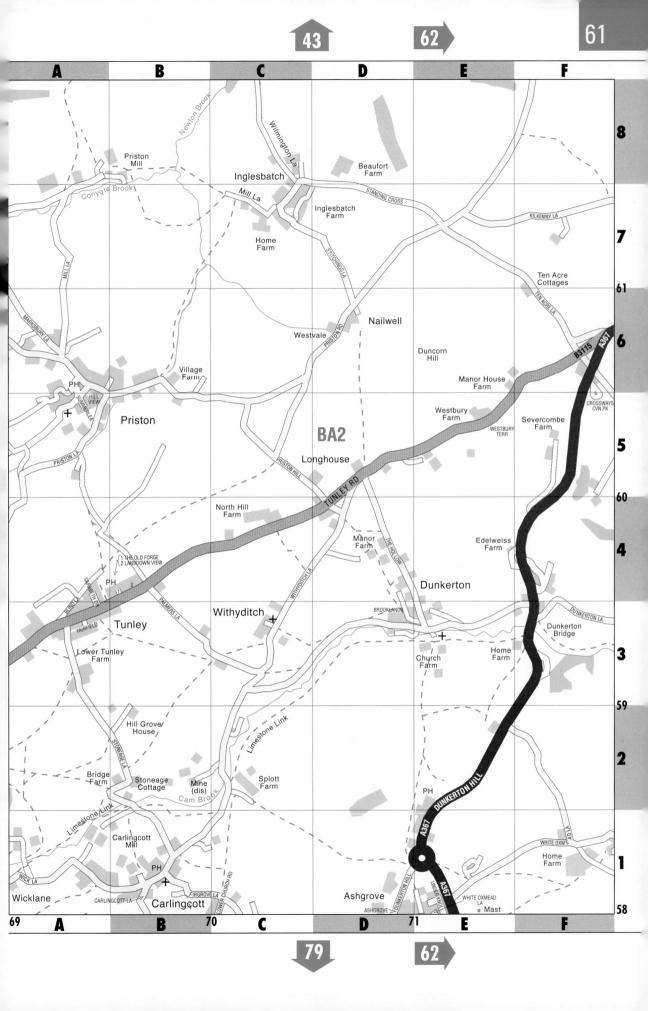

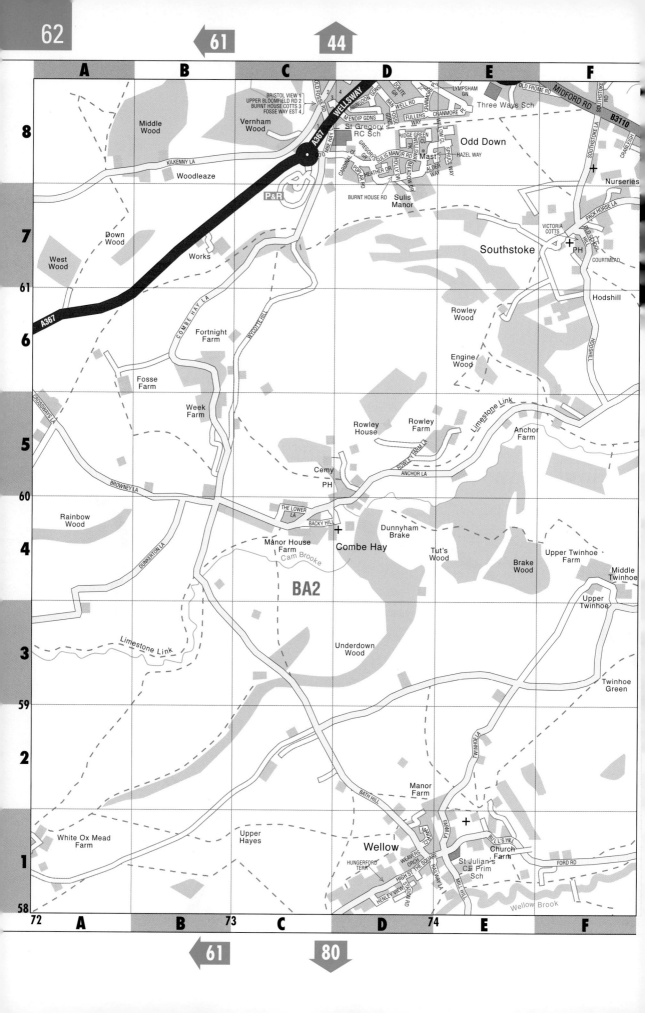

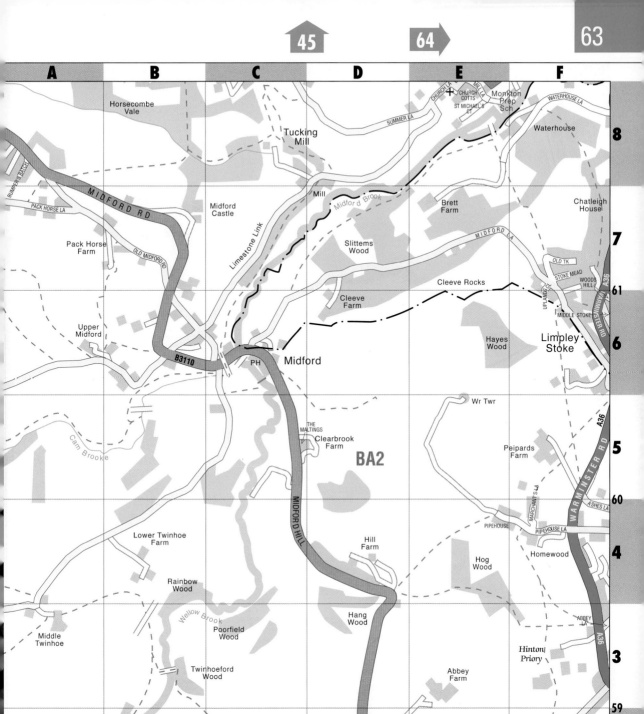

A   B   C   D   E   F

8

7

61

6

5

60

4

59

2

1

58

Horsecombe Vale

Tucking Mill

CHURCH LA
CHURCH COTTS
ST MICHAEL'S CT
Monkton Prep Sch
MILL LA
Waterhouse
WATERHOUSE LA

SUMMER LA

Mill

Midford Brook

Brett Farm

Chatleigh House

MIDFORD LA

BUMPERS PATCH

PACK HORSE LA
MIDFORD RD
Midford Castle

Limestone Link

Slittems Wood

OLD TK
Cleeve Rocks
STOKE MEAD
WOODS HILL

Pack Horse Farm

OLD MIDFORD RD

UPLANDS CL
MIDDLE STOKE

A36 WARMINSTER RD

Cleeve Farm

Upper Midford

Hayes Wood
Limpley Stoke

B3110
Midford
PH

Cam Brooke

THE MALTINGS
Clearbrook Farm

Wr Twr

Peipards Farm

WARMINSTER RD
A36

BA2

MIDFORD HILL

Hill Farm

Hog Wood

MARCHANT'S LA
ASHES LA
60
PIPEHOUSE
PIPEHOUSE LA
Homewood

Lower Twinhoe Farm

Rainbow Wood

Wellow Brook

Poorfield Wood

Hang Wood

ABBEY LA
A36

Middle Twinhoe

Twinhoeford Wood

Abbey Farm

Hinton Priory

Hankley Wood

Pennyplatt Wood

Broadfield Farm

BRANCH RD

THE GLEBE
THE BRAMBLES

Hinton House

Crewcroft Barn

Orchards Cleaves

Tytherley Farm

WELLOW LA

HIGH ST
THE BATCH
HINTON VILLAS
PO
TUGGY'S LA
Innocks Lodge
B3110

PH
GREEN LA

THE GREEN
FARLEIGH LA

Hinton Charterhouse

HINTON HILL

Lower Barn

Norton Brook

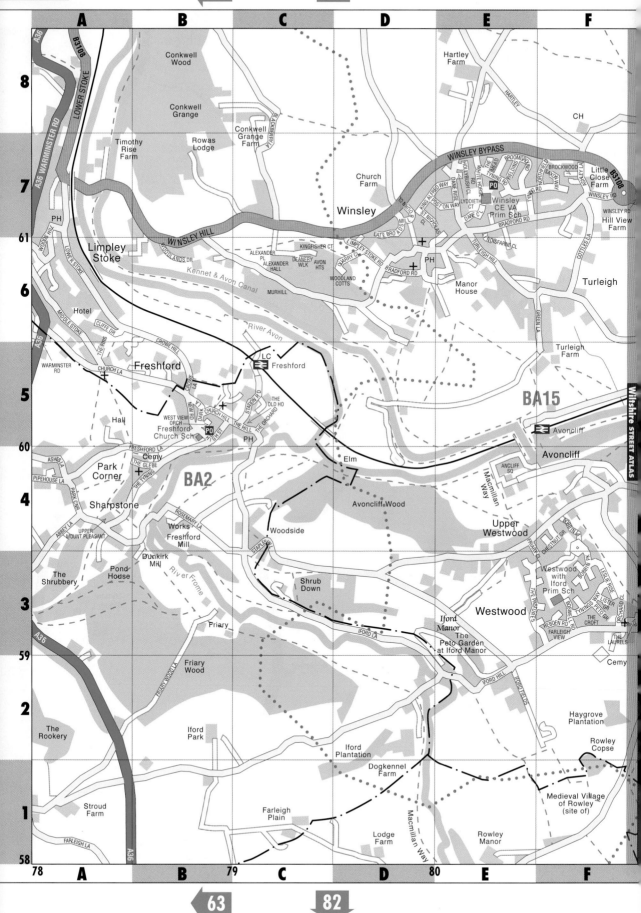

63
46

A   B   C   D   E   F

8

7

61

6

5

60

4

59

2

1

58

Wiltshire STREET ATLAS

A36 WARMINSTER RD
LOWER STOKE
B3108

Conkwell
Wood

Conkwell
Grange

Conkwell
Grange
Farm

Timothy
Rise
Farm

Rowas
Lodge

BLACKBERRY LA

Hartley
Farm

CH

HARTLEY

WINSLEY BYPASS

BROOMGROVE RD
FIELDING RD
BROCKWOOD
SAXON WAY
NORTHFIELD
Little
Close
Farm
B3108

TYNING MEAD
WHITE HORSE RD
PO
KINGSLEY LA
COTTLES LA
Winsley RD

Hill View
Farm

Church
Farm

Winsley

FOLLY RUSH CL
KING ALFRED WAY
DANE RISE
POST ON WAY
ST NICHOLAS CL
LYDDIETH CT
DANE C
Winsley
CE VA
Prim Sch
BRADFORD RD
TURLEIGH HILL
GREEN LA

LINDISFARNE CL

PH RD
LOWER STOKE
WOODS HILL
PH

Limpley
Stoke

WOODLANDS DR

WINSLEY HILL

Kennet & Avon Canal

ALEXANDER
PL
ALEXANDER
HALL

KINGFISHER CT

DEANERY
WLK
AVON
HTS

LIMPLEY STOKE RD
QUARRY CL
BRADFORD RD
PH

Turleigh

A36
Hotel

CLIFFE DR
MIDDLE STOKE
CROWE HILL
THE FIRS

MURHILL

WOODLAND
COTTS

Manor
House

Turleigh
Farm

River Avon

BA15

WARMINSTER RD
CHURCH LA
Freshford
LC
Freshford

Avoncliff

CROWE LA
NEW RD
STATION RD
THE OLD HO
THE HILL
THE ORCHARD

Hall

WEST VIEW
ORCH
Freshford
Church Sch
PO
PH

THE
GLEBE

Elm

Avoncliff

ANCLIFF
SQ

Macmillan Way

ASHER LA
PIPEHOUSE LA
Park
Corner
Cemy
BA2

Sharpstone
ABBEY LA
UPPER
MOUNT PLEASANT
PARK CNR
THE TYNING

ROSEMARY LA

Upper
Westwood

FRIARY PL
CHESTNUT GR
BOBBIN LA

Westwood
with
Iford
Prim Sch
LESLIE RISE
BOBBIN PK

The Shrubbery

Pond
House

Works
Freshford
Mill

Dunkirk
Mnl

River Frome

STAPLES HILL

Woodside

Shrub
Down

Westwood

LISTER CL
THE PASTURES
TYNINGS WAY
ORCHARD CL
THE
CROFT
THE LAURELS
Cemy
HERDEN RD
BOSWELL RD
FARLEIGH
VIEW
PETO GR

Friary

FRIARY WOOD LA
Friary
Wood

Iford
Plantation

Iford LA

Iford
Manor
The
Peto Garden
at Iford Manor

Iford Hill
FORD FIELDS

Haygrove
Plantation

The
Rookery

Iford
Park

Iford
Plantation

Dogkennel
Farm

Rowley
Copse

Medieval Village
of Rowley
(site of)

Stroud
Farm

Farleigh
Plain

Lodge
Farm

Macmillan Way

Rowley
Manor

FARLEIGH LA
A36

63
82

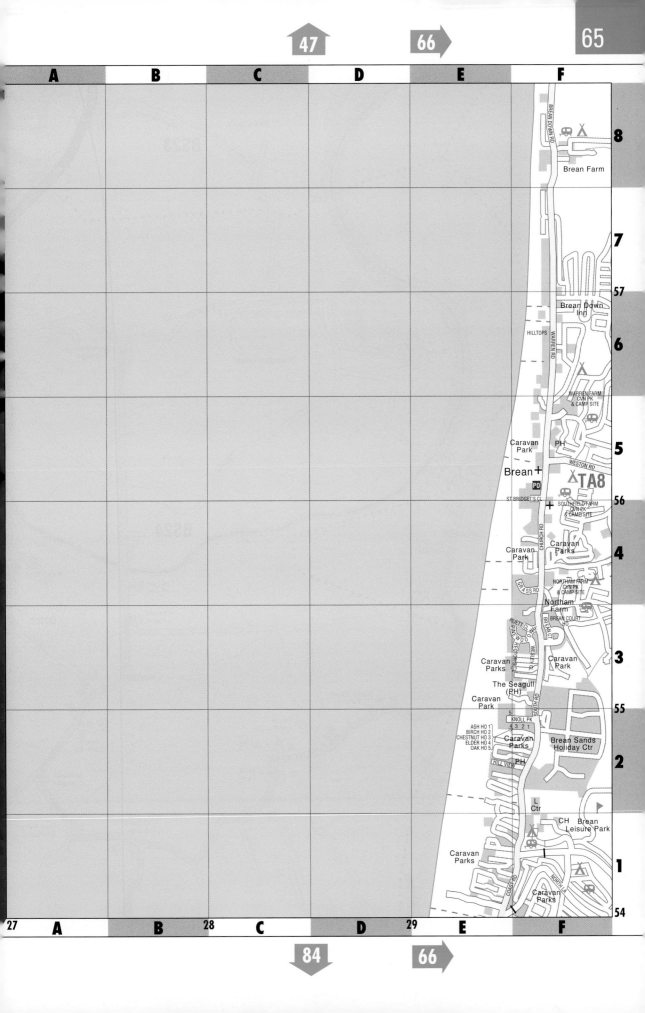

| A | B | C | D | E | F | |

8 Brean Farm

7

57 Brean Down Inn

6 HILLTOPS WARREN RD

WARREN FARM CVN PK & CAMP SITE

5 Caravan Park PH WESTON RD

Brean TA8

PO ST BRIDGET'S CL

56 SOUTHFIELD FARM CVN PK & CAMP SITE

4 Caravan Park Caravan Parks CHURCH RD GRASS RD

NORTHAM FARM CVN PK & CAMP SITE

Northam Farm

BREAN COURT HO

PUETT CL FULWOOD WAY WESLEY CL BREAN CT

3 Caravan Parks Caravan Park

The Seagull (PH) SOUTH RD

Caravan Park

55 KNOLL PK 5 4 3 2 1

ASH HO 1 BIRCH HO 2 CHESTNUT HO 3 ELDER HO 4 OAK HO 5

Caravan Parks Brean Sands Holiday Ctr

PH

HILL VIEW

2 L Ctr

CH Brean Leisure Park

1 Caravan Parks COAST RD NORTH LA

Caravan Parks

54

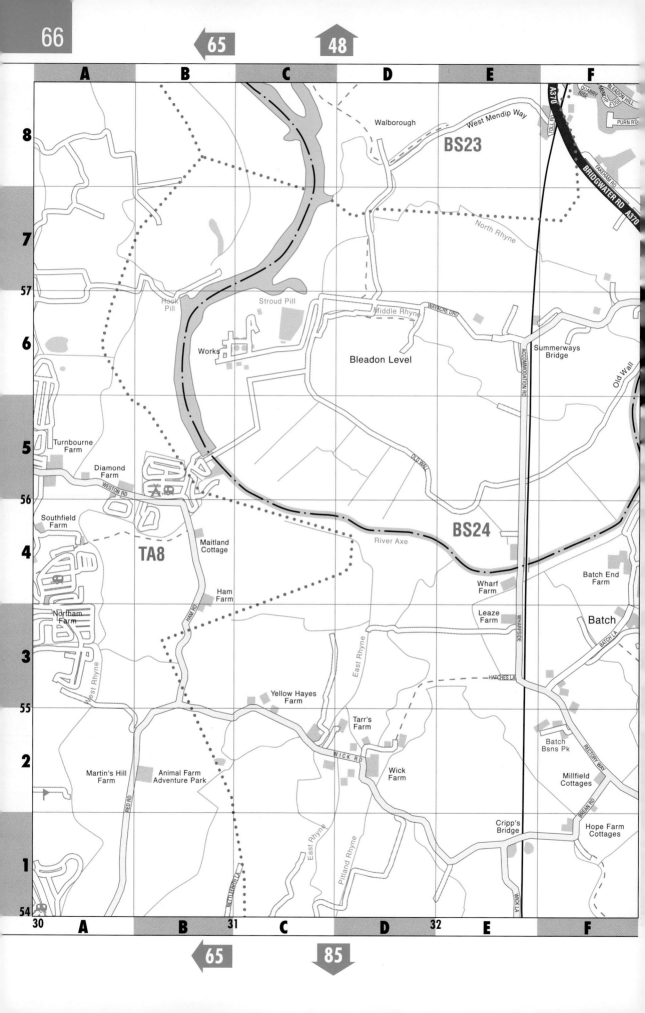

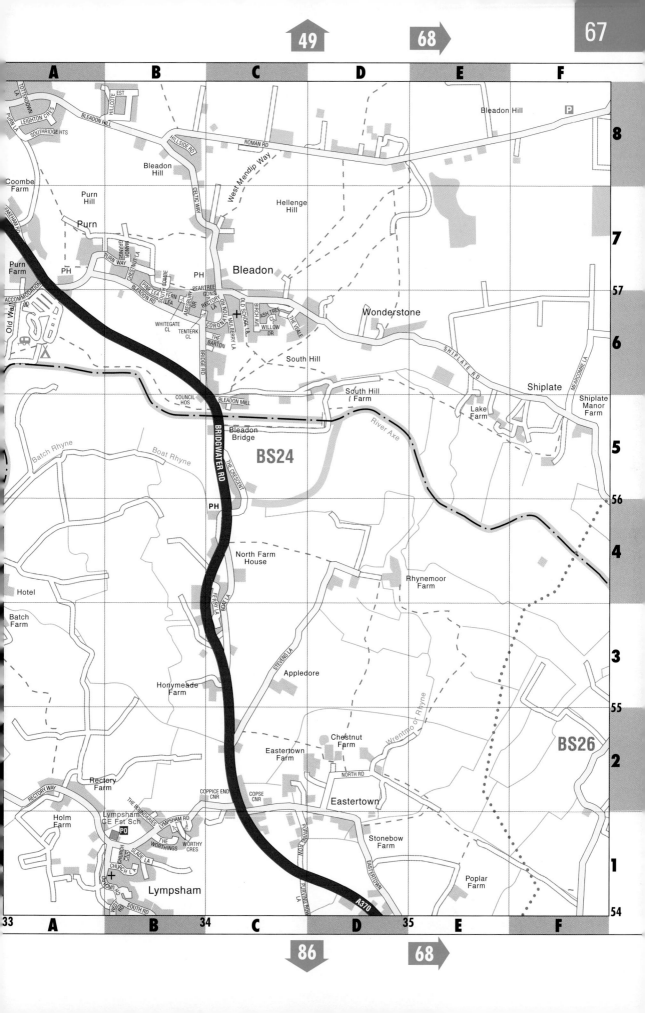

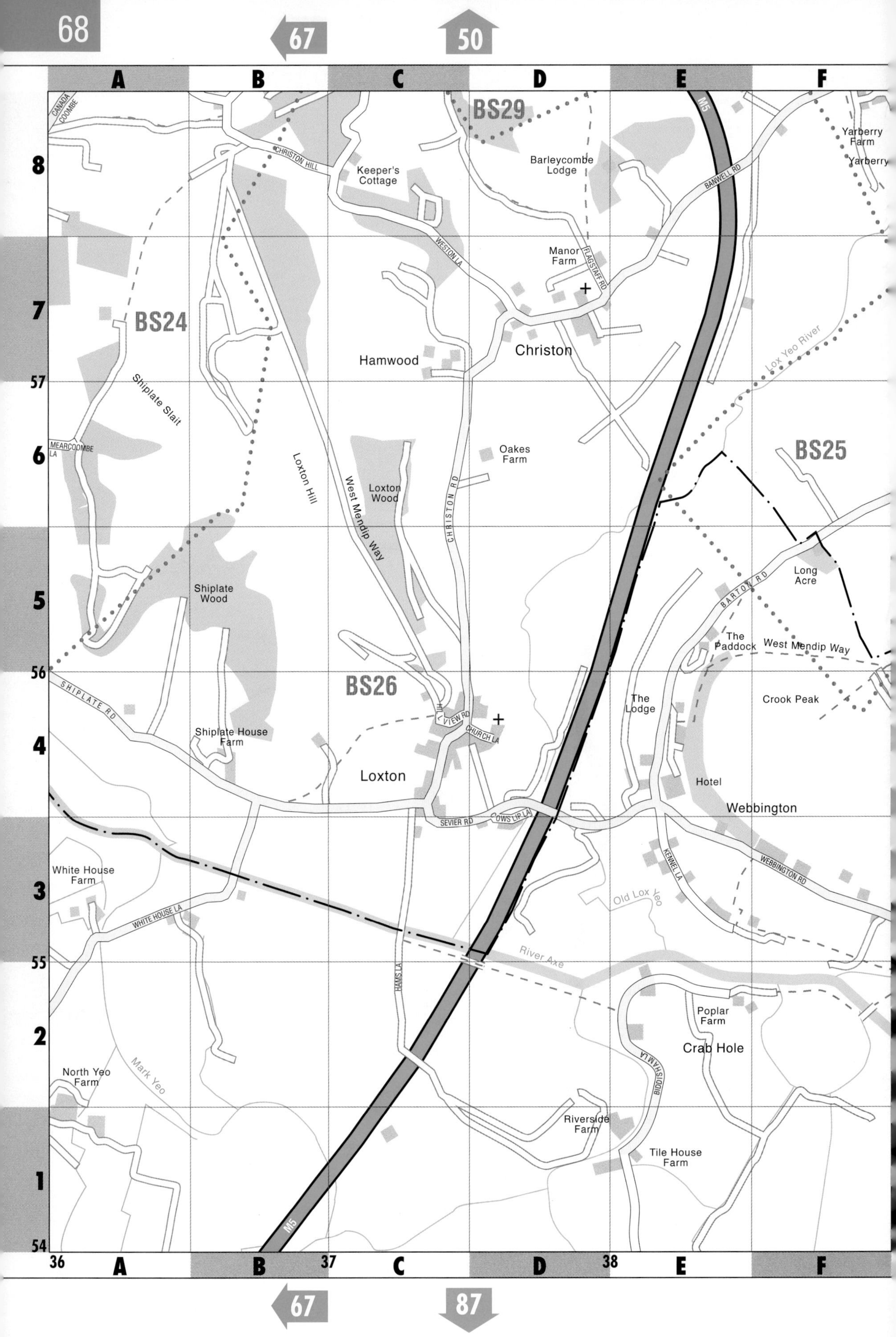

A B C D E F

8

BS29

Yarberry Farm

Yarberry

Keeper's Cottage

Barleycombe Lodge

BANWELL RD

M5

WESTON LA

Manor Farm

FLAGSTAFF RD

7

BS24

Christon

Shiplate Slait

Hamwood

Lox Yeo River

57

Oakes Farm

BS25

Loxton Hill

Loxton Wood

CHRISTON RD

6

MEARCOOMBE LA

West Mendip Way

Long Acre

BARTON RD

Shiplate Wood

The Paddock

West Mendip Way

5

Crook Peak

BS26

The Lodge

SHIPLATE RD

56

Shiplate House Farm

HILL VIEW RD

CHURCH LA

Hotel

Webbington

4

Loxton

SEVIER RD

COWS LIP LA

WEBBINGTON RD

KENNEL LA

White House Farm

3

WHITE HOUSE LA

Old Lox Yeo

HAMS LA

River Axe

55

Poplar Farm

2

Crab Hole

North Yeo Farm

Mark Yeo

BIDDISHAM LA

Riverside Farm

Tile House Farm

1

M5

54

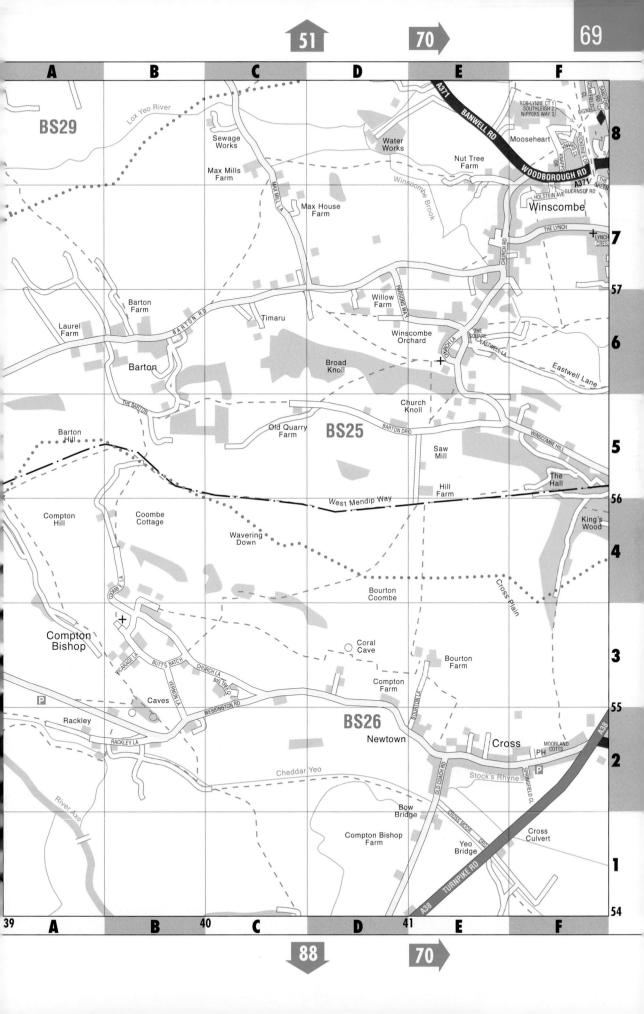

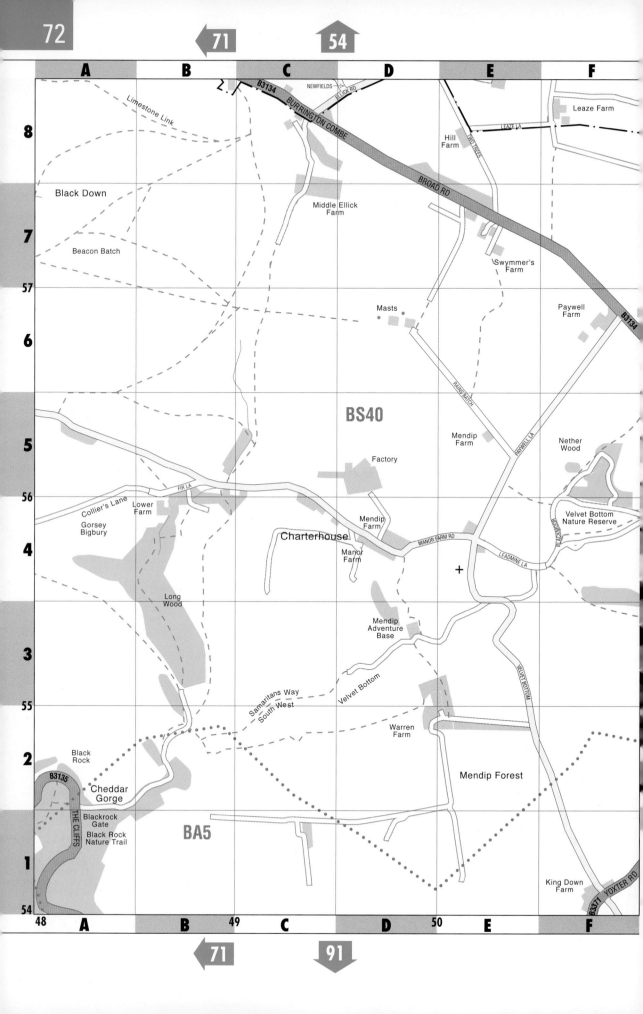

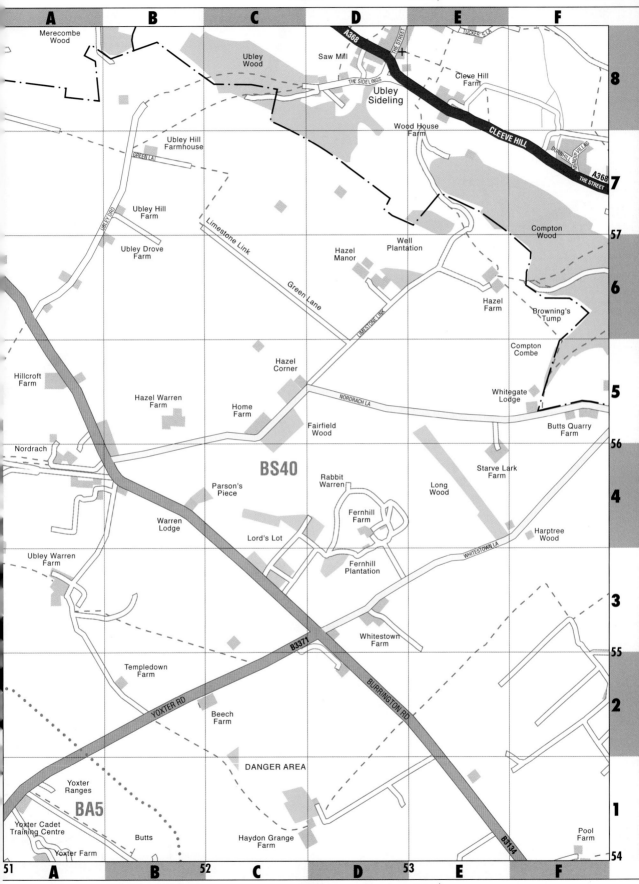

A B C D E F

Merecombe Wood

Ubley Wood

Saw Mill

THE STREET

A368

THE SIDELINGS

Ubley Sideling

Cleve Hill Farm

TUCKER'S LA

8

Wood House Farm

CLEVE HILL

DURNHILL

MENDIP VILLAS

A368

THE STREET

7

Ubley Hill Farmhouse

GREEN LA

UBLEY DRO

Ubley Hill Farm

Ubley Drove Farm

Limestone Link

Green Lane

Hazel Manor

Well Plantation

Compton Wood

57

Limestone Link

Hazel Farm

Browning's Tump

6

Compton Combe

Hillcroft Farm

Hazel Warren Farm

Hazel Corner

Home Farm

Fairfield Wood

NORDRACH LA

Whitegate Lodge

Butts Quarry Farm

5

Nordrach

BS40

Parson's Piece

Rabbit Warren

Long Wood

Starve Lark Farm

56

4

Warren Lodge

Lord's Lot

Fernhill Farm

Harptree Wood

Ubley Warren Farm

Fernhill Plantation

WHITESTOWN LA

3

B3371

Whitestown Farm

55

Templedown Farm

YOXTER RD

BURRINGTON RD

2

Beech Farm

DANGER AREA

Yoxter Ranges

BA5

1

Yoxter Cadet Training Centre

Yoxter Farm

Butts

Haydon Grange Farm

B3134

Pool Farm

54

51 A B 52 C D 53 E F

A B C D E F

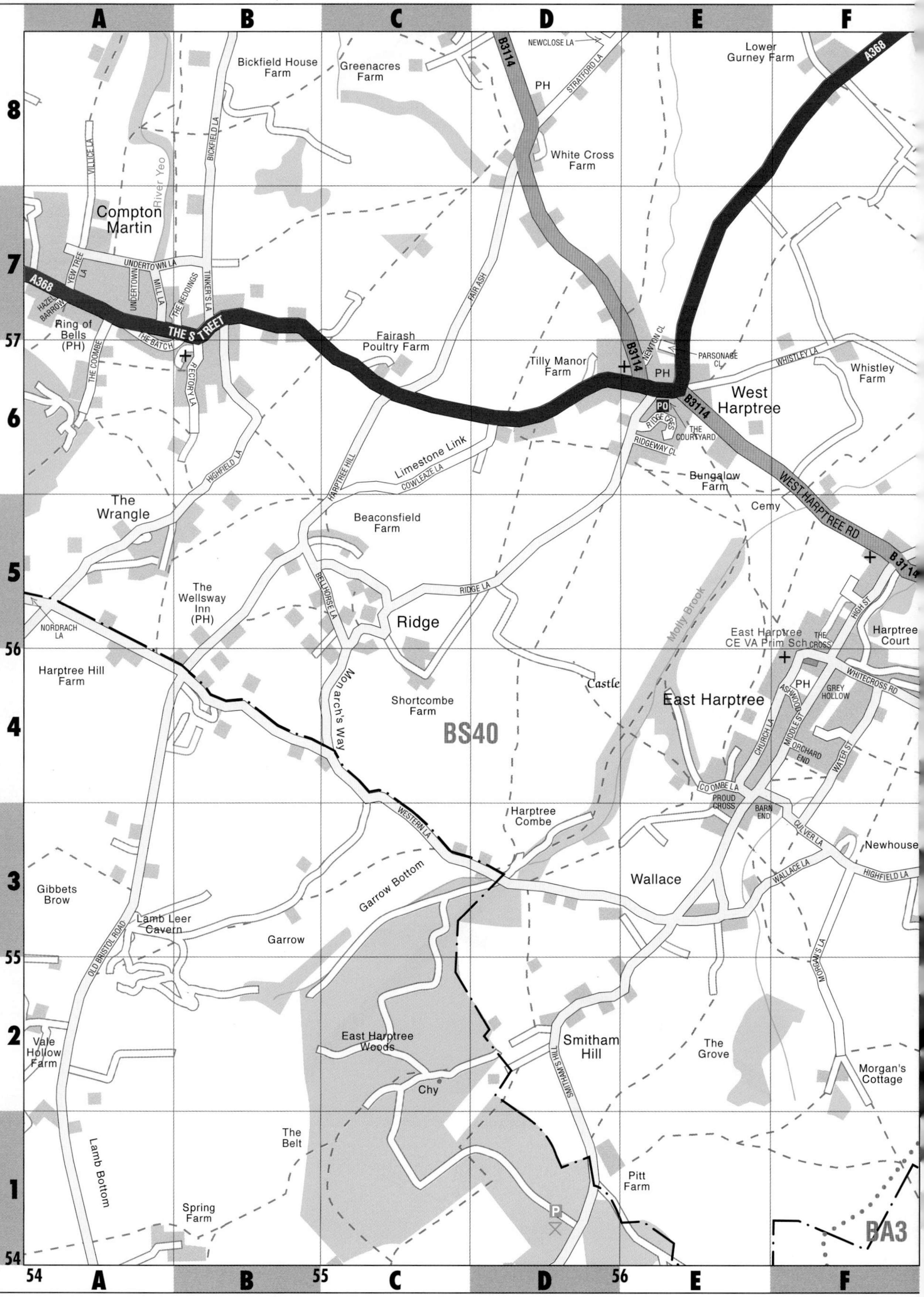

8

Bickfield House Farm
Greenacres Farm
B3114
NEWCLOSE LA
STRATFORD LA
PH
White Cross Farm
Lower Gurney Farm
A368

7

VILLICE LA
River Yeo
BICKFIELD LA
Compton Martin
A368
YEW TREE LA
UNDERTOWN LA
UNDERTOWN LA
MILL LA
THE REDDINGS
TINKER'S LA
THE STREET
HAZEL BARROW
57
Ring of Bells (PH)
THE COOMBE
THE BATCH
RECTORY LA
HIGHFIELD LA
Fairash Poultry Farm
FAIR ASH
Tilly Manor Farm
B3114
PH
PARSONAGE CL
WHISTLEY LA
Whistley Farm
West Harptree

6
HARPTREE HILL
Limestone Link
COWLEAZE LA
PO
RIDGE CROSS
RIDGEWAY CL
THE COURTYARD
Bungalow Farm
Cemy
WEST HARPTREE RD
B3114

The Wrangle
Beaconsfield Farm
BELLHORSE LA
B3114

5
The Wellsway Inn (PH)
RIDGE LA
Ridge
Molly Brook
East Harptree CE VA Prim Sch
THE CROSS
HIGH ST
Harptree Court
NORDRACH LA

56
Harptree Hill Farm
Castle
WHITECROSS RD
PH
ASHWORTH ST
GREY HOLLOW
MIDDLE LA
East Harptree
ORCHARD END
WALTER ST

4
Monarch's Way
Shortcombe Farm
BS40
CHURCH LA
COOMBE LA
PROUD CROSS
BARN END
CULVER LA
Newhouse
HIGHFIELD LA

OLD BRISTOL ROAD
Gibbets Brow
WESTERN LA
Harptree Combe
Wallace
WALLACE LA

3
Lamb Leer Cavern
Garrow Bottom
Garrow

55

2
Vale Hollow Farm
East Harptree Woods
Chy
THE SWALLOWS
Smitham Hill
The Grove
MURTRY LA
Morgan's Cottage
Lamb Bottom

The Belt
Pitt Farm

1
Spring Farm
P
BA3

54
A B C D E F
54 55 56

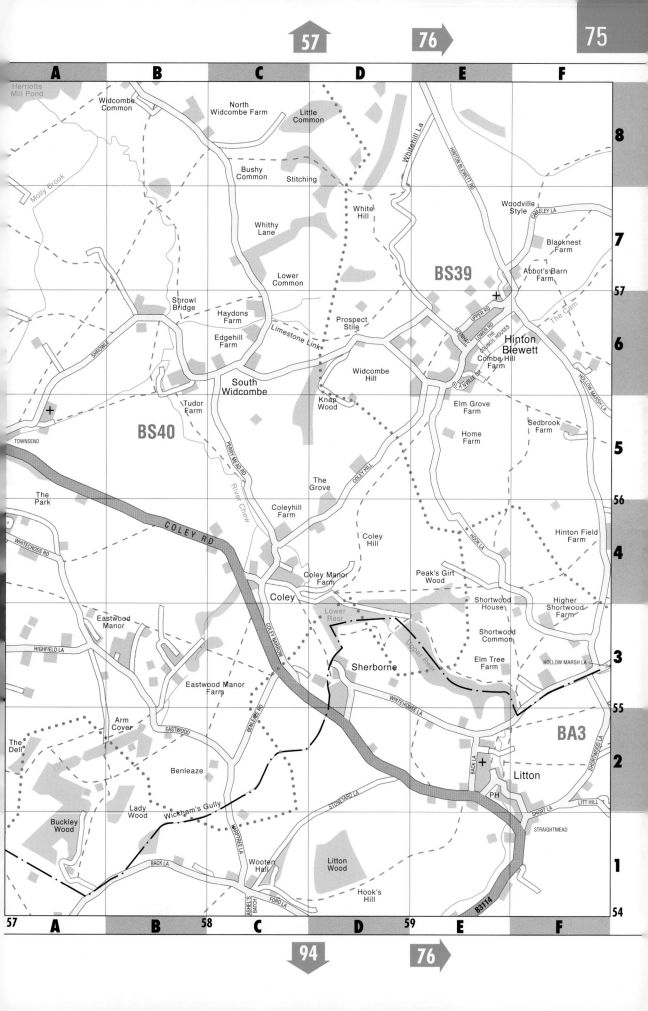

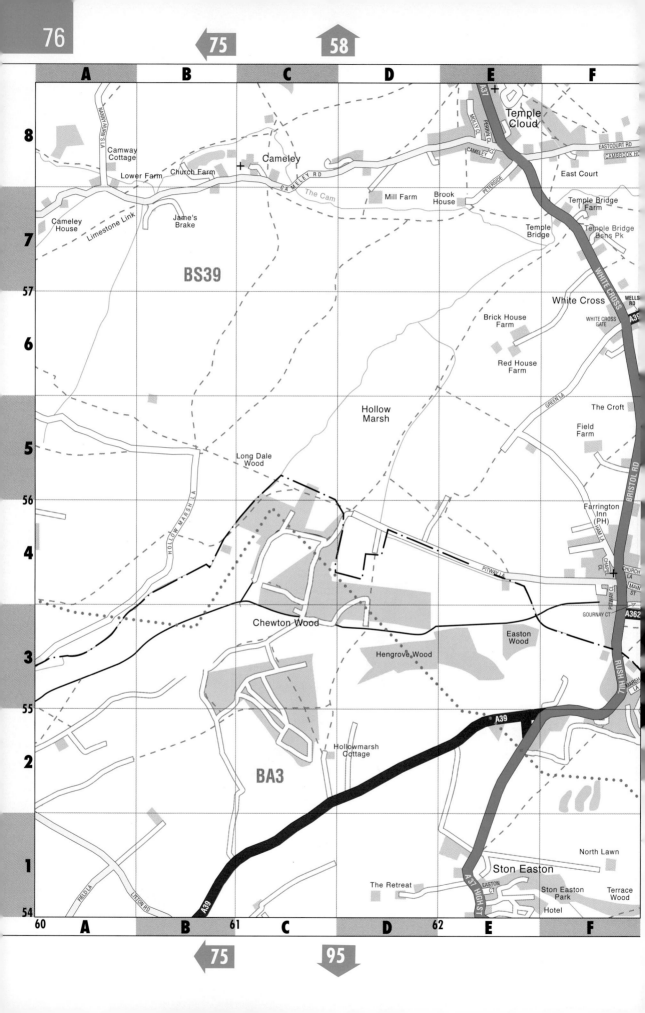

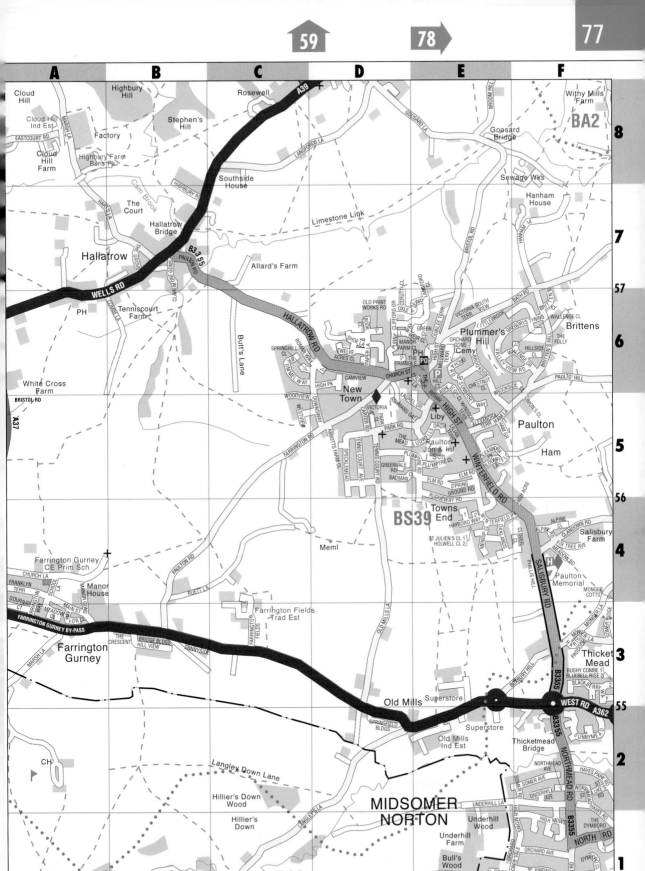

A **B** **C** **D** **E** **F**

8

Dunford Farm

Limestone Link

Upper Radford

Red House Farm

Radford

Hotel

Cam Brook

Collier

SUNNY VALE

RED HILL

CANAL VIEW

BRIDGE PLACE RD

THE HERITAGE

Camerton Court

BA2

New Barn Farm

Camerton

Abbey Farm

Camerton Park

CAMERTON HILL

SANNER'S HILL

+

7

Withymills Farm

Withy Mills

Old Hayes

RADFORD HILL

Glebe Cottage

PAULTON LA

Well Head Wood

Camerton Farm

57

BS39

6

PAULTO HILL

LOVERS LA

Starvelark Wood

EASTDOWN RD

A367

5

Broadway Cottages

BROADWAY LA

Clandown Bottom

Clan Down

BA3

NORTHDOWN RD

OVERDALE

DUCHY RD

PRINCE'S ST

SOUTH VIEW

DUCHY CL

SMALL COMBE

FOSSEWAY

56

CLANDOWN RD

WATER LA

MONGER LA

Bowlditch Farm

CRAWL LA

POW'S HILL

Clandown Farm

CHAPEL CT 1

HIGHFIELDS 2

CHAPEL RD

SMALL COMBE RD

OLD FOSSE RD

BATH NEW RD

BRISTOL RD

BATH OLD RD

4

BOWLDITCH LA

Kitley Hill

KITLEY HILL

BINCE'S LODGE LA

SPRINGFIELD HTS

SPRINGFIELD PL

CHAPEL LAWNS

FOSSE GN

Old Pit TERR

Monger

Welton Hill

OLD MILLARD'S HILL

MILLARD'S HILL

Clandown

Works

LUKE'S CL

COOMBEND

HAM PL

MEADYA WAY

3

BLACKBERRY WAY

MONGER LA

GREENHILL

HILLSIDE VIEW

MIDSOMER NORTON

Greenhill

Belle Vue

ST BARNABAS CL

GREEN TREE RD

Manor Farm

FOSSE LA

Welton Hollow

Works

MARKET PL 1

WATERLOO RD 2

Mus

55

THICKET MEAD

A362 **WEST RD**

GREENHILL RD

SPENCER RD

GELDOF RD

BEAUFORT AVE

LONG BARNABAS ST

EAST MEAD

BELLE VUE

GLADSTONE ST

MILLARDS

WELLOW BROOK CT

WELLOW BROOK

VALLEY WLK

WELLOW MDW

Midsomer Ent Pk

SOMERVALE RD

FROME RD

A362

P

Liby

P

+

2

Hayes Park

GRACE DR 1

ST CHARLES CL 2

ST ANTHONY'S CL 3

VIVIEN AVE

BERKELEY AVE

Welton

Works

STATION RD

WELTON VALE

NORTH END

BURNTON RD

Welton Prim Sch

Wheeler's Hill

RADSTOCK RD

WHEELER'S

WELTON BRO

ARCHES CL

Fosse Way Cotts

WEST HILL GDNS

WELLS RD

PINE WLK

St Nicholas CE Prim Sch

KILMERSDON RD

Bath Coll

1

B3355

CHURCH LA

THE DYMBORO

Cemy

POW'S ORCH

Midsomer Norton Prim Sch

P

THE HOLLIES

HIGH ST

Liby

RACKVERNAL RD

GULLOCK TYNING

Sp Ctr

1 HOPE TERR

2 RACKVERNAL CT

3 SOMER CT

RAILWAY VIEW

ELM TERR

FLORDA TERR

LILAC TERR

ILMINSTER MEWS

HIGHFIELDS

River Somer

SHELLEY RD

WESLEY AVE

RUSKIN RD

FOSSWAY

MILTON

WEST HILL GDNS

WEST HILL

OAK TERR

CYPRESS TERR

ACACIA

BIRCH RD

HOLLY WLK

MAPLE DR

THE DRING

WELLOW

A367

RADSTOCK

West Hill Gardens

MAY TREE RD

ROWAN CT

ASH TREE CL

WATERFORD CL

CHERRY TREE DR

CHESTNUT CL

54

ST JOHN'S CE Prim Sch

REDFIELD GR

TH

ST CHAD'S AVE

ST CHAD'S CL

FERN CL

IVY WLK

B3355

CHESTERFIELD HO

PIT RD

PRIMROSE

KINGS CL

LONGFELLOW RD

WATERSIDE RD

A367

WATERSIDE CRES

MAGNOLIA CL

Waterside

GROVE WOOD RD

66 **A** **B** **67** **C** **D** **68** **E** **F**

A1
1 MILL CT
2 SOMER HO
3 Somervale Sch

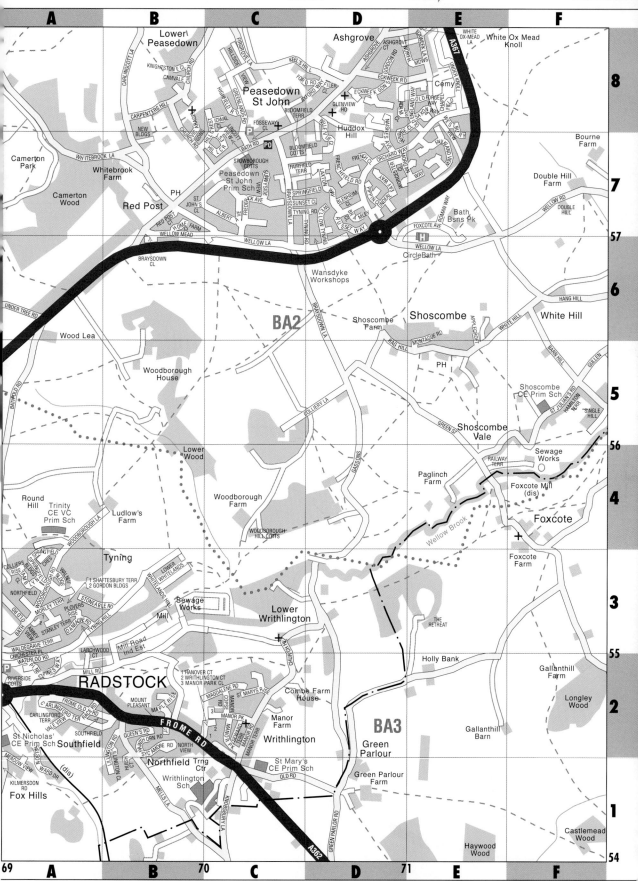

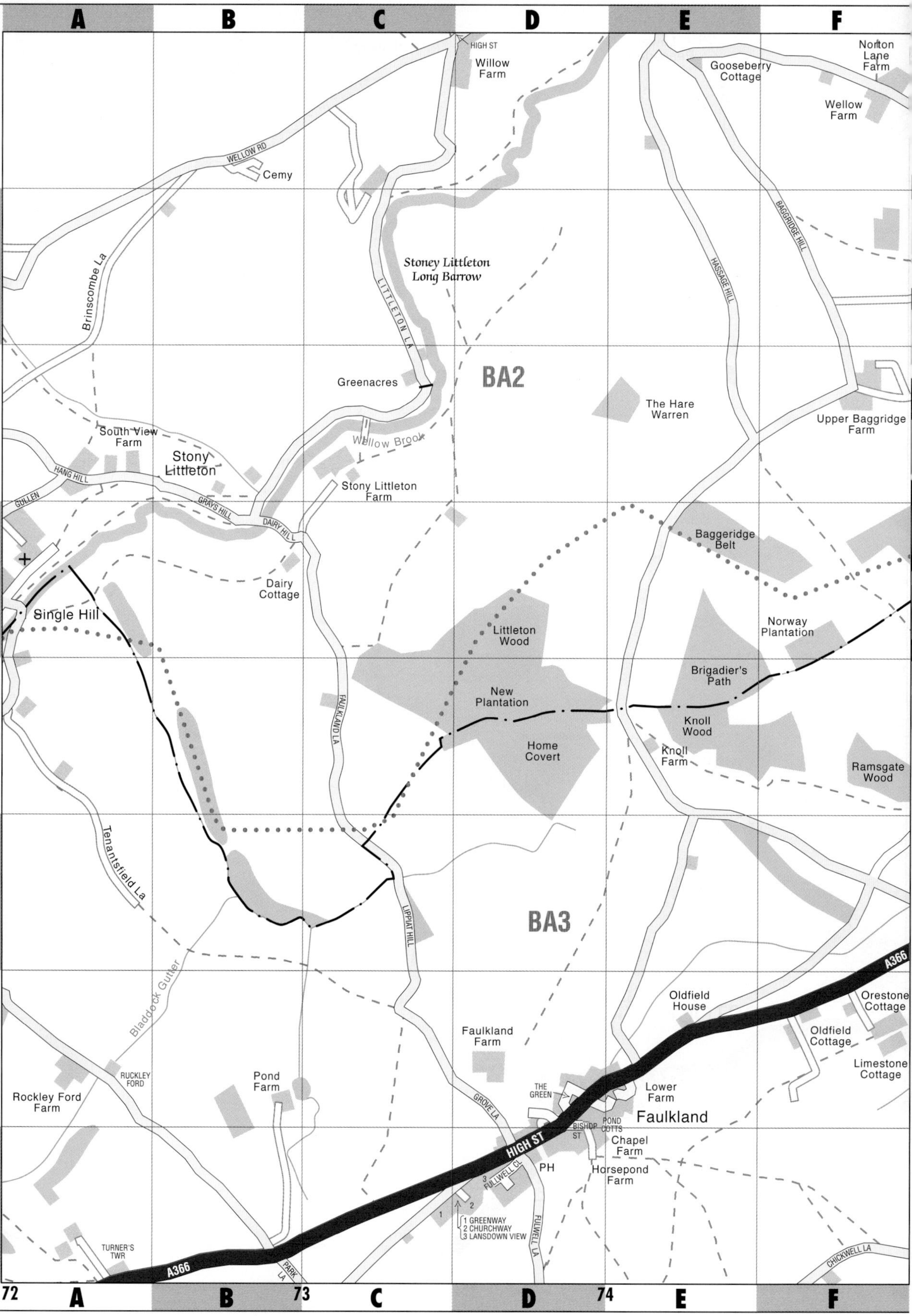

79
62

A B C D E F

8

HIGH ST
Willow Farm
Gooseberry Cottage
Norton Lane Farm
Wellow Farm

WELLOW RD
Cemy

7

Stoney Littleton Long Barrow

BAGGRIDGE HILL
HASSAGE HILL

Brinscombe La

57

BA2

Greenacres

The Hare Warren

Upper Baggridge Farm

6

South View Farm
Stony Littleton
Wellow Brook
Stony Littleton Farm

HANG HILL
GULLEN
GRAYS HILL
DAIRY HILL

Baggeridge Belt

5

Dairy Cottage

FAULKLAND LA

Littleton Wood

Norway Plantation

Brigadier's Path

Single Hill

56

New Plantation

Knoll Wood

Knoll Farm

Ramsgate Wood

4

Home Covert

Tenantsfield La

Bladdock Gutter

LIPPIAT HILL

3

BA3

55

A366

Oldfield House
Orestone Cottage

2

Faulkland Farm

Oldfield Cottage
Limestone Cottage

RUCKLEY FORD

Pond Farm

GROVE LA
THE GREEN
Lower Farm
POND COTTS
Faulkland
Chapel Farm

Rockley Ford Farm

BISHOP ST
Horsepond Farm

HIGH ST
FULLWELL CL
PH

1

1 GREENWAY
2 CHURCHWAY
3 LANSDOWN VIEW

FULLWELL LA

CHICKWELL LA

TURNER'S TWR

54

A366
PARK LA

72 A 73 B C 74 D E F

79
99

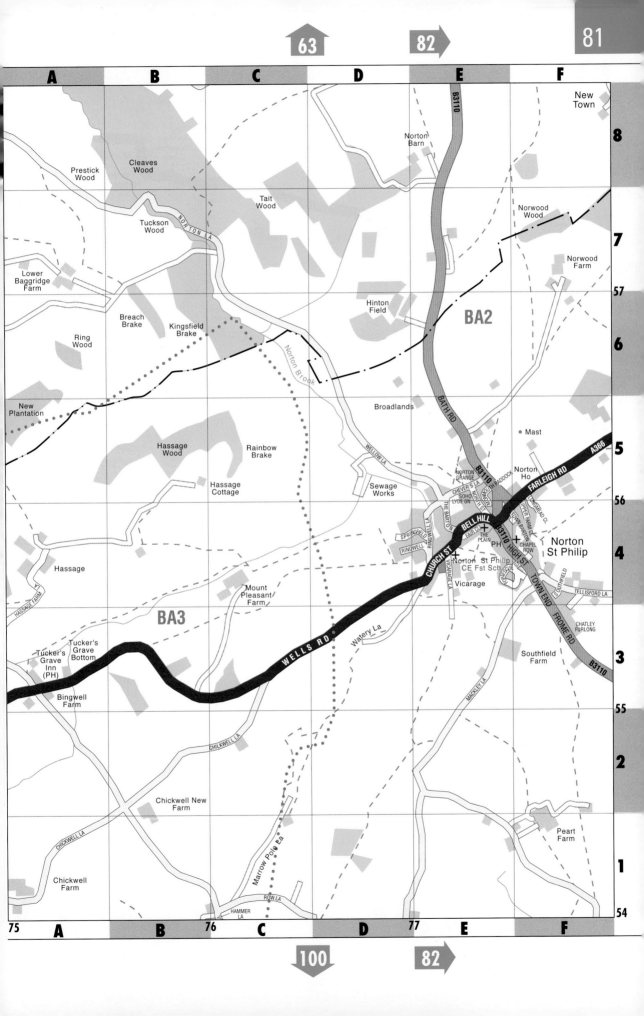

A B C D E F

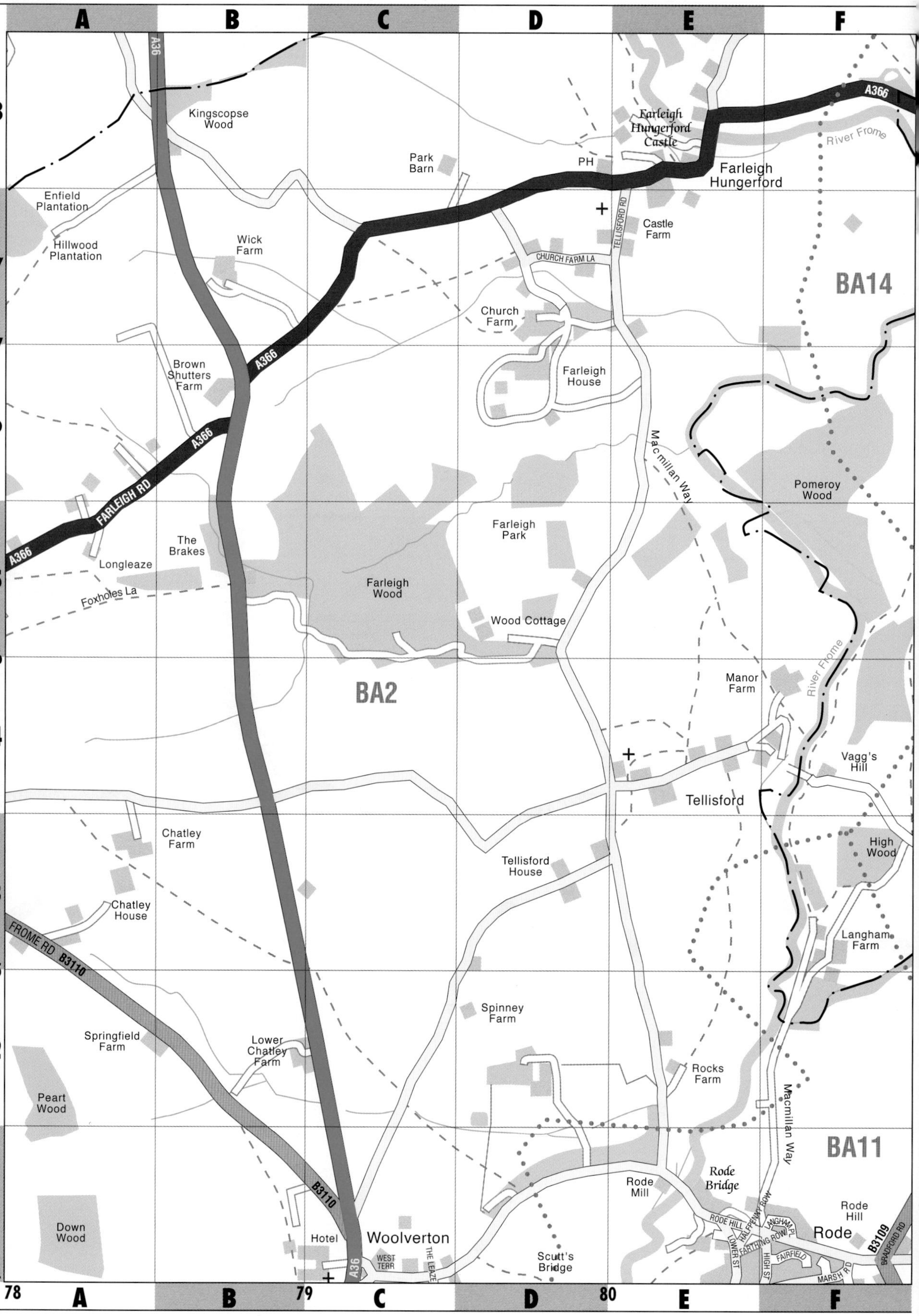

8
7
57
6
56
5
4
3
55
2
1
54

78 A B 79 C D 80 E F

Enfield Plantation
Hillwood Plantation
Kingscope Wood
Wick Farm
Brown Shutters Farm
A36
FARLEIGH RD
A366
Longleaze
The Brakes
Foxholes La
Park Barn
PH
Farleigh Hungerford Castle
Farleigh Hungerford
River Frome
BA14
CHURCH FARM LA
TELLISFORD RD
Castle Farm
Church Farm
Farleigh House
Macmillan Way
Pomeroy Wood
Farleigh Park
Farleigh Wood
Wood Cottage
BA2
Manor Farm
River Frome
Vagg's Hill
Tellisford
+
Chatley Farm
Tellisford House
High Wood
Langham Farm
Chatley House
FROME RD B3110
Spinney Farm
Springfield Farm
Lower Chatley Farm
Peart Wood
Rocks Farm
Macmillan Way
BA11
B3110
Down Wood
Hotel
WEST TERR
A36
THE LEAZE
Woolverton
Scutt's Bridge
Rode Mill
Rode Bridge
RODE HILL
HALF-PENNY ROW
LOWER ST
LANGHAM PL
CARTING ROW
HIGH ST
FAIRFIELD
MARSH RD
Rode Hill
Rode
B3109
BRADFORD RD

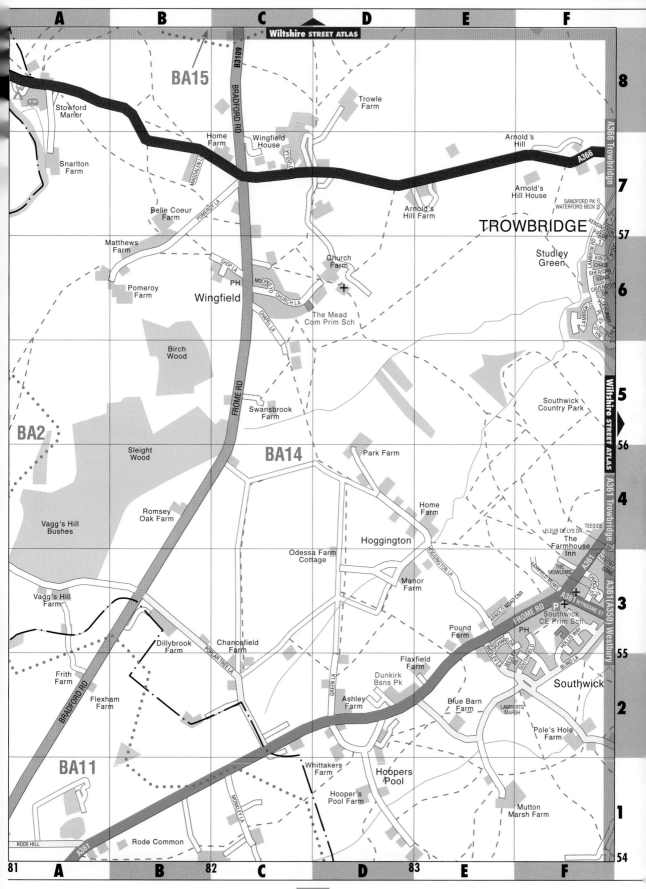

Wiltshire STREET ATLAS

A   B   C   D   E   F

BA15

B3109

BRADFORD RD

Stowford Manor

Snarlton Farm

Home Farm

Wingfield House

Trowle Farm

Arnold's Hill

A366

A366 Trowbridge

Belle Coeur Farm

POMEROY LA

MAGDALEN LA

Arnold's Hill House

TROWBRIDGE

Matthews Farm

SHOP LA

PH

MOORSYD

CHURCH LA

Arnold's Hill Farm

SANDFORD PK 1
WATERFORD BECK 2

KENSINGTON FIELDS

57

Pomeroy Farm

Wingfield

CHAPEL LA

Church Farm

The Mead Com Prim Sch

Studley Green

LAMBROK RD
KING'S CHASE
SHERIDAN GDNS
CAVENDISH DR

6

Birch Wood

FROME RD

LAMBROK CL
PL

ST

Southwick Country Park

5

BA2

Swansbrook Farm

56

Sleight Wood

BA14

Park Farm

Wiltshire STREET ATLAS

A361 Trowbridge

4

Vagg's Hill Bushes

Romsey Oak Farm

Home Farm

Odessa Farm Cottage

Hoggington

HOGGINGTON LA

FLEUR DE LYS DR
The Farmhouse Inn
TEESIDE

A361

THE MOWLEMS

COUNTRY GDNS

A361 (A350) Westbury

Vagg's Hill Farm

Manor Farm

GARFIELD MDWS

3

Dillybrook Farm

POPLAR TREE LA

Chancefield Farm

Pound Farm

ARNOLD ROAD CNR

FROME RD

WYNSOME ST

CH

Southwick CE Prim Sch

P

BRADFORD RD

Frith Farm

GREEN LA

Flaxfield Farm

WESLEY DR
ORCHARD DR

WESLEY LA

PH

HOLLIS WAY

BLIND LA

SOUTHFIELD

55

Southwick

Flexham Farm

Dunkirk Bsns Pk

Ashley Farm

Blue Barn Farm

LAMBERTS MARSH

2

Pole's Hole Farm

BA11

MONKLEY LA

Whittakers Farm

Hoopers Pool

Mutton Marsh Farm

1

Hooper's Pool Farm

RODE HILL

A361

Rode Common

54

A   B   82   C   D   83   E   F

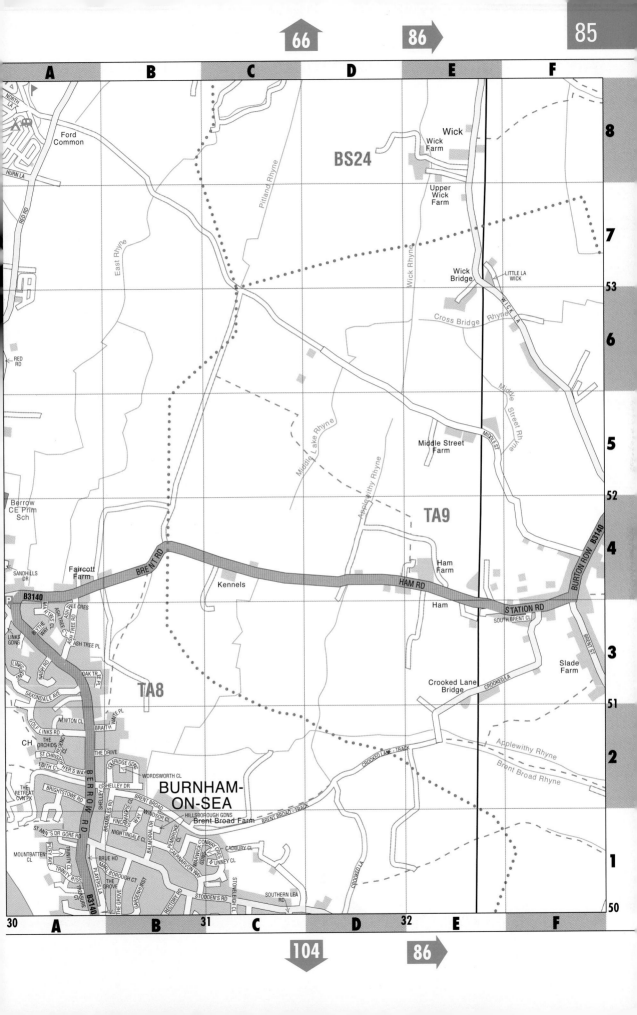

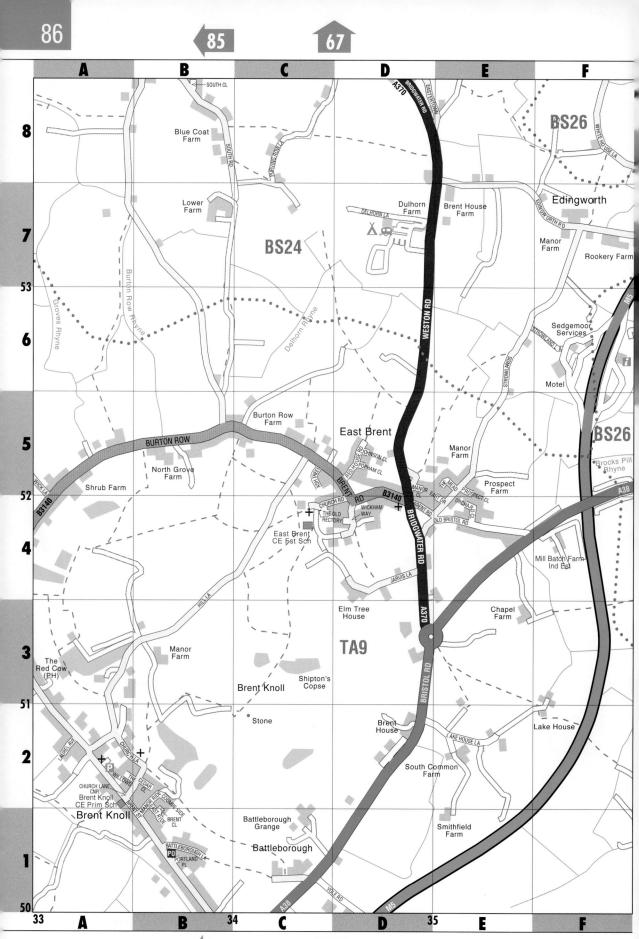

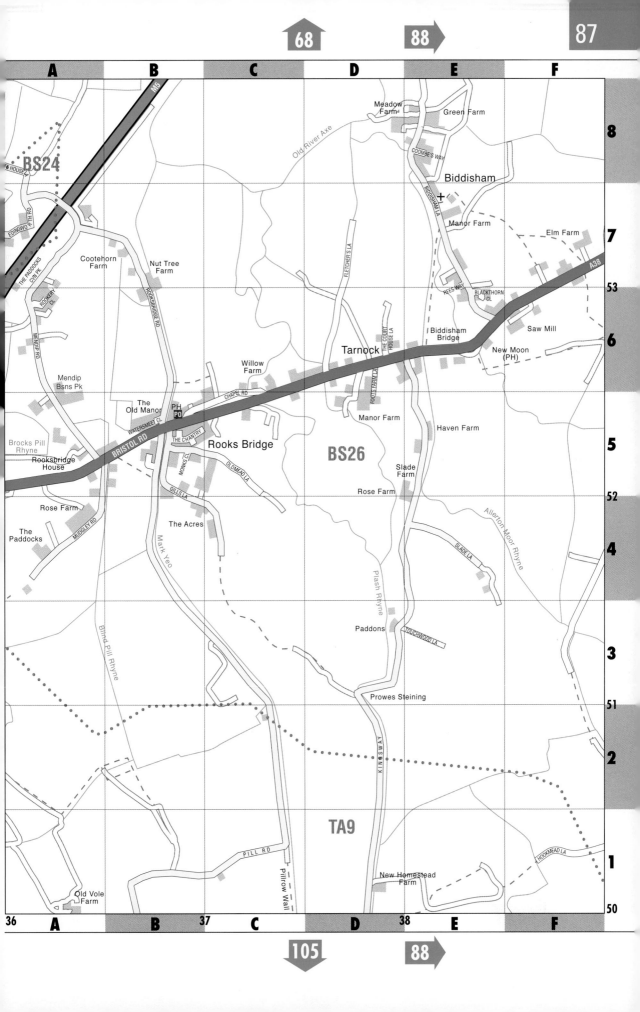

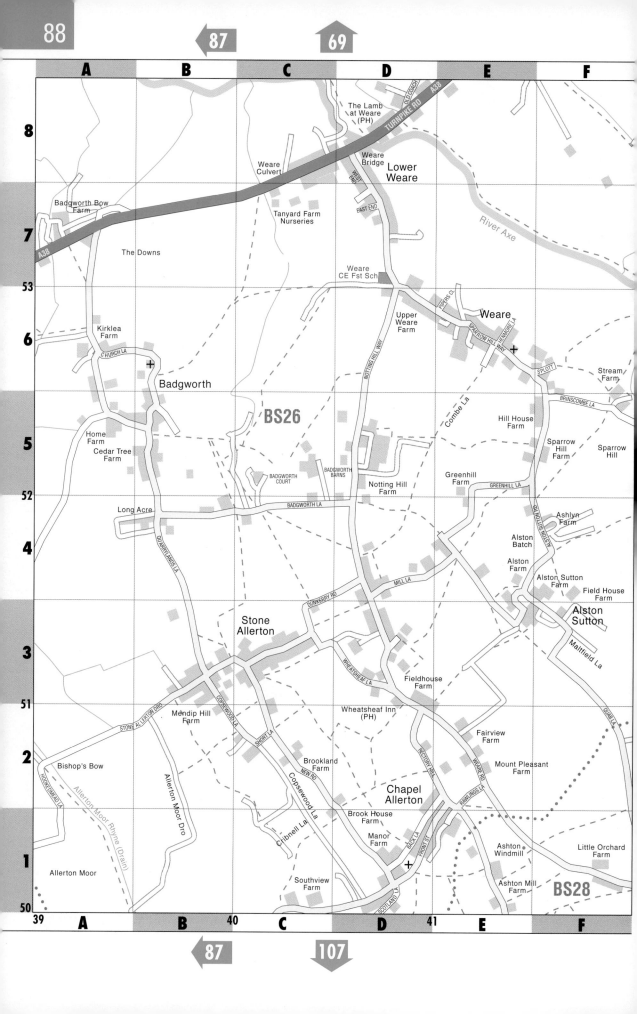

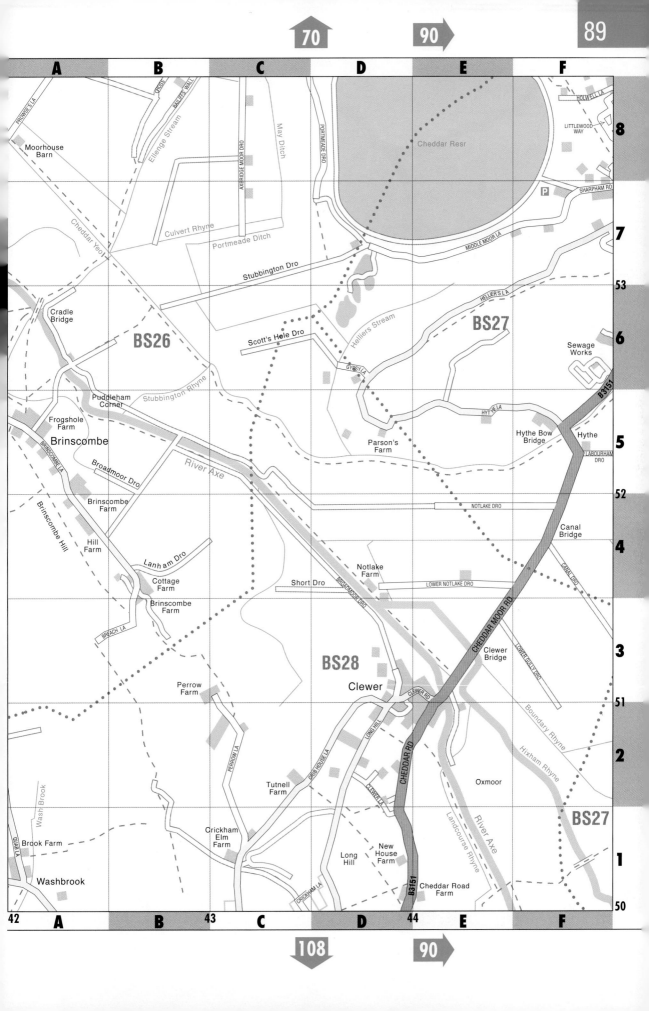

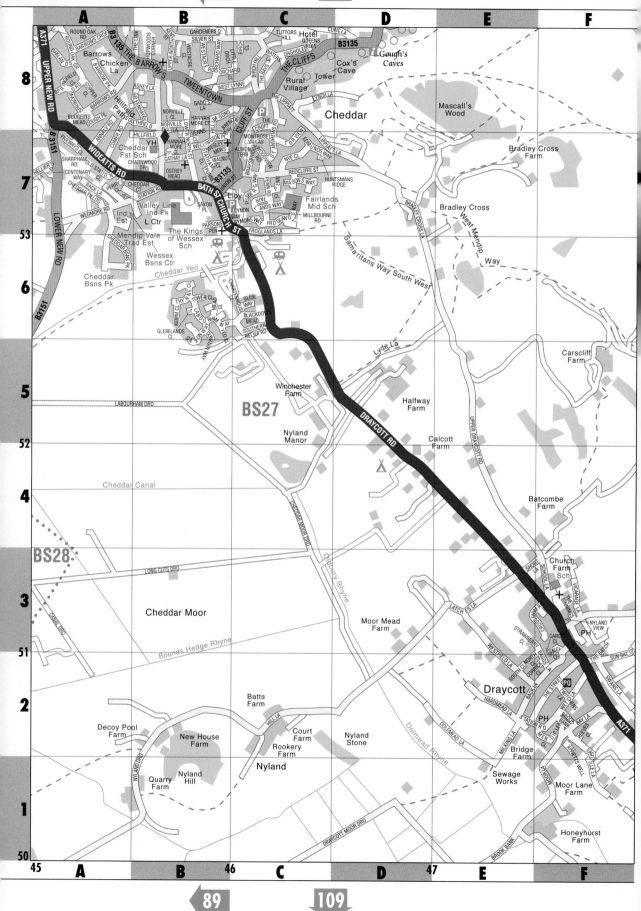

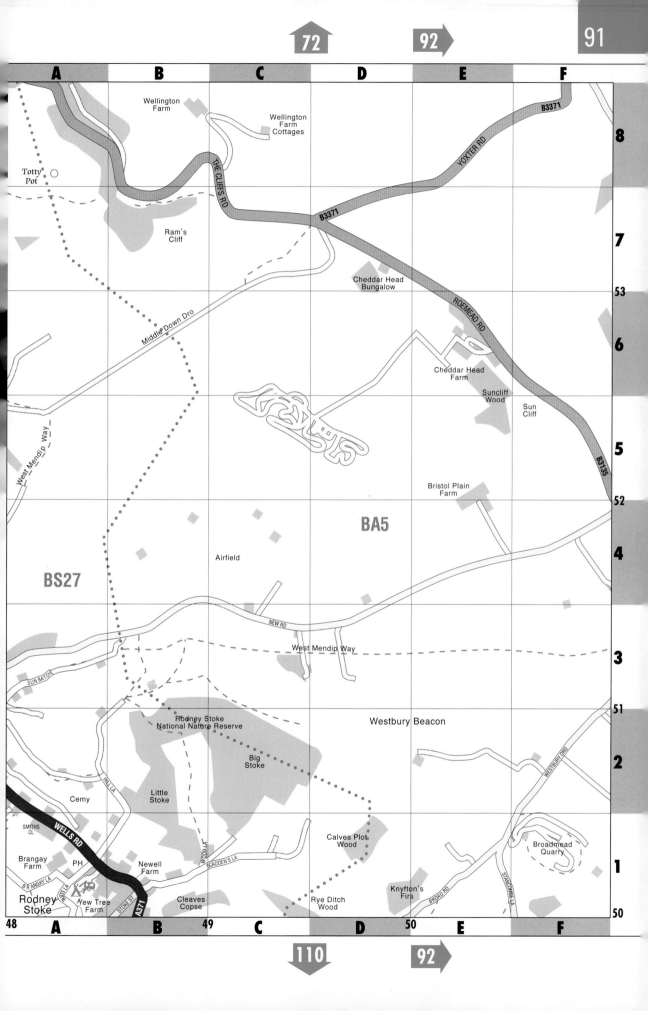

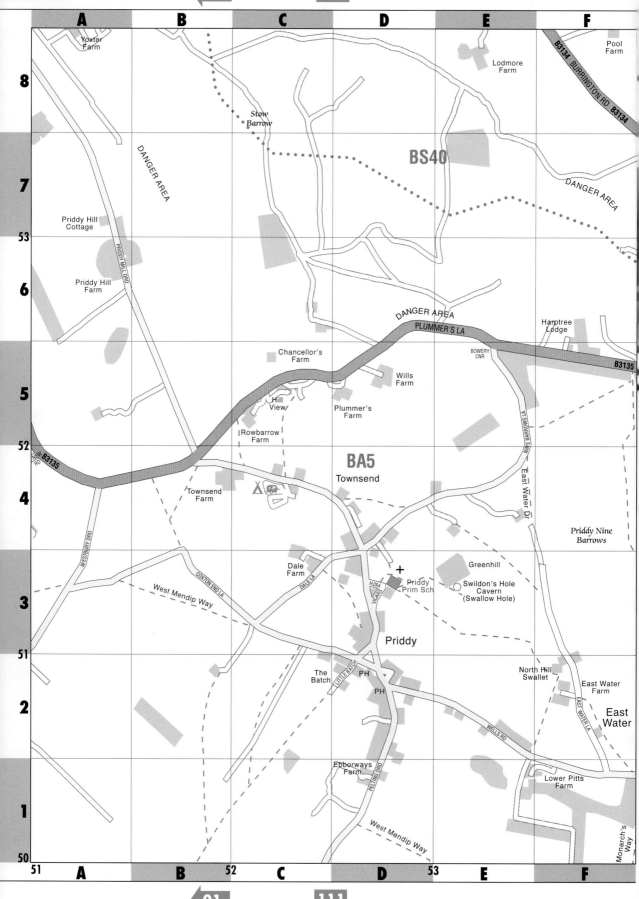

A B C D E F

8

7

53

6

53

Yoxter Farm

DANGER AREA

Priddy Hill Cottage

Priddy Hill Farm

Stow Barrow

BS40

DANGER AREA

B3134 BURRINGTON RD B3134

Pool Farm

Lodmore Farm

DANGER AREA

Harptree Lodge

PLUMMER'S LA

BOWERY CNR

B3135

PRIDDY MILL DRO

Chancellor's Farm

Hill View

Rowbarrow Farm

Wills Farm

Plummer's Farm

EAST WATER DRY

East Water Dr

5

52

NEW RD B3135

BA5

Townsend

Townsend Farm

Priddy Nine Barrows

4

WESTBURY DRO

COXTON END LA

West Mendip Way

Dale Farm

DALE LA

Priddy Prim Sch

Greenhill

Swildon's Hole Cavern (Swallow Hole)

3

51

The Batch

LITTLE BATCH

PH

PH

Priddy

North Hill Swallet

East Water Farm

2

WELLS RD

EAST WATER LA

East Water

Ebborways Farm

PELTING DRO

Lower Pitts Farm

1

West Mendip Way

Monarch's Way

50

51 A B 52 C D 53 E F

A B C D E F

8

Devil's
Punch Bowl

Swallet
Farm

Mast

Hill
Farm

Hill
Grange

Roadside
Clump

Wurt Pit
(dis)

Nett Wood
Farm

Big
Clump

SMITHAMS HILL

BS40

Niver
Hill

Greendowh Batch

OLD BRISTOL RD

B3134 BURRINGTON RD

7

53

Castle of Comfort
(PH)

Priddy
Circles

Castle
Farm

The Belt

Wigmore
Farm

Monarch's Way

EAKER HILL LA

Eaker Hill
Farm

Bendall's
Grove

West
End

BA3

6

OLD BRISTOL RD

Cranmore
View

Miners' Arms

B3134

Red Quarr
Farm

Eaker
Hill

5

TOR HOLE RD

52

BA5

4

North Hill

Priddy
Mineries

Monarch's Way

MINERY RD

P

Bendalls
Farm

B3135

3

51

Under Barrow
Farm

Stockhill

Nursery

Cuckoo
Cleeves

Tower
Hill

2

Hunters Lodge
Inn

HILLGROVE RD

Ash
Plantation

1

50

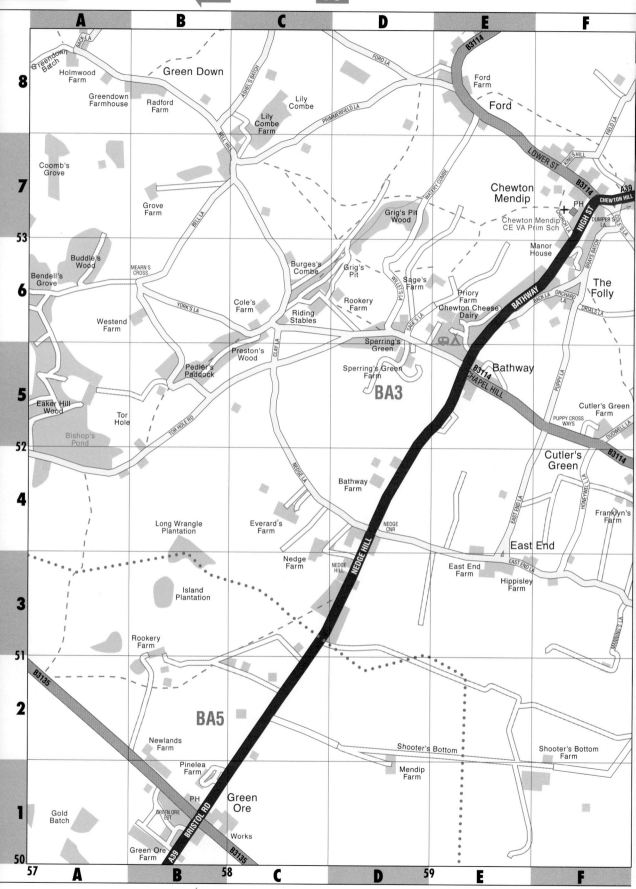

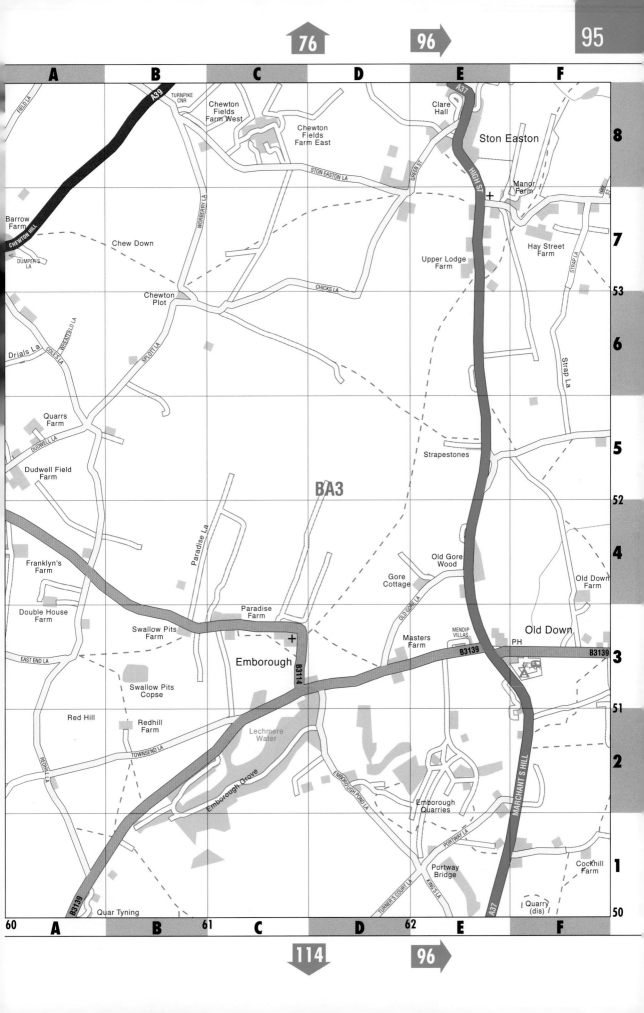

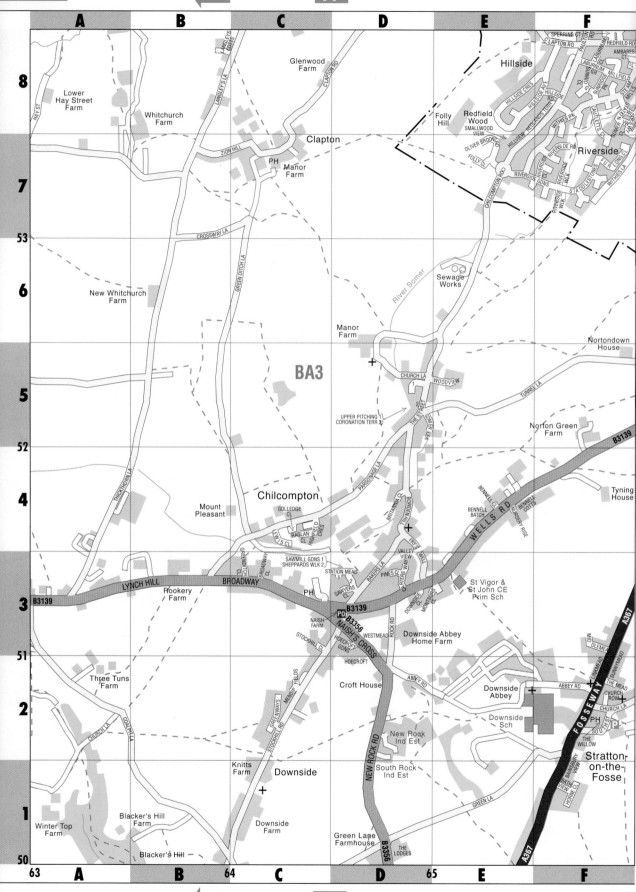

BA3

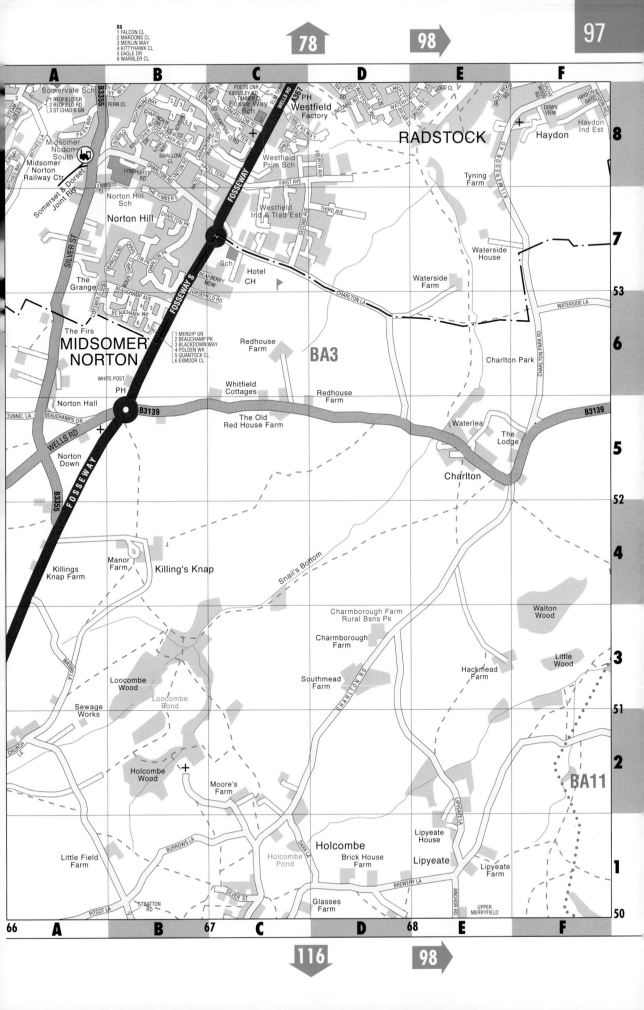

B8
1 FALCON CL
2 MARDONS CL
3 MERLIN WAY
4 KITTYHAWK CL
5 EAGLE DR
6 WARBLER CL

A   B   C   D   E   F

Somervale Sch
1 REDFIELD GR
2 REDFIELD RD
3 ST CHAD'S GN

8

Midsomer
Norton
South

Midsomer
Norton
Railway Ctr

Somerset & Dorset
Joint Rly

Norton Hill
Sch

Norton Hill

The Grange

The Firs

MIDSOMER
NORTON

White Post
PH

Norton Hall

TUNNEL LA

Norton
Down

Killings
Knap Farm

Manor
Farm

Killing's Knap

Sewage
Works

Loocombe
Wood

Loocombe
Pond

Holcombe
Wood

Little Field
Farm

Moore's
Farm

Holcombe
Pond

Burrows La

Stratton
Rd

Pitcot La

Silver St

Glasses
Farm

Holcombe

Brick House
Farm

Brewery La

Lipyeate
House

Lipyeate

Lipyeate
Farm

Upper
Merryfield

BA11

Westfield
Factory

RADSTOCK

Haydon

Haydon
Ind Est

Down
View

Tyning
Farm

Westfield
Prim Sch

Westfield
Ind & Trad Est

First Ave

Charlton La

Waterside
House

Waterside
Farm

Charlton Park

7

53

6

Hotel
CH

Sch

1 MENDIP GN
2 BEAUCHAMP PK
3 BLACKDOWN WAY
4 POLDEN WK
5 QUANTOCK CL
6 EXMOOR CL

Redhouse
Farm

BA3

Whitfield
Cottages

Redhouse
Farm

B3139

The Old
Red House Farm

Waterlea

The
Lodge

B3139

5

Charlton

52

Snail's Bottom

4

Charmborough Farm
Rural Bsns Pk

Charmborough
Farm

Walton
Wood

Southmead
Farm

Hackmead
Farm

Little
Wood

3

51

2

1

50

66   A   B   67   C   D   68   E   F

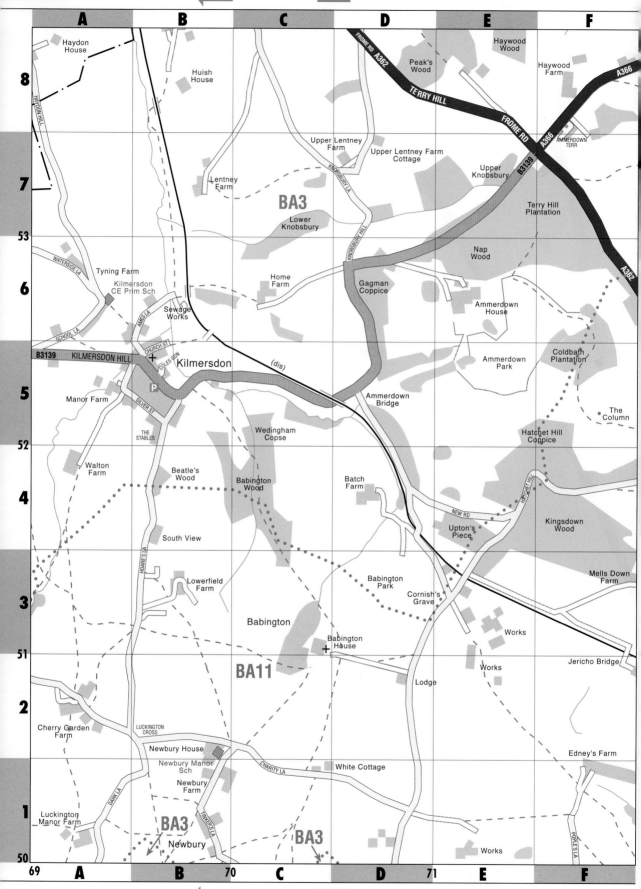

A B C D E F

Haydon
House

Huish
House

8

Upper Lentney
Farm

Peak's
Wood

Haywood
Wood

Haywood
Farm

A366

AMMERDOWN
TERR

TERRY HILL

FROME RD

A362

Upper Lentney Farm
Cottage

Upper
Knobsbury

B3139

A366

7

Lentney
Farm

BA3

Knobsbury La

Terry Hill
Plantation

53

Lower
Knobsbury

Nap
Wood

A362

Waterside La

Tyning Farm

Home
Farm

Gagman
Coppice

Ammerdown
House

Coldbath
Plantation

6

Kilmersdon
CE Prim Sch

Knobsbury Hill

Ames La

Sewage
Works

School La

Church St

Coles Don

B3139 KILMERSDON HILL

Kilmersdon

(dis)

Ammerdown
Park

Ammerdown
Bridge

The
Column

5

Manor Farm

P

Silver St

THE
STABLES

Wedingham
Copse

Hatchet Hill
Coppice

52

Walton
Farm

Beatle's
Wood

Babington
Wood

Batch
Farm

Hatchet Hill

Kingsdown
Wood

4

NEW RD

Upton's
Piece

Mells Down
Farm

Hoare's La

South View

Lowerfield
Farm

Babington
Park

Cornish's
Grave

Works

3

Babington

Jericho Bridge

51

BA11

Babington
House

Works

Lodge

2

Cherry Garden
Farm

LUCKINGTON
CROSS

Newbury House

Dark La

Tinker's La

Newbury Manor
Sch

Newbury
Farm

CHARITY LA

White Cottage

Edney's Farm

1

Luckington
Manor Farm

BA3

Newbury

BA3

Works

Pyple's La

50

69 A B 70 C D 71 E F

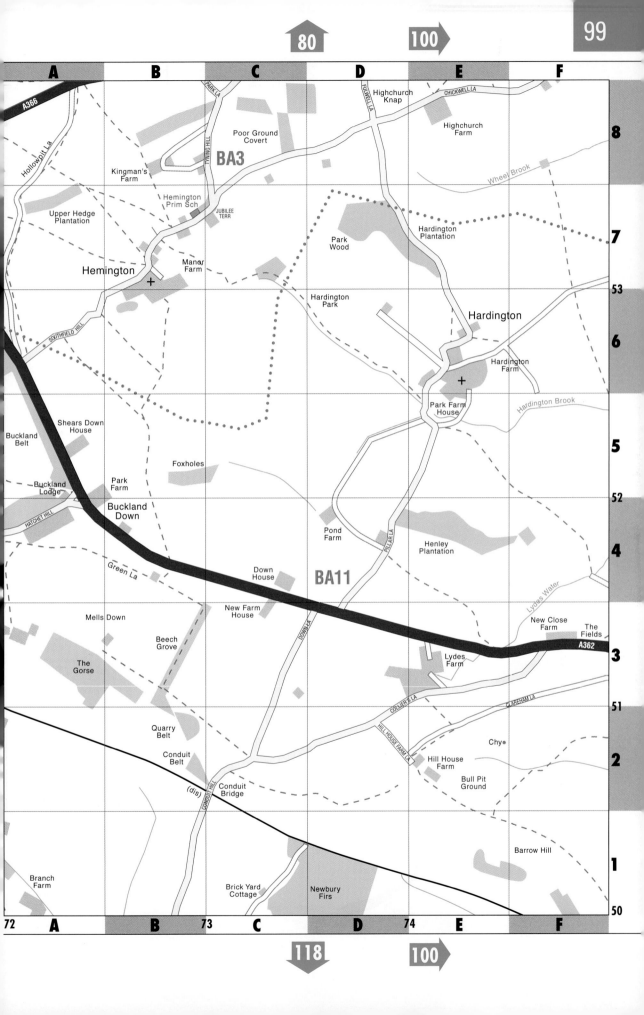

99
81

	A	B	C	D	E	F

8

Charlton Farm

Hill Brow Farm

BA3

Upper Row Farm

ROW LA

Row Farm House

Brook House Farm

7

Lower Row Farm

CHERRY GARDEN LA

STEPS LA

HAMMER LA

53

Laverton

Wheel Brook

BA2

PORT WAY

Manor Farm

6

Hardington Wood

New Barn Farm

Luxgrove Wood

Park Wood

New Barn Cottages

Cock Road Wood

5

Hardington Brook

COCK RD

Cock Road Farm

FOXHOLES LA

52

Foxholes Wood

Lydes Water

4

Buckland Wood

Orchardleigh Wood

Buckland Brook

Knacker's Hole

Macmillan Way

CH

3

BURNT HILL LA

COURT FARM 1
ST MICHAEL'S CL 2

Manor Farmhouse

Buckland Dinham

Wood Lodge

Orchardleigh House

The Bell (PH)

THE CROSS

Orchardleigh Park

A362

HIGH ST

ROGERS CL

Orchardleigh Lake

CLAREHAM LA

SANDYS CROSS LA

Church Lodge

51

The Higdens

Murtrey Hill Farm

BA11

Hope Farm

Warren Plantation

Orchardleigh Stones

2

Barrow Hill Farm

LOWER ST

Dangerfield Farm

MURTREY HILL LA

Murtrey Hill

Nightingale Lodge

Fir Plantation

The Down

Mount Pleasant Farm

Beech Plantation

Fir Wood

Longhouse Plantation

1

Murtrey Brow Plantation

Elliots

ELLIOTS LA

A362

Castle Lodge

White Mill Farm

50

99
119

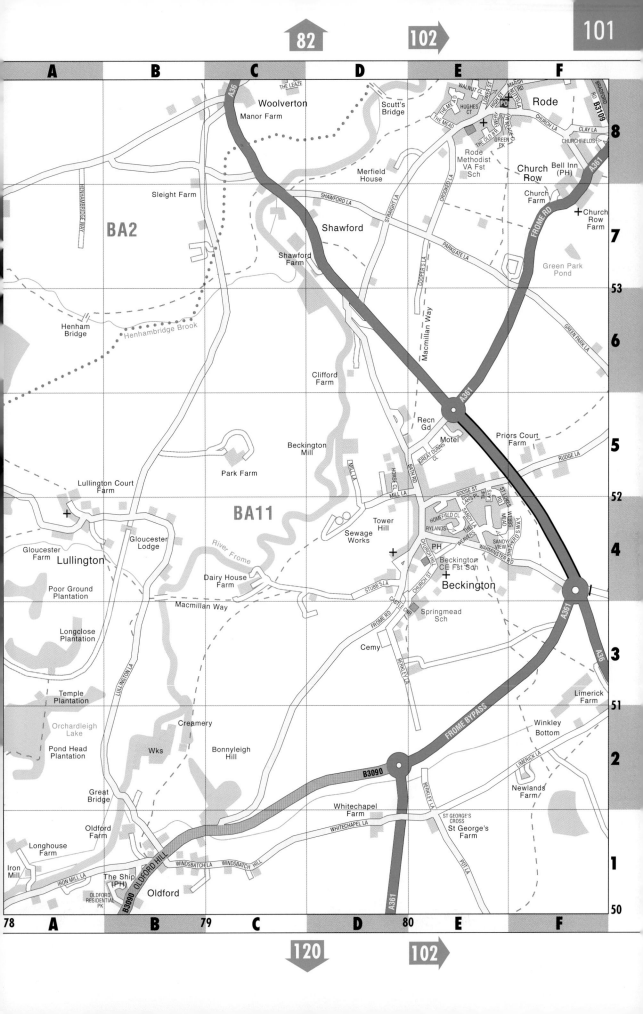

101
83

	A	B	C	D	E	F

8

BRADFORD RD
B3109
A361

Parsonage Farm

Rode Farm

Monkley La

BA14

The Devil's Bed & Bolster

7

Mount Pleasant

53

Duck Pool La

Castley Farm

Norris Hill Farm

Overcourt Farm

6

Seymour's Court

RUDGE LA

DUCK POOL LA

Duck Pool Farm

CASTLEY LA

Silver Street Farm

Brokerswood Country Pk

Hazel Wood

Upper Castley Farm

Church Farm

Round Wood

5

Waterslade

RUDGE HILL

FAIRWOOD RD

Honeybridge Farm

SCOTLAND LA

Lower Rudge Hill Farm

Rudge

Brokerswood

52

Full Moon (PH)

The Kicking Donkey (PH)

BA13

4

BA11

Lower Rudge

Carter's Bridge

White Row Farm

DADLEY LA

Stourton Bushes

3

Scotland Farm

RUDGE LA

STANDERWICK

51

Standerwick Court

Trees Farm

LC

2

Palmer's Farm

Court Farm

Bell Inn (PH)

RUDGE RD

Standerwick

TENNIS CORNER DRO

Round Wood

Fairwood Farm

Leigh Farm

STANDERWICK CROSS

Barber's Wood

Cuzner's Farm

BERKLEY ST

Frome Market

B3099

MARSH RD

A36

FOX'S DRO

1

Westbury View

A36

Five Lords Farm

CLIVEY

Clivey

Clivey Farm

B3099
DEERWOOD

50

81	A		B	82	C		D	83	E		F

Wiltshire STREET ATLAS

Stert Island

Stert Point

Fenning
Island

Bridgwater Bay
National Nature
Reserve

River Parrett

Manor
Farm

Cox's
Farm

River Parrett Trail

Collards
Farm

STEART RD

TA5

TA9

LEEKBEDS LANE - TRACK

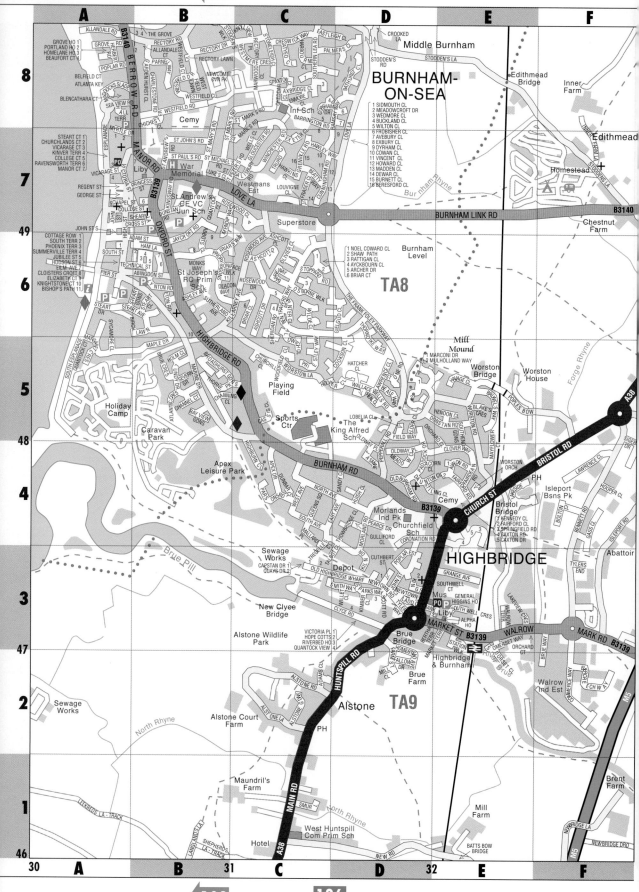

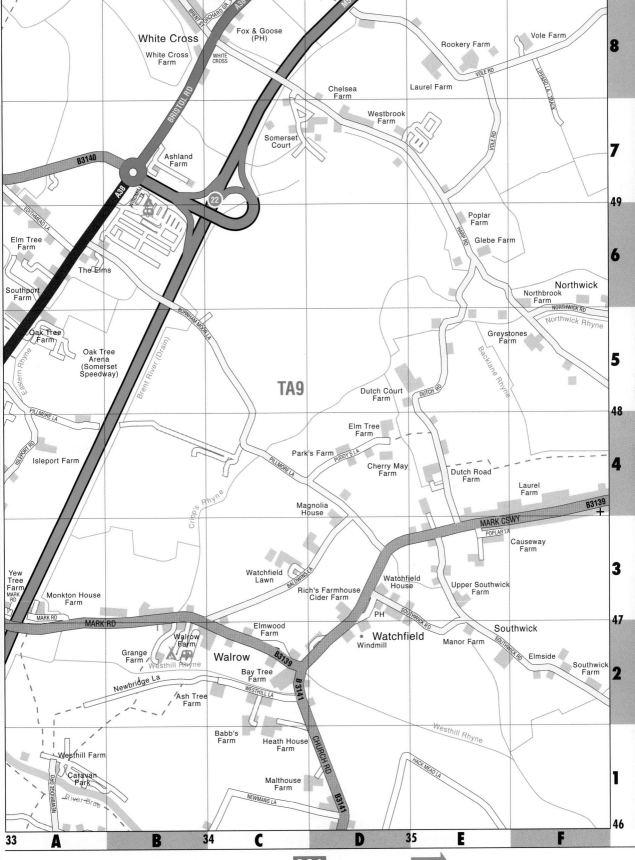

A   B   C   D   E   F

White Cross
Fox & Goose (PH)
White Cross Farm
WHITE CROSS
Ashland Farm
B3140
A38
22
BRISTOL RD
ORCHARD DR
BRENT ST
WINDMILL LA

Rookery Farm
Vole Farm
Chelsea Farm
Laurel Farm
VOLE RD
TIPPARD LA - TRACK
Westbrook Farm
Somerset Court
VOLE RD
HARP RD

8

7

49

Elm Tree Farm
The Elms
Southport Farm
EDITHMEAD LA
A38

Poplar Farm
Glebe Farm
Northwick
Northbrook Farm
NORTHWICK RD
Northwick Rhyne

6

Oak Tree Farm
Oak Tree Arena (Somerset Speedway)
Eastern Rhyne
BURNHAM MOOR LA
Brent River (Drain)

TA9

Greystones Farm
Backlane Rhyne

5

48

PILLMORE LA
Isleport Farm
ISLEPORT RD

Park's Farm
Elm Tree Farm
PUDDY'S LA
Cherry May Farm
PILLMORE LA
Dutch Court Farm
DUTCH RD
Dutch Road Farm

4

Cripp's Rhyne

Magnolia House

Laurel Farm
B3139
MARK CSWY
POPLAR LA
Causeway Farm

Watchfield Lawn
BALDWINS LA
Rich's Farmhouse Cider Farm
Watchfield House
Watchfield
Windmill
PH
SOUTHWICK RD
Upper Southwick Farm
Manor Farm
Southwick
SOUTHWICK RD
Elmside
Southwick Farm

3

47

Yew Tree Farm
MARK RD
Monkton House Farm
MARK RD
Grange Farm
Westhill Rhyne
Walrow
Walrow Farm
Elmwood Farm
B3139
Newbridge La
Bay Tree Farm
WESTHILL LA
Ash Tree Farm
B3141

2

Babb's Farm
Heath House Farm
Malthouse Farm
CHURCH RD
B3141

Westhill Farm
Caravan Park
River Brue
NEWBRIDGE DRO
NEWMANS LA

1

46

33   A   B   34   C   D   35   E   F

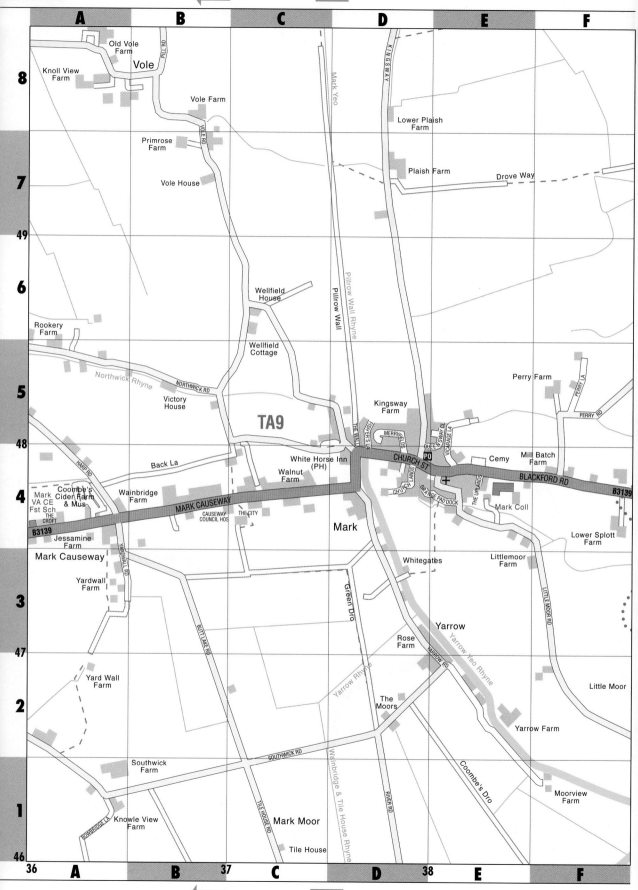

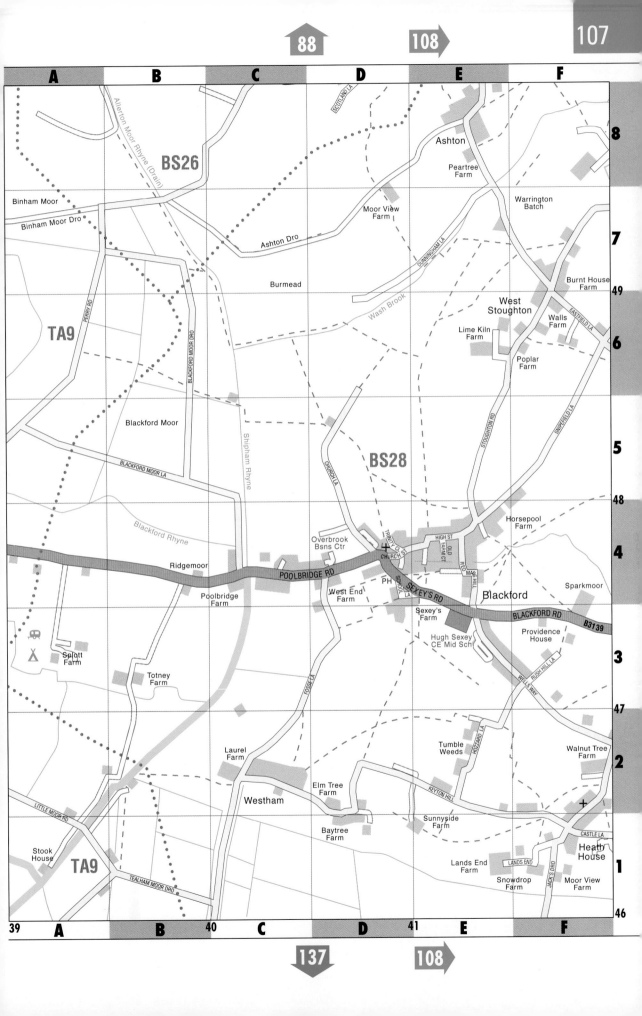

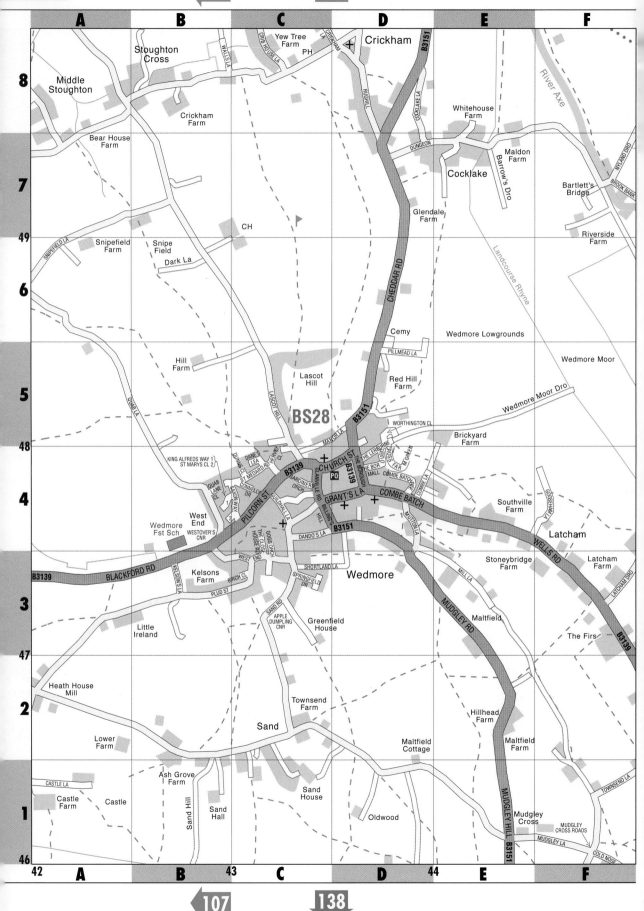

A B C D E F

8 Middle Stoughton
Stoughton Cross
Yew Tree Farm
PH
Crickham
Crickham Farm
Bear House Farm
Whitehouse Farm
Maldon Farm
River Axe

7 Cocklake
Barrow's Dro
Bartlett's Bridge
Brook Bank

49 CH
Snipefield Farm
Snipe Field
Glendale Farm
Riverside Farm

6 Dark La
Cheddar Rd
Landcourse Rhyne

5 Hill Farm
Lascot Hill
Cemy
Wedmore Lowgrounds
Wedmore Moor
Red Hill Farm
BS28
Wedmore Moor Dro

48 King Alfreds Way 1
St Marys Cl 2
Dane's Lea
Medard Rd
Brickyard Farm
Worthington Cl
Church St
The Borough
Combe Batch
Southville Farm

4 West End
Westover's Cnr
Pilcorn St
Grant's La
Combe Batch
Wells Rd
Latcham
Latcham Farm

3 Wedmore Fst Sch
Kelsons Farm
Birch Cl
Dando's La
Wedmore
Stoneybridge Farm
Latcham Dro

47 Little Ireland
Apple Dumpling Cnr
Greenfield House
Mudgley Rd
Maltfield
The Firs
B3139

2 Heath House Mill
Townsend Farm
Hillhead Farm
Maltfield Farm

Lower Farm
Sand
Maltfield Cottage

1 Castle Farm
Castle
Ash Grove Farm
Sand Hill
Sand Hall
Sand House
Oldwood
Mudgley Cross
Mudgley Cross Roads
Cold Nose

46
42 A B 43 C D 44 E F

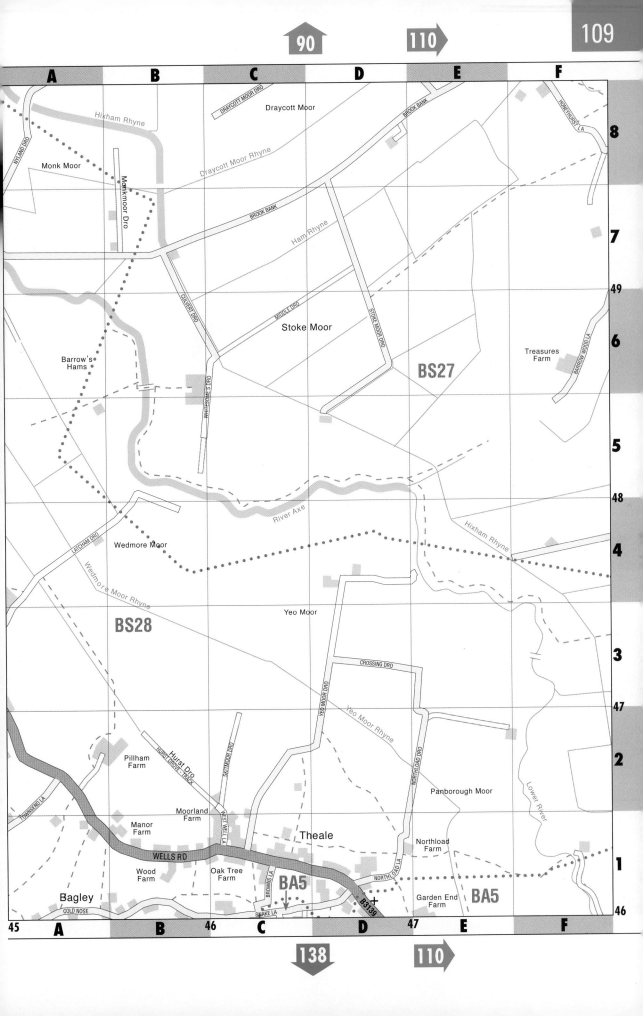

109
91

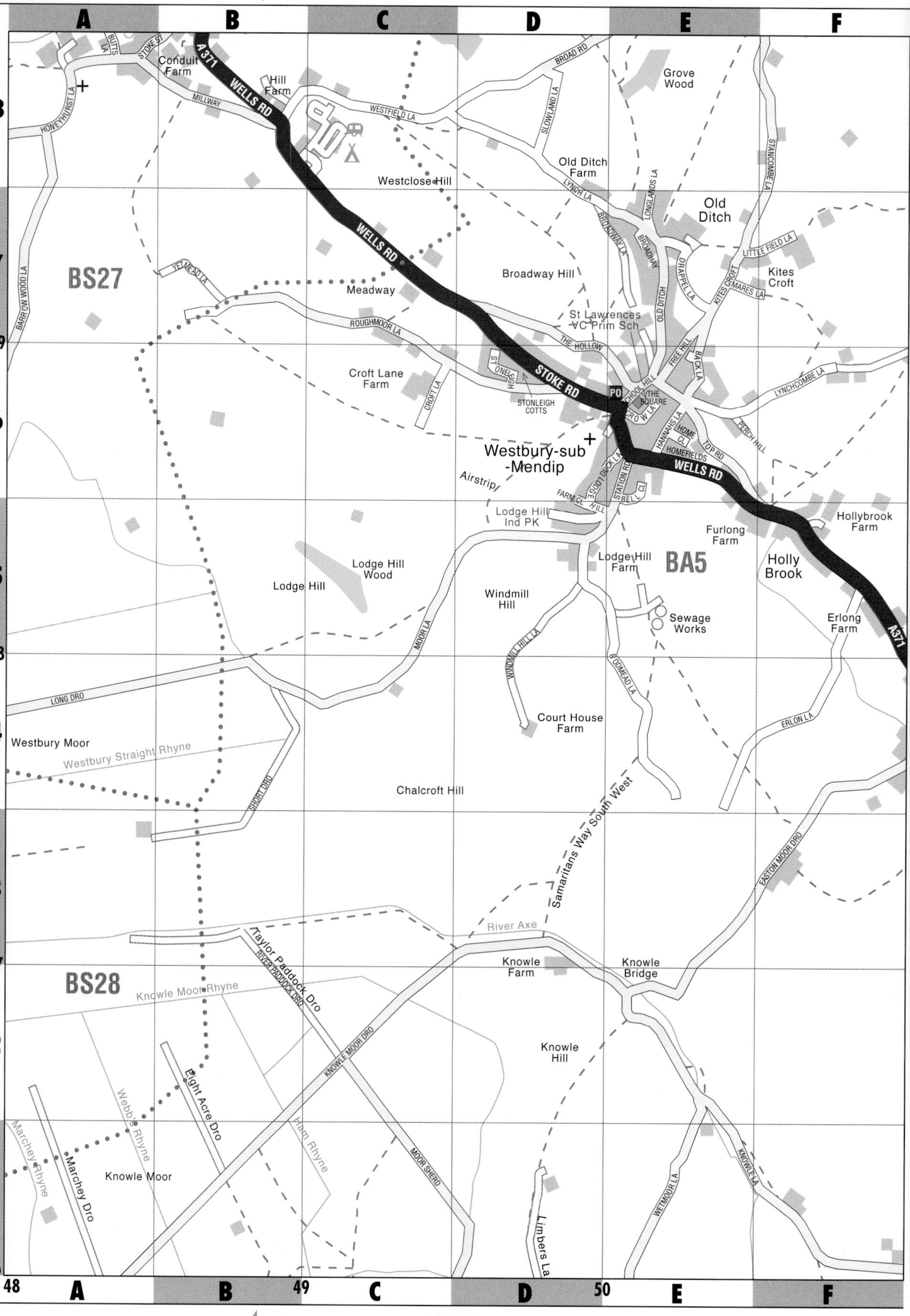

A B C D E F

8

Honeyhurst La
Butts La
Stoke St
Conduit Farm
A 371
Hill Farm
Millway
WELLS RD
Westfield La
Broad Rd
Grove Wood
Westclose Hill
Slowland La
Old Ditch Farm
Lynch La
Longlands La
Old Ditch
Stancombe La

7

BS27
Barer Wd Wood La
Yer Mead La
Meadway
WELLS RD
Broadway Hill
Broad Way La
Broad La
Drapple La
Kites Croft La
Smares La
Little Field La
Kites Croft

49

Roughmoor La
Croft Lane Farm
St Onec La
THE HOLLOW
St Lawrences VC Prim Sch
Old Ditch
Free Hill
Back La
Lynchcombe La

6

Croft La
STOKE RD
Stonleigh Cotts
PO
SCHOOL HILL
THE SQUARE
W La
Westbury-sub-Mendip
HOME CL
Mannars La
Home Cl
Homefields
TOP RD
Perch Hill

Airstrip
Lodge Hill Ind PK
FARM CL
FOOT DICK LA
HILL
Station Rd
BEL CL
WELLS RD

5

Moor La
Lodge Hill Wood
Lodge Hill
Windmill Hill
Lodge Hill Farm
Furlong Farm
Holly Brook
Hollybrook Farm
BA5
Sewage Works
Erlong Farm
A 371

48

Long Dro
Resort Dro
Westbury Moor
Westbury Straight Rhyne
Court House Farm
Windmill Hill La
Homead La
ERLON LA

4

Chalcroft Hill
Samaritans Way South West
Easton Moor Dro

3

Taylor Paddock Dro
River Paddock Dro
River Axe
Knowle Farm
Knowle Bridge

47

BS28
Knowle Moor Rhyne
Knowle Moor Dro
Knowle Hill

2

Marchey Rhyne
Webbs Rhyne
Eight Acre Dro
Ham Rhyne
Moor Sherd
Knowmea La
Homea La

1

Marchey Dro
Knowle Moor
Wetmoor La
Limbers La

46

48 A B 49 C D E 50 F

109
139

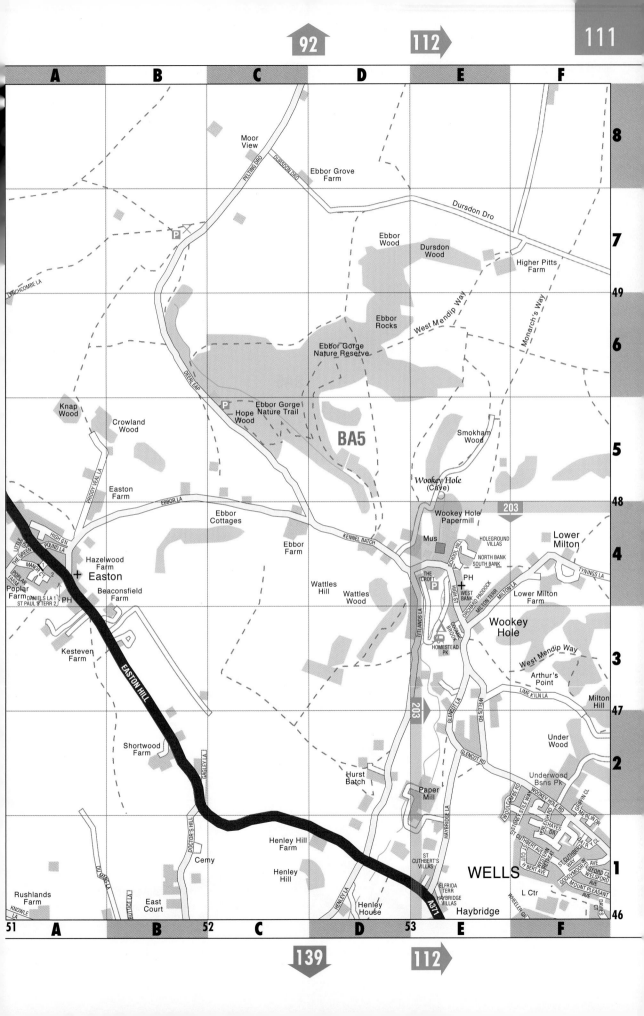

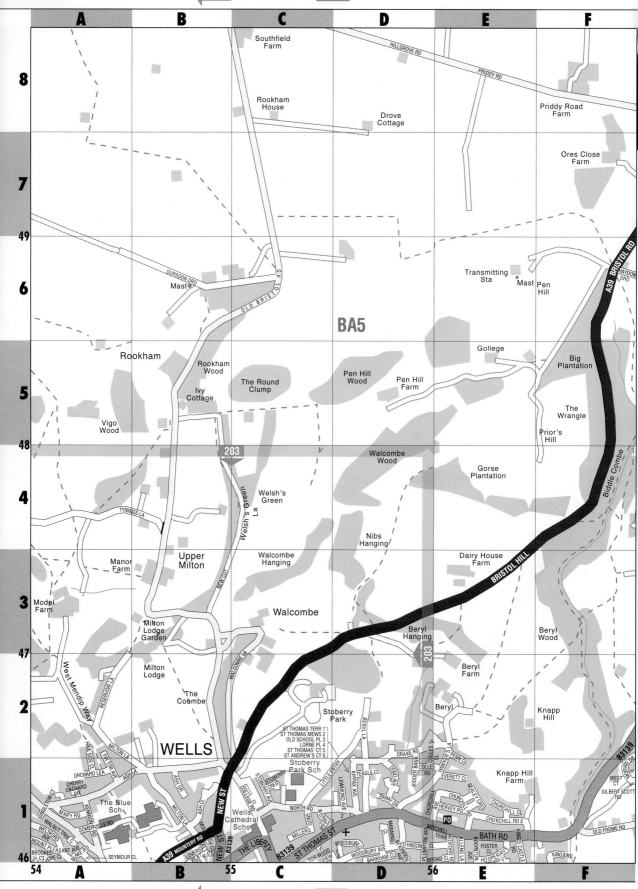

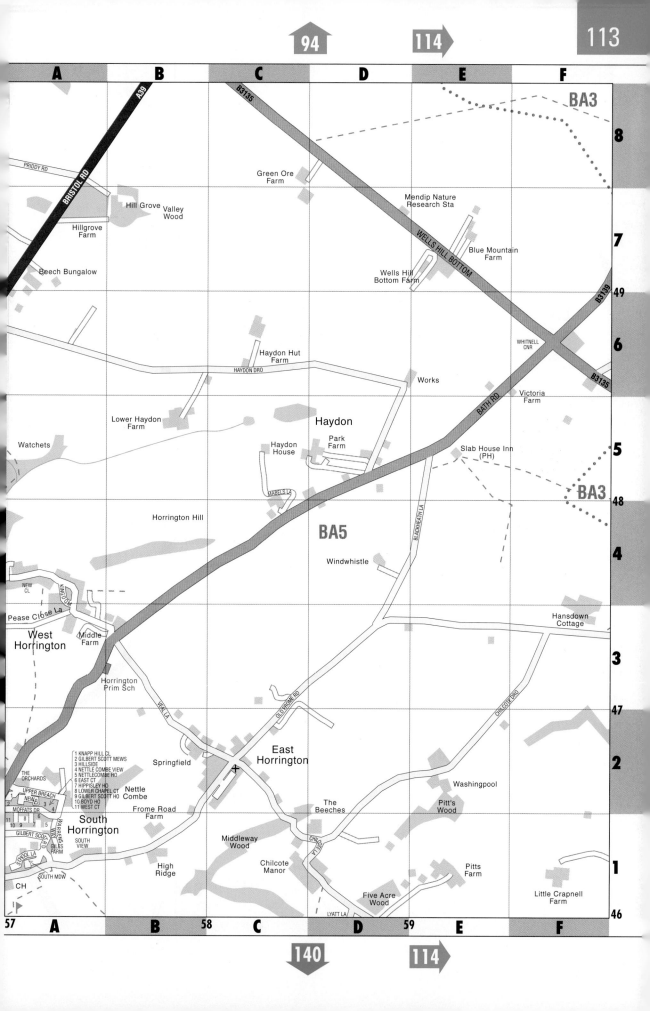

A B C D E F

BA3

8

PRIDDY RD

A39

BRISTOL RD

B3135

Green Ore Farm

Hill Grove
Valley Wood

Hillgrove Farm

Beech Bungalow

Mendip Nature Research Sta

WELLS HILL BOTTOM

Blue Mountain Farm

7

Wells Hill Bottom Farm

B3139

49

WHITNELL CNR

6

B3135

Haydon Hut Farm

HAYDON DRO

Works

BATH RD

Victoria Farm

Lower Haydon Farm

Haydon

Watchets

Haydon House

Park Farm

Slab House Inn (PH)

5

MABELS LA

48

BA3

Horrington Hill

BA5

Windwhistle

BLACKHEATH LA

4

Hansdown Cottage

NEW CL

KINGDOM

Pease Close La

West Horrington

Middle Farm

CHILCOTE DRO

3

47

Horrington Prim Sch

VEA LA

OLD FROME RD

East Horrington

1 KNAPP HILL CL
2 GILBERT SCOTT MEWS
3 HILLSIDE
4 NETTLE COMBE VIEW
5 NETTLECOMBE HO
6 EAST CT
7 HIPPISLEY HO
8 LOWER CHAPEL CT
9 GILBERT SCOTT HO
10 BOYD HO
11 WEST CT

Springfield

Nettle Combe

THE ORCHARDS

UPPER BREACH

NEW CL

MOFFATS DR

Frome Road Farm

The Beeches

CHILCOTE LA

Washingpool

Pitt's Wood

2

GILBERT SCOTT

WARRENS WAY

South Horrington

GILES FARM

SOUTH VIEW

High Ridge

Middleway Wood

Chilcote Manor

Pitts Farm

SCHOOL LA

CH

SOUTH MDW

Five Acre Wood

Little Crapnell Farm

1

LYATT LA

46

113
95

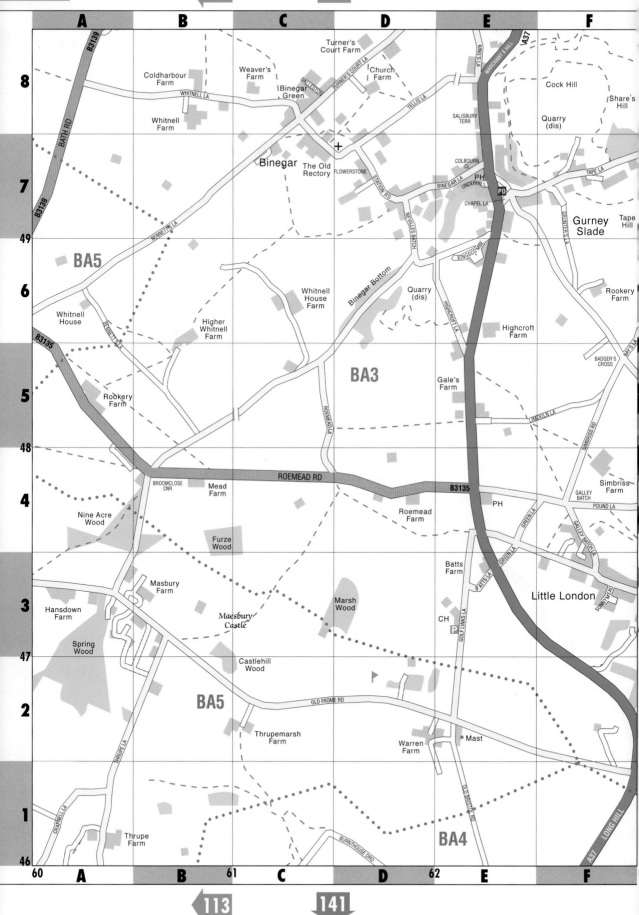

113
141

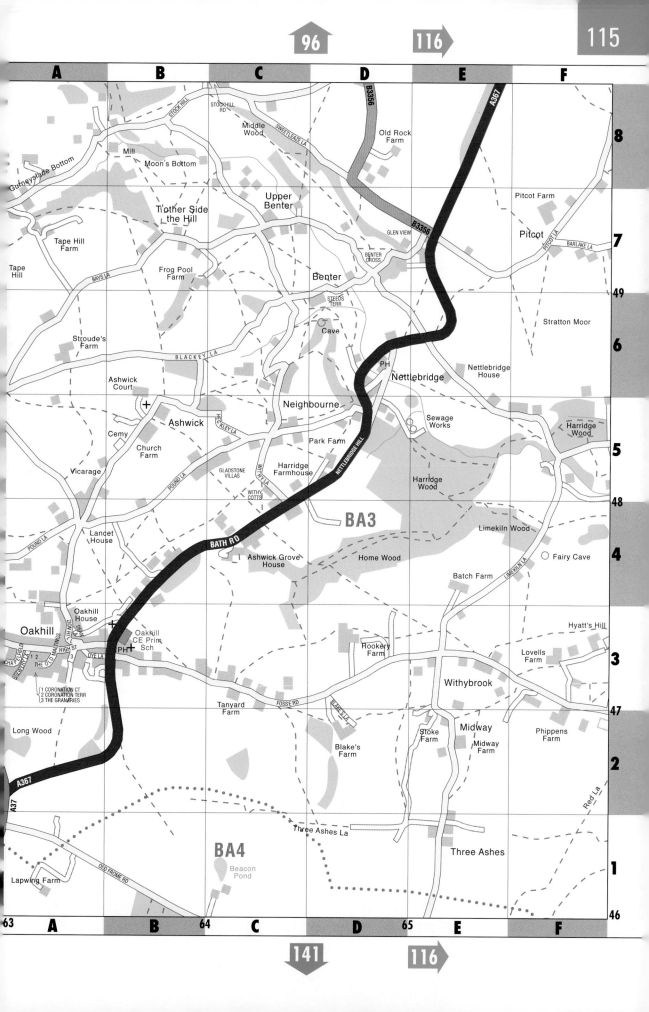

115
97

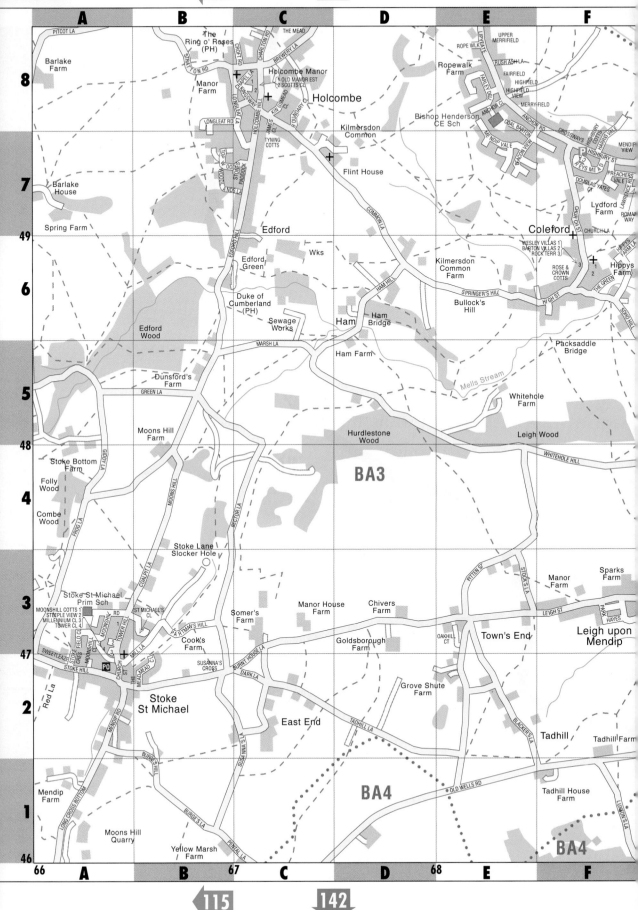

115
142

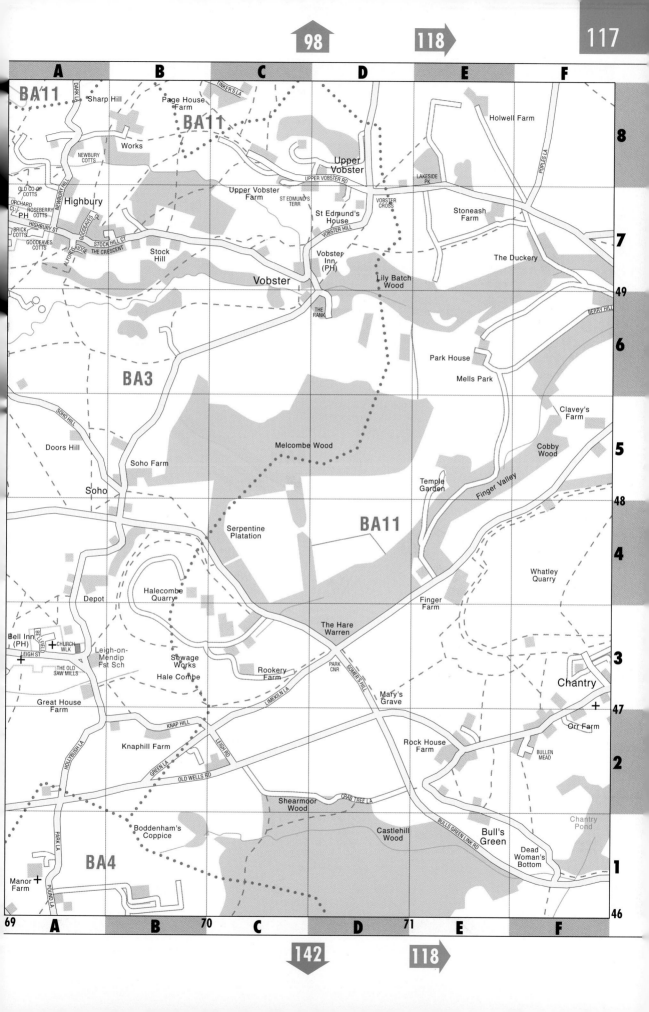

BA11

Sharp Hill

Page House Farm

TINKER'S LA

BA11

Works

NEWBURY COTTS

Holwell Farm

POPLES LA

8

OLD CO-OP COTTS

ORCHARD CL

Highbury

ROSEBERRY COTTS

PH

Upper Vobster

Upper Vobster Farm

UPPER VOBSTER RD

ST EDMUND'S TERR

St Edmund's House

Stoneash Farm

LAKESIDE PK

VOBSTER CROSS

HIGHBURY ST

BRICK COTTS

GOODEAVES COTTS

ALFORD'S RIDGE

NEWBURY HILL

DARK LA

GOODEAVES CL

STOCK HILL CT

THE CRESCENT

Stock Hill

Vobster

VOBSTER HILL

Vobster Inn (PH)

Lily Batch Wood

The Duckery

7

49

THE RANK

BERRY HILL

BA3

Park House

Mells Park

6

SOHO HILL

Doors Hill

Soho Farm

Melcombe Wood

Clavey's Farm

Cobby Wood

5

Soho

Temple Garden

Finger Valley

48

Serpentine Platation

BA11

Whatley Quarry

4

Depot

Halecombe Quarry

Finger Farm

Bell Inn (PH)

BELL FIELD

CHURCH WLK

LEIGH ST

THE OLD SAW MILLS

Leigh-on-Mendip Fst Sch

Sewage Works

Hale Combe

Rookery Farm

The Hare Warren

PARK CNR

SOMER'S HILL

LIMEKILN LA

Mary's Grave

Chantry

Orr Farm

3

47

Great House Farm

HOLLYBUSH LA

KNAP HILL

Knaphill Farm

GREEN LA

LEIGH RD

OLD WELLS RD

Rock House Farm

BULLEN MEAD

2

Boddenham's Coppice

Shearmoor Wood

CRAB TREE LA

Castlehill Wood

BULLS GREEN LINK RD

Bull's Green

Chantry Pond

PARK LA

POUND LA

BA4

Manor Farm

Dead Woman's Bottom

1

46

117
99

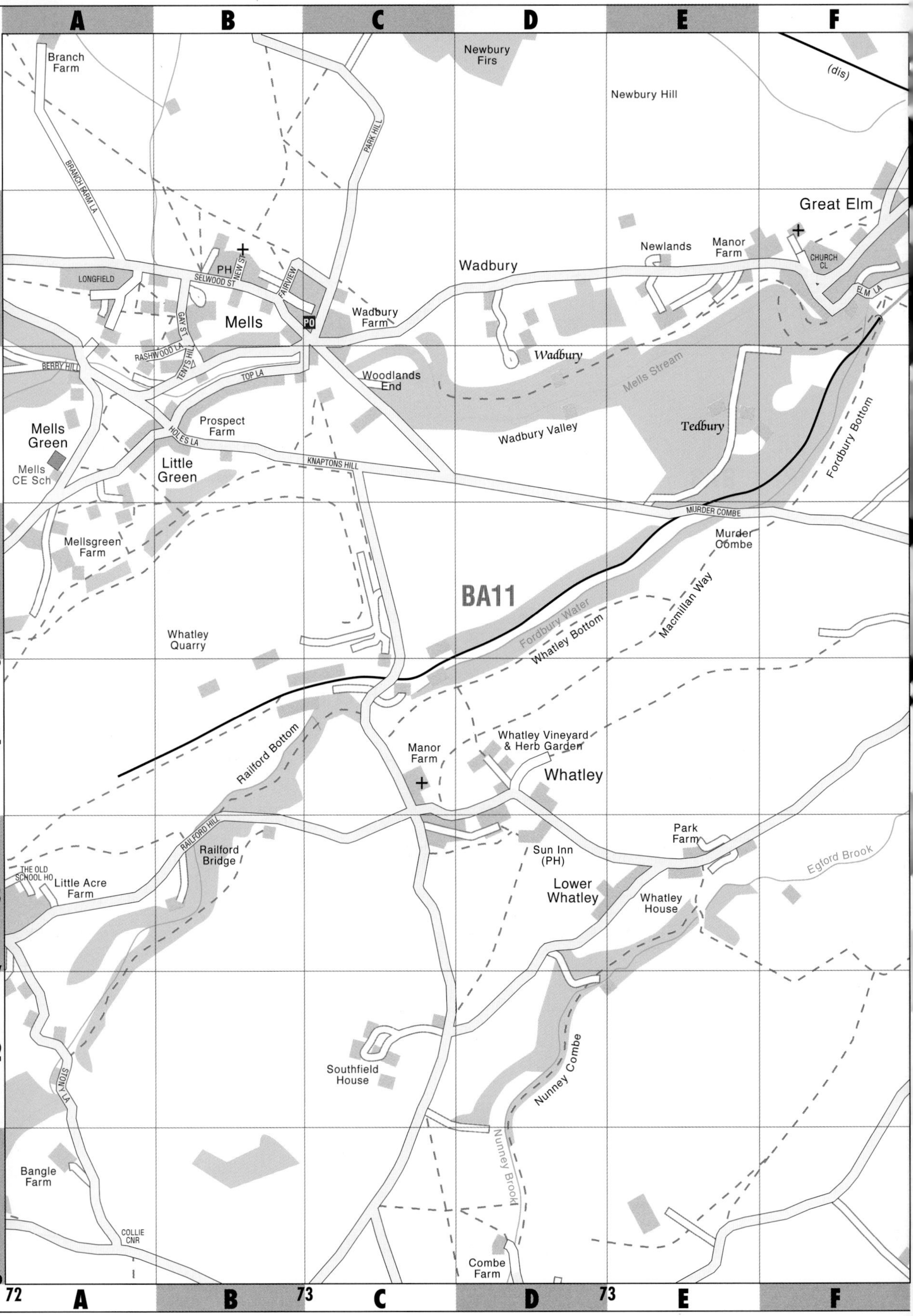

A　B　C　D　E　F

8

Branch Farm

Newbury Firs

Newbury Hill

(dis)

7

Great Elm

BRANCH FARM LA

LONGFIELD

PH

SELWOOD ST

NEW ST

FAIRVIEW

Wadbury

Newlands

Manor Farm

CHURCH CL

ELM LA

49

Mells

PO

Wadbury Farm

Wadbury

Mells Stream

GRY ST

RASHWOOD LA

TENTS HILL

TOP LA

Woodlands End

BERRY HILL

Wadbury Valley

Tedbury

Fordbury Bottom

6

Mells Green

HOLES LA

Prospect Farm

KNAPTONS HILL

Little Green

Mells CE Sch

MURDER COMBE

Murder Combe

5

Mellsgreen Farm

Whatley Quarry

BA11

Macmillan Way

Fordbury Water

Whatley Bottom

48

Railford Bottom

Manor Farm

Whatley Vineyard & Herb Garden

Whatley

4

RAILFORD HILL

Park Farm

Egford Brook

Railford Bridge

Sun Inn (PH)

THE OLD SCHOOL HO

Little Acre Farm

Lower Whatley

Whatley House

3

47

Nunney Combe

2

STONY LA

Southfield House

Nunney Brook

Bangle Farm

1

COLLIE CNR

Combe Farm

46

72　A　B　73　C　D　73　E　F

100

120

F5
1 DELTA CT
2 FOUNDRY BARTON
3 Farleigh Further
  Ed Coll

119

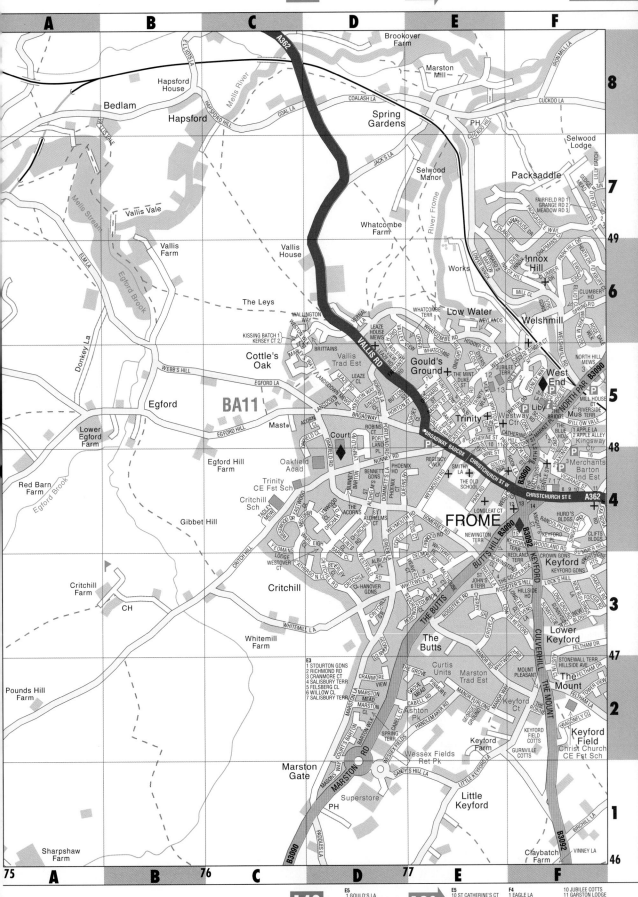

143

120

E5
1 GOULD'S LA
2 GOULD'S GROUND
3 SPININGMILL COTTS
4 WILTSHIRES BARTON
5 YORK ST
6 OLD PRINT WORKS
7 VALLIS CT
8 MORGAN'S LA
9 HOOPERS BARTON

E5
10 ST CATHERINE'S CT
11 SHEPPARD'S BARTON
12 Vallis Fst Sch
13 St Louis RC
   Prim Sch

E5
1 ST CATHERINE'S CT
2 CHURCH ST
3 MERCHANTS' BARTON
4 KNOLL VIEW
5 KNOLL HO
6 THE OLD BREWERY
7 BLINDHOUSE LA
8 VICARAGE CL
9 PLUMBER'S BARTON

F4
1 EAGLE LA

10 JUBILEE COTTS
11 GARSTON LODGE
12 WESLEY VILLAS
13 WESLEY SLOPE
14 GOREHEDGE
15 KEYFORD COTTS
16 MERCHANTS
   BARTON
17 St John's CE
   VA Fst Sch

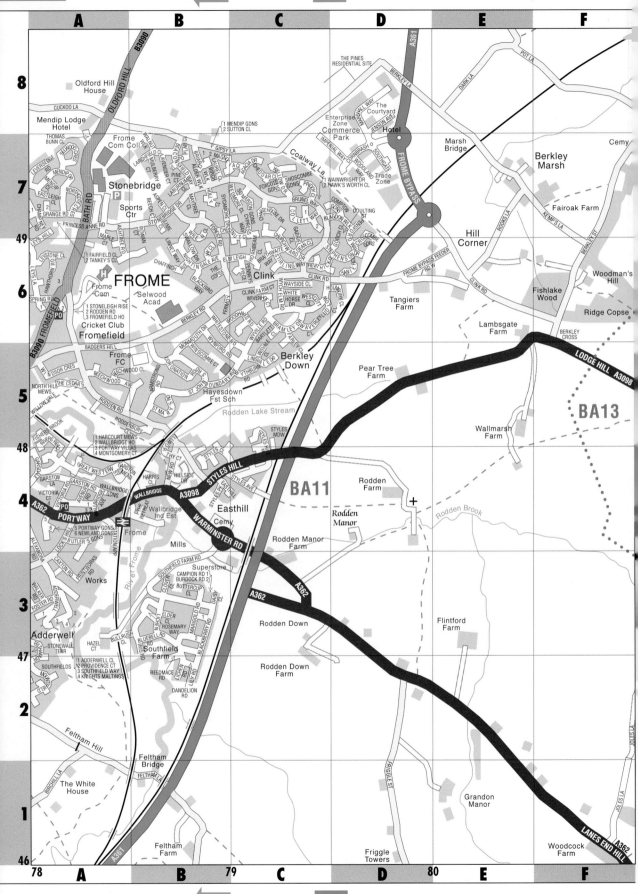

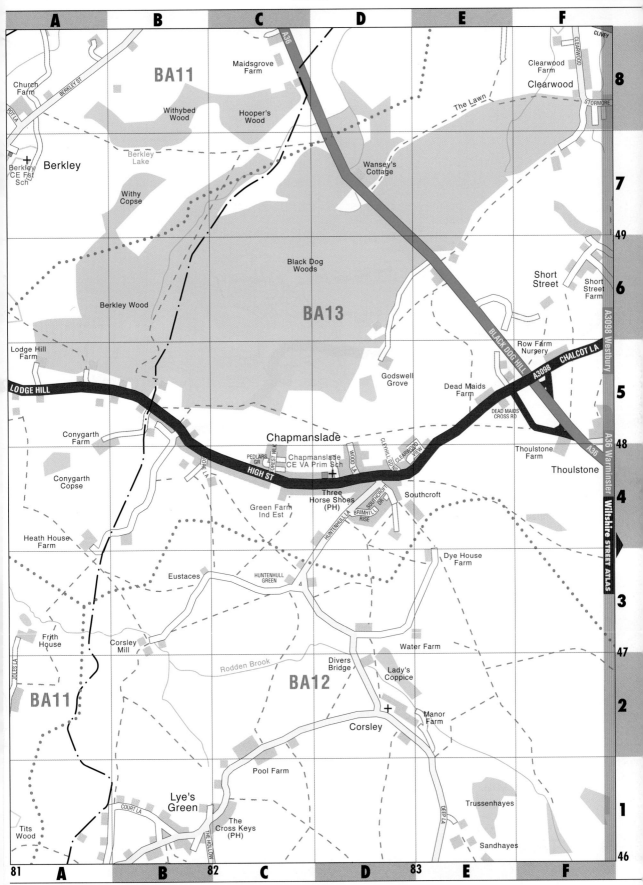

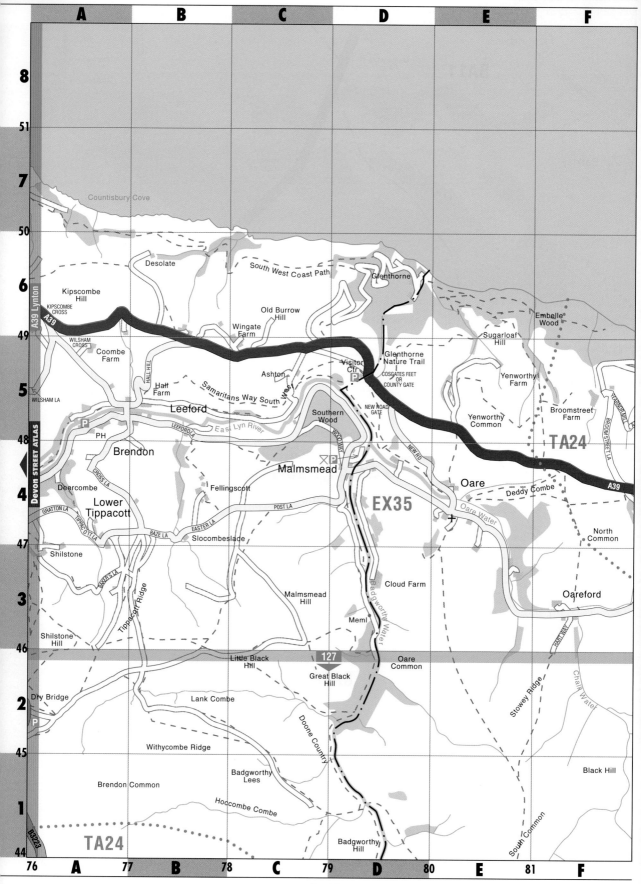

A   B   C   D   E   F

8

51

7

Countisbury Cove

50

6   Desolate   South West Coast Path   Glenthorne

Kipscombe
Hill   KIPSCOMBE
CROSS

49   Old Burrow
Hill   Embelle
Wood

Wingate
Farm   Sugarloaf
Hill

WILSHAM
CROSS   Glenthorne
Nature Trail   Yenworthy
Farm

Coombe
Farm   Ashton   Visitor
Ctr   COSGATES FEET
OR
COUNTY GATE

5   HALL HILL   Samaritans Way South   West   Yenworthy
Common   Broomstreet
Farm

WILSHAM LA   Hall
Farm   Leeford   NEW ROAD
GATE   TA24

LEEFORD LA   East Lyn River   Southern
Wood   Yenworthy
Common   BROOM STREET LA

48   P   PH   WOOD WAY   NEW RD

Brendon

Malmsmead   Oare

4   Deercombe   Fellingscott   EX35   Deddy Combe   North
Common

GRATTON LA   CROSS LA   TIPPACOTT LA   Lower
Tippacott   Slocombeslade   POST LA   Oare Water   A39

BAZE LA   EASTER LA   Oareford

Shilstone

3   BAKERS LA   Malmsmead
Hill   Cloud Farm

Tippacott Ridge   Meml   Badgworthy Water   Stowey Ridge   Chalk Water

46   Shilstone
Hill   Little Black
Hill   127   Oare
Common

Dry Bridge   Great Black
Hill   BEER WAY

2   P   Lank Combe   Doone Country   Black Hill

45   Withycombe Ridge   Badgworthy
Lees   South Common

Brendon Common

1   Hoccombe Combe

44   B3223   TA24   Badgworthy
Hill

76   A   77   B   78   C   79   D   80   E   81   F

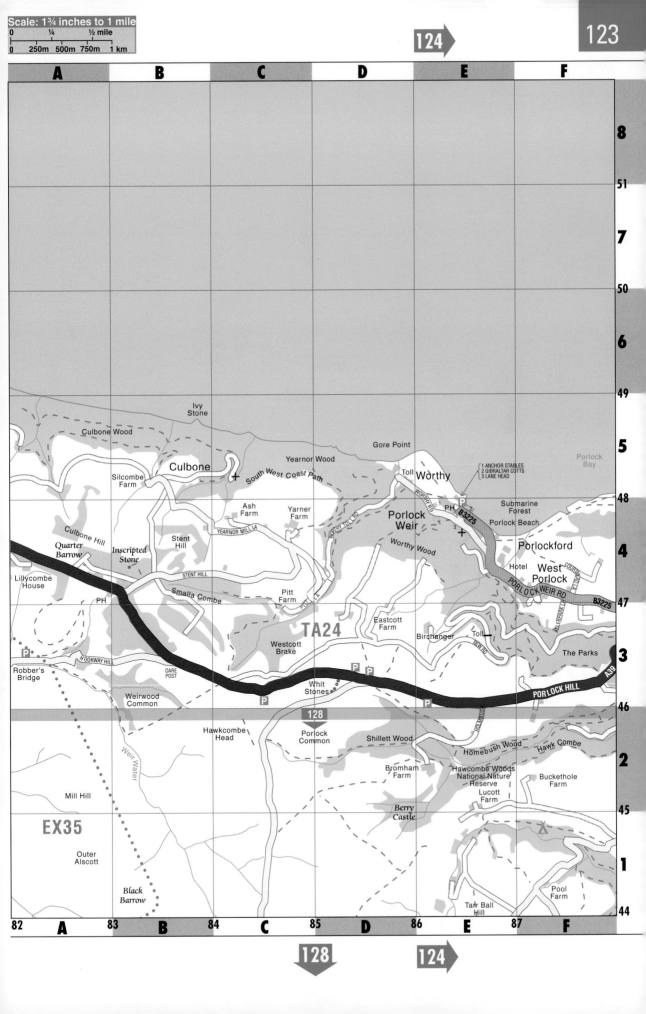

A   B   C   D   E   F

8

51

7

50

6

49

5

Ivy Stone

Culbone Wood

Culbone

Silcombe Farm

Quarter Barrow

Culbone Hill

Lillycombe House

PH

Robber's Bridge

P

HOOKWAY HILL

OARE POST

Weirwood Common

Mill Hill

EX35

Outer Alscott

Black Barrow

Weir Water

Inscripted Stone

Stent Hill

Ash Farm

YEARNOR MILL LA

STENT HILL

Smalla Combe

Yarner Farm

Yearnor Wood

South West Coast Path

Gore Point

Toll

Worthy

Porlock Weir

Worthy Wood

Westcott Brake

Pitt Farm

PITT LA

Whit Stones

P

P P

P

Hawkcombe Head

Porlock Common

128

Bromham Farm

Berry Castle

Shillett Wood

Homebush Wood

Hawcombe Woods National Nature Reserve

Lucott Farm

Tarr Ball Hill

Hawk Combe

Bucket hole Farm

Pool Farm

1 ANCHOR STABLES
2 GIBRALTAR COTTS
3 LANE HEAD

Porlock Bay

Submarine Forest

Porlock Beach

PH B3225

Porlockford

Hotel

West Porlock

PORLOCK WEIR RD

B3225

Eastcott Farm

Birchanger

Toll

NEW RD

The Parks

A39

PORLOCK HILL

COURT PLACE

ALLERBARROW

HOLLOW COMBE

TA24

48

4

47

3

46

2

45

1

44

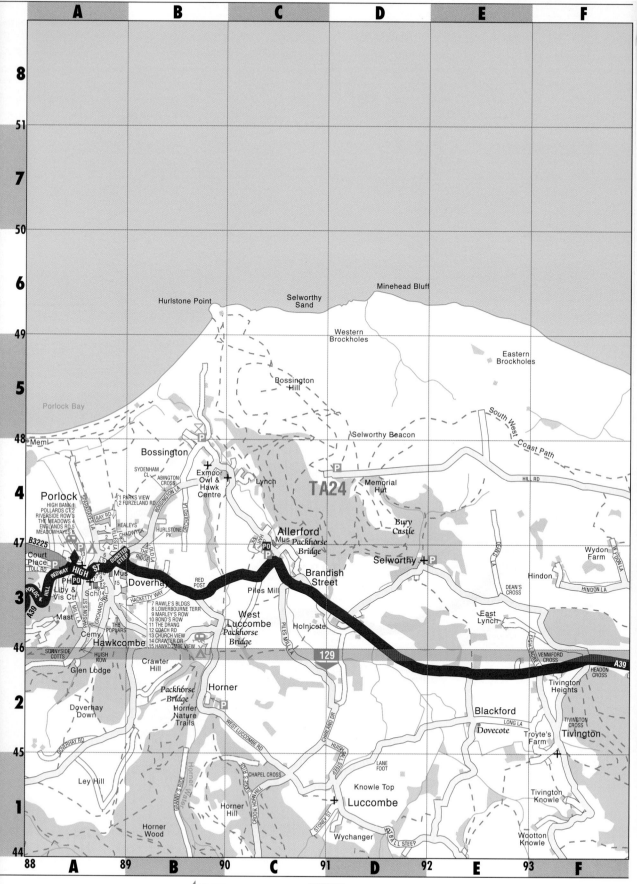

Scale: 1¾ inches to 1 mile
0   ¼   ½ mile
0   250m 500m 750m 1 km

A   B   C   D   E   F

8

51

7

50

6

Minehead Bluff

Hurlstone Point

Selworthy Sand

49

Western Brockholes

Eastern Brockholes

5

Porlock Bay

Bossington Hill

Selworthy Beacon

South West Coast Path

48

Meml

Bossington

Hill RD

Exmoor Owl & Hawk Centre

SYDENHAM CL

ABINGTON CROSS

Lynch

TA24

Memorial Hut

4

Porlock

HIGH BANK 1
POLLARDS CT 2
RIVERSIDE ROW 3
THE MEADOWS 4
ENGLANDS RD 5
MEADOWHAYES 6

1 PARKS VIEW
2 FURZELAND RD

BAY RD

HEALEYS

CHADWYCK

HURLSTONE PK

Bury Castle

Allerford
Mus

Packhorse Bridge

Wydon Farm

47

B3225

Court Place

Toll RD

PO-LOCK

HILL

REDWAY

HIGH ST

Mus

DUNSTER STEEP

THE RIDGE

OLD LA

RED POST

Brandish Street

Selworthy

Hindon

HINDON LA

PO

Lby & Vis Ctr

PH

Sch

ORCHARD LA

PARSON'S ST

Doverhay

Piles Mill

DEAN'S CROSS

3

A39

Mast

Cemy

Hawkcombe

HUISH ROW

MILL LA

THE POPLARS

HACKETTY WAY

7 RAWLE'S BLDGS
8 LOWERBOURNE TERR
9 MARLEY'S ROW
10 BOND'S ROW
11 THE DRANG
12 COACH RD
13 CHURCH VIEW
14 CRAWTER DR
15 HAWKCOMBE VIEW

West Luccombe
Packhorse Bridge

Holnicote

PILES MILL LA

East Lynch

EIGHT ACRE LA

VENNIFORD CROSS

A39

HEADON CROSS

Tivington Heights

46

SUNNYSIDE COTTS

Glen Lodge

Crawter Hill

Packhorse Bridge

Horner

Horner Nature Trails

129

Blackford

Dovecote

Troyte's Farm

Tivington

TIVINGTON CROSS

2

Doverhay Down

WEST LUCCOMBE RD

CHURCH DR

HUISH STEEP

LONG LA

LANE FOOT

HALL STEEP

Tivington Knowle

45

DOVERHAY RD

GRANNY'S RIDE

Horner Water

SOUTH HILL

CROOK HORN HILL

CHAPEL CROSS

Knowle Top

Tivington Knowle

Ley Hill

Horner Hill

Horner Wood

STONEY ST

Luccombe

Wychanger

Wootton Knowle

1

44

88   A   89   B   90   C   91   D   92   E   93   F

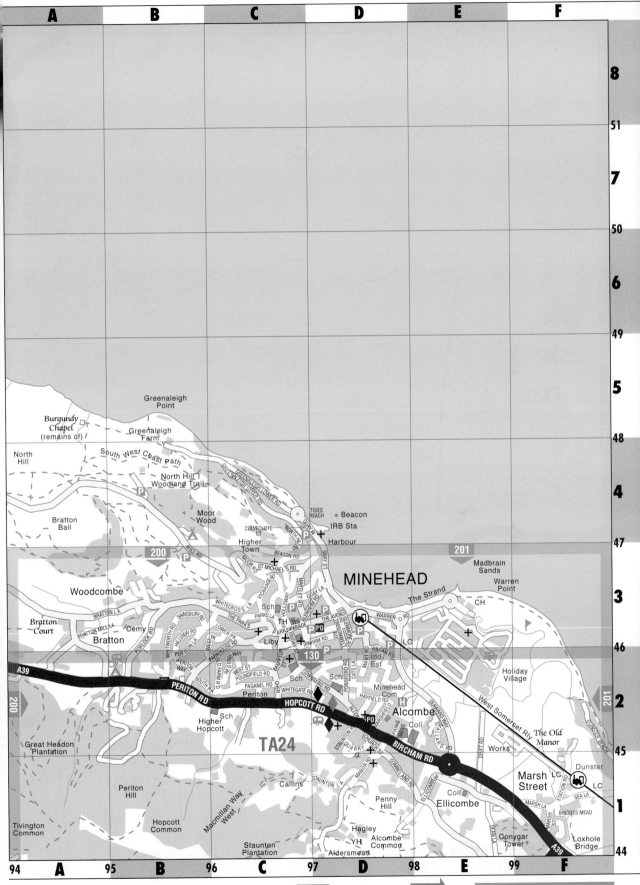

Scale: 1¾ inches to 1 mile

0   ¼   ½ mile
0 250m 500m 750m 1 km

125

A B C D E F

8
51
7
50
6
49
5
48
4
47
3
46
2
45
1
44

94 A 95 B 96 C 97 D 98 E 99 F

130 **131**

For full street detail of the highlighted areas see pages 200 and 201.

Greenaleigh Point
Burgundy Chapel (remains of)
Greenaleigh Farm
North Hill
South West Coast Path
North Hill Woodland Trail
Moor Wood
Bratton Ball
Culvecliffe Ct
Higher Town
St Michael's Rd
Beacon Rd
Tides Reach
Beacon
IRB Sta
Harbour
Woodcombe
Bratton La
Bratton Mill La
Cemy
Bratton Court
Bratton
Porlock Rd
Hillview Rd
Whitecross La
The Parks
Sainsbury Rd
Lower Rd
Peiton La
Sch
TH
Liby
The Parade
Friday St
PO
Irnham Rd
The Avenue
Blenheim Rd
Quay La
Tregonwell Rd
MINEHEAD
WARREN RD
The Strand
CH
Warren Point
Madbrain Sands
201
200
Mill Rd
Moor Rd
North Wk
Quay W
Vicarage Rd
North St
Quay St
Martlet Rd
Hollyway
P
P
LC
Ind Est
A39
200
201
Periton Rd
Regens Way
Parkhouse Rd
Old Farm Rd
West St
Poundfield Rd
Paganel Rd
South Pk
Periton Way
Sch
Cher
Whitegate Rd
Periton
130
Townsend Rd
Bancks Rd
Ponsford Rd
Cats La
Sch
Hopcott Rd
Higher Hopcott
Sch
Great Headon Plantation
Periton Hill
Higher Hopcott
TA24
Staunton Quarry
Manor Rd
Staunton Hill
Callins
Staunton La
Church St
Bircham Rd
Comeland Rd
Alcock Rd
Marshfield
Spring
PO
Hayfield Rd
Minehead Com
Seaward Way
Alcombe
Coll
H
Ballard Rd
Elicombe
Works
Deer Rd
The Old Manor
West Somerset Rly
Holiday Village
Dunster
LC
LC
Marsh Street
Station Rd
Sea La
Marsh St
Dunster Beach
Bridges Mead
Hopcott Common
Macmillan Way West
Callins
Penny Hill
Ellicombe
Coll
Ellicombe
Tivington Common
Staunton Plantation
Aldersmead
Hagley
YH
Alcombe Common
Conygar Tower
Loxhole Bridge
A39

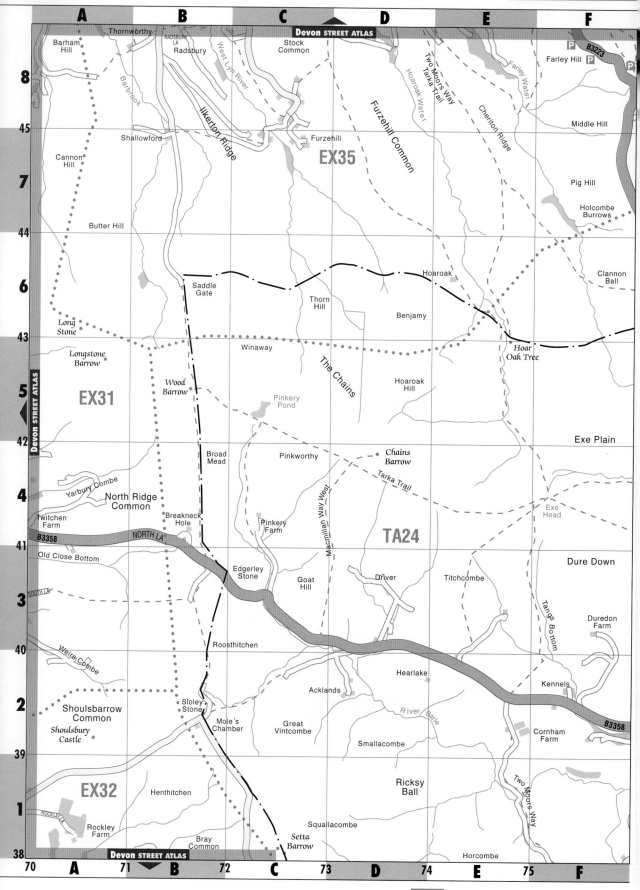

Scale: 1¾ inches to 1 mile

0   ¼   ½ mile
0   250m 500m 750m 1 km

Devon STREET ATLAS

Thornworthy
Barham Hill
RADSBURY LA
Radsbury
West Lyn River
Stock Common
B3223
P   P
Farley Hill
P

8

45
Shallowford
Furzehill
Middle Hill
EX35
Furzehill Common
Two Moors Way Tarka Trail
Hoaroak Water
Cheriton Ridge
Farley Water

Cannon Hill
Ilkerton Ridge
Barbrook

7
Pig Hill

44
Butter Hill
Holcombe Burrows

6
Saddle Gate
Hoaroak
Clannon Ball
Thorn Hill
Benjamy

Long Stone
43
Winaway
The Chains
Hoar Oak Tree

Longstone Barrow
Wood Barrow
Hoaroak Hill

5
EX31
Pinkery Pond
Exe Plain

42
Broad Mead
Pinkworthy
Chains Barrow
Tarka Trail

Yarbury Combe
North Ridge Common
Exe Head

4
Twitchen Farm
Breakneck Hole
Pinkery Farm
Macmillan Way West
TA24
Dure Down

B3358
NORTH LA
41
Old Close Bottom
Edgerley Stone
Driver
Titchcombe
Tangs Bottom
Duredon Farm

SOUTH LA
3
Goat Hill

40
Roosthitchen
Hearlake
Kennels

Weirs Combe
Acklands
River Barle
B3358

2
Shoulsbarrow Common
Sloley Stone
Mole's Chamber
Great Vintcombe
Smallacombe
Cornham Farm

Shoulsbury Castle

39
Ricksy Ball

EX32
Henthitchen
Two Moors Way

1
ROCKLEY LA
Rockley Farm
Squallacombe

38
Bray Common
Setta Barrow
Horcombe

Devon STREET ATLAS

70   A   71   B   72   C   73   D   74   E   75   F

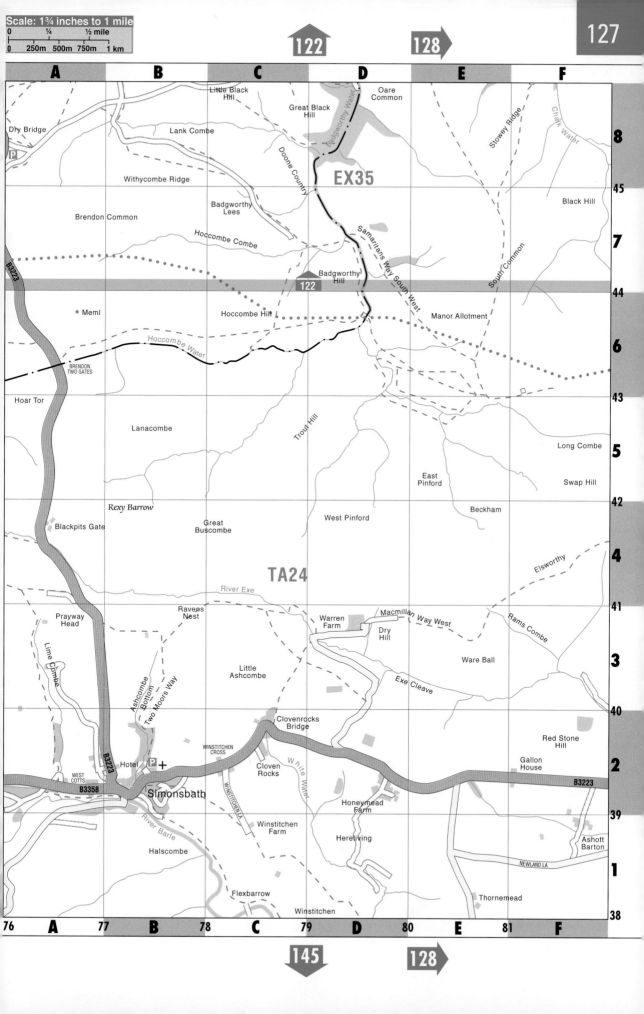

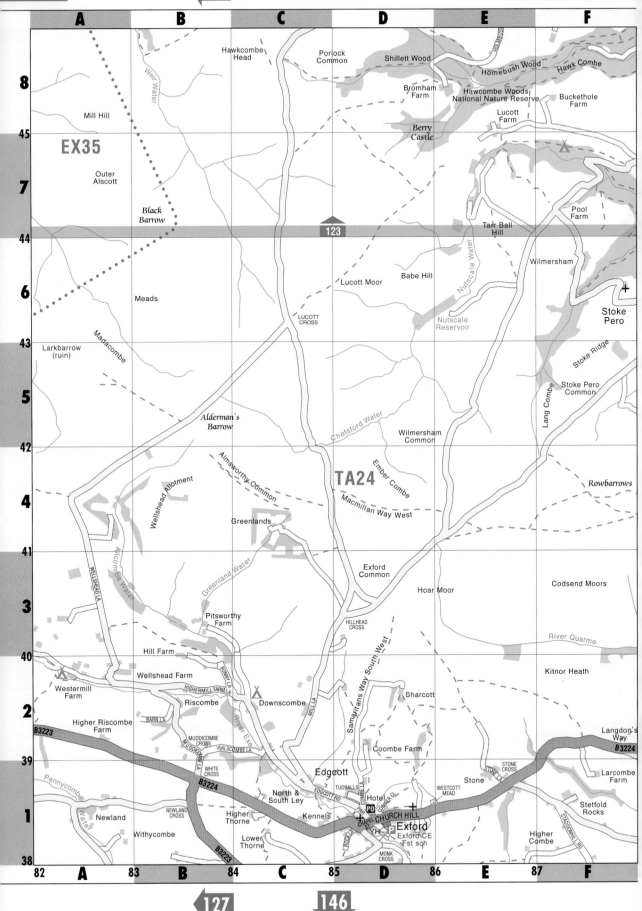

127

Scale: 1¾ inches to 1 mile

0   ¼   ½ mile
0   250m 500m 750m 1 km

A   B   C   D   E   F

8

Hawkcombe Head

Porlock Common

Shillett Wood

Homebush Wood

Hawk Combe

45

Mill Hill

EX35

Bromham Farm

Hawcombe Woods National Nature Reserve

Buckethole Farm

7

Outer Alscott

Lucott Farm

Berry Castle

44

Black Barrow

123

Pool Farm

Tarr Ball Hill

Wilmersham

6

Meads

Lucott Moor

Babe Hill

Stoke Pero

Lucott Cross

Nutscale Reservoir

43

Larkbarrow (ruin)

Madacombe

Stoke Ridge

Stoke Pero Common

Lang Combe

5

Alderman's Barrow

Chetsford Water

Wilmersham Common

42

Almsworthy Common

TA24

Ember Combe

Rowbarrows

4

Wellshead Allotment

Greenlands

Macmillan Way West

41

Greenland Water

Exford Common

Hoar Moor

Codsend Moors

River Quarme

3

Pitsworthy Farm

Hillhead Cross

Kitnor Heath

40

Hill Farm

Wellshead Farm

WELLSHEAD LA

Allcombe Water

Downscombe

Sharcott

Westermill Farm

Riscombe

HIGHERMILL FARM LA

BONNY LA

River Exe

MILL LA

Samaritans Way South West

2

Higher Riscombe Farm

BARN LA

MUDDICOMBE LA

Muddicombe Cross

YEALSCOMBE LA

Coombe Farm

Langdon's Way

B3223

White Cross

Stone

STONE LA

STONE CROSS

Larcombe Farm

B3224

39

Pennycombe Water

B3224

Edgcott

EDGCOTT RD

North & South Ley

Westcott Mead

Stetfold Rocks

1

Newland

NEWLAND CROSS

Higher Thorne

Kennels

TUDBALLS

Hotel

PO

CHURCH HILL

Exford

Exford CE Fst sch

Higher Combe

STADDONHILL RD

Withycombe

B3223

Lower Thorne

CHAPEL RD

CONNELL CL

CONNELL CL

YH

Monk Cross

FROCKLA

38

82   A   83   B   84   C   85   D   86   E   87   F

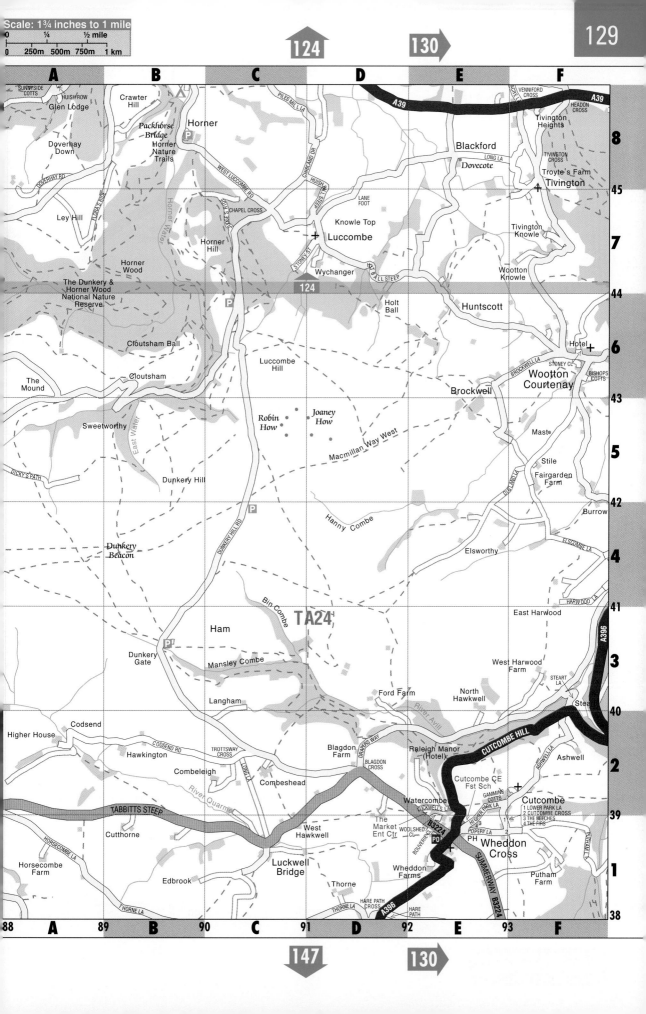

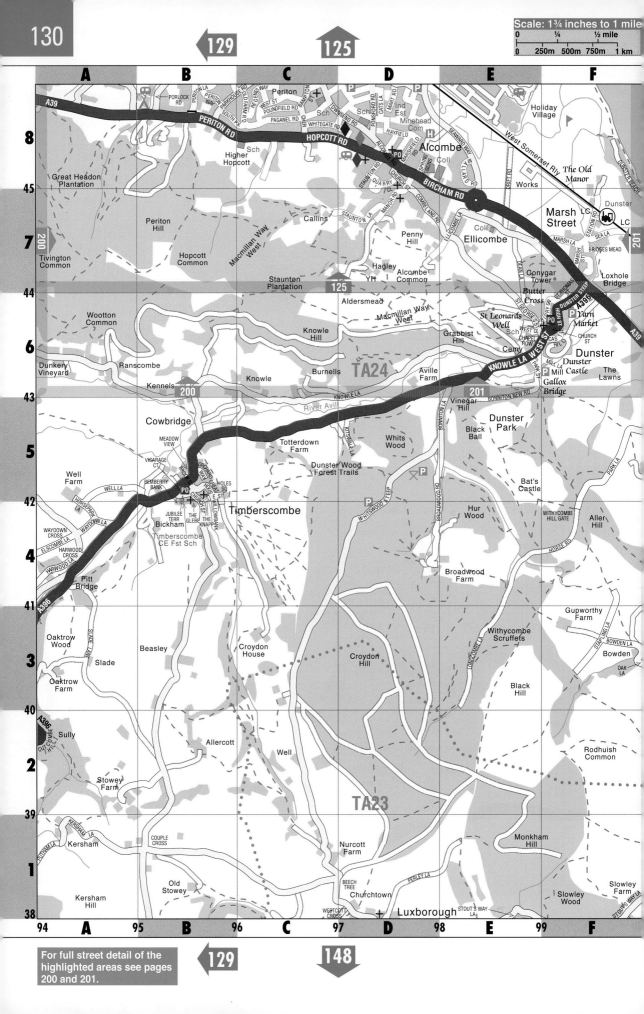

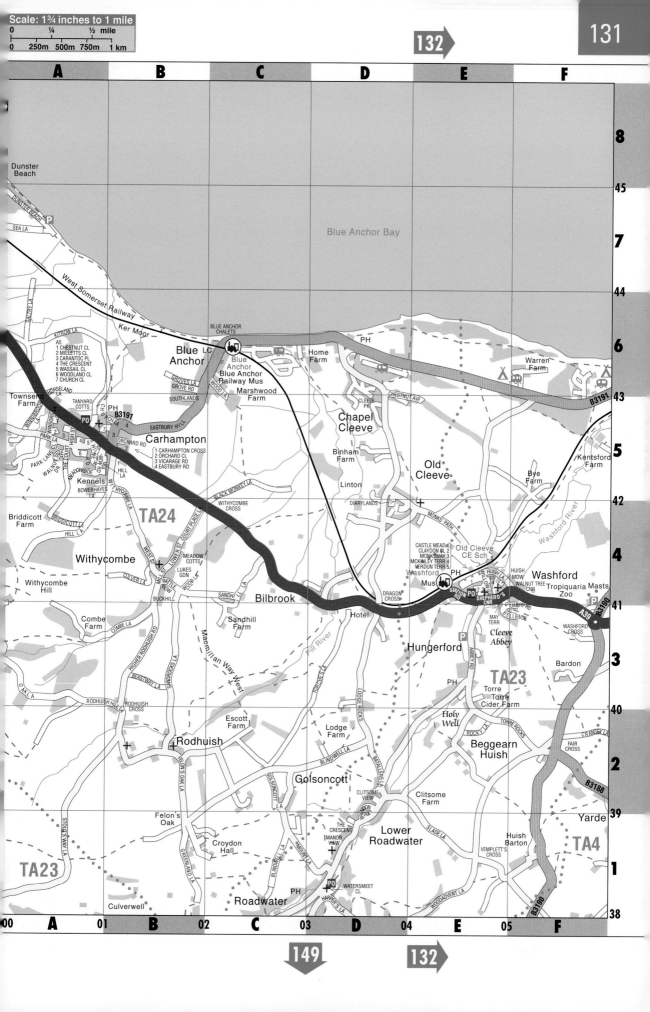

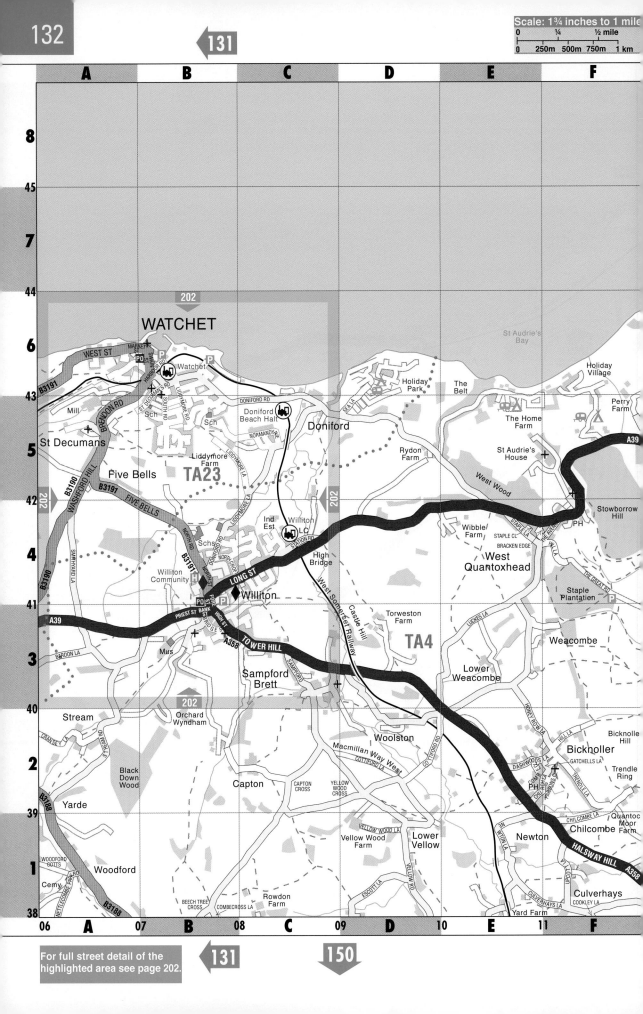

A   B   C   D   E   F

8

45

7

44

202

WATCHET

6

WEST ST
MARKET ST
PO
P
Watchet
P
SWAIN RD
HARBOUR RD

B3191

43

Mill
ST DECUMAN'S RD
SOUTH RD
Sch
LIDDYMORE RD
DONIFORD RD
Sch
Doniford
Beach Halt
Doniford

NORMANDY AVE

St Decumans
B3190
WASHFORD HILL
BRENDON RD

Five Bells
B3191
FIVE BELLS
NORTH RD
LIDDYMORE LA
Liddymore
Farm
LIDDYMORE LA

TA23

Rydon
Farm

West Wood

Holiday
Park
SEA LA
The Belt

Holiday
Village

Perry
Farm

The Home
Farm

St Audrie's
Bay

St Audrie's
House

A39

Stowborrow
Hill

42

202

B3190
SMITHYARD LA

B3191
DONIFORD RD
NORTH CROFT
Schs

Ind
Est
Williton
LC
STATION RD

202

High
Bridge

West Somerset Railway

Wibble
Farm

STAPLE LA
STAPLE CL
BRACKEN EDGE
THE AVENUE
HILL LA
PH

West
Quantoxhead

THE GREAT RD

Staple
Plantation
P

4

A39

Williton
Community
H
PRIEST ST
FORE ST
BANK ST
STRIDE GE
HIGH ST
Williton
PO

Castle Hill

Torweston
Farm

TA4

LUCKES LA

Weacombe

41

Mus

A358
TOWER HILL

Sampford
Brett

SAMPFORD

Lower
Weacombe

HONEY POW LA

Bicknolle
Hill

3

BARDON LA

Woolston

Macmillan Way West
COTTIFORD LA
COTTIFORD RD

Lower
Vellow

Bicknoller
GATCHELLS LA
DASHWOODS
COMB LA
PH
CHU RCH LA
PARSONS LA
TRENDLE LA

Trendle
Ring

202

Stream

Orchard
Wyndham

40

CRANSE LA

STREAM LA

Black
Down
Wood

Capton

CAPTON
CROSS

YELLOW
WOOD
CROSS

Chilcombe
Farm

Quantoc
Moor
Farm

Culverhays

2

B3188

Yarde

Cemy

Woodford
GOITS
NETTLECOMBE PARK RD

Woodford

B3188

BEECH TREE
CROSS
COMBECROSS LA

Rowdon
Farm

Yellow Wood
Farm

Vellow Wood
Farm

YELLOW WOOD LA

ESCOTT LA

VELLOW RD

WTON LA
3N
WYTON LA

Newton

CHILCOMBE LA
CULVERHAYS LA
CULVERHAYS LA
COOKLEY LA

HALSWAY HILL
A358

Chilcombe

PT LOGAN

1

39

38

06   A   07   B   08   C   09   D   10   E   11   F

Yard Farm

For full street detail of the
highlighted area see page 202.

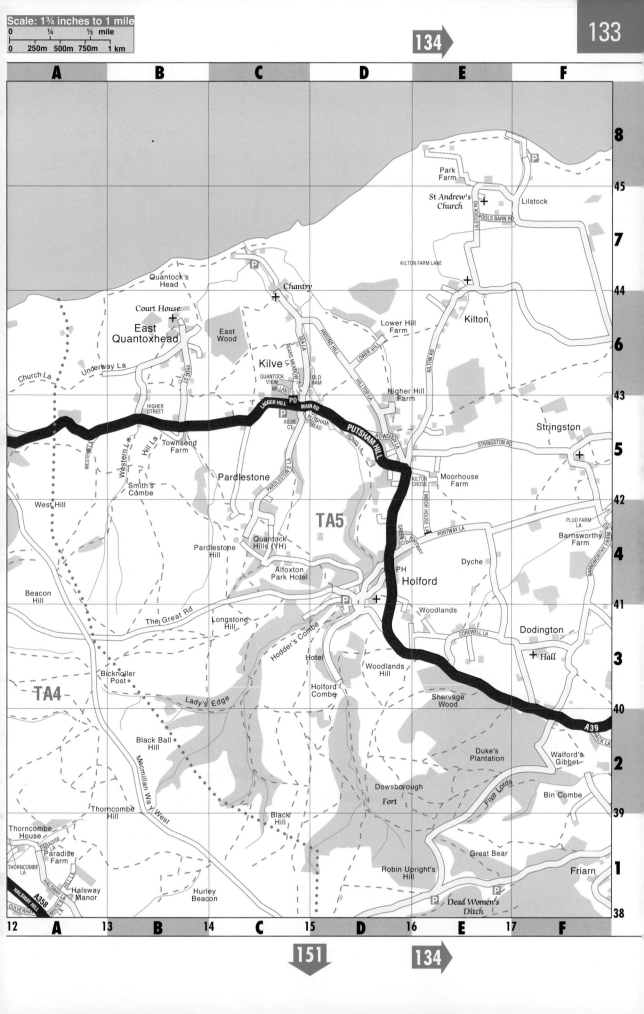

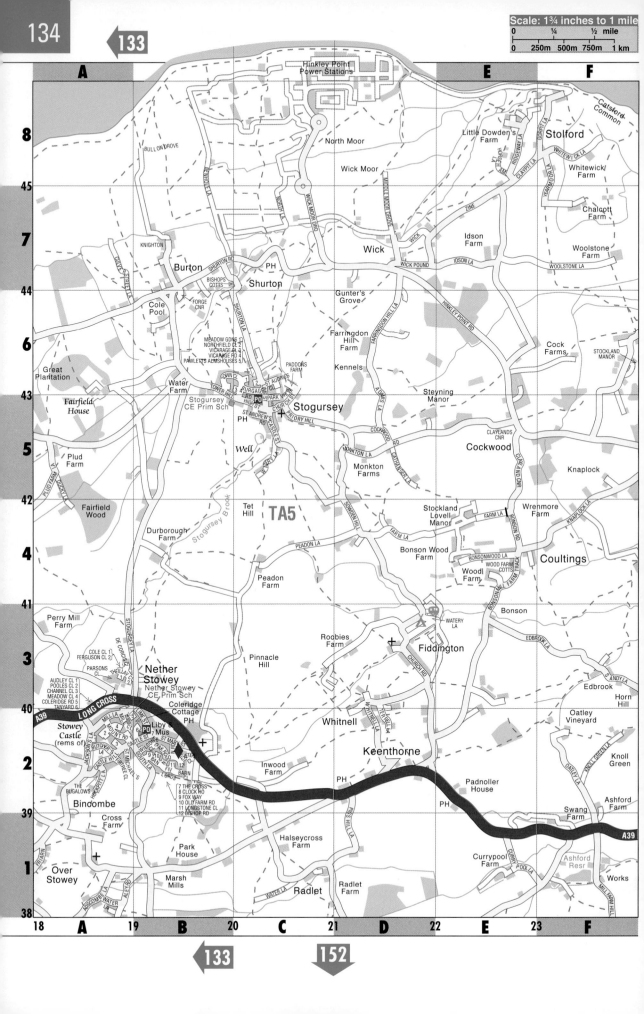

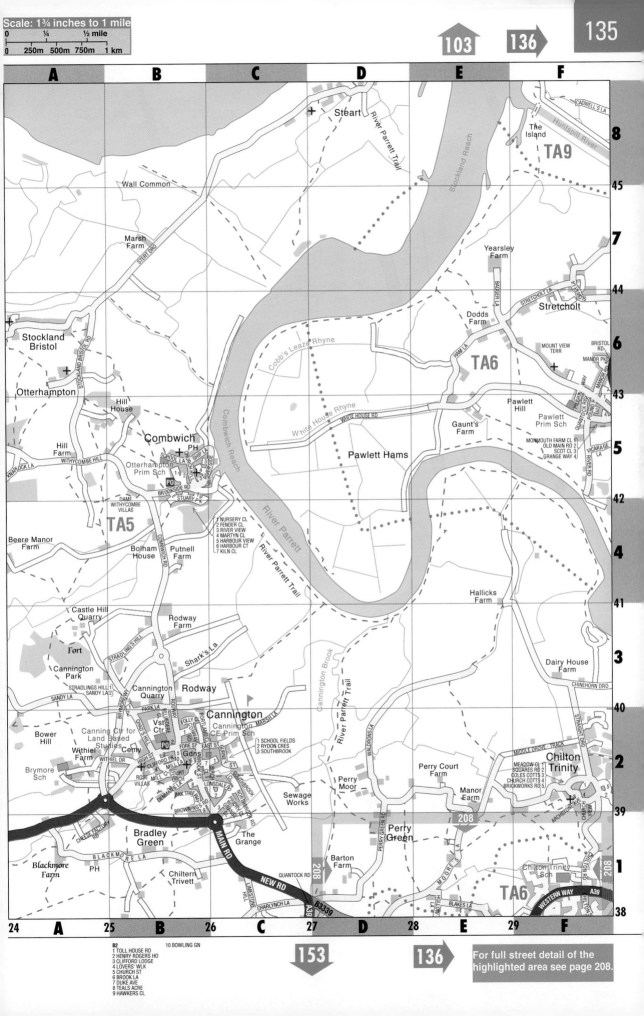

Scale: 1¾ inches to 1 mile

0 ¼ ½ mile
0 250m 500m 750m 1 km

103

136

135

A B C D E F

8
45
7
44
6
43
5
42
4
41
3
40
2
39
1
38

Steart

River Parrett Trail

Stockland Reach

Huntspill River

CADWELL'S LA

The Island

TA9

Wall Common

Marsh Farm

STERT DRO

Yearsley Farm

Dodds Farm

BADGER LA

STRETCHOLT LA

PAWLETTS

Stretcholt

Stockland Bristol

Otterhampton

STOCKLAND BRISTOL RD

Hill House

Hill Farm

WITHYCOMBE HILL

KNAPLOCK LA

Combwich

PH

Otterhampton Prim Sch

PO

SCHOOL LA
CHURCH HILL
SHIP LA
RIVERSIDE

BROOKSIDE RD

DAME WITHYCOMBE VILLAS

STUARY PK

TA5

1 NURSERY CL
2 FENDER CL
3 RIVER VIEW
4 MARTYN CL
5 HARBOUR VIEW
6 HARBOUR CT
7 KILN CL

Cobb's Leaze Rhyne

White House Rhyne

WHITE HOUSE RD

Pawlett Hams

HAM LA

TA6

Gaunt's Farm

Pawlett Hill

Pawlett Prim Sch

MOUNT VIEW TERR

PILGRIM WAY

MANOR BROOK

BRISTOL RD

MANOR PK

QUANTOCK RISE
POUND CL

VICARAGE LA

RIVER RD

MONMOUTH FARM CL 1
OLD MAIN RD 2
SCOT CL 3
GRANGE WAY 4

208

Combwich Reach

River Parrett

River Parrett Trail

Beere Manor Farm

COMBWICH RD

Bolham House

Putnell Farm

Castle Hill Quarry

Fort

Cannington Park

STRADLINGS HILL

Rodway Farm

Shark's La

Hallicks Farm

Cannington Brook

River Parrett Trail

Dairy House Farm

CHINEHORN DRO

STRAIGHT DRO

STRADLINGS HILL 1
SANDY LA 2

SANDY LA

Cannington Quarry

BROADMEAD

PARK LA

Rodway

RODWAY

Cannington

Cannington CE Prim Sch

MARSH LA

WALDRONS LA

Bower Hill

Withiel Farm

Brymore Sch

Canning Ctr for Land Based Studies

Cemy

WITHIEL DR

CHAD'S HILL

V St Ctr

PO

FOLLY
PORTLAND CL
CONWAY
FORE ST
GURNEY ST

Gdns

HIGH ST

CLIFFORD PK

ROSE VILLAS

MILL LA

BROOK ST

BIRCH

1 SCHOOL FIELDS
2 RYDON CRES
3 SOUTHBROOK

Perry Moor

Perry Court Farm

Manor Farm

MIDDLE DROVE TRACK

MEADOW CL 1
SQUARES RD 2
COLES COTTS 3
CHURCH COTTS 4
BRICKWORKS RD 5

Chilton Trinity

ARCHSTONE AVE

MANOR VIEW

CHURCH RD

CHILTON RD

208

DENMAN'S LA

OAK TREE

LONSDALE RD

BROWNING'S RD

AUSTIN RD

SOUTHBROOK

Sewage Works

PERRY GREEN RD

MOORE'S LA

Blackmore Farm

PH

CHEESE FACTORY RD

BLACKMORE LA

Bradley Green

The Grange

Chiltern Trivett

MAIN RD

NEW RD

LIMES CL

CHARLYNCH LA

QUANTOCK RD

A39

208

B3339

Barton Farm

Perry Green

WALTROTH LA

BLAKES LA

Chilton Trinity Sch

TA6

WESTERN WAY

A39

CHILTON'S

208

24 A 25 B 26 C 27 D 28 E 29 F

153

136

B2
1 TOLL HOUSE RD
2 HENRY ROGERS HO
3 CLIFFORD LODGE
4 LOVERS' WLK
5 CHURCH ST
6 BROOK LA
7 DUKE AVE
8 TEALS ACRE
9 HAWKERS CL

10 BOWLING GN

For full street detail of the highlighted area see page 208.

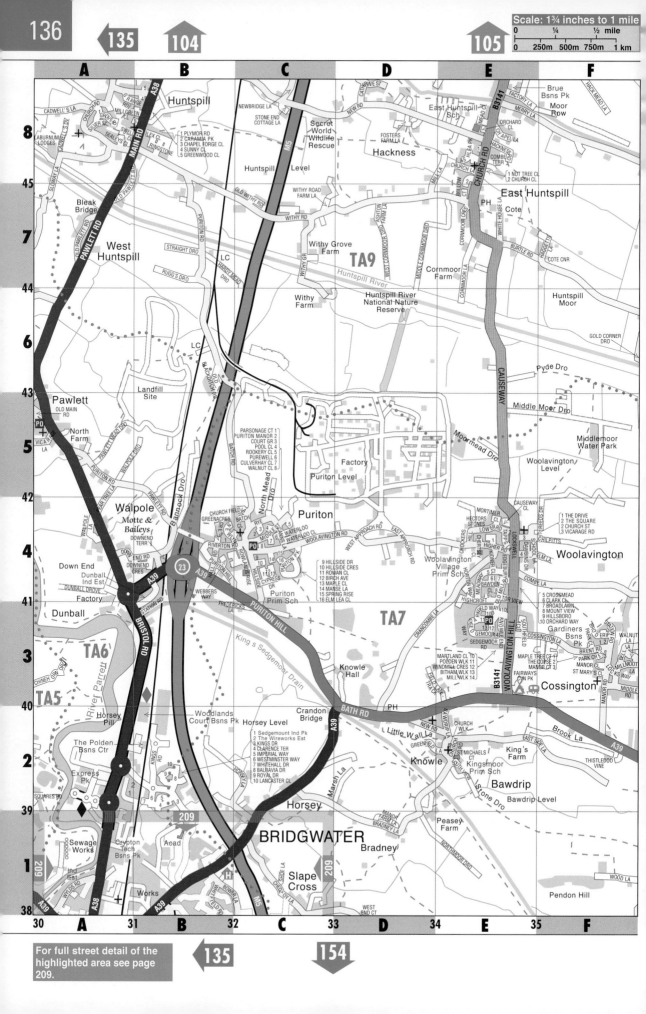

136

135
104
105

Scale: 1¾ inches to 1 mile
0   ¼   ½ mile
0 250m 500m 750m 1 km

A B C D E F

8 Huntspill
Cadwell's La Church Rd Millgreen
Laburnum Lodges
Bleak Bridge
1 PLYMOR RD
2 CARAMIA PK
3 CHAPEL FORGE CL
4 SUNNY CL
5 GREENWOOD CL
Newbridge La
Stone End Cottage La
Secret World Wildlife Rescue
East Huntspill Sch
Hackness
East Huntspill
Brue Bsns Pk
Moor Row
1 NUT TREE CL
2 CHURCH CL

45 Huntspill Level
Old Withy Rd
Withy Road Farm La
Withy Rd
Cote
PH

7 West Huntspill
Straight Dro
Rugg's Dro
Withy Grove Farm
TA9
Huntspill River
Cornmoor Farm
Huntspill Moor
Burtle Rd
Cote Cnr

44 Withy Farm
Huntspill River National Nature Reserve
Gold Corner Dro

6 Landfill Site
LC
Pyde Dro
Middle Moor Dro

43 Pawlett
Old Main Rd
North Farm
PO
Parsonage Ct 1
Puriton Manor 2
Court Gr 3
Pool Cl 4
Rookery Cl 5
Purewell 6
Culverhay Cl 7
Walnut Cl 8
Moormead Dro
Middlemoor Water Park
Woolavington Level

5 VICA LA
Puriton Level
Factory
Puriton

42 Walpole
Motte & Baileys
Downend Terr
Church Field
Greenacres
Batch
Puriton
West Approach Rd
Causeway Cl
1 THE DRIVE
2 THE SQUARE
2 CHURCH ST
3 VICARAGE RD
Woolavington

4 23 A39
Down End
Dunball Ind Est
Riverton Rd
Webbers Way
PO
9 HILLSIDE DR
10 HILLSIDE CRES
11 ROWAN CL
12 BIRCH AVE
13 MAPLE CL
14 MANSE LA
15 SPRING RISE
16 ELM LEA CL
Woolavington Village Prim Sch
5 CROSSMEAD
6 CLARK CL
7 BROADLAWN
8 MOUNT VIEW
9 HILLSBORO
10 ORCHARD WAY
Gardiners Bsns Pk

41 Dunball
Factory
Fredericks La
Puriton Hill
Puriton Prim Sch
King's Sedgemoor Drain
TA7
B3141
Woolavington Hill
MARTLAND CL 10
POLDEN WLK 11
WINDMILL CRES 12
BITHAM WLK 13
MILL WLK 14.
MAPLE TREE CT 1
THE COPSE 2
MANOR CT 3
ST MARY'S CL

3 TA6
River Parrett
Knowle Hall
Crandon Bridge
BATH RD
PH
Fairways
Cossington
Manor Rd

40 TA5
Horsey Pill
Woodlands Court Bsns Pk
Horsey Level
1 Sedgemount Ind Pk
2 The Wireworks Est
4 Kings Dr
5 Clarence Ter
5 Imperial Way
6 Westminster Way
7 Whitehall Dr
8 Balbavia Dr
9 Royal Dr
10 Lancaster Cl
Little Wall La
Church Wlk
King's Farm
Brook La
A39
Thistledoo Vine

2 The Polden Bsns Ctr
Express Pk
St Michaels Ct
Knowle
Kingsmoor Prim Sch
Bawdrip
Bawdrip Level

39 Sewage Works
209
Horsey
BRIDGWATER
Bradney
Peasey Farm
Pendon Hill

1 209
Crypton Tech Bsns Pk
Acad
Slape Cross
209
Wood La

38 209
A39
A38
A39
Works
M5
West End Ct

30 A 31 B 32 C 33 D 34 E 35 F

For full street detail of the highlighted area see page 209.

135
154

A B C D E F

8
45
7
BS28
44
6
TA9
43
5
42
BA6
4
41
3
40
2
39
1
38

36 A 37 B 38 C 39 D 40 E 41 F

Cripp's Farm
MERRY LA
Liberty Moor
TILE HOUSE RD
RIVER RD
River House Farm
Tealham Moor
North Drain
KID GATE DRO
Yellow Batches Dro
JACK'S DRO
CONGER'S DRO
TOTNEY DRO
WATT'S RD
River Brue
Liberty Farm
River Bridge
Long Moor Dro
LONG MOOR DRO
Cripps River
OUTER FURLONG DRO
Hurst Farm
MIDDLE FURLONG DRO
Burtle Hill
Burtle
Shapwick Sch
Catcott Grounds
Straight Dro
STRAIGHT DRO
GOLD CORNER DRO
WEST DRO
CHILTON DRO
PLAIN HEATH DRO
BINS LA
ROBINS DRO
MARK RD
STATION RD
BURTLE RD
WESTHAY BROAD DRO
BURTLE RD
SHAKING DRO
TA9
OLD CORNER DRO
Gold Corner Bridge
WHITCHEY DRO
NEWLANDS DRO
South Drain
Chilton Moor
JAGAAR CT
PH
BACK DRO
EAST HEATH DRO
Catcott Bridge
CATCOTT BROAD DRO
HIGH STREET DRO
BATCHKEY DRO
SKIMMERS DRO
STUBBY LAWN DRO
5
PH
Eight Acre Dro
EIGHT ACRE DRO
Edington Heath
BACK DRO
MILLARD'S DRO
EDINGTON RD
DOBBIN'S DRO
TA7
LADY'S DRO
JANE'S DRO
LOWER ROPES DRO
Catcott Heath
Westhay Heath
NEWCLOSE DRO
CHILTON RD
HIGHER ROPES DRO
WEST DRO
SUMMERCLOSE DRO
HEAD DRO
KENT DRO
Shapwick Heath National Nature Reserve
Canada Farm
COMBE LA
BELL LA
Holy Well
Nidons
MOORCLOSE DRO
SEDGE DRO
MOORHOUSE FARM LA
HEAD DRO
EAST DRO
RHYNE DRO
Millmoot LA
MILLMOOT LA
HURST LA
LANDSHIRE LA
DOLE LA
BOROUGHILL LA
GOOSE LA
BROOMEDGE LA
THE NYDON
NIDON LA
Edington
Moorgate Farm
ORCHARD CL
MOWGROUND CL
MIDDLE RD
FURLONG
PH
BARTON RISE
COMBE LA
S MNR
KEEN LA
BATES LA
CHANDLERS
THE WALLS
Holy Well
THE SQUARE
PH
LITTLE LEAZE LA
Catcott
STATION RD
ADDERMEAD LA
Kent Farm
1 ST EDWARD'S CL
2 THE GRANGE
3 WILLMOTTS CL
4 OLD VICARAGE CL
5 TOWNSEND LA
Chilton Polden
CHURCH LA
PRIORY CL
BROADWAY
CENTRE RD
HAYNE WLK
THE WALNUTS
CHURCH RD
HOLY WELL RD
SUPREMA LA
BROADMEAD LA
HUGDOLE LA
Catcott Prim Sch
Suprema Est
STEEL LA
HECTOR LA
LANGLAND LA
THE STANDARDS
Langlands Farm
THE COURTYARD 1
CHURCH CL 2
SCHOOL LA 3
LAWN LA 4
VICARAGE LA 5
NORTHBROOK DR 6
NORTHBROOK RD 7
PH
PRIORY RD
SCRUBBITT'S LA
BROADWAY AVE
CHAPEL CL
REY LANDS LA
MANOR RD
SCHOOL WAY
CHURCH RD
KING WILLIAM RD
WEARS LA
POPLAR LA
Shapwick House
KENT LA
Moorgate Farm
Ford Farm
Chilton Priory
BATH RD
A39
LOWER RD
INNSMEAD LA
MANOR RD
Cock Hill
SCOTTS LA
LIPPETTS WAY
Manor Farm
Shapwick Sch
BRIDEWELL LA
TIMBERYARD
MONKS DRO
STATION RD
ORCHARD WAY
CHURCH RD
WOOD LA
MANOR DRO
VYO DRO
CHURCH FARM CL
Stawell
STAWELL RD
MOOR RD
Shapwick

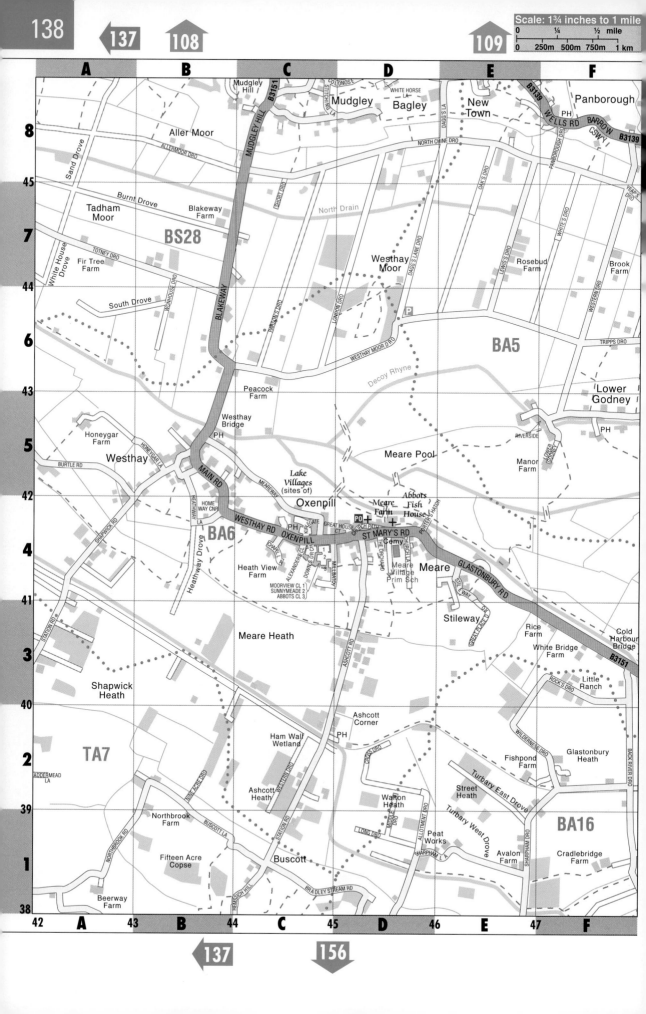

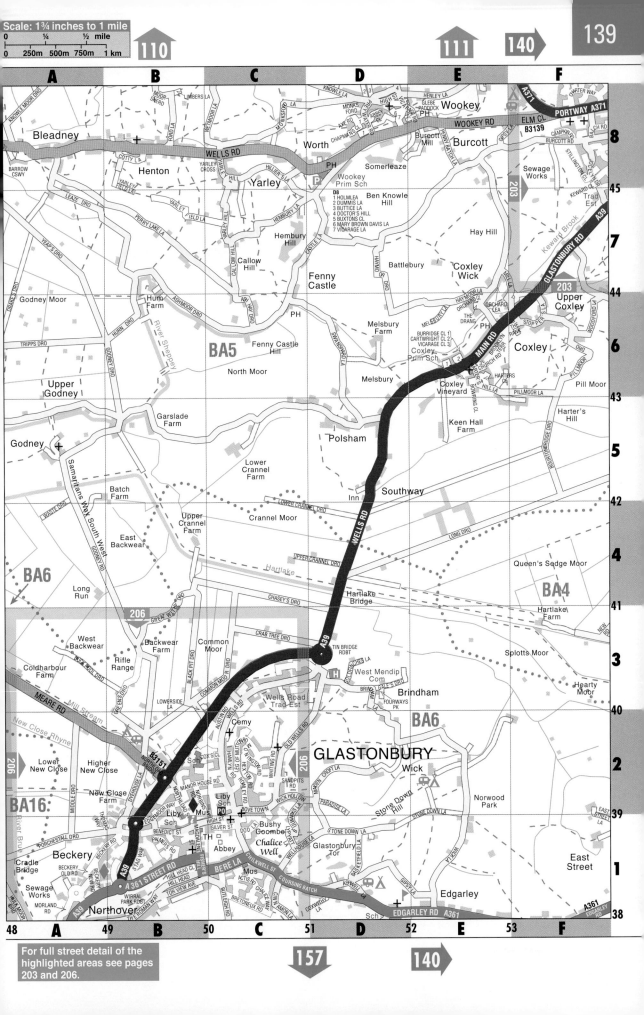

A B C D E F

8

Schs
PORTWAY
A371
STRAWBERRY WAY
A39
BURCOTT RD
CHAMBERLAIN ST
TOR ST
CATHEDRAL GN
Mus
CATH
Palace
Liby
PO
H
Sch
WELLS

1 ALLENS LA
2 KEN CL
3 CREIGHTON CL
4 KINGS RD

Cemy
King's Castle
BA5
Lyatt

Chilcote La
Crapnell Farm
Crapnell La

45

GLASTONBURY RD
Keward
A371
EAST SOMERSET WAY
The Park
Park Wood
Monarch's Way
203
Highfield
Dulcote
Sharcombe Park
Dinder Wood
Sleight La
Lyatt La
Thrupe La

7

River Sheppey
UPPER WELL ESLEY RD
BISHOPS PARK WAY
203
B3139
Dulcote Hill
Dulcote Quarry
Dinder
Croscombe
204
LONG ST
FAYRE WAY
Sch
SHEPTON RD A371
Church Hill
Riverside
Shepton Old Rd

44

Woodford
Woodford Rd
Lower
Wellesley Rd
Wellesley Farm
Dulcote Hill La
Church Hill La
Old Street La
Old Wells Rd
Dungeon La

6

Hill House Farm
Upper Wellesley Rd
Twinhills Wood
Worminster Batch
Dungeon Farm
Stump Cross
Knowle La

43

Pill Moor
Launcherley Cross
Launcherley Rd
Launcherley
Launcherley Hill
Worminster
Worminster Sleight
204
Knowle Farm
Knowle Hill
Timberwins

5

Long Dro
Wootton Vineyard
North Town
Pilton Wood
West
Back
Compton La

42

Lovell's Dro
Middle's La
Greenacres
Quaish Farm
Quaish La
High St
Dark La
North Wootton
BA4
Stoodly La
West Compton
Burford

4

New Rd
Barrow
Barrow La
Higher House La
Church View
PH
Stock's La
Chessell's La
Crossway
Northtown La
Pilton Hill
Lower Westholme Rd
Hearne House
Higher Westholme Rd
Upper Westholme
Burford Cross
Bowermead
Totterdown La
A361

41

Hearty Gate Farm
Redlake Farm
Slough La
Edwicke Farm
Mead La
Perridge Hill
Perridge House
204
WHITSTONE HILL
PO
Cemy
1 PARSON'S BATCH
2 SHOP LA
3 CUMHILL HILL
4 WEIR LA
5 ST MARY'S LA
6 ABBOTS WAY
7 SHUDWELL LA
8 BARROW STILE
9 BAKERY LA
10 JOHN BEALES HILL
11 CULVERWELL COTTS
12 OATHILL COTTS
12 JOHN BORNS COTT
13 MARGARET BONDFIELD CL

3

Pennard La
Broad Dro
Stonebridge La
Westholme La
Whitelake
Tanyard La
Steanbow Cotts
PARK HILL
Pilton Manor Vineyard
Worthy La
Bread St
Mount Pleasant
Pilton
Worthy Farm
Pylle Rd
Cockmill La

2

Hearty Moor
Ten Foot Rhyne
Gory La
Page La
Laverley Cotts
Mead
PH
Monarch's Way
Steanbow
Holt La
Holt Farm
Pilton Park
Steanbow Park Dairy Unit
Brimley La

39

East Street La
Laurels St
Newtown La
BA6
Piltown
Sticklinch Rd
Laverley
Sawpit La
Sticklinch
Sticklinch La
Manor Farm
Stickleball Hill
Ford

1

A361
PH
Mulberry Farm
Cottles La
West Pennard
West Pennard CE Prim Sch
Hillside
Lower Southtown
Church La
Green La
Castle La
Worth La
Pennard Hill
King's Hill

38

Breech La
Southtown La
Windmill La
Down La

54 A 55 B 56 C 57 D 58 E 59 F

For full street detail of the highlighted area see pages 203 and 204.

139 158

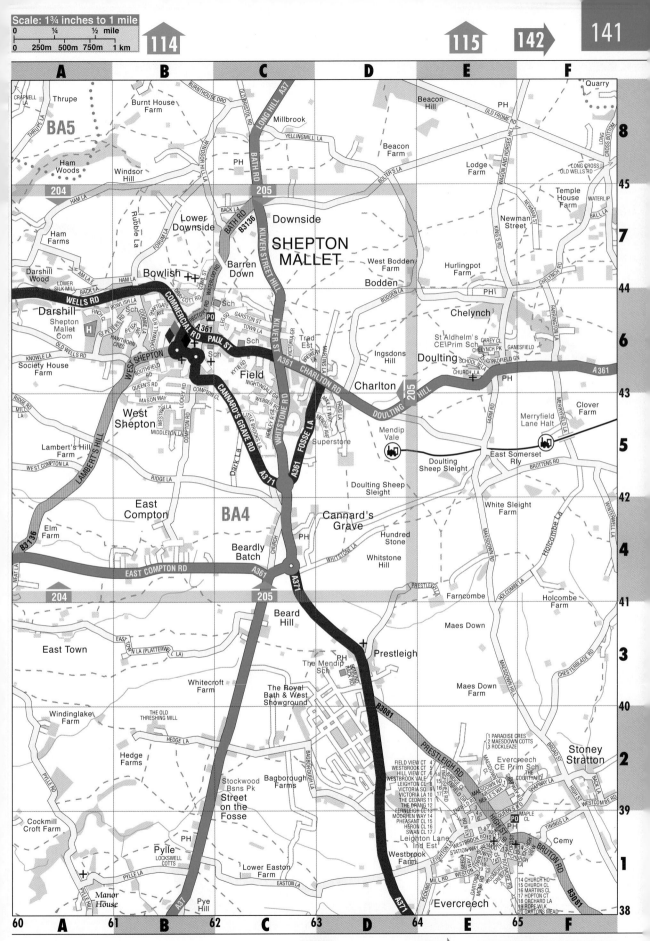

A   B   C   D   E   F

Quarry

CRAPNELL LA
Thrupe
BA5
Ham Woods
Windsor Hill
Burnt House Farm
Millbrook
YELLINGMILL LA
Downside
Beacon Hill
PH
Beacon Farm
OLD FROME RD
PH
Lodge Farm
Long Cross
Long Cross Old Wells Rd
WATERLIP
Temple House Farm
BALL LA

204   205   45

Ham Farms
Darshill Wood
Rubble La
FORUM LA
Lower Downside
SHEPTON MALLET
West Bodden Farm
Bodden
BODDEN LA
Newman Street
NEWMAN ST
KINGS RD
Hurlingpot Farm
PH
44

Darshill
Shepton Mallet Com H
WELLS RD
Bowlish
Barren Down
BATH RD B3136
KILVER STREET HILL
Downside
Chelynch
St Aldhelm's CE\Prim Sch
CAREY CL
CHELYNCH PK
GANESFIELD
7

KNOWLE LA
Society House Farm
Old Wells Rd
West Shepton
PAUL ST
CANNARD'S GRAVE RD
Field
Sch
A361
CHARLTON RD
Ingsdons Hill
Doulting
SCHOOL
CHURCH LA
PADFIELD GN
PH
A 361
6

Lambert's Hill Farm
WEST COMPTON LA
LAMBERT'S HILL
West Shepton
Mason Way
MIDDLETON LA
COMPTON RD
FOSSE LA
WHITSTONE RD
A371
A361
Charlton
DOULTING HILL
205
43

RIDGE RD
MILL LA
East Compton
RIDGE LA
Superstore
Mendip Vale
Doulting Sheep Sleight
East Somerset Rly
BROTTENS RD
Merryfield Lane Halt
MERRYFIELD LA
Clover Farm
5

Elm Farm
B3136
BA4
Cannard's Grave
Hundred Stone
Doulting Sheep Sleight
Whitstone Hill
White Sleight Farm
HOLCOMBE LA
WINTERWELL LA
42

NEAT LA
Beardly Batch
EAST COMPTON RD
A361
205
CHURCH LA
A371
PH
WHITSTONE LA
MAESDOWN RD
Farncombe
KOLCOMBE LA
Holcombe Farm
4

204   205   41

East Town
EASTON LA (PLATTERWELL LA)
Beard Hill
PRESTLEIGH RD
Maes Down
CHESTERBLADE RD
3

Windinglake Farm
THE OLD THRESHING MILL
Whitecroft Farm
The Royal Bath & West Showground
The Mendip Sch
PH
Prestleigh
Maes Down Farm
MAESDOWN HILL
40

HEDGE LA
Hedge Farms
HEDGE LA
BAGBOROUGH LA
B3081
1 Paradise Cres
2 Maesdown Cotts
3 Rockleaze
Evercreech CE Prim Sch
BROAD ST
Stoney Stratton
BACK LA
WESTCOM LA
2

Cockmill Croft Farm
PILLE RD
Stockwood Bsns Pk
Street on the Fosse
Bagborough Farms
PRESTLEIGH RD
MAESDOWN RD
Leighton Lane Ind Est
HIGH ST
PO PH
MAPLE CL
Cemy
TININGS LA
BRUTON RD
B3081
39

PYLLE LA
Manor House
Pylle
LOCKSWELL COTTS
PH
Lower Easton Farm
EASTON LA
Westbrook Farm
PECKING MILL RD
WESTBROOK RD
STATION WAY
Evercreech
1

FIELD VIEW CT 4
WESTBROOK CT 5
HILL VIEW CT 6
WESTBROOK VALE 7
LEIGHTON CL 8
VICTORIA SQ 9
VICTORIA LA 10
THE CEDARS 11
THE BRANG 12
FERNLEIGH 13
MOORHEN WAY 14
PHEASANT CL 15
HERON CL 16
SWAN CL 17

14 CHURCH HO
15 CHURCH CL
16 MARTINS CL
17 HOPTON CT
18 ORCHARD LA
19 ROPE WLK
20 GARTONS MEAD

A37
Pye Hill
A371
38

60   A   61   B   62   C   63   D   64   E   65   F

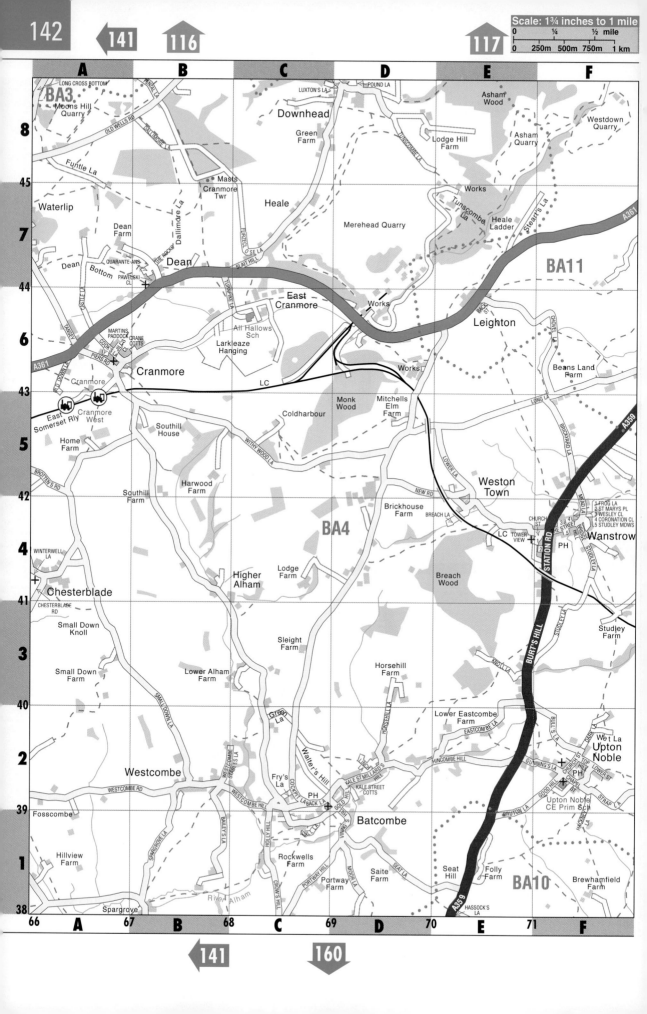

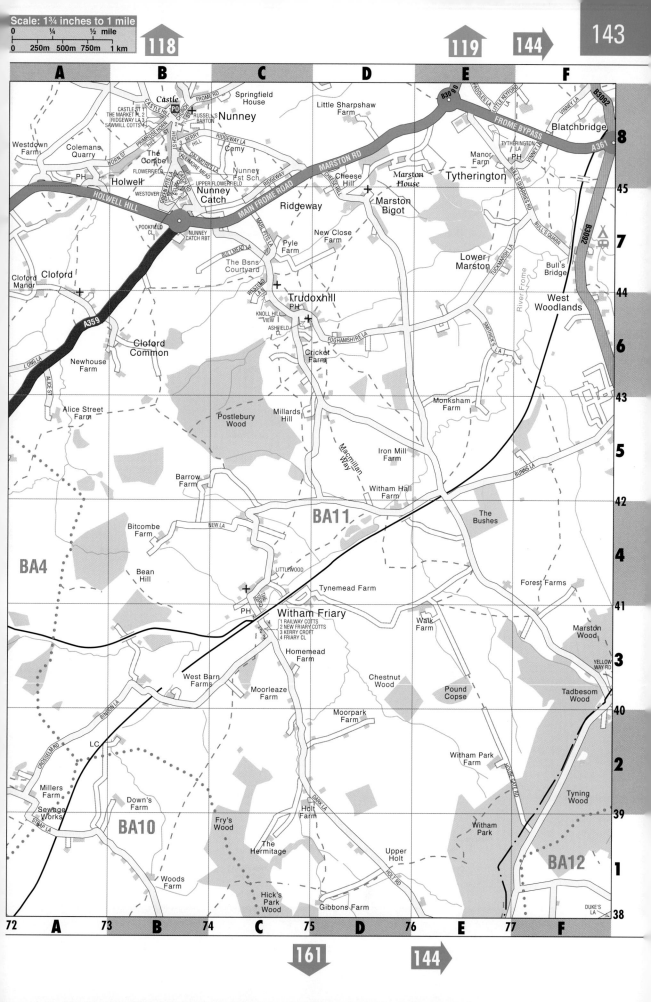

Scale: 1¾ inches to 1 mile

0   ¼   ½   mile
0   250m   500m   750m   1 km

118
119
144
143

A   B   C   D   E   F

8
45
7
44
6
43
5
42
4
41
3
40
2
39
1
38

Westdown Farm
Colemans Quarry
PH
Holwell
Castle
Castle Hill
CASTLE ST 1
THE MARKET PL 2
RIDGEWAY LA 3
SAWMILL COTTS 4
PO
RUSSELL'S BARTON
Nunney
Springfield House
Little Sharpshaw Farm
B3090
FROME RD
PADDLES LA
LITTLE KEYFORD LA
VINNEY LA
B3092
FROME BYPASS
Blatchbridge
A361
Manor Farm
PH
TYTHERINGTON LA
VINNEY LA
The Combe
HORN ST
PRIMROSE HORN
HIGH ST
BERRY HILL
DALLIMORE MEAD
Cemy
RIDGEWAY LA
MARSTON RD
Tytherington
BULL'S QUARRIES RD
45
Westover
FLOWERFIELD
UPPER FLOWERFIELD
Nunney Fst Sch
RIDGEWAY
Cheese Hill
CHEESE HILL
Marston House
Nunney Catch
Holwell Hill
HOLWELL HILL
GREEN PITS LA
Ridgeway
Marston Bigot
BULL'S QUARR
Pookfield Cl
POOKFIELD CL
Nunney Catch Rbt
NUNNEY CATCH RBT
MARL PITS LA
BULLMEAD LA
Pyle Farm
New Close Farm
Lower Marston
TUCKMARSH LA
River Frome
West Woodlands
Bull's Bridge
Cloford
Cloford Manor
A359
The Bsns Courtyard
WEST END LA
Trudoxhill
PH
KNOLL HILL VIEW
ASHFIELD CL
FOGHAMSHIRE LA
SMITH'S LA
LONG LA
ALICE ST
Newhouse Farm
Cloford Common
Cricket Farm
Monksham Farm
Postlebury Wood
Millards Hill
Iron Mill Farm
Macmillan Way
Barrow Farm
BUNNS LA
Witham Hall Farm
The Bushes
BA11
BA4
Bitcombe Farm
NEW LA
Forest Farms
Bean Hill
LITTLEWOOD
Tynemead Farm
Marston Wood
THE VZRD
PH
Witham Friary
1 RAILWAY COTTS
2 NEW FRIARY COTTS
3 KERRY CROFT
4 FRIARY CL
Walk Farm
YELLOW WAY RD
West Barn Farms
Homemead Farm
Chestnut Wood
Pound Copse
Tadbesom Wood
Moorleaze Farm
BINEGAR LA
CROSS ELM RD
LC
Millers Farm
Sewage Works
STRAP LA
BA10
Down's Farm
Moorpark Farm
DARK LA
Witham Park Farm
HOUSE COTT RD
Tyning Wood
Fry's Wood
Holt Farm
The Hermitage
Upper Holt
HOLT RD
Witham Park
BA12
Woods Farm
Hick's Park Wood
Gibbons Farm
DUKE'S LA

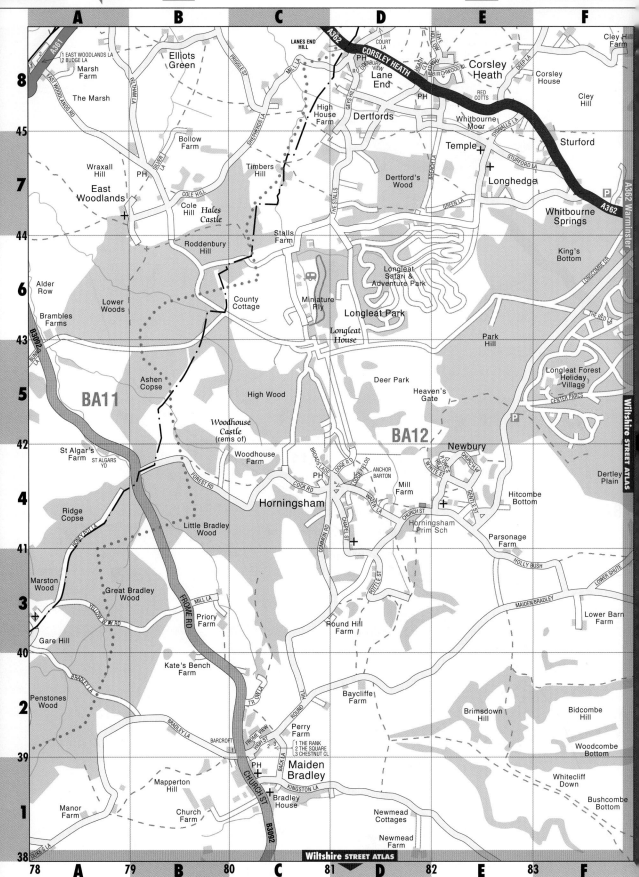

Scale: 1¾ inches to 1 mile

0   ¼   ½   mile
0 250m 500m 750m 1 km

127

146

145

E   F   G   H   J   K

Blue Gate

Great Woolcombe

TA24

Cow Castle

Pickedstones

8

37

River Barle

Two Moors Way

WINTERSHEAD RD

Wintershead Farm

Horsen Farm

7

Kinsford Water

Great Ferny Ball

Landacre Bridge

P

36

GRAVEL PIT CROSS

Long Holcombe

Horsen Hill

Ferny Ball

LANDACRE LA

Dillacombe

6

Lower Sherdon

Sherdon Water

LONG HOLCOMBE CROSS

Sherdon Farm

35

Sherdon Water

Woolcombe Allotment

Shortacombe

Barcombe

SHERDON BRIDGE

Woolcombe Farm

5

Barkman

WITHYPOOL CROSS

34

River Mole

Darlick Moors

Sandyway

Litton

4

DARLICK CNR

Longstone Wells

EX36

SANDYWAY CROSS

Sportsman's Inn (PH)

Willingford

33

Tabor Hill

126

North Molton Ridge

Litton Water

TWITCHEN BALL CNR

Twitchen Ridge

Twitchen Barrows

3

32

WHITE POST

Blindwell

TA22

2

Long Breach

76   E   77   F   78   G   79   H

Wester Emmetts

BLUE GATE

8

Comerslade

TA24

37

KINGSFORD HILL

KINGSFORD GATE CROSS

Five Barrows

Kinsford Gate

Emmett's Grange

31

7

Western Common

Kinsford Water

Hangley Cleave

Cassacombe Common

Round Hill

RIDGWAY CROSS

Black Ball

Span Head

36

1

FIVE BARROWS CROSS

CUSSACOMBE GATE

EX36

Fyldon Common

EX36

White Moor

30

A   73   B   74   C   75   D   H   80   J   81   K

Devon STREET ATLAS

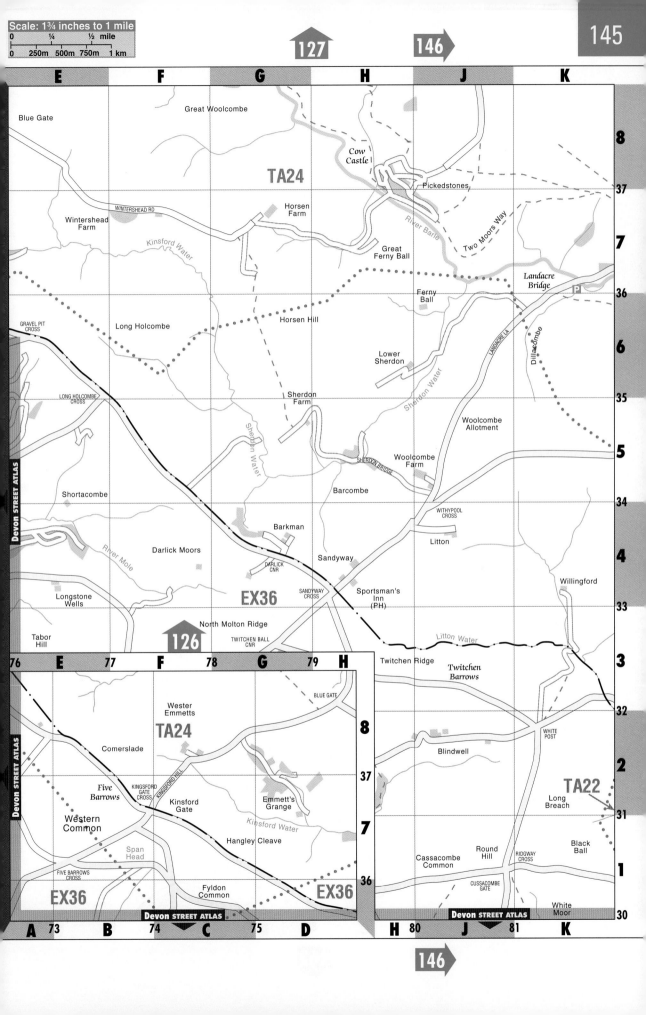

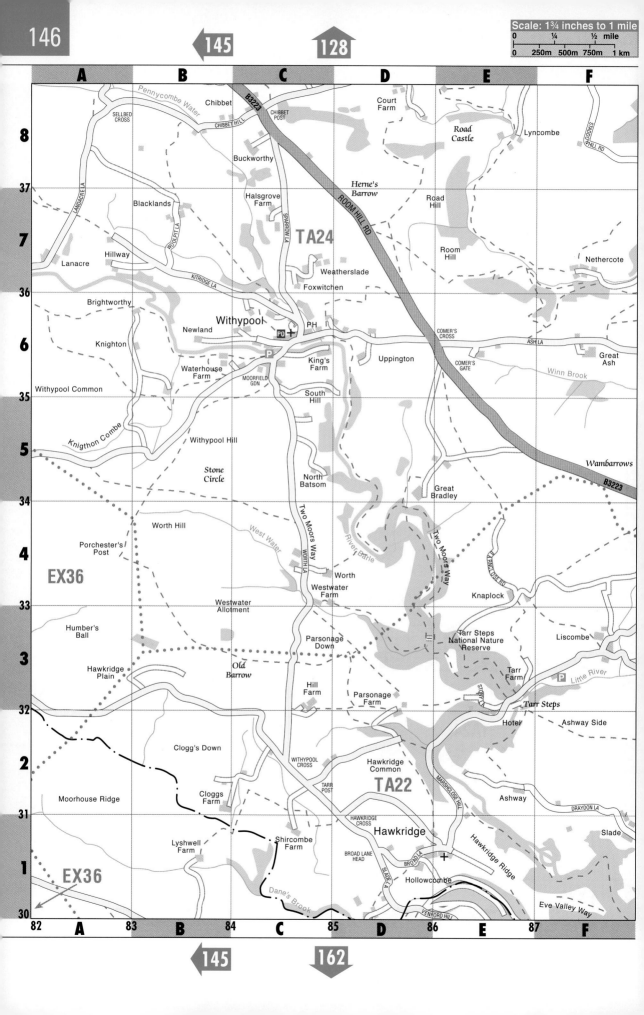

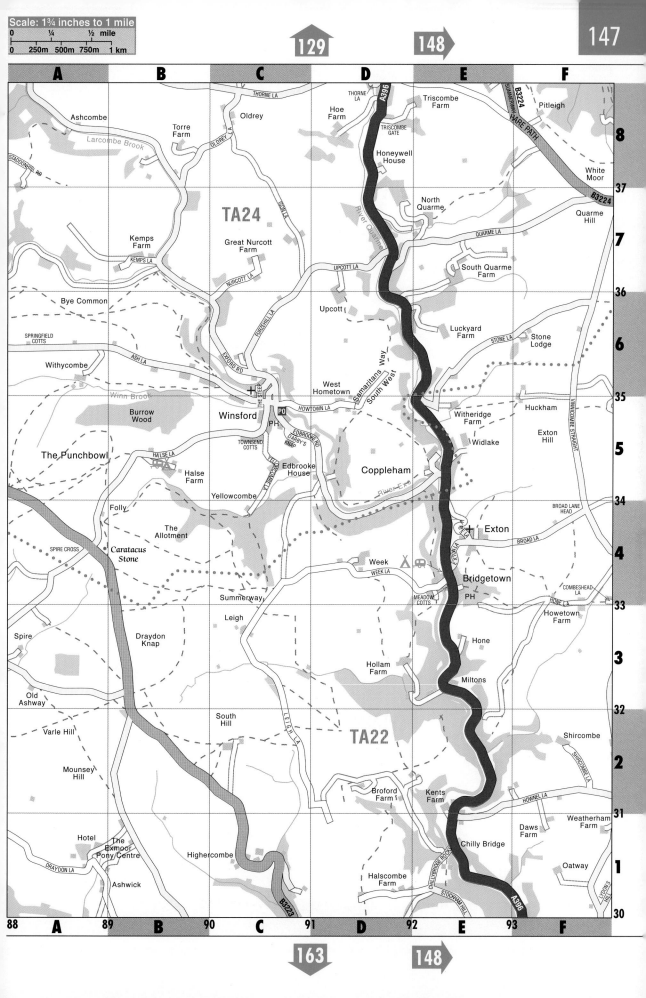

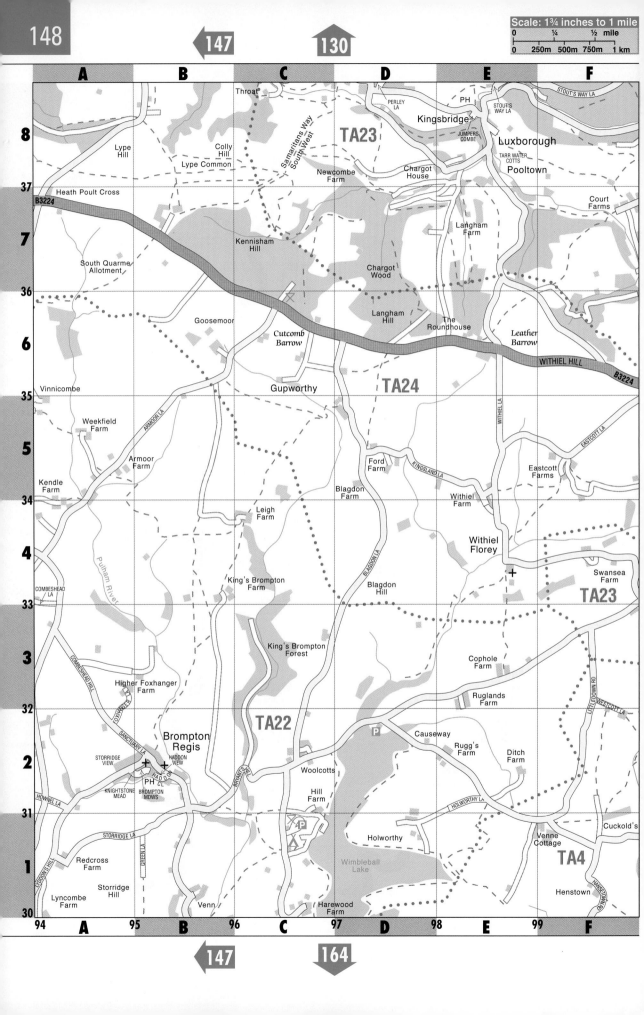

Scale: 1¾ inches to 1 mile

0   ¼   ½   mile
0   250m 500m 750m   1 km

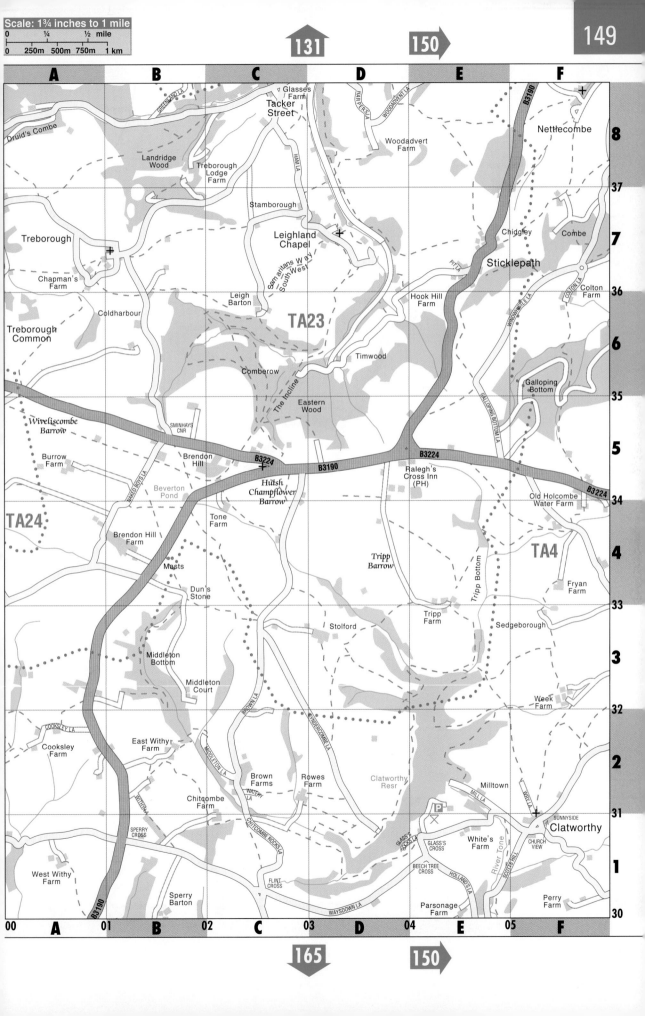

Scale: 1¾ inches to 1 mile

0 ¼ ½ mile
0 250m 500m 750m 1 km

A B C D E F

8

NETTLECOMBE PARK RD

B3188

Sheepwash La

Escott

Wayshill

Kingswood

Stogumber

ESCOTT LA

COMBER OSS LA

PH Sunny Bank

PO PH

Stogumber

Stogumber CE Prim Sch

Catford Cottage

HIGH ST

COMBECROSS HILL

BIRCHANGER LA

Monksilver

Birchanger Farm

NEVIS LA

YELLOW HO RD

SIMPIT CL

OLD WAY

STATION RD

DEANS CL

SLADE CL

PACKHORSE LA

WOOD LA

COOKLEY LA

West Somerse Rly

Stogumber RD

37

COMBE CROSS

COMBECROSS LA

Samaritans Way South West

ASHBEER HILL

Wood Farm

ARCHERS GR

Castlake Farm

Water Farm

CASTLAKE LA

WATER HILL

WATER LA

LEIGH LA

7

Bird's Hill

SILVERDOWN HILL

Mast

LOWER ASHBEER LA

Preston Cross

PRESTON LA

36

Pond Wood

Culcombe Farm

Ashbeer

Preston

Higher Vexford

Lower Vexford

HANGERLAND LN

REXTON LA

PI LA

6

MAUNSBOROUGH LA

Elworthy

Elworthy Cross

Hartrow Manor

Willett House

Rexton Farm

Plash La

REXTON LA

SHEEPSTEALING LA

35

TILSEY LA

ELWORTHY LA

Knight's

CATS CASTLE HILL

Willett Hill Cross

Coleford Water

DEAN'S LA

5

B3224

Elworthy Barrows Fort

Mast

Colwell Farmhouse

TA4

Tower

Willett

Coleford Farm

34

PARISH QUARRY RD

ASHLAND LA

Rook's Nest

TRUCKWELL LA

Willet Hill

4

Broadway Head Farm

Combe Davey

COMBE LA

SHURTLAND LA

WINTERS LA

Tolland Down

Emble Farm

Whitemoor Farm

WHITEMOOR LA

33

Battins Farm

BATTINS KNAP

PARKS LA

Tolland

Tolland Cross

Thornbush Cross

East Town

EAST TOWN LA

3

FORCHES CROSS

Hill View

Brompton Ralph

Grove Farm

GROVE LA

B3224

32

PO

Hele Farm

Westcott Farm

Manor Farm

Courtland Farm

West Deane Way

2

Hudford Farm

Bowden Farm

Middle Stone Farm

Gandstone Cross

Pitsford Hill

Moor Mill Farm

West Leigh

SANDING'S LA

31

Harwood Farm

Cording's Farm

Combe Bottom

1

CORDING'S BALL

WHITEFIELD ROCKS

Oakhampton Farm

B3188

HOCCOMBE FORD

30

06 07 08 09 10 11

A B C D E F

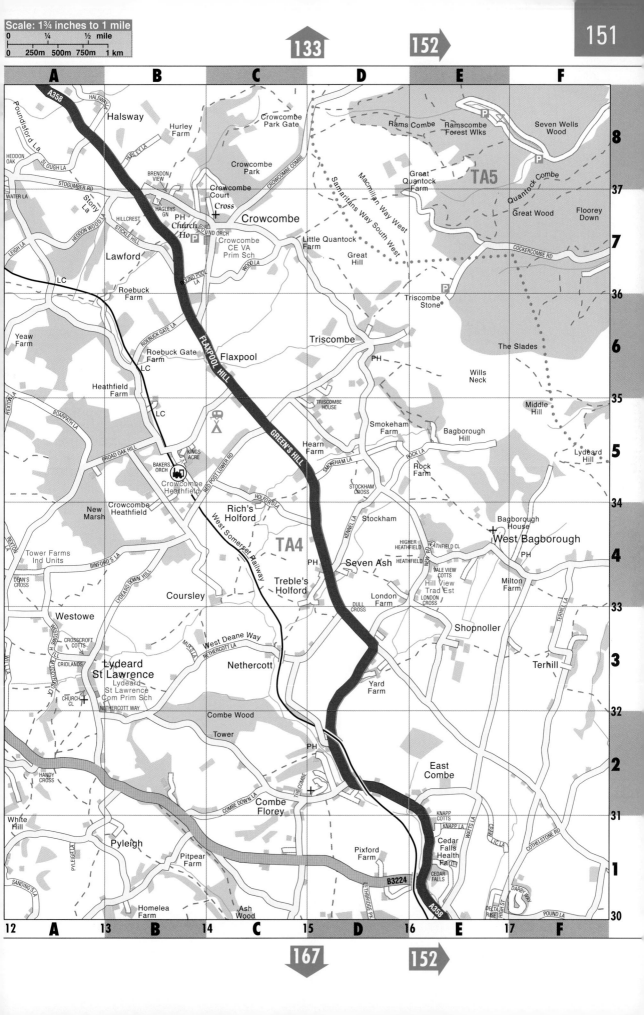

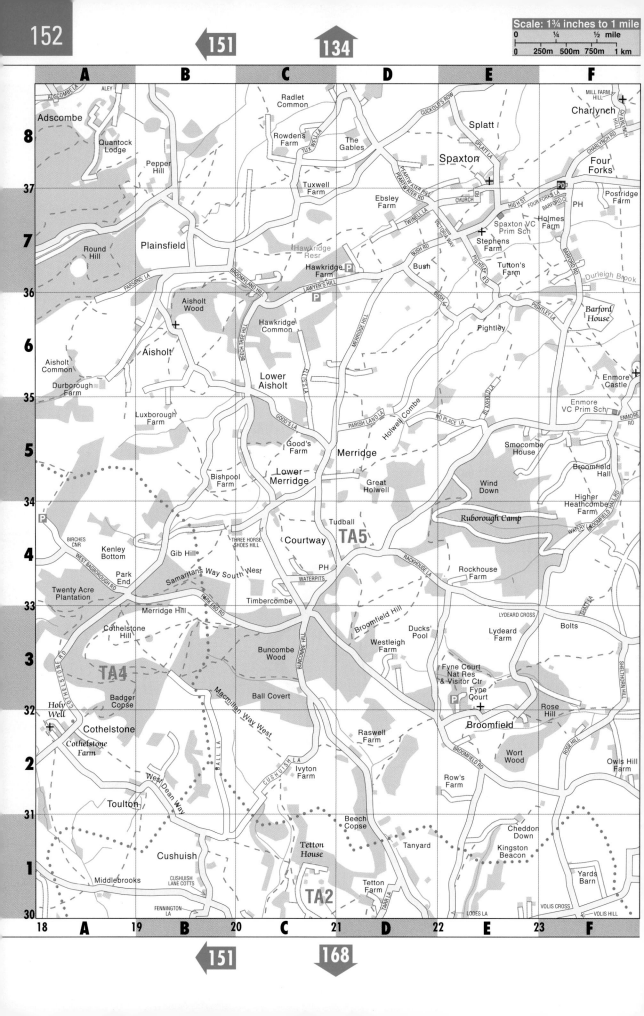

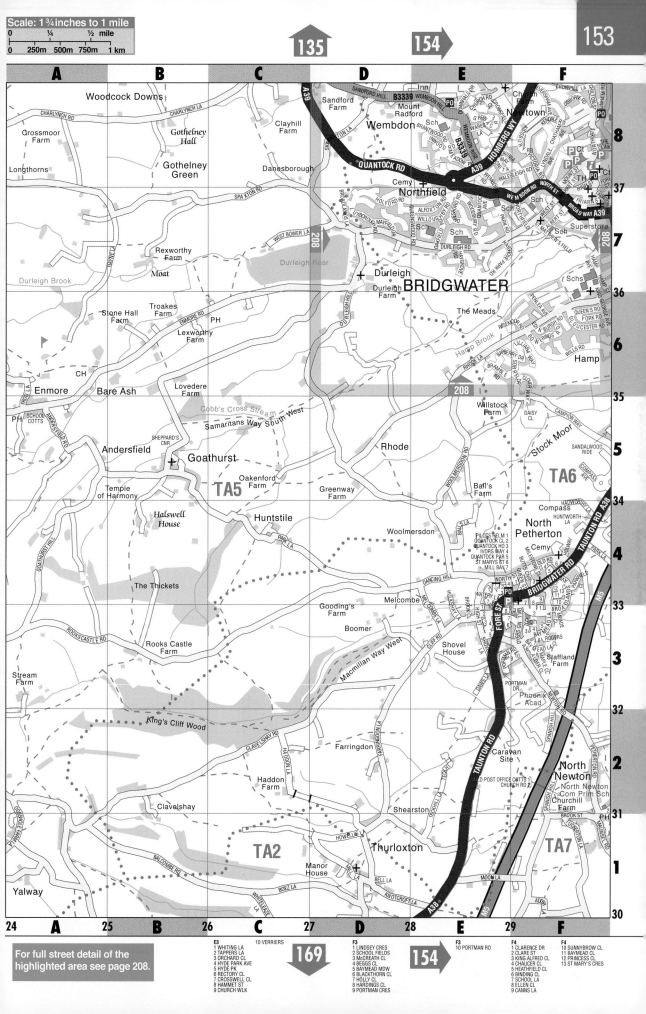

A B C D E F

Woodcock Downs

Grossmoor Farm

Longthorns

Charlynch Rd

Charlynch La

Gothelney Hall

Gothelney Green

Clayhill Farm

Danesborough

Sandford Farm

Sandford Hill

Inn

B3339

Mount Radford

Wembdon

Church Farm

Newtown

QUANTOCK RD

A39

HOMBERG WY

Cemy

Northfield

BRIDGWATER

Superstore

Rexworthy Farm

Moat

SPAXTON RD

WEST BOWER LA

Durleigh Resr

208

Durleigh

Durleigh Farm

The Meads

Hamp Brook

Hamp

8

37

7

36

Durleigh Brook

Stone Hall Farm

Troakes Farm

Lexworthy Farm

ENMORE RD

PH

DURLEIGH RD

Rhode La

BRAMBLE RD

208

6

Enmore

Bare Ash

CH

Lovedere Farm

Cobb's Cross Stream

Samaritans Way South West

Willstock Farm

DAISY CL

CAMPION WAY

Stock Moor

SANDALWOOD RIDE

35

PH

SCHOOL COTTS

ANDERSFIELD RD

Andersfield

Goathurst

Oakenford Farm

Rhode

Greenway Farm

Bafl's Farm

Compass

TA6

COMPASS

5

TA5

Temple of Harmony

Halswell House

Huntstile

PARK LA

WOOLMERSDON RD

Woolmersdon

PILOTS HELM 1
QUANTOCK CL 2
QUANTOCK HO 3
IVORS WAY 4
QUANTOCK PAR 5
ST MARYS BT 6
MILL BAY 7

North Petherton

Cemy

HUNTWORTH LA

HADWORTHY LA

TAUNTON RD A38

PARK LA

34

GOATHURST HILL

The Thickets

Gooding's Farm

Melcombe

MELCOMBE LA

BRIDGWATER RD

FOREST

33

4

ROOKSCASTLE RD

Rooks Castle Farm

Boomer

Macmillan Way West

CLIFF RD

Shovel House

Shovel

Portman Dr

Phoenix Acad

STAFFLAND FARM

M5

3

Stream Farm

King's Cliff Wood

CLAVELSHAY RD

HADDON LA

Farringdon

FARRINGDON LA

TAUNTON RD

Caravan Site

North Newton

North Newton Com Prim Sch

Churchill Farm

32

Clavelshay

Haddon Farm

Shearston

TESCHILL LA

OLD POST OFFICE COTTS 1
CHURCH RD 2

BROOK ST

PH

31

Yalway

BALCOMBE RD

TA2

BOEZ LA

WHITELEAZE LA

Manor House

MILL LA

BELL LA

Thurloxton

KNOTCROFT LA

HOWELL LA

A38

MOON LA

TA7

ADAM LA

MAUNSEL LA

30

24   25   26   27   28   29

A B C D E F

For full street detail of the highlighted area see page 208.

169   154

E3
1 WHITING LA
2 TAPPERS LA
3 ORCHARD CL
4 HYDE PARK AVE
5 HYDE PK
6 RECTORY CL
7 CROSSWELL CL
8 HAMMET ST
9 CHURCH WLK

C10 VERRIERS

F3
1 LINDSEY CRES
2 SCHOOL FIELDS
3 McCREATH CL
4 BEGGS CL
5 BAYMEAD MDW
6 BLACKTHORN CL
7 HOLLY CL
8 HARDINGS CL
9 PORTMAN CRES

F3
10 PORTMAN RD

F4
1 CLARENCE DR
2 CLARE ST
3 KING ALFRED CL
4 CHAUCER CL
5 HEATHFIELD CL
6 BINDING CL
7 SCHOOL LA
8 ELLEN CL
9 CANNS LA

F4
10 SUNNYBROW CL
11 BAYMEAD CL
12 PRINCESS CL
13 ST MARY'S CRES

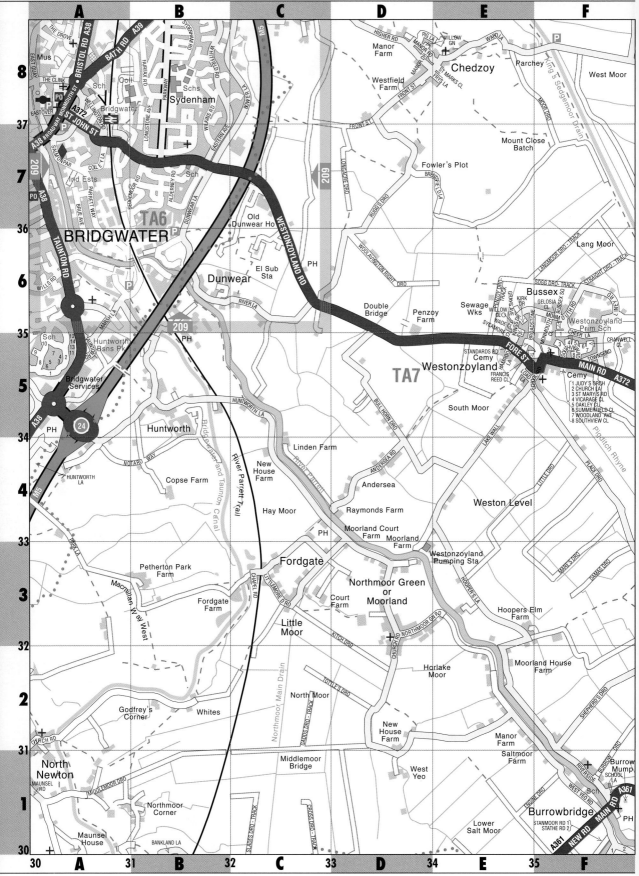

153

136

Scale: 1¾ inches to 1 mile
0   ¼   ½   mile
0   250m 500m 750m 1 km

A   B   C   D   E   F

8

37

7

36

6

35

5

34

4

33

3

32

2

31

1

30

THE DROVE
EAST QUAY
Mus
THE CLINK
PO
EASTOVER
BRISTOL RD A38
BATH RD A38
A39
A39
Sch
Coll
Bridgwater
Sydenham
FAIRFAX RD
WHITFIELD RD
SYDENHAM RD
PARKWAY
Schs
Sch
BROADWAY
MONMOUTH ST
ST JOHN ST
A38
A372
WELLINGTON RD
COL E LA
SALMON PAR
A38
209
PO
TAUNTON RD
Ind Ests
WILLS RD
PARRETT WAY
BLUE AVE
SEDGEBOR RD
ALDERNEY RD
LONGSTONE AVE
EASTERN AVE
WILKINS RD
Sch
TA6
BRIDGWATER
Old Dunwear Ho
El Sub Sta
WESTONZOYLAND RD
PH
Dunwear
RIVER LA
M5
209
HIGHER RD
PIG LA
WILLOW GRN
MANOR RD
WARD LA
Manor Farm
Westfield Farm
FRONT ST
FRYS LA
ST MARKS CL
Chedzoy
Parchey
West Moor
MOOR DRO
King's Sedgemoor Drain
FRONT ST
Mount Close Batch
Fowler's Plot
BRENSFIELD LA
LONGACRE DRO
RUGGS DRO
WOOLAVINGTON RIGHT DRO
Double Bridge
Penzoy Farm
Sewage Wks
Bussex
SOGG DRO-TRACK
LANGMOOR DRO-TRACK
STRAIGHT DRO-TRACK
Lang Moor
LINEY RD
Westonzoyland Prim Sch
KIRK DR
WILLOW CL
GRANS AVE
WADE CL
SYCAMORE CL
CHEER LA
CRANWELL CL
209
PH
Huntworth Bsns Pk
Sch
9 10 13 11
6 5 4 3 2 1
7
8
12
Bridgwater Services
A38
24
PH
Huntworth La
HUNTWORTH LA
Huntworth
MARSH LA
STANDARDS RD
Cemy
FORE ST
Westonzoyland
Cemy
FRANCIS REED CL
JARMANY HILL
LOAD LA
BROADSTONE
MONMOUTH CL
BRISTOL CL
SOUTHVIEW
MAIN RD
A372
TA7
1 JUDY'S ORCH
2 CHURCH LA
3 ST MARYS RD
4 VICARAGE CL
5 OAKLEY CL
6 SUMMERFIELD CL
7 WOODLAND AVE
8 SOUTHVIEW CL
South Moor
LAKE WALL
BULL HORN DRO
Weston Level
NOTARO WAY
Copse Farm
Linden Farm
New House Farm
ANDERSEA RD
Andersea
Raymonds Farm
RIVER PARRETT
Hay Moor
PH
Moorland Court Farm
Moorland Farm
Westonzoyland Pumping Sta
HOOPERS STA
LITTLE DRO
PLACE DRO
MARE'S DRO
DAMAS DRO
Piglitch Rhyne
Bridgwater and Taunton Canal
River Parrett Trail
CHAPEL RD
TILLBORE D RD
Fordgate
Court Farm
Northmoor Green or Moorland
NORTHMOOR GN RD
CHURCH DRO
KITCH DRO
Hoopers Elm Farm
Moorland House Farm
SHEPHERD'S DRO
Petherton Park Farm
Macmillan Wy West
Fordgate Farm
Little Moor
Horlake Moor
Northmoor Main Drain
NORTHMOOR DRO-TRACK
GAUDS DRO-TRACK
TOTTLE'S DRO
CROSS'S DRO-TRACK
North Moor
Godfrey's Corner
Whites
New House Farm
West Yeo
Manor Farm
Saltmoor Farm
RIVERSIDE
BURROW SCHOOL LA
Sch
PARK LA
MIDDLEMOOR DRO
Middlemoor Bridge
Burrow Mump
A361
North Newton
MAUNSEL RD
CHURCH RD
Northmoor Corner
Maunsel House
BANKLAND LA
Lower Salt Moor
STANMOOR RD
STATHE RD
ENGINE DRO
WEST YEO RD
A361
NEW RD
MAIN RD
Burrowbridge
A361
PH

30   A   31   B   32   C   33   D   34   E   35   F

For full street detail of the highlighted area see page 209

153

170

A5
1 MUSCOVY DR
2 ROMNEY RD
3 SAVANNAH DR
4 VIENNA WAY
5 TUNDRA WALK
6 CHEVIOT ST
7 MERINO WAY
8 CHAROLAIS DR
9 TEESWATER WAY
10 STOCKMOOR DR
11 CHAMBRAY RD
12 ANGUS WAY
13 SHIRE ST
14 CHILLINGHAM DRO

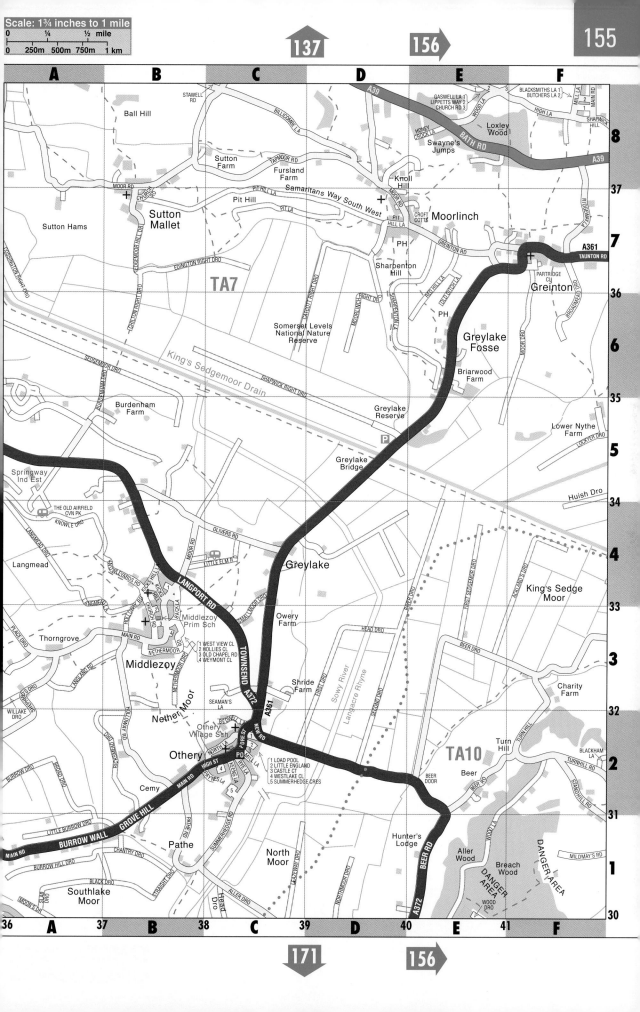

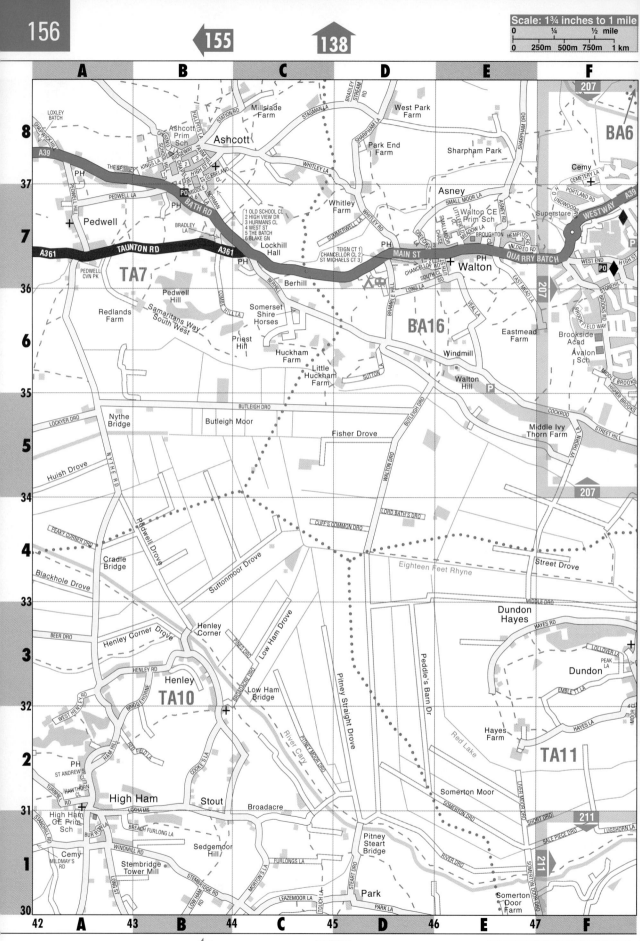

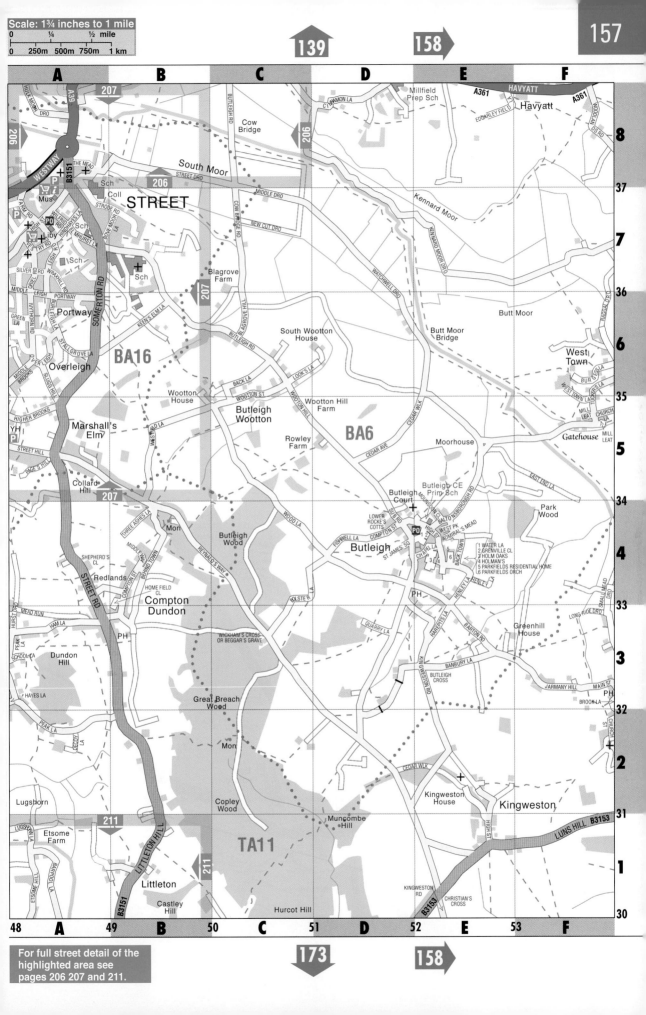

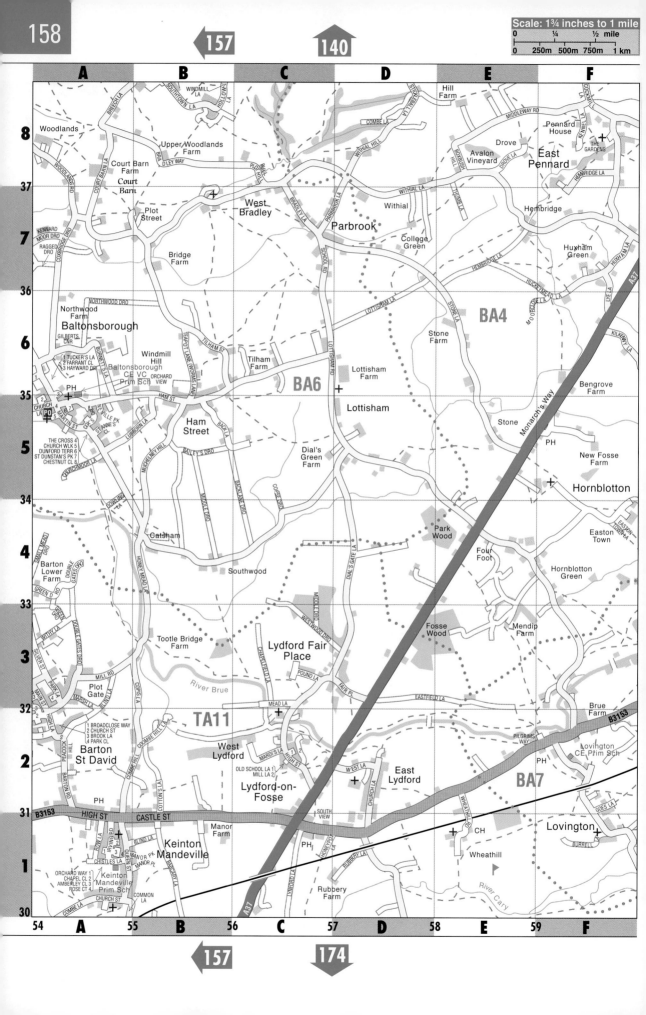

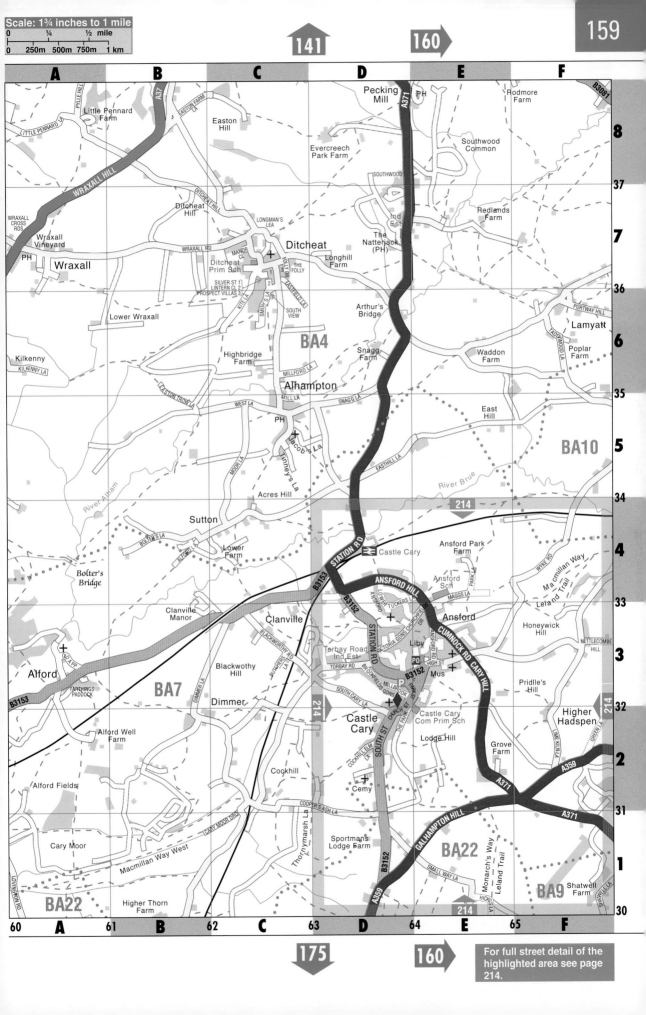

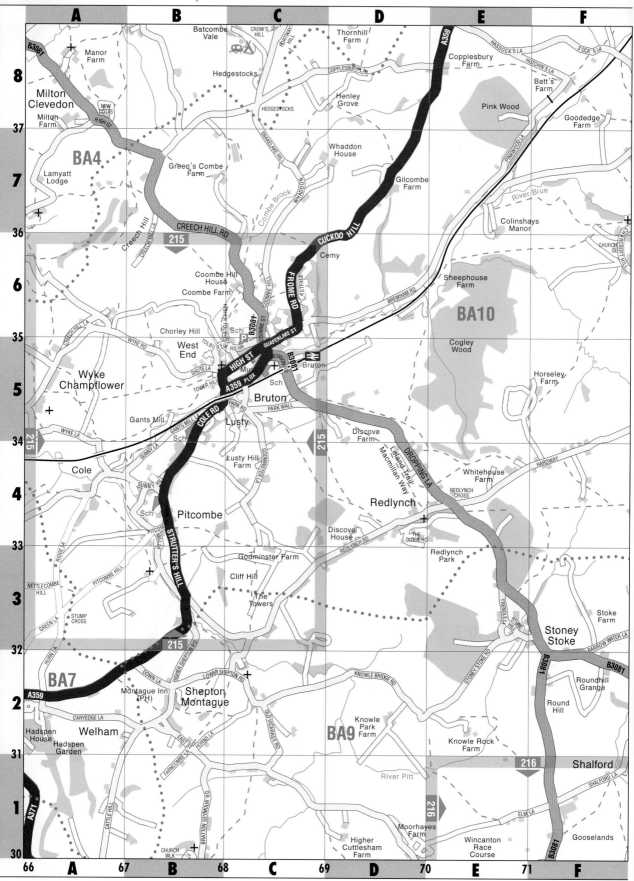

Scale: 1¾ inches to 1 mile
0   ¼   ½   mile
0   250m   500m 750m   1 km

8
37
7
36
6
35
5
34
4
33
3
32
2
31
1
30

A   B   C   D   E   F

Milton
Clevedon
Milton
Farm
Manor
Farm
NEW
COTTS
HIGH ST
B3081

BA4

Lamyatt
Lodge

Green's Combe
Farm

Batcombe
Vale
CROW'S
HILL
Hedgestocks
HEDGESTOCKS

Thornhill
Farm
Henley
Grove
Whaddon
House

Gilcombe
Farm

Copplesbury
Farm
COPPLESBURY LA
HASSOCK'S LA
HUTCHIN'S LA
S'OCK'S LA
Batt's
Farm
Pink Wood
PINKWOOD LA
Goodedge
Farm

Creech Hill
CREECH HILL LA
CREECH HILL RD
215
Combe Brook
WHADDON
SHAKELAKE HILL

CUCKOO HILL
Cemy
River Brue
CHURCH HILL
CRANROFT HILL

Chorley Hill
Coombe Hill
House
Coombe Farm
COOMBE ST
HIGHER TOLBURY
Sch
B3081
QUAPERLANE ST
A'FIELD
FROME RD
BREWHAM RD

Sheephouse
Farm

BA10

Colinshays
Manor

Cogley
Wood

CREECH HILL LA
WYKE RD
West
End
TOLBURY
HG HILL
HIGH ST
Mus
PLOX
Sch
STATION RD
B3081
Bruton
Horseley
Farm

Wyke
Champflower

Gants Mill
TOWER HILL
A359
PARK RD
Lusty
PARK WALL
Sch

215
WYKE LA
SUNNY LA
GANTS MILL LA
COLE RD
Lusty Hill
Farm
GODMINSTER LA
Discove
Farm

Whitehouse
Farm
HARDWAY
215

Cole
SUNNY LA
Sch
Pitcombe
PITCOMBE HILL
STRUTTER'S HILL
Godminster Farm
Cliff Hill
Discove
House
REDLYNCH RD
THE
CLOCK HO
Redlynch
Leland Trail
Macmillan Way
DROPPING LA
REDLYNCH
CROSS
Redlynch
Park
RIDGE LA
GREEN LA
NETTLECOMBE
HILL
STUMP
CROSS
PITCOMBE HILL
The
Towers

215
HILL LA
DOWN LA
HIGHER SHEPTON RD
LOWER SHEPTON RD
KNOWLE BRIDGE RD
TRENDLE LA
STONEY STOKE HILL
Stoke
Farm
Stoney
Stoke
BARROW WATER LA
B3081
Roundhill
Grange
Round
Hill

BA7
A359
CARYEDGE LA
Welham
Montague Inn
(PH)
Shepton
Montague
EAST LA
HORNS LA
OLD VICARAGE RD
BA9
Knowle
Park
Farm
Knowle Rock
Farm
SHALFORD LA
216
Shalford
ELM LA

Hadspen
House
Hadspen
Garden
CATTLE HILL
BRATTON SEYMOUR RD
FARNCOMBE LA
CHURCH
WLK
River Pitt
Higher
Cuttlesham
Farm
Moorhayes
Farm
216
Wincanton
Race
Course
B3081
Gooselands
A371

66   A   67   B   68   C   69   D   70   E   71   F

For full street detail of the
highlighted area see
pages 215 and 216.

159

176

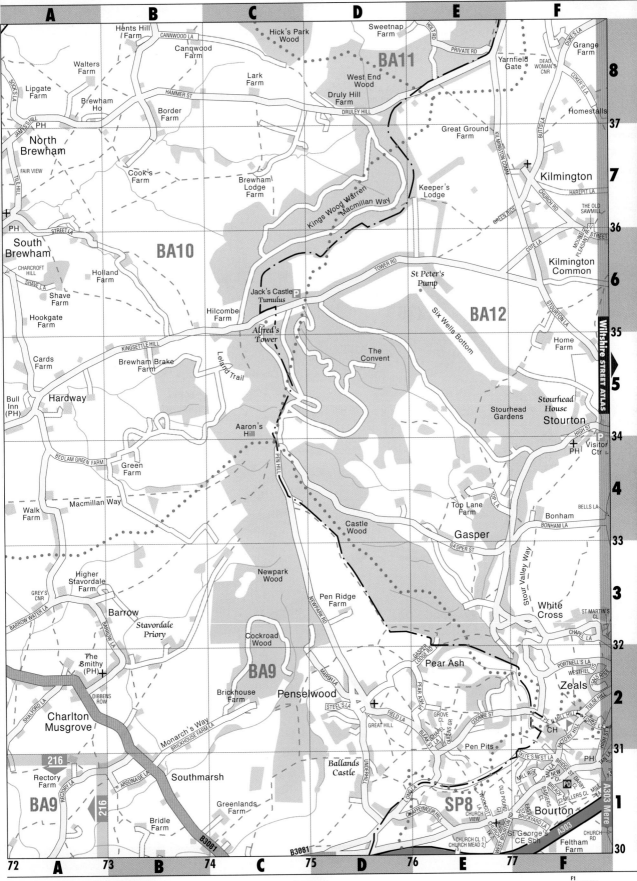

A   B   C   D   E   F

8

37

7

36

Hents Hill Farm

CANNWOOD LA

Cannwood Farm

Hick's Park Wood

Sweetnap Farm

HOLT RD

PRIVATE RD

BA11

West End Wood

Druly Hill Farm

DRULEY HILL

DUKE'S LA

Grange Farm

Yarnfield Gate

DEAD WOMAN'S CNR

Homestalls

Kilmington

Great Ground Farm

Keeper's Lodge

KILMINGTON COMM

CONEY'S LA

BUTT'S LA

CHURCH RD

HAREPIT LA

THE OLD SAWMILL

THE STREET

MOUNT PLEASANT LA

Kilmington Common

Walters Farm

Lipgate Farm

SOCK'S HILL

JAMES'S HILL

TILE HILL

PH

North Brewham

FAIR VIEW

STREET LA

PH

South Brewham

CHARCROFT HILL

SHAVE LA

Shave Farm

Hookgate Farm

Holland Farm

Lark Farm

HAMMER ST

Border Farm

Brewham Ho

Cook's Farm

Brewham Lodge Farm

BA10

Kings Wood Warren

Macmillan Way

Jack's Castle Tumulus

Hilcombe Farm

Alfred's Tower

TOWER RD

St Peter's Pump

Six Wells Bottom

BA12

The Convent

Home Farm

Cards Farm

KINGSETTLE HILL

Leland Trail

Brewham Brake Farm

Bull Inn (PH)

Hardway

BEDLAM GREEN FARM LA

Green Farm

Aaron's Hill

PEN HILL

Stourhead Gardens

Stourhead House

Stourton

HIGH ST

PH

Visitor Ctr

COTE LA

STOURTON LA

GREEN RIDGE

35

6

5

34

4

33

3

32

2

31

1

30

Walk Farm

Macmillan Way

Higher Stavordale Farm

GREY'S CNR

Barrow

BARROW LA

BARROW WATER LA

Stavordale Priory

The Smithy (PH)

DIBBENS ROW

Charlton Musgrove

SHAGFORD LA

PARSONAGE LA

216

BA9

Rectory Farm

RECTORY LA

216

Bridle Farm

Southmarsh

B3081

Brickhouse Farm

Monarch's Way

BRICKHOUSE FARM LA

Greenlands Farm

Castle Wood

Newpark Wood

Pen Ridge Farm

NEWPARK RD

Cockroad Wood

BA9

Penselwood

STEEL'S LA

MARSH LA

Ballands Castle

UNDERHILL

B3081

Top Lane Farm

GASPER ST

Gasper

BONHAM LA

Bonham

BELLS LA

TOP LA

STOUR VALLEY WAY

White Cross

ST MARTIN'S CL

CHAPEL LA

Pear Ash

GASPER LODGE RD

PEAR ASH LA

Great Hill

FIELD LA

GROVE CL

COOMBE ST

QUEEN'S GR

BLEAK ST

CHAPEL RD

Pen Pits

PORTNELL'S LA

WESTFIELD

SEAS RISE

Zeals

PEN MILL HILL

FACTORY HILL

LODGE HILL

CH

TULSE HILL

SP8

 COW DRIFFEY MOOR HILL

LONG LA

PROUT HILL

CHURCH VIEW

Bourton

CHURCH CL 1

CHURCH MEAD 2

St George's CE Sch

WTTE'S NEST LA

BRIDGE CL

NEW RD

BADGERS CL

BRICKYARD LA

MILL RISE

OLD POUND

GILLINGS CL

MILLERS CL

PO

PH

A303 Mere

A303

CHURCH RD

Feltham Farm

Wiltshire STREET ATLAS

For full street detail of the highlighted area see page 216.

F1
1 SILTON RD
2 THE MEADOWS

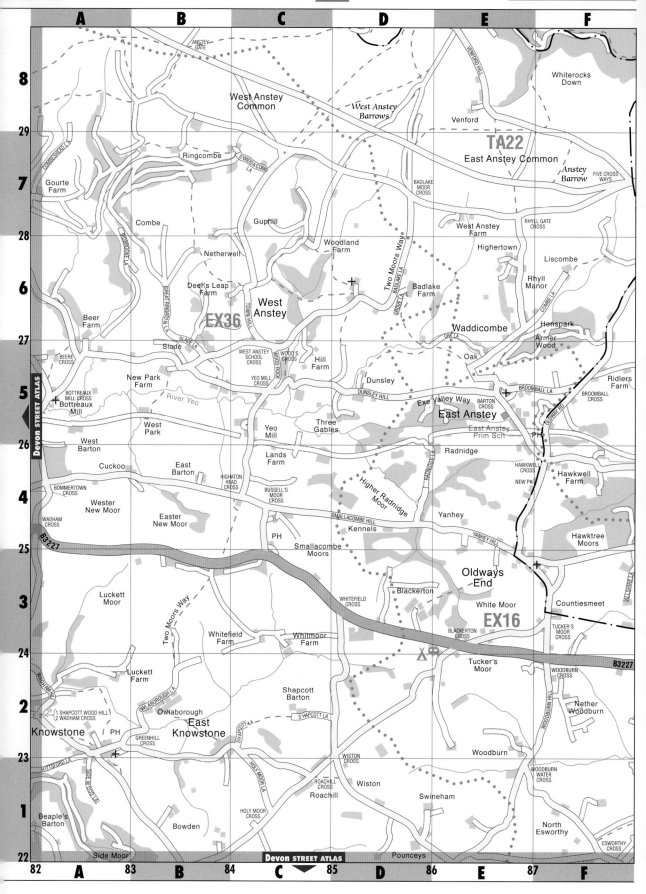

146

A   B   C   D   E   F

8

29

7

28

6

27

5

26

4

25

3

24

2

23

1

22

Whiterocks Down

West Anstey Common

West Anstey Barrows

Venford

TA22

East Anstey Common

Anstey Barrow

FIVE CROSS WAYS

ANSTEY GATE

COMBESHEAD LA

Gourte Farm

Ringcombe

S WIDDACOMB LA

Combe

Guphill

BIDBROOKE LA

Netherwell

Woodland Farm

West Anstey Farm

Highertown

RHYLL GATE CROSS

Liscombe

BADLAKE MOOR CROSS

Two Moors Way

BADLAKE LA

Rhyll Manor

GROVE LA

Deer's Leap Farm

GREAT RINGAND LA

West Anstey

EX36

TOWN HILL

Badlake Farm

Henspark

Waddicombe

Armer Wood

COMBE LA

Beer Farm

SLADE LA

Slade

WOOD ROCK

WEST ANSTEY SCHOOL CROSS

WOOD'S CROSS

Hill Farm

OAK LA

Oak

Ridlers Farm

Beere Cross

New Park Farm

YEO MILL CROSS

River Yeo

Dunsley

DUNSLEY HILL

Exe Valley Way

BARTON CROSS

BROOMBALL LA

Broomball Cross

BOTTREAUX MILL CROSS

Bottreaux Mill

Three Gables

East Anstey

PH

OLDWAY RD

West Barton

West Park

Yeo Mill

East Anstey Prim Sch

RADNIDGE LA

Radnidge

HAWKWELL CROSS

NEW PK

Hawkwell Farm

Cuckoo

East Barton

Lands Farm

Higher Radnidge Moor

Yanhey

HIGHATON HEAD CROSS

BOMMERTOWN CROSS

Wester New Moor

BUSSELL'S MOOR CROSS

SMALLACOMBE HILL

Kennels

YANHEY HILL

Hawktree Moors

WADHAM CROSS

Easter New Moor

PH

Smallacombe Moors

ALLSHIRE LA

B3227

Luckett Moor

Two Moors Way

WHITEFIELD CROSS

Blackerton

Oldways End

Countiesmeet

TUCKER'S MOOR CROSS

WADHAM HILL

Luckett Farm

Whitefield Farm

Whitmoor Farm

White Moor

EX16

BLACKERTON CROSS

Tucker's Moor

WOODBURN CROSS

B3227

OWLABOROUGH LA

Shapcott Barton

Nether Woodburn

1 SHAPCOTT WOOD HILL
2 WADHAM CROSS

Owlaborough

East Knowstone

SHAPCOTT LA

S HAPCOTT LA

WOODBURN HILL

Knowstone

PH

GREENHILL CROSS

HOLY MOOR LA

Woodburn

WOODBURN WATER CROSS

HITTSFORD LA

SIDE WOOD LA

WISTON CROSS

ROACHILL CROSS

Wiston

Swineham

North Esworthy

Beaple's Barton

Bowden

HOLY MOOR CROSS

Roachill

ESWORTHY CROSS

Side Moor

Pounceys

Devon STREET ATLAS

82   A   83   B   84   C   85   D   86   E   87   F

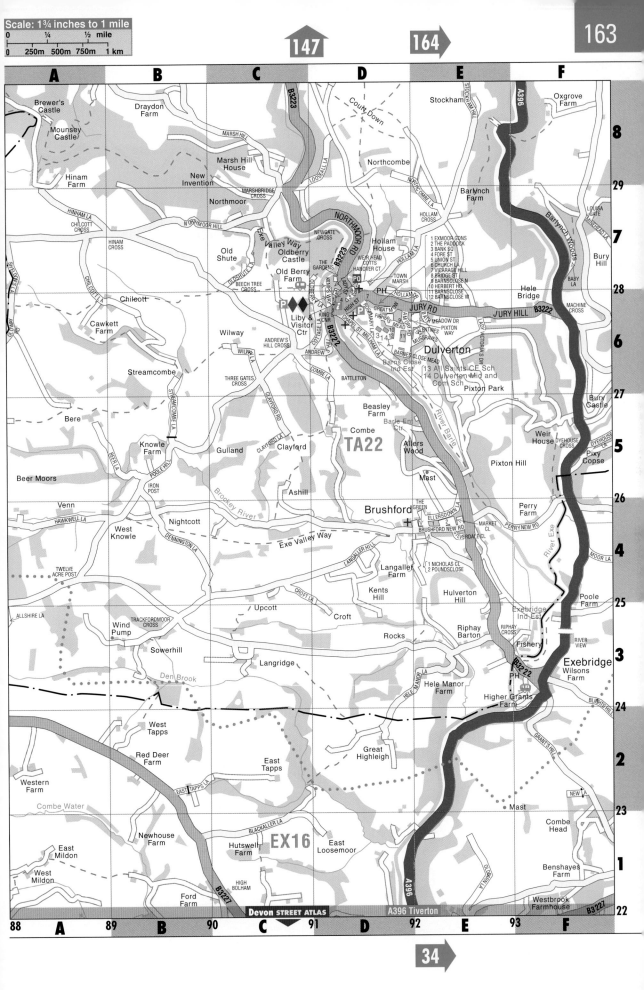

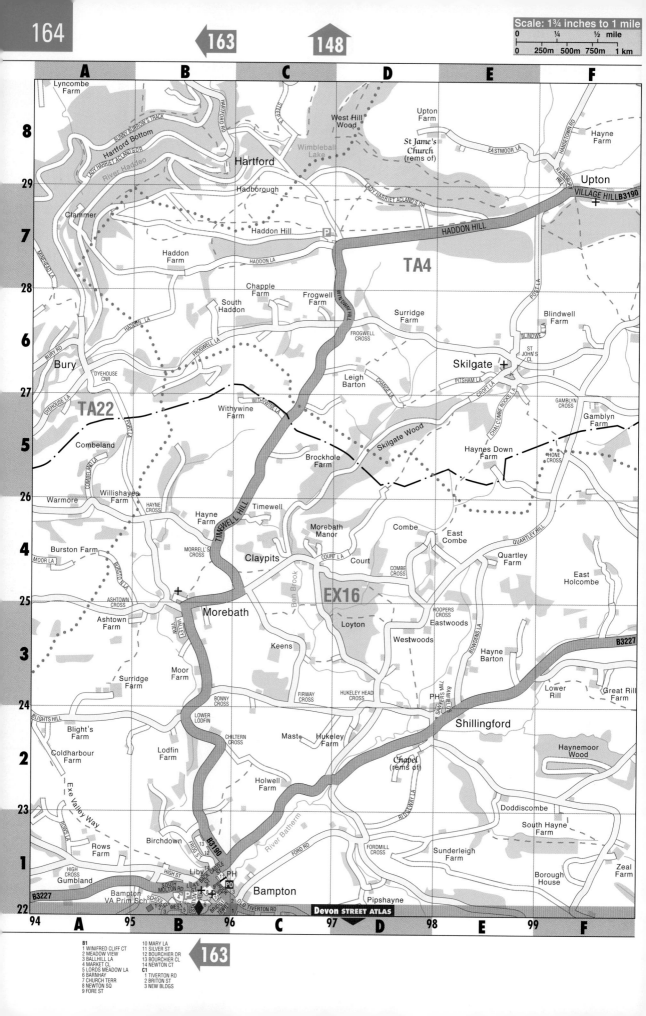

Scale: 1¾ inches to 1 mile

0 ¼ ½ mile
0 250m 500m 750m 1 km

8

Lyncombe Farm

BUNNY BURROW'S TRACK

Hartford Bottom

LADY HARRIET ACLAND'S DR

River Haddeo

Hartford

West Hill Wood

Wimbleball Lake

St Jame's Church (rems of)

Upton Farm

EASTMOOR LA

Hayne Farm

RAINSBURY RD

29

Hadborough

Clammer

Upton

VILLAGE HILL B3190

7

Haddon Hill

P

HADDON HILL

Haddon Farm

HADDON LA

LADY HARRIET ACLAND'S DR

RAINSBURY HILL

TA4

28

Chapple Farm

Frogwell Farm

WYNDWAN HILL

Surridge Farm

POST LA

Blindwell Farm

6

BURY RD

South Haddon

HADDON LA

FROGWELL LA

Frogwell Cross

Leigh Barton

CHANGE LA

Skilgate

BLINDWE

St JOHN'S CL

Bury

DYEHOUSE CNR

PITSHAM LA

CROFT LA

GAMBLYN CROSS

27

DYEHOUSE LA

TA22

WITHYWINE LA

Withywine Farm

Skilgate Wood

CHALCOMBE ROCKS LA

HONE CROSS

Gamblyn Farm

5

PORT LA

Combeland

Brockhole Farm

Haynes Down Farm

26

COMBELAND LA

Willishayes Farm

HAYNE CROSS

Hayne Farm

Timewell

TIMEWELL HILL

Morebath Manor

Combe

East Combe

QUARTLEY HILL

Warmore

4

MOOR LA

Burston Farm

BURSTON LA

MORRELL'S CROSS

Claypits

COURT LA

Court

COMBE CROSS

Quartley Farm

East Holcombe

25

ASHTOWN CROSS

Morebath

Ben Brook

EX16

HOOPERS CROSS

Eastwoods

BOWDENS LA

3

Ashtown Farm

VALLEY VIEW

Keens

Loyton

Westwoods

Hayne Barton

B3227

Surridge Farm

Moor Farm

Lower Rill

Great Rill Farm

24

BLIGHTS HILL

BONNY CROSS

LOWER LODFIN

FIRWAY CROSS

HUKELEY HEAD CROSS

PH

BANNELLS LA

SAWYERS HILL

Shillingford

Blight's Farm

CHILTERN CROSS

Mast

Hukeley Farm

2

Coldharbour Farm

Lodfin Farm

Haynemoor Wood

EXE VALLEY WAY

Holwell Farm

Chapel (rems of)

RIDGEWAY LA

Doddiscombe

South Hayne Farm

23

ROWS LA

Rows Farm

River Batherm

FORD RD

FORDMILL CROSS

Sunderleigh Farm

Zeal Farm

1

HIGH CROSS

Gumbland

HIGH ST

SOUTH MOLTON RD

B3190

FROGS ST

LUKE ST

CASTLE ST

Liby

PH

PO

Bampton

Pipshayne

Borough House

B3227

Birchdown

Bampton VA Prim Sch

SCHOOL

NEWT

BRITON TERR

OLD TIVERTON RD

Devon STREET ATLAS

22

94 95 96 97 98 99

A B C D E F

B1
1 WINIFRED CLIFF CT
2 MEADOW VIEW
3 BALLHILL LA
4 MARKET CL
5 LORDS MEADOW LA
6 BARNHAY
7 CHURCH TERR
8 NEWTON SQ
9 FORE ST
10 MARY LA
11 SILVER ST
12 BOURCHIER DR
13 BOURCHIER CL
14 NEWTON CT
C1
1 TIVERTON RD
2 BRITON ST
3 NEW BLDGS

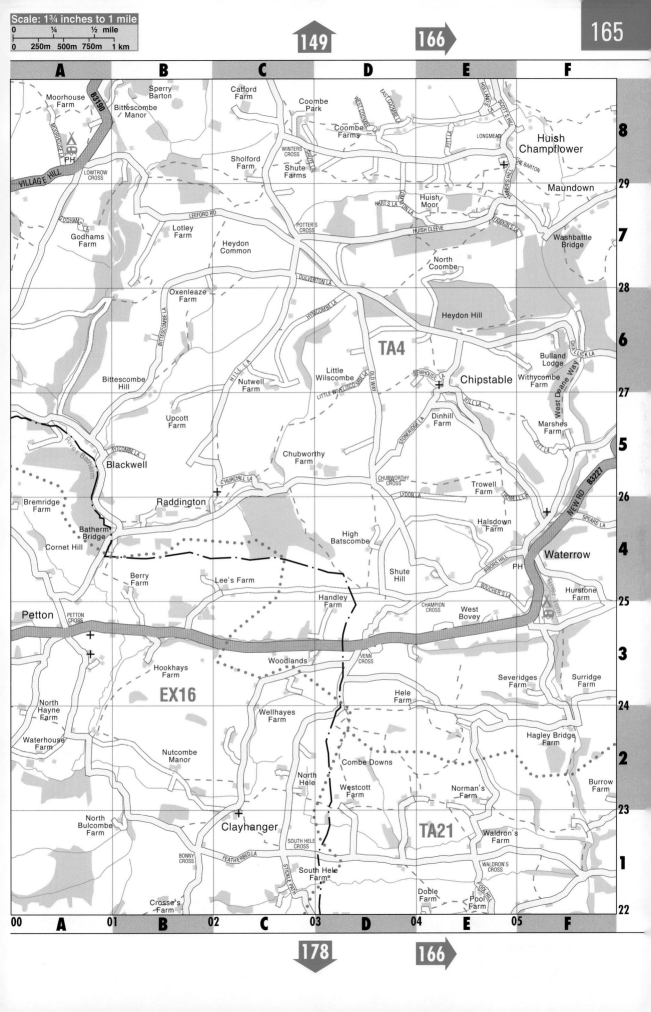

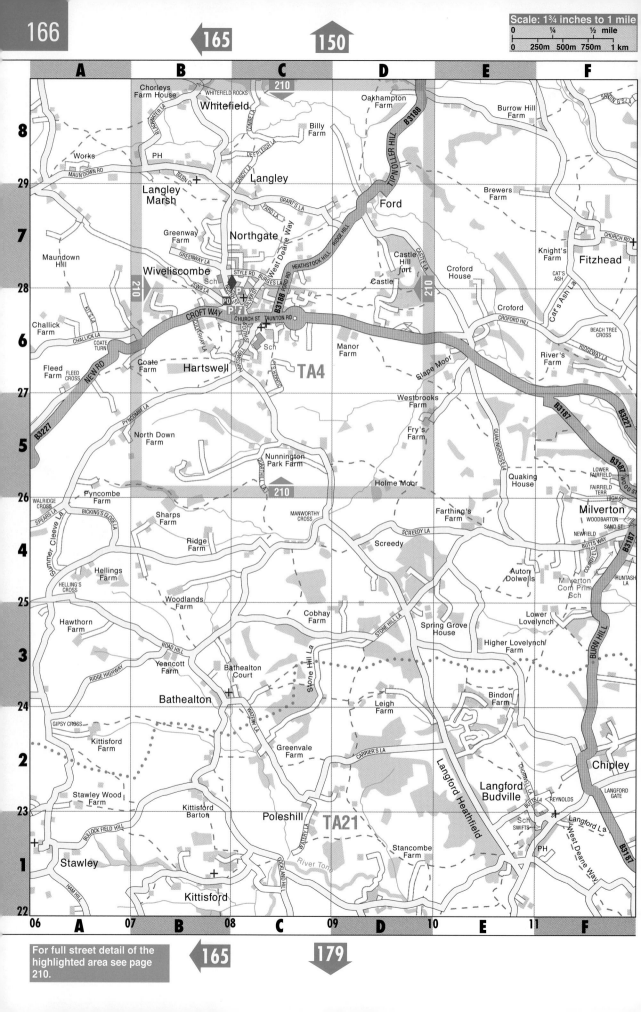

Scale: 1¾ inches to 1 mile
0   ¼   ½   mile
0   250m 500m 750m 1 km

A **B** **C** **D** **E** **F**

210

Chorleys
Farm House
WHITEFIELD ROCKS
Whitefield

Works

Billy
Farm

Oakhampton
Farm

B3188

Burrow Hill
Farm

SMITH'G'SLA

8

PH

Langley

Brewers
Farm

CHURCH RD

29
MAUNDOWN RD

Langley
Marsh

SANDY LA

GRANT'S LA

YARD LA

Ford

TIPNOLLER HILL

Knight's
Farm

Fitzhead

Maundown
Hill

Greenway
Farm

GREENWAY LA

Northgate

West Deane Way

HEATHSTOCK HILL

RIDGE HILL

FORD RD

Castle
Hill
fort

CASTLE LA

Croford
House

CAT'S
ASH

Cat's Ash La

28
Wiveliscombe

210

Sch

STYLE RD

NORTH ST

JEWS LA

BURGES LA

P

PO

B3188

Castle

Croford

CROFORD HILL

210

BEACH TREE
CROSS

Challick
Farm

KITS LA

CHALLICK LA

COATE
TURN

CROFT WAY

P

GLIDEHAM LA

CHURCH ST

TAUNTON RD

Manor
Farm

River's
Farm

RIDGEWAY LA

6

NEW RD

Coate
Farm

Hartswell

HARTSWELL

Sch

CAT'S ASH LA

TA4

Slape Moor

Fleed
Farm

FLEED
CROSS

27

PYNCOMBE LA

Westbrooks
Farm

B3187

B3227

North Down
Farm

NORTHILL LA

Fry's
Farm

QUAKINGHOUSE LA

LOWER
FAIRFIELD

B3187

WOOD ST

5

Nunnington
Park Farm

210

Holme Moor

Quaking
House

FAIRFIELD
TERR

HIGH ST

B3227

Pyncombe
Farm

Farthing's
Farm

Milverton

WALRIDGE
CROSS

Sharps
Farm

Manworthy
Cross

Screedy

SCREEDY LA

WOODBARTON

SAND ST

26
SPEARS LA

BICKING'S CLOSE LA

NEWFIELD

BUTTS WAY

B3187

4

Summer Cleeve La

Ridge
Farm

Auton
Dolwells

Milverton
Com Prim
Sch

COURTFIELD WAY

HUNTASH
LA

Hellings
Farm

HELLING'S
CROSS

Woodlands
Farm

Cobhay
Farm

STONE HILL LA

Spring Grove
House

Lower
Lovelynch

25

Hawthorn
Farm

ROAD HILL

Higher Lovelynch
Farm

BURN HILL

3

RIDGE HIGHWAY

Yeancott
Farm

Bathealton
Court

Stone Hill La

Leigh
Farm

Bindon
Farm

24
GIPSY CROSS

Bathealton

WATERY LA

Greenvale
Farm

CARRIER'S LA

Langford Heathfield

CHOLWELL LA

Chipley

2

Kittisford
Farm

Langford
Budville

BUTTS LA

Langford
Gate

Reynolds

Stawley Wood
Farm

Kittisford
Barton

Poleshill

WATERY LA

TA21

Stancombe
Farm

Sch
SWIFTS

Langford La

West Deane Way

B3187

23
BULLOCK FIELD HILL

PH

1

HAM HILL

Stawley

Kittisford

River Tone

OCKLAND HILL

22
06 **A** **07** **B** **08** **C** **09** **D** **10** **E** **11** **F**

For full street detail of the
highlighted area see page
210.

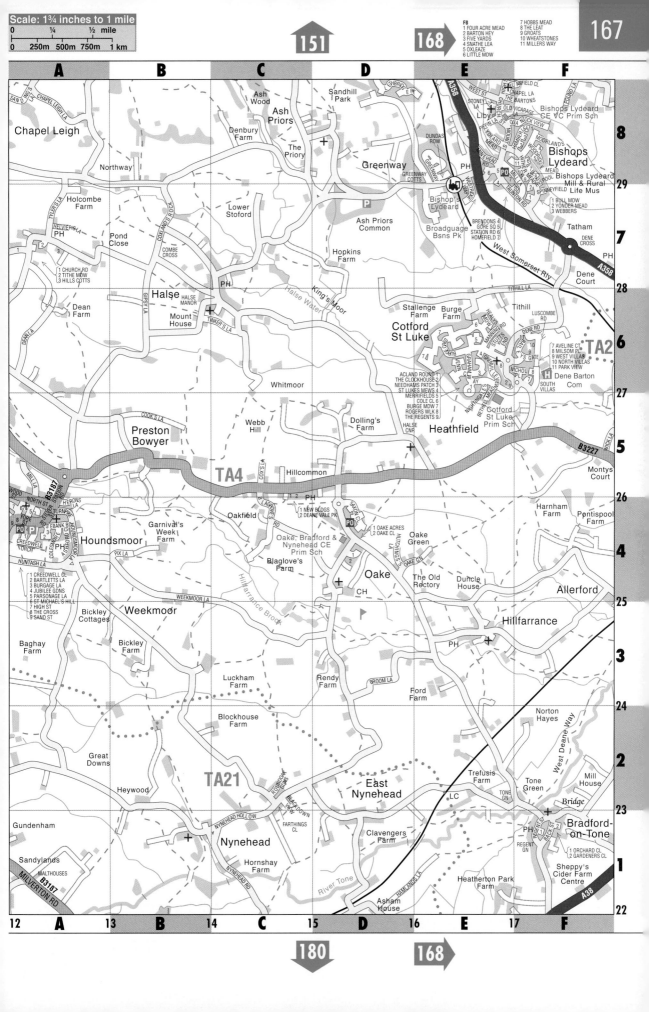

Scale: 1¾ inches to 1 mile

0   ¼   ½ mile
0   250m   500m   750m   1 km

151

168

167

F8
1 FOUR ACRE MEAD
2 BARTON HEY
3 FIVE YARDS
4 SNATHE LEA
5 OXLEAZE
6 LITTLE MDW
7 HOBBS MEAD
8 THE LEAT
9 GROATS
10 WHEATSTONES
11 MILLERS WAY

A   **B**   **C**   **D**   **E**   **F**

Chapel Leigh

Northway

Holcombe Farm

Helvier's La PH

Pond Close

Combe Cross

Dean Farm

Halse

Halse Manor

Mount House

Tinker's La

Ash Wood

Ash Priors

Denbury Farm

The Priory

Lower Stoford

Sandhill Park

Greenway

Greenway Cotts

Ash Priors Common

Hopkins Farm

King's Moor

Halse Water

Whitmoor

Webb Hill

Dolling's Farm

Halse Cnr

West St
Chapel La
The Bartons
Old Vicarage
Bishops Lydeard CE VC Prim Sch
Bishops Lydeard
Bishops Lydeard Mill & Rural Life Mus

Dundas Row

Bishops Lydeard
Broadguage Bsns Pk

West Somerset Rly

A358

Tatham
Dene Cross
PH
Dene Court

Tithill La
Stallenge Farm
Burge Farm
Tithill
Luscombe Rd

Cotford St Luke

TA2

7 AVELINE CT
8 MILSOM PL
9 WEST VILLAS
10 NORTH VILLAS
11 PARK VIEW

South Villas
Dene Barton Com

ACLAND ROUND 1
THE CLOCKHOUSE 2
NEEDHAMS PATCH 3
ST LUKES MEWS 4
MERRIFIELDS 5
COLE CL 6
BURGE MDW 7
ROGERS WLK 8
THE REGENTS 9

Cotford St Luke Prim Sch

Heathfield

B3227

Preston Bowyer

Cook's La

TA4

Hillcommon

PH

Oakfield

Oake, Bradford & Nynehead CE Prim Sch

1 NEW BLDGS
2 DEANE VALE PK

PO

1 OAKE ACRES
2 OAKE CL

Oake

Oake Green

The Old Rectory

Duncle House

Allerford

Montys Court

Harnham Farm

Pontispool Farm

Garnival's Week Farm

1 CREEDWELL CL
2 BARTLETTS LA
3 BURGAGE LA
4 JUBILEE GDNS
5 PARSONAGE LA
6 ST MICHAEL'S HILL
7 HIGH ST
8 THE CROSS
9 SAND ST

Houndsmoor

PO
PH

Pix La

Blaglove's Farm

CH

Hillfarrance

PH

Weekmoor La

Weekmoor

Bickley Cottages

Bickley Farm

Luckham Farm

Rendy Farm

Broom La

Ford Farm

Norton Hayes

West Deane Way

Baghay Farm

Blockhouse Farm

Great Downs

Heywood

TA21

Nynehead Hollow

Nynehead

Hornshay Farm

East Nynehead

Clavengers Farm

LC

Trefusis Farm

Tone Green

Tone Gn

Mill House

Bridge

Gundenham

Sandylands

Malthouses

B3187

Milverton Rd

Nynehead Rd

Farthings Cl

Blackdown Barn

River Tone

Asham House

Hamlands La

Heatherton Park Farm

Bradford-on-Tone

1 ORCHARD CL
2 GARDENERS CL

Regent Gn

Regent St
Rack St

Sheppy's Cider Farm Centre

A38

8
29
7
28
6
27
5
26
4
25
3
24
2
23
1
22

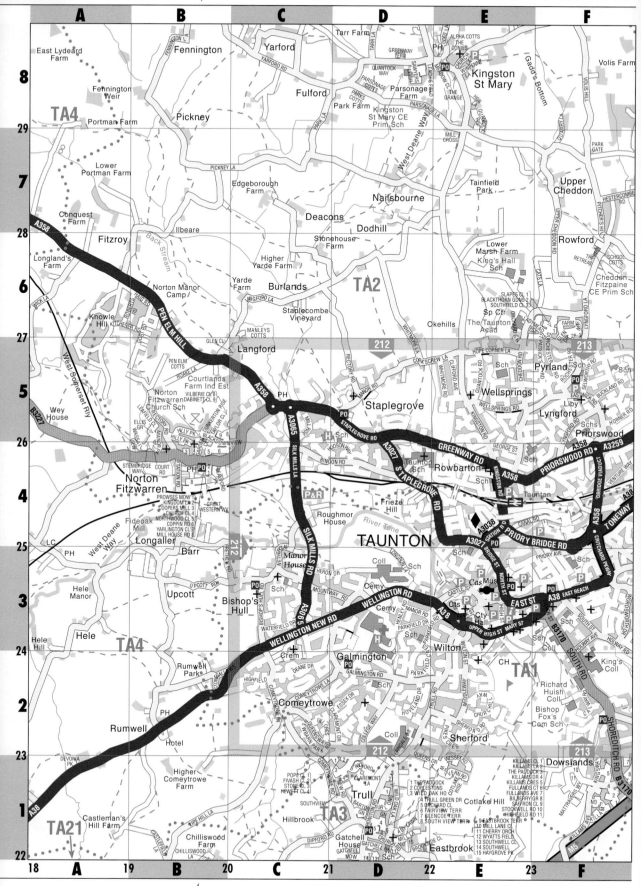

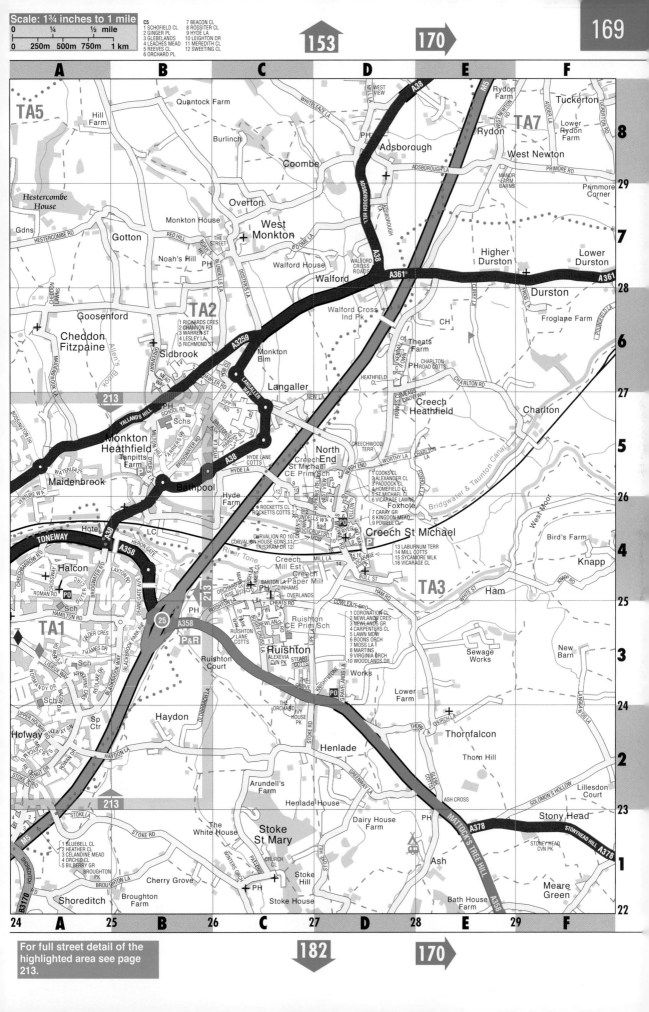

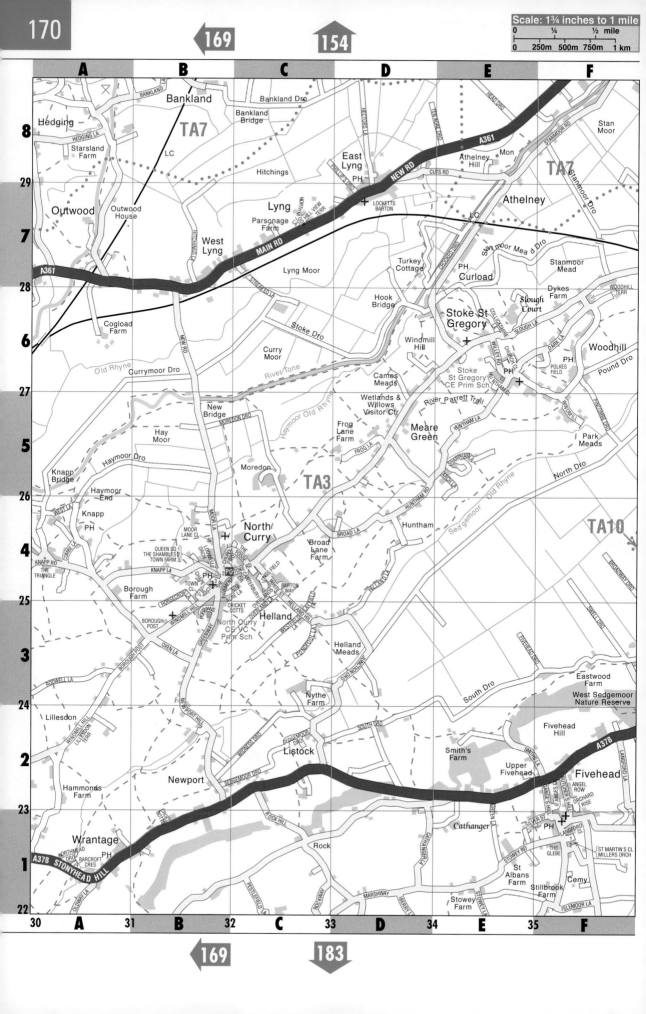

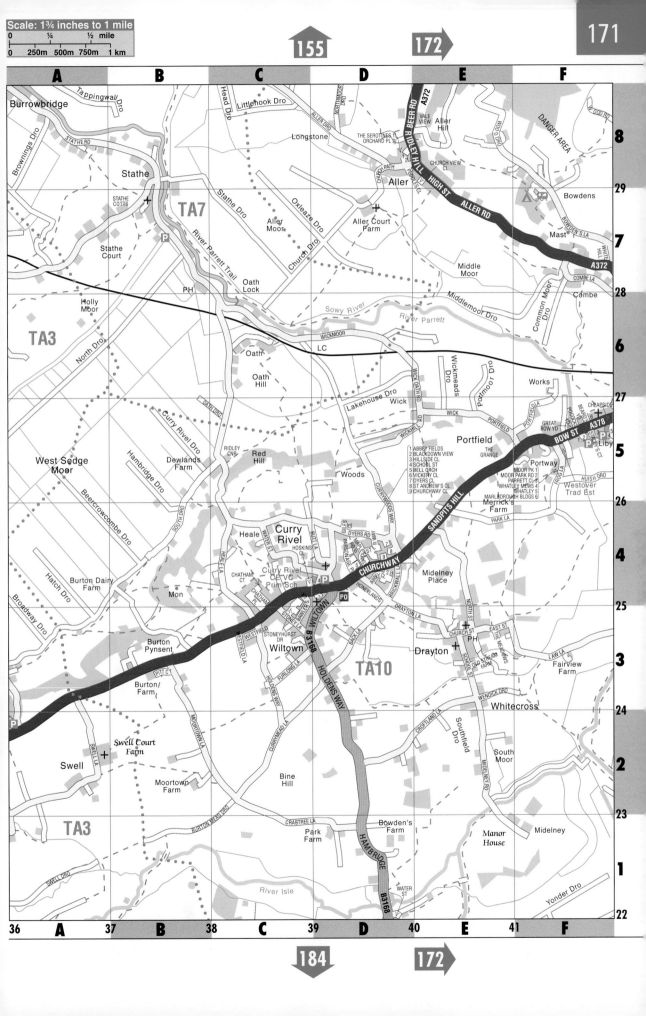

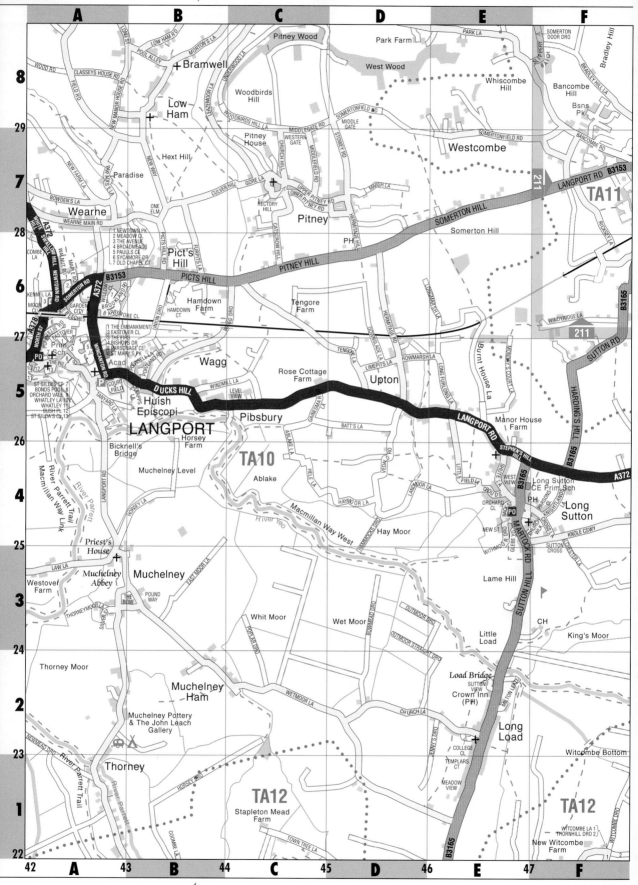

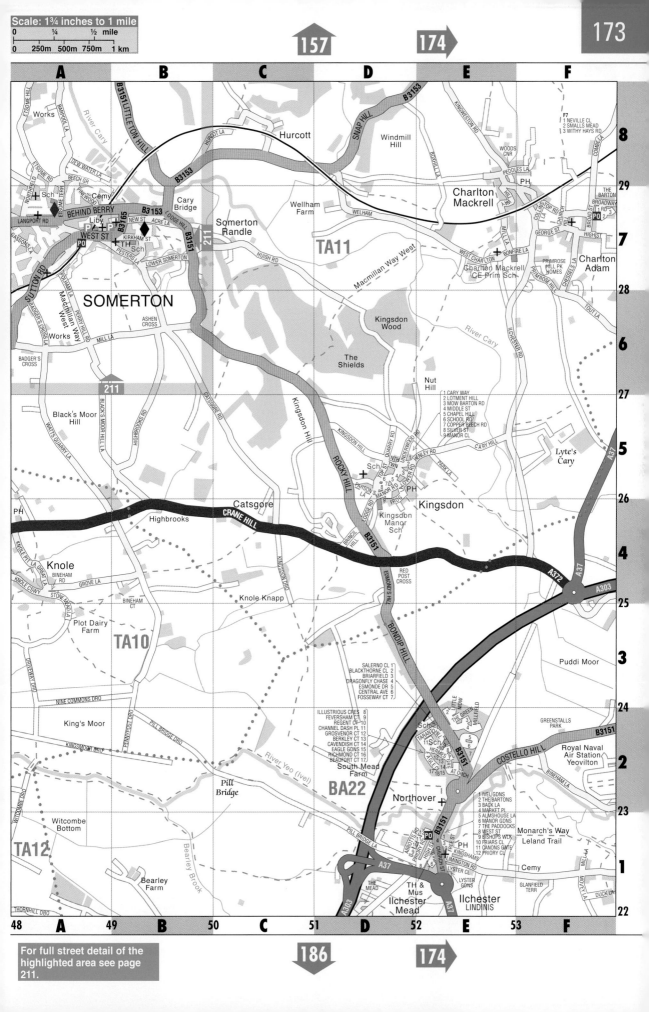

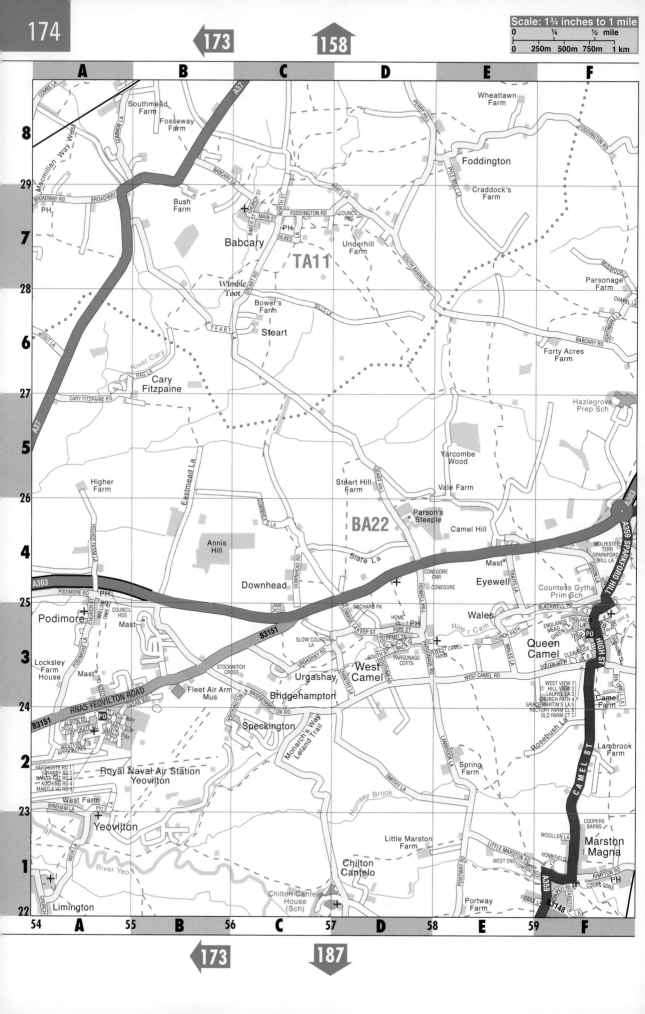

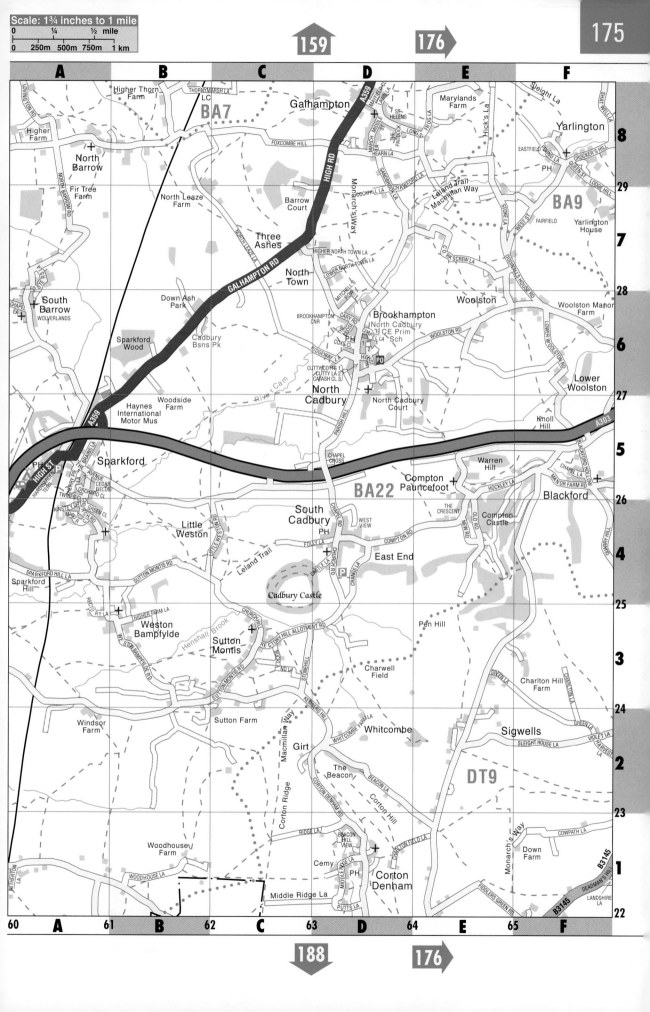

A303 · BA7 · God's Hill · Cattle Hill · Bratton Hill · Bratton Seymour · Uplands · Bratton Ho · Stickle Park La · Eastwood Farm · Lodge Hill · Jack White's Gibbet · Masts · Higher Holbrook Farm · Westleaze Farm · Suddon Grange · Wincanton Race Course · CH · Verrington · Verrington La · Windmill Hill · B3081 · Hosp · H · West Hill · Liby · P · Sch · PO · Mus · Holbrook House Hotel · WINCANTON · Cemy · Sch · Higher Clapton Farm · Lower Clapton Farm La · Gibbet Rd · Clapton La · Elliscombe Pk · Hunger Hill · 216 · Hook Valley Farm · BA9 · Southgate Rd · B3081 · A303 · Lawrence Hill · A371 · Hatherleigh Farms · Sewage Works · Brains Farm · Moor La · A303

A303 · Dancing Cross · Holton Cross · Holton St · PH · Holton · Lattiford Farm · Anchor Cnr · Higher Holton · A357 · Lattiford · Slopers La · River Cale · 216

BA22 · Maperton · North Cheriton Rd · Hook La · Shepherds Cross · The Marchant Holliday Sch · B3145 · Tower Cheriton La · Grove La · Grove Farm · Maltkin Hill Farm · Lattiford · Blackacre Hill · North Cheriton · Landseer · Wood La · Cabbage La · Monarch's Way · Marsh La · South Cheriton · Horsington Marsh · Marshbarn Farm · Charlton Hill · Silver Knap · Charn Hill · Goathill La · Hull La · Darkharbour Farm · Tower View · Coldharbour La · Higher Rd · Cheriton La · Behind Hayes · Brookside · Cemy · Horsington CE Prim Sch · Lower La · Batchpool La · Marshbarn Farm · Common La · PH · Hull Farm · Windmill Hill · Hangland's La · Horsington Rd · BA8 · Horsington · Manor · PH · Horsington Ho · Rectory La · White Cat Cotts · Duck La · Broadmoor La · Combe Throop

Charlton Horethorne · DT9 · Wilkinthroop · North Side Wood · Tower Hill · Hiscock's La · Abbas & Templecombe CE Prim Sch · Throop Rd · Slades Hill · Abbas Combe · Westwood Cotts · Templecombe · A357 · High St · Blackacre Vale Cl · B3145 · Landshire La · Waterloo Cres · Stowell · Stowell Hill

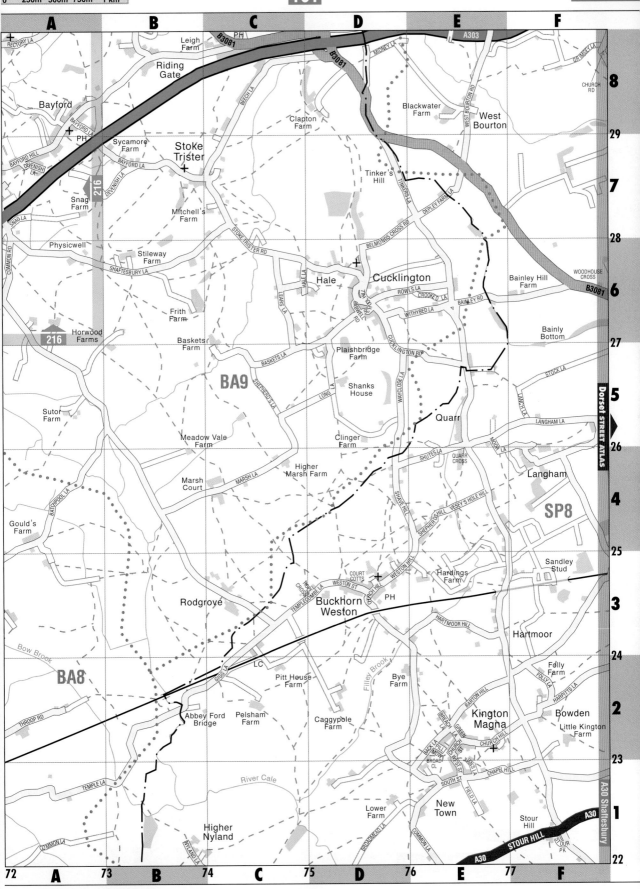

161

Scale: 1¾ inches to 1 mile

0 ¼ ½ mile
0 250m 500m 750m 1 km

A **B** **C** **D** **E** **F**

Rectory La

Bayford

Bayford La

PH

Bayford Hill

Devenish La

216

Snag Farm

Snag La

Common Rd

Physicwell

Shaftesbury La

Stileway Farm

Sycamore Farm

Mitchell's Farm

Stoke Trister Rd

Frith Farm

Horwood Farms

216

Sutor Farm

Batchpool La

Gould's Farm

BA8

Bow Brook

Throop Rd

Leigh Farm

B3081

Riding Gate

Beech La

Stoke Trister

Lears La

Hale La

Baskets Farm

Baskets La

Shepherd's La

Long La

Meadow Vale Farm

Marsh Court

Marsh La

Higher Marsh Farm

Rodgrove

Gigg La

Abbey Ford Bridge

Pelsham Farm

LC

Temple La

Higher Nyland

Nyland La

Common La

River Cale

Clapton Farm

Midney La

B3081

Tinker's Hill

Tinker's La

Belmonds Cross Rd

Hale

Rowls La

Tintock La

Brewham Rd

Crooked La

Withybed La

Cucklington

Cucklington Rd

Plaishbridge Farm

Shanks House

Waycloss La

Clinger Farm

Quarr

Shute's La

Shaft Hill

Shepherd's Hill

Vesey's Hole Hill

Temple Combe La

Imber Crossing

Weston St

Court Cotts

Church Hill

PH

Weston Hill

Buckhorn Weston

Hartmoor Hill

Pitt House Farm

Filley Brook

Bye Farm

Caggypole Farm

Broadmead La

Lower Farm

Blackwater Farm

West Bourton Rd

A303

West Bourton

Depley Farm La

Bainley Rd

Bainley Hill Farm

Woodhouse Cross

B3081

Bainly Bottom

Stock La

Lanch La

Langham La

Mdr La

Quarr Cross

Hardings Farm

Hartmoor

Sandley Stud

Langham

SP8

Folly Farm

Folly La

Harpitts La

Barton Hill

Kington Magna

Bowden

Little Kington Farm

Church Hill

Chapel Hill

Back La

Mdw

Broad Cl

Church St

West St

Field La

Jans La

South St

New Town

Stour Hill

A30

STOUR HILL

Stour Pk

A30 Shaftesbury

Dorset STREET ATLAS

BA9

8
29
7
28
6
27
5
26
4
25
3
24
2
23
1
22

A **B** **C** **D** **E** **F**

72 73 74 75 76 77

190

For full street detail of the highlighted area see page 216.

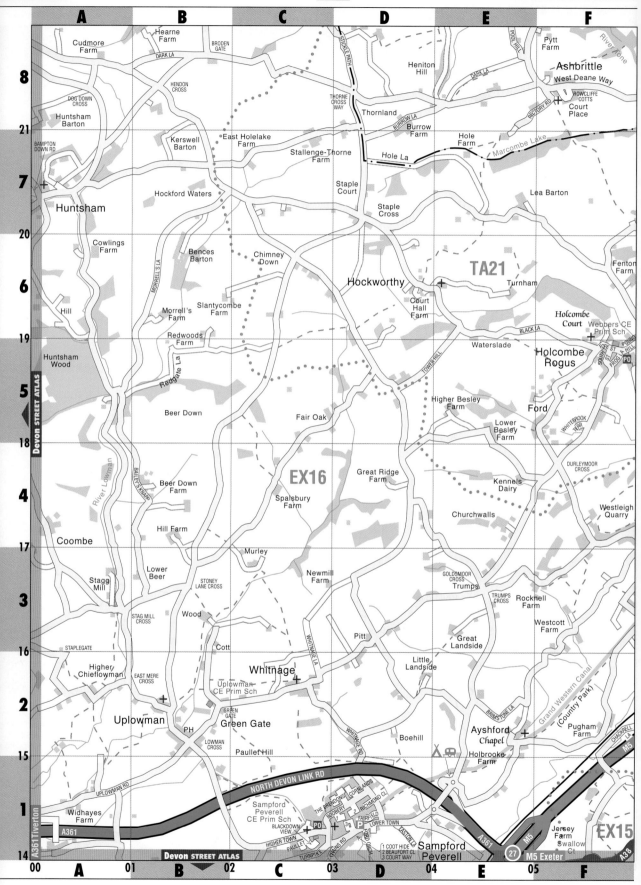

Scale: 1¾ inches to 1 mile

0   ¼   ½   mile

0   250m 500m 750m 1 km

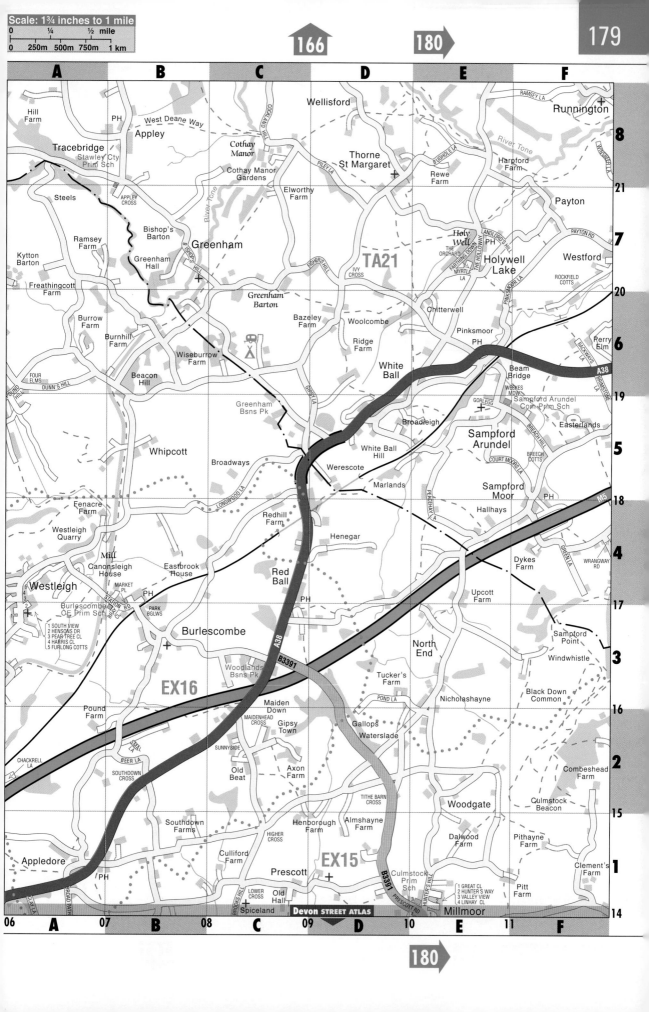

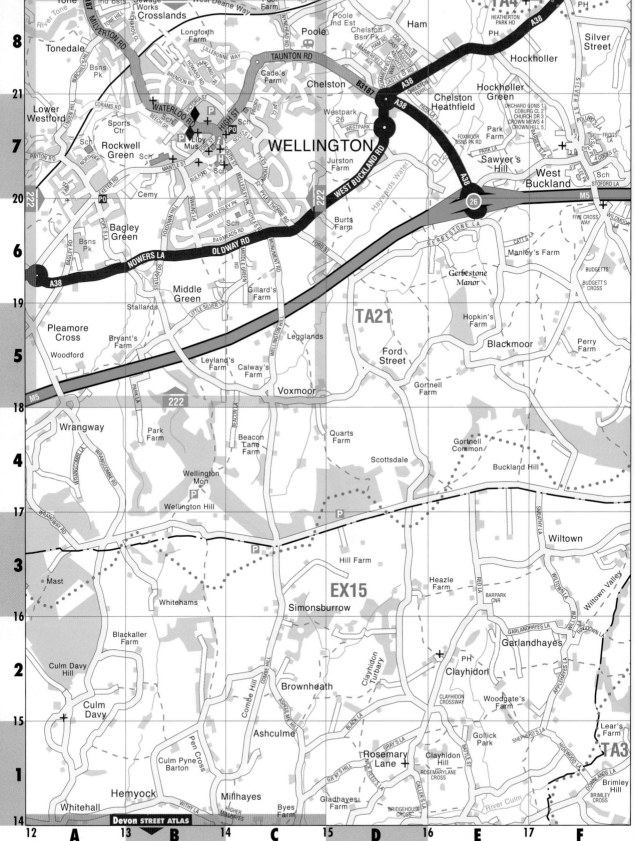

180
179
167
Scale: 1¾ inches to 1 mile
0   ¼   ½   mile
0 250m 500m 750m 1 km

A B C D E F

Tone
B3187
Ind Ests
Sewage Works
222
West Deane Way
Pool LA
Crosslands
MILVERTON RD
Longforth Farm
Poole
Poole Ind Est
Ham
TA4
HEATHERTON PARK HO
PH
PH
Silver Street
Tonedale
LILLEBONNE WAY
Cade's Farm
TAUNTON RD
Chelston Bsn Pk
COR CASTLE
Chelston
SUMMERFIELD AVE
HAM RD
CASTLE COTTS
CASTLE RD
Hockholler
21
BRENDON RD
HOWARD RD
PARKLANDS PL
Chelston
B3187
A38
KNIGHTS
CHELSTON TERR
Chelston Heathfield
Hockholler Green
ORCHARD GDNS 1
COBURG CL 2
CHURCH DR 3
CROWN NEWS 4
CROWN HILL 5
SILVER ST

Lower Westford
CORAMS RD
Waterloo Rd
VICTORIA ST
HIGH ST
PRIORY
GN CL
Westpark 26
A38
A38
Chelston
FOXMOOR BSNS PK RD
Park Farm
BARBERS PL
POLLARD'S LA
DYE'S
FROGS LA
7
Sports Ctr
Sch
P
MUS
SCOTT'S LA
PYLES THORNE
WELLINGTON
Westpark
PARK LA
Sawyer's Hill
COCKS CL
Sch
STOFORD LA
PAYTON RD
NORTHOLE
Rockwell Green
Sch
P
Liby
PO
H
Sch
Jurston Farm
WEST BUCKLAND RD
A38
West Buckland
EXETER RD
MANTLE ST
BULFORD
Sch
222
Haywards Water
20
Cemy
Cemy
SWAINS LA
WELLESLEY PK
HOLLEY'S
PYLES THORNE RD
MONUMENT RD
Burts Farm
M5
222
PO
Bagley Green
FOXDOWN HILL
BARMEADS RD
Ford St
GERBESTONE LA
Manley's Farm
BUDGETTS'
BUDGETT'S CROSS
6
POPE'S LA
Bsns Pk
NOWERS LA
OLDWAY RD
LITTLE SILVER LA
WELLINGTON HILL
Gerbestone Manor
A38
STALLARDS
Middle Green
Gillard's Farm
Hopkin's Farm
Blackmoor
Perry Farm
19
Stallards
PARK LA
222
CATT'S LA
TA21
Pleamore Cross
Bryant's Farm
Legglands
Ford Street
Gortnell Farm
5
Woodford
Leyland's Farm
Calway's Farm
Voxmoor
M5
SNEATHY LA
18
Wrangway
Park Farm
BEACON LA
Beacon Lane Farm
Quarts Farm
Gortnell Common
Wiltown
WRANGCOMBE LA
WRANGCOMBE RD
Wellington Mon
P
Scottsdale
Buckland Hill
RED LA
WILTOWN LA
4
Wellington Hill
17
WRANGWAY RD
P
P
Hill Farm
Heazle Farm
BARPARK CNR
Wiltown Valley
WILTOWN LA
APPLESHAM LA
3
Mast
EX15
Simonsburrow
GARLANDHAYES LA
Garlandhayes
RINGDOWN LA
16
Whitehams
COMBE HILL
PH
Clayhidon
WILTOWN LA
2
Blackaller Farm
ASHCULME RD
Brownheath
Clayhidon Turbary
Woodgate's Farm
CLAYHIDON CROSSWAY
Culm Davy Hill
BLACK LA
HIDEWOOD LA
Lear's Farm
15
Culm Davy
Pen Cross
Ashculme
GRAY'S HILL
Gollick Park
SHEPHERD'S LA
BATTLE ST
TA3
1
Culm Pyne Barton
GRAY'S LA
Rosemary Lane
Clayhidon Hill
ROSEMARYLANE CROSS
DOWNLANDS LA
Brimley Hill
BRIMLEY CROSS
Hemyock
WITHY LA
Millhayes
Byes Farm
Gladhayes Farm
NICKY'S HILL
CALLER'S LA
BRIDGEHOUSE CROSS
River Culm
14
Whitehall
HIGHER MILLHAYES
Devon STREET ATLAS

12   A   13   B   14   C   15   D   16   E   17   F

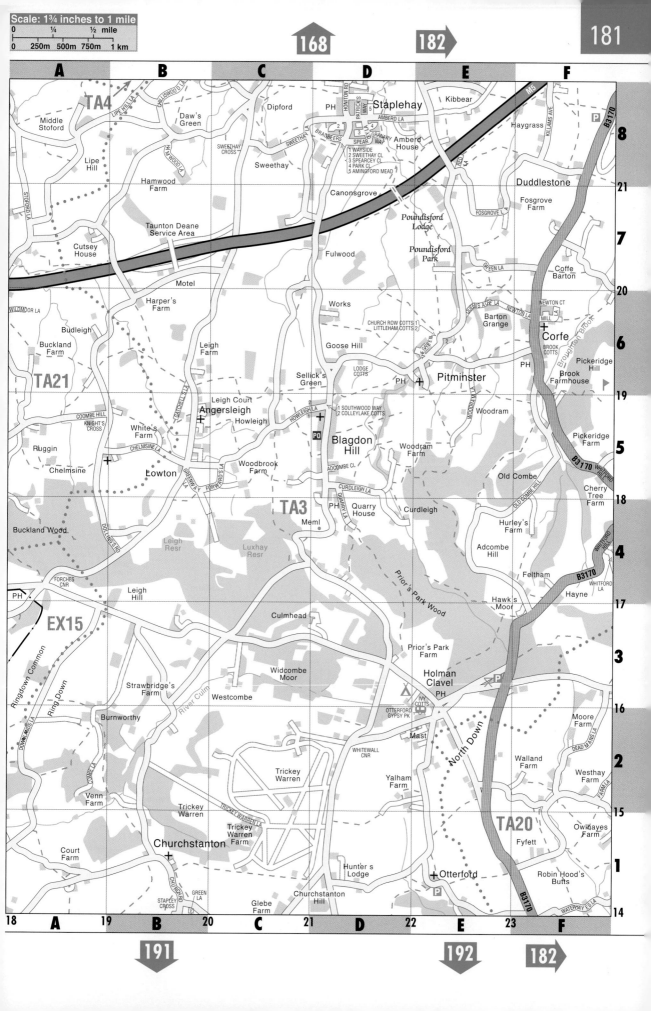

Scale: 1¾ inches to 1 mile

0 ¼ ½ mile
0 250m 500m 750m 1 km

168

182

181

A B C D E F

TA4

Middle Stoford

Lipe Hill

Hamwood Farm

CHELISWOOD LA

LIPE HILL LA

HAM WOOD LA

Daw's Green

Dipford

Sweethay

SWEETHAY CROSS

SWEETHAY

Cutsey House

Taunton Deane Service Area

Motel

Harper's Farm

Budleigh

Buckland Farm

TA21

WILDMOOR LA

Leigh Farm

Leigh Court

Angersleigh

Howleigh

COOMBE HILL

KNIGHT'S CROSS

White's Farm

Ruggin

Chelmsine

CHELMSINE LA

CRITCHELL'S LA

Lowton

GREENWAY

FORWARD'S LA

Woodbrook Farm

Buckland Wood

DOLLING'S RD

Leigh Resr

Luxhay Resr

Leigh Hill

FORCHES CNR

PH

EX15

Ringdown Common

Ring Down

DOWN MILLS LA

CORNISH LA

Venn Farm

Strawbridge's Farm

Burnworthy

Trickey Warren

TRICKEY WARREN LA

Court Farm

Churchstanton

CHURCH RD

GREEN LA

STAPLEY CROSS

Glebe Farm

Churchstanton Hill

Trickey Warren Farm

Trickey Warren

Widcombe Moor

River Culm

Westcombe

TA3

Meml

Culmhead

WHITEWALL CNR

Hunter's Lodge

Yalham Farm

Mast

OTTERFORD GYPSY PK

IVY COTTS

Holman Clavel

PH

Prior's Park Farm

Prior's Park Wood

North Down

Otterford

P

HONITON RD

PATRICKS

Staplehay

PH

BRADBEERS

SPEAR

AMBER LA

GRANARY WAY

Amber House

1 WAYSIDE
2 SWEETHAY CL
3 SPEARCEY CL
4 PARK CL
5 AMINGFORD MEAD

Canonsgrove

Fulwood

Works

CHURCH ROW COTTS 1
LITTLEHAM COTTS 2

Goose Hill

Sellick's Green

LODGE COTTS

PH

1 SOUTHWOOD WAY
2 COLLEYLAKE COTTS

HOWLEIGH LA

PO

Blagdon Hill

ADCOMBE CL

CURDLEIGH LA

QUARRY LA

PH

Quarry House

Curdleigh

Kibbear

M5

Haygrass

Duddlestone

Fosgrove Farm

FOSGROVE L

Poundisford Lodge

Poundisford Park

GREEN LA

THE GREEN

OVER'S AVE LA

NEWTON LA

Barton Grange

Pitminster

PH

Woodram

Woodram Farm

Old Combe

WOODRAM LA

OLD COMBE HILL

Hurley's Farm

Adcombe Hill

Feltham

Hawk's Moor

KILLAMS AVE

B3170

Coffe Barton

NEWTON CT

MILL

Corfe

BROOK COTTS

PH

Pickeridge Hill

Brook Farmhouse

Broughton Brook

Pickeridge Farm

B3170

WHITFORD

Cherry Tree Farm

WHITFORD HILL

B3170

WHITFORD LA

Hayne

P

Holman Clavel

Moore Farm

DEAD MAN'S LA

Walland Farm

Westhay Farm

FARM LA

TA20

Fyfett

Owl Hayes Farm

Robin Hood's Butts

WATERHAYES LA

P

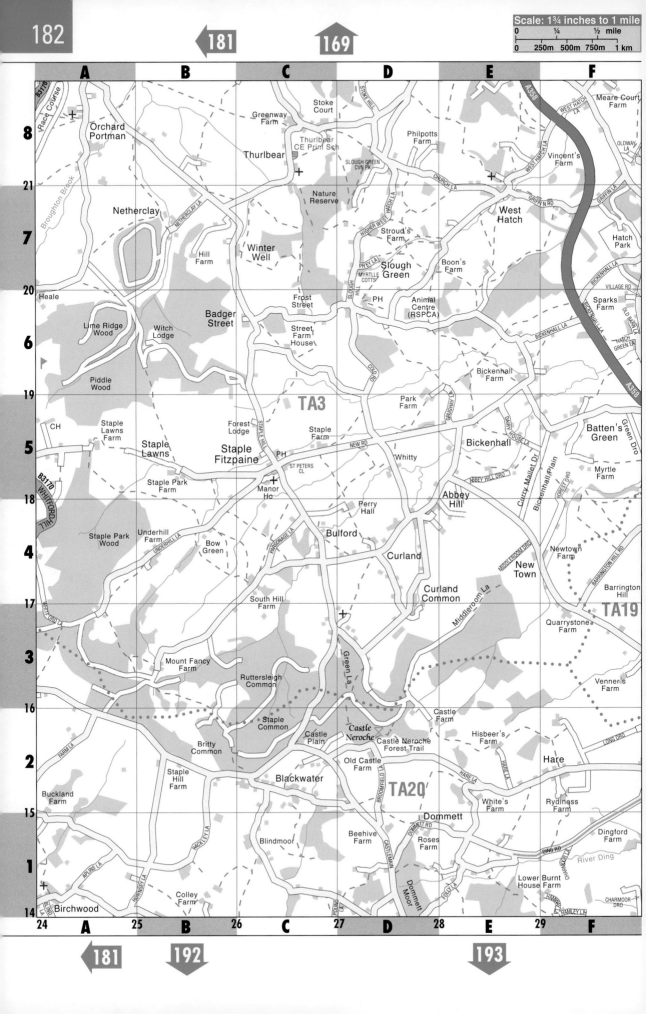

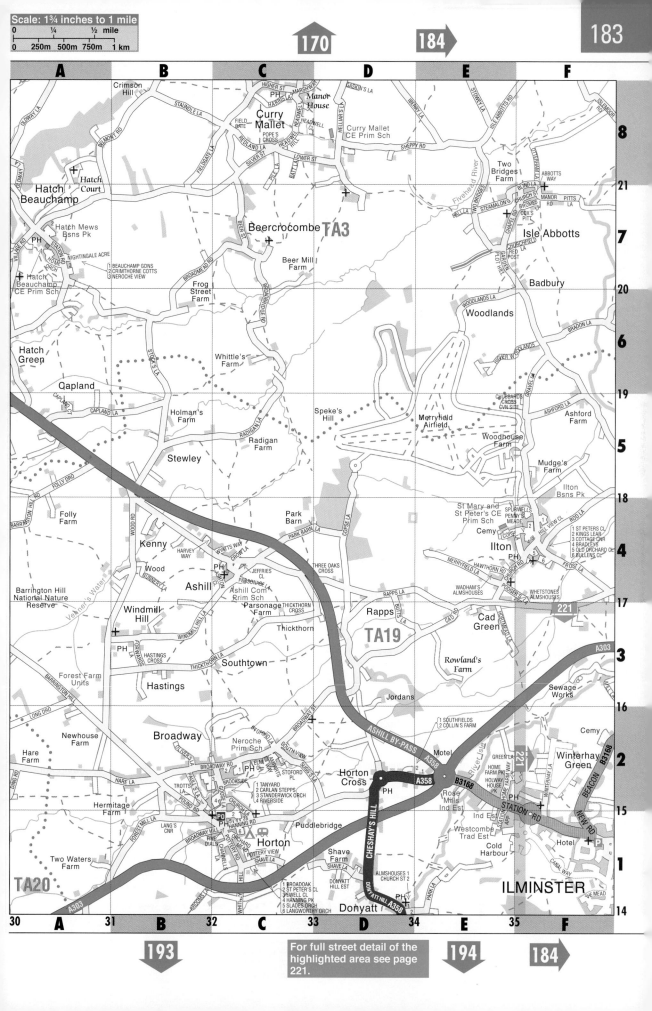

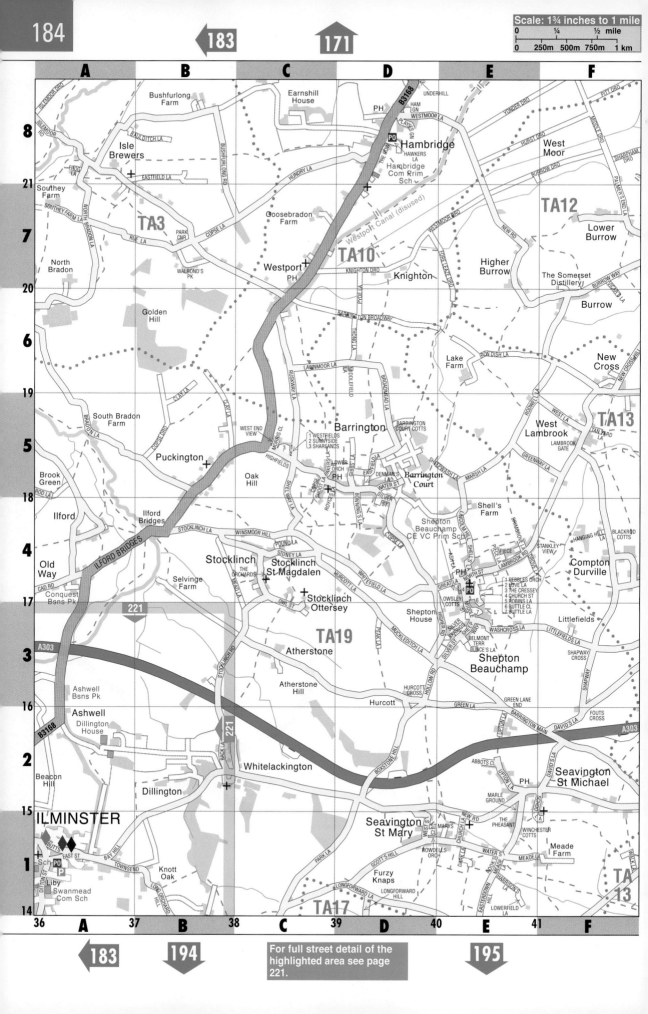

Scale: 1¾ inches to 1 mile

0   ¼   ½   mile
0 250m 500m 750m 1 km

A   B   C   D   E   F

8

21

7

6

19

5

18

4

17

3

16

2

15

1

14

Bushfurlong Farm

Earnshill House

UNDERHILL

HAM GN

WESTMOOR LA

PH

PO

Hambridge

HAWKERS LA

Hambridge Com Prim Sch

West Moor

HURST DRO

BURROW DRO

Isle Brewers

BAULDITCH LA

EASTFIELD LA

FROG LA

BUSHFURLONG RD

HUNDRY LA

YONDER DRO

PITT DRO

SHARPHAM DRO

MIDDLE DRO

PALMER'S END LA

Southey Farm

SOUTHEY FARM LA

NORTH BRADON LA

RUE LA

PARK CNR

COPSE LA

TA3

Goosebradon Farm

Westport Canal (disused)

WESTMOOR DRO

NEW RD

TA12

Lower Burrow

North Bradon

WALROND'S PK

Westport
PH

TA10

KNIGHTON DRO

Knighton

DOVE LANE DRO

Higher Burrow

The Somerset Distillery

BURROW WAY

TUCKER'S LA

Golden Hill

BARRINGTON BROADWAY

HONG LA

PYDE LA

Burrow

South Bradon Farm

BRADON LA

CLAY LA

FORD LA

LAWNMOOR LA

MIDDLEFIELD

BROADMEAD LA

Lake Farm

IRON DISH LA

RODWELL LA

WEST LA

New Cross

TAN YARD LA

TA13

Brook Green

ROD LA

COPSE DRO

WEST END VIEW

MORBIN LA

HIGHFIELDS

SHELL WAY LA

Barrington

1 WESTFIELDS
2 SUNNYSIDE
3 SHARLANDS

RUSKWAY LA

FIELD LA

BARRINGTON COURT COTTS

West Lambrook

GREENWAY LA

LAMBROOK GATE

Puckington

Oak Hill

Ilford

Ilford Bridges

STOCKLINCH LA

WINSMOOR HILL

Lower ORCH

COPSE LA

PH

PICOT LA

ROYCE'S LA

RES

DENMAN LA

WATER ST

SILVER ST

Barrington Court

SHEEPWASH LA

MARSH LA

Shell's Farm

Shepton Beauchamp CE VC Prim Sch

LINCOLN HILL

BRIMM HOLE LA

SHELL LA

STANKLEY VIEW

Hanging Hill

BLACKROD COTTS

Compton Durville

Old Way

CAD RD

Conquest Bsns Pk

ILFORD BRIDGES

Selvinge Farm

MEAD LA

THE ORCHARDS

Stocklinch

Stocklinch St Magdalen

POUND LA

STONEY LA

HURCOTT LA

WHITEFIELD LA

COPSE LA

PH

NORTH ST

WHITE LA

GREAT LA

1 REBBLES ORCH
2 LOVE LA
3 THE CRESSEY
4 CHURCH ST
5 ROBINS LA
6 BUTTLE CL
7 BUTTLE LA

PO

221

OWL ST

Stocklinch Ottersey

PEAR LA

MUCKLEDITCH LA

Shepton House

HIGHER RD

SILVER SPRINGS

OWSLEY COTTS

MIDDLE FIELD

Littlefields

A303

STOCKLINCH RD

TA19

Atherstone

Atherstone Hill

HOLLOW RD

Hurcott

HURCOTT CROSS

WASHCROSS LA

BELMONT TERR

BUNCE'S LA

Shepton Beauchamp

SHAPWAY CROSS

LITTLEFIELDS LA

Ashwell Bsns Pk

221

BACK LA

Whitelackington

BOXSTONE HILL

GREEN LA

GREEN LANE END

BARRINGTON MAIN

LIPTON LA

DAVID'S LA

FOUTS CROSS

A303

B3168

Ashwell

Dillington House

Beacon Hill

Dillington

ABBOTS CL

UPTON LA

PH

MARLE GROUND

Seavington St Michael

ILMINSTER

BUTTS

BAY HILL

TOWNSEND

Knott Oak

PARK LA

Seavington St Mary

WEST ST

ST MARYS CL

CHURCH ST

NEW RD

SCHOOL LA

SEAVINGTON

The Pheasant

Winchester Cotts

Meade Farm

Sch
PO

EAST ST

ROWDELLS ORCH

SCOTT'S HILL

WATER ST

DAPPS LA

MEADE LA

TA

DITTON ST

Liby

Swanmead Com Sch

LONG ORCHARD HILL

Furzy Knaps

LONGFORWARD LA

LONGFORWARD HILL

EASTERDOWN HILL

HARRISON'S LA

LOWERFIELD LA

WALLS LA

13

TA17

36   A   37   B   38   C   39   D   40   E   41   F

183

194

For full street detail of the highlighted area see page 221.

195

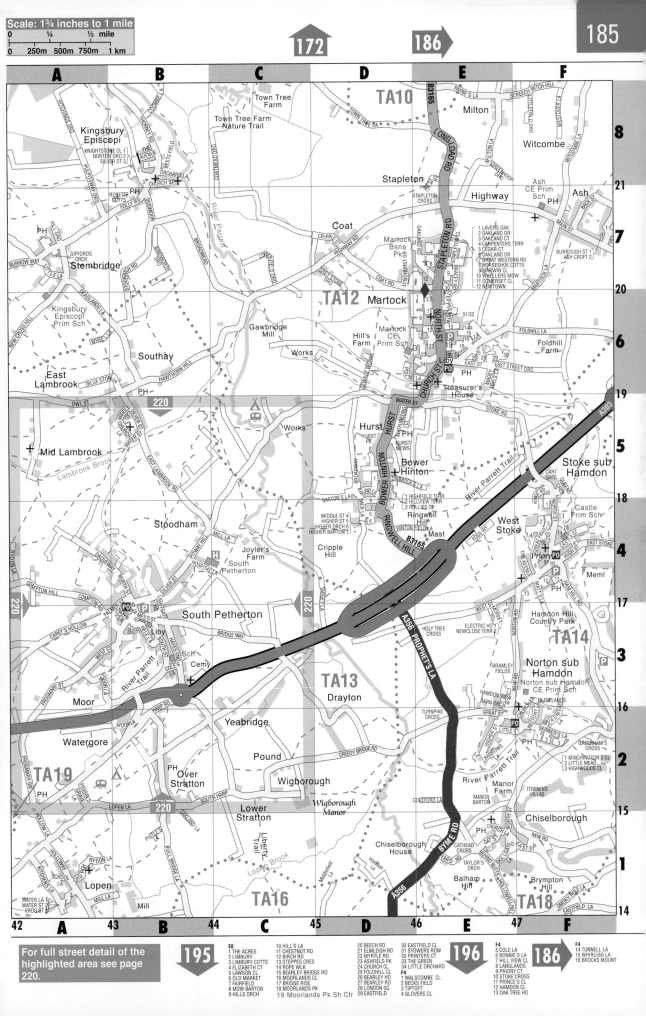

185 173

Scale: 1¾ inches to 1 mile
0   ¼   ½   mile
0   250m 500m 750m 1 km

A   B   C   D   E   F

8

21

Ash Dro
HARD LEAZE DRO
Bearley Brook
ILCHESTER MEAD DRO
A303
Burlingham's Farm
BURLINGHAM'S LA
Sock Dennis Farm
ELBOROUGH LA
Oakley Brook
Higher Oakley Farm
A37

7

Ash
BACK ST
LAVERS CT
MIDDLE LEAZE DRO
TA12
Durnfield
STONE LA
BEARLEY LA
SHERMOOR LA
Broadleaze Farm
Stonecroft Manor Farm
CHILTHORNE HILL
OAKLEY LA
Oakley Farms
Rushley Farm

20

QUEEN S LA
LITTLE TRUMPS
Tintinhull Garden
Tintinhull House
Shortland Farm
HALFWAY PH

6

FOLDHILL LA
A303
CHURCH ST
FARM ST
PH
St Margaret's Sch
SCHOOL CL
Sock Farm
KINGS HILL
ILCHESTER RD
A37
HALLETS ORCH
SOUTHCOMBE WAY 1
THE OLD GLOVE FACTORY 2
LEACHES CL 3
HEAD ST
HURLOCKS
Tintinhull
YEOVIL RD
CHILTHORNE LA
MAIN ST
FORTS ORCH
Chilthorne Domer CE Sch
Chilthorne Domer

19

P i
A3088
Halfway House Farm
PERRINS HILL RD
ST MARGARET'S RD
COLE CROSS
Monarch's Way
Leland Trail
SMEDMORE LA
Little Sammons
PH
BA21

5

A3088
Caravan Pk
Perren's Hill Farm
Wellham's Mill
MARSH LA
Axesclose Farm
Vagg
VAGG HILL
TINTINHULL RD
Vagg Farm
Vagg Pk

18

Wellhams Brook
218

4

East Stoke
MULBERRY LA
WINDSOR LA
STONEHILL LA
EAST STOKE
Sports Ctr
Stanchester Acad
LOWER HYDE RD
HYDE RD
MASON LA
INNER TOWN
Windmill Farm
WINDMILL LA
WINDMILL COTTS
BALL'S HILL
CARTGATE LINK RD
Gaundle Farm
BA22
Thorne Coffin
THORNE LA
COPSE RD
Prim Sch
WESSEX RD
ARKHILL RD

17

MONTACUTE RD
Hedgecock Hill
St Michael's Hill
ST MICHAEL'S VIEW
BISHOPSTON
P
Montacute House
SMITH'S ROW
TA15
TV, Radio & Toy Mus
Twr
PO
YEOVIL RD
Lufton Manor Coll
HIGSON CL
LUFTON LA
Boundary Way
Huish Park
P
MEMORIAL
ARTILLERY RD
Houndstone
Prim Sch
WHITE MEAD
ACER DR
SKOURTON WAY
MONKS DALE
Tithe Barn
Preston Sch

3

Ham Hill Ctry Pk
TOWNSEND
Montacute
HOLLOW LA
MIDDLE ST 1
THE BOROUGH 2
SOUTH ST 3
PARK LA
All Saints CE Prim Sch
Woodhouse Farm
NEW RD
Lufton
High Leaze Farm
BOUNDARY WAY
ROE AVE
Crem
PRESTON RD
BLUEBELL RD
LONG CL
PRESTON RD

16

TA14
Monarch's Way
Little Norton
Liberty Trail
Westbury Farm
FIVE ASHES
DRAY RD
BOUND WAY
HAM HILL RD
CHERRY LA
DONNE LA
LOWER ODCOMBE
Lower Odcombe PH
PERSON'S LA
BRYMPT LA
218
A3088
Alvington
ALVINGTON
BUNFORD LA
Preston Plucknett
Yeovil Airfield
BUNFORD LA
A3088

15

HOCKERS HILL
STREET LA
HOLLY TERR 1
ORCHARD CL 2
BROADWAY 3
CORYATE CL 4
CHURCH TERR 5
CHAPEL HILL
Higher Odcombe
LONG RD
REX RD
Odcombe
WESTBURY RD
Pye Corner Farm
Brympton House
Brympton D'Evercy
BA20
A3088
LYSANDER RD
WATERCOMBE LA
LABURNUM WAY
RUSSET WAY

1

Bagnell Farm
CHISELBOROUGH HILL LA
Chiselborough Hill
LANDSHIRE LA
EAST CHINNOCK HILL
GREEN LA
EAST CHINNOCK HILL
Cloverleaf Farm
DIBBLES LA
CAMP RD
Camp Hill
Feebarrow
GOOSEACRE LA
West Coker RD
A30
A3088
HELENA LA
NASH LA
218

14

TA18
EASTFIELD LA
Eastfield
BURYING HOLE LA

48   A   49   B   50   C   51   D   52   E   53   F

For full street detail of the highlighted area see page 218.

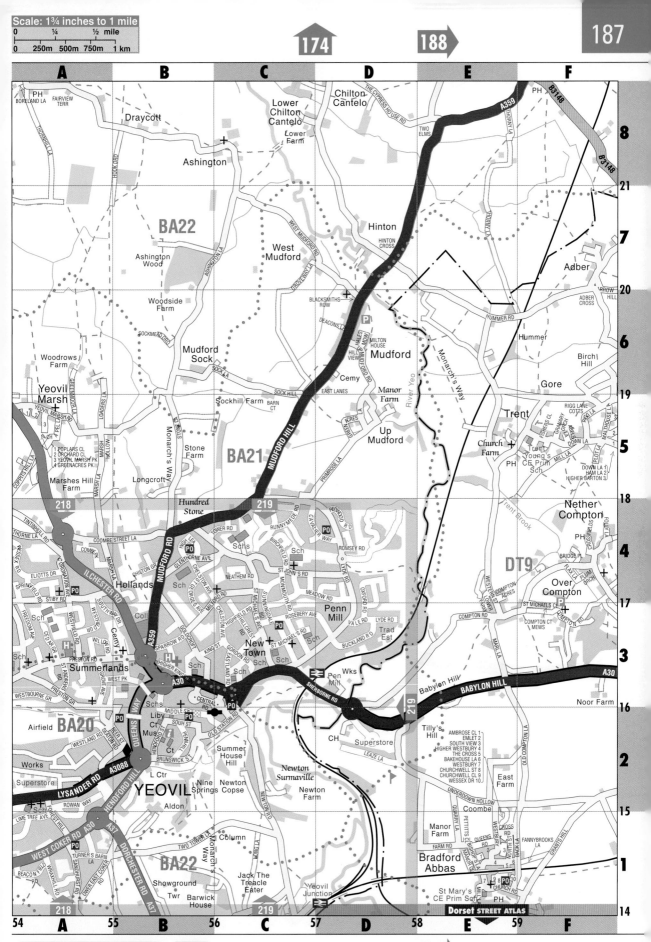

Scale: 1¾ inches to 1 mile

0   ¼   ½ mile
0   250m   500m   750m   1 km

174
188
187

A   B   C   D   E   F

PH
BORELAND LA
FAIRVIEW TERR

Draycott

Lower Chilton Cantelo
Lower Farm

Chilton Canfelo
THE CYPRESS HOUSE RD

A359
PH
B3148
B3148
THORN LA

8

Ashington

21

BA22

Ashington Wood

West Mudford

WEST MUDFORD RD
DROVEWAY LA

Hinton

Hinton Cross

Adber

7

Woodside Farm

HOOK RD

ASHINGTON LA

BLACKSMITHS ROW
DEACONS LO

HUMMER RD
THORN CL
ADBER CROSS
BARROW HILL

20

SOCKMEAD DRO

Mudford Sock

SOCK LA

HALES MDW
MILTON HOUSE

P
HILL VIEW
MANOR FARM RD

Mudford

Hummer

Birch Hill

Gore

6

Yeovil Marsh
YEOVIL MARSH RD

GREENWOOD LA
LOADERS LA

SOCK HILL

Sockhill Farm   BARN CT

East Lanes
Cemy

Manor Farm

River Yeo

Monarch's Way

Trent

RIGG LANE COTTS
FISHER CL
GRANARY BIRCH
ABELIA
ROSE LA
MALTHOUSE

19

1 POPLARS CL
2 ORCHARD CL
3 YEOVIL MARSH PK
4 GREENACRES PK

PELL CL
MARSH LA

Stone Farm

BA21

MUDFORD HILL

PRIMROSE LA
Up Mudford

REED CL
ACRES

Church Farm
PH
Trent Young's CE Prim Sch

DOWN LA
DOWN LA 1
HAM LA 2
HIGHER BARTON 3

5

COPPTS HILL
CORONATION RD

Marshes Hill Farm

Monarch's Way

Longcroft

Hundred Stone

218

Hundred Stone

219

MUDFORD RD

TONER RD
HAY LEA
GLENTHORNE AVE

RUNNYMEDE RD

REDWOOD RD
CAVALIER WAY

ROMSEY RD

PO

Trent Brook

Nether Compton

PH

18

TINTINHULL RD
THORNE LA

WESSEX RD
ELIOTTS DR

COOMBE STREET LA

COMBE

Hollands
COLL

CHILTON GR

Schs
BIRCHFIELD RD
ST JOHN S RD
Sch

LYDE RD

DT9

CROSS FIELDS
FOLLY LA
BRIDGE PL
FLAX LA
FLAM ORCH

4

SPRINGFIELD RD
STIBY RD

A359

CHELSTON AVE
ST GEORGE'S AVE
NEATHAM RD

MONMOUTH RD

MEADOW RD

OXFORD RD

Penn Mill

Over Compton
P

17

FREEDOM AVE
CEDAR GR
WILLOW RD

Sch

MILFORD RD

MILL FIELD CREST
ST MICHAEL'S AVE
ROSEBERY AVE

BUCKLAND RD

VALE RD

Trad Est
LYDE RD

COMPTON RD

St Michaels Cl
COMPTON CT MEWS

3

Sch
PRESTON RD
ST ANDREWS RD
GROVE AVE

Summerlands
WEST PK

HIGHER KING ST
A30

KING ST
GORDON RD
EASTLAND RD

NEW TOWN
ST MICHAEL'S RD

Sch

Wks
Pen Mill

Babylon Hill   BABYLON HILL
A30

Noor Farm

16

WESTBOURNE GR
PRESTON GR

SPARROW RD
OLD FORD RD

Sch

SHERBORNE RD

219
MARL LA
OLD COMPTON LA

Airfield
BA20

PO

QUEENS WAY

Liby
Ct
Mus
MIDDLE ST
SOUTH ST
CENTRAL RD
P
PO

CH
Superstore

LEAZE LA

Tilly's Hill

AMBROSE CL 1
EMLET 2
SOUTH VIEW 3
HIGHER WESTBURY 4
THE CROSS 5
BAKEHOUSE LA 6
WESTBURY 7
CHURCHWELL ST 8
CHURCHWELL CL 9
WESSEX DR 10

East Farm

2

Works
Superstore

LYSANDER RD
A3088

HENDFORD HILL

YEOVIL
Aldon

L Ctr

Nine Springs
Newton Copse

Summer House Hill

Newton Surmaville
Newton Farm

UNDERDOWN HOLLOW
Coombe

15

BEACON FIELD RD
WRAXHILL RD

WEST COKER RD
A30

SANDHURST RD
LOWER EAST COKER RD
DORCHESTER RD
A37

BA22

Showground

TWO TOWER LA
Column
Monarch's Way

Jack The Treacle Eater

Yeovil Junction

Manor Farm

QUARRY LA
PETTITTS CL
QUEENS RD
BISHOPS RD
FARM RD
WESTBURY
CROSS

Bradford Abbas

FANNYBROOKS LA
GRANTS HILL

1

218

Twr
Barwick House

219

St Mary's CE Prim Sch
PH
PO
CHURCH RD

Dorset STREET ATLAS

14

54   A   55   B   56   C   57   D   58   E   59   F

197

For full street detail of the highlighted area see pages 218 and 219.

188

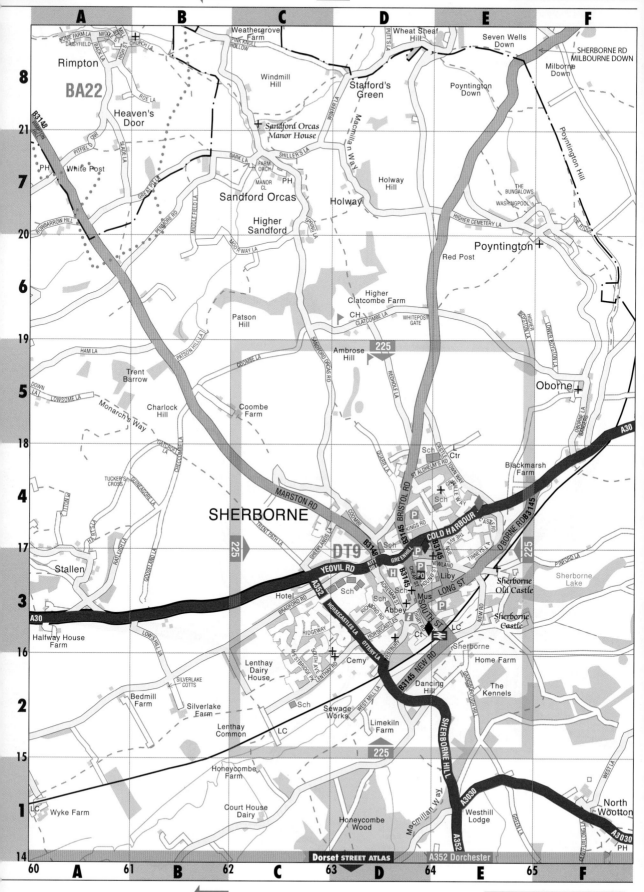

Scale: 1¾ inches to 1 mile
0   ¼   ½   mile
0   250m 500m 750m 1 km

Rimpton

BA22

Heaven's Door

White Post

PH

Weathergrove Farm

Wheat Sheaf Hill

Seven Wells Down

SHERBORNE RD
MILBOURNE DOWN

Milborne Down

Windmill Hill

Stafford's Green

Poyntington Down

Sandford Orcas Manor House

Holway Hill

Holway

Poyntington Hill

Sandford Orcas

Higher Sandford

Red Post

Poyntington

THE BUNGALOWS

WASHINGPOOL

Oborne

Patson Hill

Higher Clatcombe Farm

WHITEPOST GATE

Ambrose Hill

225

Trent Barrow

Charlock Hill

Coombe Farm

Monarch's Way

SHERBORNE

DT9

Marston Rd

YEOVIL RD

COLD HARBOUR

Blackmarsh Farm

A30

Oborne Rd B3145

Stallen

Hotel

Sherborne Old Castle

Sherborne Lake

Sherborne Castle

Halfway House Farm

Lenthay Dairy House

Abbey

Sherborne

Home Farm

Bedmill Farm

Silverlake Farm

Sewage Works

B3145 NEW RD

Dancing Hill

The Kennels

Lenthay Common

Limekiln Farm

225

SHERBORNE HILL

Honeycombe Farm

Court House Dairy

Honeycombe Wood

Macmillan Way

A3030

Westhill Lodge

North Wootton

Wyke Farm

Dorset STREET ATLAS

A352 Dorchester

A3030

For full street detail of the highlighted area see page 225.

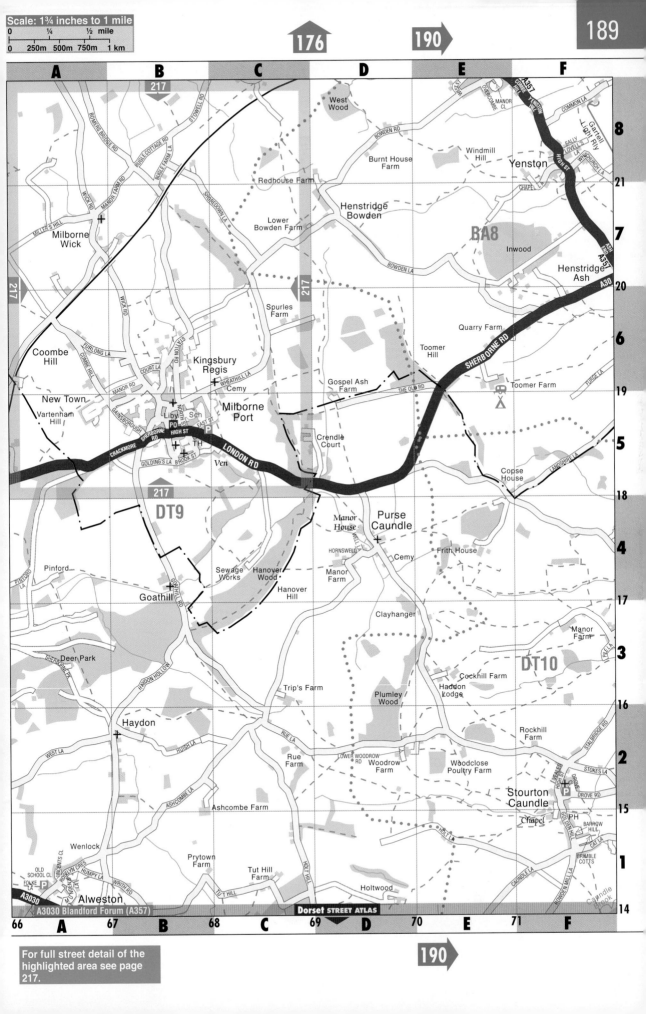

A6
1 VIRGINIA CL
2 PLAYFIELD CL
3 BROOKLAND WAY
4 ST NICHOLAS CL
5 POND CL
6 BLACKMOOR LA

7 BROOK LA
8 CHURCH ST
9 THE CROSS
10 TOWNSEND GN
11 BUGLE CT
12 WOODHAYES HO
13 COTTON CNR

14 VICTORIA TERR
15 VICTORIA GDNS
16 ELIZABETH GDNS
17 WINDSOR TERR
18 CHURCH FARM PL
19 WOODHAYES CT

189

177

Scale: 1¾ inches to 1 mile

0   ¼   ½ mile

0   250m 500m 750m 1 km

A   B   C   D   E   F

Fifehead Magdalen

Mohuns Park

Lower Nyland

NYLAND LA

Bow Brook

SHAFTESBURY RD

Coking Farm

Five Bridges

SP8

Fifehead Bsns Ctr (Manor Farm Trad Est)

Manor Farm

FIFEHEAD HILL

1 SUMMERFIELDS
2 VALE VIEW

Whitchurch

BELLMAN'S CROSS

BAZELAND'S HILL

BA8

Hackthorne Farm

Lower Marsh

Factory Farm

Strangways Farm

Hains

Henstridge Ash

Henstridge Marsh

Syles Farm

Airfield

A30

OLD STATION GDNS
MEADOW CL
STATION RD
BLACKMOOR LA

Higher Marsh

MARSH LA

PLOTT LA

VALE VALE LA
WELL LA
SOUTH
MEAD LA

Henstridge

HIGH ST STALBRIDGE RD

Towns End

Henstridge Trad Est

Gibbs Marsh Trad Est

HAM LA
MUSBURY LA
MILL LA

WOODLANDS MEAD

BURGES CE
PH
LOVELL MEAD
THE PHARMACY FLATS

BURTON ST
BURTON PH
SACKMORE

Landshire Bridge

LANDSHIRE LA

Landshire Bridge

Gibbs Marsh Farm

Marnhull Ham

West Mill

WEST MILL LA

River Stour

SACKMORE GN

Marnhull

St Gregory's CE Prim Sch

Prior's Down

Triangle Farm

Hamwood Farm

Mounters

KENTISWORTH RD
HILSEY'S
NEW LA
CHIPPEL LA
BUTTS
FINGER CNR

SILK HOUSE BARTON 1
KNIGHTSTONE CT 2
OLD MARKET MEWS 3
GROVE LANE CL 4
BARROW LEA 5
STALBRIDGE CL 6
HARDY CRES 7
BOYLE CL 8
ROBINSON HTS 9
MEADOW CL 10
SUNCLIFFE CL 11
RALEIGH RD 12
ANGLESEY COTTS 13
COPPERN WAY 14
JARVIS CL 15
WESTMINSTER COTTS 16
WESTMINSTER BLDGS 17

CHURCH HILL
DREW'S LA

Prim Sch

Station Road Bsns Pk

Gray's Farm

SHIPNEY LA

WOOD LA

Crib House Farm

Mounters CL

Works

Pleck

STALBRIDGE PK

PARK RD
POND LA
PARK
BARROW HILL

GOLD'S
HILL ST
G GROVE
PO
STATION RD
NEW RD
JOHN RD

The Sidings

Stalbridge

1 LARKS MDW
2 SPRINGFIELDS
3 THRIFT CL
4 BAGBER RD

Gomershay Farm

MILL CL
MOOR

BAT ALLEY

Yardgrove Farm

Stour Valley Way

ACKERMAN RD
VALE RD
WESSEX RD
GLOVERS RD

Hewletts Farm

King's Mill Bridge

COX HILL

MOWES LA

RING ST
THORNHILL RD
WATERLOAD LA
WOOD LA
POUND CL
GROSVENOR RD

Bibberne Farm

LOWER RD

Bungays Farm

KING'S MILL RD

MARRIAGE LA

CUTT MILL LA

Sturt Farm

CAUNDLE LA

Stalbridge Weston

Poolestown

DEACONS MILL LA

Stalbridge Common

BAGBER CROSS RDS

Marsh Farm

CARPAWAY LA

Coek's Farm

EASTOP LA

STALBRIDGE RD

HARGROVE LA

Ryalls Farm

Rushay Farm

Manor Farm

PENTRIDGE LA

STALBRIDGE LA

WOOL LA

DT10

Holtham Plantation

Obelisk

COOK'S LA

Hargrove Farm

River Lydden

Bagber Bridge

Bagber Common

Pleak House Farm

STALBRIDGE LA

WATERLOO LA
CAT LA
BRUNSELL'S KNAP
WATERLOO LA

Brunsell Knap Farm

Thornhill House

Mullins Farm

Higher Farm

Oaklea Farm

Medieval Village of Colber (site of)

Waterloo Farm

Caundle Brook

Warr Bridge

A357

Dorset STREET ATLAS

72   A   73   B   74   C   75   D   76   E   77   F

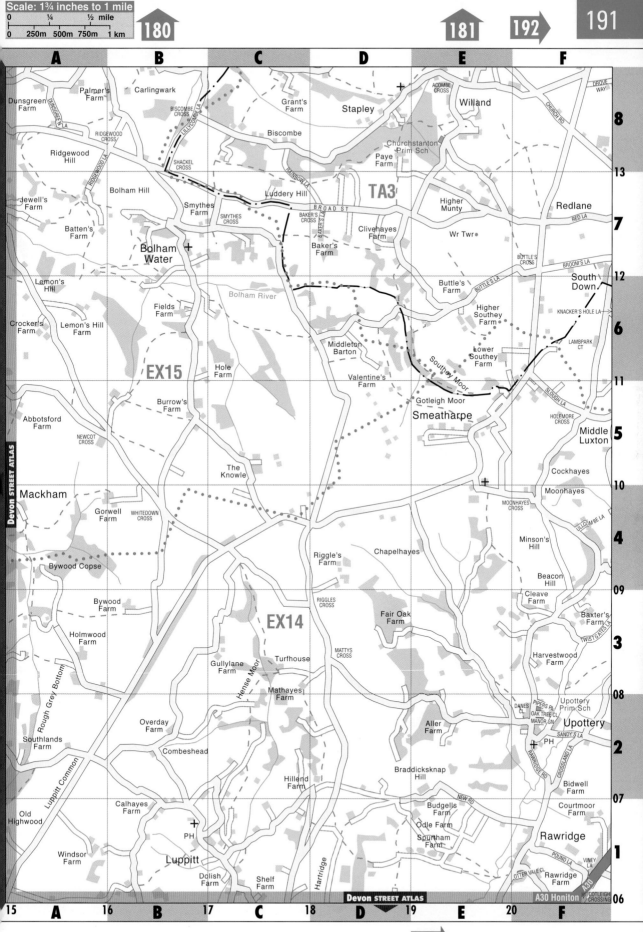

A   B   C   D   E   F

Dunsgreen Farm
Palmer's Farm
Carlingwark
Biscombe Cross
Grant's Farm
Stapley
Acombe Cross
Willand
Drove Way

Ridgewood Cross
Ridgewood Hill
Biscombe
Churchstanton Prim Sch
Church Rd

Jewell's Farm
Bolham Hill
Shackel Cross
Paye Farm
Rainbow La
TA3
Higher Munty
Redlane
Red La

Batten's Farm
Smythes Farm
Luddery Hill
Broad St
Baker's Cross
Clivehayes Farm
Wr Twr
Buttle's Cross
Broom's La

Bolham Water
Smythes Cross
Baker's La
Baker's Farm
Buttle's Farm
Buttle's La
South Down

Lemon's Hill
Fields Farm
Bolham River
Higher Southey Farm
Knacker's Hole La
Lambpark Ct

Crocker's Farm
Lemon's Hill Farm
Hole Farm
Middleton Barton
Southey Moor
Lower Southey Farm
Holemore Cross

EX15
Burrow's Farm
Valentine's Farm
Gotleigh Moor
Slough La
Middle Luxton

Abbotsford Farm
Newcot Cross
Smeatharpe
Cockhayes
Moonhayes

Mackham
Gorwell Farm
Whitedown Cross
The Knowle
Moonhayes Cross
Ullcombe La

Bywood Copse
Riggle's Farm
Chapelhayes
Minson's Hill
Beacon Hill

Bywood Farm
Riggles Cross
Fair Oak Farm
Cleave Farm
Baxter's Farm
Twist Gate La

Holmwood Farm
EX14
Turfhouse
Mattys Cross
Harvestwood Farm

Gullylane Farm
Hense Moor
Mathayes Farm
Danes Cl
Pipers Pl
Upottery Prim Sch
Oak Tree Cl
Manor Gn
Upottery

Southlands Farm
Rough Grey Bottom
Overday Farm
Aller Farm
Sandy's La
PH
Rawridge Rd
Crossland La

Combeshead
Braddicksknap Hill
Bidwell Farm

Old Highwood
Luppitt Common
Calhayes Farm
Hillend Farm
New Rd
Budgells Farm
Courtmoor Farm

Windsor Farm
PH
Odle Farm
Spurtham Farm
Rawridge

Luppitt
Dolish Farm
Shelf Farm
Hartridge
Pound La
Viney La
Otter Vale Cl
Rawridge Farm
A30

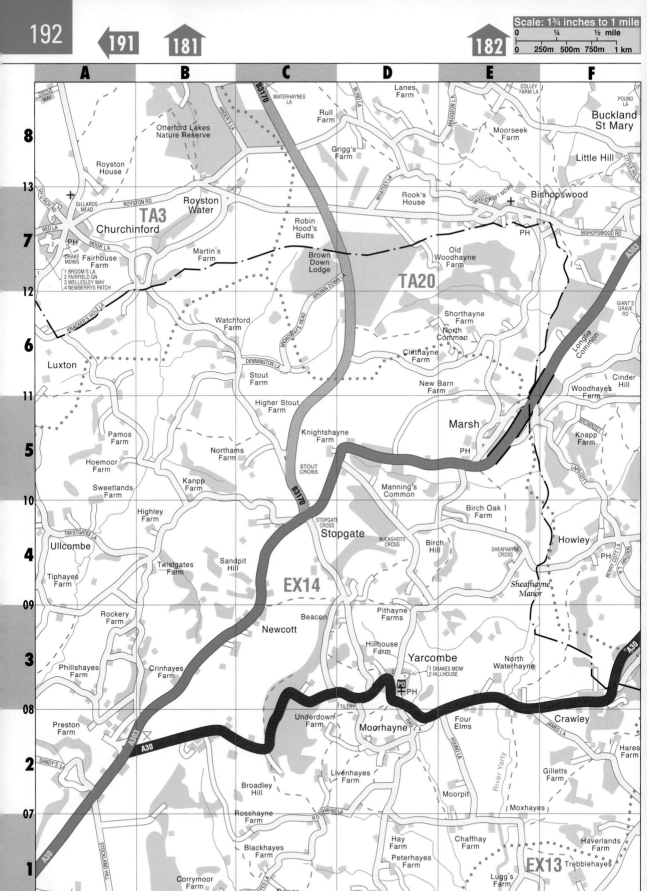

Scale: 1¾ inches to 1 mile

0   ¼   ½ mile
0   250m   500m   750m   1 km

DROVE WAY

Royston House

Otterford Lakes Nature Reserve

Buckland St Mary

COLLEY FARM LA

POUND LA

LITTLE HILL

Little Hill

GILLARDS MEAD

Royston Water

TA3

CHURCHFORD RD

Churchinford

Royston Rd

Moorseek Farm

MADGEON LA

WOODC ROFT MDWS

Bishopswood

BISHOPSWOOD RD

RED LA

PH

MOOR LA

DRAKE MDWS

Fairhouse Farm

1 BROOM'S LA
2 FAIRFIELD GN
3 WELLESLEY WAY
4 NEWBERRYS PATCH

Martin's Farm

Robin Hood's Butts

Brown Down Lodge

WATERHAYNES LA

B3170

Rull Farm

BUNDLA

Lanes Farm

WHATLEY LA

Rook's House

Old Woodhayne Farm

PH

TA20

Grigg's Farm

KNACKER'S HOLE LA

Luxton

Watchford Farm

BROADWAY'S HEAD

BROWN DOWN LA

DENNINGTON LA

Stout Farm

Higher Stout Farm

Shorthayne Farm

North Common

Cliffhayne Farm

New Barn Farm

GIANT'S GRAVE RD

Longlie Common

A303

Cinder Hill

Woodhayes Farm

BROWNSEY LA

Knapp Farm

Pamos Farm

Hoemoor Farm

Sweetlands Farm

Northams Farm

Kanpp Farm

Knightshayne Farm

STOUT CROSS

Marsh

PH

LAPSCOTT

Highley Farm

B3170

Manning's Common

STOPGATE CROSS

Stopgate

BUCKSHOTS CROSS

Birch Oak Farm

Birch Hill

SHEAFHAYNE CROSS

Howley

PH

BERRY COTT LA

JAMES LA

TWISTGATES LA

Ullcombe

Twistgates Farm

Sandpit Hill

EX14

Beacon

Pithayne Farms

Sheafhayne Manor

Tiphayes Farm

Rockery Farm

Newcott

Hillhouse Farm

Yarcombe

1 DRAKES MDW
2 HILLHOUSE

North Waterhayne

Crawley

Phillshayes Farm

Crinhayes Farm

PO

PH

Hares Farm

Preston Farm

A303

A30

Underdown Farm

TILERY

Moorhayne

RAG LA

Four Elms

JAMES LA

SANDY'S LA

Broadley Hill

Livenhayes Farm

Moorpit

POUND LA

River Yarty

Gilletts Farm

Rosshayne Farm

ROSHAYNE LA

Hay Farm

Chaffhay Farm

Moxhayes

Haverlands Farm

A30

STOCKLAND HILL

Blackhayes Farm

Peterhayes Farm

Lugg's Farm

EX13

Trebblehayes

Corrymoor Farm

BLACK HAYES LA

Rower Hill

Ley Farm

Grays Farm

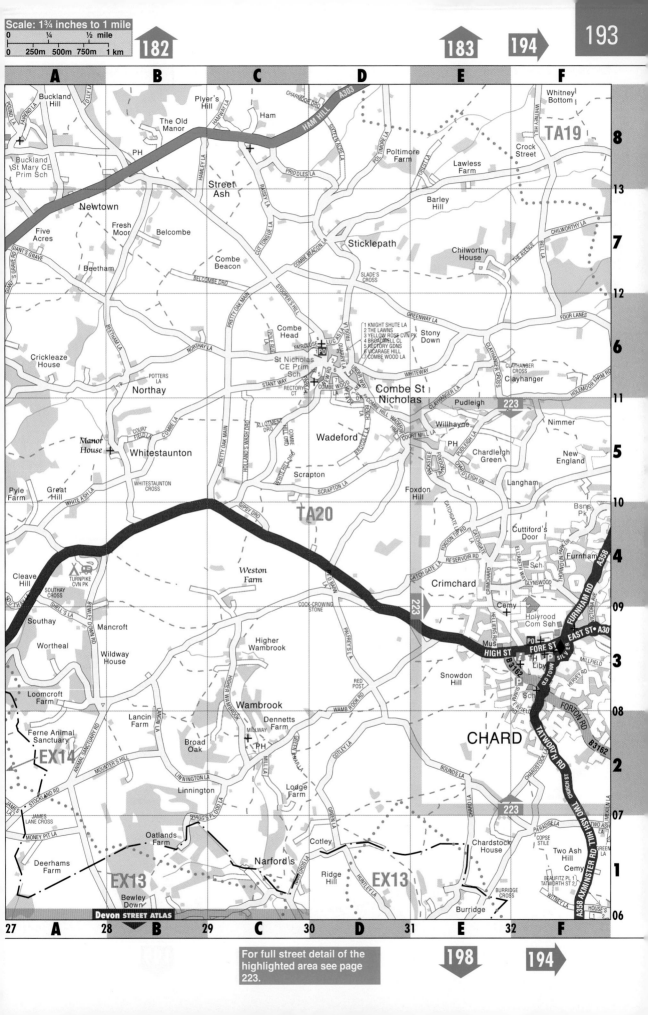

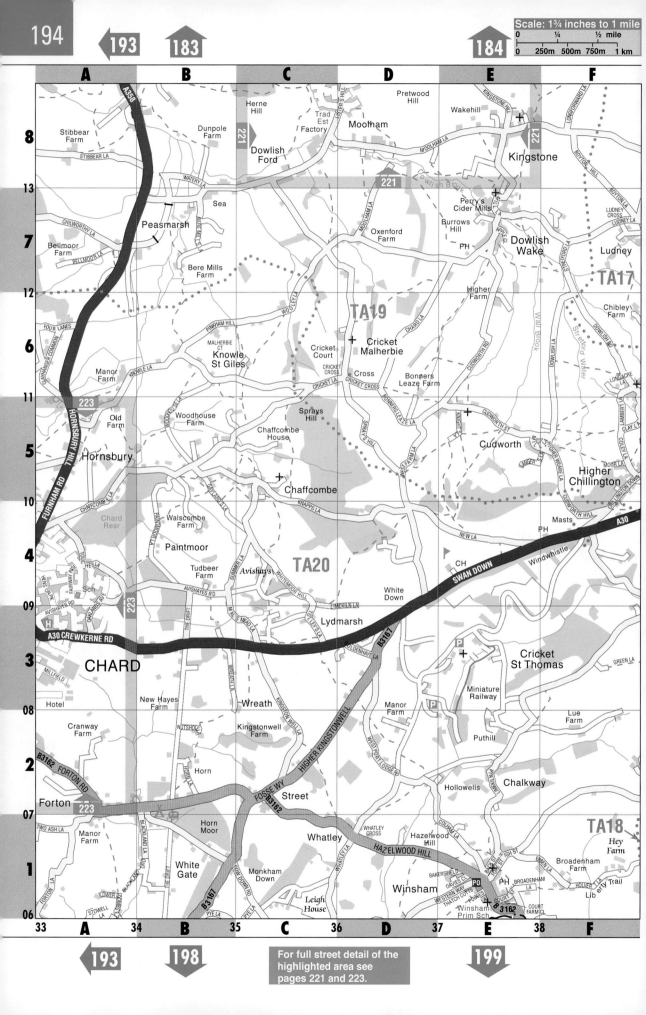

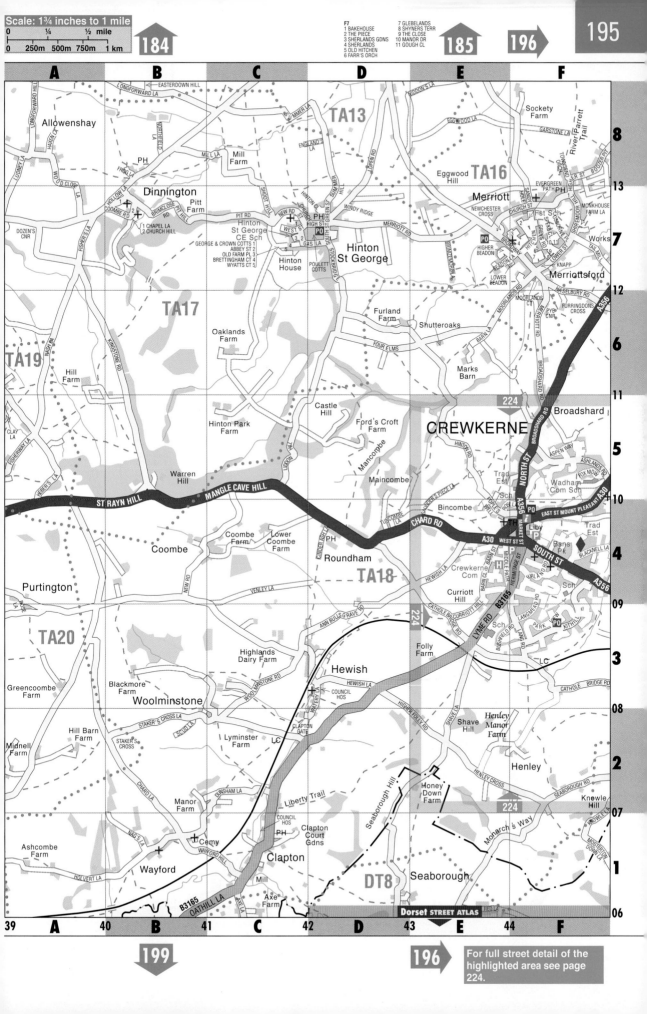

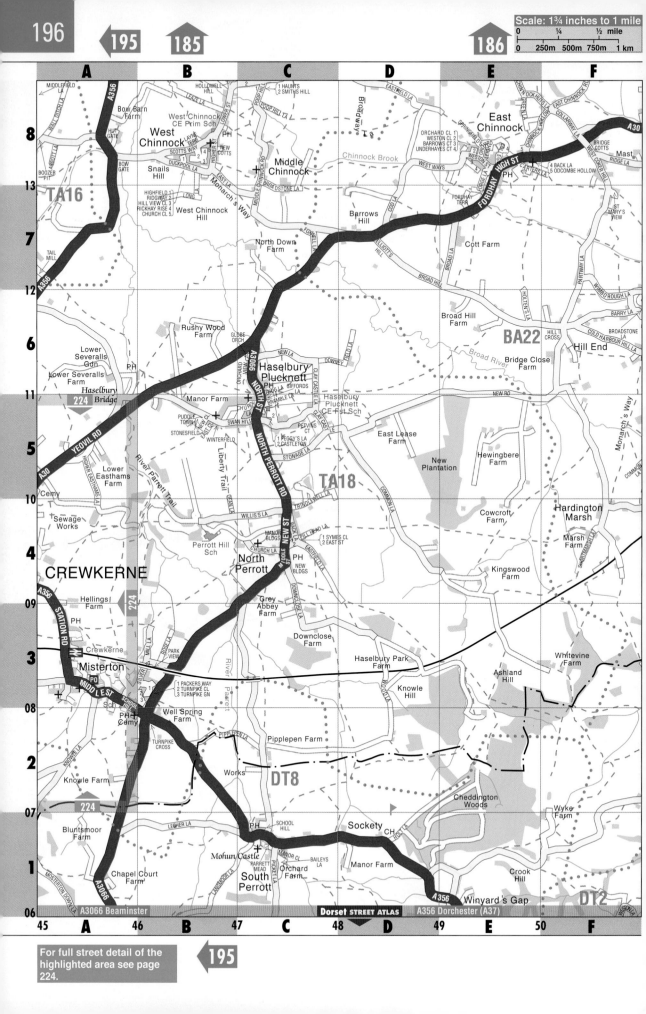

A   B   C   D   E   F

8

MIDDLEFIELD LA
A356
Bow Barn Farm
HOLLOWELL HILL
1 HAUNTS
2 SMITHS HILL
POOP HILL LA
EASTFIELD LA
Broadway
ORCHARD CL 2
WESTON CL 2
BARROWS CT 3
UNDERHAYES CT 4
SPRINGFIELD
CHINNOCK HOLLOW
COLLARWAY LA
EAST CHINNOCK HILL
A30
West Chinnock CE Prim Sch
PH
West Chinnock
LEAZE LA
SCOTTS WAY
LAYNE TERR
HIGHER
NEW COTTS
DUCKPOOL LA
EAST LA
Middle Chinnock
CHINNOCK RD
BROADSTONE LA
Chinnock Brook
WEST WAYS
WESTON ST
FORGE LA
East Chinnock
HIGH ST
FORDHAY
CARTER'S LA
4 BACK LA
5 ODCOMBE HOLLOW
West COKER HILL
BRIDGE COTTS
Mast
RIDGE LA

13

TA16

Snails Hill
Monarch's Way
HIGHFIELD 1
RIDGWAY 2
HILL VIEW CL 3
RICKHAY RISE 4
CHURCH CL 5
LONG
West Chinnock Hill
Barrows Hill
FOWELL LA
ELLIOTT'S HILL
ODD LA
FORDHAY TERR
Cott Farm
BROAD LA
PARTWAY LA
ST MARY'S VIEW

7

North Down Farm
BROAD HILL
HOLTEN'S LA
Broad Hill Farm
HILL CROSS
COLD HARBOUR HILL LA
BROADSTONE
BARRY LA
WIMBO ROUGH LA

12

A356

Rushy Wood Farm
GLOBE ORCH
A3066
NEW LA
ORCHARD
DOWNEY
BA22
Hill End
Broad River
Bridge Close Farm

6

Lower Severalls Gdn
Lower Severalls Farm
PH
Haselbury Bridge
224
Manor Farm
NORTH ST
Haselbury Plucknett
PH
ORCHARD VIEW
DRAG LA
GIFFORDS LA
BRAMBLE LA
CLAY CASTLE LA
Haselbury Plucknett CE Fst Sch
NEW RD
Hewingbere Farm
Monarch's Way
COMMON LA

11

Haselbury
PUDDLE TOWN
CHURCH CL
NORTH PERROTT RD
SWAN HILL
STONESFIELD
WINTERFIELD
PETVINS CT
1 PEGGY'S LA
2 CASTLETON
STONAGE LA
CLAY CAST
East Lease Farm
New Plantation

5

YEOVIL RD
A30
HIGHER EASTHAMS LA
Lower Easthams Farm
River Parrett Trail
Liberty Trail
TA18
Cowcroft Farm
Hardington Marsh

10

Cemy
Sewage Works
GERALD
WILLIS'S LA
NEW ST
TRINDLEWELL LA
PILL HEAD LA
1 SYMES CL
2 EAST ST
EASTFIELD A
COMMON LA
Marsh Farm

4

CREWKERNE
A3066
Perrott Hill Sch
MIDDLE LA
CHURCH LA
North Perrott
MANOR BLDGS
PH
NEW BLDGS
BUCKY LA
DOWNCLOSE LA
Kingswood Farm
SHORTMARSH LA

09

STATION RD
224
Hellings Farm
PH
ROSE LA
PARK VIEW
Grey Abbey Farm
Downclose Farm
WOOL LA
Haselbury Park Farm
Ashland Hill
Whitevine Farm

3

Crewkerne
Misterton
River Parrett
SILVER LA
MILL LA
Knowle Hill

08

PO
MIDDLE ST
SCHOOL LA
Sch
1 PACKERS WAY
2 TURNPIKE CL
3 TURNPIKE GN
PH
Cemy
Well Spring Farm
KNOWLE LA
PIPPLEPEN LA
Pipplepen Farm
Cheddington Woods
Wyke Farm

2

Knowle Farm
Turnpike Cross
Works
DT8

07

224
LEIGHER LA
Bluntsmoor Farm
SCHOOL HILL
PH
Sockety
CH
HOLT LA

1

MOSTERTON DOWN LA
A3066
Chapel Court Farm
LANGMOOR LA
Mohun Castle
PARRETT MEAD
PICKLE LA
South Perrott
MANOR CL
BAILEYS LA
Orchard Farm
Manor Farm
A356
Winyard's Gap
Crook Hill
DT12

06

45   A   46   B   47   C   48   D   49   E   50   F

For full street detail of the highlighted area see page 224.

195

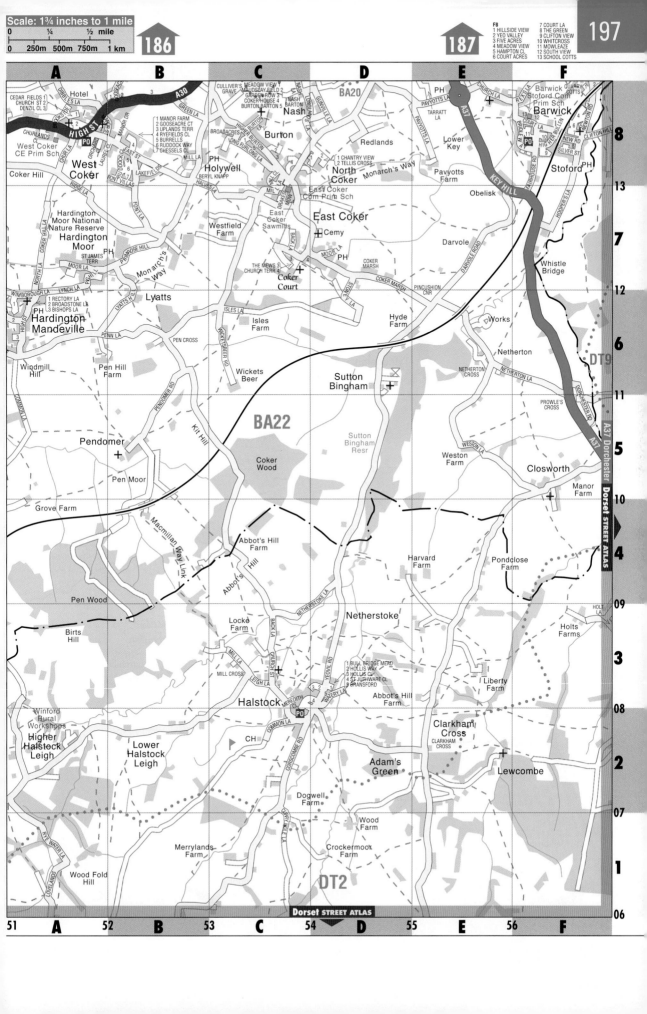

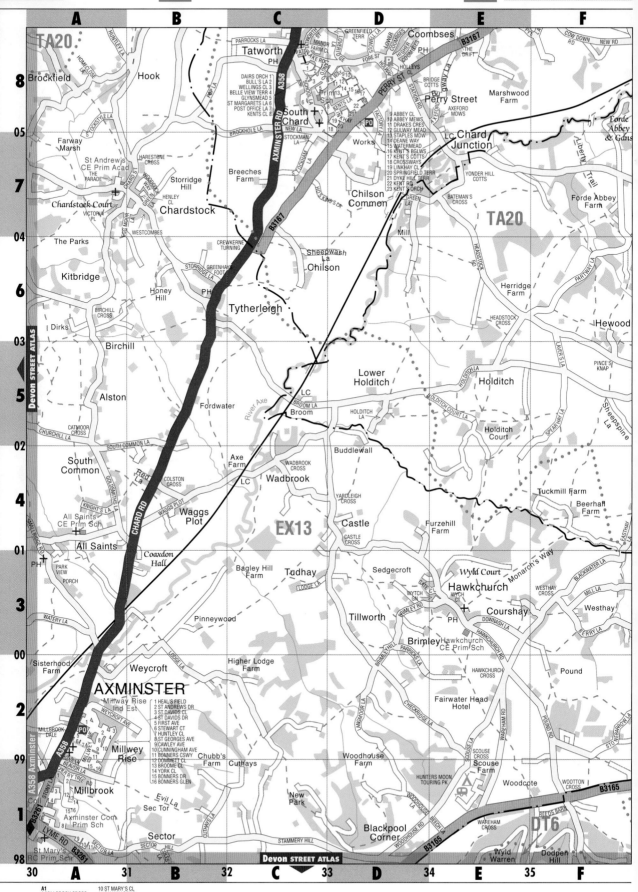

198

193

194

Scale: 1¾ inches to 1 mile
0   ¼   ½ mile
0   250m 500m 750m 1 km

TA20

Brockfield

Hook

Farway Marsh

St Andrew's CE Prim Acad
THE PARADE

Harestone Cross

Storridge Hill

Breeches Farm

Chardstock Court

Chardstock

The Parks

Westcombes

Kitbridge

Honey Hill

Dirks

Birchill Cross

Birchill

Alston

Catmoor Cross

Churchill La

South Common La

South Common

Fordwater

River Axe

Red La

Colston Cross

Waggs Plot

All Saints CE Prim Sch

All Saints

PH

Park View Porch

Coaxdon Hall

Pinneywood

Sisterhood Farm

Weycroft

Higher Lodge Farm

AXMINSTER
Millway Rise Ind Est

1 HEAL'S FIELD
2 ST ANDREWS DR
3 ST DAVIDS CL
4 ST DAVIDS DR
5 FIRST AVE
6 STEWART CT
7 HUNTLEY CL
8 ST GEORGES AVE
9 CAWLEY AVE
10 CUNNINGHAM AVE
11 BONNERS CSWY
12 DOMMETT CL
13 BROOME CL
14 YORK CL
15 BONNERS DR
16 BONNERS GLEN

Millbrook Dale

Millwey Rise

Chubb's Farm

Cuthays

Millbrook

Evil La

Sec Tor

New Park

Axminster Com Prim Sch

Sector

St Mary's RC Prim Sch

Lyme Rd

Stammery Hill

Parrocks La

Tatworth
PH

DAIRS ORCH 1
BULL'S LA 2
WELLINGS CL 3
BELLE VIEW TERR 4
GLYNSMEAD 5
ST MARGARETS LA 6
POST OFFICE LA 7
KENTS CL 8

South Chard

New La

Stockman La

Brockhole La

Crewkerne Turning

Storridge La

Greenhays Footpath

PH

Tytherleigh

Sheepwash La

Chilson

LC

Broom La

Broom

LC

Axe Farm

Wadbrook Cross

Wadbrook

Waggs Plot

Bagley Hill Farm

Lodge La

Tudhay

Higher Lodge Farm

Lodge La

Coombses
PH

B3167

Greenfield Terr

Manor Farm La

Fore St

Perry St

Station Rd

Perry Street
PH

Axeford Mdws

9 ABBEY CL
10 ABBEY MEWS
11 DRAKES CRES
12 GULWAY MEAD
13 STAPLES MDW
14 DEANE WAY
15 WATERMEAD
16 KENT'S BGLWS
17 KENT'S CDTTS
18 CROSSWAYS
19 LINKHAY CL
20 SPRINGFIELD TERR
21 DYKE HILL TERR
22 KENT RD
23 KENT'S ORCH

Chard Junction

Yonder Hill Cotts

Bateman's Cross

Green La

Mill

Chilson Common

Lower Holditch

Holditch La

Holditch Court La

Holditch

Holditch Court

Buddlewall

Yardleigh Cross

Castle

Castle Cross

Furzehill Farm

Sedgecroft

Wych Gn

Brimley Rd

Hawkchurch

Brimley

Hawkchurch CE Prim Sch

Tillworth

Woodhouse Farm

Blackpool Corner

Hunters Moon Touring Pk

Scouse Cross

Scouse Farm

Fairwater Head Hotel

Hawkchurch Cross

Pound

Wyld Court

Monarch's Way

Westhay Cross

Courshay

Westhay

Berry La

Mill La

Blackwater La

Wareham Rd

Round Rd

Woodcote

Wootton Cross

Wareham Cross

Wyld Warren

Dopden Hill

Marshwood Farm

Forde Abbey & Gdns

Liberty Trail

Forde Abbey Farm

TA20

Herridge Farm

Headstock Cross

Hewood

Pince's Knap

Sheepspine La

Tuckmill Farm

Beerhall Farm

Easthay

EX13

DT6

B3165

B3167

A358

B3167

Chard Rd

Axminster Rd

EX13

A1
1 MILLBROOK CROSS
2 CATNIP CL
3 JEFFS WAY
4 NEWBERY CL
5 LORETTO GDNS
6 MONKSTONE GDNS
7 CRIDLAKE
8 TIGERS WY
9 PRESTOR

10 ST MARY'S CL
11 SALWAY GDNS
12 FLAX MEADOW LA
13 BLEACHFIELD RI
14 LOWER MEAD
15 LINSEED DR
16 UPPER MEAD

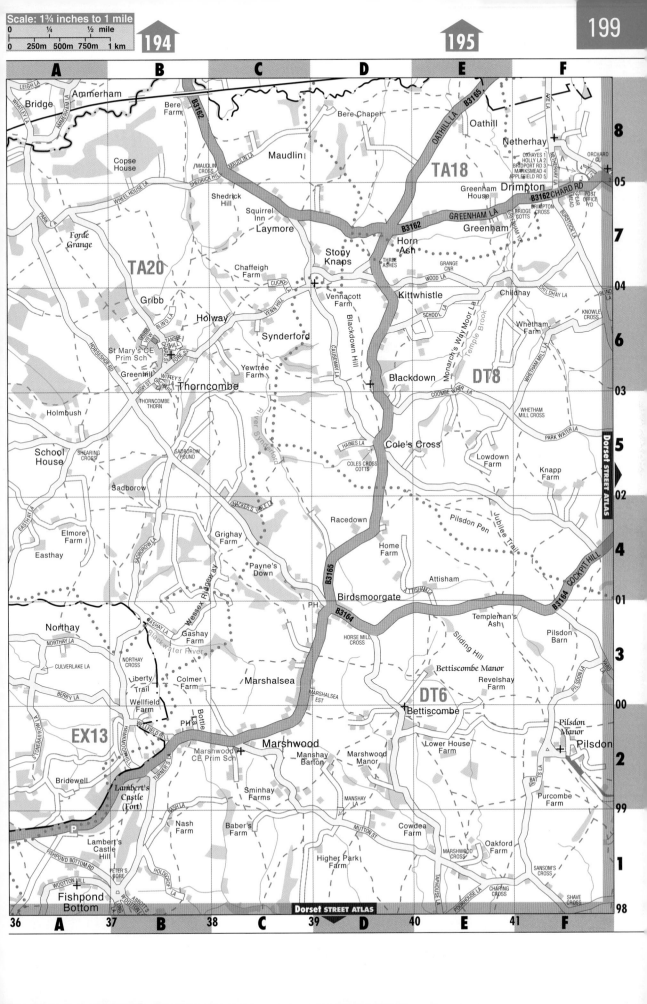

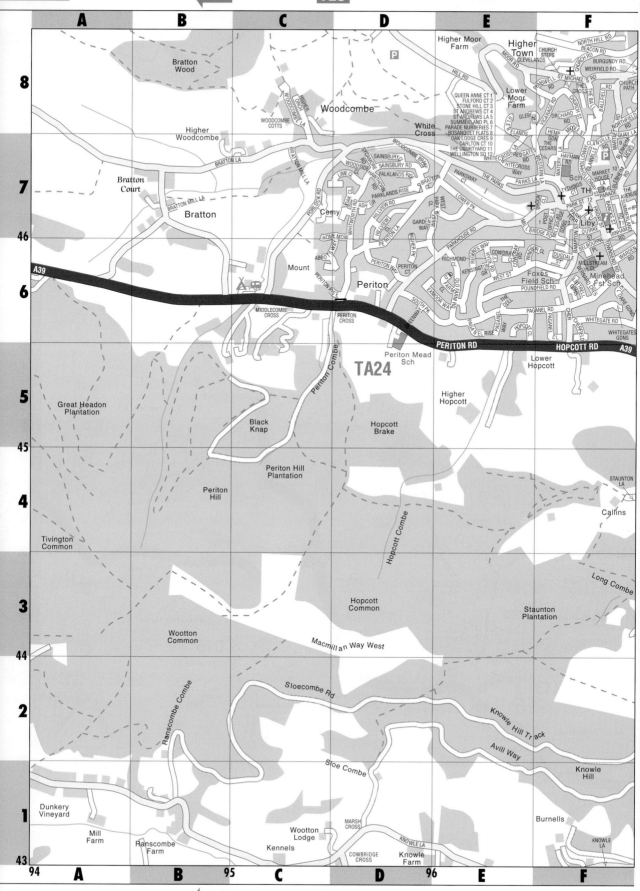

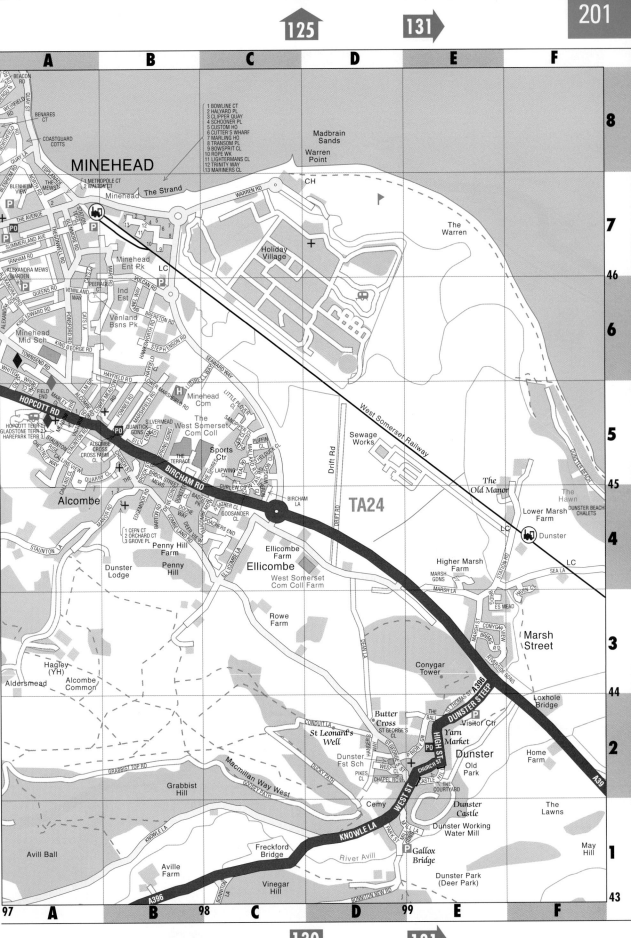

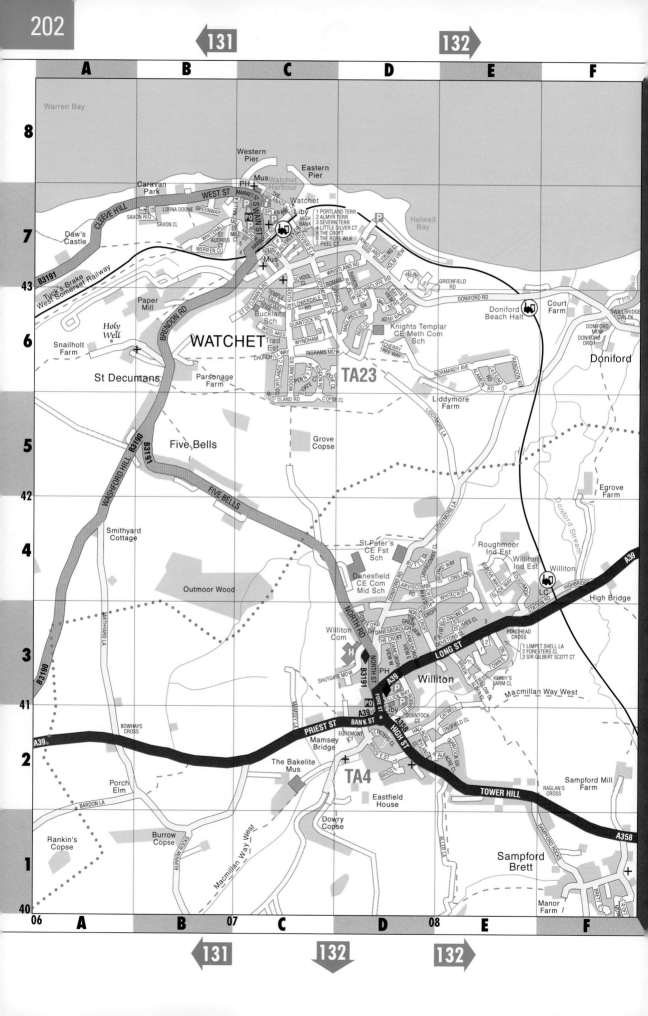

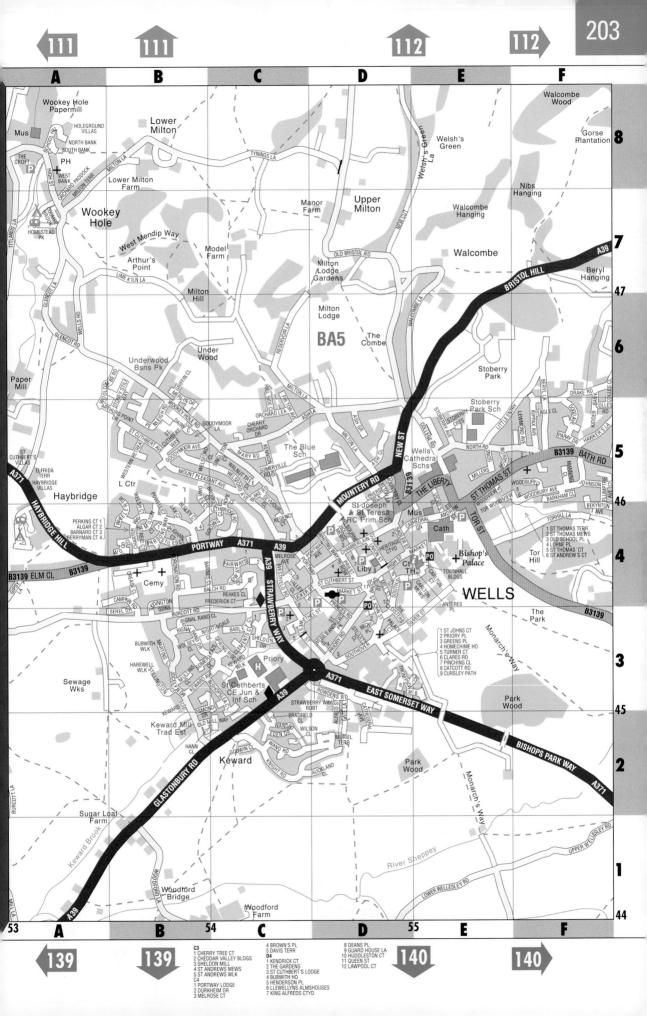

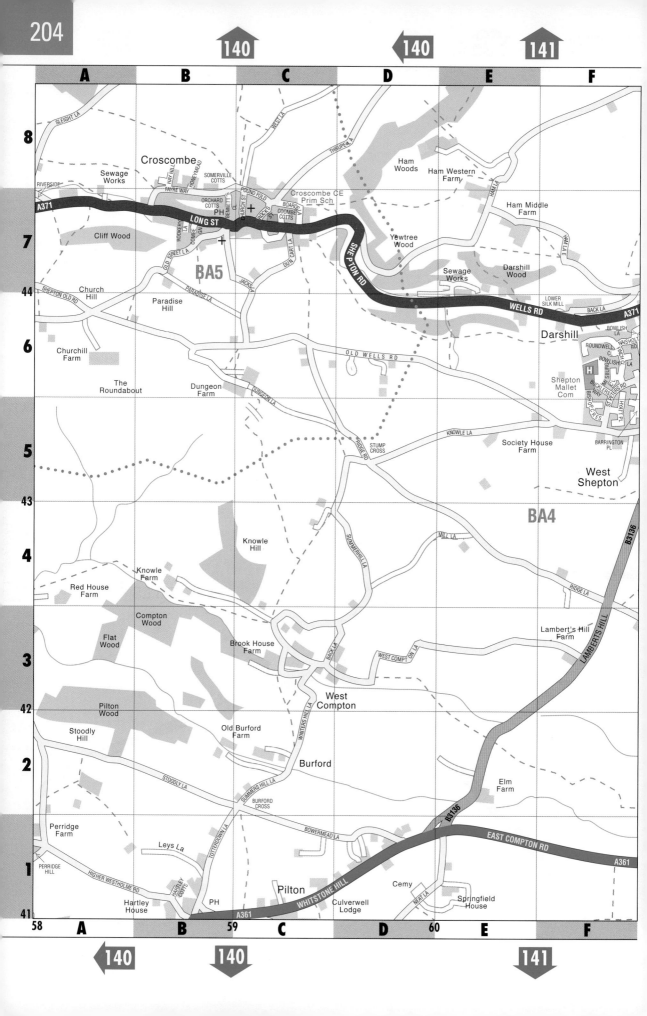

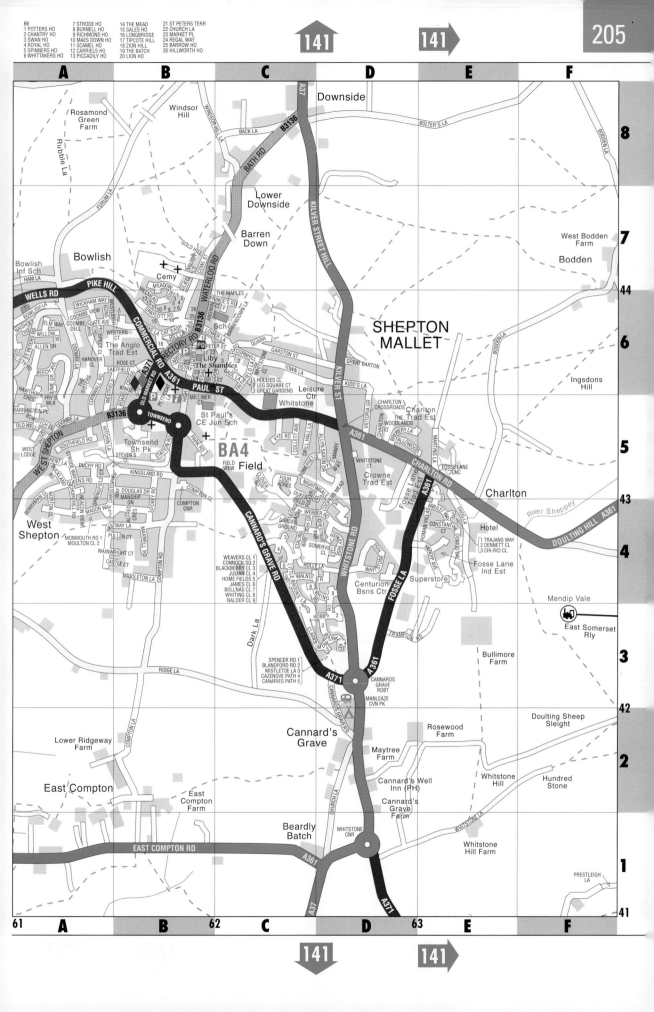

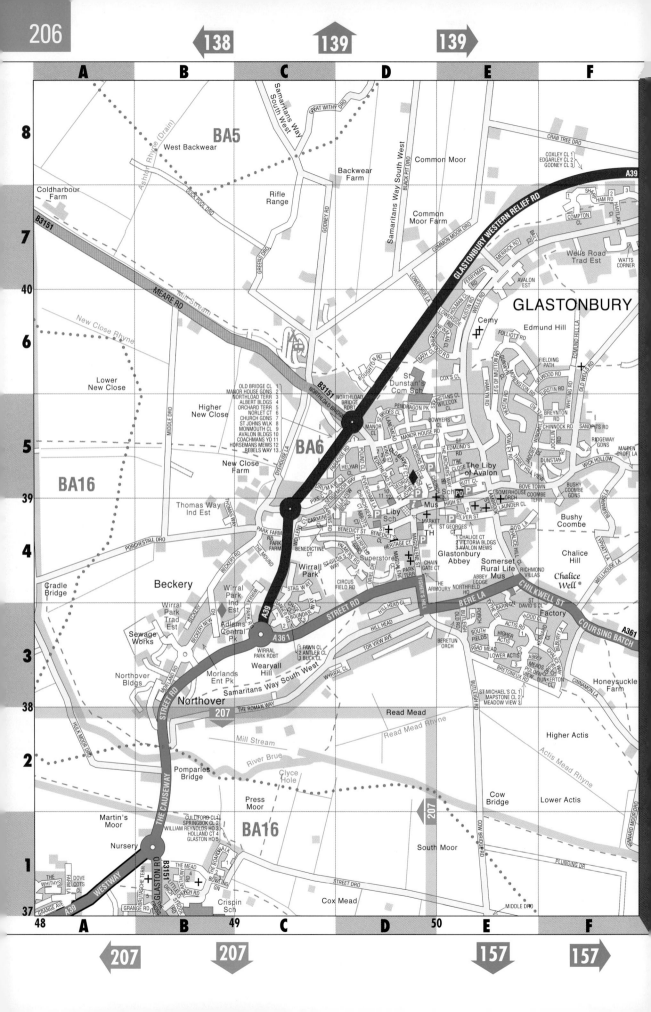

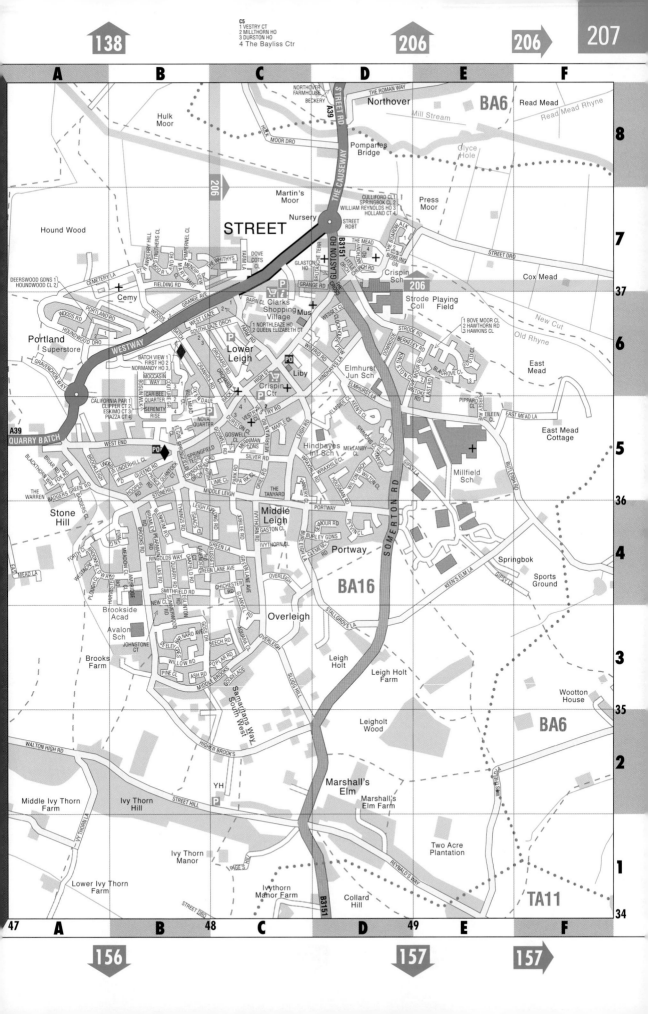

C5
1 VESTRY CT
2 MILLTHORN HO
3 DURSTON HO
4 The Bayliss Ctr

138

206

206

207

A   B   C   D   E   F

NORTHOVER
FARMHOUSE
BECKERY

THE ROMAN WAY

Northover

BA6

Read Mead

Read Mead Rhyne

STREET RD
A39

Mill Stream

8

Hulk
Moor

HULK MOOR DRO

Pomparles
Bridge

Clyce
Hole

Martin's
Moor

THE CAUSEWAY

CULLIFORD CL 1
SPRINGBOK CL 2
WILLIAM REYNOLDS HO 3
HOLLAND CT 4

Press
Moor

7

Hound Wood

Nursery

STREET

GLASTON RD

B3151

THE MEAD

STREET DRO

RAWBERRY HILL
STRUTHERS CL
TIMPERNEL CL
MENDIP VIEW

THE WHITHYS

DOVE
COTS
HO

STREET
RDBT

BOWLING
GN

Cox Mead

DEERSWOOD GDNS 1
HOUNDWOOD CL 2

CEMETERY LA

FIELDING RD

GLASTONBE TERR

BRUTASCHE TERR

LITTLE
ORCH

THE BOARDWALK

Crispin
Sch

LAND RD
MARY HART
FARM LA

GRANGE AVE

GRANGE RD

LITTLE
CROSS

THE MEAD

206

Cemy

Portland
Superstore

WOODS RD

PORTLAND RD

HOUNDWOOD DRO

GRAVENCHON WAY

WESTWAY

WOODS RD

BARN CL

BATCH

WEST LEAZE

SOUTHLEAZE ORCH

Clarks
Shopping
Village
Mus

37

1 NORTHLEAZE HO
2 QUEEN ELIZABETH CT

Strode
Coll

Strode
Playing
Field

1 BOVE MOOR CL
2 HAWTHORN RD
3 HAWKINS CL

New Cut

Old Rhyne

6

BATCH VIEW 1
FIRST HO 2
NORMANDY HO 3

Lower
Leigh

ORCHARD RD

FARM RD

WESSEX CL

GLENWORTHY'S VIEW

STRODE RD

BERKELEY RD

STRODE RD

TOWNSEND

SWIN

BLAGROVE CL

East
Mead

MOCCASIN
WAY

CARIBEE
QUARTER
SERENITY
RISE

CRANHILLS RD

ORCHARD
RD

HIGH ST
Liby

WILFRID RD

HINDHAYES LA

ELMHURST LA

ELMHURST CL

ACKEN'S CL

STONE CL

MOOR RD

EAST RD

BOSTOCK RD

PIPPARD CL

PURSEY AVE

EILEEN
CL

EAST MEAD LA

East Mead
Cottage

CALIFORNIA PAR 1
CLIPPER CT 2
ESKIMO CT 3
PIAZZA CT 4

Crispin
Ctr

NOVA
QUARTER

DURSTON RD

VESTRY CL

TRY RD

Elmhurst
Jun Sch

LEIGH RD

WRAXHILL CL

SIMMONS CL

5

A39

QUARRY BATCH

WEST END

ELGIN SPRINGFIELD RD

GOSWELL RD

GOSWELL
CL

MERRIMAN
GDNS

MERRIMAN RD

MAPLE CL

Hindhayes
Inf Sch

MELLANBY CL

WRAXHILL RD

HOUSMAN RD

WILTON CL

WILTON OROT

Millfield
Sch

BUTLEIGH RD

BLACKTHORN WAY

BRIAR RD

FOX RD

THE
WARREN

BADGERS GREEN RD

UNDERHILL CL

QUEENS RD

PRIORS RD

QUANTOCK RD

STONEHILL

SILVER RD

LIME CL

ORIEL RD

PARK RD

THE
TANYARD

TANNERY
RD

PORTWAY

GIPSY LA

36

Stone
Hill

BROOKS RD

BROADWAY

UNDERHILL
RD

HOOPER RD

LEIGH FLDS
LONG RD

JUBILEE RD

ISAAC'S

MIDDLE LEIGH

GREEN LA

Middle
Leigh

GASTON CL

IVYTHORN LA

BURLEY GDNS

MOUR CL

PEV'N CL

CLEMENT'S
RD

Portway

KEEN'S ELM LA

Springbok

Sports
Ground

GIPSY LA

4

FORD'S
BRAMLEY CL

BENHEIM RD

PEARMAN'S
DANFIELD RD

LILAC RD

QUARRY WAY

RINGOLDS WAY

SMITHFIELD
RD

EGLINTON

GREEN LANE AVE

GREEN LA

GREEN LANE AVE

GLANVILL RD

BURE LEIGH LA

STALLGROVE LA

BA16

WESTACRE
PLOUGHFIELD WAY

MEADOW CL
CAMBRIDGE

HARVESTERS
NEW CL
SUMMERWOOD
RD

CHICHESTER
RD

OVERLEIGH

OVERLEIGH
RD

AQUARA CL

Overleigh

Brookside
Acad

BARNARD MEAD

GOSS DR

BEECH RD

Leigh
Holt

Leigh Holt
Farm

3

Avalon
Sch

JOHNSTONE
CT

SEELEY

FYDES

WILLOW RD

POPLAR RD

ASH RD

PINE CL

MIDDLE BROOKS

GOOSESLADE

Samaritans Way
South West

SLUGG HILL

Leigholt
Wood

BA6

35

Brooks
Farm

Wootton
House

WALTON HIGH RD

HIGHER BROOK'S

2

Middle Ivy Thorn
Farm

Ivy Thorn
Hill

STREET HILL

YH

STREET DRO

PAGE'S HILL

Marshall's
Elm

Marshall's
Elm Farm

WEST'ND LA

REYNALD'S WAY

Ivy Thorn
Manor

Ivythorn
Manor Farm

B3151

Collard
Hill

Two Acre
Plantation

1

Lower Ivy Thorn
Farm

IVY THORN LA

STREET DRO

TA11

34

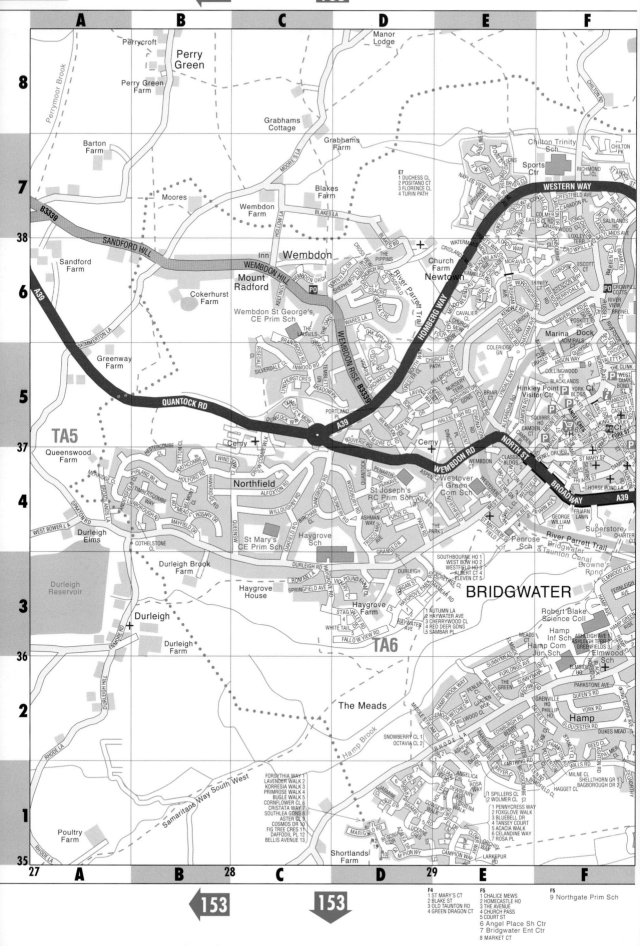

135 135

153 153

F4
1 ST MARY'S CT
2 BLAKE ST
3 OLD TAUNTON RD
4 GREEN DRAGON CT

F5
1 CHALICE MEWS
2 HOMECASTLE HO
3 THE AVENUE
4 CHURCH PASS
5 COURT ST
6 Angel Place Sh Ctr
7 Bridgwater Ent Ctr
8 MARKET CT

F5
9 Northgate Prim Sch

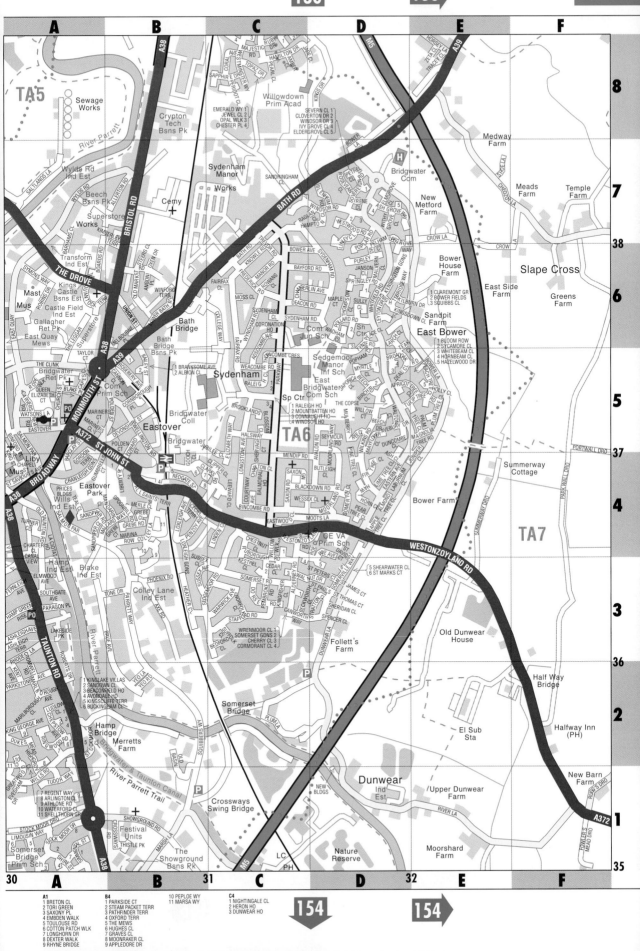

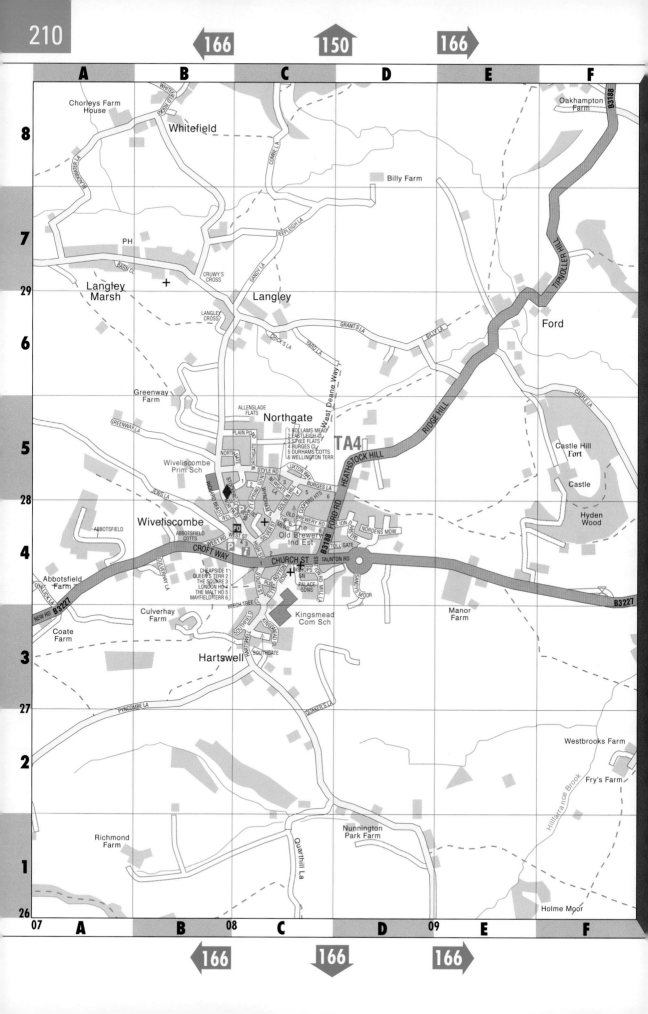

A   B   C   D   E   F

8

Chorleys Farm House
Whitefield

Billy Farm

Oakhampton Farm

B3188

7

PH

DEEPLEIGH LA

CRUWY'S CROSS

SANDY LA

COMBE LA

WHITEFIELD

BLACKWATER LA

BARN CL

29

Langley Marsh

LANGLEY CROSS

Langley

GRANT'S LA

BILLY LA

Ford

TIPNOLLER HILL

6

CRICK'S LA

YARD LA

West Deane Way

RIDGE HILL

CASTLE LA

5

Greenway Farm

GREENWAY LA

ALLENSLADE FLATS

PLAIN PO

Northgate

1 BOLLAMS MEAD
2 EASTLEIGH CL
3 STYLE FLATS
4 BURGES CL
5 DURHAMS COTTS
6 WELLINGTON TERR

TA4

HEATHSTOCK HILL

Castle Hill Fort

Castle

28

Wiveliscombe Prim Sch

NORTHGATE

STYLE RD

NEWGATE

LUXTON WAY

BURGES LA

COOPER'S HTS

Hyden Wood

JEWS LA

ABBOTSFIELD

Wiveliscombe

ABBOTSFIELD COTTS

STODDENS RD

MIDLAND BEACON

NCL

P

GOLDEN HILL

OLD BREWERY RD

FORD RD

B3188

Nordens Mdw

TOLL GATE

4

Abbotsfield Farm

CHALICK LA

NEW RD   B3227

CROFT WAY

WEST RD

CULVERHAY LA

PO   P

WEST ST

SILVER ST

4 3

i

RUSS ST

CHURCH ST

ROTTON

BISHOPS PALACE GDNS

TAUNTON RD

STATION RD

MILL LA

ST MOOR

Manor Farm

B3227

CHEAPSIDE 1
QUEEN'S TERR 2
THE SQUARE 3
LONDON HO 4
THE MALT HO 5
MAYFIELD TERR 6

BEECH TREE CL

Coate Farm

Culverhay Farm

HARTSWELL

SOUTHFIELD

KINGSMEAD RD

SOUTHGATE

Kingsmead Com Sch

3

Richmond Farm

PYNCOMBE LA

QUARKER'S LA

QUARTHILL LA

Nunnington Park Farm

Westbrooks Farm

Fry's Farm

Hillfarrance Brook

27

2

1

Holme Moor

26

07   A   B   08   C   D   09   E   F

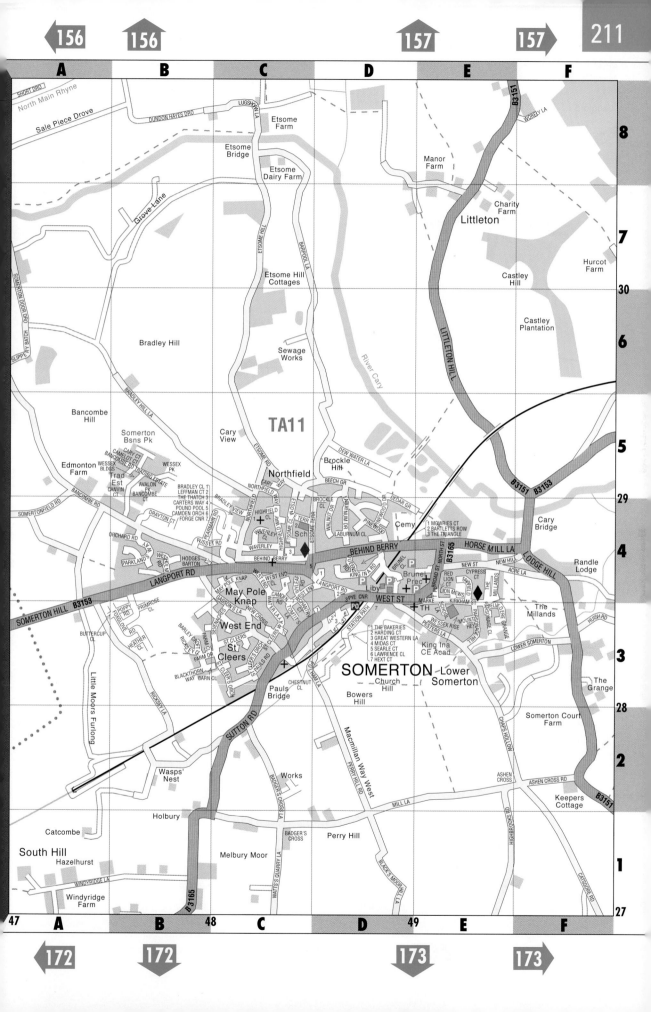

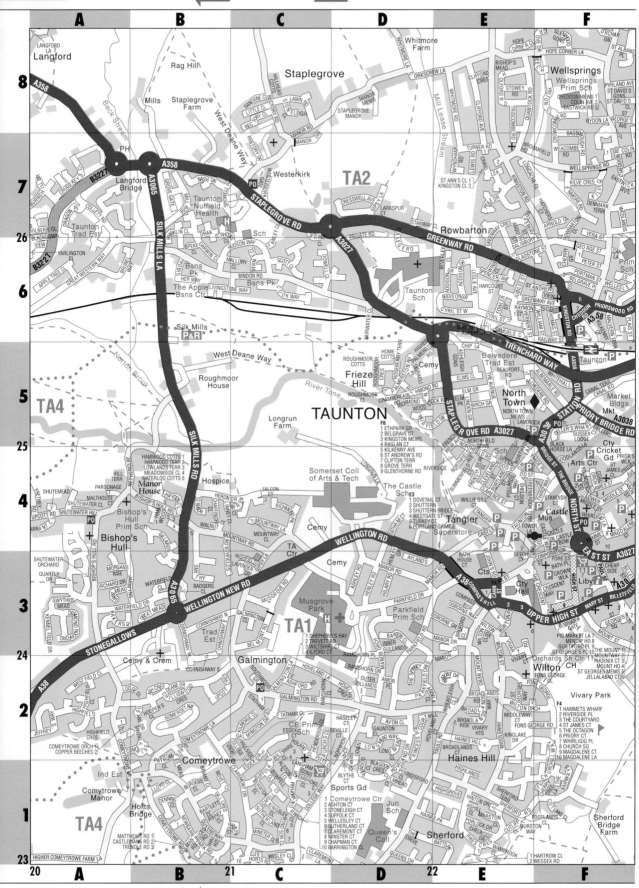

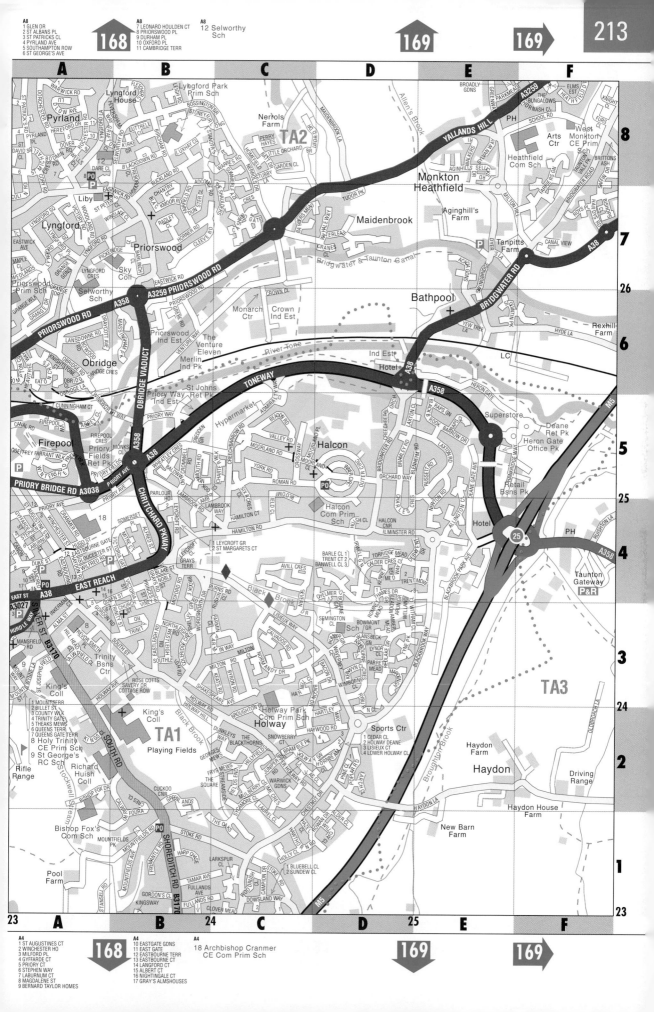

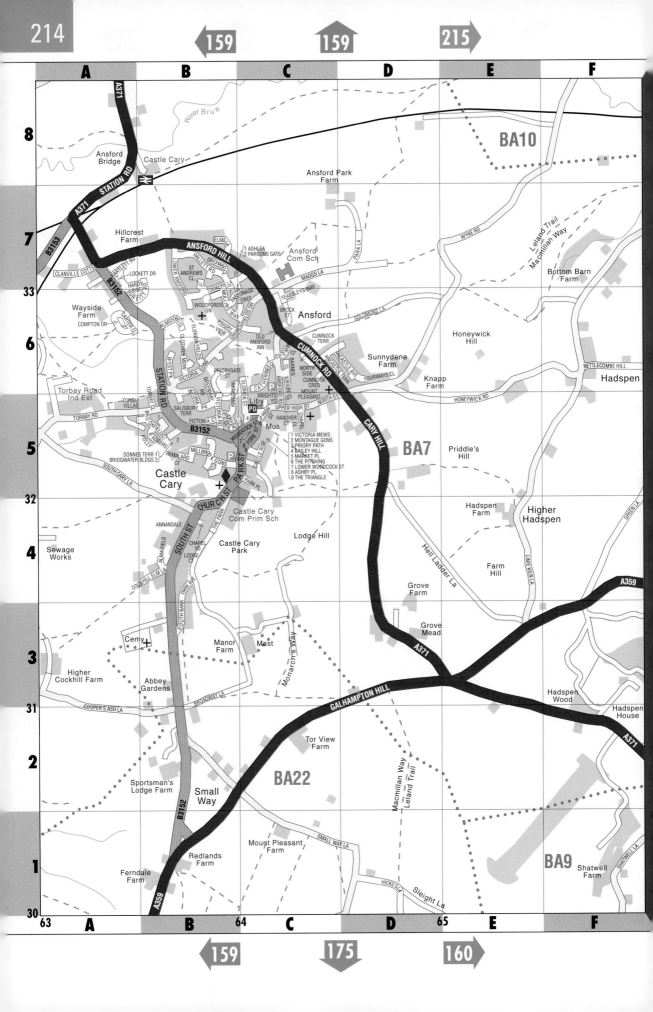

A   B   C   D   E   F

8

BA10

River Brue

Ansford Bridge

Castle Cary

Ansford Park Farm

STATION RD

A371

7

B3153

Hillcrest Farm

ANSFORD HILL

1 ASHLEA
2 PARSONS GATE

Ansford Com Sch

PARK LA

WYKE RD

Leland Trail
Macmillan Way

Bottom Barn Farm

Clanville Cotts

BARTLETT ST

LOCKETT DR

ELMS

ST ANDREWS CL

ORCHARD RD

HALLETT RD

LOWER ANSFORD

TUCKERS CL

MAWLINS WAY

PARSONAGE CRES

MAGGS LA

33

B3152

HARDY PL

Wayside Farm

COMPTON DR

CARTER CL

ALMSFORD CL

CLOTHIER MDW

FLORIDA FIELDS

WOODFORDS GN

PRIORY VIEW

CHURCHFIELDS DR

BROCK CT

Ansford

YEABSLEYS WAY

SOLOMONS LA

6

STATION RD

VICTORIA GDNS

PRIORYGATE CT

GREENWAY

CATHERINE'S CL

BARNES CL

FLORIDA TERR

JUBILEE CT

COOMBE CL

CUMNOCK RD

CUMNOCK TERR

ANCASTLE TERR

LANCASTLE AVE

Sunnydene

NORTH SIDE

Honeywick Hill

NETTLECOMBE HILL

Hadspen

Torbay Road Ind Est

TORBAY CL

TORBAY PK

Torbay Villas

VICTORIA TERR

SALISBURY PK

VICTORIA CT RD

VICTORIA RD

KNIGHTS YD

Liby

PO

UPPER HIGH ST

NORTH ST

MOUNT PLEASANT

CUMNOCK CRES

FOURWAYS CL

Knapp Farm

HONEYWICK RD

5

TORBAY RD

BROOKFIELDS

B RODGERS

POLLY

REMALARD CT

MILLBROOK GDNS

WOODCOCK ST

HANOVER CT

Mus

CHAPEL

CARY HILL

BA7

Priddle's Hill

Donnes Terr 1
Bridgwater Bldgs 2

SOUTH CARY LA

Castle Cary

PARK ST

FORE ST

CASTLE RISE

1 VICTORIA MEWS
2 MONTAGUE GDNS
3 PRIORY PATH
4 BAILEY HILL
5 MARKET PL
6 THE PITSHING
7 LOWER WOODCOCK ST
8 ASHBY PL
9 THE TRIANGLE

32

CHURCH ST

PARK PL

Castle Cary Com Prim Sch

Hadspen Farm

Higher Hadspen

GREEN LA

4

Sewage Works

ANNANDALE

THE PARK

SOUTH ST

ALMA FIELD

CHAPEL YD

LODGE CT

Castle Cary Park

Lodge Hill

Hell Ladder La

Farm Hill

LIME KILN LA

A359

COCKHILL ELM LA

SOUTH BANK

PARK AVE

Grove Farm

Grove Mead

3

Higher Cockhill Farm

Cemy

Abbey Gardens

COOPER'S ASH LA

Manor Farm

Mast

Monarch's Way

BROADWAY LA

A371

Hadspen Wood

Hadspen House

31

GALHAMPTON HILL

A371

2

B3152

Small Way

BA22

Tor View Farm

Macmillan Way
Leland Trail

Sportsman's Lodge Farm

Redlands Farm

Mount Pleasant Farm

SMALL WAY LA

BA9

1

Ferndale Farm

A359

HICKS LA

Sleight La

Shatwell Farm

SHATWELL LA

30

63   A   B   64   C   D   65   E   F

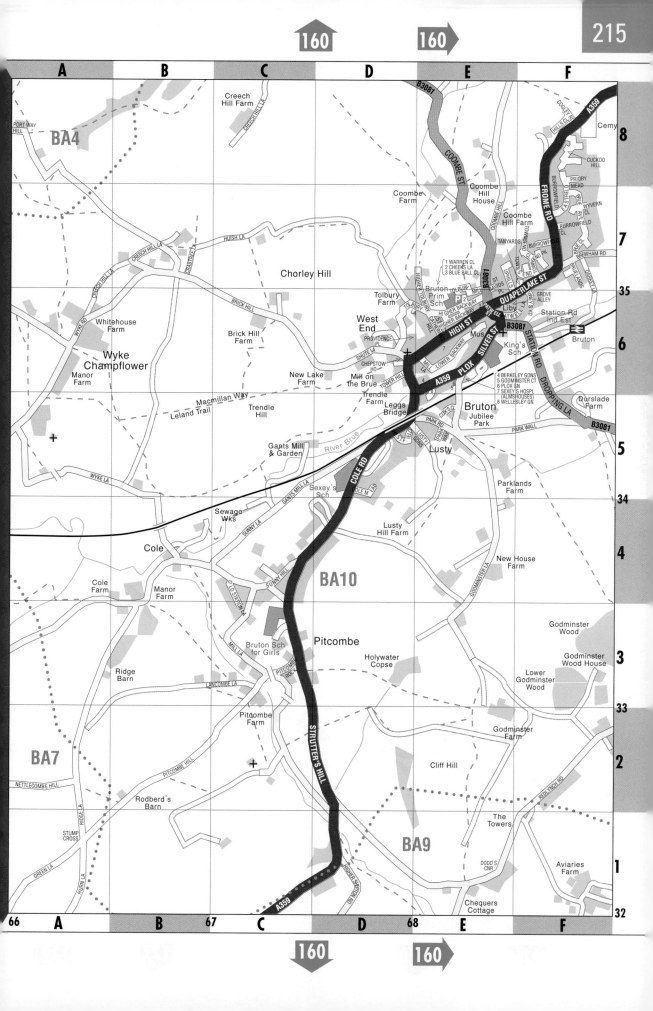

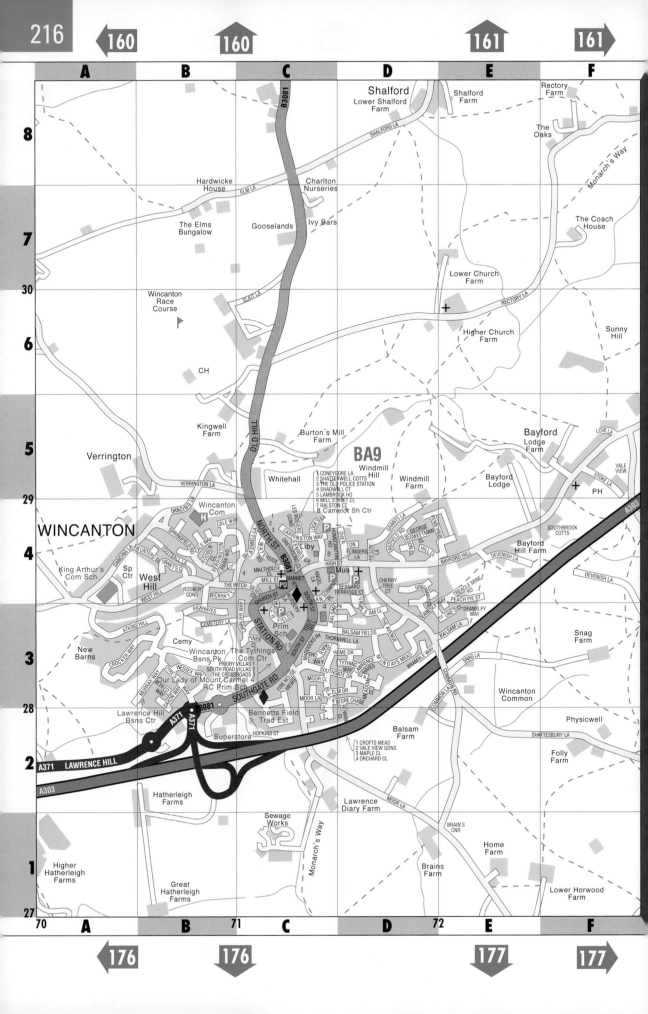

A B C D E F

8

7

30

6

5

29

4

3

28

2

1

27

Shalford
Lower Shalford Farm
Shalford Farm
Rectory Farm
The Oaks
Monarch's Way
The Coach House
Hardwicke House
ELM LA
Charlton Nurseries
Ivy Bars
Lower Church Farm
The Elms Bungalow
Gooselands
SLAIT LA
Sunny Hill
Wincanton Race Course
Higher Church Farm
RECTORY LA
CH
Kingwell Farm
Burton's Mill Farm
BA9
Windmill Hill
Bayford Lodge Farm
LOVE LA
Verrington
Whitehall
1 CONEYGORE LA
2 SHATTERWELL COTTS
3 THE OLD POLICE STATION
4 SHADWELL CT
5 LAMBROOK HO
6 MILL STREET CL
7 RALSTON CT
8 Camelot Sh Ctr
Windmill Farm
Bayford Lodge
VALE VIEW
STOKE LA
VERRINGTON LA
PH
Wincanton Com
DANCING LA
NORTH ST
Liby
GRANTS LA
CASTFIELD RD
George Sweetman Cl
Bayford Hill Farm
SOUTHBROOK COTTS
DEVENISH LA
WINCANTON
King Arthur's Com Sch
Sp Ctr
West Hill
MALTHOUSE CL
MILL ST
Market Pl
Mus
PENY VIEW
REGAL
HILL CL
Bayford Hill
DEVENISH LA
WEST HILL
PO
Angel La
Bernard Herridge Ct
CHERRY TREE CT
TREACLE MINE
PEACH PIE ST
Deansley Way
Snag Farm
Cemy
CEMETERY LA
Prim Sch
SOUTH ST
BALSAM PK
THE AVENUE
BALSAM LA
New Barns
CROCKER WAY
PINES CL
FIELDS
Balsam Fields
Wincanton Common
Wincanton Bsns. Pk
The Tythings Com Ctr
HOME DR
THORNWELL LA
SNAG LA
PRIORY VILLAS 1
SOUTH ROAD VILLAS 2
THE CROSSROADS 3
Our Lady of Mount Carmel 4
RC Prim Sch
TYTHING WAY
SOUTHGATE DR
MUN'DAYS MEAD
BRAMBLE WAY
COMMON RD
FIRE HOUSE MEWS
MOOR CL
MEADOW
ELM DR
BLACK MORE CHASE
SOUTHGATE RD
Lawrence Hill Bsns Ctr
A371
A371
B3081
Bennetts Field Trad Est
Balsam Farm
Physicwell
Superstore
HOPKINS CT
1 CROFTS MEAD
2 VALE VIEW GDNS
3 MAPLE CL
4 ORCHARD CL
SHAFTESBURY LA
Folly Farm
A371 LAWRENCE HILL
A303
Hatherleigh Farms
Sewage Works
Monarch's Way
Lawrence Diary Farm
MOOR LA
BRAIN'S CNR
Home Farm
Higher Hatherleigh Farms
Great Hatherleigh Farms
Brains Farm
Lower Horwood Farm

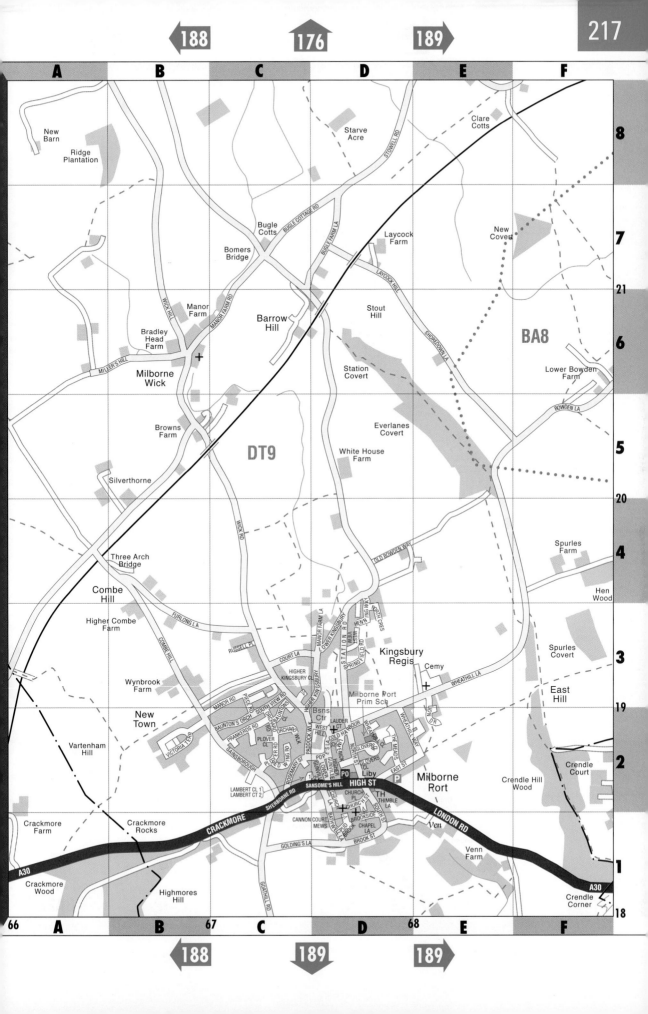

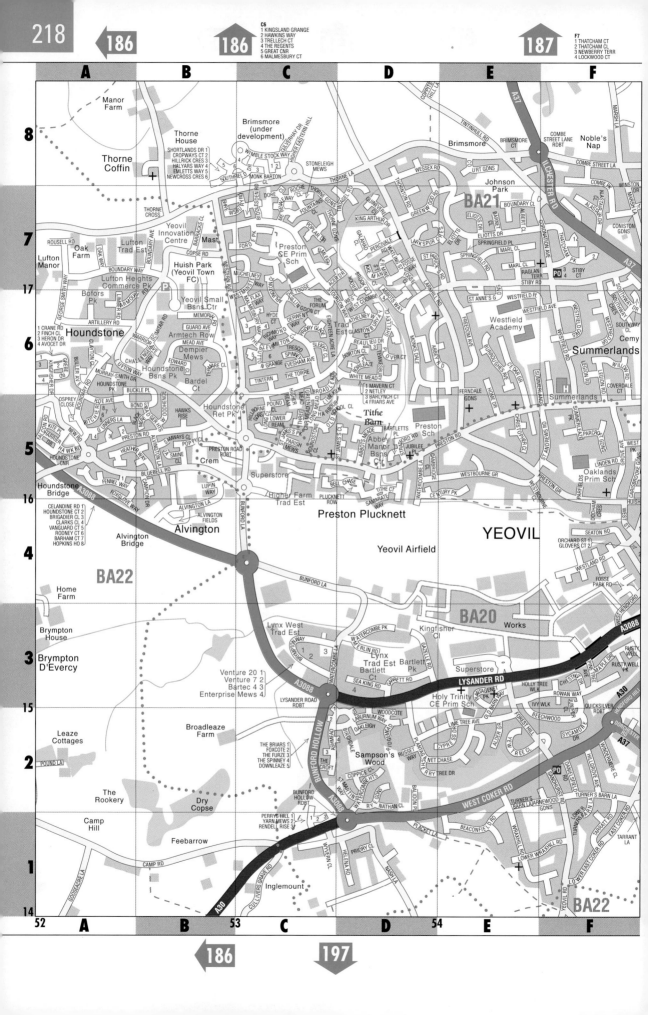

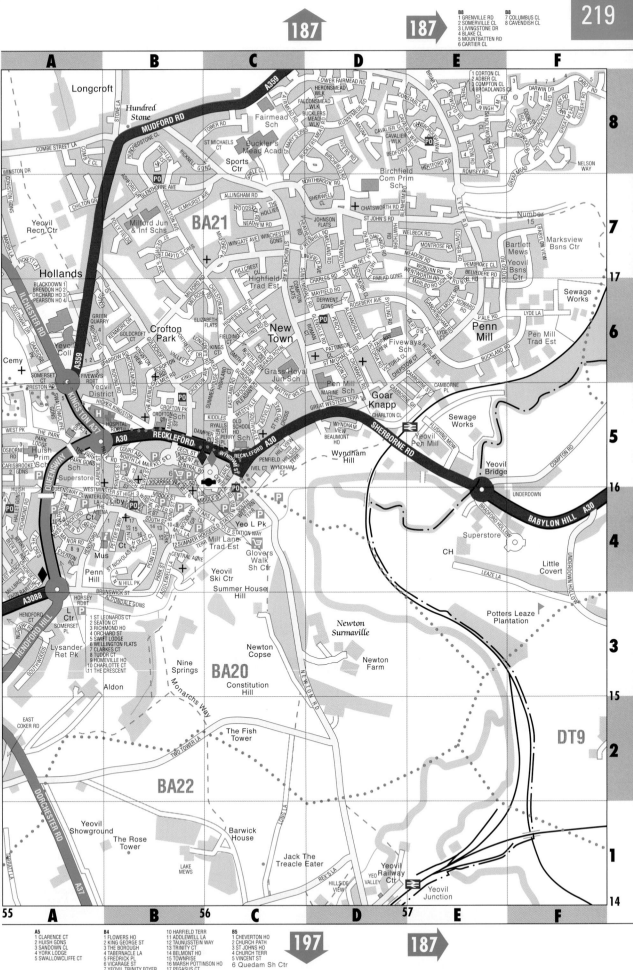

187   187

B8
1 GRENVILLE RD
2 SOMERVILLE CL
3 LIVINGSTONE DR
4 BLAKE CL
5 MOUNTBATTEN RD
6 CARTIER CL

B8
7 COLUMBUS CL
8 CAVENDISH CL

55   A   B   56   C   D   57   E   F

197   187

A5
1 CLARENCE CT
2 HUISH GDNS
3 SANDOWN CL
4 YORK LODGE
5 SWALLOWCLIFFE CT

B4
1 FLOWERS HO
2 KING GEORGE ST
3 THE BOROUGH
4 TABERNACLE LA
5 FREDRICK PL
6 VICARAGE ST
7 YEOVIL TRINITY FOYER
8 CLARENCE TERR
9 BROAD OAK
10 HARFIELD TERR
11 ADDLEWELL LA
12 TAUNUSSTEIN WAY
13 TRINITY CT
14 BELMONT HO
15 TOWNRISE
16 MARSH POTTINSON HO
17 PEGASUS CT
18 GLOVERS WLK

B5
1 CHEVERTON HO
2 CHURCH PATH
3 ST JOHNS HO
4 CHURCH TERR
5 VINCENT ST
6 QUEDAM SH CTR

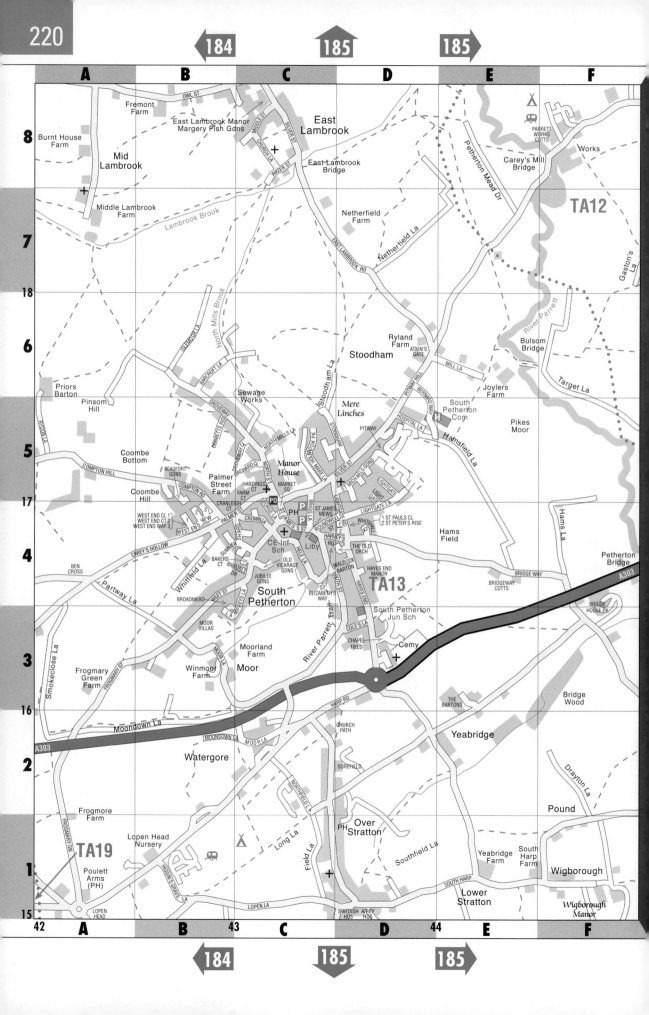

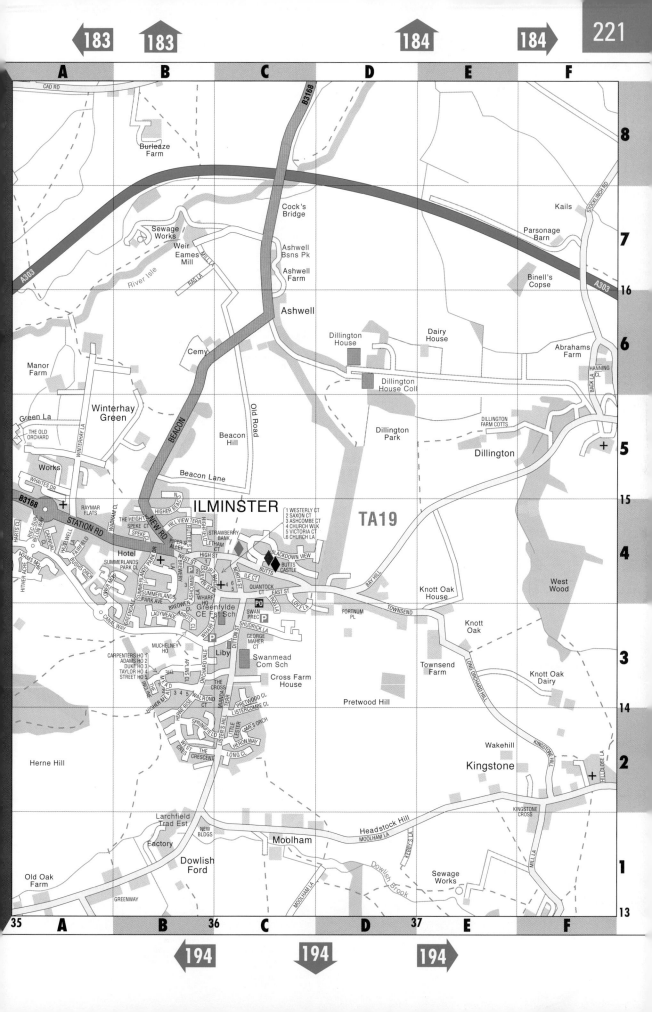

A B C D E F

8
7
16
6
5
15
4
3
14
2
1
13

CAD RD

Burleaze Farm

Sewage Works
Weir Eames Mill
RAG LA
River Isle
MILL LA

B3168

Cock's Bridge

Ashwell Bsns Pk
Ashwell Farm

Ashwell

Kails

Parsonage Barn

Binell's Copse

STOCKLINCH RD

A303

Manor Farm

Winterhay Green

Green La
THE OLD ORCHARD

BEACON

Cemy

Old Road

Beacon Hill

Dillington House

Dairy House

Dillington House Coll

Dillington Park

Dillington Farm Cotts

Dillington

Abrahams Farm

BACK LA
HANNING CL

Works

WHAITES DR

B3168

RAYMAR FLATS

STATION RD

NEW RD

Beacon Lane

HIGHER BEACON

ILMINSTER

TA19

HARTS CL
RIEC-SUR-BELON WAY
CARNIVAL

HAZELWELL LA
FAIRFIELD

WILDHAM CL
THE HEIGHTS
SPEKE CT
SPEKE CT

HILL VIEW TERR
HILL VIEW HO
BUTTS CL

Hotel
ADAMS MEAD
HITHER ACRE

SUMMERLANDS PARK CL
BUSHS ORCH
PARK DR
SUMMERLANDS PARK AVE
SUMMERLANDS

GREENDALE
INNER WAY

PIPER'S ALLEY
WEST ST
BREWERY
ASHCOMBE CL
COURT BARTON
ABBOTS CL

STRAWBERRY BANK
LETHAM CT
HIGH ST
NORTH ST
ILE CT
WHARF LA
WHARF
QUANTOCK CT

1 WESTERLY CT
2 SAXON CT
3 ASHCOMBE CT
4 CHURCH WLK
5 VICTORIA CT
6 CHURCH LA

BLACKDOWN VIEW
BUTTS CASTLE

EAST ST
FROG LA
LOVE LA

Knott Oak House

West Wood

Knott Oak

BAY HILL
TOWNSEND

LADYMEAD
CANAL WAY

Greenfylde CE Fst Sch

PO
SWAN PREC

DITTON ST
ORCHARD VALE

SHUDRICK LA
GEORGE MAHER CT

FORTNUM PL

Townsend Farm

Knott Oak Dairy

CARPENTERS HO 1
ADAMS HO 2
DUKE HO 3
TAYLOR HO 4
STREET HO 5

MUCHELNEY HO
APLINS CL
THE INCLINE

Liby

Swanmead Com Sch

Cross Farm House

LONG ORCHARD HILL

HIGHER MEAD
1 2 3 4 5
WALROND CT

THE CROSS
MANOR TERR
PRETWOOD CL
LISTERCOMBE CL

Pretwood Hill

KINGSTONE HILL

HERNE RISE
SPRINGFIELD

LISTER'S HILL
LITTLE LESTER
JAMES ORCH
HERON WAY

Wakehill

Kingstone

HILLCLOSE LA

Herne Hill

WEST CRES
THE CRESCENT

LONG CL

KINGSTONE CROSS

Larchfield Trad Est
NEW BLDGS
Factory

Headstock Hill
MOOLHAM LA

Moolham

KERRY'S LA

MILL LA

Dowlish Ford

MOOLHAM LA

Dowlish Brook

Sewage Works

Old Oak Farm

GREENWAY

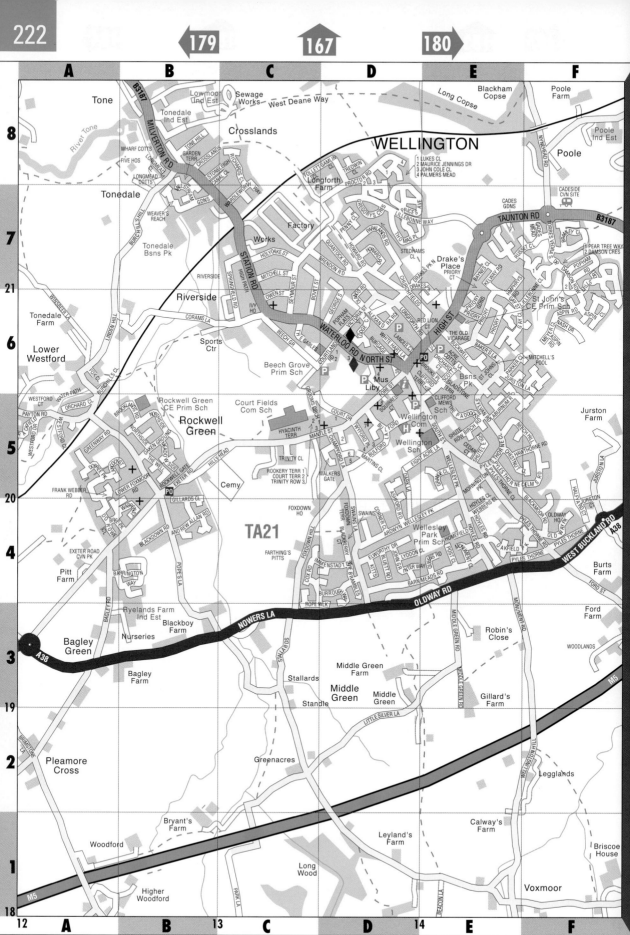

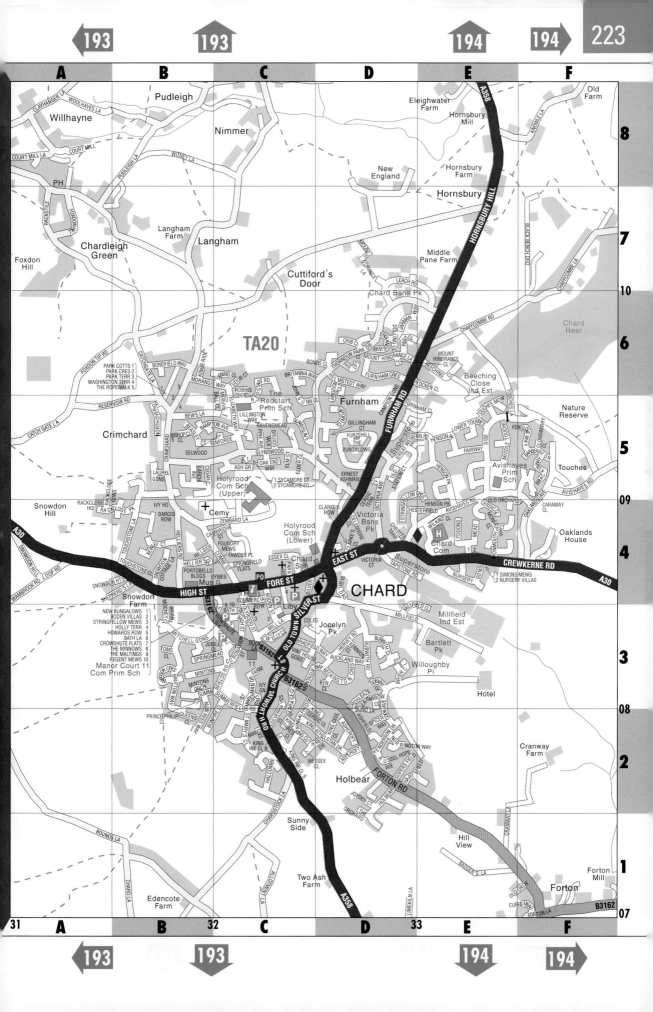

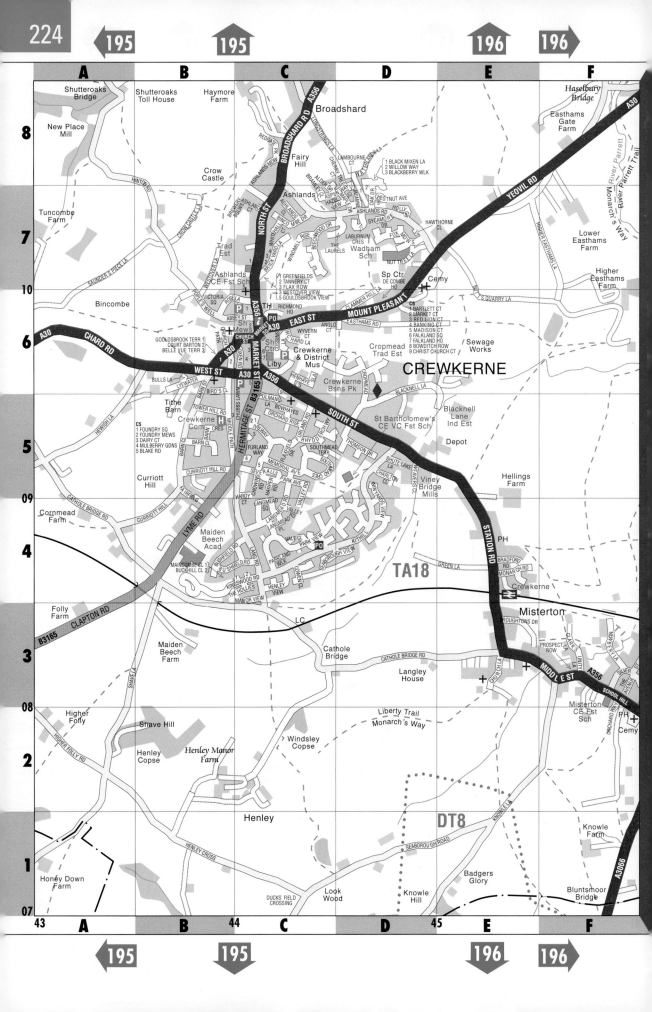

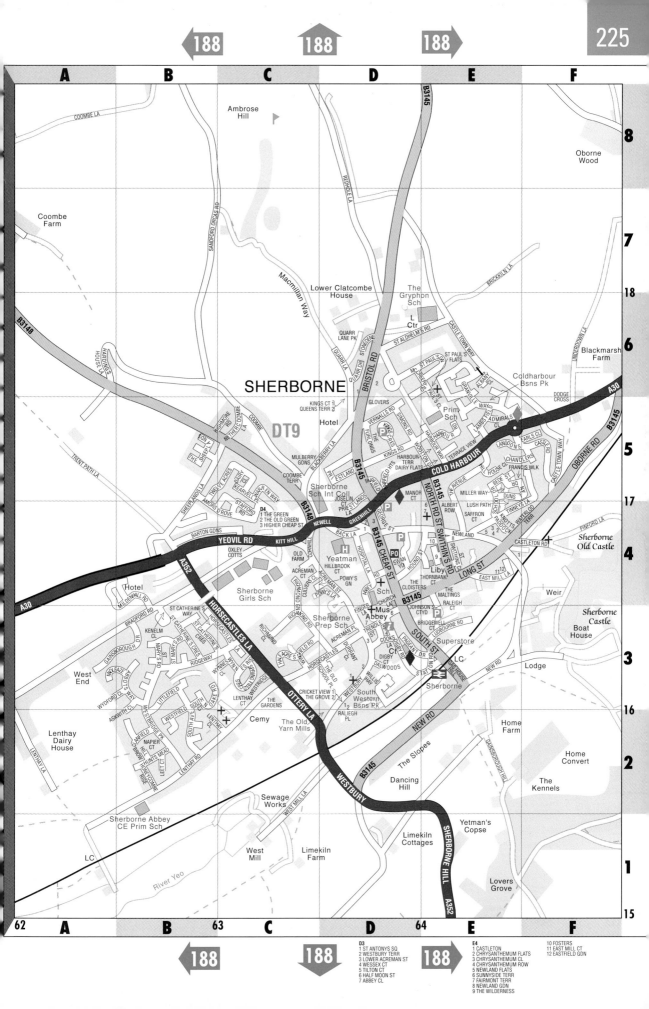

House numbers
1   59
HIGH ST

11

One-way Streets

Scale: 7 inches to 1 mile
0   110 yards 220 yards
0   125 m   250 m

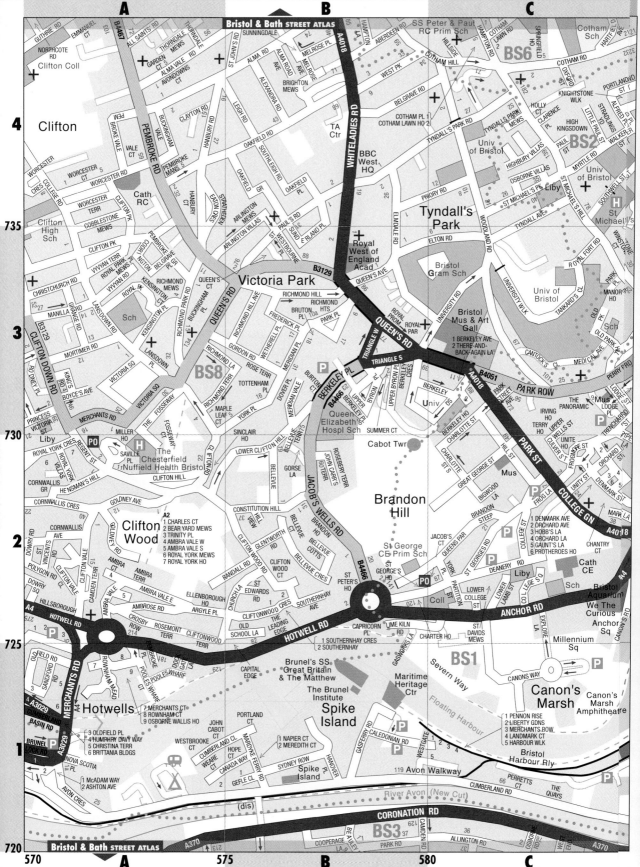

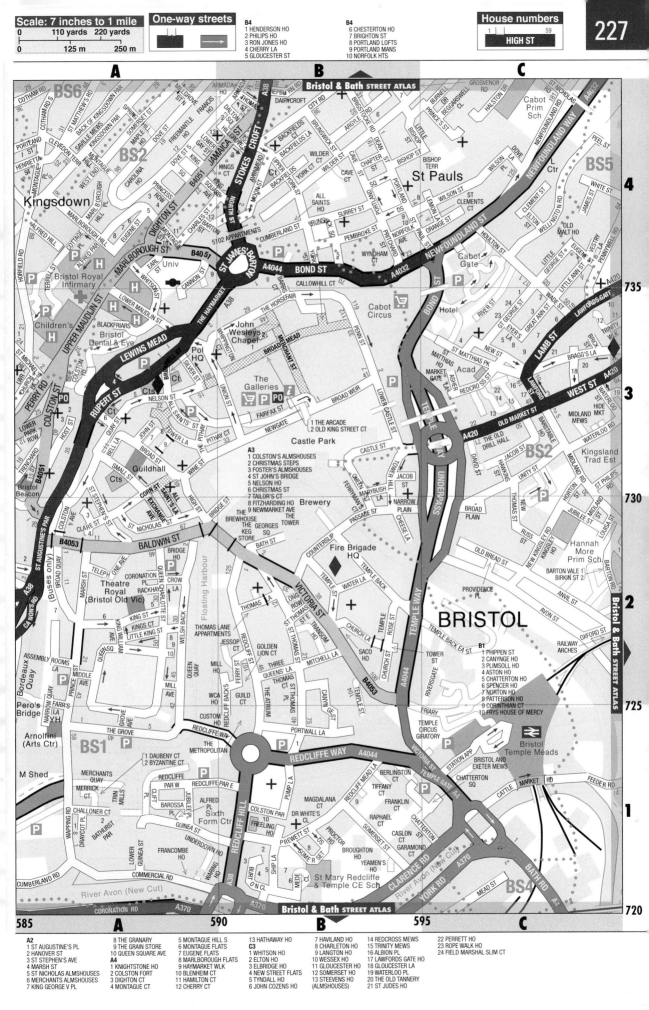

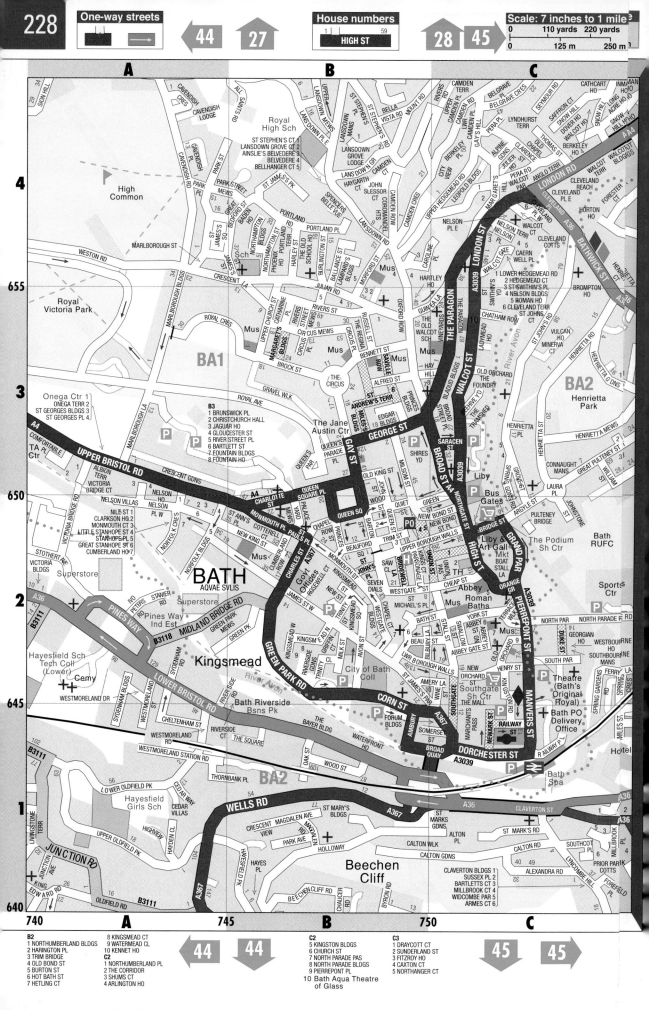

Index

Church Rd **6** Beckenham BR2..........**53** C6

Place name May be abbreviated on the map

Location number Present when a number indicates the place's position in a crowded area of mapping

Locality, town or village Shown when more than one place has the same name

Postcode district District for the indexed place

Page and grid square Page number and grid reference for the standard mapping

Cities, towns and villages are listed in CAPITAL LETTERS

Public and commercial buildings are highlighted in **magenta**   Places of interest are highlighted in blue with a star *

Abbreviations used in the index

Acad	Academy	Comm	Common	Gd	Ground	L	Leisure	Prom	Promenade
App	Approach	Cott	Cottage	Gdn	Garden	La	Lane	Rd	Road
Arc	Arcade	Cres	Crescent	Gn	Green	Liby	Library	Recn	Recreation
Ave	Avenue	Cswy	Causeway	Gr	Grove	Mdw	Meadow	Ret	Retail
Bglw	Bungalow	Ct	Court	H	Hall	Meml	Memorial	Sh	Shopping
Bldg	Building	Ctr	Centre	Ho	House	Mkt	Market	Sq	Square
Bsns, Bus	Business	Ctry	Country	Hospl	Hospital	Mus	Museum	St	Street
Bvd	Boulevard	Cty	County	HQ	Headquarters	Orch	Orchard	Sta	Station
Cath	Cathedral	Dr	Drive	Hts	Heights	Pal	Palace	Terr	Terrace
Cir	Circus	Dro	Drove	Ind	Industrial	Par	Parade	TH	Town Hall
Cl	Close	Ed	Education	Inst	Institute	Pas	Passage	Univ	University
Cnr	Corner	Emb	Embankment	Int	International	Pk	Park	Wk, Wlk	Walk
Coll	College	Est	Estate	Intc	Interchange	Pl	Place	Wr	Water
Com	Community	Ex	Exhibition	Junc	Junction	Prec	Precinct	Yd	Yard

Index of towns, villages, streets, hospitals, industrial estates, railway stations, schools, shopping centres, universities and places of interest

5102 Apartments BS1 ....227 B4

A

ABBAS COMBE 176 E1
Abbas & Templecombe CE
  Prim Sch BA8..........176 E1
Abbey Cl
  Curry Rivel TA10..........171 D4
  Firepool TA1..........213 A5
  7 Sherborne DT9 ......225 D3
  Tatworth TA20..........198 D8
  Wookey BA5..........139 D8
Abbey Ct **6** BA2 ....45 B7
Abbey Fields TA10 ....171 D4
Abbey Gate BS9..........5 E5
Abbey Gate St BA1 ....228 C2
Abbey Gdns BS22 ......49 E8
Abbey Gn BA1..........228 C2
ABBEY HILL..........182 E5
Abbey Hill Dro TA3....182 E5
Abbey La BA3..........64 A4
Abbey Lodge BA6......206 E4
Abbey Manor Bsns Ctr
  BA21..........218 D5
Abbey Meads BA6......206 E3
Abbey Mews TA20......198 D8
Abbey Pk BS31..........24 F6
Abbey Rd
  Bristol BS9..........5 F7
  Chilcompton BA3..........96 D2
  Sherborne DT9..........225 D4
  Stratton-on-t F BA3 ....96 F2
  Washford TA23..........131 E3
  Yeovil BA21..........218 D6
Abbey St
  Bath BA1..........228 C2
  Crewkerne TA18..........224 C6
  Hinton St George TA17 ..195 C7
Abbey Trad Est BA21....218 D6
Abbey View
  Bath BA2..........45 B5
  Radstock BA3..........79 A3
Abbey View Gdns BA2 ..45 B5
Abbeywood Dr BS9......5 C5
Abbot Alphege Acad
  Bath BA1..........27 E4
  Charlcombe BA1..........27 D4
Abbotsbury Rd BS48....8 D1
Abbots Cl
  Bristol BS14..........23 A3

Abbots Cl continued
  Burnham-on-S TA8 ....104 B6
  Ilminster TA19..........221 B3
  Oxenpill BA6..........138 C4
  Seavington St Michael TA19 .184 E2
Abbot's Cl BS22..........32 A3
Abbots Ct BA6..........206 D4
Abbotsfield TA4..........210 A4
Abbotsfield Cotts TA4 ..210 B4
Abbots Fish House * BA6 .138 D4
Abbots Horn BS48..........8 D2
ABBOTS LEIGH..........11 A8
Abbots Leigh Rd BS8 ....11 C7
Abbots Meade BA21....218 D5
Abbots Way
  Minehead TA24..........200 C6
  Pilton BA4..........140 E3
  Sherborne DT9..........225 B3
  Yeovil BA21..........218 D6
Abbotswood Cl BS31 ....24 D3
Abbott La TA16..........196 A8
Abbotts Farm Cl BS39 ..77 D5
Abbotts Rd BA22..........173 D1
Abbotts Way TA3..........183 F7
Abbott's Wootton La DT6 .199 B1
Ableake La DT9..........187 F5
Aberdeen Rd BS6..........226 B4
Abingdon Gdns BA2......62 D8
Abingdon St TA8..........104 B4
Abington Cross TA24....124 B4
Ablake La TA10..........172 C5
Ableton Wlk BS9..........5 C5
Abon Ho BS9..........5 C4
Abrahams Cl BS4..........22 F7
Acacia Ave BS23..........49 B8
Acacia Ct BS31..........24 C4
Acacia Dr BA11..........120 C7
Acacia Gdns TA2..........213 E7
Acacia Gr BA2..........44 C3
Acacia Rd BA3..........78 E1
Acacia Walk TA6..........208 E1
Accommodation Rd BS24 ..66 E6
Acer Dr BA21..........218 C7
Acer Village BS14..........23 C7
Achilles Path BS23..........48 E4
Ackland's Dro TA10......155 F4
Acland Round TA4......167 E6
Acombe Cross TA3......191 E8
Aconite Cl BS22..........32 B5
Acorn Cl
  Frome BA11..........119 D5
  Highbridge TA9..........104 D4
Acorn Gr BS13..........21 E6

Acre Cotts TA21..........222 E6
Acre La TA11..........211 F4
Acreman Ct DT9..........225 C4
Acreman Pl DT9..........225 D3
Acreman St DT9..........225 D4
Acresbush Cl BS13..........22 A5
Acres Ct BA22..........197 F8
Acres The **1** TA12..........185 E6
Acretree Cl TA6..........208 E3
Actis Rd BA6..........206 E3
Adams Cl
  Highbridge TA9..........104 C2
  Peasedown St John BA2..79 D8
Adams Ct **5** BS8..........11 F6
ADAM'S GREEN..........197 D2
Adams Ho TA19..........221 B3
Adam's La TA5..........134 D6
Adams Mdw TA19..........221 A4
Adam St TA8..........104 B6
Adastral Rd BS24..........50 D4
ADBER..........187 F7
Adber Cl BA21..........219 E8
Adber Cross DT9..........187 F6
Adcombe Cl TA3..........181 D5
Adcombe Rd TA2..........213 B8
Adder La TA7..........169 F8
ADDERWELL..........120 A3
Adderwell BA11..........120 A3
Adderwell Cl BA11..........120 A3
Addicott Rd BS23..........48 E6
Addiscombe Rd
  Bristol BS14..........23 B5
  Weston-super-Mare BS23 ..48 E4
Addison Gr TA2..........212 E6
Addlewell La **11** BA20 ..219 B4
Adlams Central Pk BA6 ..206 B3
Admirals Cl
  Sherborne DT9..........225 E5
  Watchet TA23..........202 D6
Admirals Ct TA6..........208 F5
Admiral's Mead BA6....157 E4
Admiral's Wlk BS20........2 B5
Admiralty Way TA1......213 C5
ADSBOROUGH..........169 D8
Adsborough Hill TA2....169 D7
Adsborough La
  Adsborough TA2..........169 E8
  West Monkton TA2..........169 D7
ADSCOMBE..........152 A8
Adscombe Ave TA6......209 C6
Adscombe La TA5......134 A1
Aelfric Mdw BS20..........2 F4
Aesop Dr BS31..........24 C3

Aginhills Dr TA2 ....213 E8
Ainslie's Belvedere BA1 ..228 B4
Ainstey Dr BA22..........175 A4
Airey Hos TA13..........220 D1
Airoh End BS24..........49 B4
Airport Rd BS14..........23 A8
Airport Rdbt BS24..........49 E7
Airport View Cvn Pk BS24..49 D7
Aisecome Way BS22......49 C6
AISHOLT..........152 B6
Akeman Cl BA21..........218 D7
Akeman Way BS11..........4 C8
Alamein Rd TA23..........202 E6
Alard Rd BS4..........22 F7
Alastair Cl BA21..........218 F7
Alastair Dr BA21..........218 F7
Albany BS23..........30 F1
Albany Cl DT9..........225 E6
Albany Ct **6** BA1..........44 B6
Albany Rd BA2..........44 C6
Albemarle Rd TA1......212 F5
Albemarle Row **9** BS8.. 11 F6
Albert Ave
  Peasedown St John BA2....79 C7
  Weston-super-Mare BS23 ..48 E6
Albert Bldgs BA6..........206 D5
Albert Cl BA21..........218 E7
Albert Ct
  Bridgwater TA6..........208 E4
  16 Taunton TA1..........213 A4
  Weston-super-Mare BS23 ..48 E6
Albert Pl
  Bath BA2..........45 C1
  Portishead BS20..........2 D4
Albert Quadrant BS23 ..48 E8
Albert Rd
  Clevedon BS21..........6 C3
  Keynsham BS31..........24 E5
  Portishead BS20..........2 D5
  Weston-super-Mare BS23 ..48 E6
Albert Row DT9..........225 E4
Albert St TA6..........208 E4
Albert Terr BA2..........44 C6
Albion Bldgs BA1..........44 D7
Albion Cl TA6..........209 B5
Albion Pl
  16 Bristol BS2..........227 C3
  Frome BA11..........119 D3
Albion Rd BA22..........174 A2
Albion Terr
  Bath BA1..........228 A3
  Cheddar BS27..........90 B7
Alburys BS40..........35 D3

Alcina Way BS31..........24 C2
ALCOMBE
  Kingsdown..........29 F7
  Minehead..........201 A4
Alcombe Cross TA24 ....201 B5
Alcombe Rd TA24..........201 A5
Aldburgh Pl BA14..........83 F6
Alder Cl
  North Petherton TA6......153 F3
  Taunton TA1..........213 D1
  Williton TA4..........202 E3
Aldercombe Rd BS9......5 C8
Alder Ct BS14..........23 B5
Alderdown Cl BS11..........5 A8
Alder Gr
  Crewkerne TA18..........224 C7
  Yeovil BA20..........218 E2
Alderley Rd BA2..........44 B4
Alderney Rd TA6..........209 C3
Alder Terr BA3..........78 E2
Alder Way BA2..........62 D8
Alder Wlk BA11..........120 B7
Aldondale Gdns BA20 ..219 B3
ALDWICK..........54 D7
Aldwick Ave BS13..........22 C3
Aldwick La BS40..........54 C7
Aldwych Cl TA8..........104 C6
Alec Ricketts Cl BA2......43 F5
Alexander Bldgs **12** BA1 .. 28 B1
Alexander Cl TA3..........169 D5
Alexander Hall BA3..........64 C6
Alexander Ho **5** BS23 ..48 F4
Alexander Mews **5** BS23 ..48 E7
Alexander Pl BA3..........64 C6
Alexanders Cl BA6......138 C4
Alexander Way BS49 ....34 B7
Alexandra Ct BS21..........6 C4
Alexandra Gdns TA24....201 A6
Alexandra Mews TA24....201 A7
Alexandra Par BS23......48 E7
Alexandra Pk BS39..........77 E5
Alexandra Pl BA2..........45 C1
Alexandra Rd
  Bath BA2..........228 C1
  Bridgwater TA6..........208 E5
  Bristol, Highridge BS13 .....21 F7
  Clevedon BS21..........6 C4
  Frome BA11..........119 F4

Alexandra Rd *continued*
Minehead TA24. . . . .**201** A6
Wellington TA21. . . . .**222** D6
Yeovil BA21 . . . .**219** D6
Alexandra Terr BS39 . . . . .**77** E5
Alexevia Cvn Pk TA3. . . . .**169** C3
Aley TA5 . . . .**152** A8
Aley Rd TA5 . . . .**134** A1
ALFORD. **159** A3
Alford La BA4, BA7. . . . . .**159** B4
Alfords Ridge BA3. . . . . . .**117** A7
Alfoxton Rd TA6. . . . .**208** C4
Alfred Cres BA4. . . . .**205** B4
Alfred Ct ⁴ BS23. . . . . . .**48** E7
Alfred Hill BS2. . . . .**227** A4
Alfred Par BS2. . . . .**227** A4
Alfred Pl
BS1. . . . .**227** A1
Bristol BS2. . . . .**226** C4
Alfred St
Bath BA1 . . . .**228** B3
Taunton TA1 . . . .**213** B4
Wells BA5. . . . .**203** D3
Weston-super-Mare BS23 . .**48** E8
Alfred's Twr ★ BA10 . . . . .**161** C6
Alfred's Way BA9 . . . .**216** B3
Algar TA5 . . . .**203** B4
ALHAMPTON. **159** C6
Alice St BA11 . . . .**143** A6
Alison Gdns BS48 . . . .**19** A7
Allandale Ct TA8 . . . .**104** B8
Allandale Rd TA8. . . . .**104** A8
Allanmead Rd BS14 . . . . . .**23** B8
Allans Way BS24 . . . .**49** F7
Allen Dr BA4. . . . .**205** A6
Allen Rd TA6. . . . .**208** F1
Allens La
Shipham BS25 . . . .**70** F8
Wells BA5. . . . .**112** E1
Allenslade Flats TA4 . . . . .**210** C5
ALLER **171** D8
Aller BS24 . . . .**49** B2
Aller Dro
Aller TA10 . . . .**171** D8
Othery TA7. . . . .**155** C1
ALLERFORD
Porlock. **124** C4
Taunton **167** F4
Aller La TA4 . . . .**202** E1
Allermoor Dro BS28 . . . . .**138** B8
Aller Par BS24 . . . .**49** B2
Allerpark La TA24 . . . .**123** F3
Aller Rd TA10 . . . .**171** E7
Allerton Cres BS14. . . . . . .**23** B4
Allerton Gdns BS14. . . . . . .**23** B5
Allerton Rd
Bridgwater TA6 . . . .**209** B7
Bristol BS14. . . . .**23** B4
All Hallows Sch BA4. . . . . .**142** C6
Allingham Rd BA21. . . . . . .**219** C7
Allington Cl TA1 . . . .**213** E4
Allington Gdns BS48. . . . . .**18** C8
Allington Rd BS3. . . . .**226** C1
Allotment Dro
Combe St Nicholas TA20. . .**193** C5
Glastonbury BA16. . . . . . .**138** D1
Allotment La
Chard TA20. . . . .**223** C1
Keynsham BS31. . . . .**24** B2
Keynsham BS31. . . . .**24** B2
Allotment Rd BA22 . . . . . .**175** C3
ALLOWENSHAY. **195** A8
ALL SAINTS. **198** A4
All Saints CE Prim Sch
Axminster EX13 . . . .**198** A4
Dulverton TA22. . . . .**163** D6
Montacute TA15. . . . .**186** B3
All Saints East Clevedon CE
Prim Sch BS21 . . . .**6** F4
All Saints Ho BS2. . . . .**227** B4
All Saints La BS21. . . . .**6** F4
All Saints' La BS1 . . . .**227** A2
All Saints Pl BA2 . . . .**45** E4
All Saints Rd BA1. . . . .**228** B4
All Saints' Rd
Bristol BS8. . . . .**226** A4
Weston-super-Mare BS23 . .**30** E1
All Saints' St BS1. . . . .**227** A3
All Saints' Terr TA6. . . . . .**209** B4
Allshire La EX16. . . . .**162** F3
Allyn Saxon Dr BA4. . . . . .**205** D5
Alma Field BA7 . . . .**214** B4
Alma Rd BS8. . . . .**226** B4
Alma Road Ave BS8 . . . . . .**226** B4
Alma St
Taunton TA1. . . . .**213** A3
Weston-super-Mare BS23 . . .**48** E7
Alma Vale Rd BS8 . . . .**226** A4
Almond Cl BS22. . . . .**32** A1
Almond Tree Cl TA6. . . . . .**209** D4
Almond Wlk BS13 . . . .**22** B6
Almsford Cl BA7 . . . .**214** B6
Almshouse La BA22 . . . . . .**173** E1
Almshouses
Donyatt TA19 . . . .**183** D1
Marshfield SN14 . . . .**13** E8
Almyr Terr TA23 . . . .**202** C7
Alpha Cotts TA2. . . . .**168** E8
Alpha Ho TA1 . . . .**104** E3
Alpine Cl BS39 . . . .**77** F4
Alpine Gdns BA1 . . . .**228** C4
Alpine Rd BS39 . . . .**77** F4
ALSTON **198** A5
Alston Cl TA1. . . . .**212** C1
Alstone Gdns TA9 . . . .**104** C2

Alstone La TA9. . . . .**104** C2
Alstone Rd TA9 . . . .**104** C2
Alstone Wildlife Pk ★ TA9 .**104** C3
ALSTON SUTTON. **88** B3
Alston Sutton Rd BS26. . . . .**88** F4
Alton Pl BA2 . . . .**228** C1
Alun Rees Way TA20 . . . . .**223** B3
Alverstoke BS14 . . . .**22** F7
Alveston Wlk BS9 . . . .**5** B7
ALVINGTON. **218** B4
Alvington Fields BA22 . . . .**218** B4
Alvington La BA22. . . . . . .**218** B5
ALWESTON. **189** A1
Alweston DT9. . . . .**189** A1
Ambares Ct BA3 . . . .**96** F8
Amber Cl TA7. . . . .**209** C8
Amberd La BA3. . . . .**181** D8
Amberey Rd BS23 . . . .**48** F5
Amberlands Cl BS48. . . . . . .**19** A7
Amberley Cl
Keinton Mandeville TA11 . .**158** A1
Keynsham BS31. . . . .**24** E4
Amberley Gdns ³ BS48. . . . .**8** D1
Amber Mead TA1 . . . .**213** D3
Ambleside Rd BA2 . . . .**44** C2
Ambra Ct BS8. . . . .**226** A2
Ambra Terr BS8. . . . .**226** A2
Ambra Vale BS8. . . . .**226** A2
Ambra Vale E BS8. . . . .**226** A2
Ambra Vale S ⁵ BS8 . . . . . .**226** A2
Ambra Vale W BS8. . . . . . .**226** A2
Ambridge BA16. . . . .**207** B4
Ambrose Cl DT9. . . . .**187** E1
Ambrose Rd BS8 . . . .**226** A2
Ambury BA1 . . . .**228** B1
Amercombe Wlk BS14. . . . .**23** D7
American Mus in Britain ★
BA2. . . . .**46** A5
Amery La BA1. . . . .**228** C2
AMESBURY. **59** F2
Amesbury Dr BS24 . . . .**67** B6
Ames La BS3. . . . .**98** B6
Ammerdown Terr BA3. . . . .**98** F7
AMMERHAM. **199** A8
Ammerham La TA20 . . . . . .**199** A8
Amor Pl TA1 . . . .**212** D2
Amors Dro DT9 . . . .**225** B4
Amory Rd TA22 . . . .**163** D6
Amulet Way BA4. . . . .**205** E4
Ancastle Ave BA7. . . . .**214** D6
Ancastle Terr BA7. . . . .**214** C6
Anchorage The BS20. . . . . . .**2** E6
Anchor Barton BA12. . . . . .**144** D3
Anchor Cl BA3 . . . .**116** E8
Anchor Cnr BA9. . . . .**176** D6
Anchor Hill BA9. . . . .**176** D6
Anchor La BA2. . . . .**62** D5
Anchor Rd
Bath BA1 . . . .**27** B1
Bristol BS1. . . . .**226** C2
Coleford BA3 . . . .**116** E8
Anchor Sq BS1. . . . .**226** C2
Anchor St TA23 . . . .**202** C7
Anchor Stables TA24 . . . . .**123** E4
Anchor Way BS20 . . . .**4** D4
Ancliff Sq BA15 . . . .**64** E4
Andalusia Acad BS2. . . . . .**227** C3
Andereach Cl BS14. . . . .**23** B8
Andersea Rd TA7. . . . .**154** D4
ANDERSFIELD. **153** B5
Andersfield Cl TA6. . . . . . .**208** A4
Andersfield Rd TA5 . . . . . .**153** A5
Ander's La TA3. . . . .**192** B8
Andrew Allan Rd TA21. . . .**222** B4
Andrew's Hill TA22 . . . . . .**163** D6
Andrew's Hill Cross TA22 .**163** C6
Andruss Dr BS41. . . . .**21** D2
Angela Cl TA1. . . . .**212** D2
Angel Cres TA6 . . . .**208** F5
Angelica Dr TA6 . . . .**208** E1
Angel La BA9 . . . .**216** C4
Angel Place Sh Ctr ⁶
TA6. . . . .**208** F5
Angel Row TA3 . . . .**170** F2
ANGERSLEIGH. **181** C5
Anglesey Cotts DT10 . . . . .**190** B4
Anglo Ct TA18 . . . .**224** C6
Anglo Terr BA1 . . . .**228** C4
Anglo Trad Est The BA4 . . .**205** B6
Angoni Pl TA6 . . . .**209** B6
Angus Way ¹² TA6. . . . . . .**154** A5
Angwin Cl BA4. . . . .**205** B6

Aplins Cl TA19 . . . .**221** B3
Aplins La TA20 . . . .**182** A1
Apple Alley BA1. . . . .**119** F5
Apple Bsns Ctr The TA2 . . .**212** B6
Appleby Wlk BS4. . . . .**22** D7
Apple Cl TA19. . . . .**194** E7
Applecroft BA2 . . . .**79** E6
APPLEDORE. **179** A1
Appledore ⁴ BS22. . . . .**31** F2
Appledore Cl BS14 . . . .**23** B8
Appledore Dr ⁹ TA6 . . . . .**209** B4
Apple Dumpling Cnr
BS28. . . . .**108** C3
Apple Farm La BA22 . . . . . .**32** B1
Applefield Rd DT8. . . . . . .**199** F8
Applehayes La EX15. . . . . .**180** F2
Applehayes Rise BS20 . . . . .**4** B3
Apple La BA11 . . . .**119** F5
Apple Tree Cl TA6. . . . .**209** D4
Appletree Ct BS22. . . . .**32** B2
Apple Tree Dr BS25 . . . .**70** A8
Appletree Mews BA22 . . . . .**32** B2
APPLEY. **179** B8
Appley Cross TA21 . . . .**179** B7
Appsley Cl BS22. . . . .**31** C1
Apricot Tree Cl TA6 . . . . . .**209** D5
Apsley Rd BA1. . . . .**44** A7
Aquara Cl BA16 . . . .**207** C3
Arbutus Dr BS9 . . . .**5** C8
Arcade The BS1. . . . .**227** B3
Appley Cross TA21 . . . .**179** B7
Arcadia TA16 . . . .**24** F8
Archbishop Cranmer CE Com
Prim Sch
¹⁸ Holway TA1 . . . .**213** A4
Taunton TA1 . . . .**213** A4
Arch Cl BS41. . . . .**10** F1
Archer Ct BS21. . . . .**6** D4
Archer Dr TA8 . . . .**104** C6
Archers Grove TA4. . . . . . .**150** E7
Archer Way The BA6 . . . . .**206** E5
Archer Wlk BS14 . . . .**23** E6
Arches The BA2. . . . .**44** A6
Archgrove BS41. . . . .**10** F1
Arch La TA3 . . . .**170** E4
Archstone Ave TA5 . . . .**135** F2
Archway St BA2. . . . .**45** B5
Arden Cl BS22 . . . .**31** F3
Ardern Cl BS9. . . . .**5** B8
Ardmore BS8 . . . .**11** D7
Ardwyn TA21. . . . .**222** D4
Arena The BA20 . . . .**219** A4
Argentia Pl BS20 . . . .**2** F7
Argyle Ave BS23 . . . .**48** F4
Argyle Pl BS8 . . . .**226** A2
Argyle Rd
Bristol BS2. . . . .**227** B4
Clevedon BS21. . . . .**6** D6
Argyle St BA2. . . . .**228** C2
Argyle Terr BA2. . . . .**44** C6
Arlington Cl
Bridgwater TA6 . . . .**209** A2
Yeovil BA21 . . . .**218** C7
Arlington Ho ⁴ BA1. . . . . .**228** C2
Arlington Mans BS8 . . . . . .**226** B4
Arlington Rd ⁴ BA2. . . . . . .**44** D5
Arlington Villas BS8. . . . . .**226** B3
Armada Ho BS2 . . . .**227** A4
Armada Pl BS1. . . . .**227** B4
Armada Rd BS14 . . . .**23** A6
Armes Ct BA2. . . . .**228** C1
Armoor Lane TA22 . . . .**148** A4
Armoury Rd BA22. . . . .**218** A6
Armoury The BA6. . . . .**206** D4
Armstrong Rd BA11. . . . . .**120** B5
Armtech Row BA22. . . . . . .**218** B6
Arnewood Gdns BA20 . . . . .**218** F2
Arnold Cl TA2. . . . .**212** F7
Arnold Noad Cnr BA14. . . . .**83** E3
Arnold's Way BS49 . . . .**17** A2
Arnolfini (Arts Ctr) ★ BS1 .**227** A1
Arnor Cl BS22. . . . .**32** A4
Arrowfield Cl BS14. . . . . . .**23** A2
Artemesia Ave BS22. . . . . . .**49** E8
Arthurs Point Dr BS3. . . . .**203** A5
Arthurswood Rd BS13. . . . .**22** A4
Artillery Rd BA22. . . . .**218** A6
Arundel Cl BS13. . . . .**22** B5
Arundell Rd BS23. . . . .**48** E8
Arundell Rd BS23 . . . .**30** E1
Arundells Way TA3. . . . . . .**169** D4
Arundel Rd
Bath BA1 . . . .**28** A1
Clevedon BS21. . . . .**6** D3
Yeovil BA21 . . . .**219** E6
Arundel Wlk BS31. . . . .**24** D5
Arun Gr TA1 . . . .**213** D4
Ascension Ho BA2. . . . .**44** D4
ASH
Martock **185** F7
Taunton **169** E1
ASHBEER. **150** C6
Ashbeer Hill TA4 . . . .**150** D7
Ashbourne Cres TA1 . . . . .**213** D3
ASHBRITTLE. **178** F8
Ash Brook BS39 . . . .**59** D1
Ashbrooke House Sch
BS23. . . . .**48** D6
Ashbury Dr BS22 . . . .**31** B2
Ashby Pl BA7 . . . .**214** C5
Ash CE Prim Sch TA12 . . . .**185** F7
Ash Cl
Bridgwater TA6 . . . .**209** D4
Wells BA5. . . . .**203** D5
Weston-super-Mare BS22 . .**32** D2
Winscombe BS25. . . . .**52** A1
Ashcombe Ct
Ilminster TA19 . . . .**221** B4
¹ Weston-super-Mare BS23 .**48** F7

Ashcombe Gdns BS23 . . . . .**49** A8
Ashcombe La
Alweston DT9. . . . .**189** B2
Ilminster TA19 . . . .**221** B4
Ashcombe Park Rd BS23. . . .**31** A1
Ashcombe Pl ⁴ BS23. . . . . .**48** F7
Ashcombe Prim Sch BS23 . .**49** A7
Ashcombe Rd BS23. . . . . . .**48** F7
ASHCOTT. **156** B8
Ashcott BS14 . . . .**22** F7
Ashcott Cl TA8 . . . .**104** C6
Ashcott Pl TA8. . . . .**104** C6
Ashcott Prim Sch TA7. . . . .**156** B8
Ashcott Rd BA6 . . . .**138** D3
Ash Cres TA1 . . . .**212** B2
Ashcroft
Chard TA20. . . . .**223** D2
Weston-super-Mare BS24 . .**49** B2
Ash Croft TA12. . . . .**185** F7
Ashcroft Ave BS31. . . . .**24** D5
Ashcroft Rd BS9. . . . .**5** C7
Ash Cross TA3 . . . .**169** E2
Ash Ct BS14. . . . .**23** A6
ASHCULME. **180** C1
Ashculme Hill EX15 . . . . . .**180** C2
Ashdene Rd BS23 . . . .**49** A8
Ashdown Ct BS9 . . . .**5** F8
Ashdown Rd BS20. . . . .**2** A6
Ashel's Batch BA3. . . . .**94** C8
Ashen Cross TA11 . . . .**211** E2
Ashen Cross Rd TA11. . . . .**211** F2
Ash End BA8. . . . .**189** F7
Asher La BA2 . . . .**227** C3
Ashes La BA3 . . . .**64** A4
Ashey La
Burrington BS40. . . . .**54** A5
Cheddar BS27 . . . .**90** B8
Ashfield TA20. . . . .**223** D2
Ashfield Cl BA11 . . . .**143** C6
Ashfield Pk ²³ TA12 . . . . . .**185** E6
Ashford Cl
Bridgwater TA6 . . . .**208** E2
Milverton TA4. . . . .**167** A4
Ashford Dr BS24. . . . .**49** A1
Ashford Gr BA21 . . . .**219** B7
Ashford La TA19 . . . .**183** F5
Ashford Rd
Bath BA2 . . . .**44** D4
Redhill BS40. . . . .**36** E4
Taunton TA1 . . . .**212** C2
Wellington TA21 . . . .**222** D4
Ash Gr
Bath BA2 . . . .**44** C4
Chard TA20. . . . .**223** C5
Clevedon BS21. . . . .**6** E4
Minehead TA24. . . . .**200** D7
Shepton Mallet BA4 . . . . .**205** C4
Wells BA5. . . . .**203** D5
Weston-super-Mare BS23 . .**48** E2
ASHGROVE. **79** D8
Ashgrove BA2 . . . .**79** D8
Ashgrove Ave BS8. . . . .**11** B7
Ashgrove Ct BA2. . . . .**79** D8
Ash Grove Way TA6 . . . . . .**209** D7
Ash Hay Dro BA5 . . . .**139** C6
Ash Hayes Dr BS48 . . . .**8** E1
Ash Hayes Rd BS48 . . . .**8** F1
Ash Ho TA8. . . . .**65** F2
ASHILL. **183** B4
Ashill Cl TA1. . . . .**212** C1
Ashill Com Prim Sch
TA19 . . . .**183** C4
ASHINGTON. **187** B8
Ashington La BA21. . . . . . .**187** B7
Ash La
Shepton Beauchamp TA19 .**184** E4
Wells BA5. . . . .**203** C5
Winsford TA24. . . . .**147** B6
Ashland Cl TA18. . . . .**224** C7
Ashland La TA4 . . . .**150** B4
Ashland Rd BS13 . . . .**22** A4
Ashlands CE Fst Sch
TA18 . . . .**224** C7
Ashlands Cl TA18. . . . .**224** C7
Ashlands Mdw TA18 . . . . .**224** C8
Ashlands Rd TA18 . . . .**224** D7
Ashlea BA7 . . . .**214** B6
Ashlea Pk TA9 . . . .**136** E8
Ashleigh Ave TA6 . . . .**209** A3
Ashleigh Cl
Paulton BS39 . . . .**77** E6
Weston-super-Mare BS23 . .**49** A8
Ashleigh Cres BS49 . . . .**34** B8
Ashleigh Gdns TA1 . . . . . .**212** E5
Ashleigh Rd
Weston-super-Mare BS23 . .**49** A8
Yatton BS49 . . . .**34** B8
Ashleigh Terr TA6. . . . .**209** A3
Ashley Ave
Bath BA1 . . . .**44** C7
Burnham-on-S TA8 . . . . . .**104** B6
Ashley Cl BS25 . . . .**70** A7
Ashley Green BA15 . . . .**46** F1
Ashley La BA15. . . . .**64** F7
Ashley Rd
Bathford BA1 . . . .**29** E3
Clevedon BS21. . . . .**6** B1
Taunton TA1 . . . .**212** D3
Ashley Terr ¹ BA1 . . . .**44** C7
Ashmans Ct BA1 . . . .**44** B6
Ashmans Gate BS39 . . . .**77** E5
Ashmans Yd BA1 . . . .**44** B6
Ashman Way TA6 . . . .**208** D4
Ashmead
Temple Cloud BS39. . . . . . .**58** E1
Yeovil BA20 . . . .**218** C2
Ashmead Rd BS31. . . . .**25** B5

Ashmead Road Ind Est
BS31. . . . .**25** B5
Ashmead Way ⁸ BS1. . . . . .**11** F5
Ashmoor Dro BA5. . . . .**139** C6
ASH PRIORS. **167** C8
Ash Rd
Banwell BS29 . . . .**50** E4
Street BA16 . . . .**207** B3
ASHTON. **107** C6
Ashton Ave BS1. . . . .**226** A1
Ashton Cl
Ashill TA19 . . . .**183** C4
Clevedon BS21. . . . .**6** B1
Ashton Court Estate ★
BS41. . . . .**11** C4
Ashton Cres BS48 . . . .**8** D1
Ashton Ct TA1 . . . .**212** C1
Ashton Dr BS3 . . . .**11** F2
Ashton Farm La TA9 . . . . .**136** D7
ASHTON GATE. **11** F4
Ashton Gate Prim Sch BS3. .**11** F4
Ashton Gate Stadium (Bristol
City FC) ★ BS3 . . . .**11** F3
Ashton Gate Trad Est BS3 . .**11** E3
Ashton Gate Underpass
BS3. . . . .**11** F3
Ashton Hill
Burnett BA2 . . . .**42** E8
Corston BA2. . . . .**43** A7
Ashton Park Sec Sch BS3 . . .**11** E3
Ashton Pk BA11. . . . .**119** E2
Ashton Rd
Bridgwater TA6 . . . .**208** F2
Bristol BS3. . . . .**11** D2
Bristol, Ashton Gate BS3 . . .**11** F4
Bristol, Bower Ashton BS3 . .**11** D3
Ashton Rise BS3 . . . .**11** F2
ASHTON VALE. **11** F2
Ashton Vale Prim Sch BS3. . .**11** F2
Ashton Vale Rd BS3 . . . .**11** E3
Ashton Vale Trad Est BS3. . .**11** F1
Ashton Way BS31 . . . .**24** E6
Ashton Windmill ★ BS28 . . .**88** E1
Ashtown Cross EX16. . . . . .**164** A3
Ash Tree Cl
Bleadon BS24. . . . .**67** C6
Burnham-on-S TA8 . . . .**85** A3
Ash Tree Cres TA8 . . . .**85** A3
Ash Tree Ct BA3. . . . .**78** E1
Ash Tree Pl TA8. . . . .**85** A3
Ashtree Rd BA11. . . . .**120** A6
Ash Tree Rd TA8 . . . .**85** A3
Ash Trees TA9 . . . .**86** C5
Ashvale Cl BS48 . . . .**9** A2
ASHWELL. **221** C6
Ashwell Bsns Pk TA19. . . . .**221** C7
Ashwell Cl BS14. . . . .**23** E6
Ashwell La
Glastonbury BA6 . . . .**139** D1
Wheddon Cross TA24 . . . . .**129** F2
ASHWICK. **115** B5
Ashwicke BS14 . . . .**23** A6
Ash Wlk BA8. . . . .**190** A6
Ashwood BS40. . . . .**74** F4
Ashwood Dr BA21 . . . .**219** B8
Askwith Cl DT9 . . . .**225** B3
ASNEY. **156** E7
Asney Rd BA16. . . . .**156** E7
Aspen Cl BA11 . . . .**120** B7
Aspen Ct TA6 . . . .**208** E4
Aspen Park Rd BS22 . . . .**49** E8
Aspen Way TA18 . . . .**224** D7
Aspin Cl TA21. . . . .**222** F6
Aspin Rd
Wellington TA21. . . . .**222** F6
Wellington TA21. . . . .**222** F6
Aspley Cl BA1. . . . .**44** B7
Asquith St TA2 . . . .**212** E6
Assembly Rooms La BS1. . .**227** A2
Astazou Dr BS24 . . . .**49** B4
Aster Cl TA6 . . . .**208** D1
Aston Ho ⁴ BS1. . . . .**227** B1
Athelney Way BA21. . . . . . .**218** D6
ATHERSTONE. **184** C3
Athlone Rd TA6. . . . .**209** A2
Atholl Cl BS22 . . . .**31** F3
Atkins Cl BS14. . . . .**23** E6
Atkin's Gate TA13 . . . .**220** D6
Atkins Hill BA9. . . . .**216** A3
Atlanta Key TA8 . . . .**104** A8
Atlantic Cres TA8 . . . .**104** B5
Atlantic Rd
Bristol BS11. . . . .**4** C8
Weston-super-Mare BS23 . .**30** C1
Atlantic Rd S BS23 . . . .**30** C1
Atlantic View BS23 . . . .**30** C1
Atlantic View Ct BS23. . . . . .**30** C1
Atlantic Way BA22. . . . . . .**174** A2
Atlay Ct BS49 . . . .**17** B1
Atrium The BS1. . . . .**227** B2
Attewell Ct BA2. . . . .**44** F4
Attisham La DT6. . . . .**199** D4
Atyeo Cl
Bristol BS3. . . . .**11** E1
Burnham-on-S TA8 . . . . . .**104** C6
Aubrey Meads BS30 . . . .**25** E8
Auckland Cl
Wells BA5. . . . .**203** C2
Weston-super-Mare BS23 . .**48** F3
Auckland Way TA20 . . . . . .**223** D3
Audley Ave BA1 . . . .**44** D7
Audley Cl
Bath BA1 . . . .**44** D7
Nether Stowey TA5. . . . . .**134** A2
Audley Gr BA1 . . . .**44** D7
Audley Lodge BA1. . . . .**44** D7
Audley Park Rd BA1 . . . .**44** D7
Augusta Pl BA1 . . . .**44** D7
Augustine's Cl BS20. . . . .**1** E4
Augustus Ave BS31. . . . .**24** F7

Aurelius Cl BS31 . . . . .24 F8
Austen Dr BS22 . . . . .32 B4
Austen Pl BS11. . . . . .4 E7
Austin Cl BA11. . . . . .119 F7
Austin Rd BA6 . . . . .206 E6
Austin Mews BS24 . . . . .50 A8
Autumn La TA6 . . . . .208 D3
Autumn Rd BS24 . . . . .50 A8
Avalon Bldgs BA6. . . . . . . .206 D5
Avalon Cl BS49. . . . . .17 A1
Avalon Est BA6. . . . . .206 E7
Avalon Ho BS48 . . . . .8 C1
Avalon Mews BA6 . . . . . . .206 E4
Avalon Pk TA11 . . . . .211 B5
Avalon Rd
  Bridgwater TA6 . . . . .209 D5
  Highbridge TA9. . . . . .104 E4
Avalon Sch BA16 . . . . .207 B3
Avalon Vineyard BA4 . . . . .158 E8
Avebury Cl TA8 . . . . .104 D8
Avebury Dr TA6 . . . . .209 D5
Avebury Rd BS3. . . . . .11 F2
Aveline Ct TA4 . . . . .167 F6
Avening Cl BS48 . . . . .19 A3
Avenue Pl BA2. . . . . .45 B1
Avenue Rd BA11 . . . . .120 A4
Avenue The
  Backwell BS48 . . . . .19 A7
  Bath, Bushey Norwood BA2 . . .45 E5
  Bath, Combe Down BA2 . . . .45 C1
  Bicknoller TA4 . . . . .132 F4
  3 Bridgwater TA6 . . . . . . .208 F5
  Bristol, Sneyd Park BS9 . . . . .5 E3
  Chard TA20. . . . . .193 F7
  Clevedon BS21. . . . . .6 E6
  Keynsham BS31 . . . . .24 E6
  Kingsbury Episcopi TA12. . . .185 B8
  Langport TA10 . . . . .172 A4
  Minehead TA24. . . . . .201 A7
  Misterton TA18. . . . . .224 F3
  Sherborne DT9. . . . . .225 E5
  Sparkford BA22 . . . . .175 A5
  Stoke sub Hamdon TA14 . . . .185 F4
  Taunton TA1. . . . . .212 E5
  Timsbury BA2. . . . . .60 B2
  Weston-super-Mare BS22 . . .32 C3
  Wincanton BA9 . . . . .216 D3
  Winscombe BS25 . . . . .70 C8
  Yatton BS49 . . . . .34 B8
  Yeovil BA21 . . . . .219 B5
Averill Ct BS21. . . . . .6 D4
Avill Cres TA1. . . . . .213 C4
Avishayes Prim Sch TA20. . .223 E5
Avishayes Rd TA20 . . . . . . .223 E4
Avocet Dr BA22 . . . . .218 A6
Avonbank Ind Est BS11. . . . . .4 B7
Avonbridge Trad Est BS11. . .4 C8
Avon Cl
  Keynsham BS31 . . . . .24 F6
  Taunton TA1. . . . . .212 D2
  Weston-super-Mare BS23 . . .48 F2
  Yeovil BA21 . . . . .219 D6
AVONCLIFF 64 F4
Avoncliff Halt BA15. . . . . . . .64 F5
Avon Cres BS1 . . . . .226 A1
Avon Ct BA1 . . . . .29 A4
Avondale Bldgs BA1. . . . . . . .28 B2
Avondale Ct
  Bath BA1 . . . . .44 B7
  Bristol, Sneyd Park BS9 . . . . .5 D3
Avondale Ho
  Bath BA2 . . . . .44 B5
  Bridgwater TA6 . . . . .209 A2
Avondale Rd BA1. . . . . .44 B6
Avondowns Ct BS8 . . . . . . .226 A4
Avon Gorge Ind Est BS11. . . .4 C7
Avon Gorge Nature Reserve ★
  BS8 . . . . .11 E7
Avon Gr BS9 . . . . .5 D2
Avon Hts BA3 . . . . .64 C6
Avon La BS31 . . . . .25 F5
Avonleaze BS9. . . . . .5 B5
Avon Livestock Ctr BS40 . . . .38 B6
Avon Mill La BS31 . . . . .24 F6
AVONMOUTH 4 B8
Avonmouth CE Prim Sch
  BS11. . . . . .4 C8
Avonmouth Dock BS11 . . . . . .4 A8
Avonmouth Rd BS11. . . . . . . .4 C8
Avon Pk BA1. . . . . .44 A7
Avon Prim Sch BS11. . . . . . . .4 D8
Avon Rd
  Bristol BS13. . . . . .22 A6
  Keynsham BS31 . . . . .24 F5
  Pill BS20. . . . . .4 C5
Avon Riverside Est BS11 . . . . .4 B7
Avon Riverside Sta ★ BS30. .25 E6
Avon Ski & Action Centre ★
  BS25. . . . . .52 C3
Avon & Somerset Pol HQ
  BS20. . . . . .1 F3
Avon St
  Bath BA1 . . . . .228 B2
  Bristol BS2. . . . . .227 C2
Avon Vale BS9 . . . . .5 D4
Avonvale Pl BA1 . . . . .28 F3
Avon Valley Adventure &
  Wildlife Pk ★ BS31. . . . . . .25 D6
Avon Valley Rly ★ BS30. . . . .25 D7
Avon Way
  Bristol, Sneyd Park BS9 . . . . .5 C4
  Portishead BS20 . . . . .2 C5
Avonwood Cl BS11. . . . . .4 E6
Awkward Hill BS40. . . . . .55 D5
AXBRIDGE 70 B1
Axbridge Bypass BS26 . . . . .70 A3
Axbridge CE Fst Sch
  BS26. . . . . .70 C1

Axbridge Cl
  Burnham-on-S TA8 . . . . . . .104 C8
  Nailsea BS48 . . . . .18 E8
Axbridge & District Mus ★
  BS26. . . . . .70 C2
Axbridge Moor Dro BS26 . . .70 C1
Axbridge Rd
  Bath BA2 . . . . .45 A2
  Cheddar BS27 . . . . .70 F2
Axe Cl BS23. . . . . .49 A5
Axeford TA20 . . . . .198 E8
Axeford Mdws TA20 . . . . . .198 E8
Axe La
  Clapton DT8 . . . . .195 C1
  Drimpton DT8. . . . . .199 F8
Axe Rd
  Bridgwater TA6 . . . . .209 B3
  Wookey BA5. . . . . .139 D8
Axe Valley Com Coll The
  EX13. . . . . .198 A1
Axford Way BA2. . . . . .79 D8
Axis BS14. . . . . .22 D5
AXMINSTER 198 B2
Axminster Com Prim Sch
  EX13. . . . . .198 A1
Axminster Rd TA20 . . . . . . .198 C7
Ayckbourn Cl TA8 . . . . .104 C6
Aycote Cl BS22. . . . . .31 C2
Ayford La SN14 . . . . .13 F4
Aylands Rd TA1. . . . . .212 D3
Aylmer Cres BS14 . . . . .23 B6
Ayr St BA2. . . . . .44 D6
AYSHFORD 178 E2
Azalea Dr TA6. . . . . .208 D1
Azalea Rd BS22 . . . . .32 A5
Azelin Ave BS13. . . . . .22 B5

B

BABCARY 174 C7
Babcary La BA22 . . . . .174 B8
Babcary Rd TA11 . . . . .174 C6
Babwell Rd BA9 . . . . .177 D6
Baby La TA12 . . . . .163 F7
Babylon Hill
  Sherborne DT9. . . . . .188 A3
  Yeovil BA21 . . . . .219 F4
Babylon View BA21. . . . . . . .219 F7
Backfields BS2. . . . . .227 B4
Backfields Ct BS2 . . . . .227 B4
Backfields La BS2 . . . . .227 B4
Back La
  Baltonsborough BA26 . . . . . .70 C2
  Baltonsborough BA6. . . . . .158 B5
  Batcombe BA4 . . . . .142 C2
  Bradford Abbas DT9. . . . . .187 F1
  Chapel Allerton BS26 . . . . . .88 D1
  Cheddar BS27 . . . . .90 A7
  Chewton Mendip BA3. . . . . .75 B1
  Curry Rivel TA10 . . . . .171 D3
  Draycott BS27 . . . . .90 F2
  East Chinnock BA22 . . . . . .196 E8
  East Coker BA22 . . . . .197 C7
  Halstock BA22 . . . . .197 C3
  Ilchester BA22 . . . . .173 E1
  Keynsham BS31 . . . . .24 E6
  Kingston Seymour BS21. . . . .16 A5
  Kington Magna SP8 . . . . . .177 E2
  Litton BA3 . . . . .75 E2
  Maiden Bradley BA12. . . . . .144 C2
  Marshfield SN14 . . . . .13 F8
  Martock TA12 . . . . .185 D4
  Middlezoy TA7. . . . . .155 B3
  Montacute TA15. . . . . .186 B3
  North Perrott TA18. . . . . . .196 C4
  Pill BS20. . . . . .4 C5
  Pilton BA4 . . . . .204 D3
  Rimpton BA22 . . . . .188 A8
  Rowberrow BS25 . . . . .53 A1
  Shepton Mallet, Darshill
    BA4. . . . . .204 F6
  Shepton Mallet, Downside
    BA4. . . . . .205 C8
  Sherborne DT9. . . . . .225 D4
  Stoney Stratton BA4. . . . . .141 F2
  Street BA16 . . . . .207 C6
  Street, Butleigh Wootton
    BA6. . . . . .207 A6
  Westbury-sub-Mendip BA5 . . .110 E6
  Whitelackington TA19. . . . . .221 F6
Backlane Dro BA6. . . . . .158 C5
Back Of Kingsdown Par
  BS6 . . . . .227 A4
Back River Dro BA16 . . . . . .138 F2
Back St
  Ash TA12 . . . . .186 A7
  Bampton EX16 . . . . .164 B1
  Bradford On Tone TA4. . . . . .167 F1
  Leighton BA11 . . . . .142 E6
  Long Sutton TA10 . . . . . . .172 E4
  Martock TA12 . . . . .185 F7
  West Camel BA22 . . . . . . .174 D3
  Winsham TA20 . . . . .194 E1
Back Stoke La BS9 . . . . .5 F6
Back Town BA6. . . . . .157 E4
Back Way TA4 . . . . .150 B8
Backways La TA21. . . . . .179 F6
BACKWELL. 19 B6
Backwell Bow BS48 . . . . .9 C1
Backwell CE Jun Sch BS48 . .19 C5
Backwell Comm 19 B8
BACKWELL COMMON 19 B8
BACKWELL GREEN 19 B6
Backwell Hill BS48. . . . . .19 B3
Backwell Hill Rd BS48 . . . . .19 E5
Backwell Sch BS48. . . . . .19 B6

Backwell Wlk BS13. . . . . .21 F8
Backy Hill BA2. . . . . .62 C4
Bacon Dr TA1. . . . . .213 D3
BADBURY 183 F7
Badcox BA11. . . . . .119 E4
Badenham Gr BS11. . . . . .4 E8
Baden Ho BA1 . . . . .228 B4
Badger Hts BA22 . . . . .218 B5
Badger Pk TA24 . . . . .201 C4
Badger Rise BS20 . . . . .1 F3
Badgers Cl
  Bourton SP8 . . . . .161 F1
  Street BA16 . . . . .207 A5
  Taunton TA1 . . . . .212 B3
Badger's Cross
  Oakhill BA3 . . . . .114 F5
  Somerton TA11 . . . . .211 C1
Badger's Cross La TA11. . . . .211 C2
Badgers Folly BA7 . . . . .214 B5
Badgers Green Rd BA6. . . . .207 A5
Badgers Hill BA11 . . . . .120 A5
Badgers Holt BS14 . . . . .23 C6
Badgers' La TA20 . . . . .223 E1
Badgers The BA22. . . . . .32 B3
BADGER STREET 182 B6
Badgers Way BS24 . . . . .49 F8
Badgers Wlk BS20. . . . . .4 B4
BADGWORTH 88 B6
Badgworth Barns BS26 . . . . .88 D5
Badgworth Ct BS26. . . . . .88 C5
Badgworth La BS26 . . . . .88 C4
Badlake La EX36 . . . . .162 D6
Badlake Moor Cross TA22 . .162 D7
Badman Cl BS39. . . . . .77 D5
Badminton Cl 17 BS23 . . . . .30 C1
Badminton Gdns BA1. . . . . . .44 C8
Bagber Cross Rds DT10 . . . .190 D3
Bagber Rd BA8. . . . . .190 C4
Bagborough Dr TA6 . . . . . . .208 F2
Bagborough La BA4 . . . . . . .141 C2
Bagborough Rd TA2. . . . . . .212 F7
Baggridge Hill BA2. . . . . .80 F7
Baggs La BS27 . . . . .90 F2
BAGLEY 109 A1
BAGLEY GREEN 222 A3
Bagley Rd TA21 . . . . .222 A3
Bagnell Cl BS14. . . . . .23 E5
Bagnell Rd BS14. . . . . .23 E5
BAILBROOK. 28 D3
Bailbrook Gr BA1 . . . . .28 C3
Bailbrook La BA1 . . . . .28 D3
Baildon Cres BS23 . . . . .49 A4
Baildon Ct 2 BS23 . . . . .48 F4
Baildon Rd BS23 . . . . .49 A4
Bailey Cl BS22 . . . . .49 E8
Bailey Ct BS20 . . . . .2 F6
Bailey Hill BA7. . . . . .214 C5
Baileys Gate TA4 . . . . .167 F6
Bailey's Knapp EX16 . . . . . .178 B4
Baileys La DT8 . . . . .196 C1
Bailey's La BA4 . . . . .142 B1
Bailey St TA6 . . . . .209 B5
Bailiffs Cl BS26 . . . . .70 C1
Bailiffs' Wall BS26 . . . . .70 B1
Baily Cl BA6 . . . . .206 E7
Bainley Rd BA9 . . . . .177 E6
Bainsbury View BA3. . . . . . . .96 F1
Bakehouse 1 TA16 . . . . . . .195 F7
Bakehouse La DT9 . . . . .187 E1
Bakelite Mus The ★ TA4 . . .202 C2
Baker Cl 8 BS21. . . . . .6 B1
Bakeries The TA11 . . . . .211 D3
Baker's Bldgs BS40. . . . . .35 D2
Bakers Cl TA1. . . . . .212 A3
Baker's Cross TA3. . . . . .191 D7
Bakers Ct TA13. . . . . .220 C4
Bakersfield TA20 . . . . .194 E1
Bakers La
  Churchinford TA3 . . . . .191 D7
  Shilstone EX35. . . . . .122 A3
  Wellington TA21 . . . . .222 E6
Bakers Orch TA4 . . . . .151 B5
Baker's Par BA2 . . . . .60 B2
Bakers Pk BS13 . . . . .22 B6
Baker St
  Babcary TA11 . . . . .174 C7
  Frome BA11. . . . . .119 E5
  Weston-super-Mare BS23 . . .48 E8
Bakery La BA4 . . . . .140 F3
Balch Rd BA5. . . . . .203 C4
Balcombe Rd TA6 . . . . .153 B1
Baldwin Rd TA1. . . . . .213 B5
Baldwins La TA9 . . . . .105 C3
Baldwin St BS1. . . . . .227 A2
Balidon Pl BA20. . . . . .218 D2
Ballance St BA1. . . . . .228 B4
Ballfield Rd TA24. . . . . .200 F8
Ballhill La EX16 . . . . .164 B1
Ball La
  Doulting BA4 . . . . .141 F7
  Isle Abbotts TA3. . . . . .183 E7
  Spaxton TA2 & TA5. . . . . . .152 B2
Balls Barn La BS24 . . . . .33 A2
Ball's Hill BA22, TA15. . . . . .186 C4
Ball's La TA5 . . . . .153 E4
Ball The
  Dunster TA24. . . . . .201 E2
  Minehead TA24. . . . . .200 F8
Balmoral Dr TA8 . . . . .85 B1
Balmoral Ho TA6. . . . . .209 C4
Balmoral Rd
  Keynsham BS31 . . . . .24 C4
  Yeovil BA21 . . . . .219 E6

Balmoral Way BS22. . . . . . . .31 D2
Balsam Cl BA9 . . . . .216 D3
Balsam Fields BA9 . . . . . . .216 D3
Balsam La BA9. . . . . .216 D3
Balsam Pk BA9. . . . . .216 C3
Baltic Pl BS20. . . . . .4 D4
BALTONSBOROUGH. 158 A6
Baltonsborough CE Prim Sch
  BA6. . . . . .158 A6
Baltonsborough CE VC Prim
  Sch BA6. . . . . .158 A6
Baltonsborough Rd BA6 . . .157 E4
Balustrade 17 BA1. . . . . .28 B1
Bamfield BS14 . . . . .23 A6
BAMPTON 164 C1
Bampton 5 BS22 . . . . .31 F2
Bampton Ave TA20 . . . . . . .223 B5
Bampton Cl BS13. . . . . .22 B7
Bampton Down Rd EX16 . . .178 A7
Bampton Prim Sch EX16. . . .164 B1
Bampton St TA24. . . . . .200 F6
Banbury La BA6. . . . . .157 E3
Bancks St TA24 . . . . .200 F7
Bancombe Rd TA11 . . . . . . .211 B5
Bancombe Rd TA11 . . . . . . .211 A4
Bancombe Rd Trading Estate
  TA11 . . . . .211 B5
Banfield Cl BS11. . . . . .5 A8
Bangers DT9. . . . . .188 F5
Bangrove Wlk BS11 . . . . .4 E8
Banister Gr BS4. . . . . .22 D7
Banking Ct 4 TA18. . . . . . .224 C6
Bankland La TA7 . . . . .154 B1
Bank Pl BS20. . . . . .4 D4
Banks Cl BS21 . . . . .16 D8
Bank Sq TA22 . . . . .163 D6
Bank St
  Highbridge TA9. . . . . .104 D3
  Williton TA4 . . . . .202 D2
Bannerdown Cl BA1 . . . . . . .29 A4
Bannerdown Dr BA1. . . . . . .29 A4
Bannerdown Rd BA1. . . . . . .29 C5
Bannerleigh La BS8 . . . . . . .11 E6
Bannerleigh Rd BS8. . . . . . .11 E6
Banneson Rd TA5 . . . . .134 B2
Bannock Cl BS4 . . . . .22 D6
Bantry Rd BS4 . . . . .22 E8
BANWELL 51 B3
Banwell Caves BS26 . . . . . . .50 E2
Banwell Cl
  Bristol BS13. . . . . .22 A8
  Keynsham BS31 . . . . .25 A2
  Taunton TA1. . . . . .213 D4
Banwell Prim Sch BS29. . . . .51 B3
Banwell Rd
  Banwell BS26, BS29. . . . . . .68 C8
  Bath BA2 . . . . .62 D8
  Locking BS24 . . . . .50 B3
  Winscombe BS25, BS29 . . . .69 E8
Banyard Rd BS20. . . . . .3 E5
Barbara Rd BA8. . . . . .176 D3
Barberry Dr
  Bridgwater TA6 . . . . .208 D1
  Chard TA20. . . . . .223 F5
Barberry Farm Rd BS49. . . .17 B1
Barber's La TA21 . . . . .180 F7
Barbers Mead TA2 . . . . .213 C2
Barbour Gdns BS13 . . . . . . .22 D3
Barbour Rd BS13 . . . . .22 D3
Barclay St TA6 . . . . .209 A5
Barcroft BA12. . . . . .144 B2
Barcroft Cres TA3 . . . . .170 A1
Barcroft La TA13 . . . . .220 B6
Bardel Ct BA22. . . . . .218 B6
Bardon La
  Williton TA4 . . . . .132 A3
  Williton TA4 . . . . .202 A2
BARE ASH 153 B6
Barford Cl TA5 . . . . .152 F7
Barford Rd TA5 . . . . .152 F7
Barham Ct BA22. . . . . .218 A5
Barhams Cl TA6. . . . . .209 A7
Barker Cl BS24. . . . . .32 C1
Barkham Cl BA5 . . . . .203 F5
Barlake La BA3 . . . . .115 F7
Barle Cl TA1. . . . . .213 D4
Barle Ent Ctr TA22 . . . . . . .163 D5
Barley Cl BA5 . . . . .203 C3
Barley Croft
  Bristol BS9. . . . . .5 F5
  Somerton TA11. . . . . .211 B3
Barley Cross BS22. . . . . .32 A5
Barley Wood Walled Garden ★
  BS40 . . . . .35 F3
Barlinch Cl TA2 . . . . .213 B7
Barlynch Ct BA21. . . . . .218 D6
Barnabas Cl BS26 . . . . .70 C2
Barnaby Cl BA3 . . . . .78 B2
Barnard Ave BA16 . . . . .207 B3
Barnard Ct BA5 . . . . .203 B4
Barnard's Cl BS49 . . . . .34 C7
Barnard Wlk BS31. . . . . .24 D4
Barn Cl
  Crewkerne TA18. . . . . .224 B5
  Frome BA11. . . . . .119 D3
  Nether Stowey TA5. . . . . . .134 B2
  Somerton TA11. . . . . .211 B3
  Street BA16 . . . . .207 C6
  Wiveliscombe TA4 . . . . . . .210 A7
Barnclose Rd TA22 . . . . . . .146 E4
Barn Cres TA18 . . . . .224 B5
Barn Ct BA21 . . . . .187 C5
Barn End BS40. . . . . .74 E3
Barnes Cl
  Castle Cary BA7. . . . . .214 C6
  Wells BA5. . . . . .203 B4
Barnes Close Mead TA22 .163 D6
Barnet Cl BA21. . . . . .218 E7

Barnetts Well BS27. . . . . . . .90 F2
Barnfield Way BA1 . . . . .29 B3
Barn Gn BA6. . . . . .206 E3
Barnhay 6 EX16 . . . . .164 B1
Barn Hill BA2 . . . . .79 F5
Barn La
  Clutton BS39. . . . . .59 A7
  Crewkerne TA18. . . . . .195 E6
  Riscombe TA24. . . . . .128 B2
Barn Meads Rd TA21 . . . . . .222 E4
Barn Orchard TA14. . . . . . . .185 E3
Barn Pool BS25 . . . . .70 F8
Barns Cl
  Barrow Gurney BS48 . . . . . .20 E4
  Nailsea BS48 . . . . .8 E2
Barnsclose TA22. . . . . .163 D6
Barnsclose N TA22 . . . . . . .163 D6
Barnsclose W TA22. . . . . . .163 D6
Barns Gd BS21 . . . . .16 E8
Barn St TA18. . . . . .224 B6
Barnstaple Ct BS4 . . . . .22 E8
Barnstaple Rd BS4 . . . . .22 E8
Barnstaple Wlk BS4 . . . . . . .22 F8
Barnsworthy Farm Rd
  TA5 . . . . .133 F4
Barnwood Ct BS48 . . . . .8 B1
Baron Cl BS30 . . . . .25 E8
Barons Cl BS3 . . . . .11 F3
Barossa Pl BS1. . . . . .227 A1
Barpark Cnr EX15. . . . . .180 E3
Barpool La TA11 . . . . .211 D6
BARR 168 B3
Barracks Cl BA22. . . . . .218 B7
Barrack's La BS11. . . . . .4 D8
BARREN DOWN 205 C6
Barrendown La BA4. . . . . . .205 C6
Barrie Way TA8 . . . . .104 C6
BARRINGTON 184 D5
Barrington Broadway
  TA10 . . . . .184 D6
Barrington Cl TA1. . . . . .212 C1
Barrington Court ★ TA19 . .184 D5
Barrington Court Cotts
  TA19 . . . . .184 D5
Barrington Hill TA19 . . . . . .183 A3
Barrington Hill National
  Nature Reserve ★ TA19. . .183 A4
Barrington Hill Rd TA19 . . . .182 F4
Barrington Main TA19 . . . . .184 E2
Barrington Pl BA4. . . . . .204 F5
Barrington Rd TA8 . . . . .104 C8
Barrington Wy TA21 . . . . . .222 B4
BARROW
  Wells 140 B4
  Wincanton 161 B3
BARROW COMMON 21 B4
Barrow Court La BS19 . . . . . .20 B5
Barrow Cswy BA5 . . . . .138 F8
Barrow Ct
  Barrow Gurney BS48 . . . . . .20 A5
  Tickenham BS21. . . . . .7 F4
Barrow Dr TA1. . . . . .213 E5
BARROW GURNEY 20 E5
Barrow Hill
  Stalbridge DT10. . . . . .190 B4
  Stourton Caundle DT10 . . . .189 F1
Barrow Hill Cres BS11. . . . . . .4 C7
Barrow Hill Rd BS11. . . . . . . .4 D6
Barrow Ho 25 BA4. . . . . . . .205 B6
Barrow La
  Charlton Musgrove BA9 . . . .161 B3
  North Wootton BA4 . . . . . . .140 B4
  Pilton BA4 . . . . .140 F3
  Winford BS40. . . . . .20 F1
Barrow Lea DT10. . . . . .190 B4
Barrowmead Dr BS11. . . . . . .4 F7
Barrow Pk BS27. . . . . .90 A8
Barrow Rd
  Bath BA2 . . . . .44 C1
  Hutton BS24. . . . . .49 E2
Barrows Cl TA6 . . . . .208 E2
Barrows Croft BS27. . . . . . . .90 A8
Barrows Ct BA22 . . . . .196 E8
Barrows La TA14 . . . . .185 E2
Barrows Rd BS27. . . . . .90 A8
Barrow St BS48 . . . . .20 D5
Barrows The
  Cheddar BS27 . . . . .90 A8
  Weston-super-Mare BS22 . . .49 C7
Barrow Stile BA4. . . . . .140 F3
BARROW VALE 59 D5
Barrow Water La BS41. . . . .161 A3
Barrow Wood La BS27. . . . .110 A7
Barrs Ct BS1 . . . . .227 B3
Barry Cl BS24. . . . . .49 A1
Barry La BA22. . . . . .196 F6
Barrymore Ct TA10 . . . . . . .172 A6
Barstable Ho BS2 . . . . .227 C3
Bartec 4 BA20. . . . . .218 C3
Bartholomew Row BA2 . . . . .60 B2
Bartlett Cl
  Frome BA11. . . . . .120 C6
  Taunton TA1. . . . . .212 B1
Bartlett Ct 1 TA18 . . . . . . .224 C6
Bartlett Ct BA20. . . . . .218 D3
Bartlett Mews BA21 . . . . . .219 F7
Bartlett Pk
  Chard TA20. . . . . .223 D3
  Yeovil BA20 . . . . .218 D3
Bartletts Ct BA2. . . . . .228 C1
Bartletts La TA4 . . . . .167 A4
Bartletts Pl BA21 . . . . .218 D5
Bartlett Sq BA7. . . . . .214 A7
Bartletts Row TA11. . . . . . .211 D4

Bartlett St **6** BA1 . . . . .228 B3
Bartletts Way BS24 . . . . . . .50 A4
BARTON 69 B6
Barton Cl
  Berrow TA8 . . . . .84 F5
  Taunton TA1 . . . . .212 D3
Barton Cross EX16 . . . . . .162 E5
Barton Dro BS25 . . . . .69 D5
Barton Gdns DT9 . . . . .225 B4
Barton Gn TA3 . . . . .168 D1
Barton Hey **2** TA4 . . . . . .167 F8
Barton Hill SP8 . . . . .177 E2
Barton La TA3 . . . . .169 C4
Barton Rd
  Barton St David TA11 . . . . .158 A2
  Berrow TA8 . . . . .84 F4
  Bristol BS2 . . . . .227 E3
  Butleigh BA6 . . . . .157 E3
  Minehead TA24 . . . . .201 B4
  Winscombe BS26 . . . . .69 C6
Barton Rise TA7 . . . . .137 B3
BARTON ST DAVID 158 A2
Barton St
  Bath BA1 . . . . .228 B2
  Bristol BS1 . . . . .227 A4
Bartons The
  Bishops Lydeard TA4 . . . . . .167 E8
  Ilchester BA22 . . . . .173 E1
  South Petherton TA13 . . . . .220 E3
Barton The
  Bleadon BS24 . . . . .67 C6
  Charlton Adam TA11 . . . . . .173 F7
  Corston BA2 . . . . .43 A7
  Huish Champflower TA4 . . . .165 E8
  Norton St Philip BA2 . . . . . . .81 E4
Barton Vale BS2 . . . . .227 C2
Barton Villas BA3 . . . . .116 F6
Barton Way TA3 . . . . .170 C4
Barton Wlk BA11 . . . . .119 D2
BARWICK 197 F8
Barwick Ho BS11 . . . . .4 E7
Barwick Stoford Com Prim
  Sch BA22 . . . . .197 F8
Barwick & Stoford Com Prim
  Sch BA22 . . . . .197 F8
Basketfield La BA6 . . . . . . .139 D1
Baskets La TA23 . . . . .131 D2
Batallers La TA23 . . . . .131 D2
Bat Alley DT10 . . . . .190 F5
BATCH 66 F3
Batch Bsns Pk BS24 . . . . . . .66 F2
Batch Cl TA7 . . . . .136 C4
Batch La
  Clutton BS39 . . . . .58 F3
  Lympsham BS24 . . . . .66 F3
Batchpool La BA8 . . . . .176 F3
Batch Rd TA7 . . . . .136 B5
Batch The
  Ashcott TA7 . . . . .156 B7
  Backwell BS48 . . . . .19 D1
  Batheaston BA1 . . . . .28 F3
  Burrington BS40 . . . . .54 B3
  Butcombe BS40 . . . . .55 B8
  Chew Magna BS40 . . . . .39 B3
  Churchill BS25 . . . . .52 F4
  Draycott BS27 . . . . .90 F2
  Farmborough BA2 . . . . .60 A6
  Hinton Charterhouse BA2 . . . .63 E1
  Saltford BS31 . . . . .25 F3
  19 Shepton Mallet BA4 . . . .205 B6
  Wincanton BA9 . . . . .216 B4
  Yatton BS49 . . . . .34 B7
Batch View BA16 . . . . .207 B6
BATCOMBE 142 D1
Bateman's Cross TA20 . . . .198 E7
BATH 228 A2
Bath Abbey ★ BA1 . . . . . . .228 C2
BATHAMPTON 28 F1
Bathampton La BA2 . . . . . . .28 F1
Bathampton Prim Sch BA2 . 28 F2
Bathampton View BA1 . . . . .29 B3
Bath Aqua Theatre of Glass ★
  BA1 . . . . .228 C3
Bath Bridge Bsns Pk TA6 . .209 B6
Bath Bsns Pk BA2 . . . . .79 E7
Bath City FC Twerton Park
  BA2 . . . . .44 B5
Bath Cl BA6 . . . . .206 D4
Bath Coll BA3 . . . . .78 F2
BATHEALTON 166 B3
BATHEASTON 28 F4
Batheaston CE Prim Sch
  BA1 . . . . .28 F4
BATHFORD 29 C1
Bathford CE Prim Sch BA1 . 29 C2
Bathford Hill
  Bathford BA1 . . . . .29 B2
  Compton Dando BS39 . . . . . .41 E5
Bathford Manor BA1 . . . . . .29 C2
Bath Foyer The BA2 . . . . . . .44 A6
Bath Hill
  Keynsham BS31 . . . . .24 F5
  Wellow BA2 . . . . .62 D2
Bath House Ct TA1 . . . . . . .212 E3
Bath La TA20 . . . . .223 C3
Bath Meadow Dr TA22 . . . .163 E6
Bath New Rd BA3 . . . . .78 F4
Bath Old Rd BA3 . . . . .78 F4
Bath Pl TA1 . . . . .212 F3
BATHPOOL 213 E6
Bath Postal Mus ★ BA1 . . . .228 C2
Bath Racecourse ★ BA1 . . . .27 A6
Bath Rd
  Ashcott TA7 . . . . .156 B7
  Bawdrip TA7 . . . . .136 D2

Bath Rd *continued*
  Beckington BA11 . . . . .101 D5
  Bitton BS30 . . . . .25 D8
  Blagdon BS40 . . . . .55 B1
  Bridgwater TA6 . . . . .209 C7
  Bristol BS2 . . . . .227 C1
  Farmborough BA2 . . . . .59 E5
  Frome BA11 . . . . .120 A7
  Horrington BA3, BA5 . . . . . .113 D5
  Kelston BA1, BS30 . . . . .26 B6
  Kingsdown SN13 . . . . .29 F5
  Moorlinch TA7 . . . . .155 E8
  Norton St Philip BA2 . . . . . . .81 E5
  Oakhill BA3 . . . . .115 B3
  Paulton BS39 . . . . .77 F6
  Peasedown St John BA2 . . . . .79 C7
  Saltford BS31 . . . . .25 D3
  Shepton Mallet BA4 . . . . . . .141 C8
  Stawell TA7 . . . . .137 B1
  Upper Langford BS40 . . . . . .53 D3
  Wells BA5 . . . . .112 E1
Bath Riverside Bsns Pk
  BA2 . . . . .228 B1
Bath's Original Theatre Royal
  & Masonic Mus ★ BA1 . . . .228 C2
Bath Spa Sta BA1 . . . . .228 C1
Bath Spa Univ Art and Design
  Bath BA1 . . . . .27 E1
  Bath BA1 . . . . .27 E1
Bath Spa Univ Coll BA1 . . . .27 E1
Bath Spa University Coll
  (Newton Pk Campus)
  BA2 . . . . .43 B5
Bath Spa University
  (Culverhey Campus) BA2 . 44 B2
Bath Sq TA20 . . . . .223 C3
Bath St
  Bath BA1 . . . . .228 C2
  Bristol BS1 . . . . .227 B2
  Chard TA20 . . . . .223 C3
  Cheddar BS27 . . . . .90 B7
  Frome BA11 . . . . .119 F4
Bathurst Cl TA8 . . . . .104 D8
Bathurst Par BS1 . . . . .227 A1
Bathurst Rd BS22 . . . . .49 C8
Bath View BA3 . . . . .96 F1
BATHWAY 94 E5
Bathwell La DT9 . . . . .217 D1
BATHWICK 45 B7
Bathwick Hill BA2 . . . . .45 C6
Bathwick Rise BA2 . . . . .45 B7
Bathwick St Mary CE Prim Sch
  Bathwick BA2 . . . . .45 C8
  Bathwick BA2 . . . . .45 C8
Bathwick St BA1, BA2 . . . . .228 C4
Batstone Cl BA1 . . . . .28 B2
Batt Dr TA2 . . . . .213 C8
BATTEN'S GREEN 182 F5
Battery La BS20 . . . . .2 D7
Battery Rd BS20 . . . . .2 D6
Battin's Knap TA4 . . . . .150 A3
Batt La TA3 . . . . .183 C8
BATTLEBOROUGH 86 C1
Battleborough La TA9 . . . . . .86 B1
Battle La BS40 . . . . .39 A3
Battle St EX15 . . . . .180 E1
Battleton TA22 . . . . .163 D6
Battle Wk BA1 . . . . .27 E4
Batts Bow Bridge TA9 . . . . .104 E1
Batts La
  Oakhill BA3 . . . . .114 E3
  Pilsdon DT6 . . . . .199 F2
Batt's La TA1 . . . . .172 D5
Battson Rd BS14 . . . . .23 E4
Batts Pk TA1 . . . . .212 E1
Bauldidch La TA3 . . . . .184 B8
Bauntons Cl DT9 . . . . .217 C2
Baunton's Orch DT9 . . . . . .217 C2
Bawden Cl TA7 . . . . .136 E4
BAWDRIP 136 E2
Bawdrip La TA7 . . . . .136 E2
Bawler Rd TA2 . . . . .169 B2
Bawler's La TA10 . . . . .171 C3
Bayer Bldg The BA2 . . . . . .228 B1
BAYFORD 216 F5
Bayford Hill BA9 . . . . .216 E4
Bayford La BA9 . . . . .177 B7
Bayford Rd TA6 . . . . .209 C6
Bay Hill TA19 . . . . .221 D4
Bay La BS27 . . . . .90 F2
Baylie Ave BS24 . . . . .32 C1
Bayliss Ctr The **4** BA16 . .207 C5
Baymead Cl **11** TA6 . . . . .153 F4
Baymead La TA6 . . . . .153 F3
Baymead Mdw **5** TA6 . . .153 F3
Baynes Cl TA21 . . . . .222 E7
Bay Rd
  Clevedon BS21 . . . . .6 D6
  Porlock TA24 . . . . .124 A4
Bay's La BA3 . . . . .115 A7
Bays The BS27 . . . . .90 C8
Baytree Ct BS22 . . . . .31 C1
Baytree Rd BS22 . . . . .31 C1
Bay Tree Rd
  Bath BA1 . . . . .28 B2
  Clevedon BS21 . . . . .6 E1
Baytree Sch BS24 . . . . .50 A8
Baytree View BS22 . . . . . . .31 D1
Bay Tree View BS22 . . . . . . .31 D1
Bay View TA23 . . . . .202 D6
Bay View Gdns TA8 . . . . . . .104 B5
Baze La EX35 . . . . .122 B4
Bazelands Hill BA8 . . . . . . .190 B7
Beach Ave BS21 . . . . .6 C2
Beach Ct BS23 . . . . .48 D6
Beach End Rd BS23 . . . . . . .48 C2
Beach Hill BS20 . . . . .2 C6
Beachlands Pk BS24 . . . . . .31 A6

Beachley Wlk BS11 . . . . .4 D7
Beach Mews BS21 . . . . .6 C4
Beach Rd
  Weston-super-Mare BS23 . . .48 D6
  Weston-super-Mare, Kewstoke
  BS22 . . . . .31 A5
Beach Rd E BS20 . . . . .2 D6
Beach Rd W BS20 . . . . .2 C6
Beach The BS21 . . . . .6 C4
Beach Tree Cross TA4 . . . . .166 F6
Beacon TA19 . . . . .221 B5
Beacon Cl **7** TA2 . . . . . . .169 C5
Beaconfield Ho TA6 . . . . . .209 A2
Beaconfield Rd BA20 . . . . .218 E1
BEACON HILL 27 F1
Beacon Hill View DT9 . . . . .175 D1
Beacon La
  Corton Denham DT9 . . . . . .175 D2
  Wellington TA21 . . . . .180 C4
Beacon Rd
  Bath BA1 . . . . .28 A1
  Minehead TA24 . . . . .200 F8
Beaconsfield Rd
  Clevedon BS21 . . . . .6 E3
  Weston-super-Mare BS23 . . .48 E7
Beaconsfield Way BA11 . . . .120 B7
Beacon View
  Coleford BA3 . . . . .116 E7
  Shepton Mallet BA4 . . . . . . .205 A4
Beadon La TA16 . . . . .195 F7
Beadon Rd TA1 . . . . .213 C5
Beafort Cl BS24 . . . . .50 C3
Beale Cl BS14 . . . . .23 E6
Beale Way TA8 . . . . .104 D5
Bean Acre The BS11 . . . . . . .4 D8
Bearbridge Rd BS13 . . . . . . .21 F4
BEARD HILL 141 C3
BEARDLY BATCH 205 C1
Beard's Yd TA10 . . . . .171 F5
BEAR FLAT 44 F4
Bearley Bridge Rd **15**
  TA12 . . . . .185 E6
Bearley Ho **26** TA12 . . . . .185 E6
Bearley La BA22 . . . . .186 B7
Bearley Rd **27** TA12 . . . . .185 E6
Bears Meadow La TA5 . . . . .133 C6
Bear Yard Mews **2** BS8. . .226 A2
Beasley Ct TA20 . . . . .223 B5
Beastway La TA24 . . . . .131 B3
Beatty Way TA8 . . . . .104 C7
Beauchamp Ave BA3 . . . . . .97 B6
Beauchamp Gdns TA3 . . . . .183 A7
Beauchamp Pk BA3 . . . . . . .97 B6
Beauchamps Dr BA3 . . . . . .97 A5
Beaufighter Rd BS24 . . . . . .49 D6
Beaufitz Pl TA20 . . . . .193 F1
Beauford Pk TA2 . . . . .168 B4
Beauford Sq BA1 . . . . .228 B2
Beaufort Ave BA3 . . . . .78 A2
Beaufort Bldgs **7** BS8. . . .11 F7
Beaufort Cl EX16 . . . . .178 D1
Beaufort Ct
  Clevedon BS21 . . . . .6 C5
  Ilchester BA22 . . . . .173 E2
Beaufort E BA1 . . . . .28 C1
Beaufort Gdns
  2 Nailsea BS48 . . . . .8 D1
  South Petherton TA13 . . . . .220 B5
Beaufort Mews
  3 Bath BA1 . . . . .28 C1
  10 Bristol BS8 . . . . .11 F7
Beaufort Pl BA1 . . . . .28 C1
Beaufort Rd
  Taunton TA1 . . . . .212 E5
  Weston-super-Mare BS23 . . .48 F7
Beaufort Villas **8** BA1. . . .28 B1
Beaufort W **11** BA1 . . . . . .28 B1
Beauley Rd BS3 . . . . .226 B1
Beaulieu Dr BA21 . . . . .218 D6
Beaumont BA1 . . . . .27 F1
Beaumont Cl BS23 . . . . .48 F4
Beaumont Ho BA21 . . . . . . .219 D5
Beau St BA1 . . . . .228 B2
Beavor La EX13 . . . . .198 A1
BECKERY 206 B4
Beckery Rd BA6 . . . . .206 B3
Beckery New Rd BA6 . . . . . .206 B3
Beckery Rd BA6 . . . . .206 B4
Becket Dr BS22 . . . . .32 A3
Becket Pl BA5 . . . . .203 D3
Becket Prim Sch BS22 . . . . .32 A2
Becket Rd BS22 . . . . .32 A4
Becket's La BS48 . . . . .18 E8
Beckford Cl **1** BA1 . . . . . .45 B7
Beckford Dr BA1 . . . . .27 E4
Beckford Gdns
  Bath BA2 . . . . .45 B8
  Bristol BS14 . . . . .23 A3
Beckford Rd BA2 . . . . .45 B7
Beckford's Twr & Mus ★
  BA1 . . . . .27 D4
Beckhampton Rd BA2 . . . . . .44 D5
BECKINGTON 101 E4
Beckington BS24 . . . . .49 A2
Beckington CE Fst Sch
  BA11 . . . . .101 E4
Beckington Cres TA20 . . . . .223 D3
Becks Bsns Pk BS31 . . . . . . .49 A7
Becks Field **2** TA14 . . . . .185 F4
Beckworth Cl TA6 . . . . .209 C3
Bector La BA3 . . . . .116 C4
Bede St DT9 . . . . .225 E5
Bedford Cl TA6 . . . . .209 C3
Bedford Ct BA1 . . . . .45 B8
Bedford Rd
  Wells BA5 . . . . .112 E1
  Weston-super-Mare BS23 . . .48 E4
  Yeovil BA21 . . . . .219 D8

Bedford St BA1 . . . . .45 B8
BEDLAM 119 B8
Bedlam Green Farm La
  BA10 . . . . .161 A4
BEDMINSTER DOWN 22 B8
Bedminster Down Sch
  Bedminster Down BS13 . . . .22 A7
  Bristol BS13 . . . . .21 F7
Bedwell La TA7 . . . . .155 C2
Bedwin Cl BS20 . . . . .1 F4
Beech Ave
  Bath BA2 . . . . .45 E5
  Shepton Mallet BA4 . . . . . . .205 A6
Beech Bsns Pk TA6 . . . . . . .209 A7
Beech Cl
  Doulting BA4 . . . . .141 E6
  Shipham BS25 . . . . .70 F8
  Taunton TA2 . . . . .212 F8
Beechcroft BS41 . . . . .21 D2
Beech Croft BS14 . . . . .23 B5
Beech Ct
  Bristol BS14 . . . . .23 A5
  Frome BA11 . . . . .120 B7
  Taunton TA1 . . . . .212 E3
  2 Wellington TA21 . . . . . .222 D6
Beech Dr
  Bridgwater TA6 . . . . .209 D5
  Nailsea BS48 . . . . .9 A3
  Shipham BS25 . . . . .70 F8
BEECHEN CLIFF 228 B1
Beechen Cliff Rd BA2 . . . . .228 B1
Beechen Cliff Sch BA2 . . . . .45 A4
Beeches The
  Bath BA2 . . . . .44 D1
  Langport TA10 . . . . .172 A6
  Sandford BS25 . . . . .52 B4
  Wheddon Cross TA24 . . . . . .129 E1
Beechfield Cl BS41 . . . . .11 C2
Beechfield Gr BS9 . . . . .5 C8
Beech Gr
  Bath BA2 . . . . .44 D4
  Somerton TA11 . . . . .211 D5
  Wellington TA21 . . . . .222 D5
Beech Grove Prim Sch
  TA21 . . . . .222 C6
Beech Hill TA21 . . . . .222 F5
Beeching Cl TA20 . . . . .223 E6
Beeching Close Ind Est
  TA20 . . . . .223 E6
Beech La
  Axminster EX13 . . . . .198 E1
  Stoke Trister BA9 . . . . .177 C8
Beechmont Dr BS24 . . . . . . .49 A1
Beechmount Cl BS24 . . . . . .48 F1
Beechmount Ct BS14 . . . . . .23 B8
Beechmount Gr BS14 . . . . . .23 B8
Beech Rd
  Bridgwater TA6 . . . . .209 D5
  20 Martock TA12 . . . . . . .185 E6
  Saltford BS31 . . . . .25 E3
  Shipham BS25 . . . . .70 F8
  Street BA16 . . . . .207 C3
  Yatton BS49 . . . . .34 C8
Beech Terr BA3 . . . . .78 E1
Beech Tree TA23 . . . . .130 D1
Beech Tree Cl TA4 . . . . .210 C4
Beech Tree Cross
  Clatworthy TA4 . . . . .149 E1
  Dulverton TA22 . . . . .163 C7
  Monksilver TA4 . . . . .132 B1
Beech Tree Hill TA5 . . . . . . .152 C6
Beech Way BA4 . . . . .141 E1
Beechwood
  Bridgwater TA6 . . . . .208 E2
  Yeovil BA20 . . . . .218 F2
Beechwood Ave
  Frome BA11 . . . . .120 A5
  Locking BS24 . . . . .50 A5
Beechwood Cl
  Bristol BS14 . . . . .23 C8
  Frome BA11 . . . . .120 A5
Beechwood Dr
  Crewkerne TA18 . . . . .224 C7
  Portishead BS20 . . . . .1 E5
Beechwood Rd
  Bath BA2 . . . . .45 B1
  Easton-in-G BS20 . . . . .4 A4
  Nailsea BS48 . . . . .8 D2
  Portishead BS20 . . . . .1 E5
Beehive Yd BA1 . . . . .228 C3
Beek's La SN14, BA1 . . . . . .13 D5
Beer Door TA10 . . . . .155 E2
Beer Dro TA10 . . . . .155 E3
Beere Cross EX36 . . . . .162 A5
Beer La
  Burlescombe EX16 . . . . .179 B2
  Dulverton TA22 . . . . .163 C6
Beer Rd TA10 . . . . .155 E1
Beer St
  Curry Mallet TA3 . . . . .183 C7
  Yeovil BA20 . . . . .219 A4
Bees Ho BS21 . . . . .6 C2
Beetham La TA20 . . . . .193 B6
Beggar Bush La BS8 . . . . . . .11 B6
Beggarswell Cl BS2 . . . . . . .227 C4
BEGGEARN HUISH 131 E2
Beggs Cl **4** TA6 . . . . .153 F3
Begonia Dr TA6 . . . . .208 D1
Behind Berry TA11 . . . . . . .211 D4
Behind Butts TA14 . . . . . . .185 E1
Behind Hayes BA8 . . . . .176 D3
Behind Town TA11 . . . . . . .157 B4
Bekynton Ave BA5 . . . . .203 F4
Belcombe Dro TA20 . . . . . .193 B7
Belfast Wlk BS4 . . . . .22 C4
Belfield Ct TA8 . . . . .104 A8
Belgrave Cres BA1 . . . . .228 C4
Belgrave Ct **2** TA2 . . . . . .212 F6

Belgrave Pl
  Bath BA1 . . . . .228 C4
  Bristol BS8 . . . . .226 A3
  Taunton TA2 . . . . .212 F6
Belgrave Rd
  Bath BA1 . . . . .28 B1
  Bristol BS8 . . . . .226 A4
  Weston-super-Mare BS22 . . .49 B8
Belgrave Terr **2** BA1. . . . .28 A1
Belgravia Rd TA6 . . . . .136 B2
Bellamy Ave BS13 . . . . .22 C4
Belland Dr BS14 . . . . .22 F4
Bella View Gdns BA6 . . . . .206 D4
Bella Vista Rd BA1 . . . . . . .228 B4
Bell Barn Rd BS9 . . . . .5 D6
Bell Chase BA20 . . . . .218 D5
Bell Cl
  Bridgwater TA6 . . . . .208 F6
  Farmborough BA2 . . . . .59 F6
  Westbury-sub-Mendip BA5 . .110 E6
Belle View Terr TA20 . . . . . .198 C8
Bellevue BS8 . . . . .226 B3
BELLE VUE 78 B3
Belle Vue
  Midsomer Norton BA3 . . . . . .78 B3
  Washford TA23 . . . . .131 E3
Belle Vue Cl BA2 . . . . .79 D7
Bellevue Cotts BS8 . . . . . . .226 B2
Bellevue Cres BS8. . . . . . . .226 B2
Bellevue Ct
  Bristol BS8 . . . . .226 B2
  Clevedon BS21 . . . . .6 D4
Bellevue Mans BS21 . . . . . . .6 D4
Bellevue Rd BS21 . . . . .6 D4
Bellevue Terr BS8. . . . . . . .226 B2
Belle Vue Terr TA18 . . . . . .224 B6
Bellfield BA3 . . . . .117 A3
Bellhanger Ct BA1 . . . . . . .228 B4
Bell Hill
  Chewton Mendip BA3 . . . . . .94 B7
  Norton St Philip BA2 . . . . . . .81 E4
Bellhorse La BS40 . . . . .74 C5
Bellifants BA2 . . . . .60 A6
Bellis Avenue TA5 . . . . .208 D1
Bell La
  Bristol BS1 . . . . .227 A3
  Chard TA19, TA20 . . . . .193 F7
  Chewton Mendip BA3 . . . . . .94 B7
  Cossington TA7 . . . . .137 A3
  Thurloxton TA2 . . . . .153 D1
Bell Language Sch The
  BA1 . . . . .44 C8
Bellman's Cross BA8 . . . . . .190 B1
Bellmoor La TA19 . . . . .194 A7
Bell Orch TA10 . . . . .171 D4
Bellotts Rd BA2 . . . . .44 C6
Bell Pit Brow BS48 . . . . .9 B2
Bell Sq BS40 . . . . .54 E3
Bellum SN14 . . . . .13 E8
BELLUTON 40 D6
Belluton La BS39 . . . . .40 D5
Belluton Villas BS39 . . . . . .40 D5
Bell Wlk BS40 . . . . .35 E2
Belmonds Cross Rd BA9 . . .177 D2
Belmont Dr
  Failand BS8 . . . . .10 B3
  Taunton TA1 . . . . .212 E2
Belmont Hill BS48 . . . . .10 B1
Belmont Ho **14** BA20 . . . .219 B4
Belmont Rd
  Bath BA2 . . . . .45 C1
  Hatch Beauchamp TA3 . . . . .183 A8
  Taunton TA1 . . . . .212 C3
  Winscombe BS25 . . . . .70 A8
Belmont Terr TA19 . . . . . . .184 E3
Belmont The BS21 . . . . .6 D3
Belmore Gdns BA2 . . . . .44 B3
Belstone Wlk BS4 . . . . .22 C8
Belton Ct BA1 . . . . .27 B2
Belton Rd BS20 . . . . .2 A6
Belvedere BA1 . . . . .228 B4
Belvedere Cl TA5 . . . . .135 B2
Belvedere Cres BS22 . . . . . .31 C1
Belvedere Ct **3** TA21 . . . .222 D6
Belvedere Grange TA11 . . . .211 E3
Belvedere Rd
  Taunton TA1 . . . . .212 F5
  Yeovil BA21 . . . . .219 E7
Belvedere Trad Est TA1 . . . .212 E5
Belvoir Rd **6** BA2 . . . . . . .44 D5
Bemberry Bank TA24 . . . . . .130 B5
Benares Ct TA24 . . . . .201 A8
Bences Cl SN14 . . . . .13 F8
Benches La BS40 . . . . .37 D3
Bench La TA20 . . . . .193 D5
Ben Cross TA13 . . . . .220 A4
Benedictine La BA6 . . . . . . .206 C4
Benedict St BA6 . . . . .206 D4
Benhole La TA5 . . . . .134 B8
Benleaze Rd BS40 . . . . .75 C2
Bennell Batch BA3 . . . . .96 E4
Bennell Cl BA3 . . . . .96 E4
Bennell Cotts BA3 . . . . .96 E4
Bennett Gdns BA11 . . . . . . .119 D4
Bennett La BA1 . . . . .28 A1
Bennett Rd TA9 . . . . .104 F4
Bennett's Cl BA5 . . . . .204 B7
Bennetts Field Trad Est
  BA9 . . . . .216 C2
Bennett's La BA3, BA5. . . . .114 A7
Bennett's Rd BA1 . . . . .28 C3
Bennett St BA1 . . . . .228 B3
Bennetts Way BS21. . . . . . . .6 E5
Bennett Way BS1, BS8. . . . .11 F5
BENTER 115 D7
Benter Cross BA3 . . . . .115 D7
Bentley Cl BS14 . . . . .22 F3

Bentley Rd BS22 . . . . 32 B3
Ben Travers Way TA8 . . . . 104 C6
Benville Ave BS9 . . . . 5 C5
Bere La BA6 . . . . 206 E4
Bere Mills La TA19 . . . . . 194 B7
Beresford Cl
  Burnham-on-S TA8 . . . . . 104 C7
  Saltford BS31 . . . . 25 E2
Beresford Gdns BA1 . . . . . 27 A3
Beretun Orch BA6 . . . . . . 206 E3
Berhill TA7 . . . . 156 C7
Berkeley Ave
  Bristol BS8 . . . . 226 C3
  Midsomer Norton BA3 . . . 78 A2
Berkeley Cres
  Bristol BS8 . . . . 226 B3
  Weston-super-Mare BS23 . . 48 C2
Berkeley Ct BA2. . . . . 45 C6
Berkeley Gdns
  Bruton BA10. . . . . 215 E6
  Keynsham BS31 . . . . 24 E4
Berkeley Ho
  Bath BA1 . . . . 228 C4
  Bristol BS1. . . . . 226 C3
Berkeley Pl
  Bath BA1 . . . . 228 C4
  Bristol BS8 . . . . 226 B3
Berkeley Rd
  Street BA16 . . . . 207 E6
  Yeovil BA20 . . . . 219 A4
Berkeley Sq BS8 . . . . 226 B3
BERKLEY 121 A7
Berkley Ave BS8 . . . . 226 B3
Berkley CE Fst Sch BA11 . . 121 A7
Berkley Cross BA11 . . . . . 120 F6
Berkley Ct BA2. . . . . 173 E2
BERKLEY DOWN. 120 C5
Berkley La
  Beckington BA11 . . . . . . 101 D3
  Frome BA11. . . . . 120 D8
BERKLEY MARSH 120 F7
Berkley Rd BA11 . . . . 120 B6
Berkley St BA11 . . . . 121 A8
Berlington Ct BS1. . . . . . . 227 B1
Bernard Cres TA24 . . . . . 200 F6
Bernard Herridge Ct BA9 . 216 D4
Bernard Ireland Ho BA1 . . 27 B1
Bernard Taylor Homes 9
  TA1 . . . . 213 A4
Bernard Way TA13 . . . . . 220 D6
Berners Cl BS4. . . . . 22 D7
BERROW 84 E5
Berrow Lodge 7 BS23. . . . 48 E5
Berrow Rd TA8. . . . . 85 A2
Berry Cl TA6 . . . . 208 E2
Berry Cott La TA20 . . . . . 192 F4
Berrydale Ave TA6 . . . . . 208 F6
Berry Hill
  Mells BA11. . . . . 118 A6
  Nunney BA11. . . . . 143 B8
Berry La EX13. . . . . 198 F3
Berryman Cl BA4. . . . . . . 205 A5
Berryman Ct BA5. . . . . . . 203 B4
Bertha Terr TA9. . . . . 104 D3
Berwick Cl TA1 . . . . 212 C1
Beryl Gr BS14. . . . . 23 C8
Beryl Knapp BA22 . . . . . . 197 B8
Beryl La BA5. . . . . 203 F6
Besley Ct BA5. . . . . 203 B4
Bests Field TA12 . . . . 185 B8
Bethell Mead TA4 . . . . . . 167 E6
BETTISCOMBE 199 E2
Bevan Rd BS30. . . . . 25 E8
Beverley Cl
  Frome BA11. . . . . 119 D3
  Taunton TA2 . . . . 212 E6
Beverley Dr TA23. . . . . . . 202 C7
Beverley Gdns BS9 . . . . 5 D7
Bewdley Rd BA2 . . . . 45 B4
Bewley Ct TA20 . . . . 223 B4
Bewley Down Rd TA20. . . 193 A3
Bews La TA20. . . . . 223 B5
Bibors Hill TA4. . . . . 165 E4
Bibury BS48. . . . . 9 A1
Bibury Ho BA1. . . . . 27 B2
BICKENHALL. 182 E5
Bickenhall La TA3. . . . . . 182 F6
Bickfield La
  Compton Martin BS40 . . . . 74 B8
  Ubley BS40. . . . . 55 F2
Bicking's Close La TA4 . . 166 A4
Bicknell Gdns BA21 . . . . . 219 B8
BICKNOLLER. 132 F2
Bidbrooke La EX36 . . . . . 162 A6
Biddiscombe Cl TA6. . . . . 208 E1
BIDDISHAM. 87 E8
Biddisham Cl 6 BS48. . . . . 8 E1
Biddisham La BS26. . . . . . . 87 E7
Biddlesden Rd BA21. . . . . 218 C7
Biddle St BS49 . . . . 34 B7
Bideford Cres BS4. . . . . . . 22 F8
Bideford Rd BS22 . . . . 31 F2
Bifield Cl BS14. . . . . 23 E5
Bifield Gdns BS14 . . . . . . 23 E5
Bifield Rd BS14. . . . . 23 E5
Bignal Rand Cl BA5. . . . . 203 B3
Bignal Rand Dr BA5 . . . . 203 B3
Bignell Cl BS25. . . . . 69 F8
Big Tree Cl BS26 . . . . 69 C3
Bigwood La BS1. . . . . 226 C2
Bilberry Cl BS9. . . . . 5 C8
Bilberry Gr TA1 . . . . 168 F1
Bilbie Cl BS40. . . . . 56 E8
Bilbie Rd
  Chew Stoke BS40. . . . . . . 56 E8
  Weston-super-Mare BS22 . . 32 B3
BILBROOK. 131 C4

Bilbury La
  Bath BA1 . . . . 228 B2
  Glastonbury BA6 . . . . . . 206 F3
Billand Cl BS13. . . . . 21 E3
Billetfield TA1 . . . . 212 F3
Billet St TA1 . . . . 212 F3
Billicombe La TA7. . . . . . 155 C8
Billing's Hill BS28 . . . . . 108 C4
Bills La TA11. . . . . 174 C6
Bince's La TA8 . . . . 42 E3
Bince's Lodge La BA3 . . . . 78 B3
BINCOMBE 134 A2
Bincombe Dr TA18 . . . . . 224 C7
Bincombe Rd TA6. . . . . . 209 C4
Binding Cl 6 TA6 . . . . . . 153 F4
Bindon La BA11. . . . . 143 B2
Bindon Rd TA2 . . . . 212 C6
Bindwell La BA22 . . . . . . 174 F3
Bindworth Dro TA12. . . . 185 A7
BINEGAR 114 C7
Binegar La BA3 . . . . 114 E7
Bineham Ct TA10. . . . . . . 173 B4
Bineham La
  Ilchester BA22. . . . . 173 F2
  Yeovilton BA22 . . . . 174 A2
Bineham Rd TA10 . . . . . . 173 A4
Binford Pl TA6 . . . . 209 A5
Binford's La TA4 . . . . 151 A4
Binhay Rd BS49 . . . . 34 C7
Binley Gr BS14. . . . . 23 D5
Binmead Gdns BS13 . . . . . 22 B4
Birbeck Chase BS24 . . . . . 50 C8
Birbeck Rd BS9 . . . . 5 E5
Bircham Cl TA6 . . . . 208 C4
Bircham La TA24 . . . . . . 201 C4
Bircham Rd
  Minehead TA24. . . . . . . 201 B5
  Taunton TA2 . . . . 213 B8
Birchanger La TA4 . . . . . 150 A8
Birch Ave
  Bleadon BS24. . . . . 67 C6
  Clevedon BS21. . . . . 6 E4
  Puriton TA7. . . . . 136 C4
Birch Cl
  Bridgwater TA6 . . . . 209 D5
  Cannington TA5 . . . . 135 B2
  Cheddar BS27. . . . . 90 C8
  Locking BS24. . . . . 50 B4
  Wedmore BS28. . . . . 108 C3
Birch Croft BS14. . . . . 23 A3
Birch Ct BS31. . . . . 24 C4
Birchdale BA20 . . . . 218 D2
Birchdale Rd BS14 . . . . . . 23 A8
Birchdene BS48. . . . . 9 A2
Birch Dr BS40. . . . . 53 A5
Birches Cnr TA4 . . . . 152 A4
Birches The BS48 . . . . 9 A2
Birchfield Com Prim Sch
  BA21. . . . . 219 D7
Birchfield Rd BA21 . . . . . 219 D8
Birch Gr
  Portishead BS20 . . . . 2 C4
  Taunton TA1 . . . . 212 E5
Birch Hill BS27. . . . . 90 C8
Birch Ho TA8 . . . . 65 F2
BIRCHILL. 198 A5
Birchill Cross EX13. . . . . 198 A6
Birchill La BA11. . . . . 120 A1
Birch Lawn TA8 . . . . 104 B6
Birch Rd
  12 Martock TA12. . . . . . 185 E6
  Radstock BA3. . . . . 78 E1
  Wellington TA21 . . . . . . 222 E5
Birch Wlk BA11. . . . . 120 B7
BIRCHWOOD. 182 A1
Birchwood Ave BS23 . . . . 49 A7
Birchwood Cl BA12. . . . . 144 E8
Birchwood Dr BS8 . . . . . . 10 B3
Birchwood La BS39. . . . . . 40 F2
Birdcombe Cl BS48. . . . . . 8 E3
Birdlip Cl BS48. . . . . 9 A1
Bird's Cl TA18. . . . . 224 B6
BIRDSMOORGATE 199 D4
Birdwell La BS41 . . . . 10 F1
Birdwell Prim Sch BS41. . 21 A8
Birdwell Rd BS41. . . . . . . 10 F1
Birkbeck Ct BS23. . . . . . . 48 D7
Birkett Rd BS23 . . . . 30 B1
Birkin St BS2. . . . . 227 C2
Birnbeck Rd BS23 . . . . . . 30 C1
Biscay Dr BS20. . . . . 2 F6
Biscombe Cross TA3 . . . . 191 B8
Bisdee Rd BS24 . . . . 49 D2
Bishop Ave BS22 . . . . 32 A3
Bishop Cl TA20. . . . . 223 B5
Bishop Cres BA4 . . . . 204 F5
Bishop Fox Dr TA1 . . . . . 213 A4
Bishop Fox's Com Sch
  TA1 . . . . 213 A1
Bishop Henderson CE Prim
  Sch
  Taunton TA1 . . . . 212 C2
  Taunton TA2 . . . . 212 C2
Bishop Henderson CE Sch
  BA3. . . . . 116 E8
Bishop Rd TA5 . . . . 134 B2
Bishops Cl
  Bristol BS9 . . . . 5 E3
  Taunton TA1 . . . . 212 C2
Bishops Cotts
  Stogursey TA5. . . . . 134 B7
  Wootton Courtenay TA24 . 129 F6
Bishops Cove BS13. . . . . . 21 F5
Bishops Ct 4 TA21 . . . . . 222 D6
Bishops Dr TA10 . . . . 172 A5
Bishops Gn TA4 . . . . 210 C4
Bishop's Hill TA21 . . . . . 179 B7

BISHOP'S HULL 212 A4
Bishop's Hull Hill TA1 . . 212 B4
Bishop's Hull Prim Sch
  TA1. . . . . 212 B4
Bishop's Hull Rd TA1 . . . 212 A3
Bishops Knoll BS9. . . . . . . 5 C3
Bishops La BA22 . . . . 197 A6
Bishop's La DT9. . . . . 187 E1
Bishopslea Cl BA5. . . . . . 203 C3
BISHOPS LYDEARD 167 F8
Bishops Lydeard CE Prim Sch
  TA4 . . . . 167 E8
Bishops Lydeard Mill & Rural
  Life Mus★ TA4 . . . . 167 F8
Bishops Lydeard Mill & Rural
  Life Mus TA4. . . . . 167 F8
Bishop's Lydeard Sta TA4 . 167 E7
Bishops Mead BS49 . . . . . 35 A8
Bishops Park Way BA5. . . 203 F2
Bishop's Path TA8. . . . . . 104 B6
Bishops Rd BS49 . . . . 35 A8
Bishop St
  Bristol BS2. . . . . 227 B4
  Faulkland BA2. . . . . 80 C2
Bishopston TA15 . . . . 186 B4
BISHOP SUTTON 57 D3
Bishop Sutton Prim Sch
  BS39. . . . . 57 D4
Bishops Wlk BA22 . . . . . . 173 D1
BISHOPSWOOD 192 E7
Bishopswood Rd TA20. . . 192 F7
BISHOPSWORTH 22 A7
Bishopsworth Rd BS13 . . . 22 A7
Bishop Terr BS2. . . . . 227 C4
Bishport Ave BS13 . . . . . . 22 C3
Bishport Cl BS13. . . . . 22 B4
Bishport Gn BS13. . . . . . . 22 C3
Bitham Wlk TA7. . . . . 136 E3
Bittern Ave BS20. . . . . 2 F7
Bittern Cl BS22. . . . . 31 F1
Bittescombe La TA4. . . . . 165 B6
Bittlemead BS13 . . . . 22 F4
BITTON 25 E7
Blackacre BS14. . . . . 23 C4
Blackacre Hill BA8 . . . . . 176 D4
Blackaller La EX16 . . . . . 163 C1
Black Bench Dro TA20. . . 223 F7
Blackberry Cl BA4. . . . . . 205 C4
Blackberry Ct TA21. . . . . 222 D4
Blackberry Dr BS22 . . . . . 32 A2
Blackberry La
  Portishead BS20 . . . . 1 F2
  Sherborne DT9. . . . . 225 D5
  Winsley BA3, BA15. . . . . . 64 C8
Blackberry Rd BA11 . . . . 120 B3
Blackberry Way BA3. . . . . 77 F3
Blackberry Wlk TA18. . . . 224 D7
Blackberry Wy BS31. . . . . 24 E3
Blackbird Cl BA3. . . . . 97 B8
Blackbird Way BA11. . . . . 120 B6
Blackbook Park Ave TA1 . 213 E4
Blackbrook Prim Sch TA1 . 213 D3
Blackbrook Rd TA1. . . . . 213 E5
Blackbook Way TA1. . . . . 213 E3
Blackburn Wy BS24. . . . . 32 C1
Blackcurrant Dr BS41 . . . 20 E8
Black Dog Hill BA13 . . . . 121 E6
BLACKDOWN. 199 D6
Blackdown BA21. . . . . 219 A6
Blackdown Bsns Pk TA21. 222 E6
Blackdown Cl BS14. . . . . . 23 B5
Blackdown Mead BS27 . . . 90 C6
Blackdown Rd
  Bridgwater TA6 . . . . 209 D4
  Portishead BS20 . . . . 2 B5
  Rockwell Green TA21 . . . 222 B4
  Taunton TA2 . . . . 213 B8
Blackdown View
  Curry Rivel TA10. . . . . . 171 D4
  Ilminster TA19 . . . . 221 C4
  Norton Fitzwarren TA2 . . 168 B5
  Nynehead TA21. . . . . . . 167 C2
  Sampford Peverell EX16 . 178 C1
Blackdown Way BA3 . . . . . 97 B6
Black Dro TA7 . . . . 155 A1
Blacker's La BA3. . . . . . . 116 E2
Blackerton Cross EX16 . . 162 E3
Blackey La BA3. . . . . 115 B6
BLACKFORD
  Minehead. 129 C6
  Wedmore. 107 E4
  Wincanton 175 F5
Blackford Hollow BA22. . . 175 F5
Blackford Moor Dro BS28,
  BS28. . . . . 107 B6
Blackford Moor La TA9,
  BS28. . . . . 107 B5
Blackford Rd
  Charlton Horethorne DT9. . 176 A2
  Mark TA9 . . . . 106 F4
  Wedmore BS28. . . . . 108 A3
Blackford Way DT9. . . . . 176 A3
Blackfriars BS1. . . . . 227 A3
Blackfriars Rd BS48 . . . . . 8 B1
Blackham La TA10 . . . . . . 155 F2
Blackhayes La EX14 . . . . 192 C1
Blackheath La BA5. . . . . . 113 E4
Black Horse Cl TA6. . . . . 208 F2
Black Horse La TA1. . . . . 212 F5
Black La
  Axbridge BS26. . . . . 70 E2
  Hemyock EX15. . . . . 180 D2
  Holcombe Rogus TA21. . . 178 E6
Blackland Dro TA20 . . . . 194 A1
Blackland La TA20. . . . . . 194 B1
Blacklands TA6 . . . . 208 F5

Black Mere BA22. . . . . . . 218 B5
Black Mixen La TA18. . . . 224 C7
Black Monkey La TA24. . . 131 C5
BLACKMOOR
  Chew Stoke 38 C3
  Churchill. 53 D6
  Wellington 180 E5
Blackmoor
  Charterhouse BS40 . . . . . 72 F4
  Clevedon BS21. . . . . 6 C1
  Lower Langford BS40. . . . . 53 C6
  3 Weston-super-Mare BS22. 31 F2
Blackmoor Cl BS40. . . . . . 53 C6
Blackmoor La 6 BA8 . . . 190 A6
Blackmoor Rd
  Abbots Leigh BS8 . . . . 4 E2
  Taunton TA2 . . . . 213 B7
  Wellington TA21 . . . . . . 222 F4
Blackmoors La BS3. . . . . . 11 E4
Blackmore Chase BA9. . . . 216 D3
Blackmore Dr BA2 . . . . . . 44 C5
Blackmore La TA5. . . . . . 135 B1
Blackmore Rd DT10 . . . . 190 B4
Blackmore Vale Cl BA8 . . 176 E1
Blacknell La TA18 . . . . . . 224 D6
Blacknell Lane Ind Est
  TA18. . . . . 224 E5
Black Nore Point BS20. . . . 1 F5
BLACKPOOL CORNER . . . 198 D1
BLACKROCK. 40 E8
Blackrock La BS39. . . . . . . 40 E7
Black Rock Nature Trail★
  BA5. . . . . 72 A1
Blackrock Villas BS20 . . . . 2 B1
Blackrod Cotts TA13. . . . . 184 F4
Blacksmith La BA1. . . . . . 28 C6
Blacksmiths La TA7 . . . . . 155 F8
Blacksmiths Row BA21 . . 187 D6
Black's Moor Hill La TA11 173 A5
Blackthorn Cl
  Biddisham BS26. . . . . 87 E6
  Bristol BS13. . . . . 22 D5
  6 North Petherton TA6. . 153 F3
Blackthorn Dr BS20 . . . . . 2 E5
Blackthorne Cl BA22 . . . . 173 E2
Blackthorn Gdns
  Taunton TA1 . . . . 168 F6
  Weston-super-Mare BS22 . . 32 A1
Blackthorn Rd BS13 . . . . . 22 D5
Blackthorn Sq BS21 . . . . . . 6 D1
Blackthorns The TA1 . . . . 213 C2
Blackthorn Terr BS22 . . . . 32 A1
Blackthorn Way
  Nailsea BS48 . . . . 9 A2
  Somerton TA11. . . . . 211 B3
  Street BA16 . . . . 207 A5
BLACKWATER. 182 C2
Blackwater La
  Axminster EX13 . . . . 198 F3
  Wiveliscombe TA4 . . . . . 210 A8
BLACKWELL. 165 B5
Blackwell Rd BA22 . . . . . 174 F3
Blackworthy Rd BA7. . . . 159 C3
Bladud Bldgs BA1. . . . . . 228 C3
BLAGDON 54 E2
Blagdon Cl BS24. . . . . 48 F1
Blagdon Cres TA1 . . . . . . 212 D1
Blagdon Cross TA24 . . . . 129 D2
BLAGDON HILL 181 D5
Blagdon La
  Blagdon BS40. . . . . 54 F6
  Brompton Regis TA22, TA24 . 148 D4
Blagdon Pk BA2. . . . . 44 A4
Blagdon Prim Sch BS40. . . 54 F2
Blagdon Wlk BA11. . . . . . 120 D7
Blagrove Cl
  Bristol BS13. . . . . 22 D4
  Street BA16 . . . . 207 B6
Blagrove Cres BS13 . . . . . 22 D4
Blagrove Hill BA6 . . . . . . 157 C6
Blagrove's Rd TA4 . . . . . 167 C4
Blaisdon BS22 . . . . 49 D7
Blaise Wlk BS9. . . . . 5 C6
Blake Cl 4 BA21 . . . . . . 219 F8
Blake End BS22 . . . . 31 E4
Blake Gn TA7 . . . . 156 B7
Blake Ind Est TA6. . . . . . 209 A3
Blake Mus The★ TA6. . . . 209 A4
Blakeney Gr BS48 . . . . . . 18 C8
Blake Pl TA6 . . . . 209 A5
Blake Rd
  5 Crewkerne TA18 . . . . 224 C5
  Wells BA5. . . . . 203 C5
Blake's Cres TA9 . . . . 104 E5
Blakes La TA5, TA6. . . . . 208 C7
Blake's La BA3. . . . . 115 D2
Blakes Rd TA6 . . . . 208 D6
Blake St
  2 Bridgwater TA6. . . . . 208 F4
  Taunton TA1 . . . . 213 B4
Blakeway BS28 . . . . 138 B6
Blandford Cl BS48. . . . . . . 8 E1
Blandford Rd BA4. . . . . . 205 D3
BLATCHBRIDGE 143 F8
Blaxhold La TA5. . . . . 152 E5
Bleachfield Rise 13 EX13. 198 A1
BLEADNEY 139 A8
BLEADON 67 C7
Bleadon Hill BS23, BS24. . 67 A8
Bleadon Mill BS24. . . . . . 67 C5
Bleadon Rd BS24. . . . . . . 67 B7
Bleak St BA9. . . . . 161 A2
Blencathra Ct TA8 . . . . . . 104 A8
Blenheim Cl
  Peasedown St John BA2. . . 79 D7

Blenheim Cl continued
  Weston-super-Mare BS22 . . 32 A2
Blenheim Ct 10 BS1 . . . . . 227 A4
Blenheim Gdns BA1 . . . . . 28 A2
Blenheim Mews TA24 . . . 200 F7
Blenheim Rd
  Bridgwater TA6 . . . . 209 D7
  Minehead TA24. . . . . . . 201 A7
  Street BA16 . . . . 207 B4
  Taunton TA1 . . . . 213 D5
  Yeovil BA21 . . . . 219 D7
Blenheim View TA24 . . . . 201 A7
Blenheim Way BS20 . . . . . 2 E5
Blew Cl BS29 . . . . 50 C7
Blights Hill EX16, TA22 . . 163 F3
Blindhouse La 7 BA11 . . 119 F4
Blind La
  Barton St David TA11 . . . 158 A2
  Bath BA1 . . . . 27 C2
  Buckland St Mary TA20. . . 182 A1
  Chard TA20. . . . . 223 D2
  Chew Stoke BS40. . . . . . . 56 E8
  Congresbury BS49 . . . . . . 34 F6
  Drimpton DT8. . . . . 199 F6
  Isle Abbotts TA3. . . . . . . 183 F8
  Keinton Mandeville TA11 . 158 B1
  Martock TA12. . . . . 185 D5
  Southwick BA14. . . . . 83 F2
  Thorncombe TA20. . . . . . 199 B6
  Tunley BA2. . . . . 61 A4
  Yatton BS49 . . . . 34 F7
Blindwell La
  Golsoncott TA23, TA24 . . 131 C1
  Skilgate TA4. . . . . 164 E6
BLOOMFIELD
  Bath 44 E3
  Timsbury 60 B4
Bloomfield BS24 . . . . 49 A2
Bloomfield Ave
  Bath BA2 . . . . 44 E4
  Timsbury BA2. . . . . 60 B3
Bloomfield Cl
  Taunton TA1 . . . . 213 C5
  Timsbury BA2. . . . . 60 B3
Bloomfield Cotts BA2 . . . . 79 C7
Bloomfield Cres BA2 . . . . 44 D2
Bloomfield Dr BA2 . . . . . . 44 D2
Bloomfield Gr BA2 . . . . . . 44 E3
Bloomfield La BS39 . . . . . 77 E5
Bloomfield Park Rd BA2 . . 60 B3
Bloomfield Pk BA2 . . . . . . 44 E3
Bloomfield Rd
  Bath BA2 . . . . 44 E3
  Timsbury BA2. . . . . 60 B3
Bloomfield Rise BA2 . . . . 44 D2
Bloomfield Rise N BA2 . . . 44 D2
Bloomfield Terr BA2 . . . . . 79 C7
Bloom Row TA6. . . . . 209 D5
Blossom Cl TA6 . . . . 209 C5
BLUE ANCHOR 131 B6
Blue Anchor Chalets
  TA24 . . . . 131 C6
Blue Anchor Railway Mus★
  TA24 . . . . 131 C6
Blue Anchor Sta TA24. . . 131 C6
Blue Ball Cl BA10. . . . . . 215 E6
Bluebell Cl
  Bristol BS9. . . . . 5 B6
  Taunton TA1 . . . . 213 C1
Bluebell Dr
  Bridgwater TA6 . . . . 208 E1
  Keynsham BS31. . . . . 24 D3
Bluebell Rd
  Frome BA11. . . . . 120 B3
  Weston-super-Mare BS22 . . 32 A6
  Yeovil BA22 . . . . 218 B5
Bluebell Rise BA3 . . . . 77 F3
Blueberry Way BS22. . . . . 31 F1
Blue Gate TA24 . . . . 145 D8
Blue Ho The BA11 . . . . . . 119 F5
Blue Reef Aquarium★
  BS1. . . . . 226 C2
Blue Sch The BA5 . . . . . . 203 C5
Blue Stone La TA13. . . . . 185 B6
Bluett Rd TA21. . . . . 222 D4
Blue Water Dr BS24 . . . . . 50 D3
Blundells La TA2 . . . . 169 C2
Blythe Ct TA1 . . . . 212 D1
Blythe Gdns BS22 . . . . . . 32 A3
Blythe Way TA8 . . . . 85 A3
BMI Bath Clinic Private Hospl
  . . . . 45 D2
Board Cross BA4 . . . . 205 B6
Boards La BA5 . . . . 204 C7
Boards Rd TA6. . . . . 209 A6
Boardwalk The BA16 . . . . 207 D7
Boarpath La TA4 . . . . 151 A5
Boat La BS24. . . . . 67 C3
Boat Stall La BA2. . . . . . . 228 C2
Bobbin La BA15. . . . . 64 F4
Bobbin Pk BA15. . . . . 64 F3
BODDEN 205 F7
Bodden La BA4 . . . . 205 E6
Boden St TA20 . . . . 223 C3
Boden Villas TA20. . . . . . 223 C3
Bodley Way BS24. . . . . . . 49 E7
Bodmin Rd TA2 . . . . 213 A8
Bodmin Wlk BS4 . . . . 22 F8
Boez La TA21 . . . . 153 D1
Bofors Pk BA22. . . . . 218 A6
Bofors Twr BS23 . . . . 49 B4
BOLHAM WATER 191 B7
Bollams Mead TA4 . . . . . 210 C5
Bollnas Cl BA4 . . . . 205 C4
Bolster La BA6. . . . . 157 C4

Bolter's La
 Alhampton BA4, BA7 . . . . **159** B4
 Shepton Mallet BA4 . . . . **141** D8
Bolton Cl TA9 . . . . **104** F4
Bomers Bridge Rd
 Charlton Horethorne DT9. . . . **176** A1
 Milborne Wick DT9 . . . . **189** A8
Bommertown Cross EX36 **162** A4
Bondfield Way TA20. . . . . **223** B6
Bondip Hill BA22, TA11 . . . . . **173** D3
Bonds Cl TA20 . . . . **223** D6
Bond's La SN14 . . . . **13** E8
Bonds Pool TA10 . . . . **172** A5
Bond's Row TA24 . . . . **124** A3
Bond St
 Bridgwater TA6 . . . . **208** F5
 Bristol BS1 . . . . **227** B3
 Yeovil BA20 . . . . **219** B4
 Yeovil, Houndstone BA22. . . . **218** B5
Bonfire Cl TA20 . . . . **223** C2
Bonfire La TA11 . . . . **173** E7
Bonham La BA12 . . . . **161** F4
Bonhill La BS39 . . . . **57** D5
Bonhill Rd BS39 . . . . **57** D5
Boniface Wlk TA8 . . . . **104** B6
Bonita Dr TA6 . . . . **208** D5
Bonners Cswy EX13 . . . . **198** A2
Bonners Dr EX13 . . . . **198** A1
Bonners Glen EX13 . . . . **198** A1
Bonners Leaze La TA20 . . . . **194** D5
Bonnie's La TA19 . . . . **185** F4
Bonning's La TA24 . . . . **184** D4
Bonniton La TA24 . . . . **130** E5
Bonniton New Rd TA24 . . . . **201** D1
Bonny Cross
 Clayhanger EX16 . . . . **165** B1
 Morebath EX16 . . . . **164** B3
Bonny La TA24 . . . . **128** B2
Bonson Hill TA5 . . . . **134** E3
Bonson Mill Farm Track
 TA5 . . . . **134** E4
Bonson Rd TA5 . . . . **134** E4
Bonsonwood La TA5 . . . . . . **134** E4
Boobery EX16 . . . . **178** D1
Book Cl BS39 . . . . **77** D6
Boome La TA2 . . . . **169** C7
Boons Orch TA3 . . . . **169** C3
Boon Villas BS11 . . . . **4** E7
Booth Way TA6 . . . . **208** D5
Boozer Pit TA16 . . . . **195** F8
Borden Gate EX16 . . . . **178** B8
Bordesley Rd BS14 . . . . **23** A3
Boreal Way 4 BS24 . . . . **49** F7
Boreland La BA22 . . . . **187** A8
Borgie Pl BS22 . . . . **31** F3
Borleyton Wlk BS13 . . . . **21** F4
Borough Mall The BS28. . . . . **108** D4
Borough Post
 Helland TA3 . . . . **170** A3
 North Curry TA3 . . . . **170** B3
Borough The
 Montacute TA15 . . . . **186** B3
 Wedmore BS28 . . . . **108** D4
 3 Yeovil BA20 . . . . **219** B4
Borver Gr BS13 . . . . **22** C4
Bosanquet Flats TA24 . . . . . **200** F7
BOSSINGTON **124** B4
Bossington Dr TA2 . . . . **213** B8
Bossington La TA24 . . . . **124** B4
Bosun Wlk BA16 . . . . **207** B6
Boswell Rd BA15 . . . . **64** F3
Botham Cl BS22. . . . . **32** A4
Bottreaux Mill Cross
 EX36. . . . . **162** A5
Boucher's La TA4 . . . . **165** E4
Boughton Rd BA6 . . . . **206** D6
Boulevard BS23. . . . . **48** E8
Boulevard The BS14. . . . . **22** E5
Boulters Rd BS13 . . . . **22** C4
Boundaries The BS24. . . . . . . **67** B1
Boundary Ave
 Frome BA11. . . . . **120** B5
 Yeovil BA22 . . . . **218** B7
Boundary Cl
 Holcombe BA3 . . . . **116** C8
 Midsomer Norton BA3 . . . . . . **97** B7
 Weston-super-Mare BS23 . . . . **48** E3
 Yeovil BA21 . . . . **218** E7
Boundary Rd
 Weston-super-Mare BS24 . . . . **50** A7
 Yeovil BA22 . . . . **218** A5
Boundary Way
 Glastonbury BA6 . . . . **206** C3
 Yeovil BA22 . . . . **218** A7
Boundhay BA22 . . . . **186** C2
Bounds La TA20. . . . . **223** A1
Bourchier Cl 13 EX16 . . . . . **164** B1
Bourchier Dr 12 EX16. . . . . . **164** B1
Bourchier Gdns BS13. . . . . . . **22** B3
Bourke Rd BA4. . . . . **205** D3
BOURNE. **54** B4
Bourne Gr TA1 . . . . **213** D4
Bourne La
 Blagdon BS40. . . . . **54** C4
 Burrington BS40. . . . . **54** B4
Bournville Prim Sch BS23. . . **48** F5
Bournville Rd BS23. . . . . **48** F4
BOURTON
 Gillingham **161** F1
 Weston-super-Mare. **32** E6
Bourtonbridge Dro BA5 . . . **139** F5
Bourton Combe BS48. . . . . . . **19** F7
Bourton La
 Cross BS26. . . . . **69** E3
 Weston-super-Mare BS22 . . . . **32** D4

Bourton Mead
 Flax Bourton BS48 . . . . **19** F8
 Long Ashton BS41 . . . . **11** A1
Bourton Wlk BS13. . . . . **22** A8
Bouverie Cl TA24. . . . . **129** E1
Bouverie Rd TA6 . . . . **208** D5
Bove Moor Cl BA16. . . . . **207** E6
Bove Moor Rd BA16. . . . . . . **207** E6
Bovet Cl TA1. . . . . **212** B1
Bove Town BA6 . . . . **206** E5
Bovet St TA21. . . . . **222** C6
Bowbridge La TA9 . . . . **106** A1
Bow Cotts BS20. . . . . **4** C4
BOWDEN **177** F2
Bowden Cl BS9 . . . . **5** C8
Bowden Hill BA3 . . . . **96** D4
Bowden La
 Milborne Port BA8 . . . . **217** F5
 Rodhuish TA24 . . . . **130** F3
 Yenston BA8. . . . . **189** D7
Bowden Rd BA8 . . . . **189** D8
Bowden's La TA10. . . . . **171** F7
Bowden Way BS8 . . . . **10** B3
Bowditch Cl BA4 . . . . **205** A5
Bowditch Row 8 TA18 . . . . . **224** C6
Bowen Rd BS24 . . . . **50** C5
BOWER ASHTON **11** E4
Bower Ashton Terr BS3. . . . . **11** F4
Bower Ave TA6 . . . . **209** C6
Bower Fields TA6. . . . . **209** D6
BOWER HINTON **185** D5
Bower Hinton TA12. . . . . **185** D5
Bowerings Rd TA6 . . . . **208** E2
Bower La TA6 . . . . **209** E6
Bowerleaze BS9 . . . . **5** C5
Bower Manor Sh Ctr TA6. . . **209** D6
Bowermead La BA4 . . . . **204** C1
Bowery Cnr BA5 . . . . **92** E5
Bowfell Cl TA1. . . . . **212** C1
Bow Gate BA18. . . . . **196** A8
Bowhayes TA18 . . . . **224** C5
Bowhays Cross TA4 . . . . **202** A2
Bowlditch La BA3 . . . . **78** B4
Bowline Cl TA6 . . . . **208** E7
Bowline Ct TA24 . . . . **201** B7
Bowling Gn
 10 Cannington TA5. . . . . **135** B2
 Street BA16. . . . . **207** D7
BOWLISH. **205** A7
Bowlish Inf Sch
 Shepton Mallet BA4 . . . . **205** A6
 Shepton Mallet BA4 . . . . **205** A6
Bowlish La BA4 . . . . **205** A6
Bowmead Dro TA10 . . . . **172** D3
Bowmont Gr TA1. . . . . **213** D3
Bowns Cl BA4. . . . . **141** E1
Bowood Rd TA2. . . . . **213** A6
Bowring Cl
 Bristol BS13. . . . . **22** C3
 Coxley BA5. . . . . **139** E6
Bowsprit Cl TA24. . . . . **201** B7
Bow St TA10 . . . . **171** F5
Bowyers Cl BA6 . . . . **206** E5
Boxbury Hill BS39 . . . . **77** F3
Boxbush Hall BA4. . . . . **158** E8
Box Bush La BS24 . . . . **33** C1
Boxhill La TA11 . . . . **173** E8
Box Rd BA1. . . . . **29** C3
Boxstone Hill TA19 . . . . **184** D2
Box Wlk BS31. . . . . **24** C4
Boyce Cl BA2 . . . . **43** F5
Boyce's Ave BS8 . . . . **226** A3
Boyd Ho BA5. . . . . **113** A1
Boyd Rd BS31. . . . . **25** D3
Boyle Cl DT10 . . . . **190** B4
Boyton Hill TA19 . . . . **194** F8
Boyton La TA19 . . . . **194** F7
Bracey Rd TA12. . . . . **185** E7
Bracken Edge TA4 . . . . **132** E4
Bracken Way TA20 . . . . **223** F5
Brackenwood Gdns★ BS20. . . **1** F5
Brackenwood Rd BS21 . . . . . . **6** E6
Bracton Dr BS14 . . . . **23** A5
Bradbeers TA3. . . . . **181** D8
Bradfield Cl
 Bridgwater TA6 . . . . **208** E1
 Wells BA5. . . . . **203** C2
Bradfield Way TA20. . . . . **223** C3
BRADFORD ABBAS **187** E1
Bradford Cl
 Clevedon BS21. . . . . **6** C1
 Taunton TA1 . . . . **168** D1
Bradford Hollow BA21. . . . . . **219** E4
BRADFORD ON TONE **167** F1
Bradford Pk BA2 . . . . **45** A2
Bradford Rd
 Bath BA2 . . . . **45** A1
 Bathford BA1. . . . . **29** B2
 Misterton TA18. . . . . **224** E4
 Rode BA11, BA14. . . . . **83** A2
 Sherborne DT9. . . . . **225** B3
 Wingfield BA14, BA15 . . . . **83** C8
 Winsley BA15. . . . . **64** D6
 Winsley BA15. . . . . **64** E7
Bradley Ave BS11 . . . . **4** E6
Bradley Cl TA11 . . . . **211** C4
Bradley Cres BS11 . . . . **4** E6
Bradley Cross La BS27. . . . . . . **90** D7
BRADLEY GREEN **135** B1
Bradley Hill La TA11 . . . . **211** B5
Bradley La
 Ashcott TA7. . . . . **156** B7
 Maiden Bradley BA11, BA12 **144** B2
 Parbrook BA6. . . . . **158** C7
Bradley Rd BS20 . . . . **3** E5

Bradleys TA19 . . . . **183** F4
Bradley Stream Rd BA16,
 TA7. **138** C1
Bradley View TA11 . . . . **211** C4
Bradley Way BA6. . . . . **158** B8
BRADNEY **136** D1
Bradney La TA7 . . . . **136** D1
Bradon La
 Isle Abbotts TA3. . . . . **183** F6
 Stocklinch TA19 . . . . **184** A5
Bradville Gdns BS41. . . . . **20** F8
Bradway BS25. . . . . **70** B8
Brae Rise BS25. . . . . **70** A8
Bragg's La BS2. . . . . **227** C3
Braikenridge Cl BS21. . . . . **6** C1
Brain's Cnr BA9 . . . . **216** E1
Brainsfield BS9 . . . . **5** F6
Brains La BA22. . . . . **175** A5
Braithwaite Pl TA8 . . . . **85** A2
Braithwaite Way TA11 . . . . . **120** C6
Brakewell Gdns BS14. . . . . . . **23** A4
Bramble Dr
 Berrow TA8. . . . . **84** F5
 Bristol BS9 . . . . **5** D3
 South Petherton TA13. . . . . . **220** C4
Bramble Hill BA16. . . . . **156** D6
Bramble La
 Bristol BS9 . . . . **5** C3
 Haselbury Plucknett TA18. . **196** C5
Bramble Pk TA1. . . . . **213** C2
Bramble Rd TA6 . . . . **208** D1
Brambles Rd TA8 . . . . **85** B1
Brambles The
 Bristol BS13. . . . . **22** C4
 Hinton Charterhouse BA2 . . . . **63** E1
 Keynsham BS31. . . . . **24** D3
 Wellington TA21. . . . . **222** D4
 Weston-super-Mare BS22 . . . . **32** D2
Bramble Way BA2. . . . . **45** B1
Bramblewood BS9 . . . . **17** B1
Bramblewood Rd BS22 . . . . . **31** E3
Bramley Cl
 Charlton Horethorne DT9. . . **176** A2
 Crewkerne TA18. . . . . **224** C7
 Locking BS24. . . . . **50** A5
 Peasedown St John BA2. . . . . **79** D7
 Pill BS20. . . . . **4** C4
 Sandford BS25. . . . . **52** A4
 Wellington TA21. . . . . **222** F7
 Yatton BS49. . . . . **34** B7
Bramley Copse BS41. . . . . **20** E8
Bramley Dr
 Backwell BS48. . . . . **19** A5
 Frome BA11. . . . . **120** C6
Bramley Fields TA14 . . . . **185** E3
Bramley Rd
 Street BA16. . . . . **207** B4
 Taunton TA1. . . . . **213** D5
Bramley Sq BS49 . . . . **34** E3
Bramleys The
 Nailsea BS48 . . . . **18** B8
 Portishead BS20 . . . . **2** F5
Brampton Ho BS20. . . . . **2** E4
Brampton Way BS20. . . . . **2** E4
Bramshill Dr BS22. . . . . **31** F3
BRAMWELL **172** B8
Branche Gr BS13. . . . . **22** D3
Branches Cross BS40 . . . . **35** E3
Branch Farm La BA11. . . . . . . **118** A7
Branch Rd BA2. . . . . **63** F2
BRANDISH STREET **124** C3
BRANDON HILL. **226** B2
Brandon Ho BS8 . . . . **226** B2
Brandon St BS1. . . . . **226** C2
Brandon Steep BS1 . . . . **226** C2
Brandown Cl BS39 . . . . **58** E1
Brangay La BS27 . . . . **91** A1
Brangwyn Sq BS22 . . . . **31** F2
Branksome Ave TA6 . . . . **209** B5
Bransby Way BS24. . . . . **50** A8
Branscombe Rd BS9 . . . . **5** C4
Branscombe Wlk BS20 . . . . . . **1** F3
Bransford BA22 . . . . **197** D3
Brantwood Rd TA6 . . . . **208** C5
BRASSKNOCKER **45** F2
Brassknocker Hill BA2. . . . . . **45** F2
Brassmill Ent Ctr BA1. . . . . . **44** A7
Brassmill La BA1. . . . . **44** A7
Brassmill Lane Trad Est
 BA1. . . . . **44** A7
BRATTON **200** B7
Bratton Cl TA24 . . . . **200** D7
Bratton Ho BA9 . . . . **176** B8
Bratton La TA24. . . . . **200** B7
Bratton Mill La
 Minehead, Bratton TA24. . . . **200** B7
 Minehead, Woodcombe
 TA24 . . . . **200** C7
Bratton Rd BS4 . . . . **22** D7
BRATTON SEYMOUR **176** C8
Bratton Seymour Rd BA9 . . **160** B1
Bray Cl EX16 . . . . **179** B3
Brays Batch BA3 . . . . **94** F6
Braysbridge BS27 . . . . **90** C7
Braysdown Cl BA2. . . . . **79** B6
Braysdown La BA2 . . . . **79** C7
BREACH. **58** F6
Breach Cl SP8 . . . . **161** F1
Breaches The BS20. . . . . **4** B5
Breach Furlong La TA10 . . **156** A1
Breach Hill TA21 . . . . **179** F5
Breach Hill Comm BS40 . . . . . **56** A5
Breach Hill La BS40 . . . . **56** C6
Breach La
 Brinscombe BS26. . . . . **89** B3
 Corsley Heath BA12. . . . . **144** E7
 Kington Magna SP8 . . . . **177** E2
 Nailsea BS48 . . . . **17** F7

Breach La continued
 Weston Town BA4. . . . . **142** E4
Breachwood View BA2 . . . . . . **44** C2
Bread And Cheese La
 Seavington St Mary TA19 . . . **184** C1
 Seavington St Mary TA19 . . . **184** C1
Bread St BA4 . . . . **140** F3
BREAN **65** F5
Brean Court Ho TA8 . . . . **65** F3
Brean Ct TA8 . . . . **65** F3
Brean Down Ave BS23 . . . . . . **48** E4
Brean Down Rd TA8 . . . . **47** F1
Brean Leisure Pk★ TA8 . . . . . **65** F1
Brean Rd BS24 . . . . **66** F1
Brecon View BS24. . . . . **49** A1
Breech Cotts TA21 . . . . **179** F5
Breech La BA6. . . . . **158** A8
Bree Cl BS22. . . . . **32** A4
Bremis Rd TA24. . . . . **201** E3
BRENDON **122** A4
Brendon Ave BS23 . . . . **48** F8
Brendon Cl TA23 . . . . **131** D2
Brendon Gdns 2 BS48 . . . . **8** E1
Brendon Ho BA21 . . . . **219** A6
Brendon Rd
 Bridgwater TA6 . . . . **208** F6
 Portishead BS20 . . . . **2** A5
 Watchet TA23. . . . . **202** B6
 Wellington TA21. . . . . **222** D7
Brendons TA4 . . . . **167** E8
Brendons The EX16 . . . . **178** D1
Brendon Two Gates TA24. . . **127** A6
Brendon View TA4 . . . . **151** B7
Brendon Way
 Bridgwater TA6 . . . . **208** F6
 Cheddar BS27 . . . . **90** C8
Brennan Cl BS4 . . . . **22** F7
Brent Broad
 Burnham-on-S TA8 . . . . **85** B2
 Burnham-on-Sea TA8 . . . . . . **85** C1
Brent Cl
 Brent Knoll TA9. . . . . **86** A1
 Weston-super-Mare BS24 . . . . **49** B2
BRENT KNOLL **86** A1
Brent Knoll CE Prim Sch
 TA9 . . . . **86** A2
Brent Rd
 Burnham-on-S TA8, TA9 . . . . . **85** B4
 Cossington TA7. . . . . **136** F3
 East Brent TA9. . . . . **86** C5
Brentsfield La TA7 . . . . **154** E7
Brent St TA9 . . . . **86** A2
Breowen Cl TA19. . . . . **221** B3
Brereton Rd TA24 . . . . **201** B6
Breton Cl 1 TA6. . . . . **209** A1
Bretoneux Rd BA6. . . . . **206** E3
Brett Cl TA4 . . . . **202** F1
Brettingham Ct TA17 . . . . . . **195** C7
Brewery Bglws TA18 . . . . **224** C7
Brewery Hill BS30 . . . . **25** F7
Brewery La
 Holcombe BA3 . . . . **97** D1
 Ilminster TA19 . . . . **221** B4
 Oakhill BA3 . . . . **115** A3
 Shepton Mallet BA4 . . . . **205** D5
Brewham Rd BA10 . . . . **160** D6
Brewhouse The BS1. . . . . **227** B2
Brewhouse Theatre & Arts
 Ctr★ TA1 . . . . **212** F4
Breynton Rd BA6. . . . . **206** F5
Brian Mooney Cl TA20 . . . . . **223** B3
Briant Cl TA1. . . . . **212** B1
Briar Cl
 Burnham-on-S TA8 . . . . **104** C6
 Frome BA11. . . . . **120** B7
 Nailsea BS48 . . . . **9** A2
 Radstock BA3. . . . . **97** D8
 Yeovil BA21 . . . . **219** E8
Briar Ct
 Bridgwater TA6 . . . . **208** E5
 Burnham-on-S TA8 . . . . **104** C6
 Pill BS20. . . . . **4** C4
Briarfield BA22 . . . . **173** E2
Briar Mead BS49 . . . . **17** A1
Briar Rd
 Hutton BS24. . . . . **49** E3
 Street BA16. . . . . **207** A5
Briars Ct BA2 . . . . **44** A4
Briars The
 Backwell BS48 . . . . **18** F7
 Yeovil BA20 . . . . **218** C2
Briarwood BS9. . . . . **5** F6
Briary Rd BS20. . . . . **2** C5
Brick Cotts BA3 . . . . **117** A7
Brick Hill BA10 . . . . **215** C6
Brickhouse Farm La BA9. . . . **161** B2
Brickkiln La DT9 . . . . **225** E7
Brick St BS2 . . . . **227** C3
Brickwall La TA10 . . . . **171** D3
Brickworks Rd TA5. . . . . **135** A2
Brickyard La
 Bourton SP8. . . . . **161** F1
 Wanstrow BA4. . . . . **142** F5
Brick Yard La TA18 . . . . **224** C7
Briddicott La TA24. . . . . **131** A4
Bridewell La
 Bath BA1. . . . . **228** B2
 Hutton BS24, BS26, BS29. . . . **50** D1
 Shapwick TA7. . . . . **137** F1
Bridewell St BS1. . . . . **227** A3
BRIDGE **199** A8
Bridge Bldgs BS39 . . . . **77** B3
Bridge Cl
 Evercreech BA4 . . . . **141** E2
 Whitchurch BS14 . . . . **23** C4
 Williton TA4 . . . . **202** D2
Bridge Cotts
 Chard Junction TA20. . . . . . . **198** D8

Bridge Cotts continued
 Drimpton DT8. . . . . **199** F7
 East Chinnock BA22 . . . . **196** F8
Bridge Farm Cl BS14. . . . . **23** A3
Bridge Farm Inf Sch BS14. . . **23** A4
Bridge Farm Jun Sch BS14 **23** A4
Bridge Farm Prim Sch
 Whitchurch BS14. . . . . **23** A4
 Whitchurch BS14 . . . . **23** A4
Bridge Farm Sq BS49 . . . . **34** D4
Bridge Gdns BA2. . . . . **60** A6
BRIDGEHAMPTON **174** C3
Bridgehampton Rd BA22. . . . **174** C3
Bridge Hill BA4 . . . . **142** E4
Bridge Ho
 11 Bath BA1. . . . . **28** C1
 Bristol BS1. . . . . **227** A2
 9 Clevedon BS21 . . . . **6** C2
 Weston-super-Mare BS23 . . . . **48** F6
Bridgehorne TA10. . . . . **156** B3
Bridgehouse Cross EX15. . . . **180** D1
Bridge House Pk TA13. . . . . . **220** F4
Bridge Learning Campus
 BS13. **22** D4
Bridge Pl DT9 . . . . **187** F4
Bridge Place Rd BA2. . . . . **78** E8
Bridge Rd
 Bath BA2 . . . . **44** C5
 Bleadon BS24. . . . . **67** B6
 Leigh Woods BS8 . . . . **11** E6
 Weston-super-Mare BS23 . . . . **48** F6
Bridge Rise 17 TA12. . . . . **185** E6
Bridges Mead TA24 . . . . **201** E3
Bridge St
 Bath BA2 . . . . **228** C2
 Bourton SP8. . . . . **161** F1
 Bristol BS1. . . . . **227** A2
 Dulverton TA22. . . . . **163** D6
 Frome BA11. . . . . **119** F5
 Taunton TA1. . . . . **212** F4
 Williton TA4 . . . . **202** D2
Bridge Terr EX16. . . . . **164** B1
Bridge The
 Frome BA11. . . . . **119** F5
 Taunton TA1. . . . . **212** F4
BRIDGETOWN **147** E4
Bridge Valley Rd BS8. . . . . . . **11** E8
Bridge Way TA13. . . . . **220** E4
Bridgeway Cotts TA13 . . . . . **220** E4
Bridgewell Ct DT9. . . . . **225** C3
BRIDGWATER **208** E3
Bridgwater TA6. . . . . **208** E4
Bridgwater Bay National
 Nature Reserve★ TA5. . . . . **103** C2
Bridgwater Bldgs BA7. . . . . . **214** B5
Bridgwater Coll TA6. . . . . . . **209** B5
Bridgwater Com Hospl
 TA6. . . . . **209** D7
Bridgwater Ct BS24 . . . . **49** A4
Bridgwater Ent Ctr 7
 TA6. . . . . **208** F5
Bridgwater Rd
 Dundry BS41, BS13, BS48. . . **21** D6
 East Brent TA9. . . . . **86** D4
 Lympsham BS24. . . . . **67** C5
 North Petherton TA6. . . . . . . **153** F4
 Taunton TA1. . . . . **213** D5
 Taunton, Bathpool TA2 . . . . . **213** F7
 Weston-super-Mare BS23,
 BS24 . . . . **48** F2
 Winscombe BS25. . . . . **70** A5
Bridgwater Ret Pk TA6. . . . . **209** A5
Bridgwater Sta TA6. . . . . **209** B4
Bridle Ave BS14. . . . . **23** D3
Bridle Way BA22 . . . . **197** E8
Bridleway The BS4 . . . . **22** D8
Bridport Rd DT8 . . . . **199** F8
Briercliffe Rd BS9. . . . . **5** D7
Briery Leaze Rd BS14. . . . . . . **23** A4
Brigadier Cl BA22 . . . . **218** A5
Brigg Cl TA6. . . . . **208** E2
Brighton Mews BS8 . . . . **226** B4
Brighton Rd BS23 . . . . **48** E6
Brighton St 7 BS2. . . . . **227** B4
Brightstowe Rd TA8 . . . . **85** A2
Brigstocke Rd BS2 . . . . **227** B4
Brimble Cotts DT10 . . . . **189** F1
Brimbleworth La BS22. . . . . . **32** C3
Brimclose Rd TA17 . . . . **195** B7
Brimgrove La TA19 . . . . **184** C4
Brimhill Rise BA13 . . . . **121** D4
BRIMLEY **198** D3
Brimley Cross TA3 . . . . **180** F1
Brimley Hill EX13 . . . . **198** D2
Brimley La BA4 . . . . **140** F2
Brimley Rd EX13 . . . . **198** D3
Brimridge Rd BS25. . . . . **70** A8
Brimsmore Ct BA21 . . . . **218** E8
Brimstone La
 Rockwell Green TA21. . . . . . . **222** A2
 Sampford Arundel TA21 . . . . **179** F6
 Sampford Peverell EX16 . . . . **178** C2
Brimzemore La TA16 . . . . **195** E6
Brincil Hill TA11. . . . . **173** D4
BRINDHAM **139** D3
Brindham La BA6. . . . . **139** D3
Brindle Cl TA2 . . . . **212** C7
Brines Orch BA8. . . . . **176** E1
Brinkworth Rd BA2. . . . . **45** B2
Brinmead Wlk BS13 . . . . **21** F3
BRINSCOMBE **89** A5
Brinscombe La BS26. . . . . **89** A5
BRINSEA **52** E8
Brinsea Batch BS49 . . . . **52** E8
Brinsea Green Farm La
 BS49 . . . . **52** F8
Brinsea La BS49. . . . . **52** F8
Brinsea Rd BS49 . . . . **34** E2

Brinsmead Cres BS20 . . . . . . 4 D4
Briscoes Ave BS13 . . . . 22 D4
BRISTOL 227 B3
Bristol Airport BS48 . . . . 36 E7
Bristol and Exeter Mews
BS1 . . . . 227 C1
Bristol Cathedral Sch
BS1 . . . . 226 C2
Bristol Dental Hospl BS1. . 227 A3
Bristol Eye Hospl BS1 . . . . 227 A3
Bristol Gate 1 BS8. . . . . 11 F5
Bristol Gram Sch BS8. . . . . 226 C3
Bristol Harbour Rly★ BS1 226 C1
Bristol Hill BA5 . . . . 112 E3
Bristol Mus & Art Gall★
BS8. . . . . 226 C3
Bristol Rd
Bridgwater TA6 . . . . 209 B7
Chew Stoke BS40. . . . . 56 E8
Chewton Mendip BA5. . . . . 113 A8
Churchill BS25 . . . . 53 A5
Congresbury BS49 . . . . 34 D5
Farrington Gurney BS39. . . . . 76 F5
Highbridge TA9. . . . . 104 F4
Horrington BA5 . . . . 112 F6
Keynsham BS31. . . . . 24 E6
Newton St Loe BA2. . . . . 43 D7
Paulton BS39 . . . . 77 E7
Pensford BS39. . . . . 40 D6
Portishead BS20 . . . . 2 E4
Radstock BA3. . . . . 78 F3
Redhill BS40. . . . . 37 A3
Rooks Bridge BS26, TA9 . . . . . 87 B5
Sherborne DT9. . . . . 225 D5
Walpole TA6 . . . . 136 B3
Weston-super-Mare BS22 . . . 32 C2
Whitchurch BS14 . . . . 23 D3
Winscombe BS25. . . . . 70 C8
Wraxall BS48. . . . . 9 D4
Bristol Rd By-pass BS40 . . . 53 C5
Bristol Rd Lower BS23. . . . . 30 F1
Bristol Road Lower BS23. . . 30 E1
Bristol Royal Hospl for
Children BS2 . . . . 227 A3
Bristol Royal Infirmary
BS2. . . . . 227 A4
Bristol Temple Meads Sta
BS1. . . . . 227 C1
Bristol View BA2. . . . . 62 C8
Bristol Zoo Gdns★ BS8 . . . . . 5 F1
Britannia Cl BA3 . . . . 96 D4
Britannia Way
Chard TA20. . . . . 223 C6
Clevedon BS21. . . . . 6 C1
Briton St 2 EX16. . . . . 164 C1
Brittains BA11 . . . . 119 D6
Brittania Bldgs BS8 . . . . . . 226 A1
Brittan Pl BS20. . . . . 3 E3
BRITTENS 77 F6
Britten's Cl BS39. . . . . 77 F6
Britten's Hill BS39. . . . . 77 F6
Brittons Ash TA2. . . . . 213 F8
Brittons Pass SN14. . . . . 13 F8
Broadacre Dro TA10. . . . . . . 156 C3
Broadacres BA22. . . . . 197 C8
Broadbridge Rd TA3. . . . . . 183 C6
Broadbury Rd BS4. . . . . 22 E8
Broad Cl
Kington Magna SP8 . . . . 177 E1
Wells BA5. . . . . 112 E1
Broadclose Way TA11 . . . . 158 A2
Broadcroft BS40 . . . . 38 F3
Broadcroft Ave BS49 . . . . 17 F1
Broadcroft Cl BS49. . . . . 17 F1
Broad Dro
Burrowbridge TA7 . . . . 155 A2
North Wootton BA4 . . . . 140 A3
Broadenham La TA20. . . . . . 194 E1
Broadfield Rd BS4 . . . . 23 A8
Broadguage Bsns Pk TA4 . 167 E7
Broadhay BA5 . . . . 110 E7
Broad Hill BA22 . . . . 196 D7
Broadhurst Gdns TA8. . . . . 104 B5
Broad La
East Chinnock BA22 . . . . 196 E7
Hawkridge TA22. . . . . 146 D1
North Curry TA3 . . . . 170 D4
Winsford TA22 . . . . 147 F4
Broadlands BS21. . . . . 6 F3
Broadlands Ave
Keynsham BS31. . . . . 24 D6
North Petherton TA6. . . . . . . 153 F4
Broadlands Cl BA21 . . . . . . 219 E8
Broadlands Ct TA1 . . . . 212 E2
Broadlands Dr BS11. . . . . 5 A8
Broadlands La TA5 . . . . 208 A4
Broadlands Rd TA1. . . . . . . 212 E2
Broadlands Rise TA1 . . . . . 212 E2
Broadlands Sch BS31. . . . . . 24 D6
Broadlands Way TA1 . . . . . 212 E2
Broad Lane Head
Hawkridge TA22. . . . . 146 D1
Winsford TA22 . . . . 147 F4
Broadlawn TA7 . . . . 136 E4
Broadleas BS13. . . . . 22 C7
Broadleaze
Bristol BS11. . . . . 4 E7
Yeovil BA21 . . . . 218 C6
Broadleaze Way BS25 . . . . . 51 F2
Broadly Gdns TA2 . . . . 213 E8
Broadmead
Bristol BS1. . . . . 227 B3
Keynsham BS31. . . . . 25 B5
Kingsbury Episcopi TA12. . . . 185 B7
South Petherton TA13. . . . . . 220 B4
Broadmead Dro TA7. . . . . . 155 F6
Broadmead La
Barrington TA19. . . . . 184 D6
Broadmead La *continued*
Catcott TA7. . . . . 137 D2
Edington TA7 . . . . 137 C3
Keynsham BS31. . . . . 25 A6
Kington Magna SP8 . . . . 177 D1
Norton Sub Hamdon TA14. . . 185 F2
Broad Mead La BS40 . . . . . . 38 A3
Broadmead Rd TA3. . . . . . . 183 B7
Broadmeads TA10. . . . . 172 A6
Broadmoor Dro BS28. . . . . . 89 D3
Broadmoor La
Bath BA1 . . . . 27 A3
Horsington BA8 . . . . 176 E2
Broadmoor Pk BA1. . . . . 27 B2
Broadmoor Vale BA1 . . . . . . 27 A3
Broadoak TA19 . . . . 183 C1
Broad Oak 9 BA20 . . . . 219 B4
Broadoak Hill BS41. . . . . 21 F2
Broad Oak Hill TA4 . . . . 151 B5
Broadoak Mathematics &
Computing Coll BS23. . . . . 48 E3
Broadoak Rd
Bridgwater TA6 . . . . 209 D5
Churchill BS40 . . . . 53 A5
Weston-super-Mare BS23 . . . 48 D3
Broad Oak Rd BS13. . . . . 21 F4
Broad Oaks BS8. . . . . 11 E6
Broad Path EX15 . . . . 179 A1
Broad Plain BS2 . . . . 227 C2
Broad Quay
Bath BA1 . . . . 228 C1
Bristol BS1. . . . . 227 A2
Broad Rd
Blagdon BS40. . . . . 72 D8
Rodney Stoke BA5 . . . . 91 E1
Broadshard Rd TA18 . . . . . 224 C8
Broadslade BA12. . . . . 144 C3
Broad St
Bath BA1 . . . . 228 C3
Bristol BS1. . . . . 227 A3
Charlton Adam TA11. . . . . . . 173 F7
Churchinford TA3 . . . . 191 D7
Congresbury BS49 . . . . 34 D4
Somerton TA11. . . . . 211 E4
Stoney Stratton BA4. . . . . . . 141 F2
Wells BA5. . . . . 203 D4
Wrington BS40. . . . . 35 D2
Broadstone TA7. . . . . 154 E6
Broadstone La
Hardington Mandeville
BA22. . . . . 197 A6
Kingston Seymour BS21. . . . . 15 F3
West Chinnock TA18. . . . . . . 196 C7
Broad Stones BA15. . . . . 46 E7
Broadstone Wlk BS13 . . . . . 22 D5
Broad Street Pl BA1 . . . . . . 228 C3
BROADWAY 183 B2
Broadway
Bath BA2 . . . . 45 B6
Bridgwater TA6 . . . . 208 F4
Charlton Adam TA11. . . . . . . 174 A7
Chilcompton BA3 . . . . 96 C3
Chilton Polden TA7 . . . . 137 B2
Frome BA11. . . . . 119 D5
Locking BS24 . . . . 50 D4
Merriott TA16. . . . . 195 F7
Odcombe BA22. . . . . 186 C2
Saltford BS31. . . . . 25 D3
Shipham BS25 . . . . 70 E8
Weston-super-Mare BS24 . . . 49 A2
Broad Way TA12 . . . . 185 D5
Broadway Acres BS27 . . . . . 70 F1
Broadway Ave TA7 . . . . 137 B2
Broadway Cl BA3. . . . . 96 C3
Broadway Dro TA3 . . . . 170 F4
Broadway Hill TA19 . . . . . . 183 B1
Broadway La
Castle Cary BA22 . . . . 214 B3
Midsomer Norton BA3 . . . . . . 78 B5
Westbury-sub-Mendip BA5 . 110 D7
Broadway Rd
Bristol, Bishopsworth BS13 . . 21 F5
Charlton Adam TA11. . . . . . . 173 F7
Horton TA19. . . . . 183 C2
Broadways Head EX14,
TA20 . . . . 192 C6
Broadway St TA19. . . . . 183 C2
Broad Weir BS1. . . . . 227 B3
Broadwell Cl TA20 . . . . 193 D6
Broadwood Rd TA24. . . . . . 130 D4
Brock Ct BA7 . . . . 214 C6
Brock End BS20. . . . . 1 F3
BROCKFIELD. 198 A8
Brockhole La EX13, TA20 . . 198 B7
Brockle Cl TA11. . . . . 211 D4
BROCKLEY 18 C2
Brockley Cl
Nailsea BS48 . . . . 8 D1
Weston-super-Mare BS24 . . . 48 F1
Brockley Combe Rd BS48 . . 19 B1
Brockley Cres BS24 . . . . 48 F1
Brockley La BS48. . . . . 18 D4
Brockley Rd BS31 . . . . 25 D3
Brockley Way BS49. . . . . 18 B3
Brockley Wlk BS13 . . . . 22 A8
Brocks La BS41 . . . . 10 F1
Brocks Mount 16 TA14. . . . 185 F4
Brocks Rd BS13 . . . . 22 C3
Brock St BA1 . . . . 228 B3
Brockway BS48 . . . . 8 F2
BROCKWELL 129 E6
Brockwell La TA24 . . . . 129 F6
Brockwood BA15. . . . . 64 F7
Brocole La TA20 . . . . 193 D5
Broderip TA7 . . . . 136 F3
BROKERSWOOD. 102 F5
Brokerswood Country Pk★
BA13. . . . . 102 F6
Bromes La TA3. . . . . 183 F7
Bromley Rd BS39. . . . . 39 F1
Brompton Ho BA2. . . . . 228 C4
Brompton Mdws TA22 . . . . 148 B2
BROMPTON RALPH 150 C3
Brompton Rd BS24 . . . . 49 A2
BROMPTON REGIS. 148 B2
Bronte Cl BS23. . . . . 49 B4
Brook Bank
Draycott BS27 . . . . 90 F2
Rodney Stoke BS27 . . . . 109 C7
Brook Cl
Long Ashton BS41 . . . . 11 B1
Minehead TA24. . . . . 200 F7
North Petherton TA6. . . . . . . 153 E3
Yeovil BA21 . . . . 218 D7
Brook Cotts
Corfe TA3 . . . . 181 F6
Corston BA2. . . . . 43 B7
Brook Ct BS13 . . . . 22 A6
Brookdale Rd BS13. . . . . 22 B6
Brooke Rd
Berrow TA8. . . . . 84 F4
Taunton TA1 . . . . 213 B4
Brookes Ct BA5 . . . . 203 C5
Brookfield Pk BA1 . . . . 27 B2
Brookfields BA7 . . . . 214 B5
Brookfield Way BA16. . . . . 207 A4
Brookfield Wlk BS21 . . . . 6 F3
Brook Gate BS3. . . . . 11 E1
Brook Gdns BS40. . . . . 53 A5
BROOKHAMPTON 175 D6
Brookhampton Cnr BA22 . 175 D6
Brooking Mdw BS48. . . . . 8 D1
Brook La
Barton St David BA6. . . . . . . 157 F3
6 Cannington TA5 . . . . 135 B2
Catcott TA7. . . . . 137 D2
7 Henstridge BA8. . . . . 190 A6
Brookland Rd
Langport TA10 . . . . 172 A6
Weston-super-Mare BS22 . . . 49 B7
Brooklands
Bridgwater TA6 . . . . 209 C5
Dunkerton BA2. . . . . 61 D3
Brooklands Rd TA21. . . . . . 222 B5
Brookland Way 3 BA8 . . . . 190 A6
Brookleaze
Bristol BS9. . . . . 5 C5
Keynsham BS31. . . . . 24 D6
Brookleaze Bldgs BA1. . . . . 28 B2
Brookleigh BA16. . . . . 207 A5
Brooklyn BS40 . . . . 35 D2
Brooklyn Rd
Bath BA1 . . . . 28 C2
Bristol BS13. . . . . 22 B8
Brooklyn Terr BA5 . . . . 139 E6
Brook Rd
Bath BA2 . . . . 44 D6
Williton TA4 . . . . 202 E3
Brook's Hill EX15. . . . . 179 C1
Brookside
Broadway TA19 . . . . 183 C2
Milborne Port DT9 . . . . 217 D1
Paulton BS39 . . . . 77 E6
Pill BS20. . . . . 4 D3
South Cheriton BA8 . . . . 176 D3
West Coker BA22. . . . . 197 A8
Brookside Acad BA16. . . . . 207 B4
Brookside Cl
Batheaston BA1. . . . . 28 F5
Paulton BS39 . . . . 77 E6
Taunton TA3 . . . . 168 D1
Brookside Dr BA2 . . . . 59 F6
Brookside Ho BA1. . . . . 27 B1
Brookside Rd TA5 . . . . 135 B5
Brooks Pl TA21 . . . . 222 E6
Brooks Rd BA16. . . . . 207 B4
Brook St
Bampton EX16 . . . . 164 B1
Cannington TA5 . . . . 135 B2
Milborne Port DT9 . . . . 217 D1
Minehead TA24. . . . . 201 B5
North Newton TA7 . . . . 153 F1
Timberscombe TA24. . . . . . . 130 B5
Brook Street Mews TA24. . 201 B5
Brookview Wlk BS13 . . . . . . 22 B7
Broomball Cross TA22. . . . 162 F5
Broomball La EX16 . . . . 162 E5
Broomclose Cnr BA3 . . . . . 114 B4
Broome Cl EX13. . . . . 198 A1
Broom Farm Cl BS48 . . . . . . 18 E8
BROOMFIELD 152 E2
Broomfield Hall Rd TA5. . . 152 F4
Broomfield Ho TA2. . . . . . . 212 E7
Broomfield La TA20 . . . . . . 182 D2
Broomfield Rd TA5. . . . . . . 152 E2
Broomground BA15 . . . . 64 E7
Broomhill La BS39 . . . . 58 E3
Broom Hill La BS39. . . . . 77 E8
Broom La
Chardstock EX13 . . . . 198 C5
Oake TA4 . . . . 167 D3
Brooms La TA19. . . . . 183 B1
Broom's La TA3. . . . . 191 F7
Broomstreet La TA24 . . . . . 122 F5
Broomyland Hill TA5 . . . . . 152 C7
Brottens Rd
Cranmore BA4 . . . . 142 A5
Doulting BA4 . . . . 141 F5
Brougham Hayes BA2 . . . . . 44 D6
Brougham Pl 2 BA1 . . . . . . 28 C2
Broughton Cl
Taunton TA1 . . . . 213 C2
Walton BA16 . . . . 156 E7
Broughton Ho BS1 . . . . 227 B1
Broughton La TA3. . . . . 169 B1
Broughton Pk TA3 . . . . 169 A1
Broughtons Dr TA18. . . . . . 224 E3
Brow Hill BA2. . . . . 28 F4
Brown Down La TA20. . . . . 192 C7
Browne Ct 4 BS8 . . . . 11 F6
Browney La BA2 . . . . 62 A5
BROWNHEATH 180 C2
Brownings Rd TA5 . . . . 135 B2
Brown La TA4, TA23. . . . . . . 149 C3
Brownlow Rd BS23 . . . . 48 E4
Browns Ct BS23. . . . . 48 E6
Brownsey La TA20. . . . . 192 F5
Brown's Folly Nature
Reserve★ BA15 . . . . 29 D1
Browns La BS28. . . . . 109 C1
Brown's Pl 4 BA5. . . . . 203 C4
Brow The
Bath BA2 . . . . 44 B5
Bath, Combe Down BA2 . . . . 45 C1
Broxholme Wlk BS11 . . . . 4 F8
Brue Ave
Bridgwater TA6 . . . . 209 B3
Bruton BA10. . . . . 215 F7
Brue Bsns Pk TA9 . . . . 136 E8
Brue Cl
Bruton BA10. . . . . 215 F7
Weston-super-Mare BS23 . . . 49 A5
Brue Cres TA8 . . . . 104 B5
Brue Ho TA8 . . . . 85 A1
Bruelands BA10. . . . . 215 F7
Brue Way TA9. . . . . 104 F3
Bruford Cl TA1. . . . . 212 E3
Bruford Dr TA2 . . . . 213 C8
Brummel Way BS39 . . . . 77 C6
Brunel Cl
Somerton TA11. . . . . 211 D4
Weston-super-Mare BS24 . . . 48 F1
Brunel Ct
Bridgwater TA6 . . . . 208 F6
Portishead BS20 . . . . 2 D6
Brunel Ho BA2. . . . . 44 A6
Brunel Institute The★
BS3. . . . . 226 B1
Brunel Lock Rd BS1 . . . . 11 F5
Brunel Prec TA11. . . . . 211 D4
Brunel Rd
Bristol BS13. . . . . 22 A8
Nailsea BS48 . . . . 8 B1
Brunel's SS Great Britain &
The Matthew★ BS1. . . . . . 226 B1
Brunel's Way TA9 . . . . 104 E5
Brunel Way
Bristol BS1, BS3. . . . . 11 F4
Frome BA11. . . . . 120 C7
Minehead TA24. . . . . 201 B6
Taunton TA2 . . . . 212 A6
Brunsell's Knap DT10. . . . . 190 A1
Brunswick Pl
1 Bath BA1. . . . . 228 B3
10 Bristol BS1 . . . . 11 F5
Brunswick Sq BS2. . . . . 227 B4
Brunswick St
1 Bath BA1. . . . . 28 B1
Bristol BS2. . . . . 227 B4
Yeovil BA20 . . . . 219 A4
BRUSHFORD. 163 D4
Brushford New Rd TA22 . . 163 E4
Brutasche Terr BA16 . . . . . 207 D7
BRUTON 215 E5
Bruton BS24 . . . . 49 A2
Bruton Ave
Bath BA2 . . . . 44 F4
Portishead BS20 . . . . 2 A5
Bruton Avenue Garages
BA2 . . . . 44 F4
Bruton Cl BS48. . . . . 18 E8
Bruton La BA4 . . . . 142 F2
Bruton Mus★ BA10. . . . . . . 215 E6
Bruton Pl BS8. . . . . 226 B3
Bruton Prim Sch BA10. . . . 215 E6
Bruton Rd BA4 . . . . 141 F1
Bruton Sch for Girls BA10 215 C3
Bruton Sta BA10 . . . . 215 F6
Brutton Way TA20. . . . . 223 B3
Bryant Ave BA3 . . . . 78 D1
Bryant Gdns BS21 . . . . 6 C1
Bryant's Hill TA22 . . . . 148 C2
Bryer Cl
Bridgwater TA6 . . . . 208 E1
Chard TA20. . . . . 223 D3
Brymore Cl TA6 . . . . 208 D5
Brymore Sch TA5. . . . . 135 A2
Brympton Ave BA22 . . . . . . 186 D2
BRYMPTON D'EVERCY 218 A3
Brympton Way BA20. . . . . 218 C3
Bsns Courtyard The BA11 . 143 C7
Bubwith Cl TA20 . . . . 223 D3
Bubwith Ho 4 BA5 . . . . 203 D4
Bubwith Rd TA20. . . . . 223 D3
Bubwith Wlk BA5 . . . . 203 B3
Buces Rd TA1. . . . . 212 B1
Buck Cl BA6 . . . . 206 C3
Buckhill TA24. . . . . 131 B4
Buckhill Cl TA18 . . . . 224 C4
BUCKHORN WESTON. 177 D3
Buckingham Cl TA6 . . . . . . 209 A2
Buckingham Pl BS8 . . . . . . 226 A3
Buckingham Rd BS24. . . . . . 49 B2
Buckingham Vale BS8. . . . . 226 A4
Buckland Cl TA8 . . . . 104 C8
BUCKLAND DINHAM 100 A3
BUCKLAND DOWN. 99 B4
Buckland Gn BS22. . . . . 32 A5
Buckland La BA22 . . . . 175 C3
Buckland Rd
Shepton Mallet BA4 . . . . 205 A5
Taunton TA2 . . . . 213 B8
Yeovil BA21 . . . . 219 E6
BUCKLAND ST MARY. 192 F8
Buckland St Mary CE Prim
Sch TA20 . . . . 193 A8
Bucklands Batch BS48. . . . . 18 F8
Buckland Sch TA23 . . . . 202 C6
Bucklands Dr BS48 . . . . 19 A8
Bucklands End BS48. . . . . . . 18 F8
Bucklands Gr BS48 . . . . 18 F8
Bucklands La BS48 . . . . 18 F8
Bucklands View BS48. . . . . . 19 A8
Buckle Path BS24 . . . . 50 C8
Buckle Pl BA22. . . . . 218 B6
Buckler's Mead Acad
BA21. . . . . 219 C8
Bucklers Mead Rd BA21 . . 219 D8
Bucklers Mead Wlk BA21 . 219 D8
Bucklers Way BA4. . . . . 204 F6
Bucklewell Cl BS11. . . . . 4 F6
Buckshots Cross EX14 . . . . 192 D4
Buckwell TA21 . . . . 222 E6
Bude Cl BS48 . . . . 9 B1
Budge La BA11. . . . . 144 A8
Budgetts TA21 . . . . 180 F6
Budgett's Cross TA21. . . . . 180 F6
Bughole La TA21 . . . . 179 E8
Bugle Cottage Rd
Barrow Hill DT9 . . . . 217 C7
Milborne Wick DT9. . . . . 189 B8
Bugle Ct 11 BA8. . . . . 190 A6
Bugle Farm La
Barrow Hill DT9 . . . . 217 D7
Milborne Wick DT9. . . . . 189 B8
Bugle Wlk TA6 . . . . 208 D1
Building of Bath Mus★
BA1. . . . . 228 C3
BULFORD 182 C4
Bulford TA21 . . . . 222 D5
Bulford La TA21. . . . . 222 D5
Bull Bridge La TA13 . . . . . . 185 B1
Bull Bridge Mead BA22 . . . 197 D3
Bullen Mead BA11. . . . . 117 F2
Bullens Cl TA19 . . . . 183 F4
Buller Ave BA22. . . . . 218 A6
Buller Rd BS29. . . . . 50 C7
Bull Horn Dro TA7. . . . . 154 D5
Bull La BS20 . . . . 4 C4
Bull Mdw TA4. . . . . 167 F7
Bullmead Cl BA16 . . . . 207 B5
Bullmead La BA11. . . . . 143 C7
Bullock Field Hill TA21 . . . 166 B2
Bullocks La BS21. . . . . 16 C4
Bullon Drove TA5 . . . . 134 B7
Bull Plot Hill BA6. . . . . 158 C8
Bullrush Cl BA11 . . . . 120 A3
BULL'S GREEN 117 E1
Bulls Green Link Rd BA11 117 E1
Bull's Hill BA2 . . . . 62 E1
Bulls La TA18 . . . . 224 B6
Bull's La
Tatworth TA20 . . . . 198 C8
Upton Noble BA4 . . . . 142 F2
Bull's Quarr BA11 . . . . 143 E8
Bull's Quarries Rd BA11 . . 143 F7
Bull St TA3 . . . . 169 D4
Bulwarks La BA6. . . . . 206 F4
Bumblebee Cl BS13 . . . . 21 E4
Bumper's Batch BA2 . . . . . . 63 A8
Bunce's La TA19 . . . . 184 E3
Buncombe Hill TA5. . . . . . . 152 C3
Bune Villas TA6 . . . . 208 E7
Bunford Hollow
Yeovil BA20 . . . . 218 C2
Yeovil, Preston Plucknett
BA20. . . . . 218 D5
Bunford Hollow Rdbt
BA20 . . . . 218 D1
Bunford La BA20, BA21 . . . 218 C4
Bungalows The
Axbridge BS26 . . . . 70 C2
Chard TA20. . . . . 223 D5
Monkton Heathfield TA2 . . . 213 F8
Nether Stowey TA5. . . . . 134 A2
Poyntington DT9. . . . . 188 E7
Bungay's Hill BA2, BS39 . . . . 59 E1
Bunker Military Mus The★
TA9 . . . . 104 D3
Bunns La
Horningsham BA11 . . . . 144 A5
Witham Friary BA11 . . . . 143 F5
Bunny Burrow's Track
TA22 . . . . 164 A8
Bunting Ct BS22. . . . . 31 E1
Bunting La BS20 . . . . 3 A6
Burchill Cl BS39. . . . . 58 F3
Burchills Cl TA21. . . . . 222 A6
Burchill's Hill TA21. . . . . . . 222 B7
Burch's Cl TA1 . . . . 212 C2
BURCOTT 139 E8
Burcott La
Coxley BA5 . . . . 139 E7
Wells BA5. . . . . 203 A3
Burcott Mill★ BA5. . . . . 139 E8
Burcott Rd BA5 . . . . 203 B3
Burdenham Dro TA7 . . . . . . 155 A6
Burdock Rd BA11 . . . . 120 B3
Burfitt Rd BA7 . . . . 214 A6
Burfoote Gdns BS14. . . . . . . 23 E4
Burfoot Rd BS14 . . . . 23 E4
BURFORD 204 C2
Burford Cl
Bath BA2 . . . . 44 B3
Portishead BS20 . . . . 2 E4
Burford Cross BA4 . . . . 204 C2
Burford Gr BS11 . . . . 4 F5
Burgage TA21 . . . . 222 D6
Burgage La TA4. . . . . 167 A4

Burgage Rd TA5 . . . . . . .134 C6
Burge Cres TA4 . . . . .167 E6
Burge Mdw TA4 . . . . .167 E6
Burges Cl
　Marnhull DT10 . . . . .190 F6
　Wiveliscombe TA4 . . . . . .210 C5
Burge's Hill BA3 . . . . .116 B1
Burges La TA4 . . . . .210 C5
Burge's La BA3 . . . . .116 B1
Burgess Cl TA1 . . . . .212 B1
Burgess La BA6 . . . . .157 F6
Burgis Rd BS14 . . . . .23 D6
Burgundy Rd TA24 . . . . . . .201 A8
BURLANDS 168 C6
Burledge Comm BS39 . . . .57 B1
Burledge La BS39 . . . . . . .57 D1
Burleigh Gdns BA1 . . . . . . .44 A8
Burleigh La BA16 . . . . .207 C4
BURLESCOMBE 179 B3
Burlescombe CE Prim Sch
　EX16 . . . . .179 B3
Burley Gdns BA16 . . . . . . .207 D4
Burlingham's La BA22 . . . .186 C8
Burlington Ct BS20 . . . . . . .2 E6
Burlington Rd
　Midsomer Norton BA3 . . . .78 C2
　Portishead BS20 . . . . .2 E7
Burlington St
　Bath BA1 . . . . .228 B4
　15 Weston-super-Mare BS23. .48 E8
Burnbush Cl BS14 . . . . .23 E6
Burnbush Prim Sch BS14 . .23 D5
Burnell Dr BS2 . . . . .227 C4
Burnell Ho **8** BA4 . . . . . . .205 B6
BURNETT 42 B7
Burnett Cl TA4 . . . . .104 C7
Burnett Hill BS31 . . . . .42 B8
Burnett Ind Est BS40 . . . . .35 E1
Burnett's La BA6 . . . . .158 A6
Burnham Cl BS24 . . . . .48 F1
Burnham Dr BS24 . . . . .48 F1
Burnham Link Rd TA8 . . . .104 E7
Burnham Moor La TA9 . . . .105 B5
BURNHAM-ON-SEA 104 D8
Burnham-on-Sea Inf Sch
　TA8 . . . . .104 C8
Burnham Rd
　Bath BA2 . . . . .44 C6
　Bristol BS11 . . . . .4 D6
　Highbridge TA8 . . . . .104 D4
Burn Hill TA4, TA21 . . . . . .166 F3
Burnshill Dr TA2 . . . . .212 A7
Burns Rd TA1 . . . . .213 C4
Burnt Hill La BA11 . . . . . . .100 A3
Burnt House Cotts BA4 . . .62 C8
Burnt House La BA3 . . . . . .116 C2
Burnt House Rd BA2 . . . . . .62 D8
Burrell La BA7 . . . . .158 F1
Burrells BA22 . . . . .197 B8
Burridge Cl BA5 . . . . .139 E6
Burridge Cross TA20 . . . . .193 E1
BURRINGTON 53 F3
Burrington Ave BS24 . . . . . .48 F1
Burrington CE Prim Sch
　BS40 . . . . .53 F3
Burrington Cl
　Nailsea BS48 . . . . .8 E1
　Weston-super-Mare BS24 . . .48 F1
Burrington Combe BS40 . . .72 C8
Burrington Coombe★
　BS40 . . . . .54 A1
Burrington La
　Burrington BS40 . . . . .54 A3
　Burrington BS40 . . . . .54 A3
Burrington Rd
　Townsend BS40 . . . . .92 F8
　Ubley Sideling BS40 . . . . . .73 D2
　West End BS40 . . . . .93 A7
Burrington Wlk BS13 . . . . . .22 A8
Burroughes Ave BA21 . . . .218 E6
Burrough St TA12 . . . . . . .185 E7
Burrough Way TA21 . . . . . .222 D4
BURROW 184 F6
BURROWBRIDGE 154 F1
Burrowbridge CE Sch
　TA7 . . . . .154 F1
Burrow Dro
　Burrowbridge TA7 . . . . . . .154 F1
　Hambridge TA12 . . . . .184 F8
Burrowfield BA10 . . . . . . .215 F7
Burrowfield Cl BA10 . . . . .215 F7
Burrow Hill Dro TA7 . . . . .155 A1
Burrow La
　Ashbrittle TA21 . . . . .178 D8
　High Ham TA10 . . . . .156 A1
Burrow Mump★ TA7 . . . . .154 F1
Burrow Rocks TA4 . . . . . . .202 B1
Burrows La BA3 . . . . .97 B1
Burrows The BS22 . . . . .32 D3
Burrow Wall TA7 . . . . .155 A1
Burrow Way
　Hambridge TA12 . . . . .184 F4
　Kingsbury Episcopi TA12. .185 A4
Burstock La DT8 . . . . .199 F7
Burston La EX16 . . . . .164 A4
BURTLE 137 D6
Burtle Rd
　Burtle TA7 . . . . .137 D6
　East Huntspill TA9 . . . . . . .136 E7
　Westhay BA6 . . . . .138 A5
BURTON
　Stogursey TA5 . . . . .134 B7
　Yeovil 197 C8

Burton Barton BA22 . . . . .197 C8
Burton Cl BS1 . . . . .227 B1
Burton Ct BS8 . . . . .226 B3
Burtonhayes DT10 . . . . . . .190 F6
Burton La BA22 . . . . .197 C8
Burton Pl TA1 . . . . .212 E3
Burton Row TA9 . . . . .86 A5
Burton St
　5 Bath BA1 . . . . .228 B2
　Marnhull DT10 . . . . .190 F6
Burt's Hill BA4 . . . . .142 F3
Burwalls Rd BS8 . . . . .11 E6
BURY 164 A6
Burying Hole La BA22 . . . .186 A1
Bury Rd TA22 . . . . .164 A6
Bury The BS24 . . . . .50 A3
Bury View BA2 . . . . .42 C5
BUSCOTT 138 C1
Buscott La TA7 . . . . .138 B1
BUSHEY NORWOOD 45 F6
Bushfield Rd TA18 . . . . . . .224 B4
Bushfurlong Rd TA3 . . . . .184 B8
Bush La
　Pilton BA4 . . . . .140 F3
　Spaxton TA5 . . . . .152 E6
Bush Pl TA10 . . . . .172 A5
Bush Rd TA5 . . . . .152 D7
Bushs Orch TA19 . . . . .221 A4
Bushy Coombe Gdns BA6 .206 F5
Bushy Combe BA3 . . . . . . .77 F3
Bushy Cross La TA3 . . . . . .169 C3
Bushy Thorn Rd BS40. . . . .56 E8
Business Pk The BS13 . . . . .22 E3
Bussell's Moor Cross
　EX36 . . . . .162 C4
BUSSEX 154 F6
Bussex Sq TA7 . . . . .154 F6
Butcher's Hill TA3 . . . . . . .170 F2
Butchers La
　Castle Cary BA7 . . . . .159 C3
　Shapwick TA7 . . . . .155 F8
Butcher's La TA5 . . . . .134 A2
BUTCOMBE 55 B8
Butcombe BS24 . . . . .49 A2
Butcombe La BS40 . . . . . . .55 B7
Butcombe Wlk BS14 . . . . . .23 B5
Butham La
　Chew Magna BS40 . . . . . . .39 A4
　Chew Magna BS40 . . . . . . .39 B3
Butlass Cl BS39 . . . . .59 D1
BUTLEIGH 157 D4
Butleigh CE Prim Sch
　Butleigh BA6 . . . . .157 E4
　Butleigh BA6 . . . . .157 E4
Butleigh Cl TA6 . . . . .209 D4
Butleigh Cross BA6 . . . . . .157 E3
Butleigh Dro
　Ashcott TA7, BA16 . . . . . .156 C5
　Walton BA16 . . . . .156 D6
Butleigh Old Rd BA6 . . . . .206 E3
Butleigh Rd
　Glastonbury BA6 . . . . .206 E3
　Street BA16 . . . . .207 E5
BUTLEIGH WOTTON 157 C5
Butler's Gdns BA11 . . . . . .120 A4
Butt Cl BA6 . . . . .206 E5
Buttercliffe Rise BS41 . . . .11 C3
Buttercup Cl
　Frome BA11 . . . . .120 B3
　Somerton TA11 . . . . .211 B3
Buttercup La
　Street BA16 . . . . .207 D6
　Street BA16 . . . . .207 D6
Butterfield Pk BS21 . . . . . . .6 C1
Buttermere Rd BS23 . . . . . .49 A5
Butterworth Ct BS4 . . . . . .22 D7
Buttice La BA5 . . . . .111 B1
Butt La TA10 . . . . .171 D4
Butt Lake Rd TA9 . . . . . . .106 B3
Buttle Cl TA19 . . . . .184 E4
Buttle La TA19 . . . . .184 E3
Buttle's Cross TA3 . . . . . . .191 F6
Buttle's La TA3 . . . . .191 E6
Button Cl BS14 . . . . .23 A6
Button St BA11 . . . . .119 D5
Butts TA19 . . . . .221 C4
BUTT'S BATCH 35 D1
Butt's Batch BS40 . . . . .35 D1
Butts Castle TA19 . . . . . . .221 C4
Butts Cl
　Marnhull DT10 . . . . .190 F5
　Williton TA4 . . . . .202 D4
Butts Cnr TA6 . . . . .153 F4
Butts Hill BA11 . . . . .119 E3
Butts La
　Ilton TA19 . . . . .183 D3
　Kilmington BA12 . . . . .161 F7
　Langford Budville TA21 . . .166 F2
　Rodney Stoke BS27 . . . . . .91 A1
Butts Orch BS40 . . . . .35 D1
Butts Quarry La TA18 . . . .224 E6
BUTTS THE 119 E3
Butts The BA11 . . . . .119 E3
Butts Way TA4 . . . . .166 F4
Buxtons Cl **5** BA5 . . . . . .139 D8
Byfield BA22 . . . . .45 B1
Byfield Pl BA2 . . . . .45 B1
Byfields BS21 . . . . .16 C8
Byme Rd TA14 . . . . .185 E1
Byron Cl
　Bath BA2 . . . . .44 F4
　Locking BS24 . . . . .50 A4
　Taunton TA1 . . . . .213 C3
Byron Cl BS24 . . . . .50 A4
Byron Ct BS23 . . . . .30 E1
Byron Pl BS8 . . . . .226 B3
Byron Rd

Byron Rd continued
　Weston-super-Mare BS23 . .49 A4
Byways Cvn Pk BS21 . . . . . .6 C1
Byzantine Ct BS1 . . . . .227 A1

C

Cabbage La BA8 . . . . .176 C3
Cabell Ct BA11 . . . . .119 D2
Cabell Rd BA11 . . . . .119 E2
Cabot Circus Sh Ctr BS1 . .227 B3
Cabot Ct BS31 . . . . .25 D2
Cabot Gate BS2 . . . . .227 C4
Cabot Prim Sch BS2 . . . . . .227 C4
Cabot Rd BA21 . . . . .219 F8
Cabot Rise BS20 . . . . .2 A5
Cabot Twr★ BS8 . . . . .226 B2
Cabot Way
　Bristol BS8 . . . . .11 F5
　Pill BS20 . . . . .4 D3
　Weston-super-Mare BS22 . . .32 A3
Cabstand BS20 . . . . .2 D6
Cadbury Bsns Pk BA22 . . .175 B6
Cadbury Camp La BS20 . . . .8 D6
Cadbury Camp La W BS21. . .7 C5
Cadbury Castle★ BA22 . . .175 C4
Cadbury Cl TA8 . . . . .85 C1
Cadbury Farm Rd BS49 . . . .34 C7
Cadbury Halt BS20 . . . . .1 F1
Cadbury Ho BS20 . . . . .2 E4
Cadbury La BS20 . . . . .1 F1
Cadbury Rd
　Keynsham BS31 . . . . .25 A2
　Portishead BS20 . . . . .2 E4
Cadbury Sq BS49 . . . . .34 E3
Cadby Ho BA2 . . . . .44 A6
Cades Cl BS14 . . . . .23 A6
Cadeside Cvn Site TA21. . .222 F7
Cades Mead TA21 . . . . . . .222 F7
Cadet Dr BS24 . . . . .49 B4
CAD GREEN 183 E3
Cadogan Rd BS14 . . . . .23 A8
Cad Rd
　Ilminster TA19 . . . . .221 A8
　Ilton TA19 . . . . .183 E3
Cadwell's Dv TA9 . . . . . . .136 A8
Cadwell's La TA9 . . . . .136 A8
Caernarvon Cl BS31 . . . . . .24 C5
Caernarvon Rd BS31 . . . . . .24 C4
Caernarvon Way TA8 . . . . . .85 B1
Caern Well Pl BA1 . . . . . . .228 C4
Cairn Cl BS48 . . . . .9 A1
Cairo Ct **18** BS23 . . . . .30 C1
Caitlin Ct BS14 . . . . .23 D6
Cala Trad Est BS3 . . . . .11 F3
Calder Cl BS31 . . . . .25 A4
Calder Cres TA1 . . . . .213 D4
Cale Cl DT10 . . . . .190 C4
Caledonia Mews BS8 . . . . .11 F6
Caledonian Rd
　Bath BA2 . . . . .44 D6
　Bristol BS1 . . . . .226 B1
Caledonia Pl BS8 . . . . .11 F7
Cale Way BA9 . . . . .216 B4
California Par BA16 . . . . . .207 B6
Caller's La EX15 . . . . .180 D1
Callins Cl TA24 . . . . .201 A5
Callins View TA24 . . . . . . .201 A5
Callow Hill BA5 . . . . .139 C7
Callowhill Ct BS1 . . . . .227 B3
Calluna Cl BS22 . . . . .32 A5
Calton Gdns BA2 . . . . .228 C1
Calton Rd BA2 . . . . .228 C1
Calton Wlk BA2 . . . . .228 B1
Calvados Rd TA1 . . . . .213 C3
Calway Rd TA1 . . . . .213 B2
Camberley Rd BS4 . . . . . . .22 D8
Camberley Wlk BS22 . . . . .49 E8
Camborne Gr BA21 . . . . . .219 E5
Camborne Rd BA21 . . . . . .219 E5
Camborne St BA21 . . . . . .219 E5
CAMBRIDGE BATCH 20 C8
Cambridge Cl BA20 . . . . . .218 D5
Cambridge Gr BS21 . . . . . . .6 D5
Cambridge Pl
　Bath BA2 . . . . .45 B5
　Weston-super-Mare BS23 . .48 D8
Cambridge Rd BS21 . . . . . . .6 D5
Cambridge St TA20. . . . . . .223 C4
Cambridge Terr
　Bath BA2 . . . . .45 B5
　11 Taunton TA2 . . . . . . .213 A8
Cam Brook Cl BA2 . . . . . . .78 D8
Cambrook Ho BS39 . . . . . . .76 F8
Camden Cres BA1 . . . . . . .228 B4
Camden Ct
　Bath BA1 . . . . .228 B4
　Bridgwater TA6 . . . . .208 E5
Camden Orch TA11 . . . . . .211 C4
Camden Pl TA6 . . . . .208 E5
Camden Rd
　Bath BA1 . . . . .28 A1
　Bridgwater TA6 . . . . .208 E5
　Bristol BS3 . . . . .226 B1
　Somerton TA11 . . . . .211 C4
Camden Row BA1 . . . . . . .228 B4
Camden Terr
　Bath BA1 . . . . .228 C4
　Bristol BS8 . . . . .226 A2
　Weston-super-Mare BS23 . .48 E7
Camel Cross BA22 . . . . . . .174 C3
CAMELEY 76 C8
Cameley CE Prim Sch BS39 .58 E1
Cameley Cl BS39 . . . . .76 E8
Cameley Gn BA2 . . . . .43 F6
Cameley La BS39 . . . . .75 F7

Cameley Rd BS39 . . . . .76 C8
Camelot Ct TA11 . . . . .211 B5
Camelot Sh Ctr BA9 . . . . . .216 C4
Camel St BA22 . . . . .174 F2
Cameroons Cl BS31 . . . . . . .24 E4
CAMERTON 78 E8
Camerton Cl BS31 . . . . .25 E3
Camerton Hill BA2 . . . . . . .78 E8
Camerton Rd BA2 . . . . .60 E1
Camomile Wlk BS20 . . . . . . .2 F5
Campian Wlk BS4 . . . . .22 D6
Campion Cl **4** BS22 . . . . .49 D7
Campion Dr
　Taunton TA1 . . . . .213 C1
　Yeovil BA22 . . . . .218 B5
Campion Gdns TA20 . . . . .223 D5
Campion Rd BA11 . . . . . . .120 B3
Campion Way TA6 . . . . . . .208 E1
Campkin Rd BA5 . . . . .203 B4
Camplins BS21 . . . . .6 C1
Camp Rd
　Bristol BS8 . . . . .11 F7
　Weston-super-Mare BS23 . .30 C1
Camp Rd N BS23 . . . . .30 B1
Camp View BS48 . . . . .8 D2
Camvale BA2 . . . . .79 B8
Camview BS39 . . . . .77 D6
Canada Coombe BS24 . . . . .50 A1
Canada Way BS1 . . . . .226 B1
Canada Way BS3 . . . . .11 F4
Canal Cl TA21 . . . . .222 B8
Canal Dro BS27, BS28 . . . . .90 A3
Canal Rd TA1 . . . . .212 F5
Canal Terr
　Bathampton BA2 . . . . .28 F1
　Taunton TA1 . . . . .212 F5
Canal View
　Bridgwater TA6 . . . . .209 A4
　Taunton TA1 . . . . .213 F7
Canal Way TA19 . . . . .221 A3
Canaries Path BA4 . . . . . . .205 D3
Canberra Cres BS24 . . . . . .50 B6
Canberra Rd BS23 . . . . . . .48 F3
Canford La BS9 . . . . .5 E8
Canford Rd BS9 . . . . .5 F8
Cannan Ct BA2 . . . . .45 A2
CANNARD'S GRAVE 205 D2
Cannard's Grave Rd BA4. .205 C4
Cannards Grave Rdbt
　BA4 . . . . .205 D3
Canning Ctr for Land Based
　Studies TA5. . . . . .135 B2
CANNINGTON 135 C2
Cannington CE Prim Sch
　TA5 . . . . .135 C2
Cannington College Gdns★
　 . . . . .135 B2
Cannington Countryside Vst
　Ctr★ TA5 . . . . .135 B2
Cannon Cl TA6 . . . . .209 B5
Cannon Court Mews
　DT9 . . . . .217 D1
Cannons Gate BS21 . . . . . .16 C8
CANNON'S MARSH 226 C1
Cannon St BS1 . . . . .227 A4
Canns La
　9 North Petherton TA6 . . .153 F4
　Puriton TA7 . . . . .136 C4
Cann St TA1 . . . . .212 E3
Cannwood La BA10 . . . . . .161 B8
Canons Cl BA2 . . . . .44 B2
Canons Gate BA22 . . . . . . .173 E1
Canon's Marsh
　Amphitheatre★
　BS1 . . . . .226 C1
Canons Rd BS1 . . . . .226 C2
Canon's Rd BS1 . . . . .226 C2
Canon St TA1 . . . . .213 A4
Canons Way BS1 . . . . .226 C1
Canons Wlk BS22 . . . . .31 D2
Cantell Gr BS14 . . . . .23 F5
Canterbury Cl BS22 . . . . . .32 B3
Canterbury Dr TA3 . . . . . .170 C4
Canterbury Rd BA2 . . . . . . .44 D5
Cantock's Cl BS8 . . . . .226 C3
Canvin Ct TA11 . . . . .211 B5
Canworth Way TA6 . . . . . .209 C3
Canynge Ho **2** BS1 . . . . .227 B1
Canynge Rd BS8 . . . . .11 F8
Canynge Sq BS8 . . . . .11 F8
Canynge St BS1 . . . . .227 B2
Capell Cl BS22 . . . . .49 B8
Capenor Cl BS20 . . . . .2 C4
Capes Cl TA6 . . . . .209 A5
Capital Edge BS8. . . . . . . .226 B1
CAPLAND 183 A6
Capland Ct TA3 . . . . .183 A5
Capland La TA3 . . . . .183 A5
Caple La BS40 . . . . .56 B5
Cappards Rd BS39 . . . . . . .57 D4
Capricorn Pl BS8. . . . . . . .226 B2
Capri Villas BS23 . . . . .30 C2
CAPTON 132 C2
Capton TA4 . . . . .132 C2
Capton Cross TA4 . . . . . . .132 C2
Caradon Pl TA6 . . . . .208 F7
Caramia Pk TA9 . . . . .136 A8
Carantoc Pl **3** TA24 . . . .131 A5
Caraway Ct TA20 . . . . .223 F5
Caray Gr TA3 . . . . .169 D4
Carberry View BS24 . . . . . .50 A8
Card Cl BS20 . . . . .2 F5
Cardigan Cres BS22 . . . . . .49 C8
Cardill Cl BS13 . . . . .22 A8
Cardinal Cl BA2 . . . . .62 D8
Carditch Dro BS49 . . . . . . .52 B8
Carey Cl BA4. . . . . .141 E6

Carey Developments **1**
　BS21 . . . . .6 C1
Carey's Cl BS21 . . . . .6 F4
Carey's Hollow TA13 . . . . .220 B4
Careys Mead BA3 . . . . . . .116 F7
Careys Way BS24 . . . . .49 E2
CARHAMPTON 131 B5
Carhampton Cross TA24 . .131 B5
Caribee Quarter BA16 . . . .207 B5
Carice Gdns BS21 . . . . .16 C8
Carisbrooke Gdns BA20. . .218 F5
Carisbrooke Rd BS4 . . . . . .22 D7
Carlan Stepps TA19 . . . . . .183 C2
CARLINGCOTT 61 B1
Carlingcott La
　Carlingcott BA2 . . . . .61 B1
　Peasedown St John BA2. . .79 B8
Carlingford Terr BA3 . . . . .79 A2
Carlingford Terrace Rd
　BA3 . . . . .79 A2
Carlow Rd BS4 . . . . .22 E8
Carlton Cl BS39 . . . . .58 F3
Carlton Ct
　Minehead TA24 . . . . .200 F7
　Wells BA5. . . . . .203 E4
Carlton Dr TA6 . . . . .208 F7
Carlton Mans BS23 . . . . . .48 E8
Carlton Mews BA5 . . . . . . .203 E4
Carlton St BS23 . . . . .48 D7
Carmine Cl BA6 . . . . .206 C4
Carnival Cl TA19 . . . . .221 A4
Carolina Ho BS2 . . . . .227 A4
Caroline Bldgs BA2. . . . . . .45 B5
Caroline Cl BS31 . . . . .24 C4
Caroline Pl BA1 . . . . .228 B4
Carpenter Cl BS23. . . . . . . .49 A7
Carpenters Cl TA3. . . . . . .169 C3
Carpenters Hill BA2 . . . . . .79 B8
Carpenters Ho TA19 . . . . .221 B3
Carpenters La BS31 . . . . . .24 E5
Carpenters Terr TA12 . . . .185 E2
Carpenters Way BA3 . . . . . .97 B8
Carraway La DT10 . . . . . . .190 F5
Carre Gdns BS22 . . . . .31 F4
Carr Ho BA2 . . . . .44 A6
Carrick Ho **7** BS8 . . . . . . .11 F6
Carriels Ho **12** BA4 . . . . . .205 B6
Carrier's La TA21. . . . . . . .166 C2
Carrington Way BA9. . . . . .216 C4
Carrs Cl BA2 . . . . .44 A6
Carrswood Vw BA2. . . . . . .43 F7
Carstons Cl BS48. . . . . .18 F6
Carter Cl BA7 . . . . .214 A6
Carter Rd BS39. . . . . .77 D5
Carters La BA22. . . . . .196 E8
Carters Way
　Chilcompton BA3 . . . . .96 D3
　Somerton TA11. . . . . .211 C4
Cart Gate TA14 . . . . .185 F5
Cartgate Link Rd TA15. . . .186 C4
Cartier Cl **6** BA21 . . . . . . .219 F8
Cartwright Cl BA5. . . . . . .139 C4
Carver Cl TA6 . . . . .208 D5
Carvers Rd TA6 . . . . .209 A5
Cary Ct TA11 . . . . .211 B5
Caryedge La BA7. . . . . . . .160 A2
CARY FITZPAINE 174 A5
Cary Fitzpaine Rd BA22. . .174 A5
Cary Hill
　Castle Cary BA7 . . . . .214 C6
　Kingsdon TA11 . . . . .173 E5
Cary Moor Dro BA7. . . . . .159 C1
Cary Rd BA22 . . . . .175 D6
Cary Way
　Kingsdon TA11 . . . . .173 D5
　Somerton TA11. . . . . .211 C4
Casey Cl BS4. . . . . .22 F7
Cashford Gate TA2 . . . . . .213 C7
Casion Cl BS1. . . . . .227 B1
Casley La BA11. . . . . .102 D6
Cassino Rd TA23 . . . . .202 E6
Cassis Cl TA8 . . . . .104 C5
Castlake La TA4. . . . . .150 F7
CASTLE 198 D4
Castle Batch Prim Sch
　BS22. . . . . .32 A5
CASTLE BOW TA1 . . . . . . .212 F4
CASTLE CARY 214 B6
Castle Cary Com Prim Sch
　BA7. . . . . .214 C4
Castle Cary Mus★ BA7. . . .214 C5
Castle Cary Sta BA7 . . . . .214 B8
Castle Cl BS48. . . . . .19 F7
Castle Cnr BA11. . . . . .101 D3
Castle Cotts TA21 . . . . . . .180 D5
Castle Cross EX13 . . . . . . .198 D4
Castle Ct
　Othery TA7. . . . . .155 C2
　Shepton Mallet BA4 . . . . .205 A4
Castle Farm La BS41. . . . . .21 B2
Castle Field Ind Est TA6. . .209 A6
Castlefield La TA4. . . . . . .168 B1
Castle Gdns BA2 . . . . .44 E3
Castle Gn TA1. . . . . .212 F4
Castle Hill
　Banwell BS29. . . . . .51 E4
　Dunster TA24. . . . . .201 E2
　Nether Stowey TA5. . . . . .134 A2
　Nunney BA11. . . . . .143 B8
Castle La
　Cranmore BA4 . . . . .142 A6
　South Cadbury BA22 . . . . .175 D4
　Wedmore BS28 . . . . .108 A1
　West Pennard BA6. . . . . . .140 C1
　Wiveliscombe TA4 . . . . . .210 F6
　Yarley BA5. . . . . .139 D7
Castlemain TA20 . . . . .182 D2
Castlemans Rd TA1. . . . . .212 B1

Castle Mead TA23 . . . . 131 E4
Castle Moat TA6 . . . . 208 F5
Castle Neroche Forest Trail★
TA20 . . . . 182 D2
Castle Prim Sch BS31 . . . . . 24 D4
Castle Rd
  Clevedon BS21 . . . . 6 E6
  Sherborne DT9 . . . . 225 F5
  Wellington TA21 . . . . 180 D8
  Weston-super-Mare BS22 . . . 31 E3
Castle Rise BA7 . . . . 214 C5
Castle Sch The TA1 . . . . 212 D4
Castle St
  Bampton EX16 . . . . 164 B1
  Bridgwater TA6 . . . . 208 F5
  Bristol BS1 . . . . 227 B3
  Frome BA11 . . . . 119 E5
  Keinton Mandeville TA11 . . 158 B1
  Nether Stowey TA5 . . . . 134 B2
  Nunney BA11 . . . . 143 B8
  Stogursey TA5 . . . . 134 C5
  Stoke sub Hamdon TA14 . . . 185 F4
  Taunton TA1 . . . . 212 E4
Castleton
  Haselbury Plucknett TA18 . . 196 C5
  ■ Sherborne DT9 . . . . 225 E4
Castleton Rd DT9 . . . . 225 E4
Castle Town Way DT9 . . . . 225 E6
Castle View ② BS24 . . . . . . 49 F8
Castle View Rd BS21 . . . . 6 D5
Castle Way TA1 . . . . 212 F4
Castlewood Cl BS21 . . . . 6 D4
Caswell Hill BS20 . . . . 3 B1
Caswell La BS20 . . . . 3 B2
Catash Cl BA22 . . . . 175 D6
Catchgate La
  Chard TA20 . . . . 193 E4
  Crimchard TA20 . . . . 223 B6
Catch Gate La TA20 . . . . 223 A5
Catch Rd BA11 . . . . 143 B7
CATCOTT 137 D2
Catcott Broad Dro TA7 . . . 137 D5
Catcott Prim Sch TA7 . . . . . 137 D2
Catcott Rd BA5 . . . . 203 E3
Catcott Right Dro TA7 . . . . 155 D6
Catemead BS21 . . . . 16 C8
Cater Rd BS13 . . . . 22 B6
Cathanger La
  Fivehead TA3 . . . . 170 D1
  Stogursey TA5 . . . . 134 D5
Catharine Pl BA1 . . . . 228 B3
Cathay La BS27 . . . . 90 B7
Cathcart Ho ⑦ BA1 . . . . 28 A1
Cathead Cross TA14 . . . . . . 185 E1
Cathedral Ave BA5 . . . . 203 D2
Cathedral Church of The Holy
  & Undivided Trinity★
  BS1 . . . . 226 C2
Cathedral Gn BA5 . . . . 203 E4
Catherine Hill BA11 . . . . . . 119 F5
Catherines Cl BA7 . . . . 214 C6
Catherine St
  Avonmouth BS11 . . . . 4 C8
  East Huntspill TA9 . . . . 136 D4
  Frome BA11 . . . . 119 E5
Catherson Cl BA11 . . . . 119 D3
Cathill La DT9 . . . . 176 A2
Cathole Bridge Rd TA18 . . . 224 A4
Cathorn La BS48 . . . . 20 C6
Cat La
  Stalbridge DT10 . . . . 190 A1
  Stourton Caundle DT10 . . . 189 F1
Catley Gr BS41 . . . . 11 B2
Catmoor Cross EX13 . . . . . 198 A5
Catnip Cl ② EX13 . . . . 198 A1
Cat's Ash
  Fitzhead TA4 . . . . 166 F7
  Shepton Mallet BA4 . . . . . . 205 B6
Cats' Castle Hill TA4 . . . . . 150 E5
Catscrow Hill TA10 . . . . 172 C6
CATSGORE 173 C4
Catsgore Rd TA11 . . . . 173 C5
Cats La
  Minehead TA24 . . . . 201 A6
  Taunton TA1 . . . . 168 F6
Cat St TA14 . . . . 185 E1
Cattle Hill
  Bratton Seymour BA9 . . . . . 176 A8
  Welham BA7 . . . . 160 A1
Cattle Market Rd BS1 . . . . . 227 C1
Catt's La TA21 . . . . 180 E6
Catwell TA4 . . . . 202 E2
Caulfield Rd BS22 . . . . 32 B4
Caundle La
  Stalbridge Weston DT10 . . . 190 A3
  Stourton Caundle DT10 . . . 189 F1
Causeway
  Nailsea BS48 . . . . 8 B3
  Woolavington TA7, TA9 . . . 136 E6
Causeway Cl TA7 . . . . 136 E4
Causeway Council Hos
  TA9 . . . . 106 B4
Causeway La DT8 . . . . 199 D6
Causeway Terr TA23 . . . . . . 202 C6
Causeway The
  Congresbury BS49 . . . . 34 D4
  Nailsea BS20 . . . . 8 F8
  Street BA16 . . . . 207 D8
  Yatton BS49 . . . . 34 C7
Causeway View BS48 . . . . 8 C2
Cautletts Cl BA3 . . . . 96 F8
Cavalier Cl
  Wembdon TA6 . . . . 208 E6
  Yeovil BA21 . . . . 219 D8
Cavalier Way
  Wincanton BA9 . . . . 216 C3
  Yeovil BA21 . . . . 219 E8
Cavalier Wlk BA21 . . . . 219 D8

Cave Ct BS2 . . . . 227 B4
Cavell Ct BS21 . . . . 6 C1
Cavendish Cl
  ⑧ Longcroft BA21 . . . . . . 219 F8
  Saltford BS31 . . . . 25 D2
Cavendish Cres BA1 . . . . . . 228 A4
Cavendish Ct BA22 . . . . 173 E2
Cavendish Dr BA14 . . . . 83 F6
Cavendish Gdns BS9 . . . . 5 C4
Cavendish Lodge BA1 . . . . . 228 A4
Cavendish Pl BA1 . . . . 228 A4
Cavendish Rd BA1 . . . . 228 A4
Caveners Ct BS22 . . . . 31 B1
Caversham Dr BS48 . . . . 9 A2
Cave St BS2 . . . . 227 B4
Cawley Ave EX13 . . . . 198 A2
Caxton Cl BA22 . . . . 228 C3
Caxton Dr ⑤ TA9 . . . . 104 E4
Caxton Rd
  Frome BA11 . . . . 120 A3
  ④ Highbridge TA9 . . . . . . 104 E4
Cazenove Path BA4 . . . . . . 205 D3
Cecil Ave
  Butleigh BA6 . . . . 157 D5
  Weston-super-Mare BS22 . . . 31 C1
Cecil St BA20 . . . . 219 B5
Cecil Terr TA6 . . . . 209 B4
Cedar Ave
  Bristol, Clifton BS8 . . . . 11 F8
  Weston-super-Mare BS23 . . . 30 E1
Cedar Cl
  Brent Knoll TA9 . . . . 86 B2
  Bridgwater TA6 . . . . 209 C3
  Chard TA20 . . . . 223 B5
  Long Ashton BS41 . . . . 10 F1
  Taunton TA1 . . . . 213 D2
Cedar Ct
  Bristol, Combe Dingle BS9 . . . 5 D7
  Bristol, Sneyd Park BS9 . . . . 5 C4
  Bristol, Westbury on T BS9 . . 5 F8
  Martock TA12 . . . . 185 E7
  Wellington TA21 . . . . 222 E5
Cedar Dr BS31 . . . . 24 D4
Cedar Falls TA4 . . . . 151 E1
Cedar Fields
  Sparkford BA22 . . . . 175 A5
  West Coker BA22 . . . . 197 A8
Cedar Gr
  Bath BA2 . . . . 44 D3
  Bristol BS9 . . . . 5 D5
  Somerton TA11 . . . . 211 D4
  Yeovil BA21 . . . . 218 E6
Cedarhurst Rd BS20 . . . . 1 E4
Cedar Pk BS9 . . . . 5 D5
Cedar Row BS11 . . . . 4 F6
Cedars The
  Chew Stoke BS40 . . . . 56 D8
  Evercreech BA4 . . . . 141 E1
  Minehead TA24 . . . . 200 F7
Cedar Terr BA3 . . . . 78 D1
Cedar Villas BA2 . . . . 228 A1
Cedar Way
  Bath BA2 . . . . 228 A1
  Nailsea BS48 . . . . 9 A2
  Portishead BS20 . . . . 2 C4
Cedar Wlk
  Butleigh BA6 . . . . 157 E5
  Kingweston TA11 . . . . 157 E2
Cedern Ave BS24 . . . . 50 C3
Cedric Cl BA1 . . . . 44 C7
Cedric Rd BA1 . . . . 44 C8
Cefn Ct TA24 . . . . 201 B4
CE Inf Sch TA13 . . . . 220 C4
Celandine Mead TA1 . . . . . 169 A1
Celandine Rd BA22 . . . . 218 A5
Celandine Way TA6 . . . . . . 208 E1
Cello St BS31 . . . . 25 B4
Celtic Way BS24 . . . . 67 B7
Cemetery La
  Street BA16 . . . . 207 A7
  Wincanton BA9 . . . . 216 B3
Centenary Cotts DT9 . . . . . 176 A1
Centenary Gdns BA8 . . . . . 190 A6
Centenary Way BS27 . . . . . . 90 A7
Center Parcs BA12 . . . . 144 F5
Central Acre BA20 . . . . 219 B4
Central Ave BA22 . . . . 173 E2
Central Pk BS14 . . . . 23 B7
Central Rd BA20 . . . . 219 B5
Central Way BS21 . . . . 6 E1
Centre Dr BS29 . . . . 50 E4
Centre Quay BS20 . . . . 2 E7
Centre Rd TA7 . . . . 137 C2
Centre The
  Keynsham BS31 . . . . 24 F5
  ⑩ Weston-super-Mare BS23 . 48 E7
Centurion Bsns Ctr BA4 . . . 205 D4
Century Pk BA20 . . . . 218 E5
Century Rd BA20 . . . . 218 C5
CE Prim Sch DT9 . . . . 176 A1
Cerdic Cl TA20 . . . . 223 E4
Cerdic Terr TA20 . . . . 223 D4
Cerney Gdns BS48 . . . . 9 A2
Cerney La BS11 . . . . 4 E5
Cerutti Cl BS39 . . . . 77 D6
CE VA Prim Sch TA6 . . . . . 209 D4
Chackrell La EX16 . . . . 178 F2
Chadleigh Gr BS4 . . . . 22 D7
Chad's Hill TA5 . . . . 135 B2
Chadwyck Cl TA24 . . . . 124 A4
CHAFFCOMBE 194 C5
Chaffcombe La TA20 . . . . . 194 B5
Chaffeymoor Hill SP8 . . . . 161 E1
Chaffinch Ave
  Frome BA11 . . . . 120 B6
  Keynsham BS31 . . . . 24 C3
Chaffinch Cl TA1 . . . . 212 B4

Chaffinch Dr BA3 . . . . 97 B8
Chaffins The BS21 . . . . 6 E2
Chain Gate Ct BA6 . . . . 206 D4
Chains Rd EX16 . . . . 178 D1
Chalcombe Rocks La TA4 . 164 E5
Chalcot La BA13 . . . . 121 F5
Chalcroft Wlk BS13 . . . . 21 E4
Chalfield Cl BS31 . . . . 25 A2
Chalfont Rd BS22 . . . . 49 C8
Chalice Cl BA6 . . . . 206 E4
Chalice Hill Cl BA6 . . . . . . 206 E4
Chalice Mews ■ TA6 . . . . . 208 F5
Chalice Way BA6 . . . . 206 F3
Chalice Well★ BA6 . . . . . . 206 F4
Chalk Farm Cl BS39 . . . . 40 A7
Chalks The BS40 . . . . 39 B3
CHALKWAY 194 E2
Challenger Way BA22 . . . . . 218 B6
Challick La TA4 . . . . 166 A6
Challoner Ct BS1 . . . . 227 A1
Challow Dr BS22 . . . . 31 B2
Chamberlain Ho TA1 . . . . . 212 D5
Chamberlain Rd BS24 . . . . . 50 C5
Chamberlain St BA5 . . . . . . 203 D4
Chamberlin Ave TA6 . . . . . 209 C6
Chambray Rd ⑪ TA6 . . . . . 154 A5
Champford La TA21 . . . . . . 222 D5
Champford Mews ②
  TA21 . . . . 222 D5
Champion Cross TA4 . . . . . 165 E3
Champion Rd BS30 . . . . 25 E8
Champney Rd BA11 . . . . . . 120 A7
Chancel Cl
  Bristol BS9 . . . . 5 D3
  Nailsea BS48 . . . . 8 D1
Chancellor Cl BA16 . . . . . . 156 D7
Chancellor Rd BA16 . . . . . . 156 D7
Chancellor's Pound BS40 . . 36 D3
Chandag Inf Sch BS31 . . . . . 25 A4
Chandag Jun Sch BS31 . . . . 25 A4
Chandag Rd BS31 . . . . 25 A4
Chandler Cl BA1 . . . . 27 B1
Chandlers DT9 . . . . 225 E5
Chandlers La TA7 . . . . 137 C3
Chandos Ct BS23 . . . . 48 D6
Chandos Rd BS31 . . . . 24 E7
Chandos St TA6 . . . . 208 F5
Change La TA4 . . . . 164 D6
Channel Cl TA5 . . . . 134 A2
Channel St
  Burnham-on-S TA8 . . . . . . 104 B5
  Weston-super-Mare BS22 . . 31 B3
Channel Dash Pl BA22 . . . . 173 E2
Channel Hts BS24 . . . . 48 F1
Channells La TA19 . . . . 183 C1
Channel Rd BS21 . . . . 6 E5
Channel View Cres BS20 . . . 2 B5
Channel View Farm La
  BS49 . . . . 35 A7
Channel View Rd BS20 . . . . . 2 B5
Channing Cl TA8 . . . . 104 B5
Channon Rd ② TA2 . . . . . . 169 B2
CHANTRY 117 F3
Chantry Cl
  Nailsea BS48 . . . . 8 C1
  Taunton TA2 . . . . 213 B7
Chantry Ct
  Bristol BS1 . . . . 226 C2
  Somerton TA11 . . . . 211 C3
Chantry Dr BS22 . . . . 32 A4
Chantry Dro TA7 . . . . 155 E1
Chantry Gdns BA14 . . . . 83 F3
Chantry Ho ② BA4 . . . . . . 205 B6
Chantry La BA22 . . . . 174 D3
Chantry Mead Rd BA2 . . . . 44 E3
Chantry The BS26 . . . . 87 B5
Chantry View BA22 . . . . . . 197 D8
CHAPEL ALLERTON 88 D2
Chapel Barton BS48 . . . . 8 C2
Chapel Cl
  Castle Cary BA7 . . . . 214 C5
  Chew Stoke BS40 . . . . 56 E8
  Chilton Polden TA7 . . . . . . 137 B2
  Farrington Gurney BS39 . . . . 76 F4
  Keinton Mandeville TA11 . . 158 A1
  Nailsea BS48 . . . . 8 E2
  North Curry TA3 . . . . 170 B4
  Winford BS40 . . . . 38 A6
CHAPEL CLEEVE 131 D5
Chapel Cross
  North Cadbury BA22 . . . . . 175 D5
  Porlock TA24 . . . . 129 C7
Chapel Ct
  Bath BA2 . . . . 228 B2
  Clandown BA3 . . . . 78 E4
  Clevedon BS21 . . . . 6 D3
Chapelfield BA3 . . . . 115 A3
Chapel Field
  Peasedown St John BA2 . . . . 79 E8
  South Petherton TA13 . . . . 220 D3
Chapelfield La TA11 . . . . . . 158 C3
Chapel Forge Cl TA9 . . . . . 136 B8
Chapel Hill
  Ashcott TA7 . . . . 156 B8
  Backwell BS48 . . . . 19 D7
  Chewton Mendip BA3 . . . . . 94 E5
  Clevedon BS21 . . . . 6 D3
  Kingsdon TA11 . . . . 173 D5
  Kington Magna SP8 . . . . . . 177 E1
  Odcombe BA22 . . . . 186 C2
  Ubley BS40 . . . . 55 C5
  Wrington BS40 . . . . 35 D3
Chapel La
  Bishops Lydeard TA4 . . . . . 167 E8
  Butleigh BA6 . . . . 157 E4
  Chew Stoke BS40 . . . . 56 D8
  Claverham BS49 . . . . 34 F8
  Cleeve BS49 . . . . 35 B7

Chapel La continued
  Dinnington TA17 . . . . 195 B7
  East Huntspill TA9 . . . . 136 E8
  Gurney Slade BA3 . . . . 114 E7
  Holcombe BA3 . . . . 116 C8
  Milborne Port DT9 . . . . 217 D2
  North Cadbury BA22 . . . . . 175 D6
  Oxenpill BA6 . . . . 138 C4
  Penselwood BA9 . . . . 161 E2
  South Cadbury BA22 . . . . . 175 F5
  Sparkford BA22 . . . . 175 A6
  Winford BS40 . . . . 38 A6
  Wingfield BA14 . . . . 83 C6
  Yenston BA8 . . . . 189 F7
  Yeovil Marsh BA21 . . . . . . 187 A5
  Zeals BA12 . . . . 161 F3
Chapel Lawns BA3 . . . . 78 E4
CHAPEL LEIGH 167 A8
Chapel Leigh La TA4 . . . . . 167 A8
Chapel Pill La BS20 . . . . 4 E4
Chapel Rd
  Bristol, Bishopsworth BS13 . 22 A6
  Clandown BA3 . . . . 78 E4
  Fordgate BA7 . . . . 154 C3
  Isle Abbotts TA3 . . . . 183 E7
  Pawlett TA6 . . . . 135 F6
  Rooks Bridge BS26 . . . . 87 C5
  South Cadbury BA22 . . . . . 175 D4
Chapel Row
  Bath BA1 . . . . 228 B2
  Bathford BA1 . . . . 29 C2
  Dunster TA24 . . . . 201 D2
  Norton St Philip BA2 . . . . . . 81 F4
  Pill BS20 . . . . 4 C4
Chapel St
  Bridgwater TA6 . . . . 209 A5
  Burnham-on-S TA8 . . . . . . 104 A7
  Dulverton TA22 . . . . 163 D6
  Exford TA24 . . . . 128 D1
  Horningsham BA12 . . . . . . 144 D4
  Upton Noble BA4 . . . . 142 F2
Chapel Yd BA7 . . . . 214 B4
Chaplains Wood BS20 . . . . . 1 E5
Chapman Ct TA1 . . . . 212 C1
Chapmans Cl
  Frome BA11 . . . . 119 F6
  Wookey BA5 . . . . 139 D8
CHAPMANSLADE 121 C5
Chapmanslade CE VA Prim
  Sch BA13 . . . . 121 D4
Chaps Hollow TA11 . . . . . . 211 D2
Chapter St BS2 . . . . 227 B4
Charbury Wlk BS11 . . . . 4 E5
Charcroft Hill BA10 . . . . . . 160 F6
CHARD 223 D4
Chard Bsns Pk TA20 . . . . . 223 D6
Chard Cl BS48 . . . . 18 F8
Chard Com Hospl TA20 . . . 223 E4
Chard Ct BS14 . . . . 23 B6
CHARD JUNCTION 198 E4
Chard La
  Chard TA20 . . . . 223 B1
  Drimpton DT8 . . . . 199 F8
  Ilminster TA19 . . . . 194 D6
  Tatworth EX13, TA20 . . . . . 193 E1
  Woolminstone TA18 . . . . . 195 B2
Chardleigh Gn TA20 . . . . . 193 E5
CHARDLEIGH GREEN 223 A7
Chard Mus★ TA20 . . . . . . 223 B4
Chard Rd
  Axminster EX13 . . . . 198 B4
  Clevedon BS21 . . . . 6 E1
  Crewkerne TA18 . . . . 224 A6
  Drimpton DT8 . . . . 199 F7
  Chard Sch TA20 . . . . 223 C4
Chard St
  Chardstock EX13 . . . . 198 B7
  Thorncombe TA20 . . . . 199 B6
CHARDSTOCK 198 B7
Chardstock Ave BS9 . . . . 5 D8
Chardstock La TA20 . . . . . . 223 C2
Chardyke Dr BS39 . . . . 58 E1
Charing Cross DT6 . . . . 199 E1
Charity La BA11 . . . . 98 C1
CHARLCOMBE 27 E3
Charlcombe La BA1 . . . . 27 F3
Charlcombe Pk BS20 . . . . . . 1 D3
Charlcombe Rise BA1 . . . . . 27 F2
Charlcombe View Rd BA1 . . 28 A2
Charlcombe Way BA1 . . . . . 27 F2
Charlcome Rise BS20 . . . . . . 1 D3
Charlecombe Ct BS9 . . . . 5 F6
Charlecombe Rd BS9 . . . . . . 5 F6
Charlecote BA1 . . . . 27 F1
Charles Cres TA1 . . . . 213 D4
Charles Cl ■ BS8 . . . . 226 A2
Charles Pl BA1 . . . . 226 A2
Charles Rd
  Frome BA11 . . . . 119 F3
  Yeovil BA21 . . . . 219 D6
Charles St
  Bath BA1 . . . . 228 B2
  Bristol BS1 . . . . 227 A4
Charlestone Rd TA8 . . . . . . 104 B8
Charleton Ho ⑧ BS2 . . . . . 227 C1
Charlock Cl ③ BS22 . . . . . . 49 D7
Charlock Rd BS22 . . . . 49 D7
Charlotte Ct BA20 . . . . 219 A4
Charlotte St S BS1 . . . . 226 C2
Charlotte St
  Bath BA1 . . . . 228 B2
  Bristol, Brandon Hill BS1 . . 226 C3
CHARLTON
  Creech St Michael 169 F5
  Radstock 97 C5
  Shepton Mallet 205 D5
CHARLTON ADAM 173 E7
Charlton Ave BS23 . . . . 48 D4

Cas–Che 237

Charlton Cl
  Bridgwater TA6 . . . . 209 C4
  Crewkerne TA18 . . . . 224 D5
  Shepton Mallet BA4 . . . . . 205 D5
  Yeovil BA21 . . . . 219 D5
Charlton Crossroads BA4 . 205 D5
Charlton Dr BS48 . . . . 9 C7
Charlton Field La DT9 . . . . 175 D1
Charlton Hill DT9, BA8 . . . 176 B3
CHARLTON
  HORETHORNE 176 B2
Charlton Horethorne CE Prim
  Sch DT9 . . . . 176 A1
Charlton La
  Creech St Michael TA3 . . . . 169 E5
  Radstock BA3 . . . . 97 D6
  Sparkford DT9 . . . . 175 F3
CHARLTON MACKRELL . . 173 E7
Charlton Mackrell CE Prim
  Sch
  Charlton Mackrell TA11 . . . 173 E7
  Charlton Mackrell TA11 . . . 173 E7
CHARLTON MUSGROVE . . 161 A2
Charlton Park Rd BA3 . . . . . 97 F6
Charlton Pk
  Keynsham BS31 . . . . 24 D5
  Midsomer Norton BA3 . . . . . 97 B7
Charlton Rd
  Creech St Michael TA3 . . . . 169 E6
  Holcombe BA3 . . . . 97 D3
  Keynsham BS31, BS14 . . . . 24 C3
  Midsomer Norton BA3 . . . . . 97 B8
  Shepton Mallet BA4 . . . . . 205 D5
  Weston-super-Mare BS23 . . 48 D4
Charlton Road Cotts TA3 . 169 D6
Charlton Trad Est BA4 . . . . 205 E5
Charlton View BS20 . . . . 2 C5
CHARLYNCH 152 F8
Charlynch Hill TA5 . . . . 152 F8
Charlynch La TA5 . . . . 153 B8
Charlynch Rd TA5 . . . . 153 A8
Charmborough Farm Rural
  Bsns Pk BA3 . . . . 97 D3
Charmoor Dro TA20 . . . . . 182 F1
Charmoor La TA20 . . . . 182 F1
Charmouth Rd BA1 . . . . 44 B2
Charn Hill DT9 . . . . 176 A2
Charnwood Cl TA6 . . . . 208 F7
Charnwood Dr BS27 . . . . . . 90 B7
Charnwood Rd BS14 . . . . . . 23 B4
Charolais Dr ⑧ TA6 . . . . . 154 A5
Charter Cl TA6 . . . . 209 A4
Charter Ho BS1 . . . . 226 B2
CHARTERHOUSE 72 C4
Charterhouse Cl
  Cheddar BS27 . . . . 90 C6
  Nailsea BS48 . . . . 8 F1
Charterhouse Dr BA11 . . . . 120 C7
Charterhouse Rd BS2 . . . . . 49 B8
Charter Way BA5 . . . . 203 B4
Charter Wlk
  Bristol BS14 . . . . 23 A6
  Taunton TA1 . . . . 213 C5
Chartley BS9 . . . . 5 D2
Chase Cl BA6 . . . . 206 C3
Chasey's Dro BA6 . . . . 139 C4
Chatham Ave TA6 . . . . 208 E6
Chatham Ct TA10 . . . . 171 C4
Chatham Pk BA2 . . . . 45 C6
Chatham Pl TA10 . . . . 171 C4
Chatham Row BA1 . . . . 228 C3
Chatley Furlong BA2 . . . . . . 81 F3
Chatsworth Rd BA21 . . . . . 219 D7
Chattenden Ho BS9 . . . . 5 F3
Chatterton Gn BS14 . . . . . . 22 F3
Chatterton Ho ⑤ BS1 . . . . 227 B1
Chatterton Sq BS1 . . . . 227 C1
Chatterton St BS1 . . . . 227 C1
Chaucer Cl ④ TA6 . . . . 153 F4
Chaucer Rd
  Bath BA2 . . . . 44 F4
  Midsomer Norton BA3 . . . . . 97 B8
  Weston-super-Mare BS23 . . 49 A4
Chaundey Gr BS13 . . . . 22 B5
Cheapside
  Bristol BS2 . . . . 227 C4
  Langport TA10 . . . . 171 F5
  Taunton TA1 . . . . 212 F3
  Wiveliscombe TA4 . . . . 210 C4
Cheap St
  Bath BA1 . . . . 228 C2
  Frome BA11 . . . . 119 F5
  Sherborne DT9 . . . . 225 D4
Cheats Rd TA3 . . . . 169 C3
Checcombe La TA19 . . . . . . 188 B4
Checkridge La EX13 . . . . . . 198 D2
CHEDDAR 90 D8
Cheddar Bsns Pk BS27 . . . . 90 A6
Cheddar Bsns Pk BS27 . . . . 90 A6
Cheddar Cl
  Burnham-on-S TA8 . . . . . . 104 C8
  Frome BA11 . . . . 120 C7
  Nailsea BS48 . . . . 18 F8
Cheddarcoombe La BS25 . . 70 E8
Cheddar Cl BS27 . . . . 90 B7
Cheddar Fields BS27 . . . . . . 90 A7
Cheddar Fst Sch BS27 . . . . 90 B7
Cheddar Gorge★ BS27 . . . . 71 E1
Cheddar Gorge Rural Village★
  BS27 . . . . 90 C8
Cheddar Gr BS13 . . . . 22 A8
Cheddar Grove Prim Sch
  BS13 . . . . 22 A8
Cheddar Gr Prim Sch ■
  BS13 . . . . 22 A8

Cheddar Moor Dro BS27 . . . 90 C4
Cheddar Moor Rd BS28 . . . 89 E3
Cheddar Rd
  Axbridge BS26 . . . . 70 E2
  Clewer BS28 . . . . 89 D2
  Wedmore BS28 . . . . 108 D6
Cheddar Valley Bldgs **2**
  BA5 . . . . 203 C3
CHEDDON FITZPAINE . . . 169 A6
Cheddon Fitzpaine CE Prim
  Sch TA2 . . . . 168 F6
Cheddon Lawns TA2 . . . . . 169 A6
Cheddon Mews TA2 . . . . . 212 F7
Cheddon Rd TA2 . . . . 212 F7
Chedworth Cl BA2 . . . . 45 F3
CHEDZOY 154 E8
Chedzoy La TA7 . . . . 209 E7
Cheeks La BA10 . . . . 215 E6
Cheer La TA7 . . . . 154 F5
Cheese Factory Rd TA5 . . 135 A1
Cheese Hill BA11 . . . . 143 D8
Cheese La BS2 . . . . 227 B2
Chelmer Cl TA1 . . . . 213 D4
Chelmer Gr BS31 . . . . 24 F4
Chelmsine La TA21 . . . . . 181 B5
Chelscombe BA1 . . . . 27 B1
Chelscombe Cl BA1 . . . . . . 27 E4
Chelsea Cl BS31 . . . . 25 A5
Chelsea Rd BA1 . . . . 44 C7
Chelsfield BS48 . . . . 19 A7
CHELSTON 180 D8
Chelston Ave BA21 . . . . . 219 B7
Chelston Bsn Pk TA21 . . . 180 D8
CHELSTON HEATHFIELD . 180 E7
Chelston Rd BS4 . . . . 22 D7
Chelston Terr TA21 . . . . . 180 D8
Chelswood Ave BS22 . . . . . 49 C8
Chelswood Gdns BS22 . . . . 49 D8
Cheltenham St BA2 . . . . . 228 A1
CHELVEY 18 D5
Chelvey Batch BS48 . . . . . 18 F3
Chelvey La BS48 . . . . 18 E4
Chelvey Rd BS48 . . . . 18 D5
Chelvey Rise BS48 . . . . 9 A1
Chelvy Cl BS13 . . . . 22 D3
CHELWOOD 59 A8
Chelwood BS23 . . . . 48 F8
Chelwood Dr
  Bath BA2 . . . . 44 D1
  Taunton TA1 . . . . 212 E1
Chelwood Rd
  Bristol BS11 . . . . 4 D7
  Saltford BS31 . . . . 25 E4
Chelwood Rdbt BS39 . . . . . 58 E8
CHELYNCH 141 E6
Chelynch Pk BA4 . . . . 141 E6
Chelynch Rd BA4 . . . . 141 F7
Chepstow Ave TA6 . . . . . . 209 A2
Chepstow Ct BA21 . . . . . . 219 D6
Chepstow Ho BA10 . . . . . 215 D6
Chepstow Rd BS4 . . . . 22 D8
Chepstow Wlk BS31 . . . . . 24 D5
Cher TA24 . . . . 200 F6
Cherfield TA24 . . . . 200 F6
Cherington Rd BS48 . . . . . . 9 A2
Cheriton St BA8 . . . . 176 D3
Cherry Ave BS21 . . . . 6 E2
Cherry Cl
  Bridgwater TA6 . . . . 209 C3
  Yatton BS49 . . . . 34 B8
Cherry Ct **12** BS1 . . . . . . 227 A4
Cherry Garden La BA2 . . . 100 D7
Cherry Gr
  Frome BA11 . . . . 119 C3
  Taunton TA2 . . . . 212 F6
  Yatton BS49 . . . . 34 B8
Cherry Hay BS21 . . . . 6 D1
Cherry La
  4 Bristol BS1 . . . . 227 B4
  Odcombe BA22 . . . . 186 C2
Cherry Orch TA3 . . . . 168 D1
Cherry Orchard Dr BA5 . . 203 C5
Cherry Pie La BA22 . . . . . 175 A5
Cherry Rd
  Long Ashton BS41 . . . . . . 10 F1
  Nailsea BS48 . . . . 8 D1
Cherry Tree Cl
  Keynsham BS31 . . . . 24 C4
  Radstock BA3 . . . . 78 E1
Cherry Tree Ct
  Crewkerne TA18 . . . . 224 D8
  Kingston Seymour BS21 . . 16 C2
  1 Wells BA5 . . . . 203 C3
  Wincanton BA9 . . . . 216 D4
Cherry Tree Dr BA20 . . . . 218 D2
Cherry Tree La TA1 . . . . . 212 F1
Cherry Tree Rd EX13 . . . . 198 A1
Cherry Tree Way TA23 . . . 202 D6
Cherrywood Cl TA6 . . . . . 208 D3
Cherrywood Rd BS22 . . . . 31 F2
Cherrywood Rise BS22 . . . 31 F2
Chertsey Cl TA7 . . . . 136 E4
Cherwell Rd BS31 . . . . 25 A4
Chescombe Rd BS49 . . . . . 34 B7
Chesham Rd N BS22 . . . . . 49 B8
Chesham Rd S BS22 . . . . . 49 B8
Cheshay's Hill TA19 . . . . . 183 D1
Cheshire Ave BS24 . . . . . . 50 C5
Chesle Cl BS20 . . . . 1 E3
Cheslefield BS20 . . . . 1 E3
Chesle Way BS20 . . . . 1 E3
Chessell La BA4 . . . . 140 C4
Chessels Cl BA22 . . . . 197 B8
Chessels La TA11 . . . . 173 F7
Chessington Ave BS14 . . . 23 B5

CHESTERBLADE 142 A4
Chesterblade Rd
  Chesterblade BA4 . . . . . . 142 A4
  Evercreech BA4 . . . . 141 F3
Chester Cl BS24 . . . . 50 A8
Chester Cres BS13 . . . . . . 22 B8
Chesterfield BS4 . . . . 223 D4
Chesterfield Cl BS29 . . . . . 50 F3
Chesterfield Ho BA3 . . . . . 78 B1
Chesterfield Nuffield Health
  Bristol Hospl The BS8 . . 226 A2
Chester Pl TA6 . . . . 209 C8
Chester Terr TA20 . . . . . . 223 D4
Chesterton Dr BS48 . . . . . . 9 A2
Chesterton Ho **6** BS2 . . . 227 B4
Chestertons The BA2 . . . . 45 F8
Chestnut Ave
  Axbridge BS26 . . . . 70 C2
  Chapel Cleeve TA24 . . . . 131 D5
  Crewkerne TA18 . . . . 224 D7
  Weston-super-Mare BS22 . 32 A1
Chestnut Barn Ind Est
  BS24 . . . . 33 D3
Chestnut Chase BS48 . . . . . 9 A3
Chestnut Cl
  Baltonsborough BA6 . . . . 158 A5
  Banwell BS29 . . . . 51 A3
  Bridgwater TA6 . . . . 209 C4
  Bristol BS14 . . . . 23 F5
  1 Carhampton TA24 . . 131 A5
  Congresbury BS49 . . . . . . 34 D4
  Frome BA11 . . . . 120 C7
  Maiden Bradley BA12 . . . 144 C2
  Paulton BS39 . . . . 77 E6
  Radstock BA3 . . . . 78 E1
  Somerton TA11 . . . . 211 C3
  Wellington TA21 . . . . 222 E5
Chestnut Ct BS13 . . . . 22 A7
Chestnut Dr
  Claverham BS49 . . . . 17 F1
  Taunton TA1 . . . . 213 C1
  Yeovil BA20 . . . . 218 F3
Chestnut Gr
  Bath BA2 . . . . 44 C4
  Clevedon BS21 . . . . 6 E4
  Westwood BA15 . . . . 64 F4
Chestnut Ho
  Brean TA8 . . . . 65 F2
  Bristol BS13 . . . . 22 D3
Chestnut La
  Ashcott TA7 . . . . 156 B8
  Bleadon BS24 . . . . 67 B7
Chestnut Par BA4 . . . . . . 205 D4
Chestnut Park Prim Sch
  BS49 . . . . 16 F2
Chestnut Rd
  Long Ashton BS41 . . . . . . 11 B2
  11 Martock TA12 . . . . . 185 E6
Chestnuts The
  Cheddar BS27 . . . . 71 A1
  Winscombe BS25 . . . . 70 A7
Chestnut Way TA24 . . . . . 201 A5
Chestnut Wlk
  Bristol BS13 . . . . 22 A6
  Saltford BS31 . . . . 25 E3
Chever's La **7** BS1 . . . . . 81 E5
Cheverton Ho **1** BA21 . . 219 B5
Cheviot Mdw BS20 . . . . . . 2 F4
Cheviot St **6** TA6 . . . . . 154 A5
Chew Cotts BS31 . . . . 24 F5
Chew Court Farm BS40 . . . 39 B3
Chew Hill BS40 . . . . 39 A4
Chew La BS40 . . . . 38 F1
CHEW MAGNA 39 C4
Chew Magna Prim Sch
  BS40 . . . . 39 B3
Chew Rd BS40 . . . . 38 C5
Chew St BS40 . . . . 39 A3
CHEW STOKE 56 D8
Chew Stoke CE Prim Sch
  BS40 . . . . 56 D8
Chewton Cheese Dairy★
  BA3 . . . . 94 E6
Chewton Hill BA3 . . . . 95 A7
CHEWTON KEYNSHAM . . . 24 E2
CHEWTON MENDIP 94 E7
Chewton Mendip CE VA Prim
  Sch BA3 . . . . 94 F7
Chewton Rd BS31 . . . . 24 E2
Cheyne Rd BS9 . . . . 5 D6
Chew Valley Sch BS40 . . . . 38 F1
Chibbet Hill TA24 . . . . . . 146 B8
Chibbet Post TA24 . . . . . . 146 C8
Chichester Cl TA8 . . . . . . 104 B8
Chichester Pl BA3 . . . . 79 A2
Chichester Rd BA16 . . . . . 207 C4
Chichester Way BS24 . . . . 50 A8
Chicks La BA3 . . . . 95 D7
Chick's La TA4 . . . . 210 C6
Chickwell La BA3 . . . . 81 A1
Chidgey Cl TA6 . . . . 208 F5
CHILCOMBE 132 F1
Chilcombe La TA4 . . . . . . 132 F1
CHILCOMPTON 96 C4
Chilcompton Rd BA3 . . . . . 96 E7
Chilcote Dro BA5 . . . . 113 E2
Chilcote La BA5 . . . . 113 D1
Chilcott Cross TA22 . . . . . 163 A7
Chilcott La TA22 . . . . 163 A7
Childhay La
  Childhay DT8 . . . . 199 F6
  Drimpton DT8 . . . . 199 F6
Chilkwell La BA3 . . . . 81 C2
Chilkwell St BA6 . . . . 206 E4
Chillingham Dro **14**
  TA7 . . . . 154 A5

Chillington Down TA19,
  TA20 . . . . 194 F4
Chilliswood Cres TA1 . . . . 212 B2
Chilliswood La
  Staplehay TA3 . . . . 181 B8
  Taunton TA3 . . . . 168 B1
Chillybridge Rocks TA22 . 147 E1
Chillyhill La BS40 . . . . 38 F2
Chilpitts TA7 . . . . 136 F4
CHILSON 198 C6
CHILSON COMMON 198 D7
Chiltern Cl BS14 . . . . 23 B4
Chiltern Cross EX16 . . . . 164 B2
CHILTHORNE DOMER . . . 186 E5
Chilthorne Domer CE Sch
  BA22 . . . . 186 E5
Chilthorne Hill BA22 . . . . 186 E6
Chilthornehill La BA22 . . 186 D6
CHILTON CANTELO 174 D1
Chilton Cantelo House (Sch)
  BA22 . . . . 174 C1
Chilton Cl TA6 . . . . 208 F7
Chilton Ct **7** BA1 . . . . . 28 B1
Chilton Dro TA7 . . . . 137 C6
Chilton Gr BA21 . . . . 219 A2
Chilton Pk TA6 . . . . 208 F7
CHILTON POLDEN 137 B2
Chilton Rd
  Bath BA1 . . . . 28 B1
  Bridgwater TA5, TA6 . . . . 208 F8
  Bristol BS4 . . . . 23 A8
  Chilton Polden TA7 . . . . . 137 B4
Chilton Right Dro TA7 . . . 155 B6
Chilton St TA6 . . . . 208 F7
CHILTON TRINITY 135 F2
Chilton Trinity Sch TA6 . . 208 F7
Chimes The BS48 . . . . 18 C8
Chinehorn Dro TA5 . . . . . 135 F3
Chinnock Hollow BA22 . . 196 E8
Chinnock Huts La TA18 . . 196 E8
Chinnock Rd BA6 . . . . 206 F5
Chip La TA1 . . . . 212 E5
CHIPLEY 166 F2
Chippel La DT10 . . . . 190 F5
Chippenham Rd
  Doynton BS30 . . . . 12 D6
  Marshfield SN14 . . . . 13 C7
Chipping Cross BS21 . . . . 16 C8
CHIPSTABLE 165 E6
Chi-Rio Cl BA4 . . . . 205 E4
CHISELBOROUGH 185 F1
Chiselborough Hill La
  TA14 . . . . 186 A1
Chisland Dr TA24 . . . . . . 129 C8
Chistles La TA11 . . . . 158 A1
Chitcombe Rocks La TA4 . 149 C1
Chivers St BA2 . . . . 45 A2
Choke Wlk BS4 . . . . 23 E8
CHOLWELL 58 D2
Cholwell Cotts BS39 . . . . . 58 D2
Chorwell La TA21 . . . . . . 166 E2
Chovel La BA11 . . . . 142 F6
Chowins Rd TA18 . . . . . . 224 C5
Christ Church CE Fst Sch
  BA11 . . . . 119 F2
Christ Church CE Prim Sch
  Bristol BS8 . . . . 226 A3
  Victoria Park BS8 . . . . . . 226 A3
  Weston-super-Mare BS23 . 48 E8
Christ Church Cl **1** BS48 . 8 E2
Christ Church Ct **9** TA18 . 224 C6
Christchurch Hall **2** BA1 . 228 B3
Christ Church Path S **12**
  BS23 . . . . 48 E8
Christchurch Rd BS8 . . . . 226 A3
Christchurch St E BA11 . . 119 F4
Christchurch St W BA11 . . 119 E4
Christian Cl BS22 . . . . 32 A3
Christian's Cross BA6 . . . 157 E1
Christina Terr BS8 . . . . . . 226 A1
Christmas St **6** BS1 . . . . 227 A3
Christmas Steps **2** BS1 . . 227 A3
CHRISTON 68 D7
Christon Hill BS26 . . . . . . 68 B8
Christon Rd
  Banwell BS29 . . . . 51 A1
  Loxton BS26 . . . . 68 C6
Christon Terr BS23 . . . . . . 48 F2
Christopher Brain St BS14 . 22 E5
Christopher Cl BA20 . . . . 218 E5
Christopher Way BA4 . . . 205 A5
Chritchard Parkway TA1 . 213 B4
Chrysanthemum Cl **3**
  DT9 . . . . 225 E4
Chrysanthemum Flats **2**
  DT9 . . . . 225 E4
Chrysanthemum Row **4**
  DT9 . . . . 225 E4
Chubbards Cross Cvn Site
  TA19 . . . . 183 E5
Chubbs Lawn TA18 . . . . . 224 C5
Chubworthy Cross TA4 . . 165 D5
Church Ave BS9 . . . . 5 E4
Church Cl
  Bathampton BA2 . . . . 28 F2
  Bathford BA1 . . . . 29 B2
  Bourton SP8 . . . . 161 E1
  7 Carhampton TA24 . . 131 A5
  Clevedon BS21 . . . . 6 A2
  East Huntspill TA9 . . . . . 136 E8
  Evercreech BA4 . . . . 141 E1
  Great Elm BA11 . . . . 118 F7
  Lydeard St Lawrence TA4 . 151 A3
  24 Martock TA12 . . . . . 185 E6
  Norton Fitzwarren TA2 . . 168 B4
  Portishead BS20 . . . . 2 D5
  Shapwick TA7 . . . . 137 F1

Church Cl continued
  South Brewham BA10 . . . 160 F6
  Stoke St Gregory TA3 . . . 170 E6
  Stoke St Mary TA3 . . . . . 169 C1
  West Chinnock TA18 . . . . 196 B8
  Yatton BS49 . . . . 34 C7
Church Cnr BS24 . . . . 67 B1
Church Cotts
  Chilton Trinity TA5 . . . . . 135 F2
  Monkton Combe BA2 . . . . 63 E8
  Newton St Loe BA2 . . . . . 43 B6
Church Ct
  Midsomer Norton BA3 . . . 78 A1
  Redhill BS40 . . . . 36 D3
Churchdown Wlk BS11 . . . 4 E5
Church Dr
  Congresbury BS49 . . . . . . 34 D4
  West Buckland TA21 . . . . 180 D7
Church Farm Bsns Pk BA2 . 43 A7
Church Farm La BA2 . . . . . 82 D7
Church Farm Pl **18** BA8 . . 190 A6
Churchfield La BA3 . . . . . 183 F7
Church Field La TA7 . . . . 136 C4
Churchfields
  Rode BA11 . . . . 101 F8
  Wellington TA21 . . . . 222 D7
Church Fields
  Wellington TA21 . . . . 222 E6
  Wincanton BA9 . . . . 216 C3
Churchfield Sch TA9 . . . . 104 D4
Churchfields Dr BA7 . . . . 214 C6
Churchfields The Village Sch
  BA15 . . . . 46 E7
Church Gdns BA6 . . . . 206 D5
Church Hayes Cl BS48 . . . 18 E8
Church Hayes Dr BS48 . . . 18 E8
Church Hill
  Beckington BA11 . . . . 101 E4
  Buckhorn Weston SP8 . . . 177 D3
  Charlton Adam TA11 . . . . 173 F7
  Combwich TA5 . . . . 135 B5
  Dinnington TA17 . . . . 195 B7
  Exford TA24 . . . . 128 D1
  Freshford BA3 . . . . 64 B5
  Kington Magna SP8 . . . . . 177 E2
  Pitney TA10 . . . . 172 C7
  Radstock BA3 . . . . 79 C3
  South Cadbury BA22 . . . . 175 C3
  Stalbridge DT10 . . . . 190 B5
  Templecombe BA8 . . . . . 176 E1
  Timsbury BA2 . . . . 60 B2
Church Ho BA4 . . . . 141 F1
Church House Rd TA8 . . . . 84 F5
CHURCHILL 52 F5
Churchill Ave
  Clevedon BS21 . . . . 6 C2
  Wells BA5 . . . . 112 E1
Churchill Batch La BA4 . . 140 D6
Churchill Bsns Pk BS23 . . 49 A7
Churchill CE VA Prim Sch
  BS40 . . . . 53 A5
Churchill Cl
  Burnham-on-S TA8 . . . . . 104 C5
  5 Clevedon BS21 . . . . . . 6 C2
  Wells BA5 . . . . 112 E1
Churchill Dr BS9 . . . . 5 D7
Churchill Gate BS25 . . . . . 52 E4
Churchill Gn BS25 . . . . . . 52 C5
CHURCHILL GREEN 52 D5
Churchill La
  Axminster EX13 . . . . 198 A5
  Chipstable TA4 . . . . 165 C5
Churchill Rd
  Frome BA11 . . . . 119 D3
  Shepton Mallet BA4 . . . . 205 A5
  Wells BA5 . . . . 112 E1
  Weston-super-Mare BS23 . 49 A7
Churchill Rd E BA5 . . . . . 112 E1
Churchill Way
  Taunton TA1 . . . . 212 F1
  Watchet TA23 . . . . 202 C6
CHURCHINFORD 192 A7
Church La
  Axbridge BS26 . . . . 70 C2
  Backwell BS48 . . . . 19 C5
  Badgworth BS26 . . . . 88 A6
  Baltonsborough BA6 . . . . 158 A5
  Bath BA2 . . . . 45 C4
  Batheaston BA1 . . . . 28 F4
  Bicknoller TA4 . . . . 132 F2
  Bishop Sutton BS39 . . . . . 57 D4
  Bitton BS30 . . . . 25 E7
  Blackford BS28 . . . . 107 D5
  Brent Knoll TA9 . . . . 86 A2
  Bristol BS1 . . . . 227 B2
  Bristol, Clifton Wood BS8 . 226 B2
  Bristol, Dundry Hill BS14 . 23 B3
  Carhampton TA24 . . . . . . 131 B5
  Chew Stoke BS40 . . . . 56 D8
  Chewton Mendip BA3 . . . 94 F7
  Chilcompton BA3 . . . . 96 D5
  Chilton Polden TA7 . . . . . 137 B2
  Churchill BS25 . . . . 52 D5
  Clutton BS39 . . . . 58 E3
  Coleford BA3 . . . . 116 F7
  Compton Bishop BS26 . . . 69 B3
  Compton Dando BS39 . . . 41 D5
  Doulting BA4 . . . . 141 E6
  Downside BA3 . . . . 96 A2
  Dulverton TA22 . . . . 163 D6
  East Coker BA22 . . . . 197 E8
  East Harptree BS40 . . . . . 74 C4
  East Huntspill TA9 . . . . . 136 E8
  East Lambrook TA13 . . . . 220 C8

Church La continued
  Evercreech BA4 . . . . 141 E1
  Farmborough BA2 . . . . . . 60 A6
  Farrington Gurney BS39 . . 77 A4
  Flax Bourton BS48 . . . . . . 19 F7
  Glastonbury BA6 . . . . 206 D5
  Haselbury Plucknett TA18 . 196 C5
  Hatch Beauchamp TA3 . . 182 E8
  Horningsham BA12 . . . . . 144 E4
  Horton TA19 . . . . 183 C2
  Hutton BS24 . . . . 49 E2
  Ilminster TA19 . . . . 221 C4
  Kingston St Mary TA2 . . . 168 E8
  Limpley Stoke BA3 . . . . . . 64 A5
  Long Ashton BS41 . . . . . . 11 C2
  Long Sutton TA10 . . . . . . 172 D2
  Loxton BS26 . . . . 68 D4
  Lympsham BS24 . . . . 67 B1
  Lynford-on-F TA11 . . . . . 158 D2
  Meare BA6 . . . . 138 D4
  Midsomer Norton BA3 . . . 78 A1
  Milborne Port DT9 . . . . . 217 D2
  Misterton TA18 . . . . 224 E3
  Monkton Combe BA2 . . . . 45 F1
  Nailsea BS21 . . . . 8 C4
  Nailsea BS48 . . . . 8 C1
  North Perrott TA18 . . . . . 196 C4
  Norton Sub Hamdon TA14 . 185 F2
  Norton Sub Hamdon,
    Chiselborough TA14 . . . 185 E1
  Paulton BS39 . . . . 77 E6
  Portbury BS20 . . . . 3 E3
  Rimpton BA22 . . . . 188 B8
  Rode BA11 . . . . 101 F8
  Ruishton TA3 . . . . 169 C4
  Ruishton, Thornfalcon TA3 . 169 C2
  Seavington St Mary TA19 . 184 E1
  22 Shepton Mallet BA4 . . 205 B6
  Shepton Mallet, Cannards Grave
    BA4 . . . . 205 D2
  Sherborne DT9 . . . . 225 D4
  Stratton-on-f F BA3 . . . . . 96 F2
  Timsbury BA2 . . . . 60 B2
  Westonzoyland TA7 . . . . . 154 F5
  West Pennard BA6 . . . . . . 140 B1
  Wingfield BA14 . . . . 83 C6
  Winscombe BS25 . . . . 69 E6
  Yatton BS49 . . . . 34 C7
Churchlands TA9 . . . . 106 D4
Churchlands Ct TA8 . . . . 104 A7
Churchland Way BS22 . . . 50 B8
Church Lane Cnr TA9 . . . . 86 A2
Church Lane End BS48 . . . 19 F8
Church Leaze BS11 . . . . . . 4 D6
Church Mdw TA6 . . . . 208 E6
Church Mdws BS14 . . . . . . 23 C4
Church Mead SP8 . . . . 161 E1
Churchmoor La BA6 . . . . 158 A5
Church Pass **4** TA6 . . . . 208 F5
Church Path
  Aller TA10 . . . . 171 D8
  Bridgwater TA6 . . . . 208 E5
  Crewkerne TA18 . . . . 224 B6
  Meare BA6 . . . . 138 D4
  Minehead TA24 . . . . 200 F8
  Queen Camel BA22 . . . . . 174 F3
  South Petherton TA13 . . . 220 C2
  2 Yeovil BA20 . . . . 219 B5
Church Path Rd BS20 . . . . 4 C4
Church Pl
  Milborne Port DT9 . . . . . 217 D2
  Pill BS20 . . . . 4 C4
Church Rd
  Abbots Leigh BS8 . . . . . . 11 A8
  Bath, Combe Down BA2 . . 45 C1
  Bath, Weston Park BA1 . . 27 C1
  Bawdrip TA7 . . . . 136 E2
  Bitton BS30 . . . . 25 E7
  Bourton SP8 . . . . 177 F8
  Bradford Abbas DT9 . . . . 187 E1
  Brean TA8 . . . . 65 F4
  Bristol, Bishopsworth BS13 . 22 A6
  Bristol, Sneyd Park BS9 . . 5 D3
  Chapel Leigh TA4 . . . . . . 167 A4
  Churchinford TA3 . . . . . . 191 F8
  Churchstanton TA3 . . . . . 181 B1
  Coxley BS14 . . . . 139 E6
  Dundry BS41 . . . . 21 D2
  East Brent TA9 . . . . 86 C4
  Easton-in-G BS20 . . . . . . 4 A4
  Edington TA7 . . . . 137 C2
  Fitzhead TA4 . . . . 166 F7
  Fordgate TA7 . . . . 154 D3
  Huntspill TA9 . . . . 136 A8
  Ilton TA19 . . . . 183 E4
  Keenthorne TA5 . . . . 134 D3
  Kilmington BA12 . . . . 161 F7
  Leigh Woods BS8 . . . . 11 D6
  Lympsham BS24 . . . . 67 B1
  Middlezoy TA7 . . . . 155 B3
  Minehead TA24 . . . . 200 F8
  North Curry TA3 . . . . 170 B4
  North Newton TA7 . . . . . 154 A2
  Peasedown St John BA2 . . 79 B8
  Pensford BS39 . . . . 40 A7
  Redhill BS40 . . . . 36 D3
  Shapwick TA7 . . . . 137 F1
  South Cadbury BA22 . . . . 175 D4
  Sparkford BA22 . . . . 175 A4
  Spaxton TA5 . . . . 152 E7
  Street BA16 . . . . 207 D7
  Sutton Mallet TA7 . . . . . 155 B7
  Taunton TA1 . . . . 168 D1
  Wembdon TA6 . . . . 208 D6
  Weston-super-Mare BS22 . 31 E4
  Whitchurch BS14 . . . . 23 C4
  Winford BS40 . . . . 38 A7
  Winscombe BS25 . . . . 69 E7

Church Rd *continued*
Yatton BS49 . . . . .34 C7
Church Rd N BS20 . . . . .2 D5
Church Rd S BS20 . . . . .2 D4
Church Rise BS40 . . . . .38 A7
CHURCH ROW 101 F8
Church Row BA3 . . . . .96 F2
Church Row Cotts TA3. . . . .181 E6
Church Sq
Clutton BS39 . . . . .58 E2
Midsomer Norton BA3 . . . . .78 A1
8 Taunton TA1 . . . . .212 F4
Church St
Babcary TA11 . . . . .174 C7
Banwell BS29 . . . . .51 B3
Barton St David BA6 . . . . . .157 F2
6 Bath BA1 . . . . .228 C2
Bathford BA1 . . . . .29 B2
Bath, Weston park BA1. . . . .27 B1
Bath, Widcombe BA2 . . . . . .45 B4
Beckington BA11 . . . . .101 E4
Bishops Lydeard TA4 . . . . . .167 E8
Blackford BS28 . . . . .107 D4
Blagdon BS40. . . . . .54 F2
Bridgwater TA6 . . . . .209 A5
Bristol BS1. . . . . .227 B2
5 Cannington TA5. . . . . . .135 B2
Castle Cary BA7 . . . . .214 B4
Chard TA20. . . . . .223 C3
Cheddar BS27 . . . . .90 B7
Coleford BA3 . . . . .116 F7
Crewkerne TA18. . . . . .224 C6
Croscombe BA5. . . . . .204 C2
Dinder BA5. . . . . .140 D7
Donyatt TA19 . . . . .183 D1
Drayton TA10 . . . . .171 E3
Dunster TA24 . . . . .201 E2
2 Frome BA11 . . . . .119 F4
Halstock BA22 . . . . .197 C3
8 Henstridge BA8. . . . . . .190 A6
Highbridge TA9. . . . . .104 E4
Hinton St George TA17 . . . . .195 C7
Horningsham BA12 . . . . . . .144 D4
Ilchester BA22. . . . . .173 E1
Isle Abbotts TA3 . . . . .183 F7
Keinton Mandeville TA11 . . .158 A1
Kilmersdon BA3 . . . . .98 B5
Kingsbury Episcopi TA12. . . .185 B8
Kington Magna SP8 . . . . . .177 E2
Lopen TA13. . . . . .185 A1
Maiden Bradley BA12. . . . . .144 C1
Mark TA9 . . . . .106 D4
Martock TA12. . . . . .185 E6
Merriott TA16 . . . . .195 F7
Milborne Port DT9 . . . . . . .217 D2
Minehead TA24. . . . . .200 F8
Minehead, Alcombe TA24 . . .201 B5
Norton St Philip BA2. . . . . .81 E4
Nunney BA11 . . . . .143 B8
Paulton BS39 . . . . .77 D6
Pensford BS39 . . . . .40 D4
Podimore BA22 . . . . .174 A3
Radstock BA3. . . . . .78 F2
Shepton Beauchamp TA19 . .184 E4
Southwick BA14. . . . . .83 F3
Stogursey TA5 . . . . .134 C5
Stoke St Michael BA3 . . . . .116 A2
Taunton TA1 . . . . .213 B3
Timberscombe TA24. . . . . .130 B5
Tintinhull BA22. . . . . .186 B6
Upton Noble BA4 . . . . .142 F2
Wanstrow BA4. . . . . .142 F4
Wedmore BS28 . . . . .108 D4
West Coker BA22 . . . . .197 A8
Wincanton BA9 . . . . .216 C4
Wiveliscombe TA4 . . . . . . .210 C4
Woolavington TA7. . . . . . . .136 E4
Woolley BA1 . . . . .27 F6
Yeovil BA20 . . . . .219 B5
Yeovilton BA22. . . . . .174 A1
CHURCHSTANTON 181 B1
Churchstanton Prim Sch
TA3 . . . . .191 E8
Church Steps TA24 . . . . . .200 F8
Church Terr
7 Bampton EX16. . . . . . .164 B1
East Coker BA22 . . . . .197 C7
Odcombe BA22. . . . . .186 C2
4 Yeovil BA20 . . . . .219 B5
Church Tk SP8 . . . . .161 E1
CHURCH TOWN 19 C5
Church Town BS48 . . . . . . .19 C5
Church View
Bourton SP8. . . . . .161 E1
Chilton Trinity TA5. . . . . . .135 F2
Clatworthy TA4. . . . . .149 F1
Evercreech BA4 . . . . .141 E1
North Wootton BA4 . . . . . .140 C4
Porlock TA24 . . . . .124 A3
Wraxall BS48 . . . . .9 B2
Church View Cl TA10 . . . . .171 E8
Churchview Ct BA6. . . . . . .206 D4
Churchward Dr BA11. . . . . .120 C6
Churchward Rd BS22 . . . . . .32 B3
Churchway
Curry Rivel TA10. . . . . . . .171 D4
Faulkland BA3. . . . . .80 D1
Church Way TA7 . . . . .137 D2
Churchway Cl TA10. . . . . . .171 D4
Churchways BS14 . . . . .23 C4
Churchwell Cl DT9 . . . . . . .187 E1
Churchwell St DT9 . . . . . . .187 E1
Church Wlk
Baltonsborough BA6 . . . . . .158 A5
Bawdrip TA7. . . . . .136 E2
Bratton Seymour BA9. . . . . .176 B8
Ilminster TA19 . . . . .221 C4
Leigh u M BA3. . . . . .117 A3

Church Wlk *continued*
Long Sutton TA10 . . . . . . .172 F4
Marston Magna BA22. . . . . .174 F1
9 North Petherton TA6. . . .153 E3
Pill BS20. . . . . .4 C4
Wrington BS40. . . . . .35 D2
Chur La BA22 . . . . .197 A8
Churlands Cl BA22 . . . . . . .197 A8
Churston Cl BS14 . . . . .23 A3
Cinder Ash La TA18. . . . . .195 D4
Cinnamon La BA6 . . . . . . .206 F3
CircleBath Hospl BA2 . . . . .79 E6
Circle The BA2. . . . . .44 B3
Circular Rd BS9. . . . . .5 E2
Circus Field Rd BA6 . . . . . .206 D4
Circus Mews BA1 . . . . . . .228 B3
Circus Pl BA1 . . . . .228 B3
Circus The BA1 . . . . .228 B3
City of Bath Coll BA1 . . . . .228 B2
City of Bristol Coll BS1 . . . .226 C2
City of Bristol Coll (South
Bristol Skills Acad) BA11 . .22 E5
City Rd BS2. . . . . .227 B4
City The TA9 . . . . .106 C4
City View BA1. . . . . .228 C4
Clammer Hill La TA18 . . . . .224 D6
Clanage Rd BS3. . . . . .11 E4
Clanders Batch BS40 . . . . . .54 D3
CLANDOWN 78 E4
Clandown Rd BS39 . . . . . . .77 F4
Clanfield DT9 . . . . .225 B2
Clan Ho BA2 . . . . .45 C7
CLANVILLE 159 C3
Clanville La TA24 . . . . .200 F7
Clanville Cotts BA7. . . . . . .214 A7
Clanville Rd TA24 . . . . . . .200 F7
CLAPTON
Crewkerne. 195 C1
Midsomer Norton. 96 C7
Clapton Court Gdns★
TA18. . . . . .195 D1
Clapton Dro BS20 . . . . .2 D1
Clapton Gate TA18 . . . . . .195 C2
CLAPTON IN GORDANO 2 E1
Clapton La
Holton BA9. . . . . .176 B6
Portishead BS20 . . . . .2 E2
Clapton Rd
Hewish TA18. . . . . .195 D2
Midsomer Norton BA3 . . . . .77 D1
CLAPTON WICK 7 E6
Clapton Wlk BS9 . . . . .5 C5
Clare Gdns BA2 . . . . .44 D1
Claremont Bldgs BA1. . . . . .28 A1
Claremont Cres BS23. . . . . .30 B1
Claremont Ct TA1 . . . . . . .212 C1
Claremont Cvn Pk TA8. . . . .84 F6
Claremont Dr TA1 . . . . . . .212 C1
Claremont Gdns
Clevedon BS21. . . . . .6 E1
Hallatrow BS39 . . . . .77 B7
4 Nailsea BS48. . . . . .8 D1
Claremont Gr TA6 . . . . . . .209 D6
Claremont Hall BS21 . . . . . .6 E4
Claremont La TA1 . . . . . . .212 C1
Claremont Pl 13 BA1 . . . . . .28 A1
Claremont Rd BA1 . . . . . . .28 B1
Claremont Wlk BA1 . . . . . . .28 A1
Clarence Ct 1 BA20. . . . . .219 A5
Clarence Dr 1 TA6. . . . . . .153 F4
Clarence Grove Rd BS23. . . .48 E5
Clarence Pl
Bath BA1 . . . . .44 B6
Bristol BS2. . . . . .226 C4
Clarence Rd BS1. . . . . .227 B1
Clarence Rd E BS23. . . . . . .48 E5
Clarence Rd N BS23 . . . . . . .48 D5
Clarence Rd S BS23 . . . . . . .48 D5
Clarence St
Bath BA1 . . . . .228 C4
Taunton TA1 . . . . .212 E4
Yeovil BA20 . . . . .219 A5
Clarence Ter TA6 . . . . .136 B2
Clarence Terr
Bath BA2 . . . . .45 D5
8 Yeovil BA20 . . . . .219 B4
Clarendon Rd
Bath BA2 . . . . .45 B5
Weston-super-Mare BS23 . . .48 F8
Clarendon Villas BA2. . . . . .45 B5
Clares Rd BA5 . . . . .203 D3
Clare St
Bridgwater TA6 . . . . .208 F5
Bristol BS1. . . . . .227 A2
2 North Petherton TA6 . . .153 F4
Clark Cl
Woolavington TA7. . . . . . .136 E4
Wraxall BS48 . . . . .9 B2
Clarken Cl BS48. . . . . .9 B3
Clarken Coombe BS41. . . . . .11 B3
Clarke's Cl TA20 . . . . .223 D4
Clarkes St BA20 . . . . .219 A4
Clarke's Row TA20 . . . . . . .223 D4
CLARKHAM CROSS 197 E2
Clarkham Cross BA22 . . . . .197 E2
Clarks Cl BA22 . . . . .218 A5
Clark's La TA18. . . . . .224 F3
Clarks Meadow BA4 . . . . . .205 C3
Clarkson Ave BS22 . . . . . . .31 C1
Clarkson Ho BA1. . . . . . . .228 A2
Clarks Rd TA6. . . . . .209 C4
Clarks Shopping Village
BA16. . . . . .207 C6
Clarks Way BA2. . . . . .44 C2
Classeys House Rd TA10. . . .172 A8
Classic Bldgs TA6. . . . . . . .208 F4
Clatcombe La DT9. . . . . . .188 D6
CLATWORTHY 149 F1

Clatworthy Dr BS14. . . . . . .23 A7
Clatworthy Resr★ TA4 . . . .149 D2
Claude Ave BA2 . . . . .44 C5
Claude Terr BA2 . . . . .44 C5
Claudius Rd BS31 . . . . .24 F7
Clavelshay Rd TA6 . . . . . . .153 C2
CLAVERHAM 17 E1
Claverham Cl BS49 . . . . . . .34 D7
Claverham Dro BS49 . . . . . .17 D5
Claverham Pk BS49 . . . . . . .34 F8
Claverham Rd BS49 . . . . . . .34 E8
CLAVERTON 46 B5
Claverton Bldgs BA2 . . . . . .228 C1
CLAVERTON DOWN 45 F3
Claverton Down Rd BA2 . . . .45 F3
Claverton Ct BA2. . . . . .45 E4
Claverton Dr BA2 . . . . .45 F3
Claverton Hill BA2 . . . . . . .46 A4
Claverton Lodge BA2. . . . . .45 C5
Claverton Pumping Sta★
BA2. . . . . .46 C5
Claverton Rd BS31 . . . . . . .25 E2
Claverton Rd W BS31 . . . . . .25 D3
Claverton St BA2. . . . . . . .228 C1
Clay Castle TA18 . . . . .196 D6
Clay Castle La TA18 . . . . . .196 C6
Claydon Cl TA23 . . . . .131 E4
Claydon Gn BS14. . . . . .22 F3
Clayford La TA22 . . . . .163 C5
Clayford Rd TA22. . . . . . . .163 C5
CLAYHANGER 165 C1
Clayhanger Common
TA19. . . . . .194 A6
Clayhanger Cross
Combe St Nicholas TA20. . . .193 E6
Combe St Nicholas TA20. . . .193 E6
Clayhanger La
Chard TA20. . . . . .223 A8
Combe St Nicholas TA20. . . .193 E6
CLAYHIDON 180 E2
Clayhidon Crossway EX15 . .180 E2
Clay La
Barrington TA19. . . . . .184 B5
Bitton BS30 . . . . .25 D8
Chewton Mendip BA3. . . . . .94 C5
Higher Chillington TA19 . . . .194 F5
Millmoor EX15 . . . . .179 A1
Rode BA11 . . . . .101 F8
Clayland Cnr TA5 . . . . .134 E5
Claylands Cnr TA5 . . . . . . .134 E5
Claypiece Rd BS13 . . . . . . .22 A4
Claypit La TA5 . . . . .134 E8
Claypit Rd BS41. . . . . .22 B1
CLAYPITS 164 C4
Claysend BA2. . . . . .43 D5
CLAYS END 43 D6
Clays End La BA2. . . . . .43 D6
Clayton Cl
Portishead BS20 . . . . .2 E4
Yeovil BA22 . . . . .218 A6
Clayton Rd BS8 . . . . .226 A4
CLEARWOOD 121 F8
Clearwood BA13 . . . . .121 F8
Clearwood View BA13 . . . . .121 E4
Cleaveside Cl BA22. . . . . . .174 F3
CLEEVE 35 B8
Cleeve Abbey★ TA23. . . . . .131 E3
Cleevedale Rd BA2. . . . . . . .45 A1
Cleeve Dr BS49 . . . . .35 B8
Cleeve Gn BA2. . . . . .44 A6
Cleeve Gr BS31. . . . . .24 D5
Cleeve Hill
Ubley BS40. . . . . .73 E8
Watchet TA23. . . . . .202 A7
Cleeve Hill Rd BS40 . . . . . . .35 C7
Cleeve Pk TA23 . . . . .131 D5
Cleeve Pl BS48. . . . . .9 A1
Cleeve Rd TA2 . . . . .213 B7
Cleeveways DT9 . . . . .176 A2
Clemence Rd BA16 . . . . . . .207 D4
Clements Cl BA5. . . . . .203 C3
Clement St BS2. . . . . .227 C4
Cleve Ct 3 BS8 . . . . .11 F6
CLEVEDON 6 B3
Clevedon Com Hospl BS21. . .6 E3
Clevedon Court★ BS21. . . . .7 A4
Clevedon Craft Ctr★ BS21. . .7 A1
Clevedon La BS21. . . . . .8 B7
Clevedon Min Rly★ BS21. . . .6 B3
Clevedon Pier★ BS21. . . . . . .6 C4
Clevedon Rd
Flax Bourton BS48 . . . . .9 F2
Midsomer Norton BA3 . . . . .78 A2
Nailsea BS21 . . . . .8 B4
Portishead BS20 . . . . .1 E1
Portishead BS20 . . . . .2 D3
Walton In Gordano BS21 . . . .7 C8
Weston-super-Mare BS23 . . .48 E6
Wraxall BS48 . . . . .9 B4
Wraxall BS48 . . . . .9 D6
Clevedon Sch BS21. . . . . . . .6 F5
Clevedon Terr BS6 . . . . . . .227 A4
Clevedon Wlk 2 BS48. . . . . .8 E2
Cleveland Cotts BA1. . . . . .228 C4
Cleveland Ct BA2. . . . . .45 C6
Cleveland Pl BA1. . . . . . . .228 C4
Cleveland Pl E BA1 . . . . . . .228 C4
Cleveland Pl W BA1. . . . . . .228 C4
Cleveland Reach BA1. . . . . .228 C4
Cleveland Row BA1. . . . . . .45 B8
Clevelands TA24 . . . . .200 F8
Cleveland St TA1. . . . . . . .212 E4
Cleveland Terr BA1. . . . . . .228 C4
Cleveland Wlk BA2. . . . . . . .45 C6
Cleve The BA21. . . . . .218 C6
CLEWER 89 D3
Clewer La BS28 . . . . .89 D2
Clewer Rd BS28. . . . . .89 D3

Clewson Rise BS14. . . . . . .22 F3
Cleyhill Gdns BA13 . . . . . .121 D4
Cliffe Dr BA3. . . . . .64 A6
Clifford Ave TA2 . . . . .212 E8
Clifford Cres TA2 . . . . .212 E8
Clifford Dr BS39 . . . . .77 D6
Clifford Gdns BS11 . . . . . . .4 E6
Clifford Ho BS23 . . . . .48 D6
Clifford Lodge 3 TA5 . . . . .135 B2
Clifford Mews TA21 . . . . . .222 E6
Clifford Pk TA5 . . . . .135 B2
Clifford Terr TA21 . . . . . . .222 E6
Cliff Rd
North Petherton TA6. . . . . .153 E3
Weston-super-Mare BS22 . . .31 A2
Cliffs Rd The BA5 . . . . .72 A1
Cliff St BS27 . . . . .90 C8
Cliffs The
Cheddar BA5. . . . . .72 A1
Cheddar BS27 . . . . .90 C8
Clift House Rd BS3. . . . . . . .11 F4
Clift House Spur BS3 . . . . . .11 F4
CLIFTON 226 A4
Clifton Ave BS23 . . . . .48 E5
Clifton Cl
1 Bristol BS8 . . . . .11 F7
Yeovil BA21 . . . . .219 E6
Clifton Coll BS8 . . . . .226 A4
Clifton College Prep Sch
BS8. . . . . .5 F1
Clifton Ct 10 BS21 . . . . .6 C2
Clifton Down BS8 . . . . .11 F7
Clifton Down Rd BS8 . . . . . .226 A3
Clifton High Gr BS9 . . . . . . .5 E5
Clifton High Sch BS8 . . . . .226 A4
Clifton Hill
Barwick BA22. . . . . .197 F8
Bristol BS8. . . . . .226 A2
Clifton Park Rd BS8 . . . . . . .11 B8
Clifton Pk BS8 . . . . .226 A3
Clifton Rd
Bristol BS8. . . . . .226 A2
Weston-super-Mare BS23 . . .48 E5
Clifton Rocks Railway★
BS8. . . . . .11 F6
Clifton St BS20. . . . . .2 C2
Clifton Suspension Bridge★
BS8. . . . . .11 F7
Clifton Suspension Bridge Rd
BS8 . . . . .11 F7
Clifton Terr 7 TA2 . . . . . . .212 F6
Clifton Vale BS8 . . . . .226 A2
Clifton Vale Cl BS8 . . . . . . .226 A2
Clifton View 9 BA22 . . . . . .197 F8
CLIFTON WOOD 226 A2
Cliftonwood Cres BS8. . . . .226 B2
Clifton Wood Ct BS8. . . . . .226 B2
Clifton Wood Rd BS8. . . . . .226 B2
Cliftonwood Terr BS8 . . . . .226 A2
Clift Pl BS1 . . . . .227 A1
Clifts Bldgs BA11. . . . . . . .119 F4
CLINK 120 C6
Clink Farm Ct BA11. . . . . . .120 C6
Clink Rd BA11. . . . . .120 D6
Clink The TA6. . . . . .209 A5
Clipper Cl TA6 . . . . .209 C4
Clipper Ct BA16. . . . . .207 B5
Clipper Quay TA24 . . . . . . .201 B7
Clitsome View TA23 . . . . . .131 D2
Clive Rd BS14. . . . . .23 C8
Clivey BA13. . . . . .102 E1
Clock Ho TA5 . . . . .134 B2
Clock Ho The BA10 . . . . . . .160 D4
Clockhouse Mews BS20 . . . . .2 D6
Clockhouse The TA4 . . . . . .167 E6
Clockhouse View BA16. . . . .207 D6
CLOFORD 143 A7
CLOFORD COMMON 143 B6
Cloisters Croft TA8. . . . . . .104 B6
Cloisters The BA5. . . . . . . .203 D3
Cloister The DT9 . . . . .225 D4
Closemead BS21 . . . . .6 D1
Close The
Glastonbury BA6 . . . . .206 E5
9 Merriott TA16 . . . . . . .195 F7
Minehead TA24. . . . . .201 B5
North Cadbury BS20 . . . . . .175 D6
Portishead BS20 . . . . .1 F1
CLOSWORTH 197 F5
Clotfurlong La DT9 . . . . . . .188 F1
Clothier Mdw BA7. . . . . . . .214 B6
Cloudberry Cl TA20. . . . . . .223 F5
Cloud Hill Ind Est BS39 . . . .77 A8
Clovelly Rd BS22 . . . . .32 A2
Clover Cl
Clevedon BS21. . . . . .6 F3
Frome BA11 . . . . .120 B3
Paulton BS39 . . . . .77 E4
Clover Ct 2 BS22 . . . . .49 D7
Clover Gd BA4 . . . . .205 C5
Clover Hill Way
Barrow Gurney BS48 . . . . . .20 F7
Bristol BS48. . . . . .21 A6
Clover Mead TA1. . . . . . . .213 C1
Clover Rd BS22 . . . . .32 A6
Cloverton Dr TA6 . . . . .209 D7
Clover Way
Bridgwater TA6 . . . . .208 E1
Highbridge TA9. . . . . .104 E4
Clumber Dr BA11. . . . . . . .119 F6
Clumber Ho BA11 . . . . . . .119 F6
CLUTTON 58 E3
CLUTTON HILL 59 B4
Clutton Hill BS39. . . . . .59 B4
Clutton Prim Sch BS39 . . . . .58 E3
Clyce Rd TA9 . . . . .104 D3
Clyde Ave BS31 . . . . .24 F4
Clyde Gdns BA2. . . . . .44 B6

Clydesdale Cl BS14. . . . . . .23 A6
Clynder Gr BS21. . . . . .6 E6
Clyntonville BS22 . . . . .31 A4
Coach House Mews BS23 . . .30 D1
Coachmans Yd BA6 . . . . . . .206 D5
Coach Rd TA24. . . . . .124 A3
Coalash La BA11 . . . . .119 D8
Coal Barton BA3. . . . . .116 E8
Coalbridge Cl BS22. . . . . . .31 F2
Coaley Rd BS11. . . . . .4 D5
Coal La BA11. . . . . .119 C8
Coal Orch TA1 . . . . .212 F4
Coalpit La
Chilcompton BA3 . . . . .96 A2
Stoke St Michael BA3 . . . . .116 B3
Coalpit Rd BA1. . . . . .29 A4
Coape Rd BS14. . . . . .23 F5
Coast Cvn Pk BS21. . . . . . . .1 B1
Coastguard Cotts TA24 . . . .201 A8
Coast Rd TA8 . . . . .84 F7
COAT 185 D7
Coates Est BS48. . . . . .8 F3
Coates Gr BS48 . . . . .9 A2
Coates Wlk BS4 . . . . .22 D6
Coate Turn TA4 . . . . .166 A6
Coatmead Dro TA12 . . . . . .185 C8
Coat Rd TA12 . . . . .185 D7
Cobbetts Rise TA13 . . . . . . .220 B5
Cobblers Way BA3 . . . . .97 C8
Cobblestone Mews BS8 . . . .226 A4
Cob Castle TA21 . . . . .180 D8
Cobhorn Dr BS13. . . . . .21 F4
Cobley Croft BS21. . . . . . . .16 C8
Cobthorn Way BS49 . . . . . . .34 E5
Coburg Cl TA21 . . . . .180 F7
Coburg Villas 11 BA1. . . . . .28 A1
Cock And Yew Tree Hill
BS40. . . . . .38 A2
Cock-Crowing Stone
TA20. . . . . .193 D4
Cockercombe Rd TA5 . . . . .151 F7
Cockers Hill BS39 . . . . .41 C5
Cockhill Elm La BA7. . . . . .214 B4
Cockhill La BA22 . . . . .175 D7
COCKLAKE 108 E7
Cocklake La BS28. . . . . . . .108 D8
Cockland Hill TA21. . . . . . .166 C1
Cockmill La BA4 . . . . .140 F1
Cockpit Hill DT6, DT8 . . . . .199 F4
Cockpit La BA4 . . . . .142 C2
Cock Rd
Buckland Dinham BA2,
BA11. . . . . .100 B5
Horningsham BA12 . . . . . . .144 C4
COCKWOOD 134 E5
Cockwood Rd TA5. . . . . . . .134 D5
Cod La BA22 . . . . .196 D7
Codrington Pl BS8 . . . . . . .226 A3
Codsend Rd TA24. . . . . . . .129 B2
Cogley Rd BA10 . . . . .215 F8
Cogsall Rd BS14 . . . . .23 F6
Coity Pl BS21 . . . . .6 C4
Coker Hill BA22 . . . . .196 F8
Coker Hill La BA22 . . . . . . .197 A7
Coker Ho BA22. . . . . .197 C8
Coker Marsh
East Coker BA22 . . . . .197 D7
East Coker BA22 . . . . .197 D7
Coker Rd BS22 . . . . .32 B2
Coker's La BA12. . . . . .161 F8
Coking La SP8. . . . . .190 E7
Colbourn Cl BA3. . . . . .114 E7
Colbourne Rd BA2 . . . . .44 D1
Colchester Cres BS4 . . . . . . .22 D7
COLD ASHTON 12 F6
Cold Harbour
Milborne Port DT9 . . . . . . .217 D2
Sherborne DT9. . . . . .225 E5
Coldharbour Bsns Pk
DT9. . . . . .225 E6
Coldharbour La BS23. . . . . .48 D3
Cold Harbour La BA22 . . . . .196 F6
Coldhills La BA8 . . . . .176 D2
Cold Nose BS28 . . . . .138 D8
Coldpark Gdns BS13. . . . . . .21 E5
Coldpark Rd BS13. . . . . . . .21 E5
Cold Rd TA3 . . . . .182 D6
Coldrick Cl BS14. . . . . .22 F3
Cole Cl
Cotford St Luke TA4 . . . . . .167 E6
Nether Stowey TA5. . . . . . .134 A3
Cole Cross BA22 . . . . .186 C6
COLEFORD 116 F7
Coleford La TA14. . . . . . . .185 E2
COLEFORD WATER 150 F4
Cole Hill BA11 . . . . .144 B7
Colehouse La BS21. . . . . . . .16 C8
Cole La 5 TA14 . . . . .185 F4
Colemead BS13 . . . . .22 B5
Cole Mead BA10 . . . . .215 D5
Cole Rd BA10 . . . . .215 D5
Coleridge Cottage★ TA5. . . .134 B2
Coleridge Cres TA1 . . . . . . .213 B3
Coleridge Gdns TA8. . . . . . .85 B2
Coleridge Gr TA6 . . . . .208 E5
Coleridge Rd
Bridgwater TA6 . . . . .208 E6
Clevedon BS21. . . . . .6 C3
Nether Stowey TA5. . . . . . .134 A2
Weston-super-Mare BS23 . . .49 A4
Coleridge Sq TA6 . . . . .208 E6
Coleridge Vale Rd E 1
BS21. . . . . .6 D2
Coleridge Vale Rd N BS21. . . .6 C2
Coleridge Vale Rd S BS21. . . .6 D2

Coleridge Vale Rd W 2
BS21 . . . . 6 C2
Coles Cotts TA5 . . . . .135 F2
COLE'S CROSS 199 D5
Coles Cross Cotts DT8 . . .199 D5
Coles Gdns BA3 . . . . .98 B5
Coleshill Dr BS13 . . . . .22 B5
Cole's La
   Chewton Mendip BA3 . . . . . .95 A6
   South Petherton TA13 . . . . .220 D3
Colesmore TA4 . . . . .167 A4
Coles Place TA20 . . . . .223 C3
Coles's La EX13 . . . . .198 B1
COLEY 75 C4
Coley Hill BS40 . . . . .75 D5
Coley La TA19 . . . . .194 F5
Coley Narrow BS40 . . . . . . .75 C3
Coley Rd BS40 . . . . .75 B4
Colham TA20 . . . . .194 E1
Colin Ave TA2 . . . . .212 F7
Colin Rd TA2 . . . . .213 A7
Collarway La BA22 . . . . . . .196 F8
College BA22 . . . . .196 E8
College Cl TA10 . . . . .172 E2
College Ct TA8 . . . . .104 A7
College Fields BS8 . . . . .11 F8
College Gn
   Bristol BS1 . . . . .226 C2
   Yeovil BA21 . . . . .219 B6
College Rd
   Bath BA1 . . . . .27 E1
   Bristol, Clifton BS8 . . . . .11 F8
   Taunton TA2 . . . . .212 D6
   Wells BA5 . . . . .203 E5
College Sq BS1 . . . . .226 C2
College St
   Bristol BS1 . . . . .226 C2
   Burnham-on-S TA8 . . . . . . .104 A7
College View
   18 Bath BA1 . . . . .28 A1
   Taunton TA1 . . . . .212 C2
College Way
   Bridgwater TA6 . . . . .209 C6
   Taunton TA1 . . . . .212 C1
Colles Cl BA5 . . . . .203 F5
Colles Rd BA5 . . . . .203 F5
Collett Ave BA4 . . . . .205 C5
Collett Cl BS22 . . . . .32 C4
Collett Rd TA2 . . . . .212 A7
Collett Way BA11 . . . . .120 C7
Colley Farm La TA20 . . . . .192 E8
Colley La TA6 . . . . .209 B4
Colleylake Cotts TA3 . . . . .181 C5
Colley Lane Ind Est TA6 . . .209 B3
Collickshire La TA3 . . . . . .170 E6
Collie La BA11 . . . . .118 A1
Collier Cl BA2 . . . . .78 D8
Colliers Gdns BS48 . . . . . . .18 F7
Colliers La BA1 . . . . .27 F4
Collier's La BA11 . . . . .99 D2
Colliers Rise BA3 . . . . .79 A3
Colliers Wlk 4 BS48 . . . . . . .8 E2
Colliery La BA2 . . . . .79 D5
Collingwood Cl
   Saltford BS31 . . . . .25 E2
   Weston-super-Mare BS22 . . .31 E4
Collingwood Ct TA6 . . . . . .208 F5
Collingwood Rd BA21 . . . .219 F8
Collin's Farm TA19 . . . . . . .183 E2
Collins' La TA11 . . . . .173 F7
Collinson Rd BS13 . . . . .22 B5
Collins St BS11 . . . . .4 B8
Colliters Way
   Bristol BS13 . . . . .21 D7
   Bristol BS13 . . . . .11 D1
Collum La BS22 . . . . .31 E6
Colman Rd TA1 . . . . .212 B1
Colmer Rd
   Bridgwater TA6 . . . . .208 F7
   Yeovil BA21 . . . . .219 B6
Colne Gn BS31 . . . . .25 A4
Colombo Cres BS23 . . . . . . .48 E3
Colston Ave BS1 . . . . .227 A2
Colston Cross EX13 . . . . . .198 B4
Colston Fort 2 BS2 . . . . . .227 B4
Colston Par BS1 . . . . .227 B1
Colston's Almshouses 1
   BS1 . . . . .227 A3
Colston St BS1 . . . . .227 A3
Colston Yd BS1 . . . . .227 A3
Colton La TA4 . . . . .149 F7
Columbus Cl 7 BA21 . . . . .219 F8
Columbus Ho BA2 . . . . .45 D8
Colyton 11 BS22 . . . . .32 A2
Combe Ave BS20 . . . . .2 C6
Combe Batch BS28 . . . . . . .108 D4
Combe Batch Rise BS28 . . .108 D4
Combe Beacon La TA20 . . .193 C7
Combe Cl
   Bicknoller TA4 . . . . .132 E2
   Yeovil BA21 . . . . .219 A8
Combe Cross
   Halse TA4 . . . . .167 B7
   Monksilver TA4 . . . . .150 C8
   Shillingford EX16 . . . . .164 D4
Combecross Hill TA4 . . . . .150 B8
Combecross La
   Monksilver TA4 . . . . .150 B8
   Stogumber TA4 . . . . .150 C8
COMBE DOWN 45 B1
Combe Down CE Prim Sch
   BA2 . . . . .45 B1
Combe Down CEVC Prim Sch
   Bathwick BA2 . . . . .45 B1
   Combe Down BA2 . . . . .45 B1

Combe Down La TA4 . . . . .151 C2
Combe Fields BS20 . . . . .2 C6
COMBE FLOREY 151 C2
Combe Gn BA5 . . . . .204 B7
Combe Gr BA1 . . . . .44 B8
COMBE HAY 62 D4
Combe Hay La BA2 . . . . .62 B6
COMBE HILL 217 A4
Combe Hill
   Barton St David TA11 . . . . .158 A2
   Combe St Nicholas TA20 . . .193 D5
   Hemyock EX15 . . . . .180 C2
   Milborne Port DT9 . . . . . . .217 B3
   Templecombe BA8 . . . . . . .176 E1
   Yenston BA8 . . . . .189 F8
Combe Hill Dro TA20 . . . . .193 C5
Combe Hill La TA7 . . . . . . .156 B7
Combe La
   Brompton Ralph TA4 . . . . .150 B3
   Charlton Adam TA11 . . . . .173 F8
   Chilton Polden TA7 . . . . . . .137 B3
   Churchstanton TA3 . . . . . .181 A2
   Combe St Nicholas TA20 . . .193 B5
   Dulverton TA22 . . . . .163 D6
   East Anstey TA22 . . . . . . .162 F6
   Exford TA24 . . . . .128 D1
   Hallatrow BS39 . . . . .77 B6
   Langport TA10 . . . . .171 F7
   North Curry TA3 . . . . .170 A4
   Parbrook BA4 . . . . .158 D8
   Rodhuish TA24 . . . . .131 B3
   Wedmore BS28 . . . . .108 D4
   Wiveliscombe TA4 . . . . . . .210 C8
   Woolavington TA7 . . . . . . .136 F4
Combeland La TA22 . . . . . .164 A5
Combeland Rd TA24 . . . . . .201 B4
Combe Pk
   Bath BA1 . . . . .44 C8
   Yeovil BA21 . . . . .218 F8
Combe Rd
   Bath BA2 . . . . .45 B1
   Portishead BS20 . . . . .2 D5
Combe Road BA2 . . . . .45 B1
COMBE ST NICHOLAS 193 D6
Combeshead Hill TA22 . . .148 A3
Combeshead La
   Brompton Regis TA22 . . . . .148 A4
   West Anstey EX36 . . . . . . .162 A7
Combeside BA2 . . . . .45 A3
Combe Side BS48 . . . . .19 A7
Combe St TA20 . . . . .223 C4
Combe Street La BA21 . . . .219 A8
Combe Street Lane Rdbt
   BA21 . . . . .218 F8
Combe Terr TA9 . . . . .136 E8
Combe The
   Burrington BS40 . . . . .53 F2
   Lydeard St Lawrence TA4 . . .151 B2
COMBE THROOP 176 F2
COMBWICH 135 B5
Combwich Rd TA5 . . . . . . .135 B4
Comer Rd BS27 . . . . .90 A7
Comer's Cross TA24 . . . . . .146 E6
Comer's Gate TA24 . . . . . .146 E6
COMEYTROWE 212 B1
Comeytrowe Ctr TA1 . . . . .212 C1
Comeytrowe La TA1, TA4 . .212 A2
Comeytrowe Orch TA1 . . . .212 A2
Comeytrowe Rd TA1 . . . . . .212 B1
Comeytrowe Rise TA1 . . . .212 B2
Comfortable BA1 . . . . .228 A3
Commerce Pk BA11 . . . . . .120 D8
Commerce Way TA9 . . . . . .104 F2
Commercial Rd
   Bristol BS1 . . . . .227 A1
   Shepton Mallet BA4 . . . . . .205 B6
Commercial Row TA20 . . . .223 C4
Commercial Way BS22 . . . .32 B2
Common La
   Charlton Adam TA11 . . . . . .174 A8
   Churchill Green BS25 . . . . . .52 B5
   Easton-in-G BS20 . . . . .4 B2
   Halstock BA22 . . . . .197 C2
   Hardington Mandeville
      BA22 . . . . .197 A5
   Holcombe BA3 . . . . .116 D7
   Huish Champflower TA4 . . .165 D7
   Kington Magna SP8 . . . . . .177 E1
   Marnhull DT10 . . . . .190 E4
   North Perrott TA18 . . . . . . .196 D4
   South Cheriton BA8 . . . . . .176 F4
   Templecombe BA8 . . . . . . .177 A1
   Wincanton BA9 . . . . .216 D3
   Yenston BA8 . . . . .189 F8
Common Moor Dro BA6 . . .206 E7
Common Rd
   Horningsham BA12 . . . . . . .144 C3
   Wincanton BA9 . . . . .216 D3
Como Ct BS20 . . . . .2 C6
Compass Ave TA6 . . . . .153 F5
Compass Hill TA1 . . . . .212 E3
Compass Rise TA1 . . . . . . .212 E3
Com Prim Sch
   Sydenham TA6 . . . . .209 B5
   Weston-super-Mare BS22 . . .32 A5
Compton Acres DT9 . . . . . .187 E4
COMPTON BISHOP 69 A3
Compton Cl
   Glastonbury BA6 . . . . .206 F1
   Shepton Mallet BA4 . . . . . .205 B5
   Taunton TA2 . . . . .213 A6
   Yeovil BA21 . . . . .219 A8
Compton Cnr BA4 . . . . .205 B5
Compton Ct Mews DT9 . . .187 F3
COMPTON DANDO 41 D6
Compton Dr
   Ansford BA7 . . . . .214 A6
   Bristol BS9 . . . . .5 C7

Compton Dr continued
   Weston-super-Mare BS24 . . .49 E7
COMPTON DUNDON 157 B4
COMPTON DURVILLE 184 F4
Compton Flats BA21 . . . . . .219 C6
Compton Gdns BA11 . . . . . .120 D7
Compton Gn BS31 . . . . .24 E4
Compton Hill TA13 . . . . . . .220 A5
Compton La
   Axbridge BS26 . . . . .70 D1
   Shepton Mallet BA4 . . . . . .205 B2
COMPTON MARTIN 74 A7
COMPTON
   PAUNCEFOOT 175 E5
Compton Rd
   Shepton Mallet BA4 . . . . . .205 B4
   South Cadbury BA22 . . . . . .175 D4
   South Petherton TA13 . . . . .220 B5
   Yeovil BA21 . . . . .187 E3
Compton St
   Butleigh BA6 . . . . .157 D4
   Compton Dundon TA11 . . . .157 B4
Comrade Ave BS25 . . . . . . .70 E8
Concorde Dr BS21 . . . . .6 B1
Condell Cl TA6 . . . . .208 F7
Condor Cl BS22 . . . . .49 D8
Conduit Hill BA11 . . . . .99 B1
Conduit La TA24 . . . . .201 D2
Conegore BA22 . . . . .174 D4
Conegore Cnr BA22 . . . . . .174 D4
Coneygree BS13 . . . . .21 F6
Conference Ave BS20 . . . . . .2 F5
Conference Cl BS20 . . . . .2 F4
CONGRESBURY 34 E4
Conies The TA2 . . . . .168 E8
Conifer Cl TA24 . . . . .128 D1
Conifer Way BS24 . . . . .49 E5
Coniston Ave BS9 . . . . .5 E6
Coniston Cres BS23 . . . . . . .48 F4
Coniston Gdns BA21 . . . . . .219 A7
CONKWELL 46 C1
Conkwell BA15 . . . . .46 C2
Connaught Ho TA4 . . . . . . .209 C5
Connaught Mans BA2 . . . . .228 C3
Connaught Pl BS23 . . . . . . .48 D8
Connaught Rd BS4 . . . . .22 E8
Connection Rd BA2 . . . . . . .44 A6
Connelly Dr BS28 . . . . .108 C4
Connock Sq BA4 . . . . .205 C4
Conquest Bsns Pk TA19 . . .184 A4
Constable Cl
   Keynsham BS31 . . . . .24 F6
   Yeovil BA21 . . . . .219 E8
Constable Dr BS22 . . . . .31 F3
Constantine Ct BA4 . . . . . . .205 E4
Constitution Hill BS8 . . . . .226 B2
Convocation Ave BA2 . . . . . .45 E5
Conway Cres TA8 . . . . .85 C1
Conway Gn BS31 . . . . .25 A3
Conway Rd TA5 . . . . .135 B2
Conygar Cl BS21 . . . . .6 F5
Conygar View TA24 . . . . . .201 E3
Conygre Gn BA2 . . . . .60 B2
Conygre Rise BA2 . . . . .59 F6
Cook Ave TA20 . . . . .223 D3
Cooke's La TA10 . . . . .156 B2
Cookley La TA4 . . . . .150 F8
Cook Rd BA21 . . . . .219 F8
Cooks Bridle Path BS48 . . . .36 D8
Cooks Cl TA3 . . . . .169 D5
Cook's Folly Rd BS9 . . . . . . .5 D3
Cooks Gdns BS48 . . . . .9 A2
Cooks Hill BS39 . . . . .58 E3
Cooks La DT9 . . . . .225 D3
Cook's La
   Banwell BS29 . . . . .51 A4
   Clevedon BS21 . . . . .7 B2
   Cranmore BA4 . . . . .142 A6
   Milverton TA4 . . . . .167 B5
   Stalbridge DT10 . . . . .190 B2
Cooksley La TA4 . . . . .149 A2
Cookson Cl TA8 . . . . .104 D5
Cook St BS11 . . . . .4 C8
Cook Way TA2 . . . . .212 C6
COOMBE
   Crewkerne 195 B4
   Sampford Peverell 178 A4
   Taunton 169 C8
Coombe DT9 . . . . .225 C5
Coombe Bridge Ave BS9 . . . .5 D6
Coombe Brook BA5 . . . . . . .203 A7
Coombe Cl BA7 . . . . .214 C6
Coombe Cotts BA5 . . . . . . .204 C7
Coombe Dale
   Backwell BS48 . . . . .37 A8
   Bristol BS9 . . . . .5 C6
Coombe Dell BA4 . . . . .205 A6
COOMBE DINGLE 5 C8
Coombe Gdns BS9 . . . . .5 E6
Coombe Hill
   Blagdon Hill TA21 . . . . .181 A5
   Bruton BA10 . . . . .215 E7
Coombe Hill La TA11 . . . . .158 A2
Coombe La
   Bristol BS9 . . . . .5 E6
   Compton Bishop BS26 . . . . .69 B4
   East Harptree BS40 . . . . . . .74 E4
   Easton-in-G BS8 . . . . .4 A2
   Kingsbury Episcopi TA12 . . .185 B8
   Shepton Mallet BA4 . . . . . .205 A6
Coomb End BA3 . . . . .78 A3
Coombend Ho BA3 . . . . .78 F3
Coombe Rd
   Dinnington TA17 . . . . .195 B7
   Nailsea BS48 . . . . .8 E1
   Weston-super-Mare BS23 . . .30 E1

Coombe Side TA9 . . . . .86 B2
Coombe St
   Bruton BA10 . . . . .215 E7
   Penselwood BA9 . . . . .161 E2
Coombe's Way BS26 . . . . . . .87 E8
Coombe Terr
   Glastonbury BA6 . . . . .206 E5
   Sherborne DT9 . . . . .225 C5
Coombe The
   Blagdon BA40 . . . . .54 C3
   Compton Martin BS40 . . . . .74 A6
Coombe View BA4 . . . . . . .205 A6
Coombe Water La DT8 . . . .199 E5
Coomb Rocke BS9 . . . . .5 D6
Cooperage La BS3 . . . . .226 B1
Cooperage The BA11 . . . . .119 F3
Cooper Rd BS9 . . . . .5 F7
Cooper's Ash La BA7,
   BA22 . . . . .214 A2
Coopers Barns BA22 . . . . . .174 F1
Coopers Hts TA4 . . . . .210 C4
Cooper's La BA11 . . . . .101 E2
Coopers Mead BA4 . . . . . . .205 D4
Coopers Mill TA2 . . . . .168 B4
Coot Hide EX16 . . . . .178 D1
Coots The BS14 . . . . .23 E6
Copeland Dr BS14 . . . . .23 B5
Copford La BS41 . . . . .11 B1
Copis La TA11 . . . . .158 B3
Coplestons TA3 . . . . .168 D1
Copley Gdns BS22 . . . . .31 F2
Coppack Ho 6 BS21 . . . . . . .6 C2
Copper Beeches TA1 . . . . . .212 A2
Copper Beech Rd TA11 . . . .173 D5
Copper Cl BS27 . . . . .90 A8
Copperfield Dr BS22 . . . . . .31 F4
Coppern Way DT10 . . . . . . .190 B4
Coppice Cl BA20 . . . . .218 D2
Coppice End Cnr BS24 . . . . .67 C2
Coppice Mews BS21 . . . . . . .6 C4
Coppice The BS13 . . . . .21 E4
Coppin Cl BA6 . . . . .206 F3
Coppin Rd TA2 . . . . .168 B4
Coppits Hill La
   Yeovil BA21 . . . . .218 D8
   Yeovil Marsh BA21 . . . . . . .187 A5
COPPLEHAM 147 D5
Copplesbury La BA4, BA10 160 D8
Copse Cl
   Watchet TA23 . . . . .202 C5
   Weston-super-Mare BS24 . . .49 A1
Copse Cnr BS24 . . . . .67 C2
Copse Dro
   Baltonsborough BA6 . . . . . .158 C5
   Barrington TA19 . . . . .184 B5
Copse End BS25 . . . . .51 F2
Copse La
   Ashill TA19 . . . . .183 D4
   Barrington TA19 . . . . .184 D4
   Hambridge TA3 . . . . .184 B7
   Ilton TA19 . . . . .183 F4
   Pilton BA4 . . . . .140 F3
Copseland BA2 . . . . .45 D5
Copse Rd
   Clevedon BS21 . . . . .6 C4
   Keynsham BS31 . . . . .25 C4
   Yeovil BA22 . . . . .218 B7
Copse Shoot La TA19 . . . . .184 C5
Copse Stile TA20 . . . . .193 F1
Copse The
   Bridgwater TA6 . . . . .209 D5
   Cossington TA7 . . . . .136 F3
   Frome BA11 . . . . .120 B6
   Weston-super-Mare BS22 . . .32 D2
Copsewood La BS28 . . . . . . .88 B2
Copthorne Cl BS14 . . . . .23 B5
Copthorn La BS40 . . . . .53 F6
Coral Ave TA6 . . . . .209 C8
Coralberry Dr BS22 . . . . . . .31 F1
Corams La TA21 . . . . .222 B6
Cording's Ball TA4 . . . . . . .150 A1
Corewell La TA5 . . . . .133 E3
CORFE 181 F6
Corfe Cl BS48 . . . . .8 D1
Corfe Cres BS31 . . . . .24 E4
Corfe Rd BS4 . . . . .22 D7
Corinthian Ct 9 BS1 . . . . . .227 B1
Cork Pl BA1 . . . . .44 D7
Corkscrew La
   North Cadbury BA22 . . . . . .175 D7
   Staplegrove TA2 . . . . .212 D8
Cork St
   Bath BA1 . . . . .44 D7
   Frome BA11 . . . . .119 F5
Cork Terr BA1 . . . . .44 D7
Cormorant Cl
   Bridgwater TA6 . . . . .209 C3
   Weston-super-Mare BS22 . . .31 F1
Cornborough Pl TA6 . . . . . .209 B5
Cornbrash BA11 . . . . .120 D7
Corner Cl TA21 . . . . .222 D4
Corner Croft BS21 . . . . .6 D1
Cornfields The BS25 . . . . . .31 F5
Cornflower Cl TA6 . . . . .208 D1
Cornhill
   Bridgwater TA6 . . . . .208 F5
   Shepton Mallet BA4 . . . . . .205 C6
   Sherborne DT9 . . . . .225 C4
   5 Wellington TA21 . . . . . .222 D6
Cornhill Dr BS14 . . . . .23 A7
Cornish Gr BS14 . . . . .23 E6
Cornishmen's Rd BA1 . . . . . .27 E4
Cornish Rd BS14 . . . . .23 E6
Cornishway E TA1 . . . . .212 B3
Cornishway N TA1 . . . . .212 B3
Cornishway S TA1 . . . . .212 B2
Cornishway W TA1 . . . . . . .212 B3
Cornish Wlk BS14 . . . . .23 E6

Cornlands EX16 . . . . .178 D1
Cornleaze BS13 . . . . .22 A5
Cornmoor Cres TA9 . . . . . . .136 E7
Cornmoor La TA9 . . . . .136 E7
Corn St
   Bath BA1 . . . . .228 B2
   Bristol BS1 . . . . .227 A3
Cornwallis Ave
   Bristol BS8 . . . . .226 A2
   Weston-super-Mare BS22 . . .31 F4
Cornwallis Cres BS8 . . . . . . .11 F6
Cornwallis Gr BS8 . . . . .226 A2
Cornwall Rd BA4 . . . . .205 A6
Cromandel Hts BA1 . . . . . . .228 B4
Coronation Ave
   Bath BA2 . . . . .44 C4
   Keynsham BS31 . . . . .24 D4
   Yeovil BA21 . . . . .218 F7
Coronation Cl
   Ruishton TA3 . . . . .169 C3
   Wanstrow BA4 . . . . .142 F4
Coronation Ct BA3 . . . . .115 A3
Coronation Est BS23 . . . . . .48 F3
Coronation Ho TA6 . . . . . . .209 C6
Coronation Pl BS1 . . . . .227 A2
Coronation Rd
   Banwell BS29 . . . . .51 A3
   Bath BA1 . . . . .44 D7
   Bleadon BS24 . . . . .67 C6
   Bridgwater TA6 . . . . .208 E5
   Bristol BS3 . . . . .226 B1
   Frome BA11 . . . . .120 B5
   Highbridge TA9 . . . . .104 D4
   Wells BA5 . . . . .203 B4
   Weston-super-Mare BS22 . . .31 A8
Coronation St TA20 . . . . . . .223 C2
Coronation Terr
   Chilcompton BA3 . . . . .96 D5
   Oakhill BA3 . . . . .115 A3
Coronation Villas BA8 . . . . .176 E1
Corondale Rd BS22 . . . . . . .49 D8
Corporate Rd BA22 . . . . . . .174 A2
Corporation St TA1 . . . . . . .212 F3
Corpus Christi RC Prim Sch
   BS23 . . . . .48 D6
Corrick Cl BS27 . . . . .90 F2
Corridor The 2 BA1 . . . . . .228 C2
Corscombe Rd BA22 . . . . . .197 C2
Corsham Dr TA8 . . . . .104 C8
CORSLEY 121 D2
Corsley Heath BA11 . . . . . .144 D8
Corsley Wlk BS4 . . . . .22 F8
CORSTON 43 B7
Corston BS24 . . . . .49 A2
Corston Dr BA2 . . . . .43 B6
Corston La BA2 . . . . .43 A8
Corston View BA2 . . . . .44 C2
Corston Wlk BS11 . . . . .4 D7
Corton Cl BA21 . . . . .219 E8
CORTON DENHAM 175 D1
Corton Denham Rd DT9 . . .175 D2
Coryate Cl BA22 . . . . .186 C2
Cory Rd TA2 . . . . .213 A4
Cosgates Feet or County Gate
   EX35 . . . . .122 C5
Cosmos Dr TA6 . . . . .208 D1
COSSINGTON 136 F3
Cossington La TA7 . . . . .136 E3
Cossington Rd BS4 . . . . .22 F8
Cossins La TA18 . . . . .224 C6
Costello Hill BA22 . . . . .173 F2
Costiland Dr BS13 . . . . .21 F6
Cote Cnr TA9 . . . . .136 F7
Cote House La BS9 . . . . .5 F5
Cote La BA12 . . . . .161 F6
Cote Paddock BS9 . . . . .5 F4
Cote Pk BS9 . . . . .5 E5
COTFORD ST LUKE 167 E6
Cotford St Luke Prim Sch
   TA4 . . . . .167 E6
Cotham Hill BS6 . . . . .226 C4
Cotham Lawn Ho BS6 . . . . .226 C4
Cotham Lawn Rd BS6 . . . . .226 C4
Cotham Pl BS6 . . . . .226 C4
Cotham Rd BS6 . . . . .226 C4
Cotham Rd S BS6 . . . . .227 A4
Cotham Sch BS6 . . . . .226 C4
Cothay Manor Gardens★
   TA21 . . . . .179 C8
COTHELSTONE 152 A2
Cothelstone Cl TA6 . . . . . . .208 B4
Cothelstone Rd TA4 . . . . . . .151 F1
Cotlake Cl TA1 . . . . .212 F1
Cotlake Rise TA1 . . . . .168 E1
Cotleigh Crossing EX14 . . .191 F1
Cotley La TA20 . . . . .193 D2
Cotman Wlk 1 BS22 . . . . . .31 F2
Cotswold Cl BS20 . . . . .2 E4
Cotswold Gdns BA3 . . . . . . .97 A6
Cotswold Rd BA2 . . . . .44 E4
Cotswold View BA2 . . . . . . .44 B5
Cotswold Way SN14 . . . . . . .13 A6
Cottage Cnr TA19 . . . . .183 F4
Cottage La TA22 . . . . .163 D4
Cottage Pl
   3 Bath BA1 . . . . .28 C3
   Bristol BS2 . . . . .227 A4
Cottage Row TA8 . . . . .104 A6
Cottages The BS40 . . . . .35 D2
Cotterell Ct BA1 . . . . .228 B2
Cottiford La TA4 . . . . .132 D2
Cottiford Rd TA4 . . . . .132 D2
Cottle Gdns BS14 . . . . .23 F6
Cottle Rd BS14 . . . . .23 F6
Cottles La
   West Pennard BA6 . . . . . . .140 B1
   Winsley BA15 . . . . .64 F6

COTTLE'S OAK 119 C5
Cotton Cnr 13 BA8. . . . . .190 A6
Cotton Mead BA2. . . . . .43 B7
Cotton Patch Wlk 6 TA6 .209 A1
Cotton's La TA11 . . . . .158 B2
Cottonwick Cl BS11 . . . . .4 D5
Cotty La BA5. . . . . .139 B8
Coulson Dr BS22 . . . . .32 B3
Coulson's Cl BS14 . . . . .23 A3
Coulson's Rd BS14 . . . . .23 A3
COULTINGS. 134 F4
Council Hos
  Babcary TA11 . . . . .174 D7
  Bleadon BS24. . . . . .67 B5
  Clapton TA18 . . . . .195 C1
  Hewish TA18. . . . . .195 D3
  Kingston Seymour BS21. . . .16 C3
  Podimore BA22 . . . . .174 A4
  Wick St Lawrence BS22 . . . .32 B8
Council Houses BA24. . . . . . .33 C3
Council Houses The
  Butcombe BS40 . . . . .55 B8
  Hinton Blewett BS39 . . . . . .75 E6
Counterslip BS1 . . . . .227 B2
Counterslip Gdns BS14 . . . .23 C6
Countess Ave TA6. . . . . .208 E7
Countess Gytha Prim Sch
  BA22. . . . . .174 F3
County Wlk TA1. . . . . .213 A3
Couple Cross TA24. . . . . . . .130 B1
COURSHAY. 198 E3
Coursing Batch BA6. . . . . . .206 F3
COURSLEY. 151 B4
Court Acres 6 BA22. . . . . . .197 F8
Court Ash BA20 . . . . .219 B5
Court Ave BS49 . . . . .34 C7
Court Barn La BA6 . . . . .158 A8
Court Barton
  Crewkerne TA18. . . . . . . .224 B6
  Ilminster TA19 . . . . .221 C4
Court Cl
  Portishead BS20 . . . . .2 D4
  Weston-super-Mare BS22 . . .32 C2
Court Cl The BS48. . . . . .19 C5
Court Cotts SP8. . . . . .177 D3
Court-de-Wyck Prim Sch
  BS49 . . . . .17 F1
Court Dr
  Sandford BS25 . . . . .52 B4
  Wellington TA21. . . . . . . .222 D5
Courtenay Cres BS4 . . . . .22 D7
Courtenay Rd BS31 . . . . .25 B2
Courtenay Wlk BS22. . . . . . . .32 A3
Court Farm BA11. . . . . .100 A3
Court Farm Cl TA6 . . . . .194 E1
Court Farm Country Park★
  Banwell BS29 . . . . .50 F5
  Weston-super-Mare BS24 . . .50 F5
Court Farm Rd BS14 . . . . .22 F3
Courtfield
  Langport TA10 . . . . .172 A5
  Milverton TA4 . . . . .166 F4
Court Field La TA20 . . . . . . .193 B6
Court Fields Com Sch
  TA21 . . . . .222 C5
Court Gdns
  Batheaston BA1. . . . . .29 A4
  Marston Magna BA22. . . . .174 F1
  Yeovil BA21 . . . . .218 E8
Court Gr TA7. . . . . .136 C4
Court Hay BS20 . . . . .4 A4
Court Hill
  Compton Dando BS39. . . . .41 D5
  Taunton TA1 . . . . .212 D2
Court Ho BS26 . . . . .70 B2
Court La
  7 Barwick BA22 . . . . .197 F8
  Bathford BA1 . . . . .29 B2
  Clevedon BS21. . . . . .7 A3
  Lye's Green BA12. . . . . . . .121 B1
  Milborne Port DT9 . . . . . .217 C3
  Morebath EX16. . . . . .164 D4
  Shipham BS25 . . . . .70 F8
Courtland Rd TA21 . . . . .222 D6
Courtlands BS31 . . . . .24 E5
Courtlands Cl TA23. . . . . . . .202 C6
Courtlands Farm Ind Est
  TA2. . . . . .168 B5
Courtlands La BS3 . . . . .11 E4
Courtlands Unit BS4. . . . . . . .22 D8
Courtmead BA2. . . . . .62 F7
Courtmead La TA24 . . . . . . .123 F4
Court Mill TA20 . . . . .223 A8
Court Mill La TA20 . . . . .223 A8
Court Moors La TA21 . . . . . .179 E5
Court Orch TA5 . . . . .135 B2
Court Pl BS22 . . . . .31 F2
Court Place La TA24. . . . . . .131 B4
Court Rd
  Norton Fitzwarren TA2. . . .168 B4
  Weston-super-Mare BS22 . . .31 A5
Court's Barton BA11. . . . . . .119 D2
Court St
  5 Bridgwater TA6. . . . . . .208 F5
  Winsham TA20 . . . . .194 E1
Court Terr TA21. . . . . .222 C5
Court The TA24 . . . . .131 A4
COURTWAY. 152 C4
Court Way EX16 . . . . .178 D1
Courtyard The
  Dunster TA24. . . . . .201 E2
  Evercreech BA4 . . . . .141 F2
  Minehead TA24. . . . . .200 F7
  Shapwick TA7 . . . . .137 F1
  3 Taunton TA1. . . . . .212 F4
  West Harptree BS40. . . . . . .74 E6
Couture Gr BA16 . . . . .207 B6

Coverdale Ct BA21 . . . . .218 F6
Cowan Cl TA8. . . . . .104 C7
COWBRIDGE. 200 D1
Cowbridge Cross TA24 . . . . .200 D1
Cow Bridge Rd BA6 . . . . . . .157 C7
Cow Down Rd TA20. . . . . . . .194 C1
Cowdray Cl TA24. . . . . .200 E6
Cowdray Rd
  Bristol BS4. . . . . .22 D7
  Minehead TA24. . . . . .200 E6
Cowen Cl TA18. . . . . .224 C4
Cowleaze La BS40. . . . . .74 C6
Cowler Wlk BS13. . . . . .21 F4
Cowling Dr BS14 . . . . .23 C5
Cowling Rd BS14. . . . . .23 D5
Cowl St BA4 . . . . .205 B7
Cowpath La DT9 . . . . .176 A1
COWSLIP GREEN 54 B8
Cowslip Green La BS40 . . . . .54 B8
Cowslip La
  East Rolstone BS22 . . . . . . .33 A2
  Loxton BS26. . . . . .68 D3
Cowslip Wlk TA6. . . . . .208 E1
Coxbridge Dro BA6. . . . . . . .158 A6
Cox Hill DT10 . . . . .190 E4
Coxland's Rock TA4 . . . . . . .167 B7
COXLEY. 139 F6
Coxley Cl BA6. . . . . .206 F7
Coxley Dr BA1 . . . . .28 B2
Coxley Prim Sch
  Coxley BA5. . . . . .139 E6
  Coxley BA5. . . . . .139 E6
COXLEY WICK. 139 E7
Cox Rd TA21. . . . . .222 C4
Coxs Cl BA22. . . . . .175 D6
Cox's Cl
  Bruton BA10. . . . . .215 E5
  Glastonbury BA6. . . . . . . .206 E6
Cox's Dr BA6. . . . . .158 A5
Cox's Gn BS40 . . . . .35 E1
COX'S GREEN. 35 E1
Cox's La TA4 . . . . .167 C5
Coxton End La BA5. . . . . .92 B3
Coxway BS21 . . . . .6 F2
Coxwithy La BA6 . . . . .139 C1
Coxwynne Cl BA3 . . . . .97 C8
Crabtree Cl BA5. . . . . .21 D1
Crab Tree Dro BA6. . . . . . . .206 F8
Crabtree La
  Curry Rivel TA10. . . . . . . .171 C1
  Dundry BS41 . . . . .21 D2
  Wyke Champflower BA10. . .215 B7
Crab Tree La BA11 . . . . .117 D2
Crackmore DT9 . . . . .217 C1
Craig Lea TA2. . . . . .212 E7
Cranberry Wlk BS9. . . . . .5 C8
Cranbourne Chase BS23. . .31 A1
Cranbourne Cl TA6. . . . . . . .208 F6
Crancombe La TA7. . . . . . . .136 D3
Crandale Rd 3 BA2. . . . . . . .44 D5
Crane Cotts BA4 . . . . .142 B6
Crane Hill TA10, TA11. . . . . .173 C4
Crane Rd BA22. . . . . .218 A6
Cranes Cl TA2. . . . . .213 D7
Cranfield Ct BS22. . . . . .31 D1
Crangs La BA22. . . . . .175 D4
Cranhill Rd
  Bath BA1. . . . . .44 D8
  Street BA16. . . . . .207 B6
Cranleigh BA2 . . . . .62 F8
Cranleigh Ct BA13 . . . . .220 B4
Cranleigh Gdns
  Bridgwater TA6. . . . . .209 A4
  Bristol BS9. . . . . .5 E4
Cranleigh Rd BS14 . . . . .23 B5
Cranmer Rd TA1 . . . . .213 A4
Cranmoor La BS49 . . . . .16 D2
CRANMORE. 142 B6
Cranmore BS24 . . . . .49 A2
Cranmore Ave BS31. . . . . . . .24 E6
Cranmore Ct 3 BA11 . . . . . .119 E3
Cranmore Pl BA2 . . . . .62 E8
Cranmore Sta★ BA4. . . . . . .142 A5
Cranmore View BA11 . . . . . .119 D2
Cranmore West Sta★
  BA4. . . . . .142 A5
Cransey La
  Washford TA4, TA23 . . . . . .131 F2
  Williton TA4 . . . . .132 A2
Crantock Ave BS13. . . . . .22 B8
Cranway La TA20. . . . . .223 F2
Cranwell Cl TA7. . . . . .154 F5
Cranwell Gr BS14 . . . . .23 A5
Cranwell Rd
  Locking BS24. . . . . .50 C5
  Locking BS24. . . . . .50 C5
Cranwells Pk BA1. . . . . .44 D8
Crapnell La BA5 . . . . .140 F8
Crawford Cl 1 BS21. . . . . . . .6 B1
Crawford La BA22 . . . . .175 D7
CRAWLEY 192 F2
Crawlic La TA4. . . . . .151 E1
Crawl La BA3 . . . . .78 C4
Crawter Dr TA24 . . . . .124 A3
Craydon Gr BS14. . . . . .23 D4
Craydon Rd BS14. . . . . .23 D5
Craydon Wlk BS14 . . . . .23 D5
Crease Cl BA5. . . . . .203 B4
Create Ctr★ BS1. . . . . .11 F5
Crediton 5 BS22. . . . . .32 A2
Creechbarrow Rd TA1. . . . . .213 C6
Creechberry Orch TA1. . . . . .213 D5
Creeches La BA16. . . . . .156 D7
CREECH HEATHFIELD. 169 E5
Creech Hill La BA10 . . . . . . .215 B7
Creech Hill Rd BA10. . . . . . .160 B7
Creech Mill Est TA3. . . . . . . .169 C4

Creech Paper Mill TA3. . . . . .169 C4
CREECH ST MICHAEL. 169 D4
Creech St Michael CE Prim
  Sch TA3. . . . . .169 D4
Creechwood Terr TA3. . . . . . .169 D5
Creedwell Cl TA4. . . . . .167 A4
Creedwell Orch TA4. . . . . . . .167 A4
Creedy Bridge Rd TA13 . . . . .185 D2
Creighton Cl BA5. . . . . .140 C8
Crescent Gdns BA1. . . . . . . .228 A3
Crescent La BA1. . . . . .228 B4
Crescent The
  Backwell BS48 . . . . .19 A6
  Bristol, Sea Mills BS9 . . . . . .5 C6
  4 Carhampton TA24 . . . . .131 A5
  Coleford BA3 . . . . .117 A7
  Farrington Gurney BS39. . . .77 B3
  Golsoncott TA23 . . . . .131 D1
  Ilminster TA19 . . . . .221 B2
  Lympsham BS24. . . . . .67 C5
  South Cadbury BA22 . . . . .175 E4
  Stanton Drew BS39 . . . . . . .39 F1
  Taunton TA1 . . . . .212 F3
  Weston-super-Mare BS22 . . .31 B1
  Yeovil BA22 . . . . .219 A4
Crescent View BA2. . . . . . . .228 B1
Crescent View Ct BS22 . . . . .31 B1
Crescent Way TA1. . . . . .212 F3
Creslands Ind Units BS24 . . .49 A3
Cressey The TA19 . . . . .184 E4
Cresswell Ave TA2 . . . . .212 D7
Cresswell Cl BS22. . . . . .32 A1
Crestfield Ave TA6 . . . . .208 F7
Crest Heights BS20. . . . . .1 E4
Creswicke Rd BS4. . . . . .22 F7
Creswick Way TA8 . . . . .104 C8
CREWKERNE. 224 D6
Crewkerne Bsns Pk TA18. . .224 D6
Crewkerne Cl BS48. . . . . .9 B1
Crewkerne Com Hospl
  TA18. . . . . .224 B5
Crewkerne & District Mus★
Crewkerne Rd TA20 . . . . . . .223 E4
Crewkerne Sta TA18 . . . . . . .224 E4
Crewkerne Turning EX13 .198 C6
Cribb's La BS40 . . . . .36 D1
Crib Cl TA20 . . . . .223 D6
Crib House La TA28 . . . . .89 C1
Crickback La
  Chew Magna BS40. . . . . . . .39 A2
  Chew Magna BS40. . . . . . . .39 A3
Cricket Cotts TA3. . . . . .170 B3
Cricket Cross
  Cricket Malherbie TA19 . . . .194 D6
  Ilminster TA19 . . . . .194 C6
Cricket Field Gn BS48 . . . . . .8 D2
Cricket La TA19, TA20 . . . . . .194 C6
CRICKET MALHERBIE 194 D6
CRICKET ST THOMAS 194 E3
Cricket St Thomas Miniature
  Rly★ TA20 . . . . .194 E3
Cricket View DT9 . . . . .225 D3
CRICKHAM. 108 D8
Crickham La BS28. . . . . .108 D8
Cricklade Ct BS48. . . . . .9 A1
Cridlake 7 EX13 . . . . .198 A1
Cridlands Mdw TA6 . . . . . . .208 E6
CRIMCHARD 223 B5
Crimchard TA20 . . . . .223 B5
Crimthorne Cotts TA3 . . . . .183 A7
Cripple St TA12. . . . . .185 D7
Crispin Ctr BA16 . . . . .207 C6
Crispin Sch BA16. . . . . .207 D7
Cristata Wy TA6. . . . . .208 D1
Critch Hill BA11 . . . . .119 C3
CRITCHILL. 119 C3
Critchill Cl BA11 . . . . .119 D3
Critchill Gr BA11 . . . . .119 D3
Critchill Rd BA11 . . . . .119 D3
Critchill Sch BA11. . . . . .119 C4
Crockerne CE Prim Sch
  BS20. . . . . .4 C4
Crockerne Dr BS20. . . . . .4 C3
Crockerne Ho BS20 . . . . .4 D4
Crockers Hill TA7 . . . . .136 E4
Crocker's Hill BA9 . . . . .175 F8
Crocker Wy BA9. . . . . .216 A3
CROCOMBE. 60 C3
Crocombe BA2. . . . . .60 C3
Crocombe La BA2. . . . . .60 C3
Croford Hill TA4 . . . . .166 C6
Croft Cl BS30 . . . . .25 D8
Croft Cotts
  Moorlinch TA7 . . . . .155 E7
  Wrantage TA3 . . . . .170 B1
Croft La
  Brushford TA22 . . . . .163 C4
  Skilgate TA4. . . . . .164 E6
  Westbury-sub-Mendip BA5 .110 C6
Croftland La TA10. . . . . .171 E2
Croft Mdw TA4. . . . . .202 C4
Crofton Ave BA21 . . . . .219 B6
Crofton Cl BA21. . . . . .219 B5
CROFTON PARK 219 B6
Crofton Pk BA21 . . . . .219 B5
Crofton Rd BA21 . . . . .219 B6
Croft Rd
  Bath BA1. . . . . .28 B1
  Holcombe BA3 . . . . .116 C8
Crofts Mead BA9. . . . . .216 C2
Croft The
  Backwell BS48. . . . . .19 A7
  Cheddar BS27. . . . . .90 C8
  Clevedon BS21. . . . . .6 F4
  Hutton BS24. . . . . .49 E3
  Mark TA9. . . . . .106 A4
  Monkton Combe BA2 . . . . . .45 D1

Croft The continued
  Watchet TA23. . . . . .202 C2
  Westwood BA15. . . . . .64 F3
  Williton TA4 . . . . .202 D3
  Wookey Hole BA5. . . . . . . .203 A8
  Yeovil BA22 . . . . .218 C2
Croft Way TA4. . . . . .210 C4
Croftways TA4. . . . . .202 D4
Cromer Ct BS21 . . . . .6 D5
Cromer Rd BS23 . . . . .48 E5
Cromwell Dr BS22. . . . . .32 A4
Cromwell Rd
  Bridgwater TA6 . . . . .209 A2
  Taunton TA1. . . . . .213 B5
  Yeovil BA21 . . . . .219 D6
Crooked Dro TA3 . . . . .170 E7
Crooked La
  Brent Knoll TA9. . . . . .85 E3
  Burnham-on-S TA8 . . . . . . .85 D1
  Cucklington SP8 . . . . .177 E6
  Rode BA11. . . . . .101 E7
Crooked Lane TA8 . . . . .85 D2
Crookes La BS22 . . . . .31 A4
Cropmead TA18. . . . . .224 D6
Cropmead Trad Est TA18 . . .224 D6
Cropways Ct BA21 . . . . .218 C5
Crosby Row BS8. . . . . .226 A2
CROSCOMBE. 204 B8
Croscombe CE Prim Sch
  BA5. . . . . .204 C7
Croscombe Gdns BA11 . . . .120 D6
CROSS. 69 E2
Crossacre TA6. . . . . .208 D6
Crosscombe Dr BS13 . . . . . .22 C3
Crosscroft Cotts TA4 . . . . . .151 A3
Cross Dro TA7 . . . . .154 C1
Crosselm Rd BA4. . . . . .143 A2
Cross La
  Axbridge BS26 . . . . .70 C4
  Brendon EX35. . . . . .122 A4
  Long Sutton TA10 . . . . . . .172 F4
Crossland La EX14 . . . . .191 F2
CROSSLANDS. 222 C8
Crosslands TA21 . . . . .222 B8
Cross Lanes BS20 . . . . .4 C4
Crossman Wlk BS21 . . . . .6 F2
Crossmead TA7. . . . . .136 E4
Cross Moor Dr BS26 . . . . . . .70 B1
Cross Moor Dro BS26. . . . . . .69 E1
Cross Moor Rd BS26. . . . . . . .70 B1
Crosspost La BA2 . . . . .42 B4
Cross Rd DT9 . . . . .187 E1
Crossroads The BA9. . . . . . .216 C3
Cross St
  Burnham-on-S TA8 . . . . . .104 A7
  Keynsham BS31. . . . . .24 F7
  3 Weston-super-Mare
  BS23. . . . . .48 E7
Cross View Rise TA6. . . . . . .208 D6
Crossway TA1. . . . . .213 C5
Cross Way DT9. . . . . .187 E1
Crossway La BA3. . . . . .96 B7
Crossways
  Coleford BA3 . . . . .116 F7
  Tatworth TA20 . . . . .198 D8
Crossways Cvn Pk BA2 . . . . .61 F5
Crossways La
  Barrow BA4 . . . . .140 C4
  Combe Hay BA2 . . . . .62 A5
Crossways Rd TA6. . . . . .209 B1
Crosswell Cl 7 TA6 . . . . . . .153 E3
Cross Wlk BS14. . . . . .23 A6
Crouds La TA10 . . . . .172 E4
Crow Castle La TA18. . . . . . .224 B7
CROWCOMBE. 151 C7
Crowcombe CE VA Prim Sch
  TA4. . . . . .151 C7
Crowcombe Combe TA4. . . .151 D7
Crowcombe Heathfield Sta★
  TA4. . . . . .151 B5
Crowcombe Rd TA2 . . . . . . .212 F8
Crowcombe Wlk TA6 . . . . . .208 C4
Crowe Hill BA3. . . . . .64 B5
Crowe La BA3. . . . . .64 B5
Crow La
  Ashill TA19 . . . . .183 D1
  Bridgwater TA7 . . . . .209 E7
  Bristol BS1. . . . . .227 A2
  Broadway TA19 . . . . .194 A4
  Slape Cross TA7 . . . . .209 E6
  Westbury-sub-Mendip BA5 .110 D6
Crown Cl TA2 . . . . .213 C6
Crowne Trad Est BA4 . . . . . .205 D5
Crown Gdns BA11 . . . . .119 F3
Crown Glass Pl 5 BS48. . . . .8 E2

Cot–Cur 241

Crown Hill
  Bath BA1 . . . . .27 C1
  West Buckland TA21. . . . . .180 F7
  Winford BS40. . . . . .38 A5
Crown Ho BS48 . . . . .8 C1
Crown Ind Est TA2 . . . . .213 C6
Crown La
  Creech St Michael TA3 . . . .169 D6
  South Petherton TA13. . . . .220 C4
Crown Mews TA21 . . . . .180 F7
Crown Rd BA1 . . . . .27 B1
Crown Wlk TA1 . . . . .212 F3
Crowpill Cotts TA6 . . . . .208 F6
Crowpill La TA6. . . . . .208 F6
Crow's Hill BA4 . . . . .142 C1
Crowshute Flats TA20 . . . . .223 C3
Crowshute Link TA20. . . . . .223 C3
Crufts Mdw TA20 . . . . .169 D4
Cruikshank Gr BS24 . . . . . . .50 B5
Crusader Cl TA6 . . . . .208 E6
Crusty La BS20. . . . . .4 C5
Cruwy's Cross TA4 . . . . .210 B7
Crypton Tech Bsns Pk
  TA6. . . . . .209 B8
Cubitt Cl BS24. . . . . .49 C4
Cuck Hill BS25 . . . . .70 E7
CUCKLINGTON 177 D6
Cucklington Rd BA9 . . . . . . .177 D6
Cuckold's Row TA5. . . . . . . .152 E8
Cuckoo Cnr TA1. . . . . .213 B2
Cuckoo Hill
  Bruton BA10. . . . . .160 D6
  Bruton BA10. . . . . .215 F8
  Frome BA11. . . . . .119 E8
Cuckoo La
  Frome BA11 . . . . .119 F8
  High Littleton BS39. . . . . . .59 B3
  Thorncombe TA20. . . . . . .199 C7
  Wraxall BS48. . . . . .9 A6
CUDWORTH. 194 E5
Cudworth Hill TA20 . . . . . . .194 F4
Cudworth Rd TA18. . . . . . . .194 E6
Cudworth St TA20. . . . . .194 E5
Cuff's Common Dro BA16 .156 D4
Cuffs Mead TA20 . . . . .223 F1
Cufic La BS27. . . . . .90 C8
CULBONE. 123 B5
Culliford Cl BA16. . . . . .207 D7
Cullimore's La BA1. . . . . .26 C4
Culliver's Grave BA22 . . . . . .197 C8
Cullivers Grave Rd BA20 . . .218 C1
CULM DAVY. 180 A2
Culmhead Cl TA1 . . . . .212 D1
Culmstock Prim Sch EX15 179 E1
Culvercliffe Ct TA24. . . . . . .125 C4
Culvercliffe Rd TA23 . . . . . .202 D7
Culverhay BS39 . . . . .41 D6
Culverhay Cl TA7. . . . . .136 C4
Culverhay Dr BA21 . . . . . . .218 C8
Culverhayes TA20 . . . . .223 C2
Culverhay La TA4 . . . . .210 B4
CULVERHAYS. 132 F1
Culverhays La TA4 . . . . .132 F1
Culverhill BA11 . . . . .119 F3
Culver Hill TA10. . . . . .172 B7
Culver La
  Carhampton TA24. . . . . . .131 B4
  East Harptree BS40 . . . . . . .74 F3
Culverlake La EX13 . . . . . . .199 A3
Culvers Cl
  Keynsham BS31. . . . . .24 E6
  Sherborne DT9. . . . . .225 C4
Culvers Rd BS31 . . . . .24 E6
Culver St BS1. . . . . .226 C2
Culver Street La TA5 . . . . . .134 A7
Culvert Dro BS27. . . . . .109 B6
Culverwell Cotts BA4. . . . . .140 F3
Culverwell Rd BS13 . . . . .22 A4
Culvery La BS39. . . . . .40 D4
Cumberland Basin Rd BS8 . .11 F5
Cumberland Cl BS1 . . . . . . .226 A1
Cumberland Ho BA1. . . . . . .228 A2
Cumberland Pl 6 BS8. . . . . .11 F6
Cumberland Rd BS1. . . . . . .226 B1
Cumberland Row BA1. . . . . .228 B2
Cumberland St BS2 . . . . . . .227 B4
Cumhill Hill BA4 . . . . .140 E3
Cumnock Cres BA7. . . . . . . .214 C6
Cumnock Rd BA7. . . . . .214 C6
Cumnock Terr BA7. . . . . . . .214 C6
Cunningham Ave EX13. . . . .198 A2
Cunningham Ct TA1. . . . . . .213 A5
Cunningham Rd TA8 . . . . . .104 C7
Cunningham Rd BA21 . . . . .219 F8
Curdleigh La TA3. . . . . .181 D5
CURLAND. 182 D4
CURLAND COMMON 182 D4
Curland Gr BS14 . . . . .23 B5
Curlew Cl TA24 . . . . .201 C4
Curlew Gdns BS22. . . . . .31 F1
Curlew Pl BS20 . . . . .2 F6
CURLOAD 170 E7
Currells La BA20 . . . . .20 B1
Curriott Hill TA18 . . . . .224 B4
Curriott Hill Rd TA18 . . . . .224 B5
Curry Hole La BA22. . . . . . . .197 C2
Curry La TA3. . . . . .169 E6
CURRY MALLET 183 C8
Curry Mallet CE Prim Sch
  TA3. . . . . .183 D8
Currymead La TA10 . . . . . . .171 C2
Currypool La TA5 . . . . .134 E1
CURRY RIVEL 171 C4
Curry Rivel CE Prim Sch
  TA10 . . . . .171 D4

Curry Rivel CE VC Prim Sch
TA10 . . . .**171** C4
Currywoods Way TA10 . .**171** D4
Cursley Path BA5 . . . .**203** D3
Curtis Units BA11 . . . .**119** E2
Curvalion House Gdns
TA3 . . . .**169** D4
Curvalion Rd TA3 . . . .**169** D4
CUSHUISH **152** B1
Cushuish La TA2 & TA5 . . .**152** C2
Cushuish Lane Cotts TA2 .**152** B1
Cussacombe Gate EX36 . .**145** J1
Cussons St BA2 . . . .**45** C8
Custom Cl BS14 . . . .**23** A7
Custom Ho
Bristol BS1. . . . .**227** A1
Minehead TA24. . . . .**201** B7
CUTCOMBE **129** F2
Cutcombe CE Fst Sch
Wheddon Cross TA24. . . . .**129** E1
Wheddon Cross TA24. . . . .**129** E2
Cutcombe Cross TA24 . . . .**129** F1
Cutcombe Hill TA24 . . . . . .**129** F2
Cuthays La EX13 . . . .**198** B1
Cuthbert St TA9 . . . .**104** D3
Cutler Rd BS13 . . . .**21** F6
CUTLER'S GREEN **94** F4
Cutliff Cl TA1 . . . .**212** E1
Cuts Rd TA3, TA7 . . . .**170** E4
Cutter's Wharf TA24 . . . . . .**201** B7
CUTTIFORD'S DOOR **223** C7
Cutt Mill La DT10 . . . .**190** F3
Cut Tongue La TA20 . . . . . .**193** C7
Cutty Cotts BA22 . . . .**175** D6
Cutty La BA22 . . . .**175** D6
Cygnet Cres BS22 . . . .**31** F1
Cynthia Rd BA2 . . . .**44** D5
Cypress Ct
Bristol BS9 . . . .**5** D3
Somerton TA11 . . . .**211** E4
Cypress Dr
Puriton TA7 . . . .**136** C4
Yeovil BA20 . . . .**218** E2
Cypress Gdns BS8 . . . .**11** C6
Cypress Terr BA3 . . . .**78** D1
Cypress Way BA11 . . . .**120** C7
Cyril St W TA2 . . . .**212** E6
Cyril St TA2 . . . .**212** E6

D

Dabinett Cl TA2 . . . .**168** B5
Dabinett Dr BS25 . . . .**52** A4
Dadley La BA11 . . . .**102** A3
Daffodil Pl TA5 . . . .**208** D1
Dafford's Bldgs BA1 . . . .**28** C2
Dafford St BA1 . . . .**28** C2
Dagg's La BS28 . . . .**138** E8
Dagg's Lane Dro BA5,
BS28 . . . .**138** D7
Daghole BS27 . . . .**90** C8
Daglands The BA2 . . . .**78** E8
Dahlia Gdns 9 BA2 . . . .**45** B7
Dairs Orch TA20 . . . .**198** C8
Dairy Cl
Horsecastle BS49 . . . .**17** A2
Sherborne DT9 . . . .**225** C5
Wells BA5. . . . .**203** B5
Dairycroft BS2 . . . .**227** B4
Dairy Ct 3 TA18 . . . .**224** C5
Dairy Flats DT9 . . . .**225** E5
Dairy Hill BA2 . . . .**80** B5
Dairy House La TA3 . . . .**182** E5
Dairylands TA24 . . . .**131** D4
Daisey Bank BA2 . . . .**45** B4
Daisy Cl
Bridgwater TA6 . . . .**153** F5
Frome BA11 . . . .**120** B3
Daisyfield BA22 . . . .**188** A8
Dakota Dr BS14 . . . .**23** A4
Dale La BA5 . . . .**92** C3
Daley Cl BS22 . . . .**32** B3
Dalimores La BA11 . . . .**143** B8
Dalleston BA3 . . . .**114** C8
Dallimore La BA4 . . . .**142** B8
Dallimore Mead BA11 . . . .**143** B8
Dalton Sq BS2 . . . .**227** B4
Dalwood 12 BA22 . . . .**32** A2
Dalwoods DT9 . . . .**225** D3
Damas Dro TA7 . . . .**154** F5
Dame Court Cl BS22 . . . .**31** F4
Dame Withycombe Villas
TA5 . . . .**135** B5
Dampier Pl BA21 . . . .**219** C5
Dampier St BA21 . . . .**219** C5
Dampiet St TA6 . . . .**208** F4
Damson Cres TA21 . . . .**222** F7
Damson Orch BA1. . . . .**29** A4
Damson Rd BS22 . . . .**49** E2
Damson Row TA21 . . . .**222** F7
Dancey Mead BS13 . . . .**21** F6
Dancing Cross BA9 . . . .**176** B5
Dancing Hill TA6 . . . .**153** E4
Dancing La BA9 . . . .**216** A4
Dandelion Rd BA11 . . . .**120** B2
DandO's La BA5 . . . .**108** C4
Dandy's Mdw BS20 . . . .**2** E4
Daneacre Rd BA3 . . . .**79** A3
Dane Cl BA15 . . . .**64** E7
Dane Rise BA15 . . . .**64** E7
Danesboro Rd TA20 . . . .**223** C4
Danesborough View TA4 .**202** D3
Danesborough View E
TA4 . . . .**202** D3

Danesborough View W
TA4 . . . .**202** D3
Danes Cl EX14 . . . .**191** D4
Danesfield CE Com Mid Sch
TA4 . . . .**202** D4
Dane's Lea BS28 . . . .**108** C4
Dangerfield Ave BS13 . . . . .**21** F6
Daniel Cl BS21 . . . .**6** F3
Daniel Mews 2 BA2 . . . .**45** B7
Danielsfield Rd BA20 . . . . .**218** F2
Daniels La BA5 . . . .**111** A4
Daniel St 3 BA2 . . . .**45** B7
Dapps Hill BS31 . . . .**24** F5
Dapwell La BS14, BS31 . . . .**24** A1
Darby Cl SP8 . . . .**161** F1
Darby's Knap TA24 . . . .**147** C5
Darby Way TA4 . . . .**151** F1
Darcis Row TA20 . . . .**223** B4
Dare Cl TA2 . . . .**213** A8
Darkey La BA10 . . . .**215** F7
Darkfield Way TA7 . . . .**136** E3
Dark La
Ashbrittle TA21 . . . .**178** E8
Backwell BS48 . . . .**19** B5
Banwell BS29 . . . .**51** C2
Berkley BA11 . . . .**120** E8
Blagdon BS40 . . . .**54** E3
Chew Magna BS40 . . . .**38** F3
Freshford BA3 . . . .**64** B5
Hockworthy EX16 . . . .**178** B8
Holcombe BA3 . . . .**97** C1
Kilmersdon BA11 . . . .**98** A1
North Wootton BA4 . . . . . .**140** C5
Sandford Orcas DT9 . . . . .**188** C7
Seavington St Mary TA19 . .**184** E1
Stoke St Gregory TA3 . . . . .**170** F6
Stoke St Michael BA3 . . . .**116** C2
Upton Noble BA4 . . . .**142** F2
Wellington TA21 . . . .**222** D5
Witham Friary BA11 . . . . .**143** D2
Darlick Cnr EX36 . . . .**145** G4
Darlington Mews 8 BA2 . . . .**45** B7
Darlington Pl BA2 . . . .**45** B6
Darlington Rd BA2 . . . .**45** B8
Darlington St BA2 . . . .**45** B7
Darmead BS24 . . . .**32** B1
DARSHILL **204** F6
Dartmouth Ave BA2 . . . .**44** C5
Dartmouth Cl BS22 . . . .**32** A2
Dartmouth Wlk BS31 . . . . . .**24** D4
Dart Rd BS22 . . . .**6** D1
Darvole Road BA22 . . . .**197** E7
Darwin Cl TA2 . . . .**212** B6
Darwin Dr BA21 . . . .**219** F8
Dashwoods La TA4 . . . .**132** E2
Daubeny Ct BS1 . . . .**227** A1
Daunton Cl TA9 . . . .**104** D4
David's La TA19 . . . .**184** F2
David's Rd BS14 . . . .**23** C6
David St BS2 . . . .**227** C3
Davies Cl
Bridgwater TA6 . . . .**208** F2
Winsham TA20 . . . .**194** E1
Davies La BS21 . . . .**16** F8
Davis Cl BA5 . . . .**203** B4
Davis Terr 5 BA5 . . . .**203** C4
Dawbins Dr TA7 . . . .**136** E4
Dawes Cl BS21 . . . .**6** D1
Daws Cl 2 BS8 . . . .**11** F6
Daws Cl TA6 . . . .**208** E2
Daws La TA6 . . . .**153** E3
Daw's La DT9 . . . .**176** A3
Daws Mead TA1 . . . .**212** A3
Day Cres BA2 . . . .**43** F6
Deacon Rd TA6 . . . .**209** C6
DEACONS **168** C7
Deacons Cl BS22 . . . .**31** E2
Deacons Cl BS22 . . . .**31** C1
Deacons La BA21 . . . .**187** D6
Deacons Mill La DT10 . . . . .**190** B3
Deacon Way TA8 . . . .**104** B6
Deadlands La TA12, TA13 . .**185** A6
Dead Maids Cross Rd
BA13 . . . .**121** E5
Deadman's Hill DT9 . . . .**176** A1
Deadmans La TA20 . . . .**181** F2
Deadmill La BA1 . . . .**28** C3
Dead Woman's Cnr BA12 . .**161** E4
Deal Cl TA6 . . . .**209** D5
DEAN **142** B7
Dean Cl
Frome BA11 . . . .**120** C6
Weston-super-Mare BS22 . .**32** B3
Deane Cl TA4 . . . .**150** D8
Deane Dr TA1 . . . .**212** B2
Deane Gate Ave TA1 . . . . . .**213** E5
Deane Ret Pk TA1 . . . .**213** F5
Deanery Rd BS1 . . . .**226** C2
Deanery Wlk BA3 . . . .**64** C6
Deanesly Way BA9 . . . .**216** D3
Deane Way TA20 . . . .**198** D8
Deanhill La BA1 . . . .**27** A2
Dean La
Crewkerne TA18 . . . .**196** B4
Dunster TA24 . . . .**201** D3
Milverton TA4 . . . .**167** A6
Oakhill BA3 . . . .**115** A3
Dean's Cross
Allerford TA24 . . . .**124** E3
Lydeard St Lawrence TA4 . .**151** A4
Dean's La
Allerford TA24 . . . .**124** E3
Brompton Ralph TA4 . . . . .**150** F4
Deansley Way BA9 . . . .**216** D3
Deans Mead BS11 . . . .**5** A8
Deans Pl 8 BA5 . . . .**203** D4

Dean St BS2 . . . .**227** B4
Deans The BS20. . . . .**2** B4
Dean Vale Pk TA4 . . . .**167** C4
Debecca's La BS20 . . . .**4** B4
De Combe Ho TA18 . . . .**224** D6
De Corcis Cl TA5 . . . .**134** A3
Decoy La TA11 . . . .**157** A2
Deep La BA12 . . . .**121** E1
Deepleigh La TA4 . . . .**210** C7
Deerleap
Easton BA5. . . . .**111** B6
Shipham BS25 . . . .**70** F8
Deer Mead BS21 . . . .**6** B1
Deerswood Gdns BA16 . . . .**207** A6
Deer View TA24 . . . .**201** C4
Delapre Rd BS23 . . . .**48** D3
Delhorn La BS24 . . . .**86** C7
Delius Gr BS4 . . . .**22** D7
Dellers Ct TA1 . . . .**212** F5
Deller's Wharf TA1 . . . .**212** F5
Dellshore Cl TA20 . . . .**223** D4
Dell The
Bristol, Westbury on T BS9 . . .**5** F5
Minehead TA24. . . . .**200** E6
Nailsea BS48 . . . .**8** D2
Weston-super-Mare BS22 . . .**31** B4
Delmore Rd BA11 . . . .**119** E3
Delta Cl BA11 . . . .**119** F5
Delta Ct 1 BA11 . . . .**119** F5
Delta Rise TA4 . . . .**151** E1
Demelza Ct BA22 . . . .**174** D3
De Montalt Pl BA2 . . . .**45** B1
Dempier Mews BA22 . . . . . .**218** B6
Dene Barton Com Hospl
TA4 . . . .**167** F6
Dene Cl BS31 . . . .**24** F3
Dene Cross TA4 . . . .**167** F7
Dene Gdns TA24 . . . .**201** B4
Dene Rd
Cotford St Luke TA4 . . . . .**167** F6
Whitchurch BS14 . . . .**23** C4
Dening Cl TA20 . . . .**223** C6
Denleigh Cl BS14 . . . .**23** A4
Denman's La
Barrington TA19 . . . .**184** D5
Cannington TA5 . . . .**135** B2
Denmark Ave BS1 . . . .**226** C2
Denmark Rd BA2 . . . .**44** D6
Denmark St BS1 . . . .**226** C2
Denmark Terr TA2 . . . .**212** F7
Dennett Cl BA4 . . . .**205** E4
Denning Cl TA1 . . . .**212** B1
Denning Ct BS22 . . . .**32** B4
Dennington La
Churchinford EX14 . . . . . .**192** C6
Dulverton EX22 . . . .**163** B4
Dennor Pk BS14 . . . .**23** B7
Denny Cl BS20 . . . .**2** A5
Denny La BS40 . . . .**39** B1
Denny View BS20 . . . .**2** A5
Dennyview Rd BS8 . . . .**10** F8
Denston Dr BS20 . . . .**2** E4
Denston Wlk BS13 . . . .**22** A7
Dentwood Gr BS9 . . . .**5** B8
Denzil Ct BA22 . . . .**197** A8
Depley Farm La BA9 . . . . . .**177** E2
Derek Mead Way BS29. . . . .**50** C7
Derham Cl BS49 . . . .**34** B8
Derham Ct BS49 . . . .**34** B8
Derham Pk BS49 . . . .**34** B8
Derham Rd BS13 . . . .**22** A5
Derricke Rd BS14 . . . .**23** F6
DERTFORDS **144** D8
Dertfords BA12 . . . .**144** D8
Derwent Gdns BA21 . . . . . .**219** D6
Derwent Gr
Keynsham BS31 . . . .**25** A5
Taunton TA1 . . . .**213** E4
Derwent Rd BS23 . . . .**49** A5
Derwent Way BA21 . . . .**218** C6
De Salis Pk BS24 . . . .**50** D8
Desmond Rochford
TA1 . . . .**212** A3
Devenish La BA9 . . . .**216** F4
Deveron Gr BS31 . . . .**25** A4
Devonia Pk TA4 . . . .**168** A1
Devonshire Bldgs BA2 . . . . .**44** F4
Devonshire Ct BS23 . . . .**48** E4
Devonshire Dr BS20 . . . .**1** F5
Devonshire Mews BA2 . . . . .**44** F3
Devonshire Pl BA2 . . . .**44** F4
Devonshire Rd
Bathampton BA2 . . . .**28** E1
Weston-super-Mare BS23 . .**48** E4
Devonshire St TA6 . . . .**209** B5
Devonshire Villas BA2 . . . . .**44** F3
Dewar Cl TA8 . . . .**104** C7
Dewberry Ave TA6 . . . .**208** E1
Dew Water La TA11 . . . .**211** D5
Dexter Wlk 8 TA6 . . . .**209** A1
Dial Hill Rd BS21 . . . .**6** D4
Dial La BS40 . . . .**20** D1
Dial's Gate La BA6, TA11 . . .**158** D4
Diamond Batch BS24 . . . . . .**32** B1
Dibbens Row BA9 . . . .**161** A2
Dibbles La BA22 . . . .**197** A8
Dickenson Rd BS23 . . . .**48** E6
Dickenson's Gr BS49 . . . .**34** E3
Dicky's Path TA24 . . . .**129** A5
Digby Ct DT9 . . . .**225** D3
Digby Rd DT9 . . . .**225** D3
Dighton Ct 3 BS2 . . . .**227** A4
Dighton St BS2 . . . .**227** A4
Digland La TA24 . . . .**129** F5
Dilkes La TA11 . . . .**174** C7
DILLINGTON **221** E5
Dillington Farm Cotts
TA19 . . . .**221** E5

Dillington House Coll
TA19 . . . .**221** D6
Dillons Rd TA3 . . . .**169** D4
DIMMER **159** C5
Dimmer La BA7 . . . .**159** B2
Dimmock's La TA12 . . . .**185** D5
DINDER **140** D7
Dinder Cl BS48 . . . .**18** E8
DINGHURST **52** E4
Dinghurst Rd BS25 . . . .**52** E4
Dingle Cl BS9 . . . .**5** D5
Dingle Cl BS13 . . . .**21** F7
Dingle Rd BS9 . . . .**5** D7
Dingle The BS9 . . . .**5** D7
Dingle View BS9 . . . .**5** C7
Dinglewood Cl BS9 . . . .**5** D7
Dingley Cl TA6 . . . .**208** E5
Ding Rd
Broadway TA19 . . . .**183** A2
Dommett TA20 . . . .**182** F1
Dinhams Cl TA3 . . . .**169** C4
Dinhay DT10 . . . .**190** F6
DINNINGTON **195** B3
Dipford Rd TA3 . . . .**168** D1
Dipland Gr BS40 . . . .**54** F2
Disraeli Pl TA1 . . . .**212** D5
DITCHEAT **159** C7
Ditcheat Hill BA4. . . . .**159** B7
Ditcheat Prim Sch BA4 . . . .**159** C7
Ditch Furlong Rd TA7 . . . . .**137** A2
Ditton St TA19 . . . .**221** C3
Dixon Gdns BA1. . . . .**27** C1
Dobree Pk TA21 . . . .**222** A4
Dobunni Cl BS14 . . . .**23** C4
Dock Gate La BS8 . . . .**226** A1
Doctor's Hill BA5 . . . .**111** B1
Dodd Ave BA5 . . . .**203** C5
Dodd's Cnr BA9 . . . .**215** E1
Dodge Cross DT9 . . . .**225** F5
Dodham Cres BA20 . . . .**218** F4
DODHILL **168** D7
Dodinalls House Rd BA22 . .**175** F7
DODINGTON **133** F3
Dod La BA6 . . . .**206** E4
Dog Down Cross EX16 . . . . .**178** A8
Doleberrow BS25 . . . .**52** F3
Dolebury Warren Nature
Reserve ★ BS25 . . . .**53** A3
Dolecroft La BS22 . . . .**32** E7
Dolemead La BS27 . . . .**90** E2
DOLEMEADS **45** B5
Dolemoor La
Congresbury BS49 . . . .**34** A4
Congresbury BS49 . . . .**34** C3
Dolling Cl TA20 . . . .**223** C6
Dolling's Rd TA3 . . . .**181** B4
Dolphin Sq BS23 . . . .**48** D7
Dominion Rd BA2 . . . .**44** A6
Dominy Cl TA20 . . . .**223** D3
DOMMETT **182** D1
Dommett Cl EX13 . . . .**198** A2
Dommett Rd TA20 . . . .**182** D1
Dommett's La BA11 . . . .**119** D4
Domus Dr BA4 . . . .**205** E4
Donald Rd BS13 . . . .**21** F7
DONIFORD **202** D3
Doniford Beach Halt TA23 .**202** E6
Doniford Dr TA4 . . . .**202** D3
Doniford Mdw TA23 . . . . . .**202** F6
Doniford Orch TA23 . . . .**202** F6
Doniford Rd
Watchet TA23 . . . .**202** E6
Williton TA4 . . . .**202** D4
Donne La TA24 . . . .**186** C2
Donnes Terr BA7 . . . .**214** B5
Donnington Wlk BS31 . . . . .**24** D4
Donstan Rd TA9 . . . .**104** E4
DONYATT **183** D1
Donyatt Hill TA19 . . . .**183** D1
Donyatt Hill Est TA19 . . . . .**183** D1
Doone Way TA24 . . . .**201** B4
Dorchester Cl 6 BS48 . . . .**8** D1
Dorchester Rd
Barwick BA22 . . . .**197** F7
East Coker BA22 . . . .**197** F5
Taunton TA2 . . . .**213** A8
Yeovil BA22 . . . .**219** A1
Dorchester St BA1 . . . .**228** C1
Dore Cl BA21 . . . .**218** C2
Dormeads View 6 BS24 . . . .**49** F7
Dorset Cl
Bath BA2 . . . .**44** D6
Frome BA11 . . . .**119** C4
Highbridge TA9 . . . .**104** E2
Dorset Ho BA2 . . . .**44** D3
Dorset Rd TA6 . . . .**209** C3
Dorset St BA2 . . . .**44** D6
Doster's La TA2 . . . .**169** C6
Double Gates Dro TA11 . . . .**158** A3
Double Hill BA2 . . . .**79** F7
Douglas Ct 3 BS23 . . . .**48** E5
Douglas Dr BA4 . . . .**205** B6
Douglas Rd BS23 . . . .**48** E5
Douglas Yates Ct BA3 . . . . .**116** F2
DOULTING **141** E6
Doulting Ct BA11 . . . .**120** C7
Doulting Hill BA4 . . . .**205** E4
Doulton Way BS14 . . . .**23** B5
Dovai Dr TA6 . . . .**208** E2
Dove Cots BA16 . . . .**207** C2
Dove La BS2 . . . .**227** C4
DOVERHAY **124** B3
Doverhay Rd
Horner TA24 . . . .**123** A1
Horner TA24 . . . .**129** A8
Dover Ho BA1 . . . .**228** C4
Dover Pl
6 Bath BA1 . . . .**28** A1

Dover Pl continued
Bristol BS8 . . . .**226** B3
Dover Rd TA2 . . . .**213** A8
Dovers La BA1 . . . .**29** C2
Dovers Pk BA1 . . . .**29** C2
Dovery Manor Mus ★
TA24 . . . .**124** A3
Dove St S BS2 . . . .**227** A4
Dove St BS2 . . . .**227** A4
Doveswell Gr BS13 . . . .**22** A4
Dovetail Ct 1 TA1 . . . .**212** E3
Dovetail Dr BS23 . . . .**49** A7
Dovetons Cl TA4 . . . .**202** E3
Dovetons Dr TA4 . . . .**202** E3
Dowding Rd BA1 . . . .**28** B1
Dowell Cl TA2 . . . .**212** C6
Dowland 13 BS22 . . . .**32** A2
Dowland Gr BS4 . . . .**22** D6
Dowling La BA6 . . . .**158** A5
Dowling Rd BS13 . . . .**22** D3
DOWLISH FORD **221** B1
Dowlish La TA19 . . . .**194** F5
Dowlish Rd TA17 . . . .**194** F6
DOWLISH WAKE **194** E7
Downash Ct EX13 . . . .**198** E3
Down Ave BA2 . . . .**45** A1
Down Cl BS20 . . . .**1** F4
Downclose La TA18 . . . .**196** C3
Downend Cres TA6 . . . .**136** B4
Downend Rd TA6 . . . .**136** B4
Downend Terr TA6 . . . .**136** B4
Downey Field La TA18 . . . . .**196** D6
Downfield
Bristol BS9 . . . .**5** C7
Keynsham BS31 . . . .**24** D5
Downhall Dr TA6 . . . .**208** D6
DOWNHEAD
Stoke St Michael. **142** C8
Yeovilton **174** C4
Downhead La BA22 . . . .**174** C5
Downhead Rd BA22 . . . .**174** C4
Down La
Bathampton BA2 . . . .**28** F1
Buckland Dinham BA11 . . . .**99** C3
Shepton Montague BA9 . . .**160** B2
Sherborne DT9 . . . .**188** A5
Trent DT9 . . . .**187** F5
West Pennard BA4, BA6. . .**140** C3
Downland Cl 5 BS48 . . . .**8** D1
Downleaze
Bristol, Stoke Bishop BS9. . . .**5** F3
Portishead BS20 . . . .**2** A5
Yeovil BA20 . . . .**218** D2
Downleaze Rd BS9 . . . .**5** F3
Down Rd BS20 . . . .**1** F4
Downs Cl BS22 . . . .**31** F1
Downs Cote Ave BS9 . . . .**5** F6
Downs Cote Dr BS9 . . . .**5** F6
DOWNSIDE
Chilcompton **96** C1
Felton. **19** D1
Shepton Mallet **205** D8
Downside
Portishead BS20 . . . .**2** C5
Street BA16 . . . .**207** D6
Downside Abbey ★ BA3 . . . .**96** E2
Downside Cl
Bathampton BA2 . . . .**28** F1
Chilcompton BA3 . . . .**96** D3
Downside Rd
Backwell BS48 . . . .**36** E8
Weston-super-Mare BS23 . .**48** F4
Weston-super-Mare Sch BA3 . . .**96** C2
Downslade La TA10 . . . .**172** D5
Down's Orch BA6 . . . .**138** C4
Downs Rd BS41 . . . .**21** D2
Downs Sch The BS48 . . . .**9** C8
Downs The BS20 . . . .**2** B4
Downsway BS39 . . . .**77** D6
Downton Rd BS13 . . . .**22** D8
Down View BA3 . . . .**97** F8
Dowry Pl 3 BS8 . . . .**11** F5
Dowry Rd BS8 . . . .**226** A2
Dowry Sq BS8 . . . .**226** A2
DOWSLANDS **168** F1
Dowsland Way TA1 . . . .**213** C1
DOYNTON **12** A8
Dozen's Cnr TA17 . . . .**195** A7
Dragon Cross TA24 . . . .**131** D3
Dragonfly Chase BA22 . . . . .**173** E2
Dragon Ri TA2 . . . .**212** A7
Dragons Hill Cl BS31 . . . .**24** F5
Dragons Hill Ct BS31 . . . .**24** F5
Dragons Hill Gdns BS31 . . . .**24** F5
Drake Ave BA2 . . . .**44** F2
Drake Cl
Saltford BS31 . . . .**25** D2
Staplegrove TA2 . . . .**212** B7
Weston-super-Mare BS22 . .**31** B4
Drake Mdws TA3 . . . .**192** A7
Drake Rd BA5 . . . .**203** F6
Drakes Cl TA6 . . . .**208** F5
Drake's Cl TA3 . . . .**169** C4
Drakes Cres TA20 . . . .**198** D8
Drake's Dro BA5 . . . .**139** A6
Drakes Mdw
East Coker BA22 . . . .**197** C2
Yarcombe EX14 . . . .**192** D3
Drakes Pk TA21 . . . .**222** D7
Drakes Pk N TA21 . . . .**222** D7
Drakes Way BS20 . . . .**2** B5
Drang The
Coxley BA5 . . . .**139** E6
Evercreech BA4 . . . .**141** E1
Porlock TA24 . . . .**124** A3
Dransfield Way BA2 . . . .**44** C4
Drapers Way TA24 . . . .**129** D2

Drappel La BA5 . . . . 110 E7
Draycot Pl BS1. . . . . 227 A1
DRAYCOTT
  Cheddar 90 E2
  Yeovil. 187 B8
Draycott Ave TA2 . . . . 213 A6
Draycott Ct **1** BA2 . . . . . . 228 C3
Draycott Moor Dro BS27 . . 90 D1
Draycott Rd
  Cheddar BS27 . . . . 90 D5
  Shepton Mallet BA4 . . . . . 205 B6
Draycott & Rodney Stoke CE
  Fst Sch BS27. . . . . 90 F3
Draydon La
  Ashwick TA22 . . . . 147 A1
  Hawkridge TA22 . . . . 146 F2
Draydon Rd BS4 . . . . 22 D8
Dray Rd BA22 . . . . 186 C2
DRAYTON
  Curry Rival 171 E3
  Southerton. 185 D3
Drayton BS24 . . . . 49 A2
Drayton Cl BS14. . . . . 23 B8
Drayton Ct TA11 . . . . 211 B4
Drayton La TA10 . . . . 171 D3
Drayton Rd BS9 . . . . 5 C8
Drew's La DT10 . . . . 190 B5
Drials La BA3 . . . . 94 F6
Drift Rd TA24 . . . . 201 D4
Drift The
  Chard TA20. . . . . 194 B3
  Chard Junction TA20. . . . 198 E8
Drill Hall La BA4 . . . . 205 C5
DRIMPTON 199 F7
Drimpton Cross DT8. . . . . 199 F7
Dring The BA3 . . . . 78 E2
Drive The
  Bristol BS14. . . . . 23 C6
  Burnham-on-S TA8 . . . . . . 85 A2
  Churchill BS25 . . . . 52 E4
  Keynsham BS31 . . . . 24 E6
  Shipham BS25 . . . . 70 E8
  Stanton Drew BS39 . . . . . . 39 F1
  Taunton TA1 . . . . 212 D1
  Weston-super-Mare BS23 . . 48 F8
  Woolavington TA7. . . . . . 136 E4
Driveway Dro TA10 . . . . . . 173 A3
Dropping La BA10 . . . . 160 D5
Drove Ct DT10 . . . . 189 F2
Drove Ct BS48 . . . . 8 E3
Drove La
  East Pennard BA4 . . . . . . 158 E8
  Shepton Beauchamp TA19 . 184 E4
Drove Rd
  Congresbury BS49 . . . . 34 D3
  Stourton Caundle DT10 . . 189 F2
  Weston-super-Mare BS23 . . 48 F5
Drove The
  Bridgwater TA6 . . . . 209 A6
  Portbury BS20. . . . . 3 D6
Droveway TA13 . . . . 220 B5
Drove Way
  Churchinford TA3 . . . . 191 F8
  Sandford BS24, BS25 . . . . . 51 E7
Droveway Cl TA13 . . . . 220 C5
Droveway La BA21 . . . . . . 187 C2
Druid Cl BS9 . . . . 5 E5
Druid Hill BS9 . . . . 5 E5
Druid Rd BS9 . . . . 5 D4
Druids Garth BA2 . . . . 28 D1
Druid Stoke Ave BS9 . . . . . . 5 D5
Druids Wlk TA20 . . . . 223 C5
Druid Woods BS9 . . . . 5 C5
Druley Hill BA10 . . . . 161 D8
Drum Ave BA6 . . . . 206 C5
Drumhead Way The BS25 . . 70 E8
Dr White's Cl BS1 . . . . 227 B1
DRY HILL 2 C6
Dryleaze BS31 . . . . 24 E7
Drysdale Cl BS2 . . . . 31 D1
Duchess Cl **1** TA6. . . . . . 208 E7
Duchy Cl BA3 . . . . 78 E5
Duchy Rd
  Clandown BA3 . . . . 78 E5
  Shepton Mallet BA4 . . . . 205 A5
Duck La
  Chard TA20. . . . . 223 C3
  Churchill BS40 . . . . 53 A8
  Horsington BA8 . . . . 176 E2
  Ilchester BA22. . . . . 173 F1
  Kenn BS21 . . . . 17 A6
  Stalbridge DT10 . . . . 190 B5
  Westbury-sub-Mendip BA5 . 110 E6
Duck Pool Dro BA6. . . . . . 206 B7
Duckpool La TA18. . . . . . . 196 B8
Duck Pool La BA11 . . . . . . 102 B6
Ducks' Field Crossing
  TA18 . . . . 224 C1
Ducks Hill TA10 . . . . 172 B5
Ducks La BS22 . . . . 32 A8
Duck St BS25 . . . . 52 C5
Ducky La TA5 . . . . 134 A5
Ducky Path TA24 . . . . 201 D2
DUDDLESTONE 181 E8
Dudley Cl BS31. . . . . 24 E4
Dudmoor TA12. . . . . 185 B7
Dudwell La BA3 . . . . 95 A5
Dugdale St TA1 . . . . 200 F6
Duke Ave **7** TA5 . . . . 135 B2
Duke Ho TA19. . . . . 221 B3
Duke's Cl BA9. . . . . 216 E3
Dukes Field BA4 . . . . 205 C5
Duke's La
  Horningsham BA12 . . . . . 144 A1
  Kilmington BA12 . . . . 161 F8
Dukes Mead TA6. . . . . 209 A2
Duke St
  Bath BA2 . . . . 228 C2

Duke St continued
  Bridgwater TA6 . . . . 208 E7
  Frome BA11. . . . . 119 C5
  Taunton TA1 . . . . 213 A4
DULCOTE. 140 C7
Dulcote Hill La BA5. . . . . . 140 C7
Dull Cross TA4. . . . . 151 D3
DULVERTON 163 E6
Dulverton La TA4 . . . . 165 D7
Dulverton Mid & Com Sch
  TA22 . . . . 163 D6
Dumfries Pl BS23 . . . . 48 E5
Dummis La BA5. . . . . 111 A1
Dumpers La BS40 . . . . 39 B2
Dumper's La BA3 . . . . 94 F7
DUNBALL. 136 A3
Dunball Drove TA6 . . . . . . 136 A4
Dunball Ind Est TA6. . . . . 136 B4
Dunball La TA9 . . . . 104 C4
Duncan Gdns BA1. . . . . 27 A3
Duncart La BA5 . . . . 204 C7
Duncliffe Cl DT10 . . . . 190 B4
Duncombe Cl TA6. . . . . . . 209 D5
Dundas Row TA4. . . . . 167 E8
DUNDON 156 F3
DUNDON HAYES. 156 F3
Dundon Hayes Dro TA11 . . 211 B8
DUNDRY 21 D2
Dundry CE Prim Sch BS41. . 21 D2
DUNDRY HILL 23 B3
Dundry La
  Dundry BS41 . . . . 21 C3
  Winford BS40. . . . . 38 A7
Dunedin Way BS22 . . . . 32 C4
Dunford Terr BA6 . . . . 158 A5
Dungarvon Rd BS24 . . . . . . 49 F7
Dungeon BS28 . . . . 108 D7
Dungeon La BS25 . . . . 204 C6
Dunkerry Rd BS26. . . . . 88 C4
DUNKERTON 61 E4
Dunkerton Cl BA6. . . . . . . 206 F3
Dunkerton Hill BA2. . . . . . . 61 E2
Dunkerton La
  Combe Hay BA2 . . . . 62 B4
  Dunkerton BA2. . . . . 61 F3
Dunkerton Rise TA2. . . . . . 168 B5
Dunkery Cl BS48 . . . . 8 E1
Dunkery Hill Rd TA24. . . . 129 C7
Dunkery & Horner Wood
  National Nature Reserve
  The ★ TA24. . . . . 129 A7
Dunkery Rd
  Bridgwater TA6 . . . . 208 D4
  Weston-super-Mare BS22 . . 32 A1
Dunkery Vineyard ★ TA24 . 200 A1
Dunkirk Bsns Pk BA14 . . . . 83 D2
Dunkleys Way TA1 . . . . . . 213 C2
Dunlin Dr **1** BS20. . . . . 2 F6
Dunningham La BS28. . . . . 107 E4
Dunns Cl BS28 . . . . 108 C4
Dunn's Hill TA21 . . . . 179 A6
Dunsford Pl BA2 . . . . 45 B6
Dunsgreen La EX15. . . . . . 191 A8
Dunsham La TA18. . . . . . . 195 C2
Dunsley Hill EX16, EX36. . 162 D5
Dunstan Dr DT9 . . . . 225 E5
Dunstan Rd
  Burnham-on-S TA8 . . . . . 104 B7
  Glastonbury BA6 . . . . 206 F5
Dunstan Way BS27 . . . . 90 B6
DUNSTER 201 E2
Dunster Beach
  Alcombe TA24. . . . . 125 F2
  Ellicombe TA24. . . . . 201 F5
Dunster Beach Chalets
  TA24 . . . . 201 F4
Dunster Castle ★ TA24 . . . 201 E1
Dunster Cl
  Minehead TA24. . . . . 201 B4
  Taunton TA2 . . . . 213 B7
Dunster Cres BS24 . . . . 49 A2
Dunster Ct BS25 . . . . 70 A8
Dunster Fst Sch
  Dunster TA24. . . . . 201 D2
  Dunster TA24. . . . . 201 D2
Dunster Gdns **5** BS48 . . . . 8 E1
Dunster Ho BA2 . . . . 45 A2
Dunster Rd
  Bristol BS4 . . . . 22 F8
  Keynsham BS31 . . . . 24 E4
Dunsters Rd BS49 . . . . 17 F1
Dunster Steep
  Dunster TA24. . . . . 201 E2
  Porlock, Doverhay TA24 . . 124 A3
Dunster Visitor Ctr ★
  TA24 . . . . 201 E2
Dunster Wood Forest Trails ★
  TA24 . . . . 130 C3
Dunster Working Water Mill ★
  TA24 . . . . 201 E1
DUNWEAR. 209 D1
Dunwear Ho **3** TA6 . . . . . 209 C4
Dunwear La TA6 . . . . 209 D3
Durban Way BS49 . . . . 17 B1
Durbin Park Rd BS21 . . . . . . 6 D5
Durcott Rd BA2 . . . . 78 D8
Durham Gr BS31 . . . . 24 D4
Durham Pl **9** BA2 . . . . . . 213 A8
Durhams Cotts TA4 . . . . . 210 C5
Durkheim Dr **2** BA5. . . . . 203 C4
DURLEIGH. 208 B3
Durleigh Cl
  Bridgwater TA6 . . . . 208 D3
  Bristol BS13. . . . . 22 A7
Durleigh Hill TA5 . . . . 208 A2
Durleigh Rd TA6 . . . . 208 C3
Durley Hill BS31. . . . . 24 C7

Durley La BS31. . . . . 24 D7
Durleymoor Cross EX16 . . 178 F4
Durley Pk BA2 . . . . 44 E4
DURNFIELD. 186 B7
Durnhill BS40 . . . . 73 F7
Durrant Cl DT9 . . . . 225 D3
Dursdon Dro
  Priddy BA5. . . . . 111 C8
  Wells BA5. . . . . 112 B6
Dursley Rd BS11 . . . . 4 E5
DURSTON 169 F6
Durston BS24 . . . . 49 A2
Durston Cl BA16 . . . . 207 C5
Durston Ho **3** BA16. . . . . 207 C5
Durston Way TA1 . . . . 212 E1
Durville Rd BS13 . . . . 22 B6
Durweston Wlk BS14 . . . . . 23 C8
Dutch Rd TA9 . . . . 105 E5
Dutton Cl BS14 . . . . 23 D6
Dutton Rd BS14 . . . . 23 D6
Dutton Wlk BS14 . . . . 23 D6
Dwelly Cl TA20 . . . . 223 C3
Dyehouse Cnr TA22 . . . . . 164 A6
Dyehouse Cross TA22 . . . . 163 F5
Dyehouse La
  Bury TA22. . . . . 164 A5
  Glastonbury BA6 . . . . 206 C5
Dye La BA3 . . . . 115 A3
Dyers Cl
  Bristol BS13. . . . . 22 D4
  Curry Rivel TA10. . . . . . . 171 D4
  West Buckland TA21. . . . . 180 F7
Dyers' Close La BA11 . . . . . 119 E5
Dyers Gn TA6 . . . . 153 F3
Dyer's La TA2 . . . . 213 E2
Dyers Rd TA10 . . . . 171 D4
Dyke Hill Terr TA20 . . . . . 198 D8
Dyke's Way BA9. . . . . 216 B3
Dymboro Ave BA3 . . . . 77 F1
Dymboro Cl BA3 . . . . 77 F1
Dymboro Gdns BA3 . . . . . . 77 F1
Dymboro The BA3. . . . . 77 F1
Dyrham Cl TA8. . . . . 104 D7
Dyson Cl BS49 . . . . 34 B8

E

Eagle Cl
  Ilchester BA22. . . . . 173 E2
  Weston-super-Mare BS22 . . 49 D8
Eagle Dr **5** BA3 . . . . 97 B8
Eagle Gdns BA22 . . . . 173 E2
Eagle La **1** BA11. . . . . . . 119 F4
Eagle Pk BA3 . . . . 28 F5
Eagle Rd BA1 . . . . 28 F5
Eagles The BS49 . . . . 34 B8
Eaker Hill La BA3. . . . . 93 F6
Eames Orch TA19 . . . . 221 C2
Earlesfield BS48 . . . . 8 C1
Earle St BA6 . . . . 219 C5
Earlham Gr BS23 . . . . 49 A7
Earls Cl
  Bridgwater TA6 . . . . 208 E7
  Sherborne DT9. . . . . 225 F5
Earl St BS1 . . . . 227 A4
EAST ANSTEY 162 E5
East Anstey Prim Sch
  EX16 . . . . 162 E5
East Approach Rd TA7. . . . 136 D4
East Ave TA9. . . . . 104 C4
Eastbourne Ave **15** BA1. . . 28 B1
Eastbourne Ct **13** TA1. . . 213 A4
Eastbourne Gate TA1. . . . . 213 A4
Eastbourne Rd TA1. . . . . . 213 A4
Eastbourne Terr **12** TA1. . 213 A4
EAST BOWER 209 E6
EAST BRENT 86 D5
East Brent CE Fst Sch TA9. . 86 C4
East Bridgwater Com Sch
  TA6 . . . . 209 C5
EASTBROOK 168 E1
Eastbrook Terr TA3 . . . . . . 168 D1
Eastbury Hill TA24. . . . . . . 131 B5
Eastbury Rd TA24 . . . . 131 B5
EAST CHINNOCK 196 E8
East Chinnock Rd
  East Chinnock TA18 . . . . . 196 F8
  Higher Odcombe TA14 . . . 186 C1
East Cl
  Bath BA2 . . . . 44 A5
  Haselbury Plucknett TA18. . 196 B5
EAST CLEVEDON 6 F3
East Clevedon Triangle
  BS21 . . . . 6 F3
Eastcliff BS20. . . . . 2 E7
EAST COKER 197 D7
East Coker Com Prim Sch
  BA22. . . . . 197 C7
East Coker Rd BA20 . . . . . 218 F2
East Coker Sawmills
  BA22. . . . . 197 C7
East Compton. 205 A2
East Compton Rd
  Pilton BA4 . . . . 204 C1
  Shepton Mallet BA4 . . . . 205 B1
East Coombe La TA4 . . . . . 165 D2
Eastcote Pk BS14 . . . . 23 B5
Eastcott La TA24 . . . . 148 F5
Eastcourt Rd BS39 . . . . 76 F8
EAST CRANMORE 142 D6
Eastcroft BS40. . . . . 54 E2
Eastcroft Cl BS40 . . . . 54 E2
East Ct BS3 . . . . 11 F3

East Ct BA5 . . . . 113 A1
Eastdown Rd BA3 . . . . 78 D5
East Dr TA9 . . . . 86 E4
EAST DUNDRY 22 A1
East Dundry La BS41 . . . . . 22 A1
East Dundry Rd BS13, BS14 . 22 F2
EAST END
  Blagdon 54 F2
  Chewton Mendip 94 E4
  Nailsea. 9 A1
  South Cadbury 175 D4
  Stoke St Michael. 116 C2
East End TA6 . . . . 88 D7
East End La
  Butleigh BA6 . . . . 157 D5
  Chewton Mendip BA3 . . . . 94 E4
Easterdown Hill
  Dinnington TA17. . . . . . . 195 B8
  Seavington St Mary TA19 . 184 E1
Easter La EX35. . . . . 122 B4
Eastermead La BS29. . . . . . 51 C3
Eastern Ave TA6 . . . . 209 D4
Eastern Ho BS23 . . . . 30 E1
EASTERTOWN. 67 D2
Eastertown BS24. . . . . 67 C1
Eastfield
  Bruton BA10. . . . . 215 F7
  20 Martock TA12 . . . . . . 185 E6
  Shepton Mallet BA4 . . . . 205 B6
  Yarlington BA9 . . . . 175 F8
Eastfield Ave BA1 . . . . 27 B2
Eastfield Cl **30** TA12 . . . . 185 E6
Eastfield Gdn **12** DT9 . . . 225 E4
Eastfield Gdns BS23 . . . . . . 30 F1
Eastfield La
  Barrington TA19 . . . . 184 D5
  Blackford BS28 . . . . 107 F6
  Ditcheat BA4 . . . . 159 C7
  East Chinnock BA22. . . . . 196 D8
  Hambridge TA3. . . . . 184 B8
  Lydford Fair Place TA11 . . 158 D3
  North Perrott TA18. . . . . 196 C4
  Norton Sub Hamdon BA22 . 185 F1
Eastfield Pk BS23 . . . . 30 F1
Eastfield Rd
  Hutton BS24. . . . . 49 E2
  Wincanton BA9 . . . . 216 D4
East Gate **11** TA1. . . . . . . 213 A4
Eastgate Gdns **10** TA1 . . . 213 A4
Easthams Rd TA18 . . . . . . 224 D6
EAST HARPTREE 74 E4
East Harptree CE VA Prim Sch
  BS40 . . . . 74 F4
Easthay La TA20. . . . . 199 A4
EAST HEWISH. 33 B6
EASTHILL. 120 B4
Easthill BA11. . . . . 120 B4
Easthill La BA7. . . . . 159 D5
EAST HUNTSPILL. 136 E7
East Huntspill Sch TA9. . . 136 E8
EAST KNOWSTONE 162 B2
East La TA18 . . . . 196 B7
EAST LAMBROOK. 220 C8
East Lambrook Manor Gdns ★
  TA13 . . . . 220 C8
East Lambrook Rd TA13 . . 220 D7
Eastland Rd BA21 . . . . 219 C5
East Lanes BA21 . . . . 187 D6
Eastlea BS21. . . . . 6 B1
East Lea Rd BA1. . . . . 44 A8
Eastleigh Cl
  Burnham-on-S TA8 . . . . . 104 C8
  Frome BA11. . . . . 120 A7
  Wiveliscombe TA4 . . . . . . 210 C5
Eastleigh Rd TA1. . . . . 213 B3
EAST LYDFORD 158 D2
EAST LYNG 170 D8
Eastlyn Rd BS13. . . . . 22 B8
East Mead BA3. . . . . 78 B2
Eastmead Ct BS9. . . . . 5 E4
Eastmead La BS9. . . . . 5 E4
East Mead La
  Street BA16. . . . . 207 F5
  Walton BA16 . . . . 156 E6
East Mere Cross EX16 . . . . 178 A2
East Mill Ct **11** DT9 . . . . . 225 E4
East Mill La DT9. . . . . 225 E4
Eastmoor La TA4. . . . . 164 E8
East Moor La TA10 . . . . . . 172 B3
Eastnor Rd BS14 . . . . 23 A3
EAST NYNEHEAD 167 D2
EASTON. 111 A4
Easton Ct BA3 . . . . 76 E1
Easton Farm La BA4 . . . . . 159 B8
Easton Hill BA5 . . . . 111 B3
Easton Ho **9** BA1. . . . . 28 C1
EASTON-IN-GORDANO. . . . 4 A4
Easton La
  Pylle BA4 . . . . 141 C1
  Sampford Peverell EX16 . . 178 D1
Easton Rd BS20 . . . . 4 C4
Easton Town La BA4 . . . . . 158 F4
Easton Trow La BA4 . . . . . 159 B5
Eastop La DT10 . . . . 190 A3
EASTOVER. 209 B5
Eastover
  Bridgwater TA6 . . . . 209 A5
  Langport TA10 . . . . 172 A6
Eastover Cl TA10 . . . . 172 A5
Eastover Com Prim Sch
  TA6 . . . . 209 B5
Eastover Gr BA2 . . . . 44 C1
Eastover Rd BS39 . . . . 59 D1
East Par BS9 . . . . 5 C6
EAST PENNARD 158 F8
EAST QUANTOXHEAD . . . 133 B6
East Quay TA6 . . . . 209 A6

East Quay Mews TA6. . . . . 209 A6
East Rd BA16 . . . . 207 E6
East Reach TA1 . . . . 213 A4
East Ride TA1 . . . . 86 B1
East Ridge Dr BS13 . . . . 21 F5
EAST ROLSTONE 33 B1
East Side La TA1. . . . . 136 F2
East Somerset Railway ★
  BA4. . . . . 205 F3
East Somerset Way BA5 . . 203 D3
East St
  Banwell BS29. . . . . 51 C3
  Bourton SP8. . . . . 161 F1
  Cannington TA5 . . . . 135 C2
  Chard TA20. . . . . 223 D4
  Crewkerne TA18. . . . . . . 224 C6
  Drayton TA10. . . . . 171 E3
  East Coker BA22 . . . . 197 B8
  Ilminster TA19 . . . . 221 C4
  Martock TA12. . . . . 185 E6
  Milborne Port DT9 . . . . . 217 D2
  North Perrott TA18. . . . . 196 C4
  Norton Sub Hamdon TA14. . 185 F1
  Shepton Montague BA9 . . 160 B2
  Taunton TA1 . . . . 212 F3
  Templecombe BA8 . . . . . . 176 F1
EAST STOKE 186 A4
East Stoke TA14. . . . . 185 F4
EAST STREET 139 F1
East Street Dro TA12 . . . . 185 E6
East Street La BA4 . . . . . . 140 A1
East Tapps La EX16 . . . . . 163 B2
EAST TOWN
  Lydeard St Lawrence 150 E3
  Shepton Mallet. 141 A3
East Town La TA4 . . . . 150 E3
East Town La (Platterwell La)
  BA4 . . . . 141 A3
EAST TWERTON 44 D7
Eastville
  Bath BA1 . . . . 28 B1
  Yeovil BA21 . . . . 219 C5
Eastville La BS27. . . . . 90 F1
EAST WATER. 92 F2
East Water La BA5 . . . . 92 F2
Eastway BS48 . . . . 8 E3
East Way BA2 . . . . 44 A5
Eastway Cl BS48 . . . . 8 D2
Eastway Sq BS48 . . . . 8 E3
Eastwell La BS25. . . . . 69 E6
Eastwick Ave TA2 . . . . 212 F7
Eastwick Rd TA2 . . . . 213 B7
Eastwood
  Bath BA2 . . . . 45 F6
  Sherborne BS40. . . . . 75 B2
Eastwood Cl
  Bridgwater TA6 . . . . 209 C4
  Frome BA11. . . . . 119 C4
  High Littleton BS39 . . . . . 59 C1
EAST WOODLANDS 144 A7
East Woodlands Rd BA11. . 144 A7
Eastwoods BA1 . . . . 29 B3
Eaton Cl BS14. . . . . 23 E5
Eaton Cres
  Bristol BS8. . . . . 226 A4
  Taunton TA2 . . . . 213 A6
Ebben La TA20 . . . . 194 F1
Ebbor Gorge Nature Reserve ★
  BA5. . . . . 111 D6
Ebbor Gorge Nature Trail ★
  BA5. . . . . 111 C5
Ebbor La BA5 . . . . 111 B5
Ebden Lo **15** BS22 . . . . 32 A2
EBDON. 32 B6
Ebdon La BS22. . . . . 32 C5
Ebdon Rd BS22. . . . . 31 F4
Ebenezer La BS9. . . . . 5 E5
Eckweek Gdns BA2. . . . . . . 79 D8
Eckweek La BA2 . . . . 79 E8
Eckweek Rd BA2 . . . . 79 D8
Ecos Ct BA11. . . . . 119 D4
Edbrooke Rd TA24 . . . . . . 147 C5
Edbrook La TA5 . . . . 134 F3
Eddington Ct BS23 . . . . 48 D7
Eden Croft BS22 . . . . 49 E8
Eden Park Cl BA1 . . . . 29 A4
Eden Park Dr BA1 . . . . 29 A4
Eden Terr BA1 . . . . 28 B2
Eden Villas **4** BA1 . . . . 28 C2
EDFORD. 116 C7
Edford Hill BA3 . . . . 116 C6
Edgar Bldgs BA1 . . . . 228 B3
EDGARLEY 139 E1
Edgarley Cl BA6. . . . . 206 F7
Edgarley Ct BS21. . . . . 6 C5
Edgarley Field La BA6 . . . . 157 E8
Edgarley Rd
  Glastonbury BA6 . . . . 139 D1
  West Pennard BA6. . . . . . 139 F1
EDGCOTT. 128 C1
Edgcott Rd TA24 . . . . 128 C1
Edgebury TA7. . . . . 136 E4
Edgecombe Ave BS22 . . . . . 31 D2
Edgecombe Mews BA1 . . . . 27 B1
Edgefield Cl BS14 . . . . 22 F3
Edgefield Rd BS14 . . . . 22 F3
Edgehill Rd BS21. . . . . 6 D6
Edgemoor Rd TA24. . . . . . 201 B4
Edgewood Cl BS14 . . . . 23 B8
Edgeworth Rd BA2 . . . . 44 C2
Edinburgh Pl **1** BS23. . . . . 48 E8
Edinburgh Rd
  Bridgwater TA6 . . . . 208 E2

Edinburgh Rd continued
Keynsham BS31 . . . . .24 E4
EDINGTON 137 C3
Edington Rd TA7 . . . . .137 D4
Edington Right Dro TA7 . .155 B7
EDINGWORTH 86 F7
Edingworth Rd BS24 . . . . . . .86 F7
Edith Cl TA8 . . . . .85 A2
EDITHMEAD 104 F7
Edmond's Hill TA11 . . . . . . .173 D4
Edmund Hill La BA6 . . . . . . .206 F6
Edmund Rd BS14 . . . . .23 A7
Edmunds Way BS27 . . . . .90 C7
Edward Cl BA22 . . . . .218 B6
Edward Ct BS31 . . . . .24 F4
Edward Rd BS21 . . . . .6 E5
Edward Rd S BS21 . . . . .6 E5
Edward Rd W BS21 . . . . .6 E6
Edward St
Bath, Bathwick BA2 . . . . . . .45 B7
Bath, Lower Weston BA1 . . .44 C7
Bridgwater TA6 . . . . .209 B5
Edwin Short Cl BS30 . . . . . . .25 E8
Egerton Rd BA2 . . . . .44 E4
EGFORD 119 B5
Egford Hill BA11 . . . . .119 C5
Egford La BA11 . . . . .119 C5
Egg Moor La EX13 . . . . .198 A7
Eggwood La TA13, TA16 . . . .195 E8
Eglin Croft BS13 . . . . .22 B4
Eglinton Rd BA16 . . . . .207 B4
Egremont Ct TA4 . . . . .202 D2
Egret Dr BS49 . . . . .16 F2
Egrove Way TA4 . . . . .202 E4
Eight Acre Dro TA7, TA9 . . .137 A5
Eight Acre La
Wellington TA21 . . . . .222 E5
Wootton Courtenay TA24 . .129 F8
Eighteen Arce La BA21 . . . .218 C6
Eighth Ave BS14 . . . . .23 A7
Eileen Cl BA16 . . . . .207 E5
Eirene Terr BS20 . . . . .4 D4
Elberton Rd BS9 . . . . .5 B7
Elborough Ave BS49 . . . . . . .34 B8
Elborough Gdns BS24 . . . . . .50 C3
Elborough La BA22 . . . . . . .186 F8
Elbridge Ho 3 BS2 . . . . . . .227 C3
Elderberry Wlk BS22 . . . . . . .31 F1
Elder Cl
Chard TA20 . . . . .223 C5
Frome BA11 . . . . .120 B3
Highbridge TA9 . . . . .104 D5
Eldergrove Cl TA6 . . . . .209 D7
Elder Ho TA8 . . . . .65 E2
Elderwood Rd BS14 . . . . .23 B7
Eldon Pl BA1 . . . . .28 B2
Eldred Cl BS9 . . . . .5 D5
Eleanor Cl BA2 . . . . .44 A5
Eleanor Cotts BA2 . . . . .44 A6
Electric Ho TA14 . . . . .185 C4
Eleven Ct TA6 . . . . .208 E4
Elfrida Terr BA5 . . . . .203 A5
Elgar Cl
Bristol BS4 . . . . .22 D6
Clevedon BS21 . . . . .6 E1
Elgin Cl BA16 . . . . .207 B5
Eliot Cl BS23 . . . . .49 A3
Eliotts Dr BA21 . . . . .218 E7
Elizabeth Cl BS24 . . . . .49 D3
Elizabeth Ct
Burnham-on-S TA8 . . . . . . .104 B6
4 Martock TA12 . . . . .185 E6
Elizabeth Flats BA21 . . . . . .219 C6
Elizabeth Gdns 16 BA8 . . . .190 A6
Elizabeth Way
Bridgwater TA6 . . . . .209 C5
Chard TA20 . . . . .223 C5
Ellbridge Cl BS9 . . . . .5 D5
Ellenborough Cres BS23 . . . .48 E6
Ellenborough Ct BS23 . . . . . .48 E6
Ellenborough Ho BS8 . . . . . .226 A2
Ellenborough Park Rd
BS23 . . . . .48 E6
Ellenborough Pk N BS23 . . . .48 D6
Ellenborough Pk S BS23 . . . .48 D6
Ellen Cl 8 TA6 . . . . .153 F4
Ellen Ho BA2 . . . . .44 A5
Ellersdown La TA22 . . . . . . .163 E4
Ellesmere Rd
Bristol BS4 . . . . .23 D8
Weston-super-Mare BS23 . . .48 D2
Ellfield Cl BS13 . . . . .21 F6
Ellick Rd BS40 . . . . .54 D1
ELLICOMBE 201 C4
Ellicombe La TA24 . . . . .201 C4
Ellicombe Mdw TA24 . . . . . .201 C4
Elliot Cl BA11 . . . . .119 F6
ELLIOTS GREEN 144 B8
Elliots La BA11 . . . . .119 B8
Elliott's Hill BA22 . . . . .196 D7
Ellis Ave BS13 . . . . .22 A8
Elliscombe Pk BA9 . . . . .176 B6
Ellis Gr TA2 . . . . .168 B5
Ellis Pk BS22 . . . . .32 C4
Ellis's La TA5 . . . . .152 C6
Elliston Dr BA2 . . . . .44 B4
Ellsbridge Cl BS31 . . . . .25 B5
Ellworthy Ct BA11 . . . . .120 B4
Elm Ave TA8 . . . . .104 B6
Elmbrook BA1 . . . . .44 D8
Elm Cl
Banwell BS29 . . . . .50 E4
Broadway TA19 . . . . .183 C2
Nailsea BS48 . . . . .8 C1

Elm Cl continued
Star BS25 . . . . .52 D1
Wells BA5 . . . . .203 A4
Yatton BS49 . . . . .34 B7
Elm Ct
Bristol BS14 . . . . .23 A6
Keynsham BS31 . . . . .24 C4
Elm Dr BA9 . . . . .216 C3
Elm Farm BS48 . . . . .9 A2
Elm Gr
Bath, Larkhill BA1 . . . . .28 C2
Bath, The Oval BA2 . . . . . . .44 C4
Locking BS24 . . . . .49 F4
Minehead TA24 . . . . .201 A5
Taunton TA1 . . . . .212 E5
Elmgrove Cl TA6 . . . . .209 D7
Elmham Way BS24 . . . . .32 B1
Elm Hayes BS13 . . . . .21 F6
Elmhurst Ave BA21 . . . . .219 B7
Elmhurst Est
Batheaston BA1 . . . . .29 A4
Batheaston BA1 . . . . .29 A5
Elmhurst Gdns BS41 . . . . . . .20 F8
Elmhurst Jun Sch BA16 . . . .207 D6
Elmhurst La BA16 . . . . .207 D6
Elmhurst Rd BS24 . . . . .49 E2
Elmhyrst Rd BS23 . . . . .48 F8
Elm La
Great Elm BA11 . . . . .119 A6
Shalford BA9 . . . . .216 B7
Woolavington TA7 . . . . . . .136 F4
Elmlea Ave BS9 . . . . .5 F5
Elm Lea Cl TA7 . . . . .136 C4
Elmlea Jun & Inf Schs BS9 . . .5 F5
Elmleigh BA21 . . . . .218 C7
Elm Leigh BA11 . . . . .120 C6
Elmleigh Rd 21 TA12 . . . . . .185 E6
Elm Lodge BS48 . . . . .9 B2
Elm Pk TA1 . . . . .212 E5
Elm Pl BA2 . . . . .44 F4
Elm Rd BS39 . . . . .77 E5
Elms Cl TA1 . . . . .212 E5
Elms Est TA2 . . . . .213 F8
Elmside Rd BA16 . . . . .207 D5
Elmslade La BA7 . . . . .214 B7
Elmsleigh Rd BS23 . . . . .48 E4
Elmsley La BS22 . . . . .31 C5
Elms Rd TA21 . . . . .222 F5
Elm St TA20 . . . . .223 C5
Elms The
Banwell BS29 . . . . .51 A4
Bath, Lambridge BA1 . . . . . .28 C2
Bath, Weston Park BA1 . . . .27 C1
Elmswood BS23 . . . . .48 F8
Elm Terr BA3 . . . . .97 C8
Elm Tree Ave
Nailsea BS48 . . . . .8 A4
Radstock BA3 . . . . .78 D1
Elmtree Dr BS13 . . . . .21 F5
Elm Tree Pk BS20 . . . . .3 D3
Elm Tree Rd
Clevedon BS21 . . . . .6 D2
Locking BS24 . . . . .50 A4
Elmvale Dr BS24 . . . . .49 F3
Elm View
Midsomer Norton BA3 . . . . .78 B1
Temple Cloud BS39 . . . . . . .58 E1
Elm Way BA4 . . . . .205 A6
Elm Wlk
Portishead BS20 . . . . .2 C4
Yatton BS49 . . . . .34 B7
Elmwood Ave TA6 . . . . .208 F3
Elmwood Sch TA6 . . . . .208 F3
Elsbert Dr BS13 . . . . .21 E6
Elscombe La
Timberscombe TA24 . . . . . .130 A4
Wootton Courtenay TA24 . .129 F4
Elton Ho 2 BS2 . . . . .227 C3
Elton Rd
Bristol BS8 . . . . .226 C3
Clevedon BS21 . . . . .6 C3
Weston-super-Mare BS22 . . .32 A4
Elton St BS2 . . . . .227 C4
Elvard Cl BS13 . . . . .22 A4
Elvard Rd BS13 . . . . .22 A4
Elwell La BS40, BS41 . . . . . . .21 A1
ELWORTHY 150 C6
Elworthy Cross TA4 . . . . . . .150 C5
Elworthy Dr TA21 . . . . .222 D4
Elworthy La TA4 . . . . .150 C5
Ely Gr BS9 . . . . .5 B7
Embankment The TA10 . . . .172 A5
Embden Walk 4 BA4 . . . . . .209 A1
Embercourt Dr BS48 . . . . . . .19 A6
Emblett La TA10 . . . . .156 F3
EMBOROUGH 95 C3
Emborough Pond La BA3 . . .95 D2
Emerald Wy TA7 . . . . .209 C8
Emery Gate BS29 . . . . .51 B3
Emlet DT9 . . . . .187 E1
Emletts Way BA21 . . . . .218 B8
Emley La BS40 . . . . .54 B6
Emlyn Cl 6 BS22 . . . . .32 B4
Emmanuel Ct BS8 . . . . .226 A4
Emmett Wood BS14 . . . . .23 B3
Empress Menen Gdns BA1 . .44 A8
Enderleigh Gdns BS25 . . . . . .52 F4
Enfield Dr BA4 . . . . .141 E2
Enfield Rd BA4 . . . . .141 E2
Engine Dro TA7 . . . . .154 F1
Engine La BS48 . . . . .18 B8
England's La TA17 . . . . .195 D8
Englands Mead BA22 . . . . . .174 F3
Englands Rd TA24 . . . . .124 A3

Englands Way TA20 . . . . . . .223 D6
ENGLISHCOMBE 43 F2
Englishcombe La BA2 . . . . . .44 C3
Englishcombe Rd BS13 . . . . .22 C3
Englishcombe Rise BA2 . . . .44 A3
Englishcombe Tithe Barn★
BA2 . . . . .43 F2
Englishcombe Way BA2 . . . .44 E3
ENMORE 153 A6
Enmore BA20 . . . . .49 A2
Enmore Cl TA8 . . . . .104 C8
Enmore Rd
Bridgwater TA5 . . . . .153 B6
Taunton TA2 . . . . .212 F7
Enmore VC Prim Sch TA5 . .152 F5
Ennerdale Cl BS23 . . . . .49 A5
Ensleigh Ave BA1 . . . . .27 E4
Enterprise Ctr The BS24 . . . .49 A3
Enterprise Mews BA20 . . . . .218 D3
Enterprise Trade Ctr BS4 . . . .22 E7
Entry Hill BA2 . . . . .44 F2
Entry Hill Dr BA2 . . . . .44 F3
Entry Hill Gdns BA2 . . . . . . .44 F2
Entry Hill Pk BA2 . . . . .44 F2
Entry Rise BA2 . . . . .44 F1
Erin Wlk BS4 . . . . .22 D8
Ermine St BA21 . . . . .218 D7
Ermine Way BS11 . . . . .4 C7
Ernest Ashman Pl TA20 . . . .223 D5
Ervine Terr BS2 . . . . .227 C4
ESCOTT 150 C8
Escott Cl TA6 . . . . .208 F6
Escott La TA4 . . . . .132 D1
Esgar Rise BS22 . . . . .31 E3
Eskdale Cl BS22 . . . . .49 D8
Eskimo Ct BA16 . . . . .207 B5
Esmonde Dr BA22 . . . . .173 E2
Esmond Gr BS21 . . . . .6 D4
Esplanade
Burnham-on-S TA8 . . . . . . .104 A7
Minehead TA24 . . . . .201 A7
Esplanade La TA23 . . . . .202 C7
Esplanade Rd BS20 . . . . .2 C7
Esplanade The TA23 . . . . . . .202 C7
Essex Cl TA20 . . . . .223 C4
Essex Ct TA1 . . . . .212 C2
Essex Dr TA1 . . . . .212 C2
Estuary Ho BS20 . . . . .2 E7
Estuary Pk TA5 . . . . .135 B5
Estune Wlk BS41 . . . . .11 A2
Esworthy Cross EX16 . . . . . .162 F1
Ethel St BA5 . . . . .203 C3
Ethpark Gr 1 TA2 . . . . .212 F6
Etonhurst BS23 . . . . .48 D6
Eton La BS29 . . . . .50 E7
Eton Rd TA8 . . . . .104 B6
Etsome Cl TA11 . . . . .211 C4
Etsome Hill TA11 . . . . .211 B3
Etsome Rd TA11 . . . . .211 C5
Etsome Terr TA11 . . . . .211 C4
Ettlingen Way BS21 . . . . .6 F2
Eugene Flats 7 BS2 . . . . . . .227 A4
Eugene St
Bristol, Kingsdown BS2 . . . .227 A4
Bristol, St Pauls BS2, BS5 . .227 C4
Eva Turner Cl BS14 . . . . .23 C6
Eveleigh Ave BA1 . . . . .28 D2
Evelyn Rd BA1 . . . . .44 B8
Evelyn Terr 12 BA1 . . . . .28 A1
Evenlode Gdns BS11 . . . . .4 F5
Evenlode Way BS31 . . . . .25 A3
EVERCREECH 141 E1
Evercreech CE Prim Sch
Evercreech BA4 . . . . .141 E2
Evercreech BA4 . . . . .141 E2
Evercreech Rd BS14 . . . . .23 B4
Evercreech Way TA9 . . . . . .104 F2
Everett Cl BA5 . . . . .112 E1
Evergreen Cl BS25 . . . . .51 F1
Evergreen Path TA16 . . . . . .195 F7
Everton Rd BS20 . . . . .219 A4
Evesham Ave BA21 . . . . .218 C6
Evesham Dr TA6 . . . . .209 A1
Ewart Rd BS22 . . . . .49 C8
Ewell Cl TA19 . . . . .183 C1
Exbourne 10 BS22 . . . . .32 A2
Exbury Cl TA8 . . . . .104 C7
Excelsior St BA2 . . . . .45 B5
Excelsior Terr BA3 . . . . .78 B1
Exchange Ave BS1 . . . . .227 A2
EXEBRIDGE 163 F3
Exebridge Ind Est TA22 . . . .163 F3
Exeter Cl
Burnham-on-S TA8 . . . . . . .104 C7
Nether Stowey TA5 . . . . . .134 B2
Exeter Rd
Portishead BS20 . . . . .2 E4
Rockwell Green TA21 . . . . .222 B5
Weston-super-Mare BS23 . . .48 E5
Exeter Road Cvn Pk TA21 . .222 A4
EXFORD 128 D1
Exford CE Fst sch TA24 . . . .128 D1
Exford Cl BS23 . . . . .48 F2
Exford Rd TA24 . . . . .147 C6
Exmoor Cl BA3 . . . . .97 B6
Exmoor Gdns TA22 . . . . .163 D6
Exmoor Owl & Hawk Centre★
TA24 . . . . .124 B4
Exmoor Pony Centre The★
TA22 . . . . .147 A1
Exmoor Rd BA2 . . . . .44 F2
Exmoor Way TA24 . . . . .200 E6
Exmouth Rd BS4 . . . . .22 F8
Explore La BS1 . . . . .226 C2
Express Pk TA6 . . . . .136 A2
EXTON 147 E4
Exton BS24 . . . . .49 A2

Exton Cl BS14 . . . . .23 B5
Exton La TA22 . . . . .147 E4
Eyer's La BS2 . . . . .227 C3
Eyers Rd BS24 . . . . .49 F7
EYEWELL 174 E4

F

Faber Gr BS13 . . . . .22 C4
Factory Hill SP8 . . . . .161 F2
Factory La
East Huntspill TA9 . . . . . . .136 E8
Tatworth TA20 . . . . .198 D8
FAILAND 10 C3
Failand Cres BS9 . . . . .5 C5
Failand La
Easton-in-G BS8 . . . . .4 A1
Portbury BS20 . . . . .3 F2
Failand Wlk BS9 . . . . .5 C6
Fairacre Cl BS24 . . . . .50 B4
Fair Ash BS40 . . . . .74 D7
Fair Cl BA2 . . . . .81 E4
Fairclose TA20 . . . . .193 D6
Fair Cross TA23 . . . . .131 F2
Faircross La SN14 . . . . .13 D8
Fairdean Rd TA9 . . . . .104 E4
Fairend La TA20 . . . . .193 A8
Fairfax Cl TA6 . . . . .209 C6
Fairfax Rd TA6 . . . . .209 C5
Fairfax St BS1 . . . . .227 B3
Fairfield
Coleford BA3 . . . . .116 E8
Crewkerne TA18 . . . . .224 B5
Ilminster TA19 . . . . .221 A4
7 Martock TA12 . . . . .185 E6
Rode BA11 . . . . .82 F1
Sampford Peverell EX16 . . .178 D1
Sherborne DT9 . . . . .225 D5
Somerton TA11 . . . . .211 E4
Tunley BA2 . . . . .61 A3
Yarlington BA9 . . . . .175 F7
Fairfield Ave BA1 . . . . .28 A2
Fairfield Cl
Backwell BS48 . . . . .19 D7
Frome BA11 . . . . .120 A7
Marshfield SN14 . . . . .13 F8
Weston-super-Mare BS22 . . .31 B1
Fairfield Dr TA4 . . . . .202 E4
Fairfield Gdns BA6 . . . . .206 D4
Fairfield Gn TA3 . . . . .192 A7
Fairfield Hts DT9 . . . . .225 D5
Fairfield Mdws BA14 . . . . . . .83 F3
FAIRFIELD PARK 28 A2
Fairfield Park Rd BA1 . . . . . .28 A2
Fairfield Rd
Bath BA1 . . . . .28 B1
Taunton TA2 . . . . .213 B7
Fairfield Sch BS48 . . . . .19 C6
Fairfield Terr
Bath BA1 . . . . .28 A1
Fitzhead TA4 . . . . .166 F5
Peasedown St John BA2 . . . .79 C7
Fairfield View BA1 . . . . .28 A2
Fairfield Way
Backwell BS48 . . . . .19 C6
Saltford BS31 . . . . .25 B4
Fairford Cl TA9 . . . . .104 E4
Fairford Rd
Bristol BS11 . . . . .4 D7
Highbridge TA9 . . . . .104 E4
Fair Furlong BS13 . . . . .22 A4
Fair Furlong Prim Sch
Bishopsworth BS13 . . . . . . .22 B4
Bristol BS13 . . . . .22 B4
Fair Hill BS25 . . . . .70 F8
Fairhouse Rd BA22 . . . . .197 F8
Fairlands Mid Sch BS27 . . . . .90 C7
Fairlands Way BS27 . . . . .90 C7
Fairmead Rd BA21 . . . . .219 C8
Fairmead Sch BA21 . . . . .219 C8
Fairmont Terr 7 DT9 . . . . . .225 E4
Fair Pl TA11 . . . . .158 D3
Fairseat Workshops BS40 . . .56 E7
Fairview
Mells BA11 . . . . .118 B7
Weston-super-Mare BS22 . . .31 F4
Fair View BA10 . . . . .161 A4
Fairview Ho BS9 . . . . .5 F8
Fairview Terr
Taunton TA1 . . . . .168 D1
Yeovilton BA22 . . . . .187 A8
Fairwater Cl TA2 . . . . .212 D6
Fairway BS4 . . . . .23 D8
Fairway Cl
Berrow TA8 . . . . .84 F4
Weston-super-Mare BS22 . . .31 B2
Fairway Rise TA20 . . . . .223 E5
Fairways
Charlcombe BA1 . . . . .27 E4
Saltford BS31 . . . . .25 E2
Wells BA5 . . . . .203 C4
Fairways Cvn Pk TA7 . . . . . .136 E3
Fairways The TA1 . . . . .212 F1
Fairway View BA21 . . . . .219 D6
Fairwood Rd BA13 . . . . .102 F5
Fairy Hill BS39 . . . . .41 D6
Fakeham Rd BS24 . . . . .66 F8
Falcon Cl
Bristol, Westbury on T BS9 . . .5 F8
Portishead BS20 . . . . .2 D4
1 Radstock BA3 . . . . .97 B8
Falcon Cres BS22 . . . . .49 D8
Falcon Ct TA1 . . . . .212 C4
Falcondale Rd BS9 . . . . .5 F7
Falconer Rd BA1 . . . . .27 A3

Falcon Rd BA22 . . . . .218 A5
Falconsmead Wlk BA21 . . . .219 D8
Falkland Ho 7 TA18 . . . . . . .224 C6
Falkland Sq 6 TA18 . . . . . . .224 C6
Falklands Rise TA24 . . . . . . .200 D7
Fallow Dr TA9 . . . . .104 D2
Fallowfield
Blagdon BS40 . . . . .54 E2
Weston-super-Mare BS22 . . .31 F3
Falmouth Cl BS48 . . . . .9 A1
Fannybrooks La DT9 . . . . . . .187 F1
Fanshawe Rd BS14 . . . . .23 A7
Faraday Rd 2 BS8 . . . . .11 F5
FARLEIGH 19 D7
Farleigh Ct BS48 . . . . .20 B8
Farleigh Further Ed Coll 3
BA11 . . . . .119 F5
FARLEIGH HUNGERFIRD 82 E8
Farleigh Hungerford Castle★
BA2 . . . . .82 E8
Farleigh La
Hinton Charterhouse BA2 . . .63 F1
Westwood BA2 . . . . .64 A1
Farleigh Rd
Backwell BS48 . . . . .19 C6
Clevedon BS21 . . . . .6 B1
Keynsham BS31 . . . . .24 D4
Norton St Philip BA2 . . . . . .81 F5
Farleigh Rise
Monkton Farleigh BA15 . . . .29 E1
Monkton Farleigh BA15 . . . .46 E8
Farleigh View BA15 . . . . .64 F3
FARLEIGH WICK 46 E4
Farleigh Wlk BS13 . . . . .22 A8
Farler's End BS48 . . . . .18 F8
FARLEY 1 B1
Farley Cl BA11 . . . . .120 C6
Farley Dell BA3 . . . . .116 E8
FARMBOROUGH 60 B6
Farmborough CE VA Prim Sch
BA2 . . . . .59 F6
Farmborough La BA2 . . . . . . .60 E6
Farm Cl
Somerton TA11 . . . . .211 B3
Westbury-sub-Mendip BA5 . .110 D6
Weston-super-Mare BS22 . . .32 C4
Farm Ct TA13 . . . . .220 C5
Farm Dr TA11 . . . . .211 B3
Farmer Rd BS13 . . . . .21 E4
Farm Hill TA7 . . . . .156 B8
Farmhouse Cl 7 BA22 . . . . . . .8 E2
Farmhouse Ct 1 BS48 . . . . . . .8 E1
Farmhouse Dr BA11 . . . . . . .119 F7
Farm La
Buckland St Mary TA20 . . . .182 A2
Coultings TA5 . . . . .134 E4
Stogursey TA5 . . . . .134 D4
Street BA16 . . . . .207 C7
Wellow BA2 . . . . .62 E1
Farm Orch DT9 . . . . .188 C7
Farm Rd
Bradford Abbas DT9 . . . . . .187 E1
Doulting BA4 . . . . .141 E5
Hutton BS24 . . . . .49 E2
Street BA16 . . . . .207 C6
Weston-super-Mare BS22 . . .31 B4
Farm St
Highbridge TA9 . . . . .104 D2
Tintinhull BA22 . . . . .186 C6
Farm View TA2 . . . . .168 F6
Farmwell Cl BS13 . . . . .22 B5
Farnaby Cl BS4 . . . . .22 C7
Farnborough Rd BS24 . . . . . .50 C4
Farncombe La BA9 . . . . .160 B1
Farndale Rd BS22 . . . . .49 D8
Farrant Cl
Baltonsborough BA6 . . . . . .158 A5
Bristol BS4 . . . . .22 D4
Taunton TA1 . . . . .212 A4
Farrant Rd BA11 . . . . .119 D5
Farrier Wy BS14 . . . . .23 D3
Farringdon Hill La TA5 . . . . .134 D6
Farringdon La TA5 . . . . .153 D2
Farrington Fields
BS39 . . . . .77 C3
Farrington Fields Trad Est
BS39 . . . . .77 C3
FARRINGTON GURNEY 77 A3
Farrington Gurney By-Pass
BS39 . . . . .77 A3
Farrington Gurney CE Prim
Sch BS39 . . . . .77 A4
Farrington La BA4 . . . . .141 C4
Farrington Rd BS39 . . . . .77 C5
Farrington Way BS39 . . . . . . .77 C4
Farrow Cl TA20 . . . . .223 D3
Farrs La BA2 . . . . .45 B2
Farr's La BS1 . . . . .227 A2
Farr's Orch 6 TA16 . . . . .195 F7
Farr St BS11 . . . . .4 B8
Farthing Combe BS26 . . . . . .70 D2
Farthing Down TA21 . . . . . . .179 E7
Farthing Rd TA6 . . . . .208 E1
Farthing Row BA11 . . . . .82 E1
Farthings Cl TA21 . . . . .167 C2
Farthings Paddock BA7 . . . .159 A3
Farthing's Pitts TA21 . . . . . .222 C4
Fashion Mus★ BA1 . . . . . . .228 B3
FAULKLAND 80 E2
Faulkland La BA2, BA3 . . . . . .80 C4
Faulkland Rd BA2 . . . . .44 D5
Faulkland View BA2 . . . . .79 E7
Faversham Dr BS24 . . . . .49 A1
Fawcus Pl TA20 . . . . .223 C4
Fawn Cl BA6 . . . . .206 C3
Fayre Way BA5 . . . . .204 B7
Fearnville Est BS21 . . . . .6 C2

Featherbed La
Chew Stoke BS40 . . . . .38 A3
Clayhanger EX16 . . . . .165 C1
Clutton BS39 . . . . .58 C6
Fedden Village BS21 . . . . . . 1 F5
Feeder Rd BS2 . . . . .227 C1
Fellowsmead DT10 . . . . . . .190 F5
Felon's Oak La TA24 . . . . . .131 B1
Felsberg Cl BA11 . . . . .119 E3
Felsberg Way BS27 . . . . . . .90 C7
Feltham Dr BA11 . . . . .120 A3
Feltham La BA11 . . . . .144 B8
FELTON 37 C8
Felton Gr BS13 . . . . .22 A8
Felton La BS40 . . . . .37 C7
Felton St BS40 . . . . .37 C7
Fender Cl TA5 . . . . .135 B5
Feniton 6 BS22 . . . . .32 A2
Fennel La BS26 . . . . .70 B2
Fennel Rd BS20 . . . . 3 A5
Fennel Way BA22 . . . . .218 A5
Fenners BS22 . . . . .32 A4
FENNINGTON 168 B8
Fennington La TA2 . . . . . . .168 B8
Fenns La BS41 . . . . .10 E1
FENNY CASTLE 139 D7
Fenshurst Gdns BS41 . . . . . 20 F8
Fenswood Cl BS41 . . . . . . .10 E1
Fenswood Ct BS41 . . . . . . .10 E1
Fenswood Mead BS41 . . . . .10 E1
Fenswood Rd BS41 . . . . . . .10 E1
Fenton Cl BS31 . . . . .25 D3
Ferenberge Cl BA2 . . . . 60 A6
Ferguson Cl TA5 . . . . .134 A3
Fermoy BA11 . . . . .120 B6
Fern Cl BA3 . . . . .78 B1
Ferndale Dr TA1 . . . . .168 D1
Ferndale Gdns BA21 . . . . .218 E6
Ferndale Rd
  Bath BA1 . . . . .28 C3
  Portishead BS20 . . . . 2 D6
Ferndown Cl
  Bristol BS11 . . . . 5 A7
  Taunton TA1 . . . . .212 D1
Ferne Animal Sanctuary*
TA20 . . . . .193 A2
Ferney Leaze La BS39 . . . . .59 C3
Fern Gr BS48 . . . . .18 C8
Fern Lea BS24 . . . . .67 B6
Fernlea Gdns BS20 . . . . 4 B4
Fernlea Rd BS22 . . . . .49 C7
Fernleigh Ave TA6 . . . . . . .209 A3
Fernleigh Cl BA4 . . . . .141 E1
Fern Lodge BS23 . . . . .48 D6
Fernside BS48 . . . . .19 A7
Fernsteed Rd BS13 . . . . . . .21 F6
Ferry Ct BA2 . . . . .45 B6
Ferry La
  Bath BA2 . . . . .45 B6
  Lympsham BS24 . . . . .67 C3
Ferryman Rd BA6 . . . . .206 E7
Ferryman's Ct BS2 . . . . . . .227 B2
Ferry St BS1 . . . . .227 B2
Fersfield BA2 . . . . .45 B3
Festival Units TA6 . . . . . . .209 B1
Feversham Ave TA6 . . . . . .208 E6
Feversham Ct BA22 . . . . . .173 E2
Feversham La BA6 . . . . . . .206 D5
Feversham Way TA2 . . . . . .213 A8
FIDDINGTON 134 D3
Fiddington Rd TA5 . . . . . . .134 D2
Fiddle La BA22 . . . . .174 F1
Fiddlers Green Rd DT9 . . . .175 E1
Fideoak Mill TA4 . . . . .168 B4
FIELD 205 C5
Field Cl BA3 . . . . .116 A3
Field End
  Axminster EX13 . . . . .198 A1
  Minehead TA24 . . . . .201 A5
Fielders The BS22 . . . . .32 B4
Fieldfare Ave BS20 . . . . 3 A6
Fieldfare Cl BS31 . . . . .24 C3
Fieldfare Gdns BS49 . . . . . .16 F2
Fieldgardens Rd BS39 . . . . .58 F1
Field Gate TA3 . . . . .183 C8
Fieldgate La TA3 . . . . .183 B8
Field Grove La BS30 . . . . . .25 C8
Fielding Ct BA21 . . . . .219 C6
Fielding Ho BA2 . . . . .44 A6
Fielding Path BA6 . . . . . . .206 E6
Fielding Rd
  Street BA16 . . . . .207 B7
  Yeovil BA21 . . . . .219 C6
Fielding's Rd BA2 . . . . .44 C6
Fieldins BA15 . . . . .64 E7
Field La
  Chewton Mendip BA3 . . . .94 F8
  Kington Magna SP8 . . . . .177 E1
  Penselwood BA9 . . . . . . .161 D2
Field Lane TA7 . . . . .136 D3
Field Marshal Slim Ct 24
BS2 . . . . .227 C3
Field Rd TA10 . . . . .156 A1
Fields End TA1 . . . . .213 C2
Fields The BS22 . . . . .32 D2
Field View BA4 . . . . .205 C5
Field View Ct BA4 . . . . . . .141 E1
Fieldway BS25 . . . . .52 B4
Field Way TA9 . . . . .104 D5
Fifehead Bsns Ctr (Manor
  Farm Trad Est) BA8 . . . . .190 F8
Fifehead Hill BA8 . . . . . . .190 F8
FIFEHEAD MAGDALEN 190 F8
Fifth Ave BS14 . . . . .23 B7
Fig Tree Cres TA6 . . . . . . .208 D1
Filer Cl BA2 . . . . .79 D8
Filers Wy BS24 . . . . .32 C1
Fillymead DT10 . . . . .190 F5

Filwood Broadway BS4 . . . .22 E8
FILWOOD PARK 22 E8
Finch Cl
  Houndstone BA22 . . . . . .218 A6
  Shepton Mallet BA4 . . . . .204 F6
  Weston-super-Mare BS22 . .49 E8
Finches The
  4 Portishead BS20 . . . . . . 2 F6
  Portishead BS20 . . . . 3 A6
Finches Way TA8 . . . . .85 B1
Finger Cnr DT10 . . . . .190 F5
Finger La DT9 . . . . .225 D3
Finisterre Parade BS20 . . . . 2 F6
Finmere Gdns BS22 . . . . . . .32 A4
Fircliff Pk BS20 . . . . 2 D7
Fire House Mews BA9 . . . . .216 C3
FIREPOOL 213 A5
Firepool Cres TA1 . . . . . . .213 A5
Firepool Vw TA1 . . . . .213 A5
Firgrove La BA2 . . . . .61 B1
Fir La BS40 . . . . .72 B5
Fir Leaze BS48 . . . . 8 B1
Firs Ct BS31 . . . . .24 C4
First Ave
  Axminster EX13 . . . . .198 A2
  Bath BA2 . . . . .44 A4
  Bristol BS14 . . . . .23 A7
  Portbury BS20 . . . . 3 E5
  Radstock BA3 . . . . .97 C8
Firs The
  Bath BA2 . . . . .45 B1
  Langport TA10 . . . . .172 A5
  Limpley Stoke BA3 . . . . . .64 A5
  Wheddon Cross TA24 . . . .129 E1
First Ho BA16 . . . . .207 B6
First Sedgemoor Dro
TA10 . . . . .155 E4
Fir Tor Ave BA5 . . . . .203 C5
Fir Tree Ave
  Paulton BS39 . . . . .77 F4
  Weston-super-Mare BS24 . .49 E4
Firtree Cl TA5 . . . . .134 A2
Fir Tree Cl TA6 . . . . .209 D4
Firway Cross EX16 . . . . . . .164 C3
Firwood Rd BA11 . . . . .119 E4
Fishers Brook BA11 . . . . . .120 A5
Fishers Cl DT9 . . . . .187 F5
Fisher's Hill
  Glastonbury BA6 . . . . . . .206 D4
  Holywell Lake TA21 . . . . .179 D7
Fisher's La
  Dinnington TA17 . . . . . . .195 A7
  Mark TA9 . . . . .106 D5
Fishers Mead TA22 . . . . . . .163 D6
Fisherway La TA19 . . . . . . .195 A5
FISHPOND BOTTOM 199 A1
Fishpond Bottom Rd DT6 .199 A1
Fishwell La BA6 . . . . .157 C7
Fitzharding Ho 8 BS1 . . . .227 A3
Fitzharding Rd BS20 . . . . . . 4 E3
FITZHEAD 166 F7
FITZROY 168 A6
Fitzroy Circ BS20 . . . . 2 F6
Fitzroy Ho 3 BA2 . . . . . . .228 C3
Fivash Cl TA1 . . . . .168 D1
Five Acres 6 BA22 . . . . . .197 F8
Five Arches Cl BA3 . . . . . . .78 C2
Five Ashes BA22 . . . . .186 C2
Five Barrows Cross EX36 . .145 B7
Five Bells TA23 . . . . .202 B5
Five Bells La TA23 . . . . . . .202 B5
Five C Bsns Ctr BS21 . . . . . . 6 B1
Five Cross Way TA21 . . . . .180 F6
Five Cross Ways TA22 . . . .162 F7
Five Dials TA19 . . . . .183 C1
FIVEHEAD 170 F2
Fivehead Dro TA3 . . . . . . .170 F3
Five Hos TA21 . . . . .222 B8
Five Lords TA5 . . . . .134 B2
Fiveways Cl BS27 . . . . .90 A7
Fiveways Rdbt BA21 . . . . . .219 A6
Fiveways Sch BA21 . . . . . .219 D6
Five Yards 3 TA4 . . . . .167 F8
Flagstaff Rd BS13 . . . . .68 D7
Flamingo Cres BS22 . . . . . .49 E8
Flat The BS39 . . . . .58 D5
Flatts La BS39 . . . . .59 C4
Flatwoods Cres BA2 . . . . . .45 F3
Flatwoods Rd BA2 . . . . .45 F3
FLAX BOURTON 19 F7
Flax Bourton CE Prim Sch
BS48 . . . . .19 F8
Flax Bourton Rd BS8 . . . . . .10 B3
Flaxfield Dr TA18 . . . . .224 C5
Flax La DT9 . . . . .187 F4
Flax Meadow La 12 EX13 . .198 A1
FLAXPOOL 151 C6
Flaxpool Hill TA4 . . . . .151 C6
Flax Row TA18 . . . . .224 C7
Flax Way BA21 . . . . .218 C6
Fleed Cross TA4 . . . . .166 A6
Fleet Air Arm Mus* BA22 .174 B3
Fletcher Ct TA2 . . . . .213 B8
Fletcher's La BS26 . . . . .87 D6
Fleur De Lys Dr BA14 . . . . .83 F4
Flingers La BA9 . . . . .216 D4
Flint Cross TA4 . . . . .149 C1
Flints Cl BA11 . . . . .119 D4
Flora's Ride TA24 . . . . .129 A7
Florence Cl 3 TA6 . . . . . . .208 E7
Florence Gr BS22 . . . . .49 B8
Florida Fields BA7 . . . . . . .214 B6
Florida St BA7 . . . . .214 C5
Florida Terr BA7 . . . . .78 C2
Flowerdale Rd TA23 . . . . . .202 C6
Flowerdown Bridge BS22 . .49 D7
Flowerdown Rd BS24 . . . . .50 D4

Flowerfield BA11 . . . . .143 B8
Flowers Hill BS4 . . . . .23 E8
Flowers Ho 1 BA2 . . . . . . .219 B4
Flowerstone BA3 . . . . .114 D7
Flowerwell Rd BS13 . . . . . .22 B5
Flushing Mdw BA21 . . . . . .219 E5
FODDINGTON 174 E8
Foddington Rd TA11 . . . . .174 F8
Foghamshire La BA11 . . . .143 D6
Foldhill 25 TA12 . . . . .185 E6
Foldhill La
  Ash BA22 . . . . .186 A6
  Martock TA12 . . . . .185 E6
Folke TA5 . . . . .189 A1
Folleigh Cl BS41 . . . . .11 B2
Folleigh Dr BS41 . . . . .11 B2
Folleigh La BS41 . . . . .11 B2
Follett Cl TA21 . . . . .222 C8
Folliott Rd BA6 . . . . .206 E6
Folly Cl
  Cannington TA5 . . . . .135 B2
  Midsomer Norton BA3 . . . .96 E7
Folly Dr BA4 . . . . .159 C7
Folly Dro TA19 . . . . .183 A5
Folly Farm Nature Reserve*
BS39 . . . . .58 B5
Folly Fields BA21 . . . . .219 B7
Folly La
  Buckland St Mary TA20 . .182 E1
  Kington Magna SP8 . . . . .177 F2
  Nether Compton DT9 . . . .187 F4
  North Wootton BA4 . . . . .140 C4
  Shipham BS25 . . . . .70 E7
  South Cadbury BA22 . . . .175 D4
  Weston-super-Mare BS23 . .48 E1
Folly Rd TA12 . . . . .185 B2
FOLLY THE 94 F6
Folly The
  Cold Ashton SN14 . . . . . .12 F6
  Ditcheat BA4 . . . . .159 C7
  Paulton BS39 . . . . .77 F6
  Saltford BS31 . . . . .25 F2
Fons George TA1 . . . . .212 F2
Fons George Cl TA1 . . . . . .212 E2
Fons George Rd TA1 . . . . .212 F2
Fonthill Rd BA1 . . . . .27 C2
Font La BA22 . . . . .197 B7
Fontmell Ct BS14 . . . . .23 D7
Font Villas BA22 . . . . .197 B8
Football La BA9 . . . . .216 B4
Footlands Cl TA1 . . . . .212 F1
Foots Farm La BS26 . . . . . . .87 D6
Forbes Fraser Hospital
BA1 . . . . .44 B8
Forches Cnr EX15 . . . . .181 A4
Forche's La TA24 . . . . .131 D3
FORD
  Chewton Mendip 94 E8
  Holcombe Rogus 178 F5
  Wiveliscombe 210 F6
Forde Abbey & Gardens*
TA20 . . . . .198 F8
Forde Pk BA21 . . . . .218 C2
FORDGATE 154 C3
Fordhay BA22 . . . . .196 E7
Fordhay Terr BA22 . . . . . . .196 E7
Ford La
  Chewton Mendip BA3 . . . .94 D8
  Pilton BA4 . . . . .140 F3
  Stawell TA7 . . . . .137 A1
  Yarley BA5 . . . . .139 B8
Fordmill Cross EX16 . . . . . .164 D1
Ford Orch EX16 . . . . .178 D1
Ford Rd
  Bampton EX16 . . . . .164 C1
  Peasedown St John BA2 . . .79 D8
  Wellow BA2 . . . . .62 F1
  Wiveliscombe TA4 . . . . . .210 C4
Ford St TA21 . . . . .222 F4
FORD STREET 180 D5
Forefield Pl BA2 . . . . .228 C1
Forefield Rise BA2 . . . . .45 B4
Forefield Terr BA2 . . . . .45 A4
Forelands BS23 . . . . .30 B1
Fore Leaze Dro TA12 . . . . .184 E7
Fore St
  9 Bampton EX16 . . . . . . .164 B1
  Bridgwater TA6 . . . . .208 F5
  Cannington TA5 . . . . .135 B2
  Castle Cary BA7 . . . . .214 C5
  Chard TA20 . . . . .223 C4
  Dulverton TA22 . . . . .163 D6
  Holcombe Rogus TA21 . . .178 F5
  Milverton TA4 . . . . .167 A4
  North Petherton TA6 . . . .153 E3
  Othery TA7 . . . . .155 C2
  Tatworth TA20 . . . . .198 D8
  Taunton TA1 . . . . .212 F3
  Thorncombe TA20 . . . . . .199 B6
  Wellington TA21 . . . . . . .222 D6
  West Camel BA22 . . . . . .174 D3
  Westonzoyland TA7 . . . . .154 E5
  Williton TA4 . . . . .202 D3
  Winsham TA20 . . . . .194 E1
Forest Dr BS23 . . . . .31 A1
Forest Dro TA3 . . . . .182 F5
Forester Ave BA2 . . . . .45 B8
Forester Cl TA6 . . . . .208 D5
Forester Ct BA2 . . . . .228 C4
Forester La BA2 . . . . .45 B8
Forester Rd
  Bath BA2 . . . . .45 B8
  Portishead BS20 . . . . 2 D4
Foresters Cl TA4 . . . . .202 E3
Forest Farm Units TA19 . . .183 A3
Forest Hill BA20 . . . . .218 E2
Forest La TA20 . . . . .193 A8
Forest Mill La TA19 . . . . . .183 B1

Forest Rd
  Frome BA11 . . . . .120 B7
  Horningsham BA11, BA12 . .144 B4
Forest Wlk BA13 . . . . .121 C4
Forge Cnr
  Somerton TA11 . . . . .211 C4
  Stogursey TA5 . . . . .134 B6
Forge End BS20 . . . . 3 E3
Forge La
  East Chinnock BA22 . . . .196 E8
  Zeals SP8, BA12 . . . . . . .161 F2
Forsythia Wy TA6 . . . . . . .208 D1
Fortescue Rd BA3 . . . . .78 F2
Fortescue St BA14 . . . . . . .81 E4
Fortfield Rd BS14 . . . . .23 B5
Forth Ave BS20 . . . . 2 F6
Forth Cl BA6 . . . . .207 A4
Fortnum Pl TA19 . . . . .221 D3
FORTON 223 F1
Forton La
  Chard TA20 . . . . .223 F1
  Tatworth TA20 . . . . .194 A1
Forton Rd TA20 . . . . .223 D2
Forts Orch BA22 . . . . .186 E6
Forum Bldgs BA1 . . . . .228 C1
Forum La BA4 . . . . .205 A7
Forum The BA21 . . . . .218 C6
Forwards La TA19 . . . . .183 B3
Forward's La TA3 . . . . .181 C5
Fosgrove La TA3 . . . . .181 E7
Fosse Barton BS48 . . . . 8 D2
Fosse Cl
  Nailsea BS48 . . . . 8 C2
  Yeovil BA21 . . . . .218 D7
Fossedale Ave BS14 . . . . . .23 C6
Fossefield Rd BA3 . . . . .97 B6
Fosse Gdns BA2 . . . . .62 D8
Fosse Gn BA3 . . . . .78 E4
Fosse La
  Batheaston BA1 . . . . .29 A4
  Blackford BS28 . . . . .107 C3
  Clandown BA3 . . . . .78 D3
  Nailsea BS48 . . . . 8 D2
  Shepton Mallet BA4 . . . . .205 D4
Fosse Lane Ind Est BA4 . . .205 E4
Fosse Lane Junc BA4 . . . . .205 D5
Fosse Lane Trad Est BA4 . .205 D5
Fosse Park Rd BA20 . . . . . .218 F4
Fosse Rd BA3 . . . . .115 C3
Fosse The TA3 . . . . .170 C4
Fosseway
  Clandown BA3 . . . . .78 E4
  Clevedon BS21 . . . . 6 C2
  Midsomer Norton BA3 . . . .97 A5
  Radstock BA3 . . . . .97 C8
Fosse Way
  Nailsea BS48 . . . . 8 C2
  Yeovil BA21 . . . . .218 D7
Fosseway Cl BA2 . . . . .79 C7
Fosse Way Cotts BA3 . . . . . .78 D2
Fosseway Ct
  Bristol BS8 . . . . .226 A2
  Ilchester BA22 . . . . .173 E2
Fosse Way Est BA2 . . . . . . .44 D1
Fosseway Gdns BA3 . . . . . .78 D1
Fosseway S BA3 . . . . .97 B7
Fosse Way Sch BA3 . . . . . .97 C8
Fosseway The BS8 . . . . . . .226 A3
Fosse Wy BA2 . . . . .194 C2
Foss La BS22 . . . . .31 D6
Foss Wy TA12 . . . . .185 E4
Foster Cl BA5 . . . . .112 E1
Foster Rd BA11 . . . . .120 A3
Fosters 10 DT9 . . . . .225 E4
Foster's Almshouses 3
BS1 . . . . .227 A3
Fosters Farm La TA9 . . . . .136 D3
Foster's La BA22 . . . . .175 A7
Foundry Barton 2 BA11 . .119 F5
Foundry Cotts BA2 . . . . . . .60 B4
Foundry Mews
  Chard TA20 . . . . .223 C4
  2 Crewkerne TA18 . . . . .224 C5
Foundry Rd TA1 . . . . .212 F4
Foundry Sq 1 TA18 . . . . . .224 C5
Foundry The BA1 . . . . .228 C3
Fountain Bldgs 7 BA1 . . . .228 B3
Fountain Ho 8 BA1 . . . . . .228 B3
Fountain La BA25 . . . . .70 B7
Fountains Cl BA22 . . . . . . .218 C7
Four Acre Mdw TA6 . . . . . .208 E6
Four Acre Mead 1 TA4 . . .167 F8
Four Acres
  Bristol BS13 . . . . .21 E4
  Shepton Mallet BA4 . . . . .205 C5
Fouracres Cl TA1 . . . . .213 B1
Four Acres Cl
  Bristol BS13 . . . . .21 E4
  Nailsea BS48 . . . . .18 E8
Four Acres Prim Sch BS13 . .21 E4
Four Elms
  Crewkerne TA17 . . . . . . .195 D6
  Holcombe Rogus TA21 . . .179 A6
FOUR FORKS 152 E7
Four Forks La TA5 . . . . . . .152 F7
Four Lanes TA20 . . . . .193 E6
Fourth Ave
  Bristol BS14 . . . . .23 B7
  Radstock BA3 . . . . .97 D8
Fourways Cl BA2 . . . . .214 D6
Fourways Pk BA6 . . . . .139 D3
Fouts Cross TA19 . . . . .184 F2
Fowen Cl BA16 . . . . .207 B4
Fowey Cl BS48 . . . . .19 A8
Fowler St TA2 . . . . .212 E6
Fownes Rd TA24 . . . . .201 B5

Foxbury Cl BA11 . . . . .119 F6
Fox Cl TA21 . . . . .222 A6
Foxcombe Hill BA22 . . . . .175 C8
Foxcombe La DT9 . . . . .176 C1
Foxcombe Rd
  Bath BA1 . . . . .44 B7
  Bristol BS14 . . . . .23 B4
FOXCOTE 79 F4
Foxcote BS20 . . . . .218 C2
Foxcote Ave BA2 . . . . .79 E7
Foxcote Gdns BA11 . . . . . .120 C7
Foxdon Hill TA20 . . . . .223 A7
Foxdon Hill
  Chard TA20 . . . . .193 E6
  Crimchard TA20 . . . . . . .223 A6
Foxdown Hill TA21 . . . . . .222 C4
Foxdown Ho TA21 . . . . . . .222 C4
Foxdown Terr TA21 . . . . . .222 D4
Foxes Field Sch TA24 . . . . .200 F6
Foxglove Cl BS22 . . . . .32 A5
Foxglove Rd TA11 . . . . . . .211 B3
Foxglove Way
  Chard TA20 . . . . .223 F5
  Yeovil BA22 . . . . .218 A5
Foxglove Wlk TA6 . . . . . . .208 E1
Foxhanger La TA22 . . . . . .148 A2
FOX HILL 45 A2
Fox Hill BA2 . . . . .45 A2
Foxhill Ho BA2 . . . . .45 A1
FOX HILLS 79 A1
Foxhole La TA3 . . . . .169 E5
Foxholes La BA2, BA11 . . .100 C5
Fox & Hounds La BS31 . . . .24 F5
Fox Mdws TA18 . . . . .224 D7
Foxmoor Bsns Pk Rd
TA21 . . . . .180 E7
Fox Rd BA16 . . . . .207 A5
Fox's Dro BA11 . . . . .102 C1
Fox Way TA5 . . . . .134 B2
Foxwell La BA22 . . . . .196 C7
Foye Ho BS8 . . . . .11 E6
Frampton Rd
  Bridgwater TA6 . . . . .208 F2
  Shepton Mallet BA4 . . . . .205 D3
Francis Cl TA3 . . . . .169 D5
Francis Fox Rd 7 BS23 . . . .48 E7
Francis Gr BA2 . . . . .45 A2
Francis Ho BS2 . . . . .227 A4
Francis Reed Cl TA7 . . . . .154 F5
Francis Wlk DT9 . . . . .225 E5
Francombe Ho BS1 . . . . . .227 A1
Frankcom Ho BA2 . . . . .45 B7
Frank Foley Parkway The
TA8 . . . . .104 D6
Frankford Mans 7 BS23 . . . .30 C1
Frankland Cl BA1 . . . . .27 B1
Frankley Bldgs BA1 . . . . . . .28 B1
Frankley Terr 6 BA1 . . . . . .28 B1
Franklin Cl TA2 . . . . .212 B7
Franklin Ct BS1 . . . . .227 B1
Franklin's Way BS49 . . . . . .17 F1
Franklyn Terr BS39 . . . . . . .77 A4
Frank Webber Rd TA21 . . .222 A5
Fraser Cl
  Burnham-on-S TA8 . . . . .104 C7
  Weston-super-Mare BS22 . .31 F4
Frederick Ave BA2 . . . . . . .79 C7
Frederick Ct BA5 . . . . .203 C4
Frederick Pl BS8 . . . . .226 B3
Frederick Rd TA6 . . . . .209 C6
Fredrick Pl 5 BS20 . . . . . .219 B4
Freedom Ave BA21 . . . . . .218 E6
Free Hill BA5 . . . . .110 E6
Freeland Pl BS8 . . . . .11 F6
Freelands BS21 . . . . .16 C8
Freeling Ho BS1 . . . . .227 B1
Freemans La BS48 . . . . . . .20 B2
Freemantle Ho BS2 . . . . . .227 A4
Free St BA22 . . . . .173 E1
Freeview Rd BA2 . . . . .44 A5
Freezinghill La BS30 . . . . . .12 B4
Fremantle Rd TA1 . . . . . . .213 B1
Frenchay Rd BS23 . . . . .48 E4
French Cl
  Nailsea BS48 . . . . 8 F3
  Peasedown St John BA2 . . .79 D7
Frenchfield Rd BA2 . . . . . . .79 D7
French Weir Ave TA1 . . . . .212 E5
French Weir Cl TA1 . . . . . .212 E4
FRESHFORD 64 B5
Freshford Church Sch BA3 .64 B5
Freshford La BA3 . . . . .64 A4
Freshford Sta BA3 . . . . . . .64 C5
Freshmoor 6 BS21 . . . . 6 F3
Frethey La TA1, TA4 . . . . . .168 B3
Friar Ave BS22 . . . . .31 E3
FRIARN 133 F1
Friarn Ave TA6 . . . . .208 F4
Friarn Lawn TA6 . . . . .208 F4
Friarn St TA6 . . . . .208 F4
Friars Ave BA22 . . . . .218 D6
Friars Cl BA22 . . . . .173 D1
Friars Way TA6 . . . . .104 B6
Friary BS1 . . . . .227 C1
Friary Cl
  Clevedon BS21 . . . . 6 C5
  Westwood BA15 . . . . .64 E4
  Witham Friary BA11 . . . .143 C3
Friary Rd BS20 . . . . 2 B5
Friary Wood La
  Freshford BA3 . . . . .64 B2
  Winsley BA15 . . . . .64 F6
Friday St TA24 . . . . .200 F7
Friendly Row BS20 . . . . 4 C5
Friendship Gr 2 BS48 . . . . . 8 F2

Friendship Rd BS48 . . . . . . 8 F3
FRIEZE HILL 212 D5
Friggle St BA11 . . . . 120 D1
Frithfield La BA4 . . . . .205 C6
Frobisher Ave BS20 . . . . 2 B5
Frobisher Cl
  Burnham-on-S TA8 . . . . . .104 D8
  Portishead BS20 . . . . 2 A5
  Weston-super-Mare BS22 . . .31 E4
Frobisher Way TA2. . . . . . . .212 B6
Frog La
  Bristol BS1 . . . . .226 C2
  Combe St Nicholas TA20 . . .193 D6
  Creech St Michael TA3 . . . .169 F6
  Dinnington TA17. . . . . .195 B8
  Enmore TA5 . . . . .153 A6
  Felton BS40 . . . . .37 C8
  Galhampton BA22 . . . . . . .175 E8
  Haselbury Plucknett TA18. .196 C6
  Holcombe Rogus TA21 . . . .178 F5
  Ilminster TA19 . . . . .221 C4
  Isle Brewers TA3 . . . . .184 A8
  Kingsdon TA11 . . . . .173 D5
  Langport TA10 . . . . .171 F5
  North Curry TA3 . . . . .170 D5
  Shepton Mallet BA4 . . . . . .205 E4
  Stoke St Michael BA3 . . . . .116 A4
  Ubley BS40. . . . . .55 D1
  Wanstrow BA4 . . . . .142 F4
  West Camel BA22. . . . . . . .174 D3
  Winford BS40. . . . . .37 F5
Froglands La BS27 . . . . .90 C7
Froglands Way BS27 . . . . . . .90 C7
Frogmary Gn TA13 . . . . . . .220 A1
Frogmary St
  South Petherton TA13. . . . .185 A3
  South Petherton TA13. . . . .220 A3
Frogmore St BS1. . . . . .226 C2
Frogs La TA21. . . . . .180 F7
Frog St
  Bampton EX16 . . . . .164 B1
  East Quantoxhead TA5 . . . .133 B6
  Lopen TA13. . . . . .185 A1
Frogwell Cross TA4 . . . . . . .164 D6
Frogwell La TA22 . . . . .164 B6
FROME. 119 E4
Frome Bypass
  Beckington BA11 . . . . .101 E2
  Tytherington BA11 . . . . . . .143 E8
Frome Bypass Feeder Rd W
  BA11 . . . . .120 D6
Frome Com Coll BA11 . . . . .120 A7
Frome Com Hospl BA11. . . .120 A6
FROMEFIELD 120 A6
Fromefield BA11 . . . . .120 A6
Fromefield Ho BA11. . . . . . .120 A6
Frome Mus★ BA11 . . . . . . .119 F5
Frome Old Rd BA3. . . . . .79 A2
Frome Rd
  Bath BA2 . . . . .44 D1
  Beckington BA11 . . . . .101 D3
  Bruton BA10. . . . . .215 F7
  Maiden Bradley BA12. . . . .144 B3
  Norton St Philip BA2. . . . . . .81 F3
  Nunney BA11 . . . . .143 B8
  Radstock BA3. . . . . .79 B2
  Rode BA11 . . . . .101 F7
  Southwick BA14. . . . . .83 F3
  Wingfield BA14 . . . . .83 C5
Frome Sta BA11. . . . . .120 A4
Frome View BA12 . . . . .144 C2
Front St
  Chapel Allerton BS26 . . . . . .88 D1
  Chedzoy TA7. . . . . .154 D8
  Churchill BS25 . . . . .52 E4
  Monksilver TA4. . . . . .150 B8
FROST HILL 34 C6
Frost Hill BS49. . . . . .34 D7
Frost La TA19 . . . . .183 F4
Fry's Bottom
  Breach BS39 . . . . .58 F7
  Chelwood BS39 . . . . .59 A6
Frys House of Mercy **11**
  BS1 . . . . .227 B1
Frys La TA7 . . . . .154 E8
Fry's La BS40 . . . . .53 F3
Frys Leaze BA1 . . . . .28 B2
Frys Mews TA1. . . . . .213 C2
Fry's Wlk BA4 . . . . .205 A5
Fryth Ho BS48 . . . . .9 D3
Fryth Way BS48 . . . . .8 C2
Fst Sch TA16 . . . . .195 F7
FULFORD. 168 C8
Fulford Cl TA24 . . . . .200 F7
Fulford Rd BS13. . . . . .22 C5
Fulford Wlk BS13. . . . . .22 B5
Fullands Ave TA1 . . . . .168 F1
Fullands Ct TA1. . . . . .168 F1
Fullands Rd TA1 . . . . .213 B1
Fullens Cl BS22 . . . . .49 D7
Fuller Cl BA4 . . . . .205 D5
Fuller Rd BA1 . . . . .28 C2
Fullers La BS25 . . . . .70 A6
Fullers Way BA2 . . . . .62 D8
Fullpits La TA7. . . . . .156 B8
Fullwell Cl BA3 . . . . .80 D1
Fulmar Rd BS22. . . . . .31 F1
Fulwell La BA3. . . . . .80 D1
Fulwood Cl TA1. . . . . .212 D1
Furge Gr BA8 . . . . .190 A6
Furge La BA8 . . . . .190 A6
Furland Rd
  Crewkerne TA18. . . . . .224 C5
  Weston-super-Mare BS22 . . .31 C2

Furland Way TA18. . . . . . . .224 C5
Furlong Cl BA3. . . . . .96 F7
Furlong Cotts EX16. . . . . . . .179 A4
Furlong Gn TA3. . . . . .168 D1
Furlong La
  Curry Rivel TA10. . . . . .171 C3
  Milborne Port DT9 . . . . . . .217 B3
Furlong Pl BS26. . . . . .70 C1
Furlongs Ave TA6 . . . . .208 E2
Furlongs La TA10 . . . . .156 C1
Furlongs The DT9 . . . . .225 D5
Furnace Way BS49 . . . . .34 E4
FURNHAM. 223 D5
Furnham Cl TA20. . . . . .223 D5
Furnham Cres TA20 . . . . . . .223 D6
Furnham Rd TA20 . . . . .223 D5
Furnleaze BS39 . . . . .58 E3
Furpits La TA10 . . . . .172 B6
Furringdons Cross TA18 . . .195 F6
Furs Cl TA2. . . . . .213 F8
Furze Cl
  Bridgwater TA6 . . . . .208 D4
  Weston-super-Mare BS22 . . .31 B2
Furzeclose La BA4 . . . . .142 C7
Furzehill TA20 . . . . .223 D5
Furzehill La TA24 . . . . .147 C6
Furzeland Rd TA24 . . . . . . .124 A4
Furze Rd BS22 . . . . .31 A3
Furze The BA20 . . . . .218 C2
Fylton Croft BS14. . . . . .23 B3
Fyne Court Nat Res & Visitor
  Ctr★ TA5 . . . . .152 E3

G

Gables Cl BS29. . . . . .51 B3
Gables The TA21 . . . . .222 C6
Gabriel Cl BA11 . . . . .120 C6
Gadds Dro TA7. . . . . .154 C2
Gadd's La BS27 . . . . .90 B8
Gagley La BA5 . . . . .111 B2
Gainesmarsh La TA10 . . . . .172 C5
Gainsborough DT9 . . . . . . .217 C2
Gainsborough Ct BA1 . . . . . .27 B1
Gainsborough Dr
  Sherborne DT9 . . . . .225 B3
  Weston-super-Mare BS22 . . .31 F3
Gainsborough Gdns BA1. . . .44 C8
Gainsborough Hill DT9 . . . .225 C2
Gainsborough Rd BS31. . . . . .24 F5
Gainsborough Way BA21 . . .219 E8
Galahad Cl BA21 . . . . .218 D7
Gale's Dro BA6. . . . . .139 D3
GALHAMPTON 175 D8
Galhampton Hill BA7,
  BA22 . . . . .214 C2
Galhampton Rd BA22. . . . . .175 C7
Galingale Way BS20 . . . . .2 F5
Gallagher Ret Pk
  TA6. . . . . .209 A6
  Weston-super-Mare BS23 . . .49 A5
Galleries The BS1 . . . . .227 B3
Galley Batch BA3. . . . . .114 F4
Galley Batch La BA3. . . . . . .114 F4
Galloping Bottom La
  TA23 . . . . .149 E5
GALMINGTON 212 C2
Galmington Cl TA1. . . . . . . .212 C3
Galmington Dr TA1. . . . . . . .212 C2
Galmington La TA1. . . . . . . .212 C2
Galmington Rd TA1 . . . . . . .212 B4
Galmington Trad Est TA1 . . .212 B3
Gamblyn Cross TA4 . . . . . . .164 F5
Gamlin Cl TA21 . . . . .222 D8
Gammins Cotts TA24 . . . . . .129 E2
Gander Cl BS13 . . . . .22 B5
Gandstone Cross TA4 . . . . .150 D2
Ganesfield BA4 . . . . .141 E6
Ganges Cl TA3 . . . . .170 F2
Gange's Hill TA3 . . . . .170 F2
Gange's La BA22. . . . . .31 F1
Gannet Mill BA22 . . . . .218 D3
Gants Mill La BA10 . . . . . . .215 D5
Gaol La BA4 . . . . .205 C6
Garamond Ct BS1 . . . . .227 B1
Garden City TA10 . . . . .172 A6
Garden Cl
  Bristol BS9. . . . . .5 C5
  Norton Fitzwarren TA2. . . . .168 B4
  Weston-super-Mare BS22 . . .31 E2
Garden Ct BS8 . . . . .226 A4
Gardener Cl BS29 . . . . .50 D8
Gardeners Cl
  Bradford On Tone TA4. . . . .167 F1
  Cheddar BS27 . . . . .90 B8
Gardeners Wlk BS41 . . . . . . .11 B1
Garden Ground BA4. . . . . . .205 C4
Gardenhurst TA8. . . . . .85 B1
Garden Hurst Cl TA8. . . . . .104 B8
Garden Plot Hill TA3 . . . . . .183 E7
Gardens Rd BS21. . . . . .6 C4
Gardens The
  Bath BA1 . . . . .27 E1
  Dulverton TA22. . . . . .163 D7
  East Pennard BA4 . . . . .158 F8
  Sherborne DT9. . . . . .225 C3
Garden Terr TA21 . . . . .222 B7
Garden Way TA24 . . . . .200 D7
Garden Wlk TA6 . . . . .208 E2
Gardiners Bsns Pk TA7. . . . .136 F3
Gardiners Orch BS28 . . . . . .108 C4
Gardner Ave BS13 . . . . .21 F7
Gardner Rd BS20. . . . . .2 D6
Garfield Terr **1** BA1. . . . . . .28 C2
Garland Ave BS24. . . . . .50 C5

GARLANDHAYES 180 F2
Garlandhayes La EX15. . . . .180 E2
Garland Ho **7** BS21 . . . . .6 C2
Garner Ct **4** BS22. . . . . .32 B4
Garonor Way BS20 . . . . .3 F5
Garre Ho BA2. . . . . .43 F5
Garrett Rd BA20. . . . . .218 D3
Garrick Rd BA2. . . . . .43 F5
Garsdale BA11 . . . . .120 A4
Garsdale Rd BS22. . . . . .49 D8
Garston Cotts BS40. . . . . . . .54 E3
Garstone La TA16 . . . . .195 F8
Garston La
  Blagdon BS40. . . . . .54 E3
  Frome BA11. . . . . .120 A4
  Marston Magna BA22. . . . .174 F1
Garston Lodge **11** BA11 . . . .119 F4
Garston Mead BA11 . . . . . . .120 A4
Garston Rd BA11. . . . . .120 A4
Garstons
  Bathford BA1. . . . . .29 C2
  7 Clevedon BS21. . . . . .6 B1
  Wrington BS40. . . . . .35 E1
Garstons Cl
  Backwell BS48. . . . . .18 F6
  Wrington BS40. . . . . .35 E2
Garstons Orch BS40. . . . . . . .35 D1
Garston St BA4 . . . . .205 C6
Garstons The BS20 . . . . .2 D4
Garth Rd BS13. . . . . .22 A8
Gartons Mead BA4 . . . . . . .141 E1
Gartons Mead Rd BA4 . . . . .141 E1
Garvins Rd BA6 . . . . .206 C4
Gashay La EX13 . . . . .199 B3
Gaskin's La TA3. . . . . .183 D8
Gas La TA17 . . . . .195 D7
Gason La BA22 . . . . .174 F4
Gasper Lodge Rd BA9 . . . . .161 E2
Gasper St BA12 . . . . .161 E3
Gass Cl TA9. . . . . .104 F4
Gassons BA2. . . . . .79 D4
Gasson's La TA11 . . . . .211 C3
Gaston Ave BS31. . . . . .24 F6
Gaston Cl BA16 . . . . .207 C4
Gaston's La TA12. . . . . .185 D5
Gastons The BS11. . . . . .5 A8
Gaswell La TA7. . . . . .155 E8
Gasworks La BS1. . . . . .226 B1
Gatchell Gn TA3. . . . . .168 D1
Gatchell Mdw TA3. . . . . . . .168 D1
Gatchells La TA4 . . . . .132 F2
Gatchell's La TA3 . . . . .181 B5
Gatcombe Farm Ind Est
  BS40. . . . . .35 D3
Gatcombe La BS48. . . . . .20 C8
Gatcombe Mill La BS48 . . . .10 C1
Gatcombe Rd BS13. . . . . . . .22 B5
Gate Cl EX13. . . . . .198 E3
Gatehouse Ave BS13. . . . . . .22 A5
Gatehouse Cl BS13 . . . . .22 A5
Gatehouse Ct BS13. . . . . . . .22 B5
Gatehouse Ctr The BS13 . . .22 B5
Gatehouse Way BS13. . . . . .22 A5
Gate La BA5 . . . . .203 D2
Gaunton Cl TA1. . . . . .212 D2
Gaunts Cl BS20 . . . . .1 F4
Gaunt's La BS1. . . . . .226 C2
Gaunts Rd TA6 . . . . .135 E6
Gay Cl TA21 . . . . .222 E6
Gay Ct BA1 . . . . .28 E3
Gay Elms Rd BS13 . . . . .22 A4
Gaylard's La TA20. . . . . . . .194 B5
Gay's Hill BA1 . . . . .228 C4
Gay St
  Bath BA1 . . . . .228 B3
  Mells BA11. . . . . .118 B7
  Wellington TA21. . . . . .222 E6
Gazelle Rd
  Weston-super-Mare BS24 . . .49 B3
  Yeovil BA20 . . . . .218 D3
Gefle Cl BS1 . . . . .226 B1
Geldof Dr BA3 . . . . .78 A2
Gelosia Cl TA7 . . . . .154 F6
General Higgins Ho TA9 . . .104 E3
Gennes Gr BA9. . . . . .216 C4
Gentle St
  Frome BA11. . . . . .119 F4
  Horningsham BA12 . . . . . . .144 E4
Geoffrey Cl BS13. . . . . .21 E6
George Cl BS48 . . . . .19 D7
George & Crown Cotts
  TA17. . . . . .195 C7
George La
  Marshfield SN14 . . . . .13 E8
  South Petherton TA13. . . . .220 C4
George Maher Ct TA19 . . . .221 C3
Georges Bldgs BA1. . . . . . . .28 C3
Georges Ground BA11. . . . .119 E2
George Sh Ctr The TA18. . . .224 C6
Georges Ho BA2 . . . . .45 B6
Georges Mews TA1. . . . . . .213 C2
George Smith Way BA22. . .218 A6
George's Pl BA2 . . . . .45 B6
George's Rd BA1 . . . . .28 A1
Georges Sq BS1. . . . . .227 B2
George St
  Bath BA1 . . . . .228 B3
  Bath, Bathwick BA2. . . . . . .45 B6
  Bridgwater TA6 . . . . .208 F5
  Burnham-on-S TA8 . . . . . .104 A4
  Charlton Adam TA11. . . . . .173 F7
  Glastonbury BA6. . . . . .206 D5
  Portishead BS20 . . . . .2 C2
  Sherborne DT9. . . . . .225 D4
  Taunton TA2 . . . . .212 F6
  Wellington TA21. . . . . .222 D6
  Weston-super-Mare BS23 . . .48 E7

George Sweetman Cl
  BA9 . . . . .216 D4
George William Ct TA6 . . . .208 F4
Georgian Ct BA11 . . . . .119 D3
Georgian Ho BA2. . . . . .228 C2
Georgian House (Mus)★
  BS1. . . . . .226 C2
Georgian View BA2. . . . . . . .44 C2
Gerard Rd BS23 . . . . .48 F8
Gerbestone La TA1. . . . . . . .180 E6
Gerrard Bldgs **5** BA2. . . . . . .45 B7
Gerrard Cl BS4. . . . . .22 D7
Geys Hill BA12 . . . . .144 D8
Giant's Grave TA20 . . . . . . .193 A7
Giant's Grave Rd TA20 . . . .193 A7
Gibbet La BS14. . . . . .23 D1
Gibbet Rd BA9 . . . . .176 B6
Gibbsfold Rd BS13 . . . . .22 C4
Gibbs' La TA19 . . . . .184 D5
Gibbs Marsh Trad Est
  DT10. . . . . .190 D6
Gibraltar Cotts TA24. . . . . .123 E4
Giddy La BA3 . . . . .116 A4
Gielgud Cl TA8. . . . . .104 D6
Gifford Cl TA20 . . . . .223 D5
Giffords La TA18 . . . . .196 C5
Giffords Orch TA12. . . . . . . .185 A7
Giffords Pl BS13 . . . . .22 A7
Gigg La SP8 . . . . .177 C2
Gilbeck Rd BS48. . . . . .8 C2
Gilbert Rd BA21 . . . . .219 F8
Gilberts Cnr BA6. . . . . .158 A6
Gilbert Scott Ho BA5 . . . . . .113 A1
Gilbert Scott Mews BA5 . . .113 A1
Gilbert Scott Rd BA5 . . . . . .113 A1
Gilberyn Dr BS22. . . . . .32 A3
Gilda Cl BS14 . . . . .23 C5
Gilda Cres BS14. . . . . .23 B6
Gilda Par BS14. . . . . .23 C5
Gilda Sq W BS14 . . . . .23 B5
Giles Cl TA10 . . . . .171 D4
Giles Farm BA5 . . . . .113 A1
Gillards TA1 . . . . .212 B4
Gillards Cl TA21. . . . . .222 B4
Gillards Mead TA3 . . . . .192 A7
Gill Cres TA1 . . . . .212 B1
Gillebank Cl BS14 . . . . .23 D5
Gillingham Ct TA20. . . . . . .223 D5
Gillingham Terr **3** BA1. . . . . .28 B1
Gill Mews BS22 . . . . .32 B4
Gillmore Cl BS22. . . . . .31 D1
Gillmore Rd BS22 . . . . .31 D1
Gills La BS26. . . . . .87 B5
Gillson Cl BS24. . . . . .49 D2
Gimblett Rd BS22 . . . . .32 B4
Ginger Pl **2** TA2 . . . . .169 C5
Gipsy Cross TA4. . . . . .166 A2
Gipsy Dro TA20 . . . . .193 C4
Gipsy La
  Burcott BA5 . . . . .139 E8
  Frome BA11. . . . . .120 B7
  Glastonbury BA6 . . . . .139 D1
  Halse TA4. . . . . .167 B6
  Sampford Arundel TA21. . . .179 D5
  Staplegrove TA2. . . . . .212 D7
  Street BA16. . . . . .207 E4
  Taunton TA1. . . . . .212 C3
  Wells BA5. . . . . .203 A4
GIRT. 175 C2
Givele Cl BA21 . . . . .219 C8
Gladstone Ct BA2 . . . . .45 C2
Gladstone Pl BA2 . . . . .45 C2
Gladstone Rd
  Bath BA2 . . . . .45 C2
  Bristol BS16 . . . . .23 B6
Gladstone St
  Midsomer Norton BA3 . . . . .78 B3
  Taunton TA2 . . . . .212 F6
Gladstone Terr
  Minehead TA24. . . . . .201 A5
  Wellington TA21. . . . . .222 E6
Gladstone Villas BA3 . . . . . .115 C5
Glanfield Villas TA4 . . . . . . .167 E8
Glanfield Terr BA22 . . . . . . .173 F1
Glanvill Ave TA20 . . . . .223 C5
Glanville Dr BS39 . . . . .75 E6
Glanville Rd BS28 . . . . .108 C4
Glanvill Rd BA16 . . . . .207 C3
Glasses Mead TA1. . . . . . . .212 B2
Glass House Hill DT9 . . . . . .225 E3
Glass's Cross TA4 . . . . .149 E1
Glass's Rocks La TA4 . . . . . .149 D1
GLASTONBURY 206 F6
Glastonbury Abbey★ BA6 . .206 E4
Glastonbury Cl BS48. . . . . . . .9 B1
Glastonbury Ct BA21 . . . . . .218 D6
Glastonbury Rd
  Meare BA6 . . . . .138 C4
  Wells BA5. . . . . .203 B2
Glastonbury Tor★ BA6 . . . .139 D1
Glastonbury Way BS22 . . . . .32 A2
Glastonbury Western Relief
  Rd BA6 . . . . .206 F2
Glaston Ho BA16 . . . . .207 D7
Glaston Rd BA16 . . . . .207 D7
Glebe Ave BS20 . . . . .2 E4
Glebe Cl BS41 . . . . .11 C2
Glebe Cotts TA3. . . . . .169 E2
Glebe Cres TA24 . . . . .200 E8
Glebe Ho
  Bath BA2 . . . . .45 B5
  Portishead BS20 . . . . .2 E4
  Weston-super-Mare BS22 . . .31 F3
Glebeland Cl TA7. . . . . .156 B8
Glebelands
  3 Langaller TA2 . . . . .169 C5
  7 Merriott TA16. . . . . .195 F7
  Minehead TA24. . . . . .200 E8

Glebelands continued
  Norton Sub Hamdon TA14. . .185 F3
  Nunney BA11 . . . . .143 B7
  Radstock BA3. . . . . .78 D1
Glebelands Cl BS27 . . . . .90 B6
Glebe Paddock BA5 . . . . . . .139 E8
Glebe Rd
  Bath BA2 . . . . .44 B4
  Clevedon BS21. . . . . .6 C2
  Long Ashton BS41 . . . . .11 C2
  Portishead BS20 . . . . .2 E4
  Weston-super-Mare BS23 . . .48 E8
Glebe The
  Fivehead TA3 . . . . .170 F1
  Freshford BA3 . . . . .64 B4
  Hinton Charterhouse BA2 . . .63 D2
  Queen Camel BA22. . . . . . .174 F3
  Timberscombe TA24. . . . . .130 B4
  Timsbury BA2. . . . . .60 B3
  Wrington BS40. . . . . .35 D2
Glebe Way BS27. . . . . .90 C6
Glebe Wlk BS31. . . . . .24 C4
Glebe Yd TA10 . . . . .172 E4
Glen Ave BS8 . . . . .10 F8
Glenavon Pk BS9. . . . . .5 C4
Glen Brook BS9 . . . . .5 D4
Glencairn Ct BA2. . . . . .45 B6
Glen Cl TA2. . . . . .168 B5
Glencoe Bsns Pk BS23. . . . . .49 A7
Glencoe Terr TA3 . . . . .168 D1
Glencot La BA5 . . . . .203 A7
Glencot Rd BA5. . . . . .203 A6
Glencroft Way BS22 . . . . . . .31 E3
Glendale
  16 BS8 . . . . .11 F6
Glendevon Rd BS14. . . . . . . .23 A3
Glen Dr
  Bristol BS9. . . . . .5 D5
  Taunton TA2 . . . . .168 F6
Gleneagles Cl
  Nailsea BS48. . . . . .9 A1
  Weston-super-Mare BS22 . . .31 F3
Glenmore Rd TA24 . . . . . . .201 A3
Glen The
  Saltford BS31. . . . . .25 F1
  Weston-super-Mare BS22 . . .31 B2
Glenthorne Nature Trail
  Gate★ EX35. . . . . .122 D5
Glenthorne Rd **9** TA2 . . . . .212 F6
Glentworth Ct **19** BS23. . . . .30 C1
Glentworth Rd BS8. . . . . . .226 B2
Glen View BA3. . . . . .115 E7
Glenview Ho BA2. . . . . .79 D8
Glenville Rd BA21 . . . . .219 D6
Glenwood Gdns TA2. . . . . . .212 F8
Glenwood Mans BS23 . . . . . .30 D1
Glenwood Rise BS20 . . . . . . .1 F5
Glen Yeo Terr BS49. . . . . . . .34 C4
Glider Ave
  Haywood Village BS24 . . . . .49 B4
  Weston-super-Mare BS24 . . .49 B4
Globe Orch TA18. . . . . .196 C6
Gloucester Ho **11** BS2 . . . . .227 C3
Gloucester La **18** BS2. . . . . .227 C3
Gloucester Rd
  Bath BA1 . . . . .28 C3
  Bridgwater TA6 . . . . .208 F2
  Burnham-on-S TA8 . . . . . .104 C7
  Upper Swainswick BA1 . . . . .28 A7
Gloucester Row **6** BS8 . . . . .11 F7
Gloucester St
  4 Bath BA1. . . . . .228 B3
  5 Bristol BS2 . . . . .227 B4
  8 Bristol, Clifton BS8 . . . . .11 F7
  Taunton TA1 . . . . .213 A4
  Weston-super-Mare BS23 . . .48 D7
Glovers DT9 . . . . .225 D5
Glovers Cl
  Milborne Port DT9 . . . . . . .217 D2
  4 Stoke sub Hamdon TA14 .185 F4
Glovers Field BS25 . . . . .70 F7
Glovers Rd BA8 . . . . .190 C4
Glovers Wlk **18** BA20. . . . . .219 B4
Glovers Wlk Sh Ctr BA20. . .219 B5
Glynsmead TA20 . . . . .198 C3
Glynswood TA20 . . . . .223 C5
Gnome Rd BS24. . . . . .49 C5
GOAR KNAPP 219 D5
GOATHILL 189 B4
Goathill La BA8 . . . . .176 C3
Goathill Rd DT9. . . . . .189 B4
GOATHURST 153 B5
Goathurst Hill TA5 . . . . .153 A4
Godhams La TA4 . . . . .165 A7
Godminster Ct BA10. . . . . . .215 E6
Godminster La BA10. . . . . . .215 E4
GODNEY 139 A5
Godney Cl BA6 . . . . .206 F7
Godney Dro BA5. . . . . .139 B6
Godney Rd BA5, BA6 . . . . . .139 A4
Godwin Cl BA5 . . . . .203 C2
Godwin Dr BS48. . . . . .9 B1
Goeffrey Farrant Wlk TA1 . .213 A5
Goes La BA7 . . . . .158 F2
Gogs Orch BS28 . . . . .108 C3
Gold Corner Dro TA9 . . . . . .137 A2
Goldcrest Way BS20 . . . . . . .2 F6
Goldcroft BA21 . . . . .219 B6
Goldcroft Ct BA21. . . . . . . .219 B6
Goldenhaye La TA20. . . . . . .194 D3
Golden Hill
  Stourton Caundle DT10 . . . .189 F1
  Wiveliscombe TA4 . . . . . . .210 C5
Golden Lion Ct BS1. . . . . . .227 B2
Golden Valley La BS30. . . . . .25 D3
Golden Valley Prim Sch
  BS48. . . . . .8 F2

Goldfinches La BA6 139 D3
Gold Hill
Batcombe BA4 142 D2
Shepton Mallet BA4 205 B7
Golding Cl BA5 203 C4
Golding's La DT9 217 C1
Goldney Ave BS8 226 A2
Goldney Cl BS39 58 F1
Goldney Rd BS8 226 A2
Goldney Way BS39 58 F1
GOLD'S CROSS 57 E6
Goldsmiths La EX13 198 A4
Goldsmoor Cross EX16 178 E3
Gold St DT10 190 B4
Golf Club La BS31 25 E2
Golf Course Rd BA2 45 D6
Golf Links La BA3 114 E3
Golf Links Rd TA8 85 A2
Golledge Cl BA3 96 C4
GOLSONCOTT 131 D2
Golsoncott La TA24 131 C2
Gooch Cl
Bridgwater TA6 209 B4
Frome BA11 120 D6
Gooch Way BS22 32 B3
Goodard Dr BS22 32 B4
Goodeaves Cl BA3 117 A7
Goodeaves Cotts BA3 117 A7
Goodeve Pk BS9 5 D3
Goodeve Rd BS9 5 D3
Good Hill BA4 142 E2
Goodlands La TA1 212 F4
Good's La TA5 152 C5
Goodwin Dr BS14 22 F4
Goodymoor Ave BA5 203 B5
Goodymoor La BA5 203 B5
Goold Cl BA2 43 A8
Goosander Cl TA24 201 C4
Goosard La BS39 77 E8
Gooseacre Ct BA22 197 B8
Gooseacre La
East Coker BA22 197 B8
Yeovil BA22 218 A1
Gooseham La BS28 108 F4
Gooseham Mead BS49 34 B4
Goose La
Chilton Polden TA7 137 B3
Horton TA19 183 C2
Gooselade BA16 207 C3
Gooseland Cl BS14 22 F3
Gooseland La DT9 188 B3
GOOSENFORD 169 A6
Goose St BA11 101 E5
Goosey La BS22 32 C2
Goosey Path TA24 201 C2
Gordano Bsns Pk BS20 2 E5
Gordano Gdns BS20 4 B4
Gordano Rd BS20 3 D7
Gordano Sch BS20 2 D3
Gordano View BS20 2 C5
Gordano Way BS20 3 F5
Gordon Bldgs BA3 79 A3
Gordon Rd
Bath BA2 45 B5
Bristol BS8 226 B3
Peasedown St John BA2 79 D8
Taunton TA1 213 A3
Weston-super-Mare BS23 48 F7
Yeovil BA21 219 C6
Gordon's Cl TA1 213 B1
Gordon Terr TA6 209 A5
GORE 187 F6
Gorefield TA13 220 D2
Gorehedge 14 BA11 119 F4
Gore La
Chapmanslade BA13 121 B4
Pitney TA10 172 C7
Gore Rd TA8 85 A1
Gores Pk BS39 59 B2
Gore Sq TA4 167 E8
Gorlangton Cl BS14 23 A7
Gorlegg TA21 179 E5
Gorpit La TA5 134 F8
Gorse La
Bristol BS8 226 B2
Cold Ashton BS30, SN14 12 D7
Gort Rd TA2 168 B6
Gory La BA6 140 A2
Gosford Mans 6 BS23 30 C1
Goshawk Dr 8 BS20 2 F6
Goslet Rd BS14 23 E5
Goss Barton BS48 8 D1
Goss Cl BS48 8 C1
Goss Dr BA16 207 B3
Goss La BS48 8 C1
Goss View BS48 8 C1
Goswell Cl BA16 207 C5
Goswell Rd BA16 207 C5
GOTHELNEY GREEN 153 B8
GOTTON 169 B7
Gough Cl 11 TA16 195 F7
Gough Pl BS27 90 A8
Gough's Caves★ BS27 90 B8
Gould Cl
Bristol BS13 22 C5
Street BA16 207 E6
Gouldsbrook Terr TA18 224 B6
Gouldsbrook View TA18 224 C7
GOULD'S GROUND 119 E5
Gould's Ground 2 BA11 119 E5
Gould's La 1 BA11 119 E5
Goulston Rd BS13 22 A5
Goulston Wlk BS13 22 A5
Gournay Ct BS39 77 A3
Governors Ho BA2 44 D6
Govier's La TA23 202 C7
Grabbist Top Rd TA24 201 B2
Grace Cl BS49 34 B8
Grace Dr BA3 78 A2
Grace Martin's La BA22 174 F3
Grace Rd BS22 32 B4
Gradwell Cl BS22 32 B3
Grafton Cl TA2 213 A8
Graham Rd BS23 48 E7
Graham Way TA4 167 E6
Grainger Ct BS11 4 E7
Grain Store The 9 BS1 227 A2
Graitney Cl BS49 35 A8
Granaries The BA3 115 A3
Granary Orch DT9 187 F5
Granary The 8 BS1 227 A2
Granary Way TA3 181 D8
Granby Hill BS8 11 F6
Granby Rd BA22 174 A2
Grand Par BA2 228 C2
Grand Pier★ BS23 48 D7
Grand Western Canal (Country Pk)★ EX16 178 F2
Granfield Gdns BS40 53 A5
Grange Ave
Highbridge TA9 104 E3
Street BA16 207 B6
Grange Bsns Pk The BS24 33 A5
Grange Cl
Cannington TA5 135 C2
Wellington TA21 222 E5
Weston-super-Mare BS23 48 E1
Grange Cnr DT8 199 E7
Grange Dr
Bridgwater TA6 208 D4
Taunton TA2 213 A6
Grange End BA3 97 B7
Grange Farm Rd BS49 17 A1
Grangefields BA16 207 D5
Grange Gdns TA2 213 A7
Grange La 6 BS13 21 F4
Grange Paddock TA9 106 E4
Grange Rd
Bristol BS8 226 A3
Bristol, Bishopsworth BS13 22 A5
Frome BA11 120 A7
Huntspill TA9 136 A8
Saltford BS31 25 C3
Street BA16 207 D7
Weston-super-Mare BS23 48 E1
Grange The
Bath BA1 27 C1
Bristol BS9 5 D7
Chilton Polden TA7 137 B2
Flax Bourton BS48 19 F7
Kingston St Mary TA2 168 E8
Langport TA10 171 E5
Grange Way TA6 135 F5
Grange Wlk TA2 213 A6
Granny's Ride TA24 123 B1
Grants Cl BA9 216 B4
Grants Hill DT9 187 F1
Grant's Hill EX16, TA22 163 F2
Grants La BA9 216 D4
Grant's La
Wedmore BS28 108 D4
Wiveliscombe TA4 210 D6
Granville Chapel 5 BS8 11 F5
Granville Rd BA1 27 E4
Granville Way DT9 225 E6
Grasmere TA6 208 C5
Grasmere Dr BS23 48 F4
Grass Meers Dr BS14 23 A4
Grassmere Rd BS49 34 B8
Grass Rd TA8 65 F4
Grass Royal BA21 219 C6
Grass Royal Jun Sch BA21 219 C6
Gratton La EX35 122 A4
Gravelands La TA3 169 D3
Gravel Hill BS40 56 B7
Gravel La TA3, TA19 183 F6
Gravel Pit Cross EX36 145 E6
Gravel Wlk BA1 228 B3
Gravenchon Way BA16 207 A6
Graves Cl 7 TA6 209 B4
Gray Hollow BS40 74 F4
Grayling Ho BS9 5 F7
Gray's Almshouses 17 TA1 213 A4
Grays Ave TA7 154 E6
Grays Hill BA2 80 B5
Gray's Hill EX15 180 D1
Gray's La EX15 180 D1
Grays Rd TA1 213 B4
Grays Terr TA1 213 B4
Great Ann St BS2 227 C3
Great Barton BA4 205 D6
Great Bedford St BA1 228 B4
Great Bow Yd TA10 171 F5
Great Brockeridge BS9 5 F6
Great Cl EX15 179 E1
Great Cnr 5 BA21 218 C6
Great Dunns Cl BA11 101 E4
GREAT ELM 118 F7
Great Field La TA14 185 F4
Great Gardens BA4 205 C6
Great George St
Bristol, Brandon Hill BS1 226 C2
Bristol, St Pauls BS2 227 C3
Great Hayles Rd BS14 23 A6
Great Hill BA9 161 D2
Great House Ct BA6 138 D4
Great House St TA24 130 B5
Great La
Knole TA10 173 A4
Shepton Beauchamp TA19 184 E4
Great Mdw TA22 163 D6
Great Mead
Taunton TA1 212 B3
Yeovil BA21 219 F7
Great Orch BA22 173 E2
Great Ostry BA4 205 B6
Great Pit La BA22, DT9 188 B7
Great Pulteney St BA2 228 C3
Great Ringaton La EX36 162 B6
Great St TA14 185 E2
Great Stanhope St BA1 228 A2
Greatstone La BS40 37 F5
Great Western La TA11 211 D3
Great Western Rd
Chard TA20 223 D5
Clevedon BS21 6 D2
Martock TA12 185 E7
Great Western St BA11 120 A4
Great Western Terr BA21 219 D5
Great Western Way TA2 212 A6
Great Western Wy TA2 168 B4
Great Withy Dro BA5 206 C8
Greatwood Cl TA6 209 A2
Great Wood Cl BS13 22 C4
Grebe Cl TA6 209 B4
Grebe Ct TA6 209 B4
Grebe Rd
Bridgwater TA6 209 B4
Taunton TA2 213 B6
Grebe Rd BA21 218 A6
Greenacre
Wembdon TA6 208 D6
Weston-super-Mare BS22 31 B2
Green Acre Rd BS14 23 A3
Greenacres
Bath BA1 27 B3
Bristol BS9 5 E7
Midsomer Norton BA3 77 E1
Puriton TA7 136 B4
Green Acres La DT9 187 D5
Greenacres Pk BA21 187 A5
Greenaleigh Lower Rd TA24 125 C4
Greenaleigh Upper Rd TA24 125 C4
Greenbank Gdns BA1 27 B1
Greenbrook Terr TA1 212 E4
Green Cl
Holford TA5 133 D4
Paulton BS39 77 E6
Sparkford BA22 175 A4
Green Cotts BA2 45 C2
Greendale TA19 221 B3
Greenditch Ave BS13 22 C5
Greenditch Cl BA3 96 C3
Green Ditch La BA3 96 B6
GREEN DOWN 94 B8
Greendown Pl BA2 45 A1
Green Dragon Ct 4 TA6 208 F4
Green Dro TA11 158 A4
Green Farm Ind Est BA13 121 C4
Greenfield Cres BS48 8 E3
Greenfield La TA7 136 D2
Greenfield Pk BS20 2 C3
Greenfield Pl BS23 48 C8
Greenfield Prim Sch BS4 22 C7
Greenfield Rd
Keynsham BS31 24 D3
WATCHET TA23 202 D6
Greenfields
Bridgwater TA6 208 F3
Crewkerne TA18 224 C7
Greenfields Ave BS29 51 A3
Greenfields Way BS23 49 B4
Greenfield Terr TA20 198 D8
Greenfield Wlk BA3 78 A3
Greenfylde CE First Sch TA19 221 C3
Greenfylde CE Fst Sch TA19 221 C3
Greengage Cl 6 BS22 49 E8
GREEN GATE 178 B2
Green Gate EX16 178 B2
GREENHAM
Drimpton 199 E7
Wellington 179 B7
Greenham Bsns Pk TA21 179 C5
Greenham La TA18 199 E7
Greenham's Cross TA14 185 F2
Greenham Yd TA18 199 E7
Greenhayes BS27 90 B8
Greenhays Foot EX13 198 B6
GREENHILL 78 A3
Greenhill DT9 225 D4
Greenhill Cl
Nailsea BS48 8 D2
Weston-super-Mare BS22 32 A3
Greenhill Croft BS25 52 B4
Greenhill Cross EX36 162 B2
Greenhill La
Alston Sutton BS26 88 E5
Sandford BS25 52 B4
Greenhill Pl BA3 78 A3
Greenhill Rd
Midsomer Norton BA3 78 A3
Sandford BS25 52 B4
Yeovil BA21 219 D7
Greenhoop Dro TA12 185 E8
Greenhouse La
Nempnett Thrubwell BS40 55 C6
Regil BS40 37 D1
Green Knap La TA20 193 C2
Green La
Bristol BS11 4 B8
Brompton Regis TA22 148 B1
Butcombe BS40 55 A7
Castle Cary BA7 214 F4
Chard TA20 193 F1
Chard Junction TA20 198 D7
Chardstock EX13 198 B7
Charlton Horethorne DT9 176 A2
Green La *continued*
Charlton Horethorne, Sigwells DT9 175 F2
Corfe TA3 181 E7
Corsley Heath BA12 144 E7
Cricket St Thomas TA20 194 F3
East Chinnock BA22 196 E8
East Coker BA22 197 B8
Failand BS8 10 C4
Farrington Gurney BS39 76 F6
Felton BS40 37 C3
Fivehead TA3 170 E2
Frome BA11 119 D4
Hinton Charterhouse BA2 63 E1
Ilminster TA19 183 E2
Kington Magna SP8 177 E2
Leigh u M BA3, BA11 117 B2
Marshfield SN14 13 E8
Misterton TA18 224 E4
Oakhill BA3 114 E4
Pitcombe BA7 215 A1
Priddy BS40 73 B7
Queen Camel BA22 174 F3
Sampford Arundel TA21 179 F4
Shepton Beauchamp TA19 184 E3
Sherborne DT9 188 E1
Southwick BA14 83 D2
Stoke St Michael BA3 116 B5
Stratton-on-t F BA3 96 E1
Street BA16 207 C4
Tatworth TA20 193 D1
West Pennard BA6 140 B1
Greenland La TA24 131 B1
Greenland Rd BS22 31 D1
Greenlands TA1 213 B2
Greenlands Rd BA2 79 C8
Green Lane Ave BA16 207 C4
Green Lane End TA19 184 E3
Green Lane Gate BA9 176 A8
Green Mead BA21 218 C5
Greenmoor La BA21 187 A5
GREEN ORE 94 C1
Green Ore Est BA5 94 B1
Green Park La BA11 101 F6
Green Park Mews BA1 228 A2
Green Park Rd BA1 228 B2
Green Parlor Rd BA3 79 D1
GREEN PARLOUR 79 D2
Green Pastures Rd BS48 9 B2
Green Patch La BA2 59 E7
Green Pits La BA11 143 B7
Green Pk
Bath BA1 228 B2
Rode BA11 101 E8
Green Quarry BA21 219 A6
Green Ride BA12 161 F7
Greenridge BS39 58 F3
Greenridge Cl BS13 21 E4
GREENSBROOK 58 F3
Green's Dro BA6 206 C7
Green's Hill TA4 151 C5
Greenslade Gdns BS48 8 D3
Greens Pl BA5 203 D3
Green St
Bath BA1 228 C2
Hinton St George TA17 195 D7
Shoscombe BA2 79 E5
Ston Easton BA3 95 E8
Greenstalls Pk BA22 173 F2
Green The
Backwell BS48 19 A5
8 Barwick BA22 197 F8
Bath BA2 44 D1
Bridgwater TA6 208 E2
Brushford TA22 163 E4
Easton BA5 111 A4
Faulkland BA3 80 D2
Hinton Charterhouse BA2 63 F1
Ilchester BA22 173 E2
Locking BS24 50 A4
33 Martock TA12 185 E6
Pill BS20 4 D4
Pitminster TA3 181 E6
1 Sherborne DT9 225 D4
Williton TA4 202 D3
Winscombe BS25 70 A7
Green Tree Rd BA3 78 B3
GREENVALE 60 B1
Greenvale Cl BA2 60 B1
Greenvale Dr BA2 60 B1
Greenvale Rd BS39 77 D5
GREENWAY 167 D8
Greenway
Bishops Lydeard TA4 167 E8
Faulkland BA3 80 C1
Ilminster TA19 221 B3
Minehead TA24 200 D6
Monkton Heathfield TA2 169 B6
North Curry TA3 170 B3
Watchet TA23 202 B7
Greenway Ave TA2 212 E6
Greenway Cl BA9 216 D4
Greenway Cotts TA4 167 E8
Greenway Cres TA2 212 E7
Greenway Ct BA2 44 F4
Greenway La
Barrington TA13 184 E5
Bath BA2 45 A4
Blagdon Hill TA3 181 B5
Cold Ashton SN14 12 D5
Combe St Nicholas TA20 193 E6
Stoke St Mary TA3 169 D2
Wiveliscombe TA4 210 A5
Greenway Pk 3 BS21 6 F3
Greenway Rd
Castle Cary BA7 214 B6
Rockwell Green TA21 222 A5
Taunton TA2 212 E6
Greenways BA3 96 C2
Greenway Terr TA2 168 D8
Greenwell La BS40 53 C7
Greenwood Cl TA9 136 B8
Greenwood Rd
Weston-super-Mare BS22 31 E2
Yeovil BA21 218 D7
Gregory Mead BS49 17 A1
Gregorys Cres TA21 222 D7
Gregorys Gr BA2 62 D8
Gregorys Tyning BS39 77 F6
GREINTON 155 F7
Greinton BS24 49 A2
Greinton Rd TA7 155 E7
Grenville Ave BS24 50 A4
Grenville Cl BA6 157 E4
Grenville Ho TA6 208 F2
Grenville Pl 7 BS1 11 F5
Grenville Rd
Burnham-on-S TA8 104 C7
1 Longcroft BA21 219 F8
Grenville View TA4 167 E6
GREYFIELD 59 C2
Greyfield Comm BS39 59 C2
Greyfield Rd BS39 59 C2
Greyfield View BS39 58 F1
Greyhound Cl BA9 216 C4
GREYLAKE 155 C4
GREYLAKE FOSSE 155 E6
Greylake Reserve★ TA7 155 D5
Greylands Rd BS13 21 F7
Grey's Cnr BA9 161 A3
Greys Rd TA16 195 F7
Greystoke Bsns Ctr BS20 2 D4
Grey Stone Dro TA12 185 D7
GRIBB 199 B6
Gribb View TA20 199 B6
Grib La BS40 54 F2
Griffen Cl TA6 208 E6
Griffen Rd BS24 49 E7
Griffin Cl
Wells BA5 203 B6
Weston-super-Mare BS22 32 B2
Griffin Ct BA1 228 B2
Griffin La TA3 182 F7
Griffin Rd
Clevedon BS21 6 E3
Hatch Beauchamp TA3 182 F7
Griggfield Wlk BS14 23 A7
Grimsey La SP8 177 F8
Grinfield Ave BS13 22 C4
Grinfield Ct BS13 22 C4
Groats 9 TA4 167 F8
Grooms Orch TA21 222 C5
GROSVENOR 28 C1
Grosvenor Bridge Rd BA1 28 C1
Grosvenor Ct BA22 173 E2
Grosvenor Pk BA1 28 C1
Grosvenor Pl BA1 28 C1
Grosvenor Rd
Bristol BS2 227 C4
Stalbridge DT10 190 B4
Grosvenor Terr BA1 28 C2
Grosvenor Villas 9 BA1 28 B1
Grove Alley BA10 215 E6
Grove Ave
Bristol BS1 227 A1
Bristol, Coombe Dingle BS9 5 C7
Yeovil BA20 218 F5
Grove Cl
Penselwood BA9 161 E2
Watchet TA23 202 C6
Grove Ct BS9 5 E5
Grove Dr
Taunton TA2 212 F8
Weston-super-Mare BS22 31 C1
Grove Gate TA2 212 B7
Grove Hill TA7 155 B1
Grove Ho
Bath BA2 45 B6
Burnham-on-S TA8 104 A8
Grove Jun Sch BS48 18 D8
Grove La
Faulkland BA3 80 D2
Frome BA11 119 E3
Knole TA10 173 A4
North Cheriton BA8 176 E5
Stalbridge DT10 190 B4
West Anstey EX36 162 D6
Weston-super-Mare BS23 48 D8
Grove Lane Cl DT10 190 B4
Grove Leaze BS11 4 D6
Grove Mead BA11 119 E2
Grove Orch BS40 54 E2
Grove Park Ct BS23 30 D1
Grove Park Rd BS23 30 D1
Grove Pl TA24 201 B4
Grove Rd
Banwell BS29 50 E4
Blue Anchor TA24 131 B6
Bristol, Coombe Dingle BS9 5 D8
Burnham-on-S TA8 104 A8
Huntspill TA9 136 A8
Weston-super-Mare BS23 48 D8
Weston-super-Mare, Milton BS22 31 C1
Groves La TA24 131 B6
Grove St BA2 228 C3
Groves The BS13 22 D4
Grove Terr 8 TA2 212 F6
Grove The
Bath BA1 27 C1
Bristol BS1 227 A1
Burnham-on-S TA8 85 B1
Frome BA11 119 E2

Grove The continued
Hallatrow BS39 . . . .**77** B7
Ruishton TA3 . . . .**169** C3
Sherborne DT9 . . . .**225** D3
Winscombe BS25 . . . .**51** F1
Wraxall BS48 . . . .**9** C3
Grove Wood Rd BA3 . . . .**78** F1
Grughay La TA3 . . . .**182** E5
Grunter's La BA3 . . . .**114** F7
Gryphon Sch The DT9 . . . . .**225** E6
Guard Ave BA22 . . . .**218** B6
Guard House La 9 BA5 . .**203** D4
Guernsey Rd BS25 . . . .**69** F7
Gug The BS39 . . . .**59** C2
Guild Ct BS1 . . . .**227** B2
Guildford Pl TA1 . . . .**212** F3
Guildhall La BS28 . . . .**108** C4
Guillemot Rd 9 BS20 . . . . . .**2** F6
Guineagore La DT9 . . . .**188** B4
Guinea La BA1 . . . .**228** C3
Guinea St BS1 . . . .**227** A1
Guinevere Cl BA21 . . . . . .**218** D7
Gullen BA2 . . . .**80** A6
Gulliford Cl TA9 . . . .**104** D4
Gulliford's Bank BS21 . . . . . .**6** F2
Gullimores Gdns BS13 . . . . .**22** B4
Gullock Tyning BA3 . . . .**78** B1
Gullons Cl BS13 . . . .**22** A6
Gullon Wlk BS13 . . . .**21** F5
Gulway Mead TA20 . . . .**198** D8
Gumbrells Ct TA6 . . . .**209** A4
Gunners La BA22 . . . .**218** A5
Gunning's La BA4 . . . .**142** F2
Gunville La
Charlton Horethorne DT9 . . .**176** A2
East Coker BA22 . . . .**197** D8
Gunwyn Cl BA6 . . . .**206** E6
GUPWORTHY **148** C6
GURNEY SLADE **114** F7
Gurney St TA5 . . . .**135** C2
Gurnville Cotts BA11 . . . . .**119** F2
Guthrie Rd BS8 . . . .**226** A4
Gwynne La TA1 . . . .**213** A3
Gwyther Mead TA1 . . . . . .**212** A3
Gyffarde Ct 4 TA1 . . . . . .**213** A4
Gyffarde St TA1 . . . .**213** A4
Gypsy La
Cheddar BS28 . . . .**89** D6
Keynsham BS31 . . . .**42** B8
Marshfield SN14 . . . .**13** F7
Gypsy Moth La BS24 . . . . . .**49** C5

H

Haberfield Hill BS8 . . . .**4** E2
Haberfield Ho 1 BS8 . . . . .**11** F6
Hacketty Way TA24 . . . . . .**124** B3
Hack La
Holford TA5 . . . .**133** F2
Nether Stowey TA5 . . . .**134** A2
Hack Mead La TA9 . . . .**105** E1
HACKNESS **136** D8
Hackness Rd TA9 . . . .**136** D8
Hackney La BA4 . . . .**142** F2
Haddon Cl TA22 . . . .**148** B2
Haddon Hill TA4 . . . .**164** E7
Haddon La
Hartford TA4 . . . .**164** C7
North Petherton TA6 . . . .**153** C2
Stalbridge DT10 . . . .**190** C5
Haddon View TA22 . . . .**148** B2
Hadley Rd BA2 . . . .**45** B2
Hadrian Cl
Bristol BS9 . . . .**5** C4
Keynsham BS31 . . . .**24** F7
HADSPEN **214** F6
Hadspen Garden ✱ BA7 . .**160** A2
Hadworthy La TA6 . . . .**153** F4
Hafner Gn BS24 . . . .**49** C4
Hagget Cl TA6 . . . .**208** F1
Haggetts La TA9 . . . .**136** E7
Hagleys Gn TA4 . . . .**151** B7
Haig Cl BS9 . . . .**5** B7
Haig Rd TA2 . . . .**168** B6
HAINES HILL **212** E2
Haines Hill TA1 . . . .**212** E2
Haines La DT8 . . . .**199** D5
Haines Pk TA1 . . . .**212** E1
Hains La DT10 . . . .**190** F7
Halcombe TA20 . . . .**223** C2
HALCON **213** D5
Halcon Cnr TA1 . . . .**213** D4
Halcon Com Prim Sch
TA1 . . . .**213** D4
HALE **177** D6
Hale La BA4 . . . .**177** C6
Halesleigh Rd TA6 . . . .**208** E5
Hale Way TA1 . . . .**213** D7
Half Acre TA4 . . . .**202** D2
Half Acre Cl
Bristol BS14 . . . .**23** A3
Williton TA4 . . . .**202** D2
Halfacre La BS14 . . . .**23** B4
Half Acres DT9 . . . .**225** C3
Half Moon St 6 BA21 . . . .**225** D3
Halfpenny Row BA11 . . . . . .**82** E1
Halfway BA22 . . . .**186** F6
Halfyard Ct TA21 . . . .**222** F4
Half Yd BS41 . . . .**53** D8
Hallam Ct BS21 . . . .**6** C4
Hallam Rd BS21 . . . .**6** C4
Hallards Cl BS11 . . . .**4** F8
HALLATROW **77** B7

Hallatrow Rd BS39 . . . .**77** C6
Hallen Dr BS9 . . . .**5** C7
Hallet Gdns BA20 . . . .**219** A4
Hallets Orch BA22 . . . .**186** B6
Hallett Rd BA7 . . . .**214** B7
Halletts Way
Axminster EX13 . . . .**198** A1
Portishead BS20 . . . .**2** D5
Hall Hill EX35 . . . .**122** B5
Halliwell Rd BS20 . . . .**1** D4
Hall La BA1 . . . .**12** B3
Hall Rd TA7 . . . .**136** B4
Hall Terr TA8 . . . .**104** A8
HALSE **167** B6
Halse Cnr TA4 . . . .**167** D5
Halse La TA24 . . . .**147** B5
Halse Manor TA4 . . . .**167** B6
HALSTOCK **197** C3
Halston Dr BS2 . . . .**227** C4
HALSWAY **151** B8
Halsway TA6 . . . .**209** C5
Halsway Hill TA4 . . . .**132** F1
Halsway La
Bicknoller TA4 . . . .**133** A1
Crowcombe TA4 . . . .**151** A8
Halswell CE Fst Sch TA4 . . .**208** E4
Halswell Gdns BS13 . . . .**22** B4
Halswell Rd BS21 . . . .**6** D1
Halt End BS14 . . . .**23** C3
Halter Path Dro TA7 . . . . .**137** C7
Halves La BA22 . . . .**197** C2
Halwyn Cl BS9 . . . .**5** D5
Halyard Dr TA6 . . . .**208** E7
Halyard Pl TA24 . . . .**201** B7
Halyard Wy BS20 . . . .**2** F7
Halyars Way BA21 . . . .**218** C8
HAM
Creech St Michael **169** E4
Holcombe **116** D6
Paulton **77** F5
Wellington **180** D8
Hamber Lea TA4 . . . .**167** F8
Hambledon Rd BS22 . . . .**32** C4
HAMBRIDGE
184 D8
Whitecross TA10 . . . .**171** D1
Hambridge Com Prim Sch
TA10 . . . .**184** D8
Ham Cl BS39 . . . .**58** F1
Hamdon Cl 12 TA14 . . . . .**185** F4
Hamdon Hill Country Pk✱
TA14 . . . .**185** F3
Hamdon View TA14 . . . . . .**185** F3
Hamdown Ct TA10 . . . .**172** B6
Ham Gn
Hambridge TA10 . . . .**184** D8
Pill BS20 . . . .**4** D3
Ham Gr BS39 . . . .**77** E5
HAM GREEN **4** E4
Ham Hill
Coleford BA3 . . . .**116** D6
Combe St Nicholas TA20 . . . .**193** D8
High Ham TA10 . . . .**156** A2
Langford Budville TA21 . . . . .**166** A1
Radstock BA3 . . . .**78** F3
Ham Hill Ctry Pk✱ TA14 . .**186** A3
Ham Hill Rd
Odcombe BA22 . . . .**186** C2
Stoke sub Hamdon TA14 . . . .**185** F4
Hamilton Ct
11 Bristol BS1 . . . .**227** A4
Taunton TA1 . . . .**213** C4
Wells BA5 . . . .**203** B4
Hamilton Dr TA6 . . . .**209** C8
Hamilton Ho BA1 . . . .**27** E3
Hamilton Rd
Bath BA1 . . . .**27** E2
Taunton TA1 . . . .**213** C4
8 Weston-super-Mare BS23 .**30** C1
Hamilton Terr BA2 . . . .**79** F5
Hamilton Wy BS14 . . . .**23** D3
Ham La
Bishop Sutton BS39 . . . .**57** C5
Burnham-on-S TA8 . . . .**104** B6
Compton Dundon TA11 . . . . .**157** A3
Croscombe BA4, BA5 . . . .**204** E7
Dundry BS41 . . . .**21** D3
Farrington Gurney BS39 . . . . .**76** F5
Kingston Seymour BS21 . . . . . .**16** B2
Marnhull DT10 . . . .**190** F6
North End BS49 . . . .**17** A3
Paulton BS39 . . . .**77** E5
Pawlett TA6 . . . .**135** E6
Rodhuish TA23 . . . .**149** C8
Shepton Mallet BA4 . . . .**205** A7
Sherborne DT9 . . . .**188** A5
Trent DT9 . . . .**187** F5
Wraxall BS48 . . . .**9** B4
Yatton BS49 . . . .**17** A3
Ham La E BA4 . . . .**204** F7
Hamlands La TA21 . . . .**167** D1
Hamlet The
Nailsea BS48 . . . .**9** A3
Templecombe BA8 . . . .**176** E1
Hamley La
Buckland St Mary TA20 . . . . .**193** B8
Combe St Nicholas TA20 . . . .**182** F1
Ham Link BS40 . . . .**53** F3
Hamlyn Cl TA1 . . . .**212** C1
Hamlyn Rd BA6 . . . .**206** E6
Ham Mdw DT10 . . . .**190** E6
Hammer La BA2, BA3 . . . . .**100** C8
Hammer St BA10 . . . .**161** B8
Hammet St
8 North Petherton TA6 . . . .**153** E3
Taunton TA1 . . . .**212** F4
Hammets Wharf 1 TA1 .**212** F4
Hammocks Dro TA10 . . . . .**172** D4

Hammond Gdns BS9 . . . .**5** E7
HAMP **208** F2
Hamp Ave TA6 . . . .**208** F3
Hamp Brook Way TA6 . . . .**208** E2
Hamp Com Jun Sch TA6 . .**208** F3
Hampden Rd BS22 . . . .**31** E2
Hamp Green Rise TA6 . . . .**209** A3
Hamp Ind Est TA6 . . . .**209** A3
Hamp Inf Sch TA6 . . . .**208** F3
Hamp St TA6 . . . .**208** F3
Hampton Cl
5 Barwick BA22 . . . .**197** F8
Bridgwater TA6 . . . .**209** D7
Hampton Cnr BS11 . . . .**4** E6
Hampton H BA2 . . . .**45** D8
Hampton Ho 10 BA1 . . . . . .**28** C1
Hampton La BS8 . . . .**226** B4
Hampton Rd BS6 . . . .**226** C4
Hampton Row BA2 . . . .**45** B8
Hampton View BA1 . . . .**28** B1
Ham Rd
Brean BS24, TA8 . . . .**66** B3
Burnham-on-S TA8 . . . .**85** E4
Creech St Michael TA3 . . . . . .**169** D4
Wellington TA21 . . . .**180** D8
Hamrod La TA7 . . . .**154** E5
Hams La BS26 . . . .**68** C3
Ham's La TA11 . . . .**174** D7
Hams Rd BS31 . . . .**24** F7
Ham St BA6 . . . .**158** B5
HAM STREET **158** B5
Hamway La TA20 . . . .**193** C8
HAMWOOD **68** C7
Hamwood TA1 . . . .**212** B4
Hamwood Cl BS24 . . . .**49** B2
Hamwood Cotts TA1 . . . . .**212** B4
Hamwood La TA1 . . . .**181** B8
Hamwood Terr TA1 . . . . . .**212** B4
Hanbury Ct BS8 . . . .**226** A4
Hanbury Rd BS8 . . . .**226** A4
Handel Rd BS31 . . . .**24** E5
Handlemaker Rd BA11 . . . .**119** E2
Handy Cross TA4 . . . .**151** A2
Hanford Ct BS14 . . . .**23** D7
Hangerland La TA4 . . . . . .**150** E6
Hanger's Way TA24 . . . . . .**201** D2
Hanger Wy BS14 . . . .**22** F5
Hang Hill BA2 . . . .**80** A6
Hanging Hill La TA13 . . . .**184** F4
Hanglands La BA8 . . . .**176** C2
Hanham La BS39 . . . .**77** F7
Hanham Way BS48 . . . .**8** B2
Hankridge Way TA1 . . . . .**213** E5
Hanna Cl BA2 . . . .**44** B6
Hannah Dr BS24 . . . .**50** C5
Hannah More Cl
Cheddar BS27 . . . .**90** B7
Wrington BS40 . . . .**35** E2
Hannah More Inf Sch BS48 .**18** D8
Hannah More Prim Sch
BS1 . . . .**227** C2
Hannah More Rd BS48 . . . . .**18** C8
Hannahs La BA5 . . . .**110** E6
Hannay Rd BS27 . . . .**71** B1
Hann Cl BA5 . . . .**203** B2
Hanning Cl TA19 . . . .**221** F6
Hanning Pk TA19 . . . .**183** C1
Hanning Rd TA19 . . . .**183** C1
Hanover Ct
Shepton Mallet BA4 . . . .**205** A6
Weston-super-Mare BS22 . . . .**32** A4
Hanover Ct
Bath BA1 . . . .**28** B2
Castle Cary BA7 . . . .**214** C5
Dulverton TA22 . . . .**163** D7
Radstock BA3 . . . .**79** C2
Hanover Gdns BA11 . . . . . .**119** D3
Hanover Ho BS20 . . . .**2** B5
Hanover Pl
Bath BA1 . . . .**45** B8
Bristol BS1 . . . .**226** B1
Hanover St
2 Bath BA1 . . . .**28** B1
2 Bristol BS1 . . . .**227** A2
Hanover Terr 5 BA1 . . . . .**28** B1
Hansetown Rd TA4 . . . . . .**148** F1
Hansford Cl BA2 . . . .**44** E1
Hansford Mews BA2 . . . . . .**44** F1
Hansford Sq BA2 . . . .**44** F1
Hanson's Way 4 BS21 . . . . .**6** C2
Hans Price Cl 18 BS23 . . . .**48** E8
Hans Price Ho 13 BS23 . . . .**48** E8
Hantone Hill BA2 . . . .**45** F8
Hapil Cl BS25 . . . .**51** F4
Happerton La BS20 . . . .**4** D2
Hapsburg Cl BS22 . . . .**32** A4
HAPSFORD **119** B8
Hapsford Hill BA11 . . . . . .**119** C8
Harbour BA21 . . . .**218** C5
Harbour Cres BS20 . . . .**2** E5
Harbour Ct TA5 . . . .**135** B5
Harbourne Cl TA8 . . . .**104** C8
Harbour Rd
Portishead BS20 . . . .**2** D6
Sherborne DT9 . . . .**225** E5
Watchet TA23 . . . .**202** C7
Harbour Road Trad Est BS20 .**2** F6
Harbour Terr DT9 . . . .**225** E5
Harbour View TA5 . . . .**135** B5
Harbour Wall BS9 . . . .**5** B4
Harbour Way DT9 . . . .**225** E5
Harbour Wlk BS1 . . . .**226** C1
Harbutts BA2 . . . .**28** F1
Harcourt Cl BS31 . . . .**25** E2
Harcourt Gdns BA1 . . . .**27** E1
Harcourt Mews BA11 . . . . .**120** A4

Harcourt St TA2 . . . .**212** E6
Harden Rd BS14 . . . .**23** E5
Harding Ct TA11 . . . .**211** D3
Harding Dr BS29 . . . .**50** C7
Hardings Cl 8 TA6 . . . . . .**153** F3
Hardings Ct TA13 . . . .**220** C5
Harding's Hill TA10, TA11 . .**172** F5
Harding's House La DT9 . . .**225** A6
Hardings La BA2 . . . .**42** A1
Harding's La BA8 . . . .**176** D4
HARDINGTON **99** E6
Hardington Dr BS31 . . . .**25** A2
HARDINGTON
MANDEVILLE **197** A6
HARDINGTON MARSH **196** F4
HARDINGTON MOOR **197** A7
Hardington Moor National
Nature Reserve✱ BA22 . . .**197** A7
Hard Leaze Dro BA22 . . . . .**186** A8
Hardmead La BS27 . . . .**90** C2
Hardwarden Terr BA22 . . . .**175** A5
HARDWAY **161** A5
Hardway Rd BA10 . . . .**160** F4
Hardwick Rd BS20 . . . .**4** C5
Hardy Cres DT10 . . . .**190** B4
Hardy Ct TA18 . . . .**224** C5
Hardy Mead Dro TA9 . . . . .**136** B7
Hardy Rise BA7 . . . .**214** A2
Hardys Rd
Langaller TA2 . . . .**169** C5
Taunton TA2 . . . .**213** F7
HARE **182** F2
Hareclive Acad BS13 . . . . . .**22** C4
Hareclive Rd BS13 . . . .**22** C4
Hare La BS20 . . . .**182** E2
Harepark Terr TA24 . . . . . .**201** A5
Hare Path TA24 . . . .**147** F8
Hare Path Cross TA24 . . . .**129** D1
Harepit La BA12 . . . .**161** F7
Harepits La BA6 . . . .**157** E3
Hare Pk TA24 . . . .**124** C4
Harestone Cross EX13 . . . .**198** B7
Harewell Wlk BA5 . . . .**203** B3
Harfield Terr 10 BA20 . . . .**219** B4
Harford Cl BS9 . . . .**5** C7
Harford Sq BS40 . . . .**39** B3
Hargrove La DT10 . . . .**190** C2
Harlech Cl BS31 . . . .**24** C4
Harley Ct 3 BS8 . . . .**11** F7
Harley La BS21 . . . .**7** C6
Harley Mews 2 BS8 . . . . . .**11** F7
Harley Pl 4 BS8 . . . .**11** F7
Harley St BA1 . . . .**228** B4
Harmony Dr BS20 . . . .**1** F4
Harnell Cl TA1 . . . .**213** C3
Harnhill Cl BS13 . . . .**22** B4
Harp Chase TA1 . . . .**213** B1
Harper's La TA23 . . . .**131** D1
Harpitts La SP8 . . . .**177** F2
Harp Rd
Brent Knoll TA9 . . . .**105** E6
South Petherton TA13 . . . . . .**220** C3
Harpsichord Way BS31 . . . . .**25** B4
Harptree BS24 . . . .**49** A2
Harptree Cl BS48 . . . .**18** C8
Harptree Hill BS40 . . . .**74** B5
Harptree La BA3 . . . .**75** C1
Harrier Dr BA22 . . . .**218** A5
Harrier Path 3 BS22 . . . . . .**49** E8
Harriets Yd BS31 . . . .**24** F5
Harrington Ave BS14 . . . . . .**23** E6
Harrington Cl BS30 . . . .**25** E8
Harrington Gr BS14 . . . .**23** E6
Harrington Rd BS14 . . . .**23** E6
Harrington Wlk BS14 . . . . . .**23** E6
Harris Cl
Frome BA11 . . . .**120** B4
Westleigh EX16 . . . .**179** A4
Harris Gr BS13 . . . .**22** B3
Harris La
Abbots Leigh BS8 . . . .**10** F8
Curry Mallet TA3 . . . .**183** C8
Harrison's La TA19 . . . .**184** E1
Harris Vale BA3 . . . .**116** F7
Hart Cl BS20 . . . .**4** E4
HARTCLIFFE **22** C4
Hartcliffe Rd BS4 . . . .**22** E8
Hartcliffe Way BS3, BS4,
BS13 . . . .**22** C7
Hartcliffe Wlk BS4 . . . .**22** F8
Harters Cl BA5 . . . .**139** E6
Harter's Hill La BA5 . . . . .**139** E6
Hartfield Ave BS6 . . . .**226** C4
HARTFORD **164** C8
Hartford Rd TA22 . . . .**164** B8
Hartgill Cl BS13 . . . .**22** B3
Hartlake Cl
Glastonbury BA6 . . . .**206** F7
Glastonbury BA6 . . . .**206** F7
Hartland 14 BS22 . . . .**32** A2
Hartley BA15 . . . .**64** E8
Hartley Cotts BA4 . . . .**204** B1
Hartley Ho BA1 . . . .**228** B3
Hartley Way TA1 . . . .**213** D2
HARTMOOR **177** F3
Hartmoor Hill SP8 . . . .**177** E3
Hartrow Cl TA1 . . . .**212** E1
Harts Cl TA19 . . . .**221** A4
Hartsfield TA20 . . . .**223** D2
Hart's La
Hallatrow BS39 . . . .**77** B7
Huish Champflower TA4 . . . .**165** D7
Sherborne DT9 . . . .**188** A3
Harts Paddock BA3 . . . .**77** F3
HARTSWELL **210** B3
Hartswell TA4 . . . .**210** C3

Hart Way EX35 . . . .**122** F3
Harvesters Dr BA16 . . . . . .**207** B4
Harvest La
Charlton Horethorne DT9 . . .**176** A2
Weston-super-Mare BS22 . . . . .**50** B8
Harvest Way BS22 . . . .**32** A5
Harvey Cl BS22 . . . .**32** A4
Harvey's Rd TA13 . . . .**220** C4
Harvey Way TA19 . . . .**183** B4
Harwood Cross TA24 . . . . .**130** A4
Harwood Gn BS22 . . . .**31** E4
Harwood La
Timberscombe TA24 . . . .**130** A4
Wootton Courtenay TA24 . . .**129** F4
HASELBURY
PLUCKNETT **196** C6
Haselbury Plucknett CE Fst
Sch
Haselbury Plucknett TA18 . . .**196** C5
Haselbury Plucknett TA18 . . .**196** C5
Haselbury Rd TA16 . . . .**195** F6
Haseley Ct TA1 . . . .**212** D2
Hassage Farm La BA3 . . . . .**81** A3
Hassage Hill BA2 . . . .**80** E7
Hassock's La BA10 . . . .**160** E8
HASTINGS **183** B3
Hastings Cross TA19 . . . . . .**183** B3
HATCH BEAUCHAMP **183** A7
Hatch Beauchamp CE Prim
Sch
Hatch Beauchamp TA3 . . . . .**183** A7
Hatch Beauchamp TA3 . . . . .**183** A7
Hatch Court✱ TA3 . . . .**183** A8
Hatcher Cl TA8 . . . .**104** D5
Hatchers Ct TA2 . . . .**212** F4
Hatches La BS24 . . . .**66** E3
Hatchet Hill BA3, BA11 . . . . .**98** C1
HATCH GREEN **183** A6
Hatch Green La TA3 . . . . . .**182** F6
Hatch Mews Bsns Pk TA3 .**183** A7
Hatfield Bldgs BA2 . . . .**45** B5
Hatfield Rd
Bath BA2 . . . .**44** F3
Weston-super-Mare BS23 . . . .**49** A8
Hathaway Ho 13 BS2 . . . . .**227** A4
Hathermead Gdns BA21 . . .**219** D7
Haugh BA15 . . . .**46** D2
Haunts TA18 . . . .**196** C8
Havage Cl TA9 . . . .**104** C5
Havage Dro BS24 . . . .**51** D8
Haven Cl TA24 . . . .**201** F3
Haven View BS20 . . . .**2** E5
Haversham Cl BS22 . . . .**31** D1
Haviland Gr BA1 . . . .**27** B3
Haviland Ho 7 BS2 . . . . . .**227** C3
Haviland Pk BA1 . . . .**27** B2
Havory BA1 . . . .**28** C1
Havyat Rd BS40 . . . .**53** C6
Havyat Road Trad Est
BS40 . . . .**35** C2
HAVYATT **157** F2
HAVYATT GREEN **53** F7
Hawarden Terr BA1 . . . .**28** B1
Hawcombe View TA24 . . . .**124** A3
Hawcombe Woods National
Nature Reserve✱ TA24 . . .**123** A3
HAWKCHURCH **198** D3
Hawkchurch CE Prim Sch
EX13 . . . .**198** D3
Hawkchurch Cross EX13 . . .**198** B3
Hawkchurch Rd EX13 . . . . .**198** D3
HAWKCOMBE **124** A3
Hawke Rd BS22 . . . .**31** E4
Hawkers Cl 9 TA5 . . . .**135** B2
Hawkers La TA10 . . . .**184** D8
Hawker's La BA5 . . . .**112** E1
Hawkfield Bsns Pk BS14 . . . .**22** C5
Hawkfield Cl BS14 . . . .**22** D5
Hawkfield Rd BS13 . . . .**22** C5
Hawkfield Way BS14 . . . . . .**22** D5
Hawkins Dr
Burnham-on-S TA8 . . . .**104** C7
Street BA16 . . . .**207** E6
Hawkin's La TA4 . . . .**165** E4
Hawkins St BS2 . . . .**227** C3
Hawkins Way 2 BA21 . . . .**218** C6
Hawkmoor Hill DT6, EX13 . .**199** B2
Hawk Rd BA22 . . . .**218** A5
HAWKRIDGE **146** D1
Hawkridge Cross TA22 . . . .**146** D1
Hawkridge Rd TA6 . . . .**208** B4
Hawksmoor Cl BS14 . . . .**23** A6
Hawks Rise BA22 . . . .**218** B5
Hawk's Worth Cl BA11 . . . .**120** C7
Hawksworth Dr BS22 . . . . . .**32** C4
Hawksworth Rd TA24 . . . . .**201** B6
Hawkwell Cross EX16 . . . . .**162** F4
Hawkwell La TA22 . . . .**163** A4
Hawley Way TA8 . . . .**104** C7
Hawthorn Cl
Bridgwater TA6 . . . .**209** D4
High Ham TA10 . . . .**156** A2
Portishead BS20 . . . .**1** F5
Hawthorn Coombe BS22 . . .**31** E3
Hawthorn Cres
Shepton Mallet BA4 . . . .**205** A6
Yatton BS49 . . . .**17** A2
Hawthorne Cl TA18 . . . .**224** D7
Hawthorne Rd TA21 . . . . . .**222** F5
Hawthorn Gdns BS22 . . . . . .**31** D2
Hawthorn Gr BA2 . . . .**45** A1
Hawthorn Hill
Kingsbury Episcopi TA13 . . . .**185** B6
Weston-super-Mare BS22 . . . . .**31** E4
Hawthorn Hts BS22 . . . .**31** D3
Hawthorn La BS22 . . . .**32** C2
Hawthorn Pk BS22 . . . .**31** E3

Hawthorn Rd
Frome BA11 120 A6
Ilton TA19 183 F4
Minehead TA24 200 D7
Radstock BA3 79 B2
Street BA16 207 E6
Taunton TA1 213 C1
Yeovil BA21 219 D7
Hawthorns La BS31 24 E5
Hawthorns The
Clevedon BS21 6 C3
Stalbridge DT10 190 C4
Hawthorn Way BS48 9 A2
Haxen La TA17 195 A8
Hayboro Way BS39 77 E4
Haybow BS24 32 E2
HAYBRIDGE 203 A5
Haybridge Hill BA5 203 A4
Haybridge La BA5 111 E1
Haybridge Villas BA5 203 A5
Haycombe BS14 22 F6
Haycombe Dr BA2 44 A4
Haycombe La BA2 44 A3
Hayden Cl BA2 228 A1
HAYDON
Milborne Port 189 B2
Radstock 97 F8
Taunton 213 E2
Wells 113 D5
Haydon Cl TA1 212 B4
Haydon Dro BA5 113 C6
Haydon Gate BA3 97 F8
Haydon Hill BA3 98 A8
Haydon Hollow DT9 189 B3
Haydon Ind Est BA3 97 F8
Haydon La TA1, TA3 213 E2
Haydon Rd TA1 213 A4
Hayesdown Fst Sch BA11 120 B5
Hayes Dr BA5 111 F1
Hayes End TA13 220 D4
Hayes End Manor TA13 220 D4
Hayesfield Girls Sch BA2 228 A1
Hayesfield Pk BA2 228 B1
Hayesfield Sch Tech Coll
BA2 44 D6
Hayes La TA11 156 F2
HAYES PARK 78 A2
Hayes Park Rd BA3 77 F2
Hayes Pl BA2 228 B1
Hayes Rd
Compton Dundon TA11 156 F3
Midsomer Norton BA3 77 F1
Hayes The BS27 90 B8
Hayeswood Farm BA15 46 F5
Hayeswood Rd BA2 59 E3
Hayfield Cl TA24 201 B6
Hayfield Rd TA24 201 B6
Haygarth Ct BA1 228 B4
Haygrove Pk TA3 168 D1
Haygrove Pk Rd TA6 208 D3
Haygrove Rd TA6 208 C3
Haygrove Sch TA6 208 C4
Hay Hill
Bath BA1 228 B3
Croscombe BA5 204 B8
Hay La BS40 37 D6
Hayleigh Ho BS13 22 C4
Hayman Rd TA24 200 F7
Haymarket The BS1 227 A3
Haymarket Wlk 9 BS1 227 A4
Haymoor Dro BA5 139 D7
Haymoor La
Coxley BA5 139 E6
Long Sutton TA10 172 D4
Hayne Cross EX16 164 B4
Hayne La TA5 153 B7
Haynes International Motor
Mus★ BA22 175 A6
Hayne Wlk TA7 137 B2
Hay St BA3 96 A8
Haytor Pk BS9 5 D6
Hayward Ave BS24 50 C8
Hayward Cl BS21 6 C1
Hayward Dr BA6 158 A6
Haywater Ave TA6 208 D3
Haywood Cl BS24 49 A1
Haywood Gdns BS24 49 B1
Haywood Rd TA1 213 D2
HAYWOOD VILLAGE 49 C4
Haywood Village Acad
BS24 49 D5
Hazel Barrow BS40 74 A7
Hazelbury Rd
Bristol BS14 23 C7
Nailsea BS48 8 D1
Hazel Cl TA1 213 C1
Hazel Cote Rd BS14 23 B4
Hazel Ct BA11 120 A3
Hazeldene Rd BS23 49 A8
Hazel Gr
Bath BA2 44 D4
Midsomer Norton BA3 97 B8
Hazell Cl BS21 6 E1
Hazel St BS14 22 E5
Hazel Terr BA3 97 C8
Hazel View TA18 224 D7
Hazel Way BA2 62 D8
Hazelwell La TA19 221 A4
Hazelwood Ct BS9 5 D3
Hazelwood Dr TA6 209 E5
Hazelwood Hill TA20 194 E1
Hazelwood Rd BS9 5 D3
Hazlegrove Prep Sch
BA22 174 F5
Hazleton Gdns BA2 45 F3
Head Croft BS48 20 B8
Head Dro
Athelney TA7 170 E8
Head Dro *continued*
Catcott TA7 137 D3
Othery TA7 155 D3
Headley Ct BS13 22 B6
Headley La BS13 22 B7
HEADLEY PARK 22 B6
Headley Park Ave BS13 22 B7
Headley Park Prim Sch
BS13 22 B6
Headley Park Rd BS13 22 A7
Headley Rd BS13 22 A6
Headley Wlk BS13 22 B7
Headon Cross TA24 129 F8
Head St BA22 186 B6
Headstock Cross TA20 198 E6
Headstock Rd TA20 198 E7
Headwell TA3 183 C8
Headwell Cl TA3 183 C8
Headwell Hill TA3 183 C8
Heal Cl TA8 104 D5
HEALE 142 C7
Heale La TA10 171 C4
Healeys TA24 124 A4
Heal's Field EX13 198 A2
Healys Mdw TA4 167 E6
Hearn La BA22 175 D8
Heart Meers BS14 23 B5
Heath Cl BA12 144 D8
Heathcombe Rd TA6 208 B4
Heath Dr BA11 119 F6
Heather Cl
Bridgwater TA6 209 B3
Minehead TA24 201 C4
Somerton TA11 211 B3
Taunton TA1 169 A1
Heatherdene BS14 22 F7
Heather Dr BA2 62 D8
Heather Rd BA21 219 D7
Heatherton Park Ho TA4 180 E8
Heather Way BA22 218 A5
HEATHFIELD 167 E5
Heathfield TA4 151 E4
Heathfield Cl
Bath BA1 27 A3
Creech St Michael TA3 169 D6
Keynsham BS31 24 C5
5 North Petherton TA6 153 F4
West Bagborough TA4 151 E4
Heathfield Com Sch TA2 213 F8
Heathfield Cres BS14 23 B4
Heathfield Dr TA2 213 F8
Heathfield Rd BS48 8 E3
Heathfield Way BS48 8 E2
Heathgate BS49 34 B8
Heathgates BS23 48 D4
HEATH HOUSE 107 F1
Heath Rd BS48 8 F3
Heath Ridge BS41 11 A2
Heathstock Hill TA4 210 D5
Heathway BA12 144 D8
Heathway La BA6 138 B4
HEAVEN'S DOOR 188 A8
Heavitree Way TA2 213 A6
Hebden Rd BA15 64 F3
Heber's La TA19 195 A5
Heckley La BA3 115 B5
Hector Cl BS24 51 A8
Hector Rd TA7 137 D2
Hectors La TA3 170 D8
Hectors Stones TA7 136 E4
Heddon Oak TA4 151 A8
Heddon Wood La TA4 151 A7
Hedge La BA4 141 B2
Hedgemead Ct BA1 228 C4
Hedges Cl 3 BS21 6 B1
Hedges The BS22 32 C3
Hedgestocks BA4 160 C8
HEDGING 170 A8
Hedging La TA7 170 A8
Heggard Cl BS13 22 A5
Heights The TA19 221 B4
HELE 168 A3
Hele La
Langport TA10 172 C4
South Petherton TA13 220 C4
Hele Manor La TA22 144 D3
Helena Rd BA20 218 D1
Helens Rd BS25 52 B4
Helicopter Mus The★ BS24 49 E5
HELLAND 170 C3
Helland Hill TA3 170 C3
Helland La TA3 170 D4
Helliar's La
Curry Mallet TA3 183 D8
Fivehead TA3 170 D1
Hellier's Cl TA20 223 B4
Hellier's La BS27 89 E6
Helliers Rd TA20 223 B4
Hellier Wlk BS13 22 C3
Helling's Cross TA4 166 A4
Helmstedt Way TA20 223 D6
Helston Rd BS48 9 A1
Helvier's La TA4 167 A7
Helwell Gn TA23 202 D6
Helwell St TA23 202 D7
Helyar Cl BA6 206 D5
Hembridge La
East Pennard BA4 158 E7
East Pennard BA4 158 F8
Hembury La BA5 139 C7
HEMINGTON 99 B7
Hemington Prim Sch BA3 99 B7
Hemming Way BS24 49 E3
Hemp Gdn TA24 200 F8
Hempitts Rd BA16 156 D7
Hemplow Cl BS14 23 D7
Hemstich Hill TA7 138 C1
HEMYOCK 180 B1
Henacre Rd BS11 4 F8
Henbury Hill BS9 5 F8
Henbury Ho BA2 45 E4
Henbury Rd BS9 5 F8
Hencliffe Rd BS14 23 D7
Henderson Cl TA1 212 C2
Henderson Dr TA20 223 D2
Henderson Ho 1 BS2 227 B4
Henderson Pl 5 BA5 203 D4
Hendford BA20 219 A4
Hendford Ct BA20 219 A3
Hendford Gr BA20 219 A4
Hendford Hill BA20 219 A3
Hendon Cl TA9 104 E5
Hendon Cross EX16 178 B8
Hengasson La BS39 57 E6
HENGROVE 23 B6
Hengrove Ave BS14 23 B8
Hengrove La BS14 23 B8
Hengrove Pk L Ctr BS14 22 E5
Hengrove Prom BS14 22 E5
Hengrove Way BS14 22 E6
Henhambridge Way BA2 101 A7
Henhayes La TA18 224 C6
Hen La BS40 37 E3
HENLADE 169 D2
HENLEY 156 B3
Henley Cl EX13 198 B7
Henley Cross
Crewkerne TA18 224 B1
Henley TA18 195 E2
Henley Gr TA1 212 D4
Henley La
Butleigh BA6 157 E4
Wookey BA5 139 E8
Yatton BS49 34 D7
Henley Lodge BS49 34 D7
Henley Pk BS49 34 C7
Henley Rd
High Ham TA10 156 B3
Kingsdon TA11 173 E5
Taunton TA1 212 D3
Henley Rise BA4 205 D4
Henley View
Crewkerne TA18 224 C4
Wellow BA2 62 D1
Henley Way BA11 119 F5
Henmore La BS26 88 E6
Hennessy Cl BS14 22 F3
Henning Way DT9 217 D3
Henrietta Ct BA2 228 C4
Henrietta Gdns BA2 228 C3
Henrietta Mews BA2 228 C3
Henrietta Pl BA2 228 C3
Henrietta Rd BA2 228 C3
Henrietta St
Bath BA2 228 C3
Bristol BS2 227 A4
Henry Butt Ho 11 BS23 48 E8
Henry Rogers Ho 2 TA5 135 B2
Henry St BA1 228 C2
Hensley Gdns BA2 44 E4
Hensley Rd BA2 44 E3
Hensman's Hill BS8 226 A2
Henson Pk TA20 223 E5
Hensons Dr EX16 179 A3
HENSTRIDGE 190 A6
HENSTRIDGE ASH 189 F7
HENSTRIDGE BOWDEN 189 D7
HENSTRIDGE MARSH 190 C7
Henstridge Trad Est BA8 190 C7
HENTON 139 B8
Hepburn Rd BS2 227 B4
Herald Cl BS9 5 D5
Herbert Gdns BA2 59 E5
Herbert Ho TA22 163 D6
Herbert Rd
Bath BA2 44 D5
Burnham-on-S TA8 104 A8
Clevedon BS21 6 D4
Herbert St TA2 212 E6
Herblay Cl BA21 219 E6
Hercules Wy BS31 24 C3
Hereford Dr TA2 213 A8
Heritage Cl BA2 79 D8
Heritage Ct BA6 206 D4
Heritage Ctyd BA5 203 D4
Heritage The BA2 78 E8
Herluin Way BS22, BS23 49 B6
Hermes Cl BS31 25 D2
Hermes Pl BA22 173 E2
Hermitage Cl BS11 4 E7
Hermitage Hill TA10 172 D6
Hermitage Rd
Bath BA1 27 E1
Langport TA10 172 D6
Hermitage St TA18 224 C5
Herne Rise TA19 221 B2
Hern La BS48 20 E5
Heron Cl
Minehead TA24 201 C4
Weston-super-Mare BS22 49 E8
Heron Ct BS21 6 C2
Heron Dr
Houndstone BA22 218 A6
Taunton TA1 212 B4
Heron Gate TA1 213 E6
Heron Gate Office Pk TA1 213 E5
Heron Gdns BS20 2 E4
Heron Ho 2 TA6 209 C4
Heron Pk TA8 84 E8
HERONS GREEN 56 C3
Herons Green La BS40 56 C4
Herons La TA4 167 A4
Heronsmead Wlk BA21 219 D8
Herons Moor Acad BS24 50 A8
Heron Way TA19 221 C2
Herridge Cl BS13 22 B4
Herridge Rd BS13 22 B4
Herschel Museum of
Astronomy★ BA1 228 B2
Hersey Gdns BS13 21 E3
Hertford Rd BA21 219 E8
Hervey Cl BS28 108 C4
Hervey Rd
Chard TA20 223 D3
Wells BA5 112 E1
Hestercombe Cl TA6 208 B4
Hestercombe House Gdns★
TA2 169 A7
Hestercombe Rd
Bristol BS13 22 B6
Taunton TA2 169 A7
Hestia Cl BS31 24 C3
Hetling Ct 7 BA1 228 B2
Hewett Cl TA3 168 D1
HEWISH
Crewkerne 195 D3
Weston-super-Mare 33 C5
Hewish Ct BS23 48 E8
Hewish La
Crewkerne TA18 224 A5
Hewish TA18 195 D3
Hext Ct TA11 211 D3
Hexton Rd BA6 206 E5
Heyron Wlk BS13 22 B4
Heywood Rd BS20 4 C4
Heywood Terr BS20 4 C4
Hibbs Cl SN14 13 F8
HICKS GATE 24 B8
Hicks's La BA22 214 D1
Hidcote Mews BS24 49 E7
Hide Mkt BS2 227 C3
Hidewood La EX15 180 F1
Higgin's Grave La TA13 220 B1
High Acre BS39 77 F4
Highaton Head Cross
EX36 162 C4
High Bank
Porlock TA24 124 A3
Watchet TA23 202 C7
High Bannerdown
Batheaston BA1 29 B4
Shockerwick BA1 29 B5
High Bolham EX16 163 C1
HIGHBRIDGE 104 E3
Highbridge TA4 202 F4
Highbridge & Burnham Sta
TA9 104 E3
Highbridge Rd TA8 104 B5
Highbrooks Rd TA11 173 B5
Highburn Cl TA8 104 C4
HIGHBURY 117 A7
Highbury Cotts
8 Bath BA1 28 A1
Coleford BA3 116 F7
Highbury Ct 15 BS23 30 C1
Highbury Farm Bsns Pk
BS39 77 A8
Highbury Par BS23 30 C1
Highbury Pl BA1 28 A1
Highbury Rd
Hallatrow BS39 77 B7
Weston-super-Mare BS23 30 C1
Highbury St BA3 117 A7
Highbury Terr 10 BA1 28 A1
Highbury Villas
9 Bath BA1 28 A1
Bristol BS2 226 C4
Highcroft
Weston-super-Mare BS23 30 F1
Woolavington TA7 136 E4
Highcroft La BA3 114 E6
High Cross EX16 164 A1
Highdale Ave BS21 6 E3
Highdale Cl BS14 23 B4
Highdale Rd BS21 6 E3
High Down Jun & Inf Schs
BS20 2 A4
Higher Actis BA6 206 E3
HIGHER ALHAM 142 C4
Higher Backway BA10 215 E6
Higher Barton
Martock TA12 185 D4
Trent DT9 187 F5
Higher Beacon TA19 221 B4
Higher Beadon TA16 195 E7
Higher Boyston La DT9 188 E6
Higher Brooks BA16 207 C2
Higher Bullen BA22 197 F8
HIGHER BURROW 184 E7
Higher Burton BA22 197 C8
Higher Cemetery La DT9 188 E7
Higher Cheap St 3 DT9 225 D4
HIGHER CHILLINGTON 194 F5
Higher Comeytrowe Farm La
TA1 212 A1
Higher Coombses TA20 198 D8
Higher Cross EX15 179 C1
HIGHER DURSTON 169 E7
Higher Eastern Hill BA21 218 C8
Higher Easthams La TA18 224 F7
Higher Farm La
Podimore BA22 174 A4
Sparkford BA22 175 B3
Higher Farm Trad Est
BA20 218 C5
Higher Folly Rd
Crewkerne TA18 224 A2
Hewish TA18 195 D2
Higher Gunville DT9 217 D2
HIGHER HADSPEN 214 E4
HIGHER HALSTOCK
LEIGH 197 A2
Higher Heathfield TA4 151 E4
Higher Kingsbury DT9 217 D3
Higher Kingsbury Cl DT9 217 C3
Higher Kingston BA21 219 B5
Higher Kingstonwell
TA20 194 C2
Higher Mead TA19 221 B3
Highermill Farm La TA24 128 B2
Higher Millhayes EX15 180 B1
Higher North Town La
BA22 175 D7
HIGHER NYLAND 177 C1
HIGHER ODCOMBE 186 C2
Higher Orch
Martock TA12 185 D4
Minehead TA24 200 C8
Higher Palmerston Rd
TA2 212 D6
Higher Park La TA24 129 E2
Higher Pk TA24 200 D6
Higher Rd
Chedzoy TA7 154 D8
Horsington BA8 176 D3
Shepton Beauchamp TA19 184 E3
Woolavington TA7 136 E4
Higher Ream BA21 218 C6
Higher Rodhuish Rd TA24 131 B3
HIGHER SANDFORD 188 C7
Higher Shepton Rd
Pitcombe BA9 215 D1
Shepton Montague BA9 160 B2
Higher St
Curry Mallet TA3 183 C8
Martock TA12 185 D4
Merriott TA16 195 F8
Norton Sub Hamdon TA14 185 E2
West Chinnock TA18 196 B8
Higher Street TA5 133 B5
Higher Tolbury BA10 215 E6
HIGHER TOWN 200 E8
Higher Town EX16 178 C1
HIGHER VEXFORD 150 E6
Higher Wambrook TA20 193 C3
Higher Weare La TA20 194 F5
Higher Westbury DT9 187 E1
Higher West Hatch La
TA3 182 D7
Higher Westholme Rd
North Wootton BA4 140 D4
Pilton BA4 204 A1
Higher Woodlands TA3 183 E6
Highfield
Coleford BA3 116 E8
Ilminster TA19 221 B4
Taunton TA1 212 A2
Taunton TA1 212 C3
Wells BA5 140 C7
West Chinnock TA18 196 B8
Highfield Cl
Bath BA2 44 B5
Somerton TA11 211 C4
Taunton TA1 212 A2
Highfield Cres
Chilcompton BA3 96 C4
Taunton TA1 212 A2
Highfield Dr BS20 1 E3
Highfield La
Compton Martin BS40 74 B6
East Harptree BS40 75 A3
Highfield Rd
Keynsham BS31 24 F2
Peasedown St John BA2 79 C8
Street BA16 207 B5
Taunton TA1 168 F4
Weston-super-Mare BS24 49 A1
Yeovil BA21 219 C6
Highfields
Barrington TA19 184 C5
Clandown BA3 78 E4
Midsomer Norton BA3 78 D2
Stanton Drew BS39 39 F1
Highfield Terr TA12 185 D5
Highfield Trad Est BA21 219 C6
Highfield View BA3 116 E8
Highfield Way TA11 211 C4
High Gn BA5 111 A4
High Gr BS9 5 B7
Highgrove TA1 212 E1
Highgrove Cl TA6 209 A2
Highgrove Wlk BS24 50 A8
HIGH HAM 156 A2
High Ham CE Prim Sch
TA10 156 A1
High Kingsdown BS2 226 C4
High La
Barton St David TA11 158 A2
Shapwick TA7 155 F8
Highland Cl BS22 31 B2
Highland Ct BA21 219 C6
Highland Rd BA2 44 B5
Highlands TA1 212 E1
Highlands La BS24 50 A8
Highlands Rd
Long Ashton BS41 11 A2
Portishead BS20 2 B5
Highland Terr BA2 44 D6
High Lea BA21 219 B8
HIGH LITTLETON 59 C1
High Littleton CE VA Prim Sch
BS39 59 C1
High Mdws BA3 77 F1
Highmead Gdns BS13 21 E4
High Mead Gdns BS39 57 D3
Highmore Rd DT9 225 C5
High Path TA21 222 C7
High Pk BS39 77 D6
High Rd BA22 175 D8

HIGHRIDGE
Bristol 21 F7
Dundry 21 D3
Highridge Cres BS13 . . . . . .21 F5
Highridge Gn BS13 . . . . . . .21 E6
Highridge Pk BS13 . . . . . . .21 F6
Highridge Rd BS13, BS41 . .21 E4
Highridge Wlk BS13 . . . . . .21 E7
High St
Aller TA10 . . . . .171 E8
Ashcott TA7 . . . . .156 B8
Axbridge BS26 . . . . .70 B2
Bampton EX16 . . . . .164 B1
Banwell BS29 . . . . .51 A2
Bath BA1 . . . . .228 C2
Bathampton BA2 . . . . .28 F1
Batheaston BA1 . . . . .28 F3
Bathford BA1 . . . . .29 D2
Bath, Twerton BA2 . . . . .44 B6
Bath, Weston BA1 . . . . .27 B1
Bishops Lydeard TA4 . . . . . .167 E8
Bitton BS30 . . . . .25 E8
Blackford BS28 . . . . .107 E4
Blagdon BS40 . . . . .54 E3
Bourton BS22 . . . . .161 F2
Bridgwater TA6 . . . . .208 F5
Bristol BS1 . . . . .227 A2
Bristol, Shirehampton BS11 . . .4 E6
Bruton BA10 . . . . .215 E6
Buckland Dinham BA11 . . . . .100 A3
Burnham-on-S TA8 . . . . .104 A6
Butleigh BA6 . . . . .157 E4
Cannington TA5 . . . . .135 B2
Carhampton TA24 . . . . .131 A5
Castle Cary BA7 . . . . .214 C5
Chapmanslade BA13 . . . . . . .121 C4
Chard TA20 . . . . .223 B4
Charlton Adam TA11 . . . . . . .173 F7
Chew Magna BS40 . . . . .39 A3
Chewton Mendip BA3 . . . . . . .94 F7
Claverham BS49 . . . . .17 F1
Coleford BA3 . . . . .116 F6
Congresbury BS49 . . . . .34 D4
Dulverton TA22 . . . . .163 D6
Dunster TA24 . . . . .201 E2
East Chinnock BA22 . . . . . . .196 E8
East Harptree BS40 . . . . .74 F5
Evercreech BA4 . . . . .141 E1
Faulkland BA3 . . . . .80 D1
Freshford BA3 . . . . .64 B5
Frome BA11 . . . . .119 E5
Glastonbury BA6 . . . . .206 E4
Hardington Mandeville
BA22 . . . . .197 A6
Henstridge BA8 . . . . .190 A6
High Littleton BS39 . . . . .59 D1
Hinton Charterhouse BA2 . . .63 E1
Hinton St George TA17 . . . . .195 D7
Ilchester BA22 . . . . .173 E1
Ilminster TA19 . . . . .221 B4
Keinton Mandeville TA11 . . . .158 A1
Keynsham BS31 . . . . .24 E6
Kingweston BA6 . . . . .157 E1
Lynford-on-F TA11 . . . . .158 C2
Maiden Bradley BA12 . . . . . .144 C2
Marshfield SN14 . . . . .13 F8
Midsomer Norton BA3 . . . . . .78 B1
Milborne Port DT9 . . . . .217 D2
Milton Clevedon BA4 . . . . . .160 A8
Milverton TA4 . . . . .166 F5
Monksilver TA4 . . . . .150 B8
Nailsea BS48 . . . . .8 F3
North Cadbury BA22 . . . . . . .175 D6
North Petherton TA6 . . . . . .153 E4
North Wootton BA4 . . . . .140 C4
Norton St Philip BA2 . . . . . . .81 E4
Nunney BA11 . . . . .143 B8
Oakhill BA3 . . . . .115 A3
Othery TA7 . . . . .155 C2
Paulton BS39 . . . . .77 E5
Paulton, Plummer's Hill BS39 . .77 E6
Pensford BS39 . . . . .40 E4
Porlock TA24 . . . . .124 A3
Portbury BS20 . . . . .3 E3
Portishead BS20 . . . . .2 D5
Queen Camel BA22 . . . . .174 F3
Rimpton BA22 . . . . .188 A8
Rode BA11 . . . . .101 E8
Saltford BS31 . . . . .25 F3
Shepton Mallet BA4 . . . . . . .205 B5
Sparkford BA22 . . . . .175 A5
Spaxton TA5 . . . . .152 E7
Stalbridge DT10 . . . . .190 B5
Stogumber TA4 . . . . .150 D8
Stogursey TA5 . . . . .134 C5
Stoke sub Hamdon TA14 . . . .185 F4
Ston Easton BA3 . . . . .95 E8
Stoney Stratton BA4 . . . . . . .141 F2
Stourton BA12 . . . . .161 F5
Stourton Caundle DT10 . . . . .189 F2
Street BA16 . . . . .207 C6
Taunton TA1 . . . . .212 F3
Templecombe BA8 . . . . .176 E1
Thorncombe TA20 . . . . .199 B6
Timsbury BA2 . . . . .60 B2
Wellington TA21 . . . . .222 E6
Wellow BA2 . . . . .62 D1
Wells BA5 . . . . .203 D4
West Coker BA22 . . . . .197 A8
Weston-super-Mare BS23 . . . .48 D8
Weston-super-Mare, Worle
BS22 . . . . .31 E2
Williton TA4 . . . . .202 D2
Wincanton BA9 . . . . .216 C4
Winford BS40 . . . . .38 A7

High St continued
Winsham TA20 . . . . .194 E1
Wiveliscombe TA4 . . . . .210 C4
Wookey BA5 . . . . .139 D8
Wookey Hole BA5 . . . . .203 A8
Woolley BA1 . . . . .27 F6
Wrington BS40 . . . . .35 D2
Yatton BS49 . . . . .34 C8
Yenston BA8 . . . . .189 F8
Yeovil BA20 . . . . .219 B4
Highview BA2 . . . . .228 A1
High View BA20 . . . . .2 A4
High View Dr TA7 . . . . .156 B8
Highwall La BS14, BS31 . . . .23 F1
HIGHWAY 185 E7
Highway Rd TA12 . . . . .185 D7
Highwoods Cl TA14 . . . . . . .185 F2
Higon Cl BA22 . . . . .186 D3
Hilary Rd TA1 . . . . .212 D3
Hildesheim Bridge BS23 . . .48 F7
Hildesheim Cl BS23 . . . . . . .48 F6
Hildesheim Ct 9 BS23 . . . . .48 E7
Hilhouse BS9 . . . . .5 C6
Hill Ave BA2 . . . . .44 F1
Hillborne Gdns BA21 . . . . . .218 C5
Hillbrook Cl DT9 . . . . .225 D4
Hill Brow DT9 . . . . .225 B2
Hill Cl BA9 . . . . .216 D4
Hillclose La TA19 . . . . .221 F2
HILL CORNER 120 E6
Hillcote Est BS24 . . . . .67 B8
Hillcrest
Crowcombe TA4 . . . . .151 B7
Peasedown St John BA2 . . . .79 C7
Pensford BS39 . . . . .40 E3
Hillcrest Cl
Bristol BS13 . . . . .22 B6
Nailsea BS48 . . . . .8 E1
Yeovil BA21 . . . . .219 C7
Hillcrest Dr BA2 . . . . .44 C4
Hillcrest Rd
Nailsea BS48 . . . . .8 E1
Portishead BS20 . . . . .1 E4
Templecombe BA8 . . . . .176 E1
Hill Crest Rd BA21 . . . . .219 C6
Hillcroft Cl BS22 . . . . .31 A2
Hill Cross BA22 . . . . .196 F6
Hill Ct BS39 . . . . .77 E6
Hilldale Rd BS48 . . . . .19 B5
Hill Dr BS8 . . . . .10 C3
Hill Dro TA12 . . . . .185 A7
Hillend BS22 . . . . .31 E3
HILL END 196 F6
HILLFARRANCE 167 E3
Hillfield BS27 . . . . .90 B7
Hill Gay Cl BS20 . . . . .1 F4
Hill Ground BA11 . . . . .119 E5
Hillgrove Ave BA20 . . . . . . .218 F2
Hillgrove Cl TA6 . . . . .208 E5
Hillgrove Rd BA5 . . . . .93 C1
Hillgrove St N BS2 . . . . .227 A4
Hillgrove St BS2 . . . . .227 B4
Hillgrove Terr BS23 . . . . . . .48 C1
Hill Head BA6 . . . . .206 D3
Hill Head Cl
Glastonbury BA6 . . . . .206 D3
Taunton TA1 . . . . .213 A3
Hillhead Cotts TA2 . . . . . . .212 C8
Hillhead Cross TA24 . . . . . .128 D3
Hillhouse EX14 . . . . .192 D3
Hill House Cl DT9 . . . . .225 E5
Hill House Farm La
Buckland Dinham BA11 . . . . .99 D2
Buckland Dinham BA11 . . . . .99 F3
Hillier's La
Churchill BS25 . . . . .52 E4
Yarley BA5 . . . . .139 C8
Hillingdon Ct BA21 . . . . . . .218 C6
Hill La
Bicknoller TA4 . . . . .132 F2
Bicknoller, Culverhays TA4 . .133 A1
Brent Knoll TA9 . . . . .86 B3
Carhampton TA24 . . . . .131 A4
Chipstable TA4 . . . . .165 C6
Clevedon BS21 . . . . .7 C4
Draycott BS27 . . . . .90 C2
Portishead BS20 . . . . .1 F1
Rodney Stoke BS27 . . . . .91 B2
Rowberrow BS25 . . . . .53 A1
Shepton Mallet BA4 . . . . . . .205 B6
Waterrow TA4 . . . . .165 E5
West Quantoxhead TA4 . . . . .132 F4
Hill Lea Gdns BS27 . . . . .90 B8
Hillmead
Churchill BS40 . . . . .53 A5
Shepton Mallet BA4 . . . . . . .205 B6
Hillmer Rise BS29 . . . . .50 F3
Hill Moor BS21 . . . . .6 E2
Hillpath BS29 . . . . .51 B2
Hill Pk BS49 . . . . .34 E5
Hill Rd
Allerford TA24 . . . . .124 E4
Clevedon BS21 . . . . .6 D4
Dundry BS41 . . . . .21 D2
Minehead TA24 . . . . .125 B4
Sandford BS25 . . . . .52 A3
Weston-super-Mare BS23 . . . .48 F8
Weston-super-Mare, Worle
BS22 . . . . .31 E2
Hill Rd E BS20 . . . . .31 E2
Hillrick Cres BA21 . . . . .218 C8
Hillsboro TA7 . . . . .136 E4
Hillsborough BS8 . . . . .226 A2
Hillsborough Gdns TA8 . . . .85 B1
Hillsborough Ho BS23 . . . . . .49 A4
Hills Cl
Chorley Hill BA10 . . . . .215 F8
Keynsham BS31 . . . . .25 A5

Hills Cotts TA4 . . . . .167 A7
Hillsdon Rd BS9 . . . . .5 F8
HILLSIDE
Axbridge 70 C2
Midsomer Norton 96 E8
Hillside
Bristol BS6 . . . . .226 C4
Chard TA20 . . . . .223 B4
Horrington BA5 . . . . .113 A2
Portbury BS20 . . . . .3 D3
Puriton TA7 . . . . .136 C4
West Pennard BA6 . . . . .140 B1
Hillside Ave
Frome BA11 . . . . .119 F2
Midsomer Norton BA3 . . . . . .96 F8
Hillside Cl
Curry Rivel TA10 . . . . .171 D4
Paulton BS39 . . . . .77 F6
Hill Side Cl BA5 . . . . .203 C5
Hillside Cres
Midsomer Norton BA3 . . . . . .96 E8
Puriton TA7 . . . . .136 C4
Hillside Dr
Frome BA11 . . . . .120 B4
Puriton TA7 . . . . .136 C4
Hillside Fst BS22 . . . . .31 E2
Hillside Gdns
Bishop Sutton BS39 . . . . .57 C3
Weston-super-Mare BS22 . . . .31 B1
Hillside Gr TA1 . . . . .212 C1
Hillside Ho BA11 . . . . .119 F3
Hillside Rd
Backwell BS48 . . . . .19 A4
Bath BA2 . . . . .44 D4
Bleadon BS24 . . . . .67 B8
Clevedon BS21 . . . . .6 D3
Long Ashton BS41 . . . . .11 B2
Midsomer Norton BA3 . . . . . .96 F8
Portishead BS20 . . . . .1 D4
Hillside Terr BA21 . . . . .219 C5
Hillside View
1 Barwick BA22 . . . . .197 F8
Midsomer Norton BA3 . . . . . .78 A3
Peasedown St John BA2 . . . .79 C8
Yeovil BA22 . . . . .219 D1
Hillside W BS24 . . . . .49 F2
Hill's La 10 TA12 . . . . .185 E6
Hills Orch 9 TA12 . . . . .185 E6
Hill St
Bristol BS1 . . . . .226 C2
Stogumber TA4 . . . . .150 D8
Hill Terr TA1 . . . . .212 A4
Hill The
Freshford BA3 . . . . .64 C5
Langport TA10 . . . . .172 A5
Hill Top BS20 . . . . .2 A4
Hilltop La TA5 . . . . .133 D6
Hill Top La BS40 . . . . .37 B3
Hilltops TA8 . . . . .65 F6
Hillview
Midsomer Norton BA3 . . . . . .96 E7
Timsbury BA2 . . . . .60 B1
Hill View
Brean TA8 . . . . .65 E2
Bristol BS8 . . . . .226 B2
Brompton Ralph TA4 . . . . . . .150 C3
Farrington Gurney BS39 . . . . .77 B3
Marksbury BA2 . . . . .42 B1
Mudford BA21 . . . . .187 D6
Priston BA2 . . . . .61 A5
Queen Camel BA22 . . . . .174 F4
Yeovil BA21 . . . . .219 C5
Hillview Ave BS21 . . . . .6 D2
Hillview Cl TA24 . . . . .200 D7
Hill View Cl
Ilton TA19 . . . . .183 F4
7 Stoke sub Hamdon TA14 .185 F4
West Chinnock TA18 . . . . . .196 B8
Hill View Ct
Evercreech BA4 . . . . .141 E1
Weston-super-Mare BS22 . . . .49 D8
Hill View Cvn Pk BS40 . . . . .20 B1
Hillview Gdns BS40 . . . . .37 C8
Hill View Park Homes
BS22 . . . . .49 D8
Hillview Rd
Loxton BS26 . . . . .68 C4
Minehead TA24 . . . . .200 D7
Hill View Rd
Bath BA1 . . . . .28 B2
Bristol BS13 . . . . .22 A8
Carhampton TA24 . . . . .131 A5
Weston-super-Mare BS23 . . . .49 A7
Hillview Terr TA12 . . . . .185 D5
Hill View Terr
Ilminster TA19 . . . . .221 B4
Lyng TA3 . . . . .170 C7
Hill View Trad Est TA4 . . . . .151 E4
Hillway TA11 . . . . .173 E7
Hillworth Ho 28 BA4 . . . . . .205 B6
Hillyfield Rd BS13 . . . . .22 A6
Hillyfields
Taunton TA1 . . . . .213 C2
Winscombe BS25 . . . . .70 B8
Hillyfields Way BS25 . . . . . . .70 A8
Hilly Head TA21 . . . . .222 B5
Hilly Pk TA2 . . . . .168 B5
Hinam Cross TA22 . . . . .163 B7
Hinckley Cl BS22 . . . . .32 C4
Hincombe Hill BA4 . . . . .142 E2
Hindhayes Inf Sch BA16 . . . .207 D5
Hindhayes La BA16 . . . . .207 D6
Hindon La TA24 . . . . .123 F3
Hind Pitts BS25 . . . . .70 F7
Hine Rd TA1 . . . . .212 B1
Hinham La TA22 . . . . .163 A7
Hinkley Point Nature Trail★
TA5 . . . . .134 C8

Hinkley Point Rd TA5 . . . . .134 E6
Hinkley Point Visitor Ctr★
TA6 . . . . .208 F4
HINTON 187 D7
Hinton BS24 . . . . .49 A2
HINTON BLEWETT 75 F6
Hinton Blewett Rd
Hinton Blewett BS39 . . . . . . .75 E8
Sutton Wick BS39 . . . . .57 E1
HINTON CHARTERHOUSE . .63 E1
Hinton Cl
Bath BA2 . . . . .43 F6
Hinton St George TA17 . . . . .195 D7
Saltford BS31 . . . . .25 E3
Hinton Cross BA22 . . . . .187 D7
Hinton Dr TA1 . . . . .212 E1
Hinton Field La TA12 . . . . . .185 D4
Hinton Hill BA2, BA3 . . . . . . .63 A1
Hinton La 12 BS8 . . . . .11 F6
Hinton Rd TA18 . . . . .224 B8
HINTON ST GEORGE 195 D7
Hinton St George CE Sch
Dinnington TA17 . . . . .195 C7
Hinton St George TA17 . . . . .195 C7
Hinton Villas BA2 . . . . .63 E1
Hippisley Dr BS26 . . . . .70 D2
Hippisley Ho BA5 . . . . .113 A1
Hippys Farm La BA3 . . . . . .116 F6
Hiscocks Dr BA2 . . . . .44 E4
Hiscocks La BA8 . . . . .176 E2
Hitchen TA16 . . . . .195 F7
Hitchen Cl SN14 . . . . .13 F8
Hitchen Hill BA4 . . . . .140 F3
Hitchings Dro TA12 . . . . . . .185 A8
Hitchings La TA3 . . . . .170 B7
Hitchin La BA4 . . . . .205 A5
Hither Acre TA19 . . . . .221 A4
Hither Bath Bridge BS4 . . . .23 E8
Hither Gn BS21 . . . . .6 F2
Hither Green Ind Est BS21 . . .6 F2
Hither Mead TA4 . . . . .167 E8
Hittsford La EX36 . . . . .162 A1
Hoare's La BA11 . . . . .98 B3
Hobart Rd BS23 . . . . .48 F3
Hobbiton Rd BS22 . . . . .32 A4
Hobbs Ct 1 BS48 . . . . .8 F2
Hobbs La BS48 . . . . .20 E3
Hobb's La BS1 . . . . .226 C2
Hobbs Mead 7 TA4 . . . . . . .167 E8
Hobbs Rd BA4 . . . . .205 D3
HOBB'S WALL 59 E5
Hob Cl TA2 . . . . .169 B2
Hob La TA2 . . . . .168 E8
Hobwell La BS41 . . . . .11 C2
Hoccombe Ford TA4 . . . . . .150 F1
Hocken Cl TA20 . . . . .223 D6
Hockers Hill BA22 . . . . .186 B2
HOCKHOLLER 180 E8
HOCKHOLLER GREEN 180 E8
Hockley Ct BA1 . . . . .27 D1
Hockley La BA22 . . . . .175 E5
Hockpitt La TA5 . . . . .134 A2
HOCKWORTHY 178 D6
Hodder's Cl BA11 . . . . .119 E5
Hodders La BS22 . . . . .32 D6
Hodges Barton TA11 . . . . . .211 C4
Hodshill BA2 . . . . .62 F6
Hoecroft BA3 . . . . .96 D2
Hoecroft Gdns BA3 . . . . .96 D3
Hogarth Mews BS22 . . . . . . .32 A3
Hogarth Wlk BS22 . . . . .32 A3
HOGGINGTON 83 D4
Hoggington La BA14 . . . . . . .83 E3
Hogues Wlk BS13 . . . . .22 B4
Holbeach Way BS14 . . . . . . .23 A2
HOLBEAR 223 D2
Holbear TA20 . . . . .223 D2
Holbrook Cres BS13 . . . . . . .22 D4
Holbrook Pk TA13 . . . . .220 C5
**Holburne Museum & Crafts
Study Ctr**★ BA2 . . . . .45 B7
Holburne Pk BA2 . . . . .45 C8
HOLCOMBE 116 C8
Holcombe Cl BA2 . . . . .28 F1
Holcombe Gn BA1 . . . . .27 B2
Holcombe Gr BS31 . . . . .24 D5
Holcombe Hill BA3 . . . . .116 C7
Holcombe La
Bathampton BA2 . . . . .28 F1
Doulting BA4 . . . . .141 E4
HOLCOMBE ROGUS 178 F5
Holcombe Vale BA2 . . . . .28 F1
Holden's Way
Curry Rivel TA10 . . . . .171 C3
Curry Rivel TA10 . . . . .171 D3
Holders Wlk BS41 . . . . .20 F8
Holdfast La TA14 . . . . .185 D1
Holditch Court La TA20 . . . .198 E5
Holditch La EX13, TA20 . . . .198 E5
Holdscroft La DT6 . . . . .199 B1
Holeground Villas BA5 . . . . .203 A8
Holemoor Farm Rd TA20 . . .193 D6
Holemore Cross EX14 . . . . .191 F5
Holes La BA11 . . . . .118 B6
Holes Sq TA24 . . . . .130 B5
HOLFORD 133 D4
Holford Cl BS48 . . . . .8 E1
Holford Ct BS14 . . . . .23 B5
Holford La TA4 . . . . .151 C5
Holford Rd
Bridgwater TA6 . . . . .208 B4
Taunton TA2 . . . . .212 B4
Hollam Cross TA22 . . . . .163 E7
Hollam Dr TA22 . . . . .163 D6
Hollam La TA22 . . . . .163 D7
Holland Ct BA16 . . . . .207 D7

Holland Rd
Bath BA1 . . . . .28 B1
Clevedon BS21 . . . . .6 B1
HOLLANDS 219 A7
Holland's La TA4 . . . . .149 E1
Holland St BS23 . . . . .49 A8
Holland's Wash Dro TA20 .193 C5
Holleys Cl TA20 . . . . .198 D8
Hollies Cl
Martock TA12 . . . . .185 D5
Middlezoy TA7 . . . . .155 B3
Shepton Mallet BA4 . . . . . . .205 C6
Hollies La BA1 . . . . .29 A6
Hollies The
Crewkerne TA18 . . . . .224 C4
Midsomer Norton BA3 . . . . . .78 A1
Yeovil BA21 . . . . .219 C7
Hollis Ave BS20 . . . . .2 C3
Hollis Cl
Halstock BA22 . . . . .197 D3
Long Ashton BS41 . . . . .21 A8
Hollis Cres BS20 . . . . .2 C3
Hollister's Dr BS13 . . . . .22 D4
Hollis Way
Halstock BA22 . . . . .197 D3
Southwick BA14 . . . . .83 F3
Holloway
Bath BA2 . . . . .228 B1
Lopen TA13 . . . . .185 A1
Minehead TA24 . . . . .200 F7
Holloway Rd TA7 . . . . .155 B2
Holloway St TA24 . . . . .200 F7
Holloway The TA21 . . . . . . .179 E7
HOLLOW BROOK 57 C6
Hollowbrook La BS39, BS40 .57 D6
Hollowell Hill
Norton Sub Hamdon TA14,
TA18 . . . . .185 E1
West Chinnock TA18 . . . . . .196 B8
Hollow La
Baltonsborough BA6 . . . . . . .158 B8
Dinnington TA17 . . . . .195 B7
Lopen TA13 . . . . .185 A1
Montacute TA15 . . . . .186 B3
Wembdon TA5, TA6 . . . . . . .208 C2
Weston-super-Mare BS22 . . . .31 F3
Hollow Marsh La BA3, BS39 .76 B4
Hollowmead BS49 . . . . .34 E8
Hollowmead Cl BS49 . . . . . . .34 E8
Hollow Rd
Shepton Beauchamp TA19 . .184 D3
Shipham BS25 . . . . .70 F8
Hollow The
Bath BA2 . . . . .44 B4
Corsley Heath BA12 . . . . . . .144 E8
Dunkerton BA2 . . . . .61 D4
Westbury-sub-Mendip BA5 . .110 D7
Hollway Cl BS14 . . . . .23 E5
Hollway Rd BS14 . . . . .23 E5
HOLLY BROOK 110 F5
Holly Bush La BA4 . . . . .144 E3
Hollybush Cl BA15 . . . . .64 E7
Hollybush La
Bristol BS9 . . . . .5 E5
Bristol BS9 . . . . .5 F4
Leigh u M BA3 . . . . .117 A2
Holly Cl
Bridgwater TA6 . . . . .209 E5
Nailsea BS48 . . . . .9 A3
7 North Petherton TA6 . . . . .153 F3
Taunton TA1 . . . . .213 C1
Weston-super-Mare BS22 . . . .32 A1
Holly Ct
Bristol BS2 . . . . .226 C4
Frome BA11 . . . . .120 B7
Holly Dr BA2 . . . . .62 D8
Holly Gr TA18 . . . . .224 D7
Holly Hill BA4 . . . . .142 C1
Hollyhock Cl TA6 . . . . .208 E2
Holly La
Clevedon BS21 . . . . .6 F5
Drimpton DT8 . . . . .199 F8
Shepton Mallet BA4 . . . . . . .205 C4
Hollyman Wlk 5 BS21 . . . . . .6 F3
Hollymead La BS9 . . . . .5 E4
Holly Ridge BS20 . . . . .2 A5
Holly Terr
Chard TA20 . . . . .223 C4
Odcombe BA22 . . . . .186 C2
Holly Tree Wlk BA20 . . . . . .218 E3
Holly Wlk
Keynsham BS31 . . . . .24 D4
Radstock BA3 . . . . .78 E1
Holman Cl BA6 . . . . .206 D3
HOLMAN CLAVEL 181 E3
Holman's BA6 . . . . .157 E4
Holmbury Cl BA11 . . . . .120 D6
Holmbush TA24 . . . . .128 E8
Holm Cl TA8 . . . . .104 B3
Holmlea
Portishead BS20 . . . . .2 F5
1 Wookey BA5 . . . . .139 D8
Holmoak Rd BS31 . . . . .24 C4
Holm Oaks BA6 . . . . .157 E4
Holm Rd BS24 . . . . .49 E2
Holms Rd BS23 . . . . .49 A5
Holm Vw TA22 . . . . .202 D7
Holsom Cl BS14 . . . . .23 F6
Holsom Rd BS14 . . . . .23 F6
Holstein Ave BS25 . . . . .69 F7
Holst Gdns BS4 . . . . .22 D7
Holt Ball Steep TA24 . . . . . .129 C8
Holten's La BA22 . . . . .196 E6
Holt Hill DT9 . . . . .189 C1
Holt La
Halstock BA22 . . . . .197 F3
South Perrott DT8 . . . . .196 D1

Holt La continued
  Stourton Candle DT9, DT10 **189** E1
  West Pennard BA6 . . . . **140** D2
HOLTON **176** C5
Holton Cross BA9 . . . . **176** C6
Holton St BA9. . . . . **176** C5
Holt Rd
  North Brewham BA11. . . . . **161** E8
  Witham Friary BA11. . . . . . . **143** D1
Holtsdown La BA1. . . . . **28** F7
Holvert La TA20 . . . . **194** F1
HOLWAY
  Sherborne **188** D7
  Taunton **213** C2
  Thorncombe. **199** C6
Holway
  North Petherton TA6. . . . . **153** F4
  Tatworth TA20 . . . . **198** D3
Holway Ave TA1. . . . . **213** B3
Holway Deane TA1 . . . . **213** C2
Holway Gn TA1 . . . . **213** C2
Holway Hill TA1 . . . . **213** B2
Holway House Pk TA19 . . . . **183** C2
Holway Park Com Prim Sch
  Holway TA1. . . . . **213** C3
  Taunton TA1 . . . . **213** C3
Holway Rd TA1. . . . . **213** B3
HOLWELL **143** B8
Holwell Cl BS39 . . . . **77** E4
Holwell Hill BA11. . . . . **143** B7
Holwell La BA11. . . . . **89** F8
Holworthy La TA22. . . . . . . **148** E2
Holy Moor Cross EX36 . . . . **162** C1
Holy Moor La EX36 . . . . **162** C1
Holyoake St TA21 . . . . **222** C7
Holyrood Com Sch (Lower)
  TA20 . . . . **223** C4
Holyrood Com Sch (Upper)
  TA20 . . . . **223** C3
Holyrood St TA20 . . . . **223** C3
Holy Tree Cross TA14. . . . . **185** E3
Holy Trinity CE Prim Sch
  Holway TA1. . . . . **213** A2
  Taunton TA1 . . . . **213** A3
  Yeovil BA20 . . . . **218** E2
HOLYWELL **197** C8
HOLYWELL LAKE **179** E7
Holy Well Rd TA7. . . . . **137** C2
Homberg Way TA6 . . . . **208** E6
Homeavon Ho BS31 . . . . **24** F5
Homecanton Ho BA9 . . . . . **216** C4
Homecastle Ho 2 TA6. . . . **208** F5
Homechime Ho BA5. . . . . . **203** D3
Home Cl
  Westbury-sub-Mendip
   BA5. . . . . **110** E6
  West Camel BA22. . . . . **174** D3
  Wrington BS40. . . . . **35** E3
Homeclose La EX13, TA20 **198** A8
Home Cotts TA1. . . . . **212** D5
Home Dr
  Wincanton BA9 . . . . **216** C3
  Yeovil BA21 . . . . **218** E5
Home Farm Cl BA2 . . . . **79** B7
Home Farm La BA22. . . . . . **188** A8
Home Farm Pk TA19. . . . . . **183** E2
Home Farm Rd BS8. . . . . **11** B8
Home Farm Way TA19 . . . . **183** E2
Homefield
  Bishops Lydeard TA4. . . . . **167** E8
  Congresbury BS49 . . . . **34** E3
  Locking BS24 . . . . **50** A5
  Timsbury BA2. . . . . **60** C2
  Wellington TA21 . . . . **222** E4
Homefield Cl
  Beckington BA11. . . . . **101** E4
  Creech St Michael TA3. . . . **169** D4
  Locking BS24. . . . . **50** A5
  Saltford BS31. . . . . **25** E3
  Winscombe BS25 . . . . **51** F1
Home Field Cl TA11. . . . . . . **157** B4
Homefield Ct BA21 . . . . **174** F1
Homefield Ind Est BS24. . . . **50** A5
Homefield Rd BS31. . . . . **25** F3
Homefields BA5. . . . . **110** C6
Home Fields BA4. . . . . **205** C6
Homeground BS21 . . . . **6** F2
Home Ground BS11 . . . . **4** D7
Homelea Pk E BA1 . . . . **44** A7
Homelea Pk W BA1. . . . . **44** A7
Home Mdw TA24. . . . . **200** D7
Homemead BA2. . . . . **43** A8
Home Mead BS4 . . . . **22** E7
Home Orch
  Chew Stoke BS40. . . . . **56** D8
  Hatch Beauchamp TA3 . . . **183** A7
Homer Wk BS31. . . . . **24** C3
Homestead BS20. . . . . **1** E3
Homestead Ave TA9. . . . . . **104** D3
Homestead Pk BA5. . . . . . . **203** A7
Homestead The
  Clevedon BS21. . . . . **6** C3
  Keynsham BS31. . . . . **24** F2
Homestead Way BS25 . . . . . **70** A8
Homeville Ho BA20. . . . . . . **219** A4
Home Way Cnr BA6 . . . . . . **138** B4
Hone Cross EX16. . . . . **164** F5
Hone La TA22. . . . . **147** F4
Honeycombe Rise DT9 . . . . **225** B2
Honey Crock La TA7. . . . . . . **155** E8
Honeygar La BA6. . . . . **138** B5
Honey Garston Cl BS13. . . . **22** B4
Honey Garston Rd BS13. . . **22** B4
HONEY HALL. **52** C7
Honeyhall La BS49 . . . . **52** D7
Honeyhurst La BS27. . . . . . **109** F8
Honeylands
  Curry Rivel TA10. . . . . **171** D4

Honeylands continued
  Portishead BS20 . . . . **2** C3
Honeymead
  Bristol BS14. . . . . **23** C6
  Croscombe BA5 . . . . **204** B8
Honey Mead La BA6, TA11. **158** B4
Honeypot La TA11. . . . . **158** C1
Honey Pot La BA11 . . . . **144** A4
Honey Row La TA4 . . . . **132** E2
Honeysuckle Pl BS24. . . . . . **50** A8
Honeywell La BA3. . . . . **94** F4
Honeywick Rd BA7 . . . . **214** E5
Honiton 9 BS22. . . . . **32** A2
Honiton Rd
  Clevedon BS21. . . . . **6** E1
  Taunton TA3 . . . . **168** D1
Hood Cl BA6 . . . . **206** E3
Hood Rd BA21 . . . . **219** F8
HOOK
  Chard. **198** B8
  Timsbury **60** D2
Hook Dro BA2. . . . . **187** B8
Hookedmead La BS26. . . . . . **88** A1
Hook Hill BA2. . . . . **60** D2
Hook La
  Hinton Blewett BA3, BS39 . . **75** E4
  North Cheriton BA9 . . . . . . **176** C5
Hooks Batch BS40. . . . . **54** C4
Hookway Hill TA24. . . . . . . **123** A3
Hooper Ave BA5. . . . . **112** E1
Hooper Cl
  Burnham-on-S TA8 . . . . . . **104** D5
  Highbridge TA9. . . . . **104** F4
Hooper Rd
  Bristol BS14. . . . . **23** D5
  Street BA16. . . . . **207** B5
Hoopers Barton 9 BA11. **119** E5
Hooper's Cl TA1 . . . . **212** B2
Hoopers Cross EX16. . . . . . **164** D3
Hooper's La
  East Coker BA22 . . . . **197** F7
  Fordgate TA7. . . . . **154** E3
HOOPERS POOL **83** D1
Hopcott Cl TA24. . . . . **200** E6
Hopcott Rd TA24. . . . . **200** F5
Hopcott Terr TA24. . . . . . . **201** A5
Hopechapel Hill 10 BS8. . . **11** F6
Hope Cl BA5 . . . . **203** C4
Hope Corner Cl TA2 . . . . . . **212** E8
Hope Corner La TA2 . . . . . . **212** F8
Hope Cote Lodge BA2 . . . . . **45** C1
Hope Cotts
  Highbridge TA9. . . . . **104** D3
  Kingston Seymour BS21. . . **16** B2
Hope Cross SP8 . . . . **177** D3
Hope Ct BS1 . . . . **226** B1
Hope Sq BS8. . . . . **11** F6
Hope Terr BA3 . . . . **78** B1
Hopewell Gdns BS11 . . . . . . **4** F7
Hopewell St TA6. . . . . **208** D5
Hopkins Cl BA9 . . . . **216** C2
Hopkins Field TA3. . . . . **169** D5
Hopkins Ho BA22. . . . . **218** A5
Hopkins St BS23 . . . . **48** E8
Hopton Cl BA4. . . . . **141** E1
Hopton Wy BA1 . . . . **27** E4
Hopwoods Corner BS27. . . . **90** B8
Horesham Gr BS13 . . . . **22** C5
Horfield Rd BS2. . . . . **227** A4
HORN ASH **199** D7
Hornbeam Cl
  Bridgwater TA6 . . . . **209** D5
  Frome BA11. . . . . **120** C6
  Taunton TA1 . . . . **213** D2
HORNBLOTTON **158** F5
Horne Cl BA3 . . . . **96** F1
HORNER **129** B8
Horner Nature Trails ★
  TA24 . . . . **129** B8
Horner Rd TA2 . . . . **213** B7
HORNINGSHAM **144** C4
Horningsham Prim Sch
  BA12. . . . . **144** D4
Horn La TA20 . . . . **194** B2
HORNSBURY. **223** E7
Hornsbury Hill TA20. . . . . . **223** E8
Hornsey La TA20. . . . . **182** B1
Horns La BA9 . . . . **160** B2
Horn's La BS26. . . . . **70** B2
Horn St BA11. . . . . **143** B8
Hornswell DT9. . . . . **189** D4
HORRINGTON **113** A1
Horrington Prim Sch BA5 **113** B3
HORSECASTLE **17** A2
Horsecastle Cl BS49 . . . . . . **17** A1
Horsecastle Farm Rd BS49 **17** A1
Horsecastle La DT9 . . . . . . **225** C3
Horsecastles DT9. . . . . **225** D3
Horsecombe Brow BA2. . . . **45** A1
Horsecombe Gr BA2. . . . . . . **45** A1
Horsecombe La TA24. . . . . **129** A1
Horsecombe Vale BA2. . . . . **45** A1
Horsecroft La TA3. . . . . **170** B4
Horsefair The BS1. . . . . **227** B3
Horseham La TA5 . . . . **134** E8
Horsehill La BA4 . . . . **142** D2
Horse La DT9 . . . . **176** A2
Horseland La TA24. . . . . . . **131** A5
Horseleaze La BS25. . . . . . . **52** D1
Horsemans Mews BA6. . . . **206** D5
Horse Mill Cross DT6 . . . . **199** D3
Horse Mill La TA11. . . . . . . **211** E4
Horsepark La TA24 . . . . **130** A4
Horse Pond La TA6. . . . . . . **208** F4
Horsepool Rd BS13. . . . . **21** E3
Horse Race La BS8 . . . . **10** A6
Horse Rd TA24 . . . . **130** F5

Horseshoe Cotts TA12 . . . . **185** E7
Horseshoe Dr BS9. . . . . **5** C4
Horseshoe Rd BA20 . . . . . . **199** A6
Horseshoe Wlk BA2 . . . . **45** B5
HORSEY. **136** C2
Horsey Dro TA10 . . . . **172** B1
Horsey La
  Horsey TA7. . . . . **136** C2
  Langport TA10. . . . . **172** A4
  Yeovil BA20 . . . . **219** A4
Horsey Rdbt BA20 . . . . **219** A3
HORSINGTON **176** D2
Horsington CE Prim Sch
  BA8. . . . . **176** D3
Horsington Ho BA8. . . . . . . **176** E2
Horsington Rd BA8. . . . . . . **176** D2
Horstmann Cl 2 BA1. . . . . . **44** B7
Hortmead La TA19 . . . . **183** E3
HORTON **183** C1
Horton Cl BA21 . . . . **218** D6
HORTON CROSS **183** D2
Horton Ho BA2. . . . . **228** C4
Horton St
  Bristol BS2. . . . . **227** C3
  Frome BA11. . . . . **119** D5
Horton Way TA7 . . . . **136** E4
Horts Rd TA1 . . . . **212** C1
Horwood Rd BS48. . . . . **8** F1
Hosegood Dr BS24. . . . . **49** C4
Hosey Wlk BS13. . . . . **22** A5
Hoskins Cl TA10. . . . . **171** C4
Hospital La
  Sherborne DT9. . . . . **225** D4
  South Petherton TA13. . . . **220** D5
Hospital Rd BS48. . . . . **20** F7
Hospital Rdbt BA20. . . . . . . **219** A5
Host St BS1. . . . . **227** A3
Hot Bath St 6 BA1 . . . . **228** B2
Hotwell Rd BS8. . . . . **226** B1
HOTWELLS **226** A1
Hotwells Prim Sch BS8 . . . . **11** F6
Houlgate Way BS26 . . . . **70** B1
Houlton St BS2. . . . . **227** C4
Houndsmill BA8. . . . . **176** E2
HOUNDSMOOR. **167** A4
Houndsmoor La TA4. . . . . . **167** A4
Hound St DT9 . . . . **225** D4
HOUNDSTONE **218** A6
Houndstone Bsns Pk
  BA22. . . . . **218** B6
Houndstone Cl BA21 . . . . . **218** C5
Houndstone Cnr BA22 . . . . **218** A5
Houndstone Ct BA22 . . . . . **218** A5
Houndstone Pk BA22 . . . . . **218** A5
Houndstone Ret Pk BA22 **218** B5
Houndwood Cl BA16. . . . . . **207** A6
Houndwood Dro BA16. . . . **207** A6
HOUNSLEY BATCH. **38** A3
House Gate Rd BA11. . . . . . **143** F2
House's La TA20 . . . . **193** F1
Housman Rd BA16 . . . . **207** D5
Houston Way BA11. . . . . . . **119** D5
Hoveland Cres TA1 . . . . **212** D2
Hoveland Ct TA1 . . . . **212** E2
Hoveland Dr TA1 . . . . **212** D1
Hoveland La TA1 . . . . **212** C2
Howard Cl
  Burnham-on-S TA8 . . . . . . **104** C7
  Saltford BS31. . . . . **25** D3
Howard Rd
  Wellington TA21 . . . . **222** D7
  Yeovil BA21 . . . . **219** E6
Howards Row TA20. . . . . . . **223** C4
Howecroft Ct BS9. . . . . **5** E4
Howecroft Gdns BS9 . . . . . . **5** E4
Howell Hill BA22. . . . . **174** D4
Howell's La TA2, TA6. . . . . . **153** D1
Howgrove Hill La BS40 . . . . **37** C2
How Hill BA2 . . . . **44** A6
Howitt Way 1 BS24 . . . . . . **49** F7
Howleigh La TA3. . . . . **181** C5
HOWLEY **192** F4
Hownel La TA22. . . . . **147** F2
Howtown La TA24. . . . . **147** D5
Hoyles Cl TA21. . . . . **222** E4
Hoyles Rd TA21. . . . . **222** E4
Hozzard La TA12 . . . . **185** E8
Huckeymead La BA4 . . . . . . **158** F7
Huddleston Ct 10 BA5 . . . . **203** D4
Hudson St TA6. . . . . **184** B6
Hudson Way TA2. . . . . **212** C6
Huett Cl TA21. . . . . **65** F3
Hugdole La TA7. . . . . **137** D2
Hughenden Rd BS23. . . . . . . **49** A8
Hughes Cl 6 TA6. . . . . **209** B4
Hughes Cl BA11. . . . . **101** E6
Hugh Sexey CE Mid Sch
  BS28 . . . . **107** C3
Hugo St TA1. . . . . **213** A4
Huish BA20 . . . . **219** A5
Huish Ball Steep TA20 . . . . **129** D7
HUISH CHAMPFLOWER. . . **165** F8
Huish Cl
  Highbridge TA9. . . . . **104** D4
  Taunton TA1 . . . . **213** D4
Huish Cleeve TA4. . . . . **165** E7
Huish Ct BA3 . . . . **79** B2
Huish Dro TA10 . . . . **171** F5
HUISH EPISCOPI. **172** B5
Huish Episcopi Acad
  TA10. . . . . **172** A5
Huish Episcopi Prim Sch
  TA10. . . . . **172** A5
Huish Gdns 2 BA20. . . . . . **219** A5
Huish La
  Alweston DT9. . . . . **189** B2
  Washford TA23. . . . . **131** E4
  Wyke Champflower BA10. . **215** C7

Huish Mdw TA23 . . . . **131** E4
Huish Park (Yeovil Town FC)
  BA22 . . . . **218** B2
Huish Prim Sch
  Crofton Park BA20 . . . . . . **219** A5
  Yeovil BA20 . . . . **219** A5
Huish Rd TA11 . . . . **173** C7
Huish Row TA24. . . . . **129** A8
Hukeley Head Cross EX16 **164** D3
Hulk Moor Dro BA16,
  BA16. . . . . **207** C8
Hulkshay La TA6. . . . . **153** E3
Hull La DT9, BA8. . . . . **176** B3
Humber Gr TA1 . . . . **213** D3
Humberstan Wlk BS11. . . . . **4** E8
Hummer Rd DT9 . . . . **187** E6
Humphreys Rd TA21. . . . . . **222** E7
Humphry Davy Way 6 BS8. **11** F5
Humpy La DT9 . . . . **189** A1
Hundredstone Cl BA21 . . . **219** B8
Hundry La TA10. . . . . **184** C8
HUNGERFORD **131** E2
Hungerford Cl BS4 . . . . **23** E8
Hungerford Gdns BS4 . . . . . **23** E8
Hungerford Rd
  Bath BA1 . . . . **44** C7
  Bristol BS4. . . . . **23** E8
Hungerford Terr BA2. . . . . . **62** D1
Hung Rd BS11 . . . . **4** E5
Hunstrete BA2. . . . . **41** D2
Hunstrete La BS39 . . . . **41** B4
Hunstrete Rd BA2. . . . . **59** F7
Huntash La TA4 . . . . **167** A4
Huntenhull Gn BA13. . . . . . **121** C3
Huntenhull La BA13 . . . . . . **121** D4
Hunter's Hill EX15. . . . . **179** E1
Hunters Moon Touring Pk
  EX13. . . . . **198** E1
Hunters Rest Miniature Rlwy ★
  BS39 . . . . **59** A5
Hunter's Way EX15 . . . . **179** E1
Huntham Cl TA3 . . . . **170** E6
Huntham La TA3. . . . . **170** E6
Huntham Rd TA3. . . . . **170** D4
Huntingham Rd BS13. . . . . . **21** F4
Huntley Cl EX13. . . . . **198** A2
Huntley Gr BS48 . . . . **9** A1
Huntley La
  Chardstock EX13 . . . . **198** A8
  Tatworth EX13, TA20 . . . . . **193** D1
HUNTSCOTT. **129** E6
HUNTSHAM **178** A7
Hunts La TA5 . . . . **133** D5
Hunt's La BS48 . . . . **34** E8
Huntsmans Ridge BS27. . . . **90** C7
Hunts Mead DT9 . . . . **225** B2
HUNTSPILL **136** B8
Huntspill Rd TA9. . . . . **104** D2
Huntspill River National
  Nature Reserve ★ TA9. . . **136** D6
HUNTSTILE **153** C4
HUNTWORTH **154** B5
Huntworth Bsns Pk TA6. . . **154** A5
Huntworth La
  Fordgate TA7. . . . . **154** C5
  North Petherton TA6. . . . . **153** F4
Hurcot La TA11 . . . . **173** C8
HURCOTT **173** C8
Hurcott Cross TA19 . . . . . . **184** D4
Hurcott La TA19. . . . . **184** D4
Hurdle Way TA1. . . . . **213** A3
Hurd's Bldgs BA11 . . . . **119** F4
Hurley La TA4 . . . . **151** B8
Hurlstone Pk TA24 . . . . **124** B3
Humans Cl TA7. . . . . **156** B8
Hurn Dro BA5. . . . . **139** B6
Hurn La
  Berrow TA8. . . . . **84** F7
  Keynsham BS31. . . . . **25** A3
  Pitcombe BA7. . . . . **215** A1
  Shepton Montague BA7. . . **160** A2
Hurn Rd BS31 . . . . **6** F2
Hursley Hill
  Bristol BS14. . . . . **40** D8
  Whitchurch BS14. . . . . **23** D1
Hursley La BS14. . . . . **23** E1
HURST **185** D5
Hurst TA12 . . . . **185** D5
Hurst Dro
  Compton Dundon TA11. . . **157** A3
  Hambridge TA10, TA12 . . . **184** E8
Hurst Drove BS28 . . . . **109** C2
Hurst Mews TA12 . . . . **185** D5
Hurston Rd BS4 . . . . **22** D7
Hurst Pk TA12 . . . . **185** D5
Hurst Rd
  Bristol BS4. . . . . **22** E8
  Weston-super-Mare BS23 . **49** A6
Hurst Wlk BS4 . . . . **22** E8
Hussey's DT10 . . . . **190** F5
Hutchings's La TA4. . . . . . . **167** D4
Hutchin's La BA10. . . . . **160** F8
HUTTON **49** E2
Hutton CE Prim Sch BA22 **49** E2
Hutton Cl
  Bristol BS9. . . . . **5** E7
  Keynsham BS31. . . . . **25** A2
Hutton Hill BA22 . . . . **49** F2
Hutton Moor La
  BS22, BS24. . . . . **49** C6
Hutton Moor Pk BS24. . . . . **49** C6
Hutton Moor Rd BS22. . . . . **49** C7
Hutton Moor Rdbt BS22. . . **49** C6
Huxham La BA4 . . . . **158** F7
Hyacinth Terr BA11. . . . . . . **222** A7
Hyatt Pl BA4. . . . . **204** F5
Hyatts Wood Rd BS48. . . . . **19** E1
Hyde Ct BA21. . . . . **218** C6

Hyde La
  9 Creech St Michael TA3. . **169** C5
  Monkton Heathfield TA2 . . **169** C5
  Taunton TA2 . . . . **213** F6
Hyde Lane Cotts TA2 . . . . . **169** C5
Hyde Park Ave 4 TA6 . . . . **153** E3
Hyde Pk 5 TA6. . . . . **153** E3
Hyde Rd
  Minehead TA24. . . . . **200** E6
  Montacute TA15. . . . . **186** B4
Hyde's La SN14 . . . . **13** A6
Hyde The
  Clevedon BS21. . . . . **16** C8
  Keynsham BS31. . . . . **24** F6
Hyland Gr BS9. . . . . **5** F8
Hylton Cl TA2 . . . . **212** F8
Hynicombe La TA4 . . . . **165** D6
Hythe La BS27. . . . . **89** E5

I

Iberry La TA3 . . . . **183** E8
ICELTON **32** C8
Idson La TA5. . . . . **134** E7
Idwal Cl BA2 . . . . **79** C3
Iford Cl BS31. . . . . **25** E3
Iford Fields BS15. . . . . **64** E2
Iford Hill BA15 . . . . **64** E2
Iford La BA3, BA15 . . . . **64** C3
IKB Academy BS31. . . . . **25** A5
ILCHESTER **173** E2
Ilchester Com Prim Sch (Inf)
  BA22. . . . . **173** E2
Ilchester Com Prim Sch (Jun)
  BA22. . . . . **173** E2
Ilchester Cres BS13 . . . . **22** B8
Ilchester La TA10. . . . . **172** F4
ILCHESTER MEAD **173** D1
Ilchester Mead BA22 . . . . . **173** D1
Ilchester Mead Dro BA22 . **186** C8
Ilchester Mus ★ BA22 . . . . **173** E1
Ilchester Rd
  Bristol BS13. . . . . **22** B8
  Charlton Mackrell TA11. . . **173** F6
  Chilthorne Domer BA21,
   BA22. . . . . **186** F6
  Yeovil BA21 . . . . **218** F8
Ile Ct TA19 . . . . **221** C4
Ilex Ave BS21 . . . . **6** E2
Ilex Cl
  Bristol BS13. . . . . **21** F6
  Huntspill TA9 . . . . **136** B8
Ilex La BS25. . . . . **51** F1
ILFORD **184** A4
Ilford Bridges TA19. . . . . . . **184** A4
Ilford Ct TA1 . . . . **212** C2
Illustrious Cres BA22 . . . . . **173** E2
ILMINSTER **221** C4
Ilminster 5 BS24 . . . . **49** A2
Ilminster Ave BS4 . . . . **22** F8
Ilminster Ave E-ACT Acad
  Bristol BS4. . . . . **23** A8
  Filwood Park BS4. . . . . **22** F8
Ilminster Cl
  Clevedon BS21. . . . . **6** E2
  Nailsea BS48. . . . . **18** D8
Ilminster Rd TA1 . . . . **213** D4
Ilsyn Gr BS14. . . . . **23** D7
ILTON **183** E4
Ilton Bsns Pk TA19. . . . . . . **183** F5
Imbercourt Cl BS14. . . . . . . **23** B8
Immenstadt Dr TA21. . . . . . **222** D4
Imperial Pk BS13. . . . . **22** C6
Imperial Rd BS14. . . . . **23** C8
Imperial Way
  Bridgwater TA6 . . . . **136** B2
  Frome BA11. . . . . **120** D7
Improvement Pl 5 TA21. . **222** D5
Inchalloch 19 BA1. . . . . **28** A1
Incline The TA19 . . . . **221** B3
Inclosures The 6 BS22. . . . **49** E8
INGLESBATCH. **61** C8
Ingleton Dr BS22. . . . . **32** A4
Ingrams Mdw TA23. . . . . . . **202** C6
Inkerman Ct TA1. . . . . **213** A3
Inman Ho BA1 . . . . **228** C4
INMAN'S BATCH. **38** A5
Inn Cotts BS11. . . . . **5** A7
Inner Circ TA1 . . . . **213** C5
Inner Elm Terr BA3. . . . . **78** C1
Inner Gullands TA1. . . . . . . **212** C3
Innicks Cl BS40 . . . . **55** D1
Innox Gdns BS13. . . . . **22** A5
Innox Gr BA2 . . . . **43** F2
INNOX HILL **119** F6
Innox Hill BA11. . . . . **119** E6
Innox La BA2. . . . . **28** B5
Innox Rd BA2. . . . . **44** B5
Inns Court Ave BS4. . . . . . . **22** D7
Inns Court Dr BS4 . . . . **22** D6
Inns Court Gn BS4. . . . . **22** D7
Innsmead La TA7. . . . . **137** B1
Instow 7 BS22. . . . . **32** A2
Instow Rd BS4 . . . . **22** E8
Instow Wlk BS4 . . . . **22** E8
International Coll Sherborne
  Sch DT9 . . . . **225** D5
Inverness Rd BA2 . . . . **44** C6
Inwood Rd TA6. . . . . **208** C5
Irene Cl TA6 . . . . **209** D7
Ireson Cl BA9. . . . . **216** D4
Ireson La BA9. . . . . **216** D4
Iris Rd BA11 . . . . **120** B3
Irnham Rd TA24. . . . . **201** A7

Iron Dish La TA13 . . . . . . .184 E6
Iron Mill La BA11 . . . . .101 A1
Ironmould La BS31 . . . . .24 A8
Iron Post TA22 . . . . .163 B5
Irons Way BS24 . . . . .50 C8
Irvine Cl TA2 . . . . .212 C6
Irving Cl BS21 . . . . 6 F3
Irving Ho BS1 . . . . .226 C3
Irving Rd TA11 . . . . .158 A1
Irwell Gn TA1 . . . . .213 D4
Isaacs Cl BA16 . . . . .207 B4
Island The BA3 . . . . .78 A1
ISLE ABBOTTS 183 F7
Isle Abbotts Rd TA3 . . . . . .183 E8
ISLE BREWERS 184 A8
Isle Brewers La TA3 . . . . . .184 B8
Islemoor Dro TA3 . . . . .184 A8
Islemoor La
  Fivehead TA3 . . . . .170 F1
  South Petherton TA13 . . . . .220 B6
Islemoor Rd TA3 . . . . .183 F8
Isleport Bsns Pk TA9 . . . . . .104 F4
Isleport Rd TA9 . . . . .104 F3
Isles La
  East Coker, Lyatts BA22 . . . .197 C6
  East Coker, Sutton Bingham
   BA22 . . . . .197 D6
Ison La TA24 . . . . .147 C2
Ivel Ct BA21 . . . . .219 C5
Ivel Gdns BA22 . . . . .173 E1
Ivel Sq BA20 . . . . .219 B5
Ivelway TA18 . . . . .224 C5
Ivo Peters Rd BA2 . . . . .228 A2
Ivors Way TA6 . . . . .153 E4
Ivy Ave BA2 . . . . .44 C4
Ivy Bank Pk BA2 . . . . .44 F2
Ivybridge 8 BS22 . . . . .32 A2
Ivy Cl BS48 . . . . .8 D1
Ivy Cotts TA3 . . . . .181 E3
Ivy Cross TA21 . . . . .179 D7
Ivy Ct BS20 . . . . .1 F5
Ivy Gn TA20 . . . . .223 C2
Ivy Gr BA2 . . . . .44 C4
Ivy Grove Cl TA6 . . . . .209 D7
Ivy Ho
  Chard TA20 . . . . .223 B4
  Wellington TA21 . . . . .222 E6
Ivy House Cotts BS29 . . . . . . .50 D7
Ivy House Pk TA3 . . . . .169 C2
Ivy La BS24 . . . . .50 A8
Ivyleaf Rd TA11 . . . . .211 C4
Ivy Pl BA2 . . . . .44 C4
Ivythorn Cl BA16 . . . . .207 C4
Ivythorn Rd BA16 . . . . .207 C4
Ivywell Rd BS9 . . . . .5 E3
Ivy Wlk
  Banwell BS29 . . . . .50 E4
  Midsomer Norton BA3 . . . . . .97 B8
  Yeovil BA20 . . . . .218 E3
IWOOD 35 A3
Iwood La BS40 . . . . .35 A2

J

Jack Price Cl BS13 . . . . .22 C3
Jack's Dro BS28 . . . . .137 F8
Jack's La
  Croscombe BA5 . . . . .204 C7
  Frome BA11 . . . . .119 D7
Jackson's La TA14 . . . . .185 D5
Jack White's Gibbet BA9 . . . .176 B8
Jacobs Cl BA6 . . . . .206 E5
Jacob's Ct BS1 . . . . .226 C2
Jacobs Mdw BS20 . . . . .2 F4
Jacob St
  Bristol BS2 . . . . .227 B3
  Bristol BS2 . . . . .227 C3
Jacob's Wells Rd BS8 . . . . . .226 B2
Jade Cl TA7 . . . . .209 C8
Jagaar Ct TA7 . . . . .137 D5
Jaguar Ho 3 BA1 . . . . .228 B3
Jamaica St BS2 . . . . .227 B4
James Cl
  Holcombe BA3 . . . . .116 C8
  Shepton Mallet BA4 . . . . . . .205 C4
James La TA14 . . . . .192 F2
James Lane Cross EX13 . . . . .193 A4
James St W BA1 . . . . .228 B2
James's Hill BA10 . . . . .161 A8
James St BS5 . . . . .227 C4
Jane Austin Centre The ★
  BA1 . . . . .228 B3
Janes Gr BA2 . . . . .45 A2
Janson Cl TA6 . . . . .209 D6
Japonica Cl TA6 . . . . .209 D5
Jarman Way TA20 . . . . .223 D6
Jarmyns TA1 . . . . .212 A3
Jarvis Cl DT10 . . . . .190 B4
Jarvis La TA4 . . . . .86 D4
Jarvis Way DT10 . . . . .190 B4
Jasmine Cl
  Bridgwater TA6 . . . . .208 D1
  Crewkerne TA18 . . . . .224 D7
  Highbridge TA9 . . . . .104 D4
  Weston-super-Mare BS22 . . . .32 A1
  Yeovil BA21 . . . . .218 B5
Jasmine Ct 8 BS23 . . . . .48 E8
Jasmine La BS49 . . . . .17 F2
Jasmine Way TA24 . . . . .32 A1
Jay Cl BA11 . . . . .120 B6
Jaycroft Rd TA8 . . . . .104 B6
Jay View BS23 . . . . .49 A5

Jeffreys' Way TA1 . . . . .212 A2
Jeffries Cl TA19 . . . . .183 C4
Jeffs Way 3 EX13 . . . . .198 A1
Jellicoe Ct TA1 . . . . .212 F3
Jellicoe Ct BS22 . . . . .31 E4
Jena Ct BS31 . . . . .25 D3
Jenson Ave BA11 . . . . .120 D8
Jesmond Rd
  Clevedon BS21 . . . . .6 C3
  Weston-super-Mare BS22 . . . .32 C4
Jesse Hughes Ct BA1 . . . . . . .28 C2
Jessop Cl BS31 . . . . .227 B2
Jessop Underpass BS3 . . . . . .11 F4
Jewel Cl TA7 . . . . .209 C8
Jews La
  Bath BA2 . . . . .44 C6
  Churchill BS25 . . . . .52 F4
  Wiveliscombe TA4 . . . . .210 B5
Jill Dando Memorial Garden ★
  8 BS23 . . . . .48 D8
Jill's Cl BA4 . . . . .142 A6
Jim O'Neil Ho BS11 . . . . .4 D7
Jocelin Dr BS22 . . . . .31 F4
Jocelin Rd BA6 . . . . .206 F5
Jocelyn Dr BS22 . . . . .203 B3
John Beales Hill BA4 . . . . . .140 F3
John Cabot Ct BS1 . . . . .226 A1
John Carr's Terr BS8 . . . . . .226 B2
John Cole Cl TA21 . . . . .222 D8
John Cozens Ho 6 BS2 . . . . .227 C3
John Grinter Way TA21 . . . . .222 D4
John Gunn Cl TA20 . . . . .223 C5
John Hall Cl BS14 . . . . .23 B7
John St S TA8 . . . . .104 A7
John Slessor Ct BA1 . . . . . . .228 B4
Johnson Cl
  East Brent TA9 . . . . .86 D5
  Wells BA5 . . . . .203 F5
Johnson Flats BA21 . . . . . . .219 C7
Johnson's Ctyd DT9 . . . . . . .225 D3
John St
  Bath BA1 . . . . .228 B3
  Bristol BS1 . . . . .227 A3
  Burnham-on-S TA8 . . . . .104 A7
  Highbridge TA9 . . . . .104 D3
Johnstone Cl BA6 . . . . .207 B3
Johnstone St BA2 . . . . .228 C2
John Wesleys Chapel ★
  .227 B3
Joles La BA11 . . . . .120 F1
Jones Cl BS49 . . . . .17 A1
Joselin Ct DT9 . . . . .225 D5
Joyden Ct TA20 . . . . .223 D2
Joy Hill BS8 . . . . .11 F6
Juan's La SP8 . . . . .177 E1
Jubilee Cl
  Bridgwater TA6 . . . . .209 C4
  Castle Cary BA7 . . . . .214 C6
  Chard TA20 . . . . .223 C3
  Midsomer Norton BA3 . . . . . .97 A8
Jubilee Cotts 10 BA11 . . . . .119 F4
Jubilee Ct
  8 Wellington TA21 . . . . . . .222 D5
  Weston-super-Mare BS23 . . . .48 F8
Jubilee Dr BS8 . . . . .10 B4
Jubilee Gdns
  Milverton TA4 . . . . .167 A4
  South Petherton TA13 . . . . . .220 C4
Jubilee La BS40 . . . . .53 A6
Jubilee Path BS22 . . . . .31 C1
Jubilee Pl
  Bristol BS1 . . . . .227 A1
  Clevedon BS21 . . . . .6 D1
  Yeovil BA21 . . . . .218 D5
Jubilee Rd
  Axbridge BS26 . . . . .70 C2
  Radstock BA3 . . . . .78 D1
  Street BA16 . . . . .207 C4
  Weston-super-Mare BS23 . . . .48 E7
Jubilee St
  Bristol BS2 . . . . .227 C2
  Burnham-on-S TA8 . . . . .104 B6
  Taunton TA1 . . . . .212 E6
Jubilee Terr
  Frome BA11 . . . . .119 E5
  Hemington BA3 . . . . .99 C7
  Paulton BS39 . . . . .77 E6
Jubilee Way BS22 . . . . .32 C3
Judge's Ride
  Luccombe TA24 . . . . .123 C1
  Luccombe TA24 . . . . .129 C7
Judy's Orch TA7 . . . . .154 F5
Julian Cl
  Bristol BS9 . . . . .5 E3
  Shepton Mallet BA4 . . . . . . .205 C4
Julian Ct BS9 . . . . .5 E3
Julian Rd
  Bath BA1 . . . . .228 B3
  Bristol BS9 . . . . .5 E3
Julian's Acres TA8 . . . . .84 F4
Julier Ho BA1 . . . . .228 C4
Julius Pl BS31 . . . . .24 F8
Jumpers Combe TA23 . . . . . .148 E8
Junction Ave BA2 . . . . .228 A1
Junction Dro TA3 . . . . .170 C2
Junction Rd BA2 . . . . .228 A1
Juniper Cl
  Bridgwater TA6 . . . . .209 E4
  Yeovil BA20 . . . . .218 F3
Juniper Pl BS22 . . . . .31 F4
Juniper Rd TA1 . . . . .213 C2
Jurston Ct TA21 . . . . .222 F4
Jurston La
  Wellington TA21 . . . . .222 E6
  Wellington TA21 . . . . .222 F5
Jury Hill TA22 . . . . .163 E6
Jury Rd TA22 . . . . .163 E6
Justice Ave BS31 . . . . .25 E3
Justice La BA11 . . . . .119 F5

K

Kale St BA4 . . . . .142 D2
Kale Street Cotts BA4 . . . . . .142 D2
Karen Cl BS48 . . . . .19 A4
Karen Dr BS48 . . . . .19 A5
Kaynton Mead BA1 . . . . .44 B7
Kearvell Pl DT9 . . . . .225 C5
Keats Ho 4 BS23 . . . . .48 F4
Keats Rd
  Radstock BA3 . . . . .97 C8
  Taunton TA1 . . . . .213 C3
Kebby's Farm Cl TA4 . . . . . .202 E3
Kebby's La TA19 . . . . .221 D1
Keble Ave BS13 . . . . .21 F5
Keeds La BS41 . . . . .10 F1
Keedwell Hill BS41 . . . . .10 F1
Keel Ave BS20 . . . . .2 F7
Keel's Hill BA2 . . . . .79 C8
Keene's Way BS21 . . . . .6 C2
Keens Cl BA16 . . . . .207 D5
Keen's Elm La BA16 . . . . . . .207 E4
Keens La TA7 . . . . .155 C2
KEENTHORNE 134 D2
Keepers Hill BA2 . . . . .43 C5
Keeper's La BA2 . . . . .42 C3
Keep St BA22 . . . . .174 D3
Keep The BS22 . . . . .32 A3
Keg Store The BS1 . . . . .227 B2
KEINTON MANDEVILLE 158 B1
Keinton Mandeville
  Prim Sch
  Keinton Mandeville TA11 . . . .158 A1
  Keinton Mandeville TA11 . . . .158 A1
Kellaway La BA2 . . . . .45 A2
Kellways BS48 . . . . .19 A4
Kelson's La BS28 . . . . .108 B3
Kelso Pl BA1 . . . . .44 D7
Kelso Villas BA1 . . . . .44 D7
KELSTON 26 C3
Kelston Cl BS31 . . . . .25 D4
Kelston Gdns BS22 . . . . .32 B5
Kelston Hill La BA1 . . . . .26 B4
Kelston Rd
  Bath BA1 . . . . .26 C3
  Keynsham BS31 . . . . .24 D5
  Weston-super-Mare BS22 . . . .32 B5
Kelston View BA2 . . . . .44 A5
Kelting Gr BS21 . . . . .6 F2
Keltings TA6 . . . . .208 C6
Kelway Rd TA21 . . . . .222 E7
Kember's Hill BA22, DT9 . . . .175 C3
Kemble Cl BS48 . . . . .9 A1
Kemble Gdns BS11 . . . . .4 F5
Kemm Cl BS27 . . . . .90 B6
Kempe's Cl BS41 . . . . .11 A2
Kempe Way BS24 . . . . .49 E7
Kemps La TA24 . . . . .147 B7
Kemp's La BA11 . . . . .120 F7
Kemps Way TA22 . . . . .163 D6
Kempthorne La BA2 . . . . .44 E1
Ken Cl
  Chard TA20 . . . . .223 D3
  Wells BA5 . . . . .140 C8
Kencot Wlk BS13 . . . . .22 B3
Kendale Rd TA6 . . . . .208 E6
Kendall Cl TA3 . . . . .169 D6
Kendrick Ct 1 BA5 . . . . . . .203 D4
Kenelm Cl DT9 . . . . .225 B3
Kenilworth Cl BS31 . . . . .24 D4
Kenilworth Ct BA1 . . . . .45 B8
Kenmare Rd BS4 . . . . .22 E8
Kenmeade Cl BS25 . . . . .70 E8
Kenmore Dr BA21 . . . . .219 B6
KENN 16 F7
Kennard Cl BA6 . . . . .206 F5
Kennard Moor Dro
  Butleigh BA6 . . . . .157 E7
  Glastonbury BA6 . . . . .206 F1
Kennaway Rd BS21 . . . . .6 E2
Kenn Bsns Pk BS21 . . . . .16 E8
Kenn Cl BS23 . . . . .49 A5
Kenn Court BS4 . . . . .22 E7
Kennedy Cl TA9 . . . . .104 E4
Kennel Batch BA5 . . . . .111 D4
Kennel Field Dr TA1 . . . . . .212 A3
Kennel La
  Compton Bishop BS26 . . . . . .68 C3
  East Pennard BA4 . . . . .158 F8
  Langport TA10 . . . . .172 A6
  West Bagborough TA4 . . . . . .151 D4
Kennel Lodge Rd BS3 . . . . . . .11 E4
Kenn Est BS21 . . . . .16 E5
Kennet Gr TA1 . . . . .213 D4
Kennet Ho 10 BA1 . . . . .228 B2
Kennet Pk BA2 . . . . .28 E1
Kennet Rd BS31 . . . . .25 A4
Kennford 6 BS22 . . . . .31 F2
Kennington Rd BA1 . . . . .44 B7
Kennion Cl TA20 . . . . .223 D3
Kennion Rd BA5 . . . . .203 C5
Kenn Moor Dr BS21 . . . . .6 E1
KENN MOOR GATE 17 F4
Kennmoor Rd BS21 . . . . .17 A6
Kenn Moor Rd BS49 . . . . . . .17 B1
Kenn Rd BS21 . . . . .16 F6
Kenn St BS21 . . . . .16 F7
KENNY 183 B4
Kensington Ct
  Bath BA1 . . . . .28 B2
  Bristol BS8 . . . . .226 A4
Kensington Fields
  BA14 . . . . .83 F7
Kensington Gdns
  Bath BA1 . . . . .28 B1
  Bridgwater TA6 . . . . .209 D6
Kensington Gr TA24 . . . . . . .200 E6

Kensington Pl
  Bath BA1 . . . . .28 B1
  Bristol BS8 . . . . .226 A4
Kensington Rd BS23 . . . . . . .48 F5
Kent Ave
  Bridgwater TA6 . . . . .209 A2
  Weston-super-Mare BS24 . . . .50 C8
  Weston-super-Mare BS24 . . . .50 D8
Kentisworth Rd DT10 . . . . . .190 F5
Kent La
  Shapwick TA7 . . . . .137 F1
  Shepton Mallet BA4 . . . . . . .205 A5
Kent Rd
  Congresbury BS49 . . . . .34 D5
  Tatworth TA20 . . . . .198 D8
Kent's Bglws TA20 . . . . .198 D8
Kents Cl TA20 . . . . .198 C8
Kent's Cotts TA20 . . . . .198 D8
Kentshare La BS40 . . . . .38 B6
Kents La TA20 . . . . .198 D8
Kent's Orch TA20 . . . . .198 D8
Kent St BS27 . . . . .71 B1
Kent Way BS22 . . . . .32 B4
Kenwyn Cl TA1 . . . . .213 D3
Keppel Cl BS31 . . . . .25 D2
Kerry Croft BA11 . . . . .143 C3
Kersey Ct BA11 . . . . .119 C5
Kersham La TA24 . . . . .130 A1
Kestrel Cl TA6 . . . . .209 C3
Kestrel Dr BS22 . . . . .31 E1
KEWARD 203 C2
Keward Ave BA5 . . . . .203 B3
Keward Cl BA5 . . . . .203 C3
Keward Mill Trad Est BA5 . . .203 B2
Keward Wlk BA5 . . . . .203 C3
Kew Rd BS23 . . . . .30 C1
Kewside BS22 . . . . .31 B4
KEWSTOKE 31 B4
Kewstoke Prim Sch BS22 . . . .31 B3
Kewstoke Rd
  Bath BA2 . . . . .45 A2
  Bristol BS9 . . . . .5 E4
  Weston-super-Mare BS22 . . . .31 C3
Kew Wlk BS4 . . . . .23 C8
Keyes Path BS22 . . . . .31 F4
KEYFORD 119 F3
Keyford BA11 . . . . .119 F3
Keyford Cotts 15 BA11 . . . .119 F4
Keyford Ct BA11 . . . . .119 F2
KEYFORD FIELD 119 F2
Keyford Field Cotts BA11 . . .119 F2
Keyford Gdns BA11 . . . . . . .119 F3
Keyford Pl BA11 . . . . .119 F4
Keyford Rdbt BA22 . . . . . . .197 E8
Keyford Terr BA11 . . . . .119 F4
Keyhaven Bglws BS22 . . . . . .31 B4
Key Hill BA22 . . . . .197 E8
KEYNSHAM 24 E3
Keynsham By-Pass BS31 . . . . .24 E7
Keynsham Rd BS30, BS31 . . . .25 A8
Keynsham Sta BS31 . . . . .24 F6
Keyton Hill BS28 . . . . .107 C2
Kicks Hill TA7 . . . . .155 B4
Kicks Hill La TA7 . . . . .155 C4
Kidder Bank BA5 . . . . .203 F5
Kiddles BA21 . . . . .219 C5
Kidd's La BA4 . . . . .205 D6
Kid Gate Dro TA9, BS28 . . . .137 D8
Kidner Cl TA7 . . . . .136 C4
Kidsbury Rd TA6 . . . . .208 E5
Kielder Dr BS22 . . . . .31 F3
Kilbirnie Rd BS14 . . . . .23 A3
Kilburn Dr TA6 . . . . .209 D6
Kildare BA2 . . . . .45 B7
Kildare Gdns TA24 . . . . .200 F6
Kildare Rd BS13 . . . . .22 C8
Kilkenny Ave 5 TA2 . . . . . . .212 F6
Kilkenny Ct TA2 . . . . .212 F6
Kilkenny La
  Bath BA2 . . . . .62 B8
  Wraxall BA4 . . . . .159 A6
Kilkenny Pl BS20 . . . . .2 C6
Killams Ave
  Staplehay TA3 . . . . .181 E8
  Taunton TA1 . . . . .168 F1
Killams Cl TA1 . . . . .168 F1
Killams Cres TA1 . . . . .168 F1
Killams Dr TA1 . . . . .168 F1
Killams Gn TA1 . . . . .168 F1
Killams La TA1 . . . . .168 F1
Killarney Ave TA8 . . . . .104 C6
Killick Way TA4 . . . . .202 D3
KILLING'S KNAP 97 B4
KILMERSDON 98 B5
Kilmersdon CE Prim Sch
  BA3 . . . . .98 A6
Kilmersdon Hill BA3 . . . . .98 A5
Kilmersdon Rd
  Bristol BS13 . . . . .22 A4
  Radstock BA3 . . . . .97 E8
KILMINGTON 161 F7
KILMINGTON COMMON 161 E6
Kilmington Common
  BA12 . . . . .161 E7
Kilminster Rd BS11 . . . . .4 D7
Kilmorie Cl TA1 . . . . .212 C2
Kiln Cl TA5 . . . . .135 B5
Kiln Dr
  Evercreech BA4 . . . . .141 E1
  Highbridge TA9 . . . . .104 D3
Kiln Pk BS23 . . . . .49 A6
KILTON 133 C6
Kilton Cross TA5 . . . . .133 C5
KILVE 133 C6
Kilve Cl TA2 . . . . .212 F7
Kilve Cres TA2 . . . . .212 F7
Kilve Cl TA5 . . . . .133 C5

Kilver St BA4 . . . . .205 D6
Kilver Street Hill BA4 . . . . . .205 D7
Kimber Cl TA9 . . . . .104 D3
Kimberley Rd BS21 . . . . .6 C2
Kimberley Terr TA6 . . . . . . .209 B7
Kinber Cl BA1 . . . . .27 A3
Kinforde TA20 . . . . .223 C5
King Alfred Cl 3 TA6 . . . . . .153 F4
King Alfred Dr TA20 . . . . . . .223 C2
King Alfred Sch The TA9 . . . .104 C5
King Alfreds Ctyd 7 BA5 . . . .203 D4
King Alfreds Way BS28 . . . . .108 A4
King Alfred Way BA15 . . . . . .64 D7
King Arthur Dr BA21 . . . . . .218 D7
King Arthur's Com Sch
  BA9 . . . . .216 A4
King Athelstan Dr TA20 . . . . .223 D2
King Ceol Cl TA20 . . . . .223 D2
King Cerdic Cl TA20 . . . . . . .223 D2
Kingcott Mill Farm Cvns
  BS48 . . . . .20 B8
King Cuthred Cl TA20 . . . . . .223 C2
King Cuthred Dr TA20 . . . . . .223 C2
Kingdom BA5 . . . . .113 A4
Kingdom La TA2 . . . . .168 B2
Kingdom Mead TA3 . . . . . . .169 D4
KINGDOWN 37 D5
Kingdown Rd BS40 . . . . .37 C5
King Edward Cl BS14 . . . . . . .23 A6
King Edward Rd
  Bath BA2 . . . . .44 D5
  Minehead TA24 . . . . .201 A6
King Edward's Jun Sch
  BA2 . . . . .45 C7
King Edward's Pre-Prep Sch
  BA1 . . . . .44 C8
King Edwards Sch BA1 . . . . . .44 C1
King Edwards Sch BA2 . . . . . .45 C7
Kingfisher Cl TA6 . . . . .209 C3
Kingfisher Cl BA20 . . . . .218 D3
Kingfisher Cl BA3 . . . . .64 C6
Kingfisher Dr
  Houndstone BA22 . . . . .218 A6
  Midsomer Norton BA3 . . . . . .97 B8
Kingfisher Rd
  Portishead BS20 . . . . .2 F7
  Portishead BS20 . . . . .3 A7
  Weston-super-Mare BS22 . . . .49 F8
Kingfisher Wy BS21 . . . . .1 B1
King George Ave TA6 . . . . . .208 F2
King George Cl TA6 . . . . . . .209 A2
King George Rd TA24 . . . . . .201 A6
King George's Rd
  Bath BA2 . . . . .44 C6
  Bristol BS13 . . . . .21 F5
  Bristol BS13 . . . . .21 F5
King George St 2 BA20 . . . . .219 B4
King George V Pl 7 BS1 . . . .227 A2
King Ina Acad TA11 . . . . . . .211 E3
King Ina Rd TA11 . . . . .211 D4
King Ine Cl N TA20 . . . . . . .223 C2
King Ine Cl S TA20 . . . . . . .223 C2
King La BS39 . . . . .58 F4
Kinglake Dr TA1 . . . . .212 E2
Kinglake Villas TA6 . . . . . . .209 A2
Kings Acre BS49 . . . . .52 E6
Kings Acre TA4 . . . . .151 B5
KINGSBRIDGE 148 E8
KINGSBURY EPISCOPI 185 A8
Kingsbury Episcopi Prim Sch
  TA12 . . . . .185 A6
KINGSBURY REGIS 217 D3
Kings Castle Bsns Est
  TA6 . . . . .209 A6
King's Castle Rd BA5 . . . . . . .112 E1
Kings Cl
  Shepton Mallet BA4 . . . . . . .205 B5
  Taunton TA1 . . . . .213 A2
Kingscliffe Terr TA6 . . . . . .209 A2
King's Cnr TA22 . . . . .163 D6
King's Coll TA1 . . . . .213 B2
Kingscombe BA3 . . . . .114 E6
Kingscourt Cl BS14 . . . . .23 A4
Kings Cres DT9 . . . . .225 D5
Kings Croft BS41 . . . . .10 E1
Kings Ct
  Bath BA1 . . . . .228 B2
  Bristol BS1 . . . . .227 A2
  Bristol, St Pauls BS1 . . . . . . .227 B4
  2 Bristol, Withywood BS13 . . .21 F4
  Sherborne DT9 . . . . .225 D5
  Yeovil BA21 . . . . .219 C6
KINGSDON 173 E4
Kingsdon CE Prim Sch
  TA11 . . . . .173 D5
Kingsdon Dro TA11 . . . . . . .173 C4
Kingsdon Hill TA11 . . . . . . .173 D5
Kingsdon Manor Sch
  TA11 . . . . .173 D4
KINGSDOWN
  Box 29 F3
  Bristol 227 A4
Kingsdown Cl TA6 . . . . .209 D6
Kingsdown Gr SN13 . . . . . . .29 F3
Kingsdown Par BS6 . . . . . . .227 A4
Kingsdown View 16 BA1 . . . .28 A1
Kings Dr
  Bridgwater TA6 . . . . .209 D8
  Westonzoyland TA7 . . . . . . .154 E6
Kingsettle Hill BA10 . . . . . . .161 B5
Kingsfield BA2 . . . . .44 C3
Kingsford Gate Cross
  TA24 . . . . .145 B7
Kingsford Hill TA24 . . . . . . .145 C7
King's Hall Sch TA2 . . . . . . .168 E6
Kingshams BA22 . . . . .173 E1
King's Head La BS13 . . . . . . .21 F7

Kingshill BS48 . . . . 8 C2
Kings Hill BA22 . . . . .186 E6
King's Hill BA3 . . . . 94 F7
Kingshill CE Prim Sch BS48 . 8 D3
Kingshill Gdns BS48 . . . . 8 C1
Kingshill La BS40 . . . . .56 C1
Kingsholme Ct BS23 . . . . . . .30 E1
Kings La TA7 . . . . .156 B8
King's La
  Binegar BA3 . . . . 95 E1
  Clevedon BS21 . . . . 6 D5
  6 Weston-super-Mare
  BS23 . . . . .48 E8
Kingsland TA23 . . . . .202 D7
Kingsland Grange **1**
  BA21 . . . . .218 C6
Kingsland La TA24 . . . . . . .148 D5
Kingsland Rd BA4 . . . . . . .205 B5
Kingsland Trad Est BS2 . . .227 C3
Kings Lear BA21 . . . . .183 F4
Kingsley Cl TA1 . . . . .212 C1
Kingsley Ho BS2 . . . . .227 C2
Kingsley Rd
  Clevedon BS21 . . . . 6 D2
  Radstock BA3 . . . . 78 C1
  Weston-super-Mare BS23 . .48 F3
KINGSMEAD 228 A2
Kingsmead BS48 . . . . 8 C2
Kingsmead Cl
  Holcombe BA3 . . . . .116 C8
  Wiveliscombe TA4 . . . . . . .210 C3
Kingsmead Com Sch BA4 .210 C5
Kingsmead Ct **8** BA1 . . . .228 B2
Kingsmead N BA1 . . . . . . .228 B2
Kingsmead Sq BA1 . . . . . .228 B2
Kingsmead St BA1 . . . . . . .228 B2
Kingsmead W BA1 . . . . . . .228 B2
Kingsmill BS9 . . . . 5 D5
King's Mill Rd DT10 . . . . . .190 D3
Kingsmoor Dro TA10 . . . . .173 A2
Kingsmoor Prim Sch TA7 .136 C6
Kings Oak Mdw BS39 . . . . .58 E2
Kings of Wessex Sch The
  BS27 . . . . .90 B7
King's Pl TA6 . . . . .208 F5
King Sq
  Bridgwater TA6 . . . . .208 F5
  Bristol BS2 . . . . .227 A4
King Square Ave BS2 . . . . .227 A4
Kings Rd
  Sherborne DT9 . . . . .225 D5
  Stoke sub Hamdon TA14 . .185 F5
  Wells BA5 . . . . .140 C8
  Wrington BS40 . . . . .35 D1
King's Rd
  Bristol BS8 . . . . .226 A3
  Clevedon BS21 . . . . 6 D5
  Doulting BA4 . . . . .141 E7
  Portishead BS20 . . . . 1 F4
Kings Ride TA20 . . . . .223 B6
King's Sch BA10 . . . . .215 E6
Kings Sq BS30 . . . . .25 D8
King St
  Bridgwater TA6 . . . . .209 A5
  Bristol BS1 . . . . .227 A2
  Frome BA11 . . . . .119 F5
  Glastonbury BA6 . . . . .206 D5
  Highbridge TA9 . . . . .104 D3
  Yeovil BA21 . . . . .219 B6
Kingston BA20 . . . . .219 A5
Kingston Ave
  Clevedon BS21 . . . . 6 E3
  Saltford BS31 . . . . 25 C3
Kingston Bldgs **5** BA1 . . .228 C2
Kingston Cl
  Street BA16 . . . . .207 D6
  Taunton TA2 . . . . .212 E7
Kingston Dr BS48 . . . . .18 C8
KINGSTONE 221 E2
Kingstone Cross TA19 . . . .221 F2
Kingstone Hill TA19 . . . . . .221 F2
Kingstone Rd TA17 . . . . . .195 B6
Kingston La
  Felton BS40 . . . . .37 F8
  Maiden Bradley BA12 . . . .144 C1
Kingston Mead BS40 . . . . . .37 F7
Kingston Mews **3** TA2 . .212 F6
Kingston Rd
  Bath BA1 . . . . .228 C2
  Nailsea BS48 . . . . .18 C8
  Taunton TA2 . . . . .212 E7
KINGSTON ST MARY 168 E8
Kingston St Mary CE Prim Sch
  TA2 . . . . .168 D8
KINGSTON SEYMOUR 16 C2
Kingston View BA21 . . . . . .219 B6
Kingston Way BS48 . . . . . . .18 C8
Kingston Well La TA20 . . . .194 C2
KINGSWAY 44 C3
Kingsway
  Bath BA2 . . . . .44 C3
  Holcombe BA3 . . . . .116 C8
  Mark BS26,TA9 . . . . .87 D3
  Portishead BS20 . . . . 1 F4
  Taunton TA1 . . . . .168 F1
Kingsway Ctr BA11 . . . . . . .119 F4
Kingsway Rd TA8 . . . . .104 B7
Kingswear **3** BS22 . . . . . .32 A2
Kings Weston Ave BS11 . . . . 4 E8
Kings Weston La BS11 . . . . . 5 A8
Kings Weston Rd BS9 . . . . . 5 B8
Kingsweston Sch BS11 . . . . 5 A8
Kings Wlk BS13 . . . . .21 E7
KINGSWOOD 150 E8
Kingswood Chase BA14 . . .83 F6
Kingswood Prep Sch BA1 . .27 E1
Kingswood Rd TA18 . . . . . .224 C4
Kingswood Sch BA1 . . . . . .27 E2

Kingswood Sch Upper Sports Fields
  Bath BA1 . . . . .27 D4
  Charlcombe BA1 . . . . .27 D4
KINGTON MAGNA 177 E2
Kington View BA8 . . . . .176 E1
Kingwell View BS39 . . . . . . .59 D2
KINGWESTON 157 E2
Kingweston Rd
  Butleigh BA6 . . . . .157 E3
  Charlton Mackrell TA11 . . .173 E8
King William Ave BS1 . . . . .227 A2
King William Rd TA7 . . . . . .137 D2
Kinsale Rd BS14 . . . . .23 C7
Kinvara Rd BS4 . . . . .22 E8
Kinver Terr TA8 . . . . .104 A7
Kipling Ave BA2 . . . . .44 F4
Kipling Cl
  Radstock BA3 . . . . .78 C1
  Weston-super-Mare BS23 . .49 A3
Kippax Ave BA5 . . . . .203 F5
Kipscombe Cross EX35 . . .122 A6
Kirk Dr TA7 . . . . .154 E6
Kirke Gr TA2 . . . . .213 B8
Kirkham St TA11 . . . . .211 E4
Kirlegate BA6 . . . . .138 C4
Kissing Batch BA11 . . . . . .119 C6
Kissmedown La BA22 . . . . .186 C5
KITBRIDGE 198 A6
Kitch Dro TA7 . . . . .154 D3
Kitchener Rd TA2 . . . . .168 A6
Kitchens La TA13 . . . . .185 A1
Kite La BA4 . . . . .159 C6
Kite Pl BA22 . . . . .218 A5
Kite's Nest La SP8 . . . . . . .161 F1
Kite Wlk **2** BS22 . . . . .49 E8
Kithill TA18 . . . . .224 D4
Kitland La BS40 . . . . .53 C8
Kitley Hill BA3 . . . . .78 C4
Kitridge La TA24 . . . . .146 B7
Kitrow La TA24 . . . . .131 A6
Kit's La TA4 . . . . .166 A6
Kitswall La TA24 . . . . .130 D5
Kitt Hill DT9 . . . . .225 C4
Kitts TA21 . . . . .222 D4
Kittwake Dr
  6 Portishead BS20 . . . . . . 2 F6
  Portishead BS20 . . . . 2 F7
KITTWHISTLE 199 D6
Kittyhawk Cl **4** BA3 . . . . .97 B8
Knacker's Hole La
  Churchinford TA3 . . . . . . .192 A6
  Thorncombe DT6,TA20 . . .199 C4
Knap Hill BA3 . . . . .117 B2
Knaplock La TA5 . . . . .134 F4
KNAPP 169 F4
Knapp TA16 . . . . .195 F7
Knapp Cotts TA5 . . . . .151 E1
Knapp Hill Cl BA5 . . . . . . .113 A2
Knapp La
  Bishops Lydeard TA4 . . . . .151 E1
  North Curry TA3 . . . . .170 B4
Knapp Rd
  Creech St Michael TA3 . . . .169 F4
  North Curry TA3 . . . . .170 A4
Knapps Cl BS25 . . . . .69 F8
Knapps Dr BS25 . . . . .69 F8
Knapp The
  Chard TA20 . . . . .194 C4
  Langport TA10 . . . . .172 B5
Knapp The TA24 . . . . .130 B4
Knapp The BA8 . . . . .176 E1
Knaptons Hill BA11 . . . . . .118 C6
Kneller Cl BS11 . . . . 5 A8
Knight Cl
  Monkton Heathfield TA2 . . .213 F8
  Weston-super-Mare BS22 . .32 A5
KNIGHTCOTT 50 F3
Knightcott Gdns BS29 . . . . .50 F3
Knightcott Ind Est BS29 . . .50 E3
Knightcott Pk BS29 . . . . . . .51 A3
Knightcott Rd
  Abbots Leigh BS8 . . . . .10 F8
  Banwell BS29 . . . . .50 F3
Knightlands La TA10 . . . . .172 F4
KNIGHTON 184 D7
Knighton TA5 . . . . .134 B7
Knighton Dro TA10 . . . . . .184 D7
Knight Rd BA5 . . . . .203 C2
Knightsbridge Pk BS13 . . . .22 E4
Knightsbridge Way TA6 . . .209 D6
Knight's Cross TA21 . . . . . .181 A5
Knight's Ct BA11 . . . . .119 F4
Knight Shute La TA20 . . . .193 D6
Knight's La
  Axminster EX13 . . . . .198 A4
  Higher Cricketham TA19 . . .194 E5
Knights Maltings BA11 . . . .120 A3
Knights Rd TA21 . . . . .180 D8
Knights Templar CE Meth
  Com Sch TA23 . . . . .202 D6
Knightstone Cl
  Axbridge BS26 . . . . .70 C1
  Kingsbury Episcopi TA12 . .185 B8
  Peasedown St John BA2 . . .79 B8
Knightstone Cswy BS23 . . . .48 C8
Knightstone Ct
  Burnham-on-S TA8 . . . . . .104 B6
  Clevedon BS21 . . . . 6 D1
  Stalbridge DT10 . . . . .190 B4
  Taunton TA2 . . . . .213 A6
  Weston-super-Mare BS23 . . .30 D1
Knightstone Gn BS23 . . . . .48 E6

Knightstone Ho
  1 Bristol BS2 . . . . .227 A4
  Weston-super-Mare BS23 . .48 D8
Knightstone Hts BA11 . . . .119 F3
Knightstone Mead TA22 . . .148 A2
Knightstone Pk **4** BS23 . . .48 E5
Knightstone Pl
  Bath BA1 . . . . .27 B1
  7 Weston-super-Mare BS22 .31 F2
Knightstone Rd BS23 . . . . . .48 C8
Knightstone Sq BS14 . . . . . .23 C5
Knightstone Wlk BS2 . . . . .226 C4
Knights Yd BA7 . . . . .214 C5
Knobsbury Hill BA3 . . . . . . .98 C6
Knobsbury La BA3 . . . . .98 D7
KNOLE 173 A4
Knole Cswy
  Knole TA10 . . . . .173 A4
  Long Sutton TA10 . . . . . . .172 F4
Knole Pit La TA10 . . . . . . .173 A4
Knoll Ct BS9 . . . . 5 D3
Knoll Green La TA5 . . . . . .134 F7
Knoll Hill BS9 . . . . 5 D3
Knoll Hill View BA11 . . . . .143 C6
Knoll Ho **5** BA1 . . . . .119 F4
Knoll La BA4 . . . . .142 E3
Knoll Pk TA8 . . . . .65 F3
Knoll The BS20 . . . . 2 D7
Knoll View
  Burnham-on-S TA8 . . . . . .104 C8
  4 Frome BA11 . . . . .119 F4
Knotcroft La TA2 . . . . .153 D1
Knotts Paddock DT9 . . . . .225 E4
KNOWLE 136 D2
Knowle Bridge Rd BA9 . . . .160 D2
Knowle Cross DT8 . . . . . . .199 F6
Knowle Dro
  Middlezoy TA7 . . . . .155 A4
  Westonzoyland TA7 . . . . . .154 F5
Knowle End TA7 . . . . .136 E3
Knowle Hill BS40 . . . . .57 C7
Knowle La
  Chard TA20 . . . . .194 B6
  Dunster TA24 . . . . .201 B1
  Misterton DT8,TA18 . . . . .224 E2
  Shepton Mallet BA4 . . . . .204 E5
  Wookey BA5 . . . . .110 E1
Knowle Moor Dro BA5 . . . .110 C2
Knowle Rd TA6 . . . . .209 C6
KNOWLE ST GILES 194 B6
Knowles Rd BS21 . . . . 6 C2
Knowleyards Rd TA7 . . . . .155 B4
KNOWSTONE 162 A4
Korresia Wlk TA6 . . . . .208 D1
Kuching BA22 . . . . .174 A2
Kylross Ave BS14 . . . . .23 B5
Kyrle Gdns BA1 . . . . .28 F3
Kyte Rd BA4 . . . . .205 C5

L

Labbott The BS31 . . . . .24 E5
Labourn Dro BS27 . . . . .90 B5
Labourham Way BS27 . . . . .90 B6
Laburnum Cl
  Bridgwater TA6 . . . . .209 D4
  Frome BA11 . . . . .120 B7
  Midsomer Norton BA3 . . . .96 F8
  Somerton TA11 . . . . .211 D4
Laburnum Cotts **7** TA21 . .222 D5
Laburnum Cres TA18 . . . . .224 D7
Laburnum Ct
  7 Taunton TA1 . . . . .213 A4
  Weston-super-Mare BS23 . .49 B7
Laburnum Dr TA11 . . . . . .211 D4
Laburnum Gr BA3 . . . . .96 F8
Laburnum Lodges TA9 . . . .136 A8
Laburnum Rd
  Wellington TA21 . . . . .222 E5
  Weston-super-Mare BS23 . .49 B7
Laburnum St TA1 . . . . .213 A4
Laburnum Terr
  Batheaston BA1 . . . . .28 F3
  Creech St Michael TA3 . . . .169 D4
Laburnum Way BA20 . . . . .218 D2
Lacey Rd BS14 . . . . .23 F6
La Ciotat Ho TA6 . . . . .209 A4
Ladd Cl TA9 . . . . .104 D3
Ladies Mile BS8 . . . . 5 F1
Ladman Gr BS14 . . . . .23 E6
Ladman Rd BS14 . . . . .23 E5
Ladycroft **5** BS21 . . . . 6 B1
Ladye Bay BS21 . . . . 6 D7
Ladye Wake BS22 . . . . .31 F4
Lady Harriet Acland's Dr
  TA22 . . . . .164 A8
Lady Lawn TA3 . . . . .168 D1
Ladymead BS20 . . . . 2 F5
Ladymead Cl TA6 . . . . .208 B4
Ladymeade
  Backwell BS48 . . . . .19 A7
  Ilminster TA19 . . . . .221 B3
Ladymead Ho BA1 . . . . . . .228 C3
Ladymead La BS40 . . . . . . .52 F5
Ladymead Rd TA2 . . . . . . .168 F6
Lady St TA22 . . . . .163 D7
Lady Victoria's Dr TA22 . . .163 E6
Ladywell BS40 . . . . .35 D2
Laggan Gdns BA1 . . . . .27 E1
Laggan Ho BA1 . . . . .27 E1
Lagger Hill TA5 . . . . .133 C5
Lahs Pl BA11 . . . . .101 E4
Lakefields BA22 . . . . .197 B8
Lakemead Gdns BS13 . . . . .21 F4
Lakemead Gr BS13 . . . . . . .21 F6
Lake Mews BA22 . . . . .219 B1
Lake Rd BS20 . . . . 2 D7

Lake Shore Dr BS13 . . . . . .22 C6
Lakeside TA9 . . . . .104 E4
Lakeside Ct BS40 . . . . .55 C5
Lakeside Ct BS24 . . . . .32 B1
Lakeside Pk
  Bridgwater TA6 . . . . .209 A3
  Vobster BA3 . . . . .117 E8
Lakeview Cres TA9 . . . . . . .104 E3
Lake Wall TA7 . . . . .154 E4
Lambert Ct DT9 . . . . .217 C2
Lambert Ct DT9 . . . . .217 D2
Lambert La TA11 . . . . .194 F5
Lambert Pl BS4 . . . . .22 D6
Lambert's Hill BA4 . . . . . . .204 F3
Lamberts Marsh BA14 . . . .83 E2
Lamb La TA6 . . . . .208 F4
Lambourne Ct TA18 . . . . . .224 D7
Lambourne Way BS20 . . . . . 2 F5
Lambourn Rd BS31 . . . . . . .25 A4
Lambpark Ct TA3 . . . . .191 F6
LAMBRIDGE 28 C2
Lambridge **6** BA1 . . . . . . .28 C1
Lambridge Bldgs **1** BA1 . .28 C1
Lambridge Grange **6** BA1 .28 C1
Lambridge Mews BA1 . . . . .28 C1
Lambridge Pl BA1 . . . . .28 C1
Lambridge St BA1 . . . . .28 C1
Lambrok Cl BA14 . . . . .83 E6
Lambrok Rd BA14 . . . . .83 E6
Lambrook Cl TA1 . . . . .213 B4
Lambrook Gate TA13 . . . . .184 F5
Lambrook Ho BA9 . . . . . . .216 C4
Lambrook La BA22 . . . . . . .174 E2
Lambrook Rd
  Shepton Beauchamp TA19 .184 E4
  Taunton TA1 . . . . .213 B4
Lambrook St BA6 . . . . .206 E4
Lambrook Way TA1 . . . . . .213 C4
Lambs Field DT9 . . . . .225 E5
Lamb St BS2 . . . . .227 C3
Lamington Cl BS13 . . . . . . .21 F6
Lamont Ho **7** BA1 . . . . . . .28 C1
Lampard's Bldgs BA1 . . . . .228 B2
Lamparts Way TA19 . . . . . .183 C2
Lampeter Rd BS9 . . . . 5 F7
Lampley Rd BS21 . . . . .16 C2
Lampreys La TA13 . . . . . . .220 C3
Lampton Ave BS13 . . . . . . .22 E3
Lampton Gr BS13 . . . . .22 E3
Lampton Rd BS41 . . . . .10 C1
LAMYATT 159 F6
Lancaster Cl TA6 . . . . .158 F6
Lancaster House Sch BS23 .48 F8
Lancer Ct TA21 . . . . .222 D6
Lanch La SP8 . . . . .177 F5
Lancin La TA20 . . . . .193 B2
Lancock St TA21 . . . . .222 A5
Landacre La TA24 . . . . . . .146 A7
Landemann Cir BS23 . . . . . .30 E1
Landemann Path **2** BS23 . .48 E8
Landing Lights BS14 . . . . . .22 C5
Landlord's Hill TA21 . . . . . .179 E7
Landmark Ct BS1 . . . . .226 C1
Landmead BA6 . . . . .206 D5
Landmoor La BS14 . . . . . . .172 D4
Landsdown Mews BA11 . . .119 D5
Landseer BA8 . . . . .176 D4
Landseer Cl BS22 . . . . .31 F3
Landseer Rd BA2 . . . . .44 B6
Lands End BS28 . . . . .107 E1
Landshire La
  Charlton Horethorne DT9 . .176 A1
  Chilton Polden TA7 . . . . . .137 A3
  Henstridge BA8 . . . . .190 C6
  Odcombe BA22 . . . . .186 C1
LANE END 144 D8
Lane End
  Corsley Heath BA12 . . . . . .144 D8
  Upper Littleton BS40 . . . . .38 C5
Lane Foot TA24 . . . . .129 D7
Lane Head TA24 . . . . .123 E4
Lanesborough Rise BS14 . .23 D7
Lanes End Hill BA11,BA12 .144 D8
Laneys Dro BS24 . . . . .49 E5
LANGALLER 169 C6
Langaller Hill TA22 . . . . . .163 D4
Langaller Way TA2 . . . . . . .169 C6
Langdon Cl TA20 . . . . .223 D6
Langdon Rd BA2 . . . . .44 B4
Langdons DT9 . . . . .225 E5
Langdons Way TA20 . . . . .198 D8
Langdown Ct BS14 . . . . . . .23 E5
Langer's La TA19 . . . . .194 E5
LANGFORD 212 A8
LANGFORD BUDVILLE 166 E2
Langford Budville CE Prim
  Sch TA21 . . . . .166 F1
Langford Cl
  Fivehead TA3 . . . . .170 D2
  Plummer's Hill BS39 . . . . . .77 D6
Langford Ct **14** TA1 . . . . .213 A4
Langford Ct Cotts BS40 . . . .53 E5
Langford Gate TA4 . . . . . . .166 F2
Langford La
  Fivehead TA3 . . . . .170 D2
  Lower Langford BS40 . . . . .53 E5
  Norton Fitzwarren TA2 . . . .168 C6
Langford Rd
  Bristol BS13 . . . . .21 F8
  Lower Langford BS40 . . . . .53 C6
  Weston-super-Mare BS23 . .49 A6
Langfords La BS39 . . . . . . .77 C3
Langford's La BS39 . . . . . . .59 D1
LANGHAM
  Chard 223 C7
  Gillingham 177 E4
Langham Dr TA1 . . . . .212 C1

Langham Gdns TA1 . . . . . .212 C1
Langham La SP8 . . . . .177 F5
Langham Pl BA11 . . . . .82 F1
Langhill Ave BS4 . . . . .22 D7
Langland La TA7 . . . . .137 C2
Langlands **8** TA14 . . . . . .185 F4
Langlands La TA7 . . . . .169 F2
Langland's La TA9 . . . . . . .104 B1
LANGLEY 210 C6
Langley Cres BS3 . . . . .11 E1
Langley Cross TA4 . . . . . . .210 B6
LANGLEY MARSH 210 C5
Langleys Cotts BA3 . . . . . . .96 B8
Langley's La BA3, BS39 . . . .77 C1
Langmead Dro
  Middlezoy TA7 . . . . .155 A4
  Westonzoyland TA7 . . . . . .154 F5
Langmead La TA7 . . . . . . .155 A4
Langmead Pl TA18 . . . . . . .224 C4
Langmead Rd TA18 . . . . . .224 C4
Langmead Sq TA18 . . . . . .224 C4
Langmoor Dro TA7 . . . . . .154 F6
Langmoor La
  Axminster EX13 . . . . .198 D2
  South Perrott DT8 . . . . . . .196 B1
LANGPORT 172 B5
Langport Gdns BS48 . . . . . .18 E8
Langport Rd
  Langport TA10 . . . . .172 A4
  Long Sutton TA10 . . . . . . .172 E5
  Middlezoy TA7 . . . . .155 B4
  Somerton TA11 . . . . .211 B4
  Weston-super-Mare BS23 . .48 E5
LANGRIDGE 27 E7
Langridge La BA1 . . . . .27 D8
Lang's Cnr TA19 . . . . .183 B1
Langton Ho **9** BS2 . . . . . .227 C3
Langworthy Orch TA19 . . . .183 C1
LANSDOWN
  Bath 27 E1
  Langridge 27 B6
Lansdown Cres
  2 Bath BA1 . . . . .27 F1
  Timsbury BA2 . . . . .60 C2
Lansdown Ct BS23 . . . . .48 F8
Lansdowne Pl BA9 . . . . . . .216 C4
Lansdowne Rd TA2 . . . . . .213 A6
Lansdown Gdns BS22 . . . . .32 B5
Lansdown Gr BA1 . . . . .228 B4
Lansdown Grove Ct BA1 . . .228 B4
Lansdown Grove Lodge
  BA1 . . . . .228 B4
Lansdown Ho BA1 . . . . .27 F1
Lansdown Hts BA1 . . . . . . .27 F1
Lansdown La
  Bath BA1 . . . . .27 B4
  Upton Cheyney BS30 . . . . .26 D8
Lansdown Mans BA1 . . . . .228 B4
Lansdown Pk BA1 . . . . .27 E3
Lansdown Pl
  Bristol BS8 . . . . .226 A3
  Frome BA11 . . . . .119 D5
  High Littleton BS39 . . . . . .59 D1
Lansdown Pl E BA1 . . . . . .228 B4
Lansdown Pl W **1** BA1 . . .27 F1
Lansdown Rd
  Bath BA1 . . . . .27 E2
  Bristol BS8 . . . . .226 A3
  Saltford BS31 . . . . .25 E3
Lansdown View
  Bath BA2 . . . . .44 C5
  Faulkland BA3 . . . . .80 D1
  Timsbury BA2 . . . . .60 C2
  Tunley BA2 . . . . .61 B4
Lanthony Cl BS24 . . . . .50 A8
Laps Cott TA20 . . . . .192 F5
Lapwing Cl
  Minehead TA24 . . . . .201 C5
  Portishead BS20 . . . . 2 F6
Lapwing Gdns BS22 . . . . . .31 F1
Larch Ave TA20 . . . . .223 B5
Larch Cl
  Bridgwater TA6 . . . . .209 D6
  Churchill BS40 . . . . .53 A5
  Nailsea BS48 . . . . 9 A2
  Taunton TA1 . . . . .213 D2
Larch Ct BA3 . . . . .97 D8
Larches The BS22 . . . . .32 A3
Larchfield Cl BA11 . . . . . . .221 B7
Larchfield Trad Est TA19 . .221 B1
Larchgrove Cres BS22 . . . . .31 F1
Larchgrove Wlk BS22 . . . . .31 F1
Larchwood Ct BA3 . . . . . . .79 A3
Lark Cl BA3 . . . . .97 B8
LARKHALL 28 C2
Larkhall Pl BA1 . . . . .28 C2
Larkhall Terr BA1 . . . . .28 C2
Larkhill Rd
  Locking BS24 . . . . .50 B6
  Yeovil BA21 . . . . .218 D7
Lark Pl BA1 . . . . .44 D7
Lark Rd BS22 . . . . .31 F1
Larks Mdw DT10 . . . . .190 C4
Larkspur Cl TA1 . . . . .213 C1
Larkspur Cres BA21 . . . . .218 D7
Larkspur Ct TA2 . . . . .212 D7
Larviscombe Cl TA4 . . . . . .202 D4
Larviscombe Rd TA4 . . . . .202 D4
Lasbury Gr BS13 . . . . .22 C5
Lascelles Ave BA21 . . . . . .219 C5
Lascelles Hill BS28 . . . . . .108 C5
LATCHAM 108 F4
Latcham Dro BS27, BS28 . .109 A4

Latches La BS27 . . . . .90 D3
Latchmoor Ho BS13 . . . . . .22 A8
Late Broads BA15 . . . . .64 D7
LATTIFORD 176 D5
Lauder Ct DT9 . . . . .217 D2
LAUNCHERLEY 140 B5
Launcherley Cross BA5 . . .140 A6
Launcherley Rd BA4, BA5 . .140 D5
Launder Ct BA6 . . . . .206 E4
Laura Pl BA2 . . . . .228 C3
Laurel Ave TA9 . . . . .86 A2
Laurel Cl
  East Coker BA22 . . . . .197 B8
  Frome BA11 . . . . .120 B7
  Taunton TA1 . . . . .213 C1
Laurel Cl
  Nailsea BS48 . . . . .8 F2
  Paulton BS39 . . . . .77 E5
  Weston-super-Mare BS23 . . .48 E2
Laurel Gdns
  Chard TA20 . . . . .223 B5
  Timsbury BA2 . . . . .60 B1
  Yatton BS49 . . . . .17 B1
Laurel La BA22 . . . . .174 F3
Laurel St BA6 . . . . .140 A1
Laurels The
  Churchill BS25 . . . . .52 F4
  Crewkerne TA18 . . . . .224 D7
  Wembdon TA6 . . . . .208 C6
  Weston-super-Mare BS23 . . .48 E2
  Westwood BA15 . . . . .64 F3
Laurel Terr BS49 . . . . .17 B1
Lavender Cl BS22 . . . . .32 A5
Lavender Ct
  Frome BA11 . . . . .120 B7
  Street BA16 . . . . .207 B4
Lavender Gr TA1 . . . . .212 C3
Lavender Wlk BA22 . . . . . . .208 D1
LAVERLEY 140 C2
Laverley Cotts BA6 . . . . . . .140 C2
Laverock Ct TA1 . . . . .212 E5
Lavers Ct TA12 . . . . .186 A7
Laver's La TA20 . . . . .198 F5
Lavers Oak TA12 . . . . .185 E7
LAVERTON 100 F7
Lavington Cl BS21 . . . . .6 B1
Lavinia Wy TA6 . . . . .208 D5
LAWFORD 151 B7
Lawfords Gate BS2 . . . . . . .227 C3
Lawfords Gate Ho [17] BS2 .227 C3
Lawford St BS2 . . . . .227 C3
Law La
  Drayton TA10 . . . . .171 F3
  Langport TA10 . . . . .172 A3
Lawn La
  Galhampton BA22 . . . . .175 D8
  Shapwick TA7 . . . . .137 F1
Lawn Mdw TA3 . . . . .169 C3
Lawnmoor La TA10 . . . . . . .184 C6
Lawn Rd TA2 . . . . .212 C8
Lawnside BS48 . . . . .19 B5
Lawns The
  Bristol BS11 . . . . .4 E7
  Combe St Nicholas TA20 . . .193 D6
  Weston-super-Mare BS22 . . .32 B3
  Yatton BS49 . . . . .17 A1
Lawn The [1] TA21 . . . . .222 D6
Lawpool Ct [12] BA5 . . . . . . .203 D4
Lawrence Cl
  Burnham-on-S TA8 . . . . . . .104 D5
  Highbridge TA9 . . . . .104 F4
  Somerton TA11 . . . . .211 D3
  Weston-super-Mare BS22 . . .31 E2
Lawrence Hayes BA9 . . . . . .216 D3
Lawrence Hill BA9 . . . . .216 A2
Lawrence Hill Bsns Ctr
  BA9 . . . . .216 B3
Lawrence Mews BS22 . . . . . .31 E2
Lawrence Rd
  Coleford BA3 . . . . .116 F7
  Weston-super-Mare BS22 . . .31 E2
  Wrington BS40 . . . . .35 E2
Laws Dr BS24 . . . . .49 F7
Lawson Cl
  [5] Martock TA12 . . . . .185 E6
  Saltford BS31 . . . . .25 C2
Lawyer's Hill TA5 . . . . .152 C7
Lax Ct BA5 . . . . .203 B4
Laxton Cl TA1 . . . . .213 D5
Laxton Rd TA1 . . . . .213 E5
Laxton Way BA2 . . . . .79 D7
Laycock Hill DT9 . . . . .217 D7
Layfield La TA3 . . . . .170 C3
LAYMORE 199 C7
Layne Terr TA18 . . . . .196 B8
Lays Bsns Ctr BS31 . . . . .24 C4
Lays Dr BS31 . . . . .24 C5
Lays La BS40 . . . . .54 D4
Lays The BA11 . . . . .101 E5
Leach Cl BS21 . . . . .6 D1
Leaches Cl BA22 . . . . .186 B6
Leaches Mead [4] TA2 . . . . .169 C5
Leach Rd TA20 . . . . .223 C4
Leach's Field TA2 . . . . .168 D8
Lea Cl BA21 . . . . .219 B8
Lea Croft BS13 . . . . .22 A4
Leading Edge The BS8 . . . . .226 B2
Leadmine La BS40 . . . . .72 E4
Leadon Gr TA1 . . . . .213 D4
Leafield Cl TA2 . . . . .168 B5
Leafy Way BS24 . . . . .50 B4
Lea Grove Rd BS21 . . . . .6 C4
Leaholme Gdns BS14 . . . . . . .23 A3
Lear's La BA9 . . . . .177 C6
Leat The [8] TA4 . . . . .167 F8

Leawood Ct [3] BS23 . . . . . . .30 C1
Leaze Cl BA11 . . . . .119 D5
Leaze Dro BA5 . . . . .139 A7
Leaze Ho BA11 . . . . .119 D5
Leaze House Mews BA11 .119 D5
Leaze La
  Blagdon BS40 . . . . .72 E8
  West Chinnock TA18 . . . . . .196 B8
  Yeovil BA21 . . . . .219 F4
Leazemoor La TA10 . . . . . . .172 B8
Leaze Rd BA11 . . . . .119 D5
Leaze The
  Radstock BA3 . . . . .97 D8
  Rode BA2 . . . . .82 C1
Leazeway Dro TA7 . . . . .155 C1
Lecher La DT8, TA18 . . . . . . .196 B1
Leda Gr BS14 . . . . .23 A7
Leedham Rd
  Locking BS24 . . . . .50 C5
  Locking BS24 . . . . .50 C5
LEEFORD 122 B5
Leeford La EX35 . . . . .122 B5
Leeford Rd TA4 . . . . .165 B7
Leekbeds La TA4 . . . . .104 A1
Leekbeds Lane TA9 . . . . . . .103 F1
Leeming Way BS11 . . . . .4 C8
Lee Pk TA21 . . . . .180 F7
Leeside BS20 . . . . .2 C5
Leet Ct DT9 . . . . .225 B2
Leeward Cl TA6 . . . . .209 C4
Leewood Rd BS23 . . . . .30 F1
Leffman Ct TA11 . . . . .211 C4
Leggar The TA6 . . . . .209 A6
Legion Rd BA21 . . . . .218 F6
Leg La BS40 . . . . .54 B3
Leg Of Mutton Rd BA6 . . . .206 E6
Leg Sq BA4 . . . . .205 C6
Leg Square Ct BA4 . . . . .205 C6
Leigh Cl BA1 . . . . .28 A2
Leigh Court Bsns Ctr BS8 . . .5 A2
Leigh Furlong Rd BA16 . . . .207 B4
Leigh La
  Cold Ashton BA1 . . . . .13 B3
  Crowcombe TA4 . . . . .151 A7
  Halstock BA22 . . . . .197 C3
  Winsford TA22 . . . . .147 C2
  Winsham TA20 . . . . .199 A8
LEIGHLAND CHAPEL 149 C7
Leigh-on-Mendip Fst Sch
  BA3 . . . . .117 A3
Leigh Rd
  Bristol BS8 . . . . .226 B4
  Leigh u M BA11 . . . . .117 C2
  Street BA16 . . . . .207 C5
  Taunton TA2 . . . . .213 B8
Leigh St BA3 . . . . .116 F3
LEIGHTON 142 E6
Leighton Cl BA4 . . . . .141 E1
Leighton Cres BS24 . . . . .67 A8
Leighton Dr [10] TA3 . . . . . .169 C5
Leighton La BA4 . . . . .141 E1
Leighton Lane Ind Est
  BA4 . . . . .141 E1
Leighton Rd BA1 . . . . .27 A3
LEIGH UPON MENDIP 116 F3
Leigh View Rd BS20 . . . . .2 E7
Leighwood Dr BS48 . . . . .8 B1
LEIGH WOODS 11 D5
Leigh Woods Forest Walks★
  BS8 . . . . .5 C1
Leigh Woods National Nature
  Reserve★ BS8 . . . . .11 D8
Leinster Ave BS4 . . . . .22 D8
Lemon La BS2 . . . . .227 C4
Lenover Gdns BS13 . . . . .22 B4
Lenthay Cl DT9 . . . . .225 C2
Lenthay Ct DT9 . . . . .225 C3
Lenthay La DT9 . . . . .225 A2
Lenthay Rd DT9 . . . . .225 B2
Leonard Houlden Ct [7]
  TA2 . . . . .213 A8
Leonard La BS1 . . . . .227 A3
Leonard's Barton BA11 . . . .119 E5
Leonides Ave BS24 . . . . .49 B4
Leopold Bldgs BA1 . . . . . . .228 C4
Lerburne The BS28 . . . . .108 D4
Lesley La TA2 . . . . .169 B2
Leslie Ave TA2 . . . . .212 E6
Leslie Rise BA15 . . . . .64 F3
Les Rosiers Gdns BA9 . . . . .216 C4
Lester Dr BS22 . . . . .32 A3
Lester La DT9 . . . . .176 A2
Letham Ct TA19 . . . . .221 B4
Lethbridge Pk TA5 . . . . .151 D1
Lethbridge Rd BA5 . . . . . . .203 C4
Level La DT9 . . . . .176 A2
Level View TA10 . . . . .172 C5
Leversedge Rd BA11 . . . . . .120 A7
LEWCOMBE 197 E2
Lewins Mead BS1 . . . . .227 A3
Lewis Cl BA3 . . . . .96 C4
Lewis Cres BA11 . . . . .119 F6
Lewisham Gr BS23 . . . . .49 A8
Lewis Rd
  Bristol BS13 . . . . .22 A8
  Taunton TA2 . . . . .212 E7
Lewis's Dro BA5 . . . . .138 E7
Lewmond Ave BA5 . . . . .203 F5
Leycroft Cl TA1 . . . . .213 B4
Leycroft Gr TA1 . . . . .213 B4
Leycroft Rd TA1 . . . . .213 B4
Leyland Wlk BS13 . . . . .21 F4
Leys Hill BA11 . . . . .120 A6
Leys La BA11 . . . . .119 F7
Leys The BS21 . . . . .6 B1
Leystone Cl BA11 . . . . .120 A6
Leyton Dr TA6 . . . . .209 D6
Lias Rd BA16 . . . . .207 B4

Liberty Gdns BS1 . . . . .226 C1
Liberty La BS40 . . . . .54 E2
Liberty Pl TA6 . . . . .209 B4
Liberty The BA5 . . . . .203 E5
Lichen Rd
  Frome BA11 . . . . .120 B2
  Frome BA11 . . . . .120 B3
Liddon Hill TA18 . . . . .195 C5
Liddymore La
  Watchet TA23 . . . . .202 D5
  Williton TA4, TA23 . . . . .202 E4
Liddymore Rd TA23 . . . . . . .202 D5
Lightgate TA13 . . . . .220 D5
Lightgate La TA13 . . . . .220 D4
Lightgate Rd TA13 . . . . .220 D4
Lilac Cl TA1 . . . . .213 C2
Lilac Terr BA3 . . . . .78 C2
Lilac Way BS22 . . . . .32 A5
Lilian Terr BS39 . . . . .77 E5
Lillebonne Cl TA21 . . . . .222 F6
Lillebonne Wy TA21 . . . . . . .222 D7
Lillesdon Terr TA3 . . . . .170 A2
Lilliana Wy TA6 . . . . .208 E1
Lillington Cl BA3 . . . . .79 B2
Lillington Rd BA3 . . . . .79 B2
Lillington Way TA20 . . . . . . .223 C5
Lilly Batch BA11 . . . . .119 F7
Lillycombe La TA3, EX15 . . .191 B8
Lily Batch BA11 . . . . .119 F7
Lilstock Rd TA5 . . . . .133 E7
Lily La BA8 . . . . .176 E1
Lily Rd BA11 . . . . .120 B2
Limber Rd BA22 . . . . .218 A6
Limbers La BA5 . . . . .139 B8
Limbury [2] TA12 . . . . .185 E6
Limbury Cotts [3] TA12 . . . .185 E6
Limebreach Wood BS48 . . . . .8 D3
Limeburn Hill BS40 . . . . .38 E5
Lime Cl
  Frome BA11 . . . . .120 B7
  Locking BS24 . . . . .50 B4
  Minehead TA24 . . . . .200 D7
  Street BA16 . . . . .207 C5
  Weston-super-Mare BS22 . . .32 A1
Lime Cres TA1 . . . . .213 C2
Lime Ct BS31 . . . . .24 C4
Lime Gr
  Bath BA2 . . . . .45 B6
  Shepton Mallet BA4 . . . . . . .205 A6
Lime Grove Gdns BA2 . . . . . .45 B6
Lime Kiln BA21 . . . . .218 C5
Limekiln La
  Bath BA2 . . . . .45 F4
  Chard, Forton TA20 . . . . . . .223 D1
  Chard, Lydmarsh TA20 . . . . .194 C3
  Cricket St Thomas TA20 . . . .194 E2
  Leigh u M BA11 . . . . .117 C3
  Oakhill BA3 . . . . .114 E5
  Stoke St Michael BA3 . . . . . .115 F4
  Tatworth TA20 . . . . .193 F1
Lime Kiln La
  Castle Cary BA7 . . . . .214 E4
  Clevedon BS21 . . . . .6 D3
  Henstridge BA8 . . . . .190 A6
  Wookey Hole BA5 . . . . .203 B7
Lime Kiln Rd BS1 . . . . .226 B2
Limekilns Cl BS31 . . . . .24 F5
Limepits La TA10 . . . . .172 D5
Limerick Cl DT9 . . . . .217 D2
Limerick La BA11 . . . . .101 F2
Limes Cl TA4 . . . . .202 E3
Lime St
  Bristol BS14 . . . . .22 E5
  Nether Stowey TA5 . . . . . . .134 B2
  Stogursey TA5 . . . . .134 C6
Limestone Hill TA5 . . . . .135 C1
Limestone Link BS40 . . . . . . .73 D6
Lime Terr BA3 . . . . .78 D1
Lime Tree Ave BA20 . . . . . . .218 E2
Lime Tree Cl TA6 . . . . .209 D4
Lime Tree Gr BS20 . . . . .4 D3
LIMINGTON 174 A1
Limington Rd BA22 . . . . . . .173 E1
Limousin Way TA6 . . . . .209 A1
Limpetshell La TA4 . . . . .202 E3
LIMPLEY STOKE 64 A6
Limpley Stoke Rd BA15 . . . . .64 D6
Linch La BA4 . . . . .142 C2
Lincoln Hill TA19 . . . . .184 E4
Lincoln Cl BS31 . . . . .24 C4
Lincoln La BS23 . . . . .49 B4
Lincombe Rd BA3 . . . . .97 D8
Lincott View BA2 . . . . .79 C8
Linden Ave BS23 . . . . .49 B8
Linden Cl
  Bridgwater TA6 . . . . .209 C4
  Bristol BS14 . . . . .23 E6
  Frome BA11 . . . . .119 D5
  Radstock BA3 . . . . .97 E8
Linden Gdns BA1 . . . . .44 D8
Linden Gr TA1 . . . . .212 E5
Linden Hill TA21 . . . . .222 A6
Linden Rd
  Clevedon BS21 . . . . .6 D4
  Yeovil BA20 . . . . .218 F5
Lindens The BS22 . . . . .31 E4
Lindisfarne Cl BA15 . . . . .64 E6
Lindsey Cl BS20 . . . . .1 F4
Lindsey Cres [1] TA6 . . . . . .153 F3
Linemere Cl BS48 . . . . .19 D6
Linen Wlk BA1 . . . . .28 C2
Lines Way BS14 . . . . .23 C3
Liney Rd TA7 . . . . .154 F6

Lingfield Ave BA21 . . . . .219 D7
Linham Rd TA6 . . . . .208 F6
Linhay Cl EX15 . . . . .179 E1
Linkhay TA20 . . . . .198 D8
Linkhay Cl TA20 . . . . .198 D8
Link La
  Burrington BS40 . . . . .53 F3
  Monkton Farleigh BA15 . . . .46 F8
Linkmead BA3 . . . . .96 F2
Link Rd
  Nailsea BS48 . . . . .8 F2
  Portishead BS20 . . . . .2 C5
Links Cl BS23 . . . . .48 C4
Links Gdns TA8 . . . . .84 F3
Linkside BS21 . . . . .6 E6
Links Rd BS23 . . . . .48 C2
Link The BS27 . . . . .90 B8
Linley Cl
  Bath BA2 . . . . .44 A5
  Bridgwater TA6 . . . . .209 D7
Linleys The BA1 . . . . .44 C7
Linne Ho BA3 . . . . .44 A5
Linnet Cl
  Taunton TA1 . . . . .212 B4
  Weston-super-Mare BS22 . . .31 E1
Linnet Gdns [5] BS20 . . . . . . .2 F6
Linnet Way
  Frome BA11 . . . . .120 B6
  Keynsham BS31 . . . . .24 C3
  Keynsham BS31 . . . . .24 C3
  Midsomer Norton BA3 . . . . . .97 B8
Linnington La TA20 . . . . .193 B2
Linseed Dr [15] EX13 . . . . . .198 A1
Linsvale Cl BA11 . . . . .120 C5
Linsvale Dr BA11 . . . . .120 C5
Lintern Cl BA4 . . . . .159 C7
Linton's Wlk BS14 . . . . .23 A7
Lion Cl BS48 . . . . .8 D2
Lion D'angers TA4 . . . . .210 D4
Lion Dr DT9 . . . . .217 E2
Lion Ho [20] BA4 . . . . .205 B6
Lion Mews TA1 . . . . .211 E4
Lipe Hill La TA3, TA4 . . . . . .168 B1
Lipe La TA3 . . . . .169 C3
Lipgate Pl BS20 . . . . .2 D3
Lippard La TA9 . . . . .105 F8
Lippetts Way TA7 . . . . .137 D1
Lippiat Hill BA3 . . . . .80 C3
Lippiatt La
  Cheddar BS27 . . . . .90 C7
  Shipham BS25 . . . . .70 F8
  Timsbury BA2 . . . . .60 B3
Lippiatt The BS27 . . . . .90 C8
LIPYEATE 97 E1
Lipyeate La BA3 . . . . .97 E2
Lisieux Cl TA1 . . . . .213 D2
Lisieux Way TA1 . . . . .213 C3
Lisle Rd BS22 . . . . .32 B4
Listercombe Cl TA19 . . . . . .221 C2
Lister Gr BA15 . . . . .64 F3
Lister's Hill TA19 . . . . .221 C2
LISTOCK 170 C2
Litfield Pl BS8 . . . . .11 F5
Litfield Rd BS8 . . . . .11 F5
Litt Hill BA3 . . . . .75 F2
Little Ann St BS2, BS5 . . . . .227 C4
Little Batch BA5 . . . . .92 D2
Little Birch Croft BS14 . . . . . .23 A3
Little Bishop St BS2 . . . . . . .227 B4
Littlebrook BS39 . . . . .77 E6
Little Brooks La BA4 . . . . . . .205 C4
Little Burrow Dro TA7 . . . . .155 A1
Little Caroline Pl [4] BS8 . . .11 F5
Little Cl TA2 . . . . .212 C8
Littledown Rd TA4 . . . . .148 F3
Little Dro TA7 . . . . .154 F4
Little Elm Rd TA7 . . . . .155 C4
Little England TA7 . . . . .155 C2
Little Entry BA5 . . . . .203 F5
Littlefield DT9 . . . . .225 B3
Littlefield Cl BA16 . . . . .156 E7
Littlefield Dro TA12 . . . . . . .185 F8
Littlefield La TA10 . . . . .172 E4
Little Field La BA5 . . . . .110 F7
Littlefields Ave BS29 . . . . . . .51 B4
Littlefields La TA19 . . . . .184 F3
Littlefields Rd BS29 . . . . .51 B3
Littlefields Rise BS29 . . . . . . .51 B3
Little George St
  Bristol BS2 . . . . .227 C4
  Weston-super-Mare BS23 . . .48 E7
Little Gn BA5 . . . . .111 A4
LITTLE GREEN 118 B6
Little Halt BS20 . . . . .1 E4
Little Ham BS21 . . . . .16 C8
Littleham Cotts TA3 . . . . . . .181 E6
Little Headley Cl BS13 . . . . . .22 B7
LITTLE HILL 192 F8
Little Hill TA20 . . . . .192 F8
LITTLE KEYFORD 119 E1
Little Keyford La BA11 . . . . .119 E1
Little King St BS1 . . . . .227 A2
Little La
  Farmborough BA2 . . . . .60 A6
  Kingsbury Episcopi TA12 . . .185 A7
Little La Wick TA9 . . . . .85 F7
Little Leaze La TA7 . . . . .137 D2
Little Lester TA19 . . . . .221 C2
Little Marston Rd BA22 . . . .174 F1
Little Mdw
  [6] Bishops Lydeard TA4 . . .167 F8
  Ilchester BA22 . . . . .173 E2
Little Mead TA14 . . . . .185 E2
Little Mead Cl BS24 . . . . .49 E3
Little Meadow End BS48 . . . .18 E8
Little Moor Rd TA9 . . . . .106 F3
Littlemore Dro TA7 . . . . .154 C3

LITTLE NORTON 186 A2
Little Orch
  Cheddar BS27 . . . . .90 C8
  Street BA16 . . . . .207 D7
  Weston-super-Mare BS23 . . .48 D1
Little Orchard [34] TA12 . . .185 E6
Little Paul St BS2 . . . . .226 C4
Little Pen TA8 . . . . .84 F5
Little Pennard La BA4 . . . . .159 A4
Little Plover Cl TA20 . . . . . .201 C5
Little Sammons BA22 . . . . . .186 E5
Little Silver Ct TA23 . . . . . . .202 C7
Little Silver La TA21 . . . . . . .222 D2
Little St TA14 . . . . .185 E2
Little Stanhope St BA1 . . . . .228 A2
Little Stoke Rd BS9 . . . . .5 E4
Little Thatch Cl BS14 . . . . . . .23 C6
LITTLETON 38 D4
Littleton Hill TA11 . . . . .211 E6
Littleton La
  Wellow BA2 . . . . .80 C7
  Winford BS40 . . . . .38 D5
Little Trumps BA22 . . . . .186 B7
LITTLE WESTON 175 B4
Little Weston Rd BS22 . . . . .175 C4
Little Withey Mead BS9 . . . . .5 F5
Little Wiveliscombe La
  TA4 . . . . .165 D6
Littlewood BA11 . . . . .143 C4
Littlewood Cl BS14 . . . . .23 B3
Littlewood La BS49 . . . . .18 C2
Littlewood Way BS27 . . . . . . .89 F8
LITTON 75 F2
Litton BS24 . . . . .49 A2
Litton Rd BA3 . . . . .76 A1
Liver Moor Dro TA11 . . . . . .156 E2
Livingstone Dr [3] BA21 . . .219 F8
Livingstone Rd BA2 . . . . .44 D5
Livingstone Terr BA2 . . . . . .228 A1
Livingstone Way TA2 . . . . . .212 B6
Llewellyns Almshouses [6]
  BA5 . . . . .203 D4
Llewellyn Way BS22 . . . . .32 B3
Lloyd Cl TA1 . . . . .212 B1
Loaders La BA21 . . . . .187 A5
Load La TA7 . . . . .154 E5
Load Pool TA7 . . . . .155 C2
Lobelia Cl TA9 . . . . .104 D5
Lockemor Rd BS13 . . . . .22 F4
Lockes Paddock BS22 . . . . . .32 C3
Lockett Dr BA7 . . . . .214 A7
Locketts Barton TA3 . . . . . . .170 D7
Lockey Rd BA4 . . . . .205 B4
Lock Gdns BS13 . . . . .21 E7
LOCKING 50 A4
Locking Farm Ind Est BS24 .50 A5
Locking Head Dro
  Locking BS24 . . . . .49 F6
  Weston-super-Mare BS24 . . .50 A6
Locking Moor Rd
  Locking BS24 . . . . .50 B5
  Weston-super-Mare BS24 . . .49 D8
Locking Prim Sch BS24 . . . . .50 B4
Locking Rd BS22, BS23 . . . . .49 D5
Lockingwell Rd BS31 . . . . . . .24 D5
LOCKSBROOK 44 B6
Locksbrook Ct [8] BA1 . . . . .44 B6
Locksbrook Rd
  Bath BA1 . . . . .44 C6
  Weston-super-Mare BS22 . . .32 B5
Locksbrook Trad Est [7]
  BA1 . . . . .44 B6
Lock's Hill BA11 . . . . .119 F3
Lockside BS20 . . . . .2 E7
Lockside Sq BS20 . . . . .2 E7
Lock's La TA9 . . . . .216 C4
Locks Way TA7 . . . . .136 F3
Lockswell TA7 . . . . .136 E4
Lockswell Cotts BA4 . . . . . .141 B1
Lockwood Ct [4] BA21 . . . . .218 F7
Lockyer Dro TA7 . . . . .156 A5
Lodes La TA2 . . . . .168 E8
Lodge Cl
  Taunton TA1 . . . . .212 A2
  Wellington TA21 . . . . .222 D2
  Yatton BS49 . . . . .34 B8
Lodge Cotts TA3 . . . . .181 D6
Lodge Ct
  Bristol BS9 . . . . .5 E4
  Castle Cary BA7 . . . . .214 B4
Lodge Dr
  Long Ashton BS41 . . . . .11 B2
  Weston-super-Mare BS23 . . .31 A1
Lodge Fields BA12 . . . . .144 D3
Lodge Gdns BA2 . . . . .44 D1
Lodge Hill
  Berkley BA11 . . . . .120 C5
  Bratton Seymour BA9 . . . . . .176 A2
  Somerton TA11 . . . . .211 F4
  Westbury-sub-Mendip BA5 . .110 D5
  Yarlington BA9 . . . . .175 F7
Lodge Hill Ind Pk BA5 . . . . .110 D5
Lodge La
  Axminster EX13 . . . . .198 B2
  Tudhay EX13 . . . . .198 C3
  Wraxall BS48 . . . . .9 B2
Lodge Pl BS1 . . . . .226 C3
Lodge Rd
  Horningsham BA12 . . . . . . .144 D4
  Kingsdon TA11 . . . . .173 D4
Lodge Rocks TA24 . . . . .131 D3
Lodge St BS1 . . . . .226 C3
Lodges The BA3 . . . . .96 D1
LODWAY 4 B5
Lodway BS20 . . . . .4 C4
Lodway Cl BS20 . . . . .4 C5
Lodway Gdns BS20 . . . . .4 C4

Lodwells Orch TA3 . . . . 170 B4
Lollover La TA10 . . . . 156 F3
Lombardy Cl 5 BS22 . . . . 49 E8
London Cross TA4 . . . . 151 E4
London Dro BA6, BS28 . . . 138 D7
London Ho TA4 . . . . 210 C4
London Rd
  Bath BA1 . . . . 228 C4
  Milborne Port DT9 . . . . . 217 E1
London Rd E BA1 . . . . 29 A3
London Rd W BA1 . . . . 28 E2
London Sq
  28 Martock TA12 . . . . . . 185 E6
  Portishead BS20 . . . . 2 E7
London St BA1 . . . . 228 C4
Longacre BS21 . . . . 16 B8
Long Acre BA4 . . . . 205 C4
Longacre Cl TA2 . . . . 212 E7
Longacre Dro TA7 . . . . 154 D7
Long Acre Ho BA1 . . . . 228 C4
Long Acre La TA19 . . . . 194 F6
Long Acre Rd BS14 . . . . 23 A3
Long Acres Cl BS9 . . . . 5 D7
LONGALLER 168 B4
LONG ASHTON 11 A1
Long Ashton Bsns Pk BS41 . 11 B1
Long Ashton By-Pass
  Barrow Gurney BS48 . . . . . 20 D7
  Bristol BS41 . . . . 11 C1
  Bristol BS41 . . . . 21 B8
Long Ashton Rd BS41 . . . . . 11 B2
Long Ave BS21 . . . . 6 B2
Long Barnaby BA3 . . . . 78 A2
Longbottom BS25 . . . . 71 A6
Longbridge 16 BA4 . . . . . . 205 B6
Longbrook Trad Est BS3 . . . 11 E3
Long Cl
  Ilminster TA19 . . . . 221 C2
  Yeovil BA21 . . . . 218 C5
Longcombe Dr BA2 . . . . . . 144 F6
Longcombe La TA24 . . . . . . 130 E3
LONGCROFT 219 A8
Longcroft Rd BA21 . . . . . . 219 C6
LONG CROSS 37 D7
Long Cross
  Bristol BS11 . . . . 4 F8
  Doulting BA4 . . . . 141 F8
  Felton BS40 . . . . 37 D7
  Nether Stowey TA5 . . . . . 134 A3
Long Cross Bottom
  Doulting BA3 . . . . 142 A8
  Stoke St Michael BA3 . . . 116 A1
Longdown Dr BS22 . . . . 32 B4
Long Dro
  Broadway TA19, TA20 . . . 183 A4
  Buckland St Mary TA20 . . 182 F2
  Glastonbury BA5 . . . . 139 E4
  Westbury-sub-Mendip BS27 110 A4
Long Eaton Dr BS14 . . . . . . 23 B7
Longfellow Ave BA2 . . . . . . 44 F4
Longfellow Rd BA3 . . . . 97 C8
Longfield BA11 . . . . 118 A7
Longfield Cl TA4 . . . . 202 E2
Longforth Rd TA21 . . . . . . 222 D6
Longforward Hill
  Dinnington TA17 . . . . 195 A8
  Seavington St Mary TA19 . . 184 D1
Longforward La
  Dinnington TA17 . . . . 195 B8
  Seavington St Mary TA19 . . 184 D1
Long Furlong La
  East Coker BA22 . . . . 197 C8
  Long Sutton TA10 . . . . . . 172 E5
Long Ground BA11 . . . . 119 F3
Long Hay Cl BA2 . . . . 44 B5
LONGHEDGE 144 E7
Long Hill
  Clewer BS28 . . . . 89 D2
  Shepton Mallet BA4 . . . . . 141 C8
Long Holcombe Cross
  EX36 . . . . 145 E6
Longhorn Dr 7 TA6 . . . . . . 209 A1
LONGHOUSE 61 D5
Long La
  Backwell BS48 . . . . 19 C2
  Barwick House BA22 . . . . 219 C1
  Bourton SP8 . . . . 161 D1
  Cucklington BA9 . . . . 177 D5
  Dinder BA5 . . . . 140 D7
  Felton BS40 . . . . 37 B5
  Fishpond Bottom DT6 . . . 199 B1
  Walton BA16 . . . . 156 D7
  Wanstrow BA4 . . . . 142 F5
  West Chinnock TA18 . . . . 196 B7
  Wheddon Cross TA24 . . . . 129 C2
  Wootton Courtenay TA24 . . 129 E8
  Wrington BS40 . . . . 36 B2
  Yeovil BA22 . . . . 187 C1
Long Lakes TA4 . . . . 202 E4
Longlands La
  East Coker BA22 . . . . 197 C8
  Westbury-sub-Mendip BA5 . 110 D8
Longleat Cl BA11 . . . . 119 F3
Longleat Ct BA11 . . . . 119 E4
Longleat Forest Holiday
  Village ★ BA12 . . . . 144 F5
Longleat House ★ BA12 . . 144 D6
Longleat La BA3 . . . . 116 C8
Longleat Rd BA3 . . . . 116 B8
Longleat Rly ★ BA12 . . . . 144 F4
Longleat Safari & Adventure
  Park ★ BA12 . . . . 144 D6
Longleaze Gdns BS24 . . . . . . 49 F3
LONG LOAD 172 E2
Long Load Rd TA12 . . . . . . 185 E8
Longman's Lea BA4 . . . . . . 159 C7
Longmarsh La TA10 . . . . . . 172 E6
Longmead TA4 . . . . 165 E8

Long Mead BA21 . . . . 218 C5
Longmead Cl
  Norton St Philip BA2 . . . . . 81 F4
  Taunton TA1 . . . . 212 D2
  Wellington TA21 . . . . 222 B8
Longmead Cotts TA21 . . . . 222 B8
Longmead Croft BS13 . . . . . 21 F4
Longmeadow Rd BS31 . . . . . 24 C4
Longmead Way TA1 . . . . . . 212 D2
Long Moor Dro TA7, TA9 . . 137 A7
Longreach Gr BS14 . . . . 23 D6
Long Ride Dro BA6 . . . . . . 157 F3
Longridge Way BS24 . . . . . . 49 F7
Long Row BS1 . . . . 227 B2
Long Run BA22 . . . . 186 C2
Longrun La TA1 . . . . 212 D4
Longs Field TA3 . . . . 170 C4
Long St
  Croscombe BA5 . . . . 204 B7
  Galhampton BA22 . . . . . . 175 E8
  High Ham TA10 . . . . 156 A1
  Sherborne DT9 . . . . 225 E4
  Williton TA4 . . . . 202 E3
Longstone Ave TA6 . . . . . . 209 C5
Longstone Cl TA5 . . . . 134 B2
Longstrings La TA18 . . . . . . 224 C8
LONG SUTTON 172 F4
Long Sutton CE Prim Sch
  Long Sutton TA10 . . . . . . 172 E4
  Long Sutton TA10 . . . . . . 172 E4
Long-Thorn BS48 . . . . 18 F6
Longthorne Pl BA2 . . . . 44 F2
Long Thorn La BS40 . . . . . . 55 E7
Longton Grove Rd 3 BS23 . 48 E8
Longton Ind Est BS23 . . . . . 48 F6
Long Valley Rd BA2 . . . . 43 F5
Longvernal BA3 . . . . 77 F1
Longvernal Prim Sch
  Midsomer Norton BA3 . . . . 77 E1
  Midsomer Norton BA3 . . . . 77 F1
Longway Ave BS13, BS14 . . . 22 F4
Longwood Ho BS8 . . . . 10 D4
Longwood La
  Burlescombe TA21 . . . . . . 179 C4
  Long Ashton BS8, BS41 . . . 10 F4
Lonsdale Ave BS23 . . . . 48 F4
Lonsdale Rd TA5 . . . . 135 C2
Look's La BA6 . . . . 157 C6
Looseall La TA22 . . . . 163 D8
LOPEN 185 A1
Lopen Head TA13 . . . . 220 A1
Lopen La TA13 . . . . 220 C1
Lopen Rd TA13, TA17 . . . . . 195 D8
Lord Bath's Dro BA16 . . . . 156 D4
Lordsleaze La TA20 . . . . . . 223 D3
Lords Meadow La 5
  EX16 . . . . 164 B1
Lords Way TA6 . . . . 208 E6
Loretto Gdns 5 EX13 . . . . 198 A1
Loretto Rd EX13 . . . . 198 A1
Lorna Doone TA23 . . . . 202 B7
Lorne Pl BA5 . . . . 203 E5
Lorne Rd BA2 . . . . 44 D6
Lotment Hill TA11 . . . . 173 D5
LOTTISHAM 158 D5
Lottisham La BA4, BA6 . . . . 158 D6
Lottisham Rd BA6 . . . . 158 C6
Lotts' Ave BS48 . . . . 19 B5
Lotus Ct BS22 . . . . 31 C1
Lotus Dr TA6 . . . . 208 D1
Louisa Gate TA22 . . . . 163 F7
Louisa St BS2 . . . . 227 C2
Louvigne Cl TA8 . . . . 104 C7
Love La
  Burnham-on-S TA8 . . . . . 104 C7
  Ilminster TA19 . . . . 221 C3
  Marnhull DT10 . . . . 190 F6
  Shepton Beauchamp TA19 . 184 E4
  Wincanton BA9 . . . . 216 F5
Lovelands DT2 . . . . 197 A1
Lovelinch Gdns BS41 . . . . . . 10 F1
Lovell Dr BS39 . . . . 57 C4
Lovell's Dro BA4 . . . . 140 A4
Lovells Mead DT10 . . . . . . 190 F6
Lovells Mill BS39 . . . . 57 D4
Lovells The BS20 . . . . 4 B4
Loveridge La TA20 . . . . 198 D8
Lovers La BA3, BS39 . . . . . . 78 A5
Lovers Wlk BA5 . . . . 203 D5
Lovers' Wlk
  4 Cannington TA5 . . . . . . 135 B2
  Weston-super-Mare BS23 . . 48 D8
Loves Hill BA2 . . . . 60 A1
Loves La BA14 . . . . 83 C7
Love's La BA2 . . . . 59 F6
LOVINGTON 158 F1
Lovington CE Prim Sch
  BA7 . . . . 158 F2
Lovington Rd
  Alford BA7 . . . . 159 A1
  Galhampton BA22 . . . . . . 175 A8
Lowbourne BS14 . . . . 22 F6
Lower Acreman St 3
  DT9 . . . . 225 D3
Lower Actis BA6 . . . . 206 E3
LOWER AISHOLT 152 C6
Lower Ansford BA7 . . . . . . 214 B7
Lower Backway BA10 . . . . . 215 E6
Lower Batch BA5 . . . . 39 B3
Lower Bath Rd TA6 . . . . . . 209 B6
Lower Beadon TA16 . . . . . . 195 F7
Lower Borough Walls
  BA1 . . . . 228 C2
Lower Bournbane Terr TA14 . 185 D2
Lower Boyston La DT9 . . . . 188 F5
Lower Bristol Rd
  Bath BA2 . . . . 44 B6

Lower Bristol Rd continued
  Clutton BS39 . . . . 58 F4
Lower Burlington Rd BS20 . . 2 E7
LOWER BURROW 184 F7
Lower Camden Pl BA1 . . . . 228 C4
LOWER CANADA 49 F2
Lower Castle St BS1 . . . . . . 227 B3
Lower Chapel Ct BA5 . . . . . 113 A1
Lower Cheriton La BA8 . . . 176 D4
LOWER CHILTON
  CANTELO 187 C8
Lower Church La BS2 . . . . . 227 A3
Lower Church Rd
  Carlingcott BA2 . . . . 61 A1
  Weston-super-Mare BS23 . . 48 D8
Lower Clapton Farm La
  BA9 . . . . 176 A6
LOWER CLAVERHAM 17 F2
Lower Claverham BS49 . . . . 17 F3
Lower Clifton Hill BS8 . . . . 226 B2
Lower College St BS1 . . . . . 226 C2
Lower Coombses TA20 . . . . 198 D8
Lower Crannel Dro BA6 . . . 139 C4
Lower Cross EX15 . . . . 179 C1
Lower Down Rd BS20 . . . . . . 2 B5
LOWER DOWNSIDE 205 C7
LOWER DURSTON 169 F7
Lower East Coker Rd
  BA20 . . . . 218 F1
Lower East Hayes BA1 . . . . . 45 B8
LOWER FAIRFIELD 10 A8
Lower Fairfield TA4 . . . . . . 166 F5
Lower Fairmead Rd BA21 . . 219 D8
Lower Fallow Cl BS14 . . . . . 22 F3
Lower Farm DT9 . . . . 187 E4
Lower Farm La BA2 . . . . 43 B7
Lower Field Dro TA12 . . . . . 185 C7
Lowerfield La TA19 . . . . . . 184 E1
Lower Foxmoor Rd TA21 . . 222 B5
Lower Gay St BS2 . . . . 227 A4
LOWER GODNEY 138 F5
Lower Guinea St BS1 . . . . . 227 A1
Lower Gully Dro BS28 . . . . . 89 F3
Lower Gunville DT9 . . . . . . 217 D2
LOWER HALSTOCK
  LEIGH 197 B2
LOWER HARMSWELL 12 C3
Lower Hedgemead Rd
  BA1 . . . . 228 C4
Lower High St BS11 . . . . 4 D7
Lower Hill TA5 . . . . 133 D6
LOWER HOLDITCH 198 D5
Lower Holway Cl TA1 . . . . . 213 D2
Lower Hyde Rd TA15 . . . . . 186 B4
Lower Innox BA11 . . . . 119 F6
Lower Kewstoke Rd BS22 . . . 31 E3
LOWER KEYFORD 119 F3
Lower Keyford BA11 . . . . . . 119 F3
Lower Kingsbury DT9 . . . . . 217 D3
Lower Kingsdown Rd SN13 . . 29 F3
Lower Knowles Rd BS21 . . . . 6 C2
Lower La
  Shepton Mallet BA4 . . . . . 205 C6
  Weston Town BA4 . . . . . . 142 C5
Lower Lamb St BS1 . . . . . . 226 C2
LOWER LANGFORD 53 C5
LOWER LEIGH 207 C6
Lower Linden Rd BS21 . . . . . 6 D3
Lower Lodfin EX16 . . . . . . 164 B2
Lower Marshfield Rd
  TA24 . . . . 201 B6
LOWER MARSTON 143 E7
Lower Maudlin St BS1 . . . . 227 A3
Lower Mdw TA19 . . . . 221 A4
Lower Mead 14 EX13 . . . . 198 A1
Lower Meadow Rd TA24 . . 201 B5
LOWER MERRIDGE 152 C5
Lower Middle St TA1 . . . . . 212 F4
LOWER MILTON 203 B8
Lower New Rd BS27 . . . . . . 90 A7
Lower Northend BA1 . . . . . . 28 E5
Lower North St BS37 . . . . . . 90 B8
Lower North Town La
  BA22 . . . . 175 D7
Lower Norton La
  Weston-super-Mare BS22 . . 31 E4
  Weston-super-Mare, Norton
  BS22 . . . . 31 C4
Lower Notlake Dro BS28 . . . 89 E4
LOWER ODCOMBE 186 D2
Lower Odcombe BA22 . . . . 186 C2
Lower Oldfield Pk BA2 . . . . 228 A1
Lower Orch TA19 . . . . 184 C5
Lower Parade Ground Rd
  BS24 . . . . 50 C5
Lower Park La TA24 . . . . . . 129 E1
Lower Park Row BS1 . . . . . 227 A3
LOWER PEASEDOWN 79 B8
Lower Pitney Rd TA10 . . . . 172 C7
Lower Pk TA24 . . . . 200 E7
Lower Queen's BS21 . . . . 6 D3
Lower Rd
  Hinton Blewett BS39 . . . . . 75 E6
  Horsington BA8 . . . . 176 B3
  Kingsdon TA11 . . . . 173 D5
  Stalbridge DT10 . . . . 190 C4
  Woolavington TA7 . . . . . . 136 E4
Lower Ream BA21 . . . . 218 C5
LOWER ROADWATER 131 D1
Lower Rocke's Cotts BA6 . . 157 D4
LOWER RUDGE 102 D4
Lower Severalls Gdn ★
  TA18 . . . . 196 A6
Lower Shepton Rd BA9 . . . 160 B2
Lower Shockerwick La
  BA1 . . . . 29 D5
Lower Shute TA3 . . . . 144 F3
Lowerside La BA6 . . . . 206 D7

Lowerside Rd BA6 . . . . 206 E6
Lower Silk Mill BA4 . . . . . . 204 F6
LOWER SOMERTON 211 E3
Lower Somerton TA11 . . . . 211 E3
Lower St
  Buckland Dinham BA11 . . . 100 A2
  Carhampton TA24 . . . . . . 131 B4
  Chewton Mendip BA3 . . . . 94 F7
  Curry Mallet TA3 . . . . . . 183 C8
  Merriott TA16 . . . . 195 F7
  Pilton BA4 . . . . 140 F3
  Rode BA11 . . . . 101 E8
  Upton Noble BA4 . . . . . . 142 F2
  West Chinnock TA18 . . . . 196 B8
Lower Stoke BA2, BA3 . . . . . 64 A8
LOWER STRATTON 220 E1
LOWER STRODE 56 A8
Lower Strode BS40 . . . . 56 A7
Lower Strode Rd BS21 . . . . . 16 A7
LOWER SWAINSWICK 28 C3
LOWER TIPPACOTT 122 A4
Lower Touches TA20 . . . . . 223 E5
Lower Town
  Montacute TA15 . . . . 186 A6
  Sampford Peverell EX16 . . 178 D1
Lower Turners Barn La
  BA20 . . . . 218 F2
LOWER VELLOW 132 D1
Lower Vellow TA4 . . . . 132 D2
LOWER VEXFORD 150 F6
LOWER WEACOMBE 132 E3
LOWER WEARE 88 D8
Lower Wellesley Rd
  Wells BA5 . . . . 140 A6
  Wells BA5 . . . . 203 F1
LOWER WESTFORD 222 A6
LOWER WESTHOLME 140 D3
Lower Westholme Rd
  BA4 . . . . 140 D3
LOWER WESTON 44 C7
LOWER WHATLEY 118 D3
Lower Whitelands BA3 . . . . 79 B3
Lower Woodcock St BA7 . . 214 C5
Lower Woodrow Rd DT10 . . 189 D2
LOWER WOOLSTON 175 F6
Lower Woolston Rd BA22 . . 175 F6
LOWER WRAXHILL BA20 . . 218 F1
LOWER WRITHLINGTON . . . 79 C3
LOW HAM 172 B8
Low Ham Rd TA10 . . . . 172 B8
Lowlands Terr TA1 . . . . 212 B4
Lowman Cross EX15 . . . . . . 178 B2
Lowmoor Ind Est TA21 . . . 222 B8
Low's Hill La DT9 . . . . 188 B3
Lowsome La TA6 . . . . 188 A5
Lowther Rd BA21 . . . . 219 E7
LOWTON 181 B5
Lowtrow Cross TA4 . . . . . . 165 A8
Low Veale La BS39 . . . . 58 A4
LOW WATER 119 E6
Loxhams TA10 . . . . 156 B2
Loxleigh Ave TA6 . . . . 209 A4
Loxleigh Gdns TA6 . . . . . . 209 A4
Loxley Batch TA7 . . . . 156 A8
Loxley Gdns BA2 . . . . 44 C4
Loxley Terr TA6 . . . . 208 F7
LOXTON 68 C4
Loxton Dr BA2 . . . . 44 B6
Loxton Rd BS23 . . . . 48 F2
Loxton Sq BS14 . . . . 23 A6
Lubborn La BA6 . . . . 158 B5
Lucas La TA20 . . . . 193 D6
LUCCOMBE 129 D7
Lucerne Cres TA6 . . . . 208 D1
Luckes La TA4 . . . . 132 E3
Luckington Cross BA11 . . . . 98 B2
Lucklands Rd BA1 . . . . 27 C1
Luckley Ave BS13 . . . . 22 C5
Lucott Cross TA24 . . . . 128 C6
Ludbourne Rd DT9 . . . . . . 225 E3
Ludlow Ave TA6 . . . . 213 A8
Ludlow Cl
  Bridgwater TA6 . . . . 209 A2
  Frome BA11 . . . . 120 C6
  Keynsham BS31 . . . . 24 D5
LUDNEY 194 F7
Ludney Cross TA19 . . . . . . 194 F7
Ludney La
  Dinnington TA17 . . . . 195 A8
  Ilminster TA19 . . . . 194 F7
Ludwells Orch BS39 . . . . . . 77 E5
LUFTON 186 D3
Lufton Heights Commerce Pk
  BA22 . . . . 218 A7
Lufton La BA22 . . . . 186 D3
Lufton Manor Coll BA22 . . 186 D4
Lufton Trad Est BA22 . . . . 218 A7
Lufton Way BA22 . . . . 218 A7
Luggard's Cross BS21 . . . . . 8 F2
Lugshorn La TA11 . . . . 211 C8
Lukes Cl TA21 . . . . 222 D8
Luke's Cl BA3 . . . . 78 F3
Lukes Gdn TA24 . . . . 131 B4
Luke St EX16 . . . . 164 B1
LULLINGTON 101 A4
Lullington La BA11 . . . . . . 101 B3
Lulsgate Bottom 37 A8
Lulsgate Rd BS13 . . . . 22 A8
Lulworth Rd BS31 . . . . 24 E4
Lundy Dr TA8 . . . . 104 B5
Luns Hill BA6 . . . . 157 F1
Lunty Mead BS48 . . . . 18 F6
Luptin Way BA22 . . . . 218 B8
LUPPITT 191 B1
Luscombe Rd TA4 . . . . 167 F6
Lush Path DT9 . . . . 225 E4

Lusty Gdns BA10 . . . . 215 E5
Luttrell Cl TA2 . . . . 213 B8
Luttrell Gdns TA24 . . . . . . 200 F6
Luttrell Wy TA24 . . . . 201 C6
Luvers La BS40 . . . . 54 D1
LUXBOROUGH 148 E8
Luxborough Rd TA6 . . . . . 208 B4
Lux Furlong BS9 . . . . 5 B7
Luxhay Cl TA2 . . . . 213 B8
LUXTON 192 A6
Luxton's La BA3, BA4 . . . . 116 F1
Luxton Way TA4 . . . . 210 C5
Lyatt La BA5 . . . . 140 E8
LYATTS 197 B6
Lyatts Hill BA22 . . . . 197 B6
Lydeale Pk BS24 . . . . 50 A4
Lyddieth Ct BA15 . . . . 64 E7
Lyddon Cl TA21 . . . . 222 D4
Lyddon Rd BS22 . . . . 32 B3
Lyddon's Hill TA22 . . . . . . 148 A1
Lyddons Mead TA20 . . . . . 223 E4
Lydeard Cross TA5 . . . . . . 152 E3
Lydeard Down Hill TA4 . . . 151 B4
Lydeard Mead TA4 . . . . . . 167 E3
LYDEARD ST LAWRENCE . . 151 B3
Lydeard St Lawrence Com
  Prim Sch TA4 . . . . 151 A3
Lyde Ct BA21 . . . . 219 E6
Lyde Gn BA2 . . . . 81 E5
Lyde La BA21 . . . . 219 F6
Lyde Rd BA21 . . . . 219 E7
LYDFORD FAIR PLACE 158 C3
LYDMARSH 194 C3
Lydon La TA4 . . . . 165 D5
LYE CROSS 36 C1
Lye Cross Rd BS40 . . . . 36 C1
Lyefield Rd BS22 . . . . 31 E4
LYE HOLE 36 E2
Lye Hole La BS40 . . . . 36 D2
Lye La BA4 . . . . 158 F6
Lye Mead BS40 . . . . 38 A6
LYE'S GREEN 121 B1
Lyes The BS49 . . . . 34 D3
Lyewater TA18 . . . . 224 B6
Lyme Gdns BA1 . . . . 44 B7
Lyme Rd
  Axminster EX13 . . . . 198 A1
  Bath BA1 . . . . 44 B7
  Crewkerne TA18 . . . . 224 B4
Lymore Ave BA2 . . . . 44 C5
Lymore Cl BA2 . . . . 44 C5
Lymore Gdns BA2 . . . . 44 C5
Lymore Terr BA2 . . . . 44 C4
LYMPSHAM 67 B1
Lympsham CE Fst Sch
  BS24 . . . . 67 B1
Lympsham Gn BA2 . . . . 62 D8
Lympsham Rd BS24 . . . . . . 67 B1
Lynbrook BS41 . . . . 10 F1
Lynbrook La BA2 . . . . 44 F3
Lynch Cl BS22 . . . . 31 F3
Lynchcombe La BA5 . . . . . 110 F6
Lynch Cres BS25 . . . . 69 F7
Lynch Hill BA3 . . . . 96 A3
Lynch La
  Cheddar BS27 . . . . 90 C8
  Hardington Mandeville
  BA22 . . . . 197 A6
  Westbury-sub-Mendip BA5 . 110 D8
Lynchmead BS25 . . . . 70 A7
Lynch The BS25 . . . . 69 F7
Lyncombe Hall BA2 . . . . . . 45 A4
LYNCOMBE HILL 45 A4
Lyncombe Hill BA2 . . . . . . 228 C1
LYNCOMBE VALE 45 A3
Lyncombe Vale BA2 . . . . . . 45 B4
Lyncombe Vale Rd BA2 . . . 45 A4
Lyndale Ave
  Bridgwater TA6 . . . . 208 E5
  Bristol BS9 . . . . 5 D5
Lynde Cl BS13 . . . . 22 B4
Lyndhurst Cres TA6 . . . . . 208 C5
Lyndhurst Gr TA12 . . . . . . 185 D7
Lyndhurst Rd
  Bath BA2 . . . . 44 C6
  Bristol BS9 . . . . 5 F7
  Keynsham BS31 . . . . 24 F3
  Midsomer Norton BA3 . . . . 97 B8
  Weston-super-Mare BS23 . . 48 E4
Lyndhurst Terr BA1 . . . . . . 228 C4
Lynfield Pk BA1 . . . . 27 C1
Lynfield Rd BA11 . . . . 119 D5
Lynford La TA11 . . . . 158 C1
LYNFORD-ON-FOSSE 158 C2
LYNG 170 C7
LYNGFORD 213 A7
Lyngford Cres TA2 . . . . . . 213 A7
Lyngford La TA2 . . . . 168 F6
Lyngford Park Prim Sch
  Priorswood TA2 . . . . 213 B8
  Taunton TA2 . . . . 213 B8
Lyngford Pl TA2 . . . . 213 A7
Lyngford Rd TA2 . . . . 213 A7
Lyngford Sq TA2 . . . . 213 A7
Lynmouth Cl BS22 . . . . 32 A2
Lynor Cl TA1 . . . . 213 D3
Lynton Cl BS20 . . . . 2 E4
Lynton Rd
  Burnham-on-S TA8 . . . . . 104 B6
  Midsomer Norton BA3 . . . . 97 B8
Lynwood Cl
  Frome BA11 . . . . 119 D4
  Midsomer Norton BA3 . . . . 97 A8
Lynx Cres BS24 . . . . 49 B2
Lynx Trad Est BA20 . . . . . 218 D3

Lynx West Trad Est BA20 . .**218** C3
Lyons Court Rd BS14 . . . . . .**23** D7
Lyons Ct BS23. . . . . **48** F7
Lype La TA22 . . . . **147** E4
Lypstone Cl BS24. . . . . **50** A8
Lypyatt La BA6. . . . . **206** F4
Lysander Rd BA20 . . . . **218** E3
Lysander Ret Pk BA20 . . . **219** A3
Lysander Road Rdbt BA20 **218** C3
Lyster Cl BA22 . . . . **173** E1
Lyster Gdns BA22 . . . . **173** E1
Lyte's Cary★ TA11. . . . . . . **173** F5
Lytes Cary Rd BS31. . . . . . . **25** A3
Lytton Gdns BA2 . . . . **44** B4
Lytton Gr BS31. . . . . **25** A5
Lyveden Gdns BS13 . . . . . . **22** B5
Lyvedon Way BS41 . . . . **11** B1

M

Mabels La BA5. . . . . **113** C5
Macaulay Bldgs BA2. . . . . . **45** C4
Macey's Rd BS13. . . . . **22** D3
Macfarlane Chase BS23 . . **49** A5
Machine Cross TA22. . . . . **163** F6
Macies The BA1. . . . . **27** B3
MACKHAM **191** A4
Mackley La BA2. . . . . **81** E3
Macleod Cl BS21. . . . . **6** A2
Macquarie Farm Cl BS49. . **17** A1
Macrae Rd BS20. . . . . **4** E4
Madam La
  Weston-super-Mare BS22 . . **31** F2
  Weston-super-Mare BS22 . . **32** A4
  Weston-super-Mare BS22 . . **32** A4
Madam's Paddock BS40 . . **39** B3
Madden Cl TA8 . . . . **104** C7
Maddocks Pk BA9. . . . . . . **216** C3
Maddocks Slade TA8 . . . . **104** A8
Madeira Ct BS23 . . . . **48** C8
Madeira Rd
  Clevedon BS21. . . . . **6** D3
  Weston-super-Mare BS23 . . **30** C1
Madey Mills La TA12. . . . . **185** E6
Madgeon La TA20 . . . . **192** E8
Madison Ct **5** TA18 . . . . **224** C6
Maesbury Rd BS31. . . . . . . **25** A2
Maesdown Cl BA4. . . . . . . **141** E2
Maesdown Cotts BA4. . . . **141** E3
Maesdown Hill BA4 . . . . . **141** E3
Maes Down Ho **10** BA4. . . **205** B6
Maesdown Rd
  Doulting BA4 . . . . **141** E4
  Evercreech BA4. . . . . **141** E2
Maesknoll La BS14, BS39 . . **40** B8
Magdalana Ct BS1. . . . . . . **227** B1
Magdalen Ave BA2 . . . . . . **228** B1
Magdalene Cl BA6. . . . . . . **206** D4
Magdalene Ct **9** TA1. . . . **212** F4
Magdalene **10** TA1. . . . . . **212** F4
Magdalene Rd BA3. . . . . . . **79** C2
Magdalene St
  Glastonbury BA6 . . . . **206** D4
  Taunton TA1 . . . . **212** F4
Magdalen La BA14 . . . . **83** B7
Magdalen Rd BA2 . . . . **228** B1
Magdalen Way BS22. . . . . . **32** A3
Magellan Cl BS22 . . . . **31** F4
Maggs Folly BS39 . . . . **59** D2
Maggs Hill BA2. . . . . **60** B2
Maggs La
  Castle Cary BA7. . . . . **214** C7
  Whitchurch BS14. . . . . **23** C4
Maglands Rd TA23 . . . . . . **202** D6
Magna Cl BA21. . . . . **219** D8
Magnolia Ave BS22. . . . . . . **32** A1
Magnolia Cl
  Frome BA11. . . . . **120** C7
  Weston-super-Mare BS22 . . **49** E7
Magnolia Rd BA3. . . . . **78** E1
Magnolia Tree Rd TA6. . . **209** E5
Magpie Cl
  Burnham-on-S TA8 . . . . . . **85** B1
  Weston-super-Mare BS22 . . **49** E8
Maiden Beech Acad
  TA18 . . . . **224** B4
MAIDEN BRADLEY **144** C1
Maiden Bradley BA12. . . . **144** E3
MAIDENBROOK **213** D7
Maidenbrook La TA2 . . . . **169** A6
Maiden Croft La BA6 . . . . **139** D2
MAIDEN HEAD **21** F1
Maidenhead Cross EX16. . **179** C2
Maidenhead Rd BS13. . . . . **22** D3
Maiden Way BS11. . . . . **4** C8
Maidstone Gr BS24. . . . . . . **49** A1
Maincombe Cl TA18 . . . . . **224** C4
MAINES BATCH **35** E3
Main Frome Road BA11. . **143** C8
Main Rd
  Brockley BS49 . . . . **18** D2
  Burrowbridge TA7 . . . . . . **154** F1
  Cannington TA5. . . . . **135** C1
  Coxley BA5. . . . . **139** E6
  Flax Bourton BS48. . . . . . . **19** F7
  Huntspill TA9 . . . . **136** B8
  Hutton BS24. . . . . **49** E2
  Kilve TA5. . . . . **133** C5
  Lyng TA3, TA7 . . . . **170** C7
  Middlezoy TA7 . . . . **155** B3
  Othery TA7. . . . . **155** B2
  Shapwick TA7. . . . . **155** F8
  Westhay BA6. . . . . **138** B5
  Westonzoyland TA7 . . . . . **154** F5

Main St
  Babcary TA11 . . . . **174** C7
  Barton St David TA11 . . . . . **158** A3
  Chilthorne Domer BA22. . . **186** E6
  Farrington Gurney BS39. . . . **77** A4
  Martock TA12 . . . . **185** F7
  Walton BA16 . . . . **156** D7
Majestic Rd TA6 . . . . **209** C8
Malago Wlk BS13 . . . . **21** E4
Malden Mead BS14. . . . . . . **23** A5
Malherbie Ct TA20 . . . . . . **194** B6
Malin Par BS20 . . . . **2** F6
Mallard Pl TA9 . . . . **104** C4
Mallard Rd TA24 . . . . **201** C5
Mallard Way TA6. . . . . **209** B4
Mallard Wlk **7** BS22 . . . . . **49** E8
Mallet Gr BA2. . . . . **45** A2
Mallory Cl TA2 . . . . **212** C6
Mallory Rd BA21 . . . . **219** F8
Mallow Cl BS21. . . . . **6** E2
Mall The
  Bath BA1. . . . . **228** C2
  Bristol, Clifton BS8. . . . . . . **11** F7
Malmesbury Ct **6** BA1. . .**218** C6
Malmesbury Way BA21 . . .**218** C6
MALMSMEAD **122** C4
Mal's Mead La TA20 . . . . . **194** C3
Malta Way BA22 . . . . **174** A2
Malt Ho The TA4 . . . . **210** C4
Malthouse Cl BA9 . . . . **216** C4
Malthouse Ct
  Frome BA11. . . . . **119** E3
  Taunton TA1. . . . . **212** A4
Malthouse La DT7. . . . . . . **187** F5
Malthouses TA21. . . . . **167** A1
Maltings Ind Est The BA1 . . **44** B6
Maltings The
  Chard TA20. . . . . **223** C3
  Frome BA11. . . . . **119** F4
  Midford BA2. . . . . **63** C5
  Sherborne DT9. . . . . **225** E4
  Weston-super-Mare BS22 . . **31** F2
Maltlands BS22 . . . . **49** D8
Malvern Bldgs BA1. . . . . . . **28** A2
Malvern Cl TA6 . . . . **209** D6
Malvern Ct BA21. . . . . **218** D6
Malvern Rd BS23. . . . . **48** E5
Malvern Terr
  4 Bath BA1. . . . . **28** A1
  Taunton TA1. . . . . **212** F6
Malvern Villas **3** BA1 . . . . **28** A1
Mamba Gr BS24. . . . . **49** B4
Mamsey La TA4 . . . . **202** C3
Manchester Cotts BS22. . . **31** E3
Mancroft Ave BS11. . . . . **4** F7
Mandarin Cl TA6 . . . . **209** B4
Mandy Mdws BA3. . . . . **77** F1
Mangle Cave Hill TA18. . **195** C5
Manilla Cres
  21 Weston-super-Mare
    BS23. . . . . **30** C1
  Weston-super-Mare BS23 . . **30** C1
Manilla Pl BS23. . . . . **30** C1
Manilla Rd BS8 . . . . **226** A3
Manleaze Cvn Pk BA4 . . . **205** D3
Manleys Cotts TA2 . . . . . . **168** C6
Manmoor La BS21. . . . . . . **203** F5
Manning Cl BA5. . . . . **203** F5
Manning Rd
  Bristol BS4. . . . . **22** F7
  Cotford St Luke TA4 . . . . . **167** E6
Manning's La BA3. . . . . **94** F3
Manor Barton TA14 . . . . . **185** E2
Manor Bldgs TA18. . . . . . . **196** C4
Manor Cl
  Berrow TA8. . . . . **84** F6
  Bradford Abbas DT9. . . . . **187** E1
  Chard TA20. . . . . **223** C2
  Charlton Horethorne DT9. . **176** A2
  Cossington TA7. . . . . **136** F3
  Ditcheat BA4 . . . . **159** C7
  East Brent TA9 . . . . **86** D5
  Easton-in-G BS20. . . . . **4** A4
  Farrington Gurney BS39. . . . **77** A3
  Glastonbury BA6 . . . . **206** D5
  Kingsdon TA11. . . . . **173** D5
  Portishead BS20. . . . . **2** A5
  Sandford Orcas DT9. . . . . **188** C7
  South Perrott DT8 . . . . . . **196** C1
  Sparkford BA22 . . . . **175** A4
  Taunton TA1 . . . . **212** E3
  Templecombe BA8 . . . . . . **189** E8
  Wellow BA2. . . . . **62** D1
Manor Cl The BS8. . . . . **11** A8
Manor Copse Rd BA3 . . . . . **79** C2
Manor Court Com Prim Sch
  Chard TA20 . . . . **223** C3
  Chard TA20. . . . . **223** C3
Manor Ct
  Backwell BS48. . . . . **19** A5
  Burnham-on-S TA8 . . . . . **104** B7
  Cossington TA7. . . . . **136** F3
  Easton BA5. . . . . **111** A4
  Horsington BA8 . . . . **176** D2
  Locking BS24. . . . . **50** B4
  Sherborne DT9. . . . . **225** D5
  Stawell TA7. . . . . **137** A1
  Weston-super-Mare BS23 . . **49** A8
Manor Dr
  Bathford BA1. . . . . **29** C2
  Berrow TA8. . . . . **84** F6
  Chedzoy TA7. . . . . **154** D8
  East Coker BA22 . . . . **197** B8
  10 Merriott TA16 . . . . . . **195** F7
  Staplegrove TA2. . . . . **212** C7
  Taunton TA1 . . . . **212** E3
Manor Farm
  Chard TA20. . . . . **223** C3

Manor Farm continued
  East Coker BA22 . . . . **197** B8
Manor Farm Barns TA7 . . **169** E8
Manor Farm Cl
  Paulton BS39 . . . . **77** D6
  Tatworth TA20 . . . . **198** C8
  Weston-super-Mare BS24 . . **49** B2
Manor Farm Cres BS24 . . . **49** B2
Manor Farm La
  Cossington TA7. . . . . **136** D1
  Milborne Port DT9 . . . . . . **217** D3
Manor Farm Rd
  Barrow Hill DT9 . . . . **217** C6
  Blackford BA22 . . . . **175** F5
  Charterhouse BA40 . . . . . . **72** D4
  Milborne Wick DT9. . . . . . **189** B7
Manor Furlong BA11 . . . . **119** E2
Manor Gdns
  Farmborough BA2 . . . . **59** F6
  Farrington Gurney BS39. . . . **77** A3
  Ilchester BA22. . . . . **173** E1
  Locking BS24 . . . . **50** A4
  Weston-super-Mare BS22 . . **31** B4
Manor Gn EX14 . . . . **191** F2
Manor Grange BS24. . . . . . **67** B7
Manor Ho BS2 . . . . **226** C3
Manor House Gdns BA6 . . **206** D5
Manor House La BS14 . . . . **23** C6
Manor House Rd BA6. . . . **206** D5
Manor La
  Abbots Leigh BS8 . . . . **10** F8
  Wedmore BS28 . . . . **108** D5
Manor Mews TA2 . . . . **212** D8
Manor Orch TA1. . . . . **212** D2
Manor Park Cl BA3. . . . . . . **79** C2
Manor Pk
  Bath BA1 . . . . **44** B8
  Keinton Mandeville TA11 . . **158** B1
  Norton Fitzwarren TA2 . . . . **168** B4
  Pawlett TA6. . . . . **135** F6
  Radstock BA3. . . . . **79** C2
  Weston-super-Mare BS23 . . **48** E1
Manor Pl TA11 . . . . **158** B1
Manor Rd
  Abbots Leigh BS8 . . . . **10** F7
  Bath BA1 . . . . **27** C1
  Bridgwater TA6. . . . . **209** C6
  Bristol, Bishopsworth BS13 . . **22** A6
  Burnham-on-S TA8 . . . . . **104** B7
  Chedzoy TA7. . . . . **154** D8
  Cossington TA7. . . . . **136** F3
  Edington TA7 . . . . **137** D2
  Frome BA11. . . . . **119** E2
  Isle Abbotts TA3. . . . . **183** F7
  Kingsdon TA11. . . . . **173** D5
  Milborne Port DT9 . . . . . . **217** C3
  Minehead TA24. . . . . **201** B4
  Pawlett TA6. . . . . **135** F6
  Radstock BA3. . . . . **79** C2
  Saltford BS31. . . . . **25** C2
  Staplegrove TA2. . . . . **212** C8
  Taunton TA1. . . . . **212** D3
  Weston-super-Mare BS23 . . **49** A8
  Yeovil BA21 . . . . **219** A4
Manor Ride TA9. . . . . **86** B2
Manor St BA22 . . . . **197** A8
Manor Terr BA3. . . . . **79** C2
Manor Valley BS23 . . . . . . **31** A1
Manor View
  Crewkerne TA18. . . . . **224** C4
  Golsoncott TA23 . . . . **131** D1
Manor Villas BA1. . . . . **27** C1
Manor Way
  Berrow TA8. . . . . **84** F6
  Failand BS8 . . . . **10** C4
  Frome BA11. . . . . **119** E2
Manse La TA7. . . . . **136** C4
Mansel Cl BS31. . . . . **25** C3
Manser Rd BS24 . . . . **50** C5
Mansfield Ave BS23 . . . . . . **49** B8
Mansfield Rd TA1 . . . . **213** A3
Manshay La DT6 . . . . **199** D1
Manship Gn BA4 . . . . **205** B4
Manston Cl BS14. . . . . **23** C7
Mantle St TA21. . . . . **222** C5
Mantle VC Rd BA22. . . . . . **174** A2
Manvers St BA1 . . . . **228** C1
Manworthy Cross TA4. . . **166** C4
MAPERTON **176** B5
Maperton Rd DT9 . . . . **176** A2
Maple Cl
  Bristol BS14. . . . . **23** D5
  Evercreech BA4 . . . . **141** F1
  North Petherton TA6. . . . . **153** F3
  Puriton TA7. . . . . **136** C4
  Street BA16 . . . . **207** C5
  Taunton TA2 . . . . **213** A7
  Weston-super-Mare BS23 . . **49** A8
  Wincanton BA9 . . . . **216** C2
Maple Ct
  Bridgwater TA6 . . . . **209** D6
  Bristol BS9. . . . . **5** F8
  Frome BA11. . . . . **120** A7
  9 Weston-super-Mare BS23 . . **30** C1
Maple Dr
  Bristol BS9. . . . . **5** C4
  Burnham-on-S TA8 . . . . . **104** B5
  Crewkerne TA18. . . . . **224** D7
  Radstock BA3. . . . . **78** E1
  Yeovil BA20 . . . . **218** F3
Maple Gdns BA2 . . . . **44** E4
Maple Gr BA2. . . . . **44** E4
Maple Ho BS2. . . . . **227** A4
Maple Leaf Ct BS8. . . . . . . **226** A3
Maple Rd
  Curry Rivel TA10 . . . . **171** D4
  Langport TA10 . . . . **172** A6
Maple Rise BA3 . . . . **79** B2

Maples The
  Nailsea BS48 . . . . **8** C1
  Shepton Mallet BA4 . . . . . **205** C6
Maplestone Rd BS14 . . . . . **23** A3
Maple Tree Ct TA7 . . . . . . **136** F3
Maple Wlk BS31. . . . . **24** D4
Mapstone Cl BA6. . . . . **206** E3
Marchant Holliday Sch The
  BA8. . . . . **176** C5
Marchant's Hill BA3. . . . . . **95** F2
Marchant's La BA2 . . . . **63** F4
Marchants Pass BA1. . . . . **228** C1
Marchfields Way BS23. . . . **49** A5
March La BA22. . . . . **175** D8
Marconi Cl BS23 . . . . **49** B7
Marconi Dr TA9. . . . . **104** D5
Marconi Rd BS20. . . . . **1** F5
Marden Gr TA1 . . . . **213** D3
Marden Rd BS31. . . . . **25** A4
Mardi's La TA11. . . . . **158** C2
Mardons Cl **2** BA3 . . . . . . **97** B8
Mardyke Ferry Rd BS1. . . **226** B1
Mare La TA13 . . . . **220** C5
Mare's Dro TA7 . . . . **154** F3
Mares La BA5 . . . . **110** E7
Margaret Cres TA4 . . . . . . **104** A5
Margaret Rd **4** BS13 . . . . . **21** F4
Margaret's Bldgs BA1 . . . . **228** B3
Margaret's Hill BA1. . . . . . **228** C4
Margery Fish Gdns★
  TA13 . . . . **220** C8
Marguerite Rd BS13 . . . . . . **21** F7
Marigold Rd
  Bridgwater TA5 . . . . **208** D1
  Frome BA11. . . . . **120** B3
Marina Row TA6 . . . . **209** B4
Marindin Dr BS22 . . . . **32** B4
Marine Ct BS21. . . . . **219** D5
Marine Dr TA8 . . . . **104** B5
Marine Hill BS21 . . . . **6** C5
Marine Par
  Clevedon BS21. . . . . **6** C4
  Pill BS20. . . . . **4** C5
  Weston-super-Mare BS23 . . **30** B1
  Weston-super-Mare BS23 . . **48** D6
Mariners Cl
  Backwell BS48 . . . . **19** A6
  Bridgwater TA6 . . . . **209** A5
  Minehead TA24. . . . . **201** B7
Mariner's Cl BS22 . . . . **31** D1
Mariners Ct TA6 . . . . **209** A5
Mariners Dr
  Backwell BS48 . . . . **19** A6
  Bristol BS9. . . . . **5** D4
Mariners Way TA23 . . . . . **202** D6
Mariner's Way BS20 . . . . **4** C5
Maritime Heritage Ctr★
  BS1. . . . . **226** B1
Marjoram Way BS20. . . . . . . **2** F5
MARK. **106** C4
MARK CAUSEWAY **106** A3
Mark Coll TA9 . . . . **106** E4
Mark Cswy TA9 . . . . **106** B4
Market Ave BS22 . . . . **32** C3
Market Cl
  4 Bampton EX16. . . . . . **164** B1
  Brushford TA22 . . . . **163** E4
Market Ct
  8 Bridgwater TA6 . . . . . **208** F5
  2 Crewkerne TA18 . . . . **224** C6
Market Ent Ctr The TA24 . . **129** E1
Market Gate BS2. . . . . **227** C3
Market House La TA24 . . . **200** F7
Market House Mus The★
  TA23 . . . . **202** C7
Market Ind Est BS49. . . . . . **17** B1
Market La BS23 . . . . **48** D8
Market Pl
  Burlescombe EX16. . . . . . **179** B4
  Castle Cary BA7 . . . . **214** C5
  Frome BA11. . . . . **119** F5
  Glastonbury BA6 . . . . **206** D4
  Ilchester BA22. . . . . **173** E1
  Radstock BA3. . . . . **78** F2
  23 Shepton Mallet BA4. . **205** B6
  Somerton TA11. . . . . **211** E4
  Wells BA5. . . . . **203** E4
  Wincanton BA9 . . . . **216** C4
  Winford BS40. . . . . **37** F7
  Wiveliscombe TA4 . . . . . . **210** C4
Market Pl The BA11 . . . . . **143** B8
Market Sq
  Crewkerne TA18. . . . . **224** C6
  South Petherton TA13. . . . **220** C4
Market St
  Bridgwater TA6. . . . . **208** F5
  Crewkerne TA18. . . . . **224** C6
  Highbridge TA9. . . . . **104** E3
  Watchet TA23. . . . . **202** C7
  Wells BA5. . . . . **203** D4
  Yeovil BA20 . . . . **219** B5
Market Terr TA9 . . . . **104** E3
Mark La BS1. . . . . **226** C2
Marklands BS9 . . . . **5** E3
Mark Rd
  Burtle TA7. . . . . **137** D6
  Highbridge TA9. . . . . **105** A2
MARKSBURY. **42** B1
Marksbury Bottom BA2. . . **42** A2
Marksbury CE Prim Sch
  BA2. . . . . **42** B2
Marksbury La
  Farmborough BA2 . . . . **60** E7
  Priston BA2 . . . . **61** A6
Marks Cl TA3 . . . . **169** C4
Marksmead DT8 . . . . **199** F8
Marksview Bsns Ctr BA21 **219** F7
Mark VA CE Fst Sch TA9 . . **106** A4

Marlborough Ave TA6 . . . .**209** A2
Marlborough Bldgs
  Bath BA1. . . . . **228** A3
  Langport TA10 . . . . **171** F5
Marlborough Ct TA6. . . . . **209** A2
Marlborough Ct TA8 . . . . . . **85** B1
Marlborough Dr BS22 . . . . **32** B2
Marlborough Flats **8**
  BS2. . . . . **227** A4
Marlborough Hill BS2. . . . **227** A4
Marlborough Hill Pl BS2. . **227** A4
Marlborough La BA1. . . . . **228** A3
Marlborough Rd BA21 . . . **219** E6
Marlborough St
  Bath BA1. . . . . **228** A4
  Bristol BS2. . . . . **227** A4
Marl Cl BA21. . . . . **218** E7
Marle Ground TA19 . . . . . **184** E2
Marlepit Gr BS13. . . . . **21** F6
Marley Cl TA24. . . . . **201** A5
Marley's Row TA24. . . . . . **124** A3
Marleys Way BA11 . . . . . . **119** C5
Marlfield Wlk BS13. . . . . . . **21** E4
Marling Ho TA24 . . . . **201** B7
Marl La DT9 . . . . **187** E3
Marlowe Ho **3** BS23 . . . . . **48** F4
Marl Pits **1** BS48. . . . . **19** A6
Marl Pits La BA11 . . . . **143** C7
Marne Cl BS14. . . . . **23** D5
MARNHULL **190** F5
Marnhull Cl DT10. . . . . **190** F6
Marriage Rd DT10 . . . . . . **190** F3
Marron Cl BS26 . . . . **70** C2
Marsa Wy **11** TA6. . . . . . . **209** B4
Marsden Rd BA2 . . . . **44** B3
MARSH **192** E5
MARSHALL'S ELM **207** D2
Marshall Way BA11. . . . . . **120** D8
Marshall Wlk BS4 . . . . **22** D7
MARSHALSEA. **199** C3
Marshalsea Est DT6. . . . . **199** C3
Marshbarn Farm La BA4. . **176** F3
Marshbridge Cross TA22. **163** C7
Marshclose Hill TA22. . . . **146** E2
Marsh Cross TA24 . . . . . . **200** D1
MARSHFIELD **13** E8
Marshfield Rd TA24 . . . . . **201** B5
Marshfield Way BA1. . . . . . **28** A1
Marsh Gdns TA24 . . . . **201** E4
Marsh Hill TA22. . . . . **163** C8
Marsh Hollow BA21. . . . . **187** A3
Marsh La
  Barrington TA19 . . . . **184** C4
  Barton St David TA11 . . . . . **158** A3
  Bridgwater TA6. . . . . **209** B3
  Buckhorn Weston BA9 . . . **177** C4
  Cannington TA5. . . . . **135** C2
  Dunster TA24 . . . . **201** E3
  Easton-in-G BS20. . . . . **4** A4
  Farrington Gurney BS39. . . . **77** A3
  Henstridge BA8 . . . . **190** B7
  Holcombe BA3 . . . . **116** C5
  Penselwood BA9 . . . . **161** D2
  Pitney TA10 . . . . **172** D7
  Portbury BS20. . . . . **3** F6
  South Cheriton BA8 . . . . . **176** E4
  Temple Cloud BS39. . . . . . **59** A1
  Tintinhull BA22. . . . . **186** A5
Marsh Lane Ind Est BS20. . . **3** F7
Marsh Pottinson Ho **16**
  BA20 . . . . **219** B4
Marsh Rd
  Bristol BS3. . . . . **11** F3
  Rode BA11. . . . . **82** F1
  Standerwick BA11 . . . . . . **102** D1
  Yatton BS49. . . . . **34** B8
Marsh St
  Avonmouth BS11. . . . . **4** C8
  4 Bristol BS1. . . . . **227** A2
  Dunster TA24 . . . . **201** E3
MARSH STREET **201** F3
Marshway TA3. . . . . **170** D1
MARSHWOOD. **199** C2
Marshwood CE Prim Sch
  DT6 . . . . **199** C2
Marshwood Cross DT6 . . . **199** E1
Marson Rd BS21 . . . . **6** D3
MARSTON BIGOT **143** C7
Marston Cl
  Frome BA11. . . . . **119** D2
  Taunton TA1. . . . . **212** E1
MARSTON GATE **119** C1
Marston La BA11 . . . . **119** D2
MARSTON MAGNA **174** F1
Marston Mead BA11. . . . . **119** D2
Marston Rd
  Frome BA11. . . . . **119** D1
  Nunney BA11. . . . . **143** D8
  Sherborne DT9. . . . . **225** B5
Marston Trad Est BA11. . . **119** E2
Martcombe Rd BS20. . . . . . . **4** C2
Martha's Orch BS13. . . . . . **21** E7
Martindale Ct BS22. . . . . . . **49** D8
Martindale Rd BS22. . . . . . **49** D8
Martingale Wy BS20. . . . . . **2** E6
Martins TA3 . . . . **169** C4
Martins Bldgs **4** TA21. . . **222** D5
Martins Cl
  Evercreech BA4 . . . . **141** E1
  Wellington TA21. . . . . **222** D6
  Wells BA5. . . . . **203** B4
Martin's Cl TA8 . . . . **85** A3
Martins Gr BS22 . . . . **31** E2
Martins La BA4 . . . . **205** D5
Martins Paddock BA4 . . . . **142** A6
Martin St BA6. . . . . **158** A5

Martins The BS20 . . . . 3 A6
Martland Cl TA7 . . . . 136 E3
Martlet Rd TA24. . . . . 200 F7
MARTOCK 185 D6
Martock BS24. . . . . 48 F2
Martock Bsns Pk TA12 . . . .185 D7
Martock CE Prim Sch
TA12 . . . . .185 D6
Martock La TA12 . . . . 185 F7
Martock Rd
Keynsham BS31 . . . . 25 A3
Long Sutton TA10 . . . . 172 E4
Mart Rd TA24 . . . . 201 B7
Mart Road Ind Est TA24 . . . 201 B6
Mart The 6 BS23 . . . . 48 E7
Martyn Cl TA5 . . . . 135 B5
Marwin Cl TA12 . . . . 185 E7
Marwood Cl TA8 . . . . 104 C8
Marwood Rd BS4. . . . . 22 E8
Mary Brown Davis La 6
BA5 . . . . 139 D8
Marybush La BS2 . . . . 227 B3
Mary Elton Prim Sch BS21 . . 6 B1
Mary Hart Cl BA16. . . . . . . 207 B7
Mary La 10 EX16. . . . . 164 B1
Mary Rd BA5. . . . . 203 C5
Mary St
Taunton TA1 . . . . 212 F3
Yeovil BA21 . . . . .219 B5
Masefield Ho BS23 . . . . 49 A4
Mason La TA15. . . . . 186 B4
Masons Way BA11. . . . . . . 119 D1
Mason's Way BS27 . . . . 90 C7
Mason Way BA4. . . . . 205 A4
Massingham Pk TA2. . . . . . 213 B6
Materman Rd BS14. . . . . 23 E5
Matfurlong Cl TA12 . . . . . .185 D5
Matthews Cl BS14. . . . . 23 F6
Matthews Rd
Taunton TA1 . . . . 212 B1
Yeovil BA21 . . . . .219 C5
Mattock's Tree Hill TA3. . .169 E1
Mattravers Wy TA1. . . . . . 168 F4
Matt's La TA14. . . . . 185 F4
Mattys Cross EX14 . . . . . . .191 D3
MAUDLIN. 199 C8
Maudlin Cross TA20 . . . . . 199 C8
Maudlin La TA20 . . . . 199 C8
Maudslay Field BA22 . . . . . 197 C8
MAUNDOWN. 165 F7
Maundown Rd TA4 . . . . . . 166 A8
Maunsell Rd BS24. . . . . 49 E7
Maunsel Rd TA7 . . . . 153 F1
Maurice Jennings Dr
TA21 . . . . .222 D8
Maximus Gdns BS30. . . . . . 24 F8
Max Mill La BS25. . . . . 69 C8
Maxwell Rd BA4. . . . . 205 B4
Maxwell St TA2 . . . . 212 E6
Maybrick Rd BA2. . . . . 44 D5
Mayfair Ave BS48 . . . . 8 F1
Mayfield Ave BS22 . . . . 31 E1
Mayfield Cl BA22 . . . . .175 D8
Mayfield Dr TA6. . . . . 208 B4
Mayfield Rd
Bath BA2 . . . . 44 D5
Yeovil BA21 . . . . .219 D6
Mayfields BS31 . . . . 24 E5
Mayfield Terr TA4. . . . . . . 210 C4
Mayflower Cl TA6 . . . . .209 D5
Mayflower Ct TA9. . . . . . . 104 E4
Mayflower Gdns BS48 . . . . . . 9 A2
May La BA1. . . . . 44 B8
Maynard Cl
Bristol BS13. . . . . 22 C5
4 Clevedon BS21 . . . . 6 F3
Maynard Rd BS13 . . . . 22 C5
Maynard Terr BS39. . . . . . . 58 F3
Maypole Cl BS39 . . . . 58 E3
MAY POLE KNAP 211 C4
May Pole Knap TA11. . . . . .211 C4
Maysfield Cl BS20. . . . . 2 D3
Maysgreen La BS24 . . . . 33 B3
May's La BS24 . . . . 33 C3
Maysmead La BS40. . . . . . . 53 C6
May Terr TA23 . . . . 131 E3
Maytree Ave BS13. . . . . 22 B7
Maytree Cl
Bristol BS13. . . . . 22 B7
Frome BA11 . . . . 120 B7
May Tree Cl BS48 . . . . 8 C1
May Tree Rd BA3. . . . . 78 E1
McAdam Way BS1. . . . . 11 F5
McCrae Rd BS24 . . . . 50 B5
McCreath Cl 3 TA6 . . . . . . 153 F3
Mc Creery Rd DT9. . . . . . . .225 D6
McKinley Terr TA23 . . . . . . 131 E4
Mdwhayes TA24. . . . . 124 A3
Mead Ave BA22 . . . . 218 B6
Mead Cl
Bath BA2 . . . . 44 E3
Bristol BS11. . . . . 4 E6
Cheddar BS27 . . . . 90 B6
East Huntspill TA9. . . . . 136 E8
Stoke St Michael BA3 . . . . . . 116 B2
Mead Com Prim Sch The
BA14. . . . . 83 C6
Meade Cl TA6. . . . . 153 F3
Meade Ho BA2. . . . . 44 A5
Meade La TA19 . . . . 184 E1
MEADGATE EAST. 60 E2
MEADGATE WEST 60 D2
Mead La
Blagdon BS40. . . . . 54 E3
Lydford Fair Place TA11 . . . . 158 C3
Saltford BS31. . . . . 25 F4
Sandford BS25. . . . . 51 E4
Stocklinch TA19 . . . . 184 C4
Mead La *continued*
Wanstrow BA4. . . . . 142 F4
West Pennard BA6. . . . . 140 C2
Meadlands BA2 . . . . 43 B7
Meadowbank BS22. . . . . 31 F3
Meadow Cl
Backwell BS48 . . . . 19 B6
Chilton Trinity TA5. . . . . 135 F2
Farrington Gurney BS39. . . . . 77 A3
Henstridge BA8 . . . . .190 A7
Highbridge TA9. . . . . .104 D4
Kingston St Mary TA2 . . . . . . 168 E8
Langport TA10 . . . . 172 A6
Nailsea BS48 . . . . 8 E3
Nether Stowey TA5. . . . . 134 A2
Stalbridge DT10. . . . . .190 B4
Street BA16 . . . . 207 B4
Wincanton BA9 . . . . .216 D3
Meadow Cotts TA24 . . . . . . 131 B4
Meadow Croft BS24 . . . . 49 B2
Meadowcroft Dr TA8 . . . . .104 C8
Meadow Ct BA1. . . . . 44 A7
Meadow Dr
Bath BA2 . . . . 62 D8
Locking BS24 . . . . 50 B4
Portishead BS20 . . . . 1 F1
Meadow Gdns
Bath BA1 . . . . 27 A1
Stogursey TA5 . . . . .134 C6
Meadow Gr BS11. . . . . 4 D7
Meadow La
Bathampton BA2 . . . . 28 D1
Walton BA16 . . . . .156 E7
Meadowland BS49 . . . . 17 A1
Meadowlands BS22 . . . . 32 C2
Meadowlands Ave TA6 . . .208 E6
Meadow Pk
Bathford BA1 . . . . 29 B3
Wembdon TA6 . . . . .208 C5
Meadow Pl BS22 . . . . 32 D3
Meadow Rd
Clevedon BS21. . . . . 6 E3
Frome BA11 . . . . .119 F7
Paulton BS39 . . . . 77 F4
Yeovil BA21 . . . . 219 E7
Meadow Rise BA4. . . . . 205 B7
Meadows Cl BS20. . . . . 1 F5
Meadows End BS25 . . . . 52 D4
Meadowside
Carhampton TA24. . . . . 131 A5
Rockwell Green TA21 . . . . . . 222 B5
Meadowside Cl TA1 . . . . . . 212 B4
Meadowside Dr BS14. . . . . . 23 A3
Meadows Prim Sch The
BS30. . . . . 25 D8
Meadow St
Axbridge BS26 . . . . 70 C2
Weston-super-Mare BS23 . . . 48 E7
Meadows The
2 Bourton SP8 . . . . 161 F1
Drayton TA10 . . . . 171 E3
Porlock TA24 . . . . 124 A3
Meadow Terr TA24. . . . . . . 201 A5
Meadow View
2 Bampton EX16. . . . . 164 B1
4 Barwick BA22 . . . . 197 F8
East Coker BA22 . . . . 197 C8
Glastonbury BA6 . . . . 206 E3
Long Sutton TA10 . . . . 172 E1
Radstock BA3. . . . . 79 A1
Timberscombe TA24. . . . . . . 130 B5
Meadow View Cl BA1. . . . . . 44 A8
Meadow Villas 14 BS23 . . . . 48 E8
Mead Rd BS20 . . . . 2 C2
Mead Run TA11 . . . . 157 A3
Meads Ct TA6. . . . . 208 E3
Meads Droveway TA3 . . . .169 D5
Mead St BS3. . . . . 227 C1
Meads The DT9 . . . . .217 D2
Mead Terr BS40. . . . . 54 E2
Mead The
Clutton BS39 . . . . 58 E3
Dundry BS41 . . . . .21 D2
East Brent TA9 . . . . 86 E5
Farmborough BA2 . . . . 60 A6
Henstridge BA8 . . . . .190 A6
Holcombe BA3 . . . . .116 C8
Ilchester BA22. . . . . .173 D1
Ilminster TA19 . . . . 221 B3
Keynsham BS31. . . . . 24 E3
Paulton BS39 . . . . 77 D5
Rode BA11 . . . . 101 E8
14 Shepton Mallet BA4. . . . . 205 B6
Shipham BS25 . . . . 70 E8
Stoke St Michael BA3 . . . . . . 116 B2
Stratton-on-t F BA3 . . . . 96 F2
Street BA16 . . . . .207 D7
Timsbury BA2. . . . . 60 C3
Winsley BA15. . . . . 64 E7
Mead Vale BS22. . . . . 49 E8
Mead Vale Prim Sch BS22 . . 31 E1
Meadway
Bristol BS9. . . . . 5 C6
Farmborough BA2 . . . . 60 A6
Temple Cloud BS39. . . . . 58 E1
Woolavington TA7. . . . . 136 E4
Mead Way TA2. . . . . 169 B6
Meadway Ave BS48. . . . . 8 D2
Mearcombe La BS24 . . . . . . 67 F6
Meardon Rd BS14 . . . . 23 E6
MEARE. 138 D4
Meare BS24 . . . . 48 F2
MEARE GREEN
Hatch Beauchamp 169 F1
Stoke St Gregory 170 D5
Meare Rd
Bath BA2 . . . . 45 A2
Glastonbury BA6 . . . . 206 B6
Meare Village Prim Sch
BA6. .138 D4
Meareway BA6. . . . . .138 C5
MEARNS 59 E2
Mearn's Cross BA3 . . . . 94 B6
Mede Cl BS1. . . . . .227 B1
Medical Ave BS2, BS8 . . . . .226 C3
Medway Cl
Keynsham BS31 . . . . 25 A3
Taunton TA1 . . . . .213 D4
Medway Dr BS31. . . . . 25 A3
Meetinghouse La BS49 . . . . 18 A1
Melbourne House Mews
BA5 . . . . .203 D4
Melbourne Pl TA6. . . . . . . .209 B6
Melbourne Terr 2 BS21 . . . . 6 D2
Melcombe Ct BA2. . . . . 44 D4
Melcombe La TA6. . . . . 153 E3
Melcombe Rd BA2 . . . . 44 D4
Mellanby Cl BA16 . . . . .207 D5
Mellent Ave BS13 . . . . 22 C3
MELLS 118 B7
Mells CE Sch BA11 . . . . . . .118 A6
Mells Cl BS31 . . . . 25 A2
MELLS GREEN. 118 A6
Mells La BA3. . . . . 79 B1
Melrose Ave
Bristol BS8. . . . . 226 B4
Wells BA5. . . . . 203 C4
Melrose Ct 3 BA5. . . . . . . .203 C4
Melrose Gr BA2 . . . . 44 B3
Melrose Pl BS8 . . . . 226 B4
Melrose Rd BA21. . . . . 219 B6
Melrose Terr BA1 . . . . 28 A2
Melsbury La BA5 . . . . 139 E6
Memorial Ave TA18 . . . . . .224 C5
Memorial Rd
Wrington BS40. . . . . 35 E2
Yeovil BA22 . . . . 218 B6
Mendip Ave
Shepton Mallet BA4 . . . . 205 E4
Weston-super-Mare BS22 . . . 31 F2
Mendip Bsns Pk BS26 . . . . . 87 A6
Mendip Cl
Axbridge BS26 . . . . 70 D2
Frome BA11 . . . . 120 A7
Keynsham BS31. . . . . 24 D5
3 Nailsea BS48. . . . . 8 E1
Paulton BS39 . . . . 77 E4
Yatton BS49 . . . . 34 B7
Mendip Dr BA11. . . . . .120 A7
Mendip Edge BS24 . . . . 66 F8
Mendip Fields BA3 . . . . 96 C2
Mendip Gdns
Bath BA2 . . . . 62 D8
Frome BA11 . . . . 120 B7
Yatton BS49 . . . . 34 B7
Mendip Gn BA3 . . . . 97 B6
Mendip Green Fst Sch
BS22 . . . . 31 E2
Mendip Ho TA1 . . . . .212 F3
Mendip Lea Cl BS27 . . . . 90 F2
Mendip Lodge BS25 . . . . 70 A8
Mendip Rd
Bridgwater TA6 . . . . .209 C4
Locking BS24 . . . . 50 D4
Portishead BS20 . . . . 2 B5
Rooks Bridge BS26. . . . . 87 A6
Stoke St Michael BA3 . . . . . . 116 A2
Weston-super-Mare BS23 . . . 49 A7
Yatton BS49 . . . . 34 B7
Mendip Rise BS24 . . . . 50 B4
Mendip Vale BA3. . . . . 116 E7
Mendip Vale Sta★ BA4 . . . . 205 F3
Mendip Vale Trad Est BS27 . 90 A7
Mendip View
Coleford BA3 . . . . 116 F7
Street BA16 . . . . 207 B7
Mendip Villas
Cheddar BS27 . . . . 71 A1
Compton Martin BS40 . . . . . . 73 F7
Emborough BA3 . . . . 95 E3
Mendip Way
Burnham-on-S TA8 . . . . 104 B7
Radstock BA3. . . . . 78 F3
Menlea BS40. . . . . 54 D3
Mercer Ct BS14 . . . . 23 B8
Merchants' Acad
Bristol BS13. . . . . 22 A4
Bristol BS13. . . . . 22 A5
Merchants Almshouses 6
BS1 .227 A2
Merchants Barton BA11 . . 119 F4
Merchants' Barton 3
BA11 . . . . 119 F4
Merchants Barton Ind Est
BA11. . . . . .119 F4
Merchants Ct BS8. . . . . . . .226 A1
Merchant Sq BS20 . . . . 2 E6
Merchants Quay BS1 . . . . .227 A1
Merchants Rd
Bristol BS8. . . . . .226 A3
Bristol, Hotwells BS8 . . . . . .226 A1
Merchants Row BS1. . . . . . .226 C1
Merchant St BS1 . . . . 227 B3
Meredith Cl
11 Creech St Michael TA3. . .169 C5
Halstock BA22 . . . . 197 C3
Meredith Ct BS1 . . . . 226 A1
Merevale Way BA21 . . . . . .218 C7
Meriden BA1 . . . . 44 D8
Meridian Pl BS8. . . . . 226 B3
Meridian Vale BS8 . . . . 226 B3
Meriet Ave BS13 . . . . 22 B4
Merino Way 7 TA6. . . . . . . 154 A5
Merle Cl TA6. . . . . 209 B4
Merlin Cl
Bristol BS9. . . . . 5 F8
Merlin Cl *continued*
1 Weston-super-Mare BS22. 49 E8
Merlin Dr BA5 . . . . .203 B5
Merlin Ind Pk TA2 . . . . .213 B6
Merlin Pk BS20 . . . . 2 A4
Merlin Rd BA20 . . . . .218 D3
Merlin Way 3 BA3 . . . . 97 B8
Merrick Ct BS1. . . . . .227 A1
Merrick Rd BA6 . . . . .206 E7
MERRIDGE 152 D5
Merridge Cl TA6 . . . . .208 A4
Merridge Hill TA5 . . . . .152 D6
Merrifields TA4 . . . . .167 E6
Merriman Gdns BA16. . . . . .207 C5
Merriman Rd BA16 . . . . . . .207 C5
Merrimans Rd BS11 . . . . 4 D8
MERRIOTT. 195 E7
Merriott Fst Sch TA16. . . . . 195 F7
Merriott Rd
Hinton St George TA17 . . . . .195 D7
Merriott TA16. . . . . .195 F6
MERRIOTTSFORD. 195 F7
Merry-field BA3 . . . . .116 E8
Merryfield La
Doulting BA4 . . . . .141 F5
Ilton TA19. . . . . 183 E4
Merryfield Lane Halt★
BA4. 141 F5
Merryfield Rd BS24. . . . . 50 B6
Merryfields TA9. . . . . .106 D5
Merry La TA9 . . . . .136 F8
Merthyr Guest Cl BA8 . . . . .176 E1
Merton Dr BS24. . . . . 50 A8
Mervyn Ball Cl TA20 . . . . . .223 C5
Methwyn Cl BS22 . . . . 49 C7
Metropole Ct TA24 . . . . . . .201 A7
Metropolitan The BS1 . . . .227 B1
Mews The
Bath BA1 . . . . 44 A8
5 Bridgwater TA6 . . . . 209 B4
East Coker BA22 . . . . .197 C7
Minehead TA24. . . . . 201 A7
Wiveliscombe TA4 . . . . 210 C4
Mewswell Dr BS27 . . . . 71 B1
Meyer Cl TA21 . . . . .222 F6
Mezellion Pl 14 BA1 . . . . 28 B1
Mianda Terr TA19. . . . . 221 C3
Michaels Mead BA1 . . . . 27 B2
Midas Ct TA11 . . . . .211 D3
Middle Ave BS1 . . . . .227 A2
Middle Brooks BA16. . . . . . .207 C3
MIDDLE BURNHAM 104 D8
MIDDLE CHINNOCK 196 C8
Middle Chinnock Rd TA18 196 C8
Middlecombe Cross TA24 200 C6
Middle Dro
Baltonsborough BA6 . . . . . . 158 B4
Compton Dundon TA11 . . . . .156 F3
Glastonbury BA6 . . . . 206 B5
Hambridge TA10, TA12 . . . . . 184 F8
Lydford Fair Place TA11 . . . . 158 C3
Rodney Stoke BS27 . . . . 109 C6
Street BA6 . . . . 157 C7
Middlefield La
Barrington TA10. . . . . .184 D6
Merriott TA16. . . . . .195 E8
Norton Sub Hamdon TA13,
TA16 . . . . .185 D1
West Chinnock TA16. . . . . . .196 A8
Middle Field La DT9. . . . . . 188 B7
Middlefield Rd TA10. . . . . . 172 C7
Middleford Ho BS13. . . . . . . 22 C4
Middle Gate TA10 . . . . .172 D8
Middlegate Rd TA10. . . . . . .172 C7
MIDDLE GREEN 222 D3
Middle Green Rd TA21. . . . .222 E3
Middle La
Bath BA1 . . . . 28 B1
Kingston Seymour BS21. . . . . 15 F4
Middle Leaze Dro TA12 . . . 185 F7
MIDDLE LEIGH 207 C4
Middle Leigh BA16 . . . . .207 C5
MIDDLE LUXTON 191 F5
Middlemead BA3. . . . . 96 F3
Middlemoor Dro TA7. . . . . .154 A1
Middle Moor Drove TA5 . . 134 D7
Middle Moor La BS27. . . . . . 89 E7
Middlemoor Water Pk★
TA7 .136 F5
Middle Path TA18 . . . . 224 B5
Middlepiece La BA2, BS31 . . 42 B7
Middle Rd TA7 . . . . .137 A3
Middle Ridge La DT9 . . . . . .175 D1
Middleroom Dro TA3 . . . . .182 E4
Middle's La BA4. . . . . .140 C4
Middle St
Ashcott TA7 . . . . .156 B7
Burnham-on-S TA9 . . . . 85 E5
East Harptree BS40 . . . . 74 F4
East Lambrook TA13. . . . . . . .220 C8
Galhampton BA22 . . . . .175 D8
Kingsdon TA11 . . . . .173 D5
Martock TA12. . . . . .185 D4
Minehead TA24. . . . . .200 F8
Misterton TA18. . . . . .224 F3
Montacute TA15. . . . . .186 B3
North Perrott TA18. . . . . .196 C4
Puriton TA7. . . . . .136 C4
Rimpton BA22 . . . . .188 A8
Shepton Beauchamp TA19 . . 184 E3
Taunton TA1 . . . . 212 F4
Yeovil BA20 . . . . .219 B4
Middle Stoke BA3. . . . . 64 A6
MIDDLE STOUGHTON 108 A8
Middle Stream Cl TA6 . . . .208 D2
Middleton La
Clatworthy TA4. . . . . 149 C2
Shepton Mallet BA4 . . . . 205 B4
Middleton Rd BS11. . . . . 4 F8
Middle Touches TA20 . . . .223 E5
Middleway TA1 . . . . .212 E2
Middle Way TA11 . . . . .157 B4
Middleway Ct TA1. . . . . . . .212 E2
Middleway Rd BA4 . . . . . . .158 E8
Middlewood Cl BA2 . . . . 44 C2
Middle Yeo Gn BS48. . . . . 8 D3
MIDDLEZOY 155 B3
Middlezoy Prim Sch
Middlezoy TA7 . . . . 155 B3
Middlezoy TA7 . . . . 155 B3
Midelney Rd TA10. . . . . . . .171 E2
MIDFORD 63 C6
Midford BS24 . . . . 48 F2
Midford Hill BA2, BA3 . . . . . . 63 C5
Midford La BA2, BA3 . . . . 63 E7
Midford Rd
Southstoke BA2 . . . . 63 B7
Taunton TA1 . . . . .213 B4
Midhaven Rise BS22. . . . . . . 31 E4
MID LAMBROOK. 220 A8
Midland Bridge Rd BA1,
BA2 .228 A2
Midland Mews BS2. . . . . . .227 C3
Midland Rd
Bath BA1 . . . . 44 D7
Bristol BS2. . . . . .227 C3
Midland St BS2 . . . . .227 C2
Midleaze DT9. . . . . .225 A3
Midney La BA9. . . . . .177 D8
Midsomer Ent Pk BA3 . . . . . 78 C2
MIDSOMER NORTON. 78 B3
Midsomer Norton Prim Sch
BA3. . . . . 78 B1
Midsomer Norton South★
BA3. . . . . 97 A8
Midsummer Bldgs BA1 . . . . 28 B2
MIDWAY 115 E2
MILBORNE PORT 217 E2
Milborne Port Bsns Ctr
DT9. .217 D2
Milborne Port Prim Sch
Milborne Port DT9 . . . . 217 D2
Milborne Port DT9 . . . . 217 D2
MILBORNE WICK 217 B6
Milburn Rd BS23. . . . . 48 F7
Milbury Gdns BS22. . . . . 31 C2
Mildenhall Rd DT9 . . . . . . .225 B4
Mildmay Dr BA22. . . . . .174 F3
Mildmay's Rd TA10. . . . . . .155 F1
Mildred Rd BA16. . . . . .156 E7
Miles Cl BS20. . . . . 4 E3
Miles's Bldgs BA1. . . . . . . .228 B3
Miles St BA2. . . . . .228 C1
Milestone Cl TA6. . . . . .153 F4
Milestone Ct BS22. . . . . 32 D2
Mile Wlk BS14 . . . . 23 A6
Milford Inf Sch BA21 . . . . .219 B7
Milford Jun Sch BA21 . . . .219 B7
Milford Pk BA21. . . . . .219 C7
Milford Pl 3 TA1. . . . . .213 A4
Milford Rd BA21 . . . . .219 C7
Milking La BS27. . . . . 90 E2
Milk St
Bath BA1 . . . . .228 B2
Frome BA11 . . . . .119 E5
Millands La TA5. . . . . .133 C6
Millands The TA11 . . . . .211 E4
Millards Ct BA3 . . . . 78 B3
Millards Hill BA3. . . . . 78 B3
Millard's Hill
Batcombe BA4 . . . . .142 D2
Midsomer Norton BA3 . . . . . . 78 C3
Mill Ave BS1. . . . . .227 A2
Millbatch BA6 . . . . .138 C4
Mill Batch Farm Ind Est
TA9. . . . . 86 F4
Mill Bay TA6 . . . . .153 E4
Millbourn Cl BA15. . . . . 64 D7
Millbourne Rd BS27 . . . . 90 C7
Millbridge Gdns TA24 . . . .200 F7
Millbridge Rd TA24. . . . . . .200 E7
MILLBROOK. 198 A1
Millbrook BA20. . . . . .219 A4
Millbrook Cross 1 EX13 . .198 A1
Millbrook Ct BA2. . . . . .228 C1
Millbrook Dale EX13. . . . . .198 A1
Millbrook Gdns BA7. . . . . .214 B5
Millbrook Pl BA2. . . . . .228 C1
Mill Cl
Cannington TA5 . . . . .135 B2
East Coker BA22 . . . . .197 C8
Frome BA11 . . . . .119 F6
Highbridge TA9. . . . . .104 D2
Nether Stowey TA5. . . . . .134 A2
Portbury BS20 . . . . 3 D2
Mill Cotts
Creech St Michael TA3 . . . . .169 D4
Saltford BS31. . . . . 25 F2
Millcross BS21. . . . . 16 C8
Mill Cross
Halstock BA22 . . . . .197 C3
Kingston St Mary TA2 . . . . . . 168 E7
Mill Ct
Midsomer Norton BA3 . . . . . . 78 A1
Watchet TA23. . . . . .202 B7
Millennium Cl BA3 . . . . . . .116 A3
Millennium Sq BS1. . . . . . . .226 C2
Miller Cl BS23. . . . . 48 F8
Miller Ho BS8. . . . . .226 A2
Millers Cl
Bourton SP8. . . . . .161 F1
Pill BS20. . . . . 4 C4
Millers Ct BS21 . . . . 16 E8

Millers Gdns BA5.........203 E5
Miller's Hill DT9.........217 A5
Millers Orch TA3.........170 F1
Millers Pl BA1.............28 E3
Millers Rise BS22.........32 A4
Millers Way **11** TA4.....167 F8
Miller Way DT9...........225 E5
Milletts Cl **2** TA24......131 A5
Mill Farm Hill TA5........134 F1
Millfield
  Chard TA20..............223 D3
  Ilchester BA22...........173 E2
  Midsomer Norton BA3.....96 F8
Millfield Cl TA20..........223 D3
Millfield Ind Est TA20....223 E3
Millfield Prep Sch BA6....139 D1
Millfield Sch BA16.........207 E5
Millford La BA4............159 C6
Mill Gdns TA24............201 D1
Millgreen Cl TA9..........136 B8
Millground Rd BS13........21 F5
Millham La TA22...........163 D6
MILLHAYES................180 C1
Mill Hill BA2...............62 E1
Mill Ho BS1...............227 A2
Mill House Ct BA11........119 F5
Mill House Rd TA2.........168 B4
Millier Rd BS49............35 B8
Milliman Cl BS13..........22 C5
Milliner Ct BA4............205 B5
Mill La
  Alhampton BA4...........159 C5
  Axminster EX13..........198 F3
  Batcombe BA4............142 C1
  3 Bath BA2............44 B6
  Bathampton BA2..........28 F2
  Beckington BA11........101 D5
  Bishops Lydeard TA4.....167 F8
  Bitton BS30...............25 E8
  Bourton SP8..............161 F1
  Bradford Abbas DT9......187 E1
  Bruton BA10.............215 E6
  Butcombe BS40...........55 A8
  Cannington TA5..........135 B2
  Chard TA20..............223 C3
  Chard, Wambrook TA20...193 C2
  Charlton Mackrell TA11...173 E2
  Chew Stoke BS40..........56 D8
  Clatworthy TA4..........149 E2
  Compton Dando BS39......41 A5
  Compton Martin BS40.....74 A7
  Congresbury BS49.........34 D4
  Corfe TA5................181 F6
  Corsley Heath BA11, BA12.144 C8
  Creech St Michael TA3....169 D4
  Crewkerne, Misterton TA18.196 B3
  Dinnington TA17.........195 B8
  Dowlish Wake TA19.......194 E7
  Dunster TA24............201 D1
  East Coker BA22..........197 C2
  East Coker, Holywell BA22.197 B8
  East Huntspill TA9.......136 D8
  Exford TA24..............128 C2
  Halstock BA22...........197 C3
  Higher Chillington TA19..194 E5
  Ilchester BA22...........173 F1
  Ilminster TA19...........221 B7
  Kingstone TA19..........221 F1
  Lopen TA13..............185 A1
  Lynford-on-F TA11........158 C2
  Maiden Bradley BA12......144 B3
  Marnhull DT10...........190 F6
  Milverton TA4............167 A5
  Monkton Combe BA2.......63 E8
  Nether Stowey TA5........134 A2
  North Wootton BA4.......140 D5
  Othery TA7...............155 C2
  Pitcombe BA10...........215 C3
  Porlock TA24.............124 A3
  Portbury BS20.............3 E3
  Priston BA2................61 A7
  Shapwick TA7.............155 F8
  Shepton Mallet BA4......204 E4
  Somerton TA11...........211 D3
  South Petherton TA13.....220 E6
  Stoke St Michael BA3.....116 B3
  Taunton TA3..............168 D1
  Thurloxton TA2...........153 D1
  Timsbury BA2..............60 B1
  Trent DT9................187 F5
  Watchet TA23.............202 C7
  Wedmore BS28............108 E3
  Wells BA5................203 A1
  West Monkton TA2........169 D8
  Wiveliscombe TA4........210 C4
  Wrington BS40............53 F8
  Yeovil BA20..............219 B4
Mill Lane EX13 TA3........168 D1
Mill La Trad Est BA20.....219 C4
Mill Leat BA6............157 F5
Mill Leg BA9..............34 D4
Millmead Ho BS13.........22 C4
Millmead Rd BA2..........44 C5
MILLMOOR................179 E1
Millmoot La TA7..........136 F3
Mill on the Brue* BA10...215 D5
Millpill Cl BS9..............5 D5
Mill Rd
  Barton St David TA11.....158 A3
  Radstock BA3..............79 B2
Mill Rise
  Bourton SP8.............161 F1
  Staplegrove TA2..........212 B7

Mill Road Ind Est BA3.....79 B3
Mills Dr TA21.............222 F7
Mill St
  Carhampton TA24.........131 A4
  North Petherton TA6......153 F3
  Rimpton BA22............188 A8
  Watchet TA23............202 C7
  Wells BA5................203 D4
  Wincanton BA9...........216 C4
Millstream Cl TA24........200 F6
Mill Stream Cl BS26........70 C1
Mill Stream Gdns TA21....222 B7
Mill Street BA9...........216 C4
Millthorn Ho **2** BA16....207 C5
Millward Terr BS39.........77 E6
Millway
  Chard TA20..............193 C2
  Rodney Stoke BS27........110 B8
Millway Rise Ind Est EX13.198 A2
Millwey Ave EX13.........198 A2
MILLWEY RISE.............198 A2
Mill Wlk TA7..............136 E3
Millwood Cl TA6..........208 E2
Milne Cl TA6.............208 F2
Milsom Pl TA4............167 F6
Milsom St BA1............228 B3
MILTON
  Martock.................185 E8
  Weston-super-Mare........31 C2
Milton Ave
  Bath BA2.................44 F4
  Weston-super-Mare BS23...49 A8
Milton Brow BS22..........31 B2
Milton Cl
  Nailsea BS48..............8 E3
  Taunton TA1.............213 C3
  Yeovil BA21.............218 C6
MILTON CLEVEDON........160 A8
Milton Ct BA4............205 B7
Milton Gn BS22............31 C1
Milton Hill
  Monkton Heathfield TA2..213 E7
  Weston-super-Mare BS22...31 B2
Milton Ho BA21...........187 D6
Milton La
  Martock TA12............185 E8
  Wells BA5................203 D5
  Wookey Hole BA5.........203 B8
Milton Leaze TA10........172 E2
Milton Lodge Gdns* BA5..203 D7
Milton Park Prim Sch BS22.31 C1
Milton Park Rd BS22.......31 C1
Milton Pl TA6............208 E4
Milton Rd
  Radstock BA3.............78 C1
  Taunton TA1.............213 C3
  Weston-super-Mare BS22,
  BS23....................49 B8
Milton Rise BS22..........31 C1
Miltons Cl BS13...........22 C4
Milton Terr BA5...........203 A8
MILVERTON..............166 F4
Milverton BS24............48 F2
Milverton Com Prim Sch
  TA4....................166 F4
Milverton Rd TA21.......222 B8
Milward Rd BS31...........24 E6
Minchinton's Cl TA14......185 F2
MINEHEAD...............201 A8
Minehead Com Hospl
  TA24...................201 B5
Minehead Ent Pk TA24....201 B5
Minehead First Sch TA24..200 F6
Minehead Fst Sch TA24....200 F6
Minehead La TA24.........164 A7
Minehead Mid Sch TA24...201 A6
Minehead Rd
  Bishops Lydeard TA4......167 F8
  Bristol BS4...............23 A8
Minehead Sta* TA24.......201 B7
Miners Cl BS41............10 F2
Minerva Ct BA2...........228 C3
Minerva Gdns BA2.........44 C4
Minery Rd BA5.............93 B3
Minnows The TA20........223 C3
Minsmere Rd BS31..........25 A4
Minster Cl TA1...........212 C1
Minster Ct TA1...........212 C1
Minster Way BA2...........45 C8
Minton Cl BS14............23 B5
Mintons TA20.............223 B3
Mintons Orch TA20........223 B3
Mint The BA11............119 E5
Misburg Cl BA4...........204 F6
MISTERTON.............224 E3
Misterton CE Fst Sch
  TA18...................224 F3
Mistletoe La BA4.........205 D3
Mitchell Gdns TA20.......223 B3
Mitchell La BS1..........227 B2
Mitchell's Pool TA21.....222 E6
Mitchell's Row BA22......175 D6
Mitchell St TA21.........222 C7
Mitchell Terr BA5........112 E1
Mitchelmore Rd BA21.....219 B5
Mitford-Slade Ct BS49....34 C7
Mitre Ct TA1.............213 B4
Mizzymead Cl **1** BS48....8 D1
Mizzymead Rd BS48.........8 E1
Mizzymead Rise BS48.......8 E1
Moccasin Way BA16.......207 B6
Moffats Dr BA5...........113 A2
Moles Rd BS40.............53 B6
Molesworth Cl BS13........22 A4
Molesworth Dr BS13........22 A4
Mollifriend La BA2.........60 B8
Molly Cl BS39.............76 E8
Monarch Ctr TA2..........213 C6

Monarch Rd TA18..........224 E4
Monday's Court La TA10...172 E5
Money Pit La EX13.........193 A1
Monger Cotts BS39.........77 F4
Monger La
  Greenhill BA3.............78 A3
  Midsomer Norton BA3.....78 A3
  Paulton BS39..............78 A4
Monington Rd BA6.........206 E6
Monk Barton Cl BA21......218 C7
Monk Cross...............128 D1
Monkhouse Farm La TA16.195 F7
Monkley La BA11...........83 C1
Monks Cl
  Rooks Bridge BS26........87 B5
  Taunton TA1.............213 B5
Monks Dale BA21..........218 D6
Monksdale Rd BA2..........44 D4
Monks Dr TA7.............137 F1
Monks Ford BA5...........139 D8
Monksford La BA5.........139 C8
Monks Hill BS22...........31 B3
MONKSILVER.............150 A8
Monks' Path TA23, TA24...131 E4
Monkstone Dr TA8.........84 F5
Monkstone Gdns **6** EX13.198 A1
Monksway TA23............131 A4
Monks Way TA8............104 B6
Monkton Ave BS24..........49 A2
MONKTON COMBE..........45 F1
MONKTON FARLEIGH.......46 F7
MONKTON HEATHFIELD...213 E8
Monkton La TA5...........134 D5
Monkton Prep Sch
  Monkton Combe BA2......63 E8
  Monkton Sen Sch BA2.....45 E1
Monmouth Cl
  Chard TA20..............223 E4
  Glastonbury BA6..........206 D5
  Portishead BS20............1 F4
  Westonzoyland TA7.......154 F6
Monmouth Ct
  Bath BA1................228 A2
  Chard TA20..............223 E4
  Pill BS20.................4 C5
Monmouth Dr BA11........120 B6
Monmouth Farm Cl TA6...135 F5
Monmouth Paddock BA2...81 E5
Monmouth Pl BA1.........228 B2
Monmouth Rd
  Keynsham BS31............24 D5
  Pill BS20.................4 C5
  Shepton Mallet BA4.......205 A5
  Taunton TA1.............213 B5
  Westonzoyland TA7.......154 F6
  Yeovil BA21.............219 D7
Monmouth St
  Bath BA1................228 B2
  Bridgwater TA6..........209 A5
Montacute BS24...........186 B3
Montacute Cir **4** BS22...49 F8
Montacute House* TA15..186 B4
Montacute Rd
  Montacute TA14, TA15....186 B4
  Tintinhull BA22.........186 B6
Montacute TV, Radio & Toy
  Mus* TA15..............186 C4
Montague Ct **4** BS2.....227 A4
Montague Flats **6** BS2...227 A4
Montague Hill BS2........227 A4
Montague Hill S **5** BS2..227 A4
Montague Ho **8** BA1......28 C1
Montague Pl BS6..........227 A4
Montague Rd
  Saltford BS31.............25 D2
  Shoscombe BA2............79 E5
Montague St BS1..........227 A4
Montague Way TA20.......223 C3
Monteclefe CE Jun Sch
  TA11...................211 E3
Montepelier BS23..........48 F8
Montgomery Ct BA11......120 A4
Montpelier E BS23.........30 F1
Montrose BS24............48 F2
Montrose Rd BA1..........219 E7
Montrose Villas BS27......90 C7
Montsurs Cl BA3...........96 D3
Monument Ct TA21........222 E4
Monument Rd TA21........222 E3
MOOLHAM................221 C1
Moolham La
  Ilminster TA19...........194 D7
  Kingstone TA19..........221 D1
Moondown La TA13........220 B2
Moonhayes Cross EX14....191 F4
Moon La TA7..............153 E1
Moonraker Cl **8** TA6......209 B4
Moon's Dro TA7...........155 A1
Moons Hill BA3...........116 A4
Moonshill Cl BA3.........116 A3
Moonshill Cotts BA3......116 A3
Moonshill Rd BA3.........116 A3
Moon St BS2..............227 B4
MOOR....................220 C3
Moor Cl
  Compton Dundon TA11....156 F2
  Langport TA10...........172 A6
  Wincanton BA9...........216 C3
Moorclose Dro TA7........137 C3
Moorclose La BA4.........158 E6
Moor Croft Rd BS24........49 E3
Moor Dro
  Chedzoy TA7.............154 F8
  Moorlinch TA7...........155 F6
Moorend Gdns BS11.........4 F7
Moor End Spout BS48.......8 D2

Moore's La TA5, TA6.......208 C7
Moores Yd BA14...........83 C6
Moorfield Gdn BA24.......146 C6
Moorfield BS48............19 A6
Moorfields Cl BA2.........44 D3
Moorfields Ct BS48.........8 D2
Moorfields Dr BA2.........44 D4
Moorfields Ho BS48.........8 D2
Moorfields Rd
  Bath BA2.................44 D4
  Nailsea BS48..............8 D2
Moor Gate BS20.............2 F4
Moor Gn BS26..............70 C1
Moor Gr BS11...............5 A8
Moorgrove Ho BS9..........5 C7
Moorham Rd BS25..........52 A1
MOORHAYNE..............192 D2
Moorhen Rd
  Kingston Seymour TA6....16 F2
  Kingston Seymour BS49...16 F2
Moorhouse La TA4........165 A8
Moor House La TA5.......133 E4
Moorings The
  Bath BA2.................45 B6
  Pill BS20.................4 C4
Moor La
  Alhampton BA4...........159 C5
  Backwell BS48............18 F6
  Batcombe BA4............142 D1
  Brushford TA22..........163 F4
  Churchinford TA3........192 A7
  Clapton in G BS20..........2 E1
  Clevedon BS21.............6 E2
  Clevedon BS21.............7 A2
  Cucklington SP8.........177 E5
  Draycott BS27............90 F1
  East Coker BA22.........197 D7
  Hardington Mandeville
    BA22.................197 A7
  Higher Chillington TA20.194 F5
  Hutton BS24..............49 D3
  North Curry TA3.........170 B4
  South Petherton TA13....220 B3
  Tickenham BS21............7 F4
  Walton in G BS21..........7 C6
  Westbury-sub-Mendip BA5.110 C5
  Weston-super-Mare BS24..49 F7
  Wincanton BA9...........216 C2
Moorland Cl TA1..........213 C5
Moorland Cotts BS26.......69 F2
Moorland Pk BS24.........33 E5
Moorland Pl TA1.........213 C5
Moorland Rd
  Bath BA2.................44 D5
  Bridgwater TA6..........209 D4
  Street BA16.............207 B7
  Taunton TA1.............213 C5
  Weston-super-Mare BS23..48 E4
MOORLANDS.............44 D3
Moorlands TA4...........167 F8
Moorlands Cl
  16 Martock TA12.......185 E6
  Nailsea BS48..............8 D2
Moorlands Ct TA16.......195 F7
Moorlands Inf Sch BA2....44 D4
Moorlands Jun Sch BA2...44 D3
Moorlands Pk **18** TA12..185 E6
Moorlands Pk Sh Ctr **19**
  TA12...................185 E6
Moorlands Rd TA16......195 E6
Moorland St BS26.........70 C1
Moorlands The BA2........44 D3
Moorland Way TA6........209 D5
Moor Lane Cl TA3.........170 B4
Moorlay Cres BS40.........37 F8
MOORLEDGE.............39 E1
Moorledge La BS39, BS40..57 F7
Moorledge Rd BS40........39 B1
MOORLINCH..............155 C7
Moorlinch Right Dro TA7.155 D6
Moor Park Rd TA19........171 F5
Moor Pk
  Clevedon BS21.............6 E2
  Langport TA10...........171 F5
Moor Rd
  Banwell BS29.............51 B5
  Middlezoy TA7...........155 B4
  Minehead TA24...........200 E8
  Moorlinch TA7...........155 D7
  Sutton Mallet TA7.......155 B8
  Yatton BS49...............17 B2
Moorsfield BS39...........58 F3
Moor Sherd BS28.........110 C1
Moorside BS40.............17 B1
Moorside Ct BS21...........6 E2
Moorside Villas BS21.......6 E2
Moortown La TA10.........171 B2
Moorview Cl BA6..........138 C4
Moor Villas TA13.........220 B3
Moorway La DT9..........188 C6
Moots La TA6.............209 D4
Morangis Way TA20.......223 B6
Moravia Cl TA6...........208 E6
Morden Wlk BS14..........23 D7
MOREBATH...............164 B3
Moredon Dro TA3.........170 C5
Moreton Cl BS14...........23 A4
Moreton La BS40...........56 A2
Moreton Mans **5** BS23...30 C1
Morford St BA1...........228 B4
Morgan Cl
  Saltford BS31.............25 D2
  Weston-super-Mare BS22..50 B8
Morgan Pl BS48............20 B7
Morgans Bldgs BS39........8 F8
Morgans Hill Cl BS48......18 D3
Morgan's La
  East Harptree BS40........74 C1

Morgan's La continued
  8 Frome BA11..........119 E5
Morgans Rise TA1.........212 A3
Morgan Sweet Pl BS25.....52 A4
Morgan Way BA2...........79 E7
Morland Rd
  Glastonbury BA6.........206 B3
  Highbridge TA9..........104 D4
Morlands Ent Pk BA6......206 B3
Morlands Ind Pk TA9......104 D4
Morley Rd TA14...........185 E3
Morley Terr
  Bath BA2.................44 D6
  Radstock BA3.............79 A3
Mornington Pk TA21......222 E5
Morpeth Rd BS4...........22 D8
Morrell's Cross EX16.....164 B4
Morrell's La EX16.........178 B6
Morris Cl TA19...........184 C5
Morris La BA1.............29 B3
Morston Ct BS22..........49 C7
Mortimer Cl
  Bath BA1.................27 B2
  Woolavington TA7........136 E4
Mortimer Rd BS8.........226 A3
Morton's La TA10.........156 C1
Moseley Gr BS23...........48 E2
Mosquito End BS23.........49 B4
Moss Cl TA6..............209 C6
Moss La TA3..............169 C3
Mosterton Down La DT8...196 A1
Mottershead Ave BS24.....50 C5
Moulton Cl BA4...........205 A4
Mound The BA6...........206 C4
Mounsdon Cl BA6.........157 E4
Mountain Ash BA1.........27 D1
Mountain's La BA2.........59 E6
Mountain Wood BA1.......29 C2
Mountbatten Cl
  Burnham-on-S TA8.........85 A1
  Weston-super-Mare BS22..31 E4
Mountbatten Ho TA6......209 C5
Mountbatten Rd **5** BA21.219 F8
Mount Beacon BA1.........28 A1
Mount Beacon Pl **3** BA1..27 F1
Mount Beacon Row **1** BA1.28 A1
Mounters Cl DT10.........190 F5
Mounter's Hill EX13, TA20.193 E4
Mountery Cl BA5..........203 D5
Mountery Rd BA5.........203 D5
Mountfields Ave TA1......213 B4
Mountfields Pk TA1.......213 B1
Mountfields Rd TA1.......213 B1
Mount Gr BA2.............44 B3
Mount Hey TA11...........211 E3
Mount Hindrance Cl TA20.223 D6
Mount Hindrance La
  TA20...................223 D6
Mount Ho TA1............212 F3
Mount La
  Charlton Horethorne DT9.176 A1
  Golsoncott TA23, TA24...131 C1
Mount Nebo TA1..........212 E2
Mount Pleasant
  Bath BA2.................45 D1
  Castle Cary BA7.........214 C5
  Crewkerne TA18.........224 D6
  Frome BA11..............119 F2
  Kilmington BA12.........161 E6
  Pill BS20.................4 D3
  Pilton BA4..............140 F3
  Radstock BA3.............79 B2
  Yeovil BA21.............219 C5
Mount Pleasant Ave BA5..203 B5
MOUNT RADFORD.........208 C6
Mount Rd
  Bath BA1................228 B4
  Bath, Southdown BA2.....44 B3
  Nether Stowey TA5.......134 A2
Mountsfield BA11.........120 A2
Mount St
  Bishops Lydeard TA4.....167 E8
  Bridgwater TA6..........208 F5
  Taunton TA1.............212 F3
Mount Terr TA1...........213 A3
MOUNT THE...............119 F2
Mount The
  Frome BA11..............119 F2
  Taunton TA1.............212 F3
  Yatton BS49...............34 C8
Mount View
  Bath, Beacon Hill BA1....28 A1
  Bath, Southdown BA2.....44 B3
  Woolavington TA7........136 E4
Mount View Terr TA6......135 F5
Mountway TA1............213 A3
Mountway Cl TA1.........212 C4
Mountway La TA1.........212 C4
Mountway Rd TA1.........212 C4
Movey La BA22............173 F1
Mow Barton
  Bristol BS13..............21 F6
  8 Martock TA12.......185 E6
New Barton Rd TA11......173 D5
Mowbray Rd BS14..........23 C7
Mowcroft Rd BS13.........22 D4
Mowes La DT10...........190 F4
Mowground La TA7........137 A3
Mowleaze **11** BA22.......197 F8
Mowlems The BA14........83 F3
Mowries Ct TA11.........211 C3
Moxham Dr BS13...........22 C4
M Shed* BS1..............227 A1
MUCHELNEY.............172 A3
Muchelney Abbey* TA10..172 A3
MUCHELNEY HAM.........172 B2
Muchelney Hill BA6......158 B5
Muchelney Ho TA19.......221 B3

Muchelney Pottery & The John Leach Gall★ TA10 172 B2
Muchelney Way BA21 218 C7
Muckleditch La TA19 184 D3
Muddicombe Cross TA24 128 B2
Muddicombe La TA24 128 B2
Muddyford La TA4 151 A3
Muddy La BS22 32 A8
MUDFORD 187 D6
Mudford Hill BA21 187 C5
Mudford Rd BA21 219 B8
MUDFORD SOCK 187 B6
MUDGLEY 138 D8
Mudgley Cross Roads BS28 108 F1
Mudgley Hill BS28 108 E1
Mudgley La BS28 108 F1
Mudgley Rd
  Rooks Bridge BS26 87 A4
  Wedmore BS28 108 E3
Mud La BS49 17 D2
Mulberry Ave BS20 2 E5
Mulberry Cl
  Backwell BS48 19 A6
  Portishead BS20 2 F5
  Taunton TA1 213 C2
  Weston-super-Mare BS22 32 A1
Mulberry Ct BA11 120 B7
Mulberry Farm BA6 140 B1
Mulberry Gdns
  4 Crewkerne TA18 224 C5
  Sherborne DT9 225 C5
Mulberry La
  Bleadon BS24 67 C6
  Stoke Sub Hamdon TA14 186 A4
Mulberry Rd BS49 34 E3
Mulberry Tree Cl TA6 209 D5
Mulberry Way BA2 45 A2
Mulberry Wlk BS9 5 C8
Mulholland Way TA9 104 D5
Mullins Cl BA5 203 B3
Mullins Way BA7 214 B6
Mundays Mead BA9 216 D3
Munden's La DT9 189 A1
Muntjac Rd BS40 53 B6
Murder Combe BA11 118 E5
Murford Ave BS13 22 B4
Murford Wlk BS13 22 B4
Murhill BA3 64 C6
Muriel Terr BA5 203 D3
Murray-Smith Dr BA22 218 A6
Murray Way BA9 216 B3
Murtry Hill La BA11 100 C2
Musbury Cl DT10 190 F6
Musbury La DT10 190 F6
Muscovy Dr 1 TA6 154 A5
Museum of Somerset★ TA1 212 F4
Museum of South Somerset★ BA20 219 B4
Musgraves TA22 163 E6
Musgrove Pk Hospl TA1 212 C3
Musgrove Rd TA1 212 C3
Musmoor La BA22 174 F7
Mus of Bath at Work★ BA1 228 B4
Mus of East Asian Art★ BA1 228 B3
Mutton La BS28 108 D4
Mutton St DT6 199 D1
Mux's La TA4 151 B3
Myrtleberry Mead BS22 32 A5
Myrtle Cl TA6 209 D5
Myrtle Dr
  Bristol BS11 4 E5
  Burnham-on-S TA8 104 A7
Myrtle Farm Rd BS22 31 C4
Myrtle Gdns BS49 34 C8
Myrtle Hill BS20 4 C5
Myrtle La TA21 179 E7
Myrtle Rd
  Bristol BS2 226 C4
  22 Martock TA12 185 E6
Myrtles The BS24 49 D2
Myrtle Tree Cres BS22 31 A6
Myrtlle Cotts TA3 182 D7

N

Nag's La TA18 195 B1
NAILSBOURNE 168 D7
NAILSEA 8 E3
Nailsea and Backwell Station BS48 18 F7
Nailsea Cl BS13 22 A7
Nailsea Moor La BS48 17 F7
Nailsea Park Cl BS48 8 F2
Nailsea Pk BS48 8 F2
Nailsea Sch BS48 8 E1
Nailsea Wall BS21 17 C8
Nailsea Wall La BS48 17 E7
NAILWELL 61 D6
Naishes Ave BA2 79 D7
Naish Farm BA3 96 D3
Naish Hill BS20 2 F1
Naish Ho BA2 44 A6
Naish La BS48 20 D3
Naisholt Rd BA4 204 F6
Naish Rd TA8 85 A3
Naish's Cross BA3 96 D3
Naish's St BA11 119 E5
Naked Boys La TA23 149 B5
Nalder Cl BA4 205 D4
Nanga-gat Rd BA22 174 A2
Nanny Hurn's La BS39 58 A1
Napier Ct
  Bristol BS1 226 B1
Napier Ct *continued*
  Sherborne DT9 225 B2
Napier Miles Rd BS11 5 A8
Napier Rd BA1 27 A3
Naples View TA6 208 E7
NARFORD'S 193 C1
Narfords La TA20 193 C1
Narrow Plain BS2 227 B2
Narrow Quay BS1 227 A2
NASH 197 C8
Nash Barton BA22 197 C8
Nash Cl BS31 25 A5
Nash Dr TA21 222 F6
Nash Gn TA2 212 B7
Nash La
  Dinnington TA17, TA19 195 A6
  East Coker BA22 197 C8
  Marshwood DT6 199 B2
  Yeovil BA20 218 D1
Nates La BS40 35 F1
Nathan Cl BA20 218 D2
Naunton Way BS22 31 B2
Neale's Way BA4 141 E2
Neathem Rd BA21 219 C7
Neat La BA4 204 D1
Nedge Cnr BA3 94 D4
Nedge Hill
  Chewton Mendip BA3 94 D3
  East End BA3 94 D3
Nedge La BA3 94 C4
Needhams Patch TA4 167 E6
NEIGHBOURNE 115 C5
Nelson Bldgs BA1 228 C4
Nelson Ct
  Bridgwater TA6 208 F5
  Weston-super-Mare BS22 31 E4
Nelson Ho
  Bath BA1 228 A3
  5 Bristol BS1 227 A3
Nelson Pl BA1 228 C4
Nelson Pl E BA1 228 C4
Nelson Pl W BA1 228 A2
Nelson St BS1 227 A3
Nelson Terr BA1 228 C4
Nelson Villas BA1 228 A2
Nelson Ward Dr BA3 79 A1
Nelson Way BA21 219 F8
Nempnett St BS40 55 D5
NEMPNETT THRUBWELL 55 D5
Neroche Prim Sch TA19 183 C2
Neroche View TA3 183 A7
Nerrols Dr TA2 213 C7
Neston Wlk BS4 22 F8
NETHERCLAY 182 B7
Netherclay TA1 212 A4
Netherclay La TA3 182 B7
NETHER COMPTON 187 F4
Nethercoombe La DT9 225 C5
NETHERCOTT 151 C3
Nethercott La TA4 151 C3
Nethercott Way TA4 151 A3
NETHERHAY 199 F8
Netherhay La DT8 199 F8
Nethermoor Rd TA7 155 B3
NETHERSTOKE 197 D3
Netherstoke La BA22 197 C3
NETHER STOWEY 134 B3
Nether Stowey CE Prim Sch
  Nether Stowey TA5 134 A2
  Nether Stowey TA5 134 A2
Netherton Cross BA22 197 E6
Netherton La
  East Coker BA22 197 F6
  Marston Magna BA22 175 A1
Netherton Rd BA21 219 D7
Netherton Wood La BS48 18 A6
Netherways BS21 6 B1
Netley BA21 218 D6
NETTLEBRIDGE 115 D6
Nettlebridge Hill BA3 115 D5
NETTLECOMBE 149 F8
Nettlecombe Hill
  Castle Cary BA7 214 F6
  Pitcombe BA7 215 A2
Nettlecombe Ho BA5 113 A1
Nettlecombe Park Rd
  Monksilver TA4 132 A1
  Sticklepath TA4 149 F7
Nettle Combe View BA5 113 A2
Nettlefrith La TA8 66 B1
Neva Rd BS23 48 E6
Neville Cl 1 TA11 173 F7
Neville Pk BA6 158 A5
Nevilles Batch BA3 114 D7
Nevys La TA4 150 E8
Newark St BA1 228 C1
Newbarn Park Rd TA1 212 B1
Newberrys Patch TA3 192 A7
Newbery Cl 4 EX13 198 A1
Newbery La TA18 224 F3
New Bldgs
  3 Bampton EX16 164 C1
  Dunwear TA7 209 D1
  Frome BA11 119 F3
  Ilminster TA19 221 B1
  North Perrott TA18 196 C4
  Oake TA4 167 C4
  Peasedown St John BA2 79 B8
New Bond St BA1 228 C2
New Bond Street Pl BA1 228 C2
Newbourne Rd BS22 49 C8
NEWBRIDGE 44 B8
Newbridge Ct BA1 44 B7
Newbridge Dro TA9 105 A1
Newbridge Gdns BA1 44 A8
Newbridge Hill BA1 44 B7
Newbridge Ho BS9 5 C4
Newbridge La TA9 104 F1
Newbridge Prim Sch BA1 44 B7
Newbridge Rd BA1, BA2 44 B7
New Bristol Rd BS22 31 E1
New Buildings La BA11 119 F3
New Bungalows TA20 223 C3
NEWBURY
  Coleford 98 B1
  Horningsham 144 E4
Newbury BA12 144 E4
Newbury Cotts BA3 117 A8
Newbury Hill BA3 117 A7
Newbury Manor Sch BA11 98 B1
Newbury Terr 3 BA21 218 F7
Newchester Cross TA16 195 E7
New Church Rd BS23 48 D2
New Cl
  Bourton SP8 161 F1
  Haselbury Plucknett TA18 196 B5
  Horrington BA5 113 A4
  Street BA16 207 B4
Newclose La BS40 56 D1
Newclose Terr TA14 185 E4
Newcombe Cvn Pk TA8 104 B8
Newcombe Dr BS9 5 C4
Newcombe La BS25 70 B7
Newcombe Rd BS9 5 F7
Newcot Cross EX15 191 A5
NEWCOTT 192 C3
New Cotts
  Milton Clevedon BA4 160 A8
  West Chinnock TA18 196 B8
NEW CROSS 184 F6
New Cross TA11 211 C3
Newcross Cres BA21 218 B8
New Cross Hill
  Barrington TA12, TA13 184 F6
  Kingsbury Episcopi TA12 185 A6
New Cut BA5 203 D7
New Cut Bow BS21 16 A6
New Cut Dro BA6 157 C7
Newditch La BS40 20 C1
Newdown La BS41 22 B2
New Ear La BS22 32 E5
Newell DT9 225 C4
New Farm La TA10 172 A7
Newfield TA4 166 F4
Newfields BS40 72 C8
New Fosseway Rd BS14 23 B6
New Fosseway Sch BS13 22 E4
Newfoundland Rd BS2 227 C4
Newfoundland St BS2 227 C4
Newfoundland Way
  Bristol BS2 227 C4
  Portishead BS20 2 E6
New Friary Cotts BA11 143 C3
Newgate BS1 227 B3
Newgate Cross TA22 163 D7
Newgate La TA4 210 C5
Newhaven Pl BS20 1 E4
Newhaven Rd BS20 1 D4
New Hill TA11 211 E4
Newhouse La TA4 165 E6
Newington Cl BA11 119 E3
Newington Terr BA11 119 E4
New Kingsley Rd BS2 227 C2
New King St BA1 228 B2
New La
  Bampton EX16 163 F2
  Charlton Horethorne DT9 176 A1
  Creech St Michael TA3 169 D5
  Cricket St Thomas TA20 194 E4
  Haselbury Plucknett TA18 196 C6
  Tatworth TA20 198 C8
  Witham Friary BA11 143 C4
Newland DT9 225 E4
Newland Cross TA24 128 B1
Newland Dr BS13 22 A4
Newland Flats 5 DT9 225 E4
Newland Gdn 8 DT9 225 E4
Newland Gdns BA11 120 A4
Newland Ho BA1 27 F1
Newland La TA24 127 F1
Newland Rd
  Bristol BS13 22 A3
  Weston-super-Mare BS23 48 F6
Newlands Cl BS20 2 C5
Newlands Cres TA3 169 C3
Newlands Gn BS21 6 E1
Newlands Gr TA3 169 C3
Newlands Hill BS20 2 C4
Newlands Rd
  Keynsham BS31 24 D4
  Ruishton TA3 169 C3
Newland Wlk BS13 22 A3
Newlyn Ave BS9 5 D5
Newlyn Cres TA7 136 B4
Newman Cl BA6 206 E6
New Manor House Rd TA10 172 A8
Newmans La
  East Huntspill TA9 105 C1
  Timsbury BA2 60 B2
Newmarket Ave 9 BS1 227 A3
New Mdws BS14 23 A6
Newmead Dro TA10 172 A2
Newnham Cl BS14 23 D7
New Orchard St BA1 228 C2
New Park Ho BS21 6 D5
Newpark Rd BA9 161 D3
New Pit Cotts BA2 60 F1
New Pk EX16 162 E4
NEWPORT 170 B2
Newport Cl
  Clevedon BS21 6 C2
  Portishead BS20 1 F4
Newport Hill TA3 170 B2
Newport Rd BS20 4 C5
Newquay Rd BS4 22 F8
New Rd
  Banwell BS29 50 E4
  Barwick BA22 197 F8
  Bathford BA1 29 D2
  Bawdrip TA7 136 D2
  Bridgwater TA6 209 A5
  Burrowbridge TA3, TA7 170 E8
  Cannington TA5 135 C1
  Carhampton TA24 131 A5
  Chapel Allerton BS26 88 C2
  Chard Junction TA20 198 F8
  Churchill BS25 52 F4
  Clevedon BS21 6 D2
  Combe St Nicholas TA20 193 D6
  Crewkerne TA18 195 B4
  Draycott BS27 91 C3
  East Huntspill TA9 136 D8
  Freshford BA3 64 B5
  Frome BA11 120 B4
  Hambridge TA12 184 E7
  Haselbury Plucknett TA18 196 E6
  High Littleton BS39 59 C3
  Hinton St George TA17 195 C7
  Ilminster TA19 221 B4
  Kilmersdon BA3 98 E4
  Lyng TA3 170 B6
  North Wootton BA4 140 A4
  Norton Sub Hamdon TA14 185 E3
  Norton Sub Hamdon, Chiselborough TA14 185 F1
  Oare EX35 122 D4
  Odcombe BA22 186 D3
  Othery TA7 155 C2
  Pensford BS39 40 D3
  Pill BS20 4 C4
  Porlock TA24 123 E3
  Rawridge EX14 191 E1
  Redhill BS40 37 A4
  Seavington St Mary TA19 184 E1
  Sherborne DT9 225 E3
  Shipham BS25 52 E1
  South Cadbury BA22 175 E4
  Stalbridge DT10 190 B4
  Staple Fitzpaine TA3 182 D5
  Taunton TA3 168 D1
  West Bagborough TA4 151 E4
  Weston Town BA4 142 D5
  Wiveliscombe TA4 166 A6
  Yeovil BA22 218 A5
New Road Gate EX35 122 D5
New Rock Ind Est BA3 96 D2
New Rock Rd BA3 96 D2
Newsome Ave BS20 4 C4
New Sq BA5 113 A2
New St
  Bath BA1 228 B2
  Bristol BS2 227 C3
  Long Sutton TA10 172 E4
  Marnhull DT10 190 F5
  Mells BA11 118 B7
  North Perrott TA18 196 C4
  Somerton TA11 211 E4
  Wells BA5 203 D5
New Street Flats 4 BS2 227 C3
New Thomas St BS2 227 C2
NEWTON
  Combe St Nicholas 193 A7
  Watchet 132 E1
Newton Cl
  Burnham-on-S TA8 85 A2
  West Harptree BS40 74 E6
Newton Ct
  14 Bampton EX16 164 B1
  Corfe TA3 181 F6
Newton Gn BS48 18 C8
Newton La
  Bicknoller TA4 132 E1
  Corfe TA3 181 F6
Newton Rd
  Barwick BA22 197 F8
  Bath BA2 43 F6
  North Petherton TA6 153 F3
  Taunton TA1 213 E4
  Weston-super-Mare BS23 48 E6
  Yeovil BA20 219 D3
NEWTON ST LOE 43 D6
Newton Sq 8 EX16 164 B1
Newton's Rd
  Weston-super-Mare BS22 31 E3
  Weston-super-Mare BS22 31 E4
NEWTOWN
  Axbridge 69 D2
  Bridgwater 208 E6
Newtown TA12 185 E7
NEW TOWN
  Bishop Sutton 57 D7
  Freshford 81 F8
  Hatch Beauchamp 182 E4
  Kington Magna 177 E1
  Milborne Port 217 B2
  Paulton 77 D6
  Wedmore 138 E8
  Yeovil 219 C6
Newtown La BA6 140 A1
Newtown Pk TA10 172 A6
Newtown Rd
  Highbridge TA9 104 D3
  Langport TA10 172 A6
New Way TA10 172 B7
Nibley Rd BS11 4 E5
Nicholas Cl TA22 163 E4
Nicholls Cl TA6 208 D4
Nichol Pl TA4 167 F6
Nichol's Rd BS20 1 F5
Nick Reed's La EX15 180 D1
Niddon's La TA13 195 E8
Nidon La TA7 137 D3
Nigel Pk BS11 4 E7
Nightingale Acre TA3 183 A7
Nightingale Ave BA11 120 B6
Nightingale Cl
  1 Bridgwater TA6 209 C4
  Burnham-on-S TA8 85 B1
  Wells BA5 203 B3
  Weston-super-Mare BS22 31 E1
Nightingale Ct
  16 Taunton TA1 213 A4
  Weston-super-Mare BS22 31 E1
Nightingale Gdns BS48 8 D2
Nightingale Gr BA4 205 C5
Nightingale La BA22 174 F6
Nightingale Rise BS20 1 F3
Nightingales TA4 167 E6
Nightingale Way BA3 97 B8
Nile St BA1 228 A2
Nimbus Rd BS24 49 C5
NIMMER 223 C8
Nine Acre Dro TA7 138 B2
Nine Acre La TA3 170 C4
Nine Barrows La BA5 92 E4
Nine Commons Dro TA10 173 A4
Nippors Way BS25 69 F8
Nithsdale Rd BS23 48 E4
Nixon Trad Units BS24 49 A3
No 1 Royal Cres Mus★ BA1 228 B3
Noah's Ark Zoo Farm★ BS48 9 B7
Noah's Hill TA2 169 B7
Noake Rd DT9 225 B3
Noble St TA1 213 B4
Noel Coward Cl TA8 104 C6
Nomis Pk BS49 34 E2
No Place La TA5 152 E5
Norbins Rd BA6 206 D5
Nordens Mdw TA4 210 D4
Nordrach La BS40 73 D5
Nore Gdns BS20 2 C6
Nore Park Dr BS20 1 F5
Nore Rd BS20 2 A6
Norfolk Ave BS2 227 B4
Norfolk Bldgs BA1 228 A2
Norfolk Cl TA6 209 C3
Norfolk Cres BA1 228 A2
Norfolk Gr BS31 24 C4
Norfolk Hts 10 BS2 227 B4
Norfolk Rd
  Portishead BS20 2 E4
  Weston-super-Mare BS23 48 F5
Norland Rd BS8 11 F8
Norlet Ct BA6 206 D5
Normandy Ave TA23 202 E6
Normandy Dr TA1 213 C3
Normandy Ho BA16 207 B6
Norman La TA7 156 B7
Norman Rd BS31 25 E3
Normans The BA2 28 F1
Normans Way BS20 3 E7
Norrington Way TA20 223 D2
Northam Farm Cvn Pk & Camp Site TA8 65 F4
Northampton Bldgs BA1 228 B4
Northampton Ho BS48 9 D3
Northampton St BA1 228 B4
Northanger Ct 5 BA2 228 C3
North Ave TA9 104 C4
NORTHAY
  Combe St Nicholas 193 B6
  Hawkchurch 199 A3
Northay Cross EX13 199 B3
Northay La
  Axminster EX13 199 A3
  Combe St Nicholas TA20 193 B6
North Bank BA5 203 A8
NORTH BARROW 175 A8
North Barrow Rd BA22 175 A6
North Bradon La TA3 184 A7
NORTH BREWHAM 161 A7
Northbrook Dr TA7 137 F1
Northbrook Rd
  Cannington TA5 135 C2
  Shapwick TA7 138 A1
  Yeovil BA21 219 D7
NORTH CADBURY 175 D6
North Cadbury CE Prim Sch BA22 175 D6
NORTH CHERITON 176 C4
North Cheriton Rd BA9 176 B5
North Chew Terr BS40 39 B3
North Chine Dro BA5 138 D8
North Cl BS27 90 F3
NORTH COKER 197 D8
Northcombe La TA22 163 E7
Northcote Cres BA11 120 A7
Northcote Rd BS8 5 F1
North Cres DT9 217 D3
North Croft TA4 202 D3
NORTH CURRY 170 C4
North Curry CE Prim Sch TA3 170 B3
North Curry CE VC Prim Sch TA3 170 B3
North Devon Link Rd EX16 178 C1
North Down Cl BS25 70 F8
North Down La BS25 70 F8
Northdown Rd BA3 78 E5
North Dro BS48 8 A2
North Elm La BS40 39 B4
NORTHEND 28 F5
NORTH END
  Clutton 58 E5
  Millmoor 179 E3
  Taunton 169 D5

NORTH END continued
Yatton **16** F3
North End
Charlton Horethorne DT9. . **176** A2
Creech St Michael TA3 . . . . . **169** D5
Midsomer Norton BA3 . . . . . . **78** B2
North End Rd BS49 . . . . **16** F3
Northern Path BS21 . . . . **6** F3
Northern Way BS21 . . . . **6** F3
NORTHFIELD
Bridgwater **208** C4
Radstock **79** B1
Somerton **211** C5
Northfield
Bridgwater TA6 . . . . **208** E4
Radstock BA3. . . . . **79** A3
Somerton TA11 . . . . **211** C4
Timsbury BA2. . . . . **60** C3
Winsley BA15 . . . . **64** F7
Northfield Ave TA1 . . . . . . **212** E4
Northfield CI TA5 . . . . **134** C6
Northfield Gdns TA1 . . . . . **212** E5
Northfield Ho
Bath BA1 . . . . **27** F1
Glastonbury BA6 . . . . **206** E4
Northfield La
Dinnington TA17 . . . . **195** B8
South Petherton TA13. . . . . . **220** C2
Northfield Rd
Minehead TA24. . . . . **201** A8
Portishead BS20 . . . . **1** E3
Taunton TA1 . . . . **212** E4
Northfields
Bath BA1 . . . . **27** F1
Taunton TA1 . . . . **212** B3
Northfields CI BA1 . . . . **27** F1
Northfield Way TA11 . . . . **211** C5
NORTHGATE **210** C5
Northgate
Bridgwater TA6 . . . . **208** F5
Wiveliscombe TA4 . . . . **210** C5
Northgate Prim Sch 🟨
TA6 . . . . **208** F5
Northgate St BA1 . . . . **228** C2
North Gr
Pill BS20 . . . . **4** C4
Wells BA5. . . . . **203** E5
North Green St 🟦 BS8 . . . . **11** F6
North Hill Mews BA11 . . . **119** F5
North Hill Rd TA24 . . . . . . **200** F8
North Hills CI BS24 . . . . **49** B2
North Hill Woodland Trail★
TA24 . . . . **125** B4
North La
Bath BA2 . . . . **45** D5
Berrow TA8. . . . . **65** F1
Challacombe EX31, TA24 . . **126** B4
East Coker BA22 . . . . **197** A7
Nailsea BS48 . . . . **8** B1
Othery TA7 . . . . **155** C2
Stogursey TA5 . . . . **134** C7
🟦 Weston-super-Mare BS23. . **48** E7
Yeovil BA20 . . . . **219** B5
Northleach Wlk BS11 . . . . . . **4** F5
North Leaze BS41 . . . . **11** B2
Northleaze CE Prim Sch
Long Ashton BS41 . . . . **11** B1
Long Ashton BS41 . . . . **11** B2
Northleaze Ho BA16 . . . . . **207** C6
North Leaze La BA22 . . . . **175** C7
Northleigh Ave BS22 . . . . . **31** C5
Northleigh Rd TA1 . . . . . . **213** B3
Northload Bridge BA6 . . . **206** C5
Northload Bridge Rdbt
BA6 . . . . **206** D5
Northload Dro BS28 . . . . . **109** E2
Northload La BS28 . . . . . . **109** D1
Northload St BA6 . . . . **206** D5
Northload Terr BA6 . . . . . . **206** D5
North Mdws BA2. . . . . **79** E8
Northmead Ave BA3. . . . . . **77** F2
Northmead CI BA3 . . . . **77** F2
Northmead Dro TA3. . . . . . **170** A1
Northmead Rd BA3. . . . . . . **77** F2
North Mills La TA13 . . . . . **220** C5
Northmoor Dro TA7 . . . . . **136** E1
Northmoor Gn Rd TA7 . . . **154** D3
Northmoor Hill TA22 . . . . **163** B7
Northmoor La TA3 . . . . . . **170** C7
Northmoor Rd
Dulverton TA22. . . . . **163** D7
Othery TA10 . . . . **155** D1
NORTH NEWTON **153** F4
North Newton Com Prim Sch
North Newton TA7 . . . . **153** F2
North Newton TA7 . . . . **153** F2
NORTHOVER
Glastonbury **206** B3
Ilchester **173** C4
Northover Bldgs BA6 . . . . **206** B3
Northover Dr TA20 . . . . . . **223** B5
Northover Farmhouse
BA6 . . . . **207** D8
North Par
Bath BA2 . . . . **228** C2
Frome BA11 . . . . **119** F5
North Parade Bldgs 🟦
BA1 . . . . **228** C2
North Parade Pas 🟦 BA1 . **228** C2
North Parade Rd BA2. . . . . **28** B2
NORTH PERROTT **196** C4
North Perrott Rd TA18 . . . **196** C4
NORTH PETHERTON **153** F4
**North Petherton Com Prim
Sch** TA6 . . . . **153** F3

North Rd
Banwell BS29 . . . . **51** A3
Bath, Bathwick BA2 . . . . **45** C4
Bath, Combe Down BA2 . . . . **45** B2
Charlton Horethorne DT9. . . **176** A2
Eastertown BS24. . . . . **67** D2
Leigh Woods BS8 . . . . **11** D7
Midsomer Norton BA3 . . . . . **78** A1
Minehead TA24. . . . . **201** A7
Sherborne DT9 . . . . **225** E5
Timsbury BA2. . . . . **60** C2
Wells BA5. . . . . **203** E5
Williton TA4 . . . . **202** D4
Northside
Castle Cary BA7 . . . . **214** C6
Rockwell Green TA21 . . . . . **222** B5
North Side Rd BS48 . . . . . . **36** F8
North Somerset Mus★
BS23 . . . . **48** E8
North St
Babcary TA11 . . . . **174** C7
Bradford Abbas DT9. . . . . . **187** E1
Bridgwater TA6 . . . . **208** E4
Bristol BS1. . . . . **227** B4
Castle Cary BA7 . . . . **214** C5
Crewkerne TA18. . . . . **224** C7
Drayton TA10 . . . . **171** E3
Haselbury Plucknett TA18. . . **196** C6
Ilminster TA19 . . . . **221** C4
Langport TA10 . . . . **172** A5
Martock TA12 . . . . **185** E6
Milborne Port DT9 . . . . **217** D2
Milverton TA4 . . . . **167** A4
Nailsea BS48 . . . . **8** B1
North Petherton TA6. . . . . . **153** E4
Norton St Philip BA2. . . . . . . **81** E4
Norton Sub Hamdon TA14. . **185** E1
Shepton Beauchamp TA19 . . **184** E4
Somerton TA11. . . . . **211** E4
South Petherton TA13. . . . . **220** C5
Stoke sub Hamdon TA14. . . **185** F4
Taunton TA1 . . . . **212** F4
Wellington TA21. . . . . **222** D6
Weston-super-Mare BS23 . . . **48** E8
Williton TA4 . . . . **202** D3
Wincanton BA9 . . . . **216** C4
Wiveliscombe TA4 . . . . **210** B4
NORTH STOKE **26** C6
North Stoke La BS30. . . . . . **26** B8
North Terr BA21 . . . . **219** C6
NORTH TOWN
North Cadbury **175** C7
North Wootton **140** D5
Taunton **212** E5
North Town TA11 . . . . **173** D5
North Town Com Prim Sch
TA1 . . . . **212** E4
Northtown La
North Wootton BA4 . . . . . . **140** C4
Taunton TA1 . . . . **212** E5
North Town Mews TA1 . . . **212** E5
Northumberland Bldgs 🟦
BA1 . . . . **228** B2
Northumberland Pl 🟦
BA1 . . . . **228** C2
North View BS21 . . . . **79** B2
North View CI BA2 . . . . **44** B5
North View Dr BS29 . . . . . . **51** A2
North Villas TA4 . . . . **167** F6
North Way
Bath BA2 . . . . **44** A5
Midsomer Norton BA3 . . . . . **78** A1
NORTH WESTON **3** F4
NORTHWICK **105** F6
NORTH WICK **39** D8
Northwick Gdns BS39 . . . . . **57** D4
Northwick Rd
Chew Magna BS39, BS41 . . . . **39** D7
Mark TA9 . . . . **106** B5
NORTH WIDCOMBE **57** B1
Northwood CI TA2 . . . . . . **168** B4
Northwood Rd BS6 . . . . . . **158** A6
NORTH WOOTTON
Sherborne **188** F1
Wells **140** C4
NORTON **31** D4
Norton CI
Chew Magna BS40 . . . . **39** B3
Shepton Mallet BA4 . . . . . . **205** A5
Norton Dro TA12 . . . . **185** B8
NORTON FITZWARREN . . . **168** B4
**Norton Fitzwarren CE Com
Prim Sch** TA2 . . . . **168** B4
Norton Grange BA2 . . . . . . **81** E5
NORTON HAWKFIELD **39** F6
NORTON HILL **97** B7
Norton Hill Sch BA3 . . . . . . **97** B8
Norton Ho 🟦 BS1 . . . . **227** B1
Norton La
Chew Magna BS39, BS40 . . . . **39** D5
Wellow BA2 . . . . **81** B7
Weston-super-Mare BS22 . . . **31** C4
Whitchurch BS14 . . . . **23** C2
NORTON MALREWARD . . . **40** B7
Norton Rd TA14 . . . . **185** E3
NORTON ST PHILIP **81** F4
Norton St Philip CE Fst Sch
BA2. . . . . **81** E4
NORTON SUB HAMDON . . **185** F3
**Norton sub Hamdon CE Prim
Sch** TA14 . . . . **185** F3
NORTON'S WOOD **7** C5
Nortons Wood La BS21 . . . . **7** A5
Norville CI BS27. . . . . **90** B8
Norville La BS27 . . . . **90** B8
Norwich CI TA1 . . . . **212** C1
Norwich Ct TA1 . . . . **212** D2
Norwood Ave BA2 . . . . **45** E5

Norwood Gr BS20 . . . . **1** F5
Notaro Wy TA7. . . . . **154** A4
Notgrove CI BS22 . . . . **31** B2
Notlake Dro BS27 . . . . **89** E4
Notting Hill Way BS26 . . . . **88** D6
Nova Quarter BA16 . . . . . . **207** B5
Nova Scotia Pl BS1. . . . . . . **226** A1
Novers Cres BS4 . . . . **22** C8
Novers Hill BS4. . . . . **22** C8
Novers La BS4 . . . . **22** D7
NOVERS PARK **22** D8
Novers Park Dr BS4 . . . . **22** C8
Novers Park Rd BS4 . . . . **22** D8
Novers Rd BS4 . . . . **22** C8
Nowers La TA21. . . . . **222** C3
Nowhere La BS48 . . . . **9** A1
Number 15 BA21 . . . . **219** F7
Nunnery La TA19 . . . . **183** B4
NUNNEY **143** C8
Nunney Barton BA11 . . . . . **119** D4
Nunney CI
Burnham-on-S TA8 . . . . **85** C1
Keynsham BS31 . . . . **25** A2
Nunney Fst Sch BA11 . . . . . **143** B8
Nunney Rd BA11 . . . . **119** D4
Nunney Castle★ BA11 . . . . . **143** B8
NUNNEY CATCH **143** B7
Nunney Catch Rbt BA11. . . **143** B7
Nurcott La TA24. . . . . **147** C7
Nursery CI TA5. . . . . **135** B5
Nursery Gdns TA20. . . . . . . **223** E4
Nursery La BA9 . . . . **216** C4
Nursery Rd BA20 . . . . **219** A3
Nursery Rise BA3 . . . . **96** E4
Nursery Terr TA8 . . . . **208** E5
Nursery Villas TA3 . . . . **223** E4
Nutgrove La BS40 . . . . **39** A4
Nutshole La TA20 . . . . **194** B2
Nut Tree CI TA9 . . . . **136** E8
Nut Tree La TA18. . . . . **224** D7
Nutts La BA11. . . . . **101** F8
Nutwell Rd BS22 . . . . **31** E2
Nutwell Sq BS22 . . . . **31** E2
Nydon The TA7. . . . . **137** D3
NYE **51** E8
Nye CI BS27 . . . . **90** C7
Nye Dro BS24 . . . . **51** E8
Nye Rd BS25 . . . . **51** F5
NYLAND **90** C1
Nyland Dro BS27 . . . . **90** B1
Nyland La BA8 . . . . **190** C8
Nyland View BS27. . . . . **90** F3
NYNEHEAD **167** C1
Nynehead Hollow TA21. . . **167** C1
Nynehead Rd
Nynehead TA21. . . . . **167** C1
Wellington TA21. . . . . **222** F8
Nythe Rd TA7 . . . . **156** A5

O

Oak Apple Dr TA6 . . . . **208** D6
Oak Ave BA2. . . . . **44** C3
Oak CI TA24. . . . . **200** D7
Oak Ct
Bristol BS14. . . . . **23** A5
Weston-super-Mare BS22 . . . **32** C3
Oakdale Gdns BS22 . . . . **31** F2
Oakdale Rd BS14. . . . . **23** A8
Oak Dr
Crewkerne TA18. . . . . **224** D7
Portishead BS20 . . . . **2** B4
OAKE **167** D4
Oake Acres TA4 . . . . **167** D4
**Oake, Bradford & Nynehead
CE Prim Sch** TA4 . . . . **167** D4
Oake CI TA4 . . . . **167** D4
Oake Gn TA4. . . . . **167** D4
Oak End Way TA20 . . . . **223** C5
Oaken Ground TA21 . . . . . **222** B5
Oakfield Acad BA11 . . . . . . **119** D4
Oakfield CI
Bath BA1 . . . . **44** D8
Frome BA11. . . . . **119** D5
Oakfield Gr BS8 . . . . **226** B4
Oakfield Pk TA21. . . . . **222** E4
Oakfield Pl BS8 . . . . **226** B4
Oakfield Rd
Bridgwater TA6 . . . . **208** C4
Bristol BS8. . . . . **226** B4
Frome BA11. . . . . **119** D4
Keynsham BS31. . . . . **24** F2
Street BA16 . . . . **207** B4
Oakford Ave BS23 . . . . **48** F8
Oakford La BA1 . . . . **29** A8
Oak Gr BS20 . . . . **4** C5
Oakgrove Way TA6 . . . . . . **209** D6
OAKHILL **115** A3
Oakhill BS24. . . . . **49** A2
Oakhill CE Prim Sch BA3. . **115** B3
Oakhill CI BS48 . . . . **9** B1
Oakhill Ct BA3. . . . . **116** E3
Oakhill Rd BA2. . . . . **44** F2
Oak Ho
Brean TA8. . . . . **65** E2
Bristol BS13. . . . . **22** D4
Oakhurst Rd BS9 . . . . **5** F5
Oak La
East Anstey TA22 . . . . **162** E6
Rodhuish TA24 . . . . **131** A3
Taunton TA2 . . . . **212** F6
Oakland Ct TA12 . . . . **185** E7
Oakland Dr
Hutton BS24. . . . . **49** E3
Martock TA12 . . . . **185** E7
Oakland La TA13 . . . . **185** B1
Oakland Rd TA12. . . . . **185** E7

Oaklands
Cheddar BS27 . . . . **90** A8
Clevedon BS21. . . . . **6** C4
Paulton BS39 . . . . **77** E4
Temple Cloud BS39. . . . . **58** E1
Oaklands Ave TA20 . . . . . . **223** F4
Oaklands Prim Sch BA20. . **218** F5
Oaklands Rd BA21 . . . . **219** D7
Oakleigh BA20 . . . . **218** D2
Oakleigh CI BS48. . . . . **19** B5
Oakley
Bath BA2 . . . . **45** E6
Clevedon BS21. . . . . **16** B8
Oakley CI TA7. . . . . **154** F5
Oakley La BA22 . . . . **186** F6
Oak Lodge Cres TA24 . . . . **200** F7
Oakmear Rd TA6. . . . . **208** E3
Oak Rd
Nether Stowey TA5. . . . . . . **134** B2
Winscombe BS25 . . . . **70** A8
Oakridge CI BS25 . . . . **70** B7
Oakridge La BS25 . . . . **70** C6
Oakridge Pk BA21 . . . . **219** A6
Oak's Dro BS25 . . . . **138** E8
Oaksey Gr BS48 . . . . **9** A1
Oak St BA2 . . . . **228** B1
Oaks The
Nailsea BS48 . . . . **9** A2
Taunton TA1 . . . . **213** C1
Wembdon TA6 . . . . **208** C6
Winford BS40. . . . . **37** F7
Oak Terr BA3 . . . . **78** D1
Oak Tree CI EX14 . . . . **191** F2
Oaktree Ct BS11 . . . . **4** E7
Oaktree Gdns BS13. . . . . . . **21** E5
Oak Tree Ho 🟥 TA14 . . . . . **185** F4
Oaktree Pk BS24 . . . . **49** E5
Oaktree Pl BS22 . . . . **32** C3
Oak Tree Pl TA8. . . . . **85** A3
Oak Tree Way TA5. . . . . . . **135** B2
Oak Tree Wlk BS13 . . . . **24** D3
Oak Vale La BA8 . . . . **190** A6
Oak Way BA22 . . . . **218** A2
OARE **122** E4
OAREFORD **122** F3
Oare Post TA24 . . . . **123** B3
Oasis Acad Brightstowe
BS11. . . . . **4** E7
Oasis Acad Brislington BS4 **23** F8
Oasis Acad John Williams
BS14. . . . . **23** B7
Oasis Acad Long Cross BS11 **4** E7
Oasis Acad New Oak BS14 . **23** B7
Oatcroft La DT9. . . . . **188** B4
Oatfield BS48. . . . . **19** F1
Oath Dro TA7. . . . . **171** B5
OATHILL **199** E8
Oathill Cotts BA4. . . . . **140** F3
Oathill La
Clapton TA18. . . . . **195** C1
Winsham TA18 . . . . **199** E8
Oatlands Ave BS14 . . . . **23** A6
Oatley La TA5. . . . . **134** F2
Oborne La DT9 . . . . **188** F5
Oborne Rd DT9 . . . . **225** F5
OBRIDGE **213** A6
Obridge CI TA2 . . . . **213** A6
Obridge Cres TA2 . . . . **213** A6
Obridge La TA2 . . . . **213** A6
Obridge Rd TA2 . . . . **213** A6
Obridge Viaduct TA2. . . . . **213** B6
Observatory Field BS25. . . . **70** B8
Observatory The BS22 . . . . **31** D3
Ocean Way BA22 . . . . **174** B3
Octagon The 🟥 TA1. . . . . . **212** F4
Octavia CI TA6. . . . . **208** E2
Octavius Rd BS31 . . . . **24** F8
ODCOMBE **186** D2
Odcombe Hollow BA22 . . . **196** E8
ODD DOWN **44** D2
Odeon Bldgs BS23. . . . . **48** E7
Odins Rd BA2 . . . . **44** D1
Oggshole Farm La TA5 . . . **153** A1
Olands Rd TA21 . . . . **222** D6
Old Acre Rd BS14 . . . . **23** A3
Old Airfield Cvn Pk The
TA7. . . . . **155** A4
Old Ansford Inn BA7. . . . . **214** C6
Old App BA7 . . . . **159** A3
Old Banwell Rd BS24 . . . . . **50** B4
Old Barn La
Bampton EX16 . . . . **163** E1
Compton Martin BS40 . . . . . **56** D1
Old Barn La
Felton BS40 . . . . **37** A5
Hatch Beauchamp TA3 . . . . **182** F6
Old Barn Way BA20. . . . . . . **218** D3
Old Barrow Hill BS11 . . . . . . **4** D7
Old Basin TA2. . . . . **209** B2
Old Blackditch Rd TA9. . . . **136** B6
Old Bond St 🟥 BA1. . . . . . . **228** B2
Old Bowden Way DT9. . . . . **217** D4
Old Bread St BS2. . . . . **227** C2
Old Brewery Ind Est The
TA4 . . . . **210** C4
Old Brewery Rd TA4. . . . . . **210** C4
Old Brewery The
🟦 Frome BA11. . . . . **119** D4
Rode BA11 . . . . **101** E8
Old Brewhouse The BA1 . . . **27** B2
Old Bridge CI BA6. . . . . **206** D4
Oldbridge Rd BS14 . . . . **23** C3
Old Bristol Rd
East Brent TA9 . . . . **86** E4
Oakhill BA3, BA4 . . . . **114** C4

Old Bristol Rd continued
Priddy BA5, BS40 . . . . **93** A6
Shepton Mallet BA4 . . . . . **141** C8
Wells BA5. . . . . **112** B5
Weston-super-Mare BS22 . . . **32** A2
Oldbroach La TA3. . . . . **213** F2
Old Bull La BA4 . . . . **141** F7
Old Burnett La BS31. . . . . . **42** A7
Old Burnham Rd TA9 . . . . . **104** D4
Old Chapel La BA1 . . . . **228** C4
Old Chapel Ct TA10. . . . . . **172** A6
Old Chapel La BS48. . . . . . . **17** F7
Old Chapel Rd TA7 . . . . . . **155** B3
Old Chelsea La BS8. . . . . . . **10** C4
Old Church Rd
Axbridge BS26 . . . . **70** C1
Clevedon BS21. . . . . **6** C3
Nailsea BS48 . . . . **18** D8
Weston-super-Mare BS23 . . . **48** D2
OLD CLEEVE **131** E5
Old Cleeve CE Sch TA23. . . **131** E4
Old Coach Rd BS26. . . . . . . **69** E2
Old Combe Hill TA3 . . . . . . **181** F5
Old Compton La DT9 . . . . . **187** F2
Old Co-op Cotts BA3 . . . . . **117** A4
Old Dairy Ct BS21 . . . . **6** E3
Old Dairy The BA2. . . . . **44** D4
OLD DITCH **110** E7
Old Ditch BA5. . . . . **110** E7
Old Ditch La TA7. . . . . **155** E7
OLD DOWN **95** F3
Old Down La BA4. . . . . **142** A6
Old Drill Hall The BS2 . . . . **227** C3
Old England Way BA2 . . . . . **79** B8
Old Farm DT9 . . . . **225** C4
Old Farm CI TA24. . . . . **200** E6
Old Farm Ct
Blackford BS28 . . . . **107** C4
Queen Camel BA22 . . . . . . **174** F3
Old Farm Pl TA17 . . . . **195** C7
Old Farm Rd
Minehead TA24. . . . . **200** E6
Nether Stowey TA5 . . . . **134** B2
Old Ferry Rd BA2. . . . . **44** C6
Oldfield BS21. . . . . **6** E1
Oldfield La BA2 . . . . **44** E4
OLDFIELD PARK **44** E4
Oldfield Park Inf Sch BA2. . **44** D6
Oldfield Park Jun Sch BA2 . **44** C4
Oldfield Park Sta BA2. . . . . **44** D6
Oldfield Pl BS8. . . . . **11** F5
Oldfield Rd
Bath BA2 . . . . **228** A1
Bristol BS8. . . . . **226** A1
Oldfield Sch BA1. . . . . **26** F1
OLDFORD **101** B1
Oldford Hill BA11 . . . . **101** B1
Oldford Residential Pk
BA11. . . . . **101** B1
Old Forge Mews BS49 . . . . . **34** B5
Old Forge The BA2. . . . . . . **61** B4
Old Forge Way BA2. . . . . . . **79** B8
Old Fosse Rd
Bath BA2 . . . . **44** C1
Clandown BA3. . . . . **78** E4
Old Frome Rd
Bath BA2 . . . . **62** E8
Doulting BA4 . . . . **141** E8
Horrington BA5. . . . . **113** D3
Oakhill BA3, BA4 . . . . **115** B1
Old Glove Factory The
BA22 . . . . **186** B6
Old Gore La BA3 . . . . **95** E3
Old Green The 🟦 DT9 . . . . **225** D4
Old Ham TA5 . . . . **133** D6
Old Hill
Wincanton BA9 . . . . **216** C5
Winford BS40. . . . . **37** D5
Wrington BS40. . . . . **35** F3
Oldhill Farm La BS40 . . . . . **37** D6
Old Hitchen 🟥 TA16. . . . . . **195** F7
Old Ho The BA3 . . . . **64** C5
Old Junction Rd BS23 . . . . . **49** B5
Old King St BA1 . . . . **228** B3
Old King Street Ct BS1. . . . **227** B1
Old La
Farmborough BA2 . . . . **60** A6
Nailsea BS21 . . . . **8** C4
Porlock TA24 . . . . **124** B3
Old Main Rd TA6 . . . . **135** C5
Old Malt Ho BS2 . . . . **227** C4
Old Maltings The BA3 . . . . **115** A3
Old Manor Est BA3 . . . . . . **116** C8
Old Market 🟥 TA12 . . . . . . **185** E6
Old Market Ct BA6. . . . . . . **206** D5
Old Market Mews DT10 . . . **190** B4
Old Market Rd
Shepton Mallet BA4 . . . . . . **205** B6
Sydenham TA6 . . . . **209** B6
Old Market Rdbt BS2. . . . . **227** C3
Old Market St BS2. . . . . . . **227** C3
Oldmead La BS26 . . . . **87** C5
Oldmead Wlk BS13 . . . . **21** E7
Old Midford Rd BA2 . . . . . . **63** B7
Old Millard's Hill BA3. . . . . **78** B3
Old Mill Rd
Portishead BS20 . . . . **2** D5
Woolavington TA7. . . . . **136** E4
Old Mill Road Ind Est BS20 . **2** E6
OLD MILLS **77** D3
Old Mills Ind Est BS39 . . . . **77** E3
Old Mills La BS39. . . . . **77** D3
Old Mill Way
Wells BA5. . . . . **203** B2
Weston-super-Mare BS24 . . . **50** A8
OLDMIXON **49** B1
Oldmixon Cres BS24. . . . . . **49** A3
Oldmixon Prim Sch BS24 . . **49** A2

Old–Par 261

Oldmixon Rd BS24 49 B1
Old Mixon Rd BS24 49 C2
Old Newbridge Hill BA1 44 A8
Old Oaks Cl TA6 208 D5
Old Orch TA20 223 F1
Old Orchard BA1 228 C3
Old Orchard Cl TA19 183 F4
Old Orchards TA20 223 E4
Old Orchard St BA1 228 C2
Old Orchard The TA19 221 A5
Old Orch The TA13 220 D4
Old Park Hill BS2 226 C3
Old Park Rd
Bristol BS11 4 D7
Clevedon BS21 6 E4
Old Pawlett Rd TA9 136 A7
Old Pensford La BS31 24 D1
Old Pit Rd BA3 97 C8
Old Pit Terr BA3 78 E4
Old Pk BS2 226 C3
Old Police Station The BA9 216 C4
Old Post Office Cotts TA7 153 F2
Old Post Office La BS23 48 D8
Old Pound Ct SP8 161 E1
Old Print Works 6 BA11 119 E5
Old Print Works Rd BS39 77 D6
Old Priory Rd BS20 4 B4
Old Quarry BA2 44 D2
Old Quarry Rd BS11 4 E7
Old Quarry Rise BS11 4 E7
Old Rd
North Petherton TA6 153 F4
Odcombe BA22 186 C2
Pensford BS39 40 E3
Radstock BA3 79 C1
South Cadbury BA22 175 E4
Old Rd The BA8 189 D6
Old Rectory The TA9 86 C4
Oldrey La TA24 147 C8
Old Saw Mills The BA3 117 A3
Old Sawmill The BA12 161 F6
Old School Cl
Alweston DT9 189 A1
Ashcott TA7 156 B8
Churchill BS25 52 F4
Yeovil BA21 218 C5
Old School Hill BA2 62 F7
Old School Ho BA21 219 C5
Old School Ho The
Bath BA1 228 B4
Whatley BA11 118 A3
Old School La
Bleadon BS24 67 C6
Catcott TA7 137 D2
Clifton Wood BS8 226 B2
Lynford-on-F TA11 158 C2
Old School Pl BA5 203 E5
Old School The BA11 119 E4
Oldshute La TA22 163 C7
Old Sneed Ave BS9 5 D4
Old Sneed Cotts BS9 5 E4
Old Sneed Pk BS9 5 D4
Old Sneed Rd BS9 5 D4
Old St BS21 6 E3
Old Station Cl
Cheddar BS27 90 A7
Wrington BS40 35 D1
Old Station Ct TA20 223 D5
Old Station Gdns BA8 190 A7
Old Station La BA10 215 C4
Old Station Rd BA20 219 C4
Old Station Way BA20 219 C4
Old Stream Farm TA10 171 E3
Old Street La BA5 204 B7
Old Tannery The 20 BS2 227 C3
Old Tarnwell BS39 40 B2
Old Taunton Rd TA6 209 A4
Old Threshing Mill The BA4 141 B2
Old Tiverton Rd EX16 164 C1
Old Tk BA2 63 F7
Old Town TA20 223 C3
Old Vicarage Cl TA7 137 B2
Old Vicarage Ct BS14 23 C4
Old Vicarage Gdns TA13 220 C4
Old Vicarage Gn BS31 24 E6
Old Vicarage La TA4 167 E8
Old Vicarage Rd BA9 160 C2
Old Vicarage The TA21 222 E6
Oldville Ave BS21 6 D2
Old Walcot Sch The BA1 228 B3
Old Wall BS24 66 D5
Old Water Gdns The BS40 54 E2
OLD WAY 184 A4
Old Way
Chipstable TA4 165 D6
Stogumber TA4 150 D8
Oldway Ho TA21 222 F4
Oldway La TA3 183 A8
Oldway Pk TA21 222 F4
Oldway Pl TA9 104 D4
Oldway Rd
East Anstey TA22 162 F5
Wellington TA21 222 E4
OLDWAYS END 162 E3
Old Wells Rd
Bath BA2 44 F3
Croscombe BA5 204 D6
Doulting BA4 142 A8
Glastonbury BA6 206 F6
Leigh u M BA3, BA4, BA11 117 B2
Shepton Mallet BA4 205 A5
Old Weston Rd
Congresbury BS49 34 B5
Flax Bourton BS48 20 B8
Old Withy Rd TA9 136 C7
Old Yarn Mills The DT9 225 D2
Oliver Brooks Rd BA3 96 E7
Oliver's La TA19 183 B2
Olivers Rd TA7 155 C4
Olivier Cl TA8 104 C6
One Elm TA10 172 B7
Onega Ctr BA1 228 A3
Onega Terr BA1 228 A3
Oolite Gr BA2 44 D1
Oolite Rd BA2 44 D1
Opal Wlk TA6 209 C8
Orange Gr BA1 228 C2
Orange St BS2 227 C4
Orchard Ave
Bristol BS1 226 C2
Midsomer Norton BA3 77 F1
Portishead BS21 7 E4
Orchard Cl
Banwell BS29 51 B3
Bishop Sutton BS39 57 C3
Bradford On Tone TA4 167 F1
Bristol, Westbury on T BS9 5 F5
Carhampton TA24 131 B5
Castle Cary BA7 214 B7
Cheddar BS27 90 B8
Coleford BA3 117 A7
Congresbury BS49 34 D4
Cossington TA7 137 A3
Coxley BA5 139 E6
Drimpton DT8 199 F8
East Brent TA9 86 E4
East Chinnock BA22 196 E8
East Huntspill TA9 136 E8
Felton BS40 37 C8
Flax Bourton BS48 20 A8
Frome BA11 119 D4
Highbridge TA9 104 E4
Keynsham BS31 24 D6
Long Sutton TA10 172 E4
3 North Petherton TA6 153 E3
Odcombe BA22 186 C2
Portishead BS20 2 D5
Queen Camel BA22 174 F3
Rockwell Green TA21 222 A5
South Petherton TA13 220 C5
Sparkford BA22 175 A5
Taunton TA3 168 D1
West Coker BA22 197 A8
Weston-super-Mare, Kewstoke BS22 31 B3
Weston-super-Mare, Worle BS22 31 F2
Westwood BA15 64 F3
Wincanton BA9 216 D3
Wrington BS40 35 E2
Yeovil Marsh BA21 187 A5
Orchard Cl The BS24 49 F4
ORCHARD COMMON 182 A8
Orchard Cotts
Croscombe BA5 204 B7
Timsbury BA2 60 F1
Orchard Cres BS11 4 D7
Orchard Ct
Claverham BS49 17 F1
Highbridge TA9 104 E3
Minehead TA24 201 B4
Street BA16 207 C6
Wellington TA21 222 E6
Orchard Dr
Bristol BS13 22 A6
Sandford BS25 52 A4
Southwick BA14 83 E3
Taunton TA1 212 A3
Orchard End BS40 74 F4
Orchard Gdns
Paulton BS39 77 E6
West Buckland TA21 180 F7
Orchard Gn TA2 212 F8
Orchard Gr TA9 105 C8
Orchard Ho
Weston-super-Mare BS22 31 F2
Yeovil BA21 219 A6
Orchard La
Allerford TA24 124 B4
Bristol BS1 226 C2
Chewton Mendip BA3 94 F6
Crewkerne TA18 224 C6
Evercreech BA4 141 E1
Kingsbury Episcopi TA12 185 B8
Thorncombe TA20 199 B6
Wembdon TA6 208 D5
Orchard Lea
Coxley BA5 139 E7
Pill BS20 4 D4
Wells BA5 203 C5
Orchardleigh BA22 196 E8
Orchardleigh View BA11 119 D6
Orchard Lodge BA2 45 F8
Orchard Mead TA19 183 C1
Orchard Paddock BA5 203 A7
Orchard Pk
Bristol BS14 23 D4
West Camel BA22 174 D3
Orchard Pl
Aller TA10 171 D8
6 Langaller TA2 169 C5
1 Weston-super-Mare BS23 48 E7
Orchard Rd
Axbridge BS26 70 C1
Backwell BS48 19 A6
Carhampton TA24 131 B5
Clevedon BS21 6 D2
Hutton BS24 49 E2
Long Ashton BS41 10 F1
Milborne Port DT9 217 C2
Minehead TA24 200 F8
Nailsea BS48 8 D1
Paulton BS39 77 E6
Somerton TA11 211 B4
Orchard Rd *continued*
Street BA16 207 C6
Orchard Rise
Crewkerne TA18 224 C5
Fivehead TA3 170 F2
Porlock TA24 124 A3
Ruishton TA3 169 C4
Orchards Sh Ctr TA1 212 F3
Orchard St
Bristol BS1 226 C2
Frome BA11 119 E5
Weston-super-Mare BS23 48 E8
Yeovil BA20 219 A4
Orchards The
Bristol, Shirehampton BS11 4 E6
Horrington BA5 113 A2
Stocklinch TA19 184 C4
Orchard Terr
5 Bath BA2 44 B6
Glastonbury BA6 206 D5
Orchard The
Banwell BS29 51 A3
Bath, Combe Down BA2 45 B1
Batheaston BA1 28 F5
Bath, Newbridge BA1 44 A7
Chard TA20 223 D2
Corston BA2 43 B8
Freshford BA3 64 C5
Holywell Lake TA21 179 E7
Locking BS24 50 A5
Meare BA6 138 D4
Pensford BS39 40 E4
Pill BS20 4 C4
Ruishton TA3 169 C2
Upper Stanton Drew BS39 40 A2
Orchard Vale
Ilminster TA19 221 B3
Langport TA10 172 A5
Midsomer Norton BA3 77 F1
Orchard View
Baltonsborough BA6 158 B6
Haselbury Plucknett TA18 196 C6
Orchard Way
Charlton Horethorne DT9 176 A2
Cheddar BS27 90 B8
Keinton Mandeville TA11 158 A1
Misterton TA18 224 F3
Peasedown St John BA2 79 D7
Shapwick TA7 137 F1
Taunton TA1 213 D5
Timberscombe TA24 130 B5
Williton TA4 202 E4
Woolavington TA7 136 E3
Orchard Wlk
Churchill BS25 52 E4
Milborne Port DT9 217 C2
Orchard Wyndham* TA4 132 B2
Orchid Cl TA1 169 A1
Orchid Dr
Bath BA2 44 C2
Keynsham BS31 24 E3
Orchids The TA8 85 A2
Orchid Wy TA6 208 E1
Oriel Dr BA6 206 D4
Oriel Gdns BA1 28 C2
Oriel Gr BA2 44 B4
Oriel Rd BA16 207 C5
Orme Dr BS21 6 D5
Ormerod Rd BS9 5 E5
Ormrod Gr BS24 50 C5
Orneage Cl BA11 101 E8
Orwell Dr BS31 25 A4
Osborne Ave BS23 48 F7
Osborne Gr TA1 212 E3
Osborne Pl TA16 195 F7
Osborne Rd
Bath BA1 44 B7
Bridgwater TA6 208 F6
Bristol BS3 226 C1
Weston-super-Mare BS23 48 F7
Yeovil BA20 219 A5
Osborne's La BA1 27 A3
Osborne Villas BS2 226 C4
Osborne Wallis Ho BS8 226 A1
Osborne Way TA1 212 E3
Osborne Wlk TA8 104 C6
Osmond Dr BA5 203 B3
Osmond Rd 2 BS24 49 F7
Osprey Ct BS14 22 D5
Osprey Gdns BS22 31 F1
Ostlings La BA1 29 B2
Ostrey Mead BS27 90 B7
Otago Terr 5 BA1 28 C2
OTHERY 155 B2
Othery Village Prim Sch TA7 155 C2
Othery Village Sch TA7 155 C2
Ottawa Rd BS23 48 F3
OTTERFORD 181 E1
Otterford Cl BS14 23 B5
Otterford Gypsy Pk TA3 181 D2
Otterford Lakes Nature Reserve* TA3 192 B8
Otterford Lakes Nature Trail* TA3 181 E1
Otterham La TA3 183 F8
OTTERHAMPTON 135 A6
Otterhampton Prim Sch TA5 135 B5
Otter Rd 1 BS21 6 E1
Otter Vale Cl EX14 191 F1
Ottery La DT9 225 C3
Our Lady of Mount Carmel RC Prim Sch
Wincanton BA9 216 C3
Wincanton BA9 216 C3
Our Lady of the Rosary RC Prim Sch BS11 5 A8
Outer Circ TA1 213 D5
Outer Gullands TA1 212 D2
Outmoor Dro TA10 172 D3
Outmoor Straight Dro TA10 172 D3
OVAL THE 44 C4
Oval The BA2 44 C4
Overbrook Bsns Ctr BS28 107 D4
Overcombe BA8 189 E8
OVER COMPTON 187 F4
Overdale
Clandown BA3 78 E5
Peasedown St John BA2 60 F3
Overhill BS20 4 D4
Over Innox BA11 119 F6
Overland La TA3 170 C3
Overlands
North Curry TA3 170 C4
Ruishton TA3 169 C4
OVERLEIGH 207 C3
Overleigh
Street BA16 207 C3
Street BA16 207 C4
Overstables La BS21 6 D3
OVER STOWEY 134 A1
OVER STRATTON 220 D1
OVERTON 169 C7
Overton BA9 216 D4
Owen Dr BS8 10 B4
Owen St TA21 222 C6
Owlaborough La EX36 162 B2
Owl St
South Petherton TA13 220 B8
Stocklinch TA19 184 C3
Owsley Cotts TA19 184 E4
Oxendale BA16 207 B5
Oxen Dr TA6 209 B6
Oxen La TA3 170 B3
OXENPILL 138 C4
Oxenpill BA6 138 C4
Oxen Rd TA18 224 C6
Oxford Pl
Bath BA2 45 C2
19 Bristol, Clifton BS8 11 F6
10 Taunton TA2 213 A8
Weston-super-Mare BS23 48 D7
Oxford Rd BA21 219 E7
Oxford Row BA1 228 B3
Oxford Sq BS24 50 B6
Oxford St
Bristol BS2 227 C2
Bristol, Tyndall's Park BS2 226 C4
Burnham-on-S TA8 104 B6
Evercreech BA4 141 E1
Weston-super-Mare BS23 48 D7
Oxford Terr 4 TA6 209 B4
Oxhayes DT8 199 F8
Oxhouse La
Failand BS8 10 B6
Winford BS40 37 D6
Oxleaze
5 Bishops Lydeard TA4 167 F8
Bristol BS13 22 D4
Oxleaze La BS41 21 E3
Oxleaze Way BS39 77 D6
Oxley Cotts DT9 225 C4
Ozenhay BS39 75 E6

P

Packers' Way TA18 196 B3
Pack Horse La BA2 62 F7
PACKSADDLE 119 F7
Packsaddle Way BA11 119 F7
Pacquet Ho BS20 4 D5
Paddles La BA11 119 D1
Paddock Cl TA3 169 D5
Paddock Dr TA9 104 D4
Paddock Gdn BS14 22 F4
Paddock Park BS22 32 B2
Paddocks Cvn Pk The BS26 87 A7
Paddocks The
Bath BA2 45 B1
Ilchester BA22 173 E1
Sandford BS25 52 C4
Wellington TA21 222 E5
Weston-super-Mare BS23 48 D2
Paddock The
Banwell BS29 51 A3
Clevedon BS21 6 D2
Corston BA2 43 B7
Dulverton TA22 163 D6
Galhampton BA22 175 D8
Portishead BS20 2 D4
Taunton, Dowsland TA1 168 F1
Taunton, Trull TA3 168 D1
Paddock Wlk DT9 217 C2
Paddock Woods BA2 45 D2
Paddons Farm TA5 134 C6
Padfield Cl BA2 44 B5
Padfield Gn BA4 141 E6
Padleigh Hill BA2 44 B2
Padstow Rd BS4 22 F8
Paganel Cl TA24 200 F6
Paganel Rd TA24 200 F6
Paganel Rise TA24 200 E6
Paganel Way TA24 200 E6
Pagans Hill BS40 38 D2
Pageant Dr DT9 225 D3
Page La BA6 140 A2
Page's Ct BS49 34 C8
Page's Hill BA16 207 C1
Pages Mead BS11 4 C8
PAINTMOOR 194 B4
Paintmoor La TA20 194 B4
Palace Ct BA5 203 D3
Palace Gdns TA4 210 C4
Palace Yard Mews BA1 228 B2
Palfrey's La TA20 193 D3
Palmer Cl TA6 208 F2
Palmer Row 7 BS23 48 E8
Palmers Cl TA8 104 D8
Palmer's Elm BS24 33 B4
Palmer's End La TA12 184 F7
Palmers La BA2 61 B3
Palmers Mead TA21 222 D8
Palmers Rd BA6 206 D4
Palmer St
Frome BA11 119 F4
South Petherton TA13 220 C4
Weston-super-Mare BS23 48 E8
Palmerston Rd TA1 212 D5
Palmer's Way BS24 49 D2
Palm Tree Cl TA6 209 E5
PANBOROUGH 138 F8
Panborough Dro BA5 138 F8
Panoramic The BS1 226 C3
Paper La BS39 77 D6
Paper Mill Gdns BS20 2 F6
Parade Nurseries TA24 200 F7
Parade The
1 Bath BA2 44 B6
Bristol, Bishopsworth BS13 22 A6
Bristol, Shirehampton BS11 4 E6
Chardstock EX13 198 A7
Minehead TA24 200 F7
Paradise Cres BA4 141 E2
Paradise La
Croscombe BA5 204 B7
Glastonbury BA6 139 D2
Langport TA10 172 A7
Tatworth TA20 193 F1
Paradise Rd BA6 206 D5
Paradise Row BS39 41 A6
Paragon Ct 13 BS23 30 C1
Paragon Pl TA6 209 A3
Paragon Rd BS23 30 C1
Paragon Sch The BA2 45 A3
Paragon The
Bath BA1 228 C3
Bristol BS8 11 F6
Paray Dr BA5 203 F5
PARBROOK 158 D7
Parbrook Ct BS14 23 B5
Parbrook La BA6 158 D7
Parcroft Gdns BA20 218 F5
PARDLESTONE 133 C5
Pardlestone La TA5 133 C5
Parfields BA20 218 F5
Parish Brook Rd BS48 8 B2
Parish Hill BA22 175 D5
Parish Land La TA5 152 D5
Parish Mews BA20 218 C5
Parish Quarry Rd TA4 150 B4
PARK 156 D1
Park Ave
Bath BA2 228 B1
Bridgwater TA6 208 D4
Castle Cary BA7 214 B4
Yatton BS49 17 B1
Park Barn La TA19 183 C4
Park Batch BS40 54 F3
Park Bglws EX16 179 B3
Park Cl
Barton St David TA11 158 A3
Cossington TA7 136 F3
Keynsham BS31 24 D5
Paulton BS39 77 D5
Staplehay TA3 181 D8
Street BA16 207 C5
Park Cnr
Hambridge TA3 184 B7
Leigh u M BA11 117 D3
Sharpstone BA2 64 A4
PARK CORNER 64 A4
Park Cotts TA20 223 B5
Park Cres
Chard TA20 223 B5
Cossington TA7 136 F3
Park Ct 5 BS23 48 E5
Park End BS29 50 E4
Park End Rd TA5 152 B4
Parker Cl TA21 222 E6
Parkes Ave BS24 50 D4
Parkes Rd BS24 50 C5
Park Farm BA6 206 C4
Park Farm Rd BA6 206 C4
Parkfield Cl TA6 153 F4
Parkfield Cres TA1 212 D2
Parkfield Dr TA1 212 D3
Parkfield Gdns BS39 57 D3
Parkfield Prim Sch TA1 212 D3
Parkfield Rd
Axbridge BS26 70 D1
Taunton TA1 212 D3
Parkfields Orch BA6 157 E4
Parkfields Residential Home BA6 157 E4
Park Gate TA2 168 F7
Parkgate La BA11 101 E7
Park Gdns
Bath BA1 44 D8
Yeovil BA20 219 A5
Park Gr DT10 190 B4
Park Hayes BA3 116 F3
Park Hill
Bristol BS11 4 F6
Mells BA11 118 C7
Pilton BA4 140 E3
Park Hill Dr BA11 119 F6
Park Ho BA2 44 E4

Parkhouse La BS31........24 C2
Parkhouse Rd TA24 .....200 E7
Parkhurst Rd BS23 .....49 A7
Park La
  Barton St David TA11 ....158 A3
  Bath BA1 ....44 D7
  Blagdon BS40...........54 F3
  Cannington TA5 ....135 B3
  Carhampton TA24.......131 A5
  Castle Cary BA7 ....214 D7
  Combe St Nicholas TA20 ..193 C6
  Downhead BA4..........117 A1
  Faulkland BA3 ....80 B1
  Goathurst TA5 ....153 C4
  Henstridge BA8 ....190 A8
  High Ham TA10 ....156 D1
  Ilminster TA19 ....183 E1
  Kingsdon TA11........173 E5
  Kingston St Mary TA2 ...168 C8
  Langport TA10 ....171 E4
  Montacute BA22, TA15 ...186 B3
  North Newton TA7 .....154 A3
  North Petherton TA6....153 F4
  Seavington St Mary TA19 ..184 C1
  Thorncombe TA20......199 A7
  Wellington TA21 ....222 C1
  West Buckland TA21 ...180 E7
  Yenston BA8 ....189 F8
Park La Cl TA24 ....131 A5
Parklands BS39.........59 D2
Parklands Ave BS22.....32 A4
Parklands Educate Together
Prim Sch BS24 ....50 B6
Parklands Rd
  Bristol BS3.............11 E4
  Wellington TA21 ....222 D7
Parklands Rise TA24 .....200 D7
Parklands Way TA11.....211 B4
Parkland Wlk TA18.......224 C4
Park Lodge BA20........219 A5
Parkmead TA2..........213 E8
Park Pl
  Bath BA1 ....228 A4
  Bristol BS2............226 C3
  Bristol BS8............226 B3
  Castle Cary BA7 ......214 C5
  Weston-super-Mare BS23 ..48 D8
Park Rd
  Bath BA1 ....44 B7
  Bridgwater TA6 ......208 D4
  Bristol BS3...........226 B1
  Bristol, Shirehampton BS11 ...4 F6
  Bruton BA10...........215 E5
  Chard TA20...........223 C4
  Clevedon BS21 ....6 D4
  Congresbury BS49 ......34 E3
  Frome BA11...........119 E4
  Henstridge BA8 ....190 A6
  Keynsham BS31........24 E6
  Paulton BS39..........77 D5
  Shepton Mallet BA4 ...205 B6
  Stalbridge DT10.......190 B4
  Street BA16 ....207 C5
  Yeovil BA20 ....219 B5
Park Row BS1..........226 C3
Park Sch The BA20 .....219 A5
Parks Cotts TA2........168 D8
Parkside Ct ◨ TA6 .....209 B4
Parks La
  Brompton Ralph TA4.....150 C3
  Minehead TA24........200 F7
Park St
  Bath BA1 ....228 A4
  Bristol BS1...........226 C3
  Castle Cary BA7 ......214 C5
  Dunster TA24 ....201 D1
  Exford TA24 ....128 D1
  Minehead TA24.........200 F7
  Taunton TA1 ....212 E3
  Yeovil BA20 ....219 B4
Parks The
  Bridgwater TA6 ......208 D4
  Minehead TA24.........200 E7
Parkstone Ave TA6......209 A2
Park Street Ave BS1.....226 C3
Park Street Mews BA1...228 A4
Parks View TA24........124 A4
Parksway Ct TA24 ....200 E7
Park Terr
  Chard TA20...........223 B6
  Glastonbury BA6 ......206 D4
  Minehead TA24.........200 F7
Park The
  Castle Cary BA7 ......214 B4
  Keynsham BS31 ....24 E6
  Portishead BS20 ....2 F5
  Yatton BS49...........17 B1
  Yeovil BA20 ....219 A5
Park Villas BS23........48 D8
Park Wall BA10.........215 F6
Park Wall Dro TA7.....209 F4
Park Water La DT8 .....199 F5
Parkway
  Bridgwater TA6 ......209 C6
  Timsbury BA2..........60 E2
Park Way
  Bruton BA10...........215 E5

Park Way continued
  Midsomer Norton BA3 ....97 A8
  Ruishton TA3 ....169 C3
Park Way BS22..........32 B1
Parkway La BA2.........60 D3
Park Wlk BS20 ....4 D4
Park Wood Cl BS14.......22 F4
Parlour Ho TA1........213 B5
Parmin Cl TA1.........213 C3
Parmin Way TA1.......213 C3
Parnell Rd BS21 ....6 D3
Parnell Way TA8 ....104 B8
Parrett Cl TA10 ....171 F5
Parrett Mead
  South Perrott DT8 .....196 C1
  Taunton TA1 ....213 D3
Parrett Way TA1.......209 B3
Parrett Works Cotts
  TA12 ....220 F8
Parricks La EX13.......198 D3
Parrocks La TA20......198 C8
Parry Cl BA2 ....44 B4
Parrys Cl BS9............5 E5
Parrys Gr BS9............5 E5
Parry's La BS9...........5 F5
Parsonage Cl
  Langport TA10 ....172 A5
  Somerton TA11.........211 E3
  West Harptree BS40 ....74 E6
  Winford BS40..........37 F6
Parsonage Cotts
  Kingston St Mary TA2 ...168 D8
  West Camel BA22.......174 D3
Parsonage Cres BA7 ...214 B6
Parsonage Ct
  Puriton TA7...........136 B4
  Taunton TA1 ....212 A4
Parsonage Hill TA11.....211 E3
Parsonage La
  Ashill TA19 ....183 C4
  Axbridge BS26 ....70 E2
  Bath BA1 ....228 B2
  Charlton Musgrove BA9 ..161 B1
  Chilcompton BA3 ....96 C4
  Kingston St Mary TA2 ...168 D8
  Milverton TA4.........167 A4
  Pensford BS39..........40 D6
  Staple Fitzpaine TA3...182 C4
  Winford BS40..........37 F6
Parsonage Pl TA10 .....171 D4
Parsonage Rd
  Berrow TA8............84 F5
  Long Ashton BS41 ......11 C2
  West Camel BA22.......174 D3
Parson's Batch BA4.....140 E3
Parsons Cl
  Bicknoller TA4........132 F2
  Long Sutton TA10 .....172 F4
  Nether Stowey TA5.....134 A3
Parson's Dro BS28......138 C2
Parsons Gate BA7......214 B7
Parsons Gn
  Clevedon BS21 ....16 C8
  Weston-super-Mare BS22 ..32 A3
Parson's La
  Houndstone BA22 ......186 D2
  Kingsdon TA11........173 D5
Parsons' La TA5........152 A7
Parsons Mead BS48 .....19 F7
Parsons Paddock BS14 ..23 A7
Parsons Pen BS27 ....90 B7
Parsons Rd TA9........104 C4
Parson's St TA24.......124 A3
Parsons Way
  Wells BA5.............203 B4
  Winscombe BS25........69 E6
Partis Coll BA1 ....44 A8
Partis Way BA1 ....44 A8
Partition St BS1.......226 C2
Partman's Hill BA3.....116 B3
Partridge Cl
  Moorlinch TA7 ....155 F7
  Weston-super-Mare BS22 ..31 F1
Partway La
  Chard Junction TA20....198 F6
  East Chinnock BA22 ....196 F7
Passage Leaze BS11.......4 D6
Passage St BS2.........227 B2
Pastures Ave BS22.......32 C3
Pastures The BA15.......64 E3
Patch Croft BS21........16 C8
Patch St BA2............42 A2
Patchwood Rd BS48......20 F7
Pathe Rd TA7..........155 B1
Pathfinder Terr ▤ TA6 ..209 B4
Patrick's Way TA3......181 D8
Patrum Cl TA1.........212 B1
Patson Hill La DT9......188 B5
Patterson Ho ▤ BS1.....227 B1
Pattinson Rd BS21.....219 D6
Pattons TA3............169 C1
Patwell Ct BA10.......215 E6
Patwell St BA10.......215 E6
Paulet EX16............178 C1
Paull's La TA19........183 B2
Paulman Gdns BS41......20 F8
Paulmont Rise BS39.....58 E1
Pauls Rd TA11.........211 C3
Paul St
  Bristol BS2...........226 C4
  Frome BA11...........119 F5
  Shepton Mallet BA4 ...205 B6
  Taunton TA1 ....212 F3
Paulto' Hill BA3, BS39....78 B6
PAULTON 77 F5
Paulton Inf Sch BS39....77 E5

Paulton Jun & Inf Sch
  BS39 ....77 E5
Paulton Jun Sch BS39 ....77 E5
Paulton La BA2, BA3 ......78 D7
Paulton Memorial Hospl
  BS39 ....77 F4
Paulton Rd
  Farrington Gurney BS39 ..77 B4
  Hallatrow BS39 ....77 B7
  Midsomer Norton BA3 ....77 F1
Paulwood Rd BS39.......58 E1
Pavement The TA3......170 B4
Pavey Cl BS13...........22 C4
Pavey Rd BS13..........22 C4
Pavyotts La BA22.......197 E8
Pawelski Cl BA4........142 B7
PAWLETT..............136 A5
Pawlett BS24............49 A2
Pawlett Mead Dro TA6...136 A5
Pawlett Prim Sch TA6....135 F5
Pawlett Rd
  Bristol BS13............22 C3
  Walpole TA6...........136 A4
  West Huntspill TA6, TA9 ..136 A4
Pawlett Wlk BS13........22 C3
Paybridge Rd BS13.......21 F4
Payne Rd BS24..........49 D2
Paynes Ho ▤ BS23.......48 E8
Paynes La TA7.........155 C2
Payne's La TA12........185 E8
PAYTON...............179 F7
Payton Rd
  Holywell Lake TA21.....179 F7
  Rockwell Green TA21....222 A5
Paywell La BS40.........72 E5
Peacehay La TA21......179 E4
Peach Tree Cl TA6......209 E5
Peacocks Cl TA21.......180 F7
Peacocks Hill TA11......158 A2
Peadon La TA5..........134 C4
Peak La
  Compton Dundon TA11 ..157 A2
  Shepton Beauchamp TA19 ..184 D3
Peaky Corner Dro TA7...156 A4
PEAR ASH 161 E2
Pear Ash La BA9........161 E2
Pearce Dr TA9..........104 D4
Pearl Cl TA6...........209 C8
Pearmain Rd
  Somerton TA11.........211 B4
  Street BA16 ....207 B4
Pearse Cl BS22..........32 B5
Pearson Ho BA21.......219 A6
Peart Cl BS13...........21 E5
Peart Dr BS13...........21 E4
Pear Tree Ave BS41......20 E8
Peartree Cl BS13........22 B4
Pear Tree Cl
  Bridgwater TA6 ......209 D4
  Westleigh EX16 ....179 A4
Peartree Field BS20.......2 F5
Peartree Gdns BS24......67 C6
Pear Tree Ind Est BS40...53 C4
Pear Tree La TA6.......136 A4
Pear Tree Way TA21.....222 F7
Peartwater Hill TA5.....152 D8
Peartwater Rd TA5......152 D7
PEASEDOWN ST JOHN 79 C8
Peasedown St John Prim Sch
  BA2....................79 C7
PEASMARSH...........194 B7
Peats Hill BS39..........40 F5
Pebbles Orch TA19......184 E4
PECKING MILL 159 D8
Pecking Mill Rd BA4....141 E1
Pedder Rd BS21 ....6 D1
Peddles Cl TA10........171 D4
Peddles La TA11........173 E8
Pedlars Gr
  Chapmanslade BA13 ...121 C4
  Frome BA11...........119 E2
PEDWELL..............156 A7
Pedwell Cvn Pk TA7....156 A7
Pedwell Hill TA7........156 A7
Pedwell La TA7.........156 A7
Peel Ct TA23...........202 C7
Peel St BS5............227 C4
Peerage Ct TA24........201 A6
Pegasus Ct ▤ BA20.....219 B4
Pegasus Pl BS25 ....51 F4
Peggy's La TA18........196 C5
Peile Dr TA2...........212 E7
Peir Cl BS20..............2 E7
Pelham Ct TA6.........209 D7
Pelican Cl BS22..........49 F8
Pelting Dro BA5.........92 D1
Pembroke Ave BS11.......4 E6
Pembroke Cl
  Burnham-on-S TA8 .....85 B1
  Taunton TA1 ....212 C1
  Yeovil BA21 ....219 E7
Pembroke Ct BS21 ....6 C4
Pembroke Gr BS8.......226 A3
Pembroke Ho ▤ BS23 ...30 C1
Pembroke Mans BS8 ....226 A4
Pembroke Pl BS8.......226 A1
Pembroke Rd
  Bridgwater TA6 ......209 C3
  Bristol BS8...........226 A4
  Bristol, Shirehampton BS11 ...4 E6
  Portishead BS20 ....1 E4
  Weston-super-Mare BS23 ..48 F4
Pembroke St BS2.......227 B4
Pembroke Vale BS8 .....226 A4
Pemswell Rd TA24......200 F8
Penarth Dr BS24.........49 A1

Penarth Rd TA6........208 D4
Pen Cross BA22........197 B6
Pendle CB25............70 A7
Pendlesham Gdns BS23 ..31 A1
PENDOMER............197 B5
Pendomer Rd BA22......197 B5
Pendragon Pk BA6......206 D5
Pen Elm Cotts TA2.....168 B5
Pen Elm Hill TA2.......168 B6
Penel Orlieu TA6.......208 F4
Penfield BA21..........219 C5
Pen Hill BA9 ....161 C4
Penlea Ave TA6........208 E2
Penlea Cl TA6..........208 E2
Penlea Ct BS11 ....4 D7
Penleigh Rd
  Wells BA5.............111 F2
  Wells BA5.............203 B6
Pen Mill Hill SP8, BA12 ..161 F2
Pen Mill Inf Sch BA21...219 D6
Pen Mill Trad Est BA21...219 F6
Penmoor Pl TA8..........84 F5
Penmoor Rd TA8.........84 F5
Penmore Rd BA22, DT9 ..188 B7
Pennant Pl BS20..........2 F7
Pennard BS24...........49 A2
Pennard Ct
  Bath BA2 ....44 A6
  Bristol BA14 ....23 B5
Pennard Gn BA2.........44 A6
Pennard La BA6.........140 A2
Penn Cl
  Cheddar BS27 ....90 C7
  Wells BA5.............112 E2
Penn Ct BS26...........70 C2
Penneys Piece BA11.....120 C6
Penn Gdns BA1..........44 A8
Penn Hill BA20.........219 B4
Penn Hill La BS31........24 C3
Penn Hill Pk BA20......219 B4
Penn Hill Rd BA1........27 A1
Pennine Gdns BS23......31 A1
Penn La BA22...........197 A6
Pennlea BS13...........22 C7
Penn Lea Ct BA1.........44 B8
Penn Lea Rd BA1.........44 B8
PENN MILL 219 E6
Pennon Rise BS1.......226 C1
Penn Rd BS27...........90 C7
Penn St BS1...........227 B3
Penns The BS21...........6 E2
PENNSYLVANIA 12 F7
Pennsylvania Vw BA1....27 E4
Penn View BA9........216 D4
Penn Way BS26..........70 C1
Penny Batch La BA5....139 E8
Penny Cl TA21.........222 D7
Pennycress BS22.........49 D7
Pennycress Wy TA6.....208 E1
Penny Lea TA23........202 C6
Pennypost Dro TA10....173 B2
Pennyquick BA2.........43 D6
Pennyquick Hill BA2.....43 F4
Pennyquick View BA2....43 F6
Penny's Meade TA19....183 F4
Pennywell Est ▤ BS21....6 D2
Pennywell Rd BS2......227 C4
Penpole Ave BS11.........4 E6
Penpole Cl BS11..........4 E7
Penpole La BS11..........4 E7
Penpole Pk BS11..........4 E7
Penpole Pl BS11..........4 E6
Penrice Cl BS22.........31 C2
Penrose BS14...........22 F7
Penrose Dr TA6........208 E4
PENSELWOOD 161 C2
PENSFORD.............40 E4
Pensford Ct BS14........23 D5
Pensford Hill BS39.......40 D5
Pensford La BS39........40 A3
Pensford Old Rd BS39....40 E3
Pensford Prim Sch BS39 ..40 D4
Pensford Way BA11.....120 D2
Pentagon The BS9 ....5 B5
Pental La BA3..........116 C1
Penthouse Hill BA1......28 F3
Pentire Ave BS13........22 A6
Pentridge La DT10......190 E2
Penzoy Ave TA6........209 B4
Penzoy Dro TA7........154 E6
Peploe Wy ▤ TA6.......209 B4
Pepperall Rd TA9.......104 D4
Peppershells La BS39....41 C6
Pepys Cl BS31...........25 D2
Pera Pl BA1............228 C4
Pera Rd BA1............228 C4
Perch Hill BA5.........110 E6
Percivale Rd BA21......218 D7
Percival Rd BS8.........11 F8
Percy Pl ▤ BA1..........28 B1
Percy Rd BA21..........219 D6
Percy Terrace BA2........44 D6
Peregrine Cl BS22.......31 F1
Perfect View BA1........28 A1
Peridot Cl TA6.........209 C8
PERITON..............200 D6
Periton Cross TA24.....200 D6
Periton Ct TA24........200 D6
Periton La TA24........200 D7
Periton Mead Sch TA24 ..200 D6
Periton Rd TA24........200 D6
Periton Rise TA24......200 D6
Periton Way TA24......200 D6
Peritrack La BS23........49 B4
Perkins Ct BA5.........203 B4
Perley La
  Luxborough TA23 ......148 D8
  Luxborough TA23 ......130 D1

Perrett Ho ▤ BS2.......227 C3
Perretts Ct BS1........226 C1
Perrett Way BS20........4 E4
Perridge Hill BA4......140 D4
Perrin Cl BS39..........76 E8
Perrings The BS48.......18 E8
Perrins Hill BA22.......186 A6
Perrott Hill Sch TA18...196 B4
Perrow La BS28..........89 C2
Perry Cl BA3............78 D1
Perry Court E-Act Acad
  BS14..................23 A6
Perrycroft Ave BS13......22 A6
Perrycroft Rd BS13......22 A6
PERRY GREEN.........208 B8
Perry Green Rd TA5.....135 D1
Perry Hill TA11.........174 D8
Perry Hill Rd TA11......211 D2
Perry La TA9...........106 F5
Perry Lake La BA5......139 B7
Perrymans Cl BS30.......12 A8
PERRYMEAD...........45 B3
Perrymead
  Bath BA2 ....45 B3
  Weston-super-Mare BS22 ..32 B5
Perrymead Ct BA2.......45 B4
Perrymead Pl BA2.......45 B4
Perry Mead Rd BS40.....75 C5
Perry New Rd TA22.....163 F4
Perry Pl BA21..........219 C5
Perry Rd
  Blackford TA9.........107 A6
  Bristol BS1...........227 A3
  Long Ashton BS41 ......20 F8
Perry's Cider Mills ★ TA19 194 E7
Perry's Cl BS27..........90 A7
Perrys Hill BA20........218 C5
Perry St TA20..........198 D8
PERRY STREET.........198 D8
Pesley Cl BS13..........22 A4
Pesters La TA11........211 E3
Pestlefield La TA3......170 C1
Petercole Dr BS13.......22 A6
Peter's Gore DT6.......199 B1
Peterside BS39..........76 E8
Peterson Ave ▤ BS13 ...22 C4
Peterson Sq BS13.......22 C3
Peter St
  Shepton Mallet BA4 ...205 B6
  Taunton TA1 ....212 F6
  Yeovil BA20 ....219 B4
Petherton Gdns BS14....23 B7
Petherton Rd
  Bristol BS14..........23 B7
  North Newton TA7 .....153 F2
Pethick Ho BS4..........22 F8
Peto Garden at Iford Manor
  The ★ BA15 ....64 E3
Peto Gr BA15...........64 F3
Petrel Cl TA6..........209 D7
Petter's Way BA20......219 B4
Petticoat La BA4.......205 B6
Pettitts Cl DT9.........187 E1
PETTON...............165 A3
Petton Cross EX16......165 A3
Petvin Cl BA16.........207 D4
Petvins Ct TA18........196 C5
Pevensey Wlk BS4.......22 D7
Pharmacy Flats The DT10 190 F6
Pheasant Row BS49......16 F2
Pheasant The TA19......184 E1
Phelps Cl TA20.........223 D6
Philippa Cl BS14........23 A7
Philips Ho ▤ BS2.......227 B4
Phillip Ho TA6.........208 F2
Phillips Cl TA6.........208 D4
Phillip's Dro TA3.......170 D7
Phillips Rd BS23.........49 A6
Phillis Hill BS39.........77 F4
Phippen St ▤ BS1.......227 B1
Phoenix Acad TA6.......153 F3
Phoenix Ct
  Frome BA11...........119 D4
  Taunton TA1 ....212 F3
Phoenix Ho
  Bath BA1 ....228 B4
  Frome BA11...........119 D4
Phoenix Rd TA6.........209 B3
Phoenix Terr TA8.......104 B6
Phoenix Way BS20........2 F6
Piazza BA16............207 B5
PIBSBURY.............172 C5
Piccadilly Pl BA1.........45 B8
Piccadilly Ho ▤ BA4....205 B6
Pickeridge Cl TA2.......213 B7
Picket La DT8..........196 C1
Pickett La BA21........219 A7
PICKNEY..............168 B8
Pickney La TA2.........168 B7
Pickpurse La TA4.......150 E8
Pickwick Rd BA1........28 A2
Picts Hill TA10.........172 B6
PICT'S HILL...........172 B6
Picts Hill Rd TA10......172 B6
Piece TA19.............184 E4
Piece La TA19..........184 E4
Piece Rd DT9..........217 C3
Piece The ▤ TA16.......195 F7
Pier Rd BS20.............2 E7
Pierrepont Pl ▤ BA1....228 C2
Pierrepont St BA1......228 C2
Piers Rd BA4...........142 A6
Pier St TA8............104 A6
Piffin La TA4...........167 E8
Pigeon House Dro BS13 ..22 D4
Pigeon La BS40..........36 E1
Pig Hill BA22...........197 A7
Pightley La TA5.........152 F6

Pightley Rd TA5 . . . . .152 E7
Pig La TA7 . . . . .154 D8
Pig Market La TA1 . . . . .212 F3
Pigott Ave BS13 . . . . .22 A4
Pigs Hill La TA5 . . . . .134 D1
Pike Cl BA6 . . . . .206 C5
Pike Hill BA4 . . . . .205 A7
Pike La BA4 . . . . .205 B6
Pikes Cres
  Dunster TA24 . . . . .201 D2
  Taunton TA1 . . . . .212 E1
Pilcorn St BS28 . . . . .108 C4
Pile La
  Curry Mallet TA3 . . . . .183 C8
  Stourton Caundle DT10 . . . . . . .189 F3
Piles Mill La
  Luccombe TA24 . . . . .129 C8
  Selworthy TA24 . . . . .123 C3
Piley La TA21 . . . . .179 D8
Pilgrims Way
  Bristol BS11 . . . . .4 C7
  Chew Stoke BS40 . . . . .56 D8
  Lovington BA7 . . . . .158 E2
  Weston-super-Mare BS22 . . . .31 E3
Pilgrim's Way TA6 . . . . .135 F5
PILL 4 C4
Pillar La BA11 . . . . .99 D4
Pill Bridge Dro TA12 . . . . .173 B2
Pill Bridge La BA22 . . . . .173 D1
Pill Head La TA18 . . . . .196 C4
Pill Mdw LA18 . . . . .177 E2
Pillmead La BS28 . . . . .108 D5
Pillmoor Dro BA5 . . . . .139 F6
Pillmoor La BA5 . . . . .139 F6
Pillmore La
  Highbridge TA9 . . . . .105 A4
  Watchfield TA9 . . . . .105 C4
Pill Rd
  Abbots Leigh BS8 . . . . .4 F1
  Pill BS20 . . . . .4 E2
  Rooks Bridge BS26, TA9 . . . . .87 C2
Pill St BS20 . . . . .4 D4
Pill Way BS21 . . . . .6 B2
Pilots Helm TA6 . . . . .153 E4
PILSDON 199 F2
Pilsdon La DT6 . . . . .199 F3
PILTON 140 F3
Pilton Hill BA4 . . . . .140 C4
Pilton Manor Vineyard★
  BA4 . . . . .140 E3
Pimms La BS22 . . . . .31 B3
Pimm's La BS22 . . . . .31 B2
Pimpernel Cl BA16 . . . . .207 B2
Pince's Knap TA20 . . . . .198 F5
Pinchay La BS40 . . . . .38 A4
Pinching Cl BA5 . . . . .203 E3
Pinckney Gn BA15 . . . . .46 E5
Pincombe Dro TA3 . . . . .170 F5
Pincushion Cnr BA22 . . . . . . .197 E6
Pine Ave TA20 . . . . .223 C6
Pine Cl
  Street BA16 . . . . .207 B3
  Taunton TA1 . . . . .213 D2
  Weston-super-Mare BS22 . . . . .31 D2
Pinecroft
  Bristol BS14 . . . . .22 F7
  Portishead BS20 . . . . .1 F6
Pine Ct
  Chew Magna BS40 . . . . .39 B3
  Frome BA11 . . . . .120 B7
  Keynsham BS31 . . . . .24 C4
  Radstock BA3 . . . . .79 A2
Pine Hill BS22 . . . . .31 D3
Pine Lea BS24 . . . . .67 B6
Pine Ridge Cl BS9 . . . . .5 C4
Pines Cl
  Chilcompton BA3 . . . . .96 D3
  Wincanton BA9 . . . . .216 C3
Pines Dro TA10 . . . . .156 C3
Pines Residential Site The
  BA11 . . . . .120 D8
Pines Way
  Bath BA2 . . . . .228 A2
  Radstock BA3 . . . . .79 A2
Pines Way Ind Est BA2 . . . . . .228 A2
Pine Tree Ave BA20 . . . . .218 F3
Pine Tree Cl TA6 . . . . .209 D4
Pinetree Rd BS24 . . . . .50 D4
Pine Wlk BA3 . . . . .78 E1
Pinewood BA11 . . . . .211 D4
Pinewood Ave BA3 . . . . .77 F1
Pinewood Dr TA11 . . . . .211 D4
Pinewood Gr BA3 . . . . .77 F1
Pinewood Rd BA3 . . . . .77 F1
Pinewood Way TA8 . . . . .65 F3
Pinford La DT9 . . . . .188 F3
Pinhay Rd BS13 . . . . .22 B6
Pinkham Hill TA20 . . . . .194 B6
Pinkhams Twist BS14 . . . . . . .23 A5
Pink Knoll Hollow DT9 . . . . . .188 C8
Pinksmoor La TA21 . . . . .179 C5
Pinkwood La BA10 . . . . .160 E2
Pinmore BA11 . . . . .119 E2
Pinney Cl TA11 . . . . .212 B1
Pinnockscroft TA8 . . . . .84 F5
Pintail Rd TA24 . . . . .201 C5
Pinter Cl TA8 . . . . .104 C6
Pioneer Ave BA2 . . . . .44 F1
Pipehouse BA2 . . . . .63 E4
Pipehouse La BA2 . . . . .63 F4
Pipe La BS1 . . . . .226 C2
Piper's Alley TA19 . . . . .221 B4
Pipers Cl BS26 . . . . .88 E6
Pipers Pl EX14 . . . . .191 F2
Pippard Cl BA16 . . . . .207 E5
Pippin Cl BA2 . . . . .79 D7
Pippin Rd TA2 . . . . .169 C5

Pippins The
  Portishead BS20 . . . . .2 F5
  Wembdon TA6 . . . . .208 D6
Pipplepen La DT8, TA18 . . . . .196 B2
Pistle's La TA13 . . . . .185 B1
Pitchcombe Gdns BS9 . . . . .5 D7
Pitcher's Hill TA2 . . . . .168 F7
Pitching The BA7 . . . . .214 C5
Pitch & Pay La BS9 . . . . .5 E3
Pitch & Pay Pk BS9 . . . . .5 E3
PITCOMBE 215 D3
Pitcombe Hill BA10 . . . . .215 B2
Pitcombe La TA4 . . . . .165 B5
Pitcombe Rock BA10 . . . . .215 C3
PITCOT 115 F7
Pitcot La BA3 . . . . .115 F7
Pitfield Cnr BA22 . . . . .188 A7
Pitfour Terr BA2 . . . . .60 B2
Pithay Ct BS1 . . . . .227 A3
Pithay The
  Bristol BS1 . . . . .227 A3
  Paulton BS39 . . . . .77 E6
Pit Hill TA17 . . . . .195 B7
Pit Hill La TA1 . . . . .155 C7
Pit La
  Backwell BS48 . . . . .19 A4
  Sticklepath TA23 . . . . .149 D7
  Sutton Mallet TA7 . . . . .155 C7
  Ubley BS40 . . . . .55 F5
Pitman Ct BA1 . . . . .28 C2
Pitman Ho BA2 . . . . .44 D4
Pitman Rd BS23 . . . . .48 E6
Pitminster La TA20 . . . . .193 D8
PITMINSTER 181 E6
PITNEY 172 C7
Pitney Hill TA10 . . . . .172 C6
Pitney Moor Dro TA10 . . . . . .156 C2
Pit Rd
  Dinnington TA17 . . . . .195 C7
  Midsomer Norton BA3 . . . . . . .78 B1
PITSFORD HILL 150 E1
Pitsham La TA4 . . . . .164 E6
Pitt Ct TA10 . . . . .171 B3
Pitten St BA3 . . . . .116 E3
Pitt La
  Huish Champflower TA4 . . . . .165 E8
  Porlock Weir TA24 . . . . .123 C3
  Waterrow TA4 . . . . .165 F5
Pitts Cl TA1 . . . . .212 C1
Pitts La TA3 . . . . .183 F7
Pitt's La BS40 . . . . .39 B1
Pitway TA13 . . . . .220 D5
Pitway TA13 . . . . .220 D5
Pitway Cl BS39 . . . . .76 F4
Pitway Hill TA13 . . . . .220 D6
Pitway La BS39 . . . . .76 F4
Pixash Bsns Ctr BS31 . . . . .25 B5
Pixash La BS31 . . . . .25 C5
Pixey Hole La BS40 . . . . .55 E3
Pix La TA4 . . . . .167 B4
Pixton Way TA21 . . . . .163 E6
Pizey Ave
  Burnham-on-S TA8 . . . . .85 A1
  Clevedon BS21 . . . . .6 B2
Pizey Ave Ind Est BS21 . . . . . . .6 C2
Pizey Cl BS21 . . . . .6 B2
Place Dro TA7 . . . . .154 F4
Placket La BA20 . . . . .218 D1
Plain Pond TA4 . . . . .210 C5
PLAINSFIELD 152 B7
Plain The BA2 . . . . .81 E4
Plais St TA2 . . . . .212 E6
Plantaganet Chase BA20 . .218 D2
Plantagenet Pk BA20 . . . . .218 E3
Platterwell La (East Town La)
  BA4 . . . . .141 B3
Players La TA4 . . . . .85 A1
Playfield Cl ② BA8 . . . . .190 A6
Playford Gdns BS11 . . . . .4 E8
Playses Gn TA10 . . . . .184 D8
PLEAMORE CROSS 222 A2
Pleasant Pl BA1 . . . . .29 D2
Pleshey Cl BS22 . . . . .31 D2
Plimsoll Ho ③ BS1 . . . . .227 B1
Plot La DT9 . . . . .187 F5
Plott La BA8 . . . . .190 B7
Plough Cl BA16 . . . . .207 A4
Ploughed Paddock BS48 . . . . .8 D1
Plover Cl
  Milborne Port DT9 . . . . .217 C2
  Minehead TA24 . . . . .201 C5
  Weston-super-Mare BS22 . . . .31 F1
Plover Ct BA21 . . . . .218 D6
Plover Rd DT9 . . . . .217 C2
Plovers Rise BA3 . . . . .79 A3
Plowage La BA22 . . . . .174 D3
Plox BA10 . . . . .215 E6
Plox Gn BA10 . . . . .215 E6
Plucknett Row BA20 . . . . .218 D5
Plud Farm La TA5 . . . . .134 A5
Plud St BS28 . . . . .108 B3
Plumber's Barton ⑨ BA11 119 F4
Plumers Cl ④ BS21 . . . . .6 E1
Plum La TA6 . . . . .209 C2
Plumley Cres BS24 . . . . .50 A4
Plumley Ct BS23 . . . . .48 D4
PLUMMER'S HILL 77 E6
Plummer's La BA5 . . . . .92 D5
Plum Orch DT9 . . . . .187 F4
Plumptre Ave BA5 . . . . .203 F5
Plumptre Cl BS39 . . . . .77 E5
Plumptre Rd BS39 . . . . .77 E5
Plumtree Cl BS25 . . . . .52 A1
Plum Tree Rd BS22 . . . . .49 E8
Plunging Dr BA6 . . . . .206 F1
Plymor Rd TA9 . . . . .136 A8
Poachers End TA24 . . . . .201 C4
Pococks Yd TA10 . . . . .171 F5

Podgers Dr BA1 . . . . .27 B2
Podger's La TA19 . . . . .183 F4
PODIMORE 174 A3
Podimore La BA22 . . . . .174 A3
Podimore Rd BA22 . . . . .174 A3
Podium Sh Ctr The BA2 . . . . .228 C2
Poets Cnr BA3 . . . . .97 C8
Polden Bsns Ctr The TA6 . .136 B2
Polden Cl BS48 . . . . .8 E1
Polden Ct TA6 . . . . .209 B5
Polden Rd
  Portishead BS20 . . . . .2 E4
  Weston-super-Mare BS23 . . . . .48 F8
Polden St TA6 . . . . .209 B5
Polden View BA6 . . . . .206 E3
Polden Wk BA3 . . . . .97 B6
Polden Wlk TA7 . . . . .136 E3
Pole Rue La TA20 . . . . .193 C6
POLESHILL 166 C1
Polestar Way BS24 . . . . .50 A8
Polham La TA11 . . . . .211 D3
Police La BS39 . . . . .40 E3
Polkes Field TA3 . . . . .170 F6
Pollard Rd
  Bridgwater TA6 . . . . .209 D6
  Weston-super-Mare BS22 . . .49 F8
Pollards Ct TA24 . . . . .124 A3
Pollard's La TA21 . . . . .180 F7
Pollards Way TA1 . . . . .212 E4
POLSHAM 139 D5
Poltimore La TA20 . . . . .193 D8
Polygon Rd BS8 . . . . .226 A2
Polygon The ⑮ BS8 . . . . .11 F6
Pomeroy La BA14 . . . . .83 B6
Pomfrett Gdns BS14 . . . . .23 E5
Pond Cl ⑤ BA8 . . . . .190 A6
Pond Cotts BA3 . . . . .80 D2
Pond Head BS20 . . . . .4 D4
Pondhead Cross TA4 . . . . . . .202 E3
Pond La TA21 . . . . .179 D3
Pond Orch TA4 . . . . .150 B8
Pondpool La TA3 . . . . .170 C3
Pond Wlk DT10 . . . . .190 B4
Ponsford Rd
  Bristol BS14 . . . . .23 B8
  Minehead TA24 . . . . .201 A6
Pookfield Cl BA11 . . . . .143 B7
Pool Alley TA10 . . . . .172 B8
Poolbridge Rd BS28 . . . . .107 C4
Pool Cl TA7 . . . . .136 C4
POOLE 222 F8
Poole Cl BS13 . . . . .22 C5
Poole Hill TA22 . . . . .163 B5
Poole Ho BA2 . . . . .43 F5
Poole Ind Est TA21 . . . . .222 F8
Poolemead Rd BA2 . . . . .43 F5
Pooles Cl TA5 . . . . .134 A2
Pooles La TA20 . . . . .194 E1
Poole St BS11 . . . . .4 B8
Pooles Wharf BS8 . . . . .226 A1
Pooles Wharf Ct BS8 . . . . . . .226 A1
Pool Hill BS21 . . . . .165 E1
Pool La BS40 . . . . .38 A2
Pools Barn Rd TA5 . . . . .133 E7
POOLTOWN 148 E8
Poop Hill TA18 . . . . .196 C8
Poop Hill La TA18 . . . . .196 C8
Poor Hill BA2 . . . . .59 F6
Poorhouse La DT6 . . . . .199 E1
Pope Cl TA1 . . . . .168 D1
Popery La TA24 . . . . .129 E1
Pope's La
  Milborne Port DT9 . . . . .217 D2
  Rockwell Green TA21 . . . . . . .222 B4
Pope's Wlk BA2 . . . . .45 B3
Popham Cl
  Bridgwater TA6 . . . . .209 D5
  East Brent TA9 . . . . .86 D5
Popham Flats TA21 . . . . .222 D6
Popham Rd TA21 . . . . .222 F7
Pop La EX13, TA20 . . . . .198 B8
Poplar Ave BS9 . . . . .5 D6
Poplar Cl
  Bath BA2 . . . . .44 D4
  Frome BA11 . . . . .120 B7
Poplar Dr BA21 . . . . .218 C7
Poplar Dro TA10 . . . . .172 C3
Poplar Est TA9 . . . . .104 D3
Poplar Farm BA5 . . . . .111 A4
Poplar La
  Catcott TA7 . . . . .137 D1
  Mark TA9 . . . . .105 E3
Poplar Pl ⑯ BS23 . . . . .48 E8
Poplar Rd
  Bath BA2 . . . . .62 D8
  Bridgwater TA6 . . . . .209 D7
  Bristol, Highridge BS13 . . . . .21 F7
  Burnham-on-S TA8 . . . . .104 A8
  Street BA16 . . . . .207 C3
  Taunton TA1 . . . . .213 D2
Poplars Cl BA21 . . . . .187 A5
Poplars The
  Easton-in-G BS20 . . . . .4 B4
  Porlock TA24 . . . . .124 A3
  Weston-super-Mare BS22 . . .32 A1
Poplar Tree La BA14 . . . . .83 C2
Poplar Wlk BS24 . . . . .49 E5
Poples Bow TA9 . . . . .104 E5
Pople's La BA11 . . . . .117 F8
Pople's Well TA18 . . . . .224 B6
Poppy Cl
  Weston-super-Mare BS22 . . .32 A5
  Yeovil BA22 . . . . .218 B5
Poppy Rd TA11 . . . . .211 B3
Porch EX13 . . . . .198 A3
Porch Cl BA6 . . . . .206 C6
Porchestall Dro BA6 . . . . .206 B4
PORLOCK 124 A4

Porlock Cl
  ③ Clevedon BS21 . . . . .6 E1
  Weston-super-Mare BS23 . . .48 F2
Porlock Dr TA1 . . . . .212 C1
PORLOCKFORD 123 F4
Porlock Gdns BS48 . . . . .8 E1
Porlock Hill TA24 . . . . .123 F3
Porlock Rd
  Bath BA2 . . . . .45 A1
  Minehead TA24 . . . . .200 C7
Porlock Visitor Ctr★
  TA24 . . . . .124 A3
PORLOCK WEIR 123 D4
Porlock Weir Rd TA24 . . . . . .123 F4
Portal Rd BS24 . . . . .50 C4
PORTBURY 3 D3
Portbury Comm BS20 . . . . . . .2 E4
Portbury Gr BS11 . . . . .4 D6
Portbury Hundreds The
  BS20 . . . . .3 C4
Portbury La BS20 . . . . .9 E7
Portbury Way BS20 . . . . .3 E5
Portbury Wlk BS11 . . . . .4 D6
Portcullis Rd TA10 . . . . .172 A6
Porter's Hatch BA6 . . . . .138 C3
PORTFIELD 171 E5
Portfield La TA10 . . . . .171 F5
PORTISHEAD 2 B4
Portishead Bsns Pk BS20 . .2 E5
Portishead Lodge BS20 . . . . . .2 D6
Portishead Prim sch BS20 . . .2 E6
Portishead Rd BS22 . . . . .32 B4
Portishead Way BS3 . . . . .11 E3
Port La TA22 . . . . .164 A5
PORTLAND 207 A6
Portland Cl
  Cannington TA5 . . . . .135 B2
  Nailsea BS48 . . . . .8 D1
Portland Ct BS1 . . . . .226 B1
Portland Dr BS20 . . . . .2 E4
Portland Grange ⑥ TA1 . . . .212 E3
Portland Lofts ⑧ BS2 . . . . . .227 B4
Portland Mans ⑨ BS2 . . . . .227 B4
Portland Pl
  Bath BA1 . . . . .228 B4
  Brent Knoll TA9 . . . . .86 B1
  Bridgwater TA6 . . . . .208 D5
  Frome BA11 . . . . .119 D5
Portland Rd
  Bath BA1 . . . . .228 B4
  Frome BA11 . . . . .119 D5
  Langport TA10 . . . . .172 B5
  Street BA16 . . . . .207 A6
Portland Sq BS2 . . . . .227 B4
Portland St
  Bristol, Clifton BS8 . . . . .11 F7
  Taunton TA1 . . . . .212 E4
Portland Terr
  Bath BA1 . . . . .228 B4
  Watchet TA23 . . . . .202 C7
Portman Cres ⑨ TA6 . . . . . .153 F3
Portman Ct BA22 . . . . .196 E8
Portman Dr TA6 . . . . .153 E3
Portman Rd TA6 . . . . .153 E3
Portmans TA3 . . . . .170 B3
Portman St TA2 . . . . .212 F6
Portmeade Dro BS26 . . . . .70 C1
Portmeirion Cl BS14 . . . . .23 B5
Portnell's La BA12 . . . . .161 F2
Portobello Bldgs TA20 . . . . .223 B4
Portreeve Dr BA21 . . . . .219 B6
Port View BS20 . . . . .4 C5
Portview Rd BS11 . . . . .4 B8
Portview Trad Est BS11 . . . . . .4 B7
Portwall Dro TA7 . . . . .209 F5
Portwall La BS1 . . . . .227 B1
PORTWAY 207 D4
Portway
  Bristol, Shirehampton BS11 . . .4 C6
  Bristol, Sneyd Park BS8 . . . . . .5 C3
  Frome BA11 . . . . .120 A4
  Holford TA5 . . . . .133 D4
  Street BA16 . . . . .207 D4
  Wells BA5 . . . . .203 C4
Port Way BA2 . . . . .100 D7
Portway Ave BA5 . . . . .203 D4
Portway Gdns BA11 . . . . .120 A4
Portway Hill
  Batcombe BA4 . . . . .142 C1
  Bruton BA4 . . . . .159 F6
Portway La
  Binegar BA3 . . . . .95 E1
  Holford TA5 . . . . .133 E4
Portway Lodge ① BA5 . . . . . .203 C4
Portway Rd BA5 . . . . .174 E1
Portway Rdbt BS11 . . . . .4 C8
Portway Villas BA11 . . . . .120 A4
Positano Ct ② TA6 . . . . .208 E7
Poskitt Ho TA6 . . . . .208 F6
Post Cl TA21 . . . . .222 E4
Post La
  Malmsmead EX35 . . . . .122 C4
  Skilgate TA4 . . . . .164 E7
Post Office La
  Blagdon BS40 . . . . .54 D3
  Flax Bourton BS48 . . . . .19 F7
  Minehead TA24 . . . . .200 F7
  Tatworth TA20 . . . . .198 C8
Post Office Rd BS24 . . . . .50 C5
Post Office Yd DT8 . . . . .199 F7
Poston Way BA15 . . . . .64 E7
Pot La BA11 . . . . .120 F8
Potter's Cross TA4 . . . . .165 C7
POTTERS HILL 20 B1
Potters Ho ① BA4 . . . . .205 B6
Potters La TA20 . . . . .193 B6
Potters View BS49 . . . . .34 E2
Potterton Cl TA6 . . . . .208 F1

Pottery Cl BS23 . . . . .49 A6
Pottery Rd TA19 . . . . .183 C1
Pottery View TA19 . . . . .183 C1
Pottle St BA12 . . . . .144 D3
Potts Cl BA1 . . . . .28 F3
Poulett Cotts TA17 . . . . .195 D7
POUND 220 F2
Pound Cl
  Glastonbury BA6 . . . . .206 D5
  Stalbridge DT10 . . . . .190 B4
  Yeovil BA21 . . . . .218 C5
Pound Farm Cl TA6 . . . . .208 D3
Poundfield La TA3 . . . . .169 F6
Poundfield Rd TA24 . . . . .200 E6
Pound Fold BA5 . . . . .204 C7
Pound Hill TA21 . . . . .179 A5
Poundisford Cl TA1 . . . . .212 D1
Pound La
  Bishops Lydeard TA4 . . . . . . .151 F1
  Buckland St Mary TA20 . . . . .193 A8
  Downhead BA4 . . . . .117 A1
  Easton BA5 . . . . .111 A4
  Lydford Fair Place TA11 . . . . .158 C3
  Martock TA12 . . . . .185 D6
  Nailsea BS48 . . . . .8 D3
  Oakhill BA3 . . . . .115 B5
  Rawridge EX14 . . . . .191 F1
  Stocklinch TA19 . . . . .184 C4
  Yarcombe EX14 . . . . .192 E2
  Yarlington BA9 . . . . .175 F8
  Yeovil BA22 . . . . .218 A2
Pound Mead BS40 . . . . .37 C8
Pound Orch TA4 . . . . .151 C7
Pound Pool TA11 . . . . .211 C4
Pound Rd
  Axminster EX13 . . . . .198 F2
  Broadway TA19 . . . . .183 B2
  Pawlett TA6 . . . . .135 F5
Poundsclose TA22 . . . . .163 E4
Pound Terr ③ TA21 . . . . .222 D5
Pound The BS40 . . . . .36 D3
Pound Way TA10 . . . . .172 B3
Pounsell La TA10 . . . . .172 B5
Powell Cl TA3 . . . . .169 D4
Powell Ct BA5 . . . . .203 B4
Powells Acres BS21 . . . . .6 E3
Powis Cl BS22 . . . . .31 C2
Powlett Ct BA2 . . . . .45 B7
Powlett Rd BA2 . . . . .45 B8
Pow's Hill BA3 . . . . .78 D5
Pow's Orch BA3 . . . . .78 A1
Powy's Gn DT9 . . . . .225 C4
Powy's La DT9 . . . . .225 C4
POYNTINGTON 188 E6
Poyntz Rd BS4 . . . . .22 F8
Prankerds Rd DT9 . . . . .217 C2
Preachers Vale BA3 . . . . .116 F7
Preanes Gn BS22 . . . . .32 A2
Precinct The BS20 . . . . .2 D5
Prescot Cl BS22 . . . . .31 B2
PRESCOTT 179 C1
Prescott Rd EX15 . . . . .179 D1
PRESTLEIGH 141 D3
Prestleigh La BA4 . . . . .141 E4
Prestleigh Rd BA4 . . . . .141 E2
PRESTON 150 E6
PRESTON BOWYER 167 B5
Preston CE Prim Sch
  BA21 . . . . .218 C7
Preston Cross TA4 . . . . .150 E6
Preston Gr BA20 . . . . .218 F5
Preston La TA4 . . . . .150 E6
PRESTON PLUCKNETT 218 D4
Preston Rd
  Yeovil BA21 . . . . .218 E5
  Yeovil, Houndstone BA22 . . . .218 B5
Preston Road Rdbt BA21 . . . .218 C5
Preston Sch BA21 . . . . .218 D5
Prestor ⑨ BA3 . . . . .198 A1
Pretwood Cl TA19 . . . . .221 C3
Prewett St BS1 . . . . .227 B1
Prey La TA3 . . . . .182 D7
Preywater Rd BA5 . . . . .139 D8
Prices Ave TA21 . . . . .222 D7
Prices Bldgs TA6 . . . . .209 A4
Priddles La TA20 . . . . .193 C8
PRIDDY 92 D3
Priddy Cl
  Bath BA2 . . . . .44 B5
  Frome BA11 . . . . .120 C7
Priddy Ct BS14 . . . . .23 B5
Priddy Dr BS14 . . . . .23 B5
Priddy Mill Dro BA5 . . . . .92 A4
Priddy Nine Barrows★ BA5 . .92 F4
Priddy Prim Sch BA5 . . . . . . .92 D3
Priddy Rd BA5 . . . . .112 E8
Priddy Veal La BA5 . . . . .111 A5
Priestlands DT9 . . . . .225 D5
Priestlands La DT9 . . . . .225 D5
Priestley Way TA8 . . . . .104 C5
Priest Row BA5 . . . . .203 D4
Priest's House★ TA10 . . . . . .172 A3
Priest St TA4 . . . . .202 C2
Priests Way BS22 . . . . .31 D2
Prigg La TA13 . . . . .220 C4
Primmerfield La BA3 . . . . .94 C8
Primore Rd TA7 . . . . .169 F8
Primrose Alley BA2 . . . . .42 D2
Primrose Cl TA11 . . . . .211 B3
PRIMROSE HILL 27 D1
Primrose Hill
  Bath BA1 . . . . .27 D1
  Charlton Mackrell TA11 . . . . .173 F7
  East Coker BA22 . . . . .197 B7
  Nunney BA11 . . . . .143 B8

Primrose Hill Pk Homes
TA11 ... 173 F7
Primrose La
Midsomer Norton BA3 ... 78 B1
Yeovil BA21 ... 187 D5
Primrose Wlk TA6 ... 208 D1
Prim Sch
Langport TA10 ... 172 A5
North Petherton TA6 ... 153 F3
Wincanton BA9 ... 216 C3
Prince Philip Cl TA20 ... 223 B3
Princes Bldgs BA1 ... 228 B3
Prince's Bldgs 17 BS8 ... 11 F6
Prince's Cl 11 TA14 ... 185 F4
Princes' La BS8 ... 11 F6
Princes Rd BA5 ... 203 D4
Prince's Rd
Clevedon BS21 ... 6 D3
Shepton Mallet BA4 ... 205 C6
Street BA16 ... 207 B5
Princess Anne Rd BA11 ... 120 A7
Princess Cl
Keynsham BS31 ... 24 E4
12 North Petherton TA6 ... 153 F4
Princess Rd TA1 ... 212 D2
Princess Row BS2 ... 227 A4
Princess St TA8 ... 104 B7
Princes St
Bath BA1 ... 228 B2
Taunton TA1 ... 213 B4
Yeovil BA20 ... 219 B5
Prince's St
Bristol BS2 ... 227 C4
Clandown BA3 ... 78 E5
Princess Victoria St BS8 ... 11 F6
Prince St BS1 ... 227 A1
Prince Street Rdbt BS1 ... 227 A2
Printers Ct 32 TA12 ... 185 E6
Printworks Rd BA11 ... 120 A3
Prior Park Bldgs BA2 ... 45 B5
Prior Park Coll BA2 ... 45 C4
Prior Park Cotts BA2 ... 228 C1
Prior Park Gdns BA2 ... 45 B5
Prior Park Landscape Gdn*
BA2 ... 45 C3
Prior Park Rd BA2 ... 45 B4
Priors Hill BA2 ... 60 A2
Prior's Wlk TA1 ... 212 F4
PRIORSWOOD ... 213 B7
Priorswood Ind Est TA2 ... 213 B6
Priorswood Pl 8 TA2 ... 213 A8
Priorswood Prim Sch
Priorswood TA2 ... 213 A6
Taunton TA2 ... 212 F6
Taunton TA2 ... 212 F6
Priorswood Rd TA2 ... 213 A6
Priory TA21 ... 222 E6
Priory Ave TA1 ... 213 A4
Priory Bridge Rd TA1 ... 213 A5
Priory Cl
Bath BA2 ... 45 B2
Cannington TA5 ... 135 C2
Castle Cary BA7 ... 214 B5
Chilton Polden TA7 ... 137 B2
Ilchester BA22 ... 173 E1
Midsomer Norton BA3 ... 78 A1
Yeovil BA20 ... 218 D1
Priory Com Sch BS22 ... 32 B3
Priory Ct
Bridgwater TA6 ... 208 F4
9 Stoke sub Hamdon TA14 ... 185 F4
5 Taunton TA1 ... 213 A4
Wellington TA21 ... 222 E7
Priory Farm Trad Est BS20 ... 3 D3
Priory Fields TA1 ... 213 A5
Priory Fields Ret Pk TA1 ... 213 A5
Priorygate Ct BA7 ... 214 B6
Priory Gdns
Bristol, Shirehampton BS11 ... 4 D7
Burnham-on-S TA8 ... 104 B6
Easton-in-G BS20 ... 4 B4
Wellington TA21 ... 222 E6
Priory Glade BA21 ... 218 C6
Priory Gn TA24 ... 201 E2
Priory Hill TA5 ... 134 C5
Priory Hospl BA5 ... 203 C3
Priory Mead BA10 ... 215 F8
Priory Mews BS23 ... 49 B7
Priory Path BA7 ... 214 C5
Priory Pl BA5 ... 203 D3
Priory Rd
Bristol BS8 ... 226 C4
Bristol, Shirehampton BS11 ... 4 D6
Chilton Polden TA7 ... 137 B2
Easton-in-G BS20 ... 4 B4
Ilchester BA22 ... 173 E1
Keynsham BS31 ... 24 E7
Portbury BS20 ... 3 D3
Wells BA5 ... 203 D3
Weston-super-Mare BS23 ... 49 A7
Priory Sch The TA2 ... 213 B7
Priory View BA7 ... 214 B6
Priory Villas BA9 ... 216 C3
Priory Way TA1 ... 213 B5
Priory Way Ind Est TA1 ... 213 B5
Priory Wlk
Portbury BS20 ... 3 D3
Taunton TA1 ... 213 A5
PRISTON ... 61 B5
Priston Cl BS22 ... 32 B5
Priston Hill BA2 ... 61 C5
Priston La
Farmborough BA2 ... 60 C7
Farmborough BA2 ... 60 C8
Priston BA2, BA3 ... 61 A5
Priston Rd BA2 ... 61 D6
Pritchard St BS2 ... 227 B4
Private Rd
North Brewham BA11 ... 161 E8
Staplegrove TA2 ... 212 D7
Privet Dr BS13 ... 22 C5
Proctor Dr BS23 ... 49 B4
Proctor Ho BS1 ... 227 B1
Proctor Rd TA21 ... 222 D8
Prophet's La TA14 ... 185 E3
Prospect Cl
East Brent TA9 ... 86 E5
Shepton Mallet BA4 ... 205 A6
Prospect Gdns BA1 ... 28 F5
Prospect Ho BS22 ... 31 E3
Prospect Pl
Bath, Beacon Hill BA1 ... 28 A1
Bathford BA1 ... 29 D2
Bath, Weston BA1 ... 27 C2
9 Weston-super-Mare BS23 ... 48 E8
Prospect Rd BA2 ... 45 C4
Prospect Row TA18 ... 224 F3
Prospect Villas BA4 ... 159 C7
Protheroes Ho BS1 ... 226 C2
Proud Cross BS40 ... 74 E4
Providence Ct BA11 ... 120 A3
Providence La BS41 ... 10 F2
Providence Pl
Bristol BS2 ... 227 C2
Bruton BA10 ... 215 D6
PROVIDENCE PLACE ... 77 F1
Providence Rise BS41 ... 10 F2
Providence View BS41 ... 11 A1
Provident Pl TA6 ... 208 E5
Prowle's Cross BA22 ... 197 F5
Prowse's La BS26 ... 70 A1
Prowses Mdw TA2 ... 168 B4
PUBLOW ... 40 F5
Publow La BS39 ... 40 E5
PUCKINGTON ... 184 B5
Pud Brook DT9 ... 217 D1
Pudding Pie Cl BS40 ... 53 A5
Pudding Pie La BS40 ... 53 A6
Puddle Town TA18 ... 196 B5
Puddy's La TA9 ... 105 D4
PUDLEIGH ... 223 B8
Pudleigh La TA20 ... 223 B8
Puffin Cl
Minehead TA24 ... 201 C5
Weston-super-Mare BS22 ... 49 F8
Pullen Ct BA4 ... 205 B4
Pulmans La TA18 ... 224 C5
Pulpitsway Dro TA12 ... 185 A8
Pulteney Ave BA2 ... 45 B6
Pulteney Bridge BA2 ... 228 C2
Pulteney Gdns BA2 ... 45 B6
Pulteney Gr BA2 ... 45 B6
Pulteney Mews 4 BA2 ... 45 B7
Pulteney Rd BA2 ... 45 B6
Pulteney Terr BA2 ... 45 B6
Pump La
Bathford BA1 ... 29 B2
Bristol BS1 ... 227 B1
Redhill BS40 ... 36 D2
Pump Sq BS20 ... 4 D5
Punnet Cl BS27 ... 90 B7
Puppy Cross Ways BA3 ... 94 F5
Puppy La BA3 ... 94 F5
Purcell Wlk BS4 ... 22 D7
Purdue Cl BS22 ... 32 B3
Purewell TA7 ... 136 C4
PURITON ... 136 C4
Puriton Hill TA7 ... 136 C3
Puriton Manor TA7 ... 136 C4
Puriton Pk TA7 ... 136 C4
Puriton Prim Sch TA7 ... 136 C4
Puriton Rd
Pawlett TA6 ... 136 A5
West Huntspill TA9 ... 136 B7
Purlewent Dr BA1 ... 27 C1
Purley Dr TA6 ... 209 D6
PURN ... 67 A7
Purnell Wy BS39 ... 77 D6
Purn La BS24 ... 67 A8
Purn Rd BS24 ... 66 F8
Purn Way BS24 ... 67 B7
PURSE CAUNDLE ... 189 D4
Purse Caundle Manor House*
DT9 ... 189 D4
Pursey Ave BA16 ... 207 E5
PURTINGTON ... 195 A4
Purving Row BS24 ... 67 C1
Purving Row La BS24 ... 67 C1
Putham La TA24 ... 129 F1
Putsham Hill TA5 ... 133 D5
Putsham Mead TA5 ... 133 D5
Puttingthorpe Dr BS22 ... 49 C7
Putts La DT9 ... 175 D1
Putt's La DT9 ... 188 D8
Puxley Cl BS14 ... 23 E6
PUXTON ... 33 D3
Puxton La BS24 ... 33 D3
Puxton Moor La BS24 ... 33 E2
Puxton Park (Adventure
Park)* BS24 ... 33 B3
Puxton Rd BS24 ... 33 C2
Pyde La TA10 ... 184 D6
Pye Cnr
Churchill BS25 ... 52 D4
Merriott TA16 ... 195 F6
Somerton TA11 ... 211 D4
Pye La TA20 ... 198 E8
PYLEIGH ... 151 B1
Pyleigh La TA4 ... 151 A1
Pyle La BA22 ... 174 A2
Pyles Thorne TA21 ... 222 F4
Pyles Thorne Cl TA21 ... 222 E5
Pyles Thorne Rd TA21 ... 222 E4
Pylewell La BS25 ... 52 D1
Pyle Well La TA11 ... 174 E8
PYLLE ... 141 B1
Pylle Hill BA4 ... 141 A1
Pylle La BA4 ... 141 B1
Pylle Rd BA4 ... 141 A2
Pyncombe La TA4 ... 210 B3
Pyne Point BS21 ... 6 C3
Pynne Cl BS14 ... 23 F5
Pynne Rd BS14 ... 23 F5
Pyracantha Wlk BS14 ... 23 A6
PYRLAND ... 213 A8
Pyrland Ave TA2 ... 212 F8
Pyrland Pl TA2 ... 213 A8
Pyrland Wlk TA6 ... 208 B4

Q

Quab La
Alston Sutton BS26 ... 88 F3
Wedmore BS28 ... 108 B5
Quab Lane Cl BS28 ... 108 B4
Quaish La BA4 ... 140 C4
Quaker's La
Hartswell TA4 ... 166 B6
Wiveliscombe TA4 ... 210 C3
Quakinghouse La TA4 ... 166 E5
Quantick Gdns TA24 ... 201 B5
Quantock Ave TA6 ... 208 D4
Quantock Cl
Burnham-on-S TA8 ... 104 B7
Midsomer Norton BA3 ... 97 B6
North Petherton TA6 ... 153 E4
Quantock Ct
Burnham-on-S TA8 ... 104 A5
Ilminster TA19 ... 221 C4
Street BA16 ... 207 B5
Williton TA4 ... 202 D2
Quantock Gr TA4 ... 202 E2
Quantock Ho TA6 ... 153 E4
Quantock Mdw TA6 ... 208 C5
Quantock Par TA6 ... 153 E4
Quantock Rd
Bridgwater TA5, TA6 ... 208 B5
Cannington TA5 ... 135 C1
Portishead BS20 ... 2 B5
Taunton TA2 ... 212 E8
Watchet TA23 ... 202 C6
Wellington TA21 ... 222 D7
Weston-super-Mare BS23 ... 48 E4
Quantock Rise
Kingston St Mary TA2 ... 168 E8
Pawlett TA6 ... 135 F5
Quantocks BA2 ... 45 A1
Quantock Terr TA6 ... 209 A6
Quantock View
Bishops Lydeard TA4 ... 167 F8
Highbridge TA9 ... 104 D3
Kilve TA5 ... 133 C6
Quantock Way
Bridgwater TA6 ... 208 C5
Kingston St Mary TA2 ... 168 D8
Quaperlake St BA10 ... 215 F7
Quarante-Ans BA4 ... 142 B7
Quarme La TA24 ... 147 E7
QUARR ... 177 E5
Quarr BA4 ... 205 C6
Quarr Cross SP8 ... 177 E4
Quarr Dr DT9 ... 225 D6
Quarr La DT9 ... 225 D6
Quarr Lane Pk DT9 ... 225 D6
Quarry Batch
Street BA16 ... 207 A5
Walton BA16 ... 156 E7
Quarry Cl
Bath BA2 ... 44 F1
Limpley Stoke BA3 ... 64 D6
Minehead TA24 ... 201 B5
Quarry Cotts BA22 ... 197 F8
Quarry Hay BS40 ... 56 D8
Quarry Hill BA22 ... 175 F4
Quarry La
Blagdon Hill TA3 ... 181 D4
Bradford Abbas DT9 ... 187 E1
Butleigh BA6 ... 157 D3
Combe St Nicholas TA20 ... 193 D6
Kingston St Mary TA2 ... 168 F7
Quarrylands La BS26 ... 88 B4
Quarrymans Ct BA2 ... 45 B1
Quarry Rd
Bath BA2 ... 45 D6
Kingsdon TA11 ... 173 D5
Portishead BS20 ... 2 C4
Sandford BS25 ... 52 A2
Street BA16 ... 207 B4
Washford TA23 ... 131 F4
Quarry Rise BS24 ... 66 F8
Quarry Rock Gdns BA2 ... 45 D4
Quarry Vale Cotts BA2 ... 45 B1
Quarry Way BS48 ... 8 D2
Quarthill La TA4 ... 166 C5
Quartley Hill EX16 ... 164 E4
Quartly Dr TA1 ... 212 A3
Quay La TA24 ... 201 A8
Quays Ave BS20 ... 2 E5
Quayside TA6 ... 208 F5
Quay St
Bristol BS1 ... 227 A3
Minehead TA24 ... 201 A8
Quays The BS1 ... 226 C1
Quay W TA24 ... 125 D4
Quebec BA2 ... 44 A6
Quedam Sh Ctr 6 BA21 ... 219 B5
Queen Anne Ct TA24 ... 200 F7
QUEEN CAMEL ... 174 F3
Queen Charlotte St BS1 ... 227 A2
QUEEN CHARLTON ... 24 B3
Queen Charlton La BS14 ... 23 E2
Queen Elizabeth Ct
Bridgwater TA6 ... 209 A5
Street BA16 ... 207 C6
Queen Elizabeth's Hospital
Sch BS8 ... 226 B3
Queen Quay BS1 ... 227 A2
Queens Acre La TA3 ... 181 E6
Queen's Ave
Bristol BS8 ... 226 B3
Portishead BS20 ... 2 C5
Queens Cl TA20 ... 223 B2
Queen's Coll TA1 ... 212 D1
Queen's Coll Jun Sch TA1 212 D1
Queenscote BS20 ... 2 F5
Queens Cres TA14 ... 185 F5
Queen's Ct BS8 ... 226 B3
Queen's Down TA3 ... 169 C4
Queens Dr TA1 ... 168 D1
Queen's Dr BA2 ... 45 A2
Queens Gate BS9 ... 5 D5
Queens Gate Terr TA1 ... 213 A3
Queens Gr BA9 ... 161 E2
Queens Par BS1 ... 226 C2
Queen's Par BA1 ... 228 B3
Queen's Parade Pl BA1 ... 228 B3
Queens Pl BA2 ... 45 B5
Queen Sq
Bath BA1 ... 228 B2
Bristol BS1 ... 227 A2
North Curry TA3 ... 170 B4
Saltford BS31 ... 25 F3
Queen Square Ave 10
BS1 ... 227 A2
Queen Square Pl BA1 ... 228 B3
Queens Rd
Banwell BS29 ... 51 A3
Bradford Abbas DT9 ... 187 E1
Frome BA11 ... 119 D4
Keynsham BS31 ... 24 D4
Minehead TA24 ... 201 A6
Nailsea BS48 ... 8 D1
Portishead BS20 ... 1 E4
Somerton TA11 ... 211 D4
Street BA16 ... 207 B5
Wellington TA21 ... 222 E4
Queen's Rd
Bridgwater TA6 ... 208 F2
Bristol BS8 ... 226 B3
Bristol, Bishopsworth BS13,
BS41 ... 21 F4
Clevedon BS21 ... 6 D3
Evercreech BA4 ... 141 E2
Radstock BA3 ... 79 B2
Shepton Mallet BA4 ... 205 A5
Weston-super-Mare BS23 ... 30 D1
Queens Row BS27 ... 90 C8
Queens Sq TA9 ... 104 C4
Queen St
Bath BA1 ... 228 B2
Bridgwater TA6 ... 208 F5
Bristol BS2 ... 227 B3
Keinton Mandeville TA11 ... 158 A1
North Petherton TA6 ... 153 F4
Taunton TA1 ... 213 B4
Tintinhull BA22 ... 186 B7
11 Wells BA5 ... 203 D4
Yarlington BA9 ... 175 F8
Queens Terr TA1 ... 213 A3
Queen's Terr
Sherborne DT9 ... 225 D6
Wiveliscombe TA4 ... 210 C4
Queensway
Taunton TA1 ... 212 B1
Yeovil BA20 ... 219 A4
Queens Way BS20 ... 1 E4
Queen's Way BS22 ... 31 F4
Queensway Cl TA9 ... 106 E5
Queensway Ctr BS22 ... 32 B2
Queensway Pl BA20 ... 219 A4
Queenswood Rd TA6 ... 208 C4
Queenwood Ave BA1 ... 28 A1
Quicksilver Rdbt BA20 ... 218 F2
Quickthorn Cl BS14 ... 23 A6
Quiet St BA1 ... 228 B2
Quilter Gr BS4 ... 22 D7
Quirke St TA24 ... 200 F7

R

Raby Mews BA2 ... 45 B7
Raby Pl BA2 ... 45 B7
Raby Villas BA2 ... 45 B7
Rackclose Gdns TA20 ... 223 A4
Rackclose Ho TA20 ... 223 A4
Rackclose Pk TA20 ... 223 B4
Rackfield TA21 ... 222 A5
Rackfield Pl BA2 ... 44 B6
Rackhay BS1 ... 227 A2
Rackhouse La TA5 ... 152 D4
Rackley La
Buckland St Mary TA20 ... 182 B1
Compton Bishop BS26 ... 69 B2
Rackstile TA20 ... 223 A7
Rackvernal Ct BA3 ... 78 B1
Rackvernal Rd BA3 ... 78 B1
RADDINGTON ... 165 B4
Raddon Cl BA4 ... 205 B6
RADFORD ... 78 C8
Radford Hill
Camerton BA2, BA3 ... 78 C7
Timsbury BA2 ... 60 C1
Radigan La TA3, TA19 ... 183 C5
RADLET ... 134 C1
Radlet Cl TA2 ... 213 B7
Radnidge La EX16 ... 162 D4
RADSTOCK ... 78 E1
Radstock & District Mus*
BA3 ... 78 F2
Radstock Rd BA3 ... 78 C2
Raggal Dro BA6 ... 157 F6
Ragged Dro BA6 ... 158 A7
Rag Hill BA3 ... 79 D5
Rag La
Babcary BA22 ... 174 B6
Ilminster TA19 ... 221 B7
Yarcombe EX14 ... 192 D2
Raglan Cl
Bridgwater TA6 ... 209 D7
Chilcompton BA3 ... 96 C4
Raglan Ct 4 TA2 ... 212 F6
Ragland La BA1 ... 28 A2
Ragland St BA1 ... 28 A2
Raglan La BS40 ... 37 E7
Raglan Pl 20 BS23 ... 30 C1
Raglan's Cross TA4 ... 202 F2
Raglan Terr
Bath BA1 ... 28 A2
Yeovil BA21 ... 218 F7
Raglan Wlk BS31 ... 24 D4
Railford Hill BA11 ... 118 B3
Railway Arches BS2 ... 227 C2
Railway Cotts BA11 ... 143 C3
Railway La BA2 ... 62 D1
Railway Pl BA1 ... 228 C1
Railway St
Bath BA1 ... 228 C1
Taunton TA2 ... 212 F6
Railway Terr BA2 ... 79 E4
Railway View Pl BA3 ... 78 B2
Rainbow La TA3 ... 191 C7
Rainham Ct 2 BS23 ... 30 C1
Rains Batch BS40 ... 72 E6
Rainsbury Hill TA4 ... 164 F8
Raisey La TA20 ... 193 C7
Raleigh Cl
Bridgwater TA6 ... 209 C5
Saltford BS31 ... 25 D2
Raleigh Ct
Sherborne DT9 ... 225 E4
3 Weston-super-Mare BS23 ... 48 E5
Raleigh Ho TA6 ... 209 C5
Raleigh Rd DT10 ... 190 B4
Raleigh Rise BS20 ... 2 B5
Raliegh Pl DT9 ... 225 D2
Ralph Allen Dr BA2 ... 45 B3
Ralph Allen Sch BA2 ... 45 E2
Ralston Ct BA9 ... 216 C4
Rambler Way TA6 ... 208 E6
Ramon Ave TA23 ... 202 D7
Ramsay Cl BS22 ... 31 E4
Ramsay Way TA8 ... 104 C8
Ramscombe Forest Wlks*
TA5 ... 151 E8
Ramscombe La BA1 ... 28 F6
Ramsey La TA21 ... 179 F8
Ramshorn Cl TA1 ... 212 C2
Ramshorn Gn TA1 ... 212 D2
Ramshorn Pl TA1 ... 212 D3
Ranchways BS20 ... 1 F4
Randall Rd BS8 ... 226 B2
Randolph Ave BS13 ... 22 B5
Randolph Cl BS13 ... 22 B5
Randolph Rd BA11 ... 119 F4
Ranger Rd BA6 ... 206 C3
Rangoon Rd TA23 ... 202 E6
Rankers La BS39 ... 41 C5
Rank The
Coxley BA5 ... 139 F6
Maiden Bradley BA12 ... 144 C2
Vobster BA3 ... 117 D6
Ranscombe Ave BS22 ... 31 D2
Ransford BS21 ... 6 B1
Raphael Ct BS1 ... 227 B1
Rapide Wy
Weston-super-Mare BS24 ... 49 B4
Weston-super-Mare BS24 ... 49 C4
RAPPS ... 183 D3
Rapps La TA19 ... 183 D4
Raps Cl TA1 ... 213 E5
Raps Gn TA1 ... 213 E5
Rashwood La BA11 ... 118 B6
Ratleigh La DT9 ... 188 A3
Rattigan Cl TA8 ... 104 C6
Rattle Row TA24 ... 131 B4
Raven Cl BS22 ... 31 E1
Raven Ct BS9 ... 5 F8
Ravenhead Dr BS14 ... 23 B8
Ravensmead TA20 ... 223 C5
Ravenswood Sch BS48 ... 8 D3
Ravensworth Terr TA8 ... 104 B7
Rawle's Bldgs TA24 ... 124 A3
Rawlings La BS26 ... 88 E2
Rawlins Ave BS22 ... 32 A5
RAWRIDGE ... 191 F1
Rawridge Rd EX14 ... 191 F2
Rayens Cl BS41 ... 10 F1
Rayens Cross Rd BS41 ... 10 F1
Rayleigh Rd BS9 ... 5 E7
Raymar Flats TA19 ... 221 A4
Raymond St TA2 ... 212 E6
Raymore Rise BS41 ... 10 F1
Rayneswood BS23 ... 48 F8
Read Mead BA6 ... 206 E3
Reakes Cl BA5 ... 203 C4
Rebels Way BA6 ... 206 D5
Reckleford BA20, BA21 ... 219 B5
Reckleford Inf Sch BA21 ... 219 C5
Rector's Cl TA8 ... 65 F3
Rector's Way BS23 ... 48 F6
Rectory Cl
Farmborough BA2 ... 60 A6
6 North Petherton TA6 ... 153 E3
Staplegrove TA2 ... 212 C8
Wraxall BS48 ... 9 A2

Rectory Ct TA20. . . . . . . .193 D6
Rectory Dr
Burnham-on-S TA8. . . . . . .104 B8
Staplegrove TA2. . . . . . . .212 C7
Yatton BS49. . . . . .34 C7
Rectory Farm Cl BA22. . . .174 F3
Rectory Farm La BA2. . . . . .43 F2
Rectory Gdns TA20. . . . . . .193 D6
Rectory Hill
Chapel Allerton BS26. . . . . .88 D2
Pitney TA10. . . . . .172 C7
South Cadbury BA22. . . . .175 C3
Rectory La
Bleadon BS24. . . . . .67 C6
Compton Martin BS40. . . . .74 B5
Hardington Mandeville
BA22. . . . . .197 A6
Horsington BA8. . . . . .176 E2
Norton Sub Hamdon TA14. .185 F2
Shalford BA9. . . . . .216 E6
Sparkford BA22. . . . . .175 A3
Timsbury BA2. . . . . .60 B2
Rectory Lawn TA8. . . . . . .104 B8
Rectory Pl TA8. . . . . .104 C8
Rectory Rd
Ashbrittle TA21. . . . . .178 F8
Burnham-on-S TA8. . . . . . .104 B8
Easton-in-G BS20. . . . . .4 B3
Norton Fitzwarren TA2. . . .168 B5
Shepton Mallet BA4. . . . . .205 B6
Staplegrove TA2. . . . . . . .212 C8
Rectory Way
Lympsham BS24. . . . . .66 F2
Yatton BS49. . . . . .34 C7
Recurium Lodge BS26. . . . .70 B2
Redacre BS40. . . . . .36 D3
RED BALL. 179 C4
Red Barn La TA20. . . . . . .193 D4
Redcliff Backs BS1. . . . . . .227 B2
REDCLIFFE BAY. 1 E4
Redcliff Cl BS20. . . . . .1 E3
Redcliff Par E BS1. . . . . . .227 A1
Redcliff Par W BS1. . . . . . .227 A1
Redcliff Sixth Form Ctr The
BS1. . . . . .227 B1
Redcliff St BS27. . . . . .90 C7
Redcliffe Way BS1. . . . . . .227 B1
Redcliff Hill BS1. . . . . .227 B1
Redcliff Mead La BS1. . . . .227 B1
Redcliff St BS1. . . . . .227 B2
Red Cotts
Blagdon BS40. . . . . .54 D6
Corsley Heath BA12. . . . . .144 E8
Redcroft BS40. . . . . .36 D3
Redcross Mews 14 BS2. . . .227 B3
Redcross St BS2. . . . . .227 C3
Red Deer Gdns TA6. . . . . .208 D3
Redding Pit La BS40. . . . . . .37 C4
Reddings The BS3. . . . . . . .74 B7
Redfield Gr BA3. . . . . .97 A8
Redfield La TA10. . . . . . . .156 A2
Redfield Rd BA3. . . . . .97 A8
Redford Cres BS13. . . . . . . .21 F3
Redford Trad Est BS3. . . . . .22 C8
Redford Wlk BS13. . . . . . . .21 F3
Redgate Pk TA18. . . . . . . .224 C8
Redgates Rd TA24. . . . . . .200 E7
Redgate St TA6. . . . . .209 B4
REDHILL. 36 D3
Red Hill
Peasedown St John BA2. . . .60 E1
Redhill BS40. . . . . .36 D2
West Monkton TA2. . . . . . .169 B7
Redhill La BA3. . . . . .95 A8
Red Hill La TA7. . . . . .155 E7
Redhole La DT9. . . . . .225 D8
Red House La BS9. . . . . .5 E6
Red House Rd TA9. . . . . . . .86 D5
Red La
Churchinford TA3. . . . . . . .191 F7
Hemyock EX15. . . . . .180 E3
Seaborough DT8. . . . . . . .195 E1
Staplehay TA3. . . . . .181 E8
Redlake Dr TA1. . . . . .213 D3
Redland Ave BS20. . . . . .3 F6
Redland La TA3. . . . . .183 C8
Redland Pk BA2. . . . . .43 F6
Redlands La TA7. . . . . . . .137 C2
Redlands Terr BA3. . . . . . . .96 F8
Redland Terr BA11. . . . . . .119 F3
REDLANE. 191 F7
Red Lion Ct
3 Crewkerne TA18. . . . . .224 C6
Somerton TA11. . . . . .211 E4
Wellington TA21. . . . . . . .222 E6
Red Lodge Bsns Pk BS24. . .32 C1
REDLYNCH. 160 E4
Redlynch Cross BA10. . . . .160 E4
Redlynch La BS31. . . . . . . .24 C2
Redlynch Rd
Pitcombe BA10. . . . . .215 F2
Redlynch BA10. . . . . .160 D3
Redmans Hill BS28. . . . . . .107 E4
Redpoll Dr BS20. . . . . .3 A6
RED POST. 79 B7
Red Post
Chard TA20. . . . . .193 D3
Isle Abbotts TA3. . . . . . . .183 E7
Porlock TA24. . . . . .124 B3
Red Post Cross TA11. . . . .173 D4
Red Post Ct BA2. . . . . .79 B7
Red Post Lower Rd TA4. . .151 C5
Red Rd
Berrow TA8. . . . . .85 A4
Brean TA8. . . . . .66 A2
Redshard La BS40. . . . . . . .53 B7
Redstart Prim Sch The
TA20. . . . . .223 C5

Redstart Rd TA20. . . . . . . .223 C6
Redway TA24. . . . . .124 A3
Red Way The BA12. . . . . . .144 F6
Redwing Dr BS22. . . . . .31 F1
Red Wing Rd DT9. . . . . . . .217 C2
Redwood Cl
Nailsea BS48. . . . . .9 A2
Radstock BA3. . . . . .97 E8
Redwood Dr BS8. . . . . .10 F4
Redwood Ho BS15. . . . . . . .22 D3
Redwood La BS48. . . . . . . .20 C7
Redwood Rd BA21. . . . . . .219 E8
Reed Cl
Bridgwater TA6. . . . . .208 F2
Chard TA20. . . . . .223 D6
Watchet TA23. . . . . .202 D6
Reedley Rd BS9. . . . . .5 F5
Reedmace Rd BA11. . . . . . .120 B2
Reedmoor Gdns TA6. . . . .208 E7
Reeds Barn EX13. . . . . . . .198 F1
Reeds Dr TA7. . . . . .136 F4
Reed Way BS22. . . . . .32 C3
Rees Way BS26. . . . . .87 E7
Reeves Cl
Draycott BS27. . . . . .90 F2
5 Langaller TA2. . . . . . . .169 C5
Regal Rd BA4. . . . . .205 B6
Regal Way 24 BA4. . . . . . .205 B6
Regency Cl TA8. . . . . .85 A2
Regency Ct BA5. . . . . .203 C4
Regency Wlk BA11. . . . . . .119 E4
Regent Ct BA22. . . . . .173 E2
Regent Gn TA4. . . . . .167 F1
Regent Mews TA20. . . . . .223 C3
Regent St
Bradford On Tone TA4. . . .167 F1
Bristol BS8. . . . . .226 A2
Burnham-on-S TA8. . . . . . .104 A7
Weston-super-Mare BS23. . .48 E7
Regents The
Cotford St Luke TA4. . . . . .167 E6
Keynsham BS31. . . . . .24 F6
4 Yeovil BA21. . . . . .218 C6
Regents Way TA24. . . . . . .200 E6
Regent Way TA6. . . . . .209 A2
REGIL. 37 F2
Regil La BS40. . . . . .38 A6
Regil Rd BS40. . . . . .37 F3
Regina The BA1. . . . . .228 B3
Reid Ct BA5. . . . . .203 B4
Remalard Ct BA7. . . . . . . .214 B5
Rendcomb Cl BS22. . . . . . . .31 B2
Rendell Rise BA20. . . . . . .218 C1
Rennison Ct BS23. . . . . . . .48 E4
Reservoir La BA5. . . . . . . .203 C6
Reservoir Rd
Chard TA20. . . . . .193 E4
Crimchard TA20. . . . . . . .223 A5
Retford Ho BA2. . . . . .45 E5
Retreat Caravan Park The
TA8. . . . . .85 A2
Retreat The
Foxcote BA3. . . . . .79 C3
Frome BA11. . . . . .120 B4
Taunton TA2. . . . . .168 F6
Weston-super-Mare BS23. . .30 C1
Reubens Ct BS22. . . . . .31 F3
Rex Rd BA22. . . . . .186 C2
Rex's La
Barwick BA22. . . . . .197 F8
Yeovil BA22. . . . . .219 C1
Rexton La TA4. . . . . .150 F5
Reynald's Way
Butleigh BA6. . . . . .157 C4
Street BA16. . . . . .207 D1
Reynolds TA21. . . . . .166 F2
Reynolds Cl BS31. . . . . .25 A5
RHODE. 153 D5
Rhode Cl BS31. . . . . .25 A3
Rhode La TA6. . . . . .208 E2
Rhodes Cl TA2. . . . . .212 C7
Rhodyate BS40. . . . . .54 D2
Rhodyate Hill BS49. . . . . . .34 F6
Rhodyate La BS49. . . . . . . .35 A7
Rhodyate The BS29. . . . . . .51 C1
Rhydderch Way TA18. . . . .224 C5
Rhyll Gate Cross TA22. . . .162 E7
Rhymes Pl BA1. . . . . .28 C3
Rhyne Bridge 9 TA6. . . . .209 A1
Rhyne Terr BS23. . . . . .48 D2
Rhyne View BS48. . . . . .8 B1
Richard Beadon Cl TA4. . . .210 B4
Richard Huish Coll TA1. . . .213 A2
Richards Cl
Wellington TA21. . . . . . . .222 C8
Weston-super-Mare BS22. . .32 B4
Richards Cres TA2. . . . . . .169 B6
Richmond Cl
Bath BA1. . . . . .27 F1
Bridgwater TA6. . . . . .208 F7
Keynsham BS31. . . . . .24 D4
Minehead TA24. . . . . .200 E6
Portishead BS20. . . . . .1 F4
Sampford Peverell EX16. . .178 D1
Sherborne DT9. . . . . .225 C3
Richmond Ct BA22. . . . . . .173 E2
Richmond Gn
Nailsea BS48. . . . . .8 F1
Sherborne DT9. . . . . .225 C4
Taunton TA1. . . . . .212 D5
Richmond Hill
Bath BA1. . . . . .27 F1
Bristol BS8. . . . . .226 B3
Richmond Hill Ave BS8. . . .226 B3
Richmond Ho
Crewkerne TA18. . . . . . . .224 C6
9 Shepton Mallet BA4. . .205 B6
Yeovil BA20. . . . . .219 A4

Richmond Hts
Bath BA1. . . . . .27 F2
Bristol BS8. . . . . .226 B3
Richmond La
Bath BA1. . . . . .27 F1
Bristol BS8. . . . . .226 B3
Richmond Mews BS8. . . . .226 A3
Richmond Park Rd BS8. . . .226 A3
Richmond Pk TA1. . . . . . . .212 C4
Richmond Pl BA1. . . . . .27 F1
Richmond Rd
Bath BA1. . . . . .27 F1
2 Frome BA11. . . . . .119 E3
Sherborne DT9. . . . . .225 C3
Taunton TA1. . . . . .212 D5
Yeovil BA20. . . . . .219 A4
Richmond St
5 Sidbmot TA2. . . . . . . .169 B2
Weston-super-Mare BS23. . .48 D7
Richmond Terr BS8. . . . . . .226 B3
Richmond Villas BA6. . . . .206 E4
Richmond Way BA21. . . . .218 C6
Rich's Farmhouse Cider
Farm ★ TA9. . . . . .105 D3
RICH'S HOLFORD. 151 C4
Ricketts La BS22. . . . . .32 A2
RICKFORD. 54 B3
Rickford La BS40. . . . . .54 A3
Rickford Rd BS48. . . . . .8 F1
Rickford Rise BS40. . . . . . . .54 A3
Rickhayes BS20. . . . . .2 C5
Rickhay Rise TA18. . . . . . .196 B8
Ricklands The BS40. . . . . . .38 A6
Ricksey Cl TA11. . . . . .211 B3
Ricksey La TA11. . . . . .211 B3
Ricksmead Dro TA7. . . . . .155 D2
Rickyard Rd BS40. . . . . . . .35 E2
RIDGE. 74 C5
Ridge Cl BS20. . . . . .2 A4
Ridge Cres BS40. . . . . .74 E6
Ridge Green Cl BA2. . . . . . .62 D8
Ridge Highway TA4. . . . . . .166 A3
Ridge Hill TA4. . . . . .210 D5
Ridge La
Corton Denham DT9. . . . . .175 D1
East Chinnock BA22. . . . . .196 F8
East Coker BA22. . . . . . . .197 A7
Pitcombe BA7, BA10. . . . .215 A2
Ridge BS40. . . . . .74 D5
Shepton Mallet BA4. . . . . .205 B4
Ridgemead BA20. . . . . . . .218 D2
Ridgemeade BS14. . . . . . . .23 B4
Ridgemount Gdns BS14. . . .23 B5
Ridge Rd
Croscombe BA4, BA5. . . . .204 D5
West Anstey TA22. . . . . . .162 D7
Ridge The
Bristol BS11. . . . . .4 E7
Porlock TA24. . . . . .124 B3
Poyntington DT9. . . . . . . .188 F7
Yatton BS49. . . . . .34 B8
Ridgeview BS41. . . . . .11 B2
Ridgeview Ho BS20. . . . . . . .2 E3
RIDGEWAY. 143 C7
Ridgeway
Ashcott TA7. . . . . .156 B8
Nailsea BS48. . . . . .8 C1
Nunney BA11. . . . . .143 C8
Sherborne DT9. . . . . .225 B3
Ridgeway Ave BS23. . . . . . .48 E6
Ridgeway Cl BS40. . . . . . . .74 E6
Ridgeway Ct BS14. . . . . . . .23 C5
Ridgeway Gdns
Bristol BS14. . . . . .23 C5
Glastonbury BA6. . . . . . . .206 F5
Ridgeway La
Bristol BS14. . . . . .23 B5
Fitzhead TA4. . . . . .166 F6
Moorlinch TA7. . . . . .155 F7
North Cadbury BA22. . . . .175 D6
Nunney BA11. . . . . .143 C8
Shillingford EX16. . . . . . . .164 D2
Stolford TA5. . . . . .134 E8
Ridgeway Rd BS41. . . . . . . .11 A2
Ridgeway The BS22. . . . . . .31 B2
Ridgewood BS9. . . . . .5 D3
Ridgewood Cross EX15. . . .191 B8
Ridgewood La EX15. . . . . . .191 A8
Ridgway TA18. . . . . .196 B8
Ridgway Cross EX36. . . . . .145 K1
RIDING GATE. 177 B8
Ridings The BS13. . . . . .21 E4
Ridley Cnr TA10. . . . . .171 C5
Ridley Hill TA10. . . . . .171 E8
Riec-Sur-Belon Way
TA19. . . . . .221 A4
Rigg La DT9. . . . . .187 F5
Rigg Lane Cotts DT9. . . . . .187 F5
Riggles Cross EX14. . . . . . .191 D3
RIMPTON. 188 A8
Rimpton Hill BA22. . . . . . .188 A7
Rimpton Rd BA22. . . . . . . .174 F1
Ringdown La EX15. . . . . . .180 F2
Ringolds Way BA16. . . . . . .207 B4
Ringspit La
Blackrock BS39. . . . . .40 E8
Bristol BS14, BS39. . . . . . . .40 E8
Ring St DT10. . . . . .190 B4
Ringstone TA9. . . . . .136 B8
Ringswell Gdns BA1. . . . . . .28 B1
Ringwell Cl BA2. . . . . .81 E4
Ringwell Hill TA12. . . . . . .185 D4
Ringwell La BA2. . . . . .81 E4
Ringwood Gr BS23. . . . . . . .31 A1
Ringwood Rd
Bath BA2. . . . . .44 C5
Bridgwater TA6. . . . . .209 A2
Riphay Cross TA22. . . . . . .163 E3

Rippleside BS20. . . . . .2 C5
Rippleside Rd BS21. . . . . . . .6 E5
Ripple The BS21. . . . . .8 D4
Risdale Rd BS3. . . . . .11 F1
Risdon Rd TA23. . . . . .202 C6
Risedale Cl TA6. . . . . .208 C5
Risedale Rd BS25. . . . . .70 A8
Risemoor Rd TA6. . . . . . . .208 D4
Ritchie Rd BA22. . . . . .218 A5
Rivendell BS22. . . . . .32 A4
Riverbed Ho TA9. . . . . .104 D3
River Dro
Dundon TA10. . . . . .156 E1
Othery TA7. . . . . .155 E4
River La TA7. . . . . .209 E1
Riverland Dr BS13. . . . . . . .21 F5
Riverleaze
Bristol BS9. . . . . .5 C5
Portishead BS20. . . . . .1 F6
River Mead BS21. . . . . .16 D8
River Paddock Dro BA5. . . .110 B2
River Pl BA2. . . . . .44 B6
River Rd
East Huntspill TA7. . . . . . .137 B8
Mark TA9. . . . . .106 D1
Pawlett TA6. . . . . .135 F5
Portbury BS20. . . . . .3 F8
Riversgate BS1. . . . . .227 C2
RIVERSIDE
Midsomer Norton. 96 F7
Wellington. 222 B6
Riverside
Banwell BS24, BS29. . . . . . .51 B5
Bridgwater TA6. . . . . .208 F7
Burrowbridge TA7. . . . . . .154 F1
Combwich TA5. . . . . .135 C5
Dinder BA5. . . . . .140 D7
Horton TA19. . . . . .183 C2
Meare BA5. . . . . .138 F5
Taunton TA1. . . . . .212 E4
Wellington TA21. . . . . . . .222 B7
Riverside Cl
Bridgwater TA6. . . . . .208 F7
Bristol BS11. . . . . .4 F5
Clevedon BS21. . . . . .6 B1
Midsomer Norton BA3. . . . .96 F7
Weston-super-Mare BS22. . .32 C3
Riverside Cotts BA3. . . . . . .79 A2
Riverside Ct BA2. . . . . .228 B1
Riverside Gdns
Bath BA1. . . . . .228 B2
Dunster TA24. . . . . .201 E3
Midsomer Norton BA3. . . . .96 F7
Riverside Pl 2 TA1. . . . . . .212 F4
Riverside Rd
Bath BA2. . . . . .228 B2
Midsomer Norton BA3. . . . .96 F7
Riverside Row TA24. . . . . .124 A3
Riverside Terr BA11. . . . . .119 F5
Riverside Wlk BA3. . . . . . . .96 F7
Rivers Rd
Bath BA1. . . . . .28 A1
Bath BA1. . . . . .228 C4
Yeovil BA21. . . . . .219 D8
Rivers Reach BA11. . . . . . .120 A5
Rivers St BA1. . . . . .228 B3
Rivers Street Mews BA1. . .228 B3
River St BS2. . . . . .227 C3
River Street Pl 5 BA1. . . . .228 B3
River Terr BS31. . . . . .24 F5
Riverton Rd TA7. . . . . .136 B4
River View
Bridgwater TA6. . . . . .208 F6
Combwich TA5. . . . . .135 B5
Exebridge TA22. . . . . .163 F3
Riverway BS48. . . . . .8 F3
River Wlk BS22. . . . . .32 D2
RNAS Yeovilton Road
BA22. . . . . .174 A2
Roachill Cross EX36. . . . . .162 C1
Road Hill
Alcombe SN13. . . . . .29 E8
Langford Budville TA4. . . .166 B3
Roads La SP8. . . . . .190 D8
Roadwater TA23. . . . . .131 C1
Roake La TA2. . . . . .168 B5
Roath Rd BS20. . . . . .2 D5
Robbins Cl BS14. . . . . .23 D6
Robert Blake Science Coll
TA6. . . . . .208 F3
Robert Ct BS8. . . . . .11 D7
Roberts Dr TA6. . . . . .209 A2
Roberts Rd TA2. . . . . .168 A6
Robert St TA4. . . . . .202 D2
Robin Cl
Bristol BS14. . . . . .23 D6
Midsomer Norton BA3. . . . .97 B8
Taunton TA1. . . . . .212 B4
Weston-super-Mare BS22. . .49 E8
Robin Dr BS24. . . . . .49 E2
Robinia Wlk BS14. . . . . . . .23 A7
Robin La BS21. . . . . .6 D5
Robin Pl BS20. . . . . .3 A6
Robins Ct
Chard TA20. . . . . .223 C6
Frome BA11. . . . . .119 D5
Robins Dr
Bridgwater TA6. . . . . .209 A6
Burtle TA7. . . . . .137 D6
Robins La
Burtle TA7. . . . . .137 C6
Frome BA11. . . . . .119 D5
Shepton Beauchamp TA19. .184 E4
Robinson Cl BS48. . . . . .19 A5
Robinson Hts TA11. . . . . . .190 B4
Robinson Way BS48. . . . . . .19 A5
Rob-Lynne Ct BS25. . . . . . . .69 F8
Roche Cl BA21. . . . . .218 C7

Rec–Rom 265
Rochester Cl BS24. . . . . . . .49 A1
Rochester Rd TA2. . . . . . . .213 A8
Rochfort Ct BA1. . . . . .45 B8
Rock Ave BS49. . . . . .8 C2
Rock Cotts BS20. . . . . .4 E3
Rockeries Dr BS25. . . . . . . .69 F8
Rockeries The BS25. . . . . . .69 F8
Rockery Pk BA2. . . . . .45 C2
Rocketts Cl TA3. . . . . .169 D4
Rocketts Cotts TA3. . . . . . .169 D4
Rockfield Cotts TA21. . . . .179 F7
Rockhall Ho 10 BS23. . . . . .30 C1
Rock Hall Ho BA2. . . . . .45 B1
Rock Hall La BA2. . . . . .45 B1
Rock Hill TA3. . . . . .170 C1
Rockhill Est BS31. . . . . .24 F4
Rockingham Gdns BS11. . . . .5 A8
Rockingham Gr BS23. . . . . .31 A1
Rock La
Bath BA2. . . . . .45 B1
Exford TA24. . . . . .128 D1
West Bagborough TA4. . . .151 E5
Rockleaze
Bristol BS9. . . . . .5 E2
Evercreech BA4. . . . . .141 E2
Rockleaze Ave BS9. . . . . . . .5 E3
Rockleaze Ct BS9. . . . . .5 E3
Rockleaze Mans 12 BS23. . .30 C1
Rockleaze Rd BS9. . . . . .5 E3
Rockliffe Ave BA2. . . . . . . .45 B8
Rockliffe Rd BA2. . . . . .45 B8
Rock Rd
Keynsham BS31. . . . . .24 E5
Midsomer Norton BA3. . . . .78 B2
Yatton BS49. . . . . .34 C7
Rock's Dro BA16. . . . . .138 F3
Rocks St BA5. . . . . .204 C7
Rocks The BA3. . . . . .142 B7
Rock Terr BA3. . . . . .116 F6
Rockway TA3. . . . . .170 C1
Rockwell Gate TA21. . . . . .222 B5
ROCKWELL GREEN. 222 B5
Rockwell Green CE Prim Sch
TA21. . . . . .222 B5
Rocky Hill TA11. . . . . .173 D5
Rocky La TA23. . . . . .131 E2
Rodber Cl BA4. . . . . .216 B4
Rodber Gdns BA9. . . . . . . .216 B4
Roddenbury Cl BA11. . . . . .120 B5
Roddenbury View BA12. . . .144 D8
Rodden Rd BA11. . . . . .120 A5
RODE. 101 F8
Rode Hill
Rode BA11. . . . . .82 E1
Southwick BA11. . . . . .83 A1
Rode Methodist VA Fst Sch
BA11. . . . . .101 E8
Rodfords Mead BS14. . . . . .23 A7
RODGROVE. 177 C3
Rodhuish Cross TA24. . . . .131 B3
Rodhuish Hill La TA24. . . .131 A3
Rod La TA19. . . . . .183 F4
Rodmead La BA5. . . . . .110 E4
Rodmead Wlk BS13. . . . . . .22 A4
Rodmoor Rd BS20. . . . . .2 D6
Rodmore Cres BA4. . . . . . .141 E1
Rodmore Rd BA4. . . . . . . .141 E1
Rodney BS24. . . . . .49 A2
Rodney Ct BA22. . . . . .218 A5
Rodney Ho BA2. . . . . .44 A6
Rodney Pl BS8. . . . . .226 A3
Rodney Rd
Backwell BS48. . . . . .19 A6
Saltford BS31. . . . . .25 E2
RODNEY STOKE. 91 A1
Rodney Stoke National Nature
Reserve ★ BS27. . . . . . . .91 B1
RODWAY. 135 B3
Rodway TA5. . . . . .135 B3
Rodwell La
Barrington TA13. . . . . .184 E5
Lillesdon TA3. . . . . .170 A3
Roe La BA22. . . . . .218 A5
Roebuck Cl BS22. . . . . .32 B4
Roebuck Gate La TA4. . . . .151 B6
Roe Cl TA6. . . . . .209 D4
Roe La BA22. . . . . .188 B8
Roemead La BA3. . . . . .114 C5
Roemead Rd
Oakhill BA3. . . . . .114 C4
Westbury Beacon BA5. . . . .91 E6
Rogers Cl
Buckland Dinham BA11. . . .100 A3
Clutton BS39. . . . . .58 E3
North Petherton TA6. . . . .153 F3
Rogers Wlk TA4. . . . . .167 E6
Roland Cl TA1. . . . . .212 C2
ROLSTONE. 32 F2
Roman Baths The ★ BA1. . .228 C2
Roman Ct BA22. . . . . .219 D6
Roman Farm Rd BS4. . . . . .22 E7
Roman Ho BA1. . . . . .228 C4
Roman La BA22. . . . . .208 C3
Roman Rd
Batheaston BA1. . . . . .29 C7
Bleadon BA3. . . . . .67 C8
Sandford BS25. . . . . .51 F4
Taunton TA1. . . . . .213 C5
Roman Villas BA4. . . . . . . .205 E4
Roman Way
Bristol BS9. . . . . .5 C4
Coleford BA3. . . . . .116 F7

Roman Way *continued*
Paulton BS39 . . . . .77 C6
Peasedown St John BA2. . . . .79 E7
Watchet TA23 . . . . .202 C7
Roman Way The BA6 . . . . . .206 C3
Romney Mead TA1 . . . . . . .213 D4
Romney Rd 2 TA6 . . . . . .154 A5
Romsey Rd BA21 . . . . .219 E8
Romulus CI BS31 . . . . .24 F7
Ron Jones Ho 3 BS1 . . . .227 B4
Rookery CI
Puriton TA7. . . . . .136 C4
Rooks Bridge BS26. . . . . . . .87 A6
Weston-super-Mare BS22 . . .31 E3
Rookery La
Croscombe BA5 . . . . .204 B7
Drimpton DT8. . . . . .199 F6
Rookery Terr TA21 . . . . . . .222 C5
Rookery The BA5. . . . . . . .140 D7
Rookery Way BS14 . . . . .22 F4
ROOKHAM 112 B5
Rook La BA11 . . . . .119 F4
ROOKS BRIDGE 87 C5
Rooksbridge Rd BS24, BS26. 87 B6
Rooksbridge Wlk BA2. . . . .44 B5
Rookscastle Rd TA5 . . . . . .153 A3
Rooks La BA11 . . . . .120 E7
Rook's Meade La TA19. . . .184 E1
ROOK'S NEST 150 C4
Room Hill Rd TA24 . . . . . . .146 D7
Roper's La BS40. . . . . .35 E3
Rope Walk Ho 23 BS2. . . .227 C3
Ropewalk The TA20 . . . . . .223 B5
Rope Wk TA24 . . . . .201 B7
Rope Wlk
Backwell BS48 . . . . .19 A5
Bridgwater TA6 . . . . .209 A5
Coleford BA3 . . . . .116 E8
Evercreech BA4 . . . . .141 E1
14 Martock TA12 . . . . .185 E6
Wellington TA21 . . . . .222 C4
Rope Wlk The TA23. . . . . .202 C7
Roping Rd BA21. . . . . .219 B6
Rosa PI TA6. . . . . .208 E1
Rosary Dr TA6 . . . . .208 B4
Rosa Wy TA6. . . . . .208 E1
Rosebank Rd TA4 . . . . .167 A4
Roseberry Cotts BA3 . . . . .117 A7
Roseberry PI BA2 . . . . .44 C6
Roseberry Rd BA2. . . . . .44 C6
Roseberry Terr TA1 . . . . . .212 D5
Rosebery Ave
Bridgwater TA6 . . . . .209 B5
Yeovil BA21 . . . . .219 D6
Rosebery St TA2 . . . . .212 E7
Rosebery Terr BS8 . . . . . . .226 B2
Rose Cotts
Taunton TA1. . . . . .213 B3
Weston-super-Mare BS22 . . .32 C2
Rose & Crown Cotts BA3. .116 F6
Rose Ct
Keinton Mandeville TA11 . . .158 A1
Shepton Mallet BA4 . . . . . . .205 B6
Rosedale Ave BS23. . . . . . . .49 A7
Rose Dale Wlk BA11 . . . . . .119 F6
Rose Gdns BS22. . . . . .32 B4
Rose Hill
Bath BA1 . . . . .28 C3
Portishead BS20 . . . . .2 C6
Spaxton TA5 . . . . .152 F2
Rose La
Crewkerne TA18. . . . . .224 B6
Crewkerne TA20. . . . . .195 A3
Crewkerne, Misterton TA18 .196 B3
Purtington TA20 . . . . .195 A3
Roseland CI BA1 . . . . .28 C3
Roselyn Cres DT9 . . . . .189 A1
Rosemary Cres BS20 . . . . . . .2 F5
Rosemary La
Dulverton TA22. . . . . .163 D6
Freshford BA3 . . . . .64 B4
ROSEMARY LANE 180 D1
Rosemarylane Cross
EX15. . . . . .180 D1
Rosemary St DT9. . . . . . . .217 C2
Rosemary Way BA11 . . . . .120 B3
Rose Meadow Vw BS3 . . . . .11 E1
Rose Meare Gdns BS13 . . . .21 E7
Rose Mills Ind Est TA19 . . .183 E2
Rosemont Terr BS8 . . . . . .226 A2
Rosemount La BA2. . . . . . . .45 B4
Rosemount Rd BS48. . . . . . .20 B8
Roseneath Ave TA8. . . . . . .84 F4
Rose Terr
Bath BA2 . . . . .45 C2
Bristol BS8. . . . . .226 B3
Rose Tree Paddock TA8 . . .84 F4
Rosette Cotts TA12 . . . . . .185 B7
Rosevean CI TA6 . . . . .209 D7
Rose Villas TA6 . . . . .135 B2
Rosewarn CI BA2. . . . . .44 A4
Rosewell Ct BA1 . . . . .228 B2
Rosewood Ave TA8 . . . . . .104 C6
Rosewood CI TA8 . . . . .104 C7
Rosewood Dr TA8. . . . . . . .104 C6
Roslyn Ave BS22 . . . . .31 C1
Rossendale CI BS22 . . . . . . .31 F3
Rosshayne La EX14. . . . . . .192 C2
Rossiter CI 8 TA2. . . . . . .169 C5
Rossiter Grange 5 BS13. . .21 F4
Rossiter Rd BA2. . . . . .228 C1
Rossiter's Hill BA11 . . . . . .119 E3
Rossiter's Rd BA11 . . . . . . .119 E3
Rosslyn CI 1 BA1 . . . . .44 B7
Rosslyn Rd BA1 . . . . .44 B7

ROTCOMBE 59 D2
Rotcombe La BS39 . . . . .59 D2
Rotcombe Vale BS39 . . . . . .59 D2
Rotton Row TA4. . . . . .210 C4
Roughmoor TA4 . . . . .202 E4
Roughmoor CI TA1 . . . . . . .212 D5
Roughmoor Cotts TA1. . . . .212 D5
Roughmoor Cres TA1. . . . . .212 D5
Roughmoor Ind Est TA4. . . .202 E4
Roughmoor La BA5 . . . . . . .110 C7
ROUNDHAM 195 D4
Round Hill BA12. . . . . .144 C2
Roundhill Gr BA2 . . . . .44 B3
Roundhill Pk BA2 . . . . .44 A4
Roundmoor CI BS31. . . . . . .25 D3
Roundmoor Gdns BS14 . . . .23 D7
Roundoak Gdns TA21. . . . . .167 C2
Round Oak Gr BS27. . . . . . . .90 A8
Round Oak Rd BS27 . . . . . . .90 A8
Round Pool La TA4. . . . . . . .151 B7
Roundwell CI BA4 . . . . .204 F6
Roundwell St TA13 . . . . . . .220 C4
Rowacres
Bath BA2 . . . . .44 B3
Bristol BS14. . . . . .22 F6
Rowan CI
Nailsea BS48. . . . . .9 A2
Puriton TA7. . . . . .136 C4
Wincanton BA9 . . . . .216 D2
Rowan Ct
Frome BA11. . . . . .120 B7
Radstock BA3. . . . . .78 E4
Rowan Dr
Berrow TA8. . . . . .84 F5
Taunton TA1. . . . . .213 D1
Rowan Ho BS13 . . . . .22 D4
Rowan PI BS24. . . . . .32 B1
Rowans CI TA6. . . . . .209 C6
Rowan St BS14. . . . . .22 E5
Rowans The BS20. . . . . .2 B4
Rowan Way
Churchill BS40 . . . . .53 A5
Yeovil BA20 . . . . .218 F3
Rowan Wlk BS31. . . . . .24 C4
Rowbarrow Hill
Rimpton DT9 . . . . .188 A7
Trent DT9 . . . . .187 F6
ROWBARTON 212 F7
Rowbarton CI TA2. . . . . . . .212 F7
ROWBERROW 53 A1
Rowberrow BS14. . . . . .22 F7
Rowberrow La BS25 . . . . . . .70 F8
Rowberrow Way BS48 . . . . . .8 E1
Rowcliffe Cotts TA21 . . . . .178 F8
Rowdells Orch TA19 . . . . . .184 D1
Rowden Mill La DT10 . . . . .189 F1
Rowdens Rd BA5. . . . . .203 D3
Rowditch La TA5 . . . . .133 D5
Rowe CI TA21. . . . . .222 A4
Rowe's Hill BA12. . . . . .144 F4
ROWFORD 168 F6
Row La
Keinton Mandeville TA11 . . .158 A1
Laverton BA2 . . . . .100 D8
Rowlands CI BA1. . . . . .29 B2
Rowlands Rise TA7. . . . . . .136 C4
Rowley Farm La BA2 . . . . . .62 D5
Rowley Rd BA6. . . . . .206 E5
Rowls La BA9 . . . . .177 C6
Rowmarsh La TA10 . . . . . . .172 D5
Rownham CI BS3. . . . . .11 A5
Rownham Ct BS8. . . . . .226 A1
Rownham Hill BS8 . . . . .11 E6
Rownham Mead BS8 . . . . . .226 A1
Row of Ashes La BS40 . . . . .36 F4
Rows La EX16. . . . . .164 A1
Rows The BS22 . . . . .31 E2
Row The
Hambridge TA10. . . . . .184 D8
Langport TA10 . . . . .172 B3
Royal Ave BA1 . . . . .228 B3
Royal Cres 2 BA1. . . . . . .219 C6
Royal Cres ★ BA1 . . . . .228 A3
Royal Cres BS23. . . . . .48 D8
Royal Ct BS23. . . . . .48 D4
Royal Dr TA6. . . . . .136 B2
Royal Fort Rd BS2, BS8 . . . .226 C4
Royal High School Bath Jun
Sch The BA1 . . . . .27 D1
Royal High School Bath The
BA1. . . . . .27 F2
Royal Ho 4 BA4 . . . . .205 B6
Royal National Hospl for
Rheumatic Diseases
BA1. . . . . .228 B2
Royal Par
Bristol BS8. . . . . .226 B3
Weston-super-Mare BS23 . . .48 D8
Royal Park Mews BA1 . . . .226 A3
Royal Pk BS8 . . . . .226 A3
Royal Portbury Dock Rd
BS20 . . . . .3 E5
Royal Prom BS8. . . . . .226 B3
Royal Sands BS23 . . . . .48 D4
Royal United Hospl BA1 . . . .44 B8
Royal West of England Acad
BS8 . . . . .226 B3
Royal York Cres BS8. . . . . . .11 F6
Royal York Ho 7 BS8. . . . .226 A2
Royal York Mews 6 BS8. . .226 A2
Royal York Villas BS8. . . . . .226 A2
Royces La TA19 . . . . .184 C5
Roynon Way BS27. . . . . .90 B7
Roys PI TA2. . . . . .213 F7
Royston Lodge BS23. . . . . . .48 D6
Royston Rd TA3 . . . . .192 A7
ROYSTON WATER 192 B7
Rozel Ho 14 BS23. . . . . .30 C1

Rubbery La TA11 . . . . .158 D1
Rubens CI BS31 . . . . .25 A5
Ruborough Rd TA6. . . . . . .209 C4
Ruby Dr TA6 . . . . .209 C8
Ruckley Ford BA3. . . . . .80 A2
Ruddock CI BA22 . . . . .197 B8
Ruddock Way BA22. . . . . . .197 B8
Ruddymead BS21 . . . . .6 D2
RUDGE 102 D5
Rudge Hill BA11. . . . . .102 D5
Rudge La
Beckington BA11. . . . . .102 B6
Standerwick BA11 . . . . .102 D3
Rudge Rd BA11. . . . . .102 B2
Rudgeway Rd BS39. . . . . . . .77 E4
Rudgewood CI BS13. . . . . . .22 D4
Rudgleigh Ave BS20. . . . . . . .4 C4
Rudgleigh Rd BS20. . . . . . . .4 C4
Rudhall Gn BS22 . . . . .32 B3
Rudmore Pk BA1. . . . . .44 A7
Rue La
Alweston DT9. . . . . .189 C2
Hambridge TA3. . . . . .184 B7
Ruett La BS39. . . . . .77 B4
Rugg's Dro
Chedzoy TA7 . . . . .154 D7
West Huntspill TA9. . . . . . .136 B7
Rugg's Hill TA22 . . . . .148 E2
Rughill BS28. . . . . .108 D8
Rugmoor La BS40. . . . . .55 D3
Rugosa Dr TA8. . . . . .84 F4
RUISHTON 169 C3
Ruishton CE Prim Sch
TA3 . . . . .169 C3
Ruishton La TA3 . . . . .169 C3
Ruishton Lane Cotts
TA3 . . . . .169 C3
RUMWELL 168 B2
RUNNINGTON 179 F8
Runnymede Rd BA21 . . . . . .219 D8
Runway The BS24 . . . . .49 C4
Rupert St
Bristol BS1. . . . . .227 A3
Taunton TA2 . . . . .212 E6
Rusham BS13. . . . . .21 F4
Rush Ash La BA3 . . . . .116 E8
Rushgrove Gdns BS39 . . . . .57 C4
RUSH HILL 44 B2
Rush Hill
Bath BA2 . . . . .44 C2
Farrington Gurney
BS39 . . . . .76 F3
Rush Hill La BS28 . . . . .107 F3
Rushmoor BS21. . . . . .6 A1
Rushmoor Gr BS48. . . . . . . .19 A5
Rushmoor La BS48 . . . . .19 A5
Rushway BS40 . . . . .53 F4
Ruskin CI TA1. . . . . .213 C4
Ruskin Rd BA3 . . . . .78 C1
Ruskway La TA10. . . . . .184 C6
Rusling La BS40. . . . . .37 A1
Russell Ave BS24. . . . . .50 C5
Russell CI BS40 . . . . .38 A6
Russell PI
Bridgwater TA6 . . . . .208 F6
Milborne Port DT9 . . . . . . .217 C3
Russell Pope Ave TA20 . . . .223 D2
Russell Rd
Clevedon BS21. . . . . .6 C3
Locking BS24. . . . . .50 C6
Russell's TA4 . . . . .210 C4
Russell's Barton BA11 . . . . .143 B8
Russell St BA1 . . . . .228 B3
Russet CI TA21 . . . . .222 F7
Russet Rd TA11 . . . . .211 B4
Russets The BS20 . . . . .2 F4
Russett CI BS48 . . . . .19 B6
Russett Gr BS48. . . . . .18 C8
Russett Rd
Street BA16 . . . . .207 C4
Taunton TA1. . . . . .213 E5
Russet Way
Peasedown St John BA2. . . . .79 D7
Yeovil BA20 . . . . .218 D2
Russ St BS2. . . . . .227 C2
Rust La BS21. . . . . .16 E4
Rusty Well BA20 . . . . .218 F3
Rusty Well Pk BA20. . . . . . .218 F3
Ruthven Rd BS4. . . . . .22 E8
Rutland CI BS22. . . . . .49 C8
Rutter's La TA19 . . . . .221 B4
Ryalls Ct BA21 . . . . .219 C5
Ryburn CI TA1. . . . . .213 D3
Rydal Ave BS24 . . . . .50 A4
Rydal Rd BS23 . . . . .48 F4
RYDON 169 E8
Rydon Cres TA5. . . . . .135 C2
Rydon La
Lopen TA13. . . . . .185 A1
South Petherton TA13. . . . .220 A5
Taunton TA2 . . . . .212 F8
Rye TA7. . . . . .136 C4
Rye CI BS13. . . . . .21 E6
Ryecroft Ave BS22. . . . . . . .31 E2
Ryecroft Rise BS41 . . . . .11 B1
Ryefields CI BA22 . . . . .197 B8
Rye Gdns BA20. . . . . .218 D2
Rye La TA7. . . . . .155 C2
Ryelands Farm Ind Est
TA21 . . . . .222 B3
Ryeleaze BS11 . . . . .4 E5
Ryepool TA4. . . . . .167 F8
Ryesland Way TA3 . . . . . . .169 D4
Rye Water La DT2 . . . . .197 A1
Rylands BA11 . . . . .101 E4
Rylands CI TA4. . . . . .202 D2
Rylestone Gr BS9 . . . . .5 F5
Rysdale Rd BS9 . . . . .5 F6

S

Sabrina Way BS9. . . . . .5 C4
Sackmore Gn DT10. . . . . . .190 F6
Sackmore La DT10 . . . . . . .190 F5
Saco Ho BS1. . . . . .227 B2
Sadborow La TA20 . . . . . . .199 B4
Sadborow Pound TA20 . . . .199 B5
Sadbury CI BS22 . . . . .32 B4
Sadler St BA5 . . . . .203 D4
Sadlier CI BS11 . . . . .5 A8
Saffin Dr TA2 . . . . .213 F8
Saffron CI TA1 . . . . .168 F1
Saffron Ct
Bath BA1 . . . . .228 C4
Sherborne DT9 . . . . .225 E4
Saffron Ho 10 BS23. . . . . . .48 E8
Saffrons The 7 BS22. . . . . .32 B4
Sage CI BS20 . . . . .1 E4
Sage's La BA3 . . . . .94 D6
Sainsbury CI TA24. . . . . . . .200 D7
Sainsbury Rd TA24 . . . . . . .200 D7
St Agnes CI BS48. . . . . .9 A1
St Albans PI TA2 . . . . .212 F8
St Aldhelm's CE Prim Sch
BA4. . . . . .141 E6
St Aldhelm's CI BA11. . . . .119 D4
St Aldhelms Ct BA11. . . . . .119 D4
St Aldhelm's Rd DT9. . . . . .225 D6
St Algars Yd BA11. . . . . . . .144 A4
St Andrew's CE Jun Sch
TA8 . . . . .104 B7
St Andrew's CE Prim Acad
EX13 . . . . .198 A7
St Andrew's CE Prim Sch
Bath BA1 . . . . .228 B4
Taunton TA2 . . . . .212 F6
St Andrews CI
Castle Cary BA7 . . . . .214 B7
Nailsea BS48. . . . . .9 A1
Weston-super-Mare BS22 . . .31 F3
St Andrew's CI
Congresbury BS49 . . . . .34 C4
Curry Rivel TA10. . . . . .171 D4
High Ham TA10. . . . . .156 A4
St Andrews Ct TA24 . . . . . .200 F7
St Andrew's Ct BA5. . . . . . .203 F5
St Andrew's Dr BS21. . . . . . .6 A2
St Andrews La TA24 . . . . . .200 F7
St Andrews Mews 4 BA5 .203 C3
St Andrew's Par 1 BS23. . .48 F4
St Andrews Pk BA5. . . . . . .203 D3
St Andrew's Prim Sch
BS49 . . . . .34 C4
St Andrews Rd
Backwell BS48 . . . . .19 B5
Cheddar BS27 . . . . .90 C7
Yeovil BA20 . . . . .218 F5
St Andrew's Rd
Burnham-on-S TA8 . . . . . . .104 C4
Stogursey TA5 . . . . .134 C5
6 Taunton TA2 . . . . .212 F6
St Andrew St BA5 . . . . .203 E4
St Andrew's Terr BA1. . . . .228 B3
St Andrews View TA1. . . . .212 F6
St Andrews Wlk 5 BA5. . .203 C3
St Anne's Ave BS24. . . . . . . .34 D6
St Anne's CE Prim Sch
BS24 . . . . .33 B5
St Anne's CI BA6. . . . . .158 A5
St Anne's CI BS31 . . . . .24 D6
St Anne's Gdns BA21. . . . . .218 E6
St Ann's CI TA2 . . . . .212 E7
St Ann's Dr TA8. . . . . .85 A1
St Ann's PI BA1. . . . . .228 B2
St Ann's Way BA2 . . . . .45 C6
St Anthony's CI BA3. . . . . . .78 A2
St Antonys Sq 1 DT9. . . . .225 D3
St Aubyn's Ave BS23. . . . . . .48 D2
St Audries CI TA5. . . . . . . .134 C6
St Audries Ct TA23. . . . . . .202 B7
St Augustine of Canterbury
Sch The TA2. . . . . .213 A7
St Augustines Ct 1 TA1 . .213 A4
St Augustine's Par BS1 . . . .227 A2
St Augustine's PI 1 BS1. . .227 A2
St Augustine St TA1 . . . . . .213 A4
St Austell CI BS48 . . . . .19 A8
St Austell Rd BS22. . . . . . . .49 B8
St Barnabas CI BA3. . . . . . . .78 B3
St Bartholomew's CE Fst Sch
TA18 . . . . .224 D5
St Bartholomew's CE VC Fst
Sch TA18 . . . . .224 D5
St Benedict's CE Jun Sch
BA6. . . . . .206 D4
St Benedict's CI BA6. . . . . .206 D4
St Benedict's RC Prim Sch
BA3. . . . . .97 C7
St Bernadette RC Prim Sch
BS14 . . . . .23 B6
St Bernadette RC Sch BS14 23 B6
St Bernard's RC Prim Sch
BS11 . . . . .4 E6
St Bernard's Rd BS11. . . . . . .4 E6
St Brides CI BA6. . . . . .206 D5
St Bridges CI BS22 . . . . .31 A6
St Bridget's CI TA8. . . . . . . .65 F5
St Cadoc Ho BS31. . . . . .24 F5
ST CATHERINE 13 F1
St Catherine La BA1. . . . . . .13 D2
St Catherine's BA2. . . . . . . .45 B8
St Catherine's Cres DT9 . . .225 B3
St Catherine's Ct 10 BA11 119 E5
St Catherines Hill BA10 . . .215 B6

St Catherine's Mead BS20 . . 4 D3
St Catherine's Way DT9. . .225 B3
St Chad's Gn BA3 . . . . .97 A8
St Charles CI BA3 . . . . .78 A2
St Christophers CI BA2 . . . . .45 C8
St Christopher's Ct BS21. . . .6 C5
St Christopher's Way TA8. . .85 C3
ST CLEERS 211 C3
St Cleers TA11 . . . . .211 C3
St Cleer's Orch TA11 . . . . . .211 C3
St Cleers Way TA11. . . . . . .211 C3
St Clements Ct
Bath BA1 . . . . .27 C1
Bristol BS2. . . . . .227 C4
Clevedon BS21. . . . . .6 C4
Keynsham BS31 . . . . .24 E6
2 Weston-super-Mare BS22 32 A2
St Clements Rd BS31 . . . . . .24 F4
St Congars Wy BS49. . . . . . .34 C4
St Cuthbert Ave BA5. . . . . .203 B5
St Cuthbert's CE Inf Sch
BA5. . . . . .203 C3
St Cuthberts CE Jun & Inf Sch
BA5. . . . . .203 C3
St Cuthbert's Lodge 3
BA5 . . . . .203 B4
St Cuthbert St BA5 . . . . . . .203 D4
St Cuthbert's Villas BA5 . . .203 A5
St Cuthbert Way BA5 . . . . .203 B5
St Davids CI EX13 . . . . .198 A2
St David's CI
Glastonbury BA6 . . . . .206 E4
Taunton TA2 . . . . .213 A8
Weston-super-Mare BS22 . . .31 B2
St David's Cres BA21 . . . . . .219 B7
St Davids Ct TA6 . . . . .209 D3
St David's Ct BS21. . . . . . . .16 E8
St David's Dr EX13 . . . . . . .198 A2
St David's Gdns TA2 . . . . . .212 F8
St Davids Mews BS1. . . . . .226 C2
St Davids PI BA10 . . . . .215 E7
ST DECUMANS 202 B6
St Decuman's Rd TA23. . . .202 C7
St Dubricius CE First Sch
TA24 . . . . .124 A3
St Dunstans CI
Glastonbury BA6 . . . . .206 D5
Keynsham BS31. . . . . .24 E6
St Dunstan's Com Sch
BA6. . . . . .206 D5
St Dunstan's Pk BA6. . . . . .158 A5
St Edmund's Rd BA6. . . . . .206 D5
St Edmund's Terr BA3 . . . . .117 C7
St Edward's CI TA7 . . . . . . .137 B2
St Edward's Rd BS8 . . . . . . .226 B2
St Edyth's Rd BS9 . . . . .5 C6
St Elizabeth's Way TA12 . .220 C4
SS Peter & Paul RC Cath★
BS8. . . . . .226 A4
SS Peter & Paul RC Prim Sch
BS8. . . . . .226 C4
St Francis RC Prim Sch
BS48. . . . . .8 F1
St Francis Rd BS31 . . . . .24 D6
St George CE Prim Sch
BS1. . . . . .226 B2
ST GEORGES 32 D3
St Georges Ave EX13 . . . . .198 A2
St George's Ave
Taunton TA2 . . . . .212 F8
Yeovil BA21 . . . . .219 B7
St Georges Bldgs BA1 . . . .228 A3
St George's CE Sch SP8. . . .161 E1
St George's CE Sch, Bourton
SP8. . . . . .161 E1
St Georges CI TA24 . . . . . . .201 D2
St George's Cross BA11. . . .101 C3
St Georges Ct BA6. . . . . . . .206 E5
St George's Hill
Bath BA2 . . . . .45 D8
Easton-in-G BS20. . . . . .4 A3
St George's La BS20. . . . . . . .4 B4
St Georges Mews TA1 . . . .212 F3
St Georges PI BA1. . . . . . . .228 A3
St George's PI TA1. . . . . . .212 F3
St Georges Prim Sch BS22 .32 C3
St George's RC Prim Sch
TA1. . . . . .213 A3
St George's RC Sch TA1. . .213 A4
St Georges Rd BS1. . . . . . .226 C2
St George's Rd
Keynsham BS31. . . . . .24 D6
Portbury BS20 . . . . .3 E7
St Georges Sq TA1. . . . . . .212 F3
St George's St TA24 . . . . . .201 D2
St Georges Way TA1. . . . . .212 E2
St Gildas TA20 . . . . .223 D4
St Gildas CI TA10 . . . . .172 A5
St Gildas Ct TA10. . . . . . . .172 A5
St Gildas RC Prim Sch
BA21. . . . . .219 D8
St Gildas's Way BA6. . . . . .206 D4
St Gregory's CE Prim Sch
Marnhull DT10 . . . . .190 F5
Marnhull DT10 . . . . .190 F5
St Gregory's RC Sch BA2. . .62 D8
St Helens BA22 . . . . .175 D8
St Hilary CI BS9 . . . . .5 D5
St Ives CI BS48 . . . . .9 A1
St Ives Rd BS23. . . . . .49 A5
St James' Barton BS1 . . . .227 B4
St James CI TA1. . . . . .212 F4
St James Ct
Bridgwater TA6 . . . . .209 D3
4 Taunton TA1. . . . . .212 F4

St James Mews TA13 . . . . .220 C4
St James's Cl BA21 . . . . . .218 D5
St James's Par BA1 . . . . . .228 B2
St James's Pk
  Bath BA1 . . . . .228 B4
  Yeovil BA20 . . . . .218 C5
St James's Sq BA6 . . . . . .157 D4
St James's Sq BA1 . . . . . .228 A4
St James's St
  Bath BA1 . . . . .228 B4
  South Petherton TA13 . . . .220 C4
St James St
  Taunton TA1 . . . . .212 E4
  Weston-super-Mare BS23 . . .48 D7
St James Terr BA22 . . . . . .197 A4
St John's BA1 . . . . .44 B8
St John & St Francis CE Prim
  Sch TA6 . . . . .209 C4
St John's Ave BS21 . . . . .6 D3
St John's Bridge 4 BS1 . . .227 A4
St John's CE Fst Sch BA11 119 F4
St John's CE Inf Sch BA1..206 E5
St John's CE Prim Sch
  Keynsham BS31 . . . . .24 E5
  Midsomer Norton BA3 . . . . .78 A1
  Midsomer Norton BA3 . . . . .78 A1
  Wellington TA21 . . . . .222 E6
  Wellington TA21 . . . . .222 E6
St John's CE VA Fst Sch
  17 Frome BA11 . . . . .119 F4
  17 Frome BA11 . . . . .119 F4
St Johns Cl TA21 . . . . .222 E6
St John's Cl
  Peasedown St John BA2. . . .79 B7
  Skilgate TA4 . . . . .164 E6
  Weston-super-Mare BS23 . . .30 D1
St John's Cres
  Midsomer Norton BA3 . . . . .78 A2
  Trowbridge BA14 . . . . .83 F6
St Johns Ct
  Axbridge BS26 . . . . .70 B2
  Bath BA2 . . . . .228 C3
  Keynsham BS31 . . . . .24 E6
  Wells BA5. . . . . .203 D5
St Johns Ho 3 BA20 . . . . .219 B5
St John's Pl BA1 . . . . .228 B2
St John's RC Prim Sch
  (Annexe) BA2. . . . . .44 A4
St Johns Rd BA2 . . . . .60 B1
St John's Rd
  Backwell BS48 . . . . .19 B5
  Bath BA2 . . . . .228 C3
  Bath, Lower Weston BA1 . . .44 C7
  Burnham-on-S TA8 . . . . . .104 B7
  Clevedon BS21. . . . . .6 D3
  Frome BA11. . . . . .120 B5
  Taunton TA1 . . . . .212 E4
  Yeovil BA21 . . . . .219 D7
St Johns Ret Pk TA1 . . . . . .213 B5
St John's Sq BA6. . . . . . . .206 D5
St John St
  Bridgwater TA6 . . . . .209 B4
  Wells BA5. . . . . .203 D4
St John's Terr BA11 . . . . . .119 E5
St Johns Wlk BA6 . . . . . . .206 D5
St John the Evangelist CE
  Prim Sch
  3 Clevedon BS21 . . . . .6 C1
  Clevedon BS21. . . . . .6 C1
St Joseph & St Teresa RC
  Prim Sch
  Wells BA5. . . . . .203 D4
  Wells BA5. . . . . .203 D4
St Josephs Field TA1 . . . . .213 A3
St Joseph's RC Prim Sch
  Bridgwater TA6 . . . . .208 D4
  Burnham-on-S TA8 . . . . . .104 B6
  Burnham-on-Sea TA8 . . . . .104 B6
  Portishead BS20 . . . . .2 D3
St Joseph's Rd BS23. . . . . . .30 E1
St Judes Ho 21 BS2. . . . . .227 C3
St Jude's Terr BA22 . . . . . . .31 C1
St Julian's CE Prim Sch
  BA2. . . . . .62 E1
St Julian's Cl BS39 . . . . . . .77 E4
St Julian's Rd BA2. . . . . . . .79 F5
St Juthware Cl BA22. . . . . .197 C3
St Katherine's Sch BS20 . . . .4 E3
St Kenya Ct BS31. . . . . .24 F5
St Keyna Prim Sch BS31 . . . .24 D5
St Keyna Rd BS31 . . . . .24 E5
St Kilda's Rd BA2. . . . . .44 D5
St Ladoc Rd BS31. . . . . .24 D6
St Laud Cl BS30 . . . . .5 D5
St Lawrence Ct BS11 . . . . . . .4 E8
St Lawrence's CE Prim Sch
  BA5. . . . . .110 E6
St Lawrences VC Prim Sch
  BA5. . . . . .110 E6
St Leonards Ct BA20. . . . . .219 A4
St Loe Cl BS14 . . . . .22 F3
St Louis RC Prim Sch
  13 Frome BA11 . . . . .119 E5
  Frome BA11. . . . . .119 E5
St Luke's Cl TA8. . . . . .104 B7
St Lukes Mews TA4. . . . . . .167 E6
St Lukes Rd BA11. . . . . . . .101 E5
St Luke's Rd
  Bath BA2 . . . . .44 F3
  Midsomer Norton BA3 . . . . .77 F2
St Margarets Cl BS48. . . . . .19 A5
St Margaret's Cl BS31 . . . . .24 D6
St Margarets Ct TA1. . . . . .213 B4
St Margarets La TA20. . . . .198 C8
St Margaret's La BS48 . . . . .19 A5
St Margaret's Rd BA22. . . .186 B6
St Margaret's Sch BA22. . . .186 C6
St Margaret's Terr BS23 . . . .48 D8

St Marks Cl
  Chedzoy TA7. . . . . .154 E8
  Keynsham BS31. . . . . .24 E6
St Marks Ct TA6. . . . . .209 D3
St Mark's Ecumenical
  CE/Methodist Prim Sch
  BS22. . . . . .31 F4
St Marks Gdns BA2. . . . . . .228 C1
St Mark's Rd
  Bath BA2 . . . . .228 C1
  Burnham-on-S TA8 . . . . . .104 B8
  Midsomer Norton BA3 . . . . .78 A2
  Weston-super-Mare BS22 . . .32 A3
St Mark's Sch BA1. . . . . . . .28 B2
St Mark's VA Prim Sch
  BS22. . . . . .31 F4
St Martins
  Clevedon BS21. . . . . .6 C5
  Long Ashton BS41 . . . . . . .11 A1
St Martin's CE Prim Sch
  BS22. . . . . .31 D2
St Martins Cl
  Fiveheald TA3 . . . . .170 F1
  Zeals BA12 . . . . .161 F3
St Martins Ct BS22 . . . . . . .31 E3
St Martin's Ct BA2. . . . . . . .44 E1
St Martin's Garden Prim Sch
  BA2. . . . . .44 D1
St Martins Hospl BA2. . . . . .44 E1
St Martin's La SN14 . . . . . .13 F8
St Martins Pk SN14 . . . . . .13 F8
St Martins Way BA20 . . . . .218 D2
St Mary CE Prim Sch BA2 . .45 C8
St Mary Redcliffe & Temple
  CE Sch BS1. . . . . .227 B1
St Mary & St Peter's CE VC
  Prim Sch
  Barrington TA19. . . . . . . .184 D5
  Ilton TA19. . . . . .183 E4
St Mary's Bldgs BA2. . . . . .228 B1
St Mary's CE Prim Sch
  Bradford Abbas DT9. . . . . .187 E1
  Bridgwater TA6 . . . . .208 C4
  Radstock BA3. . . . . .79 C1
  Thorncombe TA20. . . . . . .199 B6
  Timsbury BA2. . . . . .60 C3
St Mary's CE VA Prim Sch
  BS20. . . . . .3 E3
St Marys Cl
  Hutton BS24. . . . . .49 D2
  Seavington St Mary TA19 . .184 D1
  Wedmore BS28 . . . . .108 C4
St Mary's Cl
  10 Axminster EX13. . . . . . .198 A1
  Bath BA2 . . . . .45 B6
  Chard TA20 . . . . .223 C2
  Cossington TA7. . . . . .136 F3
  Timsbury BA2. . . . . .60 B2
St Mary's Cres
  Chard TA20 . . . . .223 C3
  13 North Petherton TA6 . . .153 E4
  Yeovil BA21 . . . . .219 C8
St Mary's Ct TA6. . . . . . . .153 E4
St Mary's Ct
  1 Bridgwater TA6 . . . . . . .208 F4
  Weston-super-Mare BS24 . . .49 A1
St Mary's Gdns BS40 . . . . . .53 B5
St Mary's Gr BS48 . . . . .18 C8
St Mary's La BA4 . . . . .140 E3
St Mary's Park Rd BS20 . . . . .2 C4
St Mary's Pk
  Langport TA10 . . . . .172 A5
  Nailsea BS48 . . . . .18 C8
St Marys Pl BA4 . . . . .142 F4
St Mary's RC Prim Sch
  Axminster EX13 . . . . .198 A1
  Bath BA1 . . . . .27 B1
St Mary's Rd
  Bristol BS11. . . . . .4 D7
  Burnham-on-S TA8 . . . . . .104 B7
  Frome BA11. . . . . .120 B5
  Hutton BS24. . . . . .49 D2
  Leigh Woods BS8 . . . . .11 D6
  Meare BA6. . . . . .138 D4
  Oxenpill BA6. . . . . .138 C4
  Portishead BS20 . . . . .2 C4
  Sherborne DT9. . . . . .225 B3
  Westonzoyland TA7 . . . . . .154 F5
St Marys Rise BA3 . . . . .79 C2
St Mary's St BS26 . . . . .70 C2
St Mary St
  Bridgwater TA6 . . . . .208 F4
  Nether Stowey TA5. . . . . . .134 B2
St Mary's View BA22 . . . . .196 F7
St Mary's Wlk BS11. . . . . . . .4 D6
St Mathew's Pl BA2 . . . . . .45 B5
St Mathias Ho BA2. . . . . . .227 C3
St Matthew's Cl BS23. . . . . .30 D1
St Matthew's Field TA6. . . .208 E4
St Matthews Gn TA6. . . . . .208 E4
St Matthew's Rd BS6 . . . . .227 A4
St Matthias Pk BS2 . . . . . .227 C3
St Medard Rd BS28. . . . . . .108 C4
St Michael Cl TA3 . . . . . . .169 D4
St Michael on the Mount CE
  Prim Sch BS2. . . . . .226 C3
St Michael Rd TA3. . . . . . .169 D4
St Michael's Ave
  Clevedon BS21. . . . . .6 D1
  Weston-super-Mare BS22 . . .32 A3
  Yeovil BA21 . . . . .219 C7
St Michael's CE First Sch
  TA24. . . . . .200 F7
St Michael's CE Jun Sch
  BA2. . . . . .44 A6
St Michaels Cl
  Nether Compton DT9 . . . . .187 F3
  Stoke St Michael BA3. . . . .116 B3

St Michael's Cl
  Buckland Dinham BA11 . . . .100 A3
  Glastonbury BA6. . . . . . . .206 E3
  Nether Stowey TA5. . . . . . .134 A2
St Michael's Cres TA2 . . . . .213 A8
St Michaels Ct
  Bawdrip TA7. . . . . .136 E2
  Walton BA16 . . . . .156 D7
  Yeovil BA21 . . . . .219 C8
St Michael's Ct BA2 . . . . . . .63 E8
St Michael's Gdns TA13. . . .220 D5
St Michael's Hill
  Bristol BS2. . . . . .226 C4
  Milverton TA4. . . . . .167 A4
St Michael's Hospl BS2. . . . .226 C4
St Michael's Pk BS2 . . . . . .226 C4
St Michael's Pl BA1 . . . . . .228 B2
St Michaels Rd BA2 . . . . . . .44 A5
St Michael's Rd
  Bath BA1 . . . . .44 D7
  Burnham-on-S TA8 . . . . . .104 B7
  Minehead TA24. . . . . .200 F8
  Yeovil BA21 . . . . .219 D6
St Michael's View TA15. . . .186 B4
St Nicholas Almshouses 5
  BS1 . . . . .227 A2
St Nicholas CE Prim Sch
  Combe St Nicholas TA20. . . .193 D6
  Henstridge BA8 . . . . .190 A7
  Radstock BA3. . . . . .78 F2
St Nicholas' CE Prim Sch
  BA3. . . . . .79 A2
St Nicholas Chantry CE Prim
  Sch BS21 . . . . .6 E3
St Nicholas Chantry CE VC
  Prim Sch BS21 . . . . .6 E3
St Nicholas Cl
  4 Henstridge BA8. . . . . . .190 A6
  Winsley BA15. . . . . .64 D7
  Yeovil BA20 . . . . .219 B4
St Nicholas Ct BA2 . . . . . . .28 F1
St Nicholas Pk BA20 . . . . .219 B4
St Nicholas Rd
  Bristol BS2. . . . . .227 C4
  Weston-super-Mare BS23 . . .48 D2
  Whitchurch BS14 . . . . .23 C4
St Nicholas St BS1 . . . . . . .227 A2
St Nicholas Way BS48 . . . . .18 D2
St Oswald's Ct BS13. . . . . . .22 A8
St Patricks Cl 3 TA2 . . . . .213 A8
St Patricks Ct BS31 . . . . . . .24 E5
St Patrick's Ct BA2 . . . . . . .45 B6
St Patrick's Rd
  Taunton TA2 . . . . .213 A8
  Yeovil BA21 . . . . .218 D7
ST PAULS 227 C4
St Paul's CE Jun Sch BA4 . .205 B5
St Pauls Cl TA13. . . . . .220 D4
St Paul's Cl DT9. . . . . .225 E6
St Pauls Ct TA6. . . . . .209 D3
St Paul's Flats DT9. . . . . . .225 E6
St Paul's Gn DT9. . . . . . . .225 E6
St Paul Pl
  Bath BA1 . . . . .228 B2
  Midsomer Norton BA3 . . . . .78 A2
St Paul's Rd
  Bristol BS8. . . . . .226 B4
  Burnham-on-S TA8 . . . . . .104 B7
  Weston-super-Mare BS23 . . .48 E5
St Paul St BS2 . . . . .227 B4
St Paul's Terr BA5. . . . . . . .111 A4
St Peter's Ave BS23 . . . . . . .30 D1
St Peter's CE Fst Sch TA4 . .202 D4
St Peters CE Prim Sch
  BS13 . . . . .21 F6
St Peter's CE Prim Sch
  BS13. . . . . .21 F6
St Peters Cl
  Ilton TA19. . . . . .183 F4
  Staple Fitzpaine TA3 . . . . .182 C5
  Williton TA4 . . . . .202 D2
St Peter's Cl
  Horton TA19. . . . . .183 C1
  Taunton TA1 . . . . .213 B7
St Peters Cres TA6 . . . . . . .209 D3
St Peter's Ho BS8 . . . . . . .226 B2
St Peters Lodge BS20. . . . . .2 D4
St Peters Rd
  Portishead BS20 . . . . .2 D4
  Shepton Mallet BA4 . . . . . .205 A6
St Peter's Rd
  Burnham-on-S TA8 . . . . . .104 B7
  Radstock BA3. . . . . .97 C8
St Peter's Rise
  Bristol BS13. . . . . .22 A7
  South Petherton TA13. . . . .220 D4
St Peters Terr 21 BA4. . . . .205 B6
St Peter's Terr BA2. . . . . . . .44 D6
St Philip's CE Prim Sch
  BA2. . . . . .44 D2
St Philips Rd BS2. . . . . . . .227 C3
St Pius X RC Prim Sch
  BS13. . . . . .22 A5
St Quintin Pk TA2 . . . . . . .213 E6
St Rayn Hill TA17. . . . . . . .195 B4
St Saviour's Ave TA6 . . . . .209 A4
St Saviour's Inf Church Sch
  BA1. . . . . .28 B2
St Saviour's Jun Church Sch
  BA1. . . . . .28 B2
St Saviour's Rd BA1 . . . . . .28 C2
St Saviour's Terr 10 BA1 . . .28 B1
St Saviours Way 4 BA1. . . .28 C1
St Stephen's Ave 3 BS1. . .227 A4
St Stephen's CE Prim Sch
  BA1. . . . . .27 F1
St Stephen's Cl BA1. . . . . . .27 F1
St Stephen's Ct BA1. . . . . .228 B4
St Stephen's Pl BA1. . . . . .228 B4

St Stephen's Rd BA1. . . . . .228 B4
St Stephen's St BS1. . . . . .227 A4
St Swithins Cl DT9 . . . . . . .225 E4
St Swithin's Pl BA1. . . . . . .228 C4
St Swithin's Rd DT9 . . . . . .225 E4
St Swithin's Yd BA2 . . . . . .228 C3
St Thomas Cross BA21. . . . .219 C5
St Thomas Ct TA6 . . . . . . .209 D3
St Thomas' Ct BA5 . . . . . . .203 E4
St Thomas Mews BA5 . . . . .203 F5
St Thomas Pl BS1 . . . . . . .227 B2
St Thomas Rd BA3 . . . . . . .78 B2
St Thomas St E BS1 . . . . . .227 B2
St Thomas St
  Bristol BS1. . . . . .227 B2
  Dunster TA24. . . . . .201 E2
  Wells BA5. . . . . .203 E5
St Thomas Terr BA5 . . . . . .203 F5
St Vigor & St John CE Prim
  Sch BA3. . . . . .96 E3
St Vincent's Rd BS8 . . . . . .226 A2
St Whites Cl BS14 . . . . .23 D3
St Whytes Rd BS4. . . . . . . .22 D8
St Winifreds Dr BA2 . . . . . .45 D2
Salcombe Gdns BS22. . . . . .32 A2
Salcombe Rd BS4 . . . . .23 A8
Sale Piece Dro TA10. . . . . .156 F1
Salerno Cl BA22 . . . . .173 E2
Sales Ho 15 BA4. . . . . . . .205 B6
Salisbury Rd
  Bath BA1 . . . . .28 B2
  Burnham-on-S TA8 . . . . . .104 C7
  Paulton BS39 . . . . .77 F4
  Weston-super-Mare BS22 . . .31 C1
Salisbury St TA2 . . . . .212 E6
Salisbury Terr
  Castle Cary BA7 . . . . .214 B5
  4 Frome BA11 . . . . .119 E3
  Frome BA11. . . . . .119 E3
  Gurney Slade BA3 . . . . . . .114 E8
  Weston-super-Mare BS23 . . .48 D7
Sally Hill BS20 . . . . .2 E7
Sally In The Wood BA1,
  BA15. . . . . .46 D6
Sally Lovell's La BA8 . . . . .189 F8
Sally Lunn's Kitchen Mus★
  BA1. . . . . .228 C2
Sallysmead Cl BS13. . . . . . .22 A4
Salmon Mead BS14. . . . . . .23 D3
Salmon Par TA6. . . . . .209 A4
SALTFORD. 25 D2
Saltford CE Prim Sch
  BS31. . . . . .25 E2
Saltford Ct BS31 . . . . .25 E3
Salthouse Ct BS21. . . . . . . .6 B2
Salthouse La BA20 . . . . . . .219 A4
Salthouse Rd BS21. . . . . . . .6 B2
Saltings Cl BS21. . . . . .6 B2
Saltlands TA6. . . . . .208 F7
Saltlands Ave TA6. . . . . . . .208 F7
Saltlands Ho TA6. . . . . . . .208 F7
Saltlands La TA6. . . . . .209 A7
Saltry La TA24 . . . . .131 A6
Saltwell Ave BS14. . . . . . . .23 C5
Salway Cl BS40 . . . . .38 E1
Salway Gdns 11 EX13 . . . . .198 A1
Samarate Way BA20 . . . . . .218 D4
Sambar Pl TA6. . . . . .208 D3
Sambourne La BS20. . . . . . .4 C4
SAMPFORD ARUNDEL. 179 E5
Sampford Arundel Com Prim
  Sch TA21 . . . . .179 E5
SAMPFORD BRETT. 202 E1
SAMPFORD MOOR. 179 F5
SAMPFORD PEVERELL 178 E1
Sampford Peverell CE Prim
  Sch EX16 . . . . .178 C1
Sampford Rocks TA4. . . . . .202 F1
Sampsons Rd BS13. . . . . . .22 A4
Samuel Ct BA8 . . . . .176 F1
Samuels Ct TA2. . . . . .212 E6
Samways Cl BA22 . . . . . . .218 B5
Sanctuary Gdns BS9. . . . . . .5 D3
Sanctuary La TA22 . . . . . . .148 A2
SAND 108 C2
Sandalwood Ride TA6. . . . .153 F5
Sandbrook La BA22 . . . . . .175 D7
Sandburrows Rd BS13. . . . . .21 F6
Sandburrows Wlk BS13. . . . .21 F6
Sandcroft BS14 . . . . .22 F6
Sandcroft Ave BS23 . . . . . . .48 D2
Sandene Ct BA2 . . . . .212 C8
Sanderling BS20 . . . . .2 F6
Sanderling Pl 7 BS20 . . . . .2 F6
Sand Farm La TA8. . . . . . . .31 A6
SANDFORD. 52 A3
SANDFORD BATCH. 51 F2
Sandford Cl 2 BS21. . . . . . .6 B1
Sandford Hill TA5, TA6 . . . .208 A6
SANDFORD ORCAS 188 C7
Sandford Orcas Manor Ho★
  DT9. . . . . .188 B7
Sandford Orcas DT9. . . . . .225 B7
Sandford Pk BA14. . . . . . . .83 F7
Sandford Prim Sch BS25. . . .52 B4
Sandford Rd
  Bristol BS8. . . . . .226 A1
  Weston-super-Mare BS23 . . .49 A7
  Winscombe BS25. . . . . . . .51 F1
Sandhill La TA24 . . . . .131 C4
Sandhills Dr TA8 . . . . .84 F4
Sandhurst Rd BA20. . . . . . .218 F1
Sanding's La
  Chapel Leigh TA4 . . . . . . .167 A8
  Fitzhead TA4. . . . . .166 F8
  Lydeard St Lawrence TA4. . .151 A1
Sandlewood Cl BA21 . . . . . .219 E8
Sandmead Rd BS25 . . . . . . .52 A4

Sandown Cl
  Bridgwater TA6 . . . . .209 A2
  3 Yeovil BA20 . . . . .219 A5
Sandpiper Cl
  Bridgwater TA6 . . . . .209 A4
  Minehead TA24. . . . . .201 C5
Sandpiper Dr BS22. . . . . . . .31 F1
Sandpiper Rd TA6. . . . . . . .209 A4
Sandpits Hill TA10. . . . . . . .171 E4
Sandpits Rd BA6 . . . . .206 F5
Sand Rd
  Wedmore BS28 . . . . .108 C3
  Weston-super-Mare BS22 . . .31 B5
Sandringham Cl TA6 . . . . . .209 C7
Sandringham Ct 2 BS23. . . .48 F5
Sandringham Rd
  1 Weston-super-Mare
    BS23. . . . . .48 F5
  Yeovil BA21 . . . . .219 E6
Sandrocks La TA24. . . . . . .131 B3
Sandscross La BA11. . . . . . .100 A3
Sand St TA4 . . . . .166 F4
Sandy Cl TA9 . . . . .104 D4
Sandy Hole TA16. . . . . . . .195 F7
Sandy La
  Beckington BA11 . . . . .101 E4
  Cannington TA5 . . . . .135 A3
  Cannington TA5 . . . . .135 B3
  Chew Magna BS40. . . . . . .39 C3
  Easton-in-G BS8 . . . . .10 A8
  Failand BS8 . . . . .10 C7
  Stanton Drew BS39, BS40. . .39 E3
  Wiveliscombe TA4 . . . . . . .210 C2
Sandyleaze BS9. . . . . .5 E7
Sandy's Hill La BA11. . . . . .119 E1
Sandy's La EX14. . . . . .191 F2
Sandys Moor TA4 . . . . .210 D4
Sandy View BA11. . . . . . . .101 E4
Sandyway Cross EX36 . . . . .145 H4
Sansome's Hill DT9 . . . . . . .217 D2
Sansom's Cross DT6. . . . . . .199 F1
Sapphire Dr TA6 . . . . .209 C8
Sarabeth Dr BA2 . . . . .61 A4
Saracen St BA1 . . . . .228 C3
Saunder's Piece La
  TA18. . . . . .224 A7
Saunters Cl BA9. . . . . .216 B4
Saunton Wlk BS4. . . . . .22 E8
Savannah Dr 3 TA6. . . . . .154 A5
Savernake Rd BS22 . . . . . . .31 F3
Savery or Cottage Row
  TA1. . . . . .213 B3
Saviano Way TA6. . . . . . . .208 E7
Saville Cres BS22 . . . . .49 C8
Saville Gate Cl BS9. . . . . . . .5 F4
Saville Mews BS6 . . . . .227 A4
Saville Pl BS8. . . . . .226 A2
Saville Rd
  Bristol BS9. . . . . .5 F3
  Weston-super-Mare BS22 . . .49 C8
Saville Row BA1 . . . . .228 B3
Savoy The BS11. . . . . .4 E6
Saw Cl BA1 . . . . .228 B2
Sawmill Cotts BA11. . . . . . .143 B8
Sawmill Gdns BA3. . . . . . . .96 D3
Sawpit La BA4 . . . . .140 C2
Sawpits Cl TA4. . . . . .150 D8
Sawyers Cl
  Chilcompton BA3 . . . . .96 D3
  Wraxall BS48 . . . . .9 A2
Sawyers Ct BS21. . . . . .6 E3
SAWYER'S HILL 180 E7
Sawyers Leigh TA2. . . . . . .168 D8
Sawyers Mill EX16. . . . . . .164 E2
Saxby Cl
  Clevedon BS21. . . . . .6 B1
  Weston-super-Mare BS22 . . .32 B4
Saxon Cl
  Oake TA4 . . . . .167 D4
  Watchet TA23. . . . . .202 B7
  Whitchurch BS14 . . . . .23 D3
Saxon Ct
  Ilminster TA19 . . . . .221 B4
  Weston-super-Mare BS22 . . .32 D3
Saxondale Ave TA8. . . . . . . .85 A3
Saxon Gn TA6. . . . . .209 C4
Saxon Pl BS27 . . . . .90 B7
Saxon Rd
  Bridgwater TA6 . . . . .209 C4
  Weston-super-Mare BS22 . . .49 C8
Saxon Ridge TA23. . . . . . . .202 B7
Saxon St BS40 . . . . .53 D6
Saxonvale BA11. . . . . .119 F4
Saxon Way
  Cheddar BS27 . . . . .90 B6
  Peasedown St John BA2. . . .79 E8
  Wedmore BS28 . . . . .108 C4
  Wincanton BA9 . . . . .216 B3
  Winsley BA15. . . . . .64 F7
Saxony Pl 3 TA6. . . . . . . .209 A1
Says La BA3. . . . . .53 B4
Scadden's La BS27. . . . . . . .91 B1
Scafell Cl
  Taunton TA1 . . . . .212 C1
  Weston-super-Mare BS23 . . .31 A1
Scamel Ho 11 BA4. . . . . . .205 B6
Scarf Dr BS24. . . . . .50 C5
Scaurs The BS22. . . . . .31 F2
Schofield Cl 1 TA2. . . . . . .169 C5
School Cl
  Bampton EX16 . . . . .164 B1
  Banwell BS29 . . . . .51 B3
  Bristol, Whitchurch BS14 . . .22 F4
  Tintinhull BA22. . . . . .186 C6
  Watchet TA23. . . . . .202 C7

School Cotts
🔢 East Coker BA22 . . . . . 197 F8
Enmore TA5 . . . . . 153 A5
Taunton TA2 . . . . . 168 F6
School Dr DT9 . . . . . 225 E5
School Fields
Cannington TA5 . . . . . 135 C2
2 North Petherton TA6 . . . 153 F3
School Hill
Ashcott TA7 . . . . . 156 B8
Cucklington BA9 . . . . . 177 D6
Misterton TA18 . . . . . 224 F3
South Perrott DT8 . . . . . 196 C1
Westbury-sub-Mendip BA5 . 110 E6
Wookey Hole BA5 . . . . . 203 A8
SCHOOL HOUSE 199 A5
School La
Barrow Gurney BS48 . . . . . 20 D5
Batheaston BA1 . . . . . 28 F4
Blackford BS28 . . . . . 107 D4
Burrowbridge TA7 . . . . . 154 F1
Chew Stoke BS40 . . . . . 56 D8
Combwich TA5 . . . . . 135 B5
Compton Dundon TA11 . . . 157 A3
Doulting BA4 . . . . . 141 E6
Draycott BS27 . . . . . 90 F3
Drimpton DT8 . . . . . 199 E6
Farrington Gurney BS39 . . . 77 A4
Horrington BA5 . . . . . 113 A1
Kilmersdon BA3 . . . . . 98 A6
Lopen TA13 . . . . . 185 A1
7 North Petherton TA6 . . . 153 F4
Rowberrow BS25 . . . . . 53 A1
Seavington St Michael TA19 . 184 E2
Shapwick TA7 . . . . . 137 F1
Somerton TA11 . . . . . 211 E3
Tatworth TA20 . . . . . 198 C8
Templecombe BA8 . . . . . 176 E1
Wick St Lawrence BS22 . . . 32 B7
Woolavington TA7 . . . . . 136 E4
School of Christ the King RC
Prim BS4 . . . . . 22 E8
School Pl BA2 . . . . . 46 B5
School Rd
Kingsdon TA11 . . . . . 173 D5
Monkton Heathfield TA2 . . . 213 F8
Parbrook BA6 . . . . . 158 C7
Westonzoyland TA7 . . . . . 154 E5
Wrington BS40 . . . . . 35 E2
School St
Curry Rivel TA10 . . . . . 171 D4
Drayton TA10 . . . . . 171 E3
School View BS48 . . . . . 9 B1
Schooner Pl TA24 . . . . . 201 B7
Scimitar Rd BA22 . . . . . 218 B6
Scobell Rise BS39 . . . . . 59 C2
Score La BS40 . . . . . 54 E2
Score The BS40 . . . . . 54 E2
Scornfield La BS40 . . . . . 56 D7
Scotch Horn Cl BS48 . . . . . 8 F2
Scotch Horn Way 5 BS48 . . . 8 F2
Scot Cl TA6 . . . . . 135 F5
Scot Elm Dr
Weston-super-Mare BS24 . . . 32 D1
Weston-super-Mare BS29 . . . 50 D8
Scot La BS40 . . . . . 38 D1
Scotland La
Axbridge BS26 . . . . . 107 D8
Chapel Allerton BS26 . . . . . 107 D8
Rudge BA11 . . . . . 102 C4
Stockwood Vale BS4, BS14 . . . 24 A7
Scots Pine Ave 3 BS48 . . . . 8 F2
Scott Cl TA2 . . . . . 212 C6
Scott Rd
Frome BA11 . . . . . 119 F5
Highbridge TA9 . . . . . 104 D3
Weston-super-Mare BS23 . . . 49 A4
Scott Road BA21 . . . . . 219 F8
Scotts Cl BA3 . . . . . 116 C8
Scotts Hill TA4 . . . . . 148 E1
Scott's Hill
Huish Champflower TA4 . . . 165 E8
Seavington St Mary TA19 . . . 184 D1
Scotts La TA7 . . . . . 137 D1
Scott's La TA21 . . . . . 222 E6
Scotts Way TA18 . . . . . 196 B8
Scouse Cross EX13 . . . . . 198 E2
Scouse La EX13 . . . . . 198 E2
Scrapton La TA20 . . . . . 193 D5
Screech Witch Hill TA12 . . 185 F8
Screedy La TA4 . . . . . 166 D4
Scruibbitts La TA7 . . . . . 137 B2
Scud La TA18 . . . . . 195 B2
Scumbrum La BS39 . . . . . 59 C2
SEABOROUGH 195 E1
Seaborough Rd TA18 . . . . . 195 F2
Seaborough Road DT8 . . . 224 D1
Seaborough View TA18 . . . 224 C4
Seabrook Rd BS22 . . . . . 31 D1
Sea King Rd BA20 . . . . . 218 D3
Sea King Way BS21 . . . . . 49 C5
Sea La
Carhampton TA24 . . . . . 131 A7
Dunster TA24 . . . . . 201 F4
Kilve TA5 . . . . . 133 C6
Watchet TA23 . . . . . 132 D5
Sealey Cl BS27 . . . . . 90 F3
Sealey Cres BA5 . . . . . 112 E1
Sealeys Cl TA9 . . . . . 136 A8
SEA MILLS 5 B6
Sea Mills Inf Sch BS9 . . . 5 C7
Sea Mills La BS9 . . . . . 5 C5
Sea Mills Prim Sch BS9 . . . 5 B5
Sea Mills Sta BS9 . . . . . 5 B4
SeaQuarium ★ BS23 . . . . . 48 D6

Searle Cres BS23 . . . . . 49 A6
Searle Ct
Clevedon BS21 . . . . . 6 E2
Somerton TA11 . . . . . 211 D3
Seat La BA4 . . . . . 142 D1
Seaton Ct BA20 . . . . . 219 A4
Seaton Rd BA20 . . . . . 218 F4
Seavale Mews BS21 . . . . . 6 C4
Seavale Rd BS21 . . . . . 6 C4
Seaview Rd
Portishead, Redcliffe Bay
BS20 . . . . . 1 F4
Portishead, West Hill BS20 . . . 1 F6
Sea View Rd TA8 . . . . . 104 A8
SEAVINGTON ST MARY . . 184 D1
SEAVINGTON ST
MICHAEL 184 F2
Seawalls BS9 . . . . . 5 D2
Seawalls Rd BS9 . . . . . 5 D2
Seaward Dr TA6 . . . . . 208 F6
Seaward Way TA24 . . . . . 201 C6
Second Ave
Axminster EX13 . . . . . 198 A2
Bath BA2 . . . . . 44 D5
Bristol BS14 . . . . . 23 B7
Radstock BA3 . . . . . 97 C7
Second Dro TA7 . . . . . 155 D3
Secret World Wildlife
Rescue ★ TA9 . . . . . 136 C8
SECTOR 198 B1
Sector Hill EX13 . . . . . 198 B1
Sector La EX13 . . . . . 198 A1
Sedge Cl TA6 . . . . . 208 F2
Sedge Dro TA7 . . . . . 137 C3
Sedge Mead BA11 . . . . . 119 F7
Sedgemoor Cl
Nailsea BS48 . . . . . 18 E8
Yeovil BA21 . . . . . 219 D7
Sedgemoor Dro
Sutton Mallet TA7 . . . . . 155 A6
Wrantage TA3 . . . . . 170 B2
Sedgemoor Hill Dr TA7 . . . 155 B7
Sedgemoor Manor Com Jun
Sch TA6 . . . . . 209 C6
Sedgemoor Manor Inf Sch
TA6 . . . . . 209 D5
Sedgemoor Rd
Bath BA2 . . . . . 44 F2
Bridgwater TA6 . . . . . 209 C3
Weston-super-Mare BS23 . . . 30 F1
Woolavington TA7 . . . . . 136 E3
Sedgemoor Way
Glastonbury BA6 . . . . . 206 D5
Woolavington TA7 . . . . . 136 E3
Sedgemount Ind Pk TA6 . . 136 A2
Sedgewick Ho BS11 . . . . . 4 E7
Seeley Cres BA16 . . . . . 207 B3
Sefton Sq BS24 . . . . . 50 A8
Selbourne Cl BA1 . . . . . 44 A8
Selbourne Pl TA24 . . . . . 200 F6
Selbourne Rd BS23 . . . . . 48 E4
Selden Rd BS14 . . . . . 23 E5
Sellbed Cross TA24 . . . . . 146 A8
Selley Wlk BS13 . . . . . 22 A5
Sellicks Rd TA3 . . . . . 213 E8
Selway Ct BA2 . . . . . 45 B2
Selwood TA20 . . . . . 223 C5
Selwood Acad BA11 . . . . . 120 B6
Selwood Cl BS22 . . . . . 49 C7
Selwood Cres BA11 . . . . . 120 A7
Selwood Rd
Frome BA11 . . . . . 119 E5
Glastonbury BA6 . . . . . 206 F6
Selwood St BA11 . . . . . 118 B7
SELWORTHY 124 D3
Selworthy Cl
Bridgwater TA6 . . . . . 208 F1
Keynsham BS31 . . . . . 24 D5
Selworthy Gdns 4 BS48 . . . 8 E1
Selworthy Ho BA2 . . . . . 44 F2
Selworthy Rd
Taunton TA2 . . . . . 213 B8
Weston-super-Mare BS23 . . . 49 A4
Selworthy Sch
Priorswood TA2 . . . . . 213 A6
12 Pyrland TA2 . . . . . 213 A8
Selworthy Specl Sch TA2 . 213 A8
Selworthy Terr BA2 . . . . . 44 F2
Semington Cl TA1 . . . . . 213 D4
Septimus Bldgs BS14 . . . . 22 D5
Serbert Cl BS20 . . . . . 2 E5
Serbert Rd BS20 . . . . . 2 E5
Serbert Way BS20 . . . . . 2 E5
Sercombe Pk BS21 . . . . . 6 E1
Serel Dr BA5 . . . . . 203 B3
Serenity Rise BA16 . . . . . 207 B5
Serlo Ct BS22 . . . . . 32 A4
Serotines The TA10 . . . . . 171 D8
Serse Cl BS31 . . . . . 24 C2
Sevenacres TA11 . . . . . 211 C3
Seven Acres La BA1 . . . . . 28 F5
Seven Acres The 3 BS24 . . . 49 F7
SEVEN ASH 151 D4
Seven Dials BA1 . . . . . 228 B2
Seventh Ave BS14 . . . . . 23 A7
Severalls Park Ave TA18 . . 224 C5
Severn Ave BS23 . . . . . 48 E5
Severn Cl TA6 . . . . . 209 D7
Severn Dr TA1 . . . . . 213 C4
Severn Gr TA8 . . . . . 104 B5
Severnleigh Gdns BS9 . . . 5 F3
Severnmeade BS20 . . . . . 1 F5
Severn Rd
Bristol BS11 . . . . . 4 D6
Pill BS20 . . . . . 4 C5
Portishead BS20 . . . . . 2 C5
Weston-super-Mare BS23 . . . 48 E5
Severn Terr TA23 . . . . . 202 C7

Severn Way BS31 . . . . . 25 A5
Severus St BS31 . . . . . 24 F8
Sevier Rd BS26 . . . . . 68 C3
Seville Ct
Portishead BS20 . . . . . 2 E7
Taunton TA1 . . . . . 212 D2
Seville Rd BS20 . . . . . 2 E7
Sewage Works La TA12 . . . 185 D6
Seward Terr BA3 . . . . . 79 C2
Sewell Ho BS25 . . . . . 70 A8
Sexey's Hospl BA10 . . . . . 215 E6
Sexey's Hospl (Almshouses)
BA10 . . . . . 215 E6
Sexey's Rd BS28 . . . . . 107 E4
Sexey's Sch BA10 . . . . . 215 D5
Seymour Cl
Clevedon BS21 . . . . . 6 E3
Uphill BA5 . . . . . 203 C5
Weston-super-Mare BS22 . . . 31 F4
Seymour Rd
5 Bath BA1 . . . . . 28 A1
Bridgwater TA6 . . . . . 209 D5
Street BA16 . . . . . 207 D4
Seymour St TA21 . . . . . 222 C6
Shackel Cross EX15 . . . . . 191 B8
Shackleton Rd BA21 . . . . . 219 F8
Shadow Wlk BS24 . . . . . 50 C3
Shadwell Ct BA9 . . . . . 216 C4
Shadwell La BA9 . . . . . 216 C4
Shaftesbury Ave 2 BA1 . . . 44 C7
Shaftesbury Cl BS48 . . . . . 18 D8
Shaftesbury La BA9 . . . . . 177 B6
Shaftesbury Mews 7 BA2 . . 44 D5
Shaftesbury Rd
Bath BA2 . . . . . 44 D5
Henstridge BA8 . . . . . 190 C8
Weston-super-Mare BS23 . . . 49 B8
Shaftesbury Terr BA3 . . . . 79 A3
Shaftgate Ave BA4 . . . . . 205 A6
Shaft Rd BA2 . . . . . 45 E1
Shaggs Flood La TA20 . . . 193 B1
Shakespeare Ave
Bath BA2 . . . . . 44 F4
Taunton TA1 . . . . . 213 C3
Shakespeare Ct BS23 . . . . 48 F2
Shakespeare Rd BA3 . . . . 78 C1
Shaking Dro TA9 . . . . . 137 B6
SHALFORD 216 D8
Shalford La
Charlton Musgrove BA9 . . . . 161 A2
Shalford BA9 . . . . . 216 D8
Shallows The BS31 . . . . . 25 F3
Shambles The TA3 . . . . . 170 B4
Sham Castle La BA2 . . . . . 45 C7
Shannon Wlk BS20 . . . . . 2 F6
Shapcott La EX36 . . . . . 162 C2
Shapcott Wood Hill EX36 . 162 A2
Shaplands BS9 . . . . . 5 F4
Shapway TA19 . . . . . 184 F3
Shapway Cross TA19 . . . . . 184 F3
Shapway La BA4 . . . . . 141 F2
Shapway Rd BA4 . . . . . 141 F2
SHAPWICK 137 F1
Shapwick Heath National
Nature Reserve ★ TA7 . . . 137 F4
Shapwick Hill TA7 . . . . . 155 F8
Shapwick Rd BA6 . . . . . 138 A4
Shapwick Right Dro TA7 . . 155 C6
Shapwick Sch
Burtle TA7 . . . . . 137 D6
Shapwick TA7 . . . . . 137 F1
Sharland Cl BS9 . . . . . 5 E3
Sharland Gr BS13 . . . . . 22 C4
Sharlands La TA19 . . . . . 184 C5
Sharpenton La TA7 . . . . . 155 D6
Sharpham Dro BA16 . . . . 138 E1
Sharpham La
Glastonbury BA16 . . . . . 138 D1
Stoke St Gregory TA3 . . . . . 170 E5
Sharpham Rd
Cheddar BS27 . . . . . 89 F7
Glastonbury BA6 . . . . . 206 F7
SHARPSTONE 64 A4
Shatterwell Cotts BA9 . . . 216 C4
Shatt La TA5 . . . . . 152 F3
Shatwell La
Castle Cary BA9 . . . . . 214 F1
Yarlington BA9 . . . . . 175 F8
Shaulders The TA2 . . . . . 213 C7
Shave Cross DT6 . . . . . 199 F1
Shave Hill SP8 . . . . . 177 D4
Shave La
Crewkerne TA18 . . . . . 224 A3
Donyatt TA19 . . . . . 183 D1
Horton TA19 . . . . . 183 C1
South Brewham BA10 . . . . . 161 A6
SHAWFORD 101 D7
Shawford La BA11 . . . . . 101 D7
Shaw Gdns BS14 . . . . . 23 A8
Shaw Path TA8 . . . . . 104 C6
Shaws Way BA2 . . . . . 43 F5
Sheafhayne Cross EX14 . . . 192 E4
Shearing Cross TA20 . . . . 199 A5
Shearn La TA8 . . . . . 104 B7
Shearwater Cl TA6 . . . . . 209 D3
Shedrick Hill TA20 . . . . . 199 B8
Sheepfair La SN14 . . . . . 13 F8
Sheephouse Cvn Pk BS20 . . . 3 E7
Sheeplands La DT9 . . . . . 225 B5
Sheeplands The DT9 . . . . . 225 B5
Sheeps Croft BS13 . . . . . 22 A5
Sheepstealing La TA4 . . . . 150 E5
Sheepwash La TA19 . . . . . 184 E5
SHEEPWAY 3 B5
Sheepway BS20 . . . . . 3 B5
Sheep Way TA19 . . . . . 184 E3
Sheepway La BS20 . . . . . 3 C5
Sheldon Cl BS21 . . . . . 6 F2

Sheldon Ct TA1 . . . . . 212 E4
Sheldon Dr BA5 . . . . . 203 C3
Sheldon Mill 3 BA5 . . . . . 203 C3
Sheldon's La BA22 . . . . . 163 A7
Shelduck Cl TA24 . . . . . 201 C5
Shelley Ave BS21 . . . . . 6 D2
Shelley Cl
Burnham-on-S TA8 . . . . . 85 A2
Yeovil BA21 . . . . . 218 D6
Shelley Dr TA8 . . . . . 85 B2
Shelley Gr TA1 . . . . . 213 B3
Shelley Rd
Bath BA2 . . . . . 44 F4
Radstock BA3 . . . . . 78 C1
Weston-super-Mare BS23 . . . 49 A4
Shell's La
Chard TA20 . . . . . 193 A3
Shepton Beauchamp TA19 . . 184 E4
Shellthorn Gr TA6 . . . . . 208 F2
Shelthorn Hill TA5 . . . . . 152 F3
Shelway La TA19 . . . . . 184 C4
Shepherds Cl TA6 . . . . . 208 D3
Shepherd's Cnr TA23 . . . . 131 E4
Shepherds Cross BA8 . . . . 176 C5
Shepherd's Dro TA7 . . . . . 155 A3
Shepherd's Hay TA1 . . . . . 212 C2
Shepherd's Hill SP8 . . . . . 177 E4
Shepherd's La
Chard TA20 . . . . . 223 B4
Cucklington BA9 . . . . . 177 C5
Frome BA11 . . . . . 144 B7
Hemyock EX15 . . . . . 180 F1
Shepherds Way
Beckington BA11 . . . . . 101 F4
Weston-super-Mare BS22 . . . 32 C2
Shepherd Wlk BA2 . . . . . 45 A1
Sheppard's Barton 11
BA11 . . . . . 119 E5
Sheppard's Cnr TA5 . . . . . 153 B5
Sheppards Gdns BA1 . . . . 27 B1
Sheppards Wlk BA3 . . . . . 96 D3
Sheppy Rd TA5 . . . . . 183 D8
Sheppy's Cider Farm Centre ★
TA4 . . . . . 167 F1
Sheppy's Mill BS49 . . . . . 34 D5
Shepton BS24 . . . . . 49 A2
SHEPTON BEAUCHAMP . 184 E3
Shepton Beauchamp CE Prim
Sch TA19 . . . . . 184 E4
Shepton Beauchamp CE VC
Prim Sch TA19 . . . . . 184 E4
SHEPTON MALLET 205 D6
Shepton Mallet Com Hospl
BA4 . . . . . 204 F6
Shepton Mallet Inf Sch
BA4 . . . . . 205 C6
SHEPTON MONTAGUE . . 160 B2
Shepton Old Rd
Croscombe BA5 . . . . . 204 A6
Dinder BA5 . . . . . 140 D7
Shepton Rd BA4, BA5 . . . . 204 D7
SHERBORNE 225 D3
Litton 75 D3
Milborne Port 225 C6
Sherborne Abbey ★ DT9 . . 225 B2
Sherborne Abbey CE Prim Sch
DT9 . . . . . 225 B2
Sherborne Castle ★ DT9 . . 225 C4
Sherborne Girls Sch DT9 . 225 C4
Sherborne Hill DT9 . . . . . 225 C1
Sherborne Mus ★ DT9 . . . 225 D4
Sherborne Old Castle ★
DT9 . . . . . 225 D5
Sherborne Pk DT10 . . . . . 189 A3
Sherborne Prep Sch
DT9 . . . . . 225 D3
Sherborne Prim Sch DT9 . 225 D4
Sherborne Rd
Milborne Port DT9 . . . . . 217 C2
Yenston BA8 . . . . . 189 E6
Yeovil BA21 . . . . . 219 D5
Sherborne Rd Milbourne
Down DT9 . . . . . 188 F8
Sherborne Sch DT9 . . . . . 225 D4
Sherborne Sch Int Coll
DT9 . . . . . 225 D5
Sherdon Bridge EX36 . . . . 145 D5
SHERFORD 212 E1
Sherford Rd TA1 . . . . . 212 E1
Sherford Terr TA1 . . . . . 212 E1
Sheridan Cl TA6 . . . . . 209 D3
Sheridan Gdns BA14 . . . . 83 F6
Sheridan Rd
Bath BA2 . . . . . 43 F5
Burnham-on-S TA8 . . . . . 104 C6
Sherlands 4 TA16 . . . . . 195 F7
Sherlands Gdns 3 TA16 . . 195 F7
Shermoor La BA22 . . . . . 186 B7
Sherring Rd BA4 . . . . . 205 D4
Sherrin Way BS13 . . . . . 21 E3
Sherston Cl BS48 . . . . . 9 A1
Shervage Ct TA6 . . . . . 209 C5
Sherwell Rd BA21 . . . . . 219 D7
Sherwood Cl BS31 . . . . . 24 E5
Sherwood Cres BS22 . . . . 31 F3
Sherwood Rd BS31 . . . . . 24 E5
Shetland Way BS48 . . . . . 9 A1
Shickle Gr BA2 . . . . . 44 D1
Shiller's La DT9 . . . . . 188 C2
SHILLINGFORD 164 E2
Shiners Elms BS49 . . . . . 34 B8
SHIPHAM 70 F7
Shipham CE Fst Sch BS25 . 70 E8
Shipham Cl
Bristol BS14 . . . . . 23 B5
Nailsea BS48 . . . . . 18 F8

Shipham Cl *continued*
Weston-super-Mare BS23 . . . 49 A7
Shipham Hill BS25 . . . . . 70 F5
Shipham La BS25 . . . . . 52 B1
Shipham Rd BS27 . . . . . 71 A3
Ship La
Bristol BS1 . . . . . 227 B1
Combwich TA5 . . . . . 135 B5
SHIPLATE 67 F6
Shiplate Rd BS24 . . . . . 67 E6
Shipney La DT10 . . . . . 190 C5
Shircombe La TA22 . . . . . 147 F2
Shire Gdns BS11 . . . . . 4 D8
SHIREHAMPTON 4 E7
Shirehampton Prim Sch
BS11 . . . . . 4 D6
Shirehampton Rd BS9 . . . 5 C6
Shirehampton Sta BS11 . . . 4 D5
Shiremoor Hill TA16 . . . . 195 F7
Shire St
Bridgwater TA6 . . . . . 209 A1
🔢 Bridgwater TA7 . . . . . 154 A5
Shires The TA24 . . . . . 201 C5
Shires Yd BA1 . . . . . 228 B3
SHOCKERWICK 29 F5
Shockerwick Farm BA1 . . . 29 E6
Shockerwick La BA1 . . . . 29 D4
Shoe La
Paulton BS39 . . . . . 77 D6
Slape Cross TA7 . . . . . 209 E7
Shoot Hill TA17 . . . . . 195 C8
Shophouse Rd BA2 . . . . . 44 B5
Shop La
Pilton BA4 . . . . . 140 E3
Wingfield BA14 . . . . . 83 C6
Shopland Ho 8 BS21 . . . . 6 C2
SHOPNOLLER 151 E3
SHOREDITCH 169 A1
Shoreditch BS40 . . . . . 56 C7
Shoreditch Rd
Stoke St Mary TA3 . . . . . 169 A1
Taunton TA1 . . . . . 213 B1
Shoredown La DT9, BA8 . . 217 E6
Short Dro
Dundon TA11 . . . . . 156 E1
Mudgley BS28 . . . . . 138 C7
Somerton TA11 . . . . . 211 A8
Westbury-sub-Mendip BA5,
BS27 . . . . . 110 B4
Short La
Draycott BS27 . . . . . 90 E3
Litton BA3 . . . . . 75 F2
Long Ashton BS41 . . . . . 11 A2
Stone Allerton BS26 . . . . . 88 C2
Shortland La BS28 . . . . . 108 C3
Shortlands Dr BA21 . . . . . 218 C8
Shortmarsh La BA22 . . . . 196 F4
SHORT STREET 121 F6
Short Way BS8 . . . . . 10 B4
Shortwood La BA3 . . . . . 75 F2
Shortwood Rd BS13 . . . . . 22 E3
Shortwood Wlk BS13 . . . . 22 E3
SHOSCOMBE 79 E6
Shoscombe CE Prim Sch
BA2 . . . . . 79 F5
Shoscombe Gdns BA11 . . . 120 C7
SHOSCOMBE VALE 79 E5
Shovel La TA6 . . . . . 153 E3
Showell Pk TA2 . . . . . 212 B7
Showering Cl BS14 . . . . . 23 D5
Showering Rd BS14 . . . . . 23 D5
Showground Bsns Pk The
TA6 . . . . . 209 B1
Showground Rd TA6 . . . . . 209 B1
Shrewsbury Bow BS24 . . . . 50 A8
Shrewsbury Rd BA22 . . . . 218 B2
Shrubbery Ave BS23 . . . . 30 D1
Shrubbery Cl TA8 . . . . . 84 E8
Shrubbery Rd BS23 . . . . . 30 D1
Shrubbery Terr 11 BS23 . . 30 C1
Shrubbery Wlk BS23 . . . . 30 D1
Shrubbery Wlk W BS23 . . . 30 D1
Shudrick La TA19 . . . . . 221 C3
Shums Ct 3 BA1 . . . . . 228 C2
Shurtland La TA4 . . . . . 150 C3
SHURTON 134 C7
Shurton La TA5 . . . . . 134 C6
Shurton Rd TA5 . . . . . 134 B7
Shute La
Bruton BA10 . . . . . 215 D6
Huish Champflower TA4 . . . 165 C8
Long Sutton TA10 . . . . . 172 E4
Shute Lake La TA18 . . . . . 224 D5
Shuteleigh TA21 . . . . . 222 E5
Shutemead TA1 . . . . . 212 A4
Shute Row TA21 . . . . . 222 E5
Shuter Rd BS13 . . . . . 21 E5
Shute's La SP8 . . . . . 177 E4
Shutewater Cl TA1 . . . . . 212 A4
Shutewater Hill TA1 . . . . . 212 A4
Shutewater Orch TA1 . . . . 212 A3
Shutgate Mdw TA4 . . . . . 202 D3
Shuttern 2 TA1 . . . . . 212 E3
Shuttern Bridge 3 TA1 . . 212 E3
Shutwell La BA4 . . . . . 140 E3
Shyners Terr 8 TA16 . . . . 195 F7
SIDBROOK 169 B6
SIDCOT 70 C7
Sidcot Dr BS25 . . . . . 70 A7
Sidcot La BS25 . . . . . 70 A7
Sidcot Sch BS25 . . . . . 70 B7
Sideland Cl BS14 . . . . . 23 E6
Sidelings The BS40 . . . . . 73 B8
Side Wood La EX36 . . . . . 162 A1
Sidings The DT10 . . . . . 190 C4
Sidmouth Cl TA8 . . . . . 104 C8
Sidney Hill Cottage Homes
BS25 . . . . . 52 E4

SIGWELLS 175 E2
Silbury Rd BS3. . . . . 11 E2
Silbury Rise BS31 . . . . 25 A2
Silcox Rd BS13. . . . . 22 C4
Silk Cl BA4 . . . . 205 B7
Silk House Barton DT10. . 190 B4
Silklands Gr BS9 . . . . 5 C6
Silk Mills La TA2 . . . . 212 B6
Silk Mills Rd TA1. . . . . 212 B4
Silton Rd 1 SP8 . . . . 161 F1
Silverberry Rd BS22 . . . . . . 32 A1
Silvercombe 1 BS23 . . . . 48 E5
Silver Ct BS48. . . . . 8 C2
Silverdale Cl
  Brushford TA22 . . . . 163 E4
  Wembdon TA6. . . . . 208 C5
Silverdown Hill TA4 . . . . . 150 C7
Silverlake Cotts DT9. . . . . 188 B2
Silverlow Rd BS48. . . . . 8 D2
Silvermead TA24 . . . . 201 B5
Silver Mead BS49 . . . . 34 D2
Silvermead Ct TA24 . . . . . . 201 B5
Silver Moor La BS29 . . . . . . 50 F7
Silver Rd BA16 . . . . 207 C5
Silver Springs TA19 . . . . . 184 E3
Silver St
  11 Bampton EX16 . . . . . . 164 B1
  Barrington TA19. . . . . 184 D5
  Barton St David TA11 . . . 158 A3
  Barwick BA22 . . . . 197 F8
  Bridgwater TA6. . . . . 208 F4
  Bristol BS1. . . . . 227 A3
  Bruton BA10 . . . . 215 E6
  Chard TA20 . . . . 223 C3
  Cheddar BS27 . . . . 90 B8
  Chew Magna BS40 . . . . . . 39 B3
  Congresbury BS49 . . . . . . 34 D2
  Crewkerne TA18. . . . . . . 196 B3
  Curry Mallet TA3. . . . . . . 183 C8
  Ditcheat BA4 . . . . 159 C7
  East Lambrook TA13. . . . 220 C8
  Fivehead TA3 . . . . 170 F1
  Glastonbury BA6 . . . . . . 206 E4
  Holcombe BA3 . . . . 97 C1
  Huntspill TA9 . . . . 136 A8
  Ilminster TA19 . . . . 221 B4
  Kilmersdon BA3 . . . . 98 B5
  Kingsbury Episcopi TA12. 185 B8
  Kingsdon TA11 . . . . 173 D5
  Langport TA10 . . . . 172 A3
  Midsomer Norton BA3 . . . 97 A7
  Milverton TA4 . . . . 167 A4
  Nailsea BS48 . . . . 8 D2
  Portishead BS20 . . . . 1 F1
  Shepton Beauchamp TA19 . 184 E3
  South Petherton TA13. . . 220 D5
  Taunton TA1. . . . . 213 A3
  Wells BA5. . . . . 203 E3
  West Buckland TA21. . . . 180 F7
  Wincanton BA9 . . . . 216 C4
  Wiveliscombe TA4 . . . . . 210 C4
  Wrington BS40. . . . . 35 E2
  Yeovil BA20 . . . . 219 B5
Silverstone Way BS49 . . . . 34 D3
SILVER STREET. 180 F8
Simbriss Rd BA3 . . . . 114 F5
Simmental St TA1 . . . . 209 A1
Simmons Cl BA16 . . . . 207 D5
SIMONSBATH. 127 B2
SIMONSBURROW 180 C3
Simons Cl BS22 . . . . 32 A2
Simon's Cl BS39 . . . . 77 F5
Simons Mews
  Chard TA20 . . . . 223 E4
  3 Weston-super-Mare BS23. 48 F7
Simons Rd DT9 . . . . 225 D5
Sinclair Ho BS8 . . . . 226 A2
Singapore Rd BS23. . . . . . . 48 E3
Singer Ct BA11 . . . . 119 F5
Singer's Knoll BA11 . . . . . 119 F4
SINGLE HILL 80 A5
Single Hill BA2. . . . . 79 F5
Singleton Ct BA5. . . . . 203 C5
SION HILL 27 E1
Sion Hill
  Bath BA1 . . . . 27 E1
  Bristol BS8. . . . . 11 F7
Sion Hill Pl BA1 . . . . 27 E1
Sion La BS8. . . . . 11 F7
Sion Pl
  Bath BA2 . . . . 45 B6
  Bristol BS8. . . . . 11 F7
Sion Rd BA1. . . . . 27 E1
Sir Bevil Grenville's Mon ★
  BA1. . . . . 12 A1
Sir Gilbert Scott Ct TA4. . 202 E3
Sirius Wood BA3 . . . . 44 B2
Siskin Wlk BS22. . . . . 49 F8
Sisters The BA4 . . . . 205 A6
Six Acres Cl TA1 . . . . 213 C5
Sixpence BS39 . . . . 59 D2
Six Streams BA1 . . . . 27 B1
Sixteen Acre La TA20 . . . . 193 D8
Sixth Ave BS14 . . . . 23 A7
Sixty Acres Cl BS8. . . . . . . 10 B4
Six Ways BS21 . . . . 6 C4
SKILGATE 164 E6
Skilgate La TA14 . . . . 185 E1
Skimmerton La TA5, TA6. 208 A5
Skinner's Hill BA2 . . . . 78 F7
Skinners La BS25. . . . . 52 F4
Skinner's La TA14 . . . . . . 185 F2
Skitmoor Dro BS28. . . . . . 109 C2
Sky Coll TA2 . . . . 213 A6
Skylark Ave BS21. . . . . 1 B1
Skylark Dr BS31. . . . . 24 C3
Skylark Cl BS49. . . . . 16 F2

Slab Dro TA7 . . . . 155 A1
Sladacre La BS40 . . . . 54 E2
Sladbrook Ct BA2. . . . . 44 C3
Sladebrook Rd BA2. . . . . . . 44 B4
Slade Cl TA4. . . . . 150 E8
Slade La
  Barrow Gurney BS48 . . . . 20 C4
  Golsoncott TA23 . . . . . . 131 E1
  Hawkridge TA22 . . . . . . 146 D1
  Lympsham BS24. . . . . 67 B1
  Rimpton BA22 . . . . 188 A7
  Rooks Bridge BS26. . . . . . 87 E4
  West Anstey EX36 . . . . . 162 B6
Slade Rd BS20 . . . . 2 D5
Slade's Cross TA20 . . . . . . 193 D7
Slades Ct 2 BS48 . . . . . . 19 A6
Slades Dro TA7 . . . . 154 C1
Slades Hill BA8 . . . . 176 E1
Slades Orch TA19 . . . . 183 C1
Slade Way TA4. . . . . 202 E4
Slait Hill BA3 . . . . 142 C7
Slait La BA9 . . . . 216 C7
Sleep La BS14. . . . . 23 D3
Sleight Cl BA21 . . . . 218 C6
Sleight House La DT9 . . . . 175 F2
Sleight La BA5 . . . . 140 E8
Slingsby Gdns BS24 . . . . . . 49 C4
Slippery Batch TA11. . . . . 211 A6
Sloe Cl BS22 . . . . 49 D8
Slopers La BA9. . . . . 176 D5
SLOUGH GREEN 182 D7
Slough Green Cvn Pk
  TA3 . . . . 182 D8
Slough Hill TA3 . . . . 182 D6
Slough La
  Cold Ashton SN14. . . . . . 12 F5
  Crowcombe TA4 . . . . 151 A8
  North Wootton BA4 . . . . 140 B3
  Stoke St Gregory TA3 . . . 170 F6
  Upottery EX14 . . . . 191 F5
Sloway La TA6, TA9 . . . . . 136 A8
Slow Court La BA22 . . . . . 174 D3
Slowland La BA5 . . . . 110 D8
Slugg Hill BA16 . . . . 207 C3
Smallacombe Hill EX16,
  EX36. . . . . 162 D4
Smallbrook La BS39. . . . . . 41 B6
Smallcombe Cl BA3. . . . . . 78 E5
Smallcombe Rd BA3. . . . . . 78 E4
Small Down End BS25 . . . . 51 F2
Small Down La BA4 . . . . . 142 B2
Small La EX16. . . . . 179 B2
Small Mead Dro BA6 . . . . 157 F4
Smallmoor Chase BA16. . 156 E7
Smallmoor Dro TA7 . . . . . 155 C3
Small Moor La BA16 . . . . . 156 E7
Smallridge Rd EX13 . . . . . 198 A4
Smalls Mead 2 TA11 . . . 173 F7
Small St BS1. . . . . 227 A3
Smallway BS49 . . . . 34 D5
SMALL WAY 214 B2
Small Way La BA22 . . . . . 214 C1
Smallways La TA7 . . . . . . 137 C1
Smallwood View BA3. . . . . 96 E7
SMEATHARPE. 191 E5
Smeathy La EX15. . . . . . . 180 F3
Smeaton Rd BS1 . . . . 11 F5
Sminhays Cnr TA23 . . . . . 149 B5
SMITHAM HILL 74 D2
Smithams Hill BS40 . . . . . . 93 C8
Smitham's Hill BS40 . . . . . 74 D2
Smithfield Rd BA16. . . . . . 207 B4
Smithick's La BA11. . . . . . 143 E6
Smithmead BS13. . . . . 22 B5
Smiths Cl BS27. . . . . 91 A1
Smith's Forge Ind Est BS49 16 F3
Smith's Hill TA18. . . . . . . 196 C8
Smiths La TA3 . . . . 170 F2
Smith's La BA4. . . . . 159 C6
Smith's Row TA15. . . . . . . 186 B4
Smith's Terr BA21. . . . . . . 219 C6
Smith Way TA9 . . . . 104 D3
Smithy TA1 . . . . 213 B3
Smithyard La TA4, TA23 . 202 A3
Smithy La
  Bridgehampton BA22. . . 174 D2
  Frome BA11. . . . . 119 E4
Smokeham La TA4 . . . . . . 151 D5
Smoky Hole La TA18. . . . . 185 F1
Smurl La TA9 . . . . 104 C1
Smythe Croft BS14. . . . . . . 23 A3
Smythes Cross EX15. . . . . 191 C7
Snagg La TA3 . . . . 159 D5
Snag La BA9 . . . . 216 E3
Snake La BS28 . . . . 109 C1
Snakelake Hill BA10. . . . . 160 C7
Snap Hill TA11 . . . . 173 D8
Snatch BS40 . . . . 55 C2
Snatch La BS40 . . . . 55 C2
Snathe Lea 4 TA4 . . . . . 167 F8
Snedden Gr TA1 . . . . 213 B5
SNEYD PK 5 D3
Snipefield La BS28 . . . . . . 108 A6
Snowberry Cl
  Bridgwater TA6. . . . . 208 E2
  Weston-super-Mare BS22 . . 32 A1
Snowberry Cl TA1. . . . . . . 213 C5
Snowdon Cottage La
  TA20 . . . . 223 B4
Snowdon Hill Loop Rd
  TA20 . . . . 223 A4
Snowdon Hts TA20 . . . . . . 223 B4
Snowdon Vale BS23 . . . . . . 31 A1
Snowdrop Cl BS22 . . . . 32 A5

Snow Hill
  Bath BA1 . . . . 28 A1
  Bath BA1 . . . . 228 C4
Snow Hill Ho BA1 . . . . 228 C4
Society Rd BA4 . . . . 205 A6
SOCKETY. 196 D1
Sock Hill BA21 . . . . 187 C6
Sock La BA21 . . . . 187 C6
Sockmead Dro BA22. . . . . 187 B6
Sock's La BA10. . . . . 160 F8
Sogg Dro TA7. . . . . 154 F6
SOHO 117 A5
Soho BA2. . . . . 81 E5
Soho Hill
  Coleford BA3 . . . . 116 F6
  Soho BA3 . . . . 117 A5
Solomon's Hollow TA3 . . 169 F2
Solomons La BA7 . . . . 214 D6
Solon CI BS13. . . . . 21 F5
Solsbury Ct BA1. . . . . 28 F3
Solsbury View 17 BA1 . . . 28 A1
Solsbury Way BA1. . . . . 28 A2
Somer Ave BA3 . . . . 77 F2
Somer Cl BA3 . . . . 96 F8
Somer Ct BA3. . . . . 78 B1
SOMERDALE 24 E7
Somerdale Ave
  Bath BA2 . . . . 44 D2
  Bristol BS4. . . . . 22 F8
  Weston-super-Mare BS22 . . 49 C8
Somerdale Cl BS22. . . . . . . 49 C8
Somerdale Rd BS31 . . . . . . 24 F7
Somerdale View BA2 . . . . . 44 C2
Somer Ho BA3. . . . . 78 A1
Somerhouse Orch BA6 . . . 206 E5
Somer Lea BA3 . . . . 96 D5
Somerleaze Cl BA5. . . . . . 203 B3
Somer Rd BA3 . . . . 77 F2
Somer Ridge BA3 . . . . 77 F3
Somerset Ave
  Taunton TA1 . . . . 212 B2
  Weston-super-Mare BS22,
  BS24. . . . . 50 A8
Somerset Brick & Tile Mus ★
  TA6 . . . . 209 A6
Somerset Bridge Prim Sch
  TA6 . . . . 209 A1
Somerset Cl
  Martock TA12 . . . . 185 E7
  Shepton Mallet BA4 . . . . 205 C5
Somerset Coll of Arts & Tech
  TA1 . . . . 212 D4
Somerset Ct BA21 . . . . . . 219 A6
Somerset Cty Cricket Gd ★
  TA1 . . . . 212 F4
Somerset Distillery The ★
  TA12 . . . . 184 F7
Somerset & Dorset Joint Rly ★
  BA3. . . . . 97 A8
Somerset & Dorset Rlwy Trust
  Mus ★ TA23 . . . . 131 E4
Somerset Fire HQ TA2 . . . 169 A7
Somerset Folly BA2 . . . . . . 60 B2
Somerset Gdns TA6 . . . . . 209 C3
Somerset Ho
  Bath BA2 . . . . 44 D3
  12 Bristol BS2. . . . . 227 C3
Somerset La BA1 . . . . 27 E1
Somerset Levels National
  Nature Reserve ★ TA7. . 155 C6
Somerset Mews BS23 . . . . 48 F6
Somerset Pl
  Bath BA1 . . . . 27 E1
  Taunton TA1 . . . . 213 B4
  Yeovil BA20 . . . . 219 A3
Somerset Rd
  Bridgwater TA6 . . . . 209 C3
  Clevedon BS21 . . . . 6 E3
  Frome BA11. . . . . 119 E4
  Portishead BS20 . . . . 1 F5
Somerset Rural Life Mus ★
  BA6. . . . . 206 E4
Somerset Shire Horses ★
  TA7 . . . . 156 C6
Somerset Sq
  Bristol BS1. . . . . 227 B1
  3 Nailsea BS48. . . . . 8 E2
Somerset St
  Bath BA1 . . . . 228 C1
  Bristol BS1. . . . . 227 B1
  Bristol, Kingsdown BS2 . . 227 A4
Somerset Way
  Highbridge TA9. . . . . 104 E3
  Paulton BS39 . . . . 77 E6
Somer's Hill BA11 . . . . 117 D3
SOMERTON 211 D3
Somerton BS24 . . . . 49 A2
Somerton Bsns Pk TA11. . 211 B5
Somerton Cl TA6. . . . . 209 D4
Somerton Door Dro
  Compton Dundon TA11 . . 156 E1
  Somerton TA11. . . . . 211 A7
Somerton Dro TA11 . . . . . 156 E1
Somertonfield Rd TA11. . 172 E7
Somerton Gdns BA11. . . . 120 C7
Somerton Hill
  Langport TA10 . . . . 172 E7
  Somerton TA11. . . . . 211 A4
Somerton Inf Sch TA11 . . 211 C4
SOMERTON RANDLE . . 173 C7
Somerton Rd
  Clevedon BS21. . . . . 6 E1
  Langport TA10 . . . . 172 A6
  Street BA16 . . . . 207 D4
Somervale Rd BA3 . . . . 78 C2
Somervale Sch
  Midsomer Norton BA3 . . . 78 A1
  3 Midsomer Norton BA3. . 78 A1

Somerville Cl
  2 Longcroft BA21. . . . . . 219 F8
  Saltford BS31. . . . . 25 E2
  Shepton Mallet BA4 . . . . 205 D4
Somerville Cotts BA5. . . . 204 B8
Somerville Rd
  Sandford BS25. . . . . 52 A4
  Wells BA5. . . . . 203 D5
Somerville Way TA6 . . . . . 209 D3
Sommerville Way BS30 . . . 25 E8
Soper Gdns BS4. . . . . 22 D7
Sopers Field TA20 . . . . . . 223 D2
Sophia Gdns BS22. . . . . . . 32 B4
Sorrel Dr TA6 . . . . 208 E1
Sorrel Gdns BS20 . . . . 2 F5
Southampton Row 5
  TA2 . . . . 213 A8
South Ave
  Bath BA2 . . . . 44 D5
  Highbridge TA9. . . . . 104 C4
  Portishead BS20 . . . . 2 D6
  Sherborne DT9 . . . . 225 B2
SOUTHAY 185 B6
Southay Cross TA20 . . . . . 193 A4
Southay La TA20 . . . . 192 F4
South Bank
  Castle Cary BA7 . . . . 214 B3
  Wookey Hole BA5. . . . . . 203 A8
SOUTH BARROW 175 A6
South Barrow Rd TA11. . . 174 A7
Southbourne Gdns BA1. . . 28 B1
Southbourne Ho 208 E4
Southbourne Mans BA2 . . 228 C2
South Brent Cl TA9 . . . . . . 85 F3
SOUTH BREWHAM 161 A6
South Bristol Bsns Pk BS4 . 22 E7
South Bristol Com Hospl
  BS14. . . . . 22 F5
South Bristol Trad Pk BS3. . 11 F3
Southbrook TA5 . . . . 135 C2
Southbrook Cl TA5 . . . . . . 135 C2
Southbrook Cotts BA9. . . 216 F4
SOUTH CADBURY. 175 C4
South Cary La BA7 . . . . . . 214 A5
SOUTH CHARD 198 C8
SOUTH CHERITON 176 B3
South Cl
  Draycott BS27 . . . . 90 E2
  Lympsham BS24. . . . . 86 B8
  Walton BA16 . . . . 156 F7
South Combe BS24 . . . . . . 67 B6
Southcombe Way BA22. . 186 B6
SOUTH COMMON 198 A4
South Common La EX13 . 198 A5
Southcot Pl BA2 . . . . 228 C1
South Croft BS25. . . . . 51 F2
Southcroft Dr BA13 . . . . . 121 D4
South Ct DT9 . . . . 225 B3
South Dene BS9. . . . . 5 E6
SOUTHDOWN 44 B4
Southdown
  Charlton Horethorne DT9 . . 176 A1
  Weston-super-Mare BS22 . . 31 F4
SOUTH DOWN 191 F6
Southdown Ave BA2. . . . . . 44 B3
Southdown Com Inf Sch
  BA2. . . . . 44 B3
Southdown Cross EX16. . . 179 B2
Southdown Jun Sch BA2. . 44 B3
Southdown Rd
  Bath BA2 . . . . 44 B4
  Bristol BS9. . . . . 5 F8
South Dro
  Curry Rivel TA10 . . . . . . 171 B4
  North Curry TA3 . . . . 170 D2
Southend Gdns TA9 . . . . . 104 E5
Southend Rd BS23 . . . . 48 E4
Southernhay BS8 . . . . 226 B2
Southernhay Ave BS8 . . . . 226 B2
Southernhay Cres BS8. . . 226 B2
Southern Lea Rd TA8 . . . . 104 C8
Southern Relief Rd BS27. . 90 C6
Southern Ring Path 4 BS21 6 C1
Southern Way BS21 . . . . . . 6 C1
South Espl TA8 . . . . 104 A5
Southey Farm La TA3. . . . 184 A7
Southey Rd BS21. . . . . 6 C3
SOUTHFIELD 79 A2
Southfield
  Cheddar BS27 . . . . 90 B8
  Norton St Philip BA2. . . . 81 F4
  Radstock BA3 . . . . 79 A2
  Southwick BA14. . . . . 83 F2
  Wiveliscombe TA4 . . . . . 210 C3
Southfield Cl
  Nailsea BS48 . . . . 8 E3
  Taunton TA2 . . . . 168 F6
  Weston-super-Mare BS23 . . 48 D2
  Woolavington TA7. . . . . . 136 E3
Southfield Dr BA21 . . . . . 218 B8
Southfield Farm Cvn Pk &
  Camp Site TA8 . . . . 65 F4
Southfield Farm Rd BA11 . 120 B3
Southfield Hill BA2. . . . . . . 99 A6
Southfield Rd
  Nailsea BS48 . . . . 8 E3
  Shepton Mallet BA4 . . . . 205 A5
Southfield Rd Trad Est BS48. 8 F3
Southfields
  Frome BA11. . . . . 120 A2
  Ilminster TA19 . . . . 183 E2
South Fields BA6. . . . . 206 E3
Southfield Way BA11. . . . 120 A3
Southgate
  Bath BA2 . . . . 228 C2
  Frome BA11. . . . . 120 D7
  Wiveliscombe TA4 . . . . . 210 C3
Southgate Ave TA6 . . . . . . 209 A3

Southgate Dr BA9 . . . . 216 C3
Southgate Rd BA9 . . . . 216 C3
Southgate Sh Ctr BA1 . . . 228 C2
South Gr BS20 . . . . 4 C4
South Green St 8 BS8. . . 11 F7
South Harp TA13 . . . . 220 E1
South Hele Cross EX16 . . 165 C1
SOUTH HILL 211 A1
South Hill BS25 . . . . 51 F2
South La
  Challacombe EX31. . . . . 126 A3
  Nether Stowey TA5. . . . . 134 B2
Southlands
  Bath BA1 . . . . 27 B1
  Carhampton TA24. . . . . . 131 B5
Southlands Dr BA2 . . . . 60 B2
Southlands Way BS49 . . . . 34 E5
South Lawn BS24 . . . . 49 F4
South Lawn Cl BS24 . . . . . 49 F4
South Lea Rd BA1. . . . . 44 A8
Southleaze BS25. . . . . 70 A6
Southleaze Orch BA16. . . 207 C6
Southleaze Rd BA16. . . . . 207 B6
Southleigh BS25. . . . . 69 F8
Southleigh Rd
  Bristol BS8. . . . . 226 B4
  Taunton TA1 . . . . 213 B3
SOUTHMARSH 161 B1
South Mdw BA5. . . . . 113 A1
South Mdws BS40 . . . . 35 E2
Southmead
  West Camel BA22. . . . . . 174 D3
  Winscombe BS25. . . . . . . 70 A8
Southmead Cres TA18. . . . 224 C5
Southmead La BA8 . . . . . . 190 A6
Southmead Rd BS22. . . . . . 49 B7
Southmead Terr TA18. . . . 224 C5
South Molton Rd EX16. . . 164 B1
South Moors La TA7 . . . . . 137 B2
Southover BA5. . . . . 203 D3
Southover Rd BS39. . . . . . . 59 D1
South Par
  Bath BA2 . . . . 228 C2
  Chew Magna BS40 . . . . . . 39 B3
  Frome BA11. . . . . 119 E4
  Weston-super-Mare BS23 . . 48 D8
South Parade Cotts BA2 . . 45 C1
SOUTH PERROTT 196 C1
SOUTH PETHERTON . . . 220 C4
South Petherton Com Hospl
  TA13 . . . . 220 D5
South Petherton Inf Sch
  TA13 . . . . 220 C4
South Petherton Jun Sch
  TA13 . . . . 220 D3
South Pk TA24 . . . . 200 D6
South Rd
  Brean TA8. . . . . 65 F3
  Lympsham BS24. . . . . 67 B1
  Midsomer Norton BA3 . . . 78 B1
  Portishead BS20 . . . . 2 D7
  Taunton TA1 . . . . 213 A2
  Timsbury BA2. . . . . 60 B2
  Watchet TA23 . . . . 202 C6
  Weston-super-Mare BS23 . . 30 C1
Southridge Hts BS24 . . . . . 67 A8
South Road Villas BA1 . . . 216 C3
South Rock Ind Est BS4. . . 96 D1
Southside BS23 . . . . 48 E8
South Side BS49 . . . . 34 E5
Southside Cl BS9. . . . . 5 B8
Southside Cres BS22 . . . . . 31 A4
South St
  Burnham-on-S TA8 . . . . . 104 A6
  Castle Cary BA7 . . . . 214 B4
  Crewkerne TA18. . . . . . . 224 D5
  Hinton St George TA17 . . 195 D7
  Holcombe Rogus TA21. . 178 F5
  Kington Magna SP8 . . . . 177 E1
  Milborne Port DT9 . . . . . 217 D2
  Montacute TA15 . . . . . . 186 B3
  Sherborne DT9. . . . . 225 E3
  South Petherton TA13. . . 220 D4
  Stratton-on-t F BA3 . . . . 96 F2
  Taunton TA1 . . . . 213 A3
  Walton BA16 . . . . 156 E7
  Wellington TA21. . . . . . . 222 E5
  Wells BA5. . . . . 203 D4
  West Camel BA22. . . . . . 174 D3
  Wincanton BA9 . . . . 216 C3
  Wiveliscombe TA4 . . . . . 210 C4
  Yeovil BA20 . . . . 219 B4
SOUTHSTOKE 62 E7
Southstoke La BA2 . . . . . . 62 F8
Southstoke Rd BA2. . . . . . . 44 F1
South Terr
  Burnham-on-S TA8 . . . . . 104 B6
  Weston-super-Mare BS23 . . 48 D8
SOUTHTOWN 183 C3
Southtown La TA6 . . . . . . 158 B8
SOUTH TWERTON 44 C5
Southview TA3. . . . . 168 C2
South View
  12 Barwick BA22 . . . . . . 197 F8
  Bawdrip TA7 . . . . 136 E2
  Bradford Abbas DT9. . . . 187 E1
  Broadway TA19 . . . . 183 C2
  Clandown BA3 . . . . 78 E5
  Ditcheat BA4 . . . . 159 C6
  Horrington BA5. . . . . 113 A1
  Lynford-on-F TA11 . . . . . 158 C1
  Monkton Combe BA2 . . . . 45 E1
  Paulton BS39 . . . . 77 E6
  Portishead BS20 . . . . 2 D7
  Queen Camel BA22. . . . . 174 F3

South View continued
Timsbury BA2. . . . . 60 B2
Westleigh EX16 . . . . .179 A3
Southview Cl
Hutton BS24. . . . . 49 E2
Westonzoyland TA7. . . . . . . .154 F5
South View Pl BA3 . . . . 78 B2
Southview Rd TA7. . . . . .154 F5
South View Rd
Bath BA2. . . . . 44 D6
Milborne Port DT9. . . . . .217 C3
South View Terr
Taunton TA3 . . . . .168 D1
Yatton BS49. . . . . 17 B1
South Villas TA4. . . . . .167 F6
Southville BA21. . . . . .219 C5
Southville Rd BS23. . . . . 48 E4
Southville Terr BA2. . . . . 45 B4
SOUTHWAY. 139 D5
Southway Cl BA21. . . . . .218 F6
Southway Cres BA21 . . . . . .218 F6
Southway Ct BS21. . . . . 6 D1
Southway Dr BA21 . . . . .218 F6
Southwell TA3. . . . . .168 D1
Southwell Cl TA3. . . . . .168 D1
Southwell Cres TA9. . . . . . .104 E3
Southwell Ct TA9. . . . . .104 E3
Southwell St BS2. . . . . .226 C4
South Western Bsns Pk
DT9. .225 D3
South Western Terr BA20 219 C4
SOUTHWICK
Trowbridge 83 F2
Watchfield 105 E2
Southwick CE Prim Sch
BA14. . . . . 83 F3
Southwick Ctry Pk★ BA14. . 83 F5
Southwick Rd TA9. . . . . .106 C1
SOUTH WIDCOMBE 75 C6
Southwood BA4. . . . . .159 D8
Southwood Ave BS9. . . . . 5 C8
Southwood Dr BS9. . . . . 5 B8
Southwood Dr E BS9 . . . . 5 C8
Southwood Gr TA1. . . . . . . .212 C2
Southwoods BA20. . . . . .219 A3
Southwood Way TA3 . . . . . .181 C5
Sovereign Rd TA6. . . . . .209 D7
Sovereign Sh Ctr BS23. . . . . 48 D8
Sowden Hill TA5. . . . . .134 D4
Spanish Hill TA6. . . . . .153 F2
Spargrove La BA4. . . . . .142 B1
SPARKFORD. 175 A5
Sparkford Hill BA22. . . . . . .174 F4
Sparkford Hill La BA22. . . .175 A4
Sparkhayes La TA24. . . . . . .124 A3
Sparks Way TA4. . . . . .104 D3
Sparrow Hill Way BS26 . . . . 88 E6
Sparrow La
Portbury Wharf BS20 . . . . 3 A6
Withypool TA24 . . . . .146 C7
Sparrow Rd BA21. . . . . .219 B6
Spartley Dr BS13. . . . . 21 F6
Spartley Wlk BS13. . . . . 21 F6
SPAXTON. 152 E8
Spaxton Cl TA8. . . . . .104 C8
Spaxton Rd TA5. . . . . .153 C7
Spaxton VC Prim Sch TA5 .152 E7
Spearcey Cl TA3. . . . . .181 D8
Spearcey La TA3. . . . . .181 D8
Spearhay La TA20 . . . . .198 F5
Spear Mead DT8 . . . . .199 F7
Spears La TA4 . . . . .166 A4
Specket La DT8 . . . . .199 E5
SPECKINGTON. 174 C2
Speckington La BA22. . . . . .174 B2
Specklemead BS39. . . . . 77 D5
Speedwell Ind Est **1** BS21 . . 6 C2
Speke Cl
Ilminster TA19 . . . . .221 B4
Merriott TA16. . . . . .195 F7
Staplegrove TA2. . . . . .212 B6
Speke Ct TA19 . . . . .221 B4
Spencer Ave TA2. . . . . .212 E6
Spencer Cl TA6. . . . . .209 D3
Spencer Dr
Midsomer Norton BA3. . . . . . 78 A2
Weston-super-Mare BS22. . . . 32 B3
Spencer Ho **6** BS1. . . . . . . .227 B1
Spencer Rd BA4. . . . . .205 C4
Spencers Belle Vue BA1. . . .228 B4
Sperring Ct BA3. . . . . 96 F8
Sperry Cross TA4 . . . . .149 B1
Spicer Way TA20 . . . . .223 D2
SPIKE ISLAND. 226 B1
Spike Island★ BS3. . . . . .226 B1
Spillers TA6. . . . . .208 E2
Spindleberry Gr BS48 . . . . . . 9 A2
Spiningmill Cotts **3** BA11 119 E5
Spinners End BS22. . . . . 32 B4
Spinners Ho **5** BA4 . . . . . . .205 B6
Spinney Croft BS13. . . . . 21 F5
Spinneyfield TA4. . . . . .167 F7
Spinney Rd BS24. . . . . 50 D4
Spinney The
Ashcott TA7. . . . . .156 A8
Portishead BS20 . . . . 2 C4
Taunton TA1. . . . . .212 D2
Weston-super-Mare BS24 . . . 48 F1
Yeovil BA20 . . . . .218 D2
Spinnings Dro BS48. . . . . 19 D2
Spire Cross TA24. . . . . .147 A4
SPLATT. 152 E8
Splatt La TA5. . . . . .152 E8
Splott BS26. . . . . 88 F6
Splott La BA3. . . . . 95 B6

Spoonbill Rd TA6. . . . . .209 B4
Spratts Bridge BS40. . . . . . . 39 A3
Sprays Hill TA20 . . . . .194 D5
Sprigg Dr BS20. . . . . 1 F1
Springbok Cl BA16. . . . . . . .207 D7
Spring Cres BA2 . . . . .228 C2
Springer's Hill BA3. . . . . . . .116 E6
Springfield
Ilminster TA19 . . . . .221 B2
Norton St Philip BA2. . . . . 81 D4
Peasedown St John BA2. . . . . 79 C7
Street BA16 . . . . .207 B5
Springfield Ave
Bridgwater TA6 . . . . .208 C3
Bristol, Shirehampton BS11. . . 4 D6
Weston-super-Mare BS22. . . . 31 D1
Springfield Bldgs
Midsomer Norton BS39. . . . . . 77 D2
Radstock BA3. . . . . 79 A3
Springfield Cl
Bath BA2. . . . . 44 B5
Cheddar BS27. . . . . 90 A8
Cross BS26. . . . . 69 F2
Springfield Cotts
Upton Cheyney BS30. . . . . . . 26 A8
Winsford TA24 . . . . .147 A6
Springfield Cres BA3. . . . . . . 79 A3
Spring Field Cres DT9 . . . . .225 C3
Springfield Ct BA4. . . . . .205 A5
Springfield Dr BS28. . . . . . . .108 C3
Springfield Flats TA20 . . . .223 C4
Springfield Gdns BS29. . . . . 51 A3
Springfield Ho
Bristol BS6. . . . . .226 C4
Portishead BS20 . . . . 2 C4
Springfield Hts BA3. . . . . 78 E4
Springfield Lawn BS11. . . . . . 4 D6
Springfield Pl
Bath BA1. . . . . 27 F1
Clandown BA3 . . . . 78 E4
Yeovil BA21 . . . . .218 E7
Springfield Rd
Cheddar BS27. . . . . 90 A8
3 Highbridge TA9 . . . . .104 E4
Highbridge TA9. . . . . .104 E4
Milborne Port DT9. . . . . .217 D3
Pill BS20. . . . . 4 C4
Portishead BS20 . . . . 2 B5
Wellington TA21. . . . . .222 C7
Wincanton BA9 . . . . .216 B4
Yeovil BA21 . . . . .218 E7
Springfields
East Chinnock BA22. . . . . . . .196 E8
Stalbridge DT10. . . . . .190 C4
Springfield Terr
Street BA16 . . . . .207 B5
Tatworth TA20 . . . . .198 D8
SPRING GARDENS. 119 D8
Spring Gardens Rd BA2. . . .228 C2
Spring Gdns
Minehead TA24. . . . . .201 B5
Wiveliscombe TA4 . . . . .210 C5
Spring Ground Rd BS39. . . . 77 E5
Spring Hill
Bristol BS2. . . . . .227 A4
Weston-super-Mare BS22 . . . 31 D2
Springhill Cl BS39. . . . . 77 C6
Spring Hill Dr BS22. . . . . 31 E1
Spring La
Bath BA1. . . . . 28 B2
Dundry BS41. . . . . 22 A1
Sandford Orcas DT9. . . . . . . .188 C7
Springley Rd TA6. . . . . .209 D6
Springmead TA20 . . . . .223 B4
Springmead Sch BA11. . . . . .101 E4
Spring Rd BA11. . . . . .119 F6
Spring Rise
Portishead BS20 . . . . 2 C3
Puriton TA7. . . . . .136 C4
Wells BA5. . . . . .203 C3
Spring Terr
Frome BA11. . . . . .119 D2
Weston-super-Mare BS22 . . . 31 C2
Spring Vale BA1 . . . . 28 B2
Spring Valley BS22. . . . . 31 C2
Springway Ind Est TA7. . . . .155 A5
Spring Wood Gdns BS24. . . 49 E3
Spruce Way
Bath BA2. . . . . 62 E8
Weston-super-Mare BS22 . . . 49 E8
Spurwells TA19 . . . . .183 F4
Squares Rd TA5. . . . . .135 F2
Square The
Axbridge BS26. . . . . 70 C2
Banwell BS29. . . . . 51 B3
Bath BA2. . . . . .228 B1
Edington TA7. . . . . .137 C2
Maiden Bradley BA12. . . . . . .144 C2
Shipham BS25 . . . . 70 E7
Taunton TA1. . . . . .213 C4
Temple Cloud BS39. . . . . 58 E1
Wellow BA2. . . . . 62 D1
Westbury-sub-Mendip BA5. .110 F8
Winscombe BS25. . . . . 69 E6
Wiveliscombe TA4 . . . . .210 C4
Woolavington TA7. . . . . .136 E4
Squibbers Wy TA6 . . . . .209 B2
Squibbs Cl TA6 . . . . .209 D5
Squibbs Ho TA6. . . . . .208 F5
Squire La BS40. . . . . 55 C1
Squirrel Ct TA21 . . . . .222 D5
Stabbins Cl BS22. . . . . 32 B5
Stables The BA3. . . . . 98 B5
Stable Yd BA2. . . . . 44 D6
Stacey's La TA10 . . . . .171 F5
Staddlestones BA3. . . . . 96 F7
Staddonhill Rd TA24. . . . . . .146 F8
Stafford Pl BS23. . . . . 48 E8

Stafford Rd
Bridgwater TA6 . . . . .209 C3
Portishead BS20 . . . . 2 E4
Sherborne DT9. . . . . .225 C4
Weston-super-Mare BS23 . . . 48 F7
STAFFORD'S GREEN. 188 D8
Stagman La TA7, BA16 . . . .156 C8
Stag Mill Cross EX16 . . . . .178 B3
Stag Way BA6. . . . . .206 C4
Stainer Cl BS4. . . . . 22 D7
Staker's Cross TA20 . . . . . .195 B2
Staker's Cross La TA18,
TA20. . . . . .195 B2
STALBRIDGE. 190 C4
Stalbridge Cl DT10 . . . . .190 B4
Stalbridge La
Marnhull DT10. . . . . .190 F2
Sturminster Newton DT10 . . .190 F1
Stalbridge Pk DT10. . . . . . . .190 A4
Stalbridge Prim Sch DT10 190 B5
Stalbridge Rd
Henstridge BA8 . . . . .190 A6
Stalbridge Weston DT10. . . . .190 A3
Stourton Caundle DT10 . . . . .189 F2
STALBRIDGE WESTON. 190 A3
Stalcombe La BA2. . . . . 42 B4
Staling Way BA4. . . . . .205 C4
Stallards TA21. . . . . .222 C3
STALLEN. 188 A3
Stallgrove La BA16 . . . . .207 D3
Stall St BA1. . . . . .228 C2
Stalls The BA12. . . . . .144 D7
Stambrook Pk BA1. . . . . 29 A5
Stammery Hill EX13. . . . . . .198 C1
Stanchester Acad TA14 . . . .186 A4
Stanchester Way TA10. . . . .171 D4
Stancombe La
Flax Bourton BS48 . . . . 19 E7
Westbury-sub-Mendip BA5. .110 F8
Standards Rd TA7. . . . . .154 E5
Standards The TA7. . . . . . . .137 D2
STANDERWICK. 102 C2
Standerwick BA13. . . . . .102 C3
Standerwick Cross BA11. . .102 B2
Standerwick Orch TA19. . . .183 C2
Standfast Pl TA2. . . . . .213 C8
Standhill Rd TA10. . . . . .155 F2
Standing Cross BA2. . . . . 61 D7
Standish Ct TA1. . . . . .212 F4
Standish St TA6. . . . . .208 F7
Stane Way BS11. . . . . 4 C7
Stanford Pl BS4. . . . . 22 D7
Stanhope Pl BA1. . . . . .228 A2
Stanhope Rd BS23 . . . . 48 E3
Stanier Cl BA11. . . . . .120 D6
Stanier Rd BA2. . . . . .228 A2
Stankley View TA19 . . . . . . .184 F4
Stanley Cl
Bridgwater TA6 . . . . .208 F2
Staplegrove TA2. . . . . .212 C6
Stanley Ct BA3. . . . . 78 B2
Stanley Gr BS23. . . . . 48 F7
Stanley Rd **2** BS23. . . . . 48 F7
Stanley Rd W BA2. . . . . 44 D5
Stanley Terr BA3. . . . . 79 A3
Stanley Villas **12** BA1 . . . . . 28 A1
Stanmoor Rd TA7 . . . . .170 F8
Stansell Rd TA1. . . . . .213 A1
Stanshalls Cl BS40. . . . . 37 C8
Stanshalls Dr BS40. . . . . 37 C8
Stanshalls La BS40. . . . . 37 C8
STANTON DREW. 39 F2
Stanton Drew Prim Sch
BS39. 40 A2
Stanton Drew Stone Circles★
BS39. 40 A3
Stanton La BS39 . . . . 40 D4
STANTON PRIOR. 42 E2
Stanton Rd BS40. . . . . 39 B3
STANTON WICK. 58 D8
Stanton Wick La BS39 . . . . . 40 B1
Stant Way TA20 . . . . .193 C6
Stanway Cl
Bath BA2. . . . . 44 D1
Taunton TA2 . . . . .212 D7
Staple Cl TA4 . . . . .132 E4
Staplecombe Vineyard★
TA2. .168 C6
STAPLE FITZPAINE. 182 C5
Staplegate EX16. . . . . .178 A3
Staple Gr BS31. . . . . 24 D5
STAPLEGROVE. 212 C8
Staplegrove CE Prim Sch
TA2. .212 C7
Staplegrove Manor TA2 . . .212 D8
Staplegrove Rd
Staplegrove TA2. . . . . .212 C7
Taunton TA1, TA2 . . . . .212 E5
STAPLEHAY. 181 D8
Staple Hill TA3. . . . . .182 C5
Staple La TA4. . . . . .132 E4
STAPLE LAWNS. 182 B5
Staples Cl BS21. . . . . 6 E1
Staples Gn BS22 . . . . 32 B3
Staples Hill BA3. . . . . 64 C4
Staples Mdw TA20 . . . . .198 D8
STAPLETON. 185 E8
Stapleton Cl TA12. . . . . .185 E7
Stapleton Cross TA12. . . . . .185 E7
Stapleton Rd TA12 . . . . .185 E7
STAPLEY. 191 B8
Stapley Cross TA3. . . . . .181 B1
Stapling La TA24. . . . . .130 F3
STAR. 52 D1
Starcross Rd BS22. . . . . 32 A2
Star La BS20. . . . . 4 D4
Starling Cl BS22. . . . . 49 E8
Starrs Cl BS26 . . . . 70 B2

Stars La BA20 . . . . .219 C4
Statham Cl
Cheddar BS27. . . . . 90 B7
Taunton TA1. . . . . .212 C2
Statham Gr TA1. . . . . .212 C2
STATHE. 171 B8
Stathe Cotts TA7. . . . . .171 B7
Stathe Rd TA7 . . . . .171 A8
Station App
Bristol BS1. . . . . .227 C1
Frome BA11. . . . . .120 A4
Ilminster TA19 . . . . .183 E1
Pensford BS39 . . . . 40 D5
Weston-super-Mare BS23 . . . 48 E7
Station Cl
Backwell BS48. . . . . 18 F7
Congresbury BS49 . . . . 34 C4
Station Lodge **8** BS23. . . . . 48 E7
Station Mead BA3. . . . . 96 D3
Station Path TA11. . . . . .211 D3
Station Rd
Ashcott TA7. . . . . .156 B8
Axbridge BS26. . . . . 70 C2
Backwell BS48. . . . . 19 A6
Bampton EX16 . . . . .164 B1
Bath BA1. . . . . 28 F2
Bath BA1. . . . . 44 C7
Binegar BA3. . . . . .114 D7
Bishops Lydeard TA4. . . . . . .167 E8
Blagdon BS40. . . . . 54 E3
Bristol, Shirehampton BS11. . . 4 D5
Bristol, Shirehampton BS11. . . 4 E6
Bruton BA10. . . . . .215 F6
Burlescombe EX16. . . . . .179 B3
Burnham-on-S TA9 . . . . 85 F3
Burtle TA7. . . . . .137 D5
Castle Cary BA7 . . . . .214 B6
Chard Junction TA20. . . . . . .198 D8
Cheddar BS27. . . . . 90 B7
Clevedon BS21. . . . . 6 D3
Clutton BS39. . . . . 58 E3
Congresbury BS49 . . . . 34 C4
Cossington TA7. . . . . .136 F3
Draycott BS27. . . . . 90 E2
Dunster TA24 . . . . .201 E4
Flax Bourton BS48 . . . . 20 A8
Freshford BA3 . . . . 64 C5
Hatch Beauchamp TA3 . . . . .183 A7
Ilminster TA19 . . . . .221 A4
Keynsham BS31. . . . . 24 E6
Meare TA7. . . . . .138 C1
Midsomer Norton BA3. . . . . . 78 B2
Milborne Port DT9. . . . . .217 D3
Milverton TA4. . . . . .167 A5
Misterton TA18. . . . . .224 E4
Nailsea BS48 . . . . 8 F2
Norton Fitzwarren TA2. . . . . .168 B4
Pill BS20. . . . . 4 C4
Portbury BS20 . . . . 3 D3
Portishead BS20 . . . . 2 D6
Sandford BS25. . . . . 51 F4
Shapwick TA7. . . . . .137 F2
Shepton Mallet BA4 . . . . . . .205 B5
Sherborne DT9. . . . . .225 C3
Stalbridge DT10. . . . . .190 B4
Stogumber TA4. . . . . .150 D8
Taunton TA1. . . . . .212 F5
Templecombe BA8 . . . . .176 E1
Walpole TA6 . . . . .136 B3
Wanstrow BA4. . . . . .142 F4
Washford TA23. . . . . .131 E4
Wellington TA21. . . . . .222 C7
Wellow BA2. . . . . 62 D1
Westbury-sub-Mendip BA5. .110 E5
Weston-super-Mare BS23 . . . 48 E7
Weston-super-Mare, St Georges
BS22. 32 D2
Weston-super-Mare, Worle
BS22. 31 F2
Williton TA4. . . . . .202 E3
Wincanton BA9 . . . . .216 C3
Wiveliscombe TA4 . . . . .210 C4
Wrington BS40. . . . . 35 D2
Yatton BS49 . . . . 17 B1
Station Rd (Blackmoor La)
BA8 .190 A7
Station Rd Ind Est BA10. . . .215 F6
Station Road Bsns Pk
DT10. . . . . .190 B5
Station Terr TA24 . . . . .201 A4
Station Vw BA3 . . . . 96 F8
Station Way BA4 . . . . .141 E5
Station Wlk TA9. . . . . .104 E3
Staundle La TA3 . . . . .183 B8
Staunton Fields BS14. . . . . . 23 C4
Staunton La
Minehead TA24. . . . . .201 A4
Whitchurch BS14 . . . . 23 D3
Staunton Rd TA24 . . . . .201 A5
Staunton Rise TA24. . . . . . . .201 A5
Staunton Way BS14 . . . . 23 D4
Stavordale Gr BS14. . . . . 23 B6
STAWELL. 137 A1
Stawell Rd TA7 . . . . .137 B1
STAWLEY. 166 A1
Stawley Cty Prim Sch
TA21. . . . . .179 B8
Stealamalong TA3 . . . . .183 E7
Steam Mills BA3. . . . . 96 F8
Steam Packet Terr **2**
TA6. .209 B4
STEANBOW. 140 D2
Steanbow Cotts BA4. . . . . . .140 D3
STEART
Babcary TA11. . . . . .174 C6
Combwich 135 D8
Steart Ave TA8. . . . . .104 B6
Steart Cl TA8 . . . . .104 B6

Steart Cotts TA3. . . . . .169 C3
Steart Ct TA8 . . . . .104 A7
Steart Dr TA8 . . . . .104 A6
Steart Dro TA10 . . . . .156 D1
Steart Gdns TA8 . . . . .104 B6
Steart Hill BA22. . . . . .174 D5
Steart La TA24 . . . . .129 F3
Steart Rd
Babcary TA11. . . . . .174 B6
Fenning Island TA5. . . . . .103 B1
Stedhams Cl TA21. . . . . .222 D7
Steeds Terr BA3 . . . . .115 D6
Steel La TA7 . . . . .137 D2
Steel Mills BS31. . . . . 24 F4
Steel's La BA9 . . . . .161 D2
Steel Well La BA8 . . . . .190 A6
Steep La TA21 . . . . .164 C8
Steeple View BA3 . . . . .116 A3
Steep The TA24 . . . . .147 C5
Steers Cl TA6 . . . . .209 B6
Steevens Ho (Almshouses) **13**
BS2. .227 C3
STEMBRIDGE. 185 A7
Stembridge Rd TA10 . . . . . .156 B1
Stembridge Tower Mill★
TA10. . . . . .156 B1
Stembridge Way TA2. . . . . . .168 B4
Stennard Gn BA2. . . . . 45 B2
Stent Hill TA24. . . . . .123 B4
Stephen's Hill TA10 . . . . . . .172 E4
Stephenson Dr BA11 . . . . . . .120 D6
Stephenson Rd TA24 . . . . . .201 B6
Stephen St TA1 . . . . .213 A4
Stephen Way **6** TA1. . . . . . .213 A4
Steppes Cres **13** TA12. . . . . .185 E6
Steppes Mdw TA12. . . . . . . .185 E6
Steps La BA2. . . . . .100 E7
Stert Dro TA5. . . . . .135 B7
Steven's Cl BA4. . . . . .205 A5
Stevens La
Frome BA11. . . . . .119 F3
Lympsham BS24. . . . . 67 C3
Stewart Ct EX13. . . . . .198 A2
Steway La BA1. . . . . 29 B6
STEWLEY. 183 B5
Stibbear La TA19. . . . . .194 A8
Stiby Ct BA21. . . . . .218 F7
Stiby Rd BA21. . . . . .218 E7
Stickland BS21. . . . . 6 C1
Stickleball La BA4, BA6.. . . .140 D1
Stickle Hill TA4 . . . . .151 B7
Sticklepark La BA9 . . . . .176 A8
STICKLEPATH
Combe St Nicholas 193 D7
Monksilver 149 E7
Stickle Path EX16 . . . . .165 C1
STICKLINCH. 140 C1
Sticklinch Rd BA6. . . . . .140 C2
Stidham La BS31. . . . . 25 B6
Stiles Ct BA5. . . . . .203 B4
STILEWAY. 138 E3
Stileway BA6. . . . . .138 E3
Stileway Bsns Pk BS21. . . . . 16 B8
Stiling Cl TA9. . . . . .104 D4
Stillingfleet Rd BS13 . . . . . . 22 C5
Stillington Cl BA5. . . . . .203 B3
Stillman Cl BS13. . . . . 21 E4
Stirling Way
Frome BA11. . . . . .120 C6
Keynsham BS31. . . . . 24 E4
Stirtingale Ave BA2. . . . . 44 C3
Stirtingale Rd BA2. . . . . 44 C3
Stitching La BS28. . . . . .138 C8
Stitchings La BA2. . . . . 61 D7
Stitchings Shord La BS39. . . 57 C4
Stoate Cl TA23. . . . . .202 C5
Stoberry Ave BA5. . . . . .203 E5
Stoberry Cres BA5 . . . . .203 E5
Stoberry Park Sch BA5 . . . .203 E5
STOCK. 53 B8
Stockbridge TA17. . . . . .195 D7
Stockbridge La BA6. . . . . . . .140 B2
Stockditch Rd TA12 . . . . . . .185 B7
Stockers Cl TA4. . . . . .210 B4
Stockham Cross TA4 . . . . . .151 D5
Stockham Hill TA22. . . . . . . .163 E8
Stock Hill BA3. . . . . .115 B8
Stockhill Cl BA3. . . . . 96 C3
Stock Hill Ct BA3. . . . . .117 B7
Stockhill Rd BA3. . . . . 96 C2
Stock La
Buckhorn Weston SP8 . . . . . .177 F5
Lower Langford BS40. . . . . 53 A7
STOCKLAND BRISTOL. 135 A6
Stockland Bristol Rd TA5 .135 A6
Stockland Hill EX14. . . . . . . .192 A1
Stockland Manor TA5 . . . . . .134 F6
Stockland Rd EX14 . . . . .193 A2
STOCKLINCH. 184 B4
Stocklinch La TA19. . . . . .184 B4
STOCKLINCH OTTERSEY. . .184 C4
Stocklinch Rd
Ilminster TA19 . . . . .221 F7
Stocklinch TA19 . . . . .184 B3
STOCKLINCH ST
MAGDALEN 184 C4
Stockman La TA20 . . . . .198 C7
Stockmead BS40. . . . . 53 B5
Stockmoor Cl TA6. . . . . .209 A2
Stockmoor Dr
10 Bridgwater TA6. . . . . . . .154 A5
Bridgwater TA6. . . . . .209 A1
Stock Moor Dro TA6. . . . . . .209 A1
Stock's La
Hatch Beauchamp TA3,
TA19 . . . . .183 B6
Leigh u M BA3. . . . . .116 E3

Stock's La continued
North Wootton BA4 . . . . .140 C4
Stockstyle La EX13 . . . . .198 A8
Stockton Cl BS14 . . . . .22 F4
Stock Way N BS48 . . . . .8 F2
Stock Way S BS48 . . . . .8 E2
Stockwell Rd TA1 . . . . . . .168 F4
Stockwitch Cross BA22 . .174 B3
STOCKWOOD 23 E5
Stockwood Bsns Pk BA4 .141 C2
Stockwood Hill BS31 . . . . .24 C7
Stockwood La BS14 . . . . . .23 E5
STOCKWOOD VALE 24 C6
Stockwood Vale BS31 . . . . .24 C6
Stodden's La TA8 . . . . . . .104 E8
Stodden's Rd TA8 . . . . .85 C1
Stodden's Wlk TA8 . . . . . .104 B8
Stodelegh Cl BS22 . . . . . . .32 B3
STOFORD 197 F8
Stoford La
Broadway TA19 . . . . .183 C2
West Buckland TA21 . . . .181 A7
Stoford Pl TA19 . . . . .183 C2
STOGUMBER 150 D8
Stogumber CE Prim Sch
TA4 . . . . .150 D8
Stogumber Rd
Kingswood TA4 . . . . .150 F8
Lawford TA4 . . . . .151 A8
Stogumber Sta★ TA4 . . . .150 E8
STOGURSEY 134 C5
Stogursey CE Prim Sch
TA5 . . . . .134 B5
Stogursey La TA5 . . . . . . .134 A3
STOKE BISHOP 5 E5
Stoke Bishop CE Prim Sch
BS9 . . . . .5 D5
Stoke Cotts BS9 . . . . .5 E4
Stoke Cres BA3 . . . . .116 A2
Stoke Cross **10** TA14 . . . .185 F4
Stoke Gr BS9 . . . . .5 E6
Stoke Hamlet BS9 . . . . .5 F6
Stoke Hill
Bristol BS9 . . . . .5 E3
Chew Stoke BS40 . . . . . . .56 D7
Stoke St Mary TA3 . . . . . .169 D1
Stoke St Michael BA3 . . . .116 A2
Stoney Stoke BA9 . . . . . . .160 E3
Stoke La
Bristol, Westbury on T BS9 . . . .5 F6
Stoke St Mary TA3 . . . . . .169 A1
Wincanton BA9 . . . . .216 F5
Yarlington BA9 . . . . .175 E7
Stokeleigh Wlk BS9 . . . . . .5 C5
Stoke Mead BA2 . . . . .63 F7
Stoke Moor Dro BS27 . . . .109 D6
Stoke Paddock Rd BS9 . . . .5 D6
Stoke Park Rd BS9 . . . . . . .5 F4
Stoke Park Rd S BS9 . . . . . .5 E3
STOKE PERO 128 F6
Stoke Rd
Bristol BS9 . . . . .5 F3
Martock TA12 . . . . .185 E5
North Curry TA3 . . . . . . .170 C4
Portishead BS20 . . . . .2 D5
Ruishton TA3 . . . . .169 C2
Stoke St Mary TA3 . . . . . .169 B1
Street BA16 . . . . .207 E6
Taunton TA1 . . . . .213 B1
Westbury-sub-Mendip BA5 .110 D6
STOKE ST GREGORY 170 E6
Stoke St Gregory CE Prim Sch
Stoke St Gregory TA3 . . . .170 E6
Stoke St Gregory TA3 . . . .170 E6
STOKE ST MARY 169 C1
STOKE ST MICHAEL 116 B2
Stoke St Michael Prim Sch
BA3 . . . . .116 A3
Stokes Croft BS1 . . . . . . .227 B4
Stokes La DT10 . . . . .189 F2
Stoke St BS27 . . . . .110 B8
STOKE SUB HAMDON . . .185 F5
Stoke sub Hamdon Castle
Prim Sch TA14 . . . . .185 F4
Stoke sub Hamdon Priory★
TA14 . . . . .185 F4
STOKE TRISTER 177 B7
Stoke Trister Rd BA9 . . . .177 C7
STOLFORD 134 F8
Stonage La TA18 . . . . . . .196 C5
Stoneable Rd BA3 . . . . . . .79 A3
Stoneage La BA2 . . . . .61 D3
STONE ALLERTON 88 C3
Stone Allerton Dro BS26 . . .88 B2
STON EASTON 95 E8
Ston Easton La BA3 . . . . . .95 D8
Stonebarrow La EX13 . . . .198 F2
Stoneberry Rd BS14 . . . . . .23 B3
STONEBRIDGE
Banwell 51 A4
Frome 120 A7
Stonebridge BS21 . . . . .6 D1
Stonebridge Dr BA11 . . . .120 B7
Stonebridge Rd BS23 . . . . .48 F4
Stonechat Green BS20 . . . . .3 A6
Stone Cl TA1 . . . . .168 D1
Stone Cross TA24 . . . . . . .128 E1
Stonedene DT9 . . . . .225 D6
Stone Down La BA6 . . . . .139 D1
STONE-EDGE BATCH 8 D4
Stone End Cottage La
TA9 . . . . .136 C8
Stonegallows TA1 . . . . . . .212 A3
Stonehenge La BS48 . . . . . .8 E4
Stonehill
South Cadbury BA22 . . . .175 C4
Stoke Sub Hamdon TA14 . .186 A4
Street BA16 . . . . .207 B5

STONE HILL 207 A4
Stone Hill Ct TA24 . . . . . .200 F7
Stone Hill La TA4 . . . . . . .166 D3
Stonehouse Cl BA2 . . . . . . .45 B2
Stonehouse La BA2 . . . . . . .45 B2
Stone La
Durnfield BA22 . . . . .186 B8
East Pennard BA4 . . . . . .158 E6
Exford TA24 . . . . .128 E1
Winsford TA24 . . . . .147 E6
Yeovil BA21 . . . . .187 B5
Stoneleigh
Chew Magna BS40 . . . . . . .39 B3
Wellington TA21 . . . . . . .222 B8
Stoneleigh Cl
Burnham-on-S TA8 . . . . .104 C8
Staplegrove TA2 . . . . . . .212 C8
Stoneleigh Ct
Bath BA1 . . . . .27 E3
Taunton TA1 . . . . .212 C1
Stoneleigh Mews BA2 . . . .218 C7
Stoneleigh Rise BA11 . . . .120 A6
Stone Mead La TA10 . . . . .173 A4
Stone Rd TA8 . . . . .104 D5
Stoneridge La TA4 . . . . . .165 D5
Stones Cross BA3 . . . . .78 B2
Stonesfield TA18 . . . . . . .196 B5
Stones Paddock BA3 . . . . .116 C7
Stonewall Terr BA11 . . . . .119 F2
Stonewell Dr BS49 . . . . . . .34 D3
Stonewell Gr BS49 . . . . . . .34 D3
Stonewell La BS49 . . . . . . .34 D3
Stonewell Park Rd BS49 . . .34 D3
Stoneyard La BA3 . . . . .75 D2
Stoney Cl TA24 . . . . .129 F6
Stoneyfield Cl BS20 . . . . . . .4 B5
Stoneyfields BS20 . . . . .4 B4
Stoney Furlong TA2 . . . . . .213 B8
Stoney Head Cvn Pk TA3 . .169 F1
Stoneyhurst Dr TA10 . . . . .171 C3
Stoney La
Bishops Lydeard TA4 . . . .167 E8
Curry Rivel TA10 . . . . . . .171 C3
East Coker BA22 . . . . . . .197 D6
Stocklinch TA19 . . . . . . .184 C4
Stoney Lane Cross EX16 . .178 B3
Stoney Littleton Long
Barrow★ BA2 . . . . .80 C7
Stoney St TA24 . . . . .129 C7
Stoney Steep
Portishead BS20 . . . . .2 C6
Wraxall BS48 . . . . .9 A5
Stoney Stile Way
Wells BA5 . . . . .111 F2
Wells BA5 . . . . .203 B6
STONEY STOKE 160 F3
Stoney Stoke Rd BA9 . . . .160 B2
STONEY STRATTON 141 F2
STONY HEAD 169 F1
Stonyhead Hill TA3 . . . . . .169 F1
STONY KNAPS 199 D7
Stony La
Axminster EX13 . . . . .198 A1
Hawkridge TA22 . . . . . . .146 E3
Whatley BA11 . . . . .118 A2
STONY LITTLETON 80 B6
Stony St BA11 . . . . .119 F5
STOODHAM 220 D6
Stoodham TA13 . . . . .220 D5
Stoodly La
North Wootton BA4 . . . . .140 A8
Pilton BA4 . . . . .204 A2
Stooper's Hill TA20 . . . . . .193 C6
STOPGATE 192 C4
Stopgate Cross EX14 . . . . .192 C4
Stoppard Rd TA8 . . . . . . .104 C6
Stopper's La BA5 . . . . . . .139 F6
Stormont Cl BS23 . . . . . . .48 F3
Stormore BA13 . . . . .121 F8
Storridge La
Axminster EX13 . . . . .198 B6
Brompton Regis TA22 . . . .148 A1
Storridge View TA22 . . . . .148 A2
Stothert Ave
Bath BA2 . . . . .228 A2
East Twerton BA2 . . . . . . .44 D6
STOUGHTON CROSS 108 B8
Stoughton Rd BS28 . . . . .107 E5
Stourhead Gardens★
BA12 . . . . .161 F5
Stourhead House★ BA12 . .161 F5
Stour Hill SP8 . . . . .177 E1
Stour Hill Pk SP8 . . . . . . .177 F1
STOURTON 161 F5
STOURTON CAUNDLE . . .189 F2
Stourton Cl BA11 . . . . . . .119 E3
Stourton Gdns **1** BA11 . . .119 E3
Stourton La BA12 . . . . . . .161 F6
Stourton View BA11 . . . . .119 E3
Stourton Way BA21 . . . . . .218 D6
STOUT 156 B2
Stout Cross EX14 . . . . . . .192 C5
Stout's Way La
Luxborough TA23 . . . . . .148 F8
Rodhuish TA24 . . . . .131 A1
Stowborough Cotts BA2 . . .79 C7
STOWELL 176 C1
Stowell Hill DT9 . . . . .176 C1
Stowell La TA20 . . . . .198 D8
Stowell Rd
Barrow Hill DT9 . . . . .217 D8
Milborne Wick DT9 . . . . .189 B8
Stowers Row **31** TA12 . . . .185 E6
STOWEY 57 F4
Stowey Bottom BS39 . . . . .57 E5
Stowey Cross Rds BS39 . . . .57 F5
Stowey La
Curry Mallet TA3 . . . . . . .183 E8

Stowey La continued
Fivehead TA3 . . . . .170 E1
Stowey Pk BS49 . . . . .34 D7
Stowey Rd
Pitney TA10 . . . . .172 D7
Taunton TA2 . . . . .212 E8
Yatton BS49 . . . . .34 C8
Stow Ho BS11 . . . . .4 E5
Stradling Ave BS23 . . . . . .48 F5
Stradling Cl TA7 . . . . .137 B2
Stradlings Hill TA5 . . . . . .135 B2
Stradling's Hill TA5 . . . . . .135 B3
Stradlings Yd BS2 . . . . . . .226 C4
Straight Dro
Burrowbridge TA7 . . . . . .155 B1
Bussex TA7 . . . . .154 F6
Chilton Trinity TA5 . . . . . .135 F2
West Huntspill TA9 . . . . .136 B7
Woolavington TA9 . . . . . .137 A6
Straight La BA11 . . . . .101 D7
Straightmead BA3 . . . . . . .75 F1
Strap La
Ston Easton BA3 . . . . .95 F7
Upton Noble BA4, BA10 . .143 A1
Stratford Cl BS14 . . . . . . .22 F3
Stratford Cl BS9 . . . . .5 F8
Stratford La BS40 . . . . . . .56 E1
Stratford Rd BA21 . . . . . .218 D5
Stratheden BS8 . . . . .226 A4
Stratton Cl TA6 . . . . .209 D3
Stratton La BS22 . . . . .31 A4
**STRATTON-ON-THE
FOSSE** 96 F1
Stratton Rd
Holcombe BA3 . . . . .116 B8
Saltford BS31 . . . . .25 E3
Strawberry Bank TA19 . . . .221 C4
Strawberry Cl BS48 . . . . . . .8 D1
Strawberry Field BS26 . . . .70 C2
Strawberry Gdns BS48 . . . .18 D8
Strawberry Hill
Clevedon BS21 . . . . .6 F4
Street BA16 . . . . .207 B7
Strawberry La BS13, BS41 . .21 E3
Strawberry Line BS49 . . . . .52 A8
Strawberry Way BA5 . . . . .203 C4
Strawberry Way Rdbt
BA5 . . . . .203 D3
Streaked La TA3 . . . . .170 C6
STREAM 132 A2
Streamcombe La TA22 . . . .163 B5
Streamcross BS49 . . . . . . .17 D1
Streamleaze BS40 . . . . . . .39 B3
Stream Rd TA4 . . . . .132 A2
Streamside
Chew Magna BS40 . . . . . . .39 B3
1 Clevedon BS21 . . . . .6 F3
Taunton TA1 . . . . .213 C2
STREET
Chard 194 C2
Glastonbury 207 C2
STREET ASH 193 C8
Street Dro
Street BA16 . . . . .207 E7
Street, Marshall's Elm BA16 207 B1
Walton BA16 . . . . .156 F5
STREET END 54 D3
Street End BA40 . . . . .54 D2
Street End La BS40 . . . . . . .54 D2
Street Hill BA16 . . . . .207 B2
Street Ho TA19 . . . . .221 B3
Street La
Odcombe BA22 . . . . .186 C2
South Brewham BA10 . . . .161 A7
STREET ON THE FOSSE . .141 C2
Street Rd
Compton Dundon TA11 . . .157 A4
Glastonbury BA6 . . . . . . .206 D3
Street BA6 . . . . .207 D8
Street Rdbt BA16 . . . . . . .207 D7
Street The
Bishop Sutton BS39 . . . . . .57 D4
Chew Stoke BS40 . . . . . . .56 B8
Chilcompton BA3 . . . . . . .96 D5
Compton Martin BS40 . . . .74 B7
Draycott BS27 . . . . .90 F2
Farmborough BA2 . . . . . . .59 F6
Kilmington BA12 . . . . . . .161 F6
Radstock BA3 . . . . .78 F2
Stowey BS39 . . . . .57 F4
Ubley BS40 . . . . .55 D1
Wanstrow BA4 . . . . .142 F4
West Monkton TA2 . . . . . .169 C7
Winford BS40 . . . . .37 F1
Stretcholt La TA6 . . . . . . .135 F6
Stretford La TA19 . . . . . . .194 F7
Stringfellow Cres TA20 . . .223 D5
Stringfellow Mews TA20 . .223 C3
STRINGSTON 133 F5
STRODE 55 E7
Strode Coll BA16 . . . . . . .207 D6
Strode Ho **7** BA4 . . . . . .205 B6
Strode La
Clevedon BS21 . . . . .6 C2
Street BA16 . . . . .207 D6
Strode Way
Clevedon BS21 . . . . .6 B1
Shepton Mallet BA4 . . . . .205 A5
Stroud Rd BS11 . . . . .4 E5
Stroud Way BS24 . . . . .49 E7
Strowland La BS24 . . . . . . .86 F6
Strowlands BS24, TA9 . . . . .86 E6
Struthers Cl BA16 . . . . . . .207 B7
Strutter's Hill BA10 . . . . . .215 D2
Stuart Ho BS23 . . . . .30 D1
Stuart Pl BA2 . . . . .44 D6
Stuart Rd BS23 . . . . .49 A5

Stuarts Cl BA5 . . . . .203 D3
Stubb's La BA11 . . . . .101 D4
Stubby La TA2 . . . . .213 C8
STUDLEY GREEN 83 F6
Studley La BA4 . . . . .142 F4
Studley Mdws BA4 . . . . . .142 F4
Stump Cross
Pitcombe BA7 . . . . .215 A1
Shepton Mallet BA4 . . . . .204 D5
STURFORD 144 F7
Sturford La BA12 . . . . . . .144 E7
Sturmey Way BS20 . . . . . . .4 E3
Sturminster Cl BS14 . . . . . .23 D6
Sturminster Lodge BS14 . . .23 D5
Sturminster Rd BS14 . . . . .23 D7
Sturt La TA3 . . . . .183 E7
Stutts End TA4 . . . . .167 E6
Style Flats TA4 . . . . .210 C5
Style Rd TA4 . . . . .210 C5
Styles Ave BA11 . . . . .120 C4
Styles Cl BA11 . . . . .120 B4
Styles Hill BA11 . . . . .120 B4
Styles Mdw BA11 . . . . . . .120 C5
Styles Pk BA11 . . . . .120 B4
Sub Rd BA6 . . . . .157 D4
Suffolk Cl TA6 . . . . .209 C3
Suffolk Cres TA1 . . . . .212 C1
Suffolk Ct TA1 . . . . .212 C1
Suffolk Ho BA1 . . . . .44 C8
Sugg's La TA19 . . . . .183 C2
Sulis Manor Rd BA2 . . . . . .62 D8
Sullivan Cl BS4 . . . . .22 D6
Sully Cl TA6 . . . . .209 D6
Sumerleaze Cres TA2 . . . .213 C8
Sumerlin Dr BS21 . . . . .6 F3
Summer Ct BS8 . . . . .226 B3
Summerfield BS22 . . . . . . .32 A3
Summerfield Ave TA1 . . . .180 D8
Summerfield Cl TA7 . . . . . .154 F5
Summerfield Ct TA1 . . . . . .212 E4
Summerfield Rd BA1 . . . . . .28 A1
Summerfields Rd TA20 . . .223 C3
Summerfield Terr BA1 . . . . .28 A1
Summerfield Way TA1 . . . .180 D8
Summer Ground Dr BS13 . .22 A5
Summerhedge Cres TA7 . .155 C2
Summerhedge Rd TA7 . . . .155 C1
Summer Hill
Frome BA11 . . . . .119 F3
Hinton St George TA17 . . .195 D7
Summerhill La
Burford BA4 . . . . .140 F5
West Shepton BA4 . . . . . .204 D4
Summerhill Rd BA1 . . . . . .27 D1
Summerhouse BS21 . . . . . . .8 D4
Summer House Terr BA20 219 B4
Summerhouse View BA21 219 C6
Summer La
Banwell BS29 . . . . .50 E5
Chard TA20 . . . . .194 C4
Hinton St George TA13,
TA17 . . . . .195 C8
Monkton Combe BA2 . . . . .63 D8
Weston-super-Mare BS22,
BS24 . . . . .32 B1
Weston-super-Mare BS29 . .50 B8
Weston-super-Mare BS29 . .50 D7
Summer La N BS22 . . . . . .32 A2
Summerland Ave TA24 . . .201 A7
Summerland Pl TA24 . . . . .200 F7
Summerland Rd TA24 . . . .200 F7
SUMMERLANDS 218 F6
Summerlands
Backwell BS48 . . . . .19 B5
Yeovil BA21 . . . . .218 F6
Summerlands Hospl BA21 218 F6
Summerlands Park Ave
TA19 . . . . .221 B4
Summerlands Park Cl
TA19 . . . . .221 B4
Summerlands Park Dr
TA19 . . . . .221 B4
Summerlands Rd BS23 . . . .49 B8
Summer Lane Cvn Pk BS29. 50 E3
Summer Lane Park Homes
BS29 . . . . .50 E4
Summerlays Ct BA2 . . . . . .45 B6
Summerlays Pl BA2 . . . . . .45 B6
Summerlea BA2 . . . . .61 A5
Summerleaze BS31 . . . . . . .24 E7
Summer Leaze BS39 . . . . . .57 D4
Summerleaze Cres TA2 . . .213 C7
Summerleaze Pk BA20 . . .218 F5
Summer Shard TA13 . . . . .220 C4
Summers Hill La BA4 . . . . .204 C2
Summerville Terr TA8 . . . .104 B6
Summerway TA24 . . . . . . .129 E1
Summerway Dro TA7 . . . . .209 E4
Summerwell La BA16 . . . . .156 D7
Summerwood Rd BA16 . . .207 B4
Sun Batch BS27 . . . . .91 A3
Sunderland Pl BS8 . . . . . .226 B3
Sunderland St **2** BA2 . . . .228 C3
Sundew Cl TA1 . . . . .213 C1
Sunfield Rd BS24 . . . . .49 E3
Sunningdale BS8 . . . . . . .226 B4
Sunningdale BS48 . . . . .9 A1
Sunningdale Rd
Weston-super-Mare BS22 . .31 F3
Yeovil BA21 . . . . .219 C6
Sunnybank BA2 . . . . .45 B4
Sunny Bank TA4 . . . . .150 B8
Sunnybank Ct BS22 . . . . . .32 B1
Sunnybank Rd TA6 . . . . . .208 E2
Sunnybank Way BS24 . . . . .32 B1
Sunnybrow Cl **10** TA6 . . . .153 F4
Sunny Cl TA9 . . . . .136 B8

Sunny Hill
Bristol BS9 . . . . .5 C7
Pitcombe BA10 . . . . .215 C4
Sunnyhill Dr BS11 . . . . .4 E6
Sunnyhill Ho E BS11 . . . . . .4 E6
Sunnyhill Ho W BS11 . . . . . .4 E6
Sunny La BA10 . . . . .215 C4
Sunnymead
Bridgwater TA6 . . . . .208 E2
Keynsham BS31 . . . . .24 F3
Midsomer Norton BA3 . . . .77 F2
Oakhill BA3 . . . . .114 F3
Stratton-on-t F BA3 . . . . . .96 F2
Sunnymeade BA6 . . . . . . .138 C4
Sunnymead La BS39 . . . . . .57 D3
Sunnymead Rd BS48 . . . . . .8 D3
Sunnyside
Barrington TA19 . . . . . . .184 C5
Bristol BS9 . . . . .5 E5
Burlescombe EX16 . . . . . .179 C2
Clatworthy TA4 . . . . .149 F1
Clutton BS39 . . . . .59 B4
Farrington Gurney BS39 . . .77 B3
Frome BA11 . . . . .119 F3
Sunnyside Cotts TA24 . . . .129 A8
Sunnyside Cres BS21 . . . . . .6 D3
Sunnyside Farm Trad Est
BS20 . . . . .4 C2
Sunnyside Gdns BA2 . . . . . .60 D2
Sunnyside Pl BA11 . . . . . .119 F3
Sunnyside Rd
Clevedon BS21 . . . . .6 D3
Weston-super-Mare BS23 . .48 E5
Sunnyside Rd N BS23 . . . . .48 E6
Sunnyside Terr **6** DT9. . . .225 E4
Sunnyside View BA2 . . . . . .79 C7
Sunnyvale
Camerton BA2 . . . . .78 C4
Clevedon BS21 . . . . .6 B1
Sunridge Cl BA3 . . . . .96 F8
Sunridge Pk BA3 . . . . .96 F8
Sunset Cl BA2 . . . . .79 C7
Sun St BA11 . . . . .119 E5
Suprema Ave TA7 . . . . . . .137 C2
Suprema Est TA7 . . . . . . .137 D2
Surrey St BS2 . . . . .227 B4
Susanna's Cross BA3 . . . . .116 B2
Susanna's La BA3 . . . . . . .116 C2
Sussex Ave TA6 . . . . .209 B3
Sussex Cl TA6 . . . . .209 B3
Sussex Lodge TA1 . . . . . . .212 F5
Sussex Pl BA2 . . . . .228 C1
Sutherland Ave TA8 . . . . .104 B6
Sutherland Cl TA1 . . . . . . .212 C1
Sutherland Ct TA1 . . . . . . .212 C1
Sutherland Dr BS24 . . . . . .49 D2
SUTTON 159 B4
SUTTON BINGHAM 197 D6
Sutton Cl
Frome BA11 . . . . .120 B7
Weston-super-Mare BS22 . .49 E8
Sutton Cross TA10 . . . . . .172 F4
Sutton Grange BA21 . . . . .218 C6
Sutton Hill
East Coker BA22 . . . . . . .197 D6
Long Sutton TA10 . . . . . .172 F4
Sutton Hill Rd BS39 . . . . . .57 D4
Sutton La
Redhill BS40 . . . . .36 F1
Walton BA16 . . . . .156 D6
SUTTON MALLET 155 B7
SUTTON MONTIS 175 C3
Sutton Montis Rd
Sparkford BA22 . . . . .175 B4
Sutton Montis BA22 . . . . .175 C3
Sutton Pk BS39 . . . . .57 D4
Sutton Rd TA11 . . . . .211 C2
Sutton St BA2 . . . . .45 B7
Sutton View TA10 . . . . . . .172 E2
SUTTON WICK 57 B2
Swains TA21 . . . . .222 D4
Swains La TA21 . . . . .222 D4
Swain St TA23 . . . . .202 C7
Swains Well BS14 . . . . .22 F6
Swainswick CE Prim Sch
BA1. . . . . .28 B5
Swainswick Gdns BA1. . . . .28 C2
Swainswick La BA1. . . . . . .28 D4
Swallow Cl BA3 . . . . .97 A8
Swallow Cl BS14 . . . . .23 F6
Swallow Cl EX16 . . . . . . .178 F1
Swallow Dr BA11 . . . . . . .120 B6
Swallow Gdns BS22 . . . . . .49 E8
Swallow Hill TA10 . . . . . . .172 A6
Swallow St BA1 . . . . .228 C2
Swallows The BS22 . . . . . .49 D7
Swan Cl BS22 . . . . .49 E8
Swancombe
Blagdon BS40 . . . . .54 E2
Clapton in G BS20 . . . . . . .8 E8
Swan Down TA20 . . . . . . .194 E4
Swane Rd BS14 . . . . .23 F6
Swan Hill TA18 . . . . .196 C5
Swan Ho **3** BA4 . . . . . . .205 B6
Swanmead Com Sch
TA19 . . . . .221 C3
Swan Prec TA19 . . . . .221 C3
Swanshard La BA5 . . . . . .139 D6
Swans La BS27 . . . . .90 F2
Swan Yd DT9 . . . . .225 D4
Swedish Hos TA13 . . . . . .220 D1
Sweetgrass Rd BS24. . . . . .50 A8
Sweethay Cl TA3 . . . . .181 D8

Sweethay Cross TA3...........181 C8
Sweethay La TA3...........181 C8
Sweeting Cl 12 TA3...........169 C5
Sweetleaze BA3...........116 A2
Sweetleaze La BA3...........115 C8
SWELL...........171 A2
Swell Cl TA9...........136 B8
Swell Dro
  North Curry TA3...........170 F3
  Swell TA3...........171 A1
Swell La TA3...........171 A2
Swiddacombe La EX36...........162 C7
Swift Cl BS22...........31 F1
Swift Lodge BA20...........219 A4
Swifts TA21...........166 F1
Swillbridge Cvn Pk TA23...202 F6
SWINEFORD...........26 A7
Swingbridge TA2...........213 E7
Swiss Ct 13 BS23...........48 E7
Swiss Dr BS3...........11 F2
Swiss Rd
  Bristol BS3...........11 F1
  Weston-super-Mare BS23...48 F1
Sycamore Cl
  Bridgwater TA6...........209 D5
  Burnham-on-S TA8...........104 A5
  Nailsea BS48...........8 E2
  Shipham BS25...........70 E8
  Taunton TA1...........213 C2
  Weston-super-Mare BS23...49 A8
  Weston-super-Mare, Locking
    BS24...........49 E5
  Westonzoyland TA7...........154 E5
Sycamore Ct TA20...........223 C5
Sycamore Dr
  Crewkerne TA18...........224 C7
  Frome BA11...........120 B7
  Langport TA10...........172 A6
  Yeovil BA20...........218 F2
Sycamore Rd
  Minehead TA24...........200 D7
  Radstock BA3...........79 B2
Sycamores BS23...........30 E1
Sycamore Sq TA20...........223 C5
Sycamore Wlk TA3...........169 C5
SYDENHAM...........209 C5
Sydenham Bldgs BA2...........228 A2
Sydenham Cl
  Bridgwater TA6...........209 C6
  Porlock TA24...........124 B4
Sydenham Rd
  Bath BA2...........228 A2
  Bridgwater TA6...........209 C6
Sydenham Terr BA2...........45 C1
Sydling Rd BA21...........219 D6
Sydnalls La BA12...........144 E8
Sydney Bldgs BA2...........45 B6
Sydney Ho BA2...........45 B7
Sydney Mews BA2...........45 B7
Sydney Pl BA2...........45 B7
Sydney Rd BA2...........45 B7
Sydney Row BS1...........226 B1
Sydney Wharf BA2...........45 B7
Sylvan Rd TA21...........222 E5
Sylvan Way
  Bristol BS9...........5 B7
  Monkton Heathfield TA2...213 E8
Symes Ave BS13...........22 C4
Symes Cl
  Chard TA20...........223 C4
  North Perrott TA18...........196 C4
Symes Pk BA1...........27 A2
Symons Way
  Bridgwater TA6...........209 A6
  Cheddar BS27...........90 C7
Syndercombe La TA4,
  TA23...........149 D2
SYNDERFORD...........199 C6

T

Tabbitts Steep TA24...........129 B2
Tabernacle La 4 BA20...........219 B4
TACKER STREET...........149 C8
Taddywood La BA4...........159 F6
TADHILL...........116 F2
Tadhill La BA3...........116 D2
TADWICK...........12 E1
Tail Mill TA16...........195 F7
Tailor's Ct 7 BS1...........227 A3
Talbot Cl TA9...........104 D3
Tallis Gr BS4...........22 D6
Tallowood BA4...........205 D5
Tamar Ave TA1...........213 B1
Tamar Dr BS31...........25 A4
Tamar Rd BS22...........32 A2
Tamblyn Cl BA3...........79 A3
Tamsin Ct BS31...........24 F5
Tamworth Rd BS31...........24 E4
Tancred St TA1...........213 A4
TANGIER...........212 E4
Tangier TA1...........212 E4
Tankard's Cl BS8...........226 C3
Tankey's Cl BA11...........120 A7
Tan La SP8...........161 F1
Tanner Cl BA3...........97 C8
Tanner Rd BS29...........50 C7
Tanner's Hill TA4...........165 E7
Tanners La SN14...........13 F8
Tanners Wlk
  Bath BA2...........43 F5
  Marshfield SN14...........13 F8
Tannery Cl BA16...........207 C5

Tannery Ct TA18...........224 C7
Tanorth Cl BS14...........23 A3
Tanorth Rd BS14...........22 F3
Tansee Hill TA20...........199 B6
Tansey BA4...........142 A6
Tansey Ct TA6...........208 E1
Tansy La BS20...........2 F5
Tanyard
  Broadway TA19...........183 C2
  Nether Stowey TA5...........134 B2
Tan Yard La TA13...........184 F5
Tanyards BA10...........215 F7
Tanyard The TA16...........207 C5
Tape La BA3...........114 F7
Taphouse La DT6...........199 E1
Tapmoor Rd TA7...........155 C8
Tappers La 2 TA6...........153 E3
Tapps La TA7...........136 E4
Tapstone Rd TA20...........223 D4
Taranto Hill BA22...........173 E2
Taranto Way BA22...........174 A2
Target La TA12...........185 D4
TARNOCK...........87 D6
Tarnock Ave BS14...........23 A7
Tarnwell BS39...........40 A2
Tarragon Pl BS20...........2 F5
Tarrant La BA20...........218 F1
Tarr La
  East Coker BA22...........197 E8
  Yeovil BA20, BA22...........219 A1
Tarratt Rd BA20...........218 F1
Tarr La
  Cushuish TA2...........152 D1
  Kingston St Mary TA2...168 D8
Tarr Post TA22...........146 C1
Tarr Steps ★ TA22...........146 E3
Tarr Steps National Nature
  Reserve ★ TA22...........146 E3
Tarr Water Cotts TA23...148 E8
Tatham St TA1...........212 D4
TATWORTH...........198 C8
Tatworth Prim Sch TA20...198 C8
Tatworth Rd TA20...........223 C2
Tatworth St TA20...........198 C8
Tauntfield Cl TA1...........213 A3
TAUNTON...........212 D5
Taunton Acad The TA2...168 E6
Taunton Nuffield Health Hospl
  TA2...........212 B7
Taunton Rd
  Ashcott TA7...........156 B7
  Bishops Lydeard TA4...........167 F7
  Bridgwater TA6...........209 A3
  North Petherton TA6...........153 F4
  Thurloxton TA6...........153 E2
  Wellington TA21...........222 E7
  Weston-super-Mare BS22...32 B4
  Wiveliscombe TA4...........210 D4
Taunton Sch TA2...........212 D6
Taunton Sta TA1...........212 F5
Taunton Third Way TA1...212 F4
Taunton Trad Est TA2...........212 A7
Taunton Vale Pk TA2...........213 F8
Taunusstein Way 12 BA20 219 B4
Taveners Wlk BS48...........8 F3
Taverner Cl BS4...........22 D7
Taverners Ct 6 BS23...........48 F4
Tavistock Rd BS22...........32 A2
Tawny Way BS22...........49 F8
Taylor Cl TA2...........168 B5
Taylor Ct
  Bridgwater TA6...........209 A5
  Weston-super-Mare BS22...32 B4
Taylor Gdns BS13...........21 F4
Taylor Ho TA19...........221 B3
Taylors Fields BS29...........51 B3
Taylor's Meade TA20...........193 D6
Taylor's Orch TA14...........185 E1
Tayman Ridge BS30...........25 D8
Teagle Cl BA5...........203 F5
Teak Cl TA6...........209 D6
Teal Cl
  Bridgwater TA6...........209 A4
  Weston-super-Mare BS22...31 F1
Tealham Moor Dro BS28...137 E8
Teal Rd TA24...........201 C5
Teals Acre 8 TA5...........135 B2
Teal Way BS20...........2 F6
Teapot Lane (Worms Lane)
  BA6...........158 B6
Teasel Wlk BS22...........49 D7
Technical St TA8...........104 B6
Teck Hill TA6...........153 E2
Teckhill La TA6...........153 E2
Teddington Cl BA2...........44 C4
Teesdale Cl BS22...........49 D8
Teeside BA14...........83 F4
Teeswater Way 9 TA6...154 A5
Teign Ct BA16...........156 D7
Teignmouth Rd BS21...........6 E3
Telephone Ave BS1...........227 A2
Telford Ho
  Bath BA2...........44 D3
  Leigh Woods BS8...........11 E7
Tellis Cross BA22...........197 D8
TELLISFORD...........82 E4
Tellisford La BA2...........81 F4
Tellisford Rd BA2...........82 E7
Tellis La BA3...........114 D8
Temblett Gn TA6...........208 C5
Templars Barton BA8...........176 E1

Templars Ct
  Long Sutton TA10...........172 E1
  1 Weston-super-Mare
    BS22...........49 D7
Templars Pl BA8...........176 E1
Templars Way BS25...........70 E7
TEMPLE...........144 E7
Temple Back BS1...........227 B2
Temple Back East BS1...227 C2
Temple Bridge Bsns Pk
  BS39...........76 F7
Temple Circus Giratory
  BS1...........227 C1
TEMPLE CLOUD...........58 E1
TEMPLECOMBE...........176 E1
Templecombe La SP8...177 C3
Templecombe Sta BA8...176 E1
Temple Ct BS31...........24 E5
Temple Field TA23...........202 C6
Temple Gate BS1...........227 B1
Temple Inn La BS39...........58 E1
Temple La BA8...........176 F1
Templeland Rd BS13...........21 F5
Temple of Harmony ★
  TA5...........153 B5
Temple Rose St BS1...227 B2
Temple St
  Bristol BS1...........227 B2
  Keynsham BS31...........24 F5
Temple Way BS2...........227 B2
Temple Way Underpass
  BS2...........227 C3
Ten Acre Dro TA7...........170 E8
Ten Acre La BA2...........61 F6
Tenby Rd BS31...........24 D4
Ten Foot Rhyne BA6...........140 A2
Tengore La TA10...........172 C6
Tennis Corner Dro BA11..102 D2
Tennis Court Ave BS39...........77 D5
Tennis Court Rd BS39...........77 D5
Tennyson Ave BS21...........6 B2
Tennyson Cl BS31...........24 F6
Tennyson Rd
  Bath BA1...........44 D7
  Weston-super-Mare BS23...49 A3
Tenterk Cl BS24...........67 B6
Tents Hill BA11...........118 B6
TERHILL...........151 F3
Terhill La TA4...........151 F3
Termare Cl BA22...........218 B6
Terrace The
  Minehead TA24...........201 A5
  Shipham BS25...........70 E8
Terrace View DT9...........225 E5
Terrace Wlk BA1...........228 C2
Terrell La TA5...........134 D2
Terrell St BS2...........227 A4
Terry Hill BA3...........98 D8
Terry Ho BS1...........226 C3
Tetbury Gdns BS48...........9 A1
Tetton Cl TA6...........208 B4
Teviot Rd BS31...........25 A4
Tewkesbury BA21...........218 D6
Tewther Rd BS13...........22 D3
Teyfant Com Sch BS13...22 E4
Teyfant Rd BS13...........22 E4
Teyfant Wlk BS13...........22 E4
Thackeray Ave BS21...........6 E4
Thackeray Ho BS23...........49 A5
Thackeray Rd BS21...........6 E4
Thames Dr TA1...........213 D4
Thatcham Cl 2 BA21...218 F7
Thatcham Cl 1 BA21...218 F7
Thatcham Pk BA21...........218 F7
Thatch Cotts TA20...........194 E1
Thatcher Cl BS20...........2 D4
Thatch The TA11...........211 C4
The Acorns BA11...........119 D4
Theaks Mews TA1...........213 A3
THEALE...........109 C1
Theatre Royal BS1...........227 A2
The Barton BS25...........69 B5
The Cliffs BS27...........71 C1
The Close House Rd BS28 108 C4
The Court House La BS26...87 D6
The Cypress House Rd
  BA22...........187 D8
The Drumway BS31...........25 B4
The Great Rd TA4...........132 F4
Theillay Cl TA5...........134 A3
The Lower La BA2...........62 C4
The Mead BS31...........24 D3
The Mendip Sch BA4...141 D3
The Old School Pl DT9...225 D3
The Pynes BS31...........25 B4
There-and-Back-Again La
  BS1...........226 C3
The Sidings BS23...........49 B4
The Uplands TA9...........106 E4
Theynes Croft BS41...........11 B1
THICKET MEAD...........77 F3
Thicket Mead BA3...........78 A2
Thickthorn Cross TA19...183 C3
Thickthorn La
  Chilcompton BA3...........96 A4
  Southtown TA19...........183 B3
Thimble La DT9...........217 D2
Third Ave
  Bath BA2...........44 D5
  Bristol BS14...........23 B7
  Radstock BA3...........97 D7
Thirlmere Rd BS23...........49 A4
Thistledoo Vine TA7...136 F2
Thistle Pk TA6...........209 B1
Thomas Bunn BA11...120 A7
Thomas Cl BS29...........51 A3
Thomas Ct BS1...........227 B2
Thomas La BS1...........227 B2

Thomas Lane Appartments
  BS1...........227 B2
Thomas Pl TA21...........222 D7
Thomas St
  Bath BA1...........228 C4
  Bristol BS2...........227 C4
  Taunton TA2...........212 F6
Thomas Way BA6...........206 B4
Thomas Way Ind Est BA6..206 B4
Thompson Cl TA6...........209 D6
Thompson Rd
  Bristol BS14...........23 E6
  Wells BA5...........203 D3
Thompson Way BS24...........50 C8
Thomson Dr TA18...........224 D5
Thong La TA10...........184 D6
Thornash Cl TA2...........213 F8
Thornbank Ct DT9...........225 E4
Thornbank Pl BA2...........228 A1
Thornbury Dr BS23...........48 E2
Thornbury Rd BS23...........48 C2
Thornbush Cross TA4...150 F3
Thorn Cl BS22...........32 B2
THORNCOMBE...........199 B6
Thorncombe Cres TA6...209 C5
Thorncombe La TA4...........133 A1
Thorncombe Thorn
  TA20...........199 B5
Thorndale BS8...........226 A4
Thorndale Cl BS22...........49 D8
Thorndale Mews BS8...........226 A4
Thorndun Park Dr TA20...223 D6
THORNE COFFIN...........218 A8
Thorne Cross BA22...........218 B7
Thorne Cross Way TA21...178 D8
Thorne Gdns BA21...........218 C7
Thorne La
  Wheddon Cross TA24...147 C8
  Winsford TA24...........147 C8
  Yeovil BA21...........218 C8
Thorne Pk TA8...........104 B5
THORNE ST MARGARET...179 D8
THORNEY...........172 A4
Thorneymoor La TA10...172 A3
Thorney Rd TA12...........185 B8
THORNFALCON...........169 E2
Thornhill Dro TA12...........173 A1
Thornhill La BA22...........187 A8
Thornhill Rd DT10...........190 B4
Thorn La TA3...........169 D2
Thornton Rd BA21...........218 D7
Thornwell La BA9...........216 D3
Thornwell Way BA9...........216 C3
Thorny La BA21...........187 E8
Thornymarsh La BA7...175 B8
THOULSTONE...........121 F4
THREE ASHES
  North Cadbury...........175 C7
  Oakhill...........115 E1
Three Ashes DT8...........199 D7
Three Ashes La TA11...157 B4
Three Corner Mead BA21 218 C5
Three Gates Cross TA22...163 C6
Three Hill View BA6...........206 E5
Three Horse Shoes Hill
  TA5...........152 C4
Three Oaks Cross TA19...183 C4
Three Queens' La BS1...227 B2
Three Ways Sch BA2...........62 E8
Three Wells Rd BS13...........21 F4
Thrift Cl DT10...........190 C4
Throgmorton Rd BS4...........22 F8
Throop Rd BA8...........176 F1
Thrubwell La BS40...........37 B4
Thrupe La BA5...........114 A2
Thrush Cl 4 BS22...........49 E8
Thumb La BA4...........158 E7
THURLBEAR...........182 C8
Thurlbear CE Prim Sch
  TA3...........182 C8
Thurlestone BS14...........23 A6
Thurlocks BA22...........186 B6
THURLOXTON...........153 C5
Thyme Cl BS20...........2 F5
Thynne Cl BS27...........90 B6
Tibbott Rd BS14...........23 D5
Tibbott Wlk BS14...........23 D5
Tiberius Rd BS31...........24 F7
Tichborne Rd BS23...........30 E1
TICKENHAM...........7 F4
Tickenham CE Prim Sch
  BS21...........7 F4
Tickenham Hill BS48...........8 E4
Tickenham Rd BS21...........7 A4
Tide Gr BS11...........5 A8
Tides Reach TA24...........125 C4
Tiffany Ct BS1...........227 B1
Tiger Moth Rd BS24...........49 C5
Tigers Wy 8 EX13...........198 A1
Tiledown BS39...........58 E1
Tiledown Cl BS39...........58 F1
Tile Hill BA10...........161 A4
Tile House Rd
  East Huntspill TA7...........137 B8
  Mark TA9...........106 C1
Tilery EX14...........192 D3
Tilham St BA6...........158 B6
Tilley Cl
  Farmborough BA2...........60 B5
  Keynsham BS31...........25 A2
Tilley La BA2...........60 A5
Tilleys Dro BA5...........138 F7
TILLWORTH...........198 D3
Tilsey La TA4...........150 C5
Tilton Ct 5 DT9...........225 D3
TIMBERSCOMBE...........130 C4
Timberscombe CE First Sch
  TA24...........130 B5

Timberscombe CE Fst Sch
  TA24...........130 B4
Timberscombe Way TA6..208 B4
Timberscombe Wlk BS14...23 C5
Timbers The BA3...........97 B7
Timberyard TA7...........137 F1
Timewell Hill EX16...........164 C4
TIMSBURY...........60 B1
TIMSBURY BOTTOM...........60 A1
Timsbury Rd
  Farmborough BA2...........60 B5
  High Littleton BS39...........59 D1
Timsbury Village Workshops
  BA2...........59 F3
Tin Bridge Rdbt BA6...139 D3
Tinkers La BS48...........19 F2
Tinker's La
  Compton Martin BS40...74 B7
  Cucklington BA9...........177 D7
  Halse TA4...........167 C6
  Kilmersdon BA11...........98 B1
Tinneys La DT9...........225 E4
Tintagel Cl BS31...........24 D4
Tintagel Rd BA21...........218 D7
Tintern BA21...........218 C6
TINTINHULL...........186 C6
Tintinhull Gdn ★ BA22...186 C6
Tintinhull Rd BA21...........186 F5
Tipcote Hill 17 BA4...........205 B6
Tipnoller Hill TA4...........210 F7
Tippacott La EX35...........122 A4
Tiptoft 3 TA14...........185 F4
Tirley Way BS22...........31 B2
Titan Barrow BA1...........29 C2
The Barn Cross EX15...179 D2
Tithe Ct BA20...........218 D5
Tithe Mdw TA4...........167 A7
Tithill La TA4...........167 F7
Titlands La BA5...........203 A7
Titus Wy BS31...........24 F7
Tiverton Gdns BS22...........32 A2
Tiverton Rd
  Bampton EX16...........164 C1
  2 Clevedon BS21...........6 E1
TIVINGTON...........129 F8
Tivington Cross TA24...129 F8
Tivoli Ho BS23...........48 E8
Tivoli La BS23...........48 E8
Tog Hill BS30...........12 B6
Toghill La BS30...........12 A8
Tolbury La BA10...........215 D6
Tolbury Mill BA10...........215 E6
TOLLAND...........150 E3
Tolland BS24...........49 A2
Tolland Cross TA4...........150 E3
Toll Bridge Rd BA1...........28 E3
Tolley's La TA20...........194 C3
Toll Gate TA4...........210 C4
Toll House Rd 1 TA5...135 B2
Toll Rd
  Porlock TA24...........124 A3
  Weston-super-Mare BS23...66 F3
Toms Cl TA20...........223 B3
Tomtit's La TA11...........211 C3
TONE...........222 A8
TONEDALE...........222 B7
Tonedale Bsns Pk TA21...222 B7
Tonedale Ind Est TA21...222 B8
Tone Dr TA6...........209 B3
Tone Gn TA4...........167 E2
Tone Hill TA21...........222 B8
Tone Rd BS21...........6 D1
Toneway TA2...........213 C6
Toose The BA21...........218 C6
Topaz Dr TA6...........209 C8
Top Hill BA4...........142 F2
Top La
  Gasper BA12...........161 E4
  Mells BA11...........118 B6
Top Rd
  Charlton Adam TA11...173 F7
  Shipham BS25...........70 F7
  Westbury-sub-Mendip BA5...110 C8
Top St
  Kingsdon TA11...........173 D5
  Pilton BA4...........140 F3
Top Wood BS3...........116 B7
Torbay Cl BA7...........214 B5
Torbay Rd BA7...........214 A5
Torbay Road Ind Est BA7..214 A5
Torbay Villas BA7...........214 A5
Tor Cl BS22...........32 A2
Torhill La BA5...........203 F4
Tor Hole Rd
  Chewton Mendip BA3...........93 F4
  Chewton Mendip BA3...........94 B4
Tori Green 2 TA6...........209 A1
Tormynton Rd BS22...........31 E3
Torre Cider Farm ★ TA23...131 E3
Torre Rocks TA23...........131 E2
Torres Vedras Dr TA21...222 F7
Torre The BA21...........218 C6
Torridge Mead TA1...........213 D4
Torridge Rd BS31...........25 A4
Torrington Ave BS4...........22 F8
Torrington Cres BS22...........32 A3
Tor St BA5...........203 E4
Tor View
  Cheddar BS27...........90 C7
  Woolavington TA7...........136 E4
Tor View Ave BA6...........206 D3
Tor Wood View BA5...........203 E4
T'OTHER SIDE THE HILL...115 B7
Totnes Cl BS22...........32 A2
Totney Dro BS28...........137 E8
Totshill Dr BS13...........22 E4
Totshill Gr BS13...........22 E4
Tottenham Pl BS8...........226 B3

Totterdown La
Pilton BA4 . . . . .204 B1
Weston-super-Mare BS24 . . . 49 A1
Totterdown Rd BS23 . . . . 48 F4
Tottle's Dro TA7 . . . . . . .154 C2
Touches CI TA20 . . . . . . .223 E5
Touches Mdw TA20 . . . . .223 E5
Touching End La SN14 . . . 13 F8
Touch La TA10 . . . . .156 C1
Touchstone CI TA20 . . . . .223 B4
Touchstone La TA20 . . . . .223 B4
Touchwood La BS26 . . . . . . 87 E3
Toulouse Rd 5 TA6 . . . . .209 A1
TOULTON 152 A2
Tout Hill BA9 . . . . .216 C3
Tout La BA22.TA11 . . . . . .174 A6
Tovey CI BS22 . . . . 31 E4
Tower CI
Cheddar BS27 . . . . 90 B6
Stoke St Michael BA3 . . . .116 A3
Tower Farms Ind Units
TA4 . . . . .151 A4
TOWERHEAD 51 D4
Towerhead Rd BS29 . . . . . 51 D3
Tower Hill
Bristol BS2 . . . . .227 B3
Bruton BA10 . . . . .215 D6
Holcombe Rogus TA21 . . .178 D5
Horsington BA8 . . . . .176 E2
Locking BS24 . . . . 50 D4
Stogursey TA5 . . . . .134 B5
Stoke St Michael BA3 . . . .116 A3
Williton TA4 . . . . .202 E2
Tower Hill Rd TA18 . . . . .224 B5
Tower House La BS48 . . . 9 A4
Tower La
Bristol BS1 . . . . .227 A3
Taunton TA1 . . . . .212 E4
Towerleaze BS9 . . . . 5 D3
Tower Rd
Kilmington BA12 . . . . . . .161 D6
Portishead BS20 . . . . 2 A4
Stawell TA7 . . . . .137 B1
Yeovil BA21 . . . . .219 C8
Tower St
Bristol BS1 . . . . .227 B2
Taunton TA1 . . . . .212 E4
Tower The BS1 . . . . .227 B2
Tower View
Frome BA11 . . . . .119 F2
South Cheriton BA8 . . . . .176 B3
Wanstrow BA4 . . . . .142 E4
Tower Wlk BS23 . . . . 30 C1
Town Barton BA2 . . . . . . 81 F4
Town CI
North Curry TA3 . . . . . . .170 B4
Stogursey TA5 . . . . .134 B6
Town End BA2 . . . . 81 F4
Townend Villas TA14 . . . .185 F2
Town Farm TA3 . . . . .170 B4
Townhall Bldgs BA5 . . . . .203 E4
Town Hill EX36 . . . . .162 C6
Town La BA4 . . . . .205 C6
Town Marsh TA22 . . . . . .163 D7
Townrise 15 BA20 . . . . . .219 B4
TOWNSEND 92 D4
Townsend
East Harptree BS40 . . . . . . 75 A5
Ilminster TA19 . . . . .221 D3
Marston Magna BA22 . . . .174 F1
Middlezoy TA7 . . . . .155 C3
Montacute TA15 . . . . . . .186 B3
Shepton Mallet BA4 . . . . .205 B5
Westonzoyland TA7 . . . . .154 F5
Williton TA4 . . . . .202 E3
TOWNS END 77 E4
TOWN'S END 116 E3
Townsend CI
Bristol BS14 . . . . 23 F5
Bruton BA10 . . . . .215 F7
Townsend Cotts TA24 . . .147 C5
Townsend Gn 10 BA8 . . .190 A6
Townsend La
Chilton Polden TA7 . . . . . .137 B2
Emborough BA3 . . . . 95 B2
Theale BS28 . . . . .109 A2
Townsend Orch
Merriott TA16 . . . . .195 F8
Street BA16 . . . . .207 B5
Townsend Pk BA10 . . . . .215 F7
Townsend Rd
Bristol BS14 . . . . 23 F5
Minehead TA24 . . . . .201 A6
Townsend Rise BA10 . . . .215 F7
Townsend Sh Pk BA4 . . . .205 B5
Townshend Rd BS22 . . . . 32 B5
Town St BA4 . . . . .205 B6
Town Tree Farm Nature
Trail ★ TA12 . . . . .185 C8
Town Tree La TA10, TA12 . .185 D8
TRACEBRIDGE 179 A8
Tracey CI TA7 . . . . .209 E4
Trackfordmoor Cross
TA22 . . . . .163 B3
Tracy CI BS14 . . . . 22 F7
Trafalgar Ct 12 BS23 . . . 48 E7
Trafalgar Rd BA1 . . . . 27 B1
Traits La BA22 . . . . .174 E4
Trajan's Way BA4 . . . . . .205 E5
Trajectus Way BS31 . . . . . 24 F7
Tramshed The BA1 . . . . . .228 C3
Transform Ind Est TA6 . . .209 A6
Transom Ho BS1 . . . . . . .228 C2
Transom PI TA24 . . . . . . .201 B7
Travers CI BS31 . . . . 24 D6
Trawden CI BS23 . . . . 31 A1
Treasure Ct TA8 . . . . 85 A1
Treasurer's Ho ★ TA12 . . .185 E6

TREBLE'S HOLFORD 151 C4
TREBOROUGH 149 A7
Tredinick CI TA2 . . . . . . .213 B8
Tredwin CI TA21 . . . . . . .222 D8
Treefield Rd BS21 . . . . . . 6 D2
Tregarth Rd BS3 . . . . 11 F1
Tregelles CI TA9 . . . . . . .104 C4
Tregonwell Rd TA24 . . . . .201 A4
Trelawn CI BS22 . . . . 32 D2
Trelissick Gdns 3 BS22 . . 49 F8
Trellech Ct 3 BA21 . . . . .218 C6
Tremes CI SN14 . . . . 13 F8
Tremlett Mews 3 BS22 . . 32 B4
Trenchard Rd
Locking BS24 . . . . 50 D4
Saltford BS31 . . . . 25 D3
Trenchard St BS1 . . . . . .226 C3
Trenchard Way TA2 . . . . .212 E5
Trendle La
Bicknoller TA4 . . . . .132 F2
Stoney Stoke BA9 . . . . . .160 E3
Trendle Rd TA1 . . . . .212 B1
Trendle St DT9 . . . . .225 D3
Trendlewood Way BS48 . . 9 A1
Trenleigh Dr BS22 . . . . . . 32 A2
TRENT 187 F5
Trent CI BA21 . . . . .219 E8
Trent Ct TA1 . . . . .213 D4
Trent Gr BS31 . . . . 25 A4
Trent Mdw TA1 . . . . .213 E4
Trent Path La DT9 . . . . . .225 A5
Trent Young's CE Prim Sch
DT9 . . . . .187 F5
Tresco Spinney BA21 . . . .218 C6
Trescothick CI BS31 . . . . . 24 E6
Trevanna Rd BS23 . . . . . . 11 F1
Trevelyan Rd BS23 . . . . . . 48 F7
Trevett Rd TA1 . . . . .212 C2
Trevithick CI BA11 . . . . . .120 C6
Trevor Rd TA6 . . . . .209 C6
Trevor Smith PI TA1 . . . . .213 A3
Trewartha CI BS23 . . . . . . 48 F8
Trewartha Pk BS23 . . . . . . 48 F8
Trewint Gdns BS4 . . . . . . 22 F8
Triangle Ct 2 BA2 . . . . . 44 D5
Triangle Ctr The BS21 . . . 6 D3
Triangle E BA2 . . . . 44 D5
Triangle N BA2 . . . . 44 D5
Triangle S BS8 . . . . .226 B3
Triangle The
Castle Cary BA7 . . . . .214 C5
Clevedon BS21 . . . . 6 D3
North Curry TA3 . . . . . . .170 A4
Paulton BS39 . . . . 77 E6
Portishead BS20 . . . . 2 B5
Somerton TA11 . . . . .211 D4
Wrington BS40 . . . . 35 D2
Triangle Villas 1 BA2 . . 44 D5
Triangle W
Bath BA2 . . . . 44 D5
Bristol BS8 . . . . .226 B3
Tribunal & Lake Village Mus ★
BA6 . . . . .206 D4
Trickey Warren La TA3 . . .181 C1
Trim Bridge 3 BA1 . . . . .228 B2
Trim St BA1 . . . . .228 B2
Trinder Rd BS20 . . . . 4 B4
Trindlewell La TA18 . . . . .196 C4
TRINITY 119 E5
Trinity Bsns Ctr TA1 . . . . .213 A3
Trinity CE Fst Sch BA11 . .119 C4
Trinity CE VC Prim Sch
BA3 . . . . 79 A4
Trinity CI
Bath BA1 . . . . .228 B2
Blackford BS28 . . . . .107 D4
Burnham-on-S TA8 . . . . . . 85 A1
Wellington TA21 . . . . . . .222 C5
Trinity Coll BS9 . . . . 5 E4
Trinity Ct
Bridgwater TA6 . . . . .208 F6
Nailsea BS48 . . . . 8 C1
13 Yeovil BA20 . . . . .219 B4
Trinity Gate TA1 . . . . . . .213 A3
Trinity Mews 15 BS2 . . . .227 C3
Trinity PI
3 Bristol BS8 . . . . .226 A2
4 Weston-super-Mare BS23 30 C1
Trinity Prim Sch BS20 . . . 2 F5
Trinity Rd
Bath BA2 . . . . 45 B2
Nailsea BS48 . . . . 8 D1
Taunton TA1 . . . . .213 B3
Weston-super-Mare BS23 . . 30 C1
Trinity Rise TA8 . . . . 85 A1
Trinity Row
Frome BA11 . . . . .119 E5
Wellington TA21 . . . . . . .222 C5
Trinity St
Bath BA1 . . . . .228 B2
Frome BA11 . . . . .119 E5
Taunton TA1 . . . . .213 B3
Trinity Way
Bridgwater TA6 . . . . .208 E6
Minehead TA24 . . . . .201 B7
Trinity Wlk
Bristol BS2 . . . . .227 C3
Frome BA11 . . . . .119 E5
Trin Mills BS1 . . . . .227 A1
Tripps Cnr BS49 . . . . 34 D7
Tripps Dro BA5 . . . . .139 A6
Tripps Row BS41 . . . . 11 A1
TRISCOMBE 151 D6
Triscombe Ave TA6 . . . . .208 D4
Triscombe Gate TA24 . . . .147 D8
Triscombe Ho TA4 . . . . . .151 D5
Triscombe Rd TA2 . . . . . .212 E8
Tristram Dr TA3 . . . . .169 D4

Trollope's Hill BA2 . . . . . . 46 A1
Tropical Bird Garden ★
TA8 . . . . 47 F2
Tropiquaria Zoo ★ TA23 . .131 F4
Trossachs Dr BA2 . . . . 45 D8
Trotts La TA19 . . . . .183 B2
Trottsway Cross TA24 . . . .129 C2
TROWBRIDGE 83 F7
Trowbridge CI TA9 . . . . . .104 D4
Trowell La TA4 . . . . .165 E4
Trow La BA12 . . . . .144 C2
Truckwell La TA4 . . . . . . .150 D4
Trudoxhill BA11 . . . . .143 C6
TRULL 168 D1
Trull CE Prim Sch TA3 . . . .168 D1
Trull Green Dr TA3 . . . . . .168 D1
Trull Rd TA1 . . . . .212 E2
Trumps Cross EX16 . . . . . .178 E3
Truro CI TA1 . . . . .104 C7
Truro Rd BS48 . . . . 9 A1
Trym Bank BS9 . . . . 5 D7
Trym Cross Rd BS9 . . . . . 5 C5
Trymleaze BS9 . . . . 5 C5
Trym Side BS9 . . . . 5 C5
Trymwood Par BS9 . . . . . 5 D6
Tucker's Cross DT9 . . . . . .188 A4
Tuckers La BA7 . . . . .214 B7
Tucker's La
Baltonsborough BA6 . . . . .157 F6
Ubley BS40 . . . . 73 E8
Tucker's Moor Cross EX16 162 F3
Tucker St BS27 . . . . .203 C4
TUCKERTON 169 F8
Tuckerton La TA7 . . . . . . .153 F1
Tuckerton Rd TA7 . . . . . .169 F8
TUCKING MILL 63 C8
Tuckingmill La BS39 . . . . . 41 E5
Tuckmarsh La BA11 . . . . .143 E7
Tuckmill BS21 . . . . 6 B1
Tudballs TA24 . . . . .128 D1
Tuddington Gdns BA5 . . .203 B4
TUDHAY 198 C3
Tudor Ct
Chard TA20 . . . . .223 C6
Yeovil BA20 . . . . .219 A4
Tudor Pk TA2 . . . . .213 D7
Tudor Rd
Portishead BS20 . . . . 2 E4
Weston-super-Mare BS22 . . 32 A4
Tudor Way TA6 . . . . .209 A1
Tufton Ave BS11 . . . . 5 A8
Tugela Rd BS13 . . . . 21 F7
Tuggy's La BA2 . . . . 63 E1
Tulip Tree Rd TA6 . . . . . .209 E5
Tulse Hill BA12 . . . . .161 F2
Tunbridge CI BS40 . . . . . . 39 B2
Tunbridge Rd BS40 . . . . . 39 B2
Tuncombe La TA18 . . . . . .195 D4
Tundra Walk 5 TA6 . . . . .154 A5
TUNLEY 61 B3
Tunley Hill BA2 . . . . 60 E2
Tunley Rd BA2, BA3 . . . . . 61 D5
Tunnel La BA3 . . . . 96 F5
Tunnell La 14 TA14 . . . . .185 F4
Tunscombe La BA4 . . . . . .142 D8
Tunstall CI BS9 . . . . 5 E4
Turin Path 4 TA6 . . . . . .208 E7
Turkey Ct 5 TA1 . . . . . . .212 E3
TURLEIGH 64 F6
Turleigh Hill BA15 . . . . . . 64 F6
Turmo Rd BS23 . . . . 49 B4
Turnbury Ave BS48 . . . . . . 9 A1
Turnbury CI BS22 . . . . 31 F3
Turner Ct
Bridgwater TA6 . . . . .209 A4
Keynsham BS31 . . . . 25 A5
Turner Rd
Wells BA5 . . . . .203 D3
Weston-super-Mare BS22 . . 31 F3
Turner Rd TA2 . . . . .212 E7
Turner's Barn La BA20 . . .218 F2
Turner's Court La BA3 . . . .114 D8
Turner's La DT6 . . . . .199 B2
Turner's Twr BA3 . . . . 80 A1
Turner Way BS21 . . . . 6 B1
Turn Hill TA10 . . . . .155 F2
Turnhill Rd TA10 . . . . . . .156 A2
Turnock Gdns BS24 . . . . . 50 D8
Turnpike
Milverton TA4 . . . . .167 A4
Sampford Peverell EX16 . . .178 C1
Turnpike CI TA18 . . . . . . .196 B3
Turnpike Cnr BA3 . . . . 95 B8
Turnpike Cross TA14 . . . . .185 E2
Turnpike Cvn Pk TA20 . . . .193 A4
Turnpike Gn TA18 . . . . . . .196 B3
Turnpike La BA4 . . . . .142 B6
Turnpike Rd
Cross BS26 . . . . 69 E1
Shipham BS25 . . . . 70 E8
Turnstone 3 BS20 . . . . . . 2 F6
Turstin Rd BA6 . . . . .206 F6
Turtlegate Ave BS13 . . . . . 21 E4
Turtlegate Wlk BS13 . . . . . 21 E4
Tut Hill DT9 . . . . .189 C1
Tutton Way BS21 . . . . 6 D1
Tuttors Hill BS27 . . . . 71 C1
Tuxwell La TA5 . . . . .152 C8
Tweed Rd BS21 . . . . 6 C1
Tweed Rd Ind Est 2 BS21 . 6 C1
Tweentown BS27 . . . . 90 B8
Twelve Acre Post TA22 . . .163 A4
Twelve Acres DT9 . . . . . . .225 B5
Twelve Acres CI BS39 . . . . 77 D6
Twelve O'clock La BA2 . . . 43 B3
TWERTON 44 A5
Twerton Farm CI 2 BA2 . . 44 B6

Twerton Inf Sch BA2 . . . . . 44 A5
Twinell La TA5 . . . . .152 C2
Twines BA22 . . . . .175 A5
Twinhoe La BA2 . . . . 62 D3
Twistgates La EX14 . . . . . .192 A4
Twitchen Ball Cnr EX36 . . .145 G3
Twitchens La BS27 . . . . . . 90 F2
Two Acres Cvn Pk BS21 . . 1 B1
Two Acres Rd BS14 . . . . . . 23 A7
Two Ash Hill TA20 . . . . . .193 F1
Two Ash La TA20 . . . . . . .194 A1
Two Bridges TA3 . . . . . . .183 E7
Two Elms BA21 . . . . .187 E8
Two Tower La BA22 . . . . .219 B2
Two Trees BA20 . . . . 72 E8
Twyford PI TA21 . . . . . . .222 D5
Tydeman Rd BS20 . . . . . . 2 F5
Tyler Gn 2 BS22 . . . . 32 B4
Tylers End TA9 . . . . .104 F3
Tyler's La TA4 . . . . .167 A7
Tyler Way TA9 . . . . .104 D3
Tyndall Ave BS8 . . . . .226 C4
Tyndall Ho 5 BS2 . . . . . .227 C3
TYNDALL'S PARK 226 C4
Tyndalls Park Mews BS2 . .226 C4
Tyndall's Park Rd BS8 . . . .226 C4
Tyne Gr 10 BS20 . . . . 2 F6
Tyne Pk TA1 . . . . .213 D3
TYNING
Radstock 79 B3
Timsbury 60 A2
Tyning CI BS14 . . . . 23 A7
Tyning Cotts BA3 . . . . . . .116 C2
Tyning End BA2 . . . . 45 B5
Tyning Hill
Hemington BA3 . . . . 99 C8
Radstock BA3 . . . . 79 B3
Tyning La BA1 . . . . 28 B1
Tyning PI BA2 . . . . 45 C2
Tyning Rd
Bath BA2 . . . . 45 C2
Bathampton BA2 . . . . 28 F2
Peasedown St John BA2 . . . 79 D7
Saltford BS31 . . . . 25 E2
Winsley BA15 . . . . 64 E7
Tynings BS39 . . . . 58 D3
Tynings La BA5 . . . . .203 C8
Tynings Mews BS23 . . . . . 48 E4
Tynings Rd BA16 . . . . . . .207 B4
Tynings The
Clevedon BS21 . . . . 6 A1
Portishead BS20 . . . . 1 F1
Tynings Way
Clutton BS39 . . . . 58 E3
Westwood BA15 . . . . 64 F3
Tyning Terr 15 BA1 . . . . . 28 A1
Tyning The
Bath BA2 . . . . 45 B5
Tynte Ave BS13 . . . . 22 E3
Tynte Rd TA6 . . . . .209 D6
Tyntesfield House (NT) ★
BS48 . . . . 9 F4
Tyntesfield Rd BS13 . . . . . 22 A8
Tyrone Wlk BS4 . . . . 22 E8
TYTHERINGTON 143 E6
Tytherington La BA11 . . . .143 E8
TYTHERLEIGH 198 C6
Tythe St BA6 . . . . .206 D3
Tythings Com Ctr The
BA9 . . . . .216 C3
Tythings Ct TA24 . . . . . . .200 F7
Tything Way BA9 . . . . . . .216 B2

UBLEY 55 E1
Ubley CE Prim Sch BS40 . . 55 D1
Ubley Dro BS40 . . . . 73 B7
UBLEY SIDELING 73 D8
Ubley La BS40 . . . . 55 D1
ULLCOMBE 192 A4
Ullcombe La EX14 . . . . . . .191 F4
Ullswater CI BS23 . . . . 49 A4
Ullswater Dr BA1 . . . . 28 A2
Uncombe CI BS48 . . . . 19 C7
Underbanks BS20 . . . . 4 D4
Underdown BA21 . . . . . . .219 F5
Underdown Ho BS1 . . . . .227 A1
Underdown Hollow
Bradford Abbas DT9 . . . . .187 E2
Yeovil BA21 . . . . .219 F4
Underdown La DT9 . . . . . .225 F6
Underhayes Ct TA18 . . . . .196 E8
Underhill
Gurney Slade BA3 . . . . . . .114 E7
Hambridge TA10 . . . . . . .184 D8
Penselwood BA9 . . . . . . .161 D1
Underhill Ave BA3 . . . . 77 F2
Underhill CI BA16 . . . . . . .207 B5
Underhill Dr BS23 . . . . 48 D1
Underhill La
Midsomer Norton BA3 . . . . 77 F2
Staple Fitzpaine TA3 . . . . .182 B4
Under Knoll BA2 . . . . 79 E8
Under La BS40 . . . . 36 D1
Underleaf Way BA2 . . . . . . 79 D7
Undertown BS40 . . . . 74 A7
Undertown La BS40 . . . . . 74 A7
Under Tree Rd BA2 . . . . . . 79 A6
Underway TA20 . . . . .193 D6
Underwood Ave BS22 . . . . 31 B1
Underwood Business Park
BA5 . . . . .203 B6
Underwood End BS25 . . . . 52 A4
Underwood La TA10 . . . . .172 C8

Underwood Rd
Glastonbury BA6 . . . . . . .206 D6
Kingsdon TA11 . . . . .173 D5
Portishead BS20 . . . . 2 C3
Union Dro TA10 . . . . .172 B6
Union Pas BA1 . . . . .228 C2
Union PI BS23 . . . . 48 D7
Union St
Bath BA1 . . . . .228 C2
Bridgwater TA6 . . . . .209 B6
Bristol BS1 . . . . .227 B3
Cheddar BS27 . . . . 90 B7
Dulverton TA22 . . . . .163 D6
Nailsea BS48 . . . . 8 C1
Wells BA5 . . . . .203 D4
Weston-super-Mare BS23 . .48 B2
Yeovil BA20 . . . . .219 B4
Unite Ho BS1 . . . . .226 C2
Unity Ct BS31 . . . . 25 A5
Unity Rd BS31 . . . . 25 A6
Unity St BS1 . . . . .226 C2
University CI BS9 . . . . 5 F4
University of Bristol Dorothy
Hodgkin Bldg BS1 . . . . . .227 A4
University Rd BS8 . . . . . .226 C3
University Wlk BS8 . . . . . .226 C3
Univ of Bath BA2 . . . . 45 E5
Univ of Bristol BS8 . . . . .226 C3
Univ of Bristol Dept of Ed
BS8 . . . . .226 C3
Univ of Bristol Langford
House Sch of Veterinary
Science BS40 . . . . 53 B6
Univ of Bristol Sch of
Veterinary Science BS2 . .226 C4
Univ of the West of England
BS3 . . . . 11 E4
Upcot Cres TA1 . . . . .212 B2
UPCOTT 168 B3
Upcott La
Bicknoller TA4 . . . . .132 F1
Winsford TA24 . . . . .147 D7
Upcott Rd TA1, TA4 . . . . . .168 B3
UPHILL 48 C2
Uphill Ct BS23 . . . . 48 D2
Uphill Dr BA1 . . . . 28 B2
Uphill Farm Cvn Pk BS23 . . 48 E1
Uphill Prim Sch BS23 . . . . 48 D1
Uphill Rd N BS23 . . . . 48 D4
Uphill Rd S BS23 . . . . 48 D2
Uphills BA10 . . . . .215 E2
Uphill Way BS23 . . . . 48 D1
Upjohn Cres BS13 . . . . 22 D3
Uplands BA5 . . . . .176 B8
Uplands CI BA2 . . . . 63 F7
Uplands Dr BS31 . . . . 25 F2
Uplands La BS31 . . . . 24 F1
Uplands Rd BS31 . . . . 25 F2
Uplands Terr BA22 . . . . . .197 B8
Uplands The BS48 . . . . 18 C8
UPLOWMAN 178 B2
Uplowman CE Prim Sch
EX16 . . . . .178 B2
UP MUDFORD 187 D5
Up Mudford Rd BA22 . . . .187 D6
UPOTTERY 191 F2
Upottery Prim Sch EX14 . .191 F2
Upper Belgrave Rd BS8 . . . 5 F1
UPPER BENTER 115 C7
Upper Berkeley PI BS8 . . .226 B3
Upper Bloomfield Rd BA2 . .44 D1
Upper Borough Walls
BA1 . . . . .228 C2
Upper Breach BA5 . . . . . .113 A2
Upper Bristol Rd
Bath BA1 . . . . 44 D7
Clutton BS39 . . . . 58 D3
Weston-super-Mare BS22 . . 31 B1
Upper Byron PI BS8 . . . . .226 B3
Upper Camden PI BA1 . . .228 C4
UPPER CHEDDON 168 F7
Upper Cheddon Rd TA2 . . .168 F7
Upper Church La BS24 . . . 49 D2
Upper Church Rd BS23 . . . 30 D1
Upper Church St BA1 . . . .228 B3
UPPER COXLEY 139 F6
Upper Crannel Dro BA6 . . .139 C4
Upper Ct BA3 . . . . 97 C8
Upper Draycott Rd BA5 . . . 90 E5
Upper East Hayes BA1 . . . 28 B1
Upper Farm CI BA2 . . . . . 81 F4
Upper Flowerfield BA11 . . .143 B7
Upper Furlong BA2 . . . . . . 60 B3
UPPER GODNEY 139 A6
Upper Green La BS40 . . . . 55 B7
Upper Hedgemead Rd
BA1 . . . . .228 B4
Upper High St
Castle Cary BA7 . . . . .214 C5
Taunton TA1 . . . . .212 E3
Upper Holway Rd TA1 . . . .213 C2
Upper Kewstoke Rd BS23 . . 30 B1
Upper Lambridge St BA1 . . 28 C2
UPPER LANGFORD 53 C3
UPPER LANGRIDGE 27 F1
Upper Lansdown Mews
BA1 . . . . 27 F1
UPPER LITTLETON 38 B6
Upper Maudlin St BS2 . . .227 A3
Upper Mead 16 EX13 . . . .198 A1
Upper Merrifield BA3 . . . .116 E8
Upper Merrifield BA3 . . . . 97 E1
UPPER MILTON 203 D7
Upper Mount Pleasant
BA3 . . . . 64 A4

Upper Myrtle Hill BS20 ..... 4 C4
Upper New Rd BS27 .... 90 A8
Upper North St BS27 ...... 90 B8
Upper Oldfield Pk BA2 .... 228 A1
Upper Pitching BA3 .... 96 D5
Upper Pitney Rd TA10 .... 172 C7
UPPER RADFORD 78 B8
Upper Radford BS39 .... 78 B7
Upper Rd BS39 .... 75 E6
Upper Stanton BS39 .... 40 A3
UPPER STANTON DREW 40 B2
Upper Strode BS40 .... 55 F7
UPPER SWAINSWICK 28 B5
Upper Town La BS40 ...... 37 C8
UPPER VOBSTER 117 C8
Upper Vobster Rd BA3 .... 117 D8
Upper Wellesley La BA5 .. 140 B6
Upper Wellesley Rd
  Wells BA5 .... 140 B7
  Wells BA5 .... 203 E1
Upper Wells St BS1 .... 226 C2
UPPER WESTHOLME 140 D4
UPPER WESTON 27 A3
UPPER WESTWOOD 64 E4
Upper Whatcombe BA11 . 119 E6
Upper Wood St TA1 .... 212 E4
Upper York St BS2 .... 227 B4
UPPOTERY 191 F2
UPTON
  Langport 172 D5
  Skilgate 164 F8
Upton BS24 .... 49 A2
UPTON CHEYNEY 26 B8
Upton Cotts BS41 .... 38 F8
Upton La
  Dundry BS41 .... 39 A8
  Seavington St Michael TA19 .184 E2
UPTON NOBLE 142 F2
Upton Noble CE Prim Sch
  BA4 .... 142 F2
Urchinwood La BS49 .... 34 F4
URGASHAY 174 C3
Urgashay Rd BA22 .... 174 C3

V

VAGG 186 F5
Vagg Hill BA22 .... 186 E5
Vagg La BA22 .... 186 F5
Vagg Pk BA22 .... 186 F5
Valda Rd BS22 .... 31 C2
Vale Cl TA18 .... 224 C4
Vale Cres BS22 .... 32 C2
Vale Ct BS8 .... 226 A4
Vale End BS48 .... 8 D1
Vale La BS3 .... 22 C8
Vale Mill Way BS24 .... 49 F8
Valentine Cl BS14 .... 23 B5
Valentines TA22 .... 163 E6
Vale Rd
  Stalbridge DT10 .... 190 B4
  Yeovil BA21 .... 219 E6
Valerian Cl BS11 .... 4 F6
Vale St BA8 .... 190 A6
Valetta Cl BS23 .... 48 F3
Valetta Pl TA6 .... 208 F5
Vale View
  Aller TA10 .... 171 E8
  Henstridge BA8 .... 190 A7
  Radstock BA3 .... 79 A2
  Wincanton BA9 .... 216 F5
Vale View Cotts TA4 ..... 151 E4
Vale View Gdns BA9 ...... 216 C2
Vale View Pl 16 BA1 ...... 28 B1
Vale View Terr BA1 .... 28 F3
Valley Cl
  6 Nailsea BS48 .... 8 E2
  Wells BA5 .... 203 C4
  Yeovil BA21 .... 219 B6
Valley Ct BS20 .... 1 E3
Valley Gdns BS48 .... 8 E2
Valley Line Ind Pk BS27 .. 90 A7
Valley Rd
  Bristol, Bedminster Down
    BS13 .... 22 A8
  Clevedon BS21 .... 6 F5
  Crewkerne TA18 .... 224 C4
  Leigh Woods BS8 .... 11 C7
  Portishead BS20 .... 2 A2
  Taunton TA1 .... 213 C5
Valley View
  Chilcompton BA3 .... 96 D3
  Clutton BS39 .... 58 E3
  Frome BA11 .... 119 D6
  Millmoor EX15 .... 179 E1
  Morebath EX16 .... 164 B3
Valley View Cl BA1 .... 28 B3
Valley View Rd
  Bath BA1 .... 28 C3
  Paulton BS39 .... 77 E6
Valley Way Rd BS48 .... 8 E3
Valley Wlk BA3 .... 78 B2
Vallis Ct 7 BA11 .... 119 E5
Vallis Fst Sch
  Frome BA11 .... 119 E5
  12 Frome BA11 .... 119 E5
Vallis Rd BA11 .... 119 D5
Vallis Trad Est BA11 .... 119 D5
Vallis Way BA11 .... 119 E5
Vanbrugh Gdns BS11 .... 4 F8
Van Diemen's La BA1 ...... 27 F2
Vandyck Ave BS31 .... 24 F6
Vane St 7 BA2 .... 45 B7
Vanguard Ct BA22 .... 218 A5

Varsity Way BS24 .... 50 B6
Vaughan Ct BA5 .... 203 B4
Veales DT10 .... 189 F2
Veale The BS24 .... 67 C6
Veal La
  Horrington BA5 .... 113 B2
  Walton BA16 .... 156 E6
Vedal Dro TA10 .... 172 D4
Vee La BS40 .... 37 D8
Vellore La BA2 .... 45 C7
Vellow Rd TA4 .... 150 D8
Vellow Wood La TA4 .... 132 D1
Velvet Bottom BS40 ...... 72 E3
Vemplett's Cross TA23 .. 131 E1
Venford Hill
  East Anstey TA22 ..... 162 E8
  Hawkridge TA22 ...... 162 E8
Venland Bsns Pk TA24 ... 201 B6
Venland Ind Pk TA24 .... 201 A6
Venley La TA18 .... 195 C4
Venn Cl TA4 .... 167 E6
Venn Cross TA4 .... 165 D3
Venn Hill DT6, TA20 .... 199 C6
Venninford Cross TA24 . 129 F8
Vennland Way TA24 ..... 201 A6
Venns Cl BS27 .... 90 B7
Venns Gate BS27 .... 71 A1
Venture 20 BA20 .... 218 C3
Venture 7 BA20 .... 218 C3
Venture Eleven The TA2 . 213 B6
Venture Way TA2 .... 213 B6
Venus La BS39 .... 58 E3
Venus St BS49 .... 34 E2
Vera St TA2 .... 212 F7
Verbena Way BS22 .... 32 A1
Verbena Wlk TA6 .... 208 E1
Vereland Rd BS24 .... 49 E3
Verlands BS49 .... 34 E5
Vernal La BA11 .... 119 D6
Vernalls Rd DT9 .... 225 D5
Vernham Gr BA2 .... 44 C1
Vernhamwood Cl BA2 .... 44 C1
Vernon Cl BS31 .... 25 D3
Vernon La BS26 .... 69 B3
Vernon Pk BA2 .... 44 C6
Vernon Terr BA2 .... 44 C6
Vernslade BA1 .... 27 A2
Verriers 10 TA6 .... 153 E3
VERRINGTON 216 A5
Verrington La BA9 ...... 216 B5
Verrington Park Rd BA9 . 216 B4
Vesey's Hole Hill SP8 ... 177 E4
Vestry Cl BA16 .... 207 C5
Vestry Ct 1 BA16 ...... 207 C5
Vestry La BA16 .... 207 C5
Vestry Rd BA16 .... 207 C5
Vian End BS22 .... 31 F4
Via Traversus BS31 .... 24 F7
Vicarage Cl
  Chard TA20 .... 223 C3
  Coxley BA5 .... 139 E6
  Creech St Michael TA3 . 169 D4
  8 Frome BA11 .... 119 F4
  Stogursey TA5 .... 134 C6
  Weston-super-Mare BS22 . 32 A3
  Westonzoyland TA7 .... 154 F5
Vicarage Ct
  Burnham-on-S TA8 .... 104 A7
  Timberscombe TA24 ... 130 B5
Vicarage Gdns BA2 .... 79 B7
Vicarage Hill
  Combe St Nicholas TA20 . 193 D6
  Dulverton TA22 .... 163 D6
Vicarage La
  Barrow Gurney BS48 ... 20 C6
  Compton Bishop BS26 .. 69 B3
  Compton Dando BS39 .. 41 D6
  Creech St Michael TA3 . 169 D4
  Draycott BS27 .... 90 F3
  Mark TA9 .... 106 E5
  Norton St Philip BA2 .. 81 E4
  Pawlett TA6 .... 135 F5
  Shapwick TA7 .... 137 F1
  7 Wookey BA5 .... 139 D8
Vicarage Lawns TA3 .... 169 D4
Vicarage Rd
  Bristol, Bishopsworth
    BS13 .... 22 A6
  Carhampton TA24 ..... 131 B5
  Leigh Woods BS8 ...... 11 D6
  Minehead TA24 .... 200 F8
  Stogursey TA5 .... 134 C6
  Wookey BA5 .... 139 E8
  Woolavington TA7 .... 136 E4
Vicarage St
  Burnham-on-S TA8 .... 104 A7
  Frome BA11 .... 119 F4
  Tintinhull BA22 ...... 186 C6
  6 Yeovil BA20 .... 219 B4
Vicarage Wlk BA20 ..... 219 B5
Vicar's Cl BA5 .... 203 E5
Vicars La TA6 .... 208 D5
Vicar's La TA12 .... 184 F7
Vicars Path BA5 .... 92 D3
Vickery Cl
  Bridgwater TA6 .... 208 D3
  Curry Rivel TA10 ..... 171 D4

Victoria Cl
  Bath BA2 .... 44 C5
  Portishead BS20 .... 2 D5
  Yeovil BA21 .... 219 D6
Victoria Cotts BA2 ...... 62 F7
Victoria Ct
  Castle Cary BA7 ...... 214 B5
  Chard TA20 .... 223 D4
  Frome BA11 .... 120 A4
  Ilminster TA19 .... 221 C4
  Portishead BS20 .... 2 D5
Victoria Gate TA1 ...... 213 B6
Victoria Gdns
  Batheaston BA1 .... 28 F3
  Castle Cary BA7 ...... 214 B6
  15 Henstridge BA8 .... 190 A6
Victoria Gr BA4 .... 205 D5
Victoria Ho
  Bath BA1 .... 44 D8
  Keynsham BS31 .... 24 F4
Victoria Jubilee Homes
  BS40 .... 53 C6
Victoria La BA4 .... 141 E1
Victoria Lodge BS22 ..... 31 E2
Victoria Mews BA7 ..... 214 B5
VICTORIA PARK 226 B3
Victoria Park Bsns Ctr BA1 44 D7
Victoria Pk
  Castle Cary BA7 ...... 214 B5
  Weston-super-Mare BS23 . 30 D1
Victoria Pl
  Bath, Combe Down BA2 .. 45 C1
  2 Bath, Lambridge BA1 . 28 C1
  Chardstock EX13 ..... 198 A7
  Highbridge TA9 .... 104 D3
  Paulton BS39 .... 77 D5
  Weston-super-Mare BS23 . 48 D8
Victoria Quadrant BS23 . 48 E8
Victoria Rd
  Avonmouth BS11 .... 4 B7
  Bath BA2 .... 44 D6
  Bridgwater TA6 .... 208 E5
  Castle Cary BA7 ...... 214 B6
  Clevedon BS21 .... 6 C3
  Frome BA11 .... 120 A4
  Minehead TA24 .... 201 A4
  Saltford BS31 .... 25 D3
  Yeovil BA21 .... 219 D6
Victoria Sh Mews TA18 . 224 C6
Victoria Sq
  Bristol BS8 .... 226 A3
  Crewkerne TA18 ...... 224 B6
  Evercreech BA4 ...... 141 E1
  Portishead BS20 .... 2 D5
  Weston-super-Mare BS23 . 48 D7
Victoria St
  Bristol BS1 .... 227 B2
  Burnham-on-S TA8 .... 104 A7
  Taunton TA1 .... 213 B4
  Wellington TA21 ..... 222 D6
Victoria Terr
  Bath BA2 .... 44 D6
  14 Bristol, Clifton BS8 . 11 F6
  14 Henstridge BA8 .... 190 A6
  Paulton BS39 .... 77 E6
Victoria Way TA5 .... 152 E7
Victory Rd TA2 .... 213 A7
Vienna Way 4 TA6 ..... 154 A5
Vigor Rd BS13 .... 22 B5
Viking Cl TA23 .... 202 D7
Vilberie Cl TA2 .... 212 A7
Village Hill
  Huish Champflower TA4 . 165 A2
  Upton TA4 .... 164 F7
Village Rd
  Hatch Beauchamp TA3 . 182 F6
  Newton St Loe BA2 .... 43 C6
Villa Rosa 16 BS23 ...... 30 C1
Villes La TA24 .... 124 A4
Villice La BS40 .... 74 A7
Vincent Cl TA4 .... 154 C7
Vincent Pl BA20 .... 219 B5
Vincents Cl DT9 .... 189 A1
Vincent St 5 BA20 .... 219 B5
Vine Gdns
  Frome BA11 .... 119 F6
  Weston-super-Mare BS22 . 32 A2
Vine Gr BA8 .... 176 E1
Vine House Gdns TA20 . 223 C3
Vinery The BS25 .... 70 A7
Vine St BA8 .... 176 E1
Vineyards BA1 .... 228 C3
Viney Bridge Mills TA18 . 224 D5
Viney La EX14 .... 191 F1
Viney St TA1 .... 213 B3
Viney's Yd BA10 .... 215 F6
Vining's Hill BA4 ...... 142 D1
Vinney La BA11 .... 143 F8
Vinnicombe Straight
  TA22 .... 147 F5
Violet La DT9 .... 176 A2
Virginia Cl 1 BA8 ..... 190 A6
Virginia Orch TA3 ..... 169 C3
Viscount Sq TA6 ...... 208 E7
Vivary Ct TA1 .... 212 E3
Vivary Gate TA1 ...... 212 F3
Vivary Hts TA1 .... 212 E2
Vivary Rd TA1 .... 212 E3
Vivien Ave BA3 .... 78 A2
Vixen Cl BA22 .... 174 A3
VOBSTER 117 C7
Vobster Cross BA3 ..... 117 D7
Vobster Hill BA3 ...... 117 D7
VOLE 106 B8
Vole Rd
  Brent Knoll TA9 .... 86 D1
  Mark TA9 .... 106 B7
Volis Cross TA5 .... 152 F1

Volis Hill TA2 .... 168 F8
Vowell Cl BS13 .... 22 B4
Vowles Cl BS48 .... 9 A3
VOXMOOR 222 F1
Vulcan Ho BA2 .... 228 C3
Vulcan Rd TA24 .... 201 B6
Vynes Cl BS48 .... 9 A1
Vynes Ind Est BS48 ..... 9 A3
Vynes Way BS48 .... 9 A1
Vyvyan Rd BS8 .... 226 A3
Vyvyan Terr BS8 ...... 226 A3

W

WADBROOK 198 C4
Wadbrook Cross EX13 .. 198 C4
WADBURY 118 D7
WADDICOMBE 162 E6
Wade Cl TA7 .... 154 E6
WADEFORD 193 D5
Wadeford Hill TA20 ... 193 D5
Wade St BS2 .... 227 C3
Wadham Cl
  Bridgwater TA6 .... 209 D6
  Ilminster TA19 .... 221 A4
Wadham Cross
  Knowstone EX36 ...... 162 A2
  West Anstey EX36 .... 162 A4
Wadham Hill EX36 ..... 162 A2
Wadham's Almshouses
  TA19 .... 183 E4
Wadham Sch TA18 ..... 224 D7
Wadham St BS23 .... 48 D8
WAGG 172 B5
Wagg Dro TA10 .... 172 B5
WAGGS PLOT 198 B4
Waggs Plot EX13 ...... 198 B4
Wagon And Horses Hill
  BA4 .... 141 E8
Wagtail Cres BS20 .... 3 A6
Wagtail Gdns BS22 ..... 49 E8
Wains Cl 3 BS21 .... 6 C2
Wainwright Cl 5 BS22 . 32 B4
Wainwright Ct BA4 .... 205 B4
Wainwright Dr BA11 .. 120 C7
Waits Cl BS29 .... 50 F3
Wakedean Gdns BS49 ... 17 A1
WALCOMBE 203 E7
Walcombe La BA5 ..... 203 E6
Walcot Bldgs
  Bath BA1 .... 45 B8
  Bath BA1 .... 228 C4
Walcot Ct BA1 .... 228 C4
Walcot Gate BA1 ...... 228 C4
Walcot Ho BA1 .... 228 C4
Walcot Par BA1 .... 228 C4
Walcot St BA1 .... 228 C4
Walcot Terr BA1 ...... 228 C4
Waldegrave Rd BA1 ..... 27 C1
Waldegrave Terr BA3 ... 79 A3
Walden Rd BS31 .... 25 A4
Waldock Barton TA13 .. 220 D4
Waldron's Cross TA21 . 165 E1
Waldrons La TA5 ...... 135 D2
WALES 174 E3
Wales La BA22 .... 174 E3
WALFORD 169 D7
Walford Ave BS22 ...... 32 C3
Walford Cross Ind Pk
  TA2 .... 169 D6
Walford Cross Roads TA2 169 D7
Waling La BA11 .... 43 D6
Walker Rd BA11 .... 120 A3
Walkers Dr BS24 .... 49 F7
Walkers Gate TA21 .... 222 D5
Walkers Ri TA2 .... 213 E8
Walker St BS2 .... 226 C4
Walk La TA13 .... 184 F1
WALLACE 74 E3
Wallace La BS40 .... 74 E3
Wallace Rd BA1 .... 28 B1
Wallace Wells Rd TA8 . 104 D5
Wallbridge BA11 ...... 120 B4
Wallbridge Ave BA11 .. 120 A4
Wallbridge Gdns BA11 . 120 A4
Wallbridge Ho BA11 ... 120 A4
Wallbridge Ind Est BA11 . 120 B4
Wall Ditch La TA16 ... 196 A8
Wallenge Cl BS39 ...... 77 F6
Wallenge Dr BS39 ..... 77 F6
Waller Gdns BA1 .... 27 C4
Walley La BS40 .... 57 B7
Wall Gn BS26 .... 70 C1
Wallingford Rd BS4 .... 22 D7
Wallington Way BA11 . 119 D6
Walliscote Grove Rd 11
  BS23 .... 48 E7
Walliscote Prim Sch BS23 . 48 E7
Walliscote Rd BS23 .... 48 D6
Walliscote Rd S BS23 . 48 D4
WALL MEAD 60 C4
Walls La BS26 .... 108 B8
Walls The TA7 .... 137 C4
Wall The TA7 .... 106 D5
Wally Court Rd BS40 ... 56 D5
Walmsley Terr 4 BA1 ... 28 B1
Walnut Bldgs BA3 ...... 79 A3
Walnut Cl
  Axbridge BS26 .... 70 B1
  Cheddar BS27 .... 90 B7
  Easton-in-G BS20 ...... 4 A3
  Keynsham BS31 .... 24 C4
  Nailsea BS48 .... 18 D1
  Puriton TA7 .... 136 C4
  Rode BA11 .... 101 D3
  Taunton TA1 .... 212 B4
  Weston-super-Mare BS24 . 49 B2

Walnut Dr
  Bath BA2 .... 44 E4
  Bridgwater TA6 ...... 209 D3
  Somerton TA11 ...... 211 D4
Walnut Gr BA4 .... 205 C4
Walnut La TA7 .... 136 F3
Walnut Rd TA10 ...... 172 A6
Walnuts The TA7 ..... 137 B2
Walnut Tree Cl
  Ubley BS40 .... 55 D1
  Wells BA5 .... 203 C5
Walnut Tree Cnr TA23 . 131 F4
Walnut Tree Cl BS49 .. 34 C4
Walnut Tree Dr TA24 . 131 A5
Walnut Wlk
  Bristol BS13 .... 22 A6
  Frome BA11 .... 120 B7
  Keynsham BS31 .... 24 C4
WALPOLE 136 B4
Walpole Dro TA9 ..... 136 A5
Walridge Cross TA4 ... 166 A4
Walrond Ct TA19 ..... 221 B4
Walrond's Pk TA3 .... 184 B7
WALROW 105 C2
Walrow TA9 .... 104 E3
Walrow Ind Est TA9 .. 104 F2
Walrow Terr TA9 ..... 104 E3
Walscombe Cl 1 TA14 . 185 F4
Walsh Ave BS14 .... 23 A7
Walsh Cl BS24 .... 49 B2
Waltham End BS24 ..... 50 A8
WALTON 156 E7
Walton Bay House Park
  Homes 1 B1
Walton CE Prim Sch BA16 156 E7
Walton Cl
  Bridgwater TA6 ...... 209 D4
  Keynsham BS31 .... 24 D4
Walton Cres BS40 ...... 37 F8
Walton Cross BS21 ...... 7 B7
Walton Ct TA24 ...... 201 A4
Walton Dro BA16 ..... 156 D5
Walton High Rd BA16 . 207 A2
WALTON IN GORDANO 7 B7
Walton Rd
  Bristol BS11 .... 4 D6
  Clevedon BS21 .... 6 D4
WALTON ST MARY 6 E5
Walton St
  Portishead BS21 .... 1 A1
  Walton in G BS21 ...... 7 A8
Walwyn Cl BA2 .... 44 A6
Walwyn Gdns BS13 ..... 22 C3
WAMBROOK 193 C3
Wambrook Rd
  Chard TA20 .... 223 A4
  Wambrook TA20 ..... 193 D3
Wand Rd BA5 .... 203 C2
Wansbeck La BA11 .... 213 D3
Wansbeck Rd BS31 ..... 25 A4
Wansbrough Rd BS22 .. 32 B4
Wansdyke Bsns Ctr BA2 . 44 D4
Wansdyke Ct BS14 ..... 23 B5
Wansdyke Prim Sch BS14 . 23 C7
Wansdyke Rd BA2 ...... 44 D1
Wansdyke Way BS14 ... 23 D3
Wansdyke Workshops
  Keynsham BS31 .... 25 A6
  Peasedown St John BA2 . 79 D6
WANSTROW 142 F4
Wapping Rd BS1 ...... 227 A1
Warbler Cl 6 BA3 ...... 97 B8
Warden Rd TA24 ..... 200 F6
Ward La TA7 .... 154 E4
Wardleworth Way TA21 . 222 C7
Wardour Rd BS4 .... 22 D8
Wareham Cl BS48 .... 8 D1
Wareham Cross EX13 .. 198 E1
Wareham Rd EX13 .... 198 E2
Wares La TA6 .... 208 D6
Waring Ho BS1 .... 227 A1
WARLEIGH 46 C6
Warleigh Cl BA11 .... 119 D4
Warleigh Dr BA1 ...... 29 A3
Warleigh La BA1 ...... 46 C5
Warleys La BS24 ...... 32 C1
Warman Cl BS14 .... 23 F6
Warman Rd BS14 ...... 23 F6
War Memorial Hospl TA8 . 104 B7
Warmington Rd BS14 ... 23 C8
Warminster Rd
  Beckington BA11 ..... 101 E4
  Claverton BA2, BA3 ... 46 B5
  Frome BA11 .... 120 B4
Warne Pk BS23 .... 49 A6
Warner Cl BS49 .... 35 A7
Warne Rd BS23 .... 49 A6
Warren Cl
  Bridgwater TA6 ...... 208 F6
  Bruton BA10 .... 215 E6
  Charlton Horethorne DT9 . 176 A2
  Fenn's Wood BS41 ..... 10 E1
  Hutton BS24 .... 49 E3
Warren Farm Cvn Pk & Camp
  Site TA8 .... 65 F5
Warren Gdns BS14 ..... 23 F5
Warren La BS41 .... 20 E8
Warren Rd
  Brean TA8 .... 65 F6
  Minehead TA24 ...... 201 B7
Warren's Cl BS27 ...... 71 B1
Warrens Hill BS27 .... 71 B1
Warrens Hill Rd BS27 . 71 D4
Warren St
  Rockwell Green TA21 . 222 A4
  3 Sidbrook TA2 ..... 169 B2

Warrens Way BA5 . . . . . . 113 A1
Warren The BA16 . . . . . . 207 A5
Warren Way DT9 . . . . . . 225 C5
Warres Rd TA2 . . . . . . 213 D8
Warrilow Cl BS22 . . . . . . 32 B5
Warrior Ave BA22 . . . . . . 218 B6
Warry Cl BS48 . . . . . . 9 B2
Warth La BS22 . . . . . . 32 A8
Warwick Ave TA6 . . . . . . 209 C3
Warwick Cl BS22 . . . . . . 49 C8
Warwick Gdns
  Burnham-on-S TA8 . . . . . . 85 B1
  Clutton BS39 . . . . . . 58 D3
  Taunton TA1 . . . . . . 213 C2
Warwick Rd
  3 Bath BA1 . . . . . . 44 B7
  Keynsham BS31 . . . . . . 24 D4
  Taunton TA2 . . . . . . 213 A8
  (was BS20 . . . . . . 31 E1
WASHBROOK 89 A1
Washcross La TA19 . . . . . . 184 E3
WASHFORD 131 F4
Washford Cross TA23 . . . . . . 131 F3
Washford Hill TA23 . . . . . . 202 A5
Washford Sta TA23 . . . . . . 131 E4
Washingpool DT9 . . . . . . 188 E7
Washing Pound La
  Bristol BS14 . . . . . . 23 B4
  Nailsea BS48 . . . . . . 8 B4
Washington Gdns TA6 . . . . . . 208 E5
Washington Terr TA20 . . . . . . 223 B5
Wash La TA15 . . . . . . 186 B4
Washpool La BA2 . . . . . . 43 F2
Wassail Cl 5 TA24 . . . . . . 131 A5
Wassail View TA2 . . . . . . 168 B4
Waste Dro BA5 . . . . . . 139 A4
WATCHET 202 B6
Watchet Boat Mus* TA23 . . . . . . 202 C7
Watchet Sta TA23 . . . . . . 202 C7
WATCHFIELD 105 D2
Watch House Pl BS20 . . . . . . 2 E7
Watch House Rd BS20 . . . . . . 4 D4
Watchill Ave BS13 . . . . . . 21 F6
Watchill Cl BS13 . . . . . . 21 F6
Watchwell Dro BA3 . . . . . . 157 D7
Waterbridge Rd BS13 . . . . . . 21 F4
Watercombe Hts BA20 . . . . . . 218 D2
Watercombe Pk BA20 . . . . . . 218 D3
Watercress Cl BS48 . . . . . . 9 B2
Waterfield Cl TA1 . . . . . . 212 B3
Waterfield Dr TA1 . . . . . . 212 B3
Waterford Beck BA14 . . . . . . 83 F6
Waterford Cl TA6 . . . . . . 209 A2
Waterford Pk BA3 . . . . . . 78 E1
Waterfront Ho BA2 . . . . . . 228 B1
WATERGORE 220 B2
Water Hill TA4 . . . . . . 150 F7
Waterhouse La BA2 . . . . . . 63 F8
Water La
  Bristol BS1 . . . . . . 227 B2
  Butleigh BA6 . . . . . . 157 E4
  Charlton Horethorne DT9 . . . . . . 176 A2
  Crowcombe TA4 . . . . . . 151 A7
  Frome BA11 . . . . . . 119 E3
  Horningsham BA12 . . . . . . 144 D4
  Keenthorne TA5 . . . . . . 134 C1
  Lopen TA13 . . . . . . 185 A1
  Nether Stowey TA5 . . . . . . 134 A1
  Paulton BA3, BS39 . . . . . . 78 A4
  Pill BS20 . . . . . . 4 C4
  Somerton TA11 . . . . . . 211 C3
  Stogumber TA4 . . . . . . 150 F7
Waterlake DT10 . . . . . . 190 B4
Waterlake Rd TA20 . . . . . . 198 C8
Waterlands La TA18 . . . . . . 224 C8
Waterleaze TA2 . . . . . . 213 D7
WATERLIP 142 A7
Waterlip BA4 . . . . . . 141 F7
Waterloo
  Frome BA11 . . . . . . 119 F5
  Puriton TA7 . . . . . . 136 C4
Waterloo Bldgs 4 BA2 . . . . . . 44 B6
Waterloo Cl TA7 . . . . . . 136 C4
Waterloo Cotts TA1 . . . . . . 212 B4
Waterloo Cres DT9 . . . . . . 176 A1
Waterloo Ho BS20 . . . . . . 4 D5
Waterloo La
  Stalbridge DT10 . . . . . . 190 A1
  Yeovil BA20 . . . . . . 219 A4
Waterloo Pl 19 BS2 . . . . . . 227 C3
Waterloo Rd
  Bristol BS2 . . . . . . 227 C3
  Radstock BA3 . . . . . . 79 A2
  Shepton Mallet BA4 . . . . . . 205 B7
  Wellington TA21 . . . . . . 222 C6
Waterloo St
  Bristol BS2 . . . . . . 227 C3
  9 Bristol, Clifton BS8 . . . . . . 11 F7
  Weston-super-Mare BS23 . . . . . . 48 E8
Waterloo Terr DT9 . . . . . . 225 F4
Watermans Mdw TA6 . . . . . . 208 E6
Watermead TA20 . . . . . . 198 D8
Watermead Cl 9 BA1 . . . . . . 228 B2
Water Path BA2 . . . . . . 222 A5
Waterpits TA5 . . . . . . 152 C4
WATERROW 165 F4
Waters Edge BS20 . . . . . . 2 E7
WATERSIDE 78 E1
Waterside Cres BA3 . . . . . . 78 D1
Waterside La BA3 . . . . . . 98 A6
Waterside Pk BS20 . . . . . . 1 D4
Waterside Rd
  Radstock BA3 . . . . . . 78 D1
  Wincanton BA9 . . . . . . 216 C4
Waters La BS27 . . . . . . 90 C8
Watersmeet Cl
  Golsoncott TA23 . . . . . . 131 D1

Watersmeet Cl continued
  Rooks Bridge BS26 . . . . . . 87 B5
Water St
  Barrington TA19 . . . . . . 184 D5
  Curry Rivel TA10 . . . . . . 171 C4
  East Harptree BS40 . . . . . . 74 F4
  East Lambrook TA13 . . . . . . 220 C8
  Hambridge TA10 . . . . . . 171 D1
  Lopen TA13 . . . . . . 185 A1
  Martock TA12 . . . . . . 185 D5
  Seavington St Michael TA19 . . . . . . 184 E1
Watery Combe BA3 . . . . . . 94 E7
Watery La
  Axminster EX13 . . . . . . 198 A3
  Bath BA2 . . . . . . 44 A6
  Broadway TA19 . . . . . . 194 B8
  Charlton Horethorne DT9 . . . . . . 176 C1
  Clatworthy TA4 . . . . . . 149 C2
  Coultings TA5 . . . . . . 134 E3
  Doynton BS30 . . . . . . 12 A8
  Halstock BA22 . . . . . . 197 D3
  Hewish TA18 . . . . . . 195 D3
  Langford Budville TA4, TA21 . . . . . . 166 C2
  Marshfield SN14 . . . . . . 13 F6
  Minehead TA24 . . . . . . 200 F7
  Nailsea BS48 . . . . . . 8 B2
  North Petherton TA6 . . . . . . 153 E4
  Spaxton TA5 . . . . . . 152 F4
  Stogursey TA5 . . . . . . 134 C5
  Stratton-on-t F BA3 . . . . . . 97 A3
  Winford BS40 . . . . . . 38 B4
Watling St BA21 . . . . . . 218 D7
Watling Way BS11 . . . . . . 4 D7
Watsons La TA6 . . . . . . 209 A5
Watts Corner BA6 . . . . . . 206 F7
Watts La TA4 . . . . . . 151 E1
Watts's Quarry La TA10, TA11 . . . . . . 173 A5
Watts's Rd TA7 . . . . . . 137 D8
Waveney Rd BS31 . . . . . . 25 A3
Wavering Down Rise BS26 . . . . . . 70 A3
Waverley Cl
  Frome BA11 . . . . . . 120 C6
  Somerton TA11 . . . . . . 211 C4
Waverley Rd
  Backwell BS48 . . . . . . 19 A7
  Bridgwater TA6 . . . . . . 208 F6
  Bristol, Shirehampton BS11 . . . . . . 4 E6
  Weston-super-Mare BS23 . . . . . . 48 E4
Waverly Ct BS49 . . . . . . 34 D3
Waverney Ct TA1 . . . . . . 213 D3
Wayacre Dro BS24 . . . . . . 66 E6
Wayclose La BA9 . . . . . . 177 D5
Waycroft Acad BS14 . . . . . . 23 E5
Waydown Cross TA24 . . . . . . 130 A4
Waydown La TA24 . . . . . . 130 A4
Wayfarer Cl BS23 . . . . . . 49 B4
Wayfield Gdns BA1 . . . . . . 28 F4
WAYFORD 195 B1
Wayford Cl BS31 . . . . . . 25 A3
Wayford Hill TA18 . . . . . . 195 C1
Wayland Rd BS22 . . . . . . 31 E3
Waysdown La TA4 . . . . . . 149 D1
Wayside
  Stapleway TA3 . . . . . . 181 D8
  Weston-super-Mare BS22 . . . . . . 31 D2
Wayside Cl BA11 . . . . . . 120 C6
Wayside Dr BS21 . . . . . . 6 E5
WAY WICK 32 E1
WCA Ho BS1 . . . . . . 227 A2
WEACOMBE 132 F3
Weacombe Rd
  Bridgwater TA6 . . . . . . 209 C5
  Taunton TA2 . . . . . . 212 F7
Weal Terr BA1 . . . . . . 27 B2
Weal The BA1 . . . . . . 27 C2
WEARE 88 E6
Weare CE Fst Sch BS26 . . . . . . 88 D7
Weare Ct BS1 . . . . . . 226 A1
Weare Rd BS26 . . . . . . 88 E2
Weares La TA7 . . . . . . 137 D2
WEARNE 172 A7
Wearne Main Rd TA10 . . . . . . 172 A7
Weatherley Dr BS20 . . . . . . 1 F3
Weatherly Ave BA2 . . . . . . 44 D2
Weavers Cl
  Crewkerne TA18 . . . . . . 224 D5
  Shepton Mallet BA4 . . . . . . 205 D4
Weavers Ct BA11 . . . . . . 119 E3
Weavers Orch BA2 . . . . . . 62 D1
Weaver's Reach TA21 . . . . . . 222 B7
Weavers The BA11 . . . . . . 101 E4
Webber Rd BA4 . . . . . . 205 D4
Webbers TA4 . . . . . . 167 F7
Webbers CE Prim Sch TA21 . . . . . . 178 F5
Webbers Cl TA21 . . . . . . 222 E4
Webbers Way TA7 . . . . . . 136 B4
WEBBINGTON 68 E4
Webbington Rd BS26 . . . . . . 69 C3
Webb's Cl BA5 . . . . . . 203 D3
Webb's Hill BA11 . . . . . . 119 B5
Webbs Mead
  Beckington BA11 . . . . . . 101 E4
  Chew Stoke BS40 . . . . . . 56 D8
Wedgwood Cl BS14 . . . . . . 23 B5
Wedgwood Rd BA2 . . . . . . 44 A5
Wedlakes TA23 . . . . . . 202 C6
Wedlands TA1 . . . . . . 212 F7
Wedlock Way BS3 . . . . . . 11 F3
WEDMORE 108 D3
Wedmore Cl
  Burnham-on-S TA8 . . . . . . 104 C8
  Frome BA11 . . . . . . 120 C7
  Weston-super-Mare BS23 . . . . . . 48 F2

Wedmore Fst Sch BS28 . . . . . . 108 B4
Wedmore Pk BA2 . . . . . . 44 A3
Wedmore Rd
  Cheddar BS27 . . . . . . 90 A7
  Clevedon BS21 . . . . . . 6 B1
  Nailsea BS48 . . . . . . 18 E8
  Saltford BS31 . . . . . . 25 D4
Weekesley La BA2 . . . . . . 60 D1
Weekes Mdw TA21 . . . . . . 179 E6
Week La TA22 . . . . . . 147 D4
WEEKMOOR 167 B3
Weekmoor La TA4 . . . . . . 167 B4
Weetwood Rd BS49 . . . . . . 34 E5
Weind The BS22 . . . . . . 31 D2
Weir Cl BS39 . . . . . . 77 D6
Weirfield Gn TA1 . . . . . . 212 D5
Weirfield Rd TA1 . . . . . . 201 A8
Weir Head Cotts TA22 . . . . . . 163 D7
Weir La
  Abbots Leigh BS8 . . . . . . 10 F5
  Marshfield SN14 . . . . . . 13 F8
  Pilton BA4 . . . . . . 140 E3
  Yeovilton BA22 . . . . . . 174 A1
Weir Rd BS49 . . . . . . 34 E3
Welbeck Rd BA21 . . . . . . 219 E7
WELHAM 160 A2
Welham TA11 . . . . . . 173 C7
Welland Cl TA1 . . . . . . 213 D4
Welland Rd
  Keynsham BS31 . . . . . . 24 F4
  Yeovil BA21 . . . . . . 219 D7
Wellard Cl 1 BS22 . . . . . . 32 B4
Well Cl
  Long Ashton BS41 . . . . . . 11 B1
  Weston-super-Mare BS24 . . . . . . 49 B2
  Winscombe BS25 . . . . . . 70 A8
Wellesley Ct TA1 . . . . . . 212 C1
Wellesley Gn BA10 . . . . . . 215 E6
Wellesley Park Prim Sch TA21 . . . . . . 222 E4
Wellesley Pk TA21 . . . . . . 222 D4
Wellesley St TA2 . . . . . . 212 F6
Wellesley Way TA1 . . . . . . 192 A7
Wellfield Hill DT6, EX13 . . . . . . 199 B2
Well House Cl BS9 . . . . . . 5 E3
Wellhouse La BA6 . . . . . . 206 F4
Wellings Cl TA20 . . . . . . 198 C8
WELLINGTON 222 D7
Wellington Bldgs BA1 . . . . . . 27 B2
Wellington Com Hospl TA21 . . . . . . 222 D5
Wellington Ct BS21 . . . . . . 6 C5
Wellington Flats BA20 . . . . . . 219 A4
Wellington Hill TA21 . . . . . . 222 E8
Wellington Jun Sch TA21 . . . . . . 222 E5
Wellington Mews BS11 . . . . . . 4 D5
Wellington Monument* TA21 . . . . . . 180 B4
Wellington Mus TA21 . . . . . . 222 D6
Wellington New Rd TA1 . . . . . . 212 B3
Wellington Pl
  Cheddar BS27 . . . . . . 90 B7
  Weston-super-Mare BS23 . . . . . . 48 D7
Wellington Rd
  Bridgwater TA6 . . . . . . 209 B5
  Bristol BS2 . . . . . . 227 C4
  Taunton TA1 . . . . . . 212 D4
Wellington Sch TA21 . . . . . . 222 E5
Wellington Sq TA24 . . . . . . 200 F7
Wellington Terr
  18 Bristol BS8 . . . . . . 11 F6
  Clevedon BS21 . . . . . . 6 D5
  Wiveliscombe TA4 . . . . . . 210 C5
WELLISFORD 179 D8
Well La
  Banwell BS29 . . . . . . 50 E3
  Purse Caundle DT9 . . . . . . 189 D4
  Timberscombe TA24 . . . . . . 130 A5
  Yatton BS49 . . . . . . 34 C8
WELLOW 62 D1
Wellow Brook Ct BA3 . . . . . . 78 B3
Wellow Brook Mdw BA3 . . . . . . 78 B2
Wellow Dr BA11 . . . . . . 120 C7
Wellow La
  Hinton Charterhouse BA2 . . . . . . 63 D1
  Norton St Philip BA2 . . . . . . 81 D5
  Peasedown St John BA2 . . . . . . 79 C6
  Shoscombe BA2 . . . . . . 79 E6
Wellow Mead BA2 . . . . . . 79 B7
Wellow Rd BA2 . . . . . . 80 B8
Wellow Sq BA2 . . . . . . 79 D7
Well Pk BS49 . . . . . . 34 E4
WELLS 203 E4
Wells Cathedral* BA5 . . . . . . 203 E4
Wells Cathedral Jun Sch BA5 . . . . . . 203 D5
Wells Cathedral Sch BA5 . . . . . . 203 E5
Wells Central CE Jun Sch BA5 . . . . . . 203 C3
Wells Cl
  Bristol BS14 . . . . . . 23 C5
  Burnham-on-S TA8 . . . . . . 104 C7
  Nailsea BS48 . . . . . . 9 B1
  Taunton TA2 . . . . . . 213 A8
Wellsea Gr BS23 . . . . . . 49 B7
Wellshead La TA24 . . . . . . 128 A3
Wells Hill Bottom BA5 . . . . . . 113 E7
Wells & Mendip Mus* BA5 . . . . . . 203 E4
WELLSPRINGS 212 F8
Wellsprings Prim Sch TA2 . . . . . . 212 F8
Wellsprings Rd TA2 . . . . . . 212 F7
Wells Rd
  Bath BA2 . . . . . . 228 B1
  Bristol BS14 . . . . . . 23 C7
  Chilcompton BA3 . . . . . . 96 F4
  Clevedon BS21 . . . . . . 6 D1

Wells Rd continued
  Corston BA2 . . . . . . 43 B7
  Dundry BS41 . . . . . . 38 F7
  Glastonbury BA6 . . . . . . 206 E6
  Glastonbury, Southway BA5, BA6 . . . . . . 139 D4
  Hallatrow BS39 . . . . . . 77 B7
  Norton St Philip BA2, BA3 . . . . . . 81 C3
  Priddy BA5 . . . . . . 92 E2
  Radstock BA3 . . . . . . 78 E2
  Rodney Stoke BS27 . . . . . . 91 B1
  Shepton Mallet BA4 . . . . . . 204 E6
  Theale BA5 . . . . . . 108 B1
  Westbury-sub-Mendip BA5 . . . . . . 110 E6
  Wookey Hole BA5 . . . . . . 203 A7
  Yarley BA5 . . . . . . 139 C8
Wells Road Trad Est BA6 . . . . . . 206 F7
Wells Sq BA3 . . . . . . 78 B1
Wellsway
  Bath BA2 . . . . . . 44 F3
  Keynsham BS31 . . . . . . 24 F3
Wells Way BA3 . . . . . . 107 F3
Wellsway Pk BA2 . . . . . . 62 D8
Wellsway Sch BS31 . . . . . . 25 A5
Well The TA21 . . . . . . 222 B5
Welsford Ave BA5 . . . . . . 203 C5
Welsford Cl BA5 . . . . . . 203 B5
Welsh Back BS1 . . . . . . 227 A2
Welsh St BA5 . . . . . . 203 B4
WELSHMILL 119 F6
Welshmill La BA11 . . . . . . 119 F5
Welshmill Rd BA11 . . . . . . 119 F5
WELTON 78 B2
Welton Gr BA3 . . . . . . 78 B3
WELTON HOLLOW 78 D2
Welton Prim Sch BA3 . . . . . . 78 C2
Welton Rd BA3 . . . . . . 78 B2
Welton Vale BA3 . . . . . . 78 B2
WEMBDON 208 C6
Wembdon Ct TA6 . . . . . . 208 E4
Wembdon Hill TA6 . . . . . . 208 D6
Wembdon Orch TA6 . . . . . . 208 C6
Wembdon Rd TA6 . . . . . . 208 E4
Wembdon Rise TA6 . . . . . . 208 D5
Wembdon St George's CE Prim Sch TA6 . . . . . . 208 C6
Wemberham Cres BS49 . . . . . . 17 A1
Wemberham La BS49 . . . . . . 33 E8
Wendick Dro TA10 . . . . . . 171 E3
Wentwood Dr BS24 . . . . . . 49 A1
Wentworth Cl BS22 . . . . . . 32 A3
Wentworth Rd BA21 . . . . . . 219 E7
Werren Cl TA23 . . . . . . 202 B7
Wesley Ave BA3 . . . . . . 78 C1
Wesley Cl
  Brean TA8 . . . . . . 65 F3
  Frome BA11 . . . . . . 119 F4
  Southwick BA14 . . . . . . 83 E2
  Taunton TA1 . . . . . . 212 C1
  Wanstrow BA4 . . . . . . 142 F4
Wesley Ct BS23 . . . . . . 48 F8
Wesley Dr BS22 . . . . . . 32 A3
Wesley La BA14 . . . . . . 83 E2
Wesley Mews BS27 . . . . . . 90 B7
Wesley Rd BA3 . . . . . . 78 C1
Wesley Slope 18 BA11 . . . . . . 119 F4
Wesley Villas
  Coleford BA3 . . . . . . 116 F6
  12 Frome BA11 . . . . . . 119 F4
Wessex Bldgs TA11 . . . . . . 211 B5
Wessex Bsns Ctr BS27 . . . . . . 90 A7
Wessex Cl
  Bridgwater TA6 . . . . . . 209 C4
  Chard TA20 . . . . . . 223 C2
  Street BA16 . . . . . . 207 D6
Wessex Ct 4 DT9 . . . . . . 225 D3
Wessex Dr DT9 . . . . . . 187 E1
Wessex Fields BA11 . . . . . . 119 D2
Wessex Fields Ret Pk BA11 . . . . . . 119 D2
Wessex Ho 10 BS2 . . . . . . 227 C3
Wessex Pk TA11 . . . . . . 211 B5
Wessex Rd
  Stalbridge DT10 . . . . . . 190 C4
  Taunton TA1 . . . . . . 168 E1
  Weston-super-Mare BS24 . . . . . . 49 B2
  Yeovil BA21 . . . . . . 218 D8
Wessex Rise TA11 . . . . . . 211 E3
Wessex Way BA9 . . . . . . 216 B3
Westacre BA16 . . . . . . 207 A4
Westacre Cl BS27 . . . . . . 90 B8
Westacre Rd BS27 . . . . . . 90 B8
WEST ANSTEY 162 C6
West Anstey School Cross EX36 . . . . . . 162 C5
West Approach Rd TA7 . . . . . . 136 D4
West Ave
  Bath BA2 . . . . . . 44 C5
  Highbridge TA9 . . . . . . 104 C4
Westaway Cl BS49 . . . . . . 34 C7
Westaway Pk BS49 . . . . . . 34 D7
WEST BAGBOROUGH 151 F4
West Bagborough Rd TA4 . . . . . . 152 A4
West Bank BA5 . . . . . . 203 A8
Westbourne Ave
  Clevedon BS21 . . . . . . 6 B2
  Keynsham BS31 . . . . . . 24 E5
Westbourne Cl BA20 . . . . . . 218 E5
Westbourne Cres BS21 . . . . . . 6 B2
Westbourne Gr BA20 . . . . . . 218 E5
Westbourne Ho BA2 . . . . . . 228 C2
Westbourne Pl BS8 . . . . . . 226 B3
WEST BOURTON 177 E8
West Bourton Rd SP8 . . . . . . 177 E8
West Bower La TA5 . . . . . . 153 C2
West Bow Ho TA6 . . . . . . 208 E4
WEST BRADLEY 158 C7
Westbridge Pk DT9 . . . . . . 225 B2

West Brook BA21 . . . . . . 218 D6
Westbrook Ct BA4 . . . . . . 141 E1
Westbrooke Ct BS1 . . . . . . 226 A1
Westbrook Pk BA1 . . . . . . 27 A2
Westbrook Rd
  Bristol BS4 . . . . . . 23 D8
  Evercreech BA4 . . . . . . 141 E1
  Weston-super-Mare BS22 . . . . . . 31 D1
Westbrook Vale BA4 . . . . . . 141 E1
WEST BUCKLAND 180 F7
West Buckland Com Prim Sch TA21 . . . . . . 180 F7
West Buckland Rd TA21 . . . . . . 180 D7
Westbury
  Bradford Abbas DT9 . . . . . . 187 E1
  Sherborne DT9 . . . . . . 225 D3
Westbury Court Rd BS9 . . . . . . 5 F7
Westbury Cres BS23 . . . . . . 48 F2
Westbury Dro
  Priddy BA5 . . . . . . 92 A3
  Westbury Beacon BA5 . . . . . . 91 F2
Westbury Gdns BA22 . . . . . . 186 C2
Westbury La BS9 . . . . . . 5 C7
WESTBURY ON TRYM 5 F7
WESTBURY-SUB-MENDIP 110 D6
Westbury Terr
  Dunkerton BA2 . . . . . . 61 E5
  2 Sherborne DT9 . . . . . . 225 D3
Westbury View BA2 . . . . . . 79 E8
WEST CAMEL 174 D3
West Camel Farm BA22 . . . . . . 174 E3
West Camel Rd BA22 . . . . . . 174 E3
West Charlton TA11 . . . . . . 173 E7
WEST CHINNOCK 196 B8
West Chinnock CE Prim Sch TA18 . . . . . . 196 B8
West Cl
  Bath BA2 . . . . . . 44 A5
  Dunster TA24 . . . . . . 201 D2
WEST COKER 197 A8
West Coker CE Prim Sch BA22 . . . . . . 197 A8
West Coker Rd BA20 . . . . . . 218 E2
WESTCOMBE
  Batcombe 142 B2
  Somerton 172 E7
Westcombe BA8 . . . . . . 176 E1
Westcombe Hill BA4 . . . . . . 142 C2
Westcombe Rd
  Evercreech BA4 . . . . . . 141 F2
  Westcombe BA4 . . . . . . 142 A2
Westcombes EX13 . . . . . . 198 B7
Westcombe Stables La BA4 . . . . . . 142 B2
Westcombe Trad Est TA19 . . . . . . 183 E1
WEST COMPTON 204 C3
West Compton La BA4 . . . . . . 204 E3
West Coombe
  Bristol BS9 . . . . . . 5 D6
  Yeovil BA21 . . . . . . 218 D6
West Coombe La TA4 . . . . . . 165 D8
West Cornmoor Dro TA9 . . . . . . 136 D7
Westcott Cl BA11 . . . . . . 120 C6
Westcott Cross TA23 . . . . . . 130 D1
Westcott La TA4 . . . . . . 148 F2
Westcott Mead TA24 . . . . . . 128 E1
West Cotts TA24 . . . . . . 127 A2
West Cres TA19 . . . . . . 221 B2
West Croft
  Blagdon BS40 . . . . . . 54 E2
  Clevedon BS21 . . . . . . 6 B2
West Ct
  Horrington BA5 . . . . . . 112 F1
  Portishead BS20 . . . . . . 2 D4
  Templecombe BA8 . . . . . . 176 E1
West Dene BS9 . . . . . . 5 E6
West Dro TA7 . . . . . . 137 D4
West Dundry La BS41 . . . . . . 21 E2
WEST END
  Blagdon 54 E3
  Chewton Mendip 93 F6
  Clevedon 6 B2
  Frome 119 F5
  Nailsea 17 F7
  Somerton 211 C3
West End
  Bristol BS3 . . . . . . 226 C1
  Bristol, Kingsdown BS2 . . . . . . 227 A4
  Frome BA11 . . . . . . 119 F5
  Lower Weare BS26 . . . . . . 88 D8
  Marston Magna BA22 . . . . . . 174 E1
  Somerton TA11 . . . . . . 211 C4
  Street BA16 . . . . . . 207 B5
  Wedmore BS28 . . . . . . 108 C3
West End Cl
  Somerton TA11 . . . . . . 211 C4
  South Petherton TA13 . . . . . . 220 B4
West End Ct
  Chedzoy TA7 . . . . . . 136 D1
  South Petherton TA13 . . . . . . 220 B4
West End Farm Cvn Pk BS24 . . . . . . 49 E4
West End La BS48 . . . . . . 18 A8
Westend La N BA11 . . . . . . 143 C6
West End Trad Est BS48 . . . . . . 8 B1
West End View
  Barrington TA19 . . . . . . 184 C5
  South Petherton TA11 . . . . . . 220 B4
West End Way TA13 . . . . . . 220 B4
Westerkirk Gate TA2 . . . . . . 212 C7
Westerleigh Rd
  Bath BA2 . . . . . . 45 B1
  Clevedon BS21 . . . . . . 6 B2

Westerly Ct TA19........221 B4
Western Approaches
BA22.................174 A2
Western Ave BA21.....218 B6
Western Ct
Clevedon BS21.............6 D3
Shepton Mallet BA4.......205 B6
Western Dr BS14.........22 E6
Western Gate TA10....172 C7
Western La
East Quantoxhead TA5....133 A5
Minehead TA24.........200 F7
Ridge BS40..............74 C3
Western Retreat BA5....203 B5
Western St DT9........187 E4
Western Way
Bridgwater TA6.........208 F7
Winsham TA20..........194 E1
Westex Ho BS23.........49 B5
West Farm La TA20.....194 D5
WESTFORD...........97 C8
Westfield
Bruton BA10............215 D5
Clevedon BS21...........16 D8
Curry Rivel TA10........171 C3
Shepton Mallet BA4......205 A6
Sherborne DT9..........225 B2
Westfield Acad BA21....218 E6
Westfield Ave BA21.....218 E6
Westfield Cl
Backwell BS48...........19 A6
Bath BA2...............44 E3
Bridgwater TA6.........208 E4
Burnham-on-S TA8.......104 B8
Keynsham BS31..........24 C5
Weston-super-Mare BS23...48 D2
West Field Cl TA1......212 A2
Westfield Cres
Banwell BS29............51 A3
Yeovil BA21.............218 F6
Westfield Ct TA8......104 B8
Westfield Dr
Backwell BS48...........19 A6
Burnham-on-S TA8.......104 B8
Westfield Gr BA21......218 F6
Westfield Ho
Bath BA2...............44 E3
Bridgwater TA6.........208 E4
Westfield Ind & Trad Est
BA3..................97 C7
Westfield La
Curry Rivel TA10........171 C3
Draycott BS27...........90 E3
North Curry TA3........170 C3
Rodney Stoke BS27......110 C8
Street BA6, BA16.......207 E2
West Field Lawn TA8...104 B8
Westfield Pk BA1........44 A7
Westfield Pk S BA1......44 A7
Westfield Pl
Bristol BS8.............11 F7
Yeovil BA21............218 E6
Westfield Prim Sch BA3...97 C8
Westfield Rd
Backwell BS48...........19 A6
Banwell BS29............51 A3
Burnham-on-S TA8.......104 B8
Frome BA11.............119 D3
Wells BA5..............203 C4
Weston-super-Mare BS23...48 D2
Yeovil BA21............218 F6
Westfields TA19.......184 C5
Westfield S BA12.......161 F2
Westfield Terr BA3.......78 D1
WESTFORD...........179 F7
Westford Cl TA21......222 A5
Westford Ct TA21......222 A5
Westford Dr TA21......222 A5
West Garston BS29......51 A3
Westgate BS1.........226 B1
Westgate Bldgs BA1....228 B2
Westgate St
Bath BA1..............228 B2
4 Taunton TA1.........212 E3
Westhall Rd BA1.........44 D7
WESTHAM...........107 C2
WEST HARPTREE......74 E6
West Harptree Rd BS40...74 E6
WEST HATCH.........182 E7
West Hatch La TA3.....182 F8
Westhaven Cl BS48......19 A6
Westhaven Sch BS23......48 D2
WESTHAY...........138 A5
Westhay Broad Dro
TA7..................137 E6
Westhay Cross EX13....198 F3
Westhay Moor Dro
BA5, BA6..............138 D6
Westhay Rd BA6.......138 C4
West Hay Rd BS40........35 C3
West Hendford BA20....218 F3
West Henley Rd TA10...156 A2
WEST HEWISH.........33 A5
WEST HILL
Nailsea................9 A5
Portishead..............2 A5
Wincanton.............216 B4
West Hill
Milborne Port DT9......217 D2
Nailsea BS48.............9 A5
Portishead BS20..........2 B5
Wincanton BA9.........216 B4
West Hill Ct BS20........2 C6
WEST HILL GARDENS....78 E1
Westhill Gdns BS20.......2 C5

West Hill Gdns
Radstock BA3...........78 D1
Radstock BA3...........78 E1
Westhill La TA9.......105 C2
West Hill Rd BA3........78 D1
Westholm Rd TA11.....211 B4
WEST HUNTSPILL.....136 A7
West Huntspill Com Prim Sch
TA9..................104 C1
West La
Alhampton BA4.........159 C5
Alweston DT9..........189 A2
Barrington TA13........184 F5
Croscombe BA5.........140 F8
Felton BS40.............37 C8
Lynford-on-F TA11......158 D2
Sherborne DT9.........188 F1
Westlake Cl TA7.......155 C2
WEST LAMBROOK.....184 F5
Westland Rd BA20.....218 F4
Westlands Distribution Pk
BS24..................49 B3
West Lea Rd BA1........27 A1
West Leaze BA16......207 B6
WESTLEIGH.........179 A4
WEST LEIGH.........150 F1
Westleigh Gdns BA4....205 A4
West Leigh Inf Sch BS18...19 A6
Westleigh Pk BS14......23 B8
Westleigh Rd TA1......213 B3
Westley Mews BS24......32 C1
West Links BS23.........48 D2
West Links Cl BS22......31 B3
West Littleton Rd SN14...13 F8
West Lodge BA4.......205 A5
WEST LUCCOMBE.....124 C3
West Luccombe Rd
Luccombe TA24.........123 C2
Luccombe TA24.........129 C8
WEST LYDFORD......158 C2
WEST LYNG..........170 B7
West Lynne BS27........90 B8
West Mall BS8..........11 F7
Westmans Est TA8.....104 C7
Westmarch Way BS22....32 A4
Westmead BA3..........96 D3
Westmead Gdns BA1.....27 A2
West Mendip Com Hospl
BA6..................139 D3
Westmere Cres TA8....104 C8
West Mill La
Marnhull DT10.........190 D6
Sherborne DT9.........225 C2
Westminster BA21......218 C7
Westminster Bldgs DT10..190 B4
Westminster Cotts DT10..190 B4
Westminster St BA20...219 A4
Westminster Way TA6...136 B2
Westminster Wy TA6....209 C8
WEST MONKTON.....169 C7
West Monkton CE Prim Sch
TA2..................213 F8
Westmoor Dro
Hambridge TA10, TA12...184 E7
Knapp TA3.............169 F4
Westmoor La TA10.....184 D8
Westmoreland Dr BA2...228 A2
Westmoreland Rd BA2...228 A1
Westmoreland St BA2...228 A2
Westmoreland Station Rd
BA2..................228 A1
WEST MUDFORD......187 C7
West Mudford Rd BA22..187 C7
WEST NEWTON......169 F8
WESTON...........27 A2
Weston All Saints CE Prim Sch
BA1..................27 A2
WESTON BAMPFYLDE..175 B3
Weston Bampfylde Rd
BA22.................175 B3
Weston Bsns Pk BS24....49 E5
Weston Cl
Bristol BS9..............5 C7
East Chinnock BA22.....196 E8
Weston Coll BS48........8 E2
Weston College BS23.....48 D8
Weston Coll South West Skills
Campus BS22...........49 C8
Weston Coll Uni Campus
BS23..................48 F2
Weston Ct BS24.........49 B3
Weston Dro BS20.........7 E8
Weston Euro Pk BS24....49 B4
Weston Express Bsns Pk
BS22..................49 C6
Weston Farm La BA1.....27 C2
Weston Gateway Tourist Pk
BS24..................32 C1
Weston General Hospl
BS23..................48 E2
Weston Hill SP8.......177 D3
Westonia BS22..........31 E2
Westonian Ct BS9........5 C4
Weston Ind Est BS24....49 B2
WESTON IN GORDANO....1 F1
Weston La
Bath BA1...............44 C8
Christon BS26...........68 C7
East Coker BA22........197 E5
Halstock DT2...........196 F1
Weston Lock Ret BA2.....44 C6
Weston Lodge BS23.....48 D8
Weston Milton Sta BS22..49 C7
Weston Miniature Rly★
BS23..................48 D5
WESTON PARK........27 C1
Weston Park Ct BA1.....27 D1
Weston Pk BA1..........27 C1

Weston Pk E BA1........27 D1
Weston Pk W BA1.......27 C1
Weston Rd
Bath BA1...............44 D8
Brean TA8..............66 A5
Congresbury BS49........34 B5
East Brent BS24, TA9.....86 D6
Failand BS8.............10 C3
Long Ashton BS41........20 D3
Weston Ret Pk BS23.....49 A6
Weston St
Buckhorn Weston SP8....177 D3
East Chinnock BA22.....196 E8
WESTON-SUPER-MARE..48 B7
Weston-super-Mare Sta
BS23..................48 E7
WESTON TOWN......142 E5
Weston Town BA4......141 E1
Weston Way BS24.......49 F2
Weston Wlk BA11......119 C6
Weston Wood Rd BS20....2 C3
WESTONZOYLAND....154 E5
Westonzoyland Prim Sch
Bussex TA6............153 F6
Westonzoyland TA7......154 F5
Westonzoyland Pumping Sta★
TA7..................154 D3
Westonzoyland Rd TA6,
TA7..................209 E4
Westover
Frome BA11............119 D4
Nunney BA11...........143 B7
Westover Ct BA11......119 D4
Westover Gdns BS9.......5 F8
Westover Gn TA6......208 E4
Westover Green Com Sch
TA6..................208 E4
Westover La
Crewkerne TA18........224 B7
Martock TA12..........185 F8
Westover Rd BS9.........5 F8
Westover's Cnr BS28....108 B4
Westover Trad Est TA18..171 F5
Westover View TA18....224 C7
WESTOWE...........151 A3
Westowe Hill TA4......151 A3
West Par BS9...........5 C7
Westpark TA21........180 D7
Westpark TA21........180 D7
Westpark 26 TA21.....180 D7
West Park Cl TA24.....200 E7
WEST PENNARD......140 B1
West Pennard CE Prim Sch
BA6..................140 B1
West Pk
Bristol BS8............226 B4
Butleigh BA6...........157 E4
Castle Cary BA7........214 B6
Minehead TA24.........200 E7
Yeovil BA20............218 F5
WEST PORLOCK......123 F4
WESTPORT..........184 C7
Westport La TA3, TA10...184 B7
West Port Lodge Rd TA20.194 D2
WEST QUANTOXHEAD..132 E4
West Quay TA6........208 F5
West Rd
East Brent BS24, TA9.....86 B7
Lympsham BS24..........67 B1
Midsomer Norton BA3.....78 A3
Wiveliscombe TA4.......210 B4
Yatton BS49............34 B7
Westridge DT9........225 C3
Westridge Way TA4....167 E7
West Rocke Ave BS9......5 D6
West Rolstone Rd BS24...33 A1
West Sedgemoor Nature
Reserve★ TA3.........170 F3
West Sedgemoor Rd TA3..170 D3
WEST SHEPTON......205 A4
West Shepton BA4.....205 A5
West Somerset Com Coll The
TA24.................201 B5
West Somerset Community
College Farm TA24......201 D4
West Somerset Railway★
TA4..................150 F7
West Somerset Rly★ TA4..151 B5
West Somerset Rural Life
Mus★ TA24............124 C4
West St
Ashcott TA7...........156 B8
Axbridge BS26...........70 B2
Bampton EX16..........164 B1
Banwell BS29............51 A3
Banwell BS29............51 B3
Bishops Lydeard TA4.....167 E8
Bridgwater TA6.........208 E4
Bristol BS2............227 C3
Carhampton TA24.......131 B4
Crewkerne TA18........224 B6
Dunster TA24..........201 D1
Hinton St George TA17...195 C7
Ilchester BA22.........173 E1
Ilminster TA19.........221 B4
Kington Magna SP8......177 E1
Martock TA12..........185 E8
Minehead TA24.........200 E6
Seavington St Mary TA19..184 D1
Somerton TA11.........211 D4
South Petherton TA13....220 B4
Stoke sub Hamdon TA14...185 E3
Templecombe BA8........189 E8
Watchet TA23..........202 B7
Wells BA5.............203 C3
Weston-super-Mare BS23...48 D8
Wiveliscombe TA4.......210 C4
Yarlington BA9.........175 F7

West St *continued*
Yeovil BA20............218 F4
WEST STOKE.........185 E4
WEST STOUGHTON...107 E6
West Terr BA2..........82 C1
WEST TOWN
Backwell................18 F5
Baltonsborough........157 F6
Ubley..................55 B6
West Town Gr BS4......23 D8
West Town La
Baltonsborough BA6.....157 F5
Bristol BS4, BS14.......23 C8
Bristol BS14............23 C8
West Town Pk BS4.......23 D8
West Town Rd
Backwell BS48...........19 A5
Bristol BS11.............4 C7
West Tyning BA2........42 B1
Westview BS39..........77 C5
West View
Creech St Michael TA3...169 D5
Long Sutton TA10.......172 E4
Milborne Port DT9......217 D3
Queen Camel BA22......174 F4
South Cadbury BA22....175 D4
West Monkton TA2......169 D8
West View Cl TA7......155 B4
Westview Orch BA3.....64 B5
West View Rd
Batheaston BA1.........29 A3
Keynsham BS31..........24 E5
West Villas TA4.......167 F6
Westville BA21........219 C5
Westward BS41.........11 B2
Westward Cl BS40........35 D2
Westward Dr BS20........4 C4
Westward Gdns BS41.....11 B2
Westward Rd BS13........21 F7
Westway
Nailsea BS48.............8 E2
Street BA16............207 B6
West Way BS21..........6 C3
Westway Ctr BA11......119 F5
Westway La BA4.......205 B4
West Ways BA22........196 E8
West Well La BS28.....109 C1
WEST WICK...........32 C1
West Wick BS24.........32 C1
West Wick Rdbt BS22, BS24.50 B8
WESTWOOD...........64 E3
Westwood BA2..........45 E6
Westwood Ave BS39......59 C2
Westwood Cl 2 BS22....31 F2
Westwood Cotts BA8....176 E1
Westwood Dro TA11....158 C3
WEST WOODLANDS...143 F6
Westwood Rd
Bridgwater TA6.........209 D7
Bristol BS4............23 D8
Westwoods BA1.........29 B3
Westwood with Iford Prim Sch
BA15..................64 F3
West Yeo Rd TA7......154 F1
Wetherell Pl BS8......226 B3
Weycroft Ave EX13.....198 A2
Weycroft Ave EX13.....198 A2
Weylands BA11........119 E6
Weymont Cl TA7.......155 B3
Weymouth Ct BA21......45 B8
Weymouth Rd
Evercreech BA4.........141 E1
Frome BA11............119 E4
Weymouth St BA1........45 B8
Whaddon Hill BA10....160 C7
Whaites Dr TA19.......221 A5
Wharf Cotts TA21.....222 B8
Wharf Ho TA19........221 B4
Wharf La
Ilminster TA19.........221 B3
Portbury BS20............3 B5
Wharf Rd BS24..........49 B4
Wharfside BS24.........66 E3
Wharncliffe Cl BS14.....23 B5
Wharncliffe Gdns BS14...23 B5
Whatcombe Rd BA11....119 D4
Whatcombe Terr BA11...119 E6
WHATLEY
Frome.................118 D4
Winsham...............194 C1
Whatley TA10.........171 F5
Whatley Cross TA20....194 C1
Whatley La
Buckland St Mary TA20..192 D7
Langport TA10.........172 A5
Tatworth TA20.........194 C1
Winsham TA20.........199 A8
Whatley Mews TA10....171 F5
Whatley Vineyard & Herb
Gdn★ BA11............118 D4
Wheatear Rd BS49......16 F2
Wheatfield Dr BS22.....32 A5
Wheatfield La BA3......95 A6
Wheathill Cl
Keynsham BS31..........24 D5
Milborne Port DT9......217 D2
Wheathill Rd TA11.....158 E2
Wheathill Way DT9....217 D2
Wheatleigh Cl TA1.....212 E2

Wheatley Cres TA1......213 B5
Wheatsheaf La
Burnett BA2.............42 C6
Stone Allerton BS26......88 D3
Wheatstones 10 TA4....167 F8
WHEDDON CROSS.....129 E1
Wheeler Gr BA5........203 B4
Wheelers Cl BA3........78 D2
Wheelers Dr BA3........78 C2
WHEELER'S HILL.......78 C2
Wheelers Rd BA3........78 D2
Wheel House La TA20...199 B7
Wheel La BA5..........185 A6
Whellers Mdw TA12....185 E7
Whetham Mill Cross DT8.199 F5
Whetham Mill La DT8....199 F6
Whetstones Almshouses
TA19.................183 F4
Whimbrel Ave 2 BS20....2 F6
WHIPCOTT..........179 B5
Whippington Ct BS1....227 B3
Whirligg 15 TA14.....185 E4
Whirligg La TA1.......212 F4
Whirligg 7 TA1........212 F4
Whistley La BS40........74 F6
Whitaker Rd BA2........45 A2
Whitbourne Moor BA12..144 E8
WHITBOURNE SPRINGS..144 F7
Whitbourne Springs BA12.144 F7
Whitchey Dro TA9......137 A5
WHITCHURCH.........23 D4
Whitchurch District Ctr
BS14..................23 D4
Whitchurch La
Bristol, Bishopsworth BS13..22 B5
Bristol, Hartcliffe BS13....22 C5
Bristol, Whitchurch BS14...22 E5
Dundry BS41............22 C1
Henstridge BA8.........190 A7
Yenston BA8...........189 F8
Whitchurch Prim Sch BS13.23 C4
Whitchurch Rd BS13.....22 A6
Whitchurch Trad Est BS14..22 F5
WHITCOMBE..........175 D2
Whitcombe Farm La DT9..175 D2
Whitcross 10 BA22.....197 F8
White Ash La TA20.....193 A5
WHITE BALL..........179 D6
Whitebeam Cl TA6.....209 D5
Whitebrook La BA2......79 A4
Whitebrook Terr TA21...178 F5
White Cats Cotts BA8...176 E3
Whitechapel La BA11...101 C1
Whitecroft TA4.........202 E4
WHITECROSS.........171 E3
WHITE CROSS
Bishop Sutton...........57 E1
Burnham-on-Sea........105 B8
Hallatrow..............76 F6
Zeals.................161 F3
White Cross
Brent Knoll TA9........105 A8
Exford TA24...........128 B1
White Cross BS39........76 F6
Whitecross Ave BS14.....23 C6
White Cross Gate BS39...76 F6
Whitecross La
Banwell BS29............51 A4
Minehead TA24.........200 F8
Whitecross Rd
East Harptree BS40......74 F4
Weston-super-Mare BS23...48 E6
Whitecross Way TA24...200 E7
Whitedown Cross EX15..191 B4
WHITEFIELD.........210 B8
Whitefield Cl BA1........29 B4
White field Cross EX36..162 D3
Whitefield La TA19.....184 D4
Whitefield Rocks TA4...150 B5
WHITE GATE.........194 B1
Whitegate Cl
Bleadon BS24...........67 B6
Minehead TA24.........201 A6
Whitegate Rd TA24.....201 A6
Whitegates Gdns TA24..200 F6
WHITEHALL..........180 A1
Whitehall
Taunton TA1............212 A5
Watchet TA23..........202 B7
Whitehall Cl TA13......220 D4
Whitehall Ct TA18......224 C7
Whitehall Rd TA6......136 B2
White Hart La TA21.....222 C1
WHITE HILL............79 F6
White Hill
Langport TA10.........172 A7
Shoscombe BA2.........79 F6
White Hill Dro TA20...193 C5
Whitehole Hill BA3.....116 E4
White Horse Dr BA11...120 C6
White Horse La BS28...138 D8
White Horse Rd BA15....64 D7
Whitehouse Ctr (PRU)
BS13..................22 C5
Whitehouse La
Litton BA3..............75 D3
Wraxall BS48.............9 A6
White House La
East Huntspill TA9......136 E7
Loxton BS26............68 A3
Whitehouse Rd BS49.....34 F8
White House Rd TA5, TA6..135 D5
WHITELACKINGTON...184 C2
Whiteladies Rd BS8....226 B4
Whitelands Hill BA3......79 B3
Whiteleaze La
Thurloxton TA2........153 C1
West Monkton TA2......169 D8

White Lodge Pk BS20......2 D6
White Mead BA21......218 D6
Whitemill La BA1......119 C3
Whitemoor Hill TA20......194 C4
Whitemoor La TA4......150 F3
Whitemore Ct BA1......29 A4
Whiteoak Way BS48......18 D8
White Oxmead La BA2......61 E1
White Ox Mead La BA2....61 F1
White Post
　Midsomer Norton BA3....97 B6
　Twitchen EX36......145 K2
Whitepost Gate DT9......188 D6
Whites Cl TA6......208 E2
White's Dro BA5......138 F7
Whitesfield Ct BS48......8 D2
Whitesfield Rd BS48......8 D1
White's La TA4......133 A1
Whitesome's Dro BS27...109 C6
White St
　Bristol BS5......227 C4
　Creech St Michael TA3...169 E4
　Horningsham BA12......144 E4
　North Curry TA3......170 C4
WHITESTAUNTON......193 B5
Whitestaunton Cross
　TA20......193 B5
Whitestone Rd BA11...120 B6
Whitestown La BS40......73 E3
Whitewall Cnr TA3......181 D2
WHITEWAY......44 A4
Whiteway TA20......193 E6
Whiteway Rd BA2......44 A3
Whitewell Pl BA11......119 C3
Whitewell Rd BA11......119 C3
Whitewells Rd BA1......28 A2
Whitewick La TA5......134 F8
Whitford Rd BS23......209 D6
Whitford Hill
　Corfe TA3......182 A4
　Pitminster TA3......181 F5
Whitford La TA3......182 A4
Whithys The BA16......207 C7
Whiting Cl BA4......205 C4
Whiting La 1 TA6......153 E3
Whiting Rd
　Bristol BS13......22 A4
　Glastonbury BA6......206 F5
Whiting Way BS13......203 D4
Whitland Ave BS13......22 B5
Whitland Rd BS13......22 B5
WHITLEY BATTS......40 F2
Whitley La BA16......156 D7
Whitley Rd TA7, BA16...156 C8
Whitling St BS40......38 A2
Whitmead Gdns BS13......22 C4
Whitmore La TA2......212 D8
Whitmore Rd TA2......212 E8
WHITNAGE......178 C4
Whitnage La EX16......178 C2
WHITNELL......134 D2
Whitnell Cnr BA5......113 F6
Whitnell La
　Binegar BA3......114 B8
　Keenthorne TA5......134 D2
Whitney Cres BS24......49 C5
Whitney Hill TA19......193 F8
Whitson Ho 1 BS2......227 C3
Whitson St BS1......227 A4
Whitstone BA4......205 C5
Whitstone Cl BA4......205 C6
Whitstone Cnr BA4......205 D1
Whitstone Ct BA4......205 D5
Whitstone Hill BA4......204 C1
Whitstone La BA4......205 E1
Whitstone Rd BA4......205 D4
Whitstone Rise BA4......205 D4
Whitswood Steep TA24...130 D4
Whittakers Ho 6 BA4...205 B6
Whitting Rd BS23......48 E4
Whittington Dr BS22......31 D2
Whittock Rd BS14......23 D6
Whittock Sq BS14......23 D7
Whittox La BA11......119 E5
Whitwell Rd BS14......23 B8
Whitworth Rd
　Frome BA11......119 F2
　Minehead TA24......200 D7
WICK
　Burnham-on-Sea......85 E8
　Glastonbury......139 E2
　Stogursey......134 D7
Wick TA10......171 E5
Wicketsbeer Rd BA22...197 C6
Wickfield BS21......6 C1
Wickham Ct BS21......6 C3
Wickham Rise BA11......119 F6
Wickham's Cross or Beggar's
　Grave BA6......157 C3
Wickham Way
　East Brent TA9......86 D4
　Shepton Mallet BA4......205 A6
Wick Hill
　Charlton Horethorne DT9...176 A1
　Milborne Port DT9......217 B6
Wickhill Rd TA10......171 D5
Wick Hollow BA6......206 F5
Wick House Cl BS31......25 D3
Wick La
　Burnham-on-S TA9......85 E6
　Glastonbury BA6......139 E2
　Lympsham BS24......66 E1
　Norton Fitzwarren TA2...168 A6
　Peasedown St John BA2, BA3 60 F1
　Pensford BS39......40 D3
　Upton Cheyney BS30......26 A8
WICKLANE......61 A1
Wicklow Rd BS4......22 E8

Wickmoor TA3......171 D6
Wick Moor Dro TA5......134 C7
Wick Oath Rd TA10......171 E6
Wick Pound TA5......134 D7
Wick Rd
　Bishop Sutton BS39......57 C3
　Lympsham BS24......66 D2
　Milborne Port DT9......217 C4
　Wick St Lawrence BS22...32 B7
WICK ST LAWRENCE......32 B7
Widcombe......45 C4
Widcombe BS14......23 A6
WIDCOMBE......45 C4
Widcombe CE Jun Sch
　BA2......45 B5
Widcombe Cres BA2......45 B5
Widcombe Hill BA2......45 C4
Widcombe Inf Sch BA2...45 B5
Widcombe Par BA2......228 C1
Widcombe Rise BA2......45 B5
Widcombe Terr BA2......45 B5
Wideatts Rd BA4......90 A7
Widmore Gr BS13......22 B5
Widness Dro TA3......170 C2
WIGBOROUGH......220 F1
Wigeon Cl TA24......201 C5
Wight Row BA20......219 B4
Wigmore Gdns BS22......31 D2
Windsor Cres TA20......223 B3
Wilbye Gr BS4......22 D7
Wildcountry La BS48......20 E6
Wilde Cl TA8......104 C6
Wilder Ct BS2......227 B4
Wilderness Dro BA16......138 E2
Wilderness The 9 DT9...225 D4
Wilder St BS2......227 B4
Wildmoor La TA21......180 F6
Wild Oak Ho TA3......168 D1
Wild Oak La TA3......168 D1
Wilfred Rd TA1......213 A4
Wilfrid Rd BA16......207 D6
Wilkins Cl TA20......223 D4
Wilkins Rd TA6......209 D5
Wilkinthroop TA10......176 C2
WILLAND......191 E8
Willan Pl BS24......32 C1
Willcocks Cl 6 TA21......222 D5
Willcox Cl BS4......206 E5
Willet Ct TA9......104 D3
Willet's La BA3......94 D6
WILLETT......150 E4
Willett Hill Cross TA4...150 D5
Willey Rd TA3......170 E6
WILLHAYNE......223 A8
William Daw Cl BS29......50 F3
William Jessop Wy BS14...22 E4
William Reynolds Ho
　BA16......207 D7
William St
　Bath BA2......228 C3
　Taunton TA2......212 F6
William's Yd BS40......38 A7
Willie Gill Ct TA1......212 E4
Willinton Rd BS4......22 F8
Willis Hay DT9......225 D3
Willis Rd BA2......45 B2
Willis's La TA18......196 C4
Will La TA4......151 A3
Willmott Cl BS14......22 F3
Willmott's Cl TA7......137 B2
Willoughby Pl BS13......22 B7
Willoughby Pl TA20......223 D3
Willoughby Rd TA6......208 C4
Willowbank TA24......130 B4
Willow Cl
　Bath BA2......62 E8
　Clevedon BS21......6 E3
　East Huntspill TA9......136 E7
　Frome BA11......119 E3
　Langport TA10......172 A6
　Long Ashton BS41......10 F1
　Portishead BS20......2 C4
　Radstock BA3......78 E2
　Taunton TA1......213 D1
　Weston-super-Mare, St Georges
　BS22......32 D2
　Weston-super-Mare, Uphill
　BS23......48 E2
　Westonzoyland TA7......154 E5
　Williton TA4......202 E3
Willow Ct TA6......209 D5
Willowdown BS22......31 E4
Willowdown Prim Acad
　TA6......209 C8
Willow Dr
　Bleadon BS24......67 C6
　Hutton BS24......49 E2
　Shepton Mallet BA4......205 A6
　Weston-super-Mare BS24...49 E5
Willowfalls BA1......28 E3
Willow Gdns BS22......32 D2
Willow Gn
　Bath BA2......44 D4
　Chedzoy TA7......154 D8
Willow Gr TA23......131 E4
Willow Ho BS13......22 D4
Willow La EX15......180 C7
Willow Rd
　Street BA16......207 B3
　Yeovil BA21......218 F6
Willows The
　Brent Knoll TA9......86 A2
　Nailsea BS48......8 F3

Willow The BA3......96 F2
Willow Tree Cl BA22......174 A4
Willow Vale BA11......119 F5
Willow Way TA18......224 D7
Willow Wlk
　Bridgwater TA6......209 C4
　Keynsham BS31......24 D4
Wills Ind Est TA9......209 A4
Wills Rd TA6......208 F1
Wills Way BS4......22 C6
Willway St BS2......227 C3
WILMINGTON......43 A1
Wilmington Hill
　Englishcombe BA2......43 C2
　Marksbury BA2......42 E1
Wilmots Way BS20......4 D4
Wilsham Cross EX35......122 A5
Wilsham La EX35......122 A5
Wilson Cl BA5......203 C2
Wilson Gdns BS24......32 C1
Wilson Pl BS2......227 C4
Wilsons Cl TA5......134 B2
Wilson St BS2......227 C4
WILSTOCK VILLAGE TA6...153 F5
Wilton Cl
　Burnham-on-S TA8......104 C8
　Street BA16......207 D5
　Taunton TA1......212 B3
Wilton Ct BS23......48 D7
Wilton Gdns BS23......48 D7
Wilton Gr TA1......212 E3
Wilton Orch
　Street BA16......207 D5
　Taunton TA1......212 E2
Wilton Rd BA21......219 E8
Wiltons BS40......35 D2
Wilton St TA1......212 E3
WILTOWN
　Curry Rivel......171 C3
　Wellington......180 F3
Wiltown TA10......171 D3
Wiltown La EX15......180 F3
Wiltshire Cl TA1......212 C2
Wiltshire Ct TA1......212 C2
Wiltshires Barton 4
　BA11......119 E5
Wiltshire Way BA1......28 A2
Wilway La TA22......163 C6
Wimble Stock Way BA21...218 C8
Wimblestone Rd BS25......51 F2
Wimborne Cl TA1......213 D3
Wimborough La BA22......196 F6
Winash Cl BS14......23 D7
WINCANTON......216 A4
Wincanton Bsns Pk BA9...216 C3
Wincanton Cl BS48......9 B1
Wincanton Com Hospl
　BA9......216 B4
Wincanton Mus * BA9...216 C3
Wincanton Prim Sch BA9...216 C3
Wincanton Rd TA10......172 A5
Winchcombe Cl BS48......19 A8
Winchcombe Gr BS11......4 F5
Winchester Cotts TA19...184 E1
Winchester Gdns BA21...219 C7
Winchester Ho 2 TA1...213 A4
Winchester Rd
　Bath BA2......44 D5
　Burnham-on-S TA8......104 C7
Winchester St TA1......213 A4
Windcliff Cres BS11......4 E7
Wind Down Cl TA6......208 C4
Windell St BA2......45 A2
Windermere Ave BS23......48 F4
Windermere Cl BA20......218 F2
Windmill TA3......170 F5
Windmill Bsns Pk BS21...16 E8
Windmill Cl TA9......105 B7
Windmill Cotts TA15......186 C4
Windmill Cres TA7......136 E3
WINDMILL HILL......183 B3
Windmill Hill
　Hutton BS24......50 A2
　Wrantage TA3......170 A2
Windmill Hill La
　Ashill TA19......183 B3
　Westbury-sub-Mendip BA5...110 D4
Windmill Hill Rd BA6......206 E5
Windmill La
　Langport TA10......172 C5
　Montacute TA15......186 C4
　West Pennard BA6......140 C1
Windmill Rd
　Clevedon BS21......16 E8
　High Ham TA10......156 A1
Windmill Rise TA18......224 C7
Windrush Cl BA2......43 F4
Windrush Gn BS31......25 A4
Windrush Rd BS31......25 A4
Windsbatch Hill BA11......101 C1
Windsbatch La BA11......101 B1
Windsor Ave BS31......24 E4
Windsor Bridge Rd BA1,
　BA2......44 D7
Windsor Castle BA1......44 D7
Windsor Cl
　Burnham-on-S TA8......85 B1
　Clevedon BS21......6 D2
　Minehead TA24......200 E6
　Taunton TA1......212 C1
Windsor Cres BA11......120 A5
Windsor Ct
　4 Bath BA1......44 C7
　13 Bristol, Clifton BS8......11 F6
Windsor Dr
　Bridgwater TA6......209 D7
　Nailsea BS48......8 E2

Windsor Hill La BA4......141 B8
Windsor Ho TA6......209 C5
Windsor La TA14......186 A4
Windsor Pl
　5 Bath BA1......44 C7
　Bristol, Clifton BS8......11 F6
Windsor Rd
　Bridgwater TA6......209 D7
　Weston-super-Mare BS22...31 C2
Windsor Terr
　Bristol, Clifton BS8......11 F6
　17 Henstridge BA8......190 A6
　Paulton BS39......77 E5
Windsor Villas 3 BA1......44 C7
Windway Hill TA4......164 D6
Windwhistle Circ BS23......48 F4
Windwhistle La
　Sticklepath TA4......149 F6
　Weston-super-Mare BS23...48 E3
Windwhistle Prim Sch
　BS23......48 F3
Windwhistle Rd BS23......48 D3
Windy Ridge TA17......195 D7
Windyridge La TA11......211 B1
Wine St
　Bath BA1......228 C2
　Bristol BS1......227 A3
　Frome BA11......119 E4
　Yeovil BA20......219 B4
WINFORD......37 F7
Winford CE Prim Sch BS40...37 F7
Winford Cl BS20......2 E4
Winford Gr BS13......22 A8
Winford La BS41......21 C1
Winford Rd BA4......38 F3
Winford Rural Workshops
　BA22......197 A2
Winford Terr
　Bridgwater TA6......209 B6
　Bristol BS41......21 C5
Wingard Cl BS23......48 D2
Wingard Cl 6 BS23......48 E5
Wingate Ave BA21......219 C2
WINGFIELD......83 C6
Wingfield Rd DT9......225 C3
Winifred Cliff Ct 1 EX16...164 B1
Winifred's La BA1......27 E1
Winkworth Way TA1, TA2...213 A5
Winnibrook La TA24......131 A5
Winnowing End BS25......52 A3
Winpenny La TA2......168 E8
Winsbeer La
　Rockwell Green TA21......222 A6
　Runnington TA21......179 F8
Winsbury View BA2......42 B1
WINSCOMBE......69 F7
Winscombe Cl BS31......24 C6
Winscombe Ct BA11......120 B5
Winscombe Dro
　Shipham BS25......70 D6
　Winscombe BS25......70 A5
Winscombe Hill BS25......69 F5
Winscombe Rd BS23......49 A7
Winscombe Woodborough
　Prim Sch BS25......70 A8
WINSFORD......147 C5
Winsham Cl BS14......23 B5
Winsham Prim Sch TA20...194 E1
Winslade Cl TA2......213 B7
WINSLEY......64 C7
Winsley Bypass BA15......64 E7
Winsley CE VA Prim Sch
　BA15......64 E7
Winsley Hill BA3......64 B6
Winsley Rd BA15......64 F7
Winsmoor Hill TA19......184 B4
Winsors La TA24......131 A5
Winstitchen Cross TA24...127 C2
Winstitchen La TA24......127 C2
Winston Cl TA2......212 E6
Winston Dr BA21......218 F8
Winstone Ct BS2......226 C3
Winstones Rd
　Barrow Gurney BS48......20 F6
　Bristol BS48......21 A6
Winterfield BA11......196 B5
Winterfield Pk BS39......77 E4
Winterfield Rd BS39......77 E5
WINTERHAY GREEN......221 A5
Winterhay La TA19......221 A5
WINTERHEAD......70 B8
Winter La DT9......188 C8
Winters Cross TA4......165 C8
Winters Field TA1......213 A5
Wintershead Rd TA24......145 F7
Winters Hill La BA4......204 C3
Winters La BS40......36 D6
Winter's La TA4......150 C3
Winters Orch TA3......169 C1
Winterstoke Commercial Ctr
　BS23......49 A6
Winterstoke Hundred Acad
　Haywood Village BA24...49 D6
　Haywood Village BS24...49 D6
Winterstoke Rd
　Bristol BS3......11 F3
　Weston-super-Mare BS23,
　BS24......49 B4
Winterstoke Underpass
　BS3......11 F4
WINTER WELL......182 C7
Winterwell La BA4......141 F4
Winter Wlk BS14......23 C6
Wint Hill BS29......51 B2
WINYARD'S GAP......196 E1
Winyards View TA18......224 D4
Wireworks Est The TA6...136 A2

Whi – Woo 277

Wirral Park Rd BA6......206 C3
Wirral Park Rdbt BA6......206 C2
Wirral Park Trad Est BA6...206 B3
Wirral Pk Ind Est BA6......206 B4
Wishford Mews BA3......78 C3
Wisley Wlk BS22......49 F7
Wisteria Ave BS24......49 D2
Wiston Cross EX36......162 D2
Witches Wlk TA6......208 E2
WITCOMBE......185 F8
Witcombe Dro
　Ilchester TA12......172 F1
　Knole TA12......173 B2
Witcombe La TA12......185 F8
Witham Cl TA1......213 D3
WITHAM FRIARY......143 C3
Witham Rd BS31......25 A3
Withers La 1 BS13......22 C4
Withey Cl E BS9......5 F6
Withey Cl W BS9......5 F5
Witheys The BS14......23 C4
Withial Hill BA4......158 D8
Withial La BA6......158 D7
Withiel Dr TA5......135 B2
WITHIEL FLOREY......148 E4
Withiel Hill TA24......148 F6
Withiel La TA24......148 E5
Withies La BA3......97 A8
Withies Pk BA3......96 F8
Withies Wy BA3......96 F8
Withmoor Dro TA10......172 E4
Withybed La BA9......177 E6
WITHYBROOK......115 E3
Withycombe Cl BS48......8 F3
WITHYCOMBE......131 B4
Withycombe Cross TA24...131 C4
Withycombe Hill TA5......135 A5
Withycombe Hill Gate
　TA24......130 F4
Withycombe La TA24......131 B5
Withy Cotts BA3......115 C5
WITHYDITCH......61 C3
Withyditch La BA2......61 C4
Withy Gr TA9......136 C7
Withy Grove Cl TA6......209 D7
Withy Hays Rd 3 TA11...173 F7
Withy La
　Barton St David TA11......158 A3
　Clatworthy TA4......149 B2
　Hemyock EX15......180 B1
　Oakhill BA3......115 C5
Withymead BS49......17 F1
WITHY MILLS......78 A7
WITHYPOOL......146 C6
Withypool Cross
　Hawkridge TA22......146 C2
　Twitchen EX36......145 J4
Withypool Gdns BS14......23 B5
Withy Rd TA9......136 C7
Withy Road Farm La TA9...136 C7
Withys The BS20......4 D4
Withywine La TA22......164 C5
WITHYWOOD......22 A4
Withywood Gdns 1 BS13...21 F4
Withy Wood La BA4......142 C5
Withywood Rd BS13......21 F4
Witney Cl BS31......25 D3
Witney La
　Chard TA20......223 B8
　Tatworth TA20......193 F1
Wittey's La TA20......199 B6
WIVELISCOMBE......210 B4
Wiveliscombe Prim Sch
　TA4......210 B5
Wivenhoe Ct BA11......120 C6
Woburn Rd BA21......219 E2
Wolfester Terr BA22......174 F4
Wollens Cl BA6......206 C4
Wolmer Cl TA6......208 E2
Wolsey Cl BA5......203 B3
Wolverlands BA22......175 A6
Wolvershill Ind Units BS29 50 C6
Wolvershill Pk BS29......51 A3
Wolvershill Rd
　Banwell BS29......50 E6
　Weston-super-Mare BS24...50 C8
WONDERSTONE......67 D6
Wonhouse Dro BS28......138 B6
Woodacre BS20......2 E7
Woodadvent La TA23......131 E1
Woodbarton TA4......166 F4
Woodbirds Hill La TA10...172 C8
WOODBOROUGH......70 B8
Woodborough Cres BS25...70 A7
Woodborough Ct BS25......70 A8
Woodborough Dr BS25......70 A8
Woodborough Hill Cotts
　BA2......79 C4
Woodborough La BA3......79 A4
Woodborough Mill La
　BS39......41 B5
Woodborough Rd
　Radstock BA3......79 A3
　Winscombe BS25......69 F8
Woodburn Cross EX16......162 F2
Woodburn Hill EX16......162 F2
Woodburn Water Cross
　EX16......162 F1
Woodbury Ave BA5......203 F5
Woodbury Cl BA5......203 F5
Woodbury Rd TA6......208 D4
Wood Cl BA5......203 B4
Woodcliff Ave BS22......31 C1
Woodcliff Rd BS22......31 C1

Wood Close La TA17......195 A8
Woodcock St BA7......214 C5
Woodcock Way EX13....198 B7
WOODCOMBE............200 C8
Woodcombe Brake TA24 .200 D7
Woodcombe Cotts TA24 .200 C8
Woodcombe La TA24....200 C8
Woodcote BA20..........218 D2
Woodcroft BS30.........57 C3
Woodcroft Mdws TA20 .192 E7
Wooddene BS25..........70 A8
Wood Dro TA10.........171 E8
Wood End Wlk BS9.......5 C6
Wood Farm Cotts TA5 .134 E4
Woodfield Cl TA8.......104 C5
WOODFORD
  Watchet................132 A1
  Wells..................140 A6
Woodford Cl BS48.......9 A1
Woodford Cotts TA4....132 A1
Woodford Ct **2** BS23....48 E5
Woodford La
  Coxley BA5............139 F6
  Wells BA5.............203 B4
Woodford Rd BA5.......140 A6
Woodfords Gn BA7......214 B6
WOODGATE............179 E2
Woodhayes BA8.........190 A6
Woodhayes Ct **19** BA8 .190 A6
Woodhayes Ho **12** BA8 .190 A6
Woodhayes Rd BA11....120 C6
Woodhenge BA22.......218 B5
WOODHILL
  Portishead.............2 D7
  Stoke St Gregory.....170 F6
Woodhill BS49..........34 E6
Woodhill Ave BS20......2 D6
Woodhill Ct BS20.......2 D6
Wood Hill Pk BS20......2 D7
Woodhill Rd BS20.......2 D7
Woodhill Terr TA3......170 F6
Woodhill Views BS48....8 F3
Woodhouse Cross SP8 .177 F6
Woodhouse La
  Axminster EX13.......198 D1
  Chard TA20............194 B6
  Marston Magna BA22...175 B1
  Montacute TA15.......186 C3
Woodhouse Rd
  Axminster EX13.......198 D1
  Bath BA2..............44 A6
Woodhurst Rd BS23.....49 A7
Woodington Rd BS21....6 C1
Wood Kilns The BS49....17 A1
Wood La
  Axbridge BS26........70 D2
  Blue Anchor TA24.....131 C6
  Butleigh BA6.........157 C4
  Carhampton TA24......131 B4
  Chapmanslade BA13...121 D4
  Clapton in G BS20.....8 E8
  Crowcombe TA4.......151 C7
  Drimpton DT8.........199 E7
  High Ham TA10........155 E1
  Marnhull DT10........190 F2
  Moorlinch TA7........155 E8
  North Perrott TA18....196 D3
  Rodney Stoke BS27....91 B1
  South Cheriton BA8...176 C4
  Stalbridge DT10.......190 B4
  Stawell TA7...........137 A1
  Stogumber TA4........150 D7
  Weston-super-Mare BS23 .30 F1
Woodland Ave TA7.....154 F5
Woodland Cl
  6 Carhampton TA24...131 A5
  Failand BS8...........10 B4
Woodland Cotts BA3....64 D6
Woodland Ct BS20......5 C3
Woodland Glade BS21....6 E5
Woodland Gr
  Bath, Bushey Norwood BA2..45 E5
  Bath, Weston Park BA1...27 C1
  Bristol BS9............5 D6
  Yeovil BA20...........219 B4
Woodland Pl BA2.......45 D5
Woodland Rd
  Bristol BS8...........226 C4
  Frome BA11...........119 F4
  Nailsea BS48..........8 E3
  Taunton TA1..........213 A7
  Watchet TA23.........202 C6
  Weston-super-Mare BS23 ..48 D4
WOODLANDS...........183 E6
Woodlands
  Axbridge BS26........70 D2
  Wellington TA21.......222 F3
  Weston-super-Mare BS23 ..30 D1
Woodlands Bsns Pk EX16 .179 C3
Woodlands Court Bsns Pk
  TA6..................136 B2
Woodlands Cl BS11......4 E5
Woodlands Dr
  Ruishton TA3.........169 C3
  Winsley BA3..........64 B6
Woodlands La
  Holcombe BA3.........116 B7
  Isle Abbotts TA3......183 E6
Woodlands Mead DT10 .190 F6
Woodlands Pk BA1......28 C2
Woodlands Rd
  Baltonsborough BA6...158 A8
  Clevedon BS21.........6 C4

Woodlands Rd *continued*
  Portishead BS20........2 D8
Woodlands The
  Peasedown St John BA2...60 F3
  Shepton Mallet BA4....205 D5
Woodland Way
  Failand BS8............10 B4
  Frome BA11...........120 D7
Woodleaze BS9..........5 B6
Woodleigh Gdns BS14...23 C6
Woodmarsh Cl BS14.....23 A4
Woodmead Gdns BS13 ..22 C4
Woodmill BS49.........17 A1
Woodpecker Ave BA3....97 B8
Woodpecker Cl BS31....24 C3
Woodpecker Dr BS22....49 E8
Woodram La TA3........181 E5
Wood Rd
  Ashill TA19...........183 B4
  High Ham TA10........172 A8
Woodridge Mead TA4 ..167 F8
Wood Rock EX36........162 C5
Woodrush Cl TA1.......213 C1
Woods Batch BA16.....207 B6
Woods Cnr TA1.........173 E8
Wood's Cross EX36.....162 C5
Woods Hill BA3.........64 A6
Woodside
  Bristol BS9............5 D3
  Midsomer Norton BA3...77 E1
Woodside Ave BS24.....49 B2
Woodside Cl TA24......200 D7
Woodside Ct BS23......49 A8
Woodside Gdns BS20....1 E5
Woodside Rd BS21......6 E5
Woodspring Ave BS22...31 B3
Woodspring Cres BS22 ..31 A3
Woodspring Mus★ BS23 .48 E8
Woodspring Priory★ BS22 .14 C1
Woods Rd BA16........207 A6
Wood St
  Bath BA1..............228 B2
  Bath, Beechen Cliff BA2 .228 B1
  Milverton TA4.........166 F5
  Taunton TA1..........212 E4
Woodstock Rd
  Taunton TA1..........212 E5
  Weston-super-Mare BS22 .49 B8
  Yeovil BA21...........219 C2
Woodview
  Chilcompton BA3......96 E5
  2 Clevedon BS21......6 F3
  Paulton BS39..........77 C5
  Wells BA5.............203 E5
Woodview Cl BS11.......4 E7
Woodview Dr BS49......35 B8
Woodview Rd BS27......90 C7
Woodview Terr
  Nailsea BS48..........8 F2
  Weston-super-Mare BS23 ..49 A6
Wood Way EX35.........122 B4
Woodwell Rd BS11......4 E5
WOOKEY.............139 E8
Wookey Cl BS48.........18 F8
WOOKEY HOLE.......203 A7
Wookey Hole Cave★ BA5 .111 E5
Wookey Hole Papermill &
  Mus★ BA5............203 A8
Wookey Hole Rd BA5...203 B5
Wookey Prim Sch
  Wookey BA5..........139 D8
  Yarley BA5............139 D8
Wookey Rd BA5........139 E8
WOOLAVINGTON.....136 F4
Woolavington Hill TA7 .136 E3
Woolavington Rd TA7 ..136 D4
Woolavington Right Dro
  TA7..................154 D6
Woolavington Village Prim
  Sch TA7.............136 E4
Woolcombe Rd
  Wells BA5.............111 F2
  Wells BA5.............203 A6
Woolcott La SP8.......161 E1
Wooler Rd BS23........48 E8
Wooley La TA19, TA20 ...194 C6
Woolhayes La TA20.....223 A8
WOOLLARD............41 A6
Woollard La
  Bristol BS14, BS39.....41 A7
  Whitchurch BS14......23 E1
WOOLLEY.............27 F5
Woolley La BA1.........28 A4
Woolley Rd BS14.......23 E5
Woolmersdon Rd TA5 ..153 E5
WOOLMINSTONE......195 B3
Woolminstone Rd TA18 .195 C3
Woolpit La TA24........146 B7
Woolshed Cl TA24......129 E1
WOOLSTON
  North Cadbury........175 E6
  Watchet...............132 D2
Woolstone La TA5......134 F7
Woolston Rd BA22.....175 E6
Woolvers Way BS24.....50 B6
WOOLVERTON.........82 C1
Wooton Hill BA6.......157 C5
WOOTTON COURTENAY .129 F6
Wootton Cross TA5....198 F1
Wootton Gr DT9........225 E5
Wootton Hill DT6......199 A1
Wootton St BA6........157 C6
Wootton Vineyard★ BA4 .140 C5
Worberry La BA3........95 B7

Worcester Bldgs BA1....28 B2
Worcester Cl BA2......79 D7
Worcester Cres BS8....226 A4
Worcester Ct BS8......226 A4
Worcester Gdns BS48 ...18 C8
Worcester Pk BA1.....28 B2
Worcester Pl BA1......28 B2
Worcester Rd BS8.....226 A4
Worcester Terr
  Bath BA1..............28 B2
  Bristol BS8...........226 A4
Wordsworth Ave BA6 ..208 E6
Wordsworth Cl TA8....85 B2
Wordsworth Dr TA1...213 B3
Wordsworth Rd
  Clevedon BS21.........6 C2
  Weston-super-Mare BS23 ..49 A3
Worely La TA11.........211 F8
Workshop La BA2......43 C6
World's End La BS31....25 C5
WORLE.................31 F2
WORLEBURY............31 A2
Worlebury Cl BS22.....31 B3
Worlebury Hill Rd BS22,
  BS23.................31 B2
Worlebury Park Rd BS22..31 A2
Worlebury St Pauls CE VA Fst
  Sch BS22............31 B3
Worle Com Sch BS22 ...31 E1
Worle Ct BS22.........31 F3
Worle Ind Est BS22....32 B2
Worle Moor Rd BS24....49 E7
Worle Sta BS22........32 B1
Worle Village Prim Sch
  BS22.................31 E2
Wormcliff La SN13.....29 F3
WORMINSTER............140 C5
Worminster Batch BA4 .140 D5
Worston La TA8........104 C5
Worston Orch TA9.....104 E4
Worston Rd TA9.......104 E5
WORTH.................139 D8
Worthings The BS24....67 B1
Worthington Cl BS28 ..108 D5
Worthy La TA22, TA24 ..146 C4
WORTHY................123 E5
Worthy Cres BS24......67 B1
Worthy La
  Creech St Michael TA3..169 D5
  Pilton BA4............140 F3
  5 Weston-super-Mare BS23.48 E8
  West Pennard BA4, BA6...140 D1
Worthy Pl **4** BS23.....48 E8
Worthy Rd TA24.......123 E5
Worthy Toll Rd TA24...123 D4
Wouldham Rd TA23....202 D6
Wrangcombe La TA21 ..180 A4
Wrangcombe Rd TA21..180 A4
Wrangle Farm Gn BS21..6 E2
WRANGLE THE..........74 A5
Wrangle The **5** BS24...49 F7
WRANGWAY.............180 A4
Wrangway Rd EX15....180 A3
WRANTAGE.............170 A1
WRAXALL
  Ditcheat..............159 A7
  Nailsea...............9 C3
Wraxall CE VA Prim Sch
  BS48.................9 B4
Wraxall Cross Rds BA4 .159 A7
Wraxall Gr BS13........22 A8
Wraxall Hill
  Ditcheat BA4.........159 A8
  Wraxall BS48..........9 C5
Wraxall Rd BS23.......49 B7
Wraxhill Cl BA16......207 D5
Wraxhill Rd
  Street BA16..........207 C5
  Yeovil BA20..........218 E1
WREATH................194 C3
Wreath La TA20........194 B3
Wren Cl
  Frome BA11..........120 B6
  Taunton TA1..........212 C4
  Weston-super-Mare BS22 .49 D8
Wren Gdns BS20.......3 A7
Wrenmoor Cl TA6.....209 C3
WRINGTON..............35 E1
Wrington CE Prim Sch
  BS40.................35 E2
Wrington Cres BS13....22 A7
Wrington Hill BS40....35 F5
Wrington La BS49......34 E5
Wrington Mead BS49...34 E5
Wrington Rd BS49.....34 F4
Wristland Rd TA23....202 D7
WRITHLINGTON.........79 C2
Writhlington Ct BA3...79 C2
Writhlington Sch BA3 ..79 C1
Writh Rd DT9..........189 B1
Wroughton Dr BS13....22 D4
Wroughton Gdns BS13 .22 D4
Wry La TA4.............149 F2
Wyatt Ave BS13........21 F5
Wyatt Cl BS13.........21 F5
Wyatt's Cl BS48........8 D2
Wyatts Ct TA17........195 C7
Wyatts Field TA3......168 D1
Wyatts Way TA19......183 C4
Wych Ct EX13..........198 E3
Wych Elm Rd BA11....120 C6
Wycotte Hill BA2......62 C6
Wydford Cl DT9.......225 B3
Wydon La TA24........124 F3
Wye Ave TA6..........209 D3

Wyedale Ave BS9.......5 C7
WYKE CHAMPFLOWER....215 A6
Wyke La
  Wyke Champflower BA10..215 A5
  Wyke Champflower BA10..215 A6
Wyke Rd
  Castle Cary BA7, BA10..214 E7
  Wyke Champflower BA10..215 C6
Wylds Rd TA6.........209 A7
Wylds Road Ind Est TA6..209 A7
Wyllie Ct BS22.........32 A5
Wymbush Cres BS13...22 C5
Wymbush Gdns BS13...22 C5
Wyndam Ct BS2.......227 B4
Wyndham Cres BS20....4 B4
Wyndham Ct BA21.....219 C5
Wyndham Rd
  Bridgwater TA6.......209 C6
  Taunton TA2..........212 E7
  Watchet TA23.........202 C6
Wyndham's TA4.......210 C4
Wyndham St BA20.....219 C5
Wyndham View BA21 ..219 D5
Wyndham Way BS20....2 E5
Wyndham Way Ret Pk BS20 .2 D4
Wynford Rd BA11.....120 B5
Wynnes Cl DT9........225 C3
Wynnes Rise DT9......225 C3
Wynsome St BA14.....83 F3
Wynter Cl BS22........32 A3
Wyrral Cl BA6.........206 D3
Wytch Gn EX13........198 E3
Wythburn Rd BA11....120 C5
Wyvern Cl
  Bruton BA10..........215 F7
  Weston-super-Mare BS23 ..48 F7
  Yeovil BA20..........218 C1
Wyvern Ct TA18.......224 C6
Wyvern Mews **5** BS23 ..48 F7
Wyvern Rd TA1........168 E1
Wyville Rd BA11.......120 C6

Y

Yadley Cl BS25.........70 A7
Yadley La BS25.........70 A6
Yadley Way BS25.......70 A7
Yallands Hill TA2......213 E8
YALWAY................153 A1
Yanel La BS25.........52 B5
Yanhey Hill EX16......162 E4
Yanleigh Cl BS13......21 C6
YANLEY................21 C8
Yanley La BS41, BS13...21 C7
Yarbury Way BS24.....32 B1
YARCOMBE.............192 D3
Yarde Pl TA1..........212 F4
Yard La
  Marshwood DT6......199 F3
  Wiveliscombe TA4....210 C6
Yardleigh Cross EX13...198 D4
Yard Rd TA14.........185 E1
Yard The BA11........143 C4
Yardwall Rd TA9......106 A3
YARFORD...............168 C8
Yarford Rd TA2.......168 C8
YARLEY................139 C8
Yarley Cross BA5......139 C8
Yarley Field La BA5....139 B7
Yarley Hill BA5........139 C8
YARLINGTON............175 F8
Yarlington Cl TA2.....168 B4
Yarnbarton BA8.......176 E1
Yarn Barton BA20.....219 A4
Yarn Mews BA20......218 C1
YARROW................106 E3
Yarrow Ct BS22.......32 A5
Yarrow Rd TA9........106 D3
YATTON................34 C8
Yatton CE VA Jun & Inf Schs
  BS49.................34 C8
Yatton Cl BS13........21 F8
Yatton Station BS49....17 A1
YEABRIDGE.............220 E2
Yeabsleys Way BA7...214 C6
Yealscombe La TA24 ..128 B2
Yeamen's Ho BS1.....227 B1
Yeap's Dro BA5........139 A7
Yearmoor La TA5......134 C6
Yearnor Mill La
  Oare TA24............122 F5
  Porlock Weir TA24....123 B5
Yeates Cl BS21.........6 E3
Yeatman Cl BS39......57 D4
Yeatman Hospl DT9 ..225 D4
Yellingmill La BA4....141 C8
Yellowcombe La TA24 .147 C5
Yellow Rose Cvn Pk TA20.193 B6
Yellow Way Rd
  Maiden Bradley BA11,
  BA12.................144 A4
  Witham Friary BA11...143 F3
Yellow Wood Cross TA4 .132 C2
YENSTON................189 F8
Yenston Hill BA8......189 F8
Yeo Bank La
  Icelton BS22..........32 D7
  Kingston Seymour BS21 ..15 F1
Yeo Cl
  Cheddar BS27........90 B6
  Weston-super-Mare BS23 ..49 A5
Yeo Ct
  Clevedon BS21.........6 C2
  Congresbury BS49....34 D4

Yeo La
  Bridgwater TA6......209 B2
  Long Ashton BS41....10 F1
Yeolands Dr BS21......6 B1
Yeo Leisure Pk★ BA20 ..219 C4
Yeomanry Way BA4 ..205 D5
Yeomans Cl BS9.......5 D5
Yeomanside Cl BS13...23 C5
Yeomans Lodge BA11 .119 C4
Yeomans Orch BS40....35 E3
Yeomead BS48.........8 F3
Yeomeads BS41........10 F1
Yeo Mill Cross EX36...162 C5
Yeo Moor BS21........6 E2
Yeo Moor Dro
  BS27, BS28..........109 D3
Yeo Moor Inf Sch BS21..6 E2
Yeo Moor Jun Sch BS21..6 E2
Yeo Moor Prim Sch BS21 ..6 E2
Yeo Rd TA6...........209 B2
Yeo Valley **2** BA22 ..197 F8
Yeo Valley Way BS48....9 B2
YEOVIL.................218 E4
Yeovil Bsns Ctr BA21 ..219 F7
Yeovil Coll BA21......219 A6
Yeovil District Hospl
  BA21.................219 B5
Yeovil Innovation Centre
  BA20.................218 B7
Yeovil Junction Sta
  BA22.................219 E1
YEOVIL MARSH.........187 A6
Yeovil Marsh Pk BA21 .187 A5
Yeovil Marsh Rd BA21 .187 A5
Yeovil Pen Mill Sta BA21 .219 E5
Yeovil Railway Ctr★
  BA22.................219 D1
Yeovil Rd
  Crewkerne TA18......224 E7
  Halstock BA22.......197 D3
  Montacute TA15.....186 B3
  Sherborne DT9.......225 C4
  Tintinhull BA22......186 C6
  Yeovil BA22..........218 F1
Yeovil Small Bsns Ctr
  BA22.................218 B6
YEOVILTON.............174 A1
Yeovil Trinity Foyer **7**
  BA20.................219 B4
Yeoward Rd BS21......6 E1
Yeo Way BS21.........6 B2
Yet Mead La BS27.....110 B7
Yevoil Coll BA20......219 A6
Yewcroft Cl BS14.....23 A4
Yewtree Batch BS40....37 A1
Yew Tree Cl
  Bishop Sutton BS39...57 D4
  Lower Langford BS40...53 E6
  Nailsea BS48..........8 C1
  Yeovil BA20..........218 E2
Yew Tree Cotts BS40...54 E3
Yew Tree Ct BS14......23 B5
Yew Tree Dr BS22......50 B8
Yew Tree Gdns
  Nailsea BS48..........8 C1
  Pill BS20..............4 C4
  Sandford BS25........52 A4
Yew Tree La
  Compton Martin BS40...74 A5
  Kingston Seymour BS21 ..16 B1
  Taunton TA2..........213 E6
Yew Tree Pk BS49......34 D3
Yomede Pk BA1........44 A7
Yonder Dro TA10.....184 E8
Yonder Hill Cotts TA20 .198 E2
Yonder Mead TA4.....167 F7
York Bldgs TA6........208 F5
York Cl
  Axminster EX13......198 A1
  Weston-super-Mare BS22 ..32 A4
York Ct BS2...........227 B4
York Gdns BS8.........11 F6
York Lodge **4** BA20 ..219 A5
York Pl
  Bath BA1..............45 B8
  Bristol, Brandon Hill BS1 .226 B3
  Bristol, Victoria Park BS8 .226 B3
  Yeovil BA20..........219 A5
York Rd
  Bridgwater TA6......208 F2
  Bristol BS2...........227 C1
  Taunton TA1..........213 C5
York's La BA3.........94 B5
York St
  Bath BA1..............228 C2
  Bristol BS2...........227 B4
  5 Frome BA11.......119 E5
  Weston-super-Mare BS23 ..48 D7
Youngwood La BS48....18 D7
Yoxter Rd
  Charterhouse BA5....72 F1
  Ubley Sideling BS40...73 B2
  Westbury Beacon BA5...91 E8

Z

ZEALS.................161 F2
Zeals Rise BA12.......161 F2
Zembard La TA20......223 C4
Zeta Cl TA7...........209 E8
Zig Zag BS21..........6 D4
Zion Hill
  Midsomer Norton BA3...96 B7
  Oakhill BA3..........115 A3
  18 Shepton Mallet BA4...205 B6